REPORTING
The Revolutionary War

BEFORE *it was*
HISTORY, *it was* NEWS

BY TODD ANDRLIK

Published by Sourcebooks, Inc.
P.O. Box 4410, Naperville, Illinois 60567-4410
(630) 961-3900
Fax: (630) 961-2168
www.sourcebooks.com

Library of Congress Cataloging-in-Publication Data

Reporting the Revolutionary War : before it was history, it was news / [compiled by] Todd Andrlik.
p. cm.
(hardcover : alk. paper) 1. United States—History—Revolution, 1775-1783—Sources. 2. United States—History—Revolution, 1775-1783—Press coverage. 3. American newspapers—History—18th century. I. Andrlik, Todd.
E203.R44 2012
973.3—dc23

2012022258

Printed and bound in the United States of America.
BG 10 9 8 7 6 5 4 3 2 1

CONTENTS

North America
Barry Lawrence Ruderman Antique Maps, raremaps.com

An early map of the British Colonies and the whole of North America, shortly after the conclusion of the French and Indian War and on the eve of revolution.

INTRODUCTION

By Todd Andrlik

THERE ARE NO PHOTOGRAPHS OF THE AMERICAN REVOLUTION. NO SNAPSHOTS EXIST TO SHOW ordinary life or depict the struggles and suffering of the late eighteenth century. Engravings and oil paintings, made long after the war ended, portray epic battles and heroism but often fail to realistically capture the moment.

Newspapers are the closest thing we have to photos of the Revolution. They transport readers back in time, providing unmatched insight about common life and life-altering events. Despite their small size and lack of headlines, eighteenth-century newspapers pack an intense, concentrated punch and demonstrate the incredible power of the printed word. Through newspapers, we realize that history is much more than a chronological list of battles as we eavesdrop on everyday life and witness everyday realities of the American Revolution through the eyes of the British and the American colonists. The eighteenth-century newspapers presented in this book help us see that history is real life, messy, and exciting. We learn firsthand what many historians claim: without newspapers, there would have been no American Revolution.

Through vivid eyewitness accounts, battlefield letters, and breaking news compiled from hundreds of newspapers—primarily printed from 1763 to 1783 on both sides of the Atlantic Ocean—this story of the American Revolution is unlike any version that has been told. It is raw and uncut, full of intense action, drama, and suspense. From start to finish, these frontline newspapers deliver incomparable insight about America's founding. As a collection, they provide one of the most reliable and comprehensive narratives of the Revolutionary Era, loaded with amazing characters, better-than-fiction plot twists, and the perfect climax. Before these famous and infamous events became the history and foundation of America, they were littered among the news of the day for colonial Americans. Mark Twain wrote "of the wide difference in interest between 'news' and 'history'; that news is history in its first and best form, its vivid and fascinating form; and that history is the pale and tranquil reflection of it."

Reporting the Revolutionary War brings to life precious first drafts of history and lets readers experience the charming rusticity of eighteenth-century newsprint, complete with stains, tears, imperfect ink and paper, typesetting mistakes, misspellings, and grammatical errors that were all typical of the era. Reading Revolution Era newspapers in their original form helps reproduce the same immediacy and uncertainty felt by those who first held them.

With each newspaper, readers gain valuable insight into the social, economic, political, and military histories of the American Revolution. Reading newspapers in their entirety—including advertisements, obituaries, and essays—provides more than a glimpse of all the obstacles and ideas of the period. It creates a 360-degree view of the American Revolution and the formation of the United States.

Another important history lesson to be gained from this book relates to journalism. We live in a time of instant and on-demand news. Journalists and bloggers work frantically around the clock, competing to break news stories before anyone else. Cable news channels and websites stream updated headlines nonstop across their screens. Using Twitter and Facebook, millions of citizen reporters scramble to share the latest news affecting their lives, practically in real time. Despite the debated endangerment of printed newspapers, it is difficult to imagine a time when media were more important. However, 250 years ago, newspapers were the fundamental form of mass media and were more important than in any other time in America's history.

Just as social media helped ignite and organize the Arab Spring revolutions of the Middle East and Northern Africa, colonial newspapers fanned the flames of rebellion, provided critical intercolonial communication during the war, sustained loyalty to the Patriot cause, and aided in the outcome of the war—all of which becomes evident after reading straight from the pages of newspapers. In *Reporting the Revolutionary War*, readers will see that Americans maintained "Liberty or Death! Join or Die!" attitudes with blood, as well as ink, on their hands. David Ramsay, who twice served as a delegate in the Continental Congress, wrote that "in establishing American independence, the pen and the press had merit equal to that of the sword."

Not only do eighteenth-century newspapers contain the exclusive essays, reports, and advertisements of the day, but they also include reprinted extracts from other primary sources such as private letters, journal entries, official government documents, and war-zone intelligence direct from merchants, travelers, soldiers, officers, and common colonists. They are a proverbial gold mine of information. Since the day the Revolutionary War ended, historians and authors have relied heavily on newspapers as the basis for their own analysis and interpretations of the course of the war. The endnotes of practically every history book about the Revolution are loaded with references to the up-close-and-personal perspectives found in newspapers.

Reporting the Revolutionary War brings to life eighteenth-century newspapers in a firsthand account of America's founding, distinct from the history we receive in high school and university texts. Never before has such a significant collection of American Revolution newspapers been made available to the general public in such color and detail. Never before has access to such an archive been made so easy. And never before has *this* version of the American Revolution been told.

THE EIGHTEENTH-CENTURY NEWSPAPER BUSINESS

By Carol Sue Humphrey

Newspapers played an important role during the American Revolution because they had already become an essential part of life for many Americans, more so than all other media (books, pamphlets, magazines, or broadsides) combined. Ever since John Campbell founded the first successful newspaper in Boston in 1704, Americans either sought out copies of the newspapers themselves or went someplace where they could hear them being read aloud. People wanted to know what was happening elsewhere, particularly in the colonies and Europe, and newspapers were the major source of such information.

Over the course of the 1700s, more newspapers appeared in the American colonies, but printing was always a difficult business. The French and Indian War had provided a major encouragement for the further growth of newspapers in the colonies because of the desire for information about the conflict. By the end of the war in 1763, each of the thirteen mainland colonies had at least one printer, and the number of newspapers had grown from eleven to twenty-three. By the time the Revolutionary War broke out in 1775, there were thirty-eight newspapers being printed on fifty presses in America. All printers looked for ways to increase business, and newspapers were a possibility. Postmasters founded the earliest newspapers in the colonies because they had easy access to information for the paper. However, they had to hire a printer if they could not produce the newssheets themselves. Many printers saw the financial possibilities and began to produce their own weekly newspapers as a way to bolster their income.

Along with an increase in the number of newspapers came an increase in the circulation of these papers. In 1750, the average newspaper circulation was about 600 copies per week. By 1770, some printers produced 1,500 copies a week, and these numbers continued to rise throughout the conflict with Great Britain. Throughout the colonies, the population of the cities did not grow as rapidly as the percentage of newspapers during the same period, indicating that more people were reading these publications. Some larger cities had several newspapers, another indication that newspaper readership was sizeable enough to sustain a growth in circulation. For example, in 1760, Philadelphia had approximately 25,000 people, and it had only grown to just over 28,000 when the first official U.S. census was taken in 1790. During the same period, the number of newspapers published in Philadelphia grew more rapidly, going from two in 1760 to seven in 1775. The total remained at seven in 1783, but there had been a number of starts and stops during the Revolution as people sought news and information and printers struggled to continue in business because of the problems created by the war.

A steady increase in literacy helped fuel the growth of publications. Newspapers were sold through subscription, but local taverns and coffeehouses often subscribed, and customers either read them directly or listened while someone else read them aloud, thus making the information available to many more people.

Delivering the newspapers to subscribers proved somewhat complicated as well. Within town, they were delivered by carrier, often a hired boy or an apprentice from the print shop. Along the coast, newspapers could be sent from one seaport to another by ship, but that would not work for inland delivery. Newspapers to outlying areas and other colonies were delivered by post riders, which could be haphazard, since the colonies did not have an organized postal system until the 1750s. There were official post roads between the colonies, but they often were not well maintained—many were more like dirt trails through the woods that were difficult to travel. It could take weeks for the post to go from one end of the colonies to the other, and that would continue to be true into the nineteenth century. Historian Frank Luther Mott determined in a 1944 study that it took six weeks for the news of the Battle of Lexington and Concord to be published throughout the colonies. The last printed account appeared in the *Georgia Gazette* in Savannah on May 31, 1775.

Printing as a trade changed very little since Johannes Gutenberg developed the press with movable type. Acquiring the necessary materials often proved difficult as well. Each item—presses, types, paper, and ink—all came from different producers, so making sure all necessary supplies were readily available could be very complicated. Most of these supplies were imported from Great Britain during the colonial era, since local production was difficult and costly and because Americans lacked the mastery of trade skills found in England.

The printing trade also could be discouraging, since it was a very slow and involved process. Most newspapers had four pages, each about ten by fifteen or eleven by seventeen inches in size. Two pages were printed on one side of a piece of paper. When both sides were printed, the newspaper would be folded in half prior to being sold. Thus, pages one and four would be on one side of the original paper while pages two and three would be on the other side. In order to produce one side of this production, thirteen separate processes had to be performed by two men operating a press. Type had to be set by hand in the page form and then locked into place in the press. It took about twenty-four to twenty-eight hours to typeset an entire four-page issue by hand. On average, this constituted about 2,400 words (13,500 type characters) on page two or three and 2,000 words (11,500 type characters) on page one (which contained fewer words because of the masthead at the top of the page). Page four was often reserved for advertisements.

After the type form was locked on the press bed, one man (the "beater") would ink the type using two large animal-skin balls. Next, he would place a piece of damp paper on the tympan (cloth padding) of the press, close the frisket (rectangular frame), and then clamp the tympan over the types. Wetting the paper ahead of time helped the ink better absorb into the paper and reduced wear on the lead types. This being done, the second man (the "puller") would turn the handle and roll the press bed under the platen (flat plate). In a quick motion, the puller would pull the bar to print the first page, turn the handle a second time, pull the bar again to print the second page, then again turn the handle in the opposite direction to roll the bed out from under the press. The beater would open the tympan and remove the printed sheet. They would repeat this two thousand times a day, each time placing freshly printed sheets on top of each other. At the end of the day, all of the sheets would be hung up to dry overnight.

The Revolution also increased many problems for printers. The war cut off access to imported supplies from Great Britain. Americans attempted to produce the needed materials but could not keep up with demand. It would not be until the 1790s that enough printing presses were produced in America to make importing them totally unnecessary. A number of people also established type foundries in the decade prior to the Revolution, but with little success. Maintaining enough type to run the print shop became increasingly difficult as the Revolution continued.

The necessary paper and ink supplies also became increasingly difficult to obtain. Printers had begun to make their own ink long before the nonimportation agreements began in the 1760s, but it seldom became more than a cottage industry for producing what an individual shop needed. Paper mills had existed since the late 1600s and more had been built in the intervening years, but the quality of the paper was not as good as imported paper, and the mills could not produce enough paper to meet the needs of American printers. In addition, importations of paper from Great Britain had been greatly reduced for a brief time following the adoption of the Stamp Act in 1765 and were totally cut off in 1775. Local production of paper became essential if print shops were to remain in operation. Consequently, many printers began to take an active interest in paper-making ventures. As the Revolution got underway, printers urged their readers to save rags for making paper to contribute to the fight for independence. However, printers often had to reduce the size of their newspaper or not publish at all because of the lack of paper and other supplies.

Printers who attempted to publish newspapers in the eighteenth century had difficulty getting content to include in their publications. Because of how time-consuming the actual printing was, newspaper printers often placed essays and advertisements on one side of the paper, since this could be printed ahead of time and allowed to dry. The inner two pages would be printed last and filled with news gleaned from other newspapers or letters. Thus, the most current and local news would typically be found on pages two and three rather than page one. The increase in the number of newspapers being published throughout the 1700s provided more information sources because printers exchanged newspapers with each other and copied materials from these traded productions on a regular basis.

Readers were most interested in international news, which generally came from London newspapers. News from other colonies proved somewhat important, while local news appeared in very small amounts. The local news in one town would be reprinted elsewhere through the exchange system, and news and information thus spread throughout the colonies. These exchanges were not always easy due to weather issues and travel problems, but the process slowly improved over the years. By the end of the French and Indian War in 1763, newspaper printers had managed to improve their business to such an extent that they had an effective system for gathering and sharing news. When the fighting in the Revolution created new problems, printers sought to replace their usual supply of information through other sources. They did this primarily by urging their readers to supply any information they received so the news could easily be shared with others through the newspapers. All printers, both Patriots and Loyalists, hoped that such information would fill the news void created by the war.

As the conflict with Great Britain escalated, Americans wanted information about what was happening. This desire encouraged some printers to try to produce more issues of their newspapers. John Mein and Thomas Fleming had founded the *Boston Chronicle* as a weekly in December

1767 and began publishing the paper semi-weekly after a year because of their readers' desire for more news. In August 1770, Zechariah Fowle and Isaiah Thomas founded the *Massachusetts Spy* in Boston as a tri-weekly publication, but the problems of acquiring needed supplies made it difficult to continue such frequent publication schedules. The *Spy* slowed to semi-weekly in November 1770 and weekly in 1771. Weekly newspapers were most common during the Revolution, but routine schedules at any frequency proved difficult to sustain.

The Revolution only exacerbated problems printers faced in acquiring supplies and information to publish their newspapers, but the Revolutionary-era printers, like their predecessors, clearly believed their news productions were important to Americans, and they worked hard to keep printing them, no matter the obstacles that stood in the way. By the time the Revolution began, newspapers were a relatively common aspect of American culture and society. They had never been easy to produce, and the Revolution did not change that reality.

EIGHTEENTH-CENTURY PRINTING PRESS
North Wind Picture Archives

REVOLUTIONARY NEWSPAPER READING TIPS

By Todd Andrlik

Eighteenth-century newspapers are a favorite source of early American scholars because they chronicle practically every event of the American Revolution, from the Stamp Act crisis through George Washington's resignation as commander in chief of the Continental Army.

Even as we approach the 250-year anniversaries of the Revolution's first events, these contemporary news accounts are well preserved, thanks in large part to the rag linen paper on which they were printed. Prior to 1870, before the transition to wood pulp, newspapers were printed on durable paper handmade with acid-free linen rags, often from clothes or ship sails. Not long after printing, some newspapers were saved and preserved by individuals for future reference, and others were bound into large volumes by libraries and museums for long-term storage.

Despite the best preservation intentions, eighteenth-century newspapers had to survive countless natural and man-made disasters, including wars, floods, fires, and deaccession (removal from an institution's collection). As a result, many still show scars such as tears, holes, stains, and tape mends. Even in the best condition, these newspapers reflect centuries-old communication obstacles and writing styles, making them an entirely different reading experience compared to today's news. Primary sources are by far the best source of information on the American Revolution, but even when original documents are well preserved, they can still sometimes be difficult to read and comprehend.

To help twenty-first-century learners better read and digest eighteenth-century newspapers, here are some important tips to consider:

1. **Put Yourself in the Period**: Toss out all preconceived notions about how we became a country. Read these papers as if it is all happening now. It will help you get inside the heads of the writers and force you to think of both sides of the issues rather than our sanitized and propagandized version of American history.

2. **Perspective**: To fully appreciate and understand differing perspectives of the Revolution, be sure to read the British newspapers as well. You may be surprised to find that British papers often presented points of view agreeable with the Americans, despite Parliament's insistence otherwise.

3. **News Time Lag**: Breaking news traveled slowly in the eighteenth century, often taking weeks to reach other colonies and countries by treacherous postal roads or ship routes, so the

first report about a major event or battle was often published after a few days or even several weeks. As such, expect to get "breaking news" in bits and pieces, even within the same newspaper. Because private correspondence from distant towns and colonies was the number one source of colonial news, new information was printed as quickly as it came to town. Sometimes conflicting information appears in the same paper or in subsequent issues. One letter with some information and a certain point of view might appear on page two, but another letter with a different perspective on the same subject may appear on page three.

4. **Old English S**: Lowercase *s* letters in eighteenth-century newspapers are still the Old English, or long *s*, version and resemble a modern-day *f*. The Old English *s* better matches the handwritten *s* letters of the period. For example, the words "last," "house," and "congress" will often appear as "laft," "houfe," and "congrefs." Under a microscope, the lowercase *f* and long *s* are different as the crossbar does not continue through, stopping at the vertical stroke. Some long *s* characters have no crossbar at all.

5. **Bias and Propaganda**: Realize that most newspapers of the time were biased, published and written by partisan Loyalists or Patriots. Regardless of the newspaper's insistence on being impartial, the paper's point of view is often apparent in the selection of material printed. This is especially noticeable prior to war breaking out. However, similar to left- or right-leaning twenty-first-century media, contemporary readers of Revolutionary newspapers were completely aware of this bias. In the battle over mind control, Revolution Era newspapers—American and British—used a variety of propaganda tactics to boost morale and increase support. Common eighteenth-century propaganda tactics included name-calling, fear mongering, selective news printing and source gathering, incompleteness, and demonizing the enemy. Sound familiar? Most of these tactics, perfected during the Revolutionary War, are still being used by some media today.

6. **Emphasis on Extracts and Excerpts:** Rather than lengthy feature stories with bold headlines, printers filled most of their newspaper pages with several excerpts (sometimes only a paragraph long) most commonly from private letters. Almost every instance of published correspondence begins with "Extract of a letter from…" Aside from letters, official dispatches, and government communications, another popular eighteenth-century news source was oral reports—sometimes rumor or hearsay—by sea captains, merchants, travelers, and soldiers. This sometimes led to conflicting stories appearing on the same page but allowed the reader to make up his or her own mind.

7. **Datelines, Not Headlines**: Eighteenth-century newspapers didn't use headlines, and most reports were separated only by a dateline or the popular "Extract of a letter from…"

8. **Struggle for Credibility**: Despite exaggeration, distortion, and the obstacles of transatlantic communication, eighteenth-century printers still needed to maintain a strong newspaper subscriber and advertiser base, so they printed news from credible sources and

often added disclaimers to unknown or unreliable sources. Frequently, newspaper printers pieced together oral, manuscript, and printed intelligence—official and unofficial—to help corroborate accounts for their own readers.

9. **News Exchange System:** Before news wire services and before professional journalists or correspondents, eighteenth-century newspaper printers relied heavily on an intercolonial newspaper exchange system to fill their pages. Printers often copied entire paragraphs or columns directly from other newspapers and frequently without attribution other than a dateline. As a result, identical reports often appeared in multiple papers throughout America. While this seems like plagiarism today, the news-swapping technique was standard operating procedure then, helping to spread the ideas of liberty and uphold the colonists' resistance to British Parliament.

10. **Evolution of Language**: Pay attention to the change in language. After all, it took a good many years to get to the point where the Americans were in real combat with the British. For example: when exactly did we become "the enemy" instead of "the Americans?"

11. **Pace of Dissent**: Pay attention to the pace by which dissent grows among the Americans. Also note that the new government quickly comes under fire, even from its supporters. This was the birth of free speech as well as a nation.

12. **Inconsistent Grammar**: Be prepared for run-on sentences with considerable comma usage and alternative word spellings—and not just the British-English difference between "color" and "colour." Prewar papers especially seemed to lack a consistency in spelling, even of common words. Also, rules regarding capitalization and punctuation were equally fluid. For example, some papers capitalized every noun, not just the proper ones.

13. **Humor and Sarcasm**: Have a sense of humor. Since much of the content is publicly printed letters addressed between anonymous authors on both sides of various issues, the tone is often snarky and sarcastic. No sword needed here. These words are often sharp, satirical, and witty.

14. **Irony**: Enjoy the ironies. It's not unusual to find the same paper discussing preparations for war and celebrating the birthday of the king. As you become absorbed by the news of the time, you will find that newspapers have the ability to make you forget the outcome. Remember, colonists were not all committed to the idea of independence, and even until early 1776, there was hope among many that things could be resolved.

15. **Read for Context**: Don't skip the ads or obits. Many of these provide insight into daily life, personal values, indentured servitude, slavery, and commerce of the time.

vage and destructive manner broke and abused his Furniture, Chairs, Tables, Desk, Glasses, China, and in short every Thing they could lay their Hands on; at the same Time purloining his Money, and dispersing his private Books and Papers, until by the Effect of Wine and the other Stores of his Cellar, they ripened in Ebriety and Madness, and became fit for the next, more desolating and barbarous Operation.

Towards Ten o'Clock they were traced by the Noise and Tumult of a numerous and confused Rabble to the Mansion-House of His Honor the Lieut. Gov. This seemed to be reserved for the utmost Violence of their diabolical Phrenzy; for immediately on the Word given, that large and stately Edifice became a Prey to the Iron Hand of Outrage and Robbery; a few Hours and the House was a meer Skeleton, and deprived of Furniture, even Wainscot and Partition, broke, hacked and mangled: and the whole by Break of Day, at once a sad Spectacle of Indignation and Wonder!

In this violent and extraordinary Desolation, besides the House and it's Furniture of very considerable Value, his Honor and his Family sustained, the loss of between … nine Hundred Pounds Sterling in Cash … Wearing Apparell, a valuable and co… Number of … as well as curio… rs and Manus… and besides the… rds, occasio… in his Honor's Po… e Claim… Title of this Provi… llen, a… faced, so that the … Conseque… may be esteem… blickly … privately, …ious.

"To bear … own Misfortune … ith Firmness, and to feel …s," (the Words o… the Occasion of an hono… worthy Gentleman, … has lately take… s) … t of true Philoso… be … med …

concern for this unhappy people: On his right hand stood the restless father of mischief with the stamp act in his hand, giving credentials to his all attentive pupil; the malignity of his heart was lively portray'd by the expressive cardinal knave at cards on his breast, accompained with a cautious memento to all placemen, that * * * * * *

"When vice prevails and impious men bear sway,
"The post of honour is a private station."

Their appearance was becoming, and procession glorious, attended by such invectives, huzza's and disdainful music as are the pure emanations of injured freedom: after passing thro' town, our hero with his companion, was conducted——————"in all the Majesty of Greece" to the height of a lofty hill, perhaps the highest summit he will e'er ascend; and there in complaisance to his fellow, committed to the flames; and a few loyal and very constitutional healths crown'd the night.

NEW-LONDON, *August* 23.

We hear that a gentleman in one of the southern provinces being advised that his son, then in London, was appointed a *STAMP-OFFICER*, for said pro… …ately …e him, that if he thought … that … detestable office, he would …

… of Stamps, … the Devil repre… They were suspe… tw…

CHAPTER I

THE CURSED STAMP ACT

Introduction

Stamp duty. When these two words touched American soil in April 1764 as a teaser of the internal tax following the Sugar Act, they set in motion a chain of events that soon united thirteen colonies, bolstered confidence, and forever altered the course of American history. First irritated by the Sugar Act, then seriously angered by the Stamp Act, colonies developed extensive intercolonial networks of resistance, chained together by independent organizations, such as the Sons of Liberty, and independent newspapers, which were widely read locally as well as raced by horseback and ship up and down the continent. The primary source of colonial communication, newspapers spread the word of mobs, violence, and boycott, which effectively prevented enforcement of the Stamp Act and led to its repeal. To avoid total humiliation, the same day Parliament passed the Stamp Act repeal, it also declared full power and authority over the colonies—a declaration it didn't hesitate to impose.

Supplement to the
Boston News-Letter
September 5, 1765

Stamp Act Riot, Boston
North Wind Picture Archives

JOIN, OR DIE.
Library of Congress

(*above*) Benjamin Franklin's cartoon in the *Pennsylvania Gazette*, May 9, 1754, urged the British North American colonists to join together against the French and the Indians. The symbol and phrase, along with other popular slogans like "Liberty or Death," "Die or Be Free," or "Don't Tread on Me" returned with new meaning—against a new enemy—during the Revolution.

KING GEORGE III, C. 1762–1764
BY ALLAN RAMSAY
The Bridgeman Art Library

(*left*) In 1760, at the age of 22, George III ascended the throne, where he served as King of Great Britain through the entire American Revolution until his death in 1820.

REPORTING THE

SUGAR ACT

By Todd Andrlik

IN 1763, THREE YEARS AFTER GEORGE III ASCENDED THE throne, Great Britain faced several serious economic challenges, including a massive national debt that skyrocketed during the Seven Years' War (1756–1763), known as the French and Indian War in North America. On the other side of the Atlantic Ocean, American colonists rejoiced after fighting alongside the mother country to defeat France. But by spring of 1764, details about new revenue-raising policies affecting colonial trade started arriving from England on packet boats, which carried the latest newspapers, private letters, and official correspondence. Immediately upon receiving word of the taxes, known as the Sugar Act because of its three-penny duty on molasses, Americans began the argument that echoed for centuries: no taxation without representation.

Printed five weeks after Parliament passed the Sugar Act, just long enough for the news' transatlantic journey, the May 10, 1764, edition of the *Pennsylvania Gazette* warned colonists that "a Scheme of Taxation of the American Colonies has for some time been in Agitation: That it had been previously debated in Parliament, whether they had Power to lay such a Tax on Colonies which had no Representatives in Parliament, and determined in the Affirmative."

From the Jamestown settlement in 1607 through 1763, Great Britain maintained an unwritten policy of salutary neglect toward its thirteen American colonies, leaving them to establish their own systems of government and taxation with the expectation that this apathetic attitude would help them flourish. A handful of regulations on colonial trade were introduced during that time, including the Navigation Act (1660) and the Molasses Act (1733), but they were not enforced or were easily evaded by bribery or smuggling.

What Americans found most upsetting about the Sugar Act of 1764 was (1) its plans for strict enforcement, essentially voiding the tranquil era of salutary neglect colonists had enjoyed since the first settlements; (2) the believed illegality of being taxed without having representatives in Parliament; and (3) the strong hint of a forthcoming stamp duty, the first internal tax on activities and transactions within the colony. At the conclusion of the same *Pennsylvania Gazette* article that delivered news of the Sugar Act was the first warning of a stamp tax:

"Besides this, an internal Tax was proposed, a Stamp Duty, &c. but many Members warmly opposing it, this was deferred till next Session; but it was feared that the Tax upon foreign Goods would pass into a Law this Session. That these Colonies are under great Disadvantages, in not having sufficient Interest in Parliament... Only, that Mr. Allen, of this Place, was indefatigable, in remonstrating to many of the Members, with whom he was acquainted, on the Illegality of an internal Tax, and had considerable Influence in preventing it."

By spring of 1764, details about new revenue-raising policies affecting colonial trade started arriving from England. Immediately upon receiving word of the taxes, Americans began the argument that echoed for centuries: no taxation without representation.

It wasn't long after news of the Sugar Act arrived in America that local newspapers began printing public concerns. According to a letter extract in the July 20, 1764, *New Hampshire Gazette*:

> *...the Destruction will be dreadful till their Eyes are open'd.——In Virginia they already feel it, Tobacco at Home, fetches little or nothing, most of their Bills are come back protested, and the Planters have no Money to pay with.——Though every one is convinced of the Unanimity amongst the Colonies, to ward off any Burden that may be intended for us; yet no Steps are taken, and all complain that they see with great Perspicnity, the Destruction that must befal us. I still flatter my self some fortunate Event will change the Face of Things, and relieve us from our Anxiety.*

MAY 10, 1764

The PENNSYLVANIA GAZETTE

PHILADELPHIA, May 10.

On Monday next the GENERAL ASSEMBLY of this Province meets here.

Our other Advices by the Packet are, that a Scheme of Taxation of the American Colonies has for some Time been in Agitation: That it had been previously debated in Parliament, whether they had Power to lay such a Tax on Colonies which had no Representatives in Parliament, and determined in the Affirmative: That on the Ninth of March Mr. ——— made a long Harrangue on the melancholy State of the Nation, overloaded with heavy Taxes, and a Debt of 146 Millions, 52 Millions of which had arisen in the four last Years: That by a Computation, which he laid before the House, 360,000 l. Sterling per Annum was expended on North-America, and therefore it was but reasonable they should support the Troops sent out for their Defence, and all the other particular Expence of the Nation on their Account. To raise this Sum, he proposed that the Drawbacks on Re-exportation of particular Goods should be discontinued: That a Duty should be laid on East-India Goods; a Duty of 7 l. Sterling per Ton on all Wines from Madeira, the Western and Canary Isles; a Duty of 3 d. per Gallon on foreign Melasses, of 10 s. Per Hundred on Sugars; a high Duty on Coffee, Cocoa, &c. and that Rum should be wholly prohibited: That Wines from Spain, Portugal, &c. first landed in England, before sent to America, should have the Duty drawn back. Besides this, an internal Tax was proposed, a Stamp Duty, &c. but many Members warmly opposing it, this was deferred till next Session; but it was feared that the Tax upon foreign Goods would pass into a Law this Session. That these Colonies are under great Disadvantages, in not having sufficient Interest in Parliament; from the Want of which, the West-Indians have been able to carry any Point against them. —— Only, that Mr. Allen, of this Place, was indefatigable, in remonstrating to many of the Members, with whom he was acquainted, on the Illegality of an internal Tax, and had considerable Influence in preventing it.

PENNSYLVANIA GAZETTE (PHILADELPHIA)

May 10, 1764

On page two, a small news report that just arrived in port was published about a "Scheme of Taxation," which included the Sugar Act and a forthcoming stamp duty. Read closely and note the origins of the "no taxation without representation" debate. Newspapers spread dramatic details of mobs, violence, and boycotts in subsequent years, but historians can point to the May 10, 1764, *Pennsylvania Gazette* as one of the printed cornerstones of revolution.

23d, will, we hope, be very pleasing to our Readers.

Two Days ago, Capt. Montour arrived with some of his Party at Johnson-Hall, brought the Scalp, &c. taken some Time since. The Indian scalped, was a Head Warrior, Nephew to the Squash-Cutter, a Chief of the Delawares. Capt. Montour brought with him likewise, a lad named Emanuel Stover, of Rariton, New-Jersey, taken last Year at Wioming, with 6 others, by the Delawares; and a Delaware who went to Johnson-Hall, on the 20th Instant, under some specious Pretences, was, on Discovery of his Villanies, apprehended. The 5 Nations (except those in Pursuit of the Enemy) are returned Home, to be in Readiness for accompanying the Troops.

The Public may confide in the following Report now in Town, viz. That by the Articles of Peace agreed on by the Five Nations, and Sir William Johnson, they are to cede to his Majesty, all the Country from Niagara to above the Great Falls, on both Sides of the River; being a Tract of 15 or 16 Miles in Length, and several in Breadth; very advantageous Concessions, equally interesting to the Public.

PHILADELPHIA, May 10.

On Monday next the GENERAL ASSEMBLY of this Province meets here.

Our other Advices by the Packet are, that a Scheme of Taxation of the American Colonies has for some Time been in Agitation: That it had been previously debated in the Parliament, whether they had Power to lay such a Tax on Colonies which had no Representatives in Parliament, and determined in the Affirmative: That on the Ninth of March Mr. ---------- made a long Harrangue on the melancholy State of the Nation, overloaded with heavy Taxes, and a Debt of 146 Millions, 52 Millions of which had arisen in the four last Years: That by a Computation, which he laid before the House, 360,000 l. Sterling per Annum was expended on North-America, and therefore it was but reasonable they should support the Troops sent out for their Defence, and all the other Expence of the Nation on their Account. To raise this Sum, he proposed that the Drawbacks on Re-exportation of particular Goods should be discontinued: That a Duty should be laid on East-India Goods; a Duty of 7 l. Sterling per Ton on all Wines from Madeira, the Western and Canary Isles; a Duty of 3 d. per Gallon on foreign Melasses, of 10 s. per Hundred on Sugars; a high Duty on Coffee, Cocoa, &c. and that Rum should be wholly prohibited: That Wines from Spain, Portugal, &c. first landed in England, before sent to America, should have the Duty drawn back. Besides this, an internal Tax was proposed, a Stamp Duty, &c. but many Members warmly opposing it, this was deferred till next Session; but it was feared that the Tax upon foreign Goods would pass into a Law this Session. That these Colonies are under great Disadvantages, in not having sufficient Interest in Parliament; from the Want of which, the West-Indians have been able to carry any Point against them.---- Only, that Mr. Allen, of this Place, was indefatigable, in remonstrating to many of the Members, with whom he was acquainted, on the Illegality of an internal Tax, and had considerable Influence in preventing it.

FORT PITT, April 26, 1764.

Extracts from the Examination of GERSHOM HICKS, (a White Man) lately with the Indians, who came in here the 14th Instant as a Spy, taken at several different times.

THAT an English Army was expected by the Indians down the Ohio this Spring. That he left Hockhocking about 30 Days ago, in Company with 7 Delaware Indians, to go to War on the Frontiers. That they came in upon Shearman's Valley, murdered and scalped one James and his Wife, and took two little Boys, their Children, Prisoners. That they came with the Children within a few Miles of this Post, when he was desired to come in here, under Pretence he had made his Escape from the Indians, and to enquire into the Strength of the Fort, Ammunition, Provisions, &c. what Guards were out each Day, and to return to them in two Nights; and that if he met with any Indians, not to let them know any thing till he got to King Beaver. That the Night they came here a Party of 8 Shawanese came to their Sleeping Place, and had two Scalps, which they

... Day of February of this Year; commanding me likewise, that, with all possible Dispatch, I should proceed on my Voyage, which I could not do so soon as I desired, for various Disappointments which happened. I arrived at Campechy the 7th Instant, and having taken Possession the 24th, I was informed of your Arrival at Balis in the Month of April, also five Vessels, and that immediately the People were dispersed as far as Rio Hondo, practising from that Time the cutting of Logwood, by Virtue of the Treaty of Peace. You did not present the Royal Schedule that my Sovereign expedited for this End, nor the Licence of the King of England for the aforesaid Effect.

This being granted, I am obliged by the King my Lord, in his Royal Confidence of the Government of this Province, and to comply entirely with the said 17th Article of the Definitive Treaty of Peace, as I said before, to dispatch the Commandant of the Fort of Bacalar, Don Joseph Rosado, with this, requiring you, that in Consideration of the Want of Instruments for your Introduction, and having extended yourselves, gathering Fruits as in your own Country, without waiting to settle the Limits with the necessary Solemnity that should have secured your Establishment, you will be pleased, with all speed, to give the necessary Advice to all your Community that are in Rio Hondo, to retire to Balis, and I expect you will present me with the Royal Schedule, that the King my Master dispatched to this End, or with Orders from the King of Great-Britain for this Effect; and there is no Doubt but I shall then attend to it with that Care and Equity I am commanded, issuing for that Purpose the necessary Orders to all the Commandants, Cabos, Military and Justiciary of all the Districts in their Jurisdiction, by which Means the Suspicion of the fatal Consequences will cease, which will be inevitable if such Conduct is continued, sufficient to destroy the good Harmony between the two Nations, and happy Tranquility that we enjoy; if the Remedy is not occurred to in time, and our Sovereigns will manifestly see how we interest ourselves, that their just and laudable Intentions take Effect, for which I am so ready on my Part, as is manifest by my Toleration, that you and all your Nation remain at Balis, and I promise myself the same on your Parts, protesting always, that for the Result of what may happen by such irregular Introduction and Excess of cutting Logwood, those who commit, or do not remedy, them, will be responsible after all. I hope you will favour me with an Answer by hand of the said Commandant of Bacalar, and other Commands most to your Satisfaction, to manifest to you the Desire I have to serve you. God guard you many Years, as he can, and I desire.

Your most humble Servant kisses your Hands,

PHILIPE REMIRES DE ESTINOS.

Merida in Jucatan, 29th December, 1763.

Sir DON JOSEPH MAUD.

DON JOSEPH ROSADO, Lieutenant of Infantry in the Battalion of Castilia, and Commandant of this Garrison and royal Fort of St. Philip, of Bacalar, and its Jurisdiction.

NOtwithstanding that the Serjeant Dionisius Chavaria, who is detatched to the Look-Out of St. Anthony, has the necessary Orders, that the English Logwood-Cutters of Rio Hondo, do retreat to Balis, without permitting them to make any Demur, because that since the 4th Instant, when the Order of the Governor and Captain General, was by me intimated to them, they have had competent Time to evacuate the River, carrying away the Utensils of their Houses: I order and command the said Serjeant, that he receive 11 Soldiers of this Garrison, well armed, which, with 4 there before, compleats the Number of 15, to remain at the said Look-Out; that with them he is not to permit any English Vessel, under any Pretext, to enter the Mouth of this River; on the Contrary, if any Flats remain in the River, they are to go out, with the Utensils of their Houses, with so much Brevity, as not to permit them to stop any where, but retire totally; as likewise those from the New-River, because in the Order intimated to them, it is expressed, that the Retreat shall be to Balis, and no other Part; and to act on the Contrary, they expose themselves to evident Danger, as by their Disobedience they lose their Negroes, and find themselves under a violent Arrest. This Order he shall manifest to as many as are not yet gone

ting Logw
ven to the
tain thems
nation of
of Vessels,
Danger of
Cargoes to
driven from
and that th
immediate
the Miserie
of the Spa
sent to you
for settling
to a State o
Method to
prehend, th
long to subs

Your Pet
will be plea
Circumstan
your Petitio

Since our
under Sente
House, for
hid under G
carried Mr.
found---The
turday next,

CUST

Sloop Fr
Branch, J.
W. Hazelto
and Snow F
dington, M
guilla. Brig
ten, Grenad
Schooner Do
ner, Nantuc
Brig Grape,

OUTWARD
er Phœnix,
Chancellor,

CLEARED
Ranger, J.
ca. Schoon
Willing-Mai
Virginia. S
E. Todd, St
Carolina. B
Allen, Lisbo

WHE
fell
due, and pre
Greenway d
and Land wi
to purchase,
JOHN EDWA

This Hous
Tavern, situa
delphia, is a
it is built of S
Acres of Lan
Woodland.

TO be so
on Tu
Brick House,
Ground, cont
with a good O
between Seco
Christopher A
and rents for

NEW YORK, July 9.

One of the Sloops that was carried into Cape Francois, in Company with Capt. Claxton, by a French Man of War, as mentioned under the Philadelphia Head, arrived here last Monday, and confirms the Account he brought; but we are since credibly informed, That an English Frigate, having Occasion to call at Turks Island, and observing the French erecting some Works there, ordered them to desist; but they not chusing to comply, the English Commander landed Part of his Crew, killed 28 Frenchmen, and took several Prisoners.

Tuesday last the Rev'd Mr. WHITEFIELD set out for the Southward, but the Day following his Servant, having drank some CYDER, and the Weather being very warm, he went into the Water at Mr. Watson's Ferry, to cool himself, and was soon after found drowned in not more than two feet of Water. This Misfortune, and the Heat of the Weather, obliged Mr. Whitefield to return to Long Island.

NEWPORT, July 2.

We hear from Providence, that Doctor Philip Bourne, of that Place, put an End to his Life, a few Days since, by a Dose of Poison.

July 9. The Sloop Elizabeth, Capt. Gardner, arrived here last Tuesday from the Coast of Africa, in 55 Days, with a Cargo of Slaves. Before he sailed, a Boat belonging to Capt. Remmington, of this Port, with a Mate and three Men on board, was overset in going into a River to the Windward of Cape Mount, by which Accident the 3 Men were drowned; but the Mate happily saved himself by swiming.

Capt. Elliot, of this Port, sailed before Captain Gardner with 160 Slaves, for the West Indies.

PROVIDENCE, July 7.

A Gentleman in a neighbouring Province, writing his Correspondent in this Town on the Scourges we are to suffer (by the late Act of Parliament) from our Mother Country, in Recompence for that Loyalty and Obedience for which this Country is so eminently destinguished, says, "Jealousy, that Bane of Society, has been the Cause of passing these Laws at Home; which will so embarrass Trade, that they will be under a Necessity to repeal what they have done in few Years, but the Destruction will be dreadful till their Eyes are open'd.——In Virginia they already feel it, Tobacco at Home, fetches little or nothing, most of their Bills are come back protested, and the Planters have no Money to pay with.——Though every one is convinced of the Unanimity amongst the Colonies, to ward off any Burden that may be intended for us; yet no Steps are taken, and all complain, that they see with great Perspicuity, the Destruction that must befal us. I still flatter myself some fortunate Event will change the Face of Things, and relieve us from our Anxiety."

came out in Company with Capt. *Mallard*, in a Mast Ship, bound to this Place; who sprung a Leak a few Days after they came away, and was obliged to put back. There was several Passengers on Board, who we hear are come in Capt. *Jarvis*.

Last Friday arrived here Capt. *Benjamin Torry*, from Fyall, having had 76 Days Passage. He spoke with Capt. *White* of Boston, off the Western Islands; who had been out five Weeks from Jamaica, bound for London; all well.

WANTED (for finishing the STATE HOUSE) a Quantity of clear Boards Laths and Lime. Likewise Joyners, Painters and Masons will be wanted immediately to compleat the Same: Any Persons inclining to furnish any or all said Materials, as well those who incline to undertake the Joyner's, Painter's, or Mason's Work; are desired to send in their Names, and lowest they will do it for, next Wednesday to the Committee appointed to get the same done, who will attend on said Day at the Sign of the King's Arms; all are desired to take Notice in making their Calculations, that nothing but the Money, will be paid them, on the Completion of any of their Agreements.

Portsmouth July 19th By Order of the Committee

MARK HUNKING WENTWORTH, *Chairman*.

Richard Champney,

NOTIFIES his Customers and others, That he has Remov'd to his Shop near Mr. *Beck's* Hatter's Shop; where he continues to Sell at the lowest Cash Price, (for Cash only) Choice Green Coffee, by the Hundred, or Quarter, Bohea Tea, Best French Indigo, and Genuine Kippen's Snuff, per Dozen or Retail, Pepper, Allspice, Nutmegs, Raisons, Loaf and Brown Sugar, Table Oyl, per Jarr or Bottle, Chesheire Cheese and Cotton Wool—— His Customers may be supply'd with all sorts of Tin Ware as usual at said Shop.

Said Champney wants a good smart LAD that inclines to learn the Tin Plate Workers Business.

TO BE SOLD

By HENRY NAGLEE,

Near Spring Hill, at Mr. JOSEPH ALCOCK's *Store, Cheap for* CASH,

PORK, Rice, Tar, Pitch, and Turpentine.

---

an half, in the house of Mr. Blackmore one
said Messengers; when after a trial of seve
his Lordship summed up the evidence in a
charge, and then the Jury went out, who
staying about three quarters of an hour, bro
their verdict against the defendants for *one t*
pounds damages. Upon the determination
Jury, there was an universal shout from a c
rable number of spectators. The council f
defendants were, the Attorney and Sollicitor
ral, Mr. Serjeants Davey and Naires, ar
Wallis; and for the plantiff, Mr. Serjeant Gl
Recorder of London, Mr. Stow, Mr. Dunni
Mr. Gardner.

At a late meeting at Newmarket, a gen
of great fortune, in one day lost ten thousan
neas; in two days more, this sum was treb
on the fourth he judiciously set out for town,
ving to tempt his stars no further for that ti
they wore so unfavourable an aspect.

We hear that a noble Personage won last
at Newmarket, no less than 40,000 l.

The spirit of gaming is now so prevalent a
the lower class of people, that a butcher in
market lost 1000l. last week at Newmar

Last week a horse was sold in Smithfi
weight at four pence per pound; the buye
seller differing on the price, they agreed
method of selling. It is said the buyer got
good bargain, as of all animals a horse is re
the lightest as to his size.

It is said above 12,000l. were depen
bets last Saturday, at Newmarket, betwe
Duke of Ancasters colt, and Lord Boling
colt, which was won by the former, and
knowing Gentlemen of the Turf were dee
ken in.

A giant, 14 feet high (who was the same
at nine years old) arrived the 14th ult. at D
from Trent, to make a shew of himself.

It has been reported, that on Thursday
————Ambassador presented a mem
our court concerning the fisheries, on whi
count the stocks fell 2 per cent.

The Order of the Bath, lately given to
Clive, was promised to Col. Draper who
his claim to accommodate his Lordship, as
add to his respect and influence with the N
Bengal.

On a gentleman's applying to Lord Cli
commission for his son, he made answer, th
had been able to give commissions to all t
applied to him, he should have had a suffic
my of officers, without needing one private

Gen. Leighton's regiment has a fine set o
scoth girls along with them; which, con
their polific nature, will, it is hoped, be an
tage in peopling our West-India colonies.

NEW-HAMPSHIRE GAZETTE (PORTSMOUTH)

July 20, 1764

Private letters were one of the top sources of colonial news and were not always very private. It was normal for a letter to be opened and read along the delivery route or to find its way to the local print shop. In this case, the extract of a gentleman's letter about the economic stresses made worse by the Sugar Act first appeared in the July 7 *Providence Gazette* (Rhode Island). As that issue circulated among the colonies, other printers published the paragraph in their newspapers like Daniel Fowle did on page three of his *New-Hampshire Gazette*.

LONDON CHRONICLE

December 6, 1764

By late 1764, Great Britain received news of America's "uneasiness" about the Sugar Act and fears of the forthcoming Stamp Act. Here, it is being communicated that the idea of being taxed internally without representation in Parliament is alarming. Less than a year later, after the Stamp Act is passed in Parliament, alarm turns to rage.

Boston, (*New England*, *Oct.* 5.

THE Members of the House of

must be supposed to determine always with wisdom and integrity, thought fit further to prorogue the Assembly to the 10th of this month.

The late act of parliament (possibly for want of a thorough understanding of it) gives some uneasiness to the people of this province, and it is said of the northern colonies in general; and the fears of being taxed, internally, by the parliament, while we have no representation on the spot, are alarming to men of the greatest penetration and judgment among us: If the jealousies and fears of the people are groundless, who can so effectually remove them, as the General Assembly, in whom, while in solemn session, the wisdom of the whole is presumed to be collected: On the other hand, if those at home, whose intentions are always upright, yet whose wisdom, being human, is not infallible, have in any respect mistaken the rights of the American subjects, and the true interest both of the colonies and the mother country, what is to be done? By no means to resist the authority of the supreme power of the nation, but humbly to remonstrate our rights and privileges: And who can do this with so much propriety, as the General Assembly? As the colonies, with regard to these matters at least, are alike affected, it is prudent for them to acquaint each other with the measures they may take: The parliament, it is said, will meet in November next, or December at farthest: Considering then, the distance of the colonies from Great Britain, the great importance of the business we have to do; and the shortness of the time prudently to effect it, even from the 5th of September, we cannot but regret, that there should be any necessity for a farther prorogation.

Boston, Oct. 7. The Surveyor-General has

Island of Cape-Breton.

Capt. Hedge, who sailed from this port yesterday se'nnight in a sloop laden with corn

Falmouth, Dec. 1. Arrived the Peggy, from Guernsey; Polly, and John and Francis, from

Lloyd, Carbery, from Newfoundland, at Malaga.

Ann Gally, Smith, from Newfoundland, at Leghorn.

Cork Packet, Evans, from Bristol, at Cork.

Sarah Ann, Clark, from Bristol, at Waterford.

Polly, Evans, from Malaga; and Forbes, Burton, from Petersburgh, at Bristol.

Prince William, Graystock, from Rotterdam, in the River.

Lovely, Scheverick; and Polly, Fagg, from New-York; and Susannah, Lockhart, from Philadelphia, at Quebec.

Banker, Kerley, from Newfoundland, at Poole.

London Packet, Califf; Hawke, Coffin; Deep Bay, Dashwood, from London; John and Sukey, Bruce, in 26 days from Land's End; and St. George, Mallard, from London and Lisbon, at Boston.

L O N D O N.

We are informed that no money will be borrowed for the service of the ensuing year.

The Account of the Capitals at the Bank, South Sea, and India Houses, November 24, 1764.

Bank Stock, ——	£. 10,780,000
4 per Cent. Consol. Ann.	20,240,000
4 per Cent. 1763, ——	3,500,000
4 per Cent. Navy, ——	3,500,000
3 one half per Cent. 1756,	1,500,000
3 one half per Cent. 1758,	4,500,000
3 per Cent. Consol, ——	33,627,821
3 per Cent. Reduced, —	17,701,323
3 per Cent. 1726, ——	1,000,100
South Sea Stock, — —	3,662,784
3 per Cent. Old Annuities,	12,404,270
3 per Cent. New, — —	8,958,255
3 per Cent. 1751, ——	2,100,000
Total,	£. 129,674,553

to the Chancery in the palace.

The English factors who reside i their correspondents here r in their letters relati ecause they were all o

ch ship, Peter Klasen, nd to Hamburg, is lost crew were saved. ports of the sailing of oned merely by orders fresh supply of ships on, which is done every articles propagated of seem calculated to serve

y the two Chief Justice s, &c. will be elegantl nsion-house, by the Ri yor, as they could not ast Friday, it being the yal Highness the Princess Wales.

The elegant cartoons, which down some time ago in the saloon i palace, to hang that room with a mask of English manufacture, are be replaced in the same apartment.

Dr. Spry, who is appointed J Court of Admiralty for the Nor district, arrived with his family a Nova Scotia, on the 23d of Septem

On Monday last the Marquis of in town from Scotland.

His Majesty has appointed Rich. den, Gent. to be Adjutant to the ment of Dragoons, in the room Knigge, who has resigned.

Thomas Sandby, Esq; is appoir to his Royal Highness the Duke land, in the room of Mr. Ford, de

Last Saturday was married a Shropshire, the Hon. Capt. Georg Miss Clive, sister to Lord Clive; young lady with a handsome fortu

Yesterday died at her house in Piccadilly, Mrs Clevland, widow Secretary Clevland, belonging miralty.

On Tuesday evening died, Mr wholesale linen-draper in Cheapsid

On Monday last came on befo Mansfield and a special jury, in th King's Bench, Guildhall, a cause foreign sailor was plaintiff, and the East-India ship defendant. The brought for the non-payment or about twenty thousand rupees, or upwards of 2000l. which the plain had been delivered, while the shi voyage from the East Indies, to th and which he denied to have rec

some time, brought in a verdict for for the value of the above amount

Yesterday morning as a countr

REPORTING THE

STAMP ACT

By Todd Andrlik

On March 22, 1765, the Stamp Act received royal assent with its fifty-five resolutions to go into effect on November 1. For the first time in 150 years of existence, Americans were going to be taxed on internal business, not external trade. Printers were to be among the hardest hit by the Stamp Act, but the effects would be felt by all colonists as it required government-issued stamps "upon every skin or piece of vellum or parchment, or sheet or piece of paper," including deeds, wills, newspapers, pamphlets, court judgments, liquor retail licenses, playing cards, etc. Among the first American newspapers to publish the Stamp Act in full was the April 18,1765, *Pennsylvania Gazette*, the same newspaper that Benjamin Franklin printed until 1748 and that continued to bear his name as printer until a partnership deal expired in 1766.

By the fall of 1765, uneasiness over the Stamp Act's internal taxes had escalated to outrage.

News of the Stamp Act spread quickly and was carried to Williamsburg, Virginia, while the House of Burgesses was still in session. The shock quickly changed the assembly's agenda as they soon found themselves debating several resolutions against the Stamp Act. Newly elected Patrick Henry delivered a passionate speech to inspire passage of more radical resolves. Despite Henry's best efforts, conservative representatives were able to successfully strike two radical resolutions from official record; however, the controversial resolves leaked to the press and were printed throughout the colonies and Great Britain, as seen in the October 17, 1765, *London Chronicle*, still making the statement Henry wanted.

By the fall of 1765, uneasiness over the Stamp Act's internal taxes escalated to outrage, as demonstrated in Boston on the morning of August 14, 1765, when two effigies were hung from a great elm tree, later called Liberty Tree, at the southern neck of town connecting Boston's 15,000 residents to the farms of Suffolk County and beyond. One effigy represented the commissioned stamp distributor Andrew Oliver and the other a green-soled "jackboot with a head and horns peeping out of the top" (*London Chronicle*, October 10, 1765) to mock George Grenville and Earl of Bute, John Stuart, whom the colonists labeled as the primary architects of the hated act.

At dusk, the effigies were lowered from the tree and paraded through town by a "great concourse of people, some of the highest reputation, and in the greatest order" until they stopped at stamp distributor Andrew Oliver's newly built stamp office on Kilby Street, not far from Long Wharf in Boston Harbor, and demolished the building. Afterward, the crowd continued to Oliver's home, where they burned his effigy and proceeded to destroy his barn, fence, garden, and, ultimately, his home. The goal was to intimidate Oliver and pressure his resignation, which it did. Oliver, who had fled his home, resigned the next day and avoided what was reported in the *London Chronicle* (October 10) as a planned second night of mob attacks against his property.

Less than two weeks later, on August 26, 1765, mobs attacked the homes of more crown-appointed officials, including Admiralty Court Deputy Register William Story, Customs Comptroller Benjamin Hallowell, and Lieutenant Governor Thomas Hutchinson. According to Massachusetts Royal Governor Francis Bernard's proclamation of August 28, reprinted in the October 19 *London Chronicle*, Hutchinson's home was left "a mere shell from top to bottom," with massive destruction to the wainscot, furniture, apparel, jewels, book, and papers, and £900 stolen from the home. Bernard's proclamation also served as a wanted poster, offering £300 for mob leaders and £100 for participants.

The intimidation of crown-appointed officials produced the result Bostonians craved. The resignation of the local stamp officer meant no one could distribute stamped paper, thereby avoiding enforcement of the Stamp Act, so businesses could proceed as usual without taxation. News of the effective revolt spread like wildfire throughout the thirteen colonies and became the tactic of choice up and down the continent with similar forced resignations taking place in Annapolis, Newport, Providence, New York, Albany, New Haven, Philadelphia, Portsmouth, Charleston, and Savannah. The Newport riot and resignation of August 27–29 is reported in detail on the back page of the *Supplement to the Boston News-Letter* on September 5, 1765, and presumably provided Bostonians with encouragement that the terror campaign they launched to help fight the Stamp Act was indeed catching on (coincidentally, a lengthy account of the August 26 attack on Story's, Hallowell's, and Hutchinson's homes in Boston was published on the front page). The episodes of Jared Ingersoll and Henry Van Schaick, appointed stamp distributors for New Haven and Albany, respectively, are well documented in the January 23, 1766, *Pennsylvania Journal.*

In October 1765, a congress of delegates from nine colonies convened in New York to author and adopt a Declaration of Resolves and Grievances; among them it was stated that Parliament could not tax the American colonies without representation.

Throughout the winter months of 1765–66, the Sons of Liberty, a term applied to both organized opposition groups as well as a generic label for any stamp tax opponent, were successful in opening correspondence channels and aligning colonial interests (see Savannah dateline in January 27, 1766, *Supplement to the Boston Gazette* containing reports originally from the *Georgia Gazette*). Using news-swapping techniques they perfected during the French and Indian War, colonial printers, among the hardest hit by the stamp duty, repurposed patriotic reports from other colonies and used their newspapers as the vehicle to lead and uphold the resistance (see Annapolis dateline in March 20, 1766, *Pennsylvania Gazette*, which was originally printed in the *Maryland Gazette* on March 6).

Beyond effigies and acts of intimidation, colonial leaders also collaborated on a joint boycott of British imports, which added financial stress to English merchants and effectively recruited them to lobby Parliament in favor of the act's repeal (see January 27 and February 17, 1766, *Boston Gazette*).

Burning of Stamp Act, Boston
Library of Congress

News of the Boston riots spread like wildfire throughout the colonies and became the tactic of choice up and down the continent.

April 18, 1765. NUMB. 1895.

The PENNSYLVANIA GAZETTE.

Containing the Freshest Advices, Foreign and Domestic.

By Captain CALEF, arrived at Boston, in a short Passage from London, we have the following Advices, viz.

EXTRACT from the VOTES of the HOUSE OF COMMONS of GREAT-BRITAIN, in Parliament assembled. Jovis, 7 Die Februarii, 1765.

MR. HUNTER (according to order) reported from the committee of the whole house, to whom it was referred to consider further of ways and means for raising the supply granted to his Majesty, the resolutions which the committee had directed him to report to the house; which he read in his place, and afterwards delivered in at the table, where the same were read, and agreed to by the house, and are as followeth, viz.

Resolved, That a stamp duty of 3 d. sterling money, be charged upon every skin or piece of vellum or parchment, or sheet or piece of paper, on which shall be ingrossed, written or printed, any declaration, plea, replication, rejoinder, demurrer, or other pleading, or any copy thereof in any court of law, within the British colonies and plantations in America.

Resolved, That a stamp duty of 2 s. sterling money, be charged upon every skin or piece of vellum or parchment, or sheet or piece of paper, on which shall be ingrossed, written or printed, any special bail, and appearance upon such bail, in any such court.

Resolved, That a stamp duty of 1 s. 6 d. sterling money, be charged upon every skin or piece of vellum or parchment, or sheet or piece of paper, on which shall be ingrossed, written or printed, any petition, bill, answer, claim, plea, replication, rejoinder, demurrer, or other pleading, in any court of chancery, or equity, within the said colonies and plantations.

Resolved, That a stamp duty of 3 d. sterling money, be charged upon every skin, or piece of vellum or parchment, or sheet or piece of paper, on which shall be ingrossed, written or printed, any copy of any petition, bill, answer, claim, plea, replication, rejoinder, demurrer, or other pleading, in any such court.

Resolved, That a stamp duty of 1 s. sterling money, be charged upon every skin or piece of vellum or parchment, or sheet or piece of paper, on which shall be ingrossed, written or printed, any monition, libel, answer, allegation, inventory, or renunciation in ecclesiastical matters, in any court of probate, court of ordinary, or other court, exercising ecclesiastical jurisdiction within the said colonies and plantations.

Resolved, That a stamp duty of 6 d. sterling money, be charged upon every skin or piece of vellum or parchment, or sheet or piece of paper, on which shall be ingrossed, written or printed, any copy of any will, other than the probate thereof, monition, libel, answer, allegation, inventory, or renunciation in ecclesiastical matters, in any such court.

Resolved, That a stamp duty of 2 l. sterling money, be charged upon every skin or piece of vellum or parchment, or sheet or piece of paper, on which shall be ingrossed, written or printed, any donation, presentation, collation, or institution, of or to any benefice, or any writ or instrument for the like purpose, or any register, entry, testimonial, or certificate, of any degree taken in any university, academy, college, or seminary of learning, within the said colonies and plantations.

Resolved, That a stamp duty of 1 s. sterling money, be charged upon every skin or piece of vellum or parchment, or sheet or piece of paper, on which shall be ingrossed, written or printed, any monition, libel, claim, answer, allegation, information, letter of request, execution, renunciation, inventory, or other pleading, in any admiralty court, within the said colonies and plantations.

Resolved, That a stamp duty of 6 d. sterling money, be charged upon every skin or piece of vellum or parchment, or sheet or piece of paper, on which any copy of any such monition, libel, claim, answer, allegation, information, letter of request, execution, renunciation, inventory, or other pleading, shall be ingrossed, written or printed.

Resolved, That a stamp duty of 10 s. sterling money, be charged upon every skin or piece of vellum or parchment, or sheet or piece of paper, on which shall be ingrossed, written or printed, any appeal, writ of error, writ of dower, ad quod damnum, cer-

Resolved, That a stamp duty of 20 s. sterling money, be charged upon every skin or piece of vellum or parchment, or sheet or piece of paper, on which shall be ingrossed, written or printed, letters of mart, or commission for private ships of war, within the said colonies and plantations.

Resolved, That a stamp duty of 10 s. sterling money, be charged upon every skin or piece of vellum or parchment, or sheet or piece of paper, on which shall be ingrossed, written or printed, any grant, appointment, or admission, of or to any public beneficial office or employment, for the space of one year, or any lesser time, of or above the value of 20 l. per annum, sterling money, in salary, fees, and perquisites, within the said colonies and plantations, except commissions of officers of the army, navy, ordnance, or militia, and of justices of the peace.

Resolved, That a stamp duty of 6 l. sterling money, be charged upon every skin or piece of vellum or parchment, or sheet or piece of paper, on which any grant of any liberty, privilege, or franchise, under the seal of any of the said colonies or plantations, or under the seal or sign manual of any governor, proprietor, or public officer, alone, or in conjunction with any other person or persons, or with any council, or any council and assembly, or any exemplification of the same, shall be ingrossed, written or printed, within the said colonies and plantations.

Resolved, That a stamp duty of 20 s. sterling money, be charged upon every skin or piece of vellum or parchment, or sheet or piece of paper, on which shall be ingrossed, written or printed, any licence for retailing of spirituous liquors, to be granted to any person who shall take out the same, within the said colonies and plantations.

Resolved, That a stamp duty of 4 l. sterling money, be charged upon every skin or piece of vellum or parchment, or sheet or piece of paper, on which shall be ingrossed, written or printed, any licence for retailing of wine, to be granted to any person who shall not take out a licence for retailing of spirituous liquors, within the said colonies and plantations.

Resolved, That a stamp duty of 3 l. sterling money, be charged upon every skin or piece of vellum or parchment, or sheet or piece of paper, on which shall be ingrossed, written or printed, any licence for retailing of wine, to be granted to any person who shall take out a licence for retailing of spirituous liquors, within the said colonies and plantations.

Resolved, That a stamp duty of 5 s. sterling money, be charged upon every skin or piece of vellum or parchment, or sheet or piece of paper, on which shall be ingrossed, written or printed, any probate of a will, letters of administration, or of guardianship for any estate, above the value of 20 l. of the same money within the British colonies and plantations upon the continent of America, the islands belonging thereto, and the Bermuda and Bahama islands, except probates of wills, and letters of administration to the effects of commom seamen or soldiers, who shall die in the public service.

Resolved, That a stamp duty of 10 s. sterling money, be charged upon every skin or piece of vellum or parchment, or sheet or piece of paper, on which shall be ingrossed, written or printed, any such probate, letters of administration, or of guardianship, within all other parts of the British dominions in America.

Resolved, That a stamp duty of 6 d. sterling money, be charged upon every skin or piece of vellum or parchment, or sheet or piece of paper, on which shall be ingrossed, written or printed, any bond, for securing the payment of any sum of money, not exceeding the sum of 10 l. of the same money, within the British colonies and plantations upon the continent of America, the islands belonging thereto, and the Bermuda and Bahama islands.

Resolved, That a stamp duty of 1 s. sterling money, be charged upon every skin or piece of vellum or parchment, or sheet or piece of paper, on which shall be ingrossed, written or printed, any bond for securing the payment of any sum of money above 10 l. and not exceeding the sum of 20 l. of the same money, within such colonies, plantations, and islands.

Resolved, That a stamp duty of 1 s. 6 d. sterling money, be charged upon every skin or piece of vellum or parchment, or sheet or piece of paper, on which shall be ingrossed, written or printed,

charged upon every skin or piece of vellum or parchment, or sheet or piece of paper, on which shall be ingrossed, written or printed, any such original grant, or any such deed, mesne conveyance, or other instrument whatsoever, by which any quantity of land above 200, and not exceeding 320 acres, shall be granted, conveyed or assigned, and in proportion for every such grant, deed, mesne conveyance, or other instrument, granting, conveying or assigning every other 320 acres, within such colonies, plantations, and islands.

Resolved, That a stamp duty of 3 s. sterling money, be charged upon every skin or piece of vellum or parchment, or sheet or piece of paper, on which shall be ingrossed, written or printed, any such original grant, or any such deed, mesne conveyance, or other instrument whatsoever, by which any quantity of land not exceeding 100 acres, shall be granted, conveyed or assigned, within all other parts of the British dominions in America.

Resolved, That a stamp duty of 4 s. sterling money, be charged upon every skin or piece of vellum or parchment, or sheet or piece of paper, on which shall be ingrossed, written or printed, any such original grant, or any such deed, mesne conveyance, or other instrument whatsoever, by which any quantity of land above 100, and not exceeding 200 acres, shall be granted, conveyed or assigned, within the same parts of the said dominions.

Resolved, That a stamp duty of 5 s. sterling money, be charged upon every skin or piece of vellum or parchment, or sheet or piece of paper, on which shall be ingrossed, written or printed, any such original grant, or any such deed, mesne conveyance, or other instrument whatsoever, whereby any quantity of land above 200, and not exceeding 320 acres, shall be granted, conveyed or assigned, and in proportion for every such grant, deed, mesne conveyance, or other instrument, granting, conveying or assigning every other 320 acres, within the same parts of the said dominions.

Resolved, That a stamp duty of 4 l. sterling money, be charged upon every skin or piece of vellum or parchment, or sheet or piece of paper, on which shall be ingrossed, written or printed, any grant, appointment or admission, of or to any public beneficial office or employment, not before mentioned to be charged, above the value of 20 l. per annum sterling money, in salary, fees and perquisites, or any exemplification of the same, within the British colonies and plantations upon the continent of America, the islands belonging thereto, and the Bermuda and Bahama islands, except commissions of officers of the army, navy, ordnance, or militia, and of justices of the peace.

Resolved, That a stamp duty of 6 l. sterling money, be charged upon every skin or piece of vellum or parchment, or sheet or piece of paper, on which shall be ingrossed, written or printed, any such grant, appointment, or admission, of or to any such public beneficial office or employment, or any exemplification of the same, within all other parts of the British dominions in America.

Resolved, That a stamp duty of 2 s. 6 d. sterling money, be charged upon every skin or piece of vellum or parchment, or sheet or piece of paper, on which shall be ingrossed, written or printed, any indenture, lease, conveyance, contract, stipulation, bill of sale, charter party, protest, articles of apprenticeship, or covenant (except for the hire of servants not apprentices; and also except such other matters as are before mentioned to be charged) within the British colonies and plantations in America.

Resolved, That a stamp duty of 5 s. sterling money, be charged upon every skin or piece of vellum or parchment, or sheet or piece of paper, on which any warrant or order for auditing any public accounts, beneficial warrant, order, grant or certificate, under any public seal, or under the seal or sign manual of any governor, proprietor, or public officer, alone, or in conjunction with any other person or persons, or with any council, or any council and assembly, not before mentioned to be charged, or any pass-port, or let-pass, surrender of office, or policy of assurance, shall be ingrossed, written or printed, within the said colonies and plantations, except warrants or orders for the service of the navy, army, ordnance, or militia, and grants of offices under 20 l. per annum, in salary, fees and perquisites.

Resolved, That a stamp duty of 2 s. 3 d. sterling money, be charged upon every skin or piece of vellum or parchment, or sheet or piece of paper, on which shall be ingrossed, written, or printed, any notarial act, bond, deed, letter of attorney, procuration, ſtrument in Writing, bearing Date the 28th Day of June 17[illegible] the Conſideration of £115 Pennſylvania Money, bargained and ſold the Subſcriber, a Tract of Land in Shrewſbury Townſhip, in York County, of which Conſideration there remains £65 to be paid in Gales of £15 per Annum, for which Bonds have been executed. And whereas it appears that the ſaid Gilleſpie, or any other Perſon (ſave the Hon. Proprietaries) had no Right, Title or Property, in the ſaid Tract of Land at the Time aforeſaid; I do therefore give this public Notice, that I will not pay any Part of the ſaid Bonds, and ſhall take legal Steps to recover the Sum advanced.

ARCHIBALD PURDY.

TO be ſold by public Vendue, at the London Coffee-Houſe, at 7 o' Clock in the Evening of Saturday, the 27th Day of April inſtant, a 3 Story Brick Houſe, with a 2 Story Brick Kitchen, and Lot of Ground, on the Eaſt-ſide of Second-ſtreet, a little above Market-ſtreet; bounded on the North and Eaſt by Ground of William Whitebread; on the South by John Head; and on the Weſt by Second-ſtreet. The Lot is 14 Feet front, by 103 Feet deep, with the Privilege of a 3 Feet Alley, from Second-ſtreet to the back End of the Lot. The Houſe is 14 Feet front by 40 deep; the Diſtance between the Houſe and Kitchen 10 Feet, with convenient Stair Ways from the Cellar to the ſecond Stories of the Houſe and Kitchen, all incloſed. The Kitchen is 20 Feet deep, which makes the whole Building 70 Feet deep, with convenient Cellars under the whole, there being an Arch under the Yard the Breadth of the Kitchen Cellar from that to the Houſe Cellar. The Houſe is well contrived and finiſhed for Shop-keeping, for which Buſineſs it is well ſituated. There is alſo a Pump near the back Door, belonging to that and the next Houſe. The Title is good, and clear of any Incumbrance, but a proportionable Part of One Shilling Sterling Quitrent on that and other Ground joining. Any Perſon inclining to view the Premiſes before the Day of Sale, may be further informed, by applying to

JOHN OR ROBERT ELTON.

TO be ſold at public Vendue, at Dover, in Kent County, upon Delaware, on Wedneſday, the 15th of May next, the following Tracts of Land, lately belonging to James Gorrell, of ſaid County, viz. One Tract of Land, containing about 90 Acres of Up-land, and 41 Acres of Marſh, being the Plantation the ſaid Gorrell now lives on, upon Jones's Creek, on which there is a good Dwelling-houſe, four Rooms on a Floor, a Store-houſe and Wharff, being a convenient Situation for a Store. One other Tract of Land, containing about 280 Acres, within Half a Mile of the above mentioned Plantation, about 100 Acres cleared, the reſt Wood-land, well timbered and watered. One other Tract of Land, containing about 125 Acres, ſituate in the Forreſt of Murtherkill Hundred, in ſaid County, diſtant 9 Miles from Dover, on which there is a Log-houſe, about 10 Acres cleared, and Half of ſaid Land may be made good Meadow, being very rich Swamp. Alſo two Thirds of one other Tract of Land, near adjoining the laſt mentioned, containing 103 Acres in the whole, on which there are two Log-houſes, about 40 Acres cleared, and ſome rich Swamp on it. Six Months Credit to be given the Purchaſers, without Intereſt, giving good Security, if required. The Titles to all the above Tracts of Land are indiſputable. Any Perſons inclining to purchaſe before the Day of Sale, may be further informed, by applying to WILLIAM KILLEN, Eſq; in Dover, or to SAMUEL PURVIANCE, JOHN SHEE, and JOHN WIKOFF, in Philadelphia, Aſſignees to ſaid Gorrell.

two Story Brick [illegible] Alley, next Door to Mr. Barnaby Barnes; they are in good Order, and compleatly finiſhed, free from Ground-rent.

RUN away from the Subſcriber, living in Weſt Nantmill Cheſter County, on the 25th of February, an Iriſh Servant Lad, named John Conner, about 19 or 20 Years of Age, 5 Feet and ſome Inches high, of a freſh Complexion, has ordinary ſhort blackiſh Hair, has a down Look, a cripling ordinary Walker, and the fore Finger of his Right Hand ſo crooked, that it ſtands almoſt ſquare, and is apt to get drunk; had on, when he went away, a whitiſh ſhort Frock Coat, almoſt new, lined with ſtriped Lincey, with flat white Metal Buttons; alſo a greyiſh Jacket, the Back blue Cloth, full large for him, old flouched Wool Hat, old Shirt and Trowſers, no Breeches, old light blue Stockings, and old Shoes, with Founders Buckles in them. Whoever ſecures ſaid Servant in any of his Majeſty's Goals, or otherwiſe, ſo as his Maſter may have him again, ſhall have Forty Shillings Reward, and reaſonable Charges, paid by JAMES M'COSKRY, or JACOB BARGE, at the Sign of the Lamb, in Philadelphia.

N. B. All Maſters of Veſſels and others are forbid to carry him off, at their Peril.

To be ſold by public Vendue, by the Subſcriber, Executor of the laſt Will and Teſtament of John Colvill, late of Fairfax County, Virginia, deceaſed, and purſuant to the ſaid Will, on the 8th Day of May next enſuing, at the Houſe of Mr. Arthur Charlton, in Frederick Town, Frederick County, Maryland, for Sterling Money, Bills of Exchange, or current Money of Pennſylvania, Maryland or Virginia, at the current Rates of Exchange;

A Very valuable Tract of Land, called Merryland, containing 6300 Acres, being and lying in the ſaid County of Frederick, along the lower Side of the Shanadore Mountain, and the Banks of Potowmack River, within 12 or 13 Miles of the ſaid Frederick Town and Court-houſe, where great Trade and Buſineſs is carried on. It is very convenient for a Dutch Settlement, as many of thoſe People live on the neighbouring Lands about it; it is well wooded and watered, and near two large Iron-works. It will be ſold all together, or in Parcels, as may beſt ſuit. A Year's Credit will be given for one Half of the purchaſe Money, if deſired, upon giving good Security, and paying Intereſt. A Plan of the ſaid Tract will be lodged at the Houſe of Mr. Charlton aforeſaid, together with an authentic Copy of the ſaid John Colvill's Will.

THOMAS COLVILL.

Exceeding good SNUFF,

To be ſold by RICHARD MORRIS, near the Court-houſe, in Market-ſtreet, Philadelphia.

WHEREAS I have been frequently applied to by Numbers of Perſons, for Snuff, which I formerly imported from London, made by Meſſieurs Goodall and Taylor: Theſe are to acquaint my former Cuſtomers, and others, that I have for Sale, a Quantity of Snuff, which far exceeds the former, and thought by the beſt Judges to be excelled by none made in England, which Snuff is manufactured by Mr. NICHOLAS POOLE, of London, Snuff-maker to Her MAJESTY, and every Bottle is diſtinguiſhed with HER ROYAL ARMS.

Said Morris continues to ſell, Spirits of Wine, Brandy, Rum, Genera, and Cordials, with all Sorts of Grocery, Glaſs and China Ware, Wholeſale and Retail, at the moſt reaſonable Rates.

N. B. A Houſe and Garden to lett, enquire as above. ⊕ 8 W.

o'Clock, [illegible]

ISAAC COOK, ſenior.

N. B. There is a good Stone Quarry on the Premiſes.

Blandfield, Eſſex County, Virginia, Feb. 5, 1765.

TO BE SOLD,

SEVERAL Thouſand Acres of Land in Auguſta County, Virginia, Part known by the Name of Beverly Manor, and the Remainder, about 5000 Acres, ſituated in the Calf Paſture. The ſaid Land will be diſpoſed of either in Parcels or otherwiſe. Any Perſon inclining to purchaſe any Part thereof, may know the Terms by applying either to Mr. Thomas Lewis, near Stanton, in Auguſta, or to the Subſcriber, who will attend at Stanton at the enſuing May Court.

ROBERT BEVERLY.

Philadelphia, April 11, 1765.

NOTICE is hereby given to the Members of the Library Company of Philadelphia, that they are to meet, purſuant to their Charter, on Monday, the Sixth Day of May next, at the Library, at Three o'Clock in the Afternoon, to chuſe Directors, and a Treaſurer, and to make their Thirty third annual Payment.

FRANCIS HOPKINSON, Secretary.

Old Church School-Houſe, April 11, 1765.

THE Proprietor returns unfeigned Thanks to thoſe Gentlemen and Ladies who have been pleaſed to attend on public Nights; but, apprehenſive that many Parents of his Pupils, as well as Numbers of his other Friends, have been fruſtrated in getting Seats, from ſuch numerous Aſſemblies, propoſes (by Advice of ſome ſelect Friends) to iſſue a convenient Number of Tickets for three public Nights, to commence on Tueſday, the 16th Inſtant, and to be continued the two ſucceeding Tueſdays. He is determined to have no more public Nights than the above this Seaſon, and therefore requeſts thoſe Gentlemen and Ladies who pleaſe to honour him with their Company, will ſend their Servants for Tickets as ſoon as poſſible; he will give out no more than the School will conveniently contain.

N. B. Tickets, at One Shilling each, to be had at the School-Houſe above-mentioned.

TO BE LETT, or SOLD,

A Commodious three Story Brick Houſe, on Society-hill, near the New Sugar Houſe, being at preſent poſſeſſed by Mr. Malcolm; there is a good Stable and Coach-houſe on the Lot, and a Garden, with a Pump of good Water at the Waſh-houſe Door, and many other Conveniencies. Any Perſon inclining to rent or purchaſe, may have it on reaſonable Terms, by applying to DAVID DEWAR, at his Houſe in Second-ſtreet, oppoſite to SAMUEL RHODES, Eſq.

For EAST and WEST FLORIDA,

THE SLOOP FLORIDA PACKET, DAVID DEWAR Maſter, will ſail ſome Time in April. For Freight or Paſſage, apply to ſaid Dewar, at his Houſe in Second-ſtreet, oppoſite to SAMUEL RHODES, Eſq. The Veſſel is Bermuda built, and has good Accommodations for Paſſengers.

Their Excellencies Governors GRANT and JOHNSTON, invite all Perſons, by Proclamation, to come and ſettle, where they may have what Lands they pleaſe for little or nothing; which, for the Fertility of the Soil, Moderation of the Climate, and Situation for Trade, certainly exceeds any Place on the Continent of North or South America, and muſt be productive of every Advantage.

PHILADELPHIA: Printed by B. FRANKLIN, POST-MASTER, and D. HALL, at the NEW PRINTING-OFFICE, near the *Market*.

PENNSYLVANIA GAZETTE (PHILADELPHIA)

April 18, 1765

This issue features one of the first full printings of the infamous Stamp Act, still more than six months from taking effect. During the summer of 1764, Benjamin Franklin, who printed the *Pennsylvania Gazette* until 1748 and remained a partner with the paper until 1766, sailed to London to protest the taxation. Franklin wrote back to a friend in Philadelphia that "we might well have hindered the sun's setting. That we could not do. But since it is down, my friend, and it may be long before it rises again, let us make as good a night of it as we can. We may still light candles." With these sentiments of moderation and compliance, Franklin's political reputation was tarnished, so he responded with a letter-writing publicity campaign to restore his image and convince colonists that he was working diligently to repeal the act.

Vol. XVIII. **The London Chronicle.** No 1377.

From TUESDAY, October 15, to THURSDAY, October 17, 1765.

To the Printer *of the* London Chronicle.

Ecce! iterum Crispinus. Hor.

Ah! what! my friend the Cobler! come again!—

Yours, good Sir, as witness O rare Ben!—

SIR,

IT has been observ'd with no less humour than truth by the ingenious Author of the first number in the *Spectator*, That the Reader of a Paper is sometimes curious and inquisitive to know *who*, and what *sort* of a man the *Writer* is: not only to his talents or abilities (if he has *any*) but also as to his *make* or *figure*, whether a short, tall, long or round-fac'd man; —in short his whole *person*—whether he wears a *peruke*, or his own *hair* frizz'd out by *Signior* Towzerano (a famous Italian hair-dresser just arrived from *Italy* with a fresh cargo of *Naples dew*, and other Italian cosmetics and essences for the *folly* of the English Ladies) or whether he wears a *buckle* in his breeches, or tied behind with one of his Landlady's old *top-knots*, with various other *particulars* of the like *importance*: I say, till the *Reader* is somewhat satisfy'd in *all* such particulars, or at least *some* of them, his judgment is at a full stop: and if ask'd his opinion of him, he proceeds with great deliberation—begs leave to suspend his judgment—shrugs his shoulders, and shakes his head, with many looks and airs of consequence—gives many significant nods, and at last ends in the formal grimace of "Why really, "Sir, as to my opinion of this Writer—I—I "—I could say—ay—that I could—now "mark what I am going to say—I don't know "what to think of him—and so, Sir, your "servant."—As to *myself*, Mr. Printer, I look upon a Cobler to be of that *vast* consequence as a *Writer*, that nobody cares a single farthing about him what *sort* of fellow he is—whether he *has* a *head* or *none* at all, or walks up and down the city with a large roundy *turnip* set between his shoulders by way of an head—whether he wears a *wig*, his own *hair*, or a tatter'd *cap* of cotton or flannel—whether a sharp *eye*, or *squints* with one—or, lastly, whether he has a good pair of *legs*, or a *wooden* one: I say, *all*, or *any one* of these things, are points of the utmost indifference to a smart, sensible Reader—the things which *he* has in view, are—can he write any thing *tolerably* clever, funny, or humourous to divert the *town*, which, like the *Athenians* of old, is daily fond of seeing and hearing *novelties*? Is he a *good* hand at bearing a part in a Review, in censuring severely what he does *not* understand, and *worrying* (like so many H—ds) the *characters* of Writers, who either can't afford, or disdain to send a *broad piece* or two, in order to court their favour? or has he any *smart* talents (like my friend ———) at assisting at a Com—n C——l in drawing up a City Address with a "*nocet empta dolore voluptas*," i. e. in plain modern English, "A Lick at the Court," or "a Sugar-Roll for *Statesmen* dipp'd in Molasses and Vinegar." I say, if he has but a *Scull* for any of these things, he'll soon find it will do—it's no matter whether the Genius is a Cobler or a Statesman, since he will want neither *Money* nor *Fame*—and with this advantage, that sometimes the Statesman is the greater *Cobler* or *Bungler* of the two, as the families of the Wrong-heads and Coblers have a very close relation and connection with each other, and have been famous for their exploits time immemorial. ----Hence, it seems, it is a common thing with us to call a Blockhead a *Wrong-headed* Whelp, or a *Cobbling* Cur, which are terms exactly of the same meaning; for when a man is fit for nothing else, he will do for a Cobler; it being observed that all *Fools* are *Coblers*, tho' it don't follow that all *Coblers* are *Fools*, as (with modesty be it spoken, and humbly hoping) witness your very humble servant,

The Cobler *of Chancery-lane.*

P. S. I shall take an opportunity to endeavour to entertain your Readers with some account of our Cobbling family, and the great Hero of it Sir Francis. And in some *future* Papers,

Quicquid agunt homines, votum, timor, ira, voluptas,
Gaudia, discursus, nostri est farrago libelli.

Which for the benefit of the Ladies, runs thus, according to *Ben Johnson*,

The *folly, vice*, and *nonsense* of the Town,
Shall in *your* Chronicle be fully shewn.

O rare Ben!

WEDNESDAY, October 16.

The London Gazette. No. 10565.

St. James's, October 15.

THE King has been pleased to grant unto the Right Rev. Dr. Frederick Keppel, Bishop of Exeter, the Deanry of the Chapel Royal in the Castle of Windsor, with the Deanry of Wolverhampton, and Registry of the Knights of the most Noble Order of the Garter, thereunto annexed, the same being void by the death of Dr. Penistone Booth.

The King has been pleased to present Richard Penneck, Clerk, M. A. to the rectory of St. John of Herslydown, Southwark, void by the resignation of Dr. James Trail.

The King has been pleased to present John Warner, Clerk, M. A. to the vicarage of West-Ham in Essex, void by the resignation of Dr. James Trail.

Lord Chamberlain's Office, Oct. 15. Orders for the Court's going out of mourning on Sunday next, the 20th instant, for the late Emperor of Germany, and the late Duke of Parma.

Bankrupt.

Thomas Ashhurst Maclane, of Lime-street, London, Merchant. To appear Oct. 22, 31, Nov. 30, at Guildhall.

Dividends to be made.

Nov. 6. William Farnworth of Cullum-street, London, Merchant and Warehouseman, at Guildhall.

Nov. 7. William Hutcheson, of Bristol, Merchant, at the Fountain Tavern in the High-street, Bristol.

Nov. 8. William Penkett, late of Chester, Grocer, at the Golden Fleece in Liverpool.

AMERICA.

Wilmington, in Virginia, August 22.

THE following are the resolutions the House of Burgesses are come to very lately with respect to the Stamp-duty, immediately on the receipt of a copy of the act of parliament from England, on which the Governor dissolved the assembly.

WHEREAS the Hon. ***** of ******* in England have of late drawn into question, how far the General Assembly of this colony hath power to enact laws for laying taxes and imposing duties, payable by the people of This his Majesty's most ancient colony: For settling and ascertaining the same to all future times, the House of Burgesses of this present General Assembly have come to the several following resolutions:

Resolved, That the first adventurers and settlers of This his Majesty's colony and dominion of Virginia, brought with them, and transmitted to their posterity, and all other his Majesty's subjects since inhabiting in this his Majesty's colony, all the privileges and immunities that have at any time been held, enjoyed and possessed by the people of Great Britain.

Resolved, That by the two royal charters granted by King James the First, the colonists aforesaid are declared entituled to all privileges and immunities of faithful Liege and natural born subjects, to all intents and purposes, as if they had been abiding and born within the realm of England.

Resolved, That his Majesty's liege people of This his most ancient colony have enjoyed the right of being thus governed by their own Assembly in the article of taxes and internal police, and that the same have never been forfeited, or any other way yielded up, but have been constantly recognized by the King and people of Great Britain.

Resolved, therefore, That the General Assembly of this colony, together with his Majesty or his Substitute, have in their representative capacity the only exclusive right and power to lay taxes and impositions upon the inhabitants of this colony; and that every attempt to vest such a power in any person or persons whatsoever other than the General Assembly aforesaid, is illegal, unconstitutional, and unjust, and has a manifest tendency to destroy British as well as American freedom.

The following RESOLVES *were not passed, only drawn up by the Committee.*

Resolved, That his Majesty's liege people, the inhabitants of this colony, are not bound to yield obedience to any law or ordinance whatsoever, designed to impose any taxation whatsoever upon them, other than the laws and ordinances of the General Assembly aforesaid.

Resolved, That any person who shall, by speaking or writing, maintain that any person or persons, other than the General Assembly of this colony, have any right or power to impose or lay any taxation whatsoever on the people here, shall be deemed an enemy to This his Majesty's colony.

Boston, New-England, August 22. The General Assembly of Virginia is, by Governor Fauquier's Proclamation, prorogued to the 17th of October next.

Governor Wentworth has prorogued the assembly of New-Hampshire to the 19th of November next.

Accounts received from several of our Whaling-Vessels on the Labrador Coast are, that they meet with some delays in regard to their fishing, in consequence of orders from the Commanding Officers on that station, a copy of which is as follows.

Memorandum,

"In pursuance of the Governor's directions, all masters of whaling-vessels, and others whom it may concern, are hereby most strictly required to observe the following particulars, viz.

"1. To carry the useless parts of such whales as they may catch, to at least three leagues from the shore, to prevent the damage that the neighbouring fishers for cod and seal sustain, by their being left on the shore.

OCTOBER 17, 1765

The

LONDON CHRONICLE

AMERICA.

Wilmington, Virginia, August 22.

THE following are the resolutions the House of Burgesses are come to very lately with respect to the Stamp-duty, immediately on the receipt of a copy of the act of parliament from England, on which the Governor dissolved the assembly

WHEREAS the Hon. ***** of ******* in England have of late drawn into question, how far the General Assembly of this colony hath power to enact laws for laying taxes and imposing duties, payable by the people of This his Majesty's most ancient colony: For settling and ascertaining the same to all future times, the House of Burgesses of this present General Assembly have come to the several following resolutions:

Resolved, That the first adventurers and settlers of This his Majesty's colony and dominion of Virginia, brought with them, and transmitted to their posterity, and all other his Majesty's subjects since inhabiting in this his Majesty's colony, all the privileges and immunities that have at any time been held, enjoyed and possessed by the people of Great Britain.

Resolved, That by the two royal charters granted by King James the First, the colonists aforesaid are declared entituled to all privileges and immunities of faithful Liege and natural born subjects, to all intents and purposes, as if they had been abiding and born within the realm of England.

Resolved, That his Majesty's liege people of This his most ancient colony have enjoyed the right of being thus governed by their own Assembly in the article of taxes and internal police, and that the same have never been forfeited, or any other way yielded up, but have been constantly recognized by the King and people of Great Britain.

Resolved, therefore, That the General Assembly of this colony, together with his Majesty or his Substitute, have in their representative capacity the only exclusive right and power to lay taxes and impositions upon the inhabitants of this colony; and that every attempt to vest such a power in any person or persons whatsoever other than the General Assembly aforesaid, is illegal, unconstitutional, and unjust, and has a manifest tendency to destroy British as well as American freedom.

The following RESOLVES *were not passed, only drawn up by the Committee.*

Resolved, That his Majesty's liege people, the inhabitants of this colony, are not bound to yield obedience to any law or ordinance whatsoever, designed to impose any taxation whatsoever upon them, other than the laws and ordinances of the General Assembly aforesaid.

Resolved, That any person who shall, by speaking or writing, maintain that any person or persons, other than the General Assembly of this colony, have any right or power to impose or lay any taxation whatsoever on the people here, shall be deemed an enemy to This his Majesty's colony.

LONDON CHRONICLE

October 17, 1765

—

On May 29, 1765, at Virginia's House of Burgesses, Patrick Henry gave a passionate speech to inspire the passage of resolutions against the Stamp Act. The two most radical resolves—including one that was intended to give Virginians the right to disobey any tax not enacted by the Virginia assembly—were struck from official record but still leaked to the public and eventually reached London newspapers.

Thursday, October 10.

SCOTLAND.

Edinburgh, October 5.

MR. William Ogilvy is elected Professor of Humanity in the King's College at Aberdeen, in place of Mr. Thomas Gordon, admitted Professor of Philosophy.

On Tuesday Night last, about five score of sheep belonging to two fleshers in Musselburgh, which were grazing a little eastward of the town, had betaken themselves for shelter from the storm, to a hollow, when they were surrounded by a high tide, carried off to the sea, and all perished. The whole number were cast ashore on Aberlady Sands.

On the 28th ult. died at Lamington, Lanerkshire, the Rev. Mr. David Blinshall, in the 47th year of his ministry there. Though in the 97th of his age, he performed all the duties of his office until about twelve months ago, retaining his memory and judgment to the last hour of his life.

Last night came down a further reprieve of fourteen days, from Wednesday next, for Lieutenant Patrick Ogilvie, now prisoner in the Tolbooth here.

COUNTRY NEWS.

Gloucester, Octob. 7. On Tuesday last died at Beckford, in this county, Benedict Wakeman, Esq; of that place.

Lately died at Rochelle in France, whither he had been for his health, George Pritchard, Esq; of Hopen, in Herefordshire.

Salisbury, Octob. 7. A few days ago, at Southampton, a girl of sixteen, being long troubled with an ague, was advised by a lad of her acquaintance to try white hellebore, of which having obtained a pennyworth, she took one half immediately, which not having the least effect, she took the remainder on the approach of the next fit, and in less than half an hour after she was seized with convulsions, and expired in a few minutes.

LONDON.

Yesterday his Majesty came from Richmond to St. James's, where there was a numerous levee, at which were present the Archbishop of Canterbury, the Duke of Newcastle, with many others of the Nobility, foreign Ministers, &c. to pay their respects to his Majesty, as being the birth-day of the Prince of Brunswick.

Neither his Royal Highness the Duke of Cumberland, nor his serene Highness the Prince of Brunswick, are yet returned from Newmarket. They are at present making several visits at the Duke of Grafton's, Duke of Rutland's, and other noble personages in Cambridge and Lincolnshires.

Extract of a Letter from Boston in New England, Aug. 26.

"Very early on Wednesday morning, the 14th instant, were discovered hanging on a limb of the great trees, so called, at the south part of this town, two effigies, one of which by the labels appeared to be designed to represent a Stamp-Officer; the other a Jackboot with a head and horns peeping out of the top: The report of the images soon spread thro' the town, brought a vast number of spectators, and had such an effect on them that scarce any could attend to the talk of day-labour; but all seemed on the wing for Freedom. About dusk the images were taken down, placed on a bier, supported in procession by six men, followed by a great concourse of people, some of the highest reputation, and in the greatest order, ecchoing forth Liberty and Property! No Stamp, &c.—Having passed thro' the town-house they proceeded down King-street, and thro' Kilby-street, where an edifice had been lately erected, which was supposed to be designed for a Stamp-Office. Here they halted, and went to work to demolish that building. This being finished, many of them loaded themselves with the wooden trophies, and proceeded (bearing the two effigies) to the top of Fort-hill, where a fire was soon kindled, in which one of them was burnt. The populace after this went to work on the barn, fence, garden, &c. And here it would have ended, had not some indiscretions, to say the least, been committed by his friends within, which so enraged the people they were not to be restrained, though hitherto no violence had been offered to any one. But it is very remarkable, though they entered the lower part of the house in multitudes, yet the damage done to it was not so great as might have been expected.

The next day the honourable gentleman who had been appointed to the duty of Distributor of the Stamps when they should arrive, supposing himself to be the object of their derision, informed the principal gentlemen of the town, that as it appeared so disagreeable to the people, he should request the liberty of being excused from that office; and in the evening the populace reassembled, erected a pyramid, intending a second bonfire; but upon hearing of the resignation, they desisted, and repaired to the gentleman's gate, gave three cheers, and took their departure without damage; but having heard it propagated that an honourable gentleman at the north part of the town, had been accessary in laying on the Stamp Duties, &c. they repaired to his house, where, upon being informed by some gentlemen of integrity and reputation, that he had not only spoke but wrote to the contrary, they retired, and having patroled the streets, returned to their respective habitations, as quietly as they had done the night before."

They write from Warsaw of the 21st ult. that the Sieur Kozlobrocki, having been guilty of murder, and had fled to the church for refuge, was taken from thence by a detachment of troops, by express orders of the supreme Court of Justice at Peterkau, where he was tried and condemned. To the breach of this privilege, the Clergy of Poland would never before submit.

Letters from Amsterdam of the 4th instant bring advice, that a further account had been received there, touching the violent hurricane which happened at St. Eustatia the 31st of last July; that the small vessels got out to sea in time, but the storm reaching to Martinico, thirty-three French, English, and Spanish ships were lost; at Guadaloupe, six ships and ten small vessels: and at Dominica, nine vessels, with a large quantity of Coffee on board, were drove on shore and lost: And on the 7th ult. another great storm happened at St. Eustatia, by which three barks and a snow were lost in the road.

Yesterday the purser of the Earl of Lincoln, Hardwick, came to the India, with the news of the above ship being safe arriv'd at Plymouth, from Fort St. George and China.

The Earl of Lincoln East-Indiaman, just arrived from China, brought home 427,500 lb. of bohea, 36,600 lb. congou, and 172,800 lb. of singlo Tea; five whole chests, 45 half ditto, and one box of china-ware; besides several other goods.

Yesterday Sir Jarvis Clifton, Bart. was introduced to his Majesty at St. James's by Lord Berkeley of Stratton, and was graciously received.

The Hon. Mr. Wallop, brother to the Earl of Portsmouth, is appointed Ensign in the 3d regiment of foot-guards, in the room of Lord Offaley, deceased.

William Newton, Gent. is appointed, by his Majesty, a Lieutenant in the 10th regiment of dragoons, in the room of Lieut. Floyer preferred. George Poyntz Ricketts, Gent. succeeds Mr. Newton, as Cornet in the said regiment.

Yesterday Col. Keene, Gentleman of horse to his Excellency the Earl of Hertford, set out for Ireland. As did likewise the Hon Col Hotham, and Lieut. Col. Paterson, to join their regiment in that kingdom.

As the alteration of the rates of postage of letters takes place this day, it may not be unacceptable to our readers to inform them, that, by an act passed the last sessions of parliament, it is enacted, that from and after the 10th day of October, 1765, the rates now payable for the postage of letters sent by the General Post not exceeding two post-stages shall cease and determine, and in place thereof the following rates shall be taken, viz. "For the conveyance of every single letter, not exceeding one whole post-stage from the office where such letter may be put in, the sum of one penny; for every double letter, two-pence; for every treble letter, three-pence; and for every ounce, four-pence; and so in proportion for every packet of deeds, writs, or other things. And for the conveyance of every single letter above one post-stage, and not exceeding two post-stages, the sum of two-pence; for every double letter, four-pence; and for every treble letter, six-pence; and for every ounce, eight-pence; and so in proportion for every pacquette of deeds, writs, or other things."

Yesterday David Durell, D. D. Principal of Hertford College, was chosen Vice-Chancellor of the university of Oxford; and Dr. Barton, Warden of Merton; Dr. Leigh, Master of Baliol; Dr. Brown, Provost of Queen's; and Dr. Randolph, President of Corpus Christi, were chosen Pro-Vice Chancellors.

Yesterday the Rev. Mr. Pearce was collated by the Dean and Chapter of St. Paul's, to the Rectory of the United Parishes of St. Mary Magdalen and St. Gregory's, Old Fish-street.

A few days ago died at Wickham, near Gosport, in Hampshire, in a very advanced age, Samuel Atkins, Esq; the second on the list of superannuated flag-officers on half-pay.

On Monday died, at his house on the Gunwharf, at Portsmouth, John Eddowes, Esq; many years storekeeper of the ordnance, &c. there.

On Tuesday last died, at Pendley hall, near Webley in Surry, Dame Margaret Estcombe, relict of Sir William Estcombe.

On Tuesday died in Lombard-street, Capt. Michael Butler, in the West-India trade.

The same day died Mr. Green, master of the Oval tavern in Grosvenor-street.

On Sunday last the Collector of the toll at Kensington Gravel-pits, was suddenly taken ill, fell down, and expired immediately.

On Tuesday the body of Mr. Parkinson, an overseer to persons employed in unloading ships, was taken up near Stone-stairs; he fell over the side of a West Indiaman last Friday-night, and was drowned.

On Monday night Mary Davers (who accused herself some years ago of the murder of her bastard child, for which she was tried and acquitted, and also charged herself with being concerned, with others, in the murder of the Turnpike man at Mary-le-bon) hanged herself in Bucket-Court, in Tottenham-Court road.

Tuesday se'nnight, at the clearing the prisoners at Guildhall, it was again argued by several eminent Counsellors, Whether a spunging-house was to be deemed a prison or not? when it was finally determined by the Court in the negative. —At the last sessions at Guildford, a Captain, who was arrested in December last, and did not surrender to the gaol before March, was cleared, the Court at that place being of opinion, that a spunging-house was a prison.

Yesterday John M'Kenzie for stealing two silver pint mugs from Mr. Abedward, a Publican in Nightingale-lane; and James Haines, for robbing Joseph Dupree, Esq; on the highway, were executed at Tyburn.

Yesterday a young fellow was carried before the Lord Mayor, being charged with forging a certificate, signed by a Captain of a Man of war, in order to receive some wages, and was committed to the Poultry-Compter.

D. L. Jealous Wife, with Fortunatus.

C. G. The Wonder, with Perseus and Andromeda.

that it would be full ſeven years before all the payments could be completed.

Letters from Stockholm adviſe, that the ſubſidy treaty between Sweden and France meets with great oppoſition.

A proclamation was publiſh'd at Boſton in New-England by his excellency the Governor Bernard on the 28th of Auguſt laſt, purporting, that "Whereas on the 26th of Auguſt, towards the evening, a great number of people unlawfully aſſembled together in the town of Boſton, arm'd with clubs, ſtaves, &c. and did firſt of all attack the dwelling houſe of William Story, Eſq; deputy regiſter of the Court of Admiralty within that province, break his windows, and enter his ſaid houſe, and the office wherein the books and files belonging to the ſaid court were lodged, and did ſcatter, burn or deſtroy the ſame, and moſt of his own papers, &c. and did deſtroy a great part of his furniture. After which the rioters did proceed to the dwelling houſe of Benjamin Hallowell, Eſq; comptroller of his Majeſty's Cuſtoms, for the port of Boſton, break down the fence before it, and enter the houſe, deſtroy the wainſcot and furniture, take away his apparel, break open his deſk and trunks, and take out all his papers, and about thirty pounds ſterling in money.

"And whereas theſe or other rioters did, on the ſame night, attack the dwelling-houſe of the Hon. Thomas Hutchinſon, Eſq; Lieutenant-Governor of the ſaid province, and deſtroy the wainſcot, leaving the houſe a mere ſhell from top to bottom, deſtroy all the furniture, deſtroy or carry off all the apparel, jewels, books, and papers of his honour and his family, drink, take away, or deſtroy eight pipes and three quarter caſks of wine, and all proviſions and ſtores of what kind ſoever in his cellars, and carry off about 900 l. ſterling in money, together with all his honour's plate, pillaging and deſtroying every thing in the ſaid houſe of what kind ſoever.

"His Excellency promiſes a reward of 300 l. for the diſcovery of the leader or leaders, of any of the parties aforeſaid, ſo that he or they may be convicted, and a reward of 100 l. for the diſcovery of any other perſon of ſuch parties. And any perſon (ſuch principal leaders only excepted) ſhall, over and above the reward aforeſaid, upon diſcovery of any of his accomplices, receive his Majeſty's gracious pardon."

Extract of a Letter from Boſton in New-England, dated Sept. 2.

"At a meeting of the freeholders and other inhabitants of the town of Boſton, on Tueſday ... The town having

appear, that he was led into an error by ſymptoms which have hitherto been always thought certain.

The French Comedians had fixed up bills at Paris for the tragedy of Phædra and Hypolitus, to be performed on the 30th ult. but when the curtain was drawn up that evening, one of the Actors appeared on the ſtage, and requeſted permiſſion to play a new comedy, which was granted by a clapping of hands; and the piece, which is called *The Guardian duped*, met with great applauſe. It is wrote by M. Caillevac de l'Etendoux, who made uſe of this ſtratagem to avoid the cabals generally attendant on a new play.

A letter from Dunkirk, dated Oct. 7, ſays, "While all are in deſpair here on account of the Engliſh miniſtry inſiſting ſo peremptorily on the deſtruction of our port, we acknowledge ſome obligations to them for being inſtrumental in having the Chevalier de Mezieres removed from being our Governor. He left this town yeſterday, to the univerſal ſatisfaction of the firſt inhabitants of the place, as well as of the meaneſt peaſants in the adjacent villages, who have equally been expoſed to his tyrannical and capricious humour. It is reported here, that the Britiſh Miniſtry made a point with our Court to recall the man who had diſtinguiſhed himſelf here in his command with ſo much violence againſt their nation. It is well known, that he extended his oppreſſion equally to the natives of the place, and acted, in every reſpect, as if tyranny was his ſole delight."

From Rome they write, that a great quantity of gold coin has been lately diſcovered in the land of Poggio-Mirleto; and that the grand treaſurer's lieutenant was gone to examine them.

It is ſaid the Prince and Princeſs of Brunſwick, with ſeveral other Royal Perſonages, will honour the City with their preſence at Guildhall next Lord Mayor's Day.

Yeſterday the Right Hon. Lady Holland was at Court at St. James's, for the firſt time ſince her arrival from France.

On Wedneſday evening the Tripoline Ambaſſador arrived in town from Portſmouth; and yeſterday he notified his arrival to the Secretaries of State.

Yeſterday ſet out for Ireland the Right Hon. —— Forteſcue, Eſq; Poſtmaſter General of that kingdom.

His Majeſty has been pleaſed to appoint Henry Baſſett, Eſq; to be a Major in the 10th regiment of foot, in the room of Major Percival. And Robert Nettle, Eſq; ſucceeds Major Baſſett

Cuckold's point, ... for the benefit of the owner. To perpetuate this circumſtance this fair is annually kept, where horn, and all toys made of horn, are publickly purchaſed.

On Tueſday laſt Capt. Hayter, of St. Martin's, was married to Miſs Millis, of Thames Ditton, in Surry.

M. Filengeri, Governor of Viterbo, died lately, and has left an immenſe fortune to the different abbeys of Sicily. Having, as he ſays in his will, got all his riches by the church, he thought himſelf therefore obliged to let them return thither.

Letters from Barbadoes of the 28th of Auguſt, bring advice of the death of Col. Edward Carleton.

On Wedneſday died, in Crutched Friars, Bartholomew Ibbot, Eſq; formerly one of the Inſpectors of the cuſtoms in the port of London.

Laſt week died at Bath, Lady Chapple, widow of the late Sir William Chapple, one of the Judges of the Court of King's Bench.

Mr. John Steers, an eminent Engliſh merchant at Liſbon, died there lately.

Yeſterday died at his houſe in Marybone-ſtreet, Piccadilly, —— Leſlie, Eſq; who ſupplied the army in Germany with wine during the late war. He died worth 20,000.

On Monday Langley and Everett, two Bargemen, who had for ſome time bore animoſity to each other, went on board a barge below Chertſey to navigate it to London, where they fought, and in the fray Everett was knocked overboard, and drowned. Langley eſcaped.

On Wedneſday John Willis, and his ſon, carpenters, pulling down ſome old houſes at Duke's Place, near Aldgate, found as much Spaniſh ſilver coin as they ſold for ſeventeen pounds and upwards.

Yeſterday the ſeſſions ended at the Old-Bailey, when 20 priſoners were tried, two of whom were capitally convicted, viz. Andrew Fitzgerald an[d] William Richardſon, for forging ſeamens wills ſeven were caſt for tranſportation, and eleve[n] acquitted. At this ſeſſions two received ſentenc[e] of death, 19 to be tranſported for ſeven year[s] one branded, and one to be fined and impriſone[d] It is remarkable there were five priſoners trie[d] this ſeſſions who were tried the September ſeſſion[s]

The next Seſſions will begin on Monday th[e] 9th of December at Guildhall, and on Wedne[ſ]day the 11th at the Old-Ba[i]l[e]y.

Wedneſday laſt a young woman was tried [at] the Old Bailey, for ſtealing, in an amour with [a] ſailor, ſeven guineas, his property; the pro[of] not being ſufficient, and the evidence of the ſ[ai]lor very favourable, ſhe was acquitted. The h[...]
caught her in his arms, a[...]
mon rapture, ſwearing
keep all, but that ſhe w[...]
e ſmacks were ſo hea[...]
Court was much ſurpriſ[...]
ling at the oddity.

plan is under conſiderat[...]
of milk, and obliging
to ſell by ſtatute meaſu[...]

K RACES.

ol. for five year-olds,
's grey horſe, Trim[...]

50l. weight for age,
bay horſe, Young Ba[...]

d, with Daphne and Amin[...]
with Perſeus and Androme[...]

LONDON CHRONICLE

October 10, 1765

Three weeks before the Stamp Act took effect, news of the August 14 riots in Boston arrived in London. English readers were likely glued to the following issues as more details of colonial anger and protest arrived by ship.

LONDON CHRONICLE

October 19, 1765

Soon after reading about the Virginia Resolves and the Boston riot of August 14, the *London Chronicle* continues to barrage its readers with terrifying American news. This time, it prints the dreadful details of the destruction of homes of Crown officials, including Lieutenant Governor Thomas Hutchinson. Here, Londoners read the proclamation by Royal Governor Francis Bernard, who offered a £300 reward for the capture of the riot leaders.

Supplement to the BOSTON News-Letter.

THURSDAY, September 5. 1765.

The following is from one of the Monday's Papers.

BOSTON, September 2.

ABOUT Twilight last Monday, a small Bonfire appeared to be kindled in King-Street, and surrounded only by a few Boys and Children; but one of the Fire-Wards perceiving it to rise to a dangerous Height, interposed and used his Endeavours to extinguish or at least to diminish it; in which salutary attempt, after several Whispers from a Person unknown, warning him of danger, he received a Blow, and such Tokens of Insult and Outrage, as obliged him to desist and take his Departure.

Soon after this, Day-light being scarce in, the Fire gradually decaying, a peculiar Hoop and Whistle was observed to be sounded from various Quarters, which instantaneously drew together a great Number of disguised Ruffians, (for this Appellation we hope not improperly applied,) armed with Clubs, Staves, &c. No sooner were they assembled, than Attack was made on the Dwelling-House of *William Story*, Esq; opposite the North side of Court-House; the lower Part of which, being his Office as Deputy-Register of the Court of Vice-Admiralty, was in a few Minutes laid open: The public Files and Records of that Court, Mr. *Story*'s private Papers, Books of Account &c. exposed to Ravage and Destruction, and improved as Fuel to revive the expiring Flames: Little more than half an Hour sufficed them here, for it seems much greater Exploits, were reserved for the Heroism of the Night.

Boisterous and intrepid, from this first Object of their Rage, they rushed onward, encreasing still in Number and Fury, to the new and elegantly finished Building of *Benjamin Hallowell*, jun. Esq; where after tearing down the Fences, breaking the Windows, &c. they at length entered the House, and in the most savage and destructive manner broke and abused his Furniture, Chairs, Tables, Desk, Glasses, China, and in short every Thing they could lay their Hands on; at the same Time purloining his Money, and dispersing his private Books and Papers, until by the Effect of Wine and the other Stores of his Cellar, they ripened in Ebriety and Madness, and became fit for the next, more desolating and barbarous Operation.

Towards Ten o'Clock they were traced by the Noise and Tumult of a numerous and confused Rabble to the Mansion-House of His Honor the Lieut. Gov. This seemed to be reserved for the utmost Violence of their diabolical Phrenzy; for immediately on the Word given, that large and stately Edifice became a Prey to the Iron Hand of Outrage and Robbery; a few Hours and the House was a meer Skeleton, and deprived of Furniture, even Wainscot and Partition, broke, hacked and mangled: and the whole by Break of Day, at once a sad Spectacle of Indigna-[...]der!

[...]t and extraordinary Desolation, be-[...]nd it's Furniture of very considera-[...]onor and his Family sustained, the [...]ight and nine Hundred Pounds Ster-[...]his Plate, Wearing Apparell, a valu-[...]ibrary, a great Number of private [...] and scarce Papers and Manuscripts, [...] large Files and Records, occasionally [...]ession, relating to the Claims and [...]ince; all dispersed, stolen, and de-[...]e Damage in it's Consequences [...] publickly as well as privately, In-[...]

[...]'s own Misfortune with Firmness, [...]thers," (the Words on the Occasion [...] and worthy Gentleman, who has [...]esidence among us) is the Part of [...] who then can blush, or be ashamed [...] those who have so severely felt the [...] a misguided and merciless Rabble.

The Sufferings of the other Gentlemen, tho' truly grievous, seems to be absorbed in the greater Misfortune of his Honor and his Family, their loss being computed at near twenty five Hundred Pounds Sterling exclusive of the Building.

The Peace and good Order of the Town has been ever since preserved by a Military Watch, which we hope in Time will have a Tendency to allay the present strange and tumultuous Spirit; tho' we would not be understood, not to distinguish this, from the truly noble Opposition to the imposition of internal Taxes, without the intervention of the respective Legislatures of the Colonies, or an equal Representation, which seems to be not only of this Province, but the united Voice of the whole British Continent.

The morning after the late Tumult and Devastation, being the Time for opening the Superiour Court of Judicature, Court of Assize, &c. His Honor the Chief Justice was obliged to attend, notwithstanding his great Distress, there not being a Quorum of the Court without him. His Brethren of the Bench, and the Gentlemen of the Bar habited in their respective Robes, and he in his only Suit! A Scene truly affecting to every humane and feeling Breast.

Several Persons were taken up and committed to Goal in this Town, last Week, on a voilent Suspicion of their being concerned in the Riot of the 26th Instant.

Since our last we have received a Number of Accounts that in the neighbouring Colonies they have gone great Lengths in their Resentment to the Stamp-Officers, some of them we here insert.

NORWICH, August 22.

The noble patriotic fire which has lighted up in one place and another, and of late shone so conspicuous at Boston, blazed here with all the vehemence and splendor of a comet, guided by the dictates of prudence and decorum. 'Twas last night our reputable STAMP-MASTER, in effigy, made his public appearance in this town, clad in a suit of white, trim'd with black, the gift of his native country, both as an emblem of his purity and innocence, and his sorrow and tender concern for this unhappy people: On his right hand stood the restless father of mischief with the stamp act in his hand, giving credentials to his all attentive pupil; the malignity of his heart was lively portray'd by the expressive cardinal knave at cards on his breast, accompained with a cautious memento to all placemen, that * * * * * *

" When vice prevails and impious men bear sway,
" The post of honour is a private station."

Their appearance was becoming, and procession glorious, attended by such invectives, huzza's and disdainful music as are the pure emanations of injured freedom: after passing thro' town, our hero with his companion, was conducted——————
" in all the Majesty of Greece" to the height of a lofty hill, perhaps the highest summit he will e'er ascend; and there in complaisance to his fellow, committed to the flames; and a few loyal and very constitutional healths crown'd the night.

NEW-LONDON, *August* 23.

We hear that a gentleman in one of the southern provinces being advised that his son, then in London, was appointed a *STAMP-OFFICER*, for said province, immediately wrote him, that if he thought proper to accept that most detestable Office, he would not expect any thing from him, and that he might never see his face more

Newport, August 26.

We hear from New London, that about 4 o'Clock last Thursday Afternoon, was exhibited, in the most public Part of the Town, the Effigies of a Distributor of Stamps, with a Boot on one of the Shoulders, and the Devil represented as looking out of the same.—They were suspended in the Air, on a Gibbet, between 20 and 30 Feet from the Ground; and after being exposed about an Hour, were taken down, and carried through the Town, attended by the principal Part of the Inhabitants. The Cannon of the Fort were repeatedly discharged during the Time of Exhibition. Between Ten and Eleven the Effigies were consumed amidst the Acclamations of the People. 'Tis said the most perfect Decorum was observed in all their Behaviour; and no Person suffered the least Injury.

SUPPLEMENT TO THE BOSTON NEWS-LETTER

September 5, 1765

This newspaper sheds light on the terror campaign that colonists launched to fight the Stamp Act. It is loaded with details about intimidation and destruction in Boston and Newport, Rhode Island. Newspapers spread the word of mobs, violence, and boycott, which forced resignations of stamp distributors, effectively preventing the enforcement of the Stamp Act and leading to its repeal.

From several Letters wrote at Newport, Rhode-Island, and from the Newport Mercury of Monday last, we have collected the following Particulars of the Populace there:

Newport, September 2.

The latter End of the Week before last, the Effigies of three Gentlemen were prepared, in order for an Exhibition, on the Tuesday following, the Day for the Choice of Deputies to represent the Town in the General Assembly; one of the Effigies represented the Distributor of the Stamps; the other two those who were suspected of countenancing the Stamp-Act.—On Monday one of the Gentlemen published the following Advertisement in the Mercury; by many thought to be a very imprudent Action at that Juncture, viz

THE Author of the Halifax Letter *gives out to the Public, That he is a Native of the Colonies, and has a Heart as warmly attached to their true Interest as any Man whatever: That the Sentiments he has adopted, in Print, have since appeared to be the Judgment of the Parliament of* Great Britain; *and the Opinion of* Nine-Tenths *of the* British *Nation; and he has published them with that Freedom, which is the Privilege, and ought to be the Boast of every* English-man. *He therefore cannot repress his Astonishment at the mistaken Notions of those, who under a Pretence of serving the Cause of Liberty, would take away the Right of private Judgment, and stop the Avenues to Truth, by instigating the Populace, and endeavouring to point their Fury against the Person and Interest of a Man, meerly because he happens to differ in Opinion from his Countrymen: And in that Instance, only exercises the same Privilege which they claim and enjoy.*

The Writer does not retract any Position contained in the Halifax Letter; *and therefore does not meanly sollicit any Favour or Exemption from the Abuse intended him, because if his Person and Interest become the Objects of popular Revenge for these Sentiments, he thinks he shall never lament the Cause, whatever may be the Consequences.*

On Tuesday Morning the 27th, between 5 and 6 o'Clock a Mob assembled, erected a Gallows near the Town House and dispers'd, and about 10 o'Clock reassembled, when the Effigies were carted up Thames Street, and then up King-street to the said Gallows where they were hung by the Neck, suspended near 15 Feet in the Air, and about 5 o'Clock in the Afternoon they made a Fire under the Gallows which consumed the Effigies and Gallows to Ashes. After the Effigies were burnt the Mob dispers'd, and no Violence was offered to the Persons or Property of any Man.

On the Effigies were the following Lables.

On the Stampman, an *S* painted on his Forehead, and *Stampman* in Capitals on his Breast.

At his Left Hand, *M--t-n H-w--d*, with an *S* on his Forehead, and on his Breast, *That fawning, insidious, infamous Parricide, Martinus Scriblerus.*—His Neck, with that of his Accomplice, connected with a Rope, to which was appended a Paper with this Inscription, *We have an hereditary, indefeasible Right to an Halter;---besides, we encouraged the Growth of Hemp you know.*—In his Right Hand he held his Halifax Letter, and on his Right Arm inscribed, *The only filial Pen.*—From his Mouth issued this Label, directed towards his Left Arm, *What avails my boasted independence---Posterity will curse my Memory.*—And on his Left Arm this Sentence, *Curs'd Ambition, accursed Clan, ye have ruined me.*

On the Right Hand of the Stampman hung, with the Letter *S* painted on his Forehead, *Dr. Murphy*, and on his Breast, *That formule, miscreated, learing Jacobite, Dr. Murphy.* Out of his mouth issued this Label, *We cannot complain Martinus, we deserve this, and more.*—In his Right Hand he held a Letter, directed, *To that Mawgawgeene of Knowledge, Dr. —— Murphy, Newport, Rhode Island.* And on his Right arm, *If I had received this Letter from the Earl of —— but a Week sooner.* And on his Left arm, *It is too late now, Martinus, to tack about, we are all aground.*

On one of the Posts out of Reach, *Whoever attempts, in any Way whatsoever, to render ineffectual this Mark of public Contempt, will be deem'd an Enemy to Liberty, and incur the Resentment of the Town.*

The same Day, at a Meeting of the Inhabitants of the Town, Metcalfe Bowler, Esq; Esq; Mr. John G. Wanton, George Hazard, Esq; Mr. Benjamin Green, Capt. Samuel Carr, and Capt. William Read, were chosen Deputies of the Town, to represent them in the General Assembly to be held in October next.—The Town also chose a Committee to prepare Instructions for their Deputies relative to the Stamp Act.

Early on Wednesday Evening, as four Gentlemen, among whom was Martin Howard, jun Esq; were walking down Queen-Street, a Person, in consequence of a private Pique, assaulted one of them, the Collector of his Majesty's Customs for that Port, the Collector soon disengaged himself, and retreated. The other Gentlemen manifested some Resentment in his Behalf; but the Return they met with, induced them to withdraw, and go towards Mr. Howard's House.—An account of this Affair immediately spread among the People, a Mob collected, and marched directly to Mr. Howard's; and not finding the Gentlemen there, they shattered some of the Windows, and went off. But not satisfied with the Mischief they had done, they soon returned to the Charge with redoubled Fury, broke the Windows and Doors all to pieces, damaged the Partitions of the House, and ruined such Furniture as was left in it, the best part being happily removed out between the attacks.—This being done, the Mob drew off, and proceeded to the hired House that Doctor Moffat lived in, where they committed Outrages equally terrible, in tearing the House to pieces, and demolishing the Furniture. The Cellars of both Houses were ravaged, and the Provisions, Wines, &c destroyed and lost—From the Doctor's they went in quest of the Gentleman first aimed at, who had luckily, by that Time, got on board the Cygnet Man of War, which lay at the back of the Fort. After this they surrounded the House of the then Stamp-Master; but upon promises of his resigning that Office, they offered no Violence to his Habitation.—It was eleven o'clock when they were about to perform this last act of devastation; but desisting from this they contented themselves with rendering more compleat the Ruin of the two Houses beforementioned.—Next Morning the Stamp Master's Resignation being publickly read, the People announced their Joy by repeated Huzza's, &c. and the Storm ceased. Things, however, did not continue long in this easy State; an Irish young Fellow, who had been but a few Days in Town, stood forth, like Massaniello, openly, declared that he was at the Head of the Mob the preceeding Night, and triumphed in the Mischief that was done. Some Gentlemen, to prevent any further Evil, thought it best to seize immediately upon this Desperadoe, and put him on board the Man of War, which they accordingly did: But this, instead of answering the designed Purpose, kindled a new Fire. The Mob began again to collect; and a Number of Persons, who it seemed, were so irritated at his being carried on board the Man of War, that it became necessary to bring him on shore again. This was done; and upon his promising immediately to quit the Government, he was released, and the Night passed without Tumult. The Morning following, Massaniello appeared again in the publick Streets, boldly declaring himself to have been the Ring-leader of the Mob, and threatning Destruction to the Town, more particularly to the Persons and Houses of those who seized him the preceding Day, unless they made him Presents agreeable to his Demands. The Attorney-General, who was the late Stamp Master, being met and insulted by him, heroically seized upon him; and some Gentlemen running to his assistance, they carried him off to Goal. This proved effectual;—nobody appeared to rescue him, nor to say a Word in his Favour. He is now under Confinement;—the Town is again in Peace, and we sincerely wish it may continue so.

The Ship Friendship, Capt. Lindsey, sailed for England Yesterday. Dr. Thomas Moffat, and Martin Howard, jun. Esq; of this Town, went Passengers.

The Lot of Land and the late Dwelling-House of Mr. Howard is advertised for Sale. His Loss sustained is computed to be about 1000£. *sterl.*

The Town of Little-Compton have given Instructions to their Deputies, but we have not Room to insert them.—In general they are like those lately given to the Members for Providence, which have been published.

PENNSYLVANIA JOURNAL (PHILADELPHIA)

January 23, 1766

The Stamp Act was technically effective from November 1, 1765, until its repeal on March 17, 1766. Despite being published within that time frame, this *Pennsylvania Journal* showed no signs of stamps as there were no stamp distributors to enforce it. This issue reports on events surrounding the intimidation of New Haven, Connecticut, and Albany, New York, stamp distributors.

The following Refolves were unanimoufly agreed to, and ordered to be printed in the New-London Gazette, viz.

1. *THAT allegiance and the ftricteft loyalty is ever due from the people of the Englifh American colonies, to our*

[...]

rights. And that every perfon who endeavours the execution of the fame, is an inveterate enemy to our public weal and tranquility.

5. *That whereas our Stampman was appointed agent for this colony at the Court of Great-Britain, in confidence that he would exert his utmoft abilities to prevent faid Act; neverthelefs he return'd, the executioner of thofe evils he was fent to defend us from. And notwithftanding his folemn engagements to the contrary, has, and ftill obftinately perfifts, by every way and means his malice and craft fuggefts, or his unbridled audacity can attempt, to plot the ruin and total overthrow of his native country, to which he is allied by the tendereft ties, and ftrongeft bonds of gratitude; and thereby has fet his own intereft in competition with the intereft of his country, and forfeited all privilege of protection from the fame,---is no longer to be believed, his friendfhip no more to be trufted,--nor his malignant defigns any longer to be endured; and that affuredly unlefs he inftantly defifts from plotting our ruin, writing, or fending any thing prejudicial to the government, or even relative to the fame, he fhall forthwith feel the weight of his injured country's righteous indignation, and know by fad experience, all the horrors of falling a defencelefs prey to the juftice of a free, injured and enraged people, whofe bofoms glow with the free fpirit of Britifh liberty, and who count not their lives dear in defence of it.*

6. *That as to the matters of charge in the aforefaid articles againft Mr. Ingerfol, we challenge him to deny, or vindicate himfelf from them, at any of our public meetings: And we do hereby give him full affurance, that if he will come, he fhall have as fair a hearing as he can defire; and fafe protection from any infult or injury to his perfon or property, while with us at our meeting.*

7. *That Mr. Ingerfol's letters be read publickly in all the counties in this colony, at their public meetings, if defired.*

8. *That copies of Mr. Ingerfol's letters be given out to fome one perfon in every county, to be kept for the benefit of the Freemen.*

9. *That we moft critically infpect every avenue and way by which the Stamp Papers may be introduced into the colony; and on appearance of danger give the moft fpeedy notice to the Freemen.*

10. *That we moft earneftly recommend to the civil authority in this colony, to proceed in bufinefs as ufual; as our ceffation and delay of bufinefs will be conftrued an implicit acknowledgement of the validity of the Stamp Act. To this purpofe we recommend a piece wrote by a mafter of reafon, and a true friend to liberty in Pennfylvania, and inferted in the New-London Gazette of the 20th inftant. Alfo we do fully concur with and adopt the Refolves of the county of New-London, of the 10th inftant.*

11. *That another meeting is appointed to be held on the firft Thurfday in March next, at the Meeting Houfe, in the firft fociety in Canterbury, at 10 o'Clock on faid day.*

NEW-HAVEN. January 19.

WHEREAS I have lately received two anonymous letters, calling on me (among other things) to give the public fome farther affurance with regard to my intentions about executing the office of diftributor of ftamps for this colony, as fome others have done fince the receiving our commiffions or deputations for that purpofe; and that I confirm the fame by oath. And altho' I don't think it beft ordiniarily to take notice of fuch letters, nor yet to take oaths upon fuch kind of occafions; yet (as I have good reafon to think that thofe

of them (efpecially of any particular detached fentences) but by me, or by mutual confent; ----that thofe paragraphs which have lately been publifhed in the New-London Gazette, I conceive to be, in fome parts, by fome miftake, differently worded from the originals, and com-

[...] what I imagine would [...] whole of my faid [...]er. This I intend [...] the papers again; [...] public will not un- [...] the matter. And [...]ofe particular letters [...] are recalled; and if, [...] was faid in them that [...]urable to the colony [...] be always ready to [...] they fhall call upon [...]t all trouble of the [...] to write no letters [...] than they now are) [...] gentlemen as, at this

J. I.

[...] *December* 30.

[...] in New-London was [...]els are cleared out there as ufual, without STAMPS: And that the juftices and Lawyers, in that county, go on with bufinefs in the old way.....

Laft Friday Se'nnight, was found in her houfe, in New Haven, lying on a fire dead, the Widow Smith:--- On examining her body, feveral wounds were found; by which it was determined that fhe had been murdered.---- Her only fon is taken up, on fufpicion of having been the perpetrator of the horrid fact, and is confined in goal for tryal.

NEW-YORK, *January* 26.

Extract of a letter from a gentleman in London, to his friend in this city, dated Nov. 9, 1765.

" I am fully fenfible of the malignity of the late meafures, and your-------has well delineated the authors. Your zeal is commendable; but you fhould not impute your grievances to the whole, which were impofed by the influence of a miniftry univerfally detefted, and now removed, and the new miniftry entirely in your favour. An entire new fyftem in your favour is adopted, and the truly noble Lord Dartmouth at the head of the Board of Trade, your friend out of judgment, being fully convinced of the mutual intereft of the colonies and their Mother Country; fo that a few months will give a new face to your affairs.

" I contributed my mite to his information, and he was fo condefcending as to call on me and thank me, and opened his fentiments without referve.----He is a charming man."

On Saturday the 4 h inftant, many of the inhabitants, of Albany, having heard that Mr. Van Schaick, of that place, merchant, had applied for the office of diftributor of the Stamps there, a number of them went to him and demanded a refignation of the office if he had it, and a folemn engagement that he nor any for him, fhould ever act in it.----That he would not enter into fuch an engagement without fome referve, in cafe the act fhould hereafter take place; which by no means fatisfying the people, feveral hundreds of them affembled the next Monday evening, and again infifted on his abfolute renunciation of the office, which he not complying with, they put a haltar about his neck, dragged him through the town, and it was thought would abfolutely have hanged him, if he had not found means to make his efcape, and take fanctuary in the fort. This fo enraged the multitude, that they returned to his houfe, and demolifhed all his furniture that they could find, to the value of 4 or 500 l.

---Two other perfons there, we hear, had alfo applied for employments in the Stamp office, one of which was very roughly ufed, and the other had fled.

The following letter from Mr. James M'Evers, of this city, to Mr. Henry Van Schaick, of Albany, is inferted by particular defire, to fatisfy the fons of Liberty in this place.

SIR, NEW-YORK, *January* 13, 1766.

I HAVE received yours of the 7th inftant, acquainting me, that through a report being propagated of your having made application to me for the diftribution of Stamps at Albany, you had incured the difpleafure of your fellow citizens, and the refentment of the populace. I am very forry that through fuch a fuppofition, you fhould meet with any infult, as it is groundlefs. I therefore (in confequence) think myfelf in duty bound, to declare that you never made any application to me

navigation ftop'd.

*** There is now at the ftore kept by WILLIAM SMITH, on the north fide of Market-ftreet, one door below Water-ftreet, between *thirty* and *forty* pieces of CLOTHS, of different colours and qualities, all our OWN Produce and Manufactory; fome of which little, if any ways, inferior to the fuper cloths imported from England; alfo home made Linens, Shalloons, Blankets, Swanfkins, Flannels, Ink Powder,&c. &c.

*** Was found, on the Lower Ferry Road, a SILVER WATCH. The Owner, by applying to John Lort, and proving his Property, may have it again.

TO BE SOLD BY

CORNELIUS BRADFORD;

Choice French INDIGO;

Alfo Green and Congo TEA.

January 23.

ABOUT twelve or thirteen years ago, a daughter of John Penfe and Maria Penfe, was fold by Adam Lynn into Pennfylvania, about fifteen miles off Philadelphia, to the weftard of it; the girls name Parvera Penfe. If the faid girl or young woman be ftill alive, her mother Maria Penfe, living in Baltimore county, at Mr. Roger Boyce's, in the fork of Gunpowder, would be glad to hear from her, or rather fee her. If fhe is alive fhe is twenty fix years old in October laft.

† MARIA PENSE.

January 23

JOHN and DAVID RHEA

Have removed their Store from their late dwelling houfe in Front Street, to the houfe of Cafper Wifter in Market Street, oppofite the Indian King tavern, where they have for fale

A LARGE and neat affortment of dry goods fuitable for the feafon, which they will difpofe of on very low terms for Cafh or fhort Credit.

All perfons indebted to them, above twelve months are defired to make immediate payment. Likewife all perfons indebted to JOHN RHEA, by bond, bill or book account, are once more requefted to make payment to prevent their debts being put into lawyers hands. the 3m.

January 23.

LOUIS DAVID LUY LAROSE,

Lately arrived from Canada, purpofes teaching the

FRENCH LANGUAGE.

ANY Ladies or Gentlemen inclinable to learn, may be waited on at their own houfes: he is to be fpoke with next door to Mr. Benjamin Loxley's in Spruce ftreet, near the Dock, where on enquiry, they may be informed of his terms. In the mean time he hopes they may meet with that fatisfaction equal to their defire.

N. B. He alfo teaches every evening at his own houfe youth of either fex and of any age.

Juft publifhed, and to be fold by WILLIAM BRADFORD, at his Book-Store in Market-Street, adjoining the London Coffee-Houfe; and SARAH TENNENT, at her Houfe in Cherry-Alley, (*Price One Shilling*)

The Bleffednefs of PEACE-MAKERS *reprefented; and the Danger of* PERSECUTION *confidered*;

IN TWO

SERMONS,

On *Mat.* v. 9.

PREACH'D at PHILADELPHIA, the 3d *Wednefday* in *May*, 1759, before the Reverend the SYNOD, of *New-York* and *Philadelphia*.

By the late Reverend

GILBERT TENNENT, A. M.

N. B. The above fermons were corrected by himfelf, and left with a defire that they might be publifhed, as foon as poffible, after his death.

Imported in the Carolina, Capt. Friend, from London, and the Tryphena capt. Smith from Liverpool, and to be fold on the loweft terms by

PHILIP BENEZET,

At his ftore in Market-ftreet, and nearly oppofite the Meal market,

RAISINS of the fun in jars of about 25 pounds wt. figs in fmall cafks, currents in ditto, fhelled almonds, and a neat affortment of merchandize, confifting of low priced broad cloths, kerfeys, plains, fcarlet ferges, camblets, fhalloons, tammies, durants, callimancoes, a large affortment of yard wide, yard and 3-8, and 7 8, cotton and linen checks, Scots handkerchiefs, red and white and Dutch pin work ditto, culgee, bandannoe and Irifh twil'd filk ditto, yard wide and 7-8 Irifh linen, flowered Swifs lawns, cotton gowns, men and women's

SUPPLEMENT TO THE BOSTON GAZETTE

January 27, 1766

Throughout the winter of 1765–66, the Sons of Liberty, a term applied to both organized opposition groups as well as a generic label for any stamp tax opponent, were successful in opening correspondence channels and aligning colonial interests. Using news-swapping techniques perfected during the French and Indian War, printers—many being Sons of Liberty and among the hardest hit by the stamp duty on paper—repurposed patriotic reports from other colonies, thereby using newspapers as the vehicle to lead and uphold the resistance. The article shown here from the January 27, 1766, *Supplement to the Boston Gazette* contains an article originally from the *Georgia Gazette*, which includes details about the Sons of Liberty meeting at Machenry's tavern in Savannah.

...very privilege we in Britain enjoy.

The colonies are so many distant provinces of the British Empire, founded upon which it will rise firm and strong, and defy the shock of ages. But if, instead of improving his accession of dominion for the purpose of strengthening the State, we make enemies of our friends, and convert this blessing of Heaven into a curse, then indeed may we have cause to weep over our late conquests, and Britain may in the end be conquered in America. But I hope better things, tho' I thus write. I trust the favourable opportunity will be eagerly embraced of uniting and incorporating the colonies with Great Britain, and that they shall be henceforth considered as one state. Never was there an ampler field for acquiring honour; never a fairer occasion of securing immortality. The man, who shall do this piece of real service to the State, will infallibly insure to himself everlasting renown, and his memory will be endeared to latest ages—Whoever he may be, who nobly undertakes it, may success accompany him in this great and good work!—My warmest wishes are for the prosperity of Britain.

WILL. ALFRED.

SAVANNAH, *in Georgia*, Oct. 24.

LAST week advice was received from Augusta, that three white men, two of them named Payne, and the other Hoggs, were killed by the Creeks, on whose lands it is said they were hunting. We also hear, that an Officer was lately killed near Pensacola, by two of these Indians, who were put to death by their father immediately on their arrival in their own country.

Oct. 31. About seven o'clock last Friday night the effigy of a Stamp-officer was carried thro' the streets and afterwards hanged and burnt, amidst the acclamations of a great concourse of people of all ranks and denominations assembled together on the occasion.

Novem. 7. One Mr. Angus we hear is appointed for this province; the stamp paper we are also told, is brought over to Charlestown, and is to be sent to this place in his Majesty's ship Speedwell.

At a meeting of the *Sons of Liberty*, on Monday night last, at Machenry's tavern, in order to consult upon the properest measures to be taken at this very alarming and critical juncture, it was unanimously agreed upon, that the Stamp-master appointed for this province, immediately on his arrival, be waited upon, and, that as that gentleman is a stranger to this place, and consequently unacquainted with the sentiments of the people, be desired to resign an office so universally disagreeable to his Majesty's American subjects, and the execution of which may be attended with very bad consequences.

Tuesday last being the anniversary of the Gun Powder Plot, the same was observed here by firing of the great guns, &c. A number of sailors having assembled together in order to parade thro' the streets, as

James Hogg, William Payne, and his brother a boy, went off to Togoolo in the Lower Cherokee, but did not own the murder. Fourteen white men, among whom are Payne's brothers, are set out from Augusta after them, who has sworn not to return without having revenge.

The miscreants who murdered the Cherokees in Virginia some time since, are fled from that province, and are said to be amongst the Paxton-boys in Pennsylvania.

They write from Pensacola, that a Dutch subject, a Native of Surrinam, having engaged to introduce the Manufacture of Cochineal in West-Florida, on promise from the Merchants of a valuable Consideration, had received his Death by Poison; and it was strongly suspected, that the Spanish Emissaries had a hand in the affair.

The Black Vomit and sweating Sickness, continued to carry off great Numbers of the French Settlers in Cayenne colony, when the last letters were received from thence.

We have the Georgia papers to the 21st of Nov. by which we find that they had no stamp paper there and that business went on as usual.

PHILADELPHIA, *January* 2.

On Thursday last an Express passed through this City, from Fort Pitt to the General, with the agreeable and important News that Capt. Stirling, and his Party, had arrived safe at Fort Chartres, in the Illinois Country, and were there received with open Arms by the Natives.------A full Confirmation this, of Colonel Croghan's Influence, and judicious Negociations, with Pondiac, and other Chiefs of many numerous Western Nations.

By Letters from Detroit of a late Date, we hear, that every Thing was in the most perfect State of Peace with the Natives.

Extract of a letter from Charlestown, South Carolina, Dec. 2, 1765.

"The Petitions which were drawn up at the Congress were agreed to, without any Alteration, and signed afterwards by our Assembly. The Members who attended at New York, have received the Thanks of the House, and are re elected again. At present every thing is very quiet here; our Liberty Boys being content to keep out the Stamps, do not injure, but protect, the Town; for some Time ago a Parcel of Sailors, having a Mind to make the most of this Suspension of Law, formed a Mob, to collect Money of the People in the Streets; but these Sons of Liberty suppressed them instantly, and committed the Ringleaders to Goal. While they act thus cooly and determinately, we have little Reason to fear they will give up the Point, especially as the Country People are all unanimous in it; besides we have had an Offer of the whole Force of North-Carolina, should it be wanted--------At Bermuda they had taken the Stamps,

...RY 27, 1766.

is usual on that day, one of them representing a stamp master, was placed upon a scaffold supported by six others, having a paper in his hand, and a rope fastened under his arms and round his neck: at certain stages they made a stand, where this pretended Stamp master was obliged by several severe blows with a cudgel to call out in a pitiful tone, *No Stamps, No riot act, Gentlemen, &c.* After having thus sufficiently exposed him to the view of the inhabitants, and used him with every indignity they could think of, they conducted him to Machenry's tavern, before which they concluded the whole by hanging him up for a little while, and afterwards cut him down, in the presence of a croud of spectators, who were highly diverted with the humour of the tars. In all the exhibitions here of this kind, private as well as public property has remained unmolested, and no outrages been committed.

Extract of a letter from a gentleman at Natchez fort to his friend in Savannah, dated 12th of Aug. last.

"I arrived here the 12th ult. and had the agreeable satisfaction to see one of the finest countries in the world; from this fort, which is built near the banks of the river Missisippi, for about 40 miles back, is absolutely delightful, the soil the richest I ever saw, though born in Old England, the oak, hickory, cedar, poplar, and beech remarkably large: It would be the greatest crime in the world to suffer this part of the river to remain unsettled, as the inhabitants would reap every advantage that could be expected from the richest lands. Every kind of grain that Europe produces would grow here in the greatest perfection."

Seven families, consisting of about 76 people, arrived here on Saturday last, from Maryland, in order to settle in this province; amongst them are a good many who have been used to farming, and tradesmen.

CHARLES-TOWN, *South-Carolina*, Oct. 23.

Five several Parties of Cherokees, are gone out to war against the Northern tribes; one of them is headed by Oucconnostora or the Great Warrior, and another by Attakullakulla

The seven Creeks who about three weeks ago killed James Hogg, William Payne, and his brother a boy, went off to Togoolo in the Lower Cherokee, but did not own the murder. Fourteen white men, among whom are Payne's brothers, are set out from Augusta after them, who has sworn not to return without having revenge.

sylvania.

They write from Pensacola, that a Dutch subject, a Native of Surrinam, having engaged to introduce the

PENNSYLVANIA GAZETTE (PHILADELPHIA)

March 20, 1766

Under the Annapolis, March 6, dateline in the *Pennsylvania Gazette* printed March 20, 1766, is another important report of the inaugural Sons of Liberty meeting in the Maryland capital.

---

nsformed that indulgence into a Right; and a general pretence parliament being only judicially ſuppoſed, is thus rendered nothing more than a legal fiction; hence the maxim prevail- ,---"that every one was a party to all acts of parliament."

ſtatute-law, or a mere act of parliament, independantly of any xiliary juriſdiction derived from the blended exertion of pre- ative in caſes of that legal Repugnancy, which in terminis are cepted by their ſaid charters; and wherein Prerogative ſingly, conjunctively with both Houſes, has and may acknowlegedly erpoſe, purſuantly to the ſame. This obedience would cer- nly be, with reſpect to him, a naked duty; an ex-parte obli- ion obtruded upon him, which is repugnant to the nature of legal ties, and deſtructive of that principle wherein Engliſh erty eſſentially conſiſts. But farther, were the Engliſh Ame- ans not only to be bound there by the acts of the Britiſh par- ment in all caſes, but alſo by thoſe of their own Aſſemblies:--- re would be a ſubjection within a ſubjection, which might ordinate their actions to alternate contrarieties and croſs penal- s! a duplicity of juriſdiction over the ſame objects, and equal- in the firſt inſtance, unknown to the law! a ſuperfetation in legiſlative ſyſtem, which ſeems monſtrous and unnatural! e delegation therefore of a legiſlative power to the colonies ſt, one would think, from its neceſſary efficacy, be conſidered only as unconcurrent with, but as excluſive of all parliamen- y participation in the proper Subjects of their legiſlation; that o ſay, in caſes not repugnant to the laws of Great-Britain. d in all ſuch caſes may not the maxim be fitly applied;--- Deſignatio unius eſt excluſio alterius, et expreſſum facit ceſſare itum?"

That ſuch a queſtion ſhould be occaſioned at this time of day, ms altogether ſurprizing; after our very parliaments having en occaſional notices of, and impliedly confirmed the acts of American Aſſemblies in local levies and aſſeſſments: And Adminiſtration itſelf having had frequent recourſes to them ſupplies in ſuch preſſing ſeaſons, when, if the Mother-coun- had a right of impoſing taxes, the importance of the occaſion uld have worthily becomed her to have done ſo, and, on the poſition of that right, ſhould have done it,---for the ſake of tainty and diſpatch.

But it has been aſſerted with more juſtice and conſiſtency, that King's Scepter is the inſtrument of power over the colonies, d Prerogative the rule by which their obedience muſt be re- lated. In this caſe, however, have not royal charters been nted, eſtabliſhing a conſtitution, and delegating to them the be- e mentioned qualified power of legiſlation? To which the wn, even for the neceſſary proviſion and maintenance of their ernment, has frequently referred itſelf, as to an eſſential prin- al concurring party; thereby recognizing that veſted right in colonies, the eſtabliſhment whereof itſelf had originally pre- bed and chartered. Moreover, is not the King a perpetual ſtituent branch of their legiſlatures; repreſentedly preſent in ry aſſembly, and an actual party to all their laws? And this ng the caſe, prerogative muſt indeed be owned to have herein pered its operations agreeably to the ſpirit of the Engliſh con- ution, and to have thus generouſly bound and limited itſelf. r could it well have happened otherwiſe: For if, as has been , the common-law followed the ſubject to America, it is pre- ed that prerogative could have only acted there conſiſtently h, and in conformity to it. Further, with particular reſpect he point in queſtion, numerous are the inſtances of money- ies and aſſeſſments enacted by the American aſſemblies, that e travelled through occaſional examinations of the ſeveral rds and cognizances here, and nevertheleſs been confirmed, received the royal approbation: And no inſtance that I can has occurred, where any ſuch act has been diſallowed merely account of its particular tendency, or of thoſe legiſlatures hav- exerciſed a power which did not appertain to them. And royal confirmation of the actual exerciſe of this power pro- ded, no doubt, from a due reſpect to, and conſideration of the

reſiduary ties which the Crown and Parliament have upon them: ---the Navigation Act, by which they are directly excluded from all foreign markets;---the power of laying duties on their ex- ports---tranſmitted to Britain;---the right of Port-entry and ...ir caſtles, fortifications, and mi- ...ſeveral officers, civil as well as ... government;---the right of ...ing their aſſemblies;---the ...e determination of appeals ...nd, as a clincher, the abſo- ... acts, when their before- ... have been exceeded. This ...hat ſupremacy, which, with ...-country has retained over ...r how little has been left ...ow taken away, how ſoon, ...e deſerted. To conclude; ...condition of our Americans ...ther Engliſh ſubject: A con- ... intemperate folly and perverſe- neſs to reduce them to! A folly and perverſeneſs, which muſt not be imputed to the policy of the Engliſh Nation!

I am, Sir, yours, &c. &c.

London, Nov. 27. ÆQUUS.

A N N A P O L I S, March 6.

On Monday, the 24th of February, a conſiderable Number of the principal Gentlemen of Baltimore County, met at the Market-Houſe in Baltimore-Town, formed themſelves into a Society for the Maintainance of Order and Protection of American LIBERTY, by the Name of the SONS OF LIBERTY, and reſolved to meet at Annapolis, on Friday laſt, to oblige the ſeveral Officers there, to open their reſpective Offices, and proceed in Buſineſs, as uſual, without ſtamped Paper: And that the Society and Application might be ſtill the more reſpectable, the SONS OF LIBERTY in Baltimore, gave the moſt ſpeedy Notice to Gentlemen of the neighbouring Counties, to form themſelves into the like Societies, and co-operate with them in this ſo laudable Work. Saturday laſt, a much greater Number of the SONS OF LIBERTY than could be expected from the Shortneſs of the Notice, met, by Adjournment, at the Court-Houſe in Annapolis; thoſe of Baltimore and Anne-Arundel Counties were preſent perſonally, and thoſe of Kent were repreſented by their Deputy; and after hearing different Propoſals, and debating thereon with great Decency, Coolneſs and Order, Reſolved, To make a written Application to the Chief Juſtice of the Provincial Court, the Secretary and Commiſſary-General, and Judges of his Lordſhip's Land Office, to open their reſpective Offices, and proceed as uſual in the Execution of their Duties, on the 31ſt Day of March inſtant, or ſooner, if a Majority of the Supreme Courts of the Northern Governments ſhould proceed in Buſineſs before that Time. And therein to propoſe, "That if the above Officers would proceed agreeable to the Requeſt, that then an Indemnification be ſigned by the SONS OF LIBERTY, and as many others as could be induced thereto, and that the reſpective Officers be requeſted to give an Anſwer in Writing under their Hands to that Propoſition." A Committee having been ordered to deliver the Requiſition of the SONS OF LIBERTY to the above mentioned Gentlemen, afterwards returned and reported the verbal Anſwer of the Chief Juſtice of the Provincial Court, and Doctor Steuart, one of the Judges of the Loan-Office, and communicated the written Anſwer of the Secretary, to this Effect; That if he ſhould continue in Office, the Clerk of the Provincial Court would receive his Directions to act as the Judges ſhould in their judicial Capacity, at the next Court, order him as their Miniſter; but before the Meeting of the Provincial Court, he could not undertake to give Directions to the Clerk, to iſſue Proceſs, whatever the Determination of the Majority of the Northern Colonies might be, whoſe Courts might ſit before ours. The Commiſſary General not being in Town, the Committee could not deliver the Requiſition to him: The verbal Anſwer of the Chief Juſtice, and that of one of the Judges of the Land-Office, were taken under Conſideration, and in Conſequence of the Order of the SONS OF LIBERTY, the Committee again waited on thoſe Gentlemen, and having informed them, "That their Refuſal to give their Anſwers in Writing, to the Propoſition aforeſaid, was deemed a great Indignity offered to the SONS OF LIBERTY, and that their Anſwers in Writing were inſtantly expected;" they received and reported their following Anſwers.

GENTLEMEN,

IN Anſwer to your Application of this Day, my Connections and Circumſtances ſpeak my Attachment to the Liberty of the Subject here. The carrying on Buſineſs at the adjourned Provincial Court will, as to myſelf, depend on the Opinion I

lately happened in the Bay, on the Eaſtern Shore. Laſt Month Mr. Jacob Bromwell, a Man of good Character, and well eſteemed, left Oxford, in his Boat (the Oxford Packet) in order to Pilot one or two Ships down the Bay: Saturday the 15th, in the Afternoon, the Packet left Captain Peacock's Ship off Sharp's Iſland, in order to work up to Captain Laing's, off the Mouth of Wye River, the Wind then being eaſterly, and very tempeſtuous, and in the Evening ſuddenly came about to Weſt, blowed extreme hard, and became very cold. The Boat being miſſing for ſome Time, and Captain Laing waiting for his Pilot, occaſioned a Suſpicion of an Accident; and after a diligent Search, they found the Boat, with a little of her Maſts to be ſeen, at the Weſtward of Poplar-Iſland, in three Fathom Water. We are told that three Perſons were in her, beſide Mr. Bromwell, viz. John Rowlandſon, and Edward Brining, both young Men, and a Dutchman, who, undoubtedly, all periſhed together.

We hear that Captain Robert Bryce, in the Brig Nancy, belonging to this Place, outward bound with a Load of Wheat, ſprung a Leak, and was obliged to put into Norfolk to ſtop it.

Trenton, March 15, 1766.

PURSUANT to an Order of William Morris, and William Clayton, Eſquires, Judges of the Inferior Court of Common Pleas for the County of Hunterdon, upon the Petition of Charles Hoff, of ſaid County, and the major Part in Value of his Creditors, Notice is hereby given to all the Creditors of the ſaid Charles Hoff, that Monday, the 14th Day of April next, is appointed by the ſaid Judges for the ſaid Creditors to meet at the Court-Houſe in Trenton, at 3 o' Clock in the Afternoon, to ſhew Cauſe, if any they have, why the ſaid Charles Hoff ſhould not aſſign over all his Eſtate and Effects, and be admitted to the Benefit of an Act of this Province of New-Jerſey, lately paſſed at Burlington, intituled, "An Act for the Relief of inſolvent Debtors."

March 20, 1766. NUMB. 1943.

The PENNSYLVANIA  GAZETTE.

Containing the Freshest Advices, Foreign and Domestic.

To the PRINTER of the LONDON CHRONICLE.

SIR,

AN ex post facto question, soon expected to be advisedly discussed is, "Whether the Mother country has a right of imposing local taxes on all her American colonies?" The precedent fact is supposed to have been ministerially preresolved, and influentially established. This necessary previous question, as to the Right, remains still to be put: And it is hoped the wisdom and equity of both Houses will not suffer it to be craftily slurred over, and much less precipitately carried;---as it were by a Coup de Main.

The proper arguments, stript of all political refinements and expediences, must turn on the consideration of two principal points, viz. the constitutional Power of the British Parliament, respecting the aforementioned fact; and the actual Exertions of royal prerogative, in the point of Right; under which it is admitted that the colonies lay claim to, and avow their respective legislative privileges.

English Liberty is a propriety attached to the individuals of the community, founded on the original frame or constitution of our government, and might be defined, "the primitive right that every freeholder had of consenting to those laws by which the Community was to be obliged." Time and change of circumstances extended this circle of comprehension, and made every subject in some respect or other a member of the legislature; his consent at first personally denoted, was afterwards allowed to be given by a proxy or representative. Usage and conveniency transformed that indulgence into a Right; and a general pretence in parliament being only judicially supposed, is thus rendered something more than a legal fiction; hence the maxim prevailed,---"that every one was a party to all acts of parliament." This privilege of becoming a Party to the laws, or of being in effect his own governor, was as it were the consideration or price of individual subjection: And from the express or implied exercise of it, the duty of our legal Obedience is inferred. But an Englishman in America has no means of being present or represented in the British Legislature, quasi a Colonist: Where then is to be found his consent to parliamentary acts operative there; and by what construction can he be said to give his voice? being thus in neither sense a party, as wanting the fundamental privilege above-mentioned; and not having been subjected to any obligation of this kind by original patent or charter; but, on the contrary, an express power being thereby granted to the colonies of enacting their own Laws, provided the same be not repugnant to those of Great-Britain. It is hard to conceive from what constitutional principle, applicable to a colony, not a conquered country, his obedience to our statute-law can be deduced. I say, to statute-law, or a mere act of parliament, independantly of any auxiliary jurisdiction derived from the blended exertion of prerogative in cases of that legal Repugnancy, which in terminis are excepted by their said charters; and wherein Prerogative singly, or conjunctively with both Houses, has and may acknowledgedly interpose, pursuantly to the same. This obedience would certainly be, with respect to him, a naked duty; an ex-parte obligation obtruded upon him, which is repugnant to the nature of all legal ties, and destructive of that principle wherein English Liberty essentially consists. But farther, were the English Americans not only to be bound there by the acts of the British parliament in all cases, but also by those of their own Assemblies:---Here would be a subjection within a subjection, which might subordinate their actions to alternate contrarieties and cross penalties! a duplicity of jurisdiction over the same objects, and equally, in the first instance, unknown to the law! a superfetation in the legislative system, which seems monstrous and unnatural!

tary participation in the proper Subjects of their legislation; that is to say, in cases not repugnant to the laws of Great-Britain. And in all such cases may not the maxim be fitly applied;---

statute, De tallagio non concedendo; or, "The prohibition of imposing any taxes or aids without the universal consent of the freemen," &c. An exemption, founded on common law, and antient English Liberty! which it seems the colonists do conceive themselves intitled to, as their birthright; that birthright, by which they are themselves tied in interest to the Mother-country, and bound to a correlative loyalty, which thus requires not any military force to be secured or vindicated. So that whether this question, of a subsisting right to impose œconomical taxes on the colonies, be applied to the British parliament, independantly as before noticed; or to the royal prerogative, exclusive of the American assemblies; in both cases it would seem, as matters are circumstanced, to be a lost point. On the other hand, should this right, so delegated to the colonies, be now considered by any after-thought as a reversible error: Be it remembered, that it was at first so delegated by solemn acts of government, that it proved the means of their vast increase and cultivation, and by consequence of those immense profits and advantages which have thence accrued to us; that it is sanctified by successive usage, grounded upon a generous reliance on English Faith and Compact, and that usage---ratified by repeated authoritative acquiescence: And lastly, that any violation of their constitutions, by what means soever executed, might unhinge the principles of their natural and civil attachment to the Mother-country; thereby opening to our foreign enemies a direct passage into our palladium itself.

Nor, this privilege being left them, let it be thought that the colonies will of course be independent. No! numerous are the residuary ties which the Crown and Parliament have upon them: ---the Navigation Act, by which they are directly excluded from all foreign markets;---the power of laying duties on their exports---transmitted to Britain;---the right of Port-entry and clearance;---the command of their castles, fortifications, and militia;---the appointment of their several officers, civil as well as military;---the executive power of government;---the right of convening, proroguing, and dissolving their assemblies;---the Governor's negative to any bill;---the determination of appeals from their Courts of Judicature;---and, as a clincher, the absolute jurisdiction of annulling their acts, when their beforementioned legislative power appears to have been exceeded. This is a general sketch of the nature of that supremacy, which, with some partial exceptions, the Mother-country has retained over her colonies.----By it, it will appear how little has been left them; and, were that little to be now taken away, how soon, at the best, they might probably be deserted. To conclude; were it not for this privilege, the condition of our Americans would be worse than that of any other English subject: A condition, that would argue the most intemperate folly and perverseness to reduce them to! A folly and perverseness, which must not be imputed to the policy of the English Nation!

I am, Sir, yours, &c. &c.

London, Nov. 27. ÆQUUS.

ANNAPOLIS, March 6.

On Monday, the 24th of February, a considerable Number of the principal Gentlemen of Baltimore County, met at the Market-House in Baltimore-Town, formed themselves into a Society for the Maintainance of Order and Protection of American LIBERTY, by the Name of the SONS OF LIBERTY, and resolved to meet at Annapolis, on Friday last, to oblige the several Officers there, to open their respective Offices, and proceed in Business, as usual, without stamped Paper: And that the Society and Application might be still the more respectable, the SONS OF LIBERTY in Baltimore, gave the most speedy Notice to Gentlemen of the neighbouring Counties, to form themselves

Shortness of the Notice, met, by Adjournment, at the Court-House in Annapolis; those of Baltimore and Anne-Arundel Counties were present personally, and those of Kent were represented by their Deputy; and after hearing different Proposals, and

have as yet to form. I shall meet my Brethren on the Day to which the Court is adjourned, and be governed by those Reasons and Principles which ought to actuate every Man who sits in Stations similar to that which is filled by

March 1, 1766. Your humble Servant, JOHN BRICE.

A PROPOSITION being this Day given in to me, requesting that Business should be done in the Land Office of this Province as usual; to which I answered, That the Land Office was open, and the Records thereof subject to the Perusal of all Persons who have Occasion to make Searches; and that Copies of the Records, authenticated by the Register, should be made out to any Person so applying, paying the usual Fees; and, as I apprehend the Sale of the Lord Proprietary's Lands, are Matters of private Concern, respecting his own Interest, he may grant Warrants, or refuse to grant them, as he shall think proper. Given under my Hand, at Annapolis, this First Day of March, 1766. GEORGE STEUART.

To the SONS OF LIBERTY, of Baltimore, Anne Arundel, and Kent Counties.

After reading of which Answers, it was ordered, that Copies of the Proceedings be transmitted to the several Counties, and their SONS OF LIBERTY invited to enter into the like Associations, and a Number, not less than Twelve, from each County, be requested to attend at Annapolis, on the 31st Instant, to see the Event of, or repeat, if necessary, the Applications already made.

We have an Account of a very melancholy Catastrophe which lately happened in the Bay, on the Eastern Shore. Last Month Mr. Jacob Bromwell, a Man of good Character, and well esteemed, left Oxford, in his Boat (the Oxford Packet) in order to Pilot one or two Ships down the Bay: Saturday the 15th, in the Afternoon, the Packet left Captain Peacock's Ship off Sharp's Island, in order to work up to Captain Laing's, off the Mouth of Wye River, the Wind then being easterly, and very tempestuous, and in the Evening suddenly came about to West, blowed extreme hard, and became very cold. The Boat being missing for some Time, and Captain Laing waiting for his Pilot, occasioned a Suspicion of an Accident; and after a diligent Search, they found the Boat, with a little of her Masts to be seen, at the Westward of Poplar-Island, in three Fathom Water. We are told that three Persons were in her, beside Mr. Bromwell, viz. John Rowlandson, and Edward Brining, both young Men, and a Dutchman, who, undoubtedly, all perished together.

We hear that Captain Robert Bryce, in the Brig Nancy, belonging to this Place, outward bound with a Load of Wheat, sprung a Leak, and was obliged to put into Norfolk to stop it.

BOSTON GAZETTE

January 27, 1766

In addition to effigies and riots, a boycott of British imports added financial stress to English merchants and effectively recruited them to lobby Parliament in favor of the act's repeal. A short paragraph in the left column of page two reports that letters from Boston merchants to England instruct them to send goods only after the Stamp Act is repealed. At the bottom of the same column is news from New York about a midnight raid of a ship with stamped papers on board. The New York Stamp Party?

... diſpatches juſt received from a gentleman in high office in America, we are credibly informed he has mentioned, that ſhould the late act of parliament be carried into execution for enforcing the ſtamp du...

... called.

A number of merchants in Boſton have wrote to England for goods to be ſent, upon condition only that the ſtamp act is repealed.

'Tis now pretty confidently aſſerted, that a great nobleman is making over all his eſtates in truſt, and intends to make a ſpeedy retreat to another country.

It is ſaid Lord Groſvenor has offered 35, 000l. for the late Duke of Cumberland's running horſes at Newmarket.

His Majeſty has conferred the honour of Knighthood on Sir William Johnſon's ſon, who lately arrived from America.

It is ſaid, that his late Royal Highneſs the Duke of Cumberland gave away near 6000l annually in private charities.

Lord Campden, we hear, will deliver his opinion concerning the legality of warrants iſſued by Secretaries of ſtate on Wedneſday next.

A letter from Madrid ſay, " The public are greatly pleaſed with the liberty which the King has granted to all his ſubjects indiſcriminately, of trading to our American colonies."

NEW-YORK, January 6.

Tueſday laſt Capt. Haviland arrived here from London, and had ten Boxes of the deteſtable ſtamp Papers on board—But about 12 a Clock laſt Night a Company of armed Men went on board his Brig, and after obliging the People to deliver up the Keys, and get Lights, they opened the Hatches, and ſeized the ſtamped Papers for this Province and Connecticut, amounting to 10 Boxes, with which they loaded a large Boat, and proceeded with them up the River to the Shipyards where they broke the Packages to Pieces, and with ſome Tar-Barrels and other Combuſtibles, made a Bonfire of them and their Contents.—When the whole was entirely conſumed, they all quietly diſperſed, without doing any MISCHIEF, or even alarming the City.

... was laudable ; but *deſtroying their Houſes, &c. no thinking ſober Man can juſtify, and if encouraged, will tend to prevent and trample upon all Order and good Government, and ... end in Murders, Anarchy, Confuſion and every ... that is dreadful to Society. The Houſe of Re... ives will be (with you I dare ſay they are ... Guardians and Defenders of the People they ... and of themſelves : the People ſhould meet ... them their Inſtructions, and they I dare ſay ... Care to guard their Liberties, and to defend ... (when obliged) from Rapine, and miniſte... ell as gubernatoral Avidity. I have ever ... by the Principles of this moſt free Govern... People could not be taxed without their Con... nothing I have lately read has altered my ... if I am miſtaken, I am open to Conviction, ... to receive Inſtruction, but not by an ipſe ... of a King.—Trials by Jury is eſtabliſh'd ... Magna Charta ; and an Act of Parliament ... Contradiction to that glorious Charter, Lord Coke tells us void.—Perhaps you may find, or I may ſee a Scot's Lawyer give his Opinion the other Way."—*

Friday laſt the Halifax Packet in 17 Days, and Yeſterday Capt Pepper, in 10 Days, arrived here from Halifax ; neither of which confirm the (pretended) Orders the Captains of the Cruizers at New-York have aſſum'd to take ; but on the contrary ſay, that Veſſels are enter'd there (without Stamps) as uſual, which may more fully appear by the following

Extract of a Letter from Halifax, dated Jan. 1. 1766.

—"IT gives us great Pleaſure to find the Port again open, ſo that an Intercourſe is not likely to be further interrupted.—The Veſſels are admitted to an Entry here as uſual, without exacting the Penalty of Ten Pounds as preſcribed in the —— Stamp Act. —The Diſtributor of the Stamps with us has received Inſtructions from the Commiſſioners of the Stamp Duties, *not* to proſecute any Perſon upon the Penalties of the Act, but only to repreſent to them who the Perſons are that refuſe Obedience, &c.——This has the Appearance of Conviction among the Learned on the other Side the Water, that the Act is unconſtitutional ; wherefore they ſeem to decline a legal and judicial Determination upon it. Surely this forbodes good Tidings——I pray God that the next Parliament may by ſome wiſe and prudent Meaſures remove every Obſtacle of Jealouſy between the Old and New-Engliſh Men, and the Benefits of Britons under the Britiſh Conſtitution for ever hereafter be mutually enjoyed"—

The public Prints brought by the Lord Hyde Packet are of no later Date than we have already publiſhed.

It was ſtrongly reported in England we ſhall very ſoon be relieved from the late grievous Impoſitions, and that Meaſures the moſt ſalutary and beneficial to the Colonies had been reſolved upon, *in ſome important Councils at the Weſt end of the Town ; as a London Paper mentions.*

The Inferiour Court of Common Pleas at Portſmouth, carry on Buſineſs as uſual, without Stamps.

... for Relief ; but it is not ſuitab... or Dignity of the Britiſh Emp... under the Pretence of redreſſi... preſume to violate the publick ...

Extract of a Letter from a ... Credit in London to a Frie... November 9 1765.

" —WE have now the Ple... our new Miniſtry ... retrieving you from the Oppreſſi... laid you under, which has rend... the People here; and a few Mon... the Face of Affairs, for they are ... take off the Stamp Duty and Du... to give you ſeveral poſitive Adva...

An Account from England ab... ſays, That They at Home have a ... with reſpect to America, they wi... to Trade, the Stamp Act they wi... relax, but will not repeal.

L O N D O N, ...

It is now again confidently aſſ... American Governor is actually ſup...

The reconciliation that has la... tween two certain great perſonage... ed this evening with a ſupper and ...

We hear that the Sun Fire Offic... by the late fire, to the amount ... pounds.

We are informed that there is ... apprehend, what the anti miniſteria... trumpet forth, that a change of a... precede, or at leaſt ſoon follow th... liament.

The right hon. the Lord Chanc... much better.

IMPORTED in the laſ... LONDON and BRISTOL, an...

Samuel Allyne...

At his Store No. 5, South Side o...

Ticklinburgs
Oznabrigs
Ruſſia Duck No. 1 to 4
Cod & Mackrel Hooks and Lines
Twine Starch
Allum Copperas
3d 4d 6d 8d 10d & 20d Nails
Pipes Glaſs
Powder Steel
Pepper Muſtard
Spices of all kinds.

ALS... ſa... Beſt ... Cordag... Quart ... Cotton ... Weſt I... Engla... Melaſſes ... Flour ... Iron Po... Mackrel ... A few C... cha...

AND ſundry other Articles at the ...

MONDAY, February 17, 1766.

BOSTON GAZETTE
February 17, 1766

Extracts of several London-to-Boston letters litter the front page of this issue. The second one down in the right column confirms that the boycotts have turned London merchants into lobbyists who "intend to apply to Parliament for some Redress with respect to the American Trade; and 'tis hoped the Government will repeal the Stamp Act, from a Conviction that the late Ministry have done wrong."

Monday Night laſt arrived here Capt. Dixcey from London, in 35 Days ; by whom we have the public Prints to the 27th of December, from which we have extracted the following Articles : viz.

From the LONDON GAZETTE.

WESTMINSTER, December 17. THIS day his Majeſty came to the Houſe of Peers, and being in his royal robes ſeated on the throne with the uſual ſolemnity, Sir Francis Molineux, Knt. Gentleman Uſher of the Black Rod, was ſent with a meſſage from his Majeſty to the Houſe of Commons, commanding their attendance in the Houſe of Peers. The Commons being come thither accordingly, His Majeſty was pleaſed to make the following moſt gracious SPEECH

My Lords and Gentlemen,

"THE preſent general ſtate of tranquility " in Europe, gave me hopes, that it " would not have been neceſſary to aſ- " ſemble my Parliament ſooner than is " uſual in times of Peace.

" BUT, as matters of importance have lately oc- " curred in ſome of my Colonies in America, which " will demand the moſt ſerious attention of Parliament " and as further informations are daily expected from " different parts of that country, of which I ſhall " order the fulleſt accounts to be prepared for your " conſideration ; I have thought fit to call you to- " gether, in order that opportunity may thereby be " given, to iſſue the neceſſary writs on the many " Vacancies that have happened in the Houſe of Com- " mons ſince the laſt Seſſion ; ſo that the Parliament " may be full, to proceed, immediately after the " uſual receſs, on the conſideration of ſuch weighty " matters as will come before you."

The Humble ADDRESS of the Right Honorable the Lords Spiritual and Temporal in Parliament aſſembled.

Moſt Gracious Sovereign,

WE, Your Majeſty's moſt dutiful and loyal Subjects, the Lords Spiritual and Temporal in Parliament aſſembled, beg Leave to return your Majeſty our humble Thanks for your moſt Gracious Speech from the Throne.

We ſhould be wanting in our Duty, not to aſſure your Majeſty, that when your Majeſty ſhall have been pleaſed to communicate to your Parliament thoſe Informations and Advices which have been, or ſhall be, received from *America*, we will proceed to the Conſideration of thoſe weighty Matters, with an Attention equal to the Importance of the Subject, and with a Reſolution to do every Thing which the Exigency of the Caſe may require.

ATTENTIVE to every Event which affects your Majeſty, permit us to congratulate your Majeſty on the Birth of a Prince. Whatever adds to your domeſtic Happineſs, and the Stability and Encreaſe of that illuſtrious Houſe from which theſe Kingdoms have received the moſt important Benefits, muſt always afford the higheſt Satisfaction to your faithful Subjects.

ANIMATED by the ſame Sentiments of Zeal and Duty to your Majeſty and your Royal Family, and under the deepeſt Impreſſions of Concern, we beg Leave to approach your Throne with our ſincere Condolence on the Loſs of His late Royal Highneſs the Duke of *Cumberland.*

THE many eminent publick and private Virtues, the Extent of Capacity, and the Magnanimity of Mind, the Affection for your Majeſty's Perſon, and the eminent Services performed for this Country, which diſtinguiſhed that great and excellent Prince, as they have left a laſting Memorial in your Royal Breaſt, ſo have they made an Impreſſion never to be eraſed from the Minds

The Humble ADDRE[...]

Moſt Graciou[...]

WE your Maje[...] the Comm[...] aſſembled, beg Le[...] Thanks of this Hou[...] from the Throne : [...] we will not fail, [...] with its Members [...] Diligence and Atte[...] cies in *America*, wh[...] our Conſideration ; [...] deavours for the H[...] ment, and the true [...] Parts of your exten[...]

Permit us, at the ſa[...] Majeſty on the late Increaſe of your Royal Family, by the Birth of a Prince. Your Majeſty's Happineſs and that of your People are one ; and every Increaſe of your Majeſty's Illuſtrious Family is conſidered by your faithful Commons, as a further Security to that Religion, and thoſe Liberties we enjoy under your Majeſty's moſt auſpicious Government.

We alſo beg Leave to offer to your Majeſty our ſincere Condolence on the great Loſs, which your Majeſty and this Kingdom have ſuſtained by the Death of his late Royal Highneſs the Duke of *Cumberland* ; whoſe private and public Virtues, whoſe Duty and Affection to your Majeſty, and whoſe diſtinguiſhed Merits and Services to this Country, as they made his Perſon dear to this Nation while he lived, ſo they cannot fail to render his Memory ſacred to the lateſt Poſterity.

The following is His Majeſty's anſwer to the addreſs of the Honourable Houſe of Commons, preſented to him on Thurſday laſt for his moſt gracious ſpeech from the Throne, viz.

" *Gentlemen,*

" I return you thanks for this loyal and dutiful addreſs.

" The ſatisfaction you expreſs in the increaſe of my family, and the affectionate ſhare you take in the great loſs I have ſuſtained by the death of the Duke of Cumberland, are freſh proofs of your zeal and loyalty.

" Your reſolution at the ſame time to ſupport the honour of my government, and to provide for the true intereſt of all my people, cannot but be acceptable to me. My conduct ſhall always ſhew, that I conſider their intereſt as inſeparable from my own."

The following is her Majeſty's anſwer to a congratulatory meſſage, ſent by the Houſe of Commons to her Majeſty, on her happy delivery of another Prince during the vacation of Parliament.

" *Gentlemen,*

" This freſh inſtance of your duty to the King and attention to Me, cannot but meet with my moſt hearty acknowledgements, and inſure a continuance of that affection I bear to this nation, whoſe welfare and proſperity will be for ever the firſt object of my wiſhes.

Laſt Sunday died at Bath, his Grace Dr. William Carmichael, Archbiſhop of Dublin.

St. James's, Dec. 21. The King has been pleaſed to conſtitue and appoint the Right Hon. John Earl of Egmont of the Kingdom of Ireland, and Lord Lovel and Holland of Enmore in the County of Somerſet in the Kingdom of Great Britain, Sir Charles Saunders, Knt. of the Bath, Auguſtus Keppel, and Charles Townſend, Eſqrs. Sir William Meredith, Bart. John Buller, and John Yorke, Eſqrs. to be Commiſſioners for executing the Office of High Ad-

[...] Manufacturers and Merchants ; by which ſuch Meaſures are pointed out, as, it is hoped, will reſtore our Commerce to its former flouriſhing State."

Extract from another Letter.

" The Diſturbances in North America about the Stamps are very alarming and cauſes great Uneaſineſs to thoſe Gentlemen who have large Sums due to them there : the Stagnation of Remittances for a few Months may be attended with bad Conſequences.---You are very right with regard to the Method of that Trade from the Body of Merchants trading to the ſeveral Provinces, who in Conjunction with thoſe concerned in the Trade thither, intend to apply to Parliament for ſome Redreſs with reſpect to the American Trade ; and 'tis hoped the Government will repeal the Stamp Act, from a Conviction that the late Miniſtry have done wrong."

Extract of a private Letter from London, dated 24th Dec. 1765.

" On Tueſday 18th December there was a warm Debate in the H—ſe of C——ns, what ſhould be done with the rebellious Americans (for 'tis the general Opinion that your Oppoſition has led you into Meaſures rather too licentious, tho' God knows I am no Friend to the Stamp-Act) Mr. G-nv--lle was exceſſively warm on the Occaſion, and urged that a large Force be ſent out to deſtroy you, to my Amazement 29 of the preſent Members concurred with him ; but there were 80 Members who as warmly oppoſed thoſe Meaſures, and you may reſt ſatisfied that every thing will be ſettled to your Satisfaction very ſoon."

Extract of a Letter from a Gentleman in London, dated Dec. 22, 1765.

" The Parliament met laſt Tueſday ; two Days they were debating the American Riots, which many called Rebellion : The preſent Miniſtry are calm and diſpaſſionate, willing to redreſs all Grievances ; and thank God, have a Majority in both Houſes. Much Heat and Altercation will ariſe to make it a long and warm Seſſions. In my next I hope to give you ſome more favourable Accounts."

Extract of another Letter of the ſame Date.

" I am now at the Court End of the Town, and have the Pleaſure to inform you, that the City and Country are all in your Favour : I make no doubt the Stamp Act will be repealed."

On the 13th of December a Deputation from the Merchants of London, trading to North-America, waited on the Miniſtry, to requeſt their Countenance and Support, in the intended Application to Parliament, for the Relief of the Colonies, and of the Trade to theſe Parts —A Liſt of the Deputation is as follows. For *Canada* Mr. John Strettel ; Mr. Anthony Vialars,

REPORTING THE

STAMP ACT REPEAL

By Todd Andrlik

By February 1766, the stamp tax crisis had become such a nuisance that Parliament passed its repeal and George III gave his royal approval on March 17. News of the repeal was instantly met with great joy and relief by London merchants, who would soon benefit from the end of boycotts on their goods. In fact, before the King and Parliament went into session to repeal the Stamp Act, measures were taken by local merchants to quickly communicate the great news with their colonial clients.

According to the March 20, 1766, *London Chronicle*, "The instant his Majesty came out of the Parliament house yesterday, an express with letters to different persons in America, set off for Falmouth; at which place, a light ship, hired and prepared by the Merchants, lay ready to set sail, the very moment the express arrives."

America's social revolution, incubated by newspapers, successfully pressured Great Britain, the world's greatest superpower, to retreat from its unprecedented legislation. Printers demonstrated the power of the press to incite political debate and influence a favorable government response, which would not soon be forgotten.

Reaching American ports in May, news of the Stamp Act repeal set off another wave of celebrations. The repeal festivities in New York quickly circulated around the colonies, such as the report from the May 29, 1766, *Pennsylvania Journal* that printed:

> *On Tuesday last we were favoured with the authenticated glorious and interesting news of the repeal from different quarters, which was instantly spread throughout the city, diffusing joy and gladness in every face : whereupon, all the bells of the different churches were rung, and the next day there was a manifestation of the greatest gratitude shewn by the True Sons of Liberty.*

One of the express letters from London, "signed by 55 of the principal Merchants trading to North America," was published in the June 16, 1766, *Boston Gazette*, addressed to "John Hancock, Esq; and the Rest of the Merchants in Boston." The letter encourages Boston merchants to support public order and gratitude toward the mother country, "which by the Repeal of this Act has given such incontestable Proof of her Moderation." It also suggests that had Americans obeyed the law and simply communicated their hardships, "[r]elief would have been more speedy."

No matter how long it took, America's social revolution, incubated by newspapers, successfully pressured Great Britain, the world's greatest superpower, to retreat from its unprecedented legislation. Printers demonstrated the power of the press to incite political debate and influence a favorable government response, which would not soon be forgotten. As Benjamin Franklin pointed out near the end of the Revolutionary War, "the same truths may be repeatedly enforced by placing them daily in different lights in newspapers, which are everywhere read… And we now find, that it is not only right to strike while the iron is hot, but that it may be very practicable to heat it by continually striking."

To save face, the Declaratory Act was passed the same day of the Stamp Act repeal and asserted Parliament's authority over the colonies as having "full power and authority, to make laws and statutes of sufficient force and validity to bind the colonies, and people of America, subjects of the Crown of Great-Britain, in all cases whatsoever."

It would not be long before Parliament picked the scab and again demonstrated its authority to tax the American colonies, stirring renewed ferment and continuing a back-and-forth struggle for power.

THE REPEAL, OR THE FUNERAL PROCESSION, OF MISS AME-STAMP, 1766
The Bridgeman Art Library

(*left*) This popular satire shows supporters of the Stamp Act gathering at a dock to carry a small coffin containing the remains of the bill toward an open vault.

ADVERTISEMENT
February 17, 1766, Boston Gazette

(*below*) In addition to the *Boston Gazette*, printers Benjamin Edes and John Gill also printed other works, including the American reprint of this anti–Stamp Act pamphlet from London.

Now in the PRESS,
And in a few Days will be Re Printed,
(From the London Edition,)
THE NECESSITY of *Repealing* the *American* STAMP-ACT demonſtrated: Or, A PROOF that GREAT-BRITAIN muſt be injured by that ACT. In a LETTER to a MEMBER of the BRITISH HOUSE of COMMONS.

condemned to be hanged; John Yemm, and George Lypiatt, were alſo condemned for ſheep-ſtealing, but have ſince been reprieved. Thomas Dee, condemned laſt aſſizes and reprieved, to be tranſported for 14 years.

LONDON.

His Majeſty was attended in the ſtate coach yeſterday to the Houſe of Peers by the Earl of Buckinghamſhire and Lord Cadogan; when the following acts, beſides thoſe mentioned in our laſt, received the royal aſſent.

An act to remove a doubt concerning ſuch part of an act made in the laſt ſeſſion of parliament, as relates to the aſcertaining of the duties upon the importation of certain linnen cloth of the manufacture of Ruſſia; and to obviate all doubts with reſpect to the importation of tea, under certain licences authorized to be granted by an act made in the 18th year of the reign of his late Majeſty.

An act to indemnify ſuch perſons as have omitted to qualify themſelves for offices and employments; and to indemnify Juſtices of the Peace, Deputy Lieutenants, and officers of the militia, or others, who have omitted to regiſter or deliver in their qualifications within the time limited by law, and for giving further time for thoſe purpoſes, &c.

An act for the better regulation of pilots for the conducting of ſhips and veſſels into and out of the port of Liverpool.

The act for repealing the American ſtamp duties, is thus intituled:—"An act to repeal an act made in the laſt ſeſſion of Parliament, intituled, An act for granting and applying certain ſtamp duties and other duties in the Britiſh Colonies and Plantations in America, towards further defraying the expences of defending, protecting, and ſecuring the ſame, and for amending ſuch parts of the ſeveral acts of Parliament relating to the trade and revenues of the ſaid Colonies and Plantations, as direct the manner of determining and recovering the penalties and forfeitures therein mentioned."

A great number of merchants met yeſterday at the King's Arms tavern, in Cornhill; from whence they went in their coaches to Weſt-

it.

King Staniſlaus of Poland has left to ea his executors, the Intendant and Farmer G ral of Lorrain, a ring worth 20,000 crown

We hear the Right Hon. Lord Cant now Earl of Delawar, will be appointed the honours his late father enjoyed.

The Court of Aldermen having lately an order, than whenever there ſhould not ſufficient number of Aldermen to make a by one o'clock, the Lord Mayor might ad the ſaid Court, without ſending to the A men's houſes, as has been lately the cuſ and yeſterday there not being a ſufficient ber of Aldermen, who attended by one o'c his Lordſhip ſoon after went away, purſua the above order of Court.

Yeſterday a diſpenſation paſſed the ſea enable the Rev. Dr. William Digby, one c Majeſty's chaplains, to hold the rector Sheldon, and alſo the vicarage of Coleſh Warwickſhire, worth 240l. per annum.

The Rev. James Fletcher, B. A. was a days ſince preſented to the vicarage of M Minſter in Norfolk, void by the ceſſion o late miniſter.

The Rev. Mr. Henry Pepperell is preſ by William Crofts, Eſq; to the rectory of Harling, with Middle Harling, in Norfolk.

A letter from Plympton in Devonſhire, "We have had nothing but rejoycings and all round the country, in every pariſh village, bells ringing, and bonfires at ni ever ſince Tueſday's poſt, which brought port that the repeal of the late Cyder-tax paſſed the Houſe of Commons. Three n bouring Juſtices of the Peace gave a t cyder each to the inhabitants of their ſe pariſhes."

On Monday died at his chambers in C Court, Gray's-Inn, Samuel Chalmers, Eſq; merly Governor of Gibraltar.

On the 7th inſtant died, at his ſeat, Stradb Hall, Pole Coſby, Eſq; by whoſe death an e of 4000l. per annum devolves to Dudley A ander Sidney Coſby, late Britiſh miniſter a court of Denmark.

On Friday died in Stanhope-Street, May- James Jeſſup Eſſup, Eſq.

and at Morpeth, it was calle and a reward offered: After man went to Mr. Turnbull delivered it, telling him ſhe before on the road near Al bull immediately ſent it to t turned her three guineas.

Tueſday died at Kirkharl land, Mr. John Brown, Ste the Duke of Portland.

Wedneſday died at Matfi land, Mr. John Armſtrong, ward Blackett, Bart.

Thurſday ſe'nnight died the county of Durham, Wm.

On the 7th inſt. died at thumberland, Rebecca Hug memory ſhe retained to th and could read without ſpect poſterity ſurvive her, viz. 6 children, and 26 great grand

Glouceſter, March 17. W of a very extraordinary inſt vengeance that happened ab Chalford in this county; Or a young man of that place, w and he moſt profanely wiſhed and his eyes never ſhut, if h next game. When he was g ſerved a black ſpot upon his l mortification began immedia over his body, ſo that he di his fleſh being quite rotten; be ſhut, notwithſtanding all friends to cloſe them. The atteſted by many of the nei with him. [*Glouceſter Jour*

At our aſſizes, which were turday, Thomas Evans and condemned to be hanged; George Lypiatt, were alſo con ſtealing, but have ſince been r Dee, condemned laſt aſſizes an tranſported for 14 years.

LONDO

His Majeſty was attended yeſterday to the Houſe of Pe Buckinghamſhire and Lord C acts, beſides thoſe ed the royal aſſent. to remove a doub ct made in the la lates to the aſcerta nportation of cer cture of Ruſſia; reſpect to the in in licences author made in the 18th ye his late Majeſty.

An act to indemnify ſuch omitted to qualify themſelve employments; and to indemn Peace, Deputy Lieutenants, militia, or others, who have o or deliver in their qualificatio

LONDON CHRONICLE

March 20, 1766

By February 1766, the stamp tax crisis had become such a nuisance that Parliament passed its repeal and King George III gave his royal approval on March 17. News of the repeal was instantly met with great joy and relief by London merchants, who would soon benefit from the end of boycotts on their goods. In fact, before the King and Parliament went into session to repeal the Stamp Act, measures were taken by local merchants to quickly communicate the great news with their colonial clients.

minſter, to expreſs their ſatisfaction on the royal aſſent being given to the bill for the repeal of the Stamp Act. The bells rang in every part of the city on the ſame occaſion; and in the afternoon the Merchants had a grand entertainment at the above Tavern, at which were preſent many perſons of diſtinction. At night many coffee-houſes and other houſes in the city were finely illuminated, and other demonſtrations of joy were ſhewn on this event.

The inſtant his Majeſty came out of the Parliament houſe yeſterday, an expreſs with letters to different perſons in America, ſet off for Falmouth; at which place, a light ſhip, hired and prepared by the Merchants, lay ready to ſet ſail, the very moment the expreſs arrives.

We are informed, that 1,800,000 l. will be granted for paying off and diſcharging the Exchequer Bills made out i[n] 1764 and 1765.

Yeſterday died at her houſe in Dover-ſtreet Mrs. Daſhwood, mother of Mrs. Daſhwood, ... of the wo[...] jeſty.

Six of the felons who were concerned in breaking Maidſtone gaol, and preſent at the murder of the keeper, were executed on Saturday ...

PENNSYLVANIA JOURNAL (PHILADELPHIA)

May 29, 1766

News of the Stamp Act repeal raced across the Atlantic, reaching American ports in May and setting off a wave of celebrations. With the help of newspapers, Americans successfully pressured the empire to retreat from its legislation. The newfound power of the printed word would be leveraged on numerous occasions in the coming years.

...rion. There may be ſome others; but theſe are the principal regulations; I hope they will all paſs, but the ſpirit of oppoſition muſt certainly overſet ſome of them."

Extract of a Letter from Briſtol, March 25.

"We have the trade bill now much at heart, and are battling it out with the London West-India merchants, and hope in the concluſion we ſhall be able to procure you in America ſuch advantages as you could wiſh yourſelves to and from the Spaniſh and French ſettlements in America.

NEW-YORK, May 26.

On Tueſday laſt we were favoured with the authenticated glorious and intereſting news of the *repeal* from different quarters, which was inſtantly ſpread throughout the city, diffuſing joy and gladneſs in every face; whereupon, all the bells of the different churches were rung, and the next day there was a manifeſtation of the greateſt gratitude ſhewn by the *True Sons of Liberty*, who could not withold any longer their open and liberal rejoicings, on a matter which ſo nearly concerned them; and in order thereto, public notice of a rejoicing was printed and diſtributed.

Accordingly, preparations being made without a moment's loſs of time, and meaſures adopted for carrying on the feſtival, a number of the Sons of Liberty repaired to Trinity Church, having been very politely acquainted by the Rector, of his intentions to preach on another ſubject, a congratulatory diſcourſe on the joyful occaſion. After which repairing to the Field of Liberty, a royal ſalute of 21 cannon was fired, and that ſucceeded by a conſiderable body of the Sons of Liberty, collecting at their uſual houſe of public reſort, where an elegant entertainment was prepared, attended with a band of muſick, and when they had dined in the moſt ſocial manner, twenty-eight loyal and conſtitutional toaſts were cheerfully drank.

The evening concluded with bonfires and other illuminations; and notwithſtanding the tranſports of our joy, and the vaſt concourſe of people which were aſſembled, the whole tranſactions of the day was conducted and finiſhed with the greateſt loyalty, harmony and good order.

The Sons of Liberty of New-York, take this early opportunity, of moſt cordially ſaluting and congratulating all their American brethren on this glorious and happy event.

A letter from London, dated March 29, ſays, The relief for the colonies, ſaid to be intended, is, reducing the duty on ſugar to one ſhilling per cent molaſſes to one penny per gallon; with liberty to import wine, fruit, and oil, from Cadiz; and perhaps the price of tea reduced.

His Majeſty's ſnow of war the Hind, arrived at Sandy-Hook from Plymouth, yeſterday afternoon, with diſpatches from the miniſtry for the different Governors on the continent, acquainting them of the total repeal of the Stamp Act; which intelligence his Excellency our Governor immediately made public at the Coffee-Houſe; and added, That the acts of trade were taken into conſideration, and 'twas hoped would terminate in favour of the colonies. The Hind left Plymouth the 7th of April, in which veſſel came paſſenger ...

6 The Doctor then delivered his eſſay, which was received with the higheſt approbation by the audience. After which the Provoſt proceeded as follows---

"Sir, as the reward of your great merit in this elegant performance, I am, in the name of the Truſtees and Faculty of this college, as well as in behalf of the worthy donor, to beg your acceptance of this *Gold Medal*--Its intrinſic value may not be an object of much conſideration to you; but the truly honourable circumſtances by which it now becomes yours, muſt render it one of the moſt valuable jewels in your poſſeſſion.

"That the firſt literary prize in this inſtitution ſhould fall to the ſhare of one of its eldeſt ſons, who to much genius and application, has joined much knowlege of the world, will not ſeem ſtrange. Yet ſtill for the honour of this ſeminary, and what will not derogate from your honor, it will appear that you have obtained this preheminence over no mean competitors.

"Some of our younger ſons (among whom we ought not to omit the name of the modeſt and candid *WATTS, with ſome others even of inferior ſtanding) have exhibited ſuch vigorous efforts of genius, and tread ſo ardently on the heels of you their ſeniors, that it will require the utmoſt exertion of all your faculties, the continual ſtraining of every nerve, if you would long wiſh to lead the way to them, in the great career of fame.-- --

"Truly delicate and difficult, we confeſs, gentlemen, was the ſubject preſcribed to you---to treat of the reciprocal advantages of a perpetual *union* between Great-Britain and her colonies, at a time when a fatal miſunderſtanding had untwiſted all the cords of that *union*, and the minds of many were too much inflamed! This difficulty was likewiſe encreaſed to us by other conſiderations.

"Great-Britain, who by her liberality has raiſed this college from a helpleſs to a flouriſhing ſtate, had an undoubted demand on us for all the returns of gratitude. Yet we could not, we durſt not, divert the ſtreams of learning from their ſacred courſe----Our country, nay all America, had a right to expect that they ſhould be directed pure along to water the goodly *Tree of* LIBERTY, nor ever be ſuffered to cheriſh any rank weed that would choak its growth.

"In this moſt difficult conjuncture, we rejoice to behold you, in your early years, exerciſing all the temper and prudence of the moſt experienced patriots. We rejoice that ever we had the leaſt ſhare in forming ſentiments, which have led you ſo powerfully to ſhow that on the everlaſting baſis of reciprocal intereſt, and a participation of conſtitutional privileges, our union ſhall be perpetuated and our bleeding wounds healed up without ſo much as a ſcar by way of remembrance-----Here you have ſhewn yourſelves entituled to the name of *true* SONS OF LIBERTY----SONS OF LIBERTY indeed! neither betraying her ſacred cauſe on the one hand, nor degenerating into licentiouſneſs on the other, &c."

This eulogium entered into ...

never lessen the Repu-
oth it need a Veil on
be found in the best
nd whatever Excesses
a, under our late dis-
lief kindly granted us
racious Sovereign and
how to distinguish the
strances of loyal Sub-
s aggrieved, from the
le. Notwithstanding
oped from your Excel-
aper generally prevails
ead the Parliament to
othing that can afford
se who were for main-
Sorrow and Concern
al.
urther to say, " When
in Form, when there
rive it of it's best and
nly Crime is their Fide-
be indifferent, but find
every legal and consti-
n the King's Authority
ill-timed Oppugnation
have been your Excel-
ording to the more ob-
sions, an heavy Charge,
or any Order of Men
Speech to both Houses
World is left to place

says, there has been an
orm, and an ill judged
the King's Authority.
er, to Truth and Jus-
the Province in which
His Majesty, oblige us to
reedom in which we are
respect to your Excel-
Occasion would merit
nay be ready from your
y upon us, and would
of the Choice that has
xcellency's Approbation.
his Province been guilty
ent in Form, or of any
Authority—We declare
of no such Thing—the
of Sovereigns, and sen-
ection with and subordi-
y, have given new and
hese happy Dispositions
upon the late Indulgence
rejoiced with the high-
ratitude to the King, to

upon Government, or an Oppugnation of the King's Authority: and should any Thing like this be ever attempted, your Excellency would find this Board zealous to defend our Sovereign's Honour, and the constitutional Power of His Representative

We beg Leave to assure your Excellency, that we shall heartily join with you in healing Divisions and burying Animosities, should they arise; and that we shall chearfully contribute all in our Power to the Peace and Honour of your Administration.

May it please your Excellency,

The Letter from the Right Honorable Mr. Secretary CONWAY to your Excellency, accompanying your second Speech from the Chair, affords us a most agreeable Occasion of repeatedly declaring the strong Sentiments of Respect and Gratitude, with which we regard the Lenity and Tenderness already so remarkably manifested on the Part of His Majesty and the Parliament, to the American Colonies, and the Prospect given us of some additional Indulgences; for all which it will be our Pleasure as it must be our Glory to make the most dutiful and affectionate Returns.—These are the Dispositions which have uniformly influenced this Board before we saw this Letter so happily adapted to confirm us in them.—And we beg Leave to assure your Excellency that from these Dispositions we shall continue to act.

There are several Paragraphs in your Excellency's Speeches that have been construed to bear hard on the Gentlemen who now constitute the Board: But your Explanation of them in Council, and your repeated Declaration, that you had no such Intention, have given Satisfaction to the Board.

We again beg Leave to assure your Excellency, that our best Abilities shall faithfully be employed, in promoting His Majesty's Honor and Interest, and in making every Part of your Administration easy and happy: And such Testimonials of your Conduct as are contained in Mr. Secretary CONWAY's Letter, will not suffer us to conclude without recognizing your Excellency in the united Character of a true Friend to the Province and a faithful Servant to the Crown.

To which ADDRESS His Excellency was pleased to return the following ANSWER.

Gentlemen,

I Thank you for your Congratulations on the Repeal of the Stamp-Act, and for your Assurances that nothing shall be wanting on your Part that may contribute towards a proper Improvement of this happy Event.

However, I doubt not but that with your Assistance, I shall soon see this Government restored to its Peace and Honour, and the Character of every Person concerned in it brought to its true Estimation.

Fra. Bernard.

THE following is the Copy of a Letter from the principal Merchants in London trading to the Colonies, sent by Express when the Act for repealing the Stamp-Act receiv'd the Royal Assent, which Express has not yet arrived that we have heard of.

To JOHN HANCOCK, Esq; *and the Rest of the Merchants in* BOSTON.

LONDON, March 18. 1766.

GENTLEMEN,

WE have now the Satisfaction of informing you by Capt Wray, sent by us Express in the Ship Dispatch, that the Bill for repealing the Stamp-Act received the Royal Assent this Day.

To enumerate the Difficulties which we have had in this Affair, would be a disagreeable Task to us; as it may seem calculated to enhance our own Merit, at the Expence of Characters whom we respect for their Situation, however they may have been induced to act a Part we could not approve, or thoroughly reconcile to the true Interests of the British Empire.

Nevertheless, we think ourselves entituled, from the Pains we have taken to serve you, to the Privilege of imparting our Sentiments on your past and future Conduct, with that Freedom and Impartiality which Observation and Experience dictate.

You must know better, than to imagine that any well regulated Government will suffer Laws, enacted with a View to public Good, to be disputed by lawless Rioters, with Impunity.

There is no Government so perfect, but that thro' Misinformation, and the Frailties even of the most elevated human Understandings, Mistakes, or at least the Appearance of such, may arise in the Conduct of Affairs, even in the wisest Legislature—but, is it just, is it tolerable, that without Proof of Inconvenience, tumultuous Force shall be encouraged by a Part, to fly in the Face of Power established for the Good of the Whole? We are persuaded, Gentlemen, that you cannot be of that Opinion, and that you will exert your utmost Endeavours to cancel the Remembrance of such flagrant Breaches of public Order, and to manifest your Gratitude and Affection to your Mother Country, which by the Repeal of this Act has given such incontestible Proof of her Moderation.

What Sentiments you ought to entertain on this Occasion, and what Conduct we would wish you to observe, will sufficiently appear from our former Letter

BOSTON GAZETTE

June 16, 1766

—

A letter from fifty-five merchants in London to John Hancock and the merchants of Boston encourages public order and gratitude toward the mother country and suggests that had Americans obeyed the law and simply communicated their hardships, "your Relief would have been more speedy."

dated 28th February laft, and fent by the firft Conveyance, the Moment we could inform you, with any Degree of Certainty what was likely to be the Fate of the Stamp-Act.

We fhall only obferve, that under Providence, you are indebted for this Event to the Clemency and paternal Regard of His Majefty for the Happinefs of his Subjects, to the publick Spirit, Abilities and Firmnefs of the prefent Adminiftration; and to the Humanity, Prudence, and Patriotifm of the Generality of thofe who compofe the Legiflature, and the moft confiderable Perfons of every Rank in this Kingdom.

We hope Gentlemen, that this Conduct in the Britifh Legiflature; provoked by the moft irritating Meafures on your Side, will forever be a Leffon to your Pofterity; as it is the moft convincing Proof, that if by any Means, Laws are, or fhould be, enacted, detrimental or feemingly oppreffive to any Part of the Britifh Subjects; the Britifh Legiflature, will at all Times, with the utmoft Tendernefs confider every Grievance, & redrefs them the Moment they are known.

We cannot but acquaint you, that had the Americans endeavoured to acquiefce with the Law, and dutifully reprefented the Hardfhips as they arofe, your Relief *would* have been more fpeedy, and we fhould have avoided many Difficulties as well as not a few *unanfwerable* mortifying Reproaches on your Account.

Such however is the Patriotifm and Magnanimity of thofe in Power, that, unaffected, by the Conduct of many on your Side the Water, and the ftrenuous Efforts of an Oppofition here to every Meafure of Lenity and Indulgence towards America; they are endeavouring to eftablifh its Commerce in particular, as well as that of the Britifh Empire in general, upon the moft folid Foundation, & the moft extenfive Plan of Utility.

On your Parts we hope that nothing will be wanting to obliterate the Remembrance of what is paffed, by fetting the Example yourfelves, and promoting the like Sentiments in others; of a dutiful Attachment to your Sovereign and the Interefts of your Mother Country, a juft Submiffion to the Laws, and refpect for the Legiflature; for in this you are moft effectually promoting your own Happinefs and Security.

By a Conduct like this, Gentlemen, you will both encourage and enable us to ferve you with Zeal on future Emergencies, fhould any fuch arife; and to fupport our mutual Interefts; the Intereft of the Colonies, which are infeparable from the common Interefts of Great-Britain, with Efficacy and Succefs.

We are, Gentlemen,
Your affured Friends,
and very humble Servants

[Signed by 55 of the principal Merchants trading to North America.]

Hartford, in Connecticut, June 9.

Laft Tuefday died at Weathersfield, in the 47th Year of his Age, Dr. Jonathan Marfh, of Norwich. He was fent for to this Town, at the Time the late unhappy Accident happened here, on Account of his great Skill in Surgery, and was very ufeful for a few Days; but one of his Arms, in which he had received a great Strain, grew fo painful that he was obliged to leave his Practice, and retire to his Brother-in-Law, (Dr. Porter of Weathersfield) where his Arm grew worfe and worfe, till it put an End to his

21, 27, 29, 35, 3
57, 63, 66, 68, 6
97, 100. Of the
raifed December 1
quent, viz. No. 5
47, 54, 68, 70, 78
7s. Tax lawful M
and to be apportion
and was laid equal
third Divifion 2s.
fecond Divifion 3d
delinquent in the f
31, 41, 42, 44, 4
In the fecond Div
46, 47, 48, 55, 5
99, 100 : In the thi
17, 18, 20, 29, 32, 42, 43, 59, 70, 74, 78, 79, 80, 81, 85, 88, 89, 92, 93, 94, 95, 118, 121, 124, 137, 162, 192. Of the 2d. 1q. Tax lawful Money Voted to be raifed May 1760, on each Acre laid out, the following Lots are delinquent, viz. In the firft Divifion, No. 6, 22, 27, 39, 41, 45, 58, 62, 68, 78, 79, 85, 88, 89, 91, 98 : In the fecond Divifion, No. 1, 4, 6, 7, 8, 9, 10, 20, 22, 25, 26, 59, 69, 94, 95, 98, 99 : In the third Divifion, No. 4, 6, 9, 11, 12, 13, 18, 20, 26, 27, 34, 35, 37, 40, 43, 51, 55, 58, 59, 60, 62, 69, 70, 73, 74, 77, 79, 80, 81, 83, 88, 91, 93, 94, 98, 108, 118, 121, 132, 138, 139, 143, 148, 158, 164, 182, 192; and alfo Fayerweather's Farm containing 500 Acres. Of the 4 d. Tax lawful Money Voted to be raifed March 1761, on each Acre laid out, the following Lots are delinquent, viz. In the firft Divifion, No. 3, 6, 27, 35, 41, 44, 45, 66, 68, 69, 80, 88, 89, 100: In the fecond Divifion, No. 10, 14, 21, 24, 25, 27, 59, 89, 94, 95, 98, 99 : In the third Divifion, No. 1, 4, 6, 9, 11, 13, 18, 20, 26, 27, 29, 40, 43, 51, 55, 58, 59, 60, 62, 69, 74, 77, 79, 83, 88, 90, 94, 95, 106, 111, 118, 121, 132, 138, 139, 143, 148, 158, 164, 182, 185, 192, and alfo Fairweather's Farm, containing 500 Acres, and Newberry's Farm in the Gore, containing 264 Acres. Of the 1d. 2q. Tax lawful Money Voted to be raifed March 1765, on each Acre of Land laid out and voted to be laid out, the following Lots are delinquent, viz. In the firft Divifion, No. 2, 3, 5, 6, 8, 11, 14, 15, 17, 19, 20, 22, 23, 24, 25, 27, 29, 30, 31, 32, 33, 35, 39, 42, 43, 45, 49, 54, 55, 62, 63, 66, 68, 69, 73, 74, 79, 81, 85, 86, 88, 89, 91, 94, 95, 96, 97, 98, 100 : In the fecond Divifion, No. 1, 2, 3, 4, 5, 6, 7, 8, 10, 11, 12, 13, 14, 15, 20, 21, 22, 23, 24, 25, 26, 27, 49, 55, 56, 57, 59, 60, 61, 62, 63, 64, 65, 69, 72, 73, 89, 91, 96, 98, 100: In the third Divifion, No. 1, 3, 4, 6, 7, 11, 12, 14, 16, 17, 18, 23, 26, 27, 29, 32, 34, 35, 36, 37, 43, 51, 52, 54, 55, 56, 59, 60, 62, 64, 68, 69, 70, 74, 76, 77, 78, 79, 80, 81, 83, 89, 90, 93, 94, 95, 96, 97, 98, 103, 104, 105, 106, 108, 111, 112, 117, 118, 120, 121, 122, 125, 128, 129, 131, 132, 133, 134, 136, 137, 138, 139, 141, 142, 144, 145, 147, 148, 153, 158, 160, 162, 163, 164, 166, 167, 169, 170, 171, 176, 178, 180, 182, 183, 184, 185, 187, 189, 192, 194, 195, 197, 198, 199, 200; alfo Fayerweather's Farm containing 500 Acres, and Colbey's and Newberry's Farm in the Gore, containing 264 Acres each.

And that every Proprietor may know the Sum he has to pay on the feveral Taxes, we would inform them, that in the firft and fecond Divifions the following Lots contain

Irifh linnens, garlix, dowlais, Ruffia linnens, Irifh fheeting, Ruffia diaper and clouting ditto, bedticks, ftriped holland, cotton gowns, filk damafcus, cotton velves, thickfetts, pillow fuftians, duroys, filk fagathies, worfted ditto, fine double allapeens, grezetts, brunetts; a fine affortment of calicoes and chints, fine broad black ruffell, brolioes, worfted grograms, calimancoes, ruffells, tammies and durants, fhalloons, plain and fprigg'd half yard and yard-wide venetian poplins, worfted and filk fprigg'd camblets, ftripped ditto, yard-wide ftuffs, mecklenburghs, fine coloured crapes, cloth coloured Englifh taffities, white & brown buckrams, yellow holland, ftay cord and braids, cambricks, 7-8 and yard wide lawns, long lawns, book muflin, plain & flower'd white and black gauze, white cat-gutt, bengalls, black, cloth, buff and crimfon worfted breeches patterns, mens, womens and childrens cotton and thread hofe, worfted caps, green and crimfon mock velvet ditto, black worfted mitts, black, pink, crimfon, blue & white pelon fattin, black, pink, crimfon and blue figur'd capuchin filks, narrow black alamode, black luteftring, yard-wide white farfnet for handkerchiefs, 3-4 black ditto, kid and lamb gloves and mittens of all forts, womens and childrens black and colour'd filk mitts, womens black and white filk gloves; a variety of womens and childrens fans, plain and drawn'd fattin hatts and bonnets, plain black ditto, chip hatts and bonnetts, half-ell and ell-wide perfians, a fine affortment of new-fafhion ribbons, tippets and turbans, linnen and filk handkerchiefs, large black gauze ditto, wax threads, Scotch and nuns threads, gimps, Englifh and French wax necklaces and earings, filk ferrets, white & black trolly lace, black bone ditto, white cap lace, tapes and pins of all forts, white chapple, common, darning & Glover's needles, *Lynn* made fhoes, black fattin ditto, children's morrocco fhoes, filk & hair, beft fcarf twift, filk twift, and basket-work'd buttons, knee garters, filk purfes, fhirt buttons, cotton and filk laces, garters, fine fhoe bindings, London qualities, bellindine filks, ivory combs, Raven's duck, &c. &c. &c.

THESE are to give Notice to the Candidates for their Second Degree this Year, That They attend at the College in this Place, on or before the 9th Day of *July* next, and if any neglect to give their Attendance accordingly, without fufficient Reafon therefor, They may not expect their Degrees this Year.

EDWARD HOLYOKE, Prefident.

Cambridge, June 5. 1766.

Life, in the 25th Year of his Age, greatly lamented, Mr. William Gardiner of this Town, Merchant; he

No. 19	55	No. 1	7	No. 24	6	No 71	6
20	60	6	6	25	6	72	7
		7	6	26	6	73	6

the Proprietors of New Framingham, *alias* Lanesborough, *in the County of* Berfhire (*legally warn'd*, *holden on the 18th of* March 1765. *Voted a Tax of*

A LIST of the Names of *those*

who AUDACIOUSLY continue to counteract the UNITED SENTIMENTS of the BODY of Merchants thro'out NORTH-AMERICA; by importing British Goods contrary to the Agreement.

John Bernard,
James McMasters & Comp'y.
John Mein,

The following is a Copy of the AGREEMENT the Merchants of this Town entered into Oct. 17. 1769.

W*HEREAS the Merchants and Traders in the Town of Boston, taking into Consideration the Deplorable Situation of the Trade, and the many Difficulties that it laboured under, did on the First Day of August* 1768, *by a Subscription under their Hands, agree, that they would not send for, or Import from Great-Britain, any Kind of Goods or Merchandize, either on their own Accounts or on Commissions, or otherwise, from the First Day of January* 1769, *to the First Day of January* 1770, *excepting, Coals, Salt, Fish-Hooks & Lines, Hemp, Duck, Bar-Lead, Shott, Wool-Cards, Card-Wire. And Whereas it appears to us the Subscribers that, as the said Agreement has been very Generally adheared to, so it has already had a good Effect, and affords a promising Prospect of answering the important Ends designed thereby, provided it should be continued, Therefore in order effectually to promote the Design of relieving the Trade, from the many Difficulties and Oppressions under which it labours, and to preserve to ourselves and Posterity, the Liberties and* ...*ileges which we were wont to enjoy, WE now* ... *and Engage with each other as follows,*

1. THAT we will not im... of Goods or Merchandize ...ritain, either on our own Accounts ...mmions, or other wise, *until the Acts im*... *America for rai*... *ing a Reve*... ...ing the A... cles of Coa... Hemp ... Wire, Clo... dicines, dye... indstones ... ol-Books ... of the ... w-York & ... ods to be ... in orde... ...er Agre...

Aug. 23. *A farmer at Granchester in Cambridgshire, was bound over to the quarter sessions by the humanity of the Rev. Dr. Plumtree, for forcing a poor woman of Caldecot into the water to prove her a witch, and otherwise maltreating her.*

Aug. 31. *The French ambassador has lately presented a memorial to the States General, in which he acquaints them that the Island of Corsica is united to the dominions of France, and hopes that in case any ships for the future shall appear under Corsican colours, their H. M. will look upon them as pirates, and treat them accordingly.*

Sept. 1. *A Correspondent says, the prodigious Increase of the French Navy is truly alarming, and should instigate the Great to lay aside Contentions and Party Squabbles, and unite in taking Care of the most essential Interests and Security of the Nation, which demand a powerful Navy well kept up and ready to defeat the Attempts of our artful and naturable Enemy.*

The French, from a Calculation lately made, reckoned in the Island of Corsica, 57 *Pieves, or Ecclesiastical Districts,* 10 *Jurisdictions,* 26,336 *Houses with Chimneys,* 32,322 *Men able to bear Arms, and* 130,680 *Souls in all.*

Aug. 31. Last Thursday died in Cavendish-square, aged 97, Edmund Hoyle, Esq; well known in the polite world for writing the celebrated treatise on the games of Whist, Quadrille, Piquet, Chess and Black-gammon, which he lived to see pass thro' no less than thirteen editions.

Yesterday several colony agents waited upon the Earls of Rochfort and Weymouth, on the subject of recent instructions from their respective colonies.

Sept...4. Saturday the Right Hon. the ... of Bute ...ontinues in a declining state ... set o... Seat at Luton Hoo, in Bedfo...

A... of artillery and ordnance ... ping... Tower and Woolwich for ...

...ay evening his Royal Highne... ...ved at his house in Gr... ...rom hi... throug... ...day ... on ... ales,

The Westminster Petition ... to different Parishes throug... been signed by a great numb... there is no time yet fixed f... his Majesty.

On Wednesday evening t... rived in Town from his Reg... and was yesterday at Court.

Wednesday several Ger... American Colonies, waited ... cers of State, on affairs ... North America.

Sept. 9. A great man has ... duct of the Bostonians, tha... now begun to prove true, ... ricans would only grow mo... were indulged."—He adde... the Revenue-Act entirely, ... of the Admiralty Courts, ... plain of, their Agents in ... the boldness to assert, that ... fied, without Concessions" ... be, is surely a matter well ... the Mother-Country.

The affairs relating to t... Bay, and also the Petition ... vernor, are postponed till ... Hilsborough from Irelanc... course of next week.

A Letter from Cante... Gentleman, just come f... that Gen. Paoli was to ... Dutch Ship, for Dover, ...

It is said that a meetin... ...ding to North America ... consider on a proper ... relative to the present stag... ...on produce the most de... ...ely remedi... ...is ... that the ... in the A... ...from H... ...n England a... ...o the farther ... ...e in North-America. ...tember 12. It is ... ...n in the Russian ... Sea, is to b... ... the Por... ...nselves ... was a... ...ps were ... eir rigg... vails he... ...ll here ... they...

CHAPTER II

FRUGALITY AND INDUSTRY

Introduction

The Declaratory Act of 1766—reiterating Great Britain's "full power and authority" over the American colonies "in all cases whatsoever"—was a hard pill for colonists to swallow following the repeal of the Stamp Act, but Americans had little to fear until Parliament enforced it, which came one year later in the form of a new tax proposal by Charles Townshend. With both sides learning valuable lessons from the Stamp Act crisis, the Townshend Acts focused on external taxes and included laws for proper enforcement. Colonists leveraged the newfound power of the newspaper press and coupled domestic manufacturing with continent-wide boycotts—tactics that helped distinguish Patriot rebels from Crown-supporting Loyalists.

Boston Gazette
November 20, 1769

Colonial American Family
North Wind Picture Archives

Charles Townshend
North Wind Picture Archives

His namesake acts included revenue-raising taxes on goods imported from England, an act establishing a new system of customs commissioners, and an act for suspending the New York assembly.

John Dickinson, a portrait by C. W. Peale, 1741–1827
The Bridgeman Art Library

Philadelphia lawyer, politician, and author of twelve letters "from a farmer" that clearly stated objections to British authority.

REPORTING THE

TOWNSHEND ACTS

By Todd Andrlik

Responsible for Britain's fiscal policies, Charles Townshend needed to defray the expense of colonial American defense and operations, which was magnified after a reduction in British property taxes left a gaping hole in the national budget. Plus, with the embarrassment of the Stamp Act repeal still fresh on the mind, new taxes would reassert imperial authority and shift the balance of power back to Great Britain.

To avoid the passionate internal tax debate from two years earlier, Townshend opted for external tariffs only. On June 29, 1767, Parliament passed the Townshend Acts, a series of laws that imposed strict revenue-raising taxes on goods imported from England, including paint, glass, lead, paper, and tea (see list of the duties in the October 12, 1767, *Pennsylvania Chronicle*). Tea had become a symbol of aristocracy in England and therefore the drink of choice among wealthy American women. The hope that external duties would be more easily stomached was quickly rejected as Americans argued that taxes on the use of paper were no different than those on the importation of it.

To ensure enforcement and payment of the new taxes, the Townshend Acts included laws for sending customs collectors to America and establishing new admiralty courts in Boston, Philadelphia, and Charleston. Yet another law dissolved New York's assembly after it had recently refused to provide housing, food, and drink for British troops.

After reading about the riots and mobs of 1765–66, Londoners, fearing further violence, cautioned friends in America about going to extremes and, thus, making more enemies. This was made evident in a letter from London, dated August 6, 1767, that was published in the *Pennsylvania Chronicle*'s October 12 issue:

> *The Opposition to America seems to increase. Every Step is taking to render the Taxation of the Colonies a popular Measure, and it is contended that they should be obliged explicitly to acknowledge that Right. I know not what to advise on this Occasion, but that the Friends of America, on both Sides the Water, should exert their utmost Endeavours to lessen the present Unpopularity of the American Cause; conciliate the Affections of the People here towards you, increase by all possible Means the Number of your Friends, and be careful not to weaken their Hands, and strengthen those of your Enemies, by rash Proceedings, the Mischiefs of which are inconceivable.*

The Townshend Acts took effect November 20, 1767, and caused a resurgence of anti-taxation prose and protests. Among the colonial chorus of dissenting voices, John Dickinson's stood out. Dickinson, a well-known Philadelphia lawyer and politician, wrote a series of twelve letters "from a farmer" that were printed and reprinted in newspapers from New Hampshire to Georgia (see the first letter in the December 21, 1767, *Boston Chronicle*). His articulate and reasonable public objections to British authority helped unite the colonies and urged nonviolent resistance. Privately, Dickinson shared copies of his letters with Boston statesman James Otis, Jr., suggesting that Massachusetts lead the charge against the Townshend Acts as it did against the Stamp Act.

With the embarrassment of the Stamp Act repeal still fresh on the mind, new taxes would reassert imperial authority and shift the balance of power back to Great Britain.

…ing the drawbacks payable on China earthen ware exported to America; and for more effectually preventing the clandeſtine running of goods in the ſaid Colonies and Plantations.

WHEREAS it is expedient that a revenue ſhould be raiſed, in your Majeſty's dominions in America, for making a more certain and adequate proviſion for defraying the charge of the adminiſtration of juſtice, and the ſupport of civil government, in ſuch provinces where it ſhall be found neceſſary; and towards further defraying the expences of defending, protecting, and ſecuring the ſaid dominions; We, your Majeſty's moſt dutiful and loyal ſubjects, the commons of Great-Britain, in parliament aſſembled, have therefore reſolved to give and grant unto your Majeſty the ſeveral rates and duties herein aftermentioned; and do moſt humbly beſeech your Majeſty that it may be enacted, and be it enacted by the King's moſt excellent Majeſty, by and with the advice and conſent of the lords ſpiritual and temporal, and commons, in this preſent parliament aſſembled, and by the authority of the ſame, that from and after the twentieth day of November, one thouſand ſeven hundred and ſixty ſeven, there ſhall be raiſed, levied, collected, and paid unto his Majeſty, his heirs, and ſucceſſors, for and upon the reſpective goods herein after mentioned, which ſhall be imported from Great-Britain into any colony or plantation in America, which now is, or hereafter may be under the dominion of his Majeſty, his heirs or ſucceſſors, the ſeveral rates or duties following; that is to ſay,

For every hundred weight avoirdupois of crown plate, flint, and white glaſs, Four ſhillings and eight-pence.

For every hundred weight avoirdupois of green glaſs, One ſhilling and two-pence.

For every hundred weight avoirdupois of red lead, Two ſhillings.

For every hundred weight avoirdupois of white lead, Two ſhillings.

For every hundred weight avoirdupois of painters colours, Two ſhillings.

For every pound weight avoirdupois of tea, Three-pence.

For every ream of paper, uſually called or known by the name of Atlas Fine, Twelve ſhillings.

For every ream of paper, called Atlas Ordinary, Six ſhillings.

For every ream of paper, called Baſtard, or double Copy, One ſhilling and ſix-pence.

For every ſingle ream of blue paper, for ſugar bakers, Ten-pence halfpenny.

For every …

…of paper, called Second Ordinary Printing Fools Cap, Six-pence three farthings.

For every ream of any other paper, called Fools Cap Fine, not made in Great-Britain, One ſhilling and ten-pence halfpenny.

For every ream of any other paper, called Fools Cap Fine Second, not made in Great-Britain, One ſhilling and ſix-pence.

For every ream of paper called Fools Cap Fine, made in Great-Britain, Nine-pence.

For every ream of paper, called Fools Cap Second, made in Great-Britain, Six-pence three farthings.

For every ream of paper, called Imperial Fine, Twelve ſhillings.

For every ream of paper, called Second Writing Imperial, Eight ſhillings and three-pence.

For every ream of paper, called German Lombard, Nine-pence.

For every ream of paper, called Medium Fine, Four ſhillings and ſix-pence.

For every ream of paper, called Genoa Medium, One ſhilling and ten-pence halfpenny.

For every ream of paper, called Second Writing Medium, Three ſhillings.

For every ream of painted paper, not made in Great-Britain, Six ſhillings.

For every ream of paper, called Fine large Poſt, One ſhilling and ten-pence halfpenny.

For every ream of paper, called Small Poſt, One ſhilling and one penny halfpenny.

For every ream of paper, called fine Genoa Pot, Six-pence three farthings.

For every ream of paper, called Second Genoa Pot, Six-pence three farthings.

For every ream of other paper, called Superfine Pot, not made in Great Britain, One ſhilling and ſix-pence.

For every ream of other paper, called Second Fine Pot, not made in Great-Britain, One ſhilling and one penny halfpenny.

For every ream of paper, called Ordinary Pot, not made in Great-Britain, Six-pence three farthings.

For every ream of paper, called Fine Pot, made in Great-Britain, Nine-pence.

For every ream of paper, called Second Pot, made in Great-Britain, Four-pence halfpenny.

For every ream of paper, called Super Royal Fine, Nine ſhillings.

For every ream of paper, called Royal Fine, Six ſhillings.

For every ream of paper, called Fine Holland Royal, Two ſhillings and five-pence farthing.

For every ream of paper, called Fine Holland Second, One ſhilling and ſix-pence.

For every …

PENNSYLVANIA CHRONICLE (PHILADELPHIA)

October 12, 1767

A series of laws, known as the Townshend Acts, were printed in this issue with the front page filled with a long list of the new taxes on paint, glass, lead, paper, tea, and more. Fresh off the Stamp Act, a general fear of politically incited violence and retaliation was common. Inside, a letter from London, dated August 6, 1767, cautions about growing opposition to America and encourages colonists to make more friends than enemies.

For every ream of paper, called German Crown, …ne-pence.

For every ream of paper, called Fine Printing …own, Nine-pence.

For every ream of paper, called Second Ordinary Printing Crown, Six-pence three farthings.

…or every ream of paper, called Crown Fine, …de in Great-Britain, Nine…

…not been printed, painted, or ſtained, and after thoſe rates reſpectively, for any greater or leſs quantity.

And it is hereby further enacted by the authority aforeſaid, That all other paper (not being particularly rated and charged in this act) ſhall pay the ſeveral and reſpective duties that are charg… ed, by this act, upon ſuch …

[W]ednesday next the GENERAL ASSEMBLY of this Province meets here.

…ay laſt at a Meeting of the Common …, ISAAC JONES, Eſq; was elected … of this City for the enſuing Year; Mr. … GIBSON was made an Alderman; …eſſieurs ANDREW and JAMES ALLEN, WILLIAM FISHER, JOSHUA …ELL, WILLIAM PARR, JOSEPH …T, GEORGE CLYMER, and JOHN …OCKS, Common Council Men.

[Ext]ract of a Letter from a Merchant in London, Auguſt 7, 1767.

…t is truly melancholy, to reflect on the preſent … of public Affairs here:—The Confuſion a… … our great men ſtill continues—who, inſtead …erting their Abilities, in this Time of Peace, … foreign Powers, to extend the Commerce of … Kingdom, pay off the National Debt, and in… … the Strength and Power of the Nation to …ort a future War, are waſting their whole …e in Party Contentions, Intrigues, and Cabals …ſtabliſh their own Power, and the Profit at…ing it; and in abuſing one another.

…ract of another Letter from London, dated Auguſt 7, 1767.

"A late Attempt to coaleſce the different Parties … a new Miniſtry, has proved ineffectual—and …ſeems probable, that the preſent Set will conti…e ſome Time longer—This ſeems not unfortu…te for America, as ſome of them who were pro…ſed to come in, were profeſſed Adverſaries of A…erica—The prevailing Diſtinction of Parties here, … thoſe who in the two laſt Seſſions of Parl—t, …ave been diſpoſed to favour America, are cal…d, by their Opponents, (by Way of Reproach) AMERICANS! while the Adherents to G——le …nd B——d, boaſt of their being true to the Inte…eſt of Britain, and zealous for maintaining its Sovereignty over the Colonies—This Declaration ſeems every Day to be more and more fixt; and it is much to be feared will be carried higher, in the next Seſſion of Parliament, for the political Purpoſes of influencing the enſuing Election—It is already ſaid, that the Act for Quartering the Soldiers at New-York, without taking Notice of its being done in Obedience to the Act of Parliament, is *evaſive* and *unſatisfactory*; that it is high Time to put the Right of taxing America out of Diſpute, by an Act of Taxation, effectually carried into Execution, &c. &c.

Extract of another Letter from London, dated Auguſt 6, 1767.

"The general Affairs of America here, bear a very diſagreeable Aſpect; the preſent Miniſtry are like to continue ſome Time longer—ſome particular Changes will happen, and I fear the principal Structure will not be of long Duration, but probably there will be another Seſſion of Parliament before a conſiderable Alteration is made.—The Oppoſition to America ſeems to increaſe. Every Step is taking to render the Taxation of the Colonies a popular Meaſure, and it is contended that they ſhould be obliged explicitly to acknowledge that Right. I know not what to adviſe on this Occaſion, but that the Friends of America, on both Sides the Water, ſhould exert their utmoſt Endeavours to leſſen the preſent Unpopularity of the American Cauſe; conciliate the Affections of the People here towards you, increaſe by all poſſible Means the Number of your Friends, and be careful not to weaken their Hands, and ſtrengthen thoſe of your Enemies, by raſh Proceedings, the Miſchiefs of which are inconceivable."

About a Month ago the young Wife of an old Gentleman, of this City, about 84 Years of Age, was ſafely delivered of a fine Daughter. They are the ſame Couple whoſe Marriage was mentioned in this Paper of the 9th of February laſt.

The Captains Adam, and Ford, from Virginia, Captain Briggs, from Rhode-Iſland, Captain Somerville, from Piſcataqua, and the Captains Che…

OCTOBER 12, 1767

The PENNSYLVANIA CHRONICLE

WHEREAS it is expedient that a revenue should be raised, in your Majesty's dominions in America, for making a more certain and adequate provision for defraying the charge of the administration of justice, and the support of civil government, in such provinces where it shall be found necessary ; and towards further defraying the expenses of defending, protecting, and securing the said dominions ; We, your Majesty's most dutiful and loyal subjects, the commons of Great-Britain, in parliament assembled, have therefore resolved to give and grant unto your Majesty the several rates and duties herein after-mentioned ; and do most humbly beseech your Majesty that it may be enacted, and be it enacted by the King's most excellent Majesty, by and with the advice and consent of the lords spiritual and temporal, and commons, in this present parliament assembled, and by the authority of the same, that from and after the twentieth day of November, one thousand seven hundred and sixty seven, there shall be raised, levied, collected and paid unto his majesty, his heirs, and successors, for and upon the respective goods herein after mentioned, which shall be imported from Great-Britain into any colony or plantation in America, which now is, or hereafter may be under the dominion of his Majesty, his heirs or successors, the several rates or duties following ; that is to say [...]

Extract of another Letter from London, dated August 7, 1767.

"A late Attempt to coalesce the different Parties in a new Ministry, has proved ineffectual—and it seems probably, that the present Set will continue some Time longer—This seems not unfortunate for America, as some of them who were proposed to come in, were professed Adversaries of America—The prevailing Distinction of Parties here, is, those who in the two last Sessions of Parl—t, have been disposed to favour America, are called, by their Opponents, (by Way of Reproach) AMERICANS ! while the Adherents to G----le and Is-------d, boast of their being true to the Interest of Britain, and zealous for maintaining its Sovereignty over the Colonies—This Declaration seems every Day to be more and more fixt ; and it is much to be feared will be carried higher, in the next Session of Parliament, for the political Purposes of influencing the ensuing Election—It is already said, that the Act for Quartering the Soldiers at New-York, without taking Notice of its being done in Obedience to the Act of Parliament, is evasive and unsatisfactory ; that it is high Time to put the Right of taxing America out of Dispute, by an Act of Taxation, effectually carried into Execution, &c. &c.

Extract of another Letter from London, dated August 6, 1767.

"The general Affairs of America here, bear a very disagreeable Aspect ; the present Ministry are like to continue some Time longer—some particular Changes will happen, and I fear the principal Structure will not be of long Duration, but probably there will be another Session of Parliament before a considerable Alteration is made.---The opposition to America seems to increase. Every Step is taking to render the Taxation of the colonies a popular Measure, and it is contended that they should be obliged explicitly to acknowledge that Right. I know not what to advise on that Occasion, but that the Friends of America, on both Sides the Water, should exert their utmost Endeavours to lessen the present Unpopularity of the American Cause ; conciliate the Affections of the People here towards you, increase by all possible Means the Number of your Friends, and be careful not to weaken their Hands, and strengthen those of your Enemies, by rash Proceedings, the Mischiefs of which are inconceivable."

To the PUBLIC.

N the firſt appearance of the Boſton Chronicle, *we ſhould think ourſelves worthy of the great encouragement we have eived, if we neglected to return thanks to Subſcribers in general whoſe number has exceeded our moſt ſanguine expectations; s, tho' an agreeable circumſtance to us, is, unattended with its cares; for as the liſt creaſed, we felt ourſelves more and more ſible of the importance of our taſk, that, of deavouring to entertain and engage the at ation of ſuch a number of gentlemen, as ap ared to encourage our undertaking.——Gra ude for this encouragement calls for our ut ſt induſtry.*

We have already mentioned, that, we conſi red the plan pointed out to us by our friends ith diffidence: We therefore hope that our aders will be candid, and not expect to ſee it lly executed either in one or a few papers: 's the winter already ſet in, will deprive us, r ſome time, of the benefit of our Britiſh nd foreign intelligence.

In this ſituation, we will endeavour, by a ariety of entertaining and inſtructive pieces o pleaſe our Subſcribers: and we will be glad we ſucceed ſometimes in making them laugh, hen we have little to intereſt them.

It is with pleaſure we inform the public, hat ſeveral gentlemen of diſtinguiſhed abili ies have promiſed us their aſſiſtance.

We ſhould eſteem it a very great favour, if entlemen of experience and knowledge (of hom we know there are many in this country) would lay before the public, their experiments and diſcoveries, as well in Huſbandry, as in the other arts and Sciences, by the channel of our paper: ſuch a correſpondence would be a be nefit to the whole——The ſocieties at home, to which are owing the late great improvements in the Arts, have been moſtly eſtabliſhed by a few public ſpirited men:—Great improve ments generally ariſe from ſmall beginnings and repeated efforts.—Here probably a few pieces in a news-paper, might be the foundation of a laſting advantage to the country.

As ſome of our Subſcribers have intimated their hopes that the Chronicle *will not be filled up with advertiſements, we ſhall explain ourſelves upon that head: we do not intend to exclude advertiſements; yet we promiſe our cuſtomers, that no one paper ſhall contain more of them than can be included into two pages.*

We beg to be excuſed for having taken up ſo much of the paper about our own affairs, as we conſider every thing of the kind an encroachment on the property of our Subſcribers; we however hope to be pardoned from our motive. Gratitude impelled us to ſpeak, as Silence might have been conſtrued into Negligence.

LETTERS

From a Farmer in Pennſylvania, to the inhabitants of the Britiſh colonies.

By John Dickinson, Esq;

LETTER I.

Beloved Countrymen,

I am a farmer, ſettled after a variety of fortunes, near the banks, of the river Delaware, in the province of Pennſylvania. I received a liberal education, and have been engaged in the buſy ſcenes of life: But am now convinced, that a man may be as happy without buſtle, as with it. My farm is ſmall, my ſervants are few, and good; I have a little money at intereſt; I wiſh for no more; my employment in my own affairs is eaſy; and and with a contented grateful mind, I am compleating the number of days allotted to me by divine goodneſs.

Being maſter of my time, I ſpend a good deal of it in a library, which I think the moſt valuable part of my ſmall eſtate, being acquainted with two or three gentlemen of abilities and learning, who honour me with their friendſhip, I believe I have acquired a greater ſhare of knowledge in hiſtory, and the laws and conſtitution of my country, than is generally attained by men of my claſs, many of them not being ſo fortunate as I have been in the opportunities of getting information.

From infancy I was taught to love humanity and liberty. Inquiry and experience have ſince confirmed my reverence for the leſſons then given me, by convincing me more fully of their truth and excellence. Benevolence towards mankind excites wiſhes for their welfare, and ſuch wiſhes endear the means of fulfiling them. Thoſe can be found in liberty alone, and therefore her ſacred cauſe ought to be eſpouſed by every man, on every occaſion, to the utmoſt of his power: as a charitable but poor perſon does not withold his mite, becauſe he cannot relieve all the diſtreſſes of the miſerable, ſo let not any honeſt man ſuppreſs his ſentiments concerning freedom, however ſmall their influence is likely to be. Perhaps he may "† touch ſome wheel" that will have an effect greater than he expects.

Theſe being my ſentiments, I am encouraged to offer to you, my countrymen, my thoughts on ſome late tranſactions, that in my opinion are of the utmoſt importance to you. Conſcious of my defects, I have waited ſome time, in expectation of ſeeing the ſubject treated by perſons much better qualified for the taſk; but being therein diſappointed, and apprehenſive that longer delays will be injurious, I venture at length to requeſt the attention of the public, praying only for one thing,—that is, that theſe lines may be read with the ſame zeal for the happineſs of Britiſh America, with which they were wrote.

With a good deal of ſurpriſe I have obſerved, that little notice has been taken of any act of Parliament as injurious in its principle to the liberties of theſe colonies, as the ſtamp-act was: I mean the act for ſuſpending the legiſlation of New-York.

The aſſembly of that government complied with a former act of parliament, requiring certain proviſions to be made for the troops in America, in every particular, I think, except the articles of ſalt, pepper, and vinegar. In my opinion they acted imprudently, conſidering all circumſtances, in not complying ſo far, as would have given ſatisfaction, as ſeveral colonies did: but my diſlike of their conduct in that inſtance, has not blinded me ſo much, that I cannot plainly perceive, that they have been puniſhed in a manner pernicious to American freedom, and juſtly alarming to all the colonies.

If the Britiſh parliament has a legal authority to order, that we ſhall furniſh a ſingle article for the troops here, and to compel obedience to that order; they have the ſame right to order us to ſupply thoſe troops with arms, cloaths, and every neceſſary, and to compel obedience to that order alſo; in ſhort, to lay any burdens they pleaſe upon us. What is this but taxing us at a certain ſum, and leaving to us only the manner of raiſing it? How is this mode more tolerable than the ſtamp-act? Would that act have appeared more pleaſing to Americans, if being ordered thereby to raiſe the ſum total of the taxes, the mighty privilege had been left to them, of ſaying how much ſhould be paid for an inſtrument of writing on paper, and how much for another on parchment.

An act of parliament commanding us to do a certain thing, if it has any validity, is a tax upon us for the expence that accrues in complying with it, and for this reaſon, I believe, every colony on the continent, that choſe to give a mark of reſpect for Great-Britain, in complying with the act relating to the troops, cautiouſly avoid the mention of that act, leaſt their conduct ſhould be attributed to its ſuppoſed obligation.

† Pope.

ed of the privileges of making laws, only for inſiſting on that excluſive privilege of taxation. If they may be legally deprived in ſuch a caſe of the privilege of making laws, why may they not, with equal reaſon, be deprived of every other privilege? Or why may not every colony be treated in the ſame manner, when any of them ſhall dare to deny their aſſent to any impoſitions that ſhall be directed? Or what ſignifies the repeal of the ſtamp-act, if theſe colonies are to loſe their other privileges, by not tamely ſurrendering that of taxation?

There is one conſideration ariſing from this ſuſpicion, which is not generally attended to, but ſhews it's importance very clearly. It was not neceſſary that this ſuſpenſion ſhould be cauſed by an act of parliament. The crown might have reſtrained the Governor of New-York, even from calling the aſſembly together, by its prerogative in the royal governments.—This ſtep, I ſuppoſe, would have been taken, if the conduct of the aſſembly of New-York, had been regarded as an act of diſobedience to the crown alone: but it is regarded as an act of "diſobedience "to the authority of the Britiſh legiſla-"ture." This gives the ſuſpenſion a conſequence vaſtly more affecting. It is a parliamentary aſſertion of the ſupreme authority of the Britiſh legiſlature over theſe colonies in the part of taxation: and is intended to compel New-York unto a ſubmiſſion to that authority. It ſeems therefore to me as much a violation of the liberty of the people of that province, and conſequently of all theſe colonies, as if the parliament had ſent a number of regiments to be quartered upon them till they ſhould comply. For it is evident, that the ſuſpenſion is meant as compulſion; and the method of compelling is totally indifferent. Is is indeed probable, that the ſight of red coats, and the beating of drums would have been moſt alarming, becauſe people are generally more influenced by their eyes and ears than by their reaſon: But whoever ſeriouſly conſiders the matter, muſt perceive, that a dreadful ſtroke is aimed at

parliament may lawfully deprive New-

Mr. Hampden's ſhip-money cauſe, for three ſhillings and four pence, was tried all the people of England, with anxious expectation, intereſted themſelves in the important deciſion; and when the ſlighteſt point touching the freedom of a ſingle colony is agitated, I earneſtly wiſh, that all the reſt may with equal ardour ſupport their ſiſter. Very much may be ſaid on this ſubject, but I hope, more at preſent is unneceſſary

With concern I have obſerved that two aſſemblies of this province have ſat and adjourned without taking any notice of this act. It may perhaps be aſked, what would have been proper for them to do? I am by no means fond of inflammatory meaſures. I deteſt them.——I ſhould be ſorry that any thing ſhould be done which might juſtly diſpleaſe our ſovereign or our mother-country. But a firm, modeſt exertion of a free ſpirit, ſhould never be wanting on public occaſions. It appears to me, that it would have been ſufficient for the aſſembly, to have ordered our agents to repreſent to the King's miniſters, their ſenſe of the ſuſpending act, and and to pray for its repeal. Thus we ſhould have borne our teſtimony againſt it; and might therefore reaſonably expect that on a like occaſion, we might receive the ſame aſſiſtance from the other colonies.

" *Concordia res parvæ creſcunt.*
Small things grow great by concord.
A FARMER.

Lord BALTIMORE's *remarks on the city of*
CONSTA
ten duri
late as

" I C
t
ous as w
more co
mic feve
" Con
one of th
is ſaid to
thouſand
ler of i
would adm
equal ground; and the ſtreets are conſequently the ſame: they are paved
not ſo dirty as thoſe were in London.—
The houſes are built of wood and plaiſter

ty, very cheap, and w
proceeds from its being
Grand Vizir himſelf, th
the Empire after the gr
who certainly is the firſt
in eminence and power,
different parts of the c
and ſhops, which he doe
month or oftner; at
followed, at a diſtance
whom he precedes, dreſ
man, enquires into the
and examines their value
bad, over-rated, or defici
meaſure, then he aſſume
calls to his attendants,
mediately the offenders
ſeldom with death.

" There are few Phy
pothecaries, and no Su
inhabitants therefore,
little of the horrid miſ
by a certain diſeaſe we
great cities.

" The religion, laws,
the Turks are, as much
them, in direct oppoſiti
eat, write, ſleep, and ſit
their dead they carry ou
foremoſt, their cloaths
ſhort; they have many wi
es allowed by law, we
have few wh—s, we a
believe in One God, we
they believe in predeſtin
our potentates ſend amb
other, the grand Signio
they ſay on this head,

in oppoſition to our faſh

* An order of the Turkiſh infantr
Signior's guard, and the main ſtrength

BOSTON CHRONICLE

December 21, 1767

—

This is the first issue of the *Boston Chronicle*, published by Scottish bookseller John Mein and his business partner, John Fleeming. Soon the *Chronicle* would be recognized as the town's most aggressively pro-Crown newspaper. The front page begins John Dickinson's first of twelve letters "from a farmer," which provided articulate anti-taxation rhetoric, helped unite the colonies, and urged nonviolent resistance.

REPORTING

Nonimportation and Nonconsumption

By Todd Andrlik

In February 1768, after petitioning King George III for a repeal of the Townshend Acts, the Massachusetts House of Representatives delivered to the other colonial legislatures a circular letter, drafted by Boston politicians Samuel Adams and James Otis, Jr. The letter, as published in the March 21, 1768, *Boston Chronicle*, encouraged harmony among the colonies and provided plenty of fodder for the other assemblies to draft their own petitions.

Boycotts of British goods were a double-edged sword. They unified all walks of life—men, women, young, old, wealthy, poor—but began driving a wedge between Patriots and Loyalists.

Furious from Massachusetts's attempt to ignite a multicolony response, Lord Hillsborough, British secretary of state for the American colonies, demanded that the body rescind the letter. In June, the House voted 92 to 17 not to rescind (see July 14, 1768, *Pennsylvania Gazette*). As a result of their disobedience to the Crown, Massachusetts's Royal Governor Francis Bernard dissolved the colonial assembly. Now with the New York and Massachusetts assemblies dissolved, the struggle for power intensified as royal executive orders were extinguishing the colonies' longstanding government by the people. Invoking the Magna Carta and Petition of Right, early English freedom documents, Americans focused their Townshend arguments on constitutional rights, liberties, and privileges.

Boycotts of British goods helped overturn the Stamp Act a couple years earlier, so mercantile abstinence was seen as a proven counterpunch to the Townshend Acts. After the unsuccessful petitions for relief, nonimportation and nonconsumption agreements were formed across the colonies and were supported, sometimes reluctantly, by various public, merchant, or mechanic organizations (see July 10, 1769, *Boston Gazette*).

American manufacturing was encouraged to help starve English merchants and simultaneously free colonists of their financial chains to the mother country by allowing them to pay off their debts to London shopkeepers and agents. New paper mills were built to supply the colonial printing industry, which was growing and gaining importance as tensions worsened. Lamb was eaten less for the purpose of increasing reserves of sheep's wool, which Daughters of Liberty used during meetings to spin hundreds of skeins of yarn at a time (see May 21, 1770, *Boston Gazette*).

The boycotts, however, were a double-edged sword. They unified all walks of life—men, women, young, old, wealthy, poor—but began driving a wedge between Patriots and Loyalists (see letter by "The Sons of Liberty" to Nathaniel Rogers, followed by "A LIST of the Names of those who AUDACIOUSLY continue to counteract the UNITED SENTIMENTS of the Body of Merchants thro'out NORTH-AMERICA; by importing British Goods contrary to the Agreement" in the May 21, 1770, *Boston Gazette*). While the strict nonimportation and nonconsumption agreements were violated by those loyal to the crown, they were also sometimes difficult to obey for wealthy Patriots, who were accustomed to the luxuries of London and made their riches by smuggling.

Loyalist printer John Mein published in his *Boston Chronicle* the names of patriotic gentlemen who broke the agreements, alleging Patriot merchant John Hancock, one of the richest men in Boston, was among the greatest offenders. Mein soon found himself in a dangerous confrontation, as described in the November 6, 1769, *New-York Gazette;* or, *Weekly Post-Boy*:

> *Last Saturday afternoon, as Mr. John Mein, publisher of the Boston Chronicle, was returning from his shop in King-street, some gentlemen then upon Change, who thought themselves ill-treated in a late publication of his, took occasion to 'catechise' him; upon which, after a few words had passed between them, he drew a pistol out of his pocket, and threatened to fire if they did not stand off; but that was so far from intimidating them, that they followed up in order to seize him...*

Tensions escalated between Loyalists and Patriots, and with British troops occupying Boston since October 1768, incidents soon became more tragic.

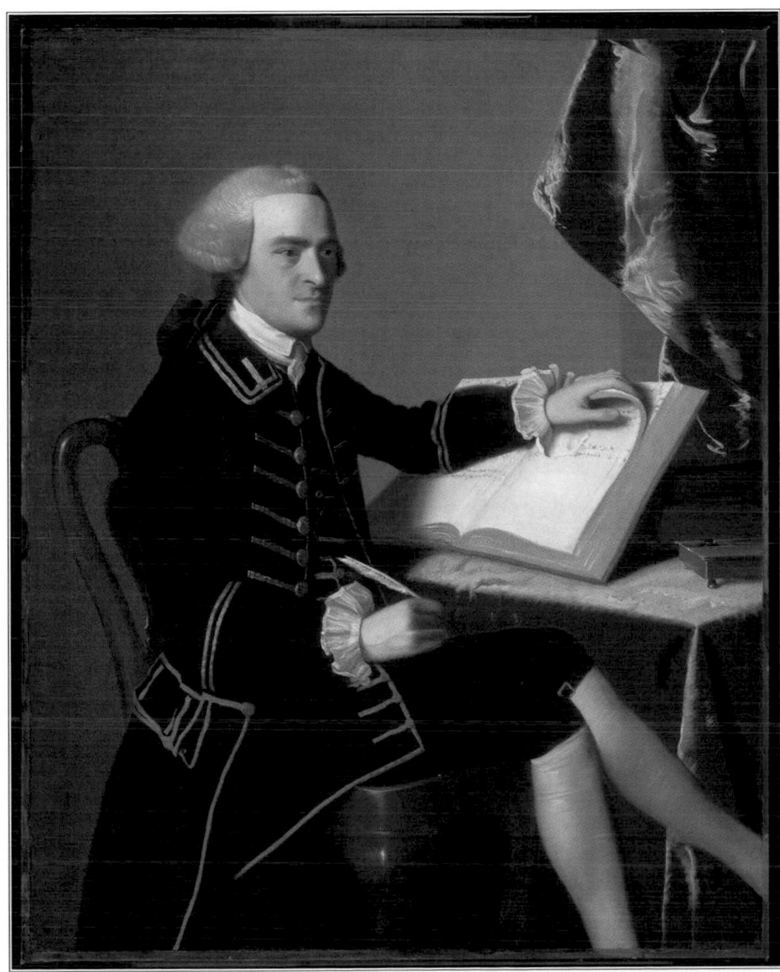

John Hancock, by John Singleton Copley, 1765
Museum of Fine Arts, Boston (current location)

(*left*) Patriot John Hancock was a prominent merchant and one of the wealthiest men in Boston. Loyalist printer John Mein accused Hancock of violating the boycott of British goods.

Daughter of Liberty
North Wind Picture Archives

(*opposite page*) Patriotic American woman spinning to avoid importing British cloth.

BOSTON CHRONICLE
March 21, 1768

Circulated to the other colonies, this letter by the Massachusetts House of Representatives served as the template for the other colonial assemblies to draft their own petitions for repeal of the Townshend Acts.

hoe they found in the vessel—
v Antigua, distant 7 leagues.

re, I connot help acquainting
affair that passed here a few
s it may be a means of pre-
ny who trade here, from be-
ey to the villany and cowar-
of our public officers. The
an English vessel now in this
ing a file of soldiers carrying
n to the fort, begged he might
erty of seeing who they were
ht know whether any of his
mong them. The corporal,
ery insolently, took him to
here the Com—d-nt treated
extreme ill language, and
him with corporal punish-
captain, not used to such
told him he was an officer as
iself, and dared him or his
him with any violence. The
immediately ordered him out
telling him, at the same time,
ld see him in the morning.
ish captain, not doubting but,
—d-nt bore a commission, he
ive him a gentleman's satis
being altogether ignorant
ous character his antagonist
s being recorded a liar, went
d next morning coming on
is sword on, met the Com—
im aside, and, told him he
wait upon him wherever he
per: that he was a gentle-
d been ill treated by him.
Com—d-nt replied, that he
im satisfaction, and turning
ed up to some gentlemen
anding at Mr. Dickson's ta-
hauled out, "Sir you have
d me, and I will complain to
nor." In this he was as good
; and aggravated his com-

prove the contrary, by which means he has recorded himself a coward. I hope this will be a caution to all gentlemen
so great a
the first of-
himself a

,) *Dec.* 22.
; hath been
e Commons
ard to Mr.
ville parish,
for making public his invention of a machine f r beating rice, which with six ordinary horses, will, in one season, beat out six hundred barrels of rice.

New York, March 4. Wednesday March second, arrived here Capt. Finglass from South-Carolina, in eight days passage, who informs us that Capt. Farrell arrived there the 13th. of February, after a disagreeable passage of 27 days; who on 29th. of January off Cape Hatteras, was struck by a violent flash of lightening, which carried away his main topmast, and the head of his main-mast: But on the 12th. of Febuary being the day before he arrived, being at anchor off Carolina, in weighing his anchor at seven o'clock in the morning, he had the most melancoly sight and accident that ever he saw, which was his mate John Studdon, killed dead on the spot, without ever making the least motion of life; It happened by the stop of the windless giving way, and the hand-spike took him under his right ear.

Providence, February 17. By Captain Joseph Tilling, from the West-Indies we are advised that Captain Pray, of this port, who sailed from hence just before the storm which happened on the 15th of December last, is arrived at St Eustatia: he had been but 14 hours from this Harbour, when, about noon, the wind met him at S. E. which increased to a violent storm, and lasted till midnight, without the least intermission: then suddenly shifting to W. S. W. blew a more terrible Hurricane than perhaps has been known in these parts for many years, which obliged him to throw over a number of horses, cattle and sheep, with a quantity of hay, stove the water on deck, and broke his boom. The extreme severity of the weather added greatly to his distress, most

it, as it was a wet season, and no rational account given how it could happen by any accident.—In the large barn, (which was 100 feet in length, and of proportionable breadth, well finish'd) there were consum'd nineteen head of neat cattle, and some swine, the flames having prevail'd so far, before the fire was discover'd that there was no possibility of saving the cattle, so much as their hides after they were dead, in the other barn some young cattle and sheep were saved—the loss is great to the public, as many milch cows and calfs were destroy'd, besides other useful stock. How much the loss is to the owner we are not able at present to say—— we wou'd only observe, that such flagrant wickedness is most amazing and alarming, as it threatens the destruction of the place where is exists; for in such cases no man's person nor property is safe; and every one would chuse to fly from such a place as fast as from one infected with the most malignant contagion, 15 load of hay was also burnt.

B O S T O N.

Copy of a letter written by the Hon. the House of Representatives, in the last Session of the General Assembly, and sent to the respective Assemblies on the continent.

Province of the Massachusetts-Bay, *Feb* 11.

To the Honourable the Speaker of the Honourable House of Representatives of the province of

S I R,

THE House of Representatives of this Province, have taken into their serious consideration, the great difficulties that must accrue to themselves and their constituents, by the operation of the several acts of parliament imposing duties and taxes on the American colonies.

As it is a subject in which every colony is deeply interested, they have no reason to doubt but your assembly is duly impress'd with its importance; and that such constitutional measures will be come into as are proper. It seems to be necessary, that all possible care should be taken that the representations of the several assemblies, upon so delicate a point, should harmonize with each other: The House therefore hope that this letter will be candidly considered in no other light than as expressing a disposition freely to communicate their mind to a sister colony, upon a common concern, in the same cannot over-leap the bounds of it, without deſtroying its own foundation: That the conſtitution aſcertains and limits both ſovereignty and allegiance; and therefore his Majeſty's American ſubjects who acknowledge themſevles bound by the ties of allegiance, have an equitable claim to the full enjoyment of the fundamental rules of the Britiſh conſtitution: That it is an eſſential unalterable right in nature, ingrafted into the Britiſh conſtitution, as a fundamental law, and ever held ſacred and irrevocable by the ſubjects within the realm, that what a man hath honeſtly acquired, is abſolutely his own, which he may freely give, but cannot be taken from him without his conſent: That the American ſubjects may therefore, excluſive of any conſideration of charter rights, with a decent firmneſs adapted to the character of free men and ſubjects aſſert this natural conſtitutional right.

It is morever their humble opinion, which they expreſs with the greateſt deference to the wiſdom of the parliament; that the acts made there, impoſing duties on the people of this province, with the ſole and expreſs purpoſe of raiſing a revenue, are infringements of their natural and conſtitutional rights; becauſe, as they are not repreſented in the Britiſh parliament, his Majeſty's commons in Britain, by thoſe acts, grant their property without their conſent.

This Houſe further are of opinion, that their conſtituents, conſidering their local circumſtances, cannot by any poſſibility, be repreſented in the parliament; and that it will for ever be inpracticable that they ſhould equally be repreſented there, and conſequently not at all; being ſeperated by an ocean of a thouſand leagues: that his Majeſty's royal predeceſſors, for this reaſon, were gaciouſly pleaſed to from a ſubordinate legiſlative here, that their ſubjects might enjoy the unalienable right of a repreſentation. And that conſidering the utter impracticability of their being fully and equally repreſented in parliament, and the great expence that muſt unavoidably attend even a partial repreſentation there, this houſe think that a taxation of their conſtituents, even without their conſent, grievous as it is, would be preferable to any repreſentation that could be admitted for them there.

Upon theſe principles, and alſo conſidering that were the right in the parlia-

to obtain redreſs.

They have alſo ſubmitted it to conſideration, whether any people can be ſaid to enjoy any degree of freedom, if the crown, in addition to its undoubted authority, of conſtituting a governor, ſhould alſo appoint him ſuch a ſtipend as it ſhall judge proper, without the conſent of the people, and at their expence: and whether, while the judges of the land, and other civil officers, hold not their commiſſions during good behaviour, their having ſalaries appointed for them by the crown, independent of the people, hath not a tendency to ſubvert the principles of equity, and endanger the happineſs and ſecurity of the ſubjects.

In addition to theſe meaſures, the houſe have wrote a letter to their agent Mr. DeBerdt, the ſentiments of which he is directed to lay before the miniſtry; wherein they take notice of the hardſhip of the act for preventing mutiny and deſertion, which requires the governor and council to provide enumerated articles for the King's marching troops, and the people to pay the expence: and alſo of the commiſſion of the gentlemen appointed commiſſioners of the cuſtoms to reſide in America, which authoriſes them to make as many appointments as they think fit, and to pay the appointees what ſums they pleaſe, for whoſe malconduct they are not accountable—From whence it may happen that officers of the crown may be multiplied to ſuch a degree, as to become dangerous to the liberty of the people, by virtue of a commiſſion which doth not appear to this houſe to derive any ſuch advantages to trade, as many have been led to expect.

Theſe are the ſentiments and proceedings of this houſe; and as they have too much reaſon to believe that the enemies of the colonies have repreſented them to his Majeſty's miniſters and parliament, as factious, diſloyal, and having a diſpoſition to make themſelves independant of the mother country, they have taken occaſion, in the moſt humble terms, to aſſure his Majeſty, and his miniſters, that with regard to the people of this provice, and as they doubt not of all the colonies, the charge is unjuſt.

The houſe is fully ſatisfied that your aſſembly is too generous and enlarged in ſentiment, to believe, that this letter proceeds from an ambition of taking the

ceptance.

AT a meeting of the free
ther inhabitants of this tow
neuil-hall, on Monday la
James Otis, Eſq; was cho
and the following Town o
enſuing year, *viz.*
Town Clerk, Mr. William
Select Men. Joſeph Jack
muel Sewall, Eſq; John R
John Hancoch, Eſq; Willia
Mr. Timothy Newell, & Jo
Town Treaſurer, Mr. Dav
Overſeers of the poor. Joh
Hon. Royal Tyler, Eſq;
Dolbeare, Mr. William
William Greenleaf, Willia
Mr. Joſeph Waldo, John
John Gore, Eſq; Capt. Sam
Thomas Tyler, Eſq; and Ca
ford.
Firewards. John Scollay
man Greenough, Eſq; Jo
Mr. William Cooper, Mr. J
dell, Thomas Marſhall,
Homes, Eſq; Mr. Joſeph T
dino Paddock, Mr. Jame
Capt. Benjamin Waldo, J
Eſq; Mr. Samuel Adams, J
ham, Eſq; Capt. Martin G
mas Dawes, Eſq;
Capt. William Downe C
ed ſerving as a fireward, b
diſpoſition of body; the
town were voted to him f
vices in that office. The
Town were alſo voted to
liams, Eſq; for his paſt
office, and in the office o
the poor.
Wardens. Henry Lloyd,
Simſon, Eſq; John Hanc
liam Blair Townſhend, Eſ
Marſton, Capt. William D
Mr. Nathan Hancock, Mr
ret, Mr. John Sweetſer jun
Capen, Mr. John May, Mr.
Committee for purchaſing
Jackſon, Eſq; William Phi
liam Homes, Eſq;
Surveyors of Wheat. Joh
Mr. John White.
Surveyor of Hemp, Mr. Jo
Aſſeſſors. Mr. William
John Kneeland, Mr. Benj
Belcher Noyes, Eſq; Mr. W
Mr. Jonathan Brown, Mr.
Collectors of Taxes. Mr.

The PENNSYLVANIA

G A Z E

Containing the Freshest Ad- vices, Foreign

To the PRINTERS of the PENNSYLVANIA GAZETTE.

Lancaster, June 28, 1768.

As the following Remarks on a Proposition of one Woods, published in the Chronicle of the 20th of June, for discovering the Longitude of a Ship at Sea, may be serviceable to the Public, so your giving them a Place in your Paper, may be acceptable to your Readers.

I APPREHEND the Gentleman is greatly mistaken, in his Notion of others attempting to measure the exact Space of a solar Day, a Thing never proposed by any that I ever understood: But what Harrison and all others mean by a Time Piece, is such an one as will measure true Time, which is the Quantity of Time any one Point, on the terraqueous Globe, takes up in revolving round from any one Point in the celestial Globe, until it intersect the same again, which is equal to the Sun's mean Motion; and as the Sun's Equation is known, consequently a Machine to measure the mean Motion, will be far preferable to any other Method yet proposed; and were not Harrison's Machines upon that erroneous Principle of Springs, they would undoubtedly answer the Intention, which he says were finished about Christmas 1765; in which he is likewise mistaken, for his Father made three, and I saw them in Motion about 18 Years since; but as to finishing, neither the Father, or his Son, will be ever able to perform that Part, though they are a curious Performance.------And as to the Gentleman's Method of measuring Time, it may answer for one Revolution of the Earth; but as the Glass must contain a large Quantity of Sand, at least three or four Pounds, let the Observer be ever so careful, the Glass cannot be turned without a considerable Loss of Time; for the Sand must all run out before it is turned, and

veral Minutes in Time.------He concludes, and says, "Thus the main Point of Navigation may be determined, without any Regard to solar Time." And above he says, "and a good Watch, or Spring Clock, will shew the Time between, &c."------So it is obvious, his Works are full of Errors, and his Writing Contradiction, and the Sea-faring Gentlemen left to their Log Line and Lead as before. C. S.

unhappy Divisions and Distractions which have operated so prejudicially to Great-Britain and the Colonies.-----After what passed in the former Part of the Sessions, and after the declared Sense of so large a Majority when the House was full-----His Majesty cannot but consider this as a very unfair Proceeding, and the Resolutions taken thereupon to be contrary to the real Sense of the Assembly, and procured by Surprise; and therefore it is the King's Pleasure, that so soon as the General Court is again assembled at the Time prescribed by the Charter, you should require of the House of Representatives, in His Majesty's Name, to to Rescind the Resolution that gave Birth to the Circular Letter from the Speaker, and to declare their Disapprobation of, and Dissent to that rash and hasty Proceeding.

"His Majesty has the fullest Reliance on the Affections of His good Subjects in the Massachusetts-Bay, and has observed with Satisfaction that Spirit of Decency, and Love of Order, which has discovered itself in the Conduct of the most considerable of its Inhabitants, and therefore His Majesty has the better Ground to hope, that the Attempt made by a desperate Faction to disturb the public Tranquility, will be discountenanced, and that the Execution of the Measure recommended to you, will not meet with any Difficulty."-----

The House by Message desired the Governor to send them the Remainder of the above Letter, also another Letter from his Lordship, which had been communicated to his Majesty's Council, and Copies of such Letters as his Excellency had wrote on the Subject contained in his Message, with the King's Instruction to him on this Matter.

In Consequence of which Message his Excellency the Governor sent the following Answer, viz.

entlemen of the House of Representatives,

D have communicated to you the whole of the llsborough's Letter relating to the Business which ou on the 21st Instant, if I had not been desirous pliance with his Majesty's Requisition might have by its appearing to be entirely dictated by a Sense but since you desire to know what my further herewith send you a Copy of the Part of the Let- this Business, which contains all my Instructions as I know you will not expect that I should dis- g's positive Commands, I must desire, that if you o oblige me to execute them, you will, previously your final Answer, prevent the Inconvenience that n the People for want of the annual Tax-Bill, derstand is not yet sent up to the Board.----If I am obliged to Dissolve the General Court, I shall not think myself at Liberty to call another, till I shall receive his Majesty's Commands for that Purpose, which will be too late to prevent the Treasurer issuing his Warrant for the whole Tax granted by the Act of the last Year.

As to the Letter of the Earl of Hillsborough which I communicated to the Council, I may beg Leave to be the proper

BY virtue of a writ, 3d day of August ne will be sold by vendue, a c or parcel of land thereun acres, more or less, situate of Chester, bounded by l Wilson, John M'Konkey, Cunningham, deceased, sei

July 9, 1768.

BY virtue of two writs Saturday, the 6th da Matthias Kerlin's tavern, i vendue, the following piec ship, to wit, a messuage, a to the south by the river De and extending back 565 fe of the street, as laid out with land of Thomas Ho lands of the widow Howell from the river to the King's piece or parcel of land, in bounded by lands of Johan mas Howell, deceased, and containing 20 acres and 60 liam Clayton, junior, Jere laid out to Marcus Hook Howell, deceased, seized in

July 9, 1768.

BY virtue of a writ, t day of August next, be sold by vendue, a certai the name of the Blue-ball 20 years past, where Thon with a good orchard, barn, land thereunto belonging, ther road leading to Marcus land, lying near the aforesa square perches; late the est in execution, and to be sold

July 9, 1768.

WHEREAS Isaac Roxborough, and having absconded from his personal Estate of him th to satisfy his Creditors, Court of Common Pleas said Court did appoint us make Distribution of the Creditors: We do herel 18th of this instant Ju

PENNSYLVANIA GAZETTE (PHILADELPHIA)

July 14, 1768

Secretary of State for the Colonies Lord Hillsborough ordered the Massachusetts circular letter to be rescinded. The Massachusetts House of Representatives defiantly voted 92 to 17 not to rescind. As a result, the governor dissolved the General Court. Later, Paul Revere commemorated the event by creating a silver bowl "to the memory of the glorious ninety-two."

…onsequence of the Earl … gh's Letter to your Excellency.

A MESSAGE from the GOVERNOR to the ASSEMBLY.

Gentlemen of the House of Representatives,

I CANNOT consistently with my Sense of my Duty, prorogue or adjourn the General Court, until I have received your Answer to his Majesty's Requisition. I must therefore repeat my Request to you to bring this Matter to a Conclusion.

Council-Chamber, June 29, 1768. F. BERNARD.

On Thursday, the 30th of June, the Committee reported a Letter to the Right Honourable the Earl of Hillsborough, setting forth to his Lordship, the several Votes and Resolutions which passed in the last House of Representatives, relating to the Circular Letter; and showing that the whole of these Matters were transacted in the Heighth of the Session, in a full House, and by a large Majority. This Letter was distinctly read several Times; and afterwards accepted by a Majority of Ninety-three *out of* One Hundred *and* five *Members present, and a fair Copy was ordered to be taken for the Speaker to sign and transmit to his Lordship as soon as might be. Then it was moved that the Question be put, whether the House will rescind the Resolution of the last House, which gave Birth to their circular Letter to the several Houses of Representatives and Burgesses of the other Colonies on the Continent? and passed in the Negative, by a Division of* Ninety-two *to* Seventeen.

Hereupon the Committee reported an Answer to the Governor's Messages of the 21st and 24th of June, which was accepted by a large Majority, and is as follows.

A MESSAGE from the ASSEMBLY to the GOVERNOR, June 30, 1768.

May it please your Excellency,

THE House of Representatives of this His Majesty's antient and loyal Province of the Massachusetts-Bay, have, with the greatest deliberation, considered your Messages of the 21st and 24th instant, with the several extracts from the letter of the Right Hon. the Earl of *Hillsborough*, His Majesty's principal Secretary of State for North-American affairs, dated the 22d of April last, which your Excellency has thought fit to communicate. We have also received the written answer which your Excellency was pleased to give the Committee of this House directed to wait on you the 29th inst. with a message, humbly requesting a recess, that the Members might be favoured with an opportunity to consult their constituents at this important crisis, when a direct and peremptory requisition is made of a new and strange constructure, and so strenuously urged, viz. That we should immediately rescind the Resolution of the last House, to transmit circular letters to the other British Colonies on the continent of North-America, barely intimating a desire that they would join in similar dutiful and loyal petitions to our most gracious Sovereign, for the redress of the grievances occasioned by sundry late Acts of Parliament, calculated for the sole purpose of raising a revenue in America. We have most diligently revised, not only the said resolution, but also the circular letter, written and sent in consequence thereof; and after all, they both appear to us, to be conceived in terms not only prudent and moderate in themselves, but respectful to the authority of that truly august body the Parliament of Great-Britain, and very dutiful and loyal in regard to His Majesty's sacred person, crown and dignity; of all which we entertain sentiments of the highest reverence and most ardent affection; and should we ever depart from these sentiments, we must stand self-condemned, as unworthy the name of British subjects, descended from British ancestors, intimately allied and connected in interests and inclination with our fellow subjects the commons of Great-Britain. We cannot but express our deep concern that a measure of the late House, in all respects so *innocent*, in most so virtuous and laudable, and as we conceive so truly patriotic, should have been represented to *Administration*, in the odious light of a party, and factious measure, and that pushed through by reverting in a thin House to, and reconsidering, what in a full Assembly had been rejected. It was, and is a matter of notoriety, that more than eighty Members were present at the re-consideration of the vote against the application to the other Colonies. The vote of reconsideration was obtained by a large majority. It is, or ought to be well known, that the presence of eighty Mem… full House, this number …

…y, or fallen under the displea- … the one, or the censure of the other.

On the whole, Sir, we will consider His most sacred Majesty under God, as our King, our best protector and common Father; and shall ever bear him true and faithful allegiance. We also regard your Excellency as the Representative of the greatest Potentate on earth, and at all times have, so far as could consist with the important purposes of preserving Life, Liberty and Property, been most ready and willing to treat you with all that respect justly due to your high rank and station. But we are constrained to say, that we are disagreeably convinced that your Excellency entertains not that parental regard for the welfare of the good people of this province, which you have sometimes been pleased to profess, and which they have at all times an irrefragible right to expect from their Governor. Your Excellency has thought fit not only to deny us a recess to consult our constituents, in regard to the present requisition, but hath assured us, in effect, that you shall take silence, at least a delay, not, as usual, for a consent, but a denial. You have also thought fit to inform us, that you cannot think yourself at liberty, in case of the Dissolution of this, to call another Assembly, without the express orders of His Majesty for that purpose: At the same time, your Excellency has been pleased to assure us, that you have communicated the whole of Lord Hillsborough's Letter, and your Instructions, so far as relate to the Requisition. In all this, however, we cannot find that your Excellency is more than directed to dissolve the present Assembly, in case of a non-compliance on the part of the House. If the Votes of the House are to be controuled by the direction of a Minister, we have left us but a vain semblance of Liberty. We know it to be the just prerogative of the Crown, at pleasure, to dissolve a Parliament: We are also sensible that, consistently with the great Charter of this Province, your Excellency, when you shall think fit, with or without the Intervention of a Minister, can dissolve the Great and General Court of this Colony, and that without the least Obligation to convene another within the Year. But should it ever grow into use, for any ill-disposed Governor of the Province, by means of a mistaken, or wilfully wrong state of facts, to procure orders for a Dissolution, that same Charter will be of no value.

We take this opportunity faithfully and firmly to represent to your Excellency, that the new Revenue Acts and Measures are not only disagreeable to, but in every view are deemed an insupportable burthen and grievance, with a very few exceptions, by all the Freeholders and other Inhabitants of this Jurisdiction: And we beg leave, once for all, to assure your Excellency, that those of this opinion are of no "*party or expiring faction.*" They have at all times been ready to devote their lives and fortunes to his Majesty's service. Of Loyalty, this Majority could as reasonably boast as any who may happen to enjoy your Excellency's smiles. Their Reputation, Rank, and Fortune, are at least equal to those, who may have been sometimes considered as the only friends to good Government; while some of the best blood of the colony, even in two Houses of Assembly, lawfully convened, and duly acting, have been openly charged with the unpardonable crime of "Oppugnation against the Royal Authority." We have now only to inform your Excellency, that this House have voted not to Rescind, as required, the Resolution of the last House; and that, on a Division on the Question, there were 92 Nays, and 17 Yeas. In all this we have been actuated by a conscientious, and finally, a clear and determined sense of Duty to God, to our King, our Country, and to our latest Posterity: And we most ardently wish, and humbly pray, that in your future conduct your Excellency may be influenced by the same Principles.

[The Governor, after having received the last foregoing Message from the House, directed their Attendance in the Council, and then and there *adjourned* the Great and General Court to Wednesday, the Third Day of August next.]

Charles-Town, South-Carolina, June 6.

A calculation having been made of the value of the produce of this province, exported since the 1st of November last, and of what remains to be shipped by the same day in the present year, at the price the planter and manufacturer has received for it at the Charles-Town market, … Million …

riors.--
uncorru
a late t
their Co
The (
admired
nihilatio
the Reso
and Unan
People, a
doubted I
Welfare o
famous N
but the N
to the late
It is said
pleased to a
Board of C
King, upon
And the H
to the same
the high Of
The Grea
The following
of Represen
which they
ING," a
Earl of Hi
Names.
William Brow
Peter Frye, E
Dr. John Cale
Jacob Fowle,
Richard Salton
Israel Williams
Mr. Jonathan
Mr. Jonathan
Capt. Joseph R
John Ashley, E
John Chadwick,
Timothy Ruggle
Chillingf. Foster
Jonathan Sayward
Mr. William Jen
Matt. Mayhew,
Josiah Edson, Es
All the free A
been prevented b
ferring Petitions a
those of the Assen
It is with great
form the King's C
asserted the Rights
Crisis, with as mu
bly.-----May Coun
public the Sentimen
by the Multitude of
What will such P
and to their God, w
ries, or any other M
to their Superiors, to
by the whole People,
be attended with an A
Consequences.
It has been conject
us by the new Duties,
tirely cover the main
York Government; b
ways equal to the Sum
its Trade, by Means of
There have been sev
through the Town and
little Foundation for the

pealed to him
pose his friend-
g manner said,
in Chester, a
rcel of damn'd
nperious inso-
struck at this
it is said he
e in Philadel-
ssinate a gen-
sooner out of
f the schooner
redoubled his
ithout offering
s fti... my
nich, with an
strike me on
did not, that
edly. " You
ow dare you
With that they
for the mate,
e commander
nner. When
hat they might
e put in irons,
e they thrust
ore he would
e light, nor to
me to Halifax.
reats and me-
the protection
lice and inso-
l, he order-
on board my
his pardon.—
e ordered his
ard my boat,
uring this in-
ome nigh the
S BEVAN.
he followed
to make up
scorn'd, and
each of the

Lisbon to his

delatory and
rious to the
that a small
will take near
terally true.)
Merchant that
his Influence
Effects of so

3.
er of Gentle-
d voluntarily
e Non-impor-
that Govern-
ered into by

Numbers of
ed at the As-
e were warm
at Patriotism

that Place, since the Troops were withdrawn, is really difficult to be described; several poor Families are in a starving Condition, and many of the Inhabitants daily deserting the Town.

SALEM, *July* 4.

WHEREAS Information has been made to the Merchants and Traders of this Town, that sundry Persons belonging to Boston, have sent Quantities of English Goods in this Town for Sale, which were imported since the General Agreement of the Merchants (not to import such Goods) took Place:— We therefore, the Merchants and Traders of the Town of Salem, at a Meeting at the King's Arms this 30th Day of June, Anno Domini 1769, do publickly DECLARE our Disapprobation thereof, and resolve, that we will do all in our Power to discourage the Sale of such Goods, by not purchasing any of them ourselves, or suffering any Person for or under us to purchase them. We think (in Justice to those Merchants and Traders who have strictly adhered to their Agreement) we ought to inform all Persons, that the Shop lately kept by Mr. John Gool, now 'tended by John Norris in this Town, is now owned and supplied by Merchants in Boston, who have taken the Advantage of others not sending for Goods, to import double the Quantity of Goods which they did at other Seasons, expecting to make their Fortunes, while others were sinking theirs for the Benefit of their Country. We hereby caution all Persons, who have the Interest of their Country at Heart, against purchasing Goods of any Persons who come from Boston and offer Goods to sale, such as Tea, Loaf-Sugar, Crates of Earhten Ware, &c. as we have great Reason to suspect, that those Goods are sent out of that Town, because of the Discouragements the Owners meet with in the Sale of them by the Friends of Liberty there. We also request the Town of Marblehead to join with their Neighbours (for the general Good) not to send for any more Goods, contrary to the Intent and Meaning of the Agreements entered into by the Inhabitants of the Town of Boston and other neighbouring Towns, which Request, if still refused, we must desire all who are real Friends to their Country, properly to take Notice of. We also request those Traders in this Town, who (it is well known) have deviated from their Contract, that they would (for the future) strictly adhere thereto; for it is determined at this Meeting, that we will make publick the Names of all those who shall hereafter break through their Engagements by purchasing Goods of those who have not subscribed the Agreements, or by any other Way.

All GENTLEMEN of NOTE, in their respective Towns, are desired to caution their Families and Neighbours from purchasing at the abovementioned Shop, or of any traveling Traders who are sent out to sell Goods imported since the Agreements aforementioned.

BOSTON, July 10.

Thursday last Major Robert Rogers came to Town from New-York; and set out the same Day for Portsmouth.

Early last Saturday Morning 4 Companies of the 64th Regiment embarked on board the Launceston, in Order to proceed to Halifax.

Same Afternoon the Body of a Man was taken up in Charles's River, suppos'd to be one Thomas Nolen, who was drowned last Tuesday Se'nnight.

Last Saturday the Viper Sloop of War arrived here

Messieurs EDES & GILL,

The following Method of grafting the Mulberry Tree is submitted to your Inspection; if you shall think it worth publishing, please to give it a Place in your valuable Gazette, and you will oblige a Friend to American Produce and Manufactures.

TAKE from the Mulberry-Tree a Root ¾ of an Inch Diameter, and 7 or 8 Feet in Length, splice the Cion, and let it be fixed into the great End of the Root after the usual Manner of grafting, wind a Woolen Thread round the Root to keep the Cion in its Place, bury the Root near the same Depth you found it, raising the great End within 3 Inches of the Surface of the Ground, which brings the Cion near perpendicular. The above Experiment was tried in April 1768. The Cion grew two Feet the first Year, and now appears very thrifty. The same Person in April 1769, grafted seven, some into shorter & smaller Roots, even to two Feet in Length; they all appear likely to do well.

CUSTOM-HOUSE, *BOSTON*.

ENTERED IN

Brooks from New-Haven; Davis from New-London; Bates fr. Canso; Childs, Murphy & Southerland fr. Virginia. Arnold from Newfoundland; Wier, Clift and Helpman from Quebec; Smith from New-York; Harman from Porto Rico; Taylor from Figuira; Somes from Turks-Island; Waters from Hispaniola; Andrews from St. Croix; Hathorn from St. Lucia; White from Dominica and St. Eustatia.

Buried in the Town of Boston since our last,
Ten Whites. No Blacks.
Baptiz'd in the several Churches, Six.

High Water at Boston, for this present Week

JULY 10, 1769

The BOSTON GAZETTE

SALEM, *July 4.*

WHEREAS Information has been made to the Merchants and Traders of this Town, that sundry Persons belonging to Boston, have sent Quantities of English Goods in this Town for Sale, which were imported since the General Agreement of the Merchants (not to import such Goods) took Place :—We therefore, the Merchants and Traders of the Town of Salem, at a Meeting at the King's Arms this 30th Day of June, Anno Domini 1769, do publickly declare our Disapprobation thereof, and resolve, that we will do all in our power to discourage the Sale of such Goods, by not purchasing any of them ourselves, or suffering any Person for or under us to purchase them. We think (in Justice to those Merchants and Traders who have strictly adhered to their Agreement) we ought to inform all Persons, that the Shop lately kept by Mr. John Gool, now 'tended by John Norris in this Town, is now owned and supplied by Merchants in Boston, who have taken the Advantage of others not sending for Goods, to import double the Quantity of Goods which they did at other Seasons, expecting to make their Fortunes, while others were sinking theirs for the Benefit of their Country. We hereby caution all Persons, who have the Interest of their Country at Heart, against purchasing Goods of any Persons who come from Boston and offer Goods to sale, such as Tea, Loaf-Sugar, Crates of Earhten Ware, &c. as we have great Reason to suspect, that those Goods are sent out of that Town, because of the Discouragements the Owners meet with in the Sale of them by the Friends of Liberty there. We also request the Town of Marblehead to join with their Neighbours (for the general Good) not to send for any more Goods, contrary to the Intent and Meaning of the Agreements entered into by the inhabitants of the Town of Boston and other neighbouring Towns, which Request, if still refused, we must desire all who are real Friends to their Country, properly to take Notice of. We also request those Traders in this Town, who (it is well known) have deviated from their Contract, that they would (for the future) strictly adhere thereto ; for it is determined at this Meeting, that we will make publick the Names of all those who shall hereafter break through their Engagements by purchasing Goods of those who have not subscribed the Agreements, or by any other Way.

ALL GENTLEMEN of NOTE, in their respective Towns, are desired to caution their Families and Neighbours from purchasing at the abovementioned Shop, or of any traveling Traders who are sent out to sell Goods imported since the Agreements aforementioned.

BOSTON GAZETTE
July 10, 1769

BOSTON GAZETTE

May 21, 1770

American manufacturing was encouraged to help starve English merchants and simultaneously free colonists of their financial chains to the mother country by allowing them to pay off their debts to London shopkeepers and agents. Lamb was eaten less for the purpose of increasing reserves of sheep's wool, which Daughters of Liberty used during meetings to spin hundreds of skeins of yarn at a time.

BOSTON, May 21.

Laſt Wedneſday Forty five Daughters of Liberty, met in the Morning at the Houſe of the Rev. Mr. MOORHEAD in this Town; in the Afternoon they exceeded Fifty. By the Evening of ſaid Day they ſpun 232 Skeins of Yarn, ſome very fine, their Labour and Materials were all generouſly given the worthy Paſtor.

Nothing appeared in their whole Conduct, but Love, Feſtivity and Application. They were, by a great Majority, of his own Congregation; the reſt of the Ladies belong'd to other Societies in the Town, who generouſly offer'd their Service. For all which, the Recipient is under great Obligations to the whole.

Their Entertainment, was wholly American Production, excepting a little Wine, &c. Many Ladies and Gentlemen were pleaſed to viſit this agreeable Collection, and appear'd highly gratified. There are above 100 Spinners in Mr. Moorhead's Society; and conſidering they are comparatively ſmall, 'tis ſuppos'd that no Congregation in the Province can produce ſo great a Number, of the ſame Number of Families.

The whole was concluded with many agreeable Tunes, Anthems and Liberty Songs, with great Judgment; fine Voices perform'd and animated on this Occaſion, in all their ſeveral Parts, by a Number of the Sons of Liberty.

Let this ſerve as a Specimen, to excite the numerous Fair in this Metropolis, and Country Towns, to exert their Parts in rendering this happy Climate opulent and flouriſhing.——*Quid Enim tentare nocebit?*

Thurſday Morning the 29th Regiment quitted the Barracks at Caſtle-Iſland, and landed at Dorcheſter-Neck, from thence they began their March for Providence, where they arrived laſt Saturday Noon, and immediately embarked on board the Tranſports then ready to proceed to the Jerſeys.

Capt. Jenkins and Capt. Hall, in Brigs, Capt. Jacobſon and Capt. Daverſon, in Ships, were to leave London ſoon after Capt. Symmes. Mr. Samuel Eliot, of this Town, Merchant, had taken his Paſſage in Capt. Jacobſon.

A Letter from London, by Capt. Burnell, mentions, that it was tho't the Eaſt-India Company would ſettle the

or three Hours.

Laſt Saturday ſail'd with a fair Wind for London, to the ſad Mortification of all the Tories Male and Female, who have been uſing all the Tricks which the grand Cabal were capable of inventing to embarraſs and hinder her Voyage, the good Ship Lydia, Capt. Scott, laden in Part

---

JUST PUBLISHE

And to be ſold by RICHARD DRA

Second EDITION: With Additi

A Plan of Exerciſe for the

TIA of the Province of the *Maſſachuſetts-B*

ed from the Plan of Diſcipline, for the NORF

Country Traders, Shopkeepers

and others, are invited to the Auction-

Queen-Street,

On *Wedneſday* and *Thurſda*

23d and 24th Inſtant,

At TEN o'Clock in the Morning, and a

the Afternoon of each Day.

At which Times and Place will be Sold by P

a large and valuable Aſſortment of GO

Among which are,

Rich blue, white, green, crim

mazarene, ſtraw, cloth color'd, ſcarlet and ties—cloth color'd Grograms,—yellow, buf green, drab, blue and cloth color'd Sattins ſtrings, black Paduſoy, pink and cloth-co —Perſian Sarſnets,——Broad Cloths, Bea Ratteens, Frize, Shalloons and Tammies Poplins, Dorſetteens, Fuſtians, Jeans, Dim ſets, Camblets, Mens and Womens cotto worſted Hoſe, Nankeens, Buckram, green crimſon and ſcarlet knit Waiſtcoat and Bre Cotton Gowns, 3 4, 7 8 & yard-wide Chec Allopeen, a few Lawns, yellow Hollands Gauze Handkerchiefs, Mens and Wome Mitts, kid and lamb ditto. A variety of bons, ſilk Ferrets, Qualities, Capuchin S nets, Blond Lace, white Wax Necklaces, T Hair, Womens & Childrens Stays, Cotton white and yellow metal Coat and Breaſt B Head ditto, &c. &c. &c.

N. B. The Sale to begin on *Wedneſday* at TEN o'Clock in the Morning, a nued till *Thurſday* Evening.

J. Ruſſell,

TO BE SOLD, B

Joſeph Peirce,

At his Shop the North Side of the To

ew *Philadelphia* FLO

nnens, ſuperfine Broad Cloths, a Vari

ALSO,

The Remains of Meſſirs. COX and B

o are embarked for England, conſiſti

ver Lace, and Bindings Gold & Silver B.

N. B. The higheſt Price given for old Lace.

On WEDNESDAY nex

Forenoon, will be Sold by PUBLI

the Houſe of MILES GREENWOO

Part of BOSTON.

---

an expreſs avowal of it

We would not *willingly* ſu

other ſecretary of ſtate eve

commend the alteration of

the province in one of its *m*

dicates himſelf by ſaying, t

of which was dictated to

"ſignified by his——

alſo when the houſe charge

ſitions to the miniſtry *priv*

denying it; but *alertly* anſ

ferred to muſt be thoſe whic

tranſmitted to his Majeſty'

Majeſty's commands ſignif

he ſays "he is ſorry that h

ſo much as *may have been e*

he receiv'd ſuch command

people to give their teſtimo

have been glad to have had

ed pains and penalties for a

cult to procure *voluntary* e

not execute the King's comm

Certain it is however tha

evidence of ſome perſons; an

poſſibly believe that Gov. B

part he did, as he declares, i

would be condemn'd, muc

adviſ'd to ſuch orders, I

have been to the people

himſelf properly enough

caſe, the charges muſt be

againſt his——'s adminiſt

wrong—This is a maxim a

niſters may, for which in for

to feel the vengeance of an i

to overthrow the conſtitution

of another, is the higheſt crim

bro't an haughty *Safford* to

Traitors will always plead *t*

Great therefore are accounta

have given them orders to *op*

are made to atone for their c

crept from the dunghill an

their ſunſhine, will retreat & r

In conſequence of this com

preſentatives, Bernard, it ſeem

vernment, tho' the Petition li

great city of London, is dee

ſcandalous.

TO BE

On THURS

By Benjami

At his uſual P

BROAD Cloths, Forreſt

Stuffs, Iriſh and Scotch H

Checks, Handkerchiefs, Mens

Sundry Articles of Houſhol

Chairs, Looking-Glaſſes, Be

Apparel, Watches, &c.

Half Pipes of choice

the Day o

wn presence.——
Lord H—— or any
Gov. Bernard to *re-*
ished constitution of
parts; tho' he vin-
of the acts, the doing
special commands
of state":——Thus
sending over depo-
, &c. he is far from
the depositions re-
y be *suppos'd* to have
in *obedience to his*
for that purpose";
done in that respect
m him", for "when
no power *to oblige*
no doubt he would
wer to have inflict-
" He found it diffi-
and therefore could
hat punctuality &c."
ocure the voluntary
he whole one could
s ordered to act the
ional to suppose he
sh'd by those *who*
rievous they may
Province; for he
that in such a
od to be directed
e King can do no
lege; but his Mi-
s some were made
ople—An attempt
ow the expression
he State——This
ely death—Little
f the great—The
unishable, if they
people; when *they*
vermin who have
themselves under
native obscurity.
he House of Re-
ed from the go-
monstrance of the
me people, to be

D
xt.
rch,
Sale;
amblets, figured
awns, Cambricks,
ts, Caps, &c. &c.
re, as Tables,
lsteads, Wearing
VINE—Samples

bances had happened there; and that the commander in chief has ordered, once more, ALL the king's ships in America before that town, as the likeliest means to awe those SONS OF LIBERTY.

PHILADELPHIA, May 10.

Extract of a Letter from London, dated March 6.

"I have had many to visit me this Morning, asking this Question, What will now be done? I answered, the Ships in the North-America Trade must go there empty; I pray the People may stand firm in the Agreement they have entered into for another Year; and it is much wished by all, who are Friends to the Liberties of free born Englishmen here, of whom there are a great Number in this Kingdom.---- Lord North, I was informed, before I got into the House of Commons, said to this Effect, That the People of Boston, who began the Association, were going on with their Importations from hence, nearly as before, having broke their Faith with New-York and Philadelphia, who had been true to their Agreement; which, tho' unwarrantable and illegal, yet their being true to their Agreements did them Honour. How it will prove, I do not pretend to say, but certain it is, that great Quantities of Goods are gone, and going to that Place.---I hope they have not been ordered by any that entered into the Non-Importation Agreement, but by Governor Bernard's Son, and those who joined in the Opposition; tho' his Father, Mein the Printer, and many others, say, that it is in a great Degree general; but be it as it may, it has much hurt the Cause of America, if not lost it, for the present Year.

"I can assure you, from all I have observed, or can learn, the most serious and sensible People in England, are much and deeply impressed with a Sense of their and our Situation; inasmuch as the Ministry, and such a one as they think it is, can carry every Point they please in Parliament, without any Regard to the constitutional Rights of the Subject. In short, unless this Nation gets engaged in a War, or something turns up which we cannot foresee, I have no Idea (nor have I heard one good Reason given by any Body, to make me think) that the present Ministry, or the Majority, which is the same Thing, will not hold their Ground, and continue their Schemes of ministerial Oppression, until their Measure is full.

On Sunday last the Rev. Mr. WHITEFIELD arrived here from Georgia, in the Georgia Packet, Capt. Souder. Monday Evening he preached at the New Presbyterian Church, and again last Night at St. Paul's Church, to very crowded Auditories.

NEW-YORK, May 14.

IT being publickly known here, that NATHANIEL ROGERS, (one of the Boston Merchants, who has all along refused to come into the Non-Importation Agreement) was in Town, and it being suspected that his Design in visiting this City, was to use his Endeavours to prevail on the Merchants here, to break thro' and put an End to their Agreement; his Effigy was exhibited (last Thursday Evening) hanging on a Gallows, with Labels on the Back and Breast of it, expressing his Crime. It was attended by some Thousand Spectators, who after parading through Part of the City, went from the Coffee-House to his Lodgings, about 9 o'Clock, in order to pay their Respects to himself, in which they were disappointed, as he din'd out of Town and had not yet returned.——They then proceeded through several of the principal

Vessels from Bristol are coming out in Ballast.

A LIST of the Names of those who AUDACIOUSLY continue to counteract the UNITED SENTIMENTS of the BODY of Merchants thro'out NORTH-AMERICA; by importing British Goods contrary to the Agreement.

JOHN GILLESPIE,
In Queen-Street, has imported a Quantity of Glass contrary to the Agreement of the Merchants, and refuses to reship them.

John Bernard,
(In King-Street, almost opposite Vernon's Head.

James McMasters,
(On Treat's Wharf.

Patrick McMasters,
(Opposite the Sign of the Lamb.

Nathaniel Rogers,
(Opposite Mr. Henderson Inches Store lower End King-Street.

William Jackson,
At the Brazen Head, Cornhill, near the Town-House.

Theophilus Lillie,
(Near Mr. Pemberton's Meeting-House, North-End.

John Taylor,
(Nearly opposite the Heart and Crown in Cornhill.

Ame & Elizabeth Cummings,
(Opposite the Old Brick Meeting House, all of Boston.

Israel Williams, Esq; *&* Son,
(Traders in the Town of Hatfield.

And, *Henry Barnes*,
(Trader in the Town of Marlboro'.

IT must evidently appear either by Importing British Goods contrary to the Agreement, or by breaking their Contract with the Merchants, that they have prefered their own little private Advantage to the Welfare of America: It is therefore highly proper that the Public should know who they are, that have at this critical Time, sordidly detached themselves from the public Interest; and as they will be deemed Enemies to their Country, by all who are well-wishers to it; so those who afford them their Countenance or give them their Custom, must expect to be considered in the same disagreeable Light.

We are desired to insert the following.

IF Mr. *Lemuel Spear* of Braintree, and Mrs. *Mary Belcher* living near the Fortification in Boston, will *desist* from purchasing Goods of the *McMasters*, IMPORTERS, nothing *further* will be said of the Matter! And Mrs. *Wingfield* and Mrs. *Curtis* are requested to desist from *visiting* the said *McMaster's* Shop, least it should be taken for granted that their Visits are *for no other End* but to purchase *unallowed Goods*. *A Hint to the Wise.*

NEW-YORK GAZETTE; OR, THE WEEKLY POST-BOY

November 6, 1769

Not long after alleging that John Hancock and other local Patriots were violating the nonimportation agreement, Boston Loyalist printer John Mein found himself in a dangerous confrontation. Shortly after the incident described here, in 1770, Hancock put Mein out of business. Just by coincidence, publishers in London asked Hancock to be their attorney in collecting debts from Mein. The Scottish printer had evidently bought books on credit to sell in Boston and hadn't paid the bill. Hancock thus got legal authority to seize Mein's property, which he did with undoubtable happiness. That took out the pro-Crown *Boston Chronicle*. Other Boston papers, including the *Post-Boy* and *News-Letter*, started receiving the Customs Office business again and became Crown mouthpieces.

Laſt Evening the following melancholy accident happened to Mr Jonathan Lowder, Poſt Rider, between Boſton and Hartford—an honeſt worthy man, extenſively known and as generally reſpected. As he was riding through the town, his horſe being touch'd by a Cart, took fright and threw his head againſt the wheel, which went over his ſhoulder and down his ſide. He was immediately carried into a houſe and ſurgeons ſent for. He had his ſenſes till they came, but died in about an hour. It was his birth day, being then 55 years of age.

Oct. 30. Tueſday laſt Mr. Robert Pierpoint, and ſeveral other inhabitants at the ſouth part of the town, made complaint to a Magiſtrate, that they had been greatly abuſed, the preceding night, and that morning, by ſome of the guard at the Fortification; likewiſe that when the guards were relieved, on their march one of the ſoldiers took his firelock off his ſhoulder, and fired it; and had not another ſoldier with his bayonet knock'd up the muzzle, the bullet which was diſcharged would have gone among a number of Perſons, that were very near ſtanding at a blackſmith's ſhop, but providentially the bullet entered the upper part of the ſhop, and hurt no perſon.---Theſe matters have ſince been examined by the magiſtrates, and ſome of the parties concerned, bound to appear at the next Court of Aſſize, to anſwer for their miſdemeanors.

Laſt Saturday afternoon, as Mr. John Mein, publiſher of the Boſton Chronicle, was returning from his ſhop in King-ſtreet, ſome gentlemen then upon Change, who thought themſelves ill-treated in a late publication of his, took occaſion to "*catechiſe*" him; upon which, after a few words had paſſed between them, he drew a piſtol out of his pocket, and threatened to fire if they did not ſtand off; but that was ſo far from intimidating them, that they followed up in order to ſeize him, and he apprehending ſome danger to himſelf from the reſentment of the people, who began to collect together pretty faſt, precipitately retreated to the main guard, which was near, with the piſtol in his hand, where, as ſoon as he entered the door, he diſcharged it at random among thoſe who cloſely followed him (tho' without doing any other damage than wounding the ſleeve of the coat of a grenadier who was upon guard) and then immediately took ſhelter in the houſe under the protection of the military conſervators of the peace:----Application was ſoon after made to Mr. Juſtice Dana, and a warrant iſſued for apprehending him, in order to anſwer for this atrocious offence; but tho' ſearch was made in the Guard-houſe and other places, by the proper civil officers, to whom the warrant was committed, they have not yet been able to ſerve it upon him.

The large French ſhip, which put in here ſome time ago in diſtreſs, having been refitted, is ſailed for France.

Saturday afternoon a perſon who lately belonged to the

Tueſday the 21ſt of November Inſtant, Circular Letters having been wrote to the reſpective Members, requiring their Attendance on that Day.

In order to amend the Breed of Sheep, if poſſible, we are aſſured, one Mr. *Deſhon*, has imported into *New-London*, from *Barbary*, two RAMS, which are much larger, and finer Wooll, than any of our *American* Sheep:——— One of thoſe Rams is ſaid to be of the true *Turkey-Breed*, the Tail of which alone generally weigh from 6 to 12 Pound weight, and are moſt delicious Mutton.——— Any Perſon bringing a Ewe to propagate from the Broad Tail Ram, pay 1s. 6d. Lawful Money.

Laſt Friday Night about 9 o'Clock, a Fire broke out in the Sugar-Houſe belonging to *John Van Cortland*, Eſq; at the North-Weſt Corner of Trinity Church-Yard; which having got to a Head when it was diſcovered, burnt with great Violence near an Hour, before it could be conquered:----But the Out Side being all of Stone, and the Night wet, the Fire was prevented from ſpreading, or doing any other Damage. Mr. *Cortland*'s Loſs is ſaid to be very conſiderable.

Laſt Monday Night one *Nicholas Lockerman*, a Shoemaker by Trade, and a ſingle Man, having been drinking at a Tavern near the Upper Barracks, kept by *James Shaw*, ---he left it about 10 o'Clock with an Intent to go home; but the next Morning was found lying at *Shaw*'s Door ſpeechleſs:---He was thereupon taken up and put into a Bed, but not recovering, he was carried next Day to the Poor Houſe, where he died, without being able to give any Account of himſelf.--The Coroner's Inqueſt brought in his Death occaſioned by exceſſive Drinking.----Whilſt he was lying on *Shaw*'s Stoop, it appeared he was robbed of his Hat, Shoes and Buckles; and it has been ſince found, that the Woman who was laſt Monday carted round the Town, in Company with two others, had ſold them to a Soldier for 1s. 6d. and a Pint of Rum;--and the three Thieves are all ſince committed to Bridewell.

CUSTOM-HOUSE, NEW-YORK, INWARD ENTRIES.

Sloop Nancy, J. Waddell from Roſcoft. Sloop John, C. Anderſon, and Sloop Polly, P. Dennis from St. Thomas. Sloop Little Betſy, B. Smith from St. Croix. Sloop Sally and Polly, W. Rhodes, and Sloop Lydia, J. Frebody jun. from Rhode-Iſland. Sloop Herring, C. Bowne from Philadelphia. Sloop Lydia, S. Clark, Sloop Newburgh, I. Belknap, and Sloop Olive, Ed. Cottle, from Nantuckett. Sloop Conway, R. Elder from Madeira.

OUTWARD.

Ship New-Hope, P. De Peyſter, for Hull. Ship Buchannan, T. Cockran for Liſbon. Brig Boon, G. Braſs for Gibraltar. Sloop Nancy, J. Rogers for Penſacola. Sloop Endeavour, G. Ellis for Philadelphia. Schooner George, T. Dent for Maryland.

CLEARED.

Ship Beaver. C. Miller, Ship Charming Polly, A. Shoemaker, and Snow General Gage, Peter Berrien to London. Brig Jeany, W. Hunter to Madeira. Brig Charlotte, H. Coupar to Antigua. Brig Polly, J. M'Con-

S is to deſire th
y, Inſolvent, to meet
Moſes Robins, in Do
rovince of Eaſt-New-J
that they may be exam
aid Eſtate, agreeable to
1769. per AAR

JOH

T O B E

RY good F
Hundred Acres, ſituate
Dutcheſs, in Rumbout
and is very handy to
e North-River. The
adow, and enough more c
Farm is about 80 Acres of good clear
which is about 40 Acres of flat low
framed double Houſe, and a Cellar a
framed Barn, with Barracks and oth
very good Orchards, one of which is
Sort, and can eaſily make between 5c
Year; beſides a great many other F
Spring nigh the Houſe, which is neve
There runs through ſaid Farm a pleaſ
Creeks leading into it.--------It is ver
as the Road leads by the Door. Said
Market, and School. Any Perſon i
may apply to the Subſcriber, who wil
the ſame. HE

T O B E

At public Vendue at the Merchants
Fourteenth Day of November, Inſta
Forenoon, by the Subſcribers.

ALL thoſe two cert
or Parcels of Land ſituate, ly
or Ulſter, and known and diſtinguiſh
Fifteen (and which ſaid two Lots N
Part of the great Lot in the Branch
the general Diviſion of Hardenbergh's
five, having Poughpacktunck River o
or Northermoſt Branch of Delaware F
Northweſt Sides thereof) and which
or Parcels of Land, are butted and bo
Number two begins at Monument I
Branch of Delaware River, (which ſ
of Stones, with a flat Stone on the T
Beach Tree marked Number 8, ſtan
South Side of the River, near the So
and is the Weſtermoſt Corner of Lot
the River the following Courſes and D
Weſt twenty Chains; then South 83
then North 78 Deg. Weſt eleven C
Weſt twelve Chains; then North 45
then North 40 Deg. Weſt fourteen C
Weſt twenty-four Chains; thence No
Chains; then North 63 Deg. Weſt nin
then South 39 Deg. Weſt twenty-one
Weſt ſeventeen Chains; then South 3
then South 50 Deg. Weſt eight Chain
five Chains; then North 38 Deg. We
40 Deg. Weſt twenty-nine Chains;
thirteen Chains; then North 8 Deg
North 5 Deg. and an half, Eaſt nin
ſixteen Deg. Eaſt nineteen Chains;
eleven Chains; then North 69 Deg.
North 58 Deg. Weſt twenty Chains;
ſeven Chains; then South 76 Deg. W
South 56 Deg. Weſt ten Chains; the
Weſt thirty five Chains; then South 5
then South 34 Deg. Weſt twenty-two
Weſt fourteen Chains and ſeventy-five
Eaſt five Chains; then South 54 Deg
fifty Links; thence South

NOVEMBER 6, 1769

The NEW-YORK GAZETTE; OR, THE WEEKLY POST-BOY

BOSTON, October 28.

[...]

Last Saturday afternoon, as Mr. John Mein, publisher of the Boston Chronicle, was returning from his shop in King-street, some gentlemen then upon Change, who thought themselves ill-treated in a late publication of his, took occasion to "*catechise*" him; upon which, after a few words had passed between them, he drew a pistol out of his pocket, and threatened to fire if they did not stand off; but that was so far from intimidating them, that they followed up in order to seize him, and he apprehending some danger to himself from the resentment of the people, who began to collect together pretty fast, precipitately retreated to the main guard, which was near, with the pistol in his hand, where, as soon as he entered the door, he discharged it at random among those who closely followed him (tho' without doing any other damage than wounding the sleeve of the coat of a grenadier who was upon guard) and then immediately took shelter in the house under the protection of the military conservators of the peace: --- Application was soon after made to Mr. Justice Dana, and a warrant issued for apprehending him, in order to answer for this atrocious offence; but tho' search was made in the Guardhouse and other places, by the proper civil officers, to whom the warrant was committed, they have not yet been able to serve it upon him.

ground, till it came to the rock, making
an opening about 24 yards broad, and a-
bout three feet deep; it then ruſhed
down the north ſide of the hill, with the
greateſt impetuoſity, hurling the largeſt
ſtones, and great quantities of earth before it, making an opening of the ſame
dimenſions all the way down the hill.
time to pay our compliments to your Excellency.
In this time of public diſtreſs, when the
General Court of the province is in a
ſtate of diſſolution; when the metropolis
is poſſeſſed by troops, and ſurrounded by
ſhips of war; and when more troops are
daily expected, it affords a general ſatisfaction that your Excellency has viſited
the province, and has now an opportunity of knowing the ſtate of it by your
obſervation and enquiry.
Your own obſervation will give you
the fulleſt evidence that the town and

CHAPTER III

THE LATE HORRID MASSACRE

Introduction

In October 1768, following multiple infractions between Patriots and Loyalists, Boston soon found itself with a ratio of one British soldier to every five inhabitants. The shock and awe of encamped redcoats and bayonets was temporarily counterattacked by calm and civility as the colonists collectively bit their lips. Frustration mounted and colonists again turned to newspapers to journal their tyrannical experiences. Bickering over boycotts and partisan loyalties escalated and incidents soon became deadly. In March 1770, as news of the Boston Massacre raced across the Atlantic to London, news from England about the repeal of the Townshend Acts headed to American ports. Americans soon read that all of the import duties were lifted with one exception—the tax on tea—and, in the wake of another tragic event in Rhode Island, colonists developed an alternative method of intercolonial communication.

Boston Chronicle
October 31, 1768

British officer harassed by boys in Boston
North Wind Picture Archives

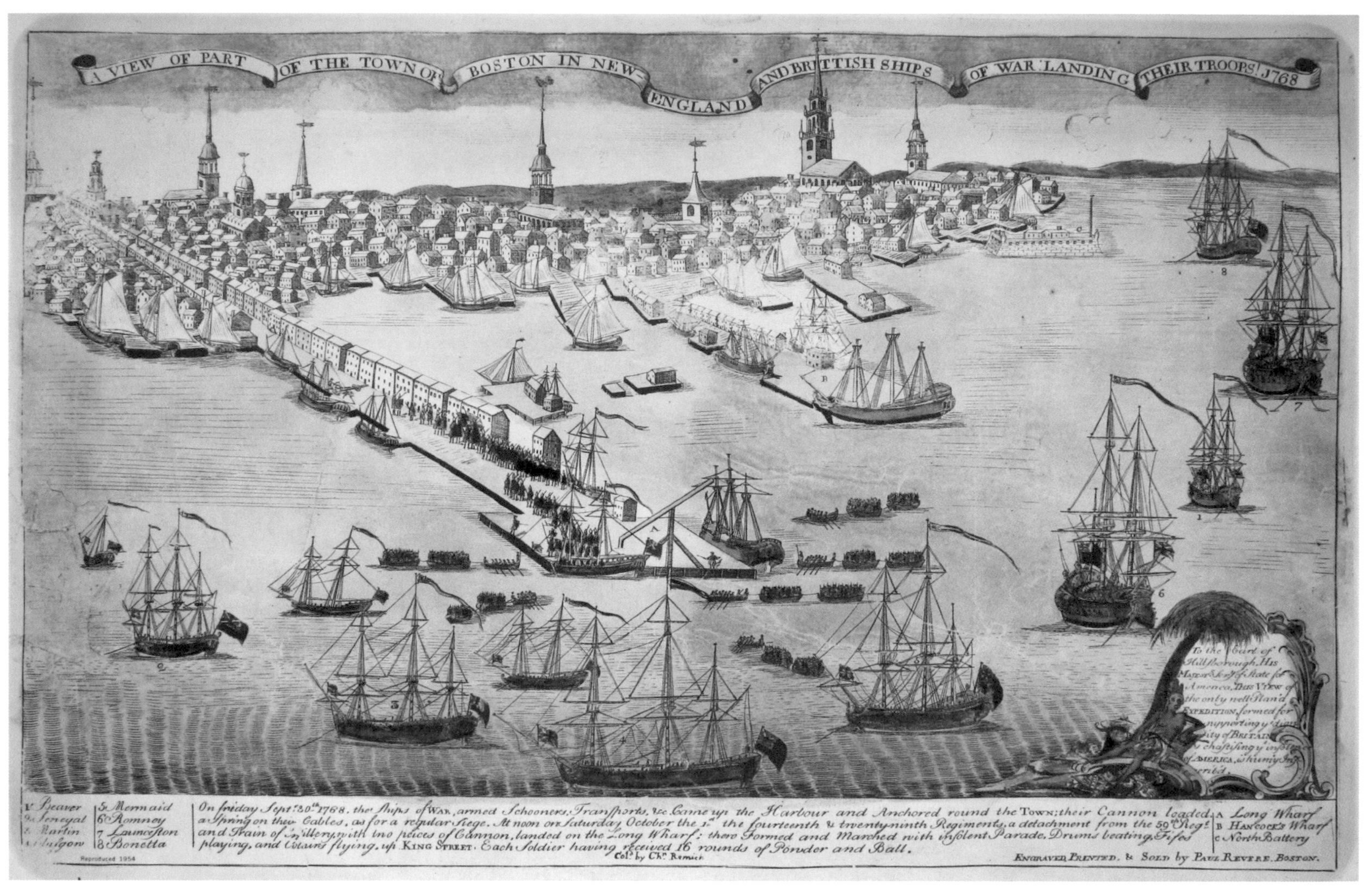

British Ships of War Landing Their Troops
Randall J. Stephens, Eastern Nazarene College

This engraving by Paul Revere states: "At noon on Saturday, October the 1st, the fourteenth & twenty-ninth Regiments, a detachment from the 59th Regiment, and Train of Artillery, with two pieces of Cannon, landed on the Long Wharf; there Formed and Marched with insolent Parade, Drums beating, Fifes playing, and Colours flying, up King Street. Each Soldier having received 16 rounds of Powder and Ball."

REPORTING THE ARRIVAL OF THE TROOPS IN BOSTON

By Robert J. Allison

Parliament created a five-member Board of Customs Commissioners in 1767 to oversee the ineffective customs apparatus, which had never raised as much in revenue as it cost to maintain. The 1767 Townshend duties on lead, paint, glass, and tea would pay the salaries of the commissioners, as well as the agents the commissioners hired to inspect cargoes. The commissioners would ensure that colonial trade, which benefitted from Britain's control of the seas, would help to pay for the fleet that controlled those seas.

Basing the board in Boston, the center of opposition to the Sugar Act and scene of riots over the Stamp Act, made less sense. The commissioners feared for their lives from the moment they arrived in Boston in late 1767.

On March 18, 1768, the anniversary of the Stamp Act repeal, mobs paraded to the houses of Governor Francis Bernard and the customs commissioners. The fifty-gun warship *Romney* arrived in June. A few days later, John Hancock's sloop *Liberty* docked, laden with Madeira wine. The crew locked the customs inspector in the hold while they quickly and illegally unloaded the cargo. When the *Romney* seized the *Liberty*, Bostonians rioted, forcing the customs commissioners to take refuge on the warship.

General Thomas Gage, the New York–based commander of British forces in North America, ordered the Fourteenth and Twenty-Ninth Regiments from Halifax to Boston. After a stormy passage, the troops reached Boston on October 1, 1768. Lord Hillsborough, British secretary of state for the colonies, sent two regiments from Ireland, which reached Boston in mid-November.

The Twenty-Ninth Regiment pitched its camp on Boston Common; Bernard knew their tents would not be adequate for the winter. The Fourteenth Regiment had no tents, but the town refused Bernard's request to quarter them. They allowed some soldiers temporarily at Faneuil Hall (where town meetings took place), and with the assembly suspended, Bernard placed others in the Old State House.

To highlight the town's seizures and sufferings, an anonymous diarist logged a day-by-day account of Boston's military occupation, which was circulated and published as the "Journal of the Times" by several colonial newspapers. "The troops still keep possession of Faneuil Hall, the court house, the representatives' chambers, &c.," the Journal of the Times reported in its October 14 entry (*Pennsylvania Chronicle*, October 31, 1768). But this was a temporary expedient. In the first two weeks, between forty and seventy soldiers deserted, encouraged by Bostonians. Officers placed guards at Boston Neck and patrolled the ferries to stop desertions, and the few deserters captured were executed to discourage others.

General Gage arrived to inspect in October. "The arrival of this gentleman from N. York at this time," the October 15 entry of Journal of the Times reported (*Pennsylvania Chronicle*, October 31, 1768), "is a very agreeable circumstance, to the friends of their country," as Gage was better able than the customs commissioners to "see and judge for himself." The Governor's Council hoped Gage would report that the troops were unnecessary. They explained to him (*Boston Chronicle,* October 31, 1768) that the June riot "appeared to have originated with those who ordered the seizure" of Hancock's ship, provoked to "furnish a plausible pretense for requesting troops." Gage did report that Boston was not in a state of rebellion, but the taxes would remain in place, and so would the customs commissioners and soldiers. Bernard rented barracks for them in empty warehouses. An uneasy peace settled on Boston, with soldiers garrisoning a town that insisted it neither needed nor wanted them. Using armed troops to keep peace in Boston, Benjamin Franklin warned, was like setting up a blacksmith forge in a gunpowder magazine.

Mr. GODDARD,

Your correſpondents furniſh you with intelligence ſo expeditiouſly, that I obſerve you have already publiſhed many of the particulars mentioned in the Journal of the Times; *nevertheleſs, as numbers of your cuſtomers would be glad to ſee the extraordinary tranſactions, &c. of the preſent day, in one comprehenſive view, in your valuable paper, on their behalf I beg the favour of you to give the following* continuation *a place, without any alteration.*

AMICUS.

B O S T O N.

JOURNAL of the TIMES.

[Continued.]

Oct. 3. TWO circular letters of Lord Hillſborough's this day ſeen in print, whereby it appears that the commiſſioners of the board of cuſtoms had repeatedly complained of being obſtructed in the execution of their office. The proceedings of council on the 27th and 29th of July laſt, which G——r B——d hitherto prevented being made public, declares to the world, that no inſult had been offered the commiſſioners;—That, "what happened on the 10th of June, ſeems to have ſprung wholly from thoſe who complain of it, and that it ſeems probable, an uproar was hoped for and intended to be ſeconded by the manner of proceeding, in making the ſeizure of the ſloop Liberty; that their quitting the town was a voluntary act, without any ſufficient ground for the ſame, and that when at the caſtle, there was no occaſion for men of war to protect them." "That it is their unanimous opinion, the civil power does not need the ſupport of troops; that it is not for his Majeſty's ſervice, nor the peace of this province, that any troops be required, or that any came into the province; and that they deem any perſons who may have made application for troops to be ſent hither, in the higheſt degree unfriendly to the peace and good order of this government, as well as to his Majeſty's ſervice and the Britiſh intereſt in America." *How deteſted and abhorred by the people muſt that G——r and thoſe men then be, who, not content with having by their miſrepreſentations introduced troops into this province, are now leaving no ſtone unturned in order*

voluntary act, without any ſufficient ground for the ſame, and that when at the caſtle, there was no occaſion for men of war to protect them." "That it is their unanimous opinion, the civil power does not need the ſupport of troops; that it is not for his Majeſty's ſervice, nor the peace of this province, that any troops be required, or that any came into the province; and that they deem any perſons who may have made application for troops to be ſent hither, in the higheſt degree unfriendly to the peace and good order of this government, as well as to his Majeſty's ſervice and the Britiſh intereſt in America." *How deteſted and abhorred by the people muſt that G——r and thoſe men then be, who, not content with having by their miſrepreſentations introduced troops into this province, are now leaving no ſtone unturned in order*

to procure quarters for them in this metropolis, to the great vexation and diſtreſs of the inhabitants, as alſo in violation of law and juſtice, which muſt be the caſe, while they are quartered in the town, to diſturb and annoy the inhabitants, and while the barracks provided by the province, at a very conſiderable expence, remain empty!——The prints of this day contain a very extraordinary advertiſement, publiſhed by order of the commiſſioners of cuſtoms, whereby it appears that the inhabitants of Nantucket, who are moſtly of the perſuaſion called Quakers, have not accommodated Mr. Samuel Procter, an officer of the cuſtoms lately ſent among them, with an office, and that therefore orders are iſſued to their ſeveral officers in America, to make ſeizure of all veſſels, and their cargoes, that ſhall arrive from that iſland, without proper documents, ſigned by the Collector and D. Comptroller of the port of Boſton.——*If quarters are to be provided by the people for cuſtom-houſe officers, who are daily increaſing upon us, as well as for his Majeſty's troops, we ſhall quickly perceive that we are without quarters ourſelves.*

Octo. 11. We have certain information, that at a full meeting of the inhabitants of Lebanon, (a large town in Connecticut) convened the 26th of September laſt, in conſequence of intelligence that troops were ſoon expected in Boſton, to be quartered upon the town; ſaid inhabitants unanimouſly expreſſed their ſentiments and reſolutions as follows, "That an union of meaſures is abſolutely neceſſary, at this important criſis, in order to maintain our liberties and immunities, and that they fully agreed with their brethren of Boſton, in the reſolves they paſſed in a late town meeting; and that conſidering themſelves connected by the ſtrongeſt ties to their fellow ſubjects, in this and the neighbouring colonies, they ſhould look upon an attack upon them, as though they themſelves were the immediate ſufferers, and that with a determinate, unalterable reſolution and firmneſs, they would aſſert and ſupport their American brethren, at the expence of their lives and fortunes; ſhould their welfare, which is ſo intimately blended with their own, demand the ſacrifice." *As it is thought the above ſhews the diſpoſition, not only of the other towns in that colony, but of the reſt of the provinces; how muſt the friends of Britain applaud the*

cuſtoms lately ſent among them, with an office, and that therefore orders are iſſued to their ſeveral officers in America, to make ſeizure of all veſſels, and their cargoes, that ſhall arrive from that iſland, without proper documents, ſigned by the Collector and D. Comptroller of the port of Boſton.——*If quarters are to be provided by the people for cuſtom-*

PENNSYLVANIA CHRONICLE (PHILADELPHIA)

October 31, 1768

Other colonies watched with great anticipation as Boston became a garrisoned town and an anonymous writer provided other colonial newspaper printers with a regular "Journal of the Times" to chronicle the military occupation.

prudence and wiſdom of the late committee of convention in Boſton, who in tenderneſs to the mother country, and loyalty to their Sovereign, under all their grievances, while they adhered ſtrictly to their rights, yet ſtrongly recommended peace and quietneſs to the people, until the effect of their laſt repreſentations and petitions could be known.

Oct. 12. Advice received that the merchants in Connecticut, have agreed as thoſe in Maſſachuſetts, and New-York, &c. had done before them, not to import any goods from Great-Britain, till the late revenue acts, &c. are repealed.—*A meaſure that muſt have the greateſt tendency to awaken the attention of the mercantile and manufactoral part of Britain to their own immediate intereſt, which they lately ſeem to have quite loſt ſight of.* The rumour of Caſtle William being delivered up by the G——r to the King's troops, aroſe from his having permitted a number of mariners from the ſhips of war, to land at Caſtle Iſland, ſix of whom it is ſaid went off in a boat laſt night.

Reports of great deſertions and a general diſpoſition to deſert from the regiments here, which it is ſaid left Halifax under great dejection of ſpirits; about 21 of the ſoldiers abſconded the laſt night, and parties from the troops with other clothing, inſtead of their regimentals are ſent after them.——*Some of the conſequences of bringing the troops into this town, in direct violation of the act of parliament, and diſregard to the advice of his Majeſty's Council, inſtead of quartering them in the barracks at Caſtle iſland, are like to be the ſcattering proper tutors through the country, to inſtruct the inhabitants in the modern way of handling the firelock, and exerciſing the men, and alſo in the various manufactures which the ingenuity and induſtry of the people of Great-Britain have hitherto furniſhed us with.*—This night a ſurgeon of one of the ſhips of war, being guilty of very diſorderly behaviour, was committed to gaol by Mr. Juſtice Quincy, as was alſo a perſon, not belonging to this province, by Mr. Juſtice Hutchinſon, on complaint of a ſoldier, that he had been enticing him to deſert; ſaid ſtranger was firſt taken and confined by Captain Willſon, in the town houſe for ſome time, without warrant or authority from any Magiſtrate.——*If the oaths of ſoldiers who are promiſed* 10 *Guineas for ſuch diſcoveries, are to be taken as ſufficient proof, we know not what proſcriptions may take place.*

Octo. 13. A private letter from Halifax contains ſome particulars relative to the Boſton expedition, not known before, viz. "That in conſequence of orders received Sept. 11th, from this place, all the workm n in the King's yard, neceſſary to equip the ſhips, were ſet to work on Sunday; a ſtrict embargo laid, and guard veſſels ſent to the mouth of the harbour to prevent intelligence being ſent, and more caution uſed than when fitting out for the Louiſbourg

to town; and that the troops embarked in as great hurry as was ever known in time of war.—*What a Tragi-comic ſcene is here preſented! and how muſt it*

has or may commit to them, as a ſecret, unleſs the B———d ſhall judge it for his Majeſty's intereſt ſo to do.

Oct. 14. The troops ſtill keep poſſeſſion of Faneuil-Hall, the court-houſe, repreſentatives' chambers, &c. Guards placed at the paſſage way into the town, near the neck. Patrolling companies near the ferry ways, and parties ſent into the country to prevent deſertions: In the forenoon one Rogers, a New-England man, ſentenced to receive one thouſand ſtripes, and a number of other ſoldiers, were ſcourged in the common by the black drummers, in a manner, which however neceſſary, was ſhocking to humanity; ſome gentlemen who had held commiſſions in the army, obſerving, that only 40 of the 170 laſhes received by Rogers, at this time, was equal in puniſhment to 500, they had ſeen given in other regiments.

Oct. 15. A deſerter from the 14th regiment was brought in laſt evening by one of the decoy parties, ſent into the country, alſo a labouring man from Roxbury, with a ſoldier's regimentals on his back, he was confined for ſome time in a tent, without lawful warrant, and afterwards committed to priſon by Mr. Juſ[illegible] Hutchinſon.—This afternoon the troops were [illegible]wn up, on the common, on the appearance of General Gage; at ſunſet there were 17 diſcharges from the field cannon; he paſſed the front of the battalion in his chariot, preceded by a number of aid de camps on horſeback. *The arrival of this gentleman from N. York, at this time, is a very agreeable circumſtance, to the friends of their country; as his mild and judicious behaviour, in that province, has been juſtly applauded; and he comes here determined to ſee and judge for himſelf.*

Oct. 16. This day Capt. Jenkins arrived from London, who brought a print of Auguſt 13th, in which there is the following article, "There are 4000 troops ordered for Boſton, which it is thought will ſufficiently intimidate thoſe people to comply with the laws enacted in England; eſpecially as the other Colonies ſeem to have deſerted them." The deſign of ſending troops among us was before fully comprehended; all the Colonies that have been permitted to meet, have united with us in humble petitions and remonſtrances, and it is hoped that the merchants of Philadelphia have, or will ſoon co-operate in a meaſure our friends at home repreſent as the moſt likely to procure a redreſs of grievances.

BOSTON, October 20.

It has been reported that the Head Quarters for the army is to be in this town.

Tueſday laſt ſailed from hence, his Majeſty's ſhip Launceſton of 40 guns, the Martin ſloop of 14 guns, and the St. Lawrence armed ſhooner, for Halifax.

gal, and Hope ſchooner.

Among the many writers in the London papers, one who ſigns *Anglo Americanus* ſays, that in the pro-

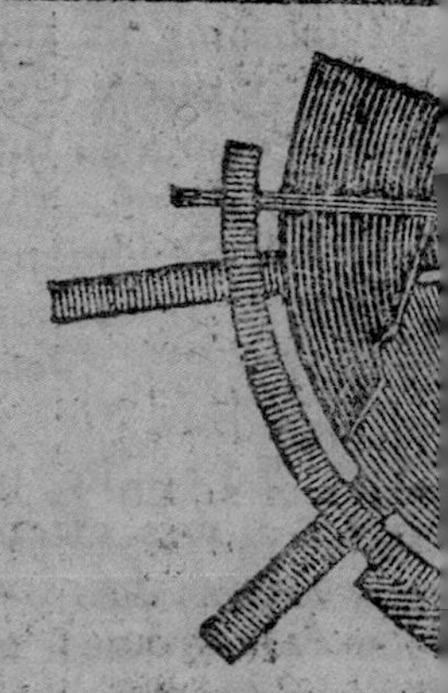

To the
THO

em from Quebec, ...hed through the ...e; and this morn- ...them was diſem- ...k the ſame rout. ...oad eleven years. ... look hearty and

The following is ...eceived here from ...uſt 2.

...2d inſtant, about ... a very uncommon ... in this neighbour- ...or large body of ...on Dungavel-hill, ...out ſix miles ſouth ... its way into the ... the rock, making ...ards broad, and a- ...; it then ruſhed ... the hill, with the ...urling the largeſt ...tities of earth be- ...ning of the ſame ...y down the hill. ...g appearance, and ... with a ſevere ſe- ... grounds on that ...d deep under wa- ...ers have loſt their ...ounds covered with ...At the ſame time ...s of water ruſhed ...f the hill, as put ... grounds in the ...d a houſe ſo in- ...ater, that had not ...eſcape by the win- ... been drowned, as ...nning through the ... after. It carried ... ſwept every thing ...a paſſage into a ...ertoun-Burn, which ... year is commonly ... ſuch an enormous ...f a houſe; and had ...ſtructions which it ...ouſe, which made ...ferent courſe, the ...ould have been in

...O N.

...n London, *Aug*. 30.

...nt of foot command-

gentlemen of the Council, in behalf of themſelves and the other members who ſubſcribed it, being all that were preſent.

To his Excellency General GAGE, *Commander in Chief of his Majeſty's forces in America.*

The Addreſs of the ſubſcribers, members of his Majeſty's Council of the province of Maſſachuſets-Bay.

SIR,

A General Council being held yeſterday gives the diſtant members of it, together with the members in the town and the neighbourhood the pleaſure of addreſſing you.—We take this firſt opportunity of doing it, and at the ſame time to pay our compliments to your Excellency.

In this time of public diſtreſs, when the General Court of the province is in a ſtate of diſſolution; when the metropolis is poſſeſſed by troops, and ſurrounded by ſhips of war; and when more troops are daily expected, it affords a general ſatisfaction that your Excellency has viſited the province, and has now an opportunity of knowing the ſtate of it by your obſervation and enquiry.

Your own obſervation will give you the fulleſt evidence that the town and province, are in a peaceful ſtate.—Your own enquiry will ſatisfy you, that tho' there have been diſorders in the town of Boſton, ſome of them did not merit notice; and that ſuch as did, have been magnified beyond the truth.

Thoſe of the 18th of March, and 10th of June are ſaid to have occaſioned the above-mentioned armament to be ordered hither.——The firſt was trivial, and could not have been noticed to the diſadvantage of the town, but by perſons inimical to it; eſpecially as it happened in the evening of a day of recreation. The other was criminal, and the actors in it were guilty of a riot: but we are obliged to ſay it had its riſe from thoſe perſons who were loudeſt in their complaints about it, and who by their overcharged repreſentations of it have been the occaſion of ſo great an armament being ordered hither. We cannot perſuade ourſelves to believe they have ſufficien evidence to ſupport ſuch repreſentations; which have moſt unjuſtly brought into queſtion the loyalty of as proceedings that have taken place in the town of Boſton. We deteſt them, and have repeatedly and publickly expreſſed that deteſtation; and in council have adviſed Governor Bernard to order the Attorney General to proſecute the perpetrators of them: but at the ſame time we are obliged to declare in juſtice to the town, that the diſorders of the 10th of June laſt, occaſioned by a ſeizure made by the officers of the cuſtoms, appeared to have originated with thoſe who ordered the ſeizure to be made. The hour of making the ſeizure (at or near ſun ſet), the threats and armed force uſed in it, the forcibly carrying the veſſel away, and all in a manner unprecedented, and calculated to irritate, juſtify the apprehenſion that the ſeizure was accompanied with theſe extraordinary circumſtances in order to excite a riot, and furniſh a plauſible pretence for requeſting troops. A day or two after the riot, and as if in proſecution of the laſt mentioned purpoſe, notwithſtanding there was not the leaſt inſult offered to the commiſſioners of the cuſtoms, either in their perſons or property, they thought fit to retire, on the pretence of ſecurity to themſelves, on board the Romney man of war, and afterwards to Caſtle William; and when there, to keep up the idea of their being ſtill in great hazard, procured the Romney and ſeveral other veſſels of war to be ſo ſtationed as to prevent an attack upon them which they affected to be afraid of.

Theſe proceedings have doubtleſs taken place, to induce a belief among the officers of the navy and army, as they occaſionally came thither, that the commiſſioners were in danger of being attacked, and to procure from thoſe officers repreſentations co-incident with their own, that they really were ſo. But their frequent landing on the main, and making excurſions to the country, where it would have been eaſy to have ſeized, if any injury had been intended them, demonſtrates the inſincerity of their declarations, that they immured themſelves at the caſtle for ſafety. This is rather to be accounted for as being an eſſential part of the concerted plan for procuring troops to be quartered here, in which they and their coadjutors have ſucceeded to their wiſh; but unhappily to the mutual detriment and uneaſi-

xcellency when you know the
' the town, which we can af-
quite peaceable, ſhall think
ſervice does not require thoſe
o continue in town, it will be
and ſatisfaction to the inha-
ou will pleaſe to order them
William, where commodious
provided for their reception;
Shirley in the neighbourhood
er of which, or in both, they
accommodated.
two regiments expected here
d, it appears by Lord Hillſbo-
er of the 30th July, they were
r a different part of North A-

xcellency ſhall think it not
with his Majeſty's ſervice that
be ſent to the place of their
ion, it will contribute to the
ppineſs of the town and pro-
ey might be ordered thither.
true and faitful ſubjects of
have an affectionate regard
er country, and a tender feel-
own, our duty to each of them
h, and we earneſtly beg your
o make a full enquiry into the
ove-mentioned, into the cau-
and the repreſentations that
made about them, in doing
Excellency will eaſily diſco-
the perſons that from lucra-
have combined againſt the
s town and province: Some
is probable, have diſcovered
lready by their own letters to
ency.

t your Excellency's repreſen-

all allow to be juſt.
Samuel Danforth,

Bradbury, Tyler, White, Pitts, *and* Dexter, *Members of his Majeſty's Council of the province of Maſſachuſetts-Bay.*

GENTLEMEN,

I Return you thanks for the honour you do me in this Addreſs, and am greatly obliged to you, for the good opinion you are pleaſed to conceive of me.

Whatever may have been the particular cauſes of the diſturbances, and riots, which have happened in the town of Boſton, theſe riots, and the reſolves which were publiſhed, have induced his Majeſty to order four regiments to this town to protect his loyal ſubjects, in their perſons and properties, and to aſſiſt the civil magiſtrates in the execution of the laws.

The diſcipline and order which will be preſerved amongſt the troops, I truſt, will render their ſtay, in no ſhape, diſtreſsful to his Majeſty's dutiful ſubjects in this town; and that the future behaviour of the people, will juſtify the beſt conſtruction of their paſt actions, which I flatter myſelf will be ſuch, as to afford me a ſufficient foundation to repreſent to his Majeſty the propriety of withdrawing the moſt part of the troops *Thomas Gage.*

Boſton, Oct. 28th, 1768.

Tueſday laſt George Erving, Eſq; of this Town, merchant, was married to Miſs Lucy Winſlow, daughter to Iſaac Winſlow, Eſq; of Roxbury.

Laſt Sunday ſe'night as Mr Turner the Coxſwain of the Pinnace belonging to his Majeſty's ſhip the Romney, was coming from the ſhip to the Long-Wharf, with three other men in a ſmall ſkiff, they accidentally overſet, when the Coxſwain

Sloop Polly, Higgins, ditto
Brig Grzel, M'Ewen, London

Sloop Hampton, ditto
Sloop Speedwell, Studſon, ditto
Sloop Nancy and Hannah, Downs, ditto

Ship Suſanna, Johnſton, London
Brig Friendſhip, Jenkins, ditto
Ship Three Friends, Robertſon, Grenada
Sloop Friendſhip, Dowman. ditto
Brig Maryland Packet, Minot, Maryland
Schooner Three Brothers, Coffin, New-York
Schooner Packet, Folgier, ditto
Brig Elizabeth, Leitch, Virginia
Sloop Ranger, Somes, Halifax

BOSTON CHRONICLE

October 31, 1768

The British fifty-gun warship *Romney* arrived in June. A few days later, John Hancock's sloop *Liberty*, laden with Madeira wine, docked. The crew locked the customs inspector in the hold while they quickly and illegally unloaded the cargo. When the *Romney* seized the *Liberty*, Bostonians rioted, forcing the customs commissioners to take refuge on the warship. The Governor's Council hoped Gage would report that the troops were unnecessary and explained to him that the June riot "appeared to have originated with those who ordered the seizure" of Hancock's ship, provoked to "furnish a plausible pretense for requesting troops." Gage did report that Boston was not in a state of rebellion. But the taxes would remain in place, and so would the customs commissioners and soldiers.

REPORTING THE

BOSTON MASSACRE

By Robert J. Allison

"Facts are stubborn things," John Adams said in his defense of the soldiers on trial for their role in the Boston Massacre. The facts of March 5, 1770, were not in dispute—eight soldiers, under command of Captain Thomas Preston, fired into a crowd of several hundred people, killing five and wounding half a dozen. But were the soldiers guilty of murder?

John's cousin Samuel Adams certainly thought so. He orchestrated the town of Boston's public response. *A Short Narrative of the Horrid Massacre*, published two weeks after the event, traces the crisis to the Stamp Act (1765) and the arrival of customs commissioners (1767). Preceding the narrative in the pamphlet was a "Report of the Committee of the Town of Boston" taken from a March 12 town meeting. The exact report was reprinted in the March 20, 1770, *Essex Gazette*.

Samuel Adams demanded removal of all soldiers from town, warning of grave danger if they stayed.

Two British regiments arriving in 1768 made the tragic conflict inevitable. Boston artist Henry Pelham sketched the scene in a print, "The Fruits of Arbitrary Power." Paul Revere copied the print, creating one of American history's most important images, showing the soldiers in line firing at unarmed townsfolk while the spires of the Town House and the First Church, symbolizing civil and spiritual power, stand impotent in the background.

John Robinson took a set of depositions to London, where a different version appeared: *A Fair Account of the Late Unhappy Disturbance at Boston.* This tells of the "Unhappy Disturbance" that began on Friday, March 2, when a group of rope workers beat an off-duty soldier; he came back with more soldiers to get revenge, but again the rope workers beat them, and all weekend Boston toughs and soldiers fought. The March 20 *Essex Gazette* (dateline Monday, March 19) said this was "stopping far short of the real source of the matter," and the May 8, 1770, *London Chronicle* talks of "repeated acts of provocation" on both sides, with the soldiers spoiling for a fight.

The evening of March 5, two hundred people tried to attack the British barracks in Brattle Square; as they were driven off, they saw sentry Hugh White defending himself in front of the Custom House from a group of harassing apprentices. The mob surrounded White. Someone alerted Captain Thomas Preston, who led seven soldiers through the crowd to White's rescue. The crowd—now three hundred or more, brandishing clubs and swords and throwing rocks—pressed them against the Custom House. Private Hugh Montgomery fired, killing Crispus Attucks, and Private Matthew Kilroy fired without aiming, blowing a hole through Samuel Gray's head. Two other soldiers fired; Benjamin Caldwell fell dead, and Samuel Maverick and Patrick Carr were mortally wounded as musket balls tore through others. Lieutenant Governor Thomas Hutchinson arrived, ordered Preston and his men to their barracks, urged the crowd to go home, and spent the rest of the night hearing witnesses. Before dawn, he ordered Preston and the soldiers arrested for murder.

Samuel Adams demanded removal of all soldiers from town, warning of grave danger if they stayed. He arranged the largest funeral North America had seen: ten thousand people followed the caskets through the streets to their common grave.

Preston and the soldiers went on trial that fall. Patriot Josiah Quincy joined John Adams in defending the soldiers, eager to prove that Bostonians would give them a fair trial. All were acquitted but Montgomery and Kilroy. Guilty of manslaughter, they pled benefit of clergy, were branded on the thumbs, and were sent to join their regiment in New Jersey.

Five witnesses testified that someone had fired from the Custom House. A servant, according to the March 12 report printed in the *Essex Gazette* (March 20), testified that his master, Manwaring, forced him to fire from the Custom House; Revere's engraving shows a musket firing from the window. After Preston's and the soldiers' trials, a jury acquitted Manwaring, then convicted the servant of perjury and had him whipped. But Samuel Adams ensured that his version of events on March 5—soldiers firing on unarmed civilians—would remain a vivid memory, with annual commemorations of the Massacre on King Street.

THE BLOODY MASSACRE
Library of Congress

This sensationalized portrayal of the Boston Massacre is titled "The bloody massacre perpetrated in King Street Boston on March 5th 1770 by a party of the 29th Regiment." It was engraved, printed, and sold by Paul Revere, but copied from a Henry Pelham print.

ESSEX GAZETTE (SALEM, MA)

March 20, 1770

The Boston Massacre was a major PR crisis with each side scrambling to control the news. Two weeks later, additional details and eyewitness accounts about the March 5 riot were published in the *Essex Gazette*, printed 15 miles north of Boston in Salem, Massachusetts. According to one report, a servant was forced to fire a gun upon the people from the Custom House, which was depicted in Paul Revere's engraving of the event.

Priſoners out of the Hand of Juſtice, and even firing upon the Inhabitants in the Street, when in the Peace of God and the King, and when we have applied for Redreſs in the Courſe of the Law of the Land, our Magiſtrates and Courts of Juſtice have appeared to be overawed by them, and ſuch a Degree of mean Submiſſion has been ſhewn to them, as has given the greateſt Diſguſt even to the cooleſt and moſt judicious Perſons in the Community. Such has been the general State of the Town.

On Friday the ſecond Inſt. a Quarrel aroſe between ſome of the Soldiers of the XXIXth, and the Ropemakers Journeymen and Apprentices, which was carried to that Length as to become dangerous to the Lives of each Party: This contentious Diſpoſition continued until the Monday Evening following, when a Party of ſeven or eight Soldiers, detached from the Main Guard under the Command of Capt. Preſton, and by his Orders fired upon the Inhabitants promiſcuouſly in King ſtreet without the leaſt warning of their Intention, and killed three on the ſpot, another has ſince died of his wounds, and others are dangerouſly not to ſay mortally wounded; Capt. Preſton and his Party are now in Goal. An Enquiry is now making into this bloody Affair; and by ſome of the Evidence there is Reaſon to apprehend that the Soldiers have been made uſe of by others as Inſtruments in executing a ſettled Plot to Maſſacre the Inhabitants. There had been but a little Time before a Murder committed in the Street by two Perſons of infamous Character, who had been employed by the Commiſſioners and Cuſtom-Houſe Officers. In the preſent Inſtance there are Witneſſes who ſwear, that, when the Soldiers fired, ſeveral Muſquets were diſcharged from

134

SALEM, March 20.

A LIST of Officers choſen at an annual Meeting of the Town of SALEM, held the 12th, and continued by Adjournment to the 19th of March, 1770.

Town-Clerk; John Higginſon, Eſq;
Town-Treaſurer; Joſeph Bowditch, Eſq;
Selectmen and Aſſeſſors; Meſſrs. Samuel Barton, jun. George Dodge, George Williams, Elias Haſket Derby, John Felt.
Overſeers of the Poor and of the Work-Houſe; Meſſrs. Joſeph Hodges, Jonathan Gardner, jun. Jonathan Ropes, jun. Richard Derby, jun. Benjamin Goodhue.
Conſtables; Meſſrs. David Smith, Robert Foſter, Benjamin Hooper, jun. William Clough.
Clerks of the Market; Meſſrs. Benjamin Oſgood, Edmund Whittemore, Joſeph Flint.
Sealers of Leather; Meſſrs. John Bray, Stephen Webb, Peter Cheever, jun.
Surveyors of Highways; Meſſrs. Joſeph Hodges, Thorndike Proctor, jun.
Hayward of the Neck and Winter Iſland; Mr. Stephen Webb.
Tything-Men; Meſſrs. Benjamin Sawyer, Jeremiah Newhall, Samuel Silſbee.
Viewers and Cullers of Staves and Hoops; Meſſrs. Joſeph Hodges, Samuel Murry, Edmund Hendfield, Arthur Jeffry, Thomas Maſon, Joſhua Phippen, Benjamin Ropes.
Surveyors and Meaſurers of Boards, and Surveyors of Shingles & Clapboards; Meſſrs. Abraham Watſon, Atwater Phippen, James Gould, David Phippen.
Meaſurers of Salt; Meſſrs. Nathaniel Archer, Edmund Hendfield, Samuel Murry.
Keeper of the Town Pound by the Alms-Houſe; Mr. Joſeph Elſon.

MARCH 20, 1770

The ESSEX GAZETTE

The following is the Substance of Letters addressed by the Committee of the Town to divers Gentlemen of the first Distinction in London.

SIR,

THE Town of Boston, now legally convened at Faneuil Hall, have directed us their Committee to acquaint you of their present miserable Situation, occasioned by the Exorbitancy of the Military Power, which, in Consequence of the Intrigues of wicked and designing Men, to bring us into a State of Bondage and Ruin, in direct Repugnance to those Rights which belong to us as Men, and as British Subjects, have long since been stationed among us.

The Soldiers ever since the fatal Day of their Arrival, have treated us with an Insolence which discovered in them an early Prejudice against us, as being that rebellious People which our implacable Enemies had maliciously represented us to be.—They landed in the Town with all the Appearance of Hostility!—They marched thro' the Town with all the Ensigns of Triumph! and evidently designed to subject the Inhabitants to the severe discipline of a Garrison. They have been continuing their Enormities by abusing the People, rescuing Prisoners out of the Hand of Justice, and even firing upon the Inhabitants in the Street, when in the Peace of God and the King, and when we have applied for Redress in the Course of the Law of the Land, our Magistrates and Courts of Justice have appeared to be overawed by them and such a Degree of mean Submission has been shewn to them, as has given the greatest Disgust even to the coolest and most judicious Persons in the Community. Such has been the general State of the Town.

On Friday the second Inst. A Quarrel arose between some of the Soldiers of the XXIXth, and the Ropemakers Journeymen and Apprentices, which was carried to that Length as to become dangerous to the Lives of each Party: this contentious Disposition continued until the Monday Evening following, when a Party of seven or eight Soldiers, detached from the Main Guard under the Command of Capt. Preston, and by his Orders fired upon the Inhabitants promiscuously in King street without the least warning of their Intention, and killed three on the spot, another has since died of his wounds, and others are dangerously not to say mortally wounded; Capt. Preston and his Party are now in Goal. An Enquiry is now making into this bloody Affair; and by some of the Evidence there is Reason to apprehend that the Soldiers have been made use of by others as Instruments in executing a settled Plot to Massacre the Inhabitants. There had been but a little Time before a Murder committed in the Street by two Persons of infamous Character, who

X GAZETTE for 1770. MARCH 13—20.

the Houſe where the Commiſſioners Board is kept, before which the ſhocking Tragedy was acted; and a Boy, Servant of one Manwaring, a petty Officer in the Cuſtoms, upon Oath accuſed his Maſter of firing a Gun upon the People out of a Window of the ſame Houſe, a number of Perſons being at the ſame Time in the Room; and he confeſſes that himſelf being threatened with Death if he refuſed, diſcharged a Gun twice by the Orders of that Company; but as it has been impoſſible for any Perſons to collect a State of Facts hitherto, we are directed by the Town to give you this ſhort Intimation of the Matter for the preſent, and to intreat your Friendſhip to prevent any ill Impreſſions from being made upon the Minds of his Majeſty's Miniſters and others againſt the Town by the Accounts which the Commiſſioners of the Cuſtoms and others our Enemies may ſend, until the Town ſhall be able to make a full Repreſentation of it; which will be addreſſed to you by the next Conveyance.

This horrible Tranſaction has occaſioned the greateſt Anxiety and Diſtreſs in the Minds of the Inhabitants, who have ever ſince been neceſſitated to keep up their own Military Watch. And his Majeſty's Coun-

the limitations of the late treaties of peace.

It is needleſs for me to recommend to the ſerious attention of my Parliament, the ſtate of my Government in America; I have endeavored, on my part, by every means, to bring back my ſubjects there, to their duty, and to a due ſenſe of lawful authority. It gives me much concern to inform you, that the ſucceſs of my endeavors has not anſwered my expectations, and that in ſome of my Colonies, many perſons have embarked in meaſures, highly unwarrantable, and calculated to deſtroy the commercial connection between them and the Mother Country.

Gentlemen of the Houſe of Commons,

I have ordered the proper eſtimates to be laid before you; I am perſuaded that your affection for my perſon and government, & your zeal for the public good, will induce you to grant ſuch ſupplies as are neceſſary; and you may be aſſured, that on my part they ſhall be managed with the ſtricteſt œconomy.

My Lords and Gentlemen,

As the welfare and proſperity of my

had been employed by the Commissioners and Custom-House Officers. In the present Instance there are Witnesses who swear, that, when the Soldiers fired, several Musquets were discharged from the House where the Commissioners Board is kept, before which the shocking Tragedy was acted; and a Boy, Servant of one Manwaring, a petty Officer in the Customs, upon Oath accused his Master of firing a Gun upon the People out of a Window of the same House, a number of Persons being at the same Time in the Room; and he confesses that himself being threatened with Death if he refused, discharged a Gun twice by the Orders of that Company; but as it has been impossible for any Persons to collect a State of Facts hitherto, we are directed by the Town to give you this short intimation of the Matter for the present, and to intreat your Friendship to prevent any ill Impressions from being made upon the Minds of his Majesty's Ministers and others against the Town by the Accounts which the Commissioners of the Customs and others our Enemies may send, until the Town shall be able to make a full Representation of it; which will be addressed to you by the next Conveyance.

This horrible Transaction has occasioned the greatest Anxiety and Distress in the Minds of the Inhabitants, who have ever since need necessitated to keep up their own Military Watch. And his Majesty's Council were so soon convinced of the imminent Danger of the Troops being any longer in the Town, that upon Application being made by the inhabitants, they immediately and unanimously advised the Lieut. Governor to effect their Removal; And Lt. Col. Dalrymple, the present commanding Officer, is now removing all the Troops to Castle William. We are With strict Truth, Sir, Your most

Faithful, and obedient Servants.

Boston, 12 March, 1770.

[...]

Extract of a Letter from a Gentleman in Boston, to his Friend in the Country, in Answer to one, desiring to be impartially informed how the late Disturbances arose.

" To trace the massacre of the 5th instant no further back than the preceding week, (a very candid account of its prelude in Mr. Gray's rope-walks, was published on that day in Fleet's paper, and since in the Essex Gazette) wou'd be stopping far short of the real source of the matter. Abundant evidence appears to warrant a very opposite conclusion! The projectors and promoters of the favorite scheme of drawing people's substance from them without their consent, have ever been the patrons of standing armies.----These must be taught to believe the people a licentious and rebellious rabble; which their lordships the common soldiery must awe into peace and good order; and if they will not be held in proper subjection by sound drubbings with lusty cudgels, heavy cutlasses, and pushes with fixed bayonets; a few discharges of powder and double quantity of lead may be occasionally necessary to disperse the people raised by the fore-mentioned gentle discipline, and learn them better manners than to huzza and whistle at their masters!

"To be serious in the enquiry, whether the outrages perpetrated by an ignorant and misinstructed soldiery originated from the provocation of a vulgar expression or stroke of a snow ball, would be solemn trifling indeed! No man, in the least acquainted with the workings of the human mind, could ever have expected, that such mortal foes as enslaving dragoons (*for the express purpose of guarding public plunderers*) and free, brave and sensible, pillaged, affronted and butchered citizens, could long live in amity together. ------I deplore the fall of my countrymen; but shall be very agreeably disappointed if these be the last victims to a bound'ess rage for lawless dominion! The inhabitants are blameless, to the amazement of their enemies! Their moderation has been mistaken for most abject timidity; & well am I assured, that a firm conviction of the fallacy of this conception will have more weight in procuring a restoration of our civil constitution than all the proofs of innocency, loyalty and affection, that could be collected from Canada to Pensacola. Your abhorrence of standing armies can be no greater than mine is of revenue officers, tho' their exportions from the people were but a bare maintenance for three tide waiters on the whole continent, and that to be independent on the people. By this entering wedge of taxing without our consent, in other terms, levying tribute at discretion, has been introduced the slavery of every state we read of in modern history. To prefer a speedy and glorious death to a lingering and shameful torture, becomes a Briton, becomes a sagacious, uncorrupted and hardly American!---------- Our friends on the Isle of Britain tell us we have no further protection to expect from them, we must therefore be madmen if we neglect to inform ourselves in every article of necessary knowledge for our own defence.---The native goodness of our Prince is as strongly presumed, and fully acknowledged in this capital as any part of his wide dominions; and none more sensibly feel the pertinency of your modest conclusion, that all those offenders may be imputed to his bad servants."

From the continuance of these, and such a force as would embolden them to hazard the fatal experiment, nothing short of carnage, devastation, and utter destruction, could be expected. Nor is there any method to escape, but the single one of convincing them that the universal voice of the colonies, at least is F r e e d o m o r D e a t h!

The accounts in this Paper and the Boston Gazette are as authentic as could then be collected; the inquiry is still continuing, and new patter turns up every day, of which, when completed, a digest will be published, which will lay open such a plot as will render the Fifth of November below the notice of even of boys and children.

The honourable John Robinson, Esq; sailed the 16th for London (it is said) with a number of depositions, to manifest that the cause of the massacre was the defence of the treasure in the custom-house, from the inhabitants, whose design the deponents verily believe was to break in and plunder it. One would think it very strange the intended robbers should take it in their heads to begin the action at Murray's barracks, at least in Boylston's alley!

The dependency of the colonies is confessedly an object long in view---Two powers independent on an inimical to their civil constitutions will soon make work enough for appeals---The expence and discouragement in which these will be involved, bids fair to dishearten the most hardy from contending, and when that becomes the case let any one determine for himself how far the British American Colonies will differ from Roman provinces, in the most corrupt era of that despotic state!

---

hereof. ...n to take ...ngthen the ...ative to the ...t; and for ...icouraging

19.

...eeding in a le... ...reat Numbers ...t is relative to ... Evidence will ... the Aggressors, ...reated by them ... Number of Evi... ...n the Custom... ...and a Track is ...e the intended ... of the perjured ...d from thence ...ng Snider was ...en clearly ap... ... and abandoned ...mploy'd by our

...Work to form ...ners and their ...ainst us---The ...r Property and ...ed; and what ... the strongest ...nfamous & de... ...not, tho' taken

there only the whole difficulty lies."

Extract of a Letter from a Gentleman in Boston, to his Friend in the Country, in Answer to one, desiring to be impartially informed how the late Disturbances arose.

" To trace the massacre of the 5th instant no further back than the preceeding week, (a very candid account of its prelude in Mr. Gray's rope-walks, was published that day in Fleet's paper, and since in the Essex Gazette) wou'd be stopping far short of the real source of the matter. Abundant evidence appears to warrant a very opposite conclusion! The projectors and promoters of the favorite scheme of drawing people's substance from them without their consent, have ever been the patrons of standing armies.---- These must be taught to believe the people a licentious and rebellious rabble; which their lordships the common soldiery must awe into peace and good order: and if they will not be held in proper subjection by sound drubbings with lusty cudgels, heavy cutlasses, and pushes with fixed bayonets; a few discharges of powder and double quantity of lead may be occasionally necessary to disperse the people raised by the fore-mentioned gentle discipline, and learn them better manners than to huzza and whittle at their masters!

" To be serious in the enquiry, whether the outrages perpetrated by an ignorant and misinstructed soldiery originated from the provocation of a vulgar expression or stroke of a snow ball, would be solemn trifling indeed! No man, in the least acquainted with the workings of the human mind, could ever have expected, that such mortal foes as enslaving dragoons *(for the express purpose of guarding publick plunderers)* and free, brave and sensible, pillaged, affronted and butchered citizens, could long live in

... Friends lament her with warm Affection; and she is mentioned with Regret, Esteem and Honor, by all her large Acquaintance.

SALEM, March 20.

By a Vessel in a short Passage from Lisbon, which arrived at Cape-Ann last Week, we are informed, that a War between the English and French was much expected and talked of at that Place.

We hear from Hampton, that a large Barn was consumed there by Fire last Friday Night, and it is said 15 Tons of Hay, and about 15 Head of Cattle, were destroyed in the Flames. The Barn and its Contents were the Property of one Mr. ----- Smith.

By Capt. George Cabot, who arrived here last Saturday in 39 Days from Bilboa, we have Advice, that the Weather, as he heard, was very tempestuous, in the Bay of Biscay, in December and January last; in which 13 Sail of Vessels were lost, and 5 of them supposed to be Fish Vessels ... foundland. It was said ... Quintals of Fish on board, ... to her all, lost.

At an annual Meeting of ... Inhabitants of the Town ... qualified to vote in Town Affairs, began and held at the Court-House (so called) in said Salem, on Monday the 12th of March, A. D. 1770.

VOTED, That JOSEPH BOWDITCH, Esq; be appointed Moderator of this Meeting.

VOTED, That the Inhabitants of this Town will use their Endeavours, that none they are con-

Whereas a Load of ...

belonging to Uriah Gibbs of Sudbury, ... the Town-House, last Night, in this Tow... some evil minded Person or Persons, dispe... the Town, and several Bundles lost: Th... fore to give Notice, that a Reward of Fi... will be given to any Person who will di... Offender or Offenders, so that he or the... brought to Justice.

N. B. As such Proceedings are a sca... Town, and ought to be discountenanced b... ber Person, it is hoped that every one w... utmost Endeavours to bring the Offender o... to condign Punishment. Salem, Ma...

Just published in Boston, and t... at the Printing-Office in Sal...

A Narrative of the C...

vity, Sufferings and Removes ... Mary Rowlandson, who was ... Prisoner by the Indians, with ...

All Persons that incli... promote our PAPER MAN... TURE, and will save Rags, ... for all clean white Linen, and ... & Linen, Two Coppers a Pou...

ESSEX GAZETTE (SALEM, MA)

March 20, 1770 (continued from previous page)

REPORTING THE

GASPEE AFFAIR

By Steven H. Park

MANY HISTORIANS HAVE REFERRED TO THE PERIOD between the Boston Massacre (or, depending upon one's perspective, the King Street Riot) and the Boston Tea Party as "the lull," a period of relative quiet in the North American colonies. One notable exception to that fleeting peace was the burning of the armed schooner *Gaspee* by a colonial mob in the Providence River in 1772. Boston attorney and later President John Adams admitted in his diary that what became known as "the *Gaspee* Affair" brought back all of his old hostile feelings against British rule. Initially, the colonial raiders seemed motivated by the desire for compensation for some illegal rum that had been seized and was being held by the *Gaspee* crew, but Patriot printers and ministers soon exploited the event for their own political purposes.

Initially, the colonial raiders seemed motivated by the desire for compensation for some illegal rum that had been seized and was being held by the Gaspee *crew, but Patriot printers and ministers soon exploited the event for their own political purposes.*

Lieutenant William Dudingston took command of the *Gaspee* in 1768. It was one of several vessels commissioned after the French and Indian War (or the Seven Years' War in Europe) to patrol the fishing waters off Canada and northern New England. When Dudingston patrolled as far south as Philadelphia in 1769 and 1771, doing basic customs enforcement with his rough manner, he made some enemies who pressed civil charges. It was not unusual for sea officers to have arrest warrants issued against them by colonials, making it difficult for them to go ashore. For this reason, and to diffuse public dislike for particular officers, the admiralty moved unpopular commanders like Dudingston around frequently. (See Davis Bevan's account from the *Pennsylvania Journal* on June 29, 1769, reprinted in the *Boston Gazette* on July 10, 1769). Sea officers and customs officials did not believe they could get a fair hearing in the courts in the thirteen colonies and would try to take colonial smugglers to a vice-admiralty "super court" in Halifax.

Rhode Island had a reputation in London for its smuggling and trading with the enemy during times of war (*London Chronicle*, July 18, 1772). All of British America could not produce enough molasses for even a small colony like Rhode Island to maintain its production of rum. Consequently, Rhode Island merchants and shipmasters went looking elsewhere to meet the demand. Lieutenant Dudingston was sent to Rhode Island by Admiral John Montagu in Boston because he was so effective at suppressing smuggling and enforcing customs regulations. When the *Gaspee* ran aground in Narragansett Bay in June 1772, a group of colonial raiders rowed out to the schooner at night, shot the commander, put the crew ashore, and burned the vessel. The *London Chronicle* report was incorrect in stating that the Lieutenant was killed, although he was so badly hurt that he did make an official statement suspecting that he would not live through the night. Dudingston did recover and was court-martialed in Great Britain for the loss of the *Gaspee,* but he continued his naval career and retired as a rear admiral.

There were several instances in the 1760s when His Majesty's Government took no administrative action following colonial attacks on customs vessels, but they could not overlook such an attack on a naval vessel like the armed schooner *Gaspee* while in active service. They could not impose a royal court on a colonial government that already had a court system in place, but they could send over a "royal commission of inquiry" to investigate. By putting Rhode Island Governor Joseph Wanton in charge of the commission, the London government virtually doomed it to failure. Wanton scheduled witnesses in such a way that no raider or *Gaspee* mariner was in Colonial House at the same time. Other commissioners thought that some of the *Gaspee* mariners could identify colonial raiders if given the opportunity. The report in the *London Chronicle* from March 25, 1773, noted that "several persons were examined." They merely asked witnesses for a physical description of the raiders and their leaders but did not bring the two parties face-to-face.

Frustrated by what seemed like colonial efforts to obstruct justice and weak excuses by witnesses for failure to appear after being summoned, the commissioners agreed to take a recess until summer. Their efforts were merely stirring up more Patriot and rebel sentiment against His Majesty's program of colonial reforms. On August 14, 1773, the *London Chronicle* reported accurately that no one was "discovered." A black slave named Aaron Biggs was the only colonial who did come forward and name the names of some powerful Rhode Island merchants. Governor Wanton worked diligently to discredit his testimony, and to this day, we do not know how much Biggs might have been "coached" by mariners aboard another British vessel, the *Beaver*.

The *Gaspee* Affair left two important Patriot developments in its wake. The Committees of Correspondence grew directly out of the frustration over the slow and inaccurate communication that followed the *Gaspee* events. It spurred direct communication between Richard Henry Lee in Virginia and Samuel Adams in Boston. Additionally, a little-known itinerant preacher named John Allen gave a highly political Thanksgiving Day sermon about the *Gaspee* Affair in Boston that became one of the most popular pre-independence pamphlets in the colonies.

Burning of the *Gaspee*
North Wind Picture Archives

Angry Rhode Island colonists burn the *Gaspee* in Providence River in 1772, before the American Revolutionary War.

tius,) on Green's Wharff, oppofite to John Rowe, Efq; where he has to fell very cheap for Cafh, a good Affortment of Englifh and India Goods, Cutlary Ware, Paper, French Indigo, &c. &c. &c.

PHILADELPHIA, June 29.

From the Pennfylvania Journal, June 29, 1769.

As the late outrageous infult and cruel treatment I have received from William Didingfton, commander of the armed fchooner Gafpey, and David Hay, captain of the Train, is become the common topic of converfation, I think I am bound in juftice to myfelf and the public, to give a full and true narrative of the whole matter.——What was my cafe yefterday, may be the cafe of every freeman, who may unfortunately fall within the power of fuch cowardly infolent officers, who difgrace the commiffions they hold, and who feem to think that their office intitles them to treat their fellow fubjects with outrage, infolence, and abufe.

On the 26th inft. going a fifhing with Mr. Thomas Pedrix, of Chefter, I faw a top-fail fchooner coming up. As I wanted to fpeak with a Pilot, who I was informed was in fuch a fchooner, I went near and hailed her, and afked what pilot was on board ? The Capt. of the fchooner replied, that the pilot did not chufe to tell his name. Such an uncivil, ungentleman-like anfwer provoked me to tell him, that a civil queftion deferved a civil anfwer, and that I thought both the Captain and Pilot *blackguards*.—Upon which the Captain ordered out his boat and five men, to bring me on board, at the fame time prefenting his firelock, and fwearing moft violently, that he would fire upon me, if I did not come along fide directly. All this time I had no apprehenfion of its being a King's armed Schooner. When the boat came up the Cockfon immediately feized me, and in a piratical manner dragged me into the boat and put me on board the fchooner, when the Captain accofted me with the moft abufive language.———Finding in what hands I had fallen, I endeavoured to mollify him, by making all the conceffions which gentlemen ought to demand. I affured him I did not know he was a King's officer; that if I had offended him I afked his pardon. Juft at this time happening to fee Capt. Hay, to whom I was known, I appealed to him for my character, expecting he would interpofe his friendly offices. But Capt. Hay in a rude infulting manner faid, "I know him very well, a tavern-keeper in Chefter, a "damned horfe-jockey. They are all a parcel of damn'd "rafcals." Tho' I heard much of the imperious infolence of the man, yet I was quite thunder ftruck at this inftance of it. He did not feem drunk, as it is faid he was when he committed the violent outrage in Philadelphia fome years ago, and attempted to affaffinate a gentleman of that city. The words were no fooner out of Capt. Hay's mouth, than the commander of the fchooner ftruck me in the face with his fift, and redoubled his ftrokes, which I endeavoured to ward off, without offering to return a blow. But in fending off his ftr[illegible], my hand happened to touch his face; on which, with an oath, he cried out, "you rafcal, will you ftrike me on "board my own veffel." I told him, I did not, that if my hand touched him, it was not defignedly. "You "lie, you rafcal," faid Capt. Hay, "how dare you "ftrike a Captain of a man of war?" With that they both fell upon me; at the fame time calling for the mate, who feized and held my hands, while the commander and Hay both beat mn in a moft cruel manner. When they had tired themfelves with beating me, that they might add infult to cruelty, they ordered me to be put in irons, and as if nothing could glut their revenge they thruft me into the hold, where the commander fwore he would keep me and would not fuffer me to fee the light, nor to have pen, ink, or paper, till he had carried me to Halifax. When the commander found that all his threats and menaces did not break my fpirit, trufting to the protection of the laws of my country, I defied his malice and infolence: His rage being fomewhat abated, he ordered the boat with five men to put me on board my boat, if I would fall on my knees and afk his pardon.—Finding he could not bring me to this, he ordered his men to carry me, bloody as I was, on board my boat, which was about half a mile diftant, and during this inhuman fcene he would not fuffer to come nigh the fchooner.

DAVIS BEVAN.

As foon as Mr. Bevan got to Chefter, he followed [illegible]

Captains.

Extract of a Letter from a Gentleman in Lifbon to his Correfpondent in this City.

THE fale of Grain here is rendered fo delatory and

[illegible] here from Bofton.

And next Day Brigadier General Pomeroy arrived here from Bofton alfo, in his Majefty's armed Schooner Sultana.

New-York, June 25, 1769.

To the PUBLIC.

AS I have juftly incurred the Refentment of my Fellow Citizens, from my Behaviour, as fet forth in an Advertifement *Of great Importance to the Public*; I beg Leave to implore the Pardon of the Public, affuring them that I am truly forry for the Part I have acted; declare and promife that I never will again attempt an Act contrary to the true Intereft and Refolutions of a People zealous in the Caufe of *Virtue* and *Liberty*; and by my future Conduct, not only convince them of my Contrition, but make it my whole Study to maintain inviolate the Refolutions they have entered into,-------befeeching the Public in general to believe me,

Their ready devoted, and moft
Obedient Humble Servant,
Alexander Robertfon.

I Alfo declare, That the Goods were returned back to Philadelphia by the Stage laft Monday, and that a Certificate of the fame fhall be produced to the Public.

The laft three Lines fworn to before me, } ELIAS DESBROSSES.

PROVIDENCE, June 24.

Saturday laft the Honourable General Affembly of this Colony adjourned to the fecond Monday in September next, then to be convened at Eaft-Greenwich.

During the Seffion a Letter was received by the Speaker from Virginia, inclofing a Copy of the Refolutions entered into by the late Houfe of Burgeffes of that Colony—to which we are told the Affembly have agreed, and a Committee is accordingly appointed for preparing an Addrefs to be prefented to his Majefty.

From Louifbourg we have Advice, that the Diftrefs of that Place, fince the Troops were withdrawn, is really difficult to be defcribed; feveral poor Families are in a ftarving Condition, and many of the Inhabitants daily deferting the Town.

SALEM, *July* 4.

WHEREAS Information has been made to the Merchants and Traders of this Town, that fundry Perfons belonging to Bofton, have fent Quantities of Englifh Goods in this Town for Sale, which were imported fince the General Agreement of the Merchants (not to import fuch Goods) took Place:—We therefore, the Merchants and Traders of the Town of Salem, at a Meeting at the King's Arms this 30th Day of June, Anno Domini 1769, do publickly DECLARE our Difapprobation thereof, and refolve, that we will do all in our Power to difcourage the Sale of fuch Goods, by not purchafing any of them ourfelves, or fuffering any Perfon for or under us to purchafe them. We think (in Juftice to thofe Merchants and Traders who have ftrictly adhered to their Agreement) we ought to inform all Perfons, that the Shop lately kept by Mr. John Gool, now 'tended by John Norris in this Town, is now owned and fupplied by Merchants in Bofton, who have taken the Advantage of others not fending for Goods, to import double the Quantity of Goods which they did at other Seafons, expecting to make their Fortunes, while others were finking theirs for the Benefit of their Country. We hereby caution all Perfons, who have the Intereft of their Country at Heart, againft purchafing Goods of any Perfons who come from Bofton and offer Goods to fale, fuch as Tea, Loaf-Sugar, Crates of Earhten Ware, &c. as we have great Reafon to fufpect, that thofe Goods are fent out of that Town, becaufe of the Difcouragements the Owners meet with in the Sale of them by the Friends of Liberty there. We alfo requeft the Town of Marblehead to join with their Neighbours (for the general Good) not to fend for any more Goods, contrary to the Intent and Meaning of the Agreements entered into by the Inhabitants of the Town of Bofton and other neighbouring Towns, which Requeft, if ftill refufed, we muft defire all who are real [illegible]

[illegible] is well known) have deviated from their Contract, that they would (for the future) ftrictly adhere thereto; for it is determined at this Meeting, that we will make publick the Names of all thofe who fhall hereafter break

[illegible] in the Barracks or Hofpital, and that it a[illegible] fhould be taken down notice fhall be given them;—the Phyficians of the Town have alfo declared, that they know not of any one Perfon, who has the Diftemper or the Symptoms of it, excepting Mrs. Tyler at the Orange Tree, Mrs. Crafts at a Houfe near Liberty Tree, and a Soldier, Sailor and two Women at the Province Hofpital at New-Bofton; at which Places a Red Flag is hung out as a fignal of the Small Pox, Guards Placed, and the Paffages ftopt, to prevent a fpread of the Infection:—A ftrict Enquiry will be continued and immediate Notice given in all the Papers if any other Perfon fhould be vifited with the Diftemper.——It is hoped that no one wil[l] conceal the Small-Pox from the Selectmen, if it fhould break out in their Family, as in fuch cafe they would b[e] profecuted to the rigor of the Law.

By Order of the Selectmen,
WILLIAM COOPER, Town-Clerk

Meffieurs EDES & GILL,

I Lately had occafion to fearch into the meaning of th[e] word BARONET, and I find it to be a *diminutiv[e]* Term, as the Grammarians fpeak, and that it denotes *little, tiny* Baron. And the word Baron is derived fro[m] the Latin *Baro*, which in its *primary* Signification a[nd] as ufed by Cicero, means a *Blockhead*, a *Sot*, a *Dolt*, *Fool*. *Vid. Ainfworth in voc.*

At a Meeting of the FREE-AMERICAN *Fire-Society, the Bunch of Grapes Tavern, July 6, 1769.*

Prefent 23 Members out of 25.

VOTED unanimoufly,

THAT Mr. ——— ——— be expelled [illegible] Society, as unworthy of being a Member of [illegible] fame, for having imported, and ftill perfifting to imp[ort] Goods from G. B. contrary to the general Agreement [of] the worthy and patriotic Merchants in this Town, [and] for having been concern'd in publifhing a partial, ev[il] and fcandalous Advertifement, tending to caft an Od[ium] on the refpectable Merchants of this Town, and fruft[rate] their good Intentions for the public Advantage.

Meffieurs EDES & GILL,

The following Method of grafting the Mulberry Tree is [sub]*mitted to your Infpection; if you fhall think it* [worth] *publifhing, pleafe to give it a Place in your val*[uable] *Gazette, and you will oblige a Friend to American* [Pro]*duce and Manufactures.*

TAKE from the Mulberry-Tree a Root ½ of an [Inch] *Diameter, and 7 or 8 Feet in Length, fplice the* [Cion] *and let it be fixed into the great End of the Root as* [the] *ufual Manner of grafting, wind a Woolen Thread* [round] *the Root to keep the Cion in its Place, bury the Root* [at] *the fame Depth you found it, raifing the great En*[d] *3 Inches of the Surface of the Ground, which brin*[gs the] *Cion near perpendicular. The above Experiment* [was] *tried in April 1768. The Cion grew two Feet th*[e same] *Year, and now appears very thrifty. The fame* [Person] *in April 1769, grafted feven, fome into fhorter &* [longer] *Roots, even to two Feet in Length; they all appea*[r] *to do well.*

On FRIDAY next,
At Ten o'Clock in the Morning,
Will be fold by PUBLIC VENDUE at the A[uction]
Room in Queen-Street.

A Variety of Goods, among whic[h]
Irifh Linens, Sheetings, Callicoes, India Patch[es], Luteftring, white Jeans, Ivory-ftick Fans, [illegible] Pieces, Mens and Boys Worfted Hofe, Womens [illegible] Cotton ditto, fpotted Bandannoes, Indigo, Snuf[f] of Pipes, &c. &c.

J. RUSSELL, Aucti[oneer]
Next Friday TEN o'Clock.

TO BE SOLD
On THURSDAY next.
By Benjamin Church
At his ufual Place of Sale;
A great Variety of valuable Artic[les]

Hollands—Bed Ticken—Irifh Holland—She[etings, Li]nens—Handkerchiefs—Mens, Womens and [Childrens] Hofe, &c. &c. Likewife fome Houfe Furnitu[re] [illegible]

BOSTON GAZETTE

July 10, 1769

Some sea officers had a lack of respect for colonials well before 1775, believing that colonials had traded with the enemy during the Seven Years' War (French and Indian War). Rhode Islanders had a very low reputation among English officers, on a par with pirates. After pieces like this one appeared in the local press, admirals would move their officers and vessels to a different city where their reputation for harsh treatment of colonials was not yet known. Since this Philadelphia story appeared in a Boston newspaper, their strategy did not work as well as they hoped.

LONDON CHRONICLE

July 18, 1772

In his haste to get information to London, Admiral Montagu mistakenly reported that Lieutenant Dudingston was dead. In fact, the commander returned to naval service in North America.

...under the command of Major General ...hotin, who has made ſome progreſs on the ...of the Black Sea, and is ſupported by the ...e Ruſſian ſquadron near Aſoph... ...led that the Princes of Cac... ...ſette, Mingrelia, Aſchaſia, ...oncert with the Ruſſians agai...

...antzick, *June* 20. Notwi... ...ſtations in Poland, the ſcarci... artificial; ſeveral perſons ... had bought it up, in order ... ...iſe of the price when called ... ...ſions have at length got int... ...nel, and a great quantity ha... is no longer a ſcarcity. Bu... another difficulty. The P... ...ike any money in exchar... except the real ducats of H... ...of gold has riſen in conſequ... ...ave an influence on the ...

...on, *June* 16. The Dos Qui... ...e 9th inſtant from Rio Jane... ...oo cruſadoes in ſpecie, and a cheſt of ...ds valued at 1,500,000 cruſadoes. The ...Dame de la Grace is alſo returned from ...e place, with effects to the amount of ...oo cruſadoes.

..., *June* 16. The Septentrion and Ruſé, ...niſh men of war, and the frigate La ...rrived here yeſterday from Lima, with cargoes.

July 13. William de Lamoignon, ...or of France, died here yeſterday, in ...year of his age.

...ve accounts from various parts of the ...of great damage done by the ſtorm on ...of laſt month.

SCOTLAND.

...gh, *July* 13. We are informed from ...authority, that a credit for 160,000l. ...s been lately granted by the Bank of ...or the uſe of a great Houſe in this ...t before this credit was granted, ...were examined into, from whence it ...at they are poſſeſſed of real eſtates ...eding all their engagements, beſides ...ne employed in different branches ...The intelligence afforded univerſal ...and the general toaſt here is, ...to the Bank of England."

...he ſilver arrow, given by the good ...burgh, was ſhot for on Bruntsfield ...e royal company of Archers, and ...John M'Pherſon.

...ay laſt died at Canaan, near th's ...bert Williamſon, Merchant of this ...e of the Directors of the Bank of

SHIP NEWS.

...16. Wind at S. W. Came down ...th all the outward-bound, the ..., Gill, for Philadelphia. Arrived ...n the Downs, with ...

...year. As ſoon as I am aſcertained of this, I ſhall be ready to give you a full anſwer to your meſſage.

Cambridge, June ...

...to be ſufficiently plain, appears to me to be doubtful and equivocal, as it may be conſtrued one way or other; ſo in complying with your deſire, founded upon this among other reaſons, I ſhould or ſhould not conform to the inſtructions of the King, whoſe ſervant I am. As reſerved as you have been in your anſwer to my meſſage, I will be unreſerved and open with you. Whilſt you diſpute the authority by which I at firſt removed the Court from Boſton, I do not intend to carry it thither again; and whenſoever I ſhall receive his Majeſty's inſtructions for exerciſing the juſt prerogative of the crown in any caſe, I will obſerve them without violation in any degree; and when your intention in any meſſage appears to me uncertain, I think it will be a ſufficient juſtification for my refuſal to do any thing in conſequence of ſuch meſſage ſo long as the uncertainty remains.

Council Chamber,
Cambridge, June 3, 1772. T. HUTCHINSON."

Thurſday his Majeſty's ſhip the Bonetta arrived expreſs from Admiral Montagu with the following diſagreeable intelligence: "That he had ſtationed the Gaſpee Schooner, Lieutenant Dudingſton, at Providence in Rhode Iſland to protect the trade, and prevent the exceſs of ſmuggling that conſtantly prevails at that place, and which by the particular activity of the Officer was ſo effectually done, that the people were determined to remove the reſtraint. Accordingly at midnight about two hundred armed men in eight boats boarded the Schooner, killed the Lieutenant, took all the people out of the veſſel, and then burnt her.

Extract of a Letter from Conſtantinople, May 10.

"There has been a diſturbance at Salonica on account of the great quantity of corn exported from thence in foreign ſhips. The people imagined it was deſigned for the Chriſtians, and were going to fall upon the Franks; but the Aga who commanded there found means to appeaſe the tum...

...crown till the legality of the extents are dete... mined, which was accordingly granted, and th... extents are to be withdrawn.

...ollows: one ...B——, a twenty thouſand pound fortune, kept joint houſe with her ſiſter in Berkley-row; about the year 1761 ſhe contracted an intimacy with the Plaintiff, whoſe huſband died inſolvent in the year 1768; during this time the Defendant frequently viſited them, and of windy nights often choſe to ſleep at their houſe. In the year 1765, the Defendant lent the Plaintiff's huſband 200l. upon bond, and after his deceaſe laid on an execution on his effects, in order to ſecure herſelf. The Plaintiff brought the preſent action to recover damages for board and lodging, at the rate of twenty guineas for twenty weeks during the whole time of their intimacy, or, more properly ſpeaking, ſo long as the evidence ſhe produced could depoſe to. The firſt evidence that was examined was the Plaintiff's Porter, (his Maſter being in the wine buſineſs) who ſwore that he knew the Defendant during the whole time ſet forth in the action, that ſhe was very frequently at his Maſter's houſe, that ſhe ſometimes lay there of ſtormy n'ghts, and that one year with another he believed ſhe might have ſpent a part of her time equal to twenty weeks. On being croſs examined, he ſaid he believed that there was no contract for board and lodging between his Maſter and her, becauſe ſhe always appeared in the houſe as a viſitor, not as a lodger, becauſe ſhe and her ſiſter kept a houſe and ſervants at the ſame time, and becauſe the place of her abode was ſo ſhort a way off, being no farther diſtant than Berkley-row, and his Maſter lived in Air-ſtreet, Piccadilly. The next and laſt witneſs was a ſervant woman who lived with the Plaintiff for two years; ſhe corroborated the teſtimony of the other witneſs, with this difference, that the young Lady ſpent full half her time at her maſter's houſe. On being croſs examined, ſhe ſaid ſhe always looked on her as a viſitor, except one time for three weeks. On being aſked her reaſons for ſelecting theſe three weeks, ſhe declared, that on the young Lady's quitt'ng her own houſe...

Thurſday, March 25.

AMERICA.

Boſton, (New-England) January 18.

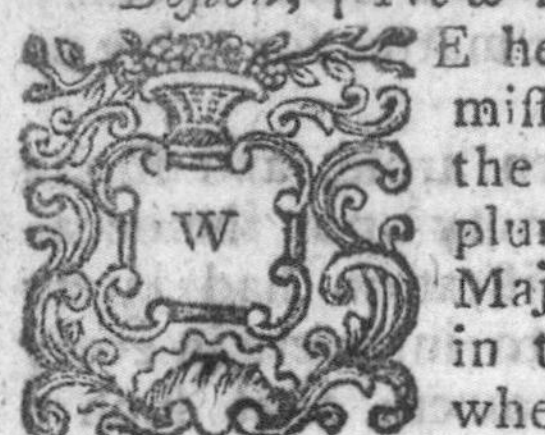

WE hear from Newport the Commiſſioners for enquiring into the circumſtances of attacking, plundering and burning his Majeſty's ſchooner Gaſpee, ſat in the Court-houſe laſt week, when ſeveral perſons were examined before them.

Boſton, Jan. 21. It is ſaid, that 45 towns and diſtricts (out of 150 towns and diſtricts that are in this Province) have had meetings, and ſent their reſolves, inſtructions to their Repreſentatives, and other proceedings, in conſequence of circular letters from this Town, to the Committee of Correſpondence, appointed by the Town, and received.

COUNTRY NEWS.

Birmingham, March 22. At the aſſizes at Shrewſbury on Monday laſt, Thomas Brinford, for ſtealing ſix horned cattle; Richard Williams, for ſtealing one weather ſheep; Francis Tipton, for ſtealing 18l. and Thomas Davies, for ſtealing a mare, received ſentence of death.

SHIP NEWS.

Deal, March 23. Wind at S. S. W. Arrived and ſailed for the River his Majeſty's ſhip the Carcaſe. Remain in the Downs the ſhips as before, and the Great Marlow, Kitchen, for Jamaica; the William and Hopewell, Fenwick, for Maryland; the Rachael, Henry, for the Granades; and the Arabella, Bryan, for Neath.

LONDON.

The latter part of the deciſion of the Houſe of Lords on Monday laſt on the appeal in which Alexander M'Clatchie was Appellant, and Mrs. Burnet, widow, Reſpondent, when their Lordſhips affirmed the interlocutors of March and

This deed was drawn up, and witneſſed by Mr. Archibald Malcolm, his ordinary Attorney;

colm's evidence, as being the adviſer of the ſettlement, and by reputation intereſted in the iſſue,

lity, it could not be pleaded in bar of his competency. Lord Mansfield was therefore fully of opinion, that Malcolm's teſtimony in the preſent caſe could not be refuſed; and that on the whole, it was an incontrovertibly juſt exception to the general rule of Law, that an Agent, Attorney, or Solicitor, was always competent to give teſtimony in any cauſe in which they might be employed, when it was impoſſible to reſort to that ſpecies of evidence in any other manner whatever.

On Tueſday the Houſe of Commons paſſed a bill for lighting, paving, and cleanſing, the ſtreets in the town of Brighthelmſtone; and a bill for making new piers, regulating ſhips, and cleanſing the harbour of Aberdeen.

Alſo the bill for making a new harbour, and for ſupplying the Inhabitants with freſh water in the town of Greenock in Scotland.

A new writ is iſſued for the election of a Member for Dover, in the room of Sir Thomas Pym Hales, deceaſed.

The election of a Member for Dover is expected to be ſtrongly conteſted.

On Tueſday, at a meeting of a number of Freeholders of the county of Huntingdon now in town, a Gentleman moved that a ſimilar engagement to that propoſed by the late Common Hall, for ſhortening the duration of Parliaments, ſhould be ſubſcribed by the Candidates at the next Election, which was unanimouſly approved of.

Orders are ſent to Woolwich for a Company of the Royal Regiment of Artillery to be in readineſs to embark for Scotland, to relieve the Company now on that ſtation.

Yeſterday arrived a Mail from Flanders, but brought nothing material.

Yeſterday Lord Stormont took leave of his Majeſty, and to-morrow will ſet out on his embaſſy to the Court of France.

The ſame day the Earl of Suffolk arrived in town from his ſeat at Charlton in Wilts, and went to Court.

The ſame day Lord Viſcount Townſhend was

under the command of Capt. Crafton, who had

party, however, put them to flight, and found five of their carcaſes in the woods, alſo ſeveral fuzees, haberſacks, &c. thrown away in their

themſelves againſt Re
have other entrench
quarter of Grand Sabl
wiſh they would ma
could truſt themſelves
numbers of the Carib
Lucia and the other
daily going, to wait
treat of the troops fr
return to their own co

Baſſeterre in St. K
which arrived here or
formed that all the me
train of artillery and
coaſt, in order effectua
that in a few days we
my's ſurrendering, or

Letters are ſaid to b
St. Vincent's, which
Infantry, under the
had come up with an
Caribbs, headed by a
regiment, when after a
laſted near an hour, th
and their ringleader
irons, and ſent to the h

Extract of a Letter
" The packet boat fr
yeſterday, and this
brought in it were carri
one directed to the C
other to the Chancellor
without any conſiderati
opened them both, and
ſeveral books not permi
Magiſtrates of the tow
to be made of them all
the Court of Juſtice."

Extract of a Letter fr
" This day ſevennig
goons arrived here, wi
quelling the mutiny an
nock and Port Glaſgow
marched on Friday, bu
heir aſſiſt
and Lig
ured a
of 40 o
vere di
ef acto
iſtrates
Inhabit
ut to fu
the lat
liſagree
iſperſed,
turned to the ſhips they

dead, and the life of ano
On Monday ſevennig

LONDON CHRONICLE
March 25, 1773

Commissioners interviewed some "witnesses" in January. Frustrated over their inability to pin anything on anybody, they took a "break" until summer, claiming that it would be easier for people to travel in the warmer weather.

LONDON CHRONICLE
August 14, 1773

Rhode Island Governor Joseph Wanton spaced the "witnesses" apart sufficiently so they never met or saw one another. Ultimately, the commissioners wrote a report where they praised their own diligence but found nothing.

uld try at a speech of my own?
e prologue, the fancy is new,
eaves, you shall judge what Tom
on can do.

time, it was in Shakespeare's days,
common sense embellish'd plays,
nglish humour turn'd buffoon,
er Operas put wit out of tune,
time, folks did not think by rules,
felt, they spoke;—our fathers were
ols.
was, mirth admit me of your crew,
s old; 'tis not the thing--'twont do.
now—We must have something

we've had, new grand illuminations,
ees, and Trips, and Installations.
Trip to-night to shew some shipping,
ight the Author a'nt caught tripping,
Play-jobbers, tho' it is surprising,
's send me on apologizing.
come o'er me. Weston, you're a soul,
ny prologue, you're so dry, so droll.
go then, I'm serv'd so to-night,
on bail for what bad poets write.
ope not—if we're brought to shame.
Author, or the Actors blame;
one request, good sirs, be friended,
give sentence till the piece is ended.

rday, August 14.

y arrived the Mail from FRANCE.

Constantinople, June 18.

THE last advices from Egypt confirm the accounts of Ali Bey's defeat and death, and mention that Mehemet Aboudaab has renewed the protestations of his zeal and fidelity to the Porte; and it is hoped that cha, the new Caimacan, who is to re-airo, will now find but little trouble ute the commission he is sent upon. was wanting to complete the triumph orte in Egypt, after defeating Ali Bey, conquering the Rebels who sided with hich their avarice has happily spared e trouble of doing; for no sooner was vs arrived of Ali's defeat, than the who were of his party, began to quar-t dividing his treasures; and the Druses, abs, and the Mutualis, took up arms. Daher, that old and renowned warrior, age of upwards of 80, full of courage our, had the grief to see some of his ildren in arms against him; upon which inted his horse, and at the head of his gave battle to his children and former , with their forces; when he had the une not only to be defeated, but killed, was fighting with amazing courage. The ccounts add, that all is in confusion in it seems as if the Pacha of

hovels these poor creatures sally forth to cultivate the earth for the use of others, which they are not permitted the enjoyment of themselves; and after having felt the intemperance of the seasons, the scorchings of the sun, cold, snow, and frost, they have no other retreats than the abovementioned, from whence they are to issue forth on the return of the day to renew their labour. Touched with this sad picture, her Imperial Majesty has given orders that this class of her subjects shall be better accommodated, by building for them more commodious habitations, wherein they may enjoy themselves with tranquillity, and no longer look on themselves as the most unfortunate class of her Majesty's subjects.

AMERICA.

Boston, New England, June 21. Last Thursday twelve persons, belonging to Salem, went from thence in a boat on a party of pleasure; but in the evening a squall of wind came up, attended with thunder and lightning, by which the boat was sunk off Marblehead, and the following persons were drowned; viz. Mr. William Ward and wife, Mr. Diggadon and wife, Mr. John Kimball and wife, the widow of Mr. Eleazar Giles, a daughter of Dr. Fairfield's, one other woman, and the wife of Mr. John Becket, Boat-builder.

Newport, (Rhode Island) June 28. The Court of Enquiry is broke up, without having been able to discover any of the parties concerned in destroying the Gaspee schooner.

New York, July 5. On Wednesday last Sir John Johnson, son of the truly worthy, gallant, and Hon. Sir William Johnson, Bart. was married to Miss Polly Watts, daughter of the Hon. John Watts, Esq; of his Majesty's Council.

SHIP NEWS.

Deal, August 12. Wind at South. Arrived and sailed for the River, the Active, Henzell, from Oporto. Came down and sailed, with the ships as per last, the Magna Charta, Maitland, for Carolina; and the Molly and Betsey, Nicholson, for Maryland. Remains in the Downs the Swift, Lante.

LONDON.

Yesterday a Mail from New York, brought by the Lord Hyde packet boat, Capt. Goddard, in 29 days to Falmouth.

The following particulars are extracted from the minutes of the Council Board of Boston in New England, which met the 21st of June last, containinig the substance of their proceedings that day.

The Council sent a message to his Excellency Thomas Hutchinson, Governor, informing him, that the House of Representatives have communicated to the Board a number of letters written from Boston to Gentlemen in England, which have occasioned great uneasiness; six of them they said appeared to be written by his Excellency. The Board referred the consideration of ... ed in the mean time de-

furnish the Lieutenant Governor, the Hon. Andrew Oliver, with copies of four letters, which appear to them to be written by him; and to desire that he will inform the Board whether he has written letters to England of the tenor of the copies aforesaid. The Lieutenant Governor returned the following answer to the Secretary:

"I have received from you a copy of a resolve of the Hon. Board, setting forth, That among the letters communicated by the House of Representatives, which have occasioned great uneasiness, and which are to come under consideration to-morrow, there are four from me, bearing date from 7th May 1767, to 12th Aug. 1769, which appear to the Board to be written and signed with my own hand, copies of which they have been pleased to cause to be sent to me, desiring that I would inform them whether I had written letters to England of the tenor of the said copies.

"I am obliged to the Board for their candour in furnishing me with those copies before they take the matter under consideration. It does not appear by the copies that either of the letters were directed to any person in England, or elsewhere. It is very material to know to whom they were wrote, for there is an essential difference between a free correspondence among friends, and letters wrote to persons in public office. I cannot therefore think it incumbent on me to authenticate imperfect copies, even if it were in my power.

"If I should be favoured with a sight of the originals, which it is to be supposed are entire and compleat, I will not deny my hand writing, if they are really such: Nor will I contest any kind of evidence which ought to be admitted in proof before the Board of their having ever been in England; although I own I should be much surprised to see any letters of mine returned from thence; for I never corresponded with any Gentleman there, whom I can suspect to be capable of so much baseness, as to betray a confidential correspondence: And it is very evident these letters are of that kind.

"I have not heard that there has been any attempt as yet to evidence so material a fact as that of the letters coming from England: I cannot therefore think that the Hon. Board will expect me to explain myself further on the subject, or that they will act upon it themselves until this has been done.

Hon. Mr. Sec. Flucker,
to be communicated AND. OLIVER."
to the Hon. Board.

Some letters from Berlin mention, that the Jews of all ranks are preparing to leave the Prussian dominions by order, on account of some of them being suspected to be concerned in the circulation of base ducats.

We hear from Dublin, that Mr. Gardiner, Mr. Leslie, Mr. Bagnelle, Mr. Dawson, and other Gentlemen of Distinction, have offered to advance, upon Government security, a sum sufficient to satisfy, for the present, the numerous ... Treasury in that kingdom.

REPORTING THE

COMMITTEES OF CORRESPONDENCE

By Carol Sue Humphrey

RELATIONS WITH GREAT BRITAIN REMAINED TENSE BUT relatively calm for most Americans in the years after the Boston Massacre of 1770. However, some people believed the fight was not over and sought ways to be prepared for future conflicts. In November 1772, Patriot leaders in Boston established a committee of correspondence to provide an organized mechanism for communication and protest when needed. Such committees had been used on a random and ad-hoc basis since 1764 to deal with specific issues, but people like Samuel Adams and Joseph Warren wanted to develop a more standardized system by tying the committees directly to the existing town meeting structure in order to provide official standing for the committee in the community and regular meetings to deal with ongoing concerns.

Other towns in Massachusetts organized similar groups. Word of the creation of Committees of Correspondence in Massachusetts soon spread to other colonies as communities in those areas organized their own groups. By March 1773, the colony of Virginia had formed a permanent colony-wide committee. They communicated this action to the other colonies and urged them to do the same. In late May, the House of Representatives of Massachusetts voted to establish its own colony-wide committee, charged with three primary duties:

> *to obtain the most early and authentic Intelligence of all such Acts and resolutions of the British Parliament, or Proceedings of Administration, as may relate to, or affect the British Colonies in America; and to keep up and maintain a Correspondence and Communication with our Sister Colonies respecting these important Considerations; and the result of such their Proceedings, from Time to Time, to lay before the House.*

On June 3, the *Massachusetts Gazette; and the Boston Weekly News-Letter* published this report and the resolutions related to the creation of the Massachusetts committee, as well as reports of the creation of similar groups in New Hampshire and Connecticut. Such detailed coverage reflected the growing awareness among many Americans that these committees were going to be increasingly important in the conflict with Great Britain. This assumption proved correct because the Committees of Correspondence became the de facto governments of the colonies when the royal institutions ceased to function properly as the arguments with Great Britain grew worse.

In each colony, these committees provided a means of communication separate from the official government that enabled the Patriots to organize to protest various British actions. In Massachusetts, for example, the committee played an important role in the events that led up to the Battle of Lexington and Concord. The Boston Committee of Correspondence worked hard to get the citizens of Boston organized to protest the shipment of East India Tea that led to the Boston Tea Party, and after the Tea Party occurred, their communication network spread the word to the rest of Massachusetts and the other colonies about what had happened in Boston.

When word of the Coercive Acts reached the colonies in the spring of 1774, the Committees of Correspondence in Massachusetts organized protests and demonstrations throughout the colony. In the wake of these events, prisoners were freed, courts were closed, and British-appointed officials were forced to resign. As a result of these revolutionary actions, the British colonial government ceased to function throughout Massachusetts, and the Committees of Correspondence stepped up to fill the gap. They eventually would provide the impetus for forming a new

THE

Massachusetts Gazette:

AND THE

Boston Weekly News-Letter.

Number 3635.

Draper's.] THURSDAY, June 3, 1773.

The Treasurer for the

County of SUFFOLK Notifies the Constables and Collectors of Taxes who are in Arrears for the Years preceding 1772, that he has received Order from the Court of General Sessions of the Peace, to issue his Warrants against them, unless they immediately pay him their respective Ballances. *May 19th. 1773.*

BOSTON, *June 3.*

Last Thursday, upon Complaint to the Honourable House of Representatives, from some of the Inhabitants of the Town of Weston, of Corruption in the Election of the Representative for that Place; the House took the Matter under Consideration, when, after examining a Number of Witnesses relative thereto, the Member was dismissed the House, and a new Precept ordered to be issued for another Choice.

The same Day after the House of Representatives had determined a contested Election, and agreed upon rules and Orders for their own Government, the Speaker communicated a Letter from the Speaker of the House of Burgesses in the Colony of Virginia, inclosing a Resolution of that Assembly, to keep up and maintain a Correspondence and free Communication with the Sister Colonies, and requesting the House to appoint a Committee to join with their Committee for that Purpose: The Speaker communicated also a Letter from the Speaker of the House of Representatives of the Colony of Rhode-Island, acquainting him that they had agreed to the salutary Measure proposed by Virginia; and the same being read, the House assigned the next Morning Nine o'Clock, to take them under Consideration, and then adjourned.

The said Letter and the Inclosures were accordingly read again on Friday Morning, and after due Consideration thereon, the House came into the following Resolutions, there being 113 Members present, and only four Dissentients.

this Continent, inclosing the aforesaid Resolves; and requesting them to lay the same before their respective Assemblies ... ly and chearfully ... the Resolves of the ...

YEAS.

Mr. Samuel Adam[s]
Hon. John Hancock
William Phillips, ...
Capt. William Hea[th]
Mr. Samuel Howe
Mr. Josiah Howe
Ebenezer Thayer, ju[n]
Mr. Nathaniel Bai...
Benjamin Lincoln, ...
Mr. Abner Ellis
Mr. Moses Bullen
Mr. Jabez Fisher
Capt. Benjamin W...
Richard Derby, jun
Mr. John Pickering
Dr. Samuel Holten
Capt. Michael Far[ley]
Hon. Joseph Gerrish
Capt. Jonathan Gr...
Mr. Elbridge Gerry
Azor Orne, Esq;
Ebenezer Burrell, E[sq;]
Mr. Moody Bridge[s]
Capt. Henry Herri[ck]
Mr. Samuel Smith
Nathaniel Allen, E[sq;]
Mr. John Gould
Aaron Wood, Esq;
Isaac Merrill, Esq;
Capt. Daniel Thur...
Capt. Thomas Gar...
Mr. Nathaniel Go...
Capt. Jonathan B...
Mr. Samuel Wyma[n]
Capt. James Barre[tt]

...ate- ...the ...nce, ...ered ...ber- ...con- ...ited ...Cor- ...st of ...e a ...the ...such ...t, or ...), or ...keep ...uni- ...im- ...their ...the ...said ...form ...Au- ...qui- ...with ...nces ...Seas ...ther ...e, a ...tters ...ouse ...the ...lony ...the ...y on

Hon. John Whitcomb, Esq;
Capt. Ephraim Doolittle
Mr. Paul Mandell
Mr. Samuel March
Mr. John Lewis
Mr. Wentworth Stewart

James McCobb, Esq;
David Ingersol, Esq;
Mr. Samuel Brown jun.
Mr. Peter Curtis
Mr. David Noble

NAYS.

Abijah White, Esq;
Thomas Gilbert, Esq;

Capt. Jeremiah Learned
John Murray, Esq;

Then the House immediately made Choice of the following Gentlemen to be the Committee of Correspondence and Communication with the other Colonies.

Mr. Speaker, Mr. Samuel Adams, Hon. John Hancock, Esq; Mr. William Phillips, Capt. William Heath, Hon. Joseph Hawley, Esq; Hon. James Warren, Esq; Richard Derby, jun. Esq; Mr. Elbridge Gerry, Jerathmeel Bowers, Esq; Jedediah Foster, Esq; Daniel Leonard, Esq; Capt. Thomas Gardner, Capt. Jonathan Greenleaf, and, James Prescott, Esq;

We hear that the Honorable House of Representatives of the Province of New-Hampshire, have taken into their wise Consideration the Plan of Union between the Colonies, as proposed by the Honourable House of Burgesses in Virginia, and have chosen a Committee of Correspondence to communicate with the other Colonies;—have wrote Letters to the Houses of Assembly in Virginia and Rhode-Island, and assured them that the House of Representatives of the Province of New-Hampshire are ready to co-operate with all their Sister Colonies to recover and perpetuate the Liberties of America.

We hear that the House of Assembly of the Colony of Connecticut, have also adopted the same Measures.

Proceedings of the Town of Barnstable.

the Water's Edge.——The Fire, ...casioned by some Coals falling fr[om] the Cabouse on to the Deck, whi[ch] pay'd over with Turpentine, and Rapidity that Nothing could be ... —The Captain, with his Wife and usually kept on board, likewise a ... ple belonging to her being ashore be taken out of the Cabin Windo[w] able to save the least Thing but ... —A report prevailing at the Tim[e] a large Quantity of Powder was ... Inhabitants in general into great ... fear of the Consequences that mi[ght] Explosion thereof; but being afte[r] none was in her, they became per[...] Hills and Wharfs were covered ... view so uncommon a Sight. Som[e] the Hold, such as Cordage, Cab[les] which were under Water befor[e] reach them, will be saved.

About the same Time a Fir[e] Goal at Cambridge, but by the ... dance of the Students, with the[ir] it was extinguished.

Yesterday Afternoon arrived ... Sloop of War from North Caroli[na]

The same Day a Schooner arriv[ed] Mole, being one of those lately ... whom we learn, that most or all th[e] detained are likewise released.

We hear from Boxford, that on ... had a terrible Storm of Hail, a ... severe Thunder and Lightning: ... that fell, we are informed, mea[sured] ... and a Half round.

MASSACHUSETTS GAZETTE;
AND THE BOSTON WEEKLY NEWS-LETTER
June 3, 1773

government structure in Massachusetts that was totally independent of the British system.

As relations with Great Britain worsened in all the colonies, the colony-wide Committees of Correspondence played a major role in the planning of the First Continental Congress and thus helped in the initial stages of establishing an intercolonial government that could successfully fight the British during the American Revolution.

are to be grounded any Instructions, that shall tend to lessen the Rights of either House, or any other Way affect the Interests of the Province?

On this Occasion it is obvious to observe that within these few Years the Ministry seem to have considered the Governors of this Province, not as Crown Officers with Commissions under the Great Seal, but as Officers within their Department and under their Direction. This remarkably appeared in the Administration of Governor Bernard, who very probably was the means of it: For there is Reason to suppose, and his Letters shew it, that he laid a Plan for depriving Americans in general, and this Province in particular, of their Liberties: And being a Volunteer in the executing it, in order to secure himself seems to have procured from the Minister Letters of Instruction from time to time, as he had occasion for them: Whereby without giving the Province an opportunity of being heard, its Rights, Interests and Character have been greatly injured. And as the same mode of proceeding has been continued, there is the same reason to complain of it. But it is humbly hoped from the Goodness and Justice of his Majesty, and the distinguished Virtues of the Earl of Dartmouth, (his Majesty's Minister for the American Department) that this Province will be made happy by the Removal of all its Grievances.

In the mean time the Board are affected with the deepest concern, that any part of their Conduct should be disapproved by his Majesty: but they humbly trust, that when his Majesty shall be informed of the Reasons on which it is grounded, it will notwithstanding be the Object of his Gracious Approbation.

Extract of the proceedings of the town of Marshfield, *on the 31st of January*, 1774.

THIS town taking into consideration the late tumultuous and as we think illegal proceedings in the town of Boston, in the detention and destruction of the teas belonging to the East India company, which we apprehend will affect our properties if not our liberties, think it our indispensible duty to show our disapprobation of such measures and proceedings:——Therefore Voted and Resolved, as the opinion of this town,——That the late measures and proceedings in the town of Boston, in the detention and destruction of the teas belonging to the East-India company, were illegal and unjust & of a dangerous tendency.—That Abijah White, Esq; the present Representative of this town, be and hereby is instructed and directed to use his utmost endeavours that the perpetrators of those mischiefs may be detected and brought to justice. And as the country has been heretofore drawn in to pay their proportionable part of the expence which accrued from the riotous and unruly proceedings and conduct of certain individuals in the town of Boston,—if application should be made to the general court by the East-India company or any other persons for a consideration for the loss of said teas, you are by no means to acquiesce, but bear your testimony against any measures by which expence may accrue to the province in general, or to the town of Marshfield

Uxbridge, purchased a male infant of one of his tenants, who had lain in a few days, and was left a widow: he gave one hundred guineas for the child, on consideration the mother was never to own it, and intends adopting it as his own son.

Nov. 15. *One Mr. Fabrigas, a resident in Minorca, on account of some very heavy oppressions from General Mostyn, his Majesty's Governor of that island, last summer, brought an action against that officer.—The cause was tried before Lord Chief Justice Mansfield, and a verdict of three thousand pounds damages was found for the plaintiff; afterwards the defendant's counsel moved the Court for a new trial, which occasioned the Governor to be summoned before a very awful tribunal, where the following particulars occurred:*

One day last week a command was sent to the culprit to attend immediately at Kew, his Majesty having business with him of the utmost importance. This command was immediately obeyed, and on the ministerial officer's arrival, he was introduced into the royal closet, where he found Lord North and Lord Mansfield, who had likewise received particular messages to attend, but were entirely ignorant of the

from Worcester goal, in the Massachusetts-Bay) was apprehended on the night of the 21st January last, for passing counterfeit dollars; also, one *Peter Hobart*, an accomplice, who has turned King's evidence, & given such a clue to Wheeler's plans, as cannot fail of the most salutary effect.

BOSTON, Thursday, February 3.

We hear that on Monday last the Corporation of Harvard-College, made Choice of the Honorable JOHN WINTHROP, Esq: LL.D. and F.R.S. to be PRESIDENT; but that he decli[ned] accepting that Office.

CHAPTER IV

THE DETESTABLE TEA

Introduction

With the Tea Act of 1773, British Parliament provided a government bailout to the East India Company, the monopoly importer of tea and one of Britain's biggest and most important businesses, which faced serious financial doom. Instead of imposing new or additional taxes, the Tea Act provided tax breaks, lowering the price of the East India Company's products and underselling American smugglers and legitimate middlemen alike. In the closing months of 1773, as tea ships sailed for America, colonists mobilized to determine exactly how the soon-arriving tea chests should be handled. With an important customs deadline looming and the threat of the tea cargo being forced into the American marketplace, a party of rebels took matters into their own hands, destroying hundreds of tea chests in Boston Harbor—a decision with revolutionary consequences.

Essex Gazette (Salem, MA)
February 8, 1774

Disguised colonists wielding axes and dumping boxes of tea into Boston Harbor
North Wind Picture Archives

REPORTING THE

TEA ACT IN AMERICA

By Benjamin L. Carp

POLITICS IN BOSTON, AND MUCH OF THE REST OF COLONIAL America, had been relatively quiet since the Boston Massacre of 1770. True, the people of Massachusetts were becoming increasingly angry with Governor Thomas Hutchinson, but the town of Boston was largely free of violent crowd action.

Then in October 1773, Boston began to learn about the provisions of the Tea Act. Parliament had passed this law on behalf of the East India Company, which had a monopoly on British tea imports from China but was deeply in debt and needed better access to the American market (see the letter in the *Boston Gazette* of March 22, 1773). The law imposed no taxes; in fact, it gave significant tax breaks to the East India Company, which would now be able to sell tea directly to designated agents, or consignees, in the American colonies. The result would be cheaper tea for colonial consumers.

The Tea Act gave privileges to a monopoly company and its consignees, which would drive other merchants out of the tea trade. Many Americans feared Parliament would extend such monopoly privileges to other commodities.

Many of the colonists were outraged, for three reasons: first, they were afraid cheap tea would seduce Americans into paying the duty (or tax) on tea that had been imposed in 1767; second, the revenue from the tea tax paid the salary of Hutchinson and other civil officials in Massachusetts—the people of Massachusetts would have preferred these salaries be paid from the coffers of the House of Representatives, so as to keep these officials accountable; and finally, the Tea Act gave privileges to a monopoly company and its consignees, which would drive other merchants out of the tea trade. Many Americans feared Parliament would extend such monopoly privileges to other commodities.

Egged on by New York City and Philadelphia (both centers for smuggling tea from foreign countries), the Bostonians protested the Tea Act in several ways. The Boston Committee of Correspondence, the local political caucus, and the newspapers coordinated protests. Crowds confronted the consignees at their homes and shops, trying to force the consignees to resign their commissions. Bostonians gathered at official town meetings on November 5, 6, and 18 to deliberate about the tea, challenge the consignees, and pass resolutions against the Tea Act.

Then the first of the tea ships hired by the East India Company, the *Dartmouth*, arrived on November 28. The next day, the people of Boston and its surrounding towns began gathering at more expansive meetings of the "body of the people." Such meetings took place November 29 and 30 and December 14 and 16. As was reported in the *Boston Evening-Post* of December 6, 1773, Faneuil Hall (the site of town meetings) was too small to contain the thousands of interested spectators, so the meetings were moved to the Old South Meeting House, the largest building in town. The meetings overtly defied Governor Hutchinson, and they continued to challenge the consignees, owners, and captains of the tea ships to send the tea back to London. The gathered subjects appointed guards to watch over the ships at night to make sure no one tried to unload the tea. Finally, the assembly announced that anyone who tried to import tea from Great Britain would be deemed "an Enemy to his Country," and everyone present agreed to prevent the tea from landing "at the Risque of their Lives and Property."

OLD SOUTH MEETING HOUSE
North Wind Picture Archives

(*at right*) The largest building in Boston, where thousands met in November and December 1773 to discuss the tea crisis.

even after they had failed.

The Houſe of P—— and B——, at Stockholm, has ſtopped payment for the ſum of *one million four hundred thouſand Dollars*, (about 313.000l. ſterl.) There is, no doubt but this failure will in its conſequences involve many other capital houſes in all the great commercial cities of Europe.

NEW-YORK, March 15.

Extract of a Letter of the 29th of January, from a Gentleman in the Weſt-Indies.

"The Caribs are reſolute, and ſeem determined that the Loſs of Liberty and Property ſhall be accompanied with that of Life;—a Determination worthy of a Briton; and as ſuch, ſhould be rever'd by one, tho' found in the Breaſt of a poor oppreſs'd Carib.—Our Troops are ſickly and appear to want that Animation, which has, hitherto always appeared on more glorious Occaſions; they ſeem ſenſible that Juſtice has not drawn the Sword.—The Expedition was ill-judged, and is condemned by every rational Being in the Weſt-Indies.—One Third of the Sum expended, given to the Caribs, would have purchaſed the Lands, and they would have retired from the Iſland.—They are by no Means Savages; many of them own 20 and 30 Negroes, and have Plantations under good Cultivation."

BOSTON, March 22.

Extract of a Letter from a Gentleman in London to his Friend in this Town, dated January 5. 1773.

"Some Circumſtances are working in Favor of America with Regard to the Duties; it is found by the laſt Year's Accounts tranſmitted by the Commiſſioners that the Balance in Favor of Britain is but about Eighty-Five Pounds, after Payment of Salaries, &c. excluſive of the Charge of a Fleet to enforce the Collection.—It is further obſerved, that the India Company is ſo out of Caſh that it cannot pay the Bills drawn upon it, and at the ſame Time ſo out of Credit that the Bank does not care to aſſiſt them; whence they find themſelves obliged to lower their Dividend, the Apprehenſion of which has ſunk their Stock from 280 to 160, whereby ſeveral Millions of Property are annihilated, occaſioning private Bankruptcies and other Diſtreſs, beſides a Loſs to the public Treaſury of £.400 000 per Ann. which the Company by Agreement are not to pay into it as heretofore, if they are not able to keep up their Dividend at 12½; and as they have at the ſame Time Tea and other India Goods in their Warehouſes, to the Amount of Four Millions as ſome ſay, for which they want a Market, and which if it had been ſold, would have kept up their Credit: This ſhews the great Importance of loſing the American Market, by keeping up the Duties on Tea, which has thrown the Trade into the Hands of Foreigners. This gives ſome Alarm, and begins to convince People more and more of the Impropriety of Quarrelling with the Americans."

Extract of a Letter from New-York, dated March 10, 1773.

"THE preſent political Tranſactions of your Province, eſpecially of your General Court, excites the Attention of all Ranks here:—Your Aſſembly's *Reply* to your Governor's late *extraordinary* Speech, meets with general Approbation; & well

any of the American Colonies. I think, however, that we ought not to be inattentive to the Subject. The Epiſcopal Clergy we know will not, and ſure we ought not.

The Comic Satiric Lecture, call'd The Times, which was to have been deliver'd this Evening at Concert-Hall, is poſtpon'd on Account of the Weather to Monday Evening next.

Folks may ſtrip us ſtark naked, and turn us out of Doors in Mid-winter, we hold the Bleſſings of Heaven on very precarious Tenu[re] ... Planners and Abettors of ſuch a[…] ſpiracy as this, and for them onl[y] ... modern *Juvenal* boaſts his De[…] maintain the Freedom of *his* Preſs.

Quere, Should not Emboweling [and] Quartering have been added to th[e] well-deſerved Puniſhments this [...] drawn up for himſelf?

On Tueſday the 30th
will be Sold at Public Auction at a Stor[e] ... ſite to the Sign of Admiral Vernon, Kin[g] ...
Fourteen Hogſheads of Choi[ce] ... *vado* SUGAR.

Loſt laſt Thurſday, a ...
ther Pocket Book, containing ſundry P[...] Ticket No. 928, in Faneuil-Hall Lottery[...] Ruddock. Whoever has found the ſa[me] ... bring it to the Printers hereof, ſhall be ... their Trouble.

A Brigantine.

Now on the Stocks at North River; a B[...] about 130 Tons, built of good Stuff and by ... (can be Launch'd in April.) To be Sol[d] ... Caſh or part Weſt-India Goods.——Alſo a fi[ne] ... Brig of three Years old, about 97 [T]ons, a p[...] and well found. Inquire of Edes & Gill.

To be Sold on Reaſonable Term[s]

A Likely Well-built B...
about 115 Tuns, ſingle Deck, 5 Years old, w[...] and a faſt Sailer. Inquire of the Printers.

N. B. A Veſſel of 70 Tuns would ſuit i[n] ...

TO BE SOLD.

The Eſtate of Capt. Edward[s] ...
late of Boſton, Mariner, deceaſed, conſiſting of [a Dwel]ling Houſe with two Rooms on a Floor, a g[...] and Garden, and fine Well of Water, pleaſ[antly situat]ed on Cambridge-Street, New-Boſton. Fo[r] Particulars, inquire of Hannah Stone, Admini[stratrix] ſaid Eſtate.

AND all Perſons that have any Demands ... Eſtate, are deſired to bring in their Accounts, the Eſtate being rendered Inſolvent.

TO-MORROW at 11 o'Clock,
Will be Sold by PUBLIC VENDUE, at the Auction-Room Foot of Royal Exchange Lane.

A Variety of *ENGLISH GOODS*,
Among which are,
30 Pieces of Iriſh Linnens, Bedticks,

Daniel Parks.

LOST at the late Fire at Mr. Ivis's, a Leather Bucket, mark'd *Wm. Homes*. If any Perſon will return it to him oppoſite the Golden Key, they ſhall be ſatisfied for their Trouble.

to this.—Theſe GOODS ...

... taken of their Education, and that good Order will be obſerv'd. The Days propos'd for public School are Mondays and Thurſdays.

N. B. Said CURTIS was Educated in *Paris*, and has taught Dancing in ſeveral Towns in this Province.—Any Perſons that are diſpoſed to employ him, are deſired to leave a Line with Capt. GORE, at the Painters Arms.

At Bowman's Dying Auction Room,
North Side of the Market,
On FRIDAY Morning next,
Sold by Public Vendue,
——Conſiſting of,
[J]erſeys, Duffils, Coating, ... Threads, Serge Denim, ... figured and plain Lawns ... 7 8 and yard-wide Iriſh Callicoes, Checks, check ... and Thread Hoſe, a ... Writing Paper, Table ... of Hard Ware, &c.— ... amongſt which are, an ... Book Caſe, one Mehogany ... Feather Beds, &c. &c. ... Ten o'Clock.

[BOS]TON, ſince our laſt, ... No Blacks. ... Churches, Fourteen.

High Water at BOSTON for this preſent Week.

Monday, 0 min. after 11		Friday, 40 m aft. 1	
Tueſday, 40 min. af. 11		Saturday, 12 m. af. 2	
Wedneſday, 10 m. aft. 12		Lord's Day 0 m. af. 3	
Thurſday 48 min. after 12		New Moon this Night.	

BOSTON GAZETTE

March 22, 1773

Parliament passed the Tea Act on behalf of the East India Company, which had a monopoly on British tea imports from China but was deeply in debt and needed better access to the American market. A letter from a gentleman in London to his friend in Boston tells "that the India Company is so out of Cash that it cannot pay the Bills drawn upon it" and that the Company has a surplus inventory of tea "to the Amount of Four Millions as some say, for which they want a Market." As the writer summarizes, this shows "the great Importance of losing the American Market, by keeping up the Duties on Tea" and suggests it will convince Great Britain to quarrel less with America.

BOSTON EVENING-POST

December 6, 1773

After the first of three tea ships arrived in Boston Harbor, thousands of concerned citizens and interested spectators packed into the Old South Meeting House to discuss how to handle the tea. The assembly concluded with the announcement that anyone who tried to import tea from Great Britain would be deemed "an Enemy to his Country," and everyone present agreed to prevent the tea from landing "at the Risque of their Lives and Property."

BOS ON, *December* 6. 1773.

At a Meeting of the PEOPLE *of*

...

rator be choſen, and

JONATHAN WILLIAMS, Eſq;

Was then choſen Moderator of the Meeting.

A MOTION was made that as the Town of Boſton had determined at a late Meeting legally aſſembled, that they would to the utmoſt of their Power prevent the landing of e Tea, the Queſtion be put, Whether is Body are abſolutely determined that the Tea ow arrived in Capt. Hall ſhall be returned to the ace from whence it came at all Events. And the ueſtion being accordingly put, it paſſed in the ffirmative. Nem. Con.

It appearing that the Hall could not contain e People aſſembled, it was Voted, that the Meet- g be immediately Adjourned to the Old South eeting-Houſe, Leave having been obtained for s Purpoſe.

The People met at the Old South according to djournment.

A Motion was made, and the Queſtion put, viz. hether it is the firm Reſolution of this Bo- that the Tea ſhall not only be ſent back, but at no Duty ſhall be paid thereon; & paſs'd in the ffirmative. Nem. Con.

It was moved, that in order to give Time to the onſignees to conſider and deliberate, before they nt in their Propoſals to this Body, as they had iven Reaſon to expect would have been done at e opening of ... there might be an Ad- ... o'Clock, P. M and the Meet- g was accordingly for that Purpoſe adjourned.

THREE o'Clock, P. M. met according to Adjournment.

A Motion was made, Whether the Tea now rrived in Captain Hall's Ship ſhall be ſent back the ſame Bottom—Paſs'd in the Affirmative, *Nem. Con.*

Mr. Rotch the Owner of the Veſſel being pre- ent, informed the Body that he ſhould enter his roteſt againſt their Proceedings.

It was then moved and voted, *nem. con.* That Mr. Rotch be directed not to enter this Tea; and hat the Doing of it would be at his Peril.

Alſo Voted, That Captain Hall the Maſter of ...

they had hitherto expend d upon them to no Pur- poſe, were prevailed upon to adjourn to the next Morning Nine o'clock.

... Nine o'Clock, ... ournment.

... ls were at length ... directed to the Mo- ... y, Eſq; one of the ... oted that the ſame ... s follow, viz.

... *v. 29th*, 1773.

... ld not return to the ... ers to their two late ... eas; we beg Leave ... ectmen that we have ... the Honorable Eaſt- ... o do all in our Power ... n, but as we under- ... Gentlemen Selectmen at Meſſ. Clarkes Interview with you laſt Saturday, that this can be effected by nothing leſs than our ſend- ing back the Teas, we beg Leave to ſay, that this is utterly out of our Power to do, but we do now declare to you our Readineſs to Store the Teas until we ſhall have Opportunity of writing to our Conſtituents and ſhall receive their further Orders reſpecting them; and we do moſt ſincerely wiſh that the Town conſi- dering the unexpected Difficulties devolved upon us will be ſatisfied with what we now offer.

We are, SIR,

Your moſt humble Servants,

Tho. & Eliſha Hutchinſon,

Benja. Faneuil, jun. for Self and

Joſhua Winſlow, Eſq;

Rich'd Clarke & Sons.

John Scollay, Eſq;

Mr. Sheriff Greenleaf came into the Meeting, and begg'd Leave of the Moderator that a Letter he had received from the Governor, requiring him to read a Proclamation to the People here aſſem- bled might be read; and it was accordingly read.

Whereupon it was moved, and the Queſtion put, Whether the Sheriff ſhould be permitted to read the Proclamation—which paſſed in the Affirma- tive, nem. con.

The Proclamation is as follows, viz.

Maſſachuſets-Bay. } By the Governor.

To JONATHAN WILLIAMS, Eſq; acting as Moderator of an Aſſembly of People in the Town of Boſton, and to the People ſo aſſembled:

WHEREAS printed Notifications were on Monday the 29th Inſtant poſted in divers Places in the Town of Boſton and publiſhed in the News-Papers of that Day calling upon the People to aſſemble toge- ther for certain unlawful Purpoſes in ſuch Notifications mentioned: And whereas great Numbers of People belonging to the Town of Boſton, and divers others belonging to ſeve- ral other Towns in the Province, did aſſemble

And the ſame bei ead by the Sheriff, there was immediately aft a loud and very general Hiſs.

A Motion was th ade, and the Queſtion put, Whether the Aſſembly would diſperſe and ſurceaſe all further Proceedings, according to the Gover- nor's Requirement——It paſs'd in the Negative, nem. con.

A Propoſal of Mr. Copley was made, that in Caſe he could prevail with the Meſſ. Clarkes to come into this Meeting, the Queſtion might now be put, Whether they ſhould be treated with Civi- lity while in the Meeting, though they might be of different Sentiments with this Body; and their Perſons be ſafe until their Return to the Place from whence they ſhould come——And the Queſ- tion being accordingly put, paſſed in the Affirma- tive, Nem. Con.

Another Motion of Mr. Copley's was put, Whether two Hours ſhall be given him, which alſo paſſed in the Affirmative.

Adjourn'd to Two o'Clock, P. M.

TWO o'Clock P. M. met according to Ad- journment.

A Motion was made and paſſed, that Mr. Rotch and Capt. Hall be deſired to give their Attendance.

Mr. Rotch appeared, and upon a Motion made the Queſtion was put, Whether it is the firm Reſolution of this Body, that the Tea brought by Capt. Hall ſhall be returned by Mr. Rotch to England in the Bottom in which it came; and whether they accordingly now require the ſame, which paſſed in the Affirmative, Nem. Con.

Mr. Rotch then informed the Meeting that he ſhould proteſt againſt the whole Proceedings as he had done againſt the Proceedings on Yeſterday, but that tho' the returning the Tea is an invo- luntary Act in him, he yet conſiders himſelf as under a Neceſſity to do it, and ſhall therefore com- ply with the Requirement of this Body.

Capt. Hall being preſent was forbid to aid or aſſiſt in unloading the Tea at his Peril, and ordered that if he continues Maſter of the Veſſel, he carry the ſame back to London; who reply'd he ſhould comply with theſe Requirements.

Upon a Motion, Reſolved, That John Rowe, Eſq; Owner of Part of Capt. Bruce's Ship expected with Tea, as alſo Mr. Timmins, Factor for Capt. Coffin's Brig, be deſired to attend.

Mr. Ezekiel Cheever was appointed Captain of the Watch for this Night, and a ſufficient Number of Volunteers gave in their Names for that Service.

VOTED, That the Captain of this Watch be deſired to make out a Liſt of the Watch for the next Night, and ſo each Captain of the Watch for the following Nights until the Veſſels leave the Harbour.

Upon a Motion made, Voted, that in Caſe it ſhould happen that the Watch ſhould be any Ways moleſted in the Night, while on Duty, they give the Alarm to the Inhabitants by the tolling of the Bells—and that if any Thing happens in the Day Time, the Alarm be by ringing of the Bells.

VOTED, That ſix Perſons be appointed to be in Readineſs to give due Notice to the Country Towns when they ſhall be required ſo to do, upon any important Occaſion. And ſix Perſons were accordingly choſen for that Purpoſe.

A Motion was made, That in Order for the ecurity of Captain Hall's Ship and Cargo, a Watch may be appointed——and it was Voted

Moderator, and to conſult, deba nd reſolve upon Ways and Means for carrying ſuch un- lawful Purpoſes into Execution ...

carry back the Tea he bro't in the ſame Bottom, & that it was the Expectation of this Body that he does the ſame by the Tea expected in Capt. Bruce; where- ...

Consignees, be in the least Degree satisfactory to this Body, & passed in the Negative. Nem. Con.

Whereas a Number of Merchants in this Province have inadvertently imported Tea from Great-Britain, while it is subject to the Payment of a Duty imposed upon it by an Act of the British Parliament for the Purpose of raising a Revenue in America, and appropriating the same without the Consent of those who are required to pay it:

RESOLVED, That in thus importing said Tea, they have justly incurr'd the Displeasure of our Brethren in the other Colonies.

And Resolved further, That if any Person or Persons shall hereafter import Tea from Great-Britain, or if any Master or Masters of any Vessel or Vessels in Great-Britain shall take the same on Board to be imported to this Place, until the said unrighteous Act shall be repeal'd, he or they shall be deem'd by this Body, an Enemy to his Country; and we will prevent the Landing and Sale of the same, and the Payment of any Duty thereon. And we will effect the Return thereof to the Place from whence it shall come.

RESOLVED, That the foregoing Vote be printed and sent to England, and all the Sea-Ports in this Province.

Upon a Motion made, Voted, That fair Copies be taken of the whole Proceedings of this Meeting, and transmitted to New-York & Philadelphia, And that Mr. SAMUEL ADAMS,
Hon. JOHN HANCOCK, Esq;
WILLIAM PHILLIPS, Esq;
JOHN ROWE, Esq;
JONATHAN WILLIAMS, Esq
Be a Committee to transmit the same.

Voted, That it is the Determination of this Body, to carry their Votes and Resolutions into Execution, at the Risque of their Lives and Property.

Voted, That the Committee of Correspondence for this Town, be desired to take Care that every other Vessel with Tea that arrives in this Harbour, have a proper Watch appointed for her—Also Voted, That those Persons who are desirous of making a Part of these Nightly Watches, be desired to give in their Names at Messieurs Edes and Gill's Printing-Office.

Voted, That our Brethren in the Country be desired to afford their Assistance upon the first Notice given; especially if such Notice be given upon the Arrival of Captain Loring, in Messieurs Clarkes' Brigantine.

Voted, That those of this Body who belong to the Town of Boston do return their Thanks to their Brethren who have come from the neighbouring Towns, for their Countenance and Union with this Body in this Exigence of our Affairs.

VOTED, That the Thanks of this Meeting be given to JONATHAN WILLIAMS, Esq; for his good services as Moderator.

VOTED, That this Meeting be Dissolved—And it was accordingly Dissolved.

of the Town of Roxbury, *legally assembled on Friday, December 3, 1773.*

After mature Deliberation, the Town came into the following Resolutions, which passed unanimously, *viz.*

WHEREAS it appears by an Act of the British Parliament passed at their last Session, That the East India Company in London, are by said Act allowed to export their Teas to America "*dischaaged from the Payment of any Customs or Duties whatsoever*" in London, *but* "*liable to the same Rules, Regulations, Penalties and Forfeitures,*" in America, as if said Act had not been passed; from which there is too much Reason to apprehend the said Act was designed to take in the Unwary, and to continue and establish the Tribute extorted from, and so much, and so justly complained of by the Americans. Upon due Consideration thereof, *Resolved*, That the Sense of this Town cannot be better express'd upon this Occasion, than in the Words of certain judicious, and truly patriotic Resolves lately entered into by the worthy Citizens of Philadelphia, & since adopted by our much respected Brethren, the Inhabitants of the Town of Boston.

And Whereas it appears that notwithstanding the repeated Application which hath been made by the Inhabitants of the Town of Boston to the Persons appointed by the East India Company, to receive and sell said Tea, to resign said Trust, they still, regardless of their own Characters, or of the Peace, Quiet and Prosperity of the People, not only of the Town of Boston, or of this Town and Province, but from the most undoubted Intelligence, America in general.

Therefore *Resolved*. That so long as said Persons appointed by the East India Company as aforesaid, shall persist in refusing to resign their Appointment to that Trust, or otherwise ease and satisfy the present Uneasiness of this People, so greatly enhanced by their repeated Refusals, they discover a want of Fellow-feeling of the Grievances under which this People are Groaning, that they prefer their own private Emolument, to the public Happiness—a Disposition to facilitate and establish the detested Tribute.—A Temper enemical to the Rights, Liberties and Prosperity of America, and that in such light they will be viewed by this Town, from whom they may not expect the least Protection.

Resolved also, That if any other of the Inhabitants of this Province shall hereafter, directly or indirectly, import any Tea into this Province, subject to a Duty in America, such Person or Persons shall be viewed by this Town as Enemies to their Country, and may not expect either Countenance or Protection.

And Whereas the Inhabitants of the Town of [Bo]ston, have repeatedly heretofore, and on the pre[sent Occasi]on in particular; given fresh proof of their [Vi]gilance and unwearied Endeavors, to recover [and pr]eserve the Rights and Liberties of America.

Resolved, That this Town look upon themselves, as in Duty bound to themselves and Posterity, to stand fast in that Liberty wherewith the Supreme Being hath made them free, & that they will readily join with the Town of Boston & other Sister Towns, in such Constitutional Measures, as shall be judged proper to preserve and hand down to Posterity inviolate, those inestimable Rights & Liberties, handed down to us (under Providence) by our worthy Ancestors. The foregoing is a true Copy,

Attest, SAMUEL GRIDLEY, Town Clerk.

AT a legal Meeting of the Freeholders and other Inhabitants of the Town of Charlestown, *Nov.* 27, 1773, *and continued by Adjournment to the 4th of December, the following* RESOLVES *were unanimously Voted*, viz.

WHEN we his Majesty's dutiful and loyal Subjects the Inhabitants of this Town, reflect on the glorious Attachment of our Ancestors to Liberty; an Attachment so strong as to induce them (during the Tyranny of the Stuarts) to quit their native Homes, and seek for Freedom in the howling Wilderness of America: When we consider that this once inhospitable Desart has by their Labor and at the Expence of their Blood and Treasure, been brought to its present flourishing Situation: When we contemplate our strong Attachment to the Person and Family of our most gracious Sovereign, & recollect that Harmony and mutual Affection that lately subsisted between our Parent State and her Colonies, the Restoration of which we most ardently wish, we cannot but have our Minds most deeply affected, and our Fears greatly alarmed at the Encroachments on our Rights and Privileges, by Administration's raising a Revenue from America without their Consent. And it adds

in the Colonies, that the retaining the Duty on Tea, for the express Purpose of raising a Revenue in America, and impowering the East India Company to send their Tea here for Sale, while subject to said Duty, is a striking Instance of their Determination to persevere in their Attacks, and thereby reduce us to the most abject State of Wretchedness and Slavery.

IV. Resolved, That whoever shall be directly or indirectly concerned in landing, receiving, buying or selling said Tea, or in importing any Tea from Great Britain, whilst subject to Duty, is an Enemy to America, and ought to be treated accordingly.

V. Resolved, That we highly approve the Vigilant, Wise and Steady Conduct of our Brethren the Inhabitants of the Town of Boston at this alarming Crisis, and beg their Acceptance of our most cordial Thanks for the same.

VI. Resolved, That we are and will be on all proper Occasions ready in Conjunction with our oppressed American Brethren to risque our Lives and Fortunes in the support of those Rights, Liberties and Privileges with which GOD, Nature and our happy Constitution has made us free.

The foregoing is a true Copy,

Attest, SETH SWEETSER, Town-Clerk.

At a Meeting of the Freeholders and other Inhabitants of the Town of Dorchester, *on the 30th of* November 1773.

THE Committee of Correspondence laid before the Town a Letter which had been agreed upon by the Committees of several Towns, to be sent to all the Towns in the Province, in order to know their Minds at this critical Juncture, and also the Votes and Proceedings of the Town of Boston thereon:

VOTED, That we highly approve of the public Conduct of the Towns of Boston and Cambridge, in their late Town-Meetings, and the Resolves they came into, in order to prevent the Act of Parliament respecting the East-India Company being allowed to send their Teas to America, to take effect.

2. But being at present engaged in private matters within the Town, and having not long since made our Minds known to the Public in sundry Resolves, which were voted unanimously, we must now cut short; but we can assure the Public, that should this Country be so unhappy as to see a day of trial, for the recovery of its Rights, by a last and solemn appeal to him who gave them, we should not be behind the bravest of our patriotic brethren, and that we will at all times be ready to assist our neighbours and friends, when they shall need us, though the greatest dangers should attend it.

3. And whereas several Persons, who are deemed Enemies to their Country, have of late by their guilty consciences been drove into this and the neighbouring Towns, to shelter themselves from the just Vengeance of their Fellow-Citizens, that we will use our endeavours, that the just indignation they there feared, shall here overtake them, and that we, though we are not all of one Town, yet are all embarked in one common Cause.

Voted, That the Town-Clerk be directed to forward a Copy hereof to the Committee of Correspondence in the Town of Boston.

A true Copy from Dorchester *Records.*

Attest. NOAH CLAP, Town-Clerk.

NEW-YORK, Nov. 25.

George Clarke, Esq; having surrendered the office of Secretary of this Province, it has been conferred, for life, upon William Knox, Esq; Under Secretary to the Earl of Dartmouth.

The Ship Grace, Capt. William Chambers, will sail for Bristol on Sunday next. This is the commander's 72d passage over the Atlantick.

Lieut. John Nordberg, of the first Battalion of the Royal Americans, now in Jamaica, is appointed Commandant of Fort George, near Lake George, with the Rank of Captain in America.

We have Advice by Capt. Couper from London, that ten Days before him sailed,

A Ship for Boston, with Tea, Chests	600
A Ship for Philadelphia, with - - -	600
A Ship for Charlestown, ready to sail, with	200
A Ship for Rhode Island, ditto, - -	200
And another for New York, taking in	600
Total,	2200

NEWPORT (*Rhode-Island*) Nov. 29.

We are assured from the best authority, that Bohea TEA in New-York is no more than Half a Dollar a pound, by wholesale, and but 3/4½ lawful, by the single Pound.

The French nation having found Bohea Tea very pernicious, have almost entirely eradicated the use of it, through the whole kingdom; and even in England, there is but very little used, there being scarcely a drop drank in any public-house in London.

Last Tuesday arrived here, from New-York, the Lady who has passed thro' several of the southern colonies under the name and character of CAROLINA MATILDA, Marchioness de WALDEGRAVE, &c.

BOSTON, December 6, 1773.

Last Saturday Capt. Shephard, in a Ship, arrived here from London: He sailed from the Downs in Company with Capt. Bruce, but has none of the obnoxious Tea on board.

We have advice by the last Vessels from England, that on the 22d of September, the Snow Duke of

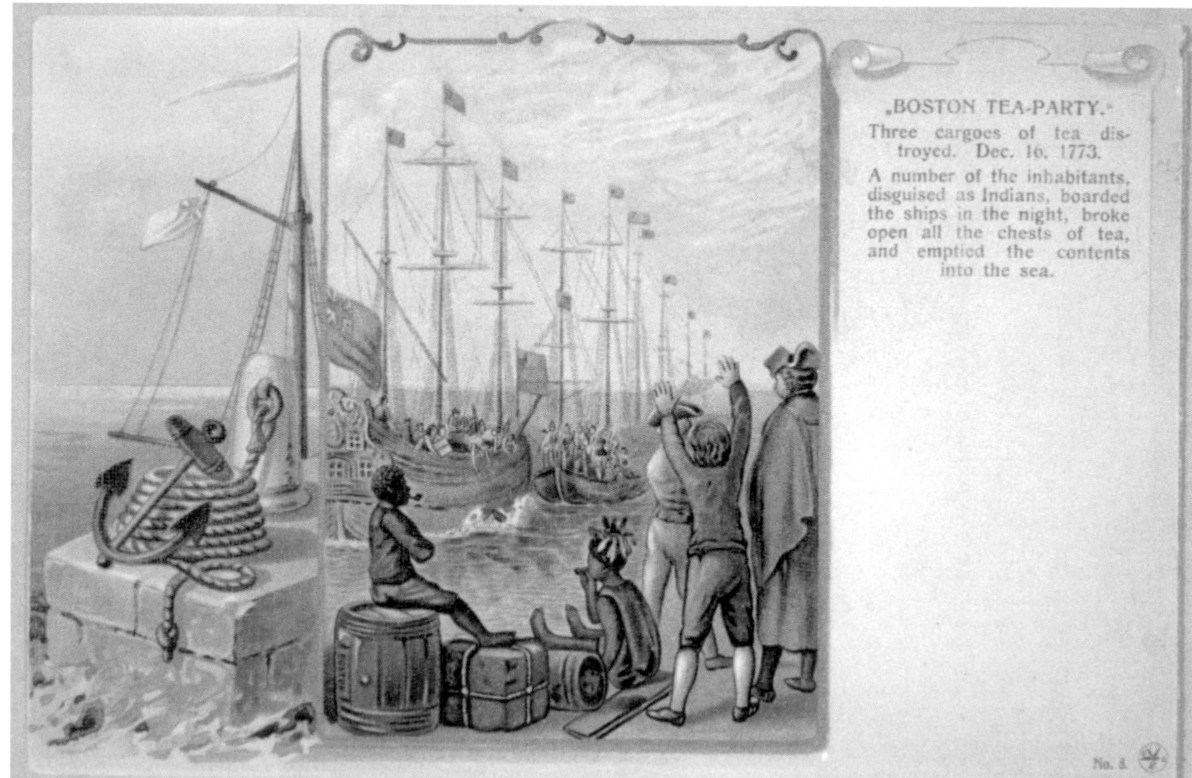

„BOSTON TEA-PARTY."
Three cargoes of tea destroyed. Dec. 16. 1773.
A number of the inhabitants, disguised as Indians, boarded the ships in the night, broke open all the chests of tea, and emptied the contents into the sea.

Destruction of the Tea
Library of Congress

(*top*) "Americans Throwing the Cargoes of the Tea Ships into the River, at Boston" from *The History of North America* (London, 1789) and (*bottom*) "Boston tea-party." Three cargoes of tea destroyed, December 16, 1773. This print, created in 1903, is a reproduction of the 1789 engraving.

REPORTING THE

BOSTON TEA PARTY

By Benjamin L. Carp

By December 16, 1773, there were three ships loaded with tea at Griffin's Wharf: the *Dartmouth*, the *Eleanor*, and the *Beaver*. The *Dartmouth* had been in Boston Harbor for almost twenty days, and when this deadline elapsed, any ship with taxable goods aboard was liable to seizure by customs officials. It was illegal for the *Dartmouth* and the other ships to return to London without unloading their cargo, but the Bostonians refused to allow the tea to land. If customs officials or the governor were willing to look the other way, then the ships might travel back across the Atlantic with the accursed tea aboard.

By December 16, customs officials had already refused to go along with the Boston crowd. So the people of Boston and the surrounding towns gathered at the Old South Meeting House and ordered Francis Rotch, owner of the *Dartmouth*, to travel to Milton and ask Governor Thomas Hutchinson to permit his ship to leave Boston Harbor. Hours later, Rotch returned to the Meeting House with the governor's refusal.

Soon afterward, the gathered Bostonians heard a war whoop, and a group of men disguised as Indians led the crowd down to Griffin's Wharf. About a hundred men boarded the three ships, lifted 340 tea chests above decks, smashed them open, and emptied their contents—over forty-six tons of tea—into the harbor. (Although the newspapers reported a figure of 342 chests, the East India Company claimed that 340 chests were destroyed.) The task took two or three hours, and the destroyers made sure not to damage anything other than the tea. The East India Company would later claim £9,659 in damages. The *Pennsylvania Packet* jokingly reported: "Letters from Boston complain much of the taste of their fish being altered."

The "Impartial Observer" whose letter was printed in the *Essex Gazette* of December 21, 1773, was anything but impartial: "I cannot but express my admiration at the conduct of this People!" he exclaimed. He insisted that the "wise and considerate body" at the Old South Meeting House "evidently tended to preserve the property of the East-India Company." Furthermore, the writer observes that it was not the gathered people from Boston and the surrounding towns who destroyed the tea, but "a number of Persons, supposed to be the Aboriginal Natives from their complections." Yet everyone knew that in reality, disguised white men, not American Indians, had destroyed the tea. In other words, the writer supported the protestors at the meetinghouse by making them blameless for the property destruction. Even the actual tea destroyers were careful to leave the rest of the ships' cargo untouched and replaced a broken lock. Meanwhile, other Boston newspapers joined the "Observer" in blaming the stubbornness of the consignees and the governor for the "fatal necessity" that "rendered this catastrophe inevitable."

The gathered Bostonians heard a war whoop, and a group of men disguised as Indians led the crowd down to Griffin's Wharf.

The *Essex Gazette* also illustrates that the people of Massachusetts were deeply interested in other American tea protests: they exulted at Philadelphia's approval, and they noted that several neighboring Massachusetts towns were publicly burning tea and pledging support for Boston.

BOSTON, December 20.

Meſſrs. PRINTERS,

HAVING accidentally arrived at Boſton upon a viſit to a Friend, the Evening before the Meeting of the Body of the People on the 29th of November, curioſity and the preſſing invitation of my moſt kind hoſt induced me to attend the Meeting; I muſt confeſs I was moſt agreeably, and I hope I ſhall be forgiven by this People if I ſay ſo unexpectedly entertained and inſtructed by the regular, reaſonable and ſenſible conduct and expreſſion of the People there collected, that I ſhould rather have entertained an idea of being tranſported to the Britiſh ſenate than to an adventitious and promiſcuous aſſembly of People of a remote Colony; were I not convinced by the genuine uncorrupted integrity and manly hardihood of the Rhetoricians of that aſſembly, that they were not yet corrupted by venality, or debauched by luxury. The conduct of that wiſe and conſiderate body in their ſeveral tranſactions, evidently tended to preſerve the property of the Eaſt-India Company: I muſt confeſs I was very diſagreeably affected with the conduct of Mr. Hutchinſon, their penſioned Governor, on the ſucceeding day, who very unſeaſonably, and as I am informed, very arbitrarily (not having the ſanction of law) framed and executed a mandate to diſperſe the People, which in my opinion, with a people leſs prudent and temperate, would have coſt him his head: The force of that body was directed to effect the return of the Teas to Great-Britain; much argument was expended, much entreaty was made uſe of to effect this deſirable purpoſe—Mr. Rotch behaved in my eſtimation very unexceptionable; his diſpoſition was ſeemingly to comport with the deſires of the People to convey the Teas to the original proprietors. The Conſignees have behaved like Scoundrels in refuſing to take the conſignment, or indemnify the owner of the ſhip which conveyed this deteſtable commodity to this port; every poſſible ſtep was taken to preſerve this property; the people being exaſperated with the conduct of adminiſtration in this affair, great pains were taken, and much policy exerted to procure a ſtated watch * for this purpoſe. The body of the people determined the Tea ſhould not be landed: the determination was deliberate, was judicious; the ſacrifice of their Rights, of the Union of all the Colonies, would have been the effect, had they conducted with leſs reſolution: On the Committee of Correſpondence they devolved the care of ſeeing their reſolutions ſeaſonably executed; that body, as I have been informed by one of their members, had taken every ſtep prudence and patriotiſm could ſuggeſt, to effect the deſirable purpoſe, but were defeated. The Body once more aſſembled, I was again preſent; ſuch a collection of the people was to me a novelty; near ſeven thouſand perſons from ſeveral towns, Gentlemen, Merchants, Yeomen and others, reſpectable for their rank and abilities, and venerable for their age and character, conſtituted the aſſembly; they decently, unanimouſly and firmly adhered to their former reſolution, that the baleful commodity, which was to rivet and eſtabliſh the duty, ſhould never be landed; to prevent the miſchief, they repeated the deſires of the committee of the Towns, that the owner of the ſhip ſhould apply for a clearance; it appeared that Mr. Rotch had been managed, and aſſembly, gave the War-Whoop, which was anſwered by a few in the galleries of the houſe where the aſſembly was convened; ſilence was commanded, and a prudent and peaceable deportment again enjoined. The Savages repaired to the ſhips which entertained the peſtilential Teas, and had began their ravage previous to the diſſolution of the meeting--they applied themſelves to the deſtruction of this commodity in earneſt, and in the ſpace of about two hours broke up 342 cheſts and diſcharged their contents into the ſea. A watch as I am informed was ſtationed to prevent embezzlement, and not a ſingle ounce of Tea was ſuffered to be purloined by the populace: One or two perſons being detected in endeavouring to pocket a ſmall quantity were ſtripped of their acquiſitions and very roughly handled—It is worthy remark that although a conſiderable quantity of goods of different kinds were ſtill remaining on board the veſſels, no injury was ſuſtained; ſuch attention to private property was obſerved that a ſmall padlock belonging to the Captain of one of the Ships being broke, another was procured and ſent to him.—I cannot but expreſs my admiration at the conduct of this People! Uninfluenced by party or any other attachment, I preſume I ſhall not be ſuſpected of miſrepreſentation.—The Eaſt-India Company muſt conſole themſelves with this reflection, that if they have ſuffered, the prejudice they ſuſtain does not ariſe from enmity to them: a fatal neceſſity has rendered this cataſtrophe inevitable—the landing the tea would have been fatal,
as it would have ſaddled the colo
impoſed without their conſe
power on earth can effect. T
numbers, ſpirit and illuminati
periment dangerous, the de
Conſignees muſt attribute to
of the property of the Eaſt-In
they ſeaſonably quieted the
by a reſignation, all had been
houſe, and the man who diſgr
preſenting him, acting in co
inveterate enemies of America
every meaſure concerted to re
That American virtue may d
to enſlave them, is the warme
I ſhall return home doubly forti
tion to prevent that deprecated calamity, the landing the teas in Rhode-Iſland, and conſole myſelf with the happieſt aſſurances that my brethren have not leſs virtue, leſs reſolution than their neighbours.

An IMPARTIAL OBSERVER.

Another Account concludes thus: "The Maſters and Owners are well pleaſed that their Ships are thus cleared; and the People are almoſt univerſally congratulating each other on this happy Event."

Capt. Loring in a Brig from London for this Place, having 58 Cheſts of the deteſted Tea on board, was caſt aſhore on the Back of Cape-Cod laſt Friday ſe'nnight: 'Tis expected the Cape Indians will give us a good Account of the Tea againſt our next.

Extract of a letter from Philadelphia, dated December 11, 1773.

—"Your Reſolutions of the 29th ult. were publickly read at our Coffee-Houſe laſt Thurſday, to a large Company of our Merchants, who gave three Cheers by Way of *Approbation*."

We hear from Philadelphia, that Capt. Ayres, in a Ship chartered by the Eaſt-India Company, Company's importing Tea into America, ſubject to a duty here; and have entered into a number of ſpirited Reſolves relative to the ſame; fully agreeing with thoſe of the Town of Boſton, and their determination to aſſiſt in carrying them into Execution, at the hazard of their Lives and Fortunes.

Immediately on the Proceedings of the People here, on the 29th ult. being received in Philadelphia, all the Bells in the City were ſet a ringing.

A CARD.

DETECTOR preſents his due reſpects to Meſſieurs A. B. C. and D. and informs thoſe dark and villainous *Aſſaſſins* that their *Conſpiracies* againſt the Lives and Liberties of a Number of the moſt worthy *Patriots* in this *Metropolis*, and the *Vicinity*, are well known; their execrable Meaſures to ſecure and tranſport them abroad, are ſeaſonably diſcovered, their Perſons are marked, and if they are diſpoſed for a concealed Plot, they may probably fall into the Pit they are digging for others. *Boſton Gaz.*

SALEM, December 21.

We are informed, that 130 Patients, who were inoculated at Salem Hoſpital laſt Thurſday ſevennight, are now broke out with the Small-Pox, and are all in a fair Way of coming out well in a few Days. Two Children, inoculated ſeveral Days after the other Patients, are not yet broke out.

Divine Service was performed at the Hoſpital laſt Sunday, when the Rev. Mr. Payſon again officiated.

and Treaſurer will attend. Dec. 20, 1773.

John White, jun.

Has to SELL,

The beſt of Saltertuda SALT,

and Grenada RUM,

Salem, Dec. 20, 1773.

William Pickman

Acquaints his Friends and the Publick, that he has juſt received in Capt. Bruce from London, and is now opening at his Store next Door to the Cuſtom-Houſe in SALEM,

A very good Aſſortment of Engliſh and India GOODS, ſuitable for the Seaſon, which he is determined to ſell at ſo low a Rate that he doubts not but he ſhall give general Satiſfaction to his good Cuſtomers.

N. B. To be ſold at ſaid Store, the beſt of Ruſſia and Ravens DUCK.

Juſt publiſhed, and to be ſold by the Printers of this Paper.

ESSEX GAZETTE (SALEM, MA)

December 21, 1773

Printed five days after the tea was destroyed in Boston Harbor, the *Essex Gazette* featured a lengthy eyewitness account from "An Impartial Observer" that was first published the previous day in the *Boston Gazette* and *Evening-Post*. This version of events is widely cited in history books.

DECEMBER 21, 1773

The

ESSEX GAZETTE

BOSTON, December 20.

Messrs. Printers,

HAVING accidentally arrived at Boston upon a visit to a Friend, the Evening before the Meeting of the Body of the People on the 29th of November, curiosity and the pressing invitation of my most kind host induced me to attend the Meeting ; I must confess I was most agreeably, and I hope I shall be forgiven by this People if I say so unexpectedly entertained and instructed by the regular, reasonable and sensible conduct and expression of the People there collected, that I should rather have entertained an idea of being transported to the British senate than to an adventitious and promiscuous assembly of People of a remote Colony ; were I not convinced by the genuine uncorrupted integrity and manly hardihood of the Rhetoricians of that assembly, that they were not yet corrupted by venality, or debauched by luxury. The conduct of that wise and considerate body in their several transactions, evidently tended to preserve the property of the East-India Company [...]

Previous to the dissolution, a number of Persons, supposed to be the Aboriginal Natives from their complection, approaching near the door of the assembly, gave the War-Whoop, which was answered by a few in the galleries of the house where the assembly was convened ; silence was commanded, and a prudent and peacable deportment again enjoined. The Savages repaired to the ships which entertained the pestilential Teas, and had began their ravage previous to the dissolution of the meeting—they applied themselves to the destruction of this commodity in earnest, and in the space of about two hours broke up 342 chests and discharged their contents into the sea. A watch as I am informed was stationed to prevent embezzlement, and not a single ounce of tea suffered to be purloined by the populace : One or two persons being detected in endeavouring to pocket a small quantity were stripped of their acquisitions and very roughly handled—It is worthy remark that although a considerable quantity of goods of different kinds were still remaining on board the vessels, no injury was sustained ; such attention to private property was observed that a small padlock belonging to the Captain of one of the Ships being broke, another was procured and sent to him.—I cannot but express my admiration at the conduct of this People ! Uninfluenced by party or any other attachment, I presume I shall not be suspected of misrepresentation.—The East-India Company must console themselves with this reflection, that if they have suffered, the prejudice they sustain does not arise from enmity to them : a fatal necessity has rendered this catastrophe inevitable—the landing the tea would have been fatal, as it would have saddled the colonies with a duty imposed without their consent, and which no power on earth can effect. Their strength and numbers, spirit and illumination render the experiment dangerous, the defeat certain: The Consignees must attribute to themselves the loss of the property of the East-India Company : had they seasonably quieted the minds of the people by a resignation, all had been well ; the custom-house, and the man who disgraces Majesty by representing him, acting in confederacy with the inveterate enemies of America, stupidly opposed every measure concerted to return the Teas.----That American virtue may defeat every attempt to enslave them, is the warmest wish of my heart. I shall return home doubly fortified in my resolution to prevent that deprecated calamity, the landing the teas in Rhode-Island, and console myself with the happiest assurances that my brethren have not less virtue, less resolution than their neighbours.

An IMPARTIAL OBSERVER

APRIL 18, 1774

The PENNSYLVANIA PACKET

Jan. 28. Letters from Boston complain much of the taste of their fish being altered: Four or five hundred chests of tea may have so contaminated the water in the harbor, that the fish may have contracted a disorder not unlike the nervous complaints of the human body. Should this complaint extend itself as far as the banks of Newfoundland, our Spanish and Portugal fish trade may be much affected by it.

[...]

It is said that the tea thrown into the Sea at Boston is valued at 18,000 l. at 1s. 6d. per pound. The whole sent to America is said to be worth about 300,000 l. which is returning home, not being suffered to be landed.

the liſt of thoſe gentlemen who were recommended by the Houſe of Commons to his Majeſty for ſome adequate employment, when the act was repealed, yet he is the only one of them who has not been provided for. All theſe circumſtances, ſo highly recommendatory of him, with a character perfectly unexceptionable, ſeem only to have operated as a bar to his preferment, till Lord Dartmouth, who has always been diſtinguiſhed for his upright and equitable conduct, rewarded his long-neglected merit. The propriety of his choice reſounds much to his Lordſhip's wiſdom, as well as to his honour; for Colonel Mercer's perfect knowledge of that country, his thorough acquaintance with the American laws, and the well-known candour, integrity, and firmneſs of his mind (excluſive of his other fair pretenſions) render him better qualified for that appointment than almoſt any other man.

Jan. 26. Advice is received from Tunis, that three Barbarian veſſels have been equipped againſt the veſſels of any chriſtian powers that ſhall approach near that port.

Letters from Peterſburgh adviſe that Admiral Spiritoff is recalled from the Mediterranean, and that Admiral Baſbaille will ſucceed him.

It is now ſaid to be ſettled by a great Perſonage for the Queen of Denmark to come to England the enſuing ſummer.

When the Duke of Glouceſter was at Paris, Morgan, the highwayman, preſented a petition to him, praying that his highneſs would procure him a pardon: The Duke gave him two guineas but told him his offences were of that nature that he could do nothing elſe for him.

It is again in agitation to appoint a commander in chief on the Britiſh eſtabliſhment; and it is generally ſuppoſed that his royal highneſs the Duke of Glouceſter will ſucceed to it.

The following ſhocking affair happened at Munich the beginning of this month:—Baron Waldeck was ſtabbed by his Valet de Chambre in his bed; the murderer was inſtantly detected, but he begged leave of the guard to go with him into his room, as he wiſhed to take along with him ſome papers of conſequence. This was granted, and the guards poſted themſelves at the doors and windows: but not minding farther what the priſoner was about, he took a well charged piſtol and ſhot himſelf. It ſince appears by ſome notes found upon him, that he was promiſed 3000 florins for that heinous action; and the hand writing appears to be that of his young maſter, the only ſon of the Baron, about ſeventeen years of age, who was immediately ſecured upon ſuſpicion.

Jan. 28. Letters from Boſton complain much of the taſte of their fiſh being altered: Four or five hundred cheſts of tea may have ſo contaminated the water in the harbour, that the fiſh may have contracted a diſorder not unlike the nervous complaints of the human body. Should this complaint extend itſelf as far as the banks of Newfoundland, our Spaniſh and Portugal fiſh trade may be much affected by it.

An act, it is ſaid, will paſs this ſeſſion, diſqualifying all perſons from voting for members of Parliament that do not poſſeſs a freehold of ten pounds a year.

Council, laſt week, only voted two regiments to America. His Majeſty has ordered five more from Ireland. The Boſtonians are to be chaſtiſed, and are to drink tea, though ever ſo great an emetic.

The Polly, Captain Ayres, is juſt arrived at Dover, returned from North-America with

Tea. On her arrival at Philadelphia, the inhabitants informed the Captain that they would not ſuffer him either to land or enter his cargo at the Cuſtom-Houſe.

It is ſaid that the tea thrown into the Sea at Boſton is valued at 18,000 l. at 1*s.* 6*d.* per pound. The whole ſent to America is ſaid to be worth about 300,000 l. which is returning home, not being ſuffered to be landed.

Extract of a letter from an Engliſh gentleman at Copenhagen, Dec. 14.

" By ſome of the Engliſh new-papers which have lately fallen into my hands, I find that you, in England, think that the King of Denmark is in a ſtate of imbecility; be that as it will, however if he is ſo, his ſubects are happy, and his actions every day prove that his mind is leſs tainted than the minds of any neighbouring Princes. He has lately ſtruck out a number of penſions which were burthenſome to his people, and has found a ſcheme himſelf to leſſen ſeveral heavy taxes very much. Are theſe actions that denote a weak mind? If they are I ſhould not be ſorry to hear that —— —— was in a ſtate of imbecility; you would perhaps then be happier than you are.—The firſt opportunity that offers, I intend writing again."

Extract of a letter from the Hague, Jan. 21.

" One of the two commiſſaries who went over to England laſt year to ſettle the differences which

PENNSYLVANIA PACKET (PHILADELPHIA)

April 18, 1774

Speculation about the cost of the destroyed tea was reported in the *Pennsylvania Packet*, but the East India Company would later claim £9,659 in damages. In the same issue, it is lightheartedly reported that "Letters from Boston complain much of the taste of their fish being altered."

ESSEX GAZETTE (SALEM, MA)

February 8, 1774

Not all colonists approved of the destruction and vandalism on the night of December 16. In late January 1774, the town of Marshfield, thirty miles south of Boston, voted and resolved that the Boston Tea Party was illegal, unjust, and "of a dangerous tendency."

and this Province in particular, of their Liberties: And being a Volunteer in the executing it, in order to secure himself seems to have procured ...

made happy by the Removal of all its Grievances.

In the mean time the Board are affected with the deepest concern, that any part of their Conduct should be disapproved by his Majesty: but they humbly trust, that when his Majesty shall be informed of the Reasons on which it is grounded, it will notwithstanding be the Object of his Gracious Approbation.

Extract of the proceedings of the town of Marshfield, *on the 31st of January*, 1774.

THIS town taking into consideration the late tumultuous and as we think illegal proceedings in the town of Boston, in the detention and destruction of the teas belonging to the East India company, which we apprehend will affect our properties if not our liberties, think it our indispensible duty to show our disapprobation of such measures and proceedings:——Therefore Voted and Resolved, as the opinion of this town,——That the late measures and proceedings in the town of Boston, in the detention and destruction of the teas belonging to the East-India company, were illegal and unjust & of a dangerous tendency.—That Abijah White, Esq; the present Representative of this town, be and hereby is instructed and directed to use his utmost endeavours that the perpetrators of those mischiefs may be detected and brought to justice. And as the country has been heretofore drawn in to pay their proportionable part of the expence which accrued from the riotous and unruly proceedings and conduct of certain individuals in the town of Boston,—if application should be made to the general court by the East-India company or any other persons for a consideration for the loss of said teas, you are by no means to acquiesce, but bear your testimony against any measures by which expence may accrue to the province in general, or to the town of Marshfield

counsel moved the Court for a new trial, which occasioned the Governor to be summoned before a very awful tribunal, where the following particulars ...

... The great personage soon appeared, and confirmed this opinion, by addressing himself to Lord Mansfield in the following manner:

"It is from you, my Lord, that we expect a clear account of the heavy charge brought lately against this gentleman, in one of our courts of justice; the relations already given us have been so partially coloured, and so indistinctively confused, that we must rely on the implicit truth of your recital, as the only means of investigating to our own satisfaction, a matter that so nearly affects ourselves, and the safety of our subjects in foreign governments. We have, my Lord (addressing himself to Lord North) desired your attendance, not alone to have the benefit of your advice, but to shew you that we will not in the least encourage or support any man, who, trusted with our delegated authority, shall use it to the worst of purposes, that of oppressing his fellow subjects. And you, Sir (speaking to the Viceroy) we thought proper to command your attendance, to bear our sincere opinion of your conduct, and to convince you, that all reliance upon our protection, assistance, or future favour is in vain, if we find you have merited by oppression and injustice, the stigma which has been thrown on your character." Lord Mansfield then entered into a minute detail of the circumstances, but eloquently palliated the most flagrant; he recited the provocations given to the Viceroy, in a stile that set them on a level with the most provoking injuries to his person and government; in which colourings he was more than once interrupted by Lord North, which set them in their true light. When his Lordship had finished, the King demanded his positive and real opinion. whether the verdict given was just and adequate? To this plain demand, enforced by a determinate voice and accent, the equivocating P—was obliged to give an affirmative reply. Lord North was then asked his opinion, who replied, that he had not the least doubt of the justness of the verdict; that the tyranny and cruelty of the Viceroy were but too palpable; though it must be confessed, some provoca-

acceptin... We ...

...Hampshi... Master: J. Malc... for want ... his Maje... tion to th... ed.—The... ally been...

Soon a... tarred and... borough, about an... *Extract of*...

"Last ... House of ... was entire... in it, the ... by the ho... full of Sm... all in a Fl... Family ex... of about ... unrelentin... moved her... and seven ... got out wi... escaped, (... dren) wen... half Leg de... they were c... being in tha... a situation ... ed: The n... by Acciden... Trees and c...

We hear ... one Day la... so much w... he expired i...

Clock, died here, the Hon.
Esq; Lieutenant-Governor of this Provi
the 68th Year of his Age.—His Remains are to
be interr'd To-Morrow Afternoon.

On the Evening of the 17th of last Month, a Pedlar, with a Budget of Tea, made his Appearance at Montague, in the County of Hampshire, and put up at the Tavern there; which taking Air, a Number of Persons (well fraught with *Tar and Feathers*) went to the Inn, determined to give him the modern Dress, thinking this a more lenient as well as ready Measure to put an immediate Stop to a Conduct so injurious to the Community, than to the *Rigour of Law*; but as the Man appeared very humble, plead Innocence, promised to return the Tea to the Place from whence it came, not to offend in the like Manner for the future, and to submit to whatever Terms they should think reasonable to impose; they dismissed him, determining to apply *an effectual Remedy* to the next Offender.

The following melancholly Accident happened on Wednesday, viz. As a Sleigh with tw
and five People, were returning from
at Haddam, and crossing Connectic
Rods above East Haddam Landing
through, when one young Wom
Gates, Daughter of Mr. Josh
Haddam, was drowned, toge
Horses, who were carried u
Current.

Saturday last the Coop
longing to Mr. Gideon
consumed by Fire, to
of Hay.

Married at New-Y
Mr. Paschal Nelson
to Miss Hester Sea
eminent Merchan

Married at H
Mr. Emerson,
chant, to Miss
muel Hobart, Esq

YEsterda
a B
have advi
Symmes,
Earl of
By Capt.
of Decem
ligence;

N,
and
etts-
ncil.
mea-
ency
Ma-
, Esq;
ature,
y over
March
Year

totidem
ent, and

oregoing
tives are
fore pray,
of all the
Governor
e said P
make An-
foregoing
and Trial
thereof, he
e forthwith
some other
ointed in his

ers, Mr. Phil-
r. Paine, Col.
reenleaf.
in the House,

m of the House.

Mr.
Capt.
Abraham F
Samuel Bancroft,
Mr. Peter Bent,
William Stickney
Capt. Josiah Stone
Mr. Jonas Stone,
Mr. Simeon Spa
Capt. Joseph Tw
Mr. Thomas P
Capt. Ebenezer
Mr. Benjamin
N A
ha Jones, E
h White,
Edson,

LIBERTY. TREE

Tea

CHAPTER V

REBELLION

Introduction

Soon after news of the Boston Tea Party arrived in London, Parliament struck back with an iron fist that included closing the Port of Boston and stripping Massachusetts of its right to self-govern. In April 1774, King George III appointed General Thomas Gage, a veteran of the French and Indian War, as commander in chief of the British forces in America and royal governor of Massachusetts, replacing the much-hated Governor Thomas Hutchinson. Tensions escalated and an arms race unfolded as New England militia and Gage's army scrambled to secure and hide powder and shot from one another. Meanwhile, Massachusetts colonists assembled their own de facto government to effectively rule the colony from the countryside. On the brink of war, a twelve-colony congress is called to discuss and debate a united resistance.

Boston Gazette
March 7, 1774

"The Bostonians
Paying the Excise-Man
or Tarring & Feathering"
Library of Congress

REPORTING THE

COERCIVE ACTS

By Ray Raphael

Colonists did not unite behind the act of political vandalism we now celebrate as the Boston Tea Party. John Adams called it "the grandest event, which has ever yet happened since the controversy with Britain opened," but George Washington chided Bostonians for "their conduct in destroying tea," and Benjamin Franklin thought the East India Company should be compensated for the ruined merchandise.

People did unite, however, around the harsh repression that followed. To punish the vandals and those who supported them, Parliament passed four acts it thought would bring rebels to their knees. People in Britain called them the Coercive Acts, but in America, they were labeled the Intolerable Acts.

The first is the best known: the Boston Port Act, which closed Boston Harbor until somebody paid for the destroyed tea. Related acts, to facilitate enforcement, permitted British soldiers to be housed in unoccupied buildings and allowed for the removal of Massachusetts residents to Britain to stand trial.

To punish the vandals and those who supported them, Parliament passed four acts it thought would bring rebels to their knees. People in Britain called them the Coercive Acts, but in America, they were labeled the Intolerable Acts.

Instead of isolating Bostonians, these measures triggered a sympathetic response from other colonies. Political groups passed supportive resolutions (posts from Connecticut House of Representatives, Newark, New York, and Philadelphia in June 20, 1774, *Pennsylvania Packet*), organized relief efforts (*Boston Evening-Post*, October 31, 1774), and selected delegates for an intercolonial assembly—the future Continental Congress—to coordinate their efforts.

The most consequential act of repression, though, was the "act for the better regulating the Government of the province of the Massachusetts Bay" (known today as the Massachusetts Government Act), which disenfranchised the province's citizens and spurred them to shed British rule. No longer could residents gather in town meetings, unless the royal governor gave his assent and approved all agenda items. The powerful council, formerly chosen by the people's representatives, would henceforth be selected by the Crown, while sheriffs and judges would be chosen by the Crown-appointed governor, not the people. Even the selection of jurors was now out of the people's hands. The very heart of the Massachusetts Charter of 1691, the provincial constitution, had been unilaterally set aside.

Resistance was immediate, widespread, and multifaceted:

- Town meetings continued despite the ban. In Salem, one block from the temporary headquarters of Governor Thomas Gage, citizens held a meeting. When Gage ordered the arrest of seven alleged ringleaders, three thousand local residents marched on the jail to force their release. In neighboring Danvers, citizens held a town meeting "and continued it two or three howers longer than was necessary, to see if he would interrupt 'em," one man reported. "He was acquainted with it, but reply'd–'Damn 'em! I won't do any thing about it unless his Majesty sends me more troops.'"

- All thirty-six Crown-appointed councilors (called "mandamus counsellors" at the time) were intimidated by groups of angry citizens and forced either to resign or to flee to Boston, where they would be protected by British troops. Timothy Ruggles, for instance, had his horse mutilated, while Abijah

Willard chose to sign a humiliating recantation to secure his safety, asking "forgiveness of all the honest, worthy gentlemen, that I have offended" by taking the oath to serve under the new act, which undermined "the Charter Rights and Liberties of this province" (August 25 Sturbridge dateline in September 5, 1774, *Massachusetts Gazette; and the Boston Post-Boy and Advertiser*).

- Finally, and most significantly, crowds numbering in the thousands closed the county courts (Barnstable dateline in October 31, 1774, *Boston Evening-Post*), the farthest reach of British imperial authority under the hated Massachusetts Government Act. More on these dramatic events in the next three sections.

THE BOSTONIANS IN DISTRESS
Library of Congress

(*above*) Depicting Boston's sufferings as a result of the Coercive Acts, this print shows three sailors feeding starving Bostonians suspended in a cage from the Liberty Tree.

THE ABLE DOCTOR, OR AMERICA SWALLOWING THE BITTER DRAUGHT
Library of Congress

(*left*) Lord North forces tea down the throat of America, represented by a Native American, and she spits it back in his face. In North's pocket is a copy of the Boston Port Bill.

B O S T O N, June …

In the Houſe of Repreſentatives of the Engliſh Colony of Connecticut.

THIS Houſe taking into their ſerious conſideration ſundry acts of the Britiſh Parliament, in which their power and right to impoſe duties and taxes upon his Majeſty's ſubjects in the Britiſh colonies and plantations in America, for the purpoſe of raiſing a revenue, are declared, attempted to be exerciſed, and in various ways enforced and carried into execution, and eſpecially a very late act, in which pains and penalties are inflicted on the capital of a neighbouring province, a precedent juſtly alarming to every Britiſh colony in America, and which being admitted, and eſtabliſhed, their lives, liberties, and properties are at the mercy of a tribunal where innocence may be puniſhed upon the accuſation and evidence of wicked men, without defence, and even without knowing the accuſer. A precedent calculated to terrify them into ſilence and ſubmiſſion whilſt they are ſtripped of their invaluable rights and liberties —do think it their duty, and expedient at this time to renew their claim to the rights, liberties and immunities of freeborn Engliſhmen, to which they are juſtly intitled by the laws of nature, by the royal grant and charter of his late Majeſty King Charles the ſecond, and by long, and uninterupted poſſeſſion, and thereupon do declare and reſolve as follows, viz.

PENNSYLVANIA PACKET (PHILADELPHIA)

June 20, 1774

—

While colonists did not unite behind the act of vandalism known as the Boston Tea Party, they did unite around the Coercive Acts that followed. The Boston Port Act triggered sympathy from other colonies, including supportive resolutions like the ones found here from the Connecticut House of Representatives, Newark, New York, and Philadelphia.

or by their repreſentatives, and are not to be unſeiſed of their liberties and free cuſtoms, ſentenced and condemned but by lawful judgement of their peers, and that the ſaid rights and immunities are recognized and confirmed to the inhabitants of the colony by the royal grant and charter aforeſaid, and are their undoubted right to all intents, conſtructions and purpoſes whatſoever.

III. That the only lawful repreſentatives of the freemen of this colony are the perſons they elect to ſerve as members of the General Aſſembly thereof.

IV. That it is the juſt right and privilege of his Majeſty's liege ſubjects of this colony to be governed by the General Aſſembly in the article of taxing, and internal police, agreeable to the powers and privileges recognized and confirmed in the royal charter aforeſaid, which they have enjoyed for more than a century paſt, and have neither forfeited nor ſurrendered, but the ſame have been conſtantly recognized by the King and Parliament of Great-Britain.

V. That the erecting new and unuſual Courts of Admiralty, and veſting them with extraordinary powers, above, and not ſubject to the common law courts in this colony, to judge and determine in ſuits relating to the duties and forfeitures contained in ſaid acts, foreign to the accuſtomed and eſtabliſhed juriſdiction of the former Courts of Admiralty in America, is, in the opinion of this Houſe, highly dangerous to the liberties of his Majeſty's American ſubjects, contrary to the great charter of Engliſh liberty, and deſtructive of one of their moſt darling rights, that of trial by juries, which is juſtly eſteemed one chief excellence of the Britiſh conſtitution, and a principle branch of Engliſh liberty.

… confident, as it is not founded on …, but has been verified in fact, and by long experience, found to produce, according to our extent, and other circumſtances, as many loyal, virtuous, induſtrious, and well governed ſubjects, as any part of his Majeſty's dominions; and as truly zealous of and warmly engaged, to promote the beſt, good and real glory of the grand whole, which conſtitutes the Britiſh empire.

XI. That it is an indiſpenſible duty, which we owe to our King, our country, ourſelves and our poſterity, by all lawful ways and means in our power, to maintain, defend and preſerve theſe our rights and liberties, and to tranſmit them entire and inviolate to the lateſt generations. And that it is our fixed, determined, and unalterable reſolution, faithfully to diſcharge this our duty.

At their ſeſſions at Hartford, on the ſecond Thurſday of May, 1774, in the 14th year of his Majeſty's reign, the foregoing reſolutions, reported to the Houſe by their committee, were unanimouſly voted and ordered to be entered on their journal or record.

June 9. Monday afternoon two young Gentlemen came into Boſton from the county of Worceſter, relating that they had been alarmed with the report that a regiment of ſoldiers had been poſted at the entrance of this city, to cut off its communication with the country.—Many reſpectable perſons, they ſaid, had aſſembled upon the occaſion, … Sabbath evening, to … intelligence as … caſe they … report, they … ſand ſtrong, … Their ex- … be the minds … of their li- … ry at all diſ- … in their act. … that by the … ſſed, and the … is utterly va- … province and … ſolved, they … in what man- … tual ſecurity. … ſail of wood … tward, bound … o unload and load again, before they are permitted to take their departure.

At a meeting of the Freeholders and Inhabitants of the county of Eſſex, in the province of New-Jerſey, at Newark in the ſaid county, on Saturday the 11*th June*, 1774.

THIS meeting taking into ſerious conſideration ſome late alarming meaſures, adopted by the Britiſh parliament, for depriving his Majeſty's American ſubjects of their undoubted and conſtitutional rights and privileges; and particularly, the act for blockading the port of Boſton, which, appears to them, pregnant with the moſt dangerous conſequences to all his Majeſty's dominions in America: do unanimouſly reſolve and agree,

I. That under the enjoyment of our conſtitutional privileges and immunities, we will ever cheerfully render all due obedience to the crown of Great-Britain, as well as full faith and allegiance to his moſt gracious Majeſty, King George the Third; and do eſteem a firm dependance on the mother-country, eſſential to our political ſecurity and happineſs.

II. That the late act of Parliament relative to Boſton, which ſo abſolutely deſtroys every idea of ſafety and confidence, appears to us, big with the moſt dangerous and alarming conſequences; eſpecially, as ſubverſive of that very dependance, which we would earneſtly wiſh to continue, as our beſt ſafeguard and protection: and that we conceive, every well-wiſher to Great-Britain and her colonies, is now loudly called upon to exert his utmoſt abilities, in promoting every loyal and pru-

The port of Boſton was on Tueſday laſt cleared of every veſſel intended for ſea, it being the day on which the late act of Parliament preſcribes, that no veſſel, except in his Majeſty's ſervice, ſhall be allowed to depart from that port until the King in Council may be pleaſed to ſuſpend its operation.

P H I L A D E L P H I A, *June* 20.

At a meeting of the Freeholders and other inhabitants of the county of Frederick, and Gentlemen practiſing at the bar, held at the town of Wincheſter, the 8th of June, 1774, to conſider of the beſt mode to be fallen upon to ſecure their liberties and properties, and alſo to prevent the dangerous tendency of an act of Parliament paſſed in the fourteenth year of his preſent Majeſty's reign, entitled, An act to diſcontinue in ſuch manner and for ſuch time as are therein mentioned, the landing and diſcharging, lading and ſhipping of goods, wares and merchandize at the town, and within the harbour of Boſton, in the province of Maſſachuſetts-Bay, in North-America, evidently has to invade and deprive us of the ſame.

The Rev. Mr. Charles M. Thruſton being voted Moderator, a Committee of the following gentlemen, viz. the Rev. Charles M. Thruſton, Iſaac Zane, George Rootes, Angus M'Donald, Alexander White, George Johnſon, and Samuel Beall 3d, were appointed to draw up Reſolves ſuitable to the ſame occaſion, who withdrawing for a ſhort time, returned with the following Votes, viz.

V O T E D,

I. THAT we will always chearfully pay due ſubmiſſion to ſuch acts of government as his Majeſty has a right by law to exerciſe over his ſubjects, as ſovereign of the Britiſh dominions, and to ſuch only.

II. That it is the inherent right of Britiſh ſubjects to be governed and taxed by Repreſentatives choſen by themſelves only; and that every act of the Britiſh Parliament reſpecting the internal policy of North America, is a daring and unconſtitutional invaſion of our ſaid rights and privileges.

III. That the act of Parliament above mentioned is not only in itſelf repugnant to the fundamental laws of natural juſtice, in condemning perſons for a ſuppoſed crime unheard, but alſo a deſpotic exertion of unconſtitutional power, calculated to enſlave a free and loyal people.

IV. That the enforcing the execution of the ſaid act of Parliament by a military power, will have a neceſſary tendency to raiſe a civil war, thereby diſſolving that union which has ſo long happily ſubſiſted between the Mother Country and her Colonies; and that we will moſt heartily and unanimouſly concur with our ſuffering brethren of Boſton, and every other part of North-America that may be the immediate victims of tyranny, in promoting all proper meaſures to avert ſuch dreadful calamities, to procure a redreſs of our grievances, and to ſecure our common liberties.

V. It is the unanimous opinion of this meeting, that a joint reſolution of all the Colonies to ſtop all importations from Great-Britain, and exportations to it, till the ſaid act be repealed, will prove the ſalvation of North-America and her liberties: On the other hand, if they continue their imports and exports, there is the greateſt reaſon to fear that fraud, power, and the moſt odious oppreſſion, will riſe triumphant over right, juſtice, ſocial happineſs and freedom.

VI. That the Eaſt-India Company, thoſe ſervile tools of arbitrary power, have juſtly forfeited the eſteem and regard of all honeſt men; and that the better to manifeſt our abhorrence of ſuch abject compliance with the will of a venal Miniſtry in miniſtering all in their power, an increaſe of the fund of peculation; we will not purchaſe Tea, or any other kind of Eaſt-India commodities, either imported now, or hereafter to be imported, except ſalt-petre, ſpices and medicinal drugs.

VII. That it is the opinion of this meeting that Committees ought to be appointed for the purpoſe of affecting a general aſſociation, that the ſame meaſures may be purſued through the whole continent: That the Committees ought to correſpond with each other, and to meet at ſuch places and times as ſhall be agreed on, in order to form ſuch general aſſociation, and that when the ſame ſhall be formed and agreed on by the ſeveral Committees, we will ſtrictly adhere thereto; and till the general ſenſe of the continent ſhall be known, we do pledge ourſelves to each other and to our country, that we will inviolably adhere to the votes of this day.

VIII. That Charles M. Thruſton, Iſaac Zane, Angus M'Donald, Samuel Beall 3d, Alexander White, and George Rootes, be appointed a Committee for

changing the charter'd conſtitution of
of Maſſachuſetts Bay into a military
and the other impoweting the Govern
tenant Governor to ſend any perſon
England to be tried for actions comm
colony, are ſubverſive of every idea o
ſerves as a prelude to the fate of ea
Britiſh colony on this continent.

4. That a congreſs of deputies fron
lonies is the moſt probable and proper
curing relief for our ſuffering Brethr
redreſs and preſerving our natural rig
ties, and the eſtabliſhing peace and mut
between the mother-country and her
conſtitutional foundation.

5. That we will concur and join w
thren of the city and county of Phila
ſiring the Speaker of the Honourable
preſentatives of this province, to wri
ral Members of Aſſembly, requeſting
in the city of Philadelphia on any
than the firſt of Auguſt next, to take
rious conſideration our very alarmin
appoint deputies to attend at a gener
the colonies, at ſuch time and pla
agreed on.

As the notice of this meeting was
agreed that a general meeting be fix
the 25th inſtant, at the dwelling h
James, at the ſign of the Turk's He
at one o'clock, P. M. in order to ch
tee of Correſpondence, and to reſolv
modes or propoſitions as may be m
tain redreſs from thoſe grievances t
now groan under; at which time
thoſe who are entitled to vote for M
ſembly, and wiſh well to their poſte
can liberty, are requeſted to attend
advice in this alarming criſis.

Laſt Saturday afternoon many t
ſpectable inhabitants of this city a
near the State-houſe, agreeable to a
take into their conſideration certain
poſitions prepared to be laid befor
as it is impoſſible to inſert the pr
meeting in this paper, we muſt defer t

CUSTOM-HOUSE, PHILA

INWARD ENTR

Ship King of Pruſſia, W. Adam
Ship Molly, G. Johnſton, Genoa.
Brig Fancy, T. Murdoch, St. Vin
Sloop Rebecca, A. Culnan, Antig
Ship Nancy and Suky, J. Robinſo
Brig Mount-Holly, G. Bayley, St
Sloop Little Welcome, J. Lamber
Sch. Felicity, A. Keeble, Virgini
Sch. Betſy, F. Savage, Virginia.
Sch. Two Brothers, B. Clark, Ne
Sloop Lively, A. Lowell, Piſcataq
Sloop Diſcovery, A. Gall, North
Sch. Happy Return, G. Simpſon,
Sloop Suſanna, T. Chadwick, N
Sch. Sally, J. Buck, North Caroli
Sloop Robert, C. Metcalf, Virgi
Sloop Polly, J. Attwood, Nova-S
Sch. North-Iſland, J. Hannah, S

OUTWARD

Brig Samuel and Charles, T. V
Ship Molly, G. Johnſton, Liſbo
Sloop Betſy, V. Wightman, Rho
Sloop Hope, T. Aſheton, Seni C
Snow John & William, W. Britto
Sloop Adventure, J. Hutchings,
Brig Chance, J. Craig, Grenado
Sloop Lively, A. Lowell, Piſcat
Ship Nancy, C. Donavan, Liſbo
Ship Clementina, P. Brown, C

CLEARE

Sch. Experiment, D. Livingſt
Sloop Induſtry, C. Gale, North
Brig Cornelia, J. Forſter, Jamai
Sch. Betſy, F. Savage, Virginia.
Sch. Polly, J. Vicary, Dominca.
Brig Induſtry, P. Hodgkinſon,
Brig Mercury, J. Trimingham,
Brig Charlotte, P. Parker, Ja
Sch. Ambroſe, J. Wooten, Ne
Sloop Robert, C. Metcalf, Virg
Sloop Friendſhip, H. Parſul, Vi
Sloop Ranger, W. Pigott, Vir
Brig Adrian, J. Duncan, St. C
Brig Ranger, C. Biddle, Jama
Sloop Betſy and Ann, P. Ligh
Brig Lucy, J. Pyner, Jamaica
Sch. Felicity, A. Moore, Jama
Schooner Mary, J. Perott, St.
Sch. Betſy, R. Alcock, Domi
Ship James and Mary Ann, W.
Sch. Peggy, J. Keogh, Domi

VI. That the apprehending and carrying persons beyond the sea, to be tried for any crime alledged to be committed within this colony; or subjecting them to be tried by commissioners, or any court constituted by act of Parliament; or otherwise within this colony, in a summary way, without a jury, is unconstitutional, and subversive of the liberties and rights of the free subjects of this colony.

VII. That any harbour or port duly opened and constituted, cannot be shut up and discharged, but by an act of the legislature of the province or colony, in which such harbour or port is situated, without subverting the rights and liberties, and destroying the property of his Majesty's subjects.

VIII. That the late act of Parliament inflicting pains and penalties on the town of Boston, by blocking up their harbour, is a precedent justly alarming to the British Colonies in America, and wholly inconsistent with, and subversive of their constitutional rights and liberties.

IX. That whenever his Majesty's service shall require the aid of the inhabitants of this colony, the same fixed principles of loyalty, as well as self preservation which have hitherto induced us fully to comply with his Majesty's requisitions, together with the deep sense we have of its being our indispensible duty (in the opinion of this House) will ever hold us under the strongest obligations, which can be given, or desired, most chearfully to grant his Majesty, from time to time, our further proportion of men and money, for the defence, protection, security and other services, of the British American dominions.

X. That we look on the well-being, and greatest security of this colony, to depend, under God, on our connections with Great-Britain, which is ardently wished, may continue to the latest posterity, and that it is the humble opinion of this House that the constitution of this colony being understood and practised upon, as it has ever since it existed (till very lately) is the surest bond of union, confidence, and mutual prosperity, of our mother-country and us, and the last foundation on which to build, the good of the whole, whether considered in a civil, military or mercantile light; and of the truth of this opinion, we are the more confident, as it is not founded on speculation only, but has been verified in fact, and by long experience, found to produce, according to our extent, and other circumstances, as many loyal, virtuous, industrious, and well governed subjects, as any part of his Majesty's dominions; and as truly zealous of and warmly engaged, to promote the best, good and real glory of the grand whole, which constitutes the British empire.

XI. That it is an indispensible duty, which we owe to our King, our country, ourselves and our posterity, by all lawful ways and means in our power, to maintain, defend and preserve these our rights and liberties, and to transmit them entire and inviolate to the latest generations. And that it is our fixed, determined, and unalterable resolution, faithfully to discharge this our duty.

At their sessions at Hartford, on the second Thursday of May, 1774, in the 14th year of his Majesty's reign, the foregoing resolutions, reported to the House by their committee, were unanimously voted and ordered to be entered on their

dential measure towards obtaining a repeal of the said act of Parliament, and all others subversive of the undoubted rights and liberties of his Majesty's American subjects.

III. That it is our unanimous opinion, that it would conduce to the restoration of the liberties of America, should the colonies enter into a joint agreement not to purchase or use any articles of British manufactory; and especially any commodities imported from the East-Indies, under such restrictions as may be agreed upon by a general congress of the said colonies hereafter to be appointed.

IV. That this county will most readily and chearfully join their brethren of the other counties in this province, in promoting such congress of deputies, to be sent from each of the colonies, in order to form a general plan of union, so that the measures to be pursued for the important ends in view, may be uniform and firm: to which plan when concluded upon, we do agree faithfully to adhere. And do now declare ourselves ready to send a committee to meet with those from the other counties, at such time and place, as by them may be agreed upon, in order to elect proper persons to represent this province in the said general congress.

V. That the freeholders and inhabitants of the other counties in this province, be requested speedily to convene themselves together, to consider the present distressing state of our public affairs; and to correspond, and consult with such other committees, as may be appointed as well as with our committee, who are hereby directed to correspond and consult with such other committees, as also with those of any other province: and particularly, to meet with the said county commitees, in order to nominate and appoint deputies to represent this province in general congress.

VI. We do hereby unanimously request the following Gentlemen, to accept of that trust; and accordingly do appoint them our committee for the purposes aforesaid, viz. Stephen Crane, Henry Garriste, Joseph Riggs, William Livingston, William P. Smith, John De Hart, John Chetwood, Isaac Ogden and Elias Boudinot, Esqrs;

N E W - Y O R K, *June* 16.

The port of Boston was on Tuesday last cleared of every vessel intended for sea, it being the day on which the late act of Parliament prescribes, that no vessel, except in his Majesty's service, shall be allowed to depart from that port until the King in Council may be pleased to suspend its operation.

P H I L A D E L P H I A, *June* 20.

At a meeting of the Freeholders and other inhabitants of the county of Frederick, and Gentlemen practising at the bar, held at the town of Winchester, the 8th of June, 1774, to consider of the best mode to be fallen upon to secure their liberties and properties, and also to prevent the dangerous tendency of an act of Parliament passed in the fourteenth year of his present Majesty's reign, entitled, An act to discontinue in such manner and for such time as are therein mentioned, the landing and discharging, lading and shipping of goods, wares and merchandize at the town, and within the harbour of Boston, in the province of Massachusetts-Bay, in North-America, evidently has to invade and deprive us of the same.

The Rev. Mr. Charles M. Thruston being voted

the purposes aforesaid; and that they, or any three of them, are hereby fully impowered to act.

Which being read, were unanimously assented to and subscribed.

On Monday the 6th instant tickets were posted up in different parts of Frederick county, Virginia, signed by the friends of liberty, requesting the Gentlemen Merchants, Freeholders, and other inhabitants of the county to meet at the Court-house, on the ensuing Wednesday, at three o'clock in the afternoon, to consider of the most proper measures to prevent the fatal consequences apprehended from the act of Parliament mentioned in the votes, and to defend and secure the rights and liberties of America. In consequence of which (though the notice did not exceed 48 hours) a great concourse assembled at the time and place appointed. The Court-house being too small to contain the company, they adjourned to the Church, where the above votes were unanimously agreed to. The general opinion of the people there seems to be, that the Boston scheme of non-importation from Great-Britain, and exportation to it, is the only probable means to obtain redress of our grievances, and shew great eagerness that it may be universally adopted.

We hear from Fort-Pitt, that the Shawanese have lately murdered eighteen White People, within nine miles of that place, and that several parties of Indians have gone forth to war against the defenceless inhabitants of the frontiers of Virginia and Pennsylvania: That it is supposed all the English traders in the Shawanese towns are killed by the Savages, and about fifteen hundred families, settled to the westward of the Allegany mountains, have deserted their habitations, and fled for sanctuary to the more interior parts of the country; and that the traders at Fort Pitt are about leaving that place as soon as they can form a party strong enough to venture forth. An Indian war seems inevitable.

At a meeting of a respectable body of the Freeholders, Inhabitants of the county of Chester, on Saturday the 18th of June, 1774. The following resolutions were deliberately and unanimously agreed on, viz.

1. THAT it is an absolute right, inherent in every English subject, to have the free use, enjoyment and disposal of all his property either by himself or representative, and that no other power on earth can legally divest him of it.

2. That we apprehend the act of Parliament for shutting up the port of Boston (until his Majesty's duties be duly collected, &c.) is highly arbitrary and oppressive to the inhabitants of that town, and, in its consequences may endanger the liberties of all the British colonies in America.

3. That the two bills mentioned in the last advices from London to be passing in Parliament, one changing the charter'd constitution of the province of Massachusetts Bay into a military government; and the other impowering the Governor, or Lieutenant Governor to send any person or persons to England to be tried for actions committed in that colony, are subversive of every idea of liberty and serves as a prelude to the fate of each charter'd British colony on this continent.

4. That a congress of deputies from the said colonies is the most probable and proper mode of procuring relief for our suffering Brethren, obtaining redress and preserving our natural rights and liberties, and the establishing peace and mutual confidence between the mother-country and her colonies on a constitutional foundation.

5. That we will concur and join with our Brethren of the city and county of Philadelphia in desiring the Speaker of the Honourable House of Representatives of this province, to write to the several Members of Assembly, requesting them to meet in the city of Philadelphia on any day, not later than the first of August next, to take into their serious consideration our very alarming situation, to appoint deputies to attend at a general congress for

cester, relating that they had been alarmed with the report that a regiment of soldiers had been posted

der White, George Johnson, and Samuel Beall 3d, were appointed to draw up Resolves suitable to the same occasion, who withdrawing for a short time,

agreed that a general meeting be fixed on Saturday the 25th instant, at the dwelling house of Jacob James, at the sign of the Turk's Head, in Goshen,

BOSTON EVENING-POST

October 31, 1774

In addition to the post from New Haven reporting on relief for "our Brethren at Boston," this issue details the closing of the Court of Common Pleas in the town of Barnstable, accomplished by "a great many people" from Barnstable, Plymouth, and Bristol counties.

BARNSTABLE, October 10, 1774.

ON Tueſday the 27th ult. the Time for the Court of General Seſſions of the Peace, and Inferior Court of Common Pleas for this County to ſit, a great number of People from this, and the neighbouring Counties of Plymouth and Briſtol, being aſſembled before the Court-Houſe door in this Town; after chooſing a Moderator, Voted and Reſolved, That it was inexpedient for ſaid Courts to ſit, under the preſent ſituation of our public affairs, until the opinion of the Continental or of a Provincial Congreſs could be known; and therefore choſe a Committee, viz. Dr. *Nathaniel Freeman* and Mr. *Stephen Nye*, of Sandwich, Capt. *Daniel Crocker* of Barnſtable, Capt. *Noah Fearing* of Wareham, and Dr. *John Pitcher* of Rocheſter, to preſent the following Addreſs to the Juſtices of ſaid Court, then convened at the Houſe of Mr. Crocker, Innholder in this Town.

To the Honorable Juſtices of his Majeſty's Inferior Court of Common Pleas, and Court of General Seſſions of the Peace, for the County of Barnſtable.

May it pleaſe your Honors,

THE Inhabitants of this Province, being greatly alarmed at the late unconſtitutional Acts of the Britiſh Parliament, conſidering them as calculated to eſtabliſh tyranny and oppreſſion inſtead of the once happy conſtitution of this Province; in conſequence of which many reſpectable Counties in the ſame have prevented the ſitting of the Inferior Courts, as well as Superior; we judge, not from an apprehenſion, merely, that they were not *conſtitutional*; but, from a ſuppoſition, that there might be appeals from *them* to the *Superior Court*, the Chief Juſtice of which receiving his ſupport from the Crown, independent of the grants of the People, cannot fail to have an unhappy bias in favor of ſaid unconſtitutional Acts; and two others, of the ſuperior Judges, having ſworn to carry the ſame Acts into execution; and judging, that by proceeding upon appeals from a Court friendly to the Conſtitution, and zealous for their Country's cauſe, to the ſaid *Superior Court*, we might in *this way*, if no other, open a door for the ſaid Chief Juſtice and his aſſiſtants to execute their Commiſſions on the plan of the ſaid oppreſſive Acts.

Wherefore a great number of the Inhabitants of the County of Barnſtable, being now convened, with ſeveral others from the ſeveral Counties in Old Plymouth Colony, taking into ſerious conſideration the neceſſity of uſing every precaution to prevent the operation of ſaid Acts, & believing the following one neceſſary, do humbly requeſt your Honors to deſiſt from all buſineſs in ſaid Courts, and from holding any Seſſions thereof, till the minds of the Continental, or of a Provincial Congreſs, be obtained:---And that your Honors would aſſure this body, that you will not, in any manner, aſſiſt in carrying ſaid unconſtitutional Acts into execution, nor hold any commiſſion in conſequence of ſaid Acts, and upon the new eſtabliſhment, or in any manner conform thereto; but that you will uſe your utmoſt endeavors to prevent the ſame from taking place.

Barnſtable, Sept. 27, 1774.	*N. Freeman, S. Nye, D. Crocker, N. Fearing, T. Pitcher,*	A Committee choſen by the Body of the People to preſent this Addreſs to your Honors in their Name.

The Addreſs being preſented accordingly, the Juſtices after taking the ſame into conſideration, returned the following Anſwer, viz.

TO Nathaniel Freeman, John Pitcher, Stephen Nye, Daniel Crocker, *and* Noah Fearing, *a Committee, as they ſay, choſen by the Body of the People, to preſent an Addreſs, this 27th of September, 1774, to the Honorable Juſtices of his Majeſty's Inferior Court of Common Pleas, and Court of General Seſſions of the Peace. ---Said Addreſs being preſented to the Juſtices of ſaid County, or at leaſt at many as are preſent: The ſaid Juſtices in anſwer thereto, ſay, That they are as much concerned at the late uncon-* [...] *provincial congreſs can be fully known, as we can by no means apprehend that any ill conſequences can attend the ſetting of ſaid Courts, until this month expires.*

		James Otis,
David Thatcher,	Kenelm Winſlow,	Thomas Smith,
Daniel Davis,	Joſeph Otis,	Edward Bacon,
Meletiah Bourn,	Iſaac Hinkley,	David Gorham,
Shearjaſhub Bourn.	Nymphas Marſton,	Solomon Otis,

The anſwer being communicated to the people, after taking the ſame into conſideration and thoroughly deliberating thereon, and juſt indignation of the people towards them for addreſſing the late infamous governor Hutchinſon, upon his departure from this province, whereby they ſaid their endeavours to ſupport, encourage and applaud, a *known Traitor*, and *inveterate Enemy*, to the country.——That ſaid addreſs was, in the apprehenſion of the people, no leſs falſe and deſigning, than flattering and fulſome, and diſcovered the unparalleled vanity, inſolence and audacity of the addreſſors, in daring, openly, to contradict the the united expreſs'd ſentiments of both houſes of the General Court, as well as of all America; by which conduct, they have forfeited the eſteem of the public, and enliſted under the banners of ſaid Hutchinſon, as enemies to the cauſe of liberty; for which they ought immediately to make ſatisfaction to the offended public.

The Juſtices and Sheriff ſigned the reſpective *declarations*, and the Addreſſors the reſpective *confeſſions* encloſed herewith, which were voted ſatisfactory. [*But the Publication of them, for want of Room, muſt be deferr'd till next Week.*]

The body of people then voted and reſolved, That the Military officers, holding commiſſions under a Captain-General, at the head of forces raiſed againſt the Rights and Properties, and conſequently the Lives of the inhabitants of this country and who is conſtantly making hoſtile preparations againſt it, muſt themſelves be conſidered as enemies to the country likewiſe, unleſs they immediately reſign their commiſſions: And therefore a committee was choſen to apply to, and acquaint them herewith, and to deſire them to reſign accordingly; and alſo to apply to the deputy-ſheriffs for them to ſign a declaration, reſpecting ſaid oppreſſive acts, ſuitable to their office.

The body of the people alſo voted to addreſs the honorable James Otis, Eſq; of this Town, as one of the conſtitutional Councellors of the Province, and pray his Honor's Attendance at the General Court, to be holden at Salem on the 5th Day of October next—The whole body accordingly marched in proceſſion to him, and preſented to him the following Addreſs, viz.

To the Honorable JAMES OTIS, Eſq;

May it pleaſe your Honour,

THE body of people aſſembled from the ſeveral counties of Barnſtable, Plymouth and Briſtol, on the 28th day of Sept. 1774, at or near the court houſe in Barnſtable, beg leave to addreſs your Honour, as one of his Majeſty's conſtitutional council of this province; and to aſſure you that we entertain a very high and grateful ſenſe of that *integrity*, and of thoſe *abilities*, which have long diſtinguiſhed you, as in every important truſt repoſed in you by the public, ſo eſpecially in the capacity we now conſider you.

And whereas his Excellency the Governor of this Province, hath iſſued writs for electing a new houſe of repreſentatives, to meet at Salem, on the 5th day of October next, and notwithſtanding a number of councellors have been appointed by mandamus from his Majeſty, in conſequence of a late act of the Britiſh parliament; but preſuming the repreſentatives of this people, yet determined to be free, never will, or ought, to conſent to do any buſineſs with them, and we look upon the council choſe laſt May by the great and general court, according to charter, to be the only conſtitutional council of this Province; we do therefore pray your Honour, that you would attend the great and general court at Salem the next ſeſſions, in ſaid capacity; and that you would continue thoſe endeavours to obtain a redreſs of the grievances ſo juſtly complained of by the People, which have long diſtinguiſhed you as an able defender of our conſtitution and liberties: And now wiſhing your Honour the ſupport of Heaven in your advanced age, that you may much longer remain a bleſſing to this Province, and enjoy the happineſs of ſeeing thoſe Rights reſtored, which have been moſt injuriouſly wreſted from us, we beg leave to ſubſcribe ourſelves, your Honour's moſt obedient

Nath'l Freeman, Stephen Nye, Joſ. Haſkel, 3d. Noah Fearing, John Pitcher,	A Committee in Behalf of the People.

[...] OTIS was pleaſed to return the [...] Anſwer, viz.

[...] *dreſs to me as a conſtitutional Coun-* [...] *ring me to attend my Duty at Salem* [...] *when the General Court is to ſet,* [...] *or putting me in Mind of my Duty;* [...] *at Salem at that Time, in caſe my* [...] *Your very humble Servant.*

[...] 74. JAMES OTIS.

[...] high eſteem of that honourable [...] of his paſt Services, their ſanguine [...] ions, and hearty approbation of his [...] eis, by giving him three cheers, and [...] ceſſion to the court-houſe.

The People voted and reſolved, that as the town of Boſton was now ſuffering in a common cauſe, they would uſe their endeavours to relieve them, by encouraging and procuring donations for their ſupport—that they would immediately provide themſelves with arms and ammunition, and hold themſelves in readineſs to aſſiſt, in defending the town of Boſton, and the rights and liberties of this country, which they never would give up, but with their lives and fortunes—that they would not import any more goods from Great-Britain, or purchaſe any imported by others, after

NEW-HAVEN, October 21.

Colony of Connecticut, October 20, 1774.

In the Houſe of Repreſentatives,

RESOLVED unanimouſly,

THAT Contributions from all the Towns in this Colony for ſupplying the Neceſſities, and alleviating the diſtreſſes of our Brethren at Boſton, ought to be continued in ſuch Manner and ſo long as their Occaſions may require. RICHARD LAW, Clerk.

From Baltimore, in Maryland, we learn that a Veſſel arrived there the 6th inſtant, ſent by General Gage to purchaſe a load of Flour, a quantity of Blankets, &c. for the Troops under his Command at Boſton; but that the Committee of Correſpondence for that Place refuſed to furniſh any of the Articles until they heard from the General Congreſs, where they had ſent an expreſs to receive directions how they ſhould act upon the Occaſion.

*** *The Notification from the* Treaſurer of the Province, *relative to the Sheriffs bringing into the* Treaſury *ſuch* Public Monies *as they now have in their Hands, &c. we received too late to be inſerted this Day; but will be in our next.*——*All* Advertiſements, *intended for Monday's Paper, muſt be ſent on Saturday Afternoon preceeding, if it is expected they have a Place therein.*——

MASSACHUSETTS GAZETTE;
AND THE BOSTON POST-BOY AND ADVERTISER

September 5, 1774

Once comprised of members elected by the people, the Massachusetts Executive Council was now appointed by the Crown under the Massachusetts Government Act. All thirty-six "mandamus counsellors" were intimidated by mobs and forced to resign or flee to the protection of British troops in Boston. Here, we read Abijah Willard's humiliating recantation in order to secure his safety.

with the declarations and reſignations aboveſaid, and paſſed in the affirmative, nem. con.

It was then moved to know whether that body would ſignify their abhorrence of mobs, riots, and the deſtruction of private property, and paſſed in the affirmative, nem. con.

Col. Phips, the high ſheriff of the county, then came before the committee of the body and complained that he had been hardly ſpoken of for the part he had acted in delivering the powder in Charleſtown magazine to the ſoldiery; which, the committee candidly conſidered and reported to the body, that it was their opinion the high ſheriff was excuſeable, as he had acted in conformity to his order from the commander in chief. Col. Phips alſo delivered the following declaration by him ſubſcribed viz.

Colonel PHIPS's *Anſwer to the Honorable body now in meeting upon the Common*, viz.

THAT I will not execute any Precept that ſhall be ſent me under the new Acts of Parliament for altering the Conſtitution of the Province of the Maſſachuſetts Bay, and that I will call in the Venires that I have ſent out under the new Eſtabliſhment.

Cambridge, Sept. 2, 1774. DAVID PHIPS.

Which was accepted as ſatisfactory.

About 8 o'clock his honor Lieut. Governor Oliver ſet off from Cambridge to Boſton, and informed Governor Gage of the true ſtate of matters, and the buſineſs of the people; which, as his honor told the Admiral, were not a mad mob, but the freeholders of the county, promiſing to return in two hours and confer further with them on his own circumſtance, as preſident of the council. On Mr. Oliver's return he came to the committee and ſignified what he had delivered to the body in the morning, viz. that as the commiſſions of Lieut. Governor, and preſident of the council, ſeemed tacked together, he ſhould undoubtedly incur his Majeſty's diſpleaſure if he reſigned the former, and pretended to hold the latter; and no body appeared to have any objection to his enjoying the place he held conſtitutionally, he begged he might not be preſſed to incur the diſpleaſure at the inſtance of a ſingle county, while any other councellor held on the new eſtabliſhment. Aſſuring them however, that in caſe the mind of the whole province collected in congreſs or otherwiſe appeared for his reſignation, he would by no means act in oppoſition to it. This ſeemed ſatisfactory to the committee, and they preparing to deliver it to the body, when Mr. commiſſioner Hallowell came through the town on his way to Boſton. The ſight of this perſon ſo inflamed the people that in a few minutes above an hundred horſemen were drawn up and proceeding in purſuit of him on the full gallop. Capt. Gardner of Cambridge firſt began a parley with one of the foremoſt. which cauſed them to halt till he delivered his mind very fully in diſſuaſion of the purſuit, and was ſeconded by Mr. Deavens, of Charleſtown, and Dr. Young, of Boſton. They generally obſerved that the object of the body's attention that day ſeemed to be the reſignation of unconſtitutional councellors, and that it might introduce confuſion into the proceedings of the day if any thing elſe was brought upon the carpet till that important buſineſs was finiſhed: And in a little time the gentlemen diſmounted their horſes and returned to the body.

But Mr. Hollowell did not entirely eſcape, as one gentleman, of a ſmall ſtature, puſhed on before the general body, and followed Mr. Hollowell, who made the beſt of his way till he got into Roxbury, where Mr. Bradſhaw overtook and ſtopped him in his chaiſe; Mr. Hollowell ſnapped his piſtols at him, but could not diſengage himſelf from him till he quitted the chaiſe, and mounted his ſervant's horſe, on which he drove into Boſton with all the ſpeed he could make; till the horſe falling within the gate, he ran on foot to the camp, through which he ſpread conſternation, telling them he was purſued by ſome thouſands, who would be in town at his heels, and deſtroy all friends of government before them.

A gentleman in Boſton, obſerving the motion in the Camp, and concluding they were on the point of marching to Cambridge, from both ends of the town, communicated the alarm to Dr. Roberts, then at Charleſtown ferry, who having a very fleet Horſe, brought the news in a few minutes to the committee, then at Dinner. The intelligence was inſtantly diffuſed, and the people whoſe arms were neareſt ſent Perſons to bring them; light horſemen were diſpatched both ways to gain more certain advice of the true ſtate of the ſoldiery. A greater fervor and reſolution probably never appeared among any troops. The diſpatches ſoon returning and aſſuring the body that the ſoldiers ſtill remained, and were likely to remain, in their camp, they reſumed their buſineſs with ſpirit, and reſolved to leave no unconſtitutional officer, within their reach, in poſſeſſion of his place. On this the committee aſſembled again, and drew up the paper, of which the following is a copy, and at the head of the body delivered it to Lieut. Governor Oliver to ſign, with which he complied, after obtaining their conſent to add the latter clauſe implying the ſource by which he was compelled, to do it. Mr. Maſon, clerk of the county of Middleſex, alſo engaged in his office to do no one thing in obediance to the new Acts of Parliament impairing our Charter.

Cambridge, Sept. 2, 1774.

of Maſſachuſetts-Bay, which being a manifeſt infringement of the charter rights and privileges of this people; I do hereby, in conformity to the commands of the body of this county now convened, moſt

the Colonel; his ſons informed them he was not at home, but had ſet off for Boſton the preceding evening; the committee made report to the company, which did not give ſatisfaction, they inſiſted upon ſearching the houſe, which was done, as alſo the barns, out houſes and ſtables, after

letter to Col. Murray, informing

office by the tenth of this mo

the Boſton news-papers, he

turn home; and then diſperſ

The ſpirit of the people, w

the firſt ſettlement of the c

in the country for hundreds

to "DIE or be FREE

MARRIED.] M

chant, to Miſs Priſcill

Scollay, Eſq; of this

Mr. William Evans,

Shilcock.

Mr. Thomas Moore,

nah Dinmore, only I

Archibald Dinmore, d

DIED.] Mrs. Sara

Tyler.---At Charleſtow

ed 82.---At Dunſtable,

Town, Merchant.---A

Crocker, aged 55.

Want of Room obliges us to om

Meeting, ſeveral Articles of Intelligence

To my worthy Town and Countrymen.

Gentlemen,

AS I have given you great Offence by ſigning an Addreſs to Governor Hutchinſon (upon his leaving the Province) and as it always gives me Pain to affront or diſoblige even a ſingle Neighbour; this has been much increaſed as the Public are ſo much concerned in it: And had I conceived that the Generality of the People ſo much diſliked an Addreſs to Mr. Hutchinſon, it ſhould not have had my Name to it, as I always place the Friendſhip and Good-will of my Fellow-Men, in the firſt Claſs of the World's Enjoyments. I am very ſorry I ever ſigned it, and hope the Public will freely forgive, Gentlemen,

Your humble Servant,

Charleſtown, Sept. 3, 1774. JOHN WHITE.

Sturbridge, Aug. 25, 1774.

WHEREAS I ABIJAH WILLARD, of Lancaſter, have been appointed, by mandamus, a Counſellor for this province, and having without due conſideration taken the oath, do now freely and ſolemnly declare that I am heartily ſorry that I have taken the ſaid oath, and do hereby ſolemnly and in good faith promiſe and engage that I will not ſit nor act in the ſaid Council, nor in any other that ſhall be appointed in ſuch manner and form, but that I will, as much as in me lies, maintain the Charter Rights and Liberties of this province, and do hereby aſk forgiveneſs of all the honeſt, worthy gentlemen, that I have offended by taking the aboveſaid oath, and deſire this may be inſerted in the public prints. Witneſs my hand,

ABIJAH WILLARD.

Meſſieurs PRINTERS,

Pleaſe to inſert the following in your next paper, and you will oblige your moſt humble ſervant, E. G.

IN the Supplement to the laſt Monday's Gazette, a writer under the ſignature of Maſſachuſettenſis, after calling me by name, plainly intimates *that I have wounded the conſtitution of my country in my department of clerk of the ſeſſions*. This cruel inſinuation not only tends to render me odious to the world of mankind, but exhibiting me to my countrymen as their enemy, at this time of public calamity, muſt render me ſingularly hateful. To one conſcious of deſerving a very different character, ſuch treatment muſt be a very ſevere trial, as it muſt affect every man of ſentiment and feeling.—Soon after the arrival of an act of Parliament, entitled an act for better regulating the government of the province of the Maſſachuſetts-Bay, in North-America, two or three clerks of the court of ſeſſions, of different counties, happening to meet; naturally fell into converſation upon the ſubject of their duty in conſequence of the requirements of that act. On this ſudden meeting, and ſhort conſultation, finding ourſelves directed by that law, we ſuppoſed ourſelves bound in duty to iſſue warrants for the return of jurors, in the manner thereby required. Upon this ſudden opinion it was, that twenty warrants were iſſued to the conſtables of the ſeveral towns in the county of Suffolk, agreeable to the directions of the ſame act; ten of which were ſigned by me, and the remaining ten by Mr. Ezekiel Price, joint clerk with me. At the time I ſigned, I did not ſuppoſe any one town in the county would take the leaſt notice of ſuch warrant, and with pleaſure I find upon enquiry, that my expectations have been anſwered.

The ſcience of the law hath never been my profeſſed ſtudy, tho' the mere mechanical buſineſs of a clerk's office hath been my employ for many years. As therefore it has not been my ſtudy *to know* any more than *to determine* what is *the law of the land*, my

give. And I now publickly declare that it was not for the leaſt inclination I had to comply with this, or any other of the acts of Parliament lately paſſed, relative to North-America, that I ſigned

To be held at PHILADELPHIA, on the firſt of September, 1774.

New Auction-Room, Dock-Square,

Beds, Tables, Chairs, Deſks, Bedſteads, &c.

WM. HUNTER, Auctioneer.

Wedneſday Morning, the Sale to begin at X o'Clock.

(By particular Deſire)

Mr. MORGAN

Informs his Friends and the Public, that on Thurſday Evening next, the 8th Inſtant, at CONCERT-HALL, will be performed

A grand CONCERT

Of Vocal and Inſtrumental MUSIC.

Firſt Violin, Mr. MORGAN.

German Flute, Mr. STIEGLITZ.

Harpſichord, Mr. SELBY.

Accompanied with Clarinets, Hautboys, Baſſoons, French Horns, Trumpets, Kettle Drums, &c. &c.

N. B. The Gentlemen Performers of the Army, Navy, and of the Town, have promiſed Mr. Morgan their Aſſiſtance in Concert; as likewiſe ſome of the beſt Perfomers from the ſeveral Bands of Muſic of the Line.

Tickets, at half a Dollar each, to be had at the Britiſh Coffee-Houſe, at Meſſieurs Cox and Berry's, and of Mr. Morgan.

☞ Said Concert was to have been this Evening, but for a particular Reaſon is poſtponed to Thurſday. The CONCERT to begin at 7 o'Clock.

James Henderſon

ACQUAINTS his Cuſtomers and others, that he has for Sale, a compleat Aſſortment of Engliſh, India and Scotch GOODS, ſuitable to all Seaſons, which he will ſell by Wholeſale and Retail, cheap for Caſh, at his Shop in Ann-ſtreet, Boſton. Amongſt which are a beautiful Aſſortment of brocaded Silks, Ducapes, ſtript, plain, and changeable Luteſtrings, Sattins and Modes of all Widths, a fine Aſſortment of the neweſt faſhioned Ribbons, to be ſold very low, plain, ſtript and flowered Muſlins, &c. &c.

WILLIAM BRECK

BEGS Leave to inform his Friends and Cuſtomers, that he has removed from his Shop, at the Golden Key, in Ann-ſtreet, to a Shop near the Hay-Market, next Door to Dr. Daniel Scott's at the Sign of the Leopard, South-End of Boſton, where he continues to ſell, as uſual,

Ware, at the loweſt Prices for Caſh.

A Few Quarter Caſks beſt

REPORTING THE

POWDER ALARM

By J. L. Bell

LATE IN AUGUST 1774, WILLIAM BRATTLE OF Cambridge, a Massachusetts militia general, wrote to Royal Governor Thomas Gage that it might be wise to secure the province's gunpowder supply. On September 1, General Gage's troops emptied a powder house outside Boston and took two small cannons from Brattle's militia unit. The people of Cambridge saw those actions as curtailing their power to defend themselves. Hearing of his neighbors' anger, Brattle fled to the protection of the Royal Army. The next day, he wrote an open letter explaining himself, published alongside his original note in the September 5, 1774, *Massachusetts Gazette; and the Boston Post-Boy and Advertiser*. But it was too late.

An exaggerated rumor that the army was attacking Boston spread west September 1. Across Massachusetts, farmers mustered in their militia companies and marched to defend the capital. By the time they reached the outskirts of Cambridge early the next morning, they knew the rumor was false—but still the men came on, leaving their guns stacked at taverns, determined to make a show of numbers.

As a rumor that the army was attacking Boston spread west, farmers mustered in their militia companies and marched to defend the capital.

Lieutenant Governor Thomas Oliver hurried from his Cambridge mansion into Boston to warn Gage not to overreact. On his way, he passed Whigs summoned by Dr. Joseph Warren heading out to Cambridge to keep people calm. Neither side's leaders wanted violence.

On Cambridge Common, the militiamen—at least three thousand strong—had called on two locals appointed to Gage's council under the Massachusetts Government Act to publicly resign. Samuel Danforth and Joseph Lee did so. Sheriff David Phips apologized for helping the army remove the militia cannon. The crowd then voted unanimously to condemn riots. Newspapers like the September 9, 1774, *New-Hampshire Gazette* printed those transactions much like the record of an official public meeting.

Colonial newspaper publishers rarely left their print shops to gather news, but Isaiah Thomas of the *Massachusetts Spy* was on Cambridge Common that day. In fact, Thomas alerted the crowd that, by coincidence, the customs commissioners were passing by. Several men on horseback began to chase Benjamin Hallowell, the least popular of those officials. A few pursued Hallowell all the way to the Boston Neck.

Now riled up, the Cambridge crowd decided to visit Lieutenant Governor Oliver, who had returned home, and demand that he resign from the council, as well. Oliver refused. The crowd's emissaries pleaded, warning they could not control four thousand angry men. Around dusk, Oliver finally signed a resignation. Rain began to fall, and the farmers dispersed to their homes. Though the rumor about Boston continued to spread through New England for days, there were no further confrontations.

No one was hurt during this event, later dubbed the "Powder Alarm," but it demonstrated three things.

First, General Gage's authority stopped at the gates of Boston. The rest of Massachusetts was beyond royal control. Prominent Loyalists like Oliver soon moved into Boston for their safety.

Second, the Massachusetts countryside was now as committed to resistance as Boston. For weeks, Whig newspapers reported, and probably overstated, how many militiamen had mustered: "FORTY THOUSAND MEN in MOTION, and under ARMS," said an item in the September 16, 1774, *New-Hampshire Gazette*. The point was not that colonists wanted war, but that they could oppose any Crown aggression with overwhelming force and unity.

Third, people saw the next stage of the conflict as a race to control artillery and gunpowder. For example, the September 23, 1774, *New-Hampshire Gazette* told its readers how General Gage and the Royal Navy had disabled batteries in Boston Harbor. Newspapers did not report that New Englanders were spiriting other cannon into the countryside, beyond the governor's reach.

The following is a *Copy* of the much-talked of Letter, wrote by Major-General Brattle, to the Commander in Chief, viz.

Cambridge, August 29, 1774.

MR. Brattle presents his Duty to his Excellency Governor Gage, he apprehends it his Duty to acquaint his Excellency from Time to Time with every Thing he hears and knows to be true, and is of Importance in these troublesome Times, which is the Apology Mr. Brattle makes for troubling the General with this Letter. Captain Minot, of Concord, a very worthy Man, this Minute informed Mr. Brattle that there had been repeatedly made pressing Applications to him to warn his Company to meet at one Minute's Warning, equipt with Arms and Ammunition, according to Law, he had constantly denied them, adding, if he did not gratify them he should be constrained to quit his Farms and Town; Mr. Brattle told him he had better do that than lose his Life, and be hanged for a Rebel; he observed that many Captains had done it, though not in the Regiment to which he belonged, which was and is under Colonel Elisha Jones, but in a neigbouring Regiment.

Mr. Brattle begs Leave humbly to quere, Whether it would not be best that there should not be one Commission Officer of the Militia in the Province.

This Morning the Select-Men of Medford, came and received their Town-Stock of Powder, which was in the Arsenal on Quarry-Hill, so that there is now therein, the King's Powder only, which shall remain there as a sacred Depositum till ordered out by the Captain General.

To his Excellency General Gage, &c. &c. &c.

TO THE PUBLIC.

Boston, September 2, 1774.

I Think it but Justice to myself to give an Account of my Conduct, for which I am blamed; and to obviate some Mistakes which are believed. His Excellency Governor Gage wrote me in the Words following: "Sir, as I am informed there are several Military Stores in your Charge, at Cambridge, I beg the Favour of you to send me a Return of them, as soon as convenient, specifying the different Sorts of each, T. Gage.---To Major General Brattle." Which Order I obeyed; the like I did to Governors Pownal, Bernard and Hutchinson: In doing of which, every Soldier will say, I did but my Duty. But it is affirmed, I advised the Governor to remove the Powder; this I positively deny, because it is absolutely false. It never so much as entered into my Mind or Thought. After I had made my Return, I never heard one Word about the Affair till the Night before last, when Sheriff Phips came to my House, with the Governor's Order to deliver him the Powder and Guns; the Keys of the Powder-House I then delivered him, and wrote to Mr. Mason, who had the Care of the Guns under me, to deliver them, which I suppose he did; both I imagine were taken, but where transported I know not. I wrote to the Governor what is contained in the above Letter; I did not write the Governor the Grounds and Reasons of the Query therein contained; but I will now mention them: They proceeded from a real Regard both to the Commission Officers and to the Province: First, to the Commission Officers; I thought, and still think, it was best for them; many of whom I thought would be unwilling to issue their Warrants, and if they did not, I apprehended they might meet with some Difficulty; and those that did, I was not convinced so great Good would result therefrom, as if another method was taken: Secondly, I thought, and still think, it would be much better for the Province; for supposing there was not one Commission Officer for the present in it, what Damage could the Province sustain? It may be answered, Commission Officers are supposed to be the most understanding in military Affairs; I grant it: But supposing their Commissions were vacated, supposing the respective Companies in the Province were disposed and determined to do any one Matter or Thing, which they imagined to be for its Safety; and proper Persons were to be employed to lead them, [illegible] their not having Commissions in the least unfit them from being employed in the particular Services they may be chosen to execute; and in this Way cannot any One conceive that some bad Consequences might be possibly prevented. Is it not easy to conceive, that the Commission Officers, leading their respective Companies, might, in the Eyes of the Judicious, be looked upon more blameable in doing such and such Things, than they would be if they were not Military Officers, and did not act under Commission? Might not the Difference with respect to the Province be looked upon very great both at home and here. It was suggested that General Gage demanded the Towns Stocks of Powder; this certainly he did not; the above Order speaks for itself. As I would not have delivered the Provincial Powder to any One but to his Excellency, or Order, so the Towns Stocks I would have delivered to none but the Selectmen, or their Order. Upon the whole the Treatment I have met with, my Banishment from my own Home, the Place of my Nativity, my House being searched, though I am informed it was without Damage, and the Sense of the People, touching my Conduct, &c. for the present cannot but be grievous, yet this Grief is much lessened by the Pleasure arising in my Mind, from a Consciousness that I am a Friend to my Country; and, in the above Instances, that I really acted according to my best Judgment for its true Interest. I am extremely sorry for what has taken Place; I hope I may be forgiven, and desire it of all that are offended, since I acted from an honest, friendly Principle, though it might be a mistaken one.

W. BRATTLE.

Messieurs MILLS and HICKS,

Taking it for granted, that a Transaction so interesting to the Community as Major General B-----'s Letter to his Excellency the Governor, and his Address to the Public in defence of the same, will be quoted in your very useful and impartial Gazette, I must insist on your accompanying the Recital of them with the subsequent QUERIES. I am, Gentlemen, your's, &c. K. D.

1. WHETHER advising the Governor to dismiss the Militia Officers of every Order through the Province, with the confessed Intention of rendering them less criminal in any Oppugnation to the present Form of Government, in which they might engage, can entitle the Advisor to *Confidence* on Account of his extraordinary *Loyalty*, in the present Acceptation of the Word with Men in Power, and agreeable to his high Expectations, both in Consequence of his previous Exertions for Promotion under the present Establishment, and Protestations of Duty [illegible]

[illegible] the Defence of it, does not fix, beyond all admissable Apology, that Character of UNEXAMPLED DUPLICITY, which bars all Confidence while it justifies its having never been placed in the Person who sustains it?

3. Whether the *Officiousness* of this Manoeuvre, [illegible]

a Slight might not have induced him to
himself, unless it had been of the last In
5. Whether the uncouth Compositio
considered as the Production of a Man of L
on any other Principle than the conscio
and some secret Fear of a Discovery, hau
Writer?
6. Whether any Part of G------l B----
REVIEW on *Cambridge Common*; c
to him, from a serious Concern for him) in

Messieurs PRINTERS,
THE freemen who were returned
at the Superior Court for this term
in the Court-House yesterday; and
bly, (Peter Oliver, Edmund Trowbrid
William Cushing and William Brown Esq
as judges,) they all to the number of twe
as Jurors for reasons which they had previ
and signed, and appointed to be read there
the above said Judges refusing to hear the
to have the reading of it to themselves, wh
the Jurymen withdrew from the Court-
tavern, where they unanimously voted tha
refusal to the world, their aforementioned r
in the public papers.———I send you a
and am your humble servant.

"BOSTON,

"COUNTY OF SUFFOLK.
"WE who are returned by the severa
to serve as Grand Jurors at the Superior
term, being actuated by a zealous regard f
and a sincere desire to promote justice, right
vernment, as being essential to the happine
would now most gladly proceed to the disch
duty required in that department, could we
by doing thus, it would tend to our own rep
welfare of our country: But when we cons
roads that have been made upon our civil c
attempts now making to alter and annul the
our Charter, granted by the most solemn fait
peatedly recognized by British Kings and pa
see the open and avowed design of establishing
system of despotism in this province, and the
born inhabitants thereof to the most abject
bondage; we feel ourselves necessarily constr
impannelled, for reasons that we are ready to
permitted, which are as follows.
"First. Because Peter Oliver, Esq; who
this Court, has been charged with high crimes
the late hon. House of Representatives, the
province; of which crimes he has never been
has been declared by that House to be unqualifi
this Court.
"Secondly. Because by a late act of the Br
altering the constitution of this province, the
present Judges of this Court, as well as the ap
from the first day of July last, is made to dep
King's pleasure, vastly different from the ten
Judges; and as we apprehend they now hold th
consequence of that act, all the judicial procee
will be taken as concessions to the validity of t
we dare not consent.
"Thirdly. Because three of the Judges, bein
the Court, namely the said Peter Oliver, Esq;
Esq; and William Brown, Esq; by taking the oa
under authority of the aforesaid act, are (as
sworn to carry into execution, all the late gri
British parliament, among the last of which is on
for the impartial administration of justice in this
we fear, really for the impunity of such perso
pretext of executing those acts murder any of the
of, which acts appear to us to be utterly repugn
of justice and common humanity, and are justl
throughout America, as highly injurious and oppr
people of this province, and manifestly destructive
as well as constitutional rights.
"Fourthly. Because we believe in our conscie
ing in concert with a Court so constituted, and un
stances, would be so far betraying the just and sa
native land, which were not the gift of Kings, bu
solely with the toil, the blood and treasure of our w
ancestors, and which we look upon ourselves unde
and inviolable obligations to maintain, and to tran
entire to our posterity.
"Therefore we the subscribers unanimously d
Grand Jurors at this Court.

"Ebenezer Hancock,	Boston,
Peter Boyer,	ditto,
Joseph Hall,	ditto,
Thomas Crafts, jun.	ditto,
James Ivers,	ditto,
Paul Revere,	ditto,
Robert Williams,	Roxbury,
William Thompson,	Brookline,
Abraham Wheeler,	Dorchester,
Joseph Jones,	Milton,
Nathaniel Belcher,	Braintree,
Samuel Hobart,	Hingham,
Joseph Poole,	Weymouth
Henry Plymton,	Medway,
Lemuel Kalloc,	Medfield,
Joseph Willet,	Wrentham,
Thomas Pratt,	Walpole,
Nicholas Rook	Chelsea,

MASSACHUSETTS GAZETTE; AND THE BOSTON POST-BOY AND ADVERTISER

September 5, 1774

Massachusetts militia general William Brattle's open letter explaining his treasonous note to Royal Governor Thomas Gage was printed in newspapers along with the original "much-talked of" note to Gage.

NEW-HAMPSHIRE GAZETTE (PORTSMOUTH)

September 9, 1774

New England newspapers from September and October 1774 are loaded with emotional content that reveal intensifying hostilities and political revolution against all royal authority.

Decks were blown up, but the Commander found Means to get her into port.

The Amount of the National DEBT, when it was stated in January last, is One Hundred Twenty-Eight Millions, Five Hundred Twenty-Four Thousand, and Three Hundred

Number of Frigates and small armed Vessels cruizing in the Mediterranean.

From the Massachusetts-Spy.

BOSTON, Sept. 1.

THE Freemen who were returned to serve as Grand Jurors at the Superior Court for this Term, made their Appearance in the Court House Yesterday; and before a numerous Assembly, (Peter Oliver. Edmund Trowbride, Foster Hutchinson, William Cushing, and William Brown, Esquires sitting on the Bench as Judges) they all to the Number of Twenty-Two declined acting as Jurors for Reasons which they had previously drawn up in Writing and signed, and appointed to be read there by their Chairman, but the above said Judges refusing to hear the same openly read, desired to have the Reading of it to themselves, which being complied with, the Jurymen withdrew from the Court House to the Exchange Tavern, where they unanimously voted that in Order to justify their Refusal to the World, their aforementioned Reasons should be printed in the public Papers.------I send you a Copy for that Purpose, and am your humble Servant.

A JURYMAN.

"BOSTON, *August* 30th, 1774.

"COUNTY OF SUFFOLK.

"WE who are returned by the several Towns in this County, to serve as Grand Jurors at the Superior Court for this present Term, being actuated by a zealous Regard for Peace and good Order, and a sincere Desire to promote Justice, Righteousness and good Government, as being essential to the Happiness of the Community; would now most gladly proceed to the Discharge of the important Duty required in that Department, could we perswade ourselves that by doing thus, it would tend to our own Reputation or promote the Welfare of our own Country: But when we consider the dangerous Inroads that have been made upon our civil Constitution, the violent Attempts now making to alter and annul the most essential Parts of our Charter, granted by the most solemn Faith of Kings, and repeatedly recognized by British Kings and Parliaments; while we see the open and avowed Design of establishing the most compleat System of Despotism in this Province, and thereby reducing the freeborn Inhabitants thereof to the most abject State of Slavery and Bondage; we feel ourselves necessarily constrained to decline being impanelled, for Reasons that we are ready to offer to the Court if permitteed, which are as follows.

"1st. Because Peter Oliver, Esq; who sits as Chief Judge of this Court, has been charged with High Crimes and Misdemeanors, by the late Hon. House of Representatives, the grand Inquest of this Province; of which Crimes he has never been legally acquitted, but has been declared by that House to be unqualified to act as Judge of this Court.

"2d. Because by a late Act of the British Parliament, for altering the Constitution of this Province, the Continuance of the present Judges of this Court, as well as the Appointment of others, from the first Day of July last, is made to depend solely on the King's Pleasure, vastly different from the Tenor of the British Judges; and as we apprehend they now hold their Places, only in Consequence of that Act, all the judicial Proceedings of the Court, will be taken as Concessions to the Validity of the same, to which we dare not consent.

"3d. Because three of the Judges, being the major Part of the Court, namely the said Peter Oliver, Esq; Foster Hutchinson, Esq; and William Brown. Esq; by taking the Oath of Counsellors, under Authority of the aforesaid Act, are (as we are informed) sworn to carry into Execution, all the late grievous Acts of the British Parliament, among the last of which is one, made ostensibly for the impartial Administration of Justice in this Province, but as we fear, really for the Impunity of such Persons, as shall under Pretext of executing those Acts, murder any of the Inhabitants thereof, which Acts appear to us to be utterly repugnant to every Idea of Justice and common Humanity, and are justly complained of throughout America, as highly injurious and oppressive to the good People of this Province, & manifestly destructive of their natural, as well as constitutional Rights.

"4th. Because we believe in our Consciences that our acting in concert with a Court so constituted and under such Circumstances, would be so far betraying the just and sacred Rights of our native Land, which were not the Gift of Kings, but were purchased solely with the Toil, the Blood and Treasure of our worthy and revered Ancestors, and which we look upon ourselves under the most sacred and inviolable obligations to maintain, and to transmit whole and entire to our Posterity.

"Therefore we the Subscribers unanimously decline serving as Grand Jurors at this Court.

"Ebenezer Hancock, Peter Boyer, Joseph Hall, Thomas Crafts, jun. James Ivers, Paul Revere, Robert Williams, Wm.

ving the Court the original Paper unless they were first permitted to read it in Court, or after Reading the Court would promise to return it to them again.

The Petit Jurors were then called for, and a List of their Names being handed to the Court they appointed Mr. Bartholomew Kneeland, Foreman, of the first Jury, and Mr. Nathan

Reasons, as aforesaid. The Chief Justice then desired the Court might peruse the Paper, which should be returned to the Jurors again; which was agreed to, read and returned. The Court then proposed the same Condition to the Grand Jury, which was complied with, and the Contents delivered, which are inserted in this Day's Paper, see the Piece signed 'A JURYMAN.'

The Reasons of the Petit Jurors were as follows.

"BOSTON, August 30, 1774.

"SUFFOLK, ss.

"*To the Honourable the Justices of the Superior* Court *of Judicature,* Court *of Assize.* &c.

"MAY IT PLEASE YOUR HONOURS,

"WE the Subscribers, returned by this County to serve as Petit Jurors this Term, beg Leave to acquaint your Honours, that as the Hon. Peter Oliver, Esq; stands impeached by the late Hon. House of Commons of this Province, in their own Name, and in the Name of the People of this Province, of high Crimes and Misdemeanors; which Impeachment, with the Reasons therefor, as they are public, would be needless for us to repeat.

"We would also beg Leave to acquaint your Honours, that as by a late Act of the British Parliament, the Continuance of the Judges of the Superior Court, is since the first of July last, made to depend upon said Act, which it is apprehended places their Dependance entirely upon the Crown, and which is esteemed a great Infringement of the Charter Rights of this Province.

"Taking the above Premises into our most serious Consideration, we beg Leave to acquaint your Honours, that we cannot in our Consciences, from a Sense of that Duty we owe to our Country, to ourselves, and to Posterity, act against the united Voice of this People:-----Therefore beg your Honours will excuse us, when we say, we decline serving as Petit Jurors for this Court.

"(*Signed*)

"Josiah Waters, Samuel Ridgeway, Nathan Frazier, Robert Wire, Bartholomew Kneeland, Thomas Chase, John Cunningham, Joseph Brewer, Jacob Sharp, Timothy Tilestone, Samuel Sprague, Ebenezer Swift, Eliphalet Sawer, Thomas White, Thomas Nash, Nathaniel Holbrook, jun, Elijah Jenning, Elisha Cushing, Ignatius Orcutt, Elijah Monk, Henry Stone, William Draper, Jonathan Parker, Ebenezer Kingsbury, Samuel Payson, Joseph Morse, Ralph Day, Nathaniel Lewis, Eliakim Cook, Joseph Lovell, Elias Thayer, Theodore Mann, James Blake."

After the Court had read the Papers, the Clerk of the Court, by Order of the Chief Justice, asked them *Seriatim*, if they would be Sworn, and every ONE refused. The Court said they would consider of their Reasons, and the Juries withdrew.---- The Court then adjourned to Ten o'Clock next Day, when they met exclusive of Mr. Oliver, and to the inexpressible Grief of their Fellow Citizens, went on to such Business as is usually transacted without Juries.

BOSTON, *Monday September* 5.

ON Wednesday last the new Council took their Seats at the Board in Boston. Their Deliberations have not hitherto transpired; and with Secrecy, on Thursday Morning at half after Four, about 260 Troops embarked on Board 13 Boats at the Long Wharfe and proceeded up Medford River, to Temple's Farm, where they landed, and went to the Powder-House on Quarry Hill, in Charlestown Bounds, whence they have taken 250 Half Barrels of Powder, the whole Store, and carried it to the Castle.

A Detachment from the Corps went to Cambridge, and brought off two Field-pieces, which had lately been sent there for Colonel Brattle's Regiment. The Preparation for this Expedition caused much Speculation, as some who were near the Governor gave out that he had sworn the Committee of Salem should recognize or be imprisoned; nay, some said they would be put on Board the Scarborough and sent to England forthwith. The Committee of Boston sent off an Express after ten on Wednesday Evening to advise their Brethren of Salem of what they apprehended was coming against them, who received their Message with great Politeness, and returned an Answer purporting their Readiness to receive any Attack they might be exposed to for acting in Pursuance to the Laws and Interest of their Country as became Men and Christians.

From these several hostile Appearances the County of Middlesex took the Alarm, and on Thursday Evening began to collect in large Bodies, with their Arms, Provision and Ammunition, determining by some Means to give a Check to a Power which so openly threatened their Destruction, and in such a clandestine Manner robb'd them of the Means of their Defence. And on Friday Morning some Thousands of them had advanced to Cambridge, armed only with Sticks, as they had left their Fire-Arms, &c. at some Distance behind them. Some indeed had collected on Thursday Evening and surrounded the Attonery-General's House, who is also Judge of Admiralty on the new

with the Charter Rights of his Country; and in confirmation of said Declaration, he delivered the following certificate drawn up by himself and sign'd with his own Hand, viz.

ALTHO' I have this Day made an open Declaration to a great Concourse of People who assembled at Cambridge, that I had resigned my Seat at the Council Board, yet for the further Satisfaction of all, I do hereby declare under my Hand, that such Resignation has actually been made. and that it is my full Purpose not to be any way concern'd as a Member of the Council, at any Time hereafter. *Sept.* 2, 1774. S. DANFORTH.

A true Copy, Attest. N. Cudworth, Cl.

Judge Lee was also on the court-house steps, and delivered his mind to the body in terms similiar to those used by Judge Danforth, and sign'd by him.

Upon this a Vote was called for to see if the Body was satisfied with the Declarations and Resignations abovesaid, & passed in the Affirmative, *nem. con.*

It was then moved to know whether that Body would signify their Abhorrence of Mobs, Riots and the Destruction of private Property, and passed in the Affirmative, *nem. con.*

Col. Phips, the High Sheriff of the County, then came before the Committee of the Body and complained that he had been hardly spoken of for the Part he had acted in delivering the Powder in Charlestown Magazine to the Soldiery; which the Committee candidly considered and reported to the Body that it was their Opinion the High Sheriff was excuseable as he had acted in Conformity to his Order from the Commander in Chief. Colonel Phips also delivered the following Declaration by him subscribed, viz.

Colonel PHIPS's Answer to the Hon. Body now in Meeting upon the Common, viz.

THAT I will not execute any Precept that shall be sent me under the new Acts of Parliament for altering the Constitution of the Province of the Massachusetts-Bay, and that I will recall all the Venires that I have sent out under the new Establishment.

Cambridge, Sept. 2d, 1774. DAVID PHIPS.

A true Copy, Test. NATH. CUDWORTH, Cl.

Which was accepted as satisfactory.

About Eight o'Clock his Honor Lieut. Governor Oliver set off from Cambridge to Boston, and informed Gov. Gage of the true State of Mattere, and the Business of the People; which as his Honor told the Admiral, were not a mad Mob, but the Freeholders of the County, promising to return in two Hours and confer further with them on his own Circumstance as President of the Council. On Mr. Oliver's Return he came to the Committee and signified what he had delivered to the Body in the Morning viz. that as the Commissions of Lieut. Governor and President of the Council, seem'd tack'd together, he should undoubtedly incur his Majesty's Displeasure if he resign'd the latter, and pretended to hold the former; and no Body appeared to have any Objection to his enjoying the Place he held constitutionally he begged he might not be pressed to incur that Displeasure at the Instance of a single County, while any other Councellor held on the new Establishment. Assuring them however, that in Case the Mind of the whole Province collected in Congress or otherwise appeared for his Resignation, he would by no Means act in Opposition to it. This seemed satisfactory to the Committee, and they were preparing to deliver it to the Body, when Commissioner Hallowell came through the Town on his Way to Boston. The Sight of that obnoxious Person so inflamed the People that in a few Minutes above 160 Horsemen were drawn up and proceeded in pursuit of him on the full Gallop. Capt. Gardner of Cambridge first began a Parley with one of the Foremost, which caused them to halt till he delivered his Mind very fully in Dissuasion of the Pursuit, & was seconded by Mr. Deavens of Charlestown, and Dr. Young of Boston. They generally observed that the Object of the Body's Attention that Day seemed to be the Resignation of unconstitutional Councellors, and that it might introduce Confusion into the Proceedings of the Day if any Thing else was brought upon the carpet till that important Business was finished; and in a little Time the Gentlemen dismounted their Horses, and returned to the Body.

But Mr. Hallowell did not entirely escape, as one Gentleman of a small Stature pushed on before the general Body and followed Hallowell, who made the best of his Way till he got into Roxbury, where Mr. Bradshaw overtook and stopped him in his chaise. Hallowell snapped his Pistols at him, but could not disengage himself from him till he quitted the chaise and mounted his Servant's Horse on which he drove into Boston with all the Speed he could make; till the Horse falling within the Gate he ran on Foot to the Camp, thro' which he spread Consternation, telling them he was pursued by some Thousands, who would be in Town at his Heels and destroy all Friends of Government before them.

A Gentleman in Boston observing the Motion in the Camp, and concluding, they were on the point of Marching to Cambridge, from both Ends of the Town, communicated the Alarm to Dr. Roberts then at Charlestown Ferry, who having a very fleet Horse brought the News in a few Minutes to the Committee, then at Dinner. The Intelligence was instantly diffused, and the People whose Arms were nearest sent Persons to bring them, while Horsemen were dispatched both Ways to gain more certain Advice of the true State of the Soldiery. A greater Fervor and Resolution probably never appeared in any Troops. The Dispatches soon returning, and assuring the Body that the soldiers still remained, and were likely to remain in their camp, they resumed their Business with Spirit, and resolved to leave no unconstitutional Officer within their Reach in Possession of his Place. On this the Committee assembled again, and drew up the Paper of which the following is a Copy, and at the Head of the Body delivered it to Lieut. Governor Oliver to sign, with which he complied, after obtaining their consent to add the latter Clause implying the Force by which he was compelled to do it. Mr. Mason, Clerk of the County of Middlesex, also engaged in his Office to do no one Thing in Obedience to the new Acts of Parliament impairing our Charter.

Cambridge, Sept. 2. 1774.

I THOMAS OLIVER being appointed by his Majesty to a Seat at the Council Board, upon and in Conformity to the

SEPTEMBER 9, 1774

The

NEW-HAMPSHIRE GAZETTE

B O S T O N, *Monday September 5.*

ON Wednesday last the new Council took their Seats at the Board in Boston. Their Deliberations have not hitherto transpired ; and with Secrecy, on Thursday Morning at half after Four, about 260 Troops embarked on Board 13 Boats at the Long Wharf and proceeded up Medford River, to Temple's Farm, where they landed, and went to the Powder-House on Quarry Hill, in Charlestown Bounds, whence they have taken 250 Half Barrels of Powder, the whole Store, and carried it to the Castle.

A Detachment from the Corps went to Cambridge, and brought off two Field-pieces, which had lately been sent there for Colonel Brattle's Regiment. The Preparation for this Expedition caused much Speculation, as some who were near the Governor gave out that he had sworn the Committee of Salem should recognize or be imprisoned ; nay, some said they would be put on Board the Scarborough and sent to England forthwith. The Committee of Boston sent off an Express after ten on Wednesday Evening to advise their Brethren of Salem of what they apprehended was coming against them, who received their Message with great Politeness, and returned an Answer purporting their Readiness to receive any Attack they might be exposed to for acting in Pursuance to the Laws and Interest of their Country as became Men and Christians.

From these several hostile Appearances the County of Middlesex took the Alarm, and on Thursday Evening began to collect in large Bodies, with their Arms, Provision and Ammunition, determining by some Means to give a Check to a Power which so openly threatened their Destruction, and in such a clandestine Manner robb'd them of the Means of their Defence. And on Friday Morning some Thousands of them had advanced to Cambridge, armed only with Sticks, as they had left their Fire-Arms, &c. at some Distance behind them. Some indeed had collected on Thursday Evening and surrounded the Attonery[sic]-General's House, who is also Judge of Admiralty on the new Plan for Nova-Scotia ; and being provoked by the Firing of a Pistol from a Window, they broke some Glass, but did little more Mischief. The Company however, concerned in this, were mostly Boys and Negroes, who soon dispersed.

On perceiving the Concourse on Friday Morning, the Committee of Cambridge sent Express to Charlestown, who communicated the Intelligence to Boston, and their respective committees proceeded to Cambridge without Delay. When the first of the Boston committee came up, they found some Thousands of People assembled round the Court-House Steps, and Judge Danforth standing upon them, speaking to the Body, declaring in Substance, that having now arrived at a very advanced Age, and spent the greater part in the Service of the public, it was a great Mortification to him to find a Step lately taken by him so disagreeable to his Country, in which he conscienciously meaned to serve them, but finding their general Sense against his holding a Seat at the Council Board on the new Establishment, he assured them that he had resigned said Office, and would never henceforth accept or act in any Office inconsistent with the Charter Rights of his Country ; and in confirmation of said Declaration, he delivered the following certificate drawn up by himself and sign'd with his own Hand, viz.

ALTHO' *I have this Day made an open Declaration to a great Concourse of People who assembled at Cambridge, that I had resigned my Seat at the Council Board, yet for the further Satisfaction of all, I do hereby declare under my Hand, that such Resignation has actually been made, and that it is my full Purpose not to be any way concern'd as a Member of the Council, at any Time hereafter. Sept. 2, 1774.* S. DANFORTH.

A true Copy, Attest. N. Cudworth, Cl.

Springfield, a great Concourse of People, judg'd to be about 3000, assembled at the Court-House in that Place, and appointed a Committee to wait on the Court, and request their Appearance among the People, which they immediately complied with, when they very willingly signed the following Engagement, viz.

WE the Subscribers, do severally Promise, and solemly engage to all People now assembled at Springfield, in the County of Hampshire on the 30th Day of Aug. 1774, that WE never will take, hold, execute, or exercise any Commission, Office, or Employment whatsoever, under, or by Virtue of, or in any Manner derived from any Authority pretended or attempted to be given by a late Act of Parliament, entitled, "An Act for the better regulating the Government of the Province of the Massachusetts Bay in New England."

Israel Williams, Oliver Partridge, Timothy Dwight, Thomas Williams, John Worthington, Joseph Hawley, William Williams, Simeon Strong, Moses Bliss, Jonathan Ashley, Elisha Porter, William Billings, John Phelps, Solomon Stoddard, Justus Ely, Caleb Strong, Samuel Fowler, Jonathan Bliss.

BOSTON, Sept. 8.

Treasurer Gray, we are credibly informed has not resigned his Office as Councellor.

Yesterday General Gage, accompanied by Lord Percy, the Admiral, and other Officers, critically surveyed the Mill Creek, which divides the Town.

By Letters from Connecticut, and by several credible Gentlemen arrived from thence, we are informed, that there were not less than FORTY THOUSAND MEN in MOTION, and under ARMS, on their Way to Boston, on Saturday, Sunday, and Monday last, having heard a false Report that the Troops had fired upon Boston, and killed several of the Inhabitants: Twelve Hundred arrived at Hartford from Farmington, & other Places Forty Miles beyond Hartford, on Sunday last, on their Way to this Place, so rapidly did the News fly. But being informed by Expresses that it was a false Report, they returned

but small Quantities of CORN *sent in, now our Ports are open: And further we have a very unpleasing Prospect of the next Year's Crop of* WHEAT. *The* POOR *are greatly oppressed, and many others much straitned.---That* BOSTON *is the Seat of* MINISTERIAL REVENGE *we too well know: The Issue we dread---How far the Colonies will yield, we know not; and if they do, how far they must they know not. The Ministry will endeavour, without Doubt, by all Means to caress one Part, while they oppress another; and if they can disunite you, they gain their End; and in Time oppress all by every* TAX *imposed upon us, for the Support of their Creatures; of this you need no Hints. We shall soon hear how Things will go down with you. May you have divine Direction. Your* LIBERTY *or* SLAVERY *are soon to be determined. Our Ministerial Tools are dogged hungry, and want to pick your Bones. The Ease with which Things passed through our Houses affords Matter for some Speculation. Whether the anti ministerial Part did not interest themselves in the Affair, or had rather the Ministry should by this Step entangle themselves, Time will probably discover.--- You will be careful how you express yourself, that neither of us be brought into Trouble, as it is very likely our Letters may be inspected."---*

PORTSMOUTH,

THURSDAY last arrived here Captain NORMAN in the Fox Mastship, with 30 Chests of TEA, consigned to Edward Parry, Esq; who refused the Consignment; upon the People's being acquainted with this repeated Insult (of the East-India Company) to the Colonies, they were greatly alarmed, and had almost absolutely determined to oblige the Ship to return to London, with the Tea only, but through the polite Behaviour of the Captain, who was ready to submit to any Thing the People thought proper upon the Occasion, he was permitted to send the Tea to Halifax, and it was put on Board Capt. Fernald, who sailed for Halifax with it last Sunday. In future no such Indulgence will be allowed to the Enemies of America.

Schooner Polly, James Tilestone, Newfoundland.
Sloop Polly, William Furnell, Halifax.
Sloop Britannia, John Gray, Nantucket.
Sloop Revenge, Benjamin Dannell, West Indies.
Brig Abigail, John Wheelwright, Ditto.
Brig Success, Edmund Freeman, Ditto.
Ship Polly, John Gregory, Ditto.

TO BE SOLD

One Half of a Right of Land,

In Rochester, originally belonging to Nicholas Harford, excepting the first Division.

Enquire of the Printer.

Whereas Mary, *the Wife of me the Subscriber, has of late run me greatly in Debt, this is therefore to forbid all Persons trusting her on my Account, as I will not pay One Penny she may contract from the date hereof.* Kittery, Sept. 14th 1774.

JOHN LILLEY.

TO BE SOLD,

For the Term of seven Years, pursuant to a Decree of Court,

George Madden,

An Excellent Weaver— Whoever inclines to purchase the said George, may hear of the Terms by enquiring at the Printing Office. …

hope, and expect this House will immediately adopt, I will be among the foremost of this illustrious Assembly, to move for such Measures as will effectually prevent a future Relapse, and make them feel what it is to provoke a fond and forgiving Parent; a Parent, my Lords, whose Welfare has ever been my greatest and most pleasing Consolation. This Declaration may seem unnecessary, but I will venture to declare, the Period is not far distant, when she will want the Assistance of her most distant Friends; but should the all disposing Hand of Providence prevent me from affording her my poor Assistance, my Prayers shall be ever for her Welfare. Length of Days be in her Right Hand, and in her left, Riches and Honor; may her Ways be Ways of Pleasantness, and all her Paths be Peace.

SALEM, *Sept.* 13, 1774.

Last Tuesday arrived here the Ship Julius Cæsar, Charles Fea, Master, from London, having on board thirty Chests and three half Chests of Tea, the Property of one Montgomery of London, consigned to Messrs. Smith and Atkinson, Merchants in Boston, who were equally surprized and offended at the Consignment, it being intirely unknown to them before the Ship's Arrival; and they solemnly declare, that Mr. Montgomery, previous to this Consignment, never had any Intercourse or commercial Correspondence with either of them. As soon as the Committee of Correspondence here had made Discovery of the Tea, the Master sent an Express to Smith and Atkinson; and the next Morning Mr. Smith came to Town, and frankly declared that the Tea should not be landed, nor any Duty paid on it here, if he … On Tuesday and Wed- …

… rations are now carrying …

NEW-PORT, Sept. 5.

Yesterday an Express arrived at Providence from Plainfield, to inquire into the Account of the Powder's being stolen by Gage's Orders, informing that there were near Ten Thousand Men in Arms, in that Part of the Country, ready to march to Boston, if needed.

About 10 o'Clock last Night an Express arrived in this Town, for Commissions for a Number of Military Officers in the wes… … and informs, that Col. Putnam had …

Home, declaring themselves ready at a Minute's Warning to arm again, and fight for their Country, and distressed Brethren of Boston.

A Number of the Poor of this Town are now employed about making Bricks at the new Yard, belonging to the Town on the Neck.

Lieutenant Governor Oliver has removed his Family and Goods from Cambridge to this Town.

In several Towns towards Connecticut, the Meeting-Houses were shut up on Sunday last, and the People all under ARMS.

We hear the Hon. Peyton Randolph, Esq; Speaker of the House of Burgesses of Virginia, is appointed President of the Congress.

Last Friday Morning one Valentine Ducket, a Deserter from the 65th Regt. now at Halifax, was shot in the Rear of the Camp in the Common, pursuant to the Sentence of a Court-Martial.

Since our last 4 24 pounders and 8 nine pounders have been transported from castle william to this town, and are now placed at the fortification on the neck.

The Hon. Mrs. GAGE, Lady of his Excellency the Governor, arrived in Town last Evening from New-York.

EXTRACT *of a* LETTER *from* GOVERNOR HUTCHINSON,
LONDON, *July* 8, 1774.

"Let the TEA be paid for by or in behalf of the TOWN, as soon as may be; and I hope you will do as much to promote this as possible.-------I find my APPLICATIONS every where to have more WEIGHT than I could EXPECT, and the PROSPECT of your speedy RELIEF to be fairer every DAY:----If finally obtained, I shall think it one of the most happy CIRCUMSTANCES of my LIFE."

LAST Monday the Select-Men of this Town waited on his … GAGE, to acquaint him that the … …ed to find that he had ordered the … Fortification on the Neck; … that he would explain to them … Movement, that they might … to quiet the Minds of the People; … the following Purpose: That … up the Avenue to the Town, or … or any of the Country People, … Town as usual; that he had … he was to protect his Majesty's … roops in this Town; and that he … hostile against the Inhabitants.

… Sept. 12.

… *Men of this Town again waited upon* … *with the following* ADDRESS, *viz* … EXCELLENCY,

… Boston, at the earnest Desire of a Number of Gentlemen of the Town and Country, again wait on your Excellency to acquaint you, that since our late Application the Apprehensions of the People not only of this but of the neighbouring Towns are greatly increased, by observing the Design of erecting a Fortress at the Entrance of the Town; & of reducing this Metropolis in other Respects to the State of a Garrison.--- This with Complaints lately made, of Abuse from some of the Guards posted in the Quarter in assaulting and forceably detaining several Persons who were peaceably passing in and out of the Town, may discourage the Market People from coming in with … Inhabitants to abandon the

Mr. PRINTER, *Please to insert the following, and you will oblige your's,* MEDICUS.

ON Saturday last was delivered of a perfect CHILD, the famous Personage Mrs. FOX, who arrived here from LONDON the 8th Instant: It was expected by many, she would have been provided with a MIDWIFE from BOSTON; as it was feared, if she was intrusted to the Unskilfulness of the *obstetric* Professors in Portsmouth, her tender Offspring might be stifled in the Birth. But as a more than ordinary Caution was observed on both Sides, the Event so much feared, has been happily prevented. The CHILD was immediately sent to Halifax, to be put under the Care of a faithful NURSE, where it will remain, until it be fit to appear in Public. The MOTHER will return to LONDON, when sufficiently recovered to venture abroad.

By a private LETTER from Boston since the Post.

The following is said to be Governor GAGE's Answer to the COMMITTEE of the County of Suffolk, who waited on his EXCELLENCY, on Account of the uneasiness of said County, occasioned by his erecting a Fortress at the Entrance of the Town, &c.

I Hoped the Assurance I gave the Selectmen of Boston on the Subject you now address me, had been satisfactory to every Body.--- I cannot possibly intercept the Intercourse between the Town and the Country; it is my Duty and Interest to encourage it, and it is as much inconsistent with my Duty and Interest to form this strange Scheme you are pleased to suggest of reducing the Inhabitants to a State of Humiliation and Vassalage, by stopping their Supplies, nor have I made it easier to effect this, than what Nature has made it. You mention the Soldiers insulting, beating and abusing Passengers as a common Thing; an Instance perhaps may be given of the bad Behaviour of some disorderly Soldiers, but I must appeal to the Inhabitants of both Town and Country for their general good Behaviour, from their first Arrival to this Time.

I would ask what Occasion there is, for such Numbers going armed in and out of the Town, and thro' the Country in an hostile Manner? Or why were the Guns removed privately in the Night from the Battery at Charlestown? The refusing Subjection to the late Acts of Parliament I find general throughout the Province, and I shall lay the same before his Majesty.

A Town-Meeting is to be held in this Town on Monday next at 3 o'Clock Afternoon, when Matters of Importance are to be transacted, therefore it is desired there may be a general Attendance.

NEW-HAMPSHIRE GAZETTE (PORTSMOUTH)

September 16, 1774

"FORTY THOUSAND MEN in MOTION and under ARMS," reported the *New-Hampshire Gazette* to show the Massachusetts countryside was committed to resistance and could oppose any Crown aggression with overwhelming force and unity.

NEW-HAMPSHIRE GAZETTE (PORTSMOUTH)

September 23, 1774

The next stage of the American Revolution was a race to arm, to control artillery and gunpowder. For example, we read here how General Gage and the Royal Navy had disabled batteries in Boston Harbor, but we do not read anything about how New Englanders were sneaking cannon into the countryside.

ligious, and for renewing that Harmony and Union between Great-Britain and the Colonies, ſo ardently wiſhed for by all good Men.

18. *Whereas the univerſal Uneaſineſs which prevails among all Orders of Men, ariſing from the wicked and oppreſſive Meaſures of the preſent Adminiſtration, may influence ſome unthinking Perſons to commit Outrage upon private Property* :——We would heartily recommend to all Perſons of this Community, not to engage in any Routs, Riots or licentious Attacks upon the Properties of any Perſon whatſoever, as being ſubverſive of all Order and Government ; but by a ſteady, manly, uniform and perſevering Oppoſition, to convince our Enemies that in a Conteſt ſo important, in a Cauſe ſo ſolemn, our Conduct ſhall be ſuch as to merit the Approbation of the Wiſe, and the Admiration of the brave and free of every Age and of every Country.

19. That ſhould our Enemies, by any ſudden Manœuvres, render it neceſſary for us to aſk the Aid and Aſſiſtance of our Brethren in the Country, ſome one of the Committee of Correſpondence, or a Selectman of ſuch Town, or the Town adjoining, where ſuch Hoſtilities ſhall commence, ſhall diſpatch Couriers with written Meſſages to the Selectmen or Committees of Correſpondence of the ſeveral Towns in the Vicinity, with a written Account of ſuch Matter, who ſhall diſpatch others to Committees more remote, 'till proper and ſufficient Aſſiſtance be obtained ; and that the Expence of ſaid Couriers be defrayed by the County, until it ſhall be otherwiſe ordered by the Provincial Congreſs.

Atteſt,

WILLIAM THOMPSON, *Clerk.*

B O S T O N, Sept. 19.

A melancholy Accident happened at Roxbury on Monday laſt, as two young Men were diverting themſelves with military Exerciſe one exchanged his Gun with the other, who gave the Words of Command ; at the Word FIRE ! his Companion diſcharged his Peice, not knowing it was loaded, and a Ball entered the Head of Mr. Henry, and killed him on the Spot.

We have received from Worceſter the Recantation of John Chandler, Eſq; and 42 others, of the Proteſtors, againſt the Proceedings of that Town, which gave ſuch Cauſe of Offence to the Public; as alſo the Acknowledgement of ſix Juſtices of that County, for having aſperſed the People in an Addreſs to General GAGE.

Laſt Wedneſday Night all the Cannon in the North Battery were ſpiked up, ſaid to be done by about 100 Men, who came in Boats from the Men of WAR.---They were, however, cleared again the next Day without much Difficulty.

The Newport Mercury of laſt Monday ſays, that "the Alarm which went thro' the Country laſt Saturday and Yeſterday ſe'nnight, reach'd New York on Monday, & had not the Accounts been ſoon contradicted, it is very certain there would have been *Sixty* or *Eighty Thouſand* Men in Arms, near Boſton, in 2 Days, not as ſome *Tories* infamouſly Inſinuate, for the Purpoſe of REBELLION ; but in Defence of ALL that's valuable, dear, holy and ſacred."

Laſt Week the Cannon at the Batteries back of Governor's Iſland were removed by Order of the General.

The TEA lately arrived in the Mary and Jane, Capt. Chapman, at Norfolk in Virginia, is to be returned in the ſame Ship by Orders of the Owners, in Conſequence of their having been waited on by the Committee of that Town.

The Phyſicians here, it is ſaid, have agreed to Innoculate no Patients for the Small Pox, during the ſitting of the Congreſs, as ſeveral of the Northern and Southern Delegates have not had that Diſorder."

We hear that Collections are making in the ſeveral Towns in the Colony of Rhode-Iſl[...] here : It is ſaid 1500 Dol[...] Newport ; and that the [...] had generouſly ſubſcrib[...]

A Correſpondent obſ[...] adviſe that the Eaſt-In[...] troyed at Boſton ; they [...] Markets in the World ; [...] Teas to ſuch Provinces, [...] pay the Duty, and they [...] vanced Price.

A great Number o[...] Barracks on the Commo[...]

Advices from L[...]

" That notwithſtandi[...] tion Aſſociation being e[...] the Continent of Ameri[...] Cuſtom Houſe in the Co[...] is not among the Liſt, th[...] about a Dozen more are n[...] is ſaid to be reſolved, at all [...] Bill, as Lord North ſays, " It will keep good for Years in America, tho' not uſed."

S A L E M, *Sept.* 20.

Letters from a Gentleman in Philadelphia, to his Friends in this Place, dated the 2d Inſt. ſay,---"The whole Attention and Converſation is wrapped up in the Congreſs, & every Mouth wiſhing them Succeſs-----they are greatly reſpected, as Men of Wiſdom, from whom the People ardently expect the Salvation of America. Every one prays for their Succeſs. The Canada Bill ſerves greatly to cement to our Welfare, and the Unanimity expected in their Councils almoſt aſſures them of it.------ What Meaſures will be adopted is as yet very uncertain ; ſome think Non-Exportation and Non-Importation to the Weſt-Indies and Great-Britain, others only to Great-Britain : But by what I can gather, it will be only with Great-Britain for the preſent, and the Weſt-Indies conditionally, at ſome future Meeting of the CONGRESS, if they find the firſt ineffectual. General Gage is moſt ſeverely handled in the Papers here and at Virginia, for his taking his Appointment. Government has not in this Place one who dares appear its Advocate. The Members from Virginia were juſt now received with Ringing of Bells, and other Marks of a moſt hearty Welcome. Upon the whole, every Thing bears the moſt promiſing Appearance for the future Welfare of America."

P H I L A D E L P H I A, Sept. 5.

Extract of a Letter from London, July 8.

" The Fox Indiaman, bound to New-England, has on board 30 Cheſts of Tea, ſhipped on the 6th Day of July, by Anthony Bacon, Eſq; of London. This Tea is generally ſuppoſed to be a Speculation of the Miniſter."

Extract of a Letter from Boſton, Auguſt 20.

" Letters by Capt. Scott have this Moment arrived :----He brings Intelligence that the People in England are rubbing up their Eyes, and begin to awake. Governor Tr---n is ſaid not a little to contribute to this : He told the Lords of Council, that it would not do to treat the Yorkers as he did the Regulators ; they were a very different kind of Men. He ſaid all the Force he had could not have ſaved the TEA, and therefore he ſent it back. He was aſked what he tho't of the preſent Meaſures adopted towards the Americans ? He anſwered, they would undoubtedly produce a Congreſs : And what would be the reſult of that ? He replied, he could not take upon him to ſay ; perhaps the Loſs of all North-America."

WILLIAMSBURG *(Virginia,) Aug.* 18.

By an Expreſe from the Frontiers, we learn that Col. M'Donald had juſt arrived from Wahatomakie, a Shawaneſe Town on the Muſkingham, which he has deſtroyed, with all the Plantations round it, taken 3 Scalps, killed ſeveral of the Indians, and made one Priſoner, with the Loſs of only two of his People, and 6 wounded ; and that an Expedition is planned againſt ſome of their other Towns, which, if ſucceſsful, will probably put an End to the War. Several Parties of Indians are daily ſeen on this Side of the Allegheny Mountains, but they have done but little Miſchief of late, except ſcalping one Family on the Head of Cedar Creek.

[...]gion of our Country ? Have they not by a partial and ignominious incloſure of Commons, deſtroyed the Cottagers who were the Supports of our Market, and (by Propagation) the Recruits of our Navy and Army ? Have they not, by a lawleſs and exorbitant Riſe of the Price of Lands, driven the Huſbandmen from [...]

[...] Country can be ſaved by you, and yet you ſuffer your Rights to be trampled on, nor turn again with the humble Spirit of a Worm. The Spirit of a Worm would ſave ye, but ye have it not ; and Ruin muſt purſue the Man, who can ſtand with his Fingers in his Mouth, and ſuffer the Slaves of Power to pick his Pockets. [...] the next Election may, in ſome Meaſure, ſnatch you from the Brink of Deſtruction, if ye can withſtand the Potations [...] you by the venal Candidates of Government. Retain yourſelves ſober, pride yourſelves in a blunt and manly Refuſal of [...], and give your Votes to ſuch honeſt Men only, who can and will ſtand by you in the Hour of Need and in the Day of Deſtruction.

Let no Intoxication warp your Reſolutions ; drink with your own M[...], nor ſwallow a Draught of Corruptions, that will moſt inevitably ruin ye all. There is ſcarce a Borough but will have Candidates of both Complexions.---You cannot be ſo blind as not to diſcern the white from the Black. Call up that antient Spunk and Virtue that ſo long diſtinguiſhed your Forefathers ; and let the World ſee that though Kings and Nobles ſtudy to ruin a People,---that Engliſhmen alone can ſave their Country, in ſpite of all the Evils of evil Men. Rouſe, Britons, rouſe from your Lethargy ; nor forget your antient Spirit, that hath ſo often reclaimed this Land in the Hours of Sorrow and Deſpair. The Virtue is alone with you---if you tamely fold your Arms and talk of Maladies, without adminiſtring a Cure, this Iſland in fifty Years will be a Colony of France, and your Children the miſerable Slaves of Arbitrary Power. Remember with Tears I give you the Caution,---remember the Prophecy ; or ſave the Land, by adopting the Advice of your ſteady and unſhaken Friend

MARVELL.

L O N D O N, July 28.

According to an Eſtimate, it is ſaid, the Navy of France at Midſummer laſt, conſiſted of 100 Ships of the Line and Frigates, ſaid to be eſteemed, upon an Average, ſuperior in Strengh to 100 Engliſh 64 Gun Ships.

It is ſaid that a French Nobleman of great Quality is in London incog. ſettling ſome Buſineſs relative to Poland. He is ſo cautious of being ſeen that he never goes out of his Lodging till late at Night, when he goes in a Chair to Down-Street, from whence he is conveyed in a Coach, attended by a certain Lord, to ſuch Places as their Buſineſs may require. 'Tis thought this will make the King of Pruſſia Sweat and Fret, when he is acquainted with it.

Orders are given for a general Survey of all the Fortifications in Great Britain, Ireland, and the Iſles of Mann, Jerſey, Guernſey and Scilly. Engineers are gone off for that Purpoſe. Every place of Strength is in future to be kept in thorough Repair.--- Some of the old Caſtles on the Sea Coaſts are to be pulled down, and the old Materials applied towards the Building new Fortifications and Barracks for Soldiers at every Place where the former are erected.

July 30. There are now fitting out, in different Yards, three Men of War deſtin'd for the Coaſt of Affrica, where they are to ſtationed for ſame Time, for the better Protection of the Trade, and are afterwards to ſail down the Coaſt, to join the Fleet on the North-American Station.

We are aſſured that ſome further, Orders and Inſtructions of an important Nature were laſt Week ſent off to General Gage, Governor of Maſſachuſet's Bay in New-England.

REPORTING THE

SUFFOLK RESOLVES

By Ray Raphael

WHILE THE RESPONSE TO THE POWDER ALARM WAS sudden and spontaneous, the lasting overthrow of British rule in all of Massachusetts outside of Boston was carefully considered. The local Committees of Correspondence, which enjoyed quasi-official status by their connection with town meetings, determined in advance to shut down the county courts after August 1, 1774, the date the Massachusetts Government Act was to take effect. (These courts, meeting quarterly, not only administered justice, but also served as the administrative arms of local government.)

The first court date was set for August 16 in Great Barrington, the "shiretown" of Berkshire County. On July 25, a local committee of correspondence told the Boston Committee it would not allow that court to sit, and on the appointed day, 1,500 people converged on the courthouse to make certain it did not. The Berkshire court would never again meet under British rule.

Springfield, in Hampshire County, was scheduled next. On August 30, before a crowd of some three thousand local citizens "in a sandy, sultry place, exposed to the sun," the Crown-appointed judges read their recantations, promising never to serve under the dreaded act (September 6 Hartford dateline in September 16, 1774, *New-Hampshire Gazette.*)

Other counties followed in turn. In the shiretown of Worcester, 4,622 militiamen from thirty-seven towns—half the adult male population of the county—assembled along both sides of Main Street as two dozen court officials slowly walked the gauntlet, hats in hand, reciting their recantations over thirty times apiece so all could hear.

In Plymouth, after some four thousand people had forced court officials to bow to their will, the victors were so enthused that they:

> *"attempted to remove a Rock (the one on which their fore-fathers first landed, when they came to this country) which lay buried in a wharfe five feet deep, up into the center of the town, near the court house. The way being up hill, they found it impracticable, as after they had dug it up, they found it to weigh ten tons at least."*

And so it went. As each county closed its courts, that county's convention of the Committees of Correspondence issued a set of resolutions explaining why the people had subverted the law. Typical of these resolutions is that of Middlesex County, which detailed item-by-item the injustices of the Massachusetts Government Act while giving only one fleeting mention to the Boston Port Act (September 8 Boston dateline in September 16, 1774, *New-Hampshire Gazette.*)

Only one of the mainland contiguous counties in Massachusetts did *not* close the courts: Suffolk, whose shiretown was Boston. There, buttressed by the presence of three thousand British soldiers, Crown-appointed officials still exerted military and political power. But Suffolk County's Committees of Correspondence still met and voiced their discontent, even if they lacked the power to overturn British authority. Hence the famous Suffolk Resolves, which resembled the resolves of other county conventions in substance but exceeded them in literary flare. Simultaneous with issuing its resolves, the Suffolk Convention sent a committee to Governor Gage to protest the cannon he positioned at the gates of Boston after the militia mobilization on September 2 (September 15 Boston dateline in September 23, 1774, *New-Hampshire Gazette.*)

Joseph Warren, on behalf of the Suffolk Convention, dispatched Paul Revere to Philadelphia with a copy of the

Suffolk Resolves, and when Revere returned September 23, he bore news that the intercolonial congress meeting there had unanimously endorsed the resolutions and would stand by the people of Massachusetts in their firm resistance to the abuses of British authority (September 26 Boston dateline in September 30, 1774, *New-Hampshire Gazette*.)

"This was one of the happiest days of my life," John Adams, one of the delegates, noted in his diary. "In Congress we had generous, noble sentiments, and manly eloquence. This day convinced me that America will support the Massachusetts or perish with her."

Historians have long noted the historic importance of the Suffolk Resolves and their endorsement by leaders from other colonies, but they have generally overlooked one key element: by sanctioning the Resolves, Congress supported deeds as well as words. It vowed to stand behind a revolution that was in full swing throughout Massachusetts.

A Map of 100 Miles Around Boston
Gentleman's Magazine, London, 1775

This map illustrates the counties of Massachusetts.

It may be depended upon, that ſome copious inſtructions reſpecting the Effectuation of a Peace between the Ruſſians and the Turks, were laſt Week ſent off to our Ambaſſadors at Peterſburgh and Conſtantinople.

BOSTON, Sept. 8.

Middleſex RESOLVES.

At a Meeting of 150 Gentlemen, being Committees from every Town and Diſtrict in the County of Middleſex, and Province if Maſſachuſetts-Bay, held at Concord in ſaid County, on the 30th and 31ſt Days of Aug. 1774. to conſult upon Meaſures proper to be taken at the preſent very important Day, viz.

The Hon. JAMES PRESCOT, Eſq; choſen Chairman.

After having read the late Act of the Britiſh Parliament entitled, An Act for the better regulating the Government of the Province of Maſſachuſetts Bay in New-England," and debated thereon;

Voted, That a Committee be appointed to take into Conſideration the ſaid Act, and report to this Meeting.

Voted, That Mr. *Jonathon Williams Auſtin*, of *Chelmſford*, Capt. *Thomas Gardner*, of Cambridge, Doctor *Iſaac Foſter*, of *Charleſtown*. Capt. *Joſiah Stone*, of *Framingham*, Mr. *Richard Deavens*, of *Charleſtown*, Doctor *Oliver Preſcott*, of *Groton*, *Henry Gardner*, Eſq; of *Stow*, Mr. *William Brown* of *Framingham*, and Mr. *Ebenezer Bridge*, jun. of *Billerica*, be the Committee.

Who reported as follows,

IT is evident to every attentive Mind, that this Province is in a very dangerous and alarming Situation. We are obliged to ſay, however painful it may be to us, that the Queſtion now is, whether by a Submiſſion to ſome late Acts of the Parliament of Great-Britain, we are contented to be the moſt abject Slaves, and entail that Slavery on Poſterity after us, or by a manly, joint and virtuous Oppoſition aſſert and ſupport our Freedom.

There is a Mode of Conduct, which in our very critical Circumſtances, we would wiſh to adopt, a Conduct, on the one Hand never tamely ſubmiſſive to Tyranny and Oppreſſion, on the other, never degenerating into Rage, Paſſion and Confuſion. This is a Spirit which we revere, as we find it exhibited in former Ages, and will command Applauſe to lateſt Poſterity.

The late Acts of Parliament pervade the whole Syſtem of Juriſprudence, by which Means, we think, the Fountains of Juſtice are fatally corrupted. Our Defence muſt therefore be immediate in Proportion to the ſuddenneſs of the Attack and vigorous in Proportion to the Danger.

We muſt NOW exert ourſelves, or all thoſe EFFORTS, which for Ten Years paſt, have brightened the Annals of this Country, will be totally fruſtrated. LIFE and DEATH, or what is more, FRREEDOM and SLAVERY are in a peculiar Senſe now before US, and the Choice and Succeſs, under God, depend greatly upon ourſelves. WE are therefore bound, as Struggling not only for ourſelves, but future Generations, to expreſs our Sentiments in the following RESOLVES; Sentiments, which we think, are founded in Truth and Juſtice, and therefore Sentiments we are determined to abide by.

RESOLVED, That as true and loyal SUBJECTS of our gracious SOVEREIGN GEORGE the THIRD, KING of Great Britain, &c. we by no MEANS intend to withdraw our ALLEGIANCE from him; but, while permitted the free Exerciſe of our natural and Charter RIGHTS, are reſolved to expend LIFE and TREASURE in his SERVICE.

RESOLVED, That when our Anceſtors emigrated from Great Britain, Charters and ſolemn Stipulations expreſſed the Conditions, and what particular Rights they yielded; what each party had to do and perform, and which each of the contradicting Parties were equally bound by.

RESOLVED, That we know of no Inſtance, in which this Province has tranſgreſſed the Rules on their Part, or any Ways forfeited their natural and chartered RIGHTS to any Power on Earth.

RESOLVED, That the Parliament of Great-Britain have exerciſed a Power contrary to the above-mentioned Charter, by paſſing Acts, which hold up their abſolute Supremacy over the Coloniſts; by another Act blocking up the Port of Boſton; and by two late Acts, the one entitled, An Act for better regulating the Government of the Province of Maſſachuſetts-Bay, the other entituled, An Act for the more impartial Adminiſtration of Juſtice in ſaid Province; and by enforcing all theſe iniquitous Acts with a large armed Force to dragoon and enſlave us.

RESOLVED, That the late Act of Parliament, entitled an Act for the better regulating the Government of the Province of the Maſſachuſetts-Bay in New England, expreſly acknowledges the Authority of the Charter, granted by their Majeſties King William and Queen Mary to ſaid Province; and that the only Rea-

of their having been forfeited, to which Charge the Province has had no Opportunity of anſwering.

RESOLVED, That a Debtor may as juſtly refuſe to pay his Debts, becauſe it is inexpedient for him, as the Parliament of

our common Rights as Engliſhmen.

RESOLVED, That every People have an abſolute Right of meeting together to conſult upon common Grievances, and to Petition, Remonſtrate and uſe every legal Method for their Removal.

RESOLVED, That the Act which prohibits theſe conſtitutional Meetings cuts away the Scaffolding of Engliſh Freedom, and reduces us to a moſt abject State of Vaſſallage and Slavery.

RESOLVED, That it is our Opinion, theſe late Acts if quietly ſubmitted to, will annihilate the laſt Veſtiges of Liberty in this Province, and therefore we muſt be juſtified by God and the World, in never ſubmitting to them.

RESOLVED, That it is the Opinion of this Body, that the preſent Act, reſpecting the Government of the Province of Maſſachuſetts-Bay, is an *artful, deep laid* Plan of Oppreſſion & Deſpotiſm, that it requires great Skill & Wiſdom to counteract it. This Wiſdom we have endeavoured to collect from the united Sentiments of the County; And although we are grieved that we are obliged to mention any Thing that may be attended with ſuch very important Conſequences, as may now enſue, yet a Senſe of our Duty as Men, as Freemen, as chriſtian Freemen, united in the firmeſt Bonds, obliges us to reſolve, that every civil Officer now in Commiſſion in this Province, and acting in conformity to the late Act of Parliament, is not an Officer agreeable to our Charter, therefore unconſtitutional, and ought to be oppoſed, in the Manner hereafter recommended.

RESOLVED, That we will obey all ſuch civil Officers, now in Commiſſion, whoſe Commiſſions were iſſued before the firſt Day of July 1774. and ſupport them in the Execution of their Offices according to the Manner uſual before the late Attempt to alter the Conſtitution of this Province; nay, even although the Governor ſhould attempt to revoke their Commiſſions.----- But that if any of ſaid Officers ſhall accept a Commiſſion under the preſent Plan of arbitrary Government, or in any Way or Manner whatever, aſſiſt the Governor or Adminiſtration in the Aſſault now making on our Rights and Liberties, we will conſider them as having forfeited their Commiſſions, and yield them no Obedience.

RESOLVED, That whereas the Hon. SAMUEL DANFORTH, and JOSEPH LEE, Eſquires; two of the Judges of the Inferior Court of common Pleas, for the County have accepted Commiſſions under the new Act by being ſworn Members of his Majeſty's Council appointed by ſaid Act: We therefore look upon them utterly incapable of holding any Office whatever.--- And whereas a Venire, on the late Act of Parliament, has iſſued from the Court of Seſſions, ſigned by the Clerk, We think they come under a preceeding Reſolve of acting in Conformity to the new Act of Parliament, We therefore Reſolve that, a Submiſſion to Courts thus acting and under theſe Diſqualifications, is a Submiſſion to the Act itſelf, and of Conſequence, as we are reſolved never to ſubmit to Courts thus conſtituted and thus acting in conformity to ſaid Act.

RESOLVED, That as, in conſequence of the former Reſolve all Buſineſs at the Inferior Court of common Pleas and Court of General Seſſions of the Peace next to be holden at Concord, muſt ceaſe; to prevent the many Inconveniences that may ariſe therefrom, we reſolve that all Actions, Writs, Suits, &c. bro't to ſaid Court, ought to remain in the ſame Condition, as at preſent, (unleſs ſettled by Conſent of Parties) 'till we know the Reſult of a Provincial and Continental Congreſs. And we reſolve, that no Plaintiff, in any Cauſe, Action or Writ aforeſaid, ought to enter ſaid Action in ſaid Court thus declared to be unconſtitutional. And we reſolve, if the Court ſhall ſet in Defiance to the Voice of the County, and default Actions and iſſue Executions accordingly, no Officer ought to ſerve ſuch Proceſs. And we are alſo determined to ſupport all Conſtables, Jurors and other Officers, who from theſe conſtitutional Principles ſhall refuſe Obedience to Courts which we have reſolved are founded on the Deſtruction of our Charter.

RESOLVED, That it is the Opinion of this Body of Delegates, that a provincial Congreſs is abſolutely neceſſary, in our preſent unhappy Situation.

Theſe are ſentiments which we are obliged to expreſs, as theſe acts are intended *immediately* to take place. We muſt *now* either oppoſe them, or tamely give up all we have been ſtrugling for. It is this that has forced us ſo ſoon on theſe very important Reſolves. However we do it with humble deference to the Provincial and Continential Congreſs, by whoſe Reſolutions we are determined to abide; to whom and the World we chearfully Appeal for the uprightneſs of our Conduct.

On the whole, theſe are "great and profound Queſtions." We are grieved to find ourſelves reduced to the Neceſſity of entering into the diſcuſſion of them. But we deprecate a State of Slavery. Our Fathers left a fair Inheritance to us, purchaſed by a waſte of Blood and Treaſure. This we are reſolved to tranſmit equally fair to our Children after us. No Danger ſhall affright, no Difficulties intimidate us. And if in Support of our Rights we are called to encounter even Death, we are yet undaunted, ſenſible that HE can never die too ſoon, who lays down

ſame, be collected by Yeas and Nays; which being done, there were 146 Yeas and 4 Nays.

Voted, That it be recommended to the ſeveral Towns and Diſtricts in this County, that each appoint one or more Delegates

have carried with them the Chains of Slavery, and Spirit of Deſpotiſm; but as they are, they ought to be remembered as great Inſtances to inſtruct the World, to what a Stretch of Liberty Mankind will naturally attain when they are left to the free Exerciſe of themſelves. And, my Lords, notwithſtanding my Intention to give my hearty Negative to the Queſtion now before you, I cannot help condemning in the ſevereſt Manner, the late turbulent and unwarrantable Conduct of the Americans in general, and the Riots in Boſton in particular. But, my Lords, the Mode which has been purſued to bring them back to a Senſe of their Duty to the parent State, has been ſo diametrically oppoſed to the fundamental Principles of ſound Policy, that Individuals poſſeſſed of common Underſtanding, muſt be aſtoniſhed at ſuch Proceedings. By blocking up the Harbour of Boſton, you have involved the innocent Trader in the ſame Puniſhment with the guilty Profligates who deſtroyed your Merchandize; and inſtead of making a well concerted Effort to ſecure the real Offenders, you clap a naval and military Extinguiſher over their Harbour; and puniſh the Sin of a few lawleſs Raparees & their Abettors upon the whole Body of the Inhabitants.

My Lords, This Country is little obliged to the Framers and Promoters of this Tea-Tax; the Americans had almoſt forgot, in their Exceſs of Gratitude for the Repeal of the Stamp-Act, any Intereſt but that of the Mother Country; there ſeemed an Emulation among the different Provinces, who ſhould be moſt dutiful and forward in their Expreſſions of Loyalty to their Royal Benefactor; as you will readily perceive by the following Extract of a Letter to from Governor Bernard to a noble Lord then in Office.

"The Houſe of Repreſentatives, (ſays he) from the Time of "opening the Seſſion to this Day, has ſhewn a Diſpoſition to "avoid all Diſpute with me; every Thing having paſſed with "as much good Humour as I could deſire. They have acted, "in all Things, with Temper and Moderation; they have a-"voided ſome Subjects of Diſpute, and have laid a Foundation "for removing ſome Cauſes of former Altercation."

This, my Lords, was the Temper of the Americans; and would have continued ſo, had it not been interrupted by your fruitleſs endeavours to tax them without their Conſent: but the Moment they perceived your Intention was renewed to tax them, through the Sides of the Eaſt-India Company, their Reſentment got the Aſcendant of their Duty, and hurried them into Actions contrary to all Laws of Policy, Civilization and Humanity, which in their cooler Hours they would have thought on with Horror; for I ſeriouſly believe, the deſtroying the Tea was much more the Effect of *Deſpair* than that of *Deſign*.

But, my Lords, from the Complexion of the whole of the Proceedings, I am apt to think, that Adminiſtration has purpoſely irritated them into thoſe late violent Acts for which they now ſo ſeverely ſmart; purpoſely to be revenged on them for the Victory they gained by the Repeal of the Stamp-Act, a Meaſure to which they ſeemingly acquieſced, but at the Bottom they were its real Enemies. For what other Motive could induce them to dreſs Taxation, that Father of American Sedition, in the Robes of an Eaſt-India Director, but to break in upon that mutual Peace and Harmony which then ſo happily ſubſiſted between them and the Mother Country? My Lords, I am an old Man, and will adviſe the noble Lords now in Office, to adopt a more gentle Mode of governing America; for the Day is not far diſtant, when America may vie with theſe Kingdoms, not only in *Arms*, but in *Arts* alſo. It is an eſtabliſhed Fact, that the principal Towns in America are *learned* and *polite*, and underſtand the Conſtitution of the Empire, as well as the noble Lords who *guide the Springs* of Government-----; and conſequently, they will have a watchful Eye over their Liberties, to prevent the leaſt encroachment of an arbitrary Adminiſtration on their hereditary Rights and Privileges.

This Obſervation ſo recently exemplified in an excellent Pamphlet which comes from the Pen of an American Gentleman,* that I ſhall take the Liberty of reading to your Lordſhips his Thoughts on the Competency of the Britiſh Parliament to tax America, which in my Opinion, ſets that intereſting Matter in the cleareſt Point of View.

"The high Court of Parliament (ſays he) is the ſupreme Legiſlative Power over the whole Empire; in all free States the Conſtitution is fixed; and as the ſupreme Legiſlative derives its Power and Authority from the Conſtitution, it cannot overleap the Bounds of it, without deſtroying it's own Foundation; for the Conſtitution aſcertains and limits both Sovereignity and Allegiance: and therefore his Majeſty's American Subjects, who acknowlege themſelves bound by the Ties of Allegiance, have an *equitable* Claim to the full Enjoyment of the fundamental Rules of the Engliſh Conſtitution; and that it is an eſſential unalterable Right in Nature, ingrafted into the Britiſh Conſtitution as a fundamental Law, and ever held ſacred and irrevocable by the Subjects within the Realm; and that what a Man has honeſtly acquired, is abſolutely his own; which he may freely give, but which cannot be taken from him without his Conſent."

This my Lords, tho' no new Doctrine, has always been my

licy, which neither the Exigencies of the State, or even the Acquieſcence in the Taxes, could juſtify upon any Occaſion whatever. Such Proceedings will never meet with their wiſhed for ſucceſs; and inſtead af adding to their Miſeries, as the Bill now

Thursday Messrs. Smith and Atkinson procured a Vessel to take the Tea on board and carry it to Halifax. That Night also a Guard was set. And the next Morning, at Day-Light, the Tea was taken out, and put on board the Vessel procured to receive it, in Presence of the Guard; who having the Marks & Numbers of the Chests, found them to agree with the Bill of Lading and the Cocket. By 7 o'Clock the Vessel, with the TEA on board, got under Sail, and before 10 was out of the Harbour, with a fair Wind.

Messrs. Smith & Atkinson in the whole Affair conducted like Men of Honour, & entirely to the Satisfaction of the Committee, having used their utmost Endeavours to dispose of the Tea in a Manner the least exceptionable.

The 59th Regiment from this Town, and two Companies of the 64th from Danvers, marched to Boston last Saturday. The former is stationed on the Neck, at the Entrance of that Town, where they are Entrenching, and where the most hostile Preparations are now carrying on.

NEW-PORT, Sept. 5.

Yesterday an Express arrived at Providence from Plainfield, to inquire into the Account of the Powder's being stolen by Gage's Orders, informing that there were near Ten Thousand Men in Arms, in that Part of the Country, ready to march to Boston, if needed.

About 10 o'Clock last Night an Express arrived in this Town, for Commissions for a Number of Military Officers in the western Parts of this Colony, and informs, that Col. Putnam had marched from Connecticut, for Cambridge, with 1500 Men, and that Col. Saltonstall was to march this Day with another Body, and that all the Country were prodigiously enraged, they having been informed that a Party of Soldiers had marched to Framingham, to seize the Powder in that Town, and had killed 6 of the Inhabitants outright.

NEW-LONDON, Sept. 2.

Last Tuesday se'nnight, Col. Willard, one of the *new Council*, came to Union to do some Business; when two Gentlemen belonging to Windham, who had been his Attornies, in a Case, met him and publickly refused to assist him any more, as they looked upon him a Traitor to his Country. The People rose, took & confined him one Night, then carried him to Brimfield, where the Province People, about 400 in Number, met them: They called a Council of themselves, and condemned Col. Willard to Newgate Prison in Symsbury, and a Number set off with and carried him 6 Miles on the Way thither. Colonel Willard then submitted to take the Oath they required, on which they dismissed him.------One Capt. Davis, of Brimfield, was present who shewing Resentment and treating the People with bad Language, they strip'd him, and give him the New-Fashion Dress of Tar and Feathers.

PHILADELPHIA, August 31.

Last Week Col. Nathaniel Folsom, and Major John Sullivan, Delegates from New-Hampshire, arrived here.

On Monday Evening the Honorable Thomas Cushing, Esq; Samuel Adams, John Adams, and Robert Treat-Paine, Esq'rs Delegates from Boston, arrived in this City.

The Gentlemen Delegates from Connecticut are expected in Town this Evening.

As are those from Virginia and Maryland on Friday.

HARTFORD, Sept. 6.

On Tuesday last, being the Day the County Court was to set at Springfield, a great Concourse of People, judg'd to be about 3000, assembled at the Court-House in that Place, and appointed a Committee to wait on the Court, and request their Appearance among the People, which they immediately complied with, when they very willingly signed the following Engagement, viz.

WE the Subscribers, do severally Promise, and solemly engage to all People now assembled at Springfield, in the County of Hampshire on the 30th Day of Aug. 1774, that WE never will take, hold, execute, or exercise any Commission, Office, or Employment whatsoever, under, or by Virtue of, or in any Manner derived from any Authority pretended or attempted to be given by a late Act of Parliament, entitled, "An Act for the better regulating the Government of the Province of the Massachusetts Bay in New England."

Israel Williams, Oliver Partridge, Timothy Dwight; Thomas Williams, John Worthington, Joseph Hawley, William Williams, Simeon Strong, Moses Bliss, Jonathan Ashley, Elisha Porter, William Billings, John Phelps, Solomon Stoddard, Justus Ely, Caleb Strong, Samuel Fowler, Jonathan Bliss.

BOSTON, Sept. 8.

Treasurer Gray, we are credibly informed has not resigned his Office as Councellor.

Yesterday General Gage, accompanied by Lord Percy, the Admiral, and other Officers, critically surveyed the Mill Creek, which divides the Town.

By Letters from Connecticut, and by several credible Gentlemen arrived from thence, we are informed, that there were not less than FORTY THOUSAND MEN in MOTION, and under ARMS, on their Way to Boston, on Saturday, Sunday, and Monday last, having heard a false Report that the Troops had fired upon Boston, and killed several of the Inhabitants: Twelve Hundred arrived at Hartford from Farmington, & other

Excellency Governor GAGE, to acquaint him that the Inhabitants were much alarmed to find that he had ordered the breaking up the Ground near the Fortification on the Neck; and requested of his Excellency that he would explain to them his Design in that extraordinary Movement, that they might thereby have it in their Power to quiet the Minds of the People; when his Excellency replied to the following Purpose: That he had no Intention of stopping up the Avenue to the Town, or of obstructing the Inhabitants or any of the Country People, coming in or going out of the Town as usual; that he had taken his Measures, and that he was to protect his Majesty's Subjects and his Majesty's Troops in this Town; and that he had no Intention of any Thing hostile against the Inhabitants.

Monday, Sept. 12.

On Friday last the Select-Men of this Town again waited upon his Excellency the GOVERNOR *with the following* ADDRESS, *viz*

MAY IT PLEASE YOUR EXCELLENCY,

THE Select-Men of Boston, at the earnest Desire of a Number of Gentlemen of the Town and Country, again wait on your Excellency to acquaint you, that since our late Application the Apprehensions of the People not only of this but of the neighbouring Towns are greatly increased, by observing the Design of erecting a Fortress at the Entrance of the Town; & of reducing this Metropolis in other Respects to the State of a Garrison.--- This with Complaints lately made, of Abuse from some of the Guards posted in the Quarter in assaulting and forceably detaining several Persons who were peaceably passing in and out of the Town, may discourage the Market People from coming in with Provisions as usual, and oblige the Inhabitants to abandon the Town.--This Event we greatly deprecate, as it will produce Miseries which may hurry the Province into Acts of Desperation.

We should therefore think ourselves happy if we could satisfy the People that your Excellency would suspend your Design, and not add to the Distresses of the Inhabitants occasioned by the PORT-BILL, that of GARRISONING the TOWN.

JOHN SCOLLAY, Chairman of the Selectmen.

§§§§§

THE GOVERNOR'S ANSWER.

GENTLEMEN,

WHEN you lately applied to me respecting my ordering some Cannon to be placed at the Entrance of the Town, which you term the erecting a Fortress; I so fully expressed my Sentiments, that I tho't you was satisfied the People had nothing to fear from that Measure, as no Use would be made thereof, unless their hostile Proceedings should make it necessary; but as you have this Day acquainted me, that your Fears are rather increased, I have thought proper to assure you, that I have no Intention to prevent the free Egress and Regress of any Person to and from the Town, or of reducing it to the State of a GARRISON, *neither shall I suffer any under my Command to injure the Person or Property of any of his Majesty's Subjects. But as it is my Duty, so it shall be my Endeavour to preserve the Peace, and promote the Happiness of every Individual; and I earnestly recommend to you, and every Inhabitant, to cultivate the same Spirit.---And heartily wish they may live quietly and happily in the Town.*

THO'S GAGE.

Boston, Sept. 9. 1774.

To the Gentlemen Selectmen of the Town of Boston.

Extract of a Letter b

PROVISIONS *are ver*
but small Quantiti
open: And further we
next Year's Crop of WH
and many others much st
MINISTERIAL REVE
dread---How far the C
they do, how far they m
endeavour, without Dou
they oppress another; a
End; and in Time opp
for the Support of thei
We shall soon hear ho
you have divine Direct
soon to be determined.
and want to pick your
passed through our Ho
Whether the anti minis
the Affair, or had rat
tangle themselves, Tim
careful how you expre
into Trouble, as it is ve

POR

THURSDAY
NORMAN in the Fox Mammp, with
30 Chests of TEA, consigned to Edward Parry, Esq; who refused the Consignment; upon the People's being acquainted with this repeated Insult (of the East-India Company) to the Colonies, they were greatly alarmed, and had almost absolutely determi-

Town, &c.

I Hoped the Assurance I gave the Selectmen of Boston on the Subject you now address me, had been satisfactory to every Body.--- I cannot possibly intercept the Intercourse between the Town and the Country; it is my Duty and Interest to encourage it, and it is as much inconsistent with my Duty and Interest to form this strange Scheme you are pleased to suggest of reducing the Inhabitants to a State of Humiliation and Vassalage, by stoping their Supplies, nor have I made it easier to effect this, than what Nature has made it. You mention the Soldiers insulting, beating and abusing Passengers as a common Thing; an Instance perhaps may be given of the bad Behaviour of some disorderly Soldiers, but I must appeal to the Inhabitants of both Town and Country for their general good Behaviour, from their first Arrival to this Time.

I would ask what Occasion there is, for such Numbers going armed in and out of the Town, and thro' the Country in an hostile Manner? Or why were the Guns removed privately in the Night from the Battery at Charlestown? The refusing Subjection to the late Acts of Parliament I find general throughout the Province, and I shall lay the same before his Majesty.

A Town-Meeting is to be held in this Town on Monday next at 3 o'Clock Afternoon, when Matters of Importance are to be transacted, therefore it is desired there may be a general Attendance.

The Customers of this Paper

are earnestly desired to pay off what they may be in Arrears immediately, as the Publisher is under a Necessity of raising Money to carry on his Business, and purchase Paper, which he does now with great Difficulty and extraordinary Charge, as it is all brought 70 Miles on Land carriage----------He hopes every Customer will send at least one Dollar, that the Paper may not be wholly stopped, as there are now the most interesting Matters depending that ever were in this Country.

The Merrimack Post-Rider, whose Year is now up, will not carry News-Papers after this Month, unless the Customers punctually pay off; Likewise the Eastern Post, and the other who Rides up Connecticut River to the College.

THE annual Convention of Ministers is to be held at the House of the Rev'd Dr. HAVEN in Portsmouth, on Wednesday the 21st of September current.

CUSTOM HOUSE, *Piscataqua*, Inward-Entries	Sept. 15. FROM.
Ship Fox, Zechariah Norman,	London.
Schooner Dolphin, Giles Pearse,	Rhode Island.
Brig Hannah, William Tresethen,	Grenada.
Clear'd Outwards	FOR.

TO BE SOLD,

For the Term of seven Years, pursuant to a Decree of Court,

George Madden,

An Excellent Weaver— Whoever inclines to purchase the said George, may hear of the Terms by enquiring at the Printing Office. Portsmouth, *Sept.* 13, 1774.

NEW-HAMPSHIRE GAZETTE (PORTSMOUTH)

September 16, 1774

After August 1, 1774, the date the Massachusetts Government Act went into effect, the local Committees of Correspondence prevented the county courts from operating. In Springfield, before a crowd of thousands, the Crown-appointed judges read their recantations, promising never to serve under the dreaded act. As each county closed its courts, the county's convention of the Committees of Correspondence issued a set of resolutions explaining why the people had subverted the law, such as those from Middlesex County.

HE Vol. XVIII.

GAZETTE,

CHRONICLE,

FOREIGN AND DOMESTIC.

NO. 935 { Weeks fince this Paper was firft Publifh'd. }

Country, Ourfelves and
al Ways and Means in
n, defend and preferve
ous Rights & Liberties
ur Fathers fought——
id to hand them down
rations.
Acts of the Britifh Par-
up the Harbour of Bof-
he eftablifhed Form of
olony ; and for fcreen-
as Violaters of the Laws
a legal Trial, are grofs
Rights to which we are
: Laws of Nature, the
and the Charter of the

ience is due from this
any Part of the Acts a-
that they be rejected
wicked Adminiftration

the Juftices of our Su-
cature, Court of Affize,
ivery, & Inferior Courts
n this County, are ap-
eir Places by any other
hich the Charter & the
e direct ; they muft be
undue Influence, & are
ionalOfficers, & as fuch
e paid them by the Peo-

Juftices of the Superior
, Court of Affize, &c.
t of Common Pleas, or
ons of the Peace, fhall
eir prefent difqualified
will fupport and bear
& their Deputies,Con-
ther Officers, who fhall
Execution the Orders of
s far as is poffible to pre-
ences that muft attend
e Courts of Juftice, we
mend it to all Creditors
nable and generous For-
btors, and to all Debtors
ft Debts with all poffible
ifputes concerning Debts

offended by accepting faid Department, and have not already, publickly refigned their Seats at the Council-Board, to make public Refignations of their Places at faid Board, on or before the TWENTIETH Day of this Inftant *September* ; and that all Perfons neglecting fo to do fhall from and after faid Day be confidered by this County, as obftinate and incorrigible Enemies to this Colony.

9. That the Fortifications begun and now carrying on upon Bofton Neck are juftly alarming to this County, and give us Reafon to apprehend fome hoftile Intention againft that Town, more efpecially as the Commander in Chief has in a very extraordinary Manner removed the Powder from the Magazine at Charleftown, and has alfo forbidden the Keeper of the Magazine at Bofton to deliver out to the Owners the Powder which they had lodged in faid Magazine.

10. That the late Act of Parliament for eftablifhing the Roman Catholic Religion, and the French Laws in that extenfive Country now called Canada, is dangerous in an extreme Degree to the Proteftant Religion, and to the civil Rights and Liberties of all America ; and therefore, as Men and Proteftant Chriftians we are indifpenfibly obliged to take all proper Means for *our* Security.

11. That whereas our Enemies have flattered themfelves that they fhall make an eafy Prey of this numerous, brave and hardy People, from an Apprehenfion that they are unacquainted with military Difcipline, We therefore for the Honor Defence and Security of this County and Province advife, as it has been recommended to take away all Commiffions from the Officers of the Militia, that thofe who now hold Commiffions or fuch other Perfons be elected in each Town as Officers in the Militia as fhall be judged of fufficient Capacity for that Purpofe, and who have evidenced themfelves the inflexible Friends to the Rights of the People, and that the Inhabitants of thofe Towns and Diftricts who are qualified do ufe their utmoft Dilligence to acquaint themfelves with the Art of War as foon as poffible, and do for that Purpofe appear under Arms at leaft once every Week.

SEPTEMBER 23, 1774

The

NEW-HAMPSHIRE GAZETTE

BOSTON, September 15, 1774.

At a Meeting of the Delegates of every Town and District in the County of *Suffolk*, on Tuesday the sixth of *September*, at the House of Mr. *Richard Woodward* of *Dedham*, and by Adjournment at the House of Mr. *Daniel Vose* of *Milton*, on Friday the Ninth Instant, JOSEPH PALMER, Esq; being chosen Moderator, and WILLIAM THOMPSON, Esq; Clerk, a Committee was chosen to bring in a Report to the Convention, and the following being several Times read and put Paragraph by Paragraph, was UNANIMOUSLY voted, *viz.*

Whereas *the Power, but not the Justice ; the Vengeance, but not the Wisdom of Great-Britain, which of old persecuted, scourged and exiled our fugitive Parents from their native Shores, now pursue us their guiltless Children with unrelenting Severity—And whereas this then savage and uncultivated Desart was purchased by the Toil and Treasure or acquired by the Valor & Blood of those our venerable Progenitors, who bequethed to us the dear bought inheritance, who consigned it to our Car & Protection ; the most sacred Obligations are upon us to transmit the glorious Purchase, unfettered by Power, unclogg'd with Shackles, to our innocent and beloved Offspring. On the Fortitude—on the Wisdom & on the Exertions of this important Day, is suspended the Fate of this New World, and of unborn Millions. If a boundless Extent of Continent, |warming with Millions, will tamely submit to live, move and have their Being at the arbitrary Will of a licentious Minister, they basely yield to voluntary Slavery, and future Generations shall load their Memories with incessant Execrations.—On the other Hand, if we arrest the Hand which would ransack our Pockets, if we disarm the Parricide who points the Dagger to our Bosoms, if we nobly defeat that fatal Edict which proclaims a* Power to frame Laws for us in all

NEW-HAMPSHIRE AND HISTORICAL

CONTAINING the Freſheſt ADVICES

Friday *Sept.* 23, 1774.

BOSTON, September 15. 1774.

At a Meeting of the Delegates

of every Town and Diſtrict in the County of *Suffolk*, on Tueſday the ſixth of *September*, at the Houſe of Mr. *Richard Woodward* of Dedham, and by Adjournment at the Houſe of Mr. *Daniel Voſe* of *Milton*, on Friday the Ninth Inſtant, JOSEPH PALMER, Eſq; being choſen Moderator, and WILLIAM THOMPSON, Eſq; Clerk, a Committee was choſen to bring in a Report to the Convention, and the following being ſeveral Times read and put Paragraph by Paragraph, was UNANIMOUSLY voted, *Viz.*

WHEREAS *the Power, but not the Juſtice; the Vengeance, but not the Wiſdom of Great-Britain, which of old perſecuted, ſcourged and exiled our fugitive Parents from their native Shores, now purſue us their guiltleſs Children with unrelenting Severity—And whereas this then ſavage and uncultivated Deſart was purchaſed by the Toil and Treaſure or acquired by the Valor & Blood of thoſe our venerable Progenitors, who bequeathed to us the dear bought Inheritance, who conſigned it to our Care & Protection; the moſt ſacred Obligations are upon us to tranſmit the glorious Purchaſe, unfettered by Power, unclogg'd with Shackles, to our innocent and beloved Offspring. On the Fortitude—on the Wiſdom & on the Exertions of this important Day, is ſuſpended the Fate of this New World, and of unborn Millions. If a boundleſs Extent of Continent, ſwarming with Millions, will tamely ſubmit to live, move and have their Being at the arbitrary Will of a licentious Miniſter, they baſely yield to voluntary Slavery, and future Generations ſhall load their Memories with inceſſant Execrations.—On the other Hand, if we arreſt the Hand which would ranſack our Pockets, if we diſarm the Parricide who points the Dagger to our Boſoms, if we nobly defeat that fatal Edict which proclaims a* Power to frame Laws for us in all Caſes whatſoever, *thereby entailing the endleſs and numberleſs Curſes of Slavery upon Us, our Heirs and their Heirs forever; if we ſucceſsfully reſiſt that unparrallelled Uſurpation of unconſtitutional Power, whereby our Capital is robbed of the Means of Life, whereby the Streets of Boſton are thronged with Military Executioners, whereby our Coaſts are lined, & Harbours crowded with Ships of War, whereby the Charter of the Colony, that ſacred Barrier againſt the Encroachments of Tyranny, is mutilated, and in Effect annihilated; whereby a murderous Law is framed to ſhelter Villains from the Hand of Juſtice; whereby that unalienable and ineſtimable Inheritance, which we derived from Nature, the Conſtitution of Britain, which was covenanted to us in the Charter of the Province, is totally wrecked, annulled and vacated;—Poſterity will acknowledge that Virtue which preſerved them free and happy; and while we enjoy the Rewards and Bleſſings of the Faithful, the Torrent of Panegyrick will roll down our Reputations to that lateſt Period, when the Streams of Time ſhall be abſorbed in the Abyſs of Eternity.*

Therefore, WE HAVE RESOLVED, AND DO RESOLVE,

1ſt. THAT whereas his Majeſty GEORGE the Third is the rightful Succeſſor to the Throne of Great-Britain, & juſtly entitled to the Allegiance of the Britiſh Realm and agreeable to *Compact*, of the Engliſh Colonies in America.—Therefore we the Heirs and Succeſſors of the firſt Planters of this Colony, do chearfully acknowledge the ſaid GEORGE the Third to be our rightful Sovereign, and that ſaid Covenant is the Tenure and Claim on which are founded our Allegiance and Submiſſion.

2. That it is an indiſpenſable Duty which

NEW-HAMPSHIRE GAZETTE (PORTSMOUTH)

September 23, 1774

Suffolk County, whose shiretown was Boston, was the only county in Massachusetts not to close the courts because it was occupied by three thousand British soldiers. Still, the county's Committees of Correspondence met and documented their discontent, which resulted in the famous Suffolk Resolves, "which resembled the resolves of other county conventions in substance but exceeded them in literary flare."

Cases whatsoever, *thereby entailing the endless and numberless Curses of Slavery upon Us, our Heir and their Heirs forever ; if we successfully resist that unparrallelled Usurpation of unconstitutional Power, whereby our Capital is robbed of the Means of Life, whereby the Streets of Boston are thronged with Military Executioners, whereby our Coasts are lined, & Harbours crowded with Ships of War, whereby the Charter of the Colony, that sacred Barrier against the Encroachments of Tyranny, is mutilated, and in effect annihilated ; whereby a murderous Law is framed to shelter Villains from the Hand of Justice ; whereby that unalienable and inestimable Inheritance, which we derived from Nature, the Constitution of Britain, which was covenanted to us in the Charter of the Province, is totally wrecked, annulled and vacated;----Posterity will acknowledge that Virtue which preserved them free and happy ; and while we enjoy the Rewards and Blessings of the Faithful, the Torrent of Panegyrick will roll down our Reputations to that latest Period, when the Streams of Time shall be absorbed in the Abyss of Eternity.*

Therefore, WE HAVE RESOLVED, and DO RESOLVE,

1st. That whereas his Majesty George the Third is the rightful Successor to the Throne of Great-Britain, & Justly entitled to the Allegiance of the British Realm and agreeable to *Compact*, of the English Colonies in America.—Therefore we the Heirs and Successors of the first Planters of this Colony, do chearfully acknowledge the said GEORGE the Third to be our rightful Sovereign, and that said Covenant is the Tenure and Claim on which are founded our Allegiance and Submission.

2. That it is an indispensable Duty which we owe GOD, our Country, Ourselves and Posterity, by all lawful Ways and Means in our Power, to maintain, defend and preserve those civil and religious Rights & Liberties for which many of our Fathers fought----bled----and died : and to hand them down entire to future Generations.

3. That the late Acts of the British Parliament for blocking up the Harbour of Boston, and for altering the established Form of Government in this Colony ; and for screening the most flagitious Violaters of the Laws of the Province from a legal Trial, are gross Infractions of these Rights to which we are justly entitled by the Laws of Nature, the British Constitution, and the Charter of the Province.

4. That no Obedience is due from this Province to either or any Part of the Acts abovementioned ; but that they be rejected as the Attempts of a wicked Administration to enslave America.

5. That so long as the Justices of our Superior Courts of Judicature, Court of Assize, & General Goal Delivery, & Inferior Courts of Common Please in this County, are appointed, or hold their Places by any other Tenure than that which the Charter & the Laws of the Province direct; they must be considered as under undue Influence, & are therefore unconstitutional Officers, & as such no Regard ought to be paid them by the People of this County.

6. That if the Justices of the Superior Court of Judicature, Court of Assize, &c. Justices of the Court of Common Please, or of the General Sessions of the Peace, shall sit and act during their present disqualified State, this County will support and bear harmless all Sheriffs & their Deputies, Constables, Jurors and other Officers, who shall refuse to carry into Execution the Orders of the said Courts : And as far as is possible to prevent the Inconveniences that must attend the Suspension of the Courts of Justice, we do earnestly recommend it to all Creditors to exercise all reasonable and generous Forbearance to their Debtors, and to all Debtors to discharge their just Debts with all possible Speed, and if any Disputes concerning Debts or Trespasses shou'd arise, which cannot be settled by the Parties or either of them shall refuse so to do, they ought to be considered as co-operating with the Enemies of this Country.

NEW-HAMPSHIRE GAZETTE (PORTSMOUTH)

September 30, 1774

Between 1773 and 1775, Paul Revere had two dozen revolutionary rides. One such ride was to share the Suffolk Resolves with the Continental Congress and return with their response, which was documented here.

BOSTON Sept. 22.

Upon receiving the last Answer of his Excellency, the Committee met together, and having carefully perused the same, were unanimously of Opinion, That his Excellency's Answer could not be deemed satisfactory to the County.----And further, that his Excellency in his Reply had been pleased to propose several Questions, which if unanswered by the Committee would leave on the Minds of People not fully acquainted with the State of Facts some very disagreeable Impressions concerning the Conduct and Behaviour of the People in the County and Province. And the following Address was unanimously voted to be presented to his Excellency.

May it please your Excellency,

THE Answer you have been pleased to favour us with to the Address this Day presented to you, gives us Satisfaction so far as it relates to your own Intentions; and we thank your Excellency for the Declaration which you have made, that it is your Duty & Interest to encourage an Intercourse between Town and Country; and we intreat your Indulgence while we modestly reply to the Questions proposed in your Answer. Your Excellency is too well acquainted with the Human Heart not to be sensible that it is natural for the People to be soured by Oppression, and jealous for their personal Security, when their Exertions for the Preservation of their Rights are construed into Treason and Rebellion. Our Liberties are invaded by Acts of the British Parliament, troops are sent to inforce those Acts. They are now erecting Fortifications at the Entrance of the Town of Boston, upon the compleating those, the Inhabitants of the Town of Boston will be in the Power of a Soldiery who must implicitly obey the Orders of an Administration who have hitherto evidenced no singular Regard to the Liberties of America. The Town is already greatly impoverished and distressed by the Operations of the barbarous Port-Bill. Your Excellency, we are perswaded from Principles of Humanity, would refuse to be an Actor in the tragical Scene that must ensue upon shutting up the Avenues to the Town, and reducing the Inhabitants by Distress and Famine, to a disgraceful and slavish Submission; but that cruel Work may possibly be reserved for a Successor, disposed and instructed thereto. Daily Supplies of Provisions are necessary for the Subsistence of the Inhabitants of the Town. The Country disgusted and jealous at the formidable Operations now carrying on, survey with Horror, a Plan concerted---whereby the Inhabitants of the Town of Boston may be imprisoned and starved at the Will of a Military Command. They kindly invite them to abandon the Town, and earnestly solicit them to share the homely Banquet of Peace in the Country. Should their Refusal involve them in Miseries hitherto unheard of, and hardly conceiv'd of, the Country must stand acquitted, and will not hold their Liberties so loosely as to sacrifice them to the Obstinacy of their Brethren in Boston.

Your Excellency has been pleased to order the Powder from the Magazine in Charlestown, to forbid the Delivery of the Powder in the Magazine of Boston to the legal Proprietors, to seize the Cannon at Cambridge, and bring a formidable Number from Castle William, which are now placed at the Entrance of the Town of Boston. And have likewise in Addition to the Troops now here, been pleased to send for Reinforcements to Quebec and other Parts of the Continent. These Things, Sir, together with the Disposition of the Ships of War, we humbly think sufficiently justify the Proceedings for which your Excellency seems to be at a Loss to account.

Your Excellency has suggested that Nature has made it easy to cut off the Communication between Town and Country.---Our only Request is, that the Entrance into the Town may remain as Nature has formed it.

If the Security to his Majesty's Troops is the only Design in the late Manœuvres, we beg leave to assure your Excellency that the most certain, and by far the most honorable Method of making them secure and safe, will be to give the People of the Province the strongest Proof that no Design is forming against their Liberties. And we again solicit your Excellency with that Earnestness which becomes us on this important Occasion to desist from every Thing which has a Tendency to alarm them, and particularly from fortifying the Entrance into the Town of Boston

We rely on your Excellency's Wisdom and Candor that, in your proposed Representation to our common Sovereign, you will Endeavour to redeem us from the Distresses which we apprehend were occasioned by the grossest Misinformation, and that you will assure his Majesty that no Wish of Independency, no adverse Sentiments or Designs towards his Majesty or his Troops now here, actuate his good Subjects in this Colony; but that their sole Intention is to preserve pure and inviolate those Rights to which, as Men, and English Americans, they are justly entitled, and which have been guaranteed to them by his Majesty's Royal Predecessors. By Order of the Committee,

JOSEPH WARREN, Chairman.

A COPY of the above was delivered to Mr. Sec'ry *Flucker*, by the Chairman, with a Desire that he would as soon as convenient, present it to the Governor, & request his Excellency

BOSTON, Sept. 26.

By Mr. PAUL REVERE, *who returned Express from Philadelphia last Friday Evening, we have the following Important* Intelligence.

PHILADELPHIA, Sept. 17, 1774.

SIR,

WE received your Favour of the 11th Inst. together with the Resolutions of the County of Suffolk, and communicated the same to the Congress: In Consequence of which they passed the several Resolutions which will be delivered to you by Mr. Revere, together with a Letter from the President. They highly applaud the wise, temperate and spirited Conduct of our People, in their Opposition to the late Act for altering our Constitution. These Resolves will, we trust, support and comfort our Friends, and confound our Enemies. In Behalf of myself and Brethren, I am with Respect,

Your most humble Servant,

JOSEPH WARREN, Esq; THOMAS CUSHING.

PHILADELPHIA, 17th Sept. 1774.

SIR,

YOUR Letter of the 11th Inst. directed "To the Hon'ble *Thomas Cushing*, Esq; and the other Gentlemen of the Congress, Members for Massachusetts Bay," together with the Resolutions entered into by the Delegates of the several Towns in the County of Suffolk, and their Address to his Excellency Governor GAGE, were communicated to the Congress, whereupon the Congress came into the following unanimous RESOLVES, which by their Order I transmit to you to be communicated to the Committee of Correspondence for the Town of Boston.

I am, SIR,

your most obedient Servant,

JOSEPH WARREN, Esq; PEYTON RANDOLPH.

IN CONGRESS, *Saturday*, Sept. 17, 1774.

A LETTER from Dr. JOSEPH WARREN, and sundry Resolutions entered into by the County of SUFFOLK, on Tuesday the 6th of this Instant, and an Address from the Delegates of the said County to his Excellency Governor GAGE, dated the 9th Instant, were read. Whereupon,

RESOLVED *unanimously*, That this Assembly deeply feels the suffering of their Countrymen in the Massachusetts-Bay, under the Operation of the late unjust, cruel and oppressive Acts of the British Parliament---that they most thoroughly approve the Wisdom and Fortitude with which Opposition to these wicked ministerial Measures has hitherto been conducted, & they earnestly recommend to their Brethren a Perseverance in the same firm and temperate Conduct, as expressed in the Resolutions determined upon at a Meeting of the Delegates for the County of Suffolk, on Tuesday the 6th Inst. trusting that the Effect of the united Efforts of North-America in their Behalf, will carry such Conviction to the British Nation, of the unwise, unjust, and ruinous Policy of the present Administration, as quickly to introduce better Men and wiser Measures.

RESOLVED *unanimously*, That Contributions from all the Colonies for supplying the Necessities and alleviating the Distresses of our Brethren at Boston, ought to be continued, in such Manner and so long as their Occasions may require.

A true Extract from the Minutes,

CHARLES THOMPSON, Secr.

DELEGATES who attend the CONGRESS.

From New Hampshire.

Major John Sullivan, and Col. Nathaniel Folsom.

From Massachusetts Bay.

Hon'ble Thomas Cushing, Esq; Mr. Samuel Adams, John Adams, and Robert Treat Paine, Esqs;

From Rhode-Island.

Hon. Stephen Hopkins, Esq; Hon. Samuel Ward, Esq;

From Connecticut.

Hon. Eliphalet Dyer, Silas Deane, and Roger Sherman, Esq'rs.

From New York.

James Duane, John Jay, Philip Livingston, Isaac Low, Col. William Floyd, and Henry Wesner, Esq'rs.

From New-Jersey.

James Kinsey, William Livingston, John D'Hart, Stephen Crane, and Richard Smith, Esq'rs.

From Pennsylvania.

Hon. Joseph Galloway, Samuel Rhoads, Thomas Mifflin, Charles Humporys, John Morton, Edward Biddle, and George Ross, Esq'rs.

From Newcastle, Kent, and Sussex Governments.

Cæsar Rodney, Thomas M'Kean, and George Read, Esq'rs.

From Maryland.

Mathew Tilgham, Thomas Johnson, jr. Robert Gouldsborough, William Paca, and Samuel Chase, Esq'rs.

From Virginia.

Hon. Peyton Randolph, Richard Henry Lee, George Washington, Patrick Henry, Richard Bland, Benjamin Harrison, and Edmund Pendleton, Esq'rs.

From North Carolina.

19. The virtuous Few in both Houses of Parliament.
20. The CITY of London. 21. Lord Chatham. 22. Lord Cambden. 23. Bishop of St. Asaph. 24. Duke of Richmond. 25. Sir George Saville. 26. Mr. Burke. 27. General Conway. 28. Mr. Dunning. 29. Mr. Sawbridge. 30. Dr. Franklin. 31. Mr. Dulany. 32. Mr. Hancock.

The Acclamations with which several of them were received, not only testified the Sense of the Honor conferred by such worthy Guests, but the fullest Confidence in their Wisdom and Integrity, and a firm Resolution to adopt and support such Measures as they shall direct for the public Good at this alarming Crisis.

BOSTON Sept. 26.

Thursday last, being the Anniversary of his Majesty's Coronation, the Guns at Castle William, and of the Batteries in this Town, also on board the Men of War in the Harbour were fired at Noon.-----His Excellency the Governor received the Compliments of the Gentlemen of the Army and Navy, &c. at the Council Chamber.

We hear the Town of Hartford in Connecticut, have contributed 1400 Bushels of Grain, Middletown about the same Quantity---Kensington 600---Middle Haddam 600, and other Towns in that Colony are doing the same for the Relief of the Poor in this Town.

Wednesday last the Freeholders and other Inhabitants of Boston met at Faneuil-Hall, for the Choice of Representatives to serve in the Great and General Court to be convened at Salem the 5th of next Month, when the following Gentlemen were chosen, viz. The Hon. *Thomas Cushing*, Esq; Mr. *Samuel Adams*, Hon. *John Hancock*, Esq; and *William Philips*, Esq;

Last Friday the Town made Choice of Dr. *Joseph Warren*, Dr. *Benjamin Church*, and Mr. *Nathaniel Appleton*, to serve as Delegates in the Provincial Congress, to be held at Concord on the second Tuesday of October next, in Addition to the four Representatives of this Town---and the following Instructions for our Representatives were voted, viz.

GENTLEMEN,

AS we have now chosen you to represent us in the Great and general Court to be holden at Salem on Wednesday the 5th Day of October next ensuing: we do hereby instruct you that in all your Doings as Members of the House of Representatives you adhere firmly to the Charter of this Province granted by their Majesty's King William and Queen Mary, and that you do no Act which can possibly be construed into an Acknowlegement of the Act of the British Parliament for altering the Government of the Massachusetts Bay, more especially that you acknowledge the Hon. Board of Councellors elected by the General Court at their Session in May last, as the only rightful and constitutional Council of this Province. And as we have Reason to believe that a conscientious Discharge of your Duty will produce your Dissolution as an House of Representatives, We do hereby impower and instruct you to join with the Members who may be sent from this and the Neighbouring Towns in the Province, and to meet with them at a Time to be agreed on in a general Provincial Congress, to act upon such Matters as may come before you in such a Manner as shall appear to be most conducive to the true Interest of this Town and Province, and most likely to preserve the Liberties of all America.

At a Meeting of the Select-Men and Committee of Correspondence, Sept. 24, 1774.

OUR Friends in the Neighbouring Towns and the Country in general, having expressed their Uneasiness lest the Workmen in this Town, by assisting the Army in building Barracks should give Occasion of Umbrage to their Friends who dwell more remote, whether in this or the neighbouring Colonies, particularly to our Brethren of New York, who have nobly rejected the Application of the Barrack-Master for Mechannicks and other Assistants from that place; ----Therefore having debated this Matter in Compliance with the Application of our Friends in the Country,------It is the Opinion of this joint Committee that should the Mechanicks or other Inhabitants of this Town, assist the Troops by furnishing them with Artificers, Labourers, or Materials of any Kind to build Barracks or other Places of Accomodation for the Troops they will probably incur the Displeasure of their Brethren, who may withhold their Contributions for the Relief of the Town, and deem them as Enemies to the Rights and Liberties of America, by furnishing the Troops with Conveniences for their Residence and accomodation in this Town.

By the public Papers and Letters from London, to the 30th of July we are informed, that Governor Hutchinson's Representation of the State of our Affairs were very pleasing to the Ministry, who were led to expect a Payment of the Tea, and a Submission to, and acquiescence in, the late Acts of the British Parliament, by the Friendship and Zeal of the Addressers to Governor Hutchinson, who have been represented as a Majority of the Men of Property, and Consequence in this Town----that the Operation of the Boston Port Act would greatly contribute

REPORTING THE

Massachusetts Provincial Congress

By Ray Raphael

Worcester, Springfield, Plymouth—the revolution that swept through Massachusetts in 1774 was a decentralized grassroots movement without any command post. Initially, this made it difficult to stop. "The flames of sedition," Governor Gage complained, had "spread universally throughout the Country beyond Conception." But how could the revolution be sustained without any central coordinating body?

On August 26 and 27, at the request of activists from Worcester, delegates from four counties convened in Boston for the first multicounty meeting of the Committees of Correspondence. Hoping to provide a more enduring structure to the movement, that meeting suggested that a Provincial Congress convene in Concord on the second Tuesday of October, and all the county committees, as they closed the courts, echoed this call.

For protocol, the towns also elected representatives to the official General Court, which had been scheduled to meet on October 5. This body convened in Salem, then the provincial capital, to demonstrate a willingness to work within the 1691 Provincial Charter—but not the Massachusetts Government Act. Governor Gage, though, had discontinued the General Court in advance. After waiting a full day for the governor to show up, knowing of course he would not, representatives transformed themselves into a new Provincial Congress, not beholden to any British authority. They then adjourned until October 11, the date set by the county conventions for a Provincial Congress to meet in Concord (October 10 Boston dateline in October 13, 1774, *Massachusetts Gazette; and the Boston Weekly News-Letter*).

The response to the call for the Provincial Congress was overwhelming: 209 of the province's 260 towns and districts sent representatives, a far greater showing than the General Court had ever mustered. The meeting was too large for Concord to host, so it moved to Cambridge instead.

Delegates differed on how to proceed from there. The town of Worcester had instructed its representative to "raise from the dissolution of the old constitution, as from the ashes of the Phenix, a new form, where all officers shall be dependent on the suffrages of the people." A new government? Were people ready to make such a dramatic break with Britain in October 1774? Many were, particularly from the western towns, but others were not. While western radicals might have comprised the majority, leadership positions went primarily to the better educated and more experienced political figures from Boston and other eastern towns. The push to declare "independency," form a new government, and raise an army to attack the British stronghold in Boston stalled in the Provincial Congress.

Even if it did not move as quickly as radicals would have liked, the Provincial Congress did take definitive steps to prepare Massachusetts for the counterrevolution British officials were expected to stage. The Congress proceeded on several fronts, as witnessed by entries from its journal reprinted in the October 31, 1774, issue of the *Boston Evening-Post*. On October 26, it recommended that militia companies choose officers and that these men reorganize their regiments, form battalions, and select field officers; this was to be a democratic army, top to bottom. Further, they encouraged the companies to arm and train. Then, since an army costs money, the Provincial Congress chose its own receiver general and recommended that all sheriffs pay the taxes they had collected to him rather than to the official tax collector.

The Provincial Congress did not claim to be a government, however, for that would amount to a declaration of independence. This meant it could not *require* towns to send it money, but it "earnestly recommended" and "strongly recommended" they do so. The army it raised, too, remained unofficial for months. Not until April 1775, as the British army prepared for its inevitable offensive, did the Provincial Congress formally sponsor an army.

After Lexington and Concord, the illusion of a government-that-is-not-a-government became more difficult to sustain. On May 16, the Provincial Congress asked the Continental Congress for "your most explicit advice, respecting the taking up and exercising the power of civil government," and the Continental Congress, which itself had no official standing, instructed the Provincial Congress to set elections for a new government and then disband. On July 19, 1775, the Massachusetts Provincial Congress dissolved itself, but the following day, the new government declared that all the "resolves, doings, and transactions" of the Provincial Congress be "confirmed and established, as lawful and valid."

THE

Maſſachuſett

AND

Boſton Weekly

Draper's.] THU

BOSTON, October 10, 1774.

WEDNESDAY laſt the Members choſen in Conſequence of Governor GAGE's Writ for calling a General Aſſembly, met at the Court-Houſe in Salem purſuant to the Precepts; and after waiting a Day without being admitted to the uſual Oaths, which ſhould have been adminiſtred by the Governor or other conſtitutional Officers; and having choſen the Honorable JOHN HANCOCK, Eſq; to be their Chairman, and BENJAMIN LINCOLN, Eſq; Clerk, they proceeded to Buſineſs, and paſſed the following Reſolves.

Province of the MASSACHUSETTS-BAY.

In the Court-Houſe at Salem, *October* 7, 1774.

WHEREAS ... *Writs bearing Date the Firſt of September laſt, for the Election of Members to ſerve as Repreſentatives in a Great and General Court, which he did "think fit and appoint" to be convened and holden the 5th Day of October Inſtant, at the Court-Houſe in this Place: And whereas a Majority of Members duly elected in conſequence of ſaid Writs, did attend at ſaid Court-Houſe the Time appointed, there to be qualified according to Charter for taking Seats and acting as Repreſentatives in ſaid Great and General Court; but were not met by the Governor, or other conſtitutional Officer or Officers by him appointed for adminiſtring the uſual Oaths, and qualifying them thereto. And whereas a Proclamation bearing date the 28th of September laſt, and publiſhed in ſundry News Papers, with the Signature of his Excellency, contains many Reflections on this Province, as being in a tumultuous and diſorderly State; and appears to have been conſidered by his Excellency as a conſtitutional Diſcharge of all ſuch Perſons as have been elected in Conſequence of his Excellency's ſaid Writ.——The Members aforeſaid ſo attending, having conſidered the Meaſures which his Excellency has been pleaſed to take by his ſaid Proclamation, and finding them to be unconſtitutional, unjuſt, and diſreſpectful to the Province, think it their Duty to paſs the following Reſolves.* Therefore,

RESOLVED, as the Opinion of ſaid Members,

I. THAT by the Royal Charter of the Province, the Governor for the Time being, is expreſly obliged to convene "upon every laſt Wedneſday in the Month of May, every Year for ever, and at ſuch other *Times* as he ſhall *think fit and appoint,* a Great and General Court." And therefore that, as his Excellency *had thought fit, and by his Writ appointed* a Great and General Court to be convened on the 5th Day of October Inſtant, his Conduct in preventing the ſame is againſt the expreſs Words, as well as

adjourn, prorogue and diſſolve all Great and General Courts," ...

II. That the Conſtitutional Government of the Inhabitants of

MASSACHUSETTS GAZETTE; AND THE BOSTON WEEKLY NEWS-LETTER

October 13, 1774

Despite Royal Governor Gage's cancellation of the Massachusetts General Court meeting, it still met in Salem and voted to "resolve themselves into a Provincial Congress" with John Hancock as its chairman.

ed than Hostilities with Great Britain—notwithstanding the Province has not the most distant Design of attacking, annoying, or molesting his Majesty's Troops aforesaid, but on the other Hand will consider and treat every Attempt of the Kind, as well as all Measures tending to prevent a Reconciliation between Britain and the Colonies as the highest degree of Enmity to the Province.——Nevertheless there is great Reason from the Considerations aforesaid to be apprehensive of the most fatal Consequences; and that the Province may be in some Degree provided against the same, and under full Persuasion that the Measures expressed in the following Resolves are perfectly consistent with such Resolves of the Continental Congress as have been communicated to us,

It is *Resolved* and hereby recommended to the several Companies of Militia in this Province, who have not already chosen and appointed Officers, that they meet forthwith and elect Officers to command their respective Companies; and that the Officers so chosen assemble as soon as may be; and where the said Officers shall judge the Limits of the present Regiments too extensive, that they divide them and settle and determine their Limits, and proceed to elect Field Officers to command the respective Regiments so formed; and that the Field Officers so elected, forthwith endeavour to enlist one Quarter at the least of the Number of the respective Companies, and form them into Companies of fifty Privates at the least, who shall equip & hold themselves in Readiness to march at the shortest Notice; and that each and every Company so formed, choose a Captain and two Lieutenants to command them on any necessary and emergent Service: And that the said Captain and Subalterns so elected, form the said Companies into Battalions to consist of nine Companies each; and that the Captains and Subalterns of each Battalion so formed, proceed to elect Field Officers to command the same. And this Congress doth most earnestly recommend that all the aforesaid Elections be proceeded in and made with due Deliberation and general Regard to the public Service.

Also *Resolved*, That as the Security of the Lives, Liberties and Properties of the Inhabitants of this Province depends under Providence on their Knowledge and Skill in the Art Military, and in their being properly and effectually armed and equipt; if any of said Inhabitants are not provided with Arms and Ammunition according to Law, they immediately provide themselves forthwith; and that they use their utmost Diligence to perfect themselves in Military Skill; and that if any Town or District within the Province is not provided with the full Town Stock of Arms and Ammunition according to Law, the Selectmen of such Town or District take effectual Care without Delay to provide the same.

A true Extract from the Minutes,

BENJAMIN LINCOLN, Sec'ry.

In Provincial Congress, Octo. 28. 1774.

WHEREAS this Province has not as yet received from the Continental Congress such explicit directions, respecting Non-Importation and Non-Consumption Agreements as are expected; And whereas the greatest Part of the Inhabitants of this Colony have entered into Non-Importation & Consumption Agreements, the good Effects of which are very conspicuous.——Therefore,

RESOLVED, That this Congress approve of the said Agreements, and earnestly recommend to all the Inhabitants of this Colony, strictly to conform to the same, until the further Sense of the Continental or of this Provincial Congress is made public. And further, this Congress highly applaud the Conduct of those Patriotic Merchants who have generously refrained from Importing British Goods since the Commencement of the cruel Boston Port-Bill; at the same Time reflect with Pain on the Conduct of those, who have sordidly preferred their private Interest to the Salvation of their suffering Country, by continuing to Import as usual; and recommend it to the Inhabitants of the Province that they discourage the Conduct of said Importers by refusing to purchase any Article whatever of them.

A true Extract from the Minutes,

BENJAMIN LINCOLN, Sec'ry.

In Provincial Congress, October 28. 1774.

IT has been recommended by the Congress, That whereas the Monies heretofore granted and ordered to be assessed by the General Court of this Province, and not paid into the Province Treasury, the same should not be paid to the Hon. Harrison Gray, Esq; for Reasons most obvious:

Therefore, *Resolved*, That Henry Gardner, Esq; of Stow, be and hereby is appointed Receiver-General, until the further Order of this or some other Congress, or House of Representatives of this Province; whose Business it shall be to receive all such Monies as shall be offered to be paid into his Hands, to the Use of the Province, by the several Constables, Collectors or other Persons, by Order of the several Towns or Districts, and to give his Receipt for the same.——And it is hereby recommended to the several Towns and Districts within this Province, that they immediately call Town and District Meetings, and give Directions to all Constables, Collectors and other Persons, who may have any Part of the Province Tax of such Town or District ... the Purpose aforesaid. And it is also recommended, that the several Towns and Districts in said Directions signify and expressly engage to such Constable, Collector or other Person, as shall have their said Monies in their Hands, that their paying the same ...

in that manner to levy the Contents of such Assessments; and that they do oblige and compel the said Constables and Collectors to comply with and execute the Directions of this Resolve, in as much as the present alarming Situation and Circumstances of this Province do make it necessary for the Safety thereof.

A true Extract from the Minutes,

BENJAMIN LINCOLN, Sec'ry.

In Provincial Congress, Octo. 29, 1774.

RESOLVED, That it be recommended to the Inhabitants of this Province, that in Order to their perfecting themselves in the Military Art, they proceed in the Method ordered by his Majesty in the Year 1764; it being in the Opinion of this Congress, the best calculated for Appearance and Defence.

A true Extract from the Minutes,

BENJAMIN LINCOLN, Sec'ry.

*** The Manual Exercise, recommended to be practised by the above Resolve of the Congress, is to be had only of T. and J. FLEET, at the Heart and Crown in Cornhill, Boston.——

Extract of a Letter from a Gentleman in the Country, to his Friend in Boston, dated Oct. 26, 1774.

"I Thank you for your last favor, of the 13th inst. and I think I can subscribe to your creed in every thing except where you say you believe that General B--tt--e *is sorry* for what has happen'd, that is, he is sorry he is found out, and am apt to think that is your meaning; he is *semper idem*. All these disturbances and altercations are in consequence of his officious impertinent Letter to G. G. but as he is an original, the best way is to dispise him, and let him alone; if he asks pardon, and replaces a similar quantity of Gun-powder at Quarry-hill, in the room of what he most surreptitiously took therefrom, *but nothing less*. I could decypher him, but it is loss of time, pen, ink, paper and breath.——I join with you, I think the troops ought to be supplied with straw, &c. As to our Courts being shut up, I entirely acquiesce with you, it is WRONG, VERY WRONG.——Pray Sir, have not our Clerks of the Pleas, and Sessions of the Peace witnessed a good confession under their hands publickly? That man who holds up his hand for obedience to these late, most cruel and inhuman Acts of P———t, ought to have it cut off: Well, Sir, if our Courts can go on in the old channel, pray what hinders? I think, Sir, with you, that the shutting up our Courts is rather a compliance with those Acts, and will by our enemies be so construed, as it has brought us to a pause; for let us think but one minute, have not our Sheriffs, Deputies, Grand and Petit Jurors, openly and repeatedly abjured these infamous acts? Where is the Attorney (show me the man) who dare, being left of Heaven, to countenance these, I had almost said, accursed Acts? but if that epithet is too harsh I recall it——Mark the end of that man, for I prophesy it will not be peace; nay, there are only some seeking tools who do appear on that side of the question.—If any of our Judges (and some there are) remain so abandoned, from the necessity of the thing, *they must be paddled aside and good men put in their place*. When justice departs from, injustice enters a land, the precedent is alarming, it is hard, very hard, to come to rights after we have been accustomed to do wrong, and to live without law and justice, I foresee a thousand unconquerable difficulties arising! All nature will be inverted! The man who has the least, or no property, will direct and controul the man of property: What prostitution and inversion is this? I also deprecate with you the ignorance and blindness of the more common people in the Mother Country. If the truth of facts was not wickedly hid from them by wicked men, Bute, Mansfield and North would have been on the other side of the ferry long ago; and I am also very sensible that truth is industriously hid by the same set of men from the eyes of our King, or the prejudices of his education are great. The people of England are honest, but they are wretchedly imposed on, they will see it anon, and will rise like Thunder and make publick examples of wicked men. Which God grant."——

THE Printers hereof have received the Declarations and Acknowledgments of several Deputy Sheriffs, and other Persons, who by signing an Address to Governor Hutchinson had rendered themselves obnoxious to the People; but have not Room to publish them this Week:——Tho' had the Recantations of the few who have lately taken Refuge in this Town, and obstinately persist in their new and unconstitutional Appointments, been offered us, we should have taken Pleasure in postponing other Matters in order to insert them, that so those Exiles might return in Peace to their respective Families, and again enjoy that social Domestic Happiness and Friendship of their Fellow-Citizens, which by most People is esteemed one of the greatest Blessings that can be enjoyed in this Life, and which we wish to contribute what is in our Power to put all Mankind in the Possession of.——The two following Acknowledgments, however, are so concise we can't omit obliging our Readers with them, as they may serve for a Specimen to other Addressers whose Principles are such as not to incline them to make long Confessions, even when they know they were to blame.——

WHereas I the Subscriber signed an Address to the late Governor Hutchinson——I wish the Devil had had said Address before I had seen it.

Marblehead, Oct. 24, 1774. J. FOWLE.

... tica on board the ships of war that have been fitted out there; and that 8000 Men went on board the Esquial, Angalo, &c. which sailed the first of August for America.—The reasons of all their preparations, *they say*, may be easily guessed at, France and Spain certainly intend to attack the British Colonies in America, and to take advantage of the present disputes between them and the mother-country, while they are so irritated against the British Government."

A Letter from Lisbon, as late as Sept. 6th, makes no mention of a War between them & the Spaniards.

Extract of a Letter from a Gentleman in London, *to his Friend at* New-York.

"In reply to your Paragraph respecting the conduct of Philadelphia and your City, in regard to the Tea-Ships: I have not heard that Administration has cast the least reflection on either of those Provinces or their conduct therein. Boston is the present object of their resentment, and should they succeed therein, every other Province will have their resentment in course, as opportunity offers."

Tuesday last being the anniversary of his Majesty's Accession to the Throne, the same was observed here by the firing of the Guns at the Castle, at the Batteries in this Town, and of those on board the Men of War in the Harbour.—At Noon the Piquet Guards of the several Regiments here marched into King-Street, where they fired three Vollies on the Occasion.

The Provincial Congress is adjourned to the 23d Day of November next.

The two Whaling Vessels, outward bound, lately mentioned to have been lost on Nantucket Shoals and 21 Persons left on board supposed to have perished, we have since the satisfaction to hear were all saved: One of whom gives the following account of their remarkable Preservation, viz. That they lay on the Shoal two Nights and one Day, in which time one of the Vessels went to pieces, the other beat over the Shoal and overset; they then made a Raft of the Vessel's Spars, and 13 of the People got on the same, and there being a light Breeze of Wind, they happily drifted on Nantucket Island, after being 24 hours on the Raft in the most perilous Situation, as it was scarcely able to support them above Water: The other 8 of the Crew got on the Quarter-deck of the Vessel which beat to Pieces, and also drove on Nantucket Island. For three Days they had no other Provision than three Cod-Fish to subsist on.

The General Assembly of Pennsylvania has met, and after choosing Edward Biddle, Esq; Speaker, they added John Dickinson, Esq; to the general Congress.

Last Friday arrived a Transport Ship from Quebec, and Yesterday two more with Troops on board from the same Place.

Last Saturday se'nnight the Dwelling House of Aaron Wood, Esq; of Boxford, was consumed by Fire, together with part of the Furniture.

ON Wednesday last died at Charlestown, after a tedious Illness, Mrs. *Mary Foster*, relict of the late *Richard Foster*, Esq;——She was a Person of a truly Christian disposition, and peculiarly solicitous to discharge the several duties of life, *without partiality and without hypocrisy*:—very discrete, humane and charitable; calm and unmoved at the various and inevitable events of Providence, and grieved only at the sufferings of the meek and innocent, the wickedness of the wicked, and the evils of sin; the loss of such a Christian, such a Mother, such a Relative, Neighbour and Friend, will always deeply affect the virtuous and good. She descended from ancestors of the first characters in the Province, whom she hath honour'd in the conduct of her life: and the voice of all remind us that

"The sweet remembrance of the just,
Shall flourish when they sleep in dust."

MARRIED.] Capt. *Callahan* to Miss *Lucretia Greene*, Daughter of Mr. *Benja. Greene*, Merchant.

DIED] Mr. *Watts*, Malster, aged 79.——Miss ...

In the Alms-House, Miss *Mary Cook*, aged 81.

At Leicester, Colonel *Thomas Denny*, aged 50: He represented that Town and the Districts of Spen-

L O N D O N, February 21.

Every impartial person will admit, that the Minister, by making the Parliament take such contradictory Resolutions within a few days, and without any intervening events that might occasion them, hath let down the dignity of Parliament to the lowest degree, and rendered the legal authority of the nation ridiculous. The minister has hereby shewn that he is absolute master of the Parliament, and can make the members of it jump backwards and forwards, like a parcel of Spaniels over a stick, just as he pleases?—What a contemptible idea must the people of England, from such inconsistent proceedings, entertain of their legislators?

When the three General Officers kissed his Majesty's hand, previous to their departure for America, he enjoined them in expressions the most affecting, to let humanity influence them more than courage, and to avoid an engagement with those deluded people, if it can be done with safety to his person and crown. From this we may rest satisfied, that neither their lives nor fortunes will be endangered, if their behaviour does not amount to that pitch of villainy that appeared in the Scotch Rebels in 1745.

The loss of Lord Coventry and the Duke of Northumberland to Government, has made a great turn in the scale of politics.

Several patriotic Gentlemen have actually entered into an agreement to embark for America, as soon as the present session is concluded.

House of Commons, March 1.

At three o'clock the House went into a Committee on the Bill for restraining the Commerce, and prohibiting the New-England Provinces from fishing on the Banks of Newfoundland. A strong opposition was expected on the part of the minority; but the field was left to Administration entirely clear; not a syllable being offered by way of either amendment or reprobation. The Victors however designed to make a few alterations, or what they pleased to call amendments, and to be reported on Monday.

The new Plan respecting America, proposed by the ostensible Agent, is one of the most insidious that ever entered the depraved heart of a corrupt Minister: being at once calculated to set the people here against their brethren in the Colonies, by a *seeming* proposals of conciliatory measures, and at the same time to sow divisions among the Americans, by holding out a deceitful lure to them to come in, if any one among them shall be found weak enough to swallow the bait.

...tious Firings, &c. with a Precision seldom exceeded by any regular troops.

B O S T O N, *April* 17. 1775.

In Capt. Collins came one of the Hands who sailed with Capt. Calef, to London: He informs, that the latter had a tedious P...

In Provincial Congress, Concord, *April* 14. 1775.

WHEREAS Numbers of Persons from their unhappy situation in the Town of Boston, are removing with their Effects.——It is recommended to the good People of this Province, that they would rent their Houses, and assist such Persons with Teams for their removal, Provisions for their Support, and all other Necessaries upon as easy and cheap Terms as they can possibly afford; and that all Goods and Merchandize be sold in like Manner, agreeable to the Spirit of the Continental Association.

By Order of the Provincial Congress,
JOHN HANCOCK, President.

In Provincial Congress, *Concord*, April 15, 1775.

WHEREAS it has pleased the righteous Sovereign of the Universe, in just Indignation against the Sins of a People long blessed with inestimable Privileges, civil and religious, to suffer the Plots of wicked Men on both Sides of the Atlantic, who for many Years have incessantly laboured to sap the Foundation of our public Liberties, so far to succeed, that we see the New-England Colonies reduced to the ungrateful Alternative of a tame Submission to a state of absolute Vassalage to the Will of a despotic Minister—or of preparing themselves speedily to defend, at the hazard of Life, the unalienable Rights of themselves and Posterity, against the avowed Hostilities of their parent State, who openly threatens to wrest them from their Hands by Fire and Sword.

In Circumstances dark as these, it becomes us, as Men and Christians, to reflect that, whilst every prudent Measure should be taken to ward off the impending Judgments, or prepare to act a proper Part under them when they come; at the same Time, all Confidence must be with-held from the Means we use; and reposed only on that God who rules in the Armies of Heaven, and without whose Blessing the best human Counsels are but Foolishness—and all created Power Vanity.

It is the Happiness of his Church that, when the Powers of Earth and Hell combine against it, and those who should be nursing Fathers become its Persecutors—then the Throne of Grace is of the easiest Access—and its Appeal thither is graciously invited by the Father of Mercies, who has assured it, that when his Children ask Bread he will not give them a Stone:

THEREFORE, in Compliance with the laudable Practice of the People of God in all Ages, with humble Regard to the Steps of divine Providence towards this oppressed, threatned and endangered People, and especially in Obedience to the Command of Heaven, that binds us *to call on him in the Day of Trouble*,—

Resolved, That it be, and hereby is recommended to the good People of this Colony, of all Denominations, that THURSDAY the Eleventh Day of *May* next be set apart as a Day of Public Humiliation, Fasting and Prayer; that a total Abstinence from servile Labor and Recreation be observed, and all their religious Assemblies solemnly convened, to humble themselves before God under the heavy Judgments felt and feared, to confess the Sins that have deserved them, to implore the forgiveness of all...

We learn from Concord, that on Saturday last the Provincial Congress, which had been sitting there, adjourned to the 10th of May next; tho' if necessary, to be summoned to meet earlier:—We also have it from undoubted authority, that a perfect Unanimity...

DONATION... MASS...
From unknown Ha...
Monson, 2C. oqr...
Meal, 2...
Hanover, From a ...
SO...
From Mess'rs *Cha*...
Bill on Mr. *Na*...
Part of nett Pr...
at New-York, ...
N. B. *The Donati*... *the 27th of Mar*...

Elizab...
At her Shop two ...
House, North-Sid...
An Assortment ...
Ware, among wh...
Sizes, and ...
A few Crates o...
Also Groce...
Capers by the B...
Keg, or Pound, ...
Anchovies, do. do. ...
Choice Durham Mu...
in Bottles of various ...
Flask Oil, ...
Double & single re...
Loaf Sugar, ...
Coffee, Chocola...
Spermaceti Candles ...
Hard Soap, Crown ...
Castile ditto, ...
Poland Starch, ...
Patent Sago, Ci...
Most of the above ... *Retail, with* ...

For L...

At TEN oCl...
Will be Sold by ...
At *RUSSELL*'s A...
—A Variety ...

BOSTON EVENING-POST
October 31, 1774

Soon after forming, the Provincial Congress proceeded on several fronts, including the October 26 resolve that local militia companies meet, elect officers, form and arm themselves, and perfect their "Military Skill."

BOSTON EVENING-POST
April 17, 1775

Printed on the eve of the Battle of Lexington and Concord, this issue of the *Boston Evening-Post* features the official reports and resolves from the final Massachusetts Provincial Congress meetings before war breaks out. We also learn that the Provincial Congress adjourned to May 10.

REPORTING THE

FIRST CONTINENTAL CONGRESS

By Benjamin H. Irvin

On March 31, 1774, Parliament enacted the Port Bill, a severe piece of legislation intended to punish Bostonians for flagrantly destroying East India Company tea. The first of four detested Coercive Acts, the Port Bill closed Boston Harbor to maritime trade, depriving the town's fifteen thousand inhabitants of their subsistence. When news of the Port Bill reached the colonies in early May, it provoked an immediate outcry. In town meetings and provincial conventions, dismayed Americans pled for unified resistance. Many proposed that the colonists elect delegates to a general congress, as several colonial assemblies had done during the Stamp Act crisis nearly ten years before.

Delegates to the "Grand Continental Congress" journeyed to Philadelphia early that autumn. Representing twelve colonies—Georgia did not send delegates—their ranks included many of the most prominent statesmen in British North America. Among them were Peyton Randolph, speaker of the Virginia House of Burgesses; Joseph Galloway, speaker of the Pennsylvania Assembly; Stephen Hopkins and Samuel Ward, both former governors of Rhode Island; merchant Philip Livingston, the scion of a manorial New York family; the brothers John and Edward Rutledge, distinguished planter-lawyers from South Carolina; the cousins Samuel and John Adams, the former a firebrand assemblyman, the latter a prominent attorney of the Boston Massacre trials; and numerous other individuals of comparable stature and wealth.

On September 5, the delegates gathered at the City Tavern to address preliminary matters. For their meeting place, they chose Carpenters' Hall, a two-story brick building owned by a Philadelphia trade guild. To serve as secretary, they selected Charles Thomson, a local Patriot who had helped organize tea boycotts. The delegates then agreed to conduct their deliberations in secrecy. What historians know of the First Continental Congress comes chiefly from the delegates' private papers and from Congress's official resolutions, which were published as complete journals and also as piecemeal entries in colonial newspapers, as in the February 17, 1775, edition of the *New-Hampshire Gazette*.

Most congressmen resented Parliament's repeated efforts to tax the colonists and to subordinate their legislative assemblies, but delegates disagreed over the wisest course of resistance. More radical delegates, like Samuel Adams and Richard Henry Lee, favored the establishment of trade boycotts to exert economic pressure on Great Britain, as some American communities had intermittently done during the taxation controversies of the 1760s and early 1770s. Champions of economic resistance carried a forceful popular mandate. Throughout that summer, indignant colonists had urged their representatives to implement a strategy of commercial opposition. Virginia's provincial convention, for example, resolved to cease importation from Great Britain, as reported in the August 26, 1774, edition of the *New-Hampshire Gazette*. Nevertheless, several congressmen doubted that economic resistance would sway British policymakers. Joseph Galloway, Isaac Low, and others feared that boycotts would instead devastate American trade.

Before Congress could deliberate such matters, a dire report from Massachusetts disrupted its proceedings. On September 6, an express rider brought an urgent message: British soldiers had marched on Charlestown, a bloody skirmish had ensued, and naval vessels had cannonaded the town of Boston all through the night. This desperate account, dispatched at the height of the Powder Alarm, proved mostly untrue, but it distressed the inhabitants of Philadelphia and cast a somber tone over the delegates' affairs.

In the weeks that followed, Congress progressed steadily toward a platform of aggressive resistance. On September 17, it endorsed the incendiary Suffolk Resolves, delivered by the courier Paul Revere, which declared that no obedience was due to the Coercive Acts and that the people of Massachusetts ought diligently "to acquaint themselves with the art of war." In mid-October, Congress issued a statement of grievances that predicated American rights on "the immutable laws of nature." The following week, it composed addresses to the people of Great Britain and to the inhabitants of the British colonies, including Quebec, St. John's, and Nova Scotia. In those addresses, one of which appeared in the November 29, 1774, edition of the *Essex Gazette*, Congress recited a history of tyrannical British government. Exercising a right preserved by the Magna Carta, Congress also composed a petition to King George III. Published in the February 3, 1775, edition of the *New-Hampshire Gazette*, this petition implored the king to disavow "designing and dangerous" ministers.

Most significantly, before adjourning, Congress framed the Articles of Association, a comprehensive scheme of nonimportation, nonexportation, and nonconsumption boycotts. Circulated throughout the colonies and enforced by local committees of observation and inspection, the Association called upon Americans to withdraw from the transatlantic trade and to forgo expensive leisure activities. By pinching British pocketbooks, the Association might have compelled the Royal Ministry to pursue a peaceful resolution to the imperial conflict. But in April 1775, months before nonexportation went into effect, war broke out in Massachusetts, dashing hopes of reconciliation.

DELEGATES who attend the CONGRESS.

From New Hampſhire.

Major John Sullivan, and Col. Nathaniel Folſom.

From Maſſachuſetts Bay.

Hon'ble Thomas Cuſhing, Eſq; Mr. Samuel Adams, John Adams, and Robert Treat Paine, Eſqs;

From Rhode-Iſland.

Hon. Stephen Hopkins, Eſq; Hon. Samuel Ward, Eſq;

From Connecticut.

Hon. Eliphalet Dyer, Silas Deane, and Roger Sherman, Eſq'rs.

From New York.

James Duane, John Jay, Philip Livingſton, Iſaac Low, Col. William Floyd, and Henry Weſner, Eſq'rs.

From New-Jerſey.

James Kinſey, William Livingſton, John D'Hart, Stephen Crane, and Richard Smith, Eſq'rs.

From Pennſylvania.

Hon. Joſeph Galloway, Samuel Rhoads, Thomas Mifflin, Charles Humporys, John Morton, Edward Biddle, and George Roſs, Eſq'rs.

From Newcaſtle, Kent, and Suſſex Governments.

Cæſar Rodney, Thomas M'Kean, and George Read, Eſq'rs.

From Maryland.

Mathew Tilgham, Thomas Johnſon, jr. Robert Gouldſborough, William Paca, and Samuel Chaſe, Eſq'rs.

From Virginia.

Hon. Peyton Randolph, Richard Henry Lee, George Waſhington, Patrick Henry, Richard Bland, Benjamin Harriſon, and Edmund Pendleton, Eſq'rs.

From North Carolina.

William Hooper, and Joſeph Hewes, Eſq'rs.

From South-Carolina.

Hon. Henry Middleton, John Rutledge, Thomas Lynch, Chriſtopher Gadſden, and Edward Rutledge, Eſq'rs.

NEW-HAMPSHIRE GAZETTE (PORTSMOUTH)
September 30, 1774

Shortly after the First Continental Congress convened in Philadelphia, this list of delegates was published.

Continental Congreſs continu'd

Tueſday, October 18th, 1774:

The congreſs reſumed the conſideration of the plan of aſſociation, &c. and after ſundry amendments the ſame was agreed to and ordered to be tranſcribed that it may be ſigned by the ſeveral Members.

The committee appointed to prepare an addreſs to the people of Great-Britain, bro't in a draught which was read and ordered to lie on the table for the peruſal of the members and to be taken into conſideration to-morrow.

Wedneſday, October 19th, 1774.

The congreſs reſumed the conſideration of the addreſs to the people of Great-Britain, and the ſame being debated by paragraphs, and ſundry amendments made, the ſame was recommitted in order that the amendments may be taken in.

The committee appointed to prepare a memorial to theſe colonies reported a draught which was read and order'd to lie on the table. Ordered that this memorial be taken into conſideration to-morrow.

Thurſday, October 20th, 1774,

The aſſociation being copied, was read and ſigned at the table and is as follows,

See the Aſſociation in this Paper, Novem. 11.

The congreſs then reſumed the conſideration of the memorial to the inhabitants of theſe colonies, and after debates thereon, adjourned till to morrow.

...by paragraphs was approved & is as follows,

See the Memorial in this Paper, Novem. 18.

Resolved, That an addreſs be prepared to the people of Quebec and letters to the colonies of St. Johns, Nova-Scotia, Eaſt and

The committee appointed to prepare a letter to the colonies of St. John's, &c. reported a draught which was read, and being amended was approved and is as follows,

PHILADELPHIA, October 22, 1774.

Gentlemen,

THE preſent critical and truly alarming ſtate of American affairs, having been conſidered in a general congreſs of deputies from the colonies of New-Hampſhire, Maſſachuſetts-Bay, Rhode-Iſland, Connecticutt, New-York, New-Jerſey, Pennſylvania, the lower counties on Delaware, Maryland, Virginia, North-Carolina, and South-Carolina, with that attention and mature deliberation which the important nature of the caſe demand, they have determined for themſelves and the colonies they repreſent, on the meaſures contained in the incloſed papers, which meaſures, they recommend to your colony, to be adopted with the earneſtneſs, that a well directed zeal for American liberty can prompt, ſo rapidly violent & unjuſt has been the late conduct of the Britiſh adminiſtration againſt the colonies, that either a baſe and ſlaviſh ſubmiſſion, under the loſs of this ancient, juſt and conſtitutional liberty muſt quickly take place, or an adequate oppoſition be formed.

We pray to God to take you under his protection, and to preſerve the freedom and happineſs of the whole Britiſh empire.

We are, &c.

Monday, October 24, 1774,

The committee appointed to prepare an ... to the people of Quebec, which was ... after debate recommitted.

... committee to whom the addreſs was ...itted, brought in a draught which ... and ordered to be taken into conſi... to-morrow.

Tueſday, October 25,

... congreſs reſumed the conſideration ... debated by paragraphs was approved and ordered to be engroſſed.

Ordered, That the addreſs to the King, be encloſed to the ſeveral colony agents in

that ſerved like ad
to be added to the A
ing your Favours
from the pureſt C
diſſembled Patrio
acknowledged.
tion, when it was
of Muſtard. I ha
it has become a g
that crawl upon
the Root, the fou
on its Branches.
work immediatel
and cut it down ;
cauſe it is a Peſt
led ſuddenly by a
Thouſands in the
An Apprehenſio
of Great-Britain
told you was the S
Week I endeavou
Neceſſity of her re
hing ſome Gover
now to point out
upon which the b
was the violent A
the Eaſt-India Co
of their Tea. In
ment of that Tra
back & view the C
As the Governmen
Spirit or Genius o
narchical, ariſtocra
and commercial.
which is the moſt
it is worthy of Re
Britiſh Nation upo
like injuring a Fr
Honor. Commer
tional Wealth, fo
by all Orders of M
Cottage. In ſom
held in Contempt
they reſpect him.
in the State, often
the firſt Families i
Blood flows in th
Trade is founded
mutually ſupplyin
dundances. Thus
enriched, the Arp
away, and Manki
Huſbandr Manu
are its tre Sup
theſe, it would ce

NEW-HAMPSHIRE GAZETTE (PORTSMOUTH)

February 17, 1775

Most of what historians know about the First Continental Congress comes from the delegates' private papers and Congress's official resolutions, which were published as complete journals and also as piecemeal entries in colonial newspapers.

NEW-HAMPSHIRE GAZETTE (PORTSMOUTH)

August 26, 1774

In the summer of 1774, the Virginia provincial convention protested Parliament's Coercive Acts by boycotting British goods. That autumn, the Continental Congress adopted an even more comprehensive scheme of economic resistance known as the Articles of Association.

At a very full Meeting of DELEGATES *from the different Counties in the Colony and Dominion of* VIRGINIA, *begun in* Williamsburg *the first Day of August* 1774; *and continued by several Adjournments to Saturday the* 6th *of the same Month, when a Number of* RESOLVES *were passed and signed by* 108 *Persons, being an* ASSOCIATION *unanimously resolved upon and agreed to. At the same Time the following* INSTRUCTIONS *were given for the* DEPUTIES *appointed to meet in* GENERAL CONGRESS *on the Part of the Colony.*

THE unhappy Disputes between Great Britain and her American Colonies, which began about the third Year of his Majesty's Reign, and since, continually increasing, have proceeded to Lengths so dangerous and alarming as to excite just Apprehensions in the Minds of his Majesty's faithful Subjects of this Colony that they are in Danger of being deprived of their natural, ancient, constitutional, and chartered Rights, have compelled them to take the same into their most serious Consideration; and, being deprived of their usual and accustomed Mode of making known their Grievances, have appointed us their Representatives to consider what is proper to be done in this dangerous Crisis of American Affairs. It being our Opinion that the united Wisdom of North America should be collected in a General Congress of all the Colonies, we have appointed the Hon. PEYTON RANDOLPH, Esq; RICHARD HENRY LEE, GEORGE WASHINGTON, PATRICK HENRY, RICHARD BLAND, BENJAMIN HARRISON, and EDMUND PENDLETON, Esquires, Deputies to represent this Colony in the said Congress to be held at Philadelphia on the first Monday in September next.

And that they may be the better informed of our Sentiments touching the Conduct we wish them to observe on this important Occasion, we desire that they will express, in the first Place our Faith and true Allegiance to his Majesty King George the Third, our lawful and rightful Sovereign; and that we are determined, with our Lives and Fortunes, to support Him in the legal Exercise of all his just Rights and Prerogatives. And however misrepresented, we sincerely approve of a constitutional Connexion with Great-Britain, and wish most ardently a Return of that Intercourse of Affection and commercial Connexion that formerly united both Countries, which can only be effected by a Removal of those Causes of Discontent which have of late unhappily divided us.

It cannot admit of a Doubt but that British Subjects in America are entitled to the same Rights and Privileges as their Fellow Subjects possess in Britain; and therefore, that the Power assumed by the British Parliament to bind America by their Statutes, in all Cases whatsoever, is unconstitutional, and the Source of these unhappy Differences.

The End of Government would be defeated by the British

their local Circumstances, cannot, be there represented. Of this Nature we consider the several Acts of Parliament for raising a Revenue in America, for extending the Jurisdiction of the

ESSEX GAZETTE (SALEM, MA)

November 29, 1774

Congress composed addresses to the people of Great Britain and to the inhabitants of British colonies, including Quebec. In the address printed in this edition of the *Essex Gazette*, Congress recited a history of tyrannical British government.

ESSEX GAZ

both foreig

NU

From TUESDAY, *November* 22, to TUESDAY,

SALEM: Printed by *Samuel* and *Ebenezer Hall*, at their Printing-Office nea

American Continental CONGRESS, *Oct.* 1774.

To the INHABITANTS of the COLONIES Of *New-Hampshire, Massachusetts-Bay, Rhode-Island and Providence* Plantations; *Connecticut, New-York, New-Jersey, Pennsylvania,* the Counties of *New-Castle, Kent* and *Sussex* on Delaware; *Maryland, Virginia, North-Caroli-na* and *South-Carolina.*

Friends and Fellow Countrymen,

WE, the Delegates appointed by the good people of the above Colonies to meet at Philadelphia in September last, for the purposes mentioned by our respective Constituents, have in pursuance of the trust reposed in us, assembled and taken into our most serious consideration the important matters recommended to the Congress. Our resolutions thereupon will be herewith communicated to you. But as the situation of public affairs grows daily more and more alarming; and as it may be more satisfactory to you to be informed by us in a collective body, than in any other manner, of those sentiments that have been approved, upon a full and free discussion by the Representatives of so great a part of America, we esteem ourselves obliged to add this Address to these Resolutions.

In every case of opposition by a people to their rulers, or of one state to another, duty to Almighty God, the Creator of all, requires that a true and impartial judgment be formed of the measures leading to such opposition; and of the causes by which it has been provoked, or can in

permitted to give a wrong bias to reason, it may be enabled to take a dispassionate view of all the

The inhabitants of these colonies, confiding in the justice of Great-Britain, were scarcely allowed *sufficient* time to receive and consider this act, before another, well known by the name of the *stamp-act*, and passed in the fifth year of this reign, engrossed the whole of their attention. By this statute the British Parliament exercised in the most explicit manner a power of *taxing* us, and extending the jurisdiction of Courts of *Admiralty* and *Vice-Admiralty* in the Colonies, to matters arising within the body of a county, directed the numerous penalties and forfeitures, thereby inflicted, to be recovered in the said Courts.

In the same year a tax was imposed upon us, by an act, establishing several new fees in the customs. In the next year the stamp-act was repealed; not because it was founded on an erroneous principle, but, as the repealing act recites, because "the continuance thereof would be attended with many inconveniencies, and might be productive of consequences greatly detrimental to the commercial interest of Great-Britain."

In the same year, and by a subsequent act, it was declared, "that his Majesty in Parliament, "of right, had a power to bind the people of these "Colonies by statutes *in all cases whatsoever.*"

In the same year, another act was passed, for imposing rates and duties payable in these colonies. In this statute the Commons avoiding the terms of *giving* and *granting*, "humbly besought his Majesty that it might be enacted, &c." But from a declaration in the preamble, that the rates and duties were "in lieu of" several others grant-

pears, that these duties were intended *for that purpose.*

liament made in
House of Represen
hibited by a statut
tioned, from mak
or vote, except for a
until provision sho
bly for furnishing
not only with all
the statute *which*
but also with those
statutes, which w
the twenty-fourth

These statutes o
prehensions and di
sided on the repea
the just fears and
statute w...
lish Courts of *Ad*
new model, expres
recovering the pe
by acts of Parlian
raising a revenue i

The immediate
subvert the right
by rendering Asse
perty, by taking t
out their consent;
substituting in the
Vice-Admiralty C
side, holding thei
and unduly to infl
Law, by rendering
pendant on the C

other, will be fou
system, in which

pare an addreſs to the people of Great-Britain, and a memorial to the inhabitants of Britiſh America, and 3d, to prepare a loyal addreſs to his Majeſty agreeable to reſolutions already entered into.

¶ To be continu'd.

The following is the PETITION of the CONTINENTAL CONGRESS, To the KING's moſt excellent MAJESTY.

TO a ſovereign, who "*glories in the name of Briton*," the bare recital of theſe acts muſt we preſume, juſtify the loyal ſubjects who fly to the foot of his throne and implore his clemency for protection againſt them.

From this deſtructive ſyſtem of colony adminiſtration, adopted ſince the concluſion of the late war, have flowed thoſe diſtreſſes, dangers, fears, & jealouſies, that overwhelm your Majeſty's dutiful coloniſts with affliction; and we defy our moſt ſubtle & inveterate enemies to trace the unhappy differences between Great Britain and theſe colonies, from an earlier period, or from other cauſes than we have aſſigned; had they proceeded on our part from a reſtleſs levity of temper, unjuſt impulſes of ambition, or artful ſuggeſtions of ſeditious perſons, we ſhould merit the opprobrious terms frequently beſtowed on us by thoſe we revere. But, ſo far from promoting innovations, we have only oppoſed them, and can be charged with no offence, unleſs it be one to receive injuries and be ſenſible of them.

Had our Creator been pleaſed to give us exiſtence in a land of ſlavery, the ſenſe of our condition might have been mitigated by ignorance and habit; but, thanks be to his adorable goodneſs, we were born the heirs of freedom, and ever enjoyed our rights under the auſpices of your royal anceſtors, whoſe family was ſeated on the Britiſh throne to reſcue and ſecure a pious & gallant nation from the popery and deſpotiſm of a ſuperſtitious & inexorable tyrant. Your Majeſty, we are confident, juſtly rejoices, that your title to the crown is thus founded on the title of your people to liberty; and therefore we doubt not but your royal wiſdom muſt approve the ſenſibility that teaches your ſubjects anxiouſly to guard the bleſſings they received from divine providence, & thereby to prove the performance of that compact which elevated the illuſtrious houſe of Brunſwick to the imperial

ly was ſeated on the Britiſh throne to reſcue and ſecure a pious & gallant nation from the popery and deſpotiſm of a ſuperſtitious & inexorable tyrant. Your Majeſty, we are confident, juſtly rejoices, that your title to the crown is thus founded on the title of your people to liberty; and therefore we doubt not but your royal wiſdom muſt approve the ſenſibility that teaches your ſubjects anxiouſly to guard the bleſſings they received from divine providence, & thereby to prove the performance of that compact which elevated the illuſtrious houſe of Brunſwick to the imperial dignity it now poſſeſſes.

The apprehenſion of being degraded into a ſtate of ſervitude from the pre-eminent rank of Engliſh freemen, while our minds retain the ſtrongeſt love of liberty, and clearly foreſee the miſeries preparing for us and our poſterity, excites emotions in our hearts which, though we cannot deſcribe, we ſhould not wiſh to conceal. Feeling as men, and thinking as ſubjects, in the manner we do, ſilence would be diſloyalty. By giving this faithful information we do all in our power to promote the great objects of your royal care, the tranquility of your government, and the welfare of your people.

Duty to your Majeſty, and regard for the preſervation of ourſelves and our poſterity, the primary obligations of nature and of ſociety, command us to entreat your royal attention, and, as your Majeſty enjoys the ſignal diſtinction of reigning over freemen, we apprehend the language of freemen cannot be diſpleaſing. Your royal indignation, we hope, will rather fall on thoſe deſigning and dangerous men who daringly interpoſing themſelves between your royal perſon and your faithful ſubjects, and for ſeveral years paſt inceſſantly employed to diſſolve the bonds of ſociety, by

bunal before which all mankind

NEW-HAMPSHIRE GAZETTE (PORTSMOUTH)
February 3, 1774

In its 1774 petition to George III, the Continental Congress professed loyalty and dutifulness to the king, but it also proclaimed "the strongest love of liberty."

Filled with ſentiments of duty to your Majeſty, & of affection to our parent ſtate, deeply impreſſed by our education, and ſtrongly confirmed by our reaſon; & anxious to evince the ſincerity of theſe diſpoſitions, we preſent

REPORTING THE

RAID ON FORT WILLIAM AND MARY

By J. Dennis Robinson

According to New Hampshire history, the American Revolution began four months before the famous Battle of Lexington and Concord. Royal Governor John Wentworth was well liked in his hometown of Portsmouth, New Hampshire, and saw his subjects as "more moderate" than those to the south in Boston. But by early December 1774, his effort to mollify the growing unrest was failing, and his friendly relations with the royal governors of Massachusetts angered locals. On December 13, Paul Revere rode his horse through frigid weather from Boston to alert citizens of Portsmouth that the Royal Navy was coming. Revere said British command was sending reinforcements to secure Fort William and Mary in nearby New Castle. Strategically located on an island at the mouth of New Hampshire's only seaport, the fort's armory held a major supply of gunpowder and weapons. The British and local authorities had recently taken or disabled guns from shore batteries and forts in Massachusetts and Rhode Island. Worse yet, as Revere told the Committee of Safety, the mother country now planned to ban the export of weapons to all her rowdy American children. The fuse was lit.

Roused by fife and drum the following morning, December 14, 1774, a crowd of about four hundred citizens from Portsmouth and nearby towns made its way to Fort William and Mary. Captain John Cochran commanded only five soldiers at the fort, which was in poor condition. Shots were fired. In his report to Governor Wentworth, Cochran wrote:

Had anyone been killed, American history texts would tell a different version of the start of the Revolution.

> *I immediately ordered three four-pounders to be fired on them, and then the small arms; and, before we could be ready to fire again, we were stormed on all quarters, and they immediately secured both me and my men.*

Local rebels lowered the British colors and stole the king's munitions. Cochran and one of his men were injured in the battle. Had anyone been killed, American history texts would tell a different version of the start of the Revolution.

Governor Wentworth certainly recognized the significance of the raid as seen by his stern proclamation read at the Portsmouth State House on December 26 and reprinted in the January 9, 1775, *Boston Evening-Post.* As Wentworth reported, the crowd overpowered the guards, made treasonous insults, and stole over one hundred barrels of gunpowder and other munitions in a "most daring and rebellious manner." Despite his demands, none of the "high-handed offenders" were captured. Two of the supposed insurgent leaders, John Langdon and John Sullivan, became key figures in the Revolution and were both early governors of the state of New Hampshire. The gunpowder was hidden in several towns to make sure the royal authorities would not recover it, and according to local legend, it was later used at the Battle of Bunker Hill.

The details, including the presence of Paul Revere, were reported by Wentworth in a letter to General Gage the same day as the raid. In the letter, the governor blamed "the imbecility of this government" for not sending ships of war to Portsmouth to protect the fort. Contrary to his proclamation, it is clear from his private correspondence that he knew the names of the "popular leaders" who organized the raid. On December 15, Wentworth attempted to find thirty local men to protect the fort but without luck, as it was again invaded by a much larger force that carried away many light cannons and sixty muskets.

Delayed by a slow start, tides, and bad weather, British

warships HMS *Canceaux* and HMS *Scarborough* arrived well after the raids. On December 28, two days after his official proclamation, the governor sent a brief letter to his friend Lord Dartmouth in England to warn that the citizens of Portsmouth "are arming and exercising men as if for immediate war." Wentworth's family had been among the most powerful leaders of the colony since 1717. Despite his empathy for the protestors, he was unable to cool their outrage. John Wentworth and his family were forced from their home by an armed mob on June 13, 1775. After a brief stay at the fort and aboard HMS *Scarborough*, they fled to England, never to return under penalty of death. John Wentworth became governor of Nova Scotia, where he died in 1808. His ruined fort, renamed Fort Constitution, still stands as mute evidence of the revolutionary New Hampshire shots not heard around the world.

BOSTON, in NEW-ENGLAND.

On Monday the 26th of December his Excellency Governor WENTWORTH, of New-Hampſhire iſſued the following Proclamation, viz.

By the GOVERNOR,

A PROCLAMATION

WHereas ſeveral Bodies of Men did, in the Day time of the 14th and Night of the 15th of this inſtant December, in the moſt daring and rebellious Manner inveſt, attack and forcibly enter into his Majeſty Caſtle William and Mary in this Province, and overpowering and confining the Captain and Garriſon, did, beſides committing many treaſonable Inſults and Outrages, break open the Magazine of ſaid Caſtle and plunder it of above 100 Barrels of Gunpowder, with upwards of 60 Stand of Small Arms, and did alſo force from the Ramparts of ſaid Caſtle and carry off 16 Pieces of Cannon, and other Military Stores, in open Hoſtility and direct Oppugnation of his Majeſty's Government, and in the moſt attrocious Contempt of his Crown and Dignity:

I DO, by Advice and Conſent of his Majeſty's Council, iſſue this Proclamation, ordering and requiring in his Majeſty's Name, all Magiſtrates and other Officers, whether Civil or Military, as they regard their Duty to the KING and the Tenor of the Oaths they have ſolemnly taken and ſubſcribed, to exert themſelves in detecting and ſecuring in ſome of *his Majeſty's Goals* in this Province the ſaid Offenders, in Order to their being brought to condign Puniſhment: And from Motives of Duty to the KING and Regard to the Welfare of the good People of this Province: I do in the moſt earneſt and ſolemn Manner, exhort and enjoin you, his Majeſty's liege Subjects of this Government, to beware of ſuffering yourſelves to be ſeduced by the falſe Arts or Menaces of abandoned Men, to abet, protect, or ſcreen from Juſtice any of the ſaid high-handed Offenders, or to withhold or ſecrete his Majeſty's Munition forcibly taken from his Caſtle; but that each and every of you will uſe your utmoſt Endeavours to detect and diſcover the Perpetrators of theſe Crimes to the civil Magiſtrate, and aſſiſt in ſecuring and bringing them to Juſtice, and in recovering the King's Munition: This Injunction it is my bounden Duty to lay ſtrictly upon you, and to require your Obedience thereto, as you value individually your Faith and Allegiance to his Majeſty, as you wiſh to preſerve that Reputation to the Province in general; and as you would avert the dreadful but moſt certain Conſequences of a contrary Conduct to yourſelves and Poſterity.

Given at the Council Chamber in Portſmouth the 26th Day of December, in the 15th Year of the Reign of our Sovereign Lord GEORGE the Third, by the Grace of GOD, of Great Britain, France, and Ireland, KING, Defender of the Faith, &c. and in the Year of our Lord CHRIST, 1774.

By His Excellency's Command, with Advice of Council,
J. WENTWORTH.
THEODORE ATKINSON, Sec'ry.

GOD ſave the KING.

By Capt. Sinclair, *who is arrived at Marblehead in* 40 *Days from* Falmouth, *we have the following Advices from* London.

LONDON, October 22.

To LORD NORTH.

GOvernment hath a long time formed the plan for eſtabliſhing epiſcopacy in America, and a conſiderable ſum been left by private gentlemen for its ſupport. The eſtabliſhment is neceſſay, on ac-

Oct. 29. The letters received on Friday from Boſton, dated the 21ſt of September, are of the moſt alarming nature. They aſſert that the inhabitants of Boſton, and of the province of Maſſachuſetts-Bay, are now in arms. They have put themſelves into conſtant exerciſe, and obſerve the moſt regular diſcipline. The Governor (General Gage) alarmed to the laſt degree at this ſtate of things, ſent to New-York for more troops, but the people of New-York refuſed to furniſh tranſports to convey the troops.—Theſe ſteps have been taken without waiting for the deliberations of the congreſs.——It is very ſtrange, and muſt very ſoon excite more than aſtoniſhment, that thoſe men are continued in office, who have brought the public affairs to this horrid ſituation.

The ſtate or importance of the American colonies is ſo little underſtood or regarded by the *cunning people* at the weſt end of the town, that we are told they have univerſally agreed that if all our ſettlements there were at the bottom of the ſea, it would be much better for England, Theſe to be ſure are very pretty concluſions ... thoſe dominions which have brought in ſo ... lions to England; about thoſe dominions ... conſtantly employed an infinite number of ſhipping; about thoſe dominions, which rendered this natio...
the laſt war. From thi...
tance of our colonies ...
capable they are of ma...
and we may alſo gueſs ...
of the exerciſe or ſuch ...
hoves every Engliſhm...
welfare of the Americ...
ſuch a great dependanc...
Extract of a Letter f...
on board the True ...
September 30, *to* ...
"On Wedneſday l...
the Glorious Memory ...
form Briſtol bound fo...
inſt. met with a viole...
loſt her mizen maſt, ...
people waſhed overbo...
the cargoe ſhifted, a...
above the cargoe in the ...
juſt keep her up with the pumps conſtantly at work as the people was very much jadod, what with pumping and getting her as upright as they could (which indeed was but very indifferent at beſt) however the Captain deſired I would keep him company till we either ſaw land or near a port, which I readily complied with and kept him company till ſix o'clock the next morning, w... finding by ſounding we

Nov. 3. The proclamation againſt ſending guns and gunpowder out of this kingdom will be of very little uſe or effect, becauſe the Americans will certainly procure whatever quantity of them they want from Holland, France, and Spain; and if orders were given to ſtop and ſeize ſuch ſhips as were laden with the above commodities by thoſe nations, it would bring on an immediate war with them: An event which the preſent miniſtry dare not hazard with any foreign power, though they aſſume courage ſufficient to ſend fleets and armies to cut the throats of our American brethren.

No leſs than ten acts of parliament have been made to teaze and perſecute the Americans, ſince the acceſſion of George III.

This morning the Lord Mayor elect went up in his new private coach, with a pair of cream coloured horſes, attended by Alderman Croſby, Thomas, and Hayley, and the two ſheriffs, and was preſented to the Lord Chancellor, who expreſſed the uſual approbation.

An Evening Paper ſays, the People were ſo enraged at Hereford with Alderman Harley that they burnt his Coach.

Nov. 5. When the Lord Mayor elect was preſented ...

... are ſubmitted to and eſtabliſhed.

By the laſt letters from America we have the melancholy account of the burning of the town of Boſton; and that this fire had been occaſioned by a general ſkirmiſh between the army and the inhabitants, in conſequence of the General's iſſuing preſs warrants to man the ſhips which are ſhort of complement, through ... epidemical diſtemper. The General

BOSTON EVENING-POST

January 9, 1775

—

Four months before the Battle of Lexington and Concord, and the "shot heard round the world," the first armed exchange between American and British military units took place in Portsmouth, New Hampshire, about 50 miles north of Boston. To some historians, this confrontation signaled the start of the Revolutionary War because it was the first deliberate confrontation of the war and first use of deadly force to seize territory and ordnance.

injury of the experiment is irre-
reaſon, I think, to apprehend that
eſent conteſt with America.
e bravery of our troops; what men
a country furniſhed with faſtneſſes
ntimately known to the enemy you
is unavailing or embarraſſing, and
than human power to ſucceed to
en forbid that the bravery of ſuch
ſo vainly, ſo fatally employed;
verthrow of BRADDOCK by a
rthrow incurred by the very diſci-
truſt, will be apt to doubt the fa-
by military force; they who re-
efforts of all the colonies were
arms in the late war againſt the
oubtful of this expedient.
ng been already ſaid on the ſub-
your valuable moments, which I
employed; indulge me, how-
moſt ſerious attention to the true
try, and to the welfare of our bre-
revered and eſteemed by all good
ferred with honour to poſterity,
fection, and eſteem, be echoed
nd extenſive empire.

MEMENTO.

WN, *July* 31.

y Connonade at Roxbury ſince
We have not yet heard the par-
urnt.
granted to the inhabitants of
number of perſons have ſince
permitted to bring their effects.
ning two priſoners were taken
rleſtown, and ... to he...
hey were taken
e ſentry ma...
it i...

it. The breaſtwork about two hundred. The rail fence ſtuffed with ſtraw four or five hundred. The reaſon why the ſquare was ſo thinly manned on the ſide toward Boſton, was becauſe the fire from Cop's hill poured in ſo thick that there was no living in it. The regulars when they found the fire ſlacked for want of ammunition, puſhed over the walls with their guns in their left hand, and their ſwords in the right, for it was ſuch an unfiniſhed piece of work that they ran over it. Part of them had come round on the ſide next Charleſtown, ſo as to fire on the back of our people, when they began to leave the entrenchment, and it was then we loſt our men. The ſhips and floating batteries prevented any aſſiſtance, or ſupport of conſequence, being given to our men; the fire from Cop's hill ceaſed when that with ſmall arms began, but that from a ſhip off New Boſton killed and raked our men quite up to the Sun tavern. —— thinks there was more than three thouſand of the regulars landed. They advanced in open order, the men often twelve feet apart in the front, but very cloſe after one another in extraordinary deep or long files. As faſt as the front man was ſhot down, the next ſtepped forward into his place; but our men dropt them ſo faſt, they were a long time coming up. It was ſurpriſing how they would ſtep over their dead bodies, as though they had been logs of wood. Their officers, it is ſaid, were obliged to puſh them on behind, notwithſtanding which they once ran and filled ſome of the boats, the fire was ſo hot. One of ———'s Captains told me he fired about thirty five times, and after that threw ſtones. ——— ſays when they puſhed over the breaſtwork, what with the ſmoke and duſt, it was ſo dark in the ſquare that he was obliged to feel about for the outlet, the earth, which they threw up for a breaſtwork, being very dry and looſe, for they had only one of theſe ſhort nights to execute it in.

Extract of a letter from LONDON, *June* 1.

"IT is my indiſpenſable duty to inform my countrymen on your ſide the water, of whatever reſolutions are form... this ſide injurious to your ſa...red rights, that you... on your guard to defe... ...rnicious... and t...annical...

...ſiſt of 8000 men, in order to co-operate
in forcing a relinquiſhment of the preſent
in ſupporting conſtitutional liberty through
nions."

SPEECH *of the Hon.* TEMPLE LUTTRELL,
mons, on the conduct of Adminiſtration wit
affairs.

IT is but too viſible, from the raſh mea
Miniſters of your government here in En
temper and ſituation of your American colon
will be inevitable.

Gentlemen on the other ſide of the Houſe h
favourite propoſition, that protection and obe
duties; and, of courſe, that the withdrawing
the other. Now, Sir, by theſe bills you ar
protection to ſome purpoſe; I therefore preſu
no longer to be treated as rebels, but, whatſo
zard of battle, will be entitled to the ſame n
the ſame acts of clemency and of grace that a
according to the modern ſyſtem of war, by ev
in the world. You have a ſtriking examp
conduct from ancient time, in the moſt flagran
all the wars the Romans ever waged: I me
their own countrymen, commonly called the
that, in many of it's circumſtances, bears ſo
to the preſent unhappy æra in our hiſtory,
aſking leave of the Houſe to ſay a fe...
ſions of mankind, ...
nearly ali...
look...

CHAPTER VI

BLOODY NEWS

Introduction

On the morning of April 19, 1775, war erupted along a country road west of Boston as colonial forces stood their ground and exchanged deadly fire with the world's largest and most feared army, the British regulars (soldiers). Bloody news about Lexington and Concord ignites the colonies as a swarm of militia and minutemen from all over New England race to surround Boston, trapping the British. The Continental Congress urgently reconvenes in Philadelphia to manage the hostilities while militia units capture heavy artillery from Fort Ticonderoga and prove their strength and steadfast determination at Bunker Hill. George Washington is appointed commander in chief of the Continental Army, helping to lay siege to Boston while an invasion of Canada is soon approved.

Virginia Gazette
(Williamsburg)
(Dixon and Hunter)
August 26, 1775

Battle of Bunker Hill
North Wind Picture Archives

REPORTING THE BATTLE OF LEXINGTON AND CONCORD

By J. L. Bell

News of the first full battle of the Revolutionary War spread gradually. For Massachusetts militia officers in towns along the roads from Boston to Concord, it came on April 18, 1775, as neighbors reported seeing British army officers on horseback, cloaks over their uniforms and pistols. That night, provincial riders, alarm bells, and signal guns transmitted the warning that eight hundred infantrymen had crossed the Charles River and were marching west. Militia companies began to muster.

On the morning of April 19, the news grew grim: royal troops had fired on a militia company on Lexington common, killing eight. At midday, people learned that those British regulars were searching Concord, destroying the Provincial Congress's supplies and cannons. Another exchange of fire at Concord's North Bridge left dead on both sides. Meanwhile, a reinforcement column had marched out of Boston.

As soon as the royal troops left the center of Concord, the Middlesex County militia began a concerted counterattack. The regulars met their reinforcements in Lexington, and the combined force struggled east to Charlestown through growing hostile fire. By the end of the day, about 3,800 militiamen had seen action against about 1,500 regulars. More than 270 British were left dead, wounded, or missing; for the Americans, only ninety-four.

On April 21, the New-Hampshire Gazette *published a front-page article on the "BLOODY NEWS" from Massachusetts, reflecting the regional importance of the battle.*

On April 21, the *New-Hampshire Gazette* published a front-page article on the "BLOODY NEWS" from Massachusetts. A collection of rumors, this early printed report on the battle was wrong in several major details, but it reflected the regional importance of the event. Normally, colonial newspapers started with foreign news set in type over the preceding week; in this one paper, the battle in Massachusetts pushed those columns aside.

The Massachusetts Provincial Congress worked to shape the news of the battle, issuing a detailed report that portrayed the militiamen as victims of aggression. Magistrates gathered eyewitness accounts favorable to the provincials; some even came from captured British soldiers, as John Dixon and William Hunter reprinted in the June 3, 1775, *Virginia Gazette*.

The legislature also commissioned John Derby of Salem to sail his family's schooner *Quero* to Britain with no cargo except a few copies of the April 21 and 28, 1775, *Salem Gazette*, containing Congress's report on the battle. Derby arrived in London on the evening of May 28. His news was soon discussed all over the capital. The Secretary of State's office had to issue a reminder, published in the June 1, 1775, *London Chronicle*, that there was still no official word from Massachusetts.

General Thomas Gage's report finally arrived in London on June 9. As quoted in the June 13, 1775, *London Chronicle*, Gage stated that the fight at Lexington began when "guns were fired upon the King's troops from behind a stone wall." He suggested the rebels had suffered "very considerable" losses and did not mention how his army was now besieged in Boston. Reflecting British army priorities, the general named casualties among the officers but merely numbered the enlisted men. The *Chronicle* continued to print news from America culled from newspapers, official dispatches, and private letters.

Back in Massachusetts, the printers of the *Essex Gazette* moved their press to Cambridge, headquarters of the new New England army, and began issuing the *New-England Chronicle*. They published letters between

General Gage and Governor Jonathan Trumbull of Connecticut (who sided with the resistance), soldiers' letters intercepted on their way to England, and Gage's widely derided proclamation of amnesty for rebels who surrendered.

American newspapers formed a consensus that one goal of the British army's march had been to arrest Massachusetts's political leaders, particularly John Hancock and Samuel Adams. General Gage described his aim as destroying rebel supplies in Concord; his orders and private files, made available in the twentieth century, confirm this. But the early American assumptions still shape how historians retell the event.

One part of the Battle of Lexington and Concord that did not appear in newspapers of the day was the story of Paul Revere. As dramatic as his experiences were, they had a limited effect on the fight, and Massachusetts officials did not wish to publicize how they had prepared for war. It took almost a century before Henry W. Longfellow's poem "Paul Revere's Ride" made the silversmith into an American icon. On April 19, 1775, he was just one of thousands of men caught up in the start of the war.

The Fight on Lexington Common
North Wind Picture Archives

(*right*) British regulars fire on a militia company, killing eight and starting the first full battle of the Revolutionary War.

British Retreat from Concord, MA
North Wind Picture Archives

(*left*) By the end of the royal troops' retreat from Concord to Boston, more than 270 British were left dead, wounded, or missing; for the Americans, only ninety-four.

FRIDAY *April* 21, 1775.

DIEU ET MON DROIT

No. 96

BLOODY NEWS.

PORTSMOUTH, April 20, 1775.

Early this Morning, we were alarmed, with an Expreſs from Newbury-Port, with the following Letter, to the Chairman of the Committee of Correſpondence in this Town.

SIR, Newbury-Port, April 19, 1775.

THIS Town has been in a continual Alarm ſince Mid-day, with Reports of the TROOPS having marched out of Boſton to make ſome Attack in the Country—The Reports in general concur, in part, in having been at Lexington.—And it is very generally ſaid they have been at Concord.—— We ſent off an Expreſs this Afternoon, who went as far as Simons's at Danvers, before he could get Information that he thought might be depended upon— he there met two or three Gentlemen who affirmed, the Regular *Troops* and our Men had been engaged chief of the Morning, and that it is ſuppoſed we had Twenty-five Thouſand Men engaged againſt Four Thouſand Regulars; that the Regulars had begun a Retreat—— Our Men here are ſetting off immediately——And as the *Sword is now drawn,* and *firſt drawn on the Side of the Troops,* we ſcruple not, you will give the *readieſt and fulleſt Aſſiſtance in your Power*—— And ſend this Information further on—— In Behalf of the Committee for this Town,

Your humble Servant,

JAMES HUDSON, Chairman.

By the Expreſs who brought the above Letter, we hear the Attack began at Lexington,

NEW-HAMPSHIRE GAZETTE (PORTSMOUTH)

April 21, 1775

One of the biggest stories of the eighteenth century, and only two colonial newspapers carried the breaking news on the front page. This is one of those two. This is also the only newspaper to use an actual headline, not a dateline, for its first report of Lexington and Concord.

bers had been ſlain on both Sides. A Rein-

leaving one Thouſand only to guard the Town.

Thurſday One o'Clock. Another Expreſs

By the Nautilus and Falcon Ships of War, arrived at Boſton from London, we have the following important Advices, viz.

LONDON, *February* 16.

ORDERS are ſent to Commanders of his Majeſty's Guard Ships at Portſmouth & Plymouth, to take on board an extra Number of Hands to be ready to man the Ships fitting out for Sea.

The Miniſtry complain very loudly of the Alteration in the Temper of a certain American Governor, ſince his being made Commander in Chief of the Forces in that Quarter; An Addition of Power it was expected would have produced additional Zeal; But they ſay, like all others, he is dwindled into the tame Magiſtrate.

Orders are given from the War Office, for the Lord Lieutenants of every County in England to give in Accounts of the State and Condition of the Militia, as well Officers as private Men.

Not a Commiſſion has been lately beſtowed either at the War-Office or the Admiralty for the American Service, but to Perſons whoſe Opinions with Reſpect to the Oppoſition of the Colonies have been firſt very ſcrupulouſly canvaſſed.

Orders are ſent to the commanding Officers of Marines, at Chatham and Portſmouth, to raiſe a Number of Recruits to compleat the ſeveral Companies to their full Compliment of Men, to ſupply the Draughts that have been made for Boſton.

We learn that in Virginia they have now 15000 Troops under Arms, 1000 Horſe, and 5000 free Negroes.

Feb. 21. All the Deſerters from the Troops on the other Side the Atlantic, we are aſſured, are Engliſh and Iriſh; not a Scotchman having yet flinched from his Duty, or betrayed the leaſt Deſire to depart from the very Letter of his Commiſſion.

Is is not ſomewhat remarkable, ſays a Correſpondent, that our Quarrels with Spain and France ſhould be ſettled by drawing our Purſe Strings; but thoſe with America, by Fire and Sword.

A Morning Paper obſerves, that a Spaniſh Fleet is abſolutely cruizing off Boſton, and it is added, that the Americans have refuſed to ſupply the Troops under General Gage with any kind of Proviſions, for which Purpoſe ſeveral Regiments of Provincials were encamped near that City, who have cut off all Communication between the Soldiers and the Country People.

Upwards of 3000l. have been raiſed privately in London ſince the Meeting of Parliament, for the Relief of the diſtreſſed Americans, and tranſmitted there.

Among the many Reaſons aſſigned to account for Monday's American Motion, are the certain Loſs of the Revenue of Trade and Commerce, the Uncertainty whether the Troops would act [...]ſt their Fellow-Subjects, the utter impracticability of enſla[...] [...]e Americans, and laſtly, an almoſt certainty of the Mili[...] [...]ng ſoon wanted nearer Home, to oppoſe European Invaders. [...] Adam Gordon, in the late Debate in Parliament, was for [...]ng the American Acts with Vigour. His Reaſons he begged [...]o read from a Diary he himſelf had written when in Ame[...] [...]d which Diary, as he confeſſed, the Miniſtry did him the [...] to conſult, as a Guide in their Proceedings againſt the Ame[...] [...]---The Subſtance of this Diary was, "That the People of [...]n were naturally ſenſible and extremely polite, but very [...] inclined to Faction; that Governor Hutchinſon was the [...]of Men, but rendered very uneaſy in his Office by the tur[...] [...]t Spirit of the People; that the Colony Governments in[...] [...]ined too much to the popular Scale, and therefore Lord Adam "urges in this Diary the abſolute Neceſſity of altering the Char" "ters, in order to conſtitute a Government of a more Royal Na-

gland, ſhe meditates a more ſerious Blow, by ſecuring America againſt her natural Friend.

The ſpirited Behaviour of the People of Jamaica, has thrown a

are to be bro't to for
any Merchandize,
to the ſaid Province
ſaid Provinces or C
Great-Britain, or f
and that no other M
the ſaid Provinces
been imported into
ſhipped from any of
cept Great Britain
dies, on Forfeiture

"Alſo, that after
of Wines, Salt, or
Horſes, Victual, an
of Ireland, and Go
for his Majeſty's F
tiſh Iſlands in the
tence whatſoever, u
and carried directly
Veſſel.

"Likewiſe, tha
or Ireland, or the
after the limited T
North America, or
leſs the Maſter do
jeſty's Ships of W
American Fiſheries
vernor of the Colo
Nova-Scotia, New
Virginia, N. Caroli
Florida, ſetting fort
one of the ſaid Colo
jeſty's Subjects, In
ful for any of the C
ſtationed for the P
America to ſeize, a
That nothing here
longing to the Fren
not carrying on any

"Theſe reſtraints
Laws ſhall be reſto
declared incapable
pains and Penalties.

From the St. JA

AN Opinion hav
Lord has mad
with the Addreſs of
made laſt Monday in
the following auther

See the Motion

This Motion, Sir,
heres in every Thin
Offer of Lives and F
cies, by Parliament,
nies return to their I
Legiſlature, their re
Application, be remo
nire, the noble Lord
define the utmoſt Co
the Mother Country
above Motion. The
ſon to complain, tha

this Country over A
ned Firmneſs by his
to know, that a grea

VIRGINIA GAZETTE (WILLIAMSBURG) (DIXON AND HUNTER)

June 3, 1775

As part of its effort to steer public opinion, the Massachusetts Provincial Congress gathered one-sided eyewitness accounts, including some from captured British soldiers, which were published in newspapers up and down the continent.

---

opposition to our engagements, may not escape, [illegible] those ships, on hearing how things are at your Capes, do not land their dry goods in some part of the Bay. All goods on board should be taken possession of by the committee, and ship and all should be sent back, the salt at least thrown into the sea, and the goods returned by the ship."

WILLIAMSBURG, *June* 3.

LAST Monday morning a detachment of cavalry from [the] WILLIAMSBURG VOLUNTEERS, in their uniforms, [well] mounted and equipped, with a waggon containing their bag[gage] and provisions, set out in a regular military procession, to [meet] the Hon. PEYTON RANDOLPH, Esq; late President of [the] Grand Continental Congress, on the way hither from Phila[del]phia, his presence being requisite at our General Assembly [now] sitting here. On Tuesday, about noon, the troop of horse [met] that Gentleman at Ruffin's ferry, accompanied by Col. CART[ER] BRAXTON, and escorted them to Williamsburg, after ha[ving] been joined by a company of infantry, who marched out th[e dis]tance of two miles for the same purpose. They arrived he[re at] sunset, and were attended to the honourable Gentleman's ho[use] by the whole body of cavalry and infantry, whose very martial ap[pearance] gave great satisfaction to the spectators. The bells began to ring as our worthy Delegate entered the city, and the unfeigned joy of the inhabitants, on this occasion, was visible in every countenance; there were illuminations in the evening, and the volunteers, with many other respectable Gentlemen, assembled at the Raleigh, spent an hour or two in harmony and cheerfulness, and drank several patriotic toasts.

Yesterday the Honourable House of Burgesses appointed committees to proceed on the ordinary business of the country.

We hear from King and Queen, that on Monday the 22d ult. a most dreadful whirlwind happened in that county. It seemed to rise from two thunder clouds meeting in the west; about one o'clock its course was easterly, and tore up every thing in its way near a quarter of a mile wide. Many poor people have felt its direful effects; no less than eight plantations are swept in as many miles, some not having a house left; 4 persons, viz. a young man, a woman, a boy, and a child in its mother's arms, were crushed to death, and several so much bruised and wounded that their recovery is doubtful. In short, such a scene of horrour and devastation was never seen before by winds in this country.

Extract of a letter from PHILADELPHIA, *May* 23.

"A Gentleman from Rhode Island brings an account that a Captain of a man of war at Boston had sent out a cutter to take a sloop arrived in a river there, with provisions for the provincial army, which was done; but the people collected in armed boats, regained their own, and took the other vessel, sending the crew prisoners into the country. Accounts from England and Ireland are, that the troops at the former are said to be countermanded, and at the latter an unwillingness to embark had produced a skirmish, in which many were killed, and the embarkation stopped."

In a late Philadelphia paper have been published, by order of the Congress, affidavits and depositions of sundry persons of Lexington, Concord, &c. by which it appears that the provincials were first attacked at both places by the King's troops. The following are depositions of three of the wounded regulars, which were published with those of the provincials.

LINCOLN, *April* 23, 1775.

"I JOHN BATEMAN, belonging to the 52d regiment, commanded by Col. Jones, on Wednesday morning the 19th day of April instant, was in the party marching to Concord; being at Lexington, in the county of Middlesex, and being nigh the meeting-house in said Lexington, there was a small party of men gathered together in that place when our said troops marched by; and I testify and declare, that I heard the word of command given to the troops to fire, and some of said troops did fire, and I saw one of said small party lay dead on the ground, nigh said meeting-house; and I testify that I never heard any of the inhabitants so much as fire one gun on said troops. JOHN BATEMAN."

CONCORD, *April* 23, 1775.

"I JAMES MARR, of lawful age, testify and say, that in the evening of the 18th instant I received orders from George

---

House of Commons [illegible] I hope, auspicious advance on the part of the parent state.

It must now be manifest, to all dispassionate people, that the Parliament, the high and supreme legislature of the empire, far from having entertained thoughts so inconsistent with the wisdom [illegible]

[illegible] to their full scope, and that your gift, if you should [illegible] to offer any, may be, in the completest manner, free. The civil government of this country being already provided for, you will only have to declare what proportion, and by what means, you are willing to contribute towards the public burthens of the state, burthens to which the mother country hath cheerfully submitted to secure the colonies from the encroachments of a dangerous and vigilant enemy: And I am warranted to say, that as it is never intended to require you to tax yourselves, without Parliament's taxing the subjects of Great Britain on the same occasion, in a far greater proportion, no prudence which you shall think necessary to observe for your security in that particular can be disapproved of.

And I can likewise assure you, that if you should judge fit to adopt the principle, and imitate the example of justice, equity, and moderation, in your proposals, which actuated the House of Commons in their resolution, declaring at once what was ultimately expected of you; such a compliance on your part will be considered by his Majesty not only as a testimony of your reverence for Parliament, but also as a mark of your duty and attachment to your Sovereign, who has no object nearer his heart than the peace and prosperity of his subjects in every part of his dominions.

I must recommend to you to fall upon means of paying the officers and private men employed in repelling the late invasion and incursions of the Indians, as I make no doubt you will think their services on that occasion deserving of your attention.

Gentlemen of the COUNCIL, *Mr.* SPEAKER, *and Gentlemen of the* HOUSE *of* BURGESSES,

You may be assured of my cheerful concurrence in all measures, and ready assent to all laws, which it may be found expedient to adopt for the present peace, tranquillity, and advantage of the country; and I hope you will think it necessary to these ends, that the courts of justice should forthwith be opened, in order that the laws may again have their due course.

I cannot conclude without exhorting you in the most earnest manner, to enter upon the subject matter, now recommended to you, with that patience, calmness, and impartiality, which its great importance requires, and to reflect upon the benefits this country hath received from the support given to it by the parent state, which I hope will animate your zeal, now you have it in your power, to restore that harmony and mutual confidence which rendered both countries so flourishing, and, in short, to pursue your true interest, which will convert our present gloomy apprehensions into prospects of peace, happiness, and lasting security.

AT a general meeting of the freeholders of Mecklenburg county, convened on Monday the 8th day of May 1775, at the courthouse of said county, in order to elect a committee, pursuant to a resolution of the American Continental Congress, the better to secure a due observation of the association entered into by the said Congress, the freeholders then proceeded to the choice of

JUNE 1, 1775

The LONDON CHRONICLE

For the London Chronicle.

To the P U B L I C. [...]

AS a doubt of the authenticity of the account from Salem, touching an engagement between the King's Troops and the Provincials in the Massachusetts Bay, may arise from a paragraph in the Gazette of this evening, I desire to inform all those who wish to see the original affidavits which confirm that account, that they are deposited at the Mansion House with the Right Hon. the Lord Mayor for their inspection.

ARTHUR LEE [...]

ADVICES from AMERICA.

The following Affidavits and other Particulars, relative to the late Skirmish between his Majesty's Troops and the Provincials in Massachusett's Bay, were received on Monday last. Lexington, April 23, 1775.

WE John Hoar, John Whithed, Abraham Gearfield, Benjamin Munroe, Isaac Park, William Hosmer, John Adams, Gregory Stone, all of Lincoln, in the county of Middlesex, Massachusett's Bay, all of lawful age, do testify and say, that on Wednesday last we were assembled at Concord in the morning of said day, in consequence of information received, that a brigade of regular troops were on their march to the said town of Concord, who had killed six men at the town of Lexington ; about an hour afterward we saw them approaching, to the number of 1200 ; on which we retreated to a hill about 80 rods back ; and the said troops then took possession of the hill where we were first posted. Presently after this, we saw the troops moving towards the North Bridge, about one mile from the said Concord Meetinghouse. We then immediately went before them, and passed the bridge, just before a party of them, to the number of about 200, arrived. They there left about one half of their 200 at the Bridge, and proceeded with the rest towards Col. Barrett's, about two miles from the said Bridge. We then seeing several fires in the town, thought the houses in Concord were in danger, and marched towards the said Bridge ; and the troops who were stationed there, observed our approach, marched back over the Bridge, and then took up some of the planks. We then hastened our march towards the Bridge ; and when we had got near the Bridge they fired on our men first, three guns one after the other ; they also fired a considerable number more ; and then, and not before (having orders from our commanding officer not to fire till we were fired upon) we fired upon the regulars, and they retreated. On their retreat through this town, Lexington, to CharlesTown, they ravaged and distressed private property, and burnt three houses, one barn, and one shop.

The above affidavit was signed by the persons whose names are mentioned at the beginning of it, and sworn before William Reed, John Cuming, Jonathan Hastings, and Duncan Ingraham, Esqrs. four of his Majesty's Justices of the Peace. And Nathaniel Gorham, Notary Public, certifies that full faith is to be given to the transactions of the said Justices.

Lexington, April 23. I James Barrett, of Concord, Colonel of a regiment of militia in the county of Middlesex, do testify and say, that on Wednesday morning last, about day-break, I was informed of the approach of a number of the regular troops to the town of Concord, where were some magazines belonging to this province, and where there were assembled some of the militia of this and the neighbouring towns, when I ordered them to march to the North Bridge (so called) which they had passed, and were taking up. I ordered said militia to march to said Bridge, and pass the same, but not to fire on the King's troops unless they were first fired upon. We advanced near said bridge, when the said troops fired upon our militia, and killed two men dead on the spot, and wounded several others, which was the first firing of guns in the town of Concord. My detachment then returned the fire, which killed and wounded several of the said King's troops.

JAMES BARRET.

Vol. XXXVII. **The London Chronicle.** N° 2883.

From TUESDAY, MAY 30, to T

LONDON CHRONICLE

June 1, 1775

News of Lexington and Concord, via copies of the *Salem Gazette*, arrived in London on the evening of May 28. For nearly two weeks, Londoners only knew the rebel version of events.

For the London Chronicle.

To the PUBLIC.

Tuesday, May the 30th, 1775.

As a doubt of the authenticity of the account from Salem, touching an engagement between the King's Troops and the Provincials in the Massachusetts Bay, may arise from a paragraph in the Gazette of this evening, I desire to inform all those who wish to see the original affidavits which confirm that account, that they are deposited at the Mansion House with the Right Hon. the Lord Mayor for their inspection.

ARTHUR LEE,
Agent for the House of Representatives of the Massachusetts Bay.

ADVICES FROM AMERICA.

The following Affidavits and other Particulars, relative to the late Skirmish between his Majesty's Troops and the Provincials in Massachusett's Bay, were received on Monday last.

Lexington, April 23, 1775.

We John Hoar, John Whithed, Abraham Gearfield, Benjamin Munroe, Isaac Park, William Hosmer, John Adams, Gregory Stone, all of Lincoln, in the county of Middlesex, Massachusett's Bay, all of lawful age, do testify and say, that on Wednesday last we were assembled at Concord in the morning of said day, in consequence of information received, that a brigade of regular troops were on their march to the said town of Concord, who had killed six men at the town of Lexington; about an hour afterward we saw them approaching, to the number of 1200; on which we retreated to a hill about 80 rods back; and the said troops then took possession of the hill where we were first posted. Presently after this, we saw the troops moving towards the North Bridge, about one mile from the said Concord Meeting-house. We then immediately went before them, and passed the bridge, just before a party of them, to the number of about 200, arrived. They there left about one half of their 200 at the Bridge, and proceeded with the rest towards Col. Barrett's, about two miles from the said Bridge. We then seeing several fires in the town, thought the houses in Concord were in danger, and marched towards the said Bridge; and the troops who were stationed there, observing our approach, marched back over the Bridge, and then took up some of the planks. We then hastened our march towards the Bridge; and when we had got near the Bridge they fired on our men first, three guns one after the other; they also fired a considerable number more; and then, and not before, (having orders from our commanding officer not to fire till we were fired upon) we fired upon the regulars, and they retreated. On their retreat through this town, Lexington, to Charles-Town, they ravaged and distressed private property, and burnt three houses, one barn, and one shop.

The above affidavit was signed by the persons whose names are mentioned at the beginning of it, and sworn before William Reed, John Cuming, Jonathan Hastings, and Duncan Ingraham, Esqrs. four of his Majesty's Justices of the Peace. And Nathaniel Gorham, Notary Public, certifies that full faith is to be given to the transactions of the said Justices.

Lexington, April 23. I James Barrett, of the county of Middlesex, d… on Wednesday morning la… I was informed of the appr… the regular troops to the… where were some magazin… province, and where there… of the militia of this an… towns, when I ordered them… North Bridge (so called) which … and were taking up. I ordered said militia to march to said Bridge, and pass the same, but not to fire on the King's troops unless they were first fired upon. We advanced near said bridge, when the said troops fired upon our militia, and killed two men dead on the spot, and wounded several others, which was the first firing of guns in the town of Concord. My detachment then returned the fire, which killed and wounded several of the said King's troops.

JAMES BARRETT.

Sworn before Wm. Reed, Jonathan Hastings, and Duncan Ingraham, Justices of the Peace.

Lexington, April 23. We Bradbury Robinson, Samuel Spring, Thaddeos Bancroft, all of Concord, and James Adams, of Lincoln, all in the county of Middlesex, all of lawful age, do testify and say, that on Wednesday morning last, near ten of the clock, we saw near one hundred of regular troops, being in the town of Concord, at the North Bridge in the said town (so called) and having passed the same, they were taking up the said bridge, when about three hundred of our militia were advancing towards the said bridge, in order to pass the said bridge, when without saying any thing to us, they discharged a number of guns on us, which killed two men dead on the spot, and wounded several others, when we returned the fire on them, which killed two of them, and wounded several, which was the beginning of hostilities in the town of Concord.

Sworn before W. Reed, W. Stickney, and Jon. Hastings, his Majesty's Justices of the Peace.

Lincoln, April 23. I John Bateman, belonging to the fifty-second regiment, commanded by Colonel Jones, on Wednesday morning, on the 19th of April instant, was in the party marching for Concord, being at Lexington in the county of Middlesex; being nigh the meeting house in said Lexington, there was a small party of men gathered together in that place, when our said troops marched by; and I testify and declare, that I heard the word of command given to the troops to fire, and some of the said troops did fire, and I saw one of the said small party lie dead on the ground, nigh the said meeting house; and I testify, that I never heard any of the inhabitants so much as fire one gun on the said troops.

Sworn before John Cuming and Duncan Ingraham, Justices of the Peace.

Concord, April 23. I James Marr, of lawful age, testify and say, that in the evening of the 18th instant, I received orders from George Hutchinson, Adjutant of the fourth regiment of regular troops stationed at Boston, to prepare and march, to which orders I attended, and marched to Concord, where I was ordered by an officer, with about one hundred men, to guard a certain bridge there; while attending that service, a number of people came along, in order, as I suppose, to cross the said bridge, at which time a number of the regular troops first fired upon them.

Sworn before Duncan I…ham and Jonas

… place, we saw a body of provincial troops armed, to the number of about sixty or seventy men. On our approach they dispersed, and soon after firing began; but which party fired first I cannot exactly say, as our troops rushed on shouting and huzzaing, previous to the firing, which was continued by our troops so long as any of the provincials were to be seen. From thence we marched to Concord. On a hill near the entrance of the town, we saw another body of provincials assembled. The light infantry companies were ordered up the hill to disperse them. On our approach they retreated towards Concord. The grenadiers continued the road under the hill towards the town. Six companies of light infantry were ordered down to take possession of the bridge, which the provincials retreated over. The company I commanded was one. Three companies of the above detachment went forward about two miles. In the mean time, the provincial troops returned, to the number of about three or four hundred. We drew up on the Concord side of the bridge. The Provincials came down upon us, upon which we engaged and gave the first fire. This was the first engagement after the one at Lexington: A continued firing from both parties lasted through the whole day. I myself was wounded at the attack of the bridge, and am now treated with the greatest humanity, and taken all possible care of …

… above is a true copy … by express from … Newhaven, and attested by the committee of correspondence from town to town. Test. Jon. Sturges, And. Rowland, Silleck Silliman, Thad. Burr, Job Bartram.

WEDNESDAY, MAY 31.

The London Gazette. No. 11565.

Secretary of State's Office, Whitehall, May 30, 1775.

A Report having been spread, and an account having been printed and published, of a skirmish between some of the people in the Province of Massachuset's Bay and a detachment of his Majesty's troops; it is proper to inform the Public, that no advices have as yet been received in the American department of any such event.

There is reason to believe, that there are dispatches from General Gage on board the Sukey, Capt. Brown, which, though she sailed four days before the vessel that brought the printed account, is not yet arrived.

Warsaw, May 13.

The very uncommonly dry and cold weather, which we have had for some time past, has occasioned a great mortality in and about this town.

Copenhagen, May 16. On the 13th a placart was published here, by Government, containing the report lately propagated of an intention to suppress or reduce the Bank Notes of one rixdollar, and promising a reward of 1000 rixdollars for discovering the author of … and on the 15th, the Magistrates

Chelmsford, June 9. M. Lingard, at Writtle, ſowed three wheat kernels in his garden early this ſpring, which have produced what is hardly credible, not leſs than 151 ſtalks of wheat, which are all in a thriving ſtate.

LONDON.

From the LONDON GAZETTE.

Whitehall, June 10. Lieutenant Nunn, of the Navy, arrived this morning at Lord Dartmouth's office, and has brought letters from General Gage, Lord Percy, and Lieutenant Colonel Smith, containing the following particulars of what paſſed on the 19th of April laſt, between a detachment of the King's troops in the province of Maſſachuſett's Bay, and ſeveral parties of Rebel Provincials, viz.

General Gage having received inteligence of a large quantity of military ſtores beig collected at Concord, for the avowed purpoſe of ſupplying a body of troops to act in oppſition to his Majeſty's government, detached, on the 18th of April, at night, the Grenadiers of his army, and the Light Infantry, under the command of Lieutenant Colonel Smith of the 10th regiment, and Major Pitcairne of the Maines, with orders to deſtroy the ſaid ſtores; and the next morning eight companies of the 4th, the ſame number of the 23d and 49th, and ſome Marines, marched under the command of Lord Percy, to ſupport the other detachment.

Lieutenant Colonel Smith finding, after he had advanced ſome miles on his march, that the country had been alarmed by the firing of guns, and ringing of bells, diſpatched ſix companies of Light Infantry, in order to ſecure two bridges on different roads beyond Concord, who, upon their arrival at Lexington, found a body of the country people drawn up under arms on a green, cloſe to the road; and, upon the King's troops marching up to them, in order to inquire the reaſon of their being ſo aſſembled, they went off in great confuſion, and ſeveral guns were fired upon the King's troops from behind a ſtone wall, and alſo from the Meeting-houſe and other houſes, by which one man was wounded, and Major Pitcairne's horſe ſhot in two places. In conſequence of this attack by the rebels, the troops returned the fire, and killed ſeveral of them; after which the detachment marched on to Concord, without any thing further happening, where they effected the purpoſe for which they were ſent, having knocked off the trunnions of three pieces of iron ordnance, burnt ſome new gun carriages, and a great number of carriage wheels, and thrown into the river a conſiderable quantity

...lonel Smith and Major Pitcairne did every...ing that men coul... general; and th... ual intrepidity.

...turn of the ... Officers, Drum... and wounded, ... 19th of April...

4th, or King's ... Knight, killed. ... and priſoner. ... wounded. 7 rank... 8 miſſing.

5th regiment. ... Lieutenant William Cox, Lieutenant Thomas Hawkſhaw, wounded. 5 rank and file killed, 15 wounded, 1 miſſing.

10th regiment. Lieutenant Colonel Francis Smith, Captain Lawrence Parſons, Lieutenant Wald. Kelly, Enſign Jeremiah Leſter, wounded. 1 rank and file killed, 13 wounded, 1 miſſing.

18th regiment. 1 rank and file killed, 4 wounded, 1 miſſing.

23d regiment. Lieut. Colonel Bery Bernard, wounded. 4 rank and file killed, 26 wounded, 6 miſſing.

38th regiment. Lieut. William Sutherland wounded, 1 Serjeant wounded. 4 rank and file killed, 11 wounded.

43d regiment. Lieut. Hull wounded and priſoner. 4 rank and file killed, 5 wounded, 2 miſſing.

47th regiment. Lieut. Donald M'Cloud, Enſign Henry Baldwin, wounded. 1 Serjeant wounded. 5 rank and file killed, 21 wounded.

52d regiment. 1 Serjeant miſſing. 3 rank and file killed. 2 wounded.

59th regiment. 3 rank and file killed, 3 wounded.

Marines. Captain Souter, Second Lieutenant M'Donald, wounded. Second Lieutenant Iſaac Potter miſſing. 1 Serjeant killed, ... wounded, 1 miſſing. 1 Drummer killed. 5 rank and file killed, 36 wounded, 5 miſſing.

T O T A L.

1 Lieutenant killed.
2 Lieutenant-Colonels wounded.
2 Captains wounded.
9 Lieutenants wounded.
1 Lieutenant miſſing.
2 Enſigns wounded.
1 Serjeant killed, 7 wounded, 2 miſſing. 1 Drummer killed, 1 wounded. 62 rank and file killed, 157 wounded, 24 miſſing.

N. B. Lieutenant Iſaac Potter reported to be wounded and taken priſoner.

Signed THO. GAGE.

Extract of a Letter from Edinbur...

... where the lives of ſo many men de... as the ſecurity of the nation.

" The ſmugglers upon this co... ſeized from them within this mo... wards of 1200 ankers of brandy, ... beſides teas, by the cuſtom-houſe...

" The crops of graſs, barley, ... like to turn out very bad, owing... dry ſpring; the wheat is thin and...

" We have had great plenty of ... this coaſt this ſeaſon, which have ... to 1s. 6d. per dozen.

" His Majeſty's ſhip Kent, Cap... is ordered to join the grand fleet ... Portſmouth; the Romney of 50 g... Duff, is at anchor in the Sound ... Dublin, Albion, Raiſonable, and T... ſhips, are at their moorings in the H... Hunter ſloop of war hath been ... ſheathed for the American ſtatio... ſloop of war is going into dock; ... and Fame are in the docks repai... Prudent, late from the Eaſt Indies ... being very leaky."

Extract of a Letter from Chath...

" Sunday arrived here the Au... with Lord Sandwich, &c. on boar... ſhip was ſaluted with 15 guns f... jeſty's ſhip Ramillies, Commodore ... Vernon, which compliment was ... the Auguſta yacht, with ſeven ... Sandwich did not come on ſhore t...

" Monday morning his Lordſ... ſhore at the dock-yard, accompai... Seaford, Sir Hugh Palliſer, Dr. ... Omiah, the native of Otaheite; t... ceived in the yard by Col. M'K... Marines, Maurice Suckling, Eſq; ... Sir John Williams, Surveyor, Wi... Eſq; Comptroller of the victuallin... his Majeſty's navy, Commiſſioner... the principal officers of the do... Grenadier company of Marines w...

LONDON CHRONICLE
June 13, 1775

On June 9, General Gage's official report about the battle of April 19 arrived in London. According to Gage, the first shot came when "guns were fired upon the King's troops from behind a stone wall."

great numbers of the rebels aſſembled in many parts, and a conſiderable body of them attacked the Light Infantry poſted on one of the bridges.

de Guines arrived at his houſe in Great George-ſtreet, from France. His Excellency, immediately on his arrival, was viſited by all the foreign

Their Lordſhips, &c. walked rou... and took a view of the ſhips buil...

NEW-ENGLAND CHRONICLE (CAMBRIDGE, MA)

May 12, 1775

The printers of the *Essex Gazette* moved their press from Salem to Cambridge, the headquarters of the new New England army, and began publishing the *New-England Chronicle*. This is the first issue after the move and title change.

We are constantly stating the great obligation we have conferred on the Colonies by our former behaviour towards them; if it was ever so good, we can claim no merit from hence in private or public concerns, to do injury in future; they do not complain of your *former* behaviour, but they say, you have altered this very system from whence you would now derive their submission.

There are two arguments of the noble Lord which I must remark upon before I sit down; the first is, "the comparative view of "Taxation between this country and the Colonies, according to "the number of inhabitants." His Lordship says, "we pay about "twenty-five shillings a head, and they pay about six-pence." Who is there so unacquainted with political arithmetic as not to know that the small sum people pay in Taxation is often a proof of their poverty, and the large sum a proof of their prosperity, by demonstrating the riches from the greatness of the consumption? Let this kind of reasoning be applied to Ireland or Scotland, where we know the multitude to be poor in comparison to the inhabitants of London, whom we know to be rich; besides, if the Colonist does not pay in *palpable Cash* from his own hand, does not he pay all the *Taxes* on the four millions of *Manufactures* he receives, and part of those Taxes on the raw materials he sends hither.

The other argument is still more extraordinary. The noble Lord says, "if we fail in our attempt of forcing America, we shall "still be in the same situation we are in at present." What! after our armies have been disgraced, our fellow-subjects destroyed, all the irritation of a civil war, public confidence, and fair opinion lost!---Does the noble Lord think he will be in the same situation *himself?*---I really speak it with regret, for *personally* I have much regard for the noble Lord, and particularly because I perceive, from his *faint* manner of stating his propositions, that they are not the dictates of his own mind, and that they are forced on him.

I cannot see my other memorandums, and therefore I shall conclude by *heartily concurring* with the noble Lord who moved for the recommitment of this Address.

CAMBRIDGE, May 12.

Copy of a Letter to his Excellency General GAGE, from the Hon. JONATHAN TRUMBULL, Esq; Governor of his Majesty's Colony of Connecticut, in behalf of the General Assembly of said Colony.

SIR, Dated HARTFORD, April 28th, 1775.

THE alarming situation of public affairs in this country, and the late unfortunate transactions in the province of the Massachusetts Bay, have induced the General Assembly of this colony, now sitting in this place, to appoint a committee of their body to wait upon your Excellency, and to desire me, in their name, to write to you relative to these very interesting matters.

The inhabitants of this colony are intimately connected with the people of your province, and esteem themselves bound by the strongest ties of friendship, as well as of common interest, to regard with attention whatever concerns them. You will not therefore be surprized that your first arrival at Boston, with a body of his Majesty's troops, for the declared purpose of carrying into execution certain acts of parliament, which, in their apprehension, were unconstitutional and oppressive, should have given the good people of this colony a very just and general alarm; your subsequent proceedings in fortifying the town of Boston, and other military preparations, greatly increased their apprehensions for the safety of their friends and brethren; they could not be unconcerned spectators of their sufferings in that which they esteemed the common cause of this country; but the late hostile and secret inroads of some of the troops under your command into the heart of the country, and the violences they have committed, have driven them almost into a state of desperation. They feel now not only for their friends, but for themselves, and their dearest interests & connections. We wish not to exaggerate, we are not sure of every part of our information; but, by the best intelligence that we have yet been able to obtain, the late transaction was a most unprovoked attack upon the lives and property of his Majesty's subjects; and it is represented to us, that such outrages have been committed as would disgrace even barbarians, and much more Britons, so highly famed for humanity as well as bravery: It is feared therefore that we are devoted to destruction, and that you have it in command and intention, to ravage and desolate the country. If this is not the case, permit us to ask, why have these outrages been committed? Why is the town of Boston now shut up? And to what end are all the hostile preparations that are daily making, and why do we continually hear of fresh destinations of troops for this country? The people of this colony, you may rely upon it, abhor the idea of taking arms against the troops of their Sovereign, and dread nothing so much as the horrors of civil war; but at the same time we beg leave to assure your Excellency, that as they apprehend themselves justified by the principle of self-defence, so they are most firmly resolved to defend their rights and privileges to the last extremity; nor will they be restrained from giving aid to their brethren, if any unjustifiable attack is made upon them. Be so good, therefore, as to explain yourself upon this most important subject, as far as is consistent with your duty to our common Sovereign.---Is there no way to prevent this unhappy dispute from coming to extremities? Is there no alternative but absolute submission, or the

happy for them if they had sought relief, only in the way which the constitution, their reason, and their interest pointed out.

You cannot wonder at my fortifying the town of Boston, or making any other military preparations, when you are assured, that previous to my taking these steps, such was the open threats, and such the warlike preparations thoughout this province as rendered it my indispensable duty to take every precaution in my power, for the protection of his Majesty's troops under my command, against all hostile attempts. The intelligence you seem to have received, relative to the late excursion of a body of troops into the country, is altogether injurious and contrary to the true state of facts; the troops disclaim, with indignation, the barbarous outrages of which they are accused, so contrary to their known humanity. I have taken the greatest pains to discover if any were committed, and have found examples of their tenderness both to the young and the old, but no vestige of cruelty or barbarity: It is very possible that in firing into houses, from whence they were fired upon, that old people, women or children, may have suffered, but if any such thing has happened it was in their defence, and undesigned. I have no command to ravage and desolate the country, and were it my intention I have had pretence to begin it, upon the sea ports, who are at the mercy of the fleet. For your better information, I inclose you a narrative of that affair, taken from gentlemen of indisputable honor and veracity, who were eye-witnesses of all the transactions of that day. The leaders here have taken pains to prevent any account of this affair getting abroad, but such as they have thought proper to publish themselves; and to that end the post has been stopped, the mails broke open, and letters taken out; and by these means the most injurious and inflammatory accounts have been spread throughout the continent, which has served to deceive and inflame the minds of the people.

When the resolves of the Provincial Congress breathed nothing but war, when those two great and essential prerogatives of the King, the levying of troops, and disposing of the public monies, were wrested from him; and when magazines were forming by an assembly of men, unknown to the constitution, for the declared purpose of levying war against the King, you must acknowledge it was my duty, as it was the dictate of humanity to prevent, if possible, the calamities of civil war, by destroying such magazines.--- This, and this alone, I attempted. You ask why is the town of Boston now shut up? I can only refer you, for an answer, to those bodies of armed men, who now surround the town, and prevent all access to it. The hostile preparations you mention, are such as the conduct of the people of this province has rendered it prudent to make, for the defence of those under my command.

You assure me the people of your colony abhor the idea of taking arms against the troops of their Sovereign, I wish the people of this province, for their own sakes, could make the same declaration. You enquire, is there no way to prevent this unhappy dispute from coming to extremities? Is there no alternative, but absolute submission, or the desolations of war? I answer, I hope there is; the King and Parliament seem to hold our terms of reconciliation, consistent with the honor and interest of Great-Britain, and the rights and privileges of the colonies; they have mutually declared their readiness to attend to any real grievances of the colonies, and to afford them every just and reasonable indulgence, which shall, in a dutiful and constitutional manner, be laid before them; and his Majesty adds, it is his ardent wish that this disposition may have a happy effect, on the temper and conduct of his subjects in America: I must add likewise the resolution of the 27th February, on the grand dispute of taxation and revenue, leaving it to the colonies to tax themselves, under certain conditions; here is surely a found
people who wish a reconciliation
tween countries so nearly conn
terest; but I fear that the lead
still are, intent only on shedding

I am much obliged by your fa
character, and assure you, as it
deavour hitherto, so I shall con
protect all his Majesty's liege su
sons and property. You ask, w
my duty to suspend the operatio
menced no operations of war b
me to suspend, while I am fur
have already begun, and threat
war, and are now violently da
many others of the King's sub
tion, of all the conveniences a
the country abounds; but it mu
able people, when I assure you, th
jure or molest quiet and peaceable subjects; but on the contrary, shall esteem it my greatest happiness to defend and protect them, against every species of violence and oppression.

I am, Sir, &c. THO. GAGE.

Hon. Governor Trumbull.

The following is an exact Copy of a Letter which was intercepted at Roxbury last Week.

Boston, 4th May, 1775.

tants, till on the Night of the 18th of April, twenty-one Companies of Granadiers and Light-Infantry were ordered into the Country about 18 Miles; where, between 4 and 5 o'Clock in the Morning, we met an incredible Number of People of the Country in Arms against us. *Col. Smyth of the 10th Regiment ordered us to rush on them with our Bayonets fixed*; at which Time some of the Peasants fired on us, and our Men returning the Fire, the Engagement begun; they did not fight us like a regular Army, only like Savages, behind Trees and Stone Walls, and out of the Woods and Houses, where in the latter we killed Numbers of them, as well as in the Woods and Fields. The Engagement began between 4 and 5 in the Morning, and lasted till 8 at Night. I can't be sure when you'll get another Letter from me, as this extensive Continent is all in Arms against us: These People are very numerous, and full as bad as the Indians for *scalping and cutting the dead Men's Ears and Noses off, and those they get alive, that are wounded and can't get off the Ground.*"

April 28, 1775.

"The Granadiers and Light Infantry marched for Concord, where were Powder and Ball, Arms, and Cannon mounted on Carriages; but before we could destroy them all, we were fired on by the Country People, who are not brought up in our military Way as ourselves, were surrounded always in the Woods; the Firing was very hot on both Sides; about 2 in the Afternoon the 2d Brigade came up, which was 4 Regiments and Part of the Artillery, which were of no Use to us, as the Enemy were in the Woods, and when we found they fired from Houses, we set them on Fire, and they ran to the Woods like Devils. We were obliged to retreat to Boston again, over Charles-River, our Ammunition being all fired away. We had 150 wounded and killed, and some taken Prisoners; we were forced to leave some behind, who were wounded. We got back to Boston about 2 o'Clock next Morning, and them that were able to walk were forced to mount Guard and lie in the Field. I never broke any Fast for 48 Hours, for we carried no Provisions, and thought to be back next Morning. I had my Hat shot off my Head 3 Times, 2 Balls through my Coat, and carried away my Bayonet by my Side, and near being killed. The People of Boston are in great Trouble, for G. Gage will not let the Town's People go out. Direct for me to Chatham's Division of Marines."

"*Dear Parents*, *April 30, 1775.*

"Before this reaches you, you may hear that our Regiment has been engaged with the Provincials. The Granadiers and Light Infantry marched about 9 at night. At 6 next Morning 423 Soldiers and 47 Marines, in all 1500, marched to reinforce the Granadiers and Light Infantry; joined about 1 o'Clock, and found them not engaged, which they had been 8 Hours before; for we had 2 Pieces Cannon, which made us march very slow.--- As soon as we came up we fired the Cannon, which brought them from behind the Trees, for we did not fight as you did in Germany, for we could not see above 10 in a Body, for they were behind Trees and Walls, and fired at us, and then loaded on their Bellies. We had but 36 Rounds, which obliged us to go Home that Night, and as we came along they got before us and fired at us out of the Houses and killed and wounded a great many of us, but we *levelled their Houses* as we came along. It was thought there were about 6000 at first, and at Night double that Number. The King's Troops lost in killed and wounded 150, and the Americans 500 Men, Women and Children, for there was *a Number of Women and Children burnt in their Houses.* Our Regiment has 5 killed and 31 wounded, particularly Col. Bernard, in the Thigh, which all the Regiment is sorry for. The Shot flew thick. I got a wounded Man's Gun, and killed two of them, as I am sure of.---

much, by cutting down their Liberty Poles and Alarm Posts. We have had a great many died in our Regiment last Winter, so that what with wounded Men and what has deserted, we have not 300 Men, and Duty is so hard that we come off Guard in the Morning and mount Pickets at Night."

"*Honour'd Mother*, *April 25, 1775.*

"*The Rebels, when we came to Concord, burnt their Stores, fired upon the King's Troops, and a smart Engagement ensued.* About two

REPORTING THE

WILLIAMSBURG GUNPOWDER INCIDENT

By Neal Thomas Hurst

Williamsburg was the capital of Virginia at the outbreak of the American Revolution. The city was home to many prominent Virginians who supported the cause of American liberty, including Peyton Randolph, later the president of the first Continental Congress, and George Wythe, signer of the Declaration of Independence.

After the Port of Boston's closing, the House of Burgesses called for a day of fasting, humiliation, and prayer in support of the people of Massachusetts. John Murray, the Fourth Earl of Dunmore and governor of Virginia, quickly denounced this act and dissolved Virginia's representative body. The Burgesses moved their session to the Raleigh Tavern and commenced the First Virginia Convention on August 1, 1774. Taking matters into their own hands, the Burgesses, along with merchants in the city, decided to stop importing goods from England. By the fall of 1774, independent companies formed across the colony. These men kept watch over the colony as tensions ran high and helped to enforce the nonimportation agreement. Only a month after the Second Virginia Convention and Patrick Henry's infamous "Liberty or Death" speech, Lord Dunmore made a decision that forever changed the course of the colonies' history.

Only a month after the Second Virginia Convention and Patrick Henry's infamous "Liberty or Death" speech, Lord Dunmore made a decision that forever changed the course of the colonies' history.

On the morning of Friday, April 21, 1775, Lord Dunmore gave orders to Captain Henry Collins of the armed schooner *Magdalen* to remove fifteen barrels of gunpowder from the magazine at Williamsburg. Under the cover of darkness, plans were executed successfully between 3:00 and 4:00 a.m., losing only a bayonet scabbard when the sailors returned. Later that morning, the citizens of Williamsburg were outraged and immediately armed and mobilized the Independent Company.

The news of the powder being taken spread across Virginia rapidly. Editors William Hunter and John Dixon printed in their newspaper, the *Virginia Gazette*, an address from the mayor of Williamsburg on April 22, 1775. They wrote "that the inhabitants of this city were this morning exceedingly alarmed by a report that a large quantity of gunpowder was in the preceding night, while they were sleeping in their beds, removed from the public magazine in this city." The citizens requested:

> *... as guardians of this city, we therefore humbly desire to be informed by your Excellency, upon what motives, and for what particular purpose, the powder has been carried off [...]*

Militia and independent companies across Virginia mustered and prepared to march on Williamsburg to forcibly, if necessary, take the powder back. The *Pennsylvania Evening Post* reported on May 9, 1775, that Mann Page Jr., Esq., rode from Fredericksburg to Williamsburg to find out if the powder was returned. The newspaper reported that the taking of the powder "had spread a general alarm, and greatly exasperated all ranks of people." Patrick Henry publicly demanded that Dunmore either return the gunpowder or pay £330 for it. Thousands of armed men marched on Williamsburg under the command of Henry. Lord Dunmore, enraged over Henry's request, demanded his arrest. While camped at Doncastle's Ordinary, nearly fifteen miles from the capital, word was received that the governor paid the treasury for the powder. This stalled armed conflict in Virginia.

Many of the organized militia companies continued and camped in Williamsburg, setting the tone for the next several months. A continuous guard was placed on the capital and magazine. The homes of Robert Carter Nicholas, treasurer of the colony of Virginia, and Peyton Randolph were also placed under guard. News of the first shots at Lexington arrived in Williamsburg by express rider on the evening of April 28. The Revolution had already begun. The Williamsburg gunpowder incident prompted the Third Virginia Convention, which established an interim government and allowed the raising of regiments within the colony. This posture of defense allowed Virginia to prepare and organize for their first major battle against the British at Great Bridge.

Patrick Henry
North Wind Picture Archives

Patrick Henry publicly demanded that Lord Dunmore, royal governor of Virginia, return the gunpowder he had removed from the Williamsburg magazine or pay £330.

VIRGINIA GAZETTE (WILLIAMSBURG) (DIXON AND HUNTER)

April 22, 1775

There were three *Virginia Gazettes* being printed in Williamsburg the day the first shot was fired on Lexington Green. Typically, they are distinguished by their publishers: Alexander Purdie, John Pinkney, and John Dixon and William Hunter.

... of New York, gives us the following account ... unhappy diſturbance which happened in that place:—On the 13th inſtant a number of people, to the amount of about 50, collected ... to oppoſe the ſitting of the Court. The Court party, to ...

... went armed to the courthouſe, with an intent to kill the ſheriff and clerk of the Court, but finding the Court reinforced by a number of men from New Hampſhire, they deſiſted from their purpoſe. The Court then adjourned to the next ſeſſions. No Courts have been eſtabliſhed in the county till within theſe three years paſt; and the people were very uneaſy, and exclaimed highly againſt the eſtabliſhment; in ſo much that in March 1774 a militia was raiſed in the county to ſuppreſs riots and diſturbances among them. It muſt be obſerved that the Court party were enemies to diſorder, and zealous aſſertors of the rights and liberties of the people, and were ſenſible how neceſſary to the peace and happineſs of ſociety is the regular adminiſtration of juſtice; and have ſhewn the ſame readineſs in oppoſing any forms of government not known by the conſtitution, as in erecting and defending legal Courts of juſtice.

NEWPORT, *March* 27.

WE are well informed that General Gage has four hundred of Rivington's papers regularly ſent him every week by the poſt, which are diſtributed among the army, navy, and ſuch others as are thought moſt proper to promote the infamous plan of enſlaving this country. Theſe papers are doubtleſs paid for out of the American revenue: Thus, Americans, you already begin to ſee your own money employed for enſlaving yourſelves and your children.

It is confidently aſſerted that 60,000 pounds ſterling, has been remitted from the treaſury in England, to be diſtributed among ſome hungry d—gs at New York.

We are well aſſured that his Honour our Governor has received a circular letter from Lord Dartmouth, of January 4th, in which ...

Common Council of the city of Williamſburg.

My Lord,

WE his Majeſty's dutiful and loyal ſubjects, the Mayor, Recorder, Aldermen, and Common Council, of the city of Williamſburg, in Common Hall aſſembled, humbly beg leave to repreſent to your Excellency, that the inhabitants of this city were this morning exceedingly alarmed by a report that a large quantity of gunpowder was in the preceding night, while they were ſleeping in their beds, removed from the public magazine in this city, and conveyed, under an eſcort of marines, on board one of his Majeſty's armed veſſels lying at a ferry on James river.

We beg leave to repreſent to your Excellency, that as this magazine was erected at the public expence of this colony, and appropriated to the ſafe keeping of ſuch munition as ſhould be there lodged from time to time, for the protection and ſecurity of the country, by arming thereout ſuch of the militia as might be neceſſary in caſes of invaſions and inſurrections, they humbly conceive it to be the only proper repoſitory to be reſorted to in times of imminent danger.

We further beg leave to inform your Excellency, that, from various reports at preſent prevailing in different parts of the country, we have too much reaſon to believe that ſome wicked and deſigning perſons have inſtilled the moſt diabolical notions into the minds of our ſlaves, and that therefore the utmoſt attention to our internal ſecurity is become the more neceſſary.

The circumſtances of this city, my Lord, we conſider as peculiar and critical. The inhabitants, from the ſituation of the magazine, in the midſt of their city, have, for a long tract of time, been expoſed to all thoſe dangers which have happened in many countries from exploſions, and other accidents. They have, from time to time, thought it incumbent on them to guard the magazine. For their ſecurity they have, for ſome time paſt, judged it neceſſary to keep ſtrong patrols on foot; in their preſent circumſtance, then, to have the chief and neceſſary means of their defence removed, cannot but be extremely alarming. Conſidering ourſelves as guardians of the city, we therefore humbly deſire to be informed by your Excellency, upon what motives, and for what particular purpoſe, the powder has been carried off in ſuch a manner; and we earneſtly entreat your Excellency to order it to be immediately returned to the magazine.

To which his EXCELLENCY *returned this verbal anſwer:*

THAT, hearing of an inſurrection in a neighbouring county he had removed the powder from the magazine, where he did not think it ſecure, to a place of perfect ſecurity; and that upon his word and honour, whenever it was wanted on any inſurrection, it ſhould be delivered in half an hour; that he had removed it in the night time to prevent any alarm, and that Captain Collins had his expreſs commands for the part he had acted; he was ſurpriſed to hear the people were under arms on this occaſion, and that he ſhould not think it prudent to put powder into their hands in ſuch a ſituation.

The John, Capt. Taylor, from Liverpool, is arrived in James river, by whom we have received London advices to the 21ſt of February. Captain Taylor ſailed on the 27th, and ſays that a ...

... actually taken place, which, it was generally thought, would occaſion a turn of meaſures in favour of the Americans.

Laſt Saturday, and this week, the following perſons were put ...

FREDERICKSBURG, *April* 12, 1775.

ALL Perſons indebted to *William Houſton* either by Bond or open Accounts, are deſired to ſettle, and pay their reſpective Balances to *John Holladay*, Junior, who is properly authoriſed to receive them.

2|| WILLIAM HOUSTON.

To be SOLD *by the Subſcriber, at her Sto*...

... and well choſen Aſſortment of

GOODS.

PENNSYLVANIA EVENING POST (PHILADELPHIA)

May 9, 1775

… beg leave further to repreſent, that there is now due from the ſaid provinces and colonies, to the city of London only, one million ſterling and upwards.

That their remittances are almoſt intirely made by means of the fiſheries, and conſequently the ruin brought on thoſe colonies will deeply injure the commercial intereſt of Great-Britain, and ultimately fall on the landed property of theſe kingdoms.

That among other grievances, of which our fellow ſubjects in America ſo generally complain, is their being deprived of trial by jury in particular caſes, and the extenſion of the juriſdiction of the Admiralty Courts; which grievances, your Petitioners with much concern find, are not only continued, but extended by the preſent bill; and they think it their duty to repreſent it as their firm opinion to this Right Honourable Houſe, and the diſquietudes which univerſally prevail in the minds of their fellow ſubjects in America, will be increaſed and confirmed by this bill; which is, unjuſt as they conceive, becauſe it involves the puniſhment of thoſe who are allowed to be innocent, with thoſe who are ſuppoſed to be guilty; and that theſe diſquietudes will never be removed, unleſs lenient meaſures are purſued, and their grievances redreſſed.

Your Petitioners, therefore, moſt humbly pray, that the ſaid bill may not paſs into a law.

Publiſhed by order of the Committee.

THOMAS LANE, *Chairman.*

CHARLESTOWN (*South-Carolina*) *April* 17.

By a veſſel which was 22 days ago at Havannah, we learn, that harbour was then full of men of war; and that the Spaniards were very inquiſitive concerning the preſent diſpute between Great-Britain and her colonies; alſo, that a fleet with troops, from old Spain, had arrived there about Chriſtmas.

The General Aſſembly of this Province met here laſt week and is now ſitting.

WILLIAMSBURG, *April* 28.

Yeſterday, about ten o'clock, Mann Page, jun. Eſq; one of the Repreſentatives for Spotſylvania, arrived here in twenty-four hours from Frederickſburg; being charged by a number of people of the different counties, now aſſembling there, to inquire whether the gunpowder had been replaced in the public magazine, the removal of which had ſpread a general alarm, and greatly exaſperated all ranks of people. Expreſſes had been ſent into ſeveral counties, and it was expected that upwards of 2000 men would be aſſembled in Frederickſburg by this evening; and the militia of Caroline were ordered to meet to-morrow, at ten o'clock, to be in readineſs to join thoſe of the upper counties. Mr. Page returned again in the evening, and carried a letter from the Hon. the Speaker, to endeavor to pacify the people; and as that gentleman ſets out to-morrow, by land, to attend the General Congreſs, we hear he propoſes meeting them, and it is hoped, from his great influence, that he will be able to prevail on them to return home, and reſt ſatisfied with the Governor's promiſe that the powder ſhall be given up when there is occaſion for it.—The independent companies of Caroline and

---

NEWPORT, *May* 1.

Laſt Wedneſday, as Mr. John Brown, of Providence, merchant, was going from this town to Providence, in one of the packets, the packet was ſtopped, by order of Captain Wallace, of the ſhip Roſe, and Mr. Brown taken on board the ſhip Swan; ſoon after which another packet was ſtopped as ſhe was going up. Theſe packets had on board a quantity of flour, which Mr. Brown had purchaſed for a number of veſſels he was fitting out. Part, or all, of the flour was taken on board the ſhip; and the next day Mr. Brown was ſent off in one of the packets, to be carried to Admiral Graves, at Boſton, without having a ſingle reaſon given for his being thus violently ſeized and carried out of this colony, contrary to all law, equity and juſtice.

Extract of a letter from Roxbury, dated April 28.

"Notwithſtanding your many neglects, notwithſtanding my many avocations, I once more ſalute you—*jacta eſt alea.* What folly could induce Gen. Gage to act a part ſo fatal to Britain.—It is all over with them—their withering laurels will ſoon be plucked from their brows by the rapacious Bourbon.—I pity the madneſs which effected their deſtruction.—You have, no doubt, been informed of the affair of laſt Wedneſday.—Is it not truly amazing, that ſuch a body of regulars, ſo thoroughly appointed, with artillery, &c. ſhould be defeated, and put to flight, by a handful of raw, undiſciplined peaſants?—We have loſt but forty one, and but few, not exceeding ten, wounded—they have near three hundred killed, wounded and miſſing.—Our countrymen ſwarm to our defence from all quarters—we are buſily organizing our troops, and ſhall ſoon have a well conſtructed army in the field, of 30,000 men.—Gage and his troops are immured within the walls of Boſton; and what is a delay to our ſatisfaction, our friends are entrapped by them:—We have ſome hopes they will be liberated this day; Gen. Gage has propoſed, upon their ſurrendering their arms, that they may march out; they ſurrendered their arms yeſterday.

"Poor Quincy, alas, he is no more! He returned to his native country, preſſed the beloved ſoil, and died—We did not ſee him; he breathed his laſt, the night before laſt, at Cape Ann.

"We have had an expreſs, by the way of Connecticut, incloſing tranſcripts from letters ſent lately to New-York,—ſuch a vile ſyſtem of ſlavery is preparing for us, as might make a Domitian bluſh.—Thank God, our enemies will aſſuredly be defeated."

NEW-YORK, M[illegible]

[illegible] in lat. 45, 39, lon. 35, 23, with ſix ſhips and a brig, from Plymouth, bound to Boſton with troops.

Thurſday laſt the Harriot Packet, Captain Lee, ſailed with the mail for Falmouth, in whom went paſſengers, the Hon. John Watts, and Roger Morris, Eſqrs, Members of his Ma-

REPORTING THE SECOND CONTINENTAL CONGRESS

By Benjamin H. Irvin

The Continental Congress reconvened on May 10, 1775, scarcely three weeks after British regulars and Massachusetts militiamen clashed at Lexington and Concord. News of the battle spread quickly across the Atlantic seaboard, provoking thousands of men and boys to turn out in defense of their liberties. As they journeyed back to Philadelphia, through every town they passed, members of Congress observed scores of volunteers performing military exercises to the music of fife and drum. At the outskirts of New York City, a corps of nearly one thousand soldiers waited to escort the New England delegates—including John Hancock and the cousins Samuel and John Adams—into town. "[T]he roads were lined with greater numbers of people than were ever known on any occasion before," reported the *Pennsylvania Evening Post* on May 9: "Their arrival was announced by the ringing of bells."

The Second Continental Congress met in the Pennsylvania State House and immediately began sifting through eyewitness accounts of the skirmishes in Massachusetts. Turning its attention to New York City, where shiploads of British reinforcements were daily expected, Congress admonished inhabitants to "act on the defensive, so long as may be consistent with their safety." But, in an alarming resolution reprinted in the *Pennsylvania Gazette* of May 24, 1775, it further advised them to "repel force by force" and to prepare "places of retreat" for women and children. Two weeks later, Congress dispatched an inflammatory address to "the oppressed Inhabitants of Canada," urging them to join the fight against a "licentious" British ministry.

Momentously, in anticipation of the war's escalation, Congress voted in mid-June to provision the New England militias that had gathered outside of Boston with flour and gunpowder. It determined to augment those troops by raising ten companies of riflemen. It commissioned George Washington, a war-seasoned colonel in the Virginia militia, to command American troops. And it appointed a committee to draft rules to govern the military. By these measures, Congress established the Continental Army, or, as the *Virginia Gazette* boasted on July 29, 1775, "the forces of *the united colonies of North America*."

No sooner had Congress voted to build this army than British and American forces again clashed. The desperately hard-fought Battle of Bunker Hill left little doubt that a deadly war had begun. Nevertheless, Congress wished to justify Americans' military preparations, so on July 6, it issued the Declaration on Taking Arms. Drafted in its final form by the Pennsylvania congressman John Dickinson, this declaration rebuked Parliament's "cruel and impolitic" efforts to subjugate the colonists. The American people had been driven to arms not by a desire for independence, but rather, as the declaration proclaimed, by Parliament's "intemperate rage."

Though vigilant of his liberty, Dickinson fervently hoped the American colonies and the British Empire would soon be reconciled. Even as he revised the Declaration on Taking Arms, Dickinson prevailed upon Congress to assure King George III of Americans' allegiance. The so-called Olive Branch Petition—adopted by Congress on July 8 and widely reprinted, as in *Lloyd's Evening Post* of September 6, 1775—once again beseeched the king to protect the colonists from his ministers' "delusive pretences, fruitless terrors, and unavailing severities." To the dismay of the Crown's loyal subjects, the king not only rejected the Olive Branch Petition, but also, by a proclamation issued August 23, commanded that the American rebellion be suppressed.

In the months that followed, Anglo-American relations

deteriorated rapidly. On November 7, Lord Dunmore, the royal governor of Virginia, offered freedom to all slaves and indentured servants who took arms against their rebel masters. In December, Parliament passed the Prohibitory Act, casting American ships out of the Royal Navy's protection. On January 1, 1776, Dunmore ordered a British man-of-war to bombard Norfolk, Virginia's largest port. Soon after, King George secured treaties with numerous German sovereigns to provide auxiliary soldiers for the war. And on March 23, as reported in the May 2, 1776, edition of the *New-England Chronicle*, the Continental Congress authorized American privateers to raid British vessels. Thus, long before Congress declared independence in July 1776, Great Britain and the United Colonies began treating each other as enemies.

As the Revolution unfolded, Congress struggled to provision the Continental Army. Because it possessed no power to tax, Congress financed much of the war by printing unbacked paper dollars. It also aggressively pursued diplomatic relations with King Louis XVI of France, who provided essential military and financial assistance. To strengthen the United States, Congress drafted the Articles of Confederation, formally ratified in 1781. By the time Franco-American forces compelled Cornwallis's surrender at Yorktown, the power of Congress had greatly declined. The failure of its military procurement policies and the collapse of the continental currency weakened Congress, as did the stringent, supermajority voting requirements adopted under the Articles of Confederation. After the war, aside from the notable land ordinances of the mid-1780s, the states left the federal union in precarious drift. Not until the Constitutional Convention of 1787 did Americans take up federal governance in earnest again.

Second Continental Congress
North Wind Picture Archives

Congress leaves the Pennsylvania State House in Philadelphia to hear the first public reading of the Declaration of Independence.

PENNSYLVANIA EVENING POST (PHILADELPHIA)

May 9, 1775

In Philadelphia, the journey and arrival of the delegates of the Second Continental Congress was big news as the who's who from around the colonies gathered for the first time since bloodshed in Massachusetts.

their way for Philadelphia, to attend the Continental Congress, the Hon. John Hancock, and Thomas Cushing, Esqrs. Samuel Adams, John Adams, and Robert Treat Paine, Esqrs. Delegates for the province of Massachusetts-Bay; and the Hon. Eliphalet Dyer, and Roger Sherman, Esqrs. and Silas Dean, Esq; Delegates for the colony of Connecticut. They were met a few miles out of town by a great number of the principal gentlemen of the place, in carriages and on horseback, and escorted into the city by near a thousand men under arms; the roads were lined with greater numbers of people than were ever known on any occasion before. Their arrival was announced by the ringing of bells, and other demonstrations of joy. They have double centries placed at the doors of their lodging.

We hear the above gentlemen, accompanied by the Delegates for this city, set out this day for Philadelphia.

PHILADELPHIA, *May* 9.

We hear from Charlestown, South-Carolina, that on the 21st of March, at night, about eight hundred stand of small arms, two hundred cutlasses, and all the cartouch boxes, fit for service, with several bundles of match and some flints, were taken out of the public armoury in the state-house; and on the same night the public powder magazine, built about four miles from the town, was broke open, and all the powder carried off, being about five hundred weight. The Governor has offered a reward of one hundred pounds sterling for apprehending the offenders.

Saturday last Gen. Lee arrived in town from the Southren Colonies.

Last night the brig Charlestown Packet, Capt. Barton, arrived from Charlestown. In this vessel came passengers the Hon. Henry Middleton, Christopher Garsden, John Rutledge, and Edward Rutledge, Esqs. Delegates for South-Carolina.

Thomas Lynch, Esq; the other Delegate, sailed the day before in a schooner. It is said she is in the river.

And this day arrived the Hon. Peyton Randolph, Esq; George Washington, Patrick Henry, Richard Henry Lee, Edmund Pendleton, Benjamin Harrison, and Richard Bland, Esquires, Delegates for Virginia.——Richard Casswell, and Joseph Hewes, Esquires, Del. for North-Carolina. Also Samuel Chace, Thomas Johnson, and John Hall, Esquires, Del. for Maryland.

This afternoon the brig Chance, Craig, arrived from Grenada.

The Delegates for Massachuestts-Bay, Connecticut, and New-York, are expected here to-morrow about noon.

Capt. Wright, of the brig Charlestown Packet, died the 21st of April, off Cape Fear, on his passage to Charlestown.

---

ed from giving aid to their brethren, if any unjuſtifiable attack is made upon them. Be ſo good, therefore, as to explain yourſelf upon this moſt important ſubject, as far as is conſiſtent with your duty to our common Sovereign. Is there no way to prevent this unhappy diſpute from com ing to extremities? Is there no alternative but abſolu ſubmiſſion, or the deſolations of war? By that humani which conſtitutes ſo amiable a part of your character, f the honour of our Sovereign, and by the glory of th Britiſh empire, we intreat you to prevent it, if it be po ſible; ſurely it is to be hoped that the temperate wiſdo of the empire might, even yet, find expedients to reſto peace, that ſo all parts of the empire may enjoy their pa ticular rights, honours and immunities: Certainly this an event moſt devoutly to be wiſhed for; and will it n be conſiſtent with your duty, to ſuſpend the operatio of war on your part, and enable us on ours to quiet th minds of the people, at leaſt, till the reſult of ſome further deliberations may be known. The importance of the occaſion will, we doubt not, ſufficiently apologize for the earneſtneſs with which we addreſs you, and any ſeeming impropriety which may attend it, as well as induce you to give us the moſt explicit and favourable anſwer in your power. *I am, with great eſteem and reſpect,*

In behalf of the General Aſſembly, Sir, &c.

(Signed) JON. TRUMBULL.

His Excellency THOMAS GAGE, *Eſq;*

His Excellency General GAGE's *Anſwer, to the foregoing Letter.*

SIR, *Dated Boſton, May 3, 1775.*

I Am to acknowledge the receipt of your letter of the 28th of April laſt, in behalf of the General Aſſembly of your colony, relative to the alarming ſituation of public affairs in this country, and the late tranſactions in this province: That this ſituation is greatly alarming, and that theſe tranſactions are truly unfortunate, are truths to be regretted by every friend to America, and by every well-wiſher for the peace, proſperity and happineſs of this province. The intimate connections and ſtrong ties of friendſhip, between the inhabitants of your colony and the deluded people of this province, cannot fail of inducing the former to interpoſe their good offices, to convince the latter of the impropriety of their paſt conduct, and to perſuade them to return to their allegiance, and to ſeek redreſs of any ſuppoſed grievances in thoſe decent and conſtitutional methods, in which alone they can hope to be ſucceſsful.

That troops ſhould be employed for the purpoſe of protecting the Magiſtrates in the execution of their duty, when oppoſed with violence, is not a new thing in the Engliſh or any other government: That any acts of the Britiſh Parliament are unconſtitutional or oppreſſive, I am not to ſuppoſe; if any ſuch there are, in the apprehenſion of the people of this province, it had been happy for them if they had ſought relief, only in the way which the conſtitution, their reaſon, and their intereſt pointed out.

You cannot wonder at my fortifying the town of Boſton, or making any other military preparations, when you are aſſured, that previous to my taking theſe ſteps, ſuch was the open threats, and ſuch the warlike preparations throughout this province, as rendered it my indiſpenſable duty to take every precaution in my power, for the protection of his Majeſty's troops under my command, againſt all hoſtile attempts. The intelligence you ſeem to have received, relative to the late excurſion of a body of troops into the country, is altogether injurious and contrary to the true ſtate of facts; the troops diſclaim, with indignation, the barbarous outrages of which they are ac-

tinue to exert my utmoſt efforts to protect all his Majeſty's liege ſubjects under my care, in their perſons and property. You aſk whether it will not be conſiſtent with my duty to ſuſpend the operations of war

PENNSYLVANIA GAZETTE (PHILADELPHIA)

May 24, 1775

In an alarming resolution reprinted in this *Pennsylvania Gazette*, the Second Continental Congress advised inhabitants of New York, where shiploads of British reinforcements were expected soon, to "repel force by force" and to prepare "places of retreat" for women and children.

NEW-PORT, May 15.

A gentleman, who left Roxbury, near Boſton, on Wedneſday laſt, ſays, that juſt before he came away letters were received there from England, by a veſſel in a ſhort paſſage to Salem, one was dated the 3d, and the other the 9th of April; both of which gave an account, that moſt of the troops, which had been ſeveral times ordered to embark and couutermanded, were, on account of the great diſturbances among the people, finally ſtopped.

The whole regiment of light dragoons, to a man, has refuſed to come over to fight againſt this country; this we have from a Gentleman who left Liverpool the 30th of March.

NEW-YORK, May 18.

In CONGRESS, *at* Philadelphia, *May 15, 1775.*

THE City and County of New-York having through Delegates applied to the Congreſs for their advice how to conduct themſelves with regard to the troops expected there, the Congreſs took the matter into their moſt ſerious deliberation, and came to the following reſolution:

"That it be recommended for the preſent to the inhabitants of New-York, that if the troops which are expected ſhould arrive, the ſaid colony act on the defenſive, ſo long as may be conſiſtent with their ſafety and ſecurity: That the troops may be permitted to remain in the barracks, ſo long as they behave peaceably and quietly, but that they be not ſuffered to erect fortifications, or take any ſteps for cutting off the communication between the town and country; and that if they commit hoſtilities, or invade private property, the inhabitants ſhould defend themſelves, and their property, and repel force by force:—That the warlike ſtores be removed from the town:—That places of retreat, in caſe of neceſſity, be provided for the women and children of New-York; and a ſufficient number of men be embodied, and kept in conſtant readineſs for protecting the inhabitants from inſult and injury."

A true copy from the Minutes,

CHARLES THOMPSON, Secretary.

Gentlemen,

Incloſed, we ſend you the advice of the Congreſs, on the ſubject on which you requeſted it, and leſt the advice to remove the military ſtores might be conſtrued to extend to thoſe belonging to the Crown, we think it prudent to ſuggeſt to you, that the contrary conſtruction is the true one.

You would have received this advice before, had not ſundry circumſtances not material, or perhaps not proper to explain, concurred in deferring it till now.

We are, Gentlemen, Your humble ſervants,

James Duane, Francis Lewis, John Jay, Lewis Morris, Philip Livingſton, John Alſop.

We hear that orders are sent down to Scotland for the officers to fill up their regiments to the full complement of men, as soon as possible.

A report prevails, that the King of Denmark is dangerously ill, some say dead.

Extract of a letter from PORTSMOUMH, *May* 17.

"Every sloop of war and small vessel at this port and Plymouth is now put into commission, and various services; but we have not yet received any particular orders for large ships, though war is talked of as strong here as in London."

A morning paper says: A letter just received from Copenhagen says, every thing in that city is in the greatest confusion; the Queen Dowager durst not appear in public, and the King, on account of the death of the Queen, is almost distracted. The popopulace, many of whom were the Queen's enemies when living, now say she was innocent, and that her death was occasioned by the false accusations brought against her by the Queen Dowager's party.

There are now living in the parish of St. Bees, Cumberland, two brothers, and three sisters, whose ages are 71, 81, 83, 85, and 87.

CAMBRIDGE, *June* 26.

NONE of the men who have been raised by this, and several other colonies, are, in future, to be distinguished as the troops of any particular colony, but as the forces of *the united colonies of North America,* into whose joint service they have been taken by the Continental Congress, and are to be paid and supported accordingly.

We hear from Exeter, New Hampshire, that a committee from the Congress sitting there waited on the province treasurer for what money he had by him belonging to the province, and received from him 1500l. which was safely conveyed to Exeter.

Last monday night died of the wounds he received in the battle of the 17th ult. the amiable, the gallant Colonel Thomas Gardner, of this place.

The following is thought to contain a true account of the loss of the enemy, including those who died of their wounds; taken June 29th, 1775.

Return of the killed at Charelstown the 17th of June, taken from an orderly serjeant in Boston.

Commission officers 92, serjeants 102, corporals 100, rank and file 753, total of killed 1047; wounded, 445. Total of killed and wounded, 1492.

HARTFORD, *July* 10.

Extract of a letter from FORT GEORGE *(near* TICONDEROGA*) dated June 29, 1775.*

THE reports from the northward are various. It is thought, from the best accounts, that the Canadians will be very reluctant to enter into the service against the colonies, and it is

THE following is the most accurate list of the killed and

Dutton, of the 38th; Lieutenant Gould, and Lieutenant Hilliard, of the 47th; Major Williams, Capt. Addison, Capt. Davidson, and Capt. Smith, of the 52d; Lieutenant Dalrymple, of the 63d;

VIRGINIA GAZETTE (WILLIAMSBURG) (DIXON AND HUNTER)

July 29, 1775

In anticipation of the war's escalation, Congress established the Continental Army, or, as printed here, "the forces of *the united colonies of North America.*"

An intermission of three weeks between our two last publications, is the reason why the following important Resolves did not appear sooner.

AMERICAN UNITED COLONIES.

IN CONGRESS, *March* 23. 1776.

WHEREAS the Petitions of these United Colonies to the King, for the Redress of great and manifest Grievances, have not only been rejected, but treated with Scorn and Contempt; and the Opposition to Designs evidently formed to reduce them to a State of servile Subjection, and their necessary Defence against hostile Forces actually employed to subdue them, declared Rebellion: And Whereas an unjust War hath been commenced against them, which the Commanders of the British Fleets and Armies have prosecuted and still continue to prosecute with their utmost Vigour and in a cruel Manner; wasting, spoiling and destroying the Country, burning Houses and defenceless Towns, and exposing the helpless Inhabitants to every Misery from the Inclemency of the Winter, and not only urging Savages to invade the Country, but instigating Negroes to murder their Masters: And Whereas the Parliament of Great-Britain hath lately passed an Act, affirming these Colonies to be in open Rebellion; forbidding all Trade and Commerce with the Inhabitants thereof, until they shall accept Pardons and submit to despotic Rule; declaring their Property, wherever found upon the Water, liable to Seizure and Confiscation; and enacting that what had been done there, by Virtue of the Royal Authority, were just and lawful Acts, and shall be so deemed: From all which it is manifest, that the iniquitous Scheme, concerted to deprive them of the Liberty they have a right to by the Laws of Nature and the English Constitution, will be pertinaciously pursued. It being, therefore, necessary to provide for their Defence and Security, and justifiable to make Reprisals upon their Enemies, and otherwise to annoy them, according to the Laws and Usages of Nations; the CONGRESS, trusting that such of their Friends in Great-Britain (of whom it is confessed there are many intitled to Applause and Gratitude for their Patriotism and Benevolence, and in whose Favour a Discrimination of Property cannot be made) as shall suffer by Captures, will impute it to the Authors of our common Calamities, DO DECLARE AND RESOLVE as followeth, *to wit*:

RESOLVED, That the Inhabitants of these Colonies be permitted to fit out Armed Vessels to cruise on the Enemies of these United Colonies.

RESOLVED, That all Ships and other Vessels, their Tackle, Apparel, and Furniture, and all Goods, Wares and Merchandizes belonging to any Inhabitant or Inhabitants of Great-Britain, taken on the high Seas, or between high and low water Mark, by any Armed Vessel fitted out by any private Person or Persons to whom Commissions shall be granted, and being libelled and prosecuted in any of these ... the Trial of Maritime Affairs ... lawful Prize, and after ... Mariners on ... Vessels shall be ... until the ... for the Use of ... Mariners of ... portions as they ... lution shall not ... nging Settlers, ... the Use of these ... Friends to the ... the Effects of ... such Settlers.

RESOLVED, That all Ships or Vessels, with their Tackle, Apparel ... Wares and Merchandizes belonging ... which shall be taken by any ... be deemed forfeited, one third, after ... to the Officers and ... Wages of Seamen and Mariners, as aforesaid, to the use of the United Colonies, and two thirds to the ... Vessels with their Tackle, Ap-

NEW-ENGLAND CHRONICLE (BOSTON)

May 2, 1776

The Second Continental Congress authorized American privateers to raid British vessels.

Lloyd's EVENING POST

VOL. XXXVII.] From MONDAY, SEPTEMBER 4, to WEDNESDAY, SEPTEMBER 6, 1775. [Numb. 28

Copy of the PETITION *from the* GENERAL CONGRESS *in* AMERICA *to his* MAJESTY, *which was delivered to Lord* DARTMOUTH *the first of this Month, and to which, his Lordship said, no Answer would be given.*

RICHARD PENN.

Sept. 4, 1775. ARTHUR LEE.

To the KING's *Moſt Excellent* MAJESTY.

Moſt Gracious SOVEREIGN,

E your Majeſty's faithful Subjects of the Colonies of New Hampſhire, Maſſachuſetts Bay, Rhode Iſland and Providence Plantations, Connecticut, New York, New Jerſey, Pennſylvania, the Counties of New Caſtle, Kent and uſſex in Delaware, Maryland, Virginia, Iorth and South Carolina, in Behalf of urſelves and the Inhabitants of theſe Coonies, who have deputed us to repreſent hem in General Congreſs, entreat your Iajeſty's gracious Attention to this our umble Petition.

The Union between our Mother Country nd theſe Colonies, and the Energy of mild nd juſt Government, produced Benefits ſo emarkably important, and afforded ſuch Aſſurance of their Permanency and Increaſe, hat the Wonder and Envy of other Nations vere excited, while they beheld Great Briain riſing to a Power the moſt extraordinary he World had ever known. Her Rivals oberving that there was no Probability of this appy Connection being broken by Civil Diſſentions, and apprehending its future Effects, if left any longer undiſturbed, reolved to prevent her receiving ſo continual nd formidable an Acceſſion of Wealth and trength, by checking the Growth of theſe ettlements, from which they were to be erived.

In the Proſecution of this Attempt, Events unfavourable to the Deſign took place, hat every Friend to the Intereſt of Great ritain and theſe Colonies, entertained leaſing and reaſonable Expectations of ſeeng an additional Force and Extenſion imnediately given to the Operations of the Jnion hitherto experienced, by an Enlarge-

o a greater Diſtance.

At the Concluſion, therefore, of the late

by domeſtic Dangers in their Judgement of a more dreadful Kind.

Nor were their Anxieties alleviated by any Tendency in this Syſtem to promote the Welfare of the Mother Country: For though its Effects were more immediately felt by them, yet its Influence appeared to be injurious to the Commerce and Proſperity of Great Britain.

We ſhall decline the ungrateful Taſk of deſcribing the irkſome Variety of Artifices practiſed by many of your Majeſty's Miniſters; the deluſive Pretences, fruitleſs Terrors, and unavailing Severities, which have from Time to Time been dealt out by them in their Attempts to execute this impolitic Plan, or of tracing through a Series of Years paſt the Progreſs of the unhappy Differences between Great Britain and theſe Colonies, which have flowed from this fatal Source. Your Majeſty's Miniſters perſevering in their Meaſures, and proceeding to open Hoſtilities for enforcing them, have compelled us to arm in our own Defence, and have engaged us in a Controverſy ſo peculiarly abhorrent from the Affections of your ſtill faithful Coloniſts, that when we conſider whom we muſt oppoſe in this Conteſt, and if it continues, what may be the Conſequence; our own particular Misfortunes are accounted by us only as Parts of our Diſtreſs.

Knowing to what violent Reſentments and incurable Animoſities civil Diſcords are apt to exaſperate and in Parties, we think ou diſpenſable Obligat to your Majeſty, t and ourſelves, imm Means in our Power our Safety, for ſto ſion of Blood, and ing Calamities that pire. Thus called Majeſty on Affairs o rica, and probably we are earneſtly deſi Office with the utn Majeſty; and we th Royal Magnanimity a make the moſt favou of our Expreſſions on ſo uncommon an

the Sentiments which agitate the Minds of us, your dutiful Subjects, we are perſuaded

Generations in both Countries; and to tra mit your Majeſty's Name to Poſterity, ado ed with that ſignal and laſting Glory t has attended the Memory of thoſe illuſtri Perſonages, whoſe Virtues and Abilities h extricated States from dangerous Conv ſions, and by ſecuring Happineſs to othe have erected the moſt noble and dura Monuments to their own Fame.

We beg Leave further to aſſure your M jeſty, that notwithſtanding the Sufferings your loyal Coloniſts, during the Courſe the preſent Controverſy, our Breaſts ret too tender a Regard for the Kingdom fr which we derive our Origin, to requeſt ſu a Reconciliation, as might in any Man be inconſiſtent with *her dignity or her Welfa* Theſe, related as we are to her, Honour a Duty, as well as Inclination, induce us ſupport and advance; and the Apprehenſi that now oppreſs our Hearts, with unſpe able Grief, being once removed, your M jeſty will find your faithful Subjects, on t Continent, *ready and willing*, at all Tim as they have ever been, with their *Lives Fortunes, to aſſert and maintain the Rights Intereſts of your Majeſty and of our Mo Country.*

We therefore beſeech your Majeſty, t your Royal Authority and Influence may graciouſly interpoſed, to procure us Re from our afflicting Fears and Jealouſi occaſioned by the Syſtem before mention

your American People, we are convin your Majeſty would receive ſuch ſatisfa

that the wiſhed-for Opportunity would ſ be reſtored to them, of evincing the Si

LLOYD'S EVENING POST (LONDON)

September 6, 1775

The Olive Branch Petition, adopted by the Second Continental Congress on July 8, took almost two months to reach London. Letters to the editor and advertisements for *Lloyd's Evening Post* were received at Lloyd's Coffee Shop, located above the Royal Exchange, which was a prominent interchange of port news, and its reports often fed other London newspapers.

REPORTING THE

CAPTURE OF FORT TICONDEROGA

By William P. Tatum III

On May 10, 1775, American forces struck the first of a series of blows that nearly unraveled British control of Canada by seizing Fort Ticonderoga. Built by the French in 1756, Ticonderoga had been the focus of two major battles in 1758 and 1759. After the conclusion of the French and Indian War, the fort acted as a secure storage facility for cannons and other military stores. By 1775, it was a sleepy backwater located well within the defensive perimeter of Britain's North American holdings.

In the spring of 1775, Fort Ticonderoga became the focus of several competing American expeditions. Connecticut, Massachusetts, and the contested Hampshire Grants (modern Vermont) sought to seize the fort for themselves. Massachusetts retained the services of Benedict Arnold, a native of Connecticut, who proceeded west from the siege of Boston in early May to raise militia volunteers for an attack on the fort. Ethan Allen, leader of the frontier force known as "The Green Mountain Boys," was making preparations for his own assault on Ticonderoga to secure territorial claims for Vermont. The two officers met at a council of war in Castleton, where Arnold was appointed the titular head of the force, though the majority of the soldiers owed their allegiance to Allen.

By the evening of May 9, 1775 (a day earlier than what was noted in the *Pennsylvania Gazette* article of May 24, 1775), the Arnold-Allen expedition was assembled across Lake Champlain from the fort. A scarcity of boats delayed the crossing until the early hours of May 10 and forced the Americans to send several detachments over instead of advancing en masse. As the *Pennsylvania Gazette* reported, Allen and Arnold rushed the fort with only a handful of soldiers, which nevertheless outnumbered the oblivious British garrison. Ignorant of the events at Lexington and Concord, as well as of the larger American rebellion, the British forces were quickly overwhelmed, with many of the soldiers and their officers captured while still asleep in their barracks. While no one was killed in the engagement, Allen's undisciplined troops immediately set to looting the garrison, an act that led to their eventual dismissal. Allen eventually sent the British troops to Connecticut as a gift to Governor John Trumbull.

The capture of Fort Ticonderoga had a number of short- and long-term effects on the course of the American Revolution. As noted in the article, the fort contained large amounts of military stores, particularly cannons, which played a crucial role in supplying American forces. Henry Knox transported several of the larger cannons to Boston, where they were employed in the final stages of the siege. Its capture by American forces also returned Fort Ticonderoga to its former glory as a vital frontier post. In August 1775, Continental General Richard Montgomery launched his invasion of Quebec from the fort. His expedition quickly rolled up a string of British border posts, captured Montreal, and laid siege to Quebec City, where the campaign stalled and ultimately collapsed in early 1776. In the summer and autumn of the same year, the fort became the front line of American defenses against a British invasion from Canada, as well as the base of Benedict Arnold's American fleet on Lake Champlain. Ticonderoga's formidable appearance played a vital role in British General Guy Carleton's decision not to continue his attacks after the Battle of Valcour Island in October. While captured by British troops under General John Burgoyne the following year, the fort quickly fell back into American hands following the British surrender at Saratoga, serving out the remainder of the war as a relatively quiet American base.

John Lawrence, arrived here from Falmouth, in 6 weeks; by him we learn, that all the acts depending in Parliament, relative to American affairs, had received the Royal aſſent; and that the packet for this port was to ſail the day after him.

PHILADELPHIA, May 24.

On Wedneſday evening laſt arrived here, John Brown, Eſq; from Ticonderoga, expreſs to the General Congreſs; from whom we learn, that on the beginning of this inſtant, a company of about fifty men, from Connecticut, and the weſtern part of Maſſachuſetts, and joined by upwards of one hundred from Bennington, *in New-York government*, and the adjacent towns, proceeded to the eaſtern ſide of Lake Champlain, and on the night before the 11th current, croſſed the Lake with 85 men (not being able to obtain craft to tranſport the reſt) and about day-break inveſted the fort, whoſe gate, contrary to expectation, they found ſhut, but the wicker open, through which, with the Indian war whoop, all that could, entered one by one, others ſcaling the wall on both ſides of the gate, and inſtantly ſecured and diſarmed the centries, and preſſed into the parade, where they formed the hollow ſquare; but immediately quitting that order, they ruſhed into the ſeveral barracks on three ſides of the fort, and ſeized on the garriſon, conſiſting of two officers, and upwards of forty privates,* whom they brought out, diſarmed, put under guard, and have ſince ſent priſoners to Hartford, in Connecticut. All this was performed in about ten minutes, without the loſs of a life, or a drop of blood on our ſide, and but very little on that of the King's troops.

In the fort were found about thirty barrels of flour, a few barrels of pork, ſeventy odd cheſts of leaden ball, computed at three hundred tons, about ten barrels of powder in bad condition, near two hundred pieces of ordnance of all ſizes, from eighteen pounders downwards, at Ticonderoga and Crown-point, which laſt place, being held only by a corporal and eight men, falls of courſe into our hands.

By this ſudden expedition, planned by ſome principal perſons in the four neighbouring colonies, that important paſs is now in the hands of the Americans, where we truſt the *wiſdom* of the Grand Continental Congreſs, will take effectual meaſures to ſecure it, as it may be depended on that adminiſtration means to form an army in Canada, compoſed of Britiſh regulars, French and Indians, to attack the colonies on that ſide.

Mr. Brown brought intercepted letters from Lieut. Malcom Fraſer, to his friends in New-England, from which appear, that Gen. Carleton has almoſt unlimited powers, civil and military, and has iſſued orders for raiſing a Canadian regiment, in which Mr. Fraſer obſerves, the officers find difficulty, as the common people are by no means fond of the ſervice. He likewiſe remarks, that all the King's European ſubjects are diſaffected at the partial preference given to the late converts to loyalty, as he phraſes it, to their utter excluſion from all confidence, or even common civility. Matters are indeed in ſuch a ſituation, that many, if not moſt of the merchants talk of leaving the province.

Mr. Brown alſo relates, that two regular officers of the 26th regiment, now in Canada, applied to two Indians, one a head warrior of the Caughanawaga ...

... farther and farther on ſaid courſe, they at length arrived at Cohaſs, where the Indians ſay they were ſtopt and interrogated by the inhabitants ...

College of Philadelphia, May 17, 1775.

THIS day the public Commencement for Graduates in the Arts was held here, in the preſence of the moſt illuſtrious aſſembly this Seminary ever beheld.

About half an hour after nine o'clock, agreeable to an invitation previouſly given to them, the Honorable Members of the CONTINENTAL CONGRESS were pleaſed to proceed in a body from the State-Houſe to the College, where they were received at the gate by the Provoſt, and conducted to the places prepared for their reception in the *Hall*. As ſoon as they were ſeated, the *Truſtees*, with the Governor as Preſident at their head, followed by the Provoſt, Vice-provoſt, Profeſſors, Graduates and other Students, in their proper habits, entered the Hall, and took their places, the Galleries and other parts of the houſe being filled with as many of the reſpectable inhabitants of the city as could find room. The buſineſs then proceeded in the following ORDER, viz.

1. Part of the Church Service, and an occaſional Prayer, by the Provoſt.
2. An Anthem, accompanied with the organ and other inſtrumental muſic.
3. Latin Salutatory Oration, de Amicitia, by Henry Ridgely.
4. On the *Education of young Ladies*, by Francis Brown Sappington.
5. Latin Syllogiſtic Diſpute, Utrum detur Senſus Moralis? Reſpondent, William Moore Smith; Opponents, Benjamin Chew and John Mifflin.
6. On *Ancient Eloquence*, by Thomas Ennals.
7. On *Politeneſs*, by John Mifflin.
8. On the *Fall of Empires*, by William Moore Smith.
9. The degrees were then conferred as follows, viz.

BACHELORS OF ARTS.

Benjamin Chew, *Townſend Eden, *Thomas Ennals, John Farrel, John Mifflin, *Henry Ridgely, *Francis Brown Sappington, and William Moore Smith.

MASTERS OF ARTS.

Samuel Armor, John Park and John Thomas.

Honorary Maſter of Arts, James Roſs.

10. A Dialogue and two Odes ſet to muſic. The ſpeakers in the Dialogue were John Farrel, F. B. Sappington, and W. M. Smith.
11. Valedictory Oration, by B. Chew.
12. CHARGE to the Graduates, by the Provoſt.
13. *Concluding Pr*...

... lic nature, are herewith communicated.

* *The young Gentleman* ...

[*To be concluded in our next.*]

** The Officers belonging to the ...

A ... Hea ... She ... hereof.

W ... A ... a ... he now li ... reading, th ... and ſeveral ... geometry, ... practice in ... war; which ... any of his ... him. He w ... the firſt of ... will be for ...

WHE ... my ... Preſbyterians ... went to relea ... public manne ... the propagato ... malicious a ſ ... to my hurt. ... approved the ... juſt rights and ... the capacities ... the riſque of ... aſſert the cauſe ... greſs and Com ... or inadvertentl ... report.

N. B. I am ... further ſatisfa ... report, and my ... ſhould not prov ...

THIS is ... HEES, p ... ton, that they ... Eſq; and the H ... Supreme Court ... Perth-Amboy, ... ſhew cauſe (if a ... diſcharged ...

... one named Eben ... ſandy complexion ... round the edges ... brecches, &c. St ... which it is expe ...

PENNSYLVANIA GAZETTE (PHILADELPHIA)

May 24, 1775

This version of the capture of Fort Ticonderoga was widely circulated among American newspapers. Months later, the artillery captured there would be used to fortify Dorchester Heights and help force the British to evacuate Boston.

REPORTING THE

BATTLE OF NODDLE'S ISLAND

By James L. Nelson

By the end of May 1775, the American army surrounding Boston was feeling pretty good about itself—and they had reason. On April 19, they had battered the redcoats at Lexington and Concord, chased them into Boston, and cut off all interaction with the countryside. Confidence was not so high, however, that anyone wanted to launch a frontal assault on Boston, so the Americans contented themselves with depriving the British of food, hay, straw, and firewood. The two articles shown here, one from the *New-York Journal* and the other from the *New-England Chronicle*, describe the Battle of Noddle's Island, the sharpest fight between American and British forces to take place between Lexington and Concord and the Battle of Bunker Hill. It was a fight for sheep and hay.

Noddle's and Hog Islands, a chief source for hay and grazing land, sat just across the mouth of the Charles and Mystic rivers from Boston. Today, they are a great jumble of urban sprawl, but in 1775, they were just humps of pasture, home to hundreds of sheep, hayfields, and a few houses.

The two newspaper articles describe, with varying degrees of accuracy, two different parts of the same battle. In the predawn hours of May 27, 1775, about six hundred American troops splashed across the narrow river that separated Hog Island from the shore. For most of the morning, they drove livestock from the islands unseen by the British. It was only in the afternoon, when they set fire to the hayfields, that the redcoats took notice.

The British landed marines and some field artillery on the island and tried to flank the American troops by boat. Oddly, neither article mentions the fighting that took place on shore, perhaps because the most dramatic fighting took place on the water. The sloop mentioned in the *New-England Chronicle*'s article is no doubt the *Britannia*, which was mauled by American small arms and artillery. Worse off was the schooner *Diana*, featured prominently in both articles. *Diana* found herself caught between Noddle's Island and the mainland with no wind and a falling tide. Once aground, she was pounded into a near wreck by men under the command of Israel Putnam, abandoned by the British, and burned the next morning by the Yankees.

The *New-York Journal* article is quite accurate in its description of events, insofar as it closely matches other accounts and official reports of the action. In both cases, the American victory is greatly exaggerated. It is unlikely the British were as frightened as the *New-England Chronicle* suggests, and the claim that the British "killed and wounded exceed 300" is way off the mark. The British had two men who died; the Americans, none. It was only a few weeks after this that the British and the Americans would get a taste of how formidable their enemies really were on the slopes of nearby Bunker Hill.

NEW-ENGLAND CHRONICLE (CAMBRIDGE, MA)

June 15, 1775

—

rom St. Kitts, ad-
e news of the en-
fected in much the
s of St. Euſtatia.
hiladelphia, at their
ed the laſt Thurſday
Congregations under
d Prayer on account
c Affairs. Should
Faſt, the Synod have
eference to the Day
it is not more than
urſday of June ;—
e ordered both Days

he Congregations in
n of the laſt Thurſ-
yer, during the Con-

June 5.
phia, of a late date.
talions, conſiſting of
ade ſuch rapid pro-
e able to go through
reat eaſe and quick-
ndered at, when we
ſt they have been un
day not always ex
large company well
mpany of about 100
ear, have one extra-
lmiſſion of every man
fers to enroll himſelf
her he can hit a cir-
imes out of 6, at the
ot, he is put by until.
What will not a
fect? Every county
ir forces."
don, 1756, entitled
et in the Mediterra-
letter to a member
hor, ſpeaking of the
ſs of the lives an
d army, has this re
r Peter Warren re
Breton he happene
of land and Sea offi-

...ters to deſtroy the truly pious, juſt and humane General, and the virtuous Attendants aſſembled above) in Conſ quence of which Application was made (by him) for the Keys, belonging to the ſame; but not being able through Impatience to obtain them, a Bayonet, together with his ferocious Countenance, and a Centry penetrated theſe otherwiſe impregnable Vaults, and gave ... to a moſt thorough Examination of their Contents; ... overturning and re-overturning all that could conceal ... Combuſtibles, without diſcovering any Thing capable of ... on by Fire, except a few empty Powdering-Tubs, or ... Fawks's except an half famiſhed Rat or two, the might... ...ation began to ſubſide, and the Gentry aloft to enter f... the important buſineſs of the day. Whether the ſame tremor took poſſeſſion of the troops (poſted in Kingſtreet on the occaſion) as of their Maſters, we cannot preciſely inform our Readers; but this is certain, no ſooner was the word Preſent given, than a moſt hideous and irregular popping was heard thro' their whole Ranks, which ſounded neither like Gun, Drum, Trumpet, Blunderbuſs or Thunder. This frightful Noiſe, was once or twice heard to the no ſmall Aſtoniſhment of many Eye and Ear Witneſſes to the whole.

CAMBRIDGE, June 15.

Extract of a Letter from Falmouth, Caſco-Bay, dated June 4, 1775.

"Capt. -----, (who on his Paſſage to New-York from this Place with a Load of Spars, was lately ſeized by Admiral Greaves and carried into Boſton) returned here laſt Thurſday Evening.---- He ſays he was at the Wharf at Noddle's-Iſland when the Battle began, and has given us a particular Account of the ſame. He ſays the Sloop near Winniſimmit, that had the firſt Bruſh, cut or ſlipped her Cables, and came and faſtened to his Stern: He was ſhocked to ſee the Blood running out of the Scuppers; there was a Number of Dead and Wounded lying on the Deck, but the Survivors did not care to tell how many. The Diana Schooner next engaged, and the Maſter of her told Capt. -----, that Guns never were better ſerved than ours were, that not a Shot miſſed him.--- I have not Time to write you all he ſays: One Man was carried on board for dead, but next Morning came too, and had not the leaſt Wound about him; others were frighted almoſt to Death, &c. and that there was an amazing Difference in the Looks and Behaviour of the Enemy after the Battle, from what there was before; before there was nothing but Noiſe and Confuſion, afterwards all were ſtill and quiet, inſomuch that you could hardly perceive that there was any Fleet or Army there. From the General down to the common Soldier, they ſeemed to be in a great Panic, were afraid to go to Bed, for fear the Yankees ſhould kill them before Morning."

In one of our late Papers, a Captain of the Militia was ſaid to be killed, in the Battle at Concord, by our own People, owing to their firing at too great a Diſtance. We are ſince well aſſured, by a Perſon who was very near him at the Time, that the ſaid Captain was killed by the Regulars, before a Gun was diſcharged on our Side. However, as Accidents of that Kind *may* happen, it is hoped the Caution againſt firing at too great Diſtance, in any future Engagement, will be duly obſerved.

Laſt Tueſday a Soldier belonging to the New-Hampſhire Troops, bathing in Miſtick River, was unfortunately drowned.

The patriotic Ladies of the Town of Concord are deſired to accept the unfeigned Thanks of the Publick for their Care and Kindneſs in collecting and ſending to the Hoſpital a Cheſt of old Linen Rags, &c. This Inſtance of their Humanity and publick Spirit does Honour to the Town, and will we hope induce others to imitate ſo good an Example.

THE Printers of this Paper requeſt their Cuſtomers at *Salem* and *Marblehead* to pay the Amount of their reſpective Accounts to Mr. JOSEPH HILLER, of Salem, Watchmaker.

... thority, Poſt-Rider from CAMBRIDGE to EXETER; and that he is under Oath for the faithful Performance of his Truſt. He ſets out from the Poſt-Office here every Thurſday, and returns the Saturday following. All Perſons who may pleaſe to ...

... Month, unleſs for thoſe Perſons who ſhall ſignify, either to himſelf or the Printers, their Willingneſs to pay the Poſtage, agreeable to the above Prices.

LOST by the Subſcriber, on the Morning of the 19th April, a ſilver WATCH, with a ſteel Chain, and ſilver Seal engraved E. G.; alſo a few Days after, an outſide Garment uſually called a French great Coat, with a crimſon velvet Cape. Any Perſon who will cauſe the ſame to be returned, ſhall be rewarded therefor, by ELBRIDGE GERRY.

P. S. The Watch is marked on the Face "Ellis London", if the Owner rightly remembers. *Watertown, May 25, 1775.*

STOLEN out of the Houſe of Samuel Shepard, Innholder in Haverhill, on the Night following the 11th of this Inſtant, 1 patch Gown; 1 bengal brown Gown, coffed up with Perſian; 2 black Cloaks; 2 Aprons, one black; 2 Handkerchiefs; 2 pair of Stockings; 2 pair of Women's black Everlaſting Shoes; a Holland Shift; a Pair of ſtone Buttons, and a Number of other Articles. Whoever ſhall recover and deliver the ſame to the Subſcriber, ſhall have the Reward of Ten Dollars.

Haverhill, June 13, 1775. SAMUEL SHEPARD.

STRAYED or ſtolen from the Subſcriber, of Enfield, in Connecticut, on the Night of the 13th Inſtant, out of a Paſture in Brookline, a ſmall Mare, almoſt black, a natural Pacer, her Mane hanging on the near Side, the Hair wore off on her left Side and right Thigh, carries her Head low, 7 Years old, and ſhod all round. Whoever will take up ſaid Mare and return her to Capt. Hezekiah Parſons, of ſaid Enfield, now in Roxbury, in Col. Pitkin's Regiment, ſhall have one Dollar Reward, and all neceſſary Charges paid. JOHN PARSONS.

In Provincial Congreſs, at the City of New-York,
May 25, 1775.

WHEREAS the Enemies of American Liberty are indefatigable in their Endeavours to diſ unite theſe Colonies; and in proſecuting of this Meaſure, evil-minded Perſons may inſinuate that the northern Colonies have hoſtile intentions againſt our Fellow-Subjects in Canada.

Reſolved, *That this Congreſs do moſt earneſtly recommend it to all Perſons, whatſoever, not to commit any Hoſtilities againſt the People of that Country, and do hereby declare to the World, that we do conſider every ſuch Step as infamous and highly inimical to all the Colonies.*

Ordered, *That the above Reſolution be publiſhed.*

A true Copy from the Minutes,

ROBERT BENSON, Secretary.

NEW-YORK JOURNAL

June 15, 1775

The two articles printed in the *New-England Chronicle* and *New-York Journal* describe the Battle of Noddle's Island, the sharpest fight between American and British forces to take place between Lexington and Concord and the Battle of Bunker Hill. It was a fight for sheep and hay.

GRESS, and several thou... ong whom were a great ...st respectable inhabitants ... who have since marched the important fortresses ...d Crown Point.

...4th regiment of troops, ...ny of Connecticut, under ...Col. Hinman, marched for ...conderoga.

...returned from the east- ...n Goddard, who has been ...oliciting the establishment ...constitutional principles, ...last succeeded, the mat- ...aken up by the Commit- ...Congresses, or Assemblies, ...New Hampshire, Massa- ...de Island, and Connecti- ...hich, offices, post masters, ...of postage are established, ...fore the Continental Con- ...approved, or altered as ...pedient—It is hoped this, ...ernments, will come into ...the rates of postage have ...before. In our next, it is ...particular account of this

...May last, the new Provin- ...e Massachusetts Bay, met ...fore whom the Rev. Dr. ...nt of the College, preach- ...adapted to the occasion, ...in Isaiah i. 26. "And I ...udges as at the first, and ...at the beginning: after- ...called, the city of righte- ...al city."

Association, until two vessels shall arrive from London with goods into this Colony, after a general importation from Great Britain to ... worth of goods, to be shipped on board his Majesty's April Packet as baggage.—I now give you a hint that seven persons from America are in Scotland, ordering goods in the ship Lilly, Capt. Thomas Cochran, from Greenock; as he does not sail before the tenth of April, you will receive this first. Capt. Cochran sails for New-York, and not for Philadelphia."

In consequence of the above letter having been published in one of the Philadelphia papers, a sub-committee was appointed to wait on Captain Cockran, who declared that Messrs. George and John Buchanan, owners of the ship Lilly, had been so particularly careful to prevent any goods being ship'd on board said ship; that they gave strict orders to Capt. Cockran, that no trunks, chests, or packages should be shipp'd without strict examination: And Captain Cockran further declared, he was ready to make oath, that no goods, wares, or merchandize was shipp'd on board said ship to his knowledge.

On the 13th day of June, 1775, personally appeared before me David Matthews, Esq; Alderman, of the East Ward, in the city of New York, Thomas Cockran, commander of the ship Lilly, who being duly sworn on the holy evangelists of almighty God; deposeth and saith, that having seen the above extract of a letter relative to goods being ordered to be shipped in the ship Lilly, whereof he is master, published in one of the Philadelphia news papers; the same is false and groundless: That not

which were from officers of the army at Boston. That those letters in general are full of complaints and expressions of uneasiness. Some of the officers desire and entreat to sell out, others say they are fighting in a bad cause, and apprehensive of a mutiny, others mention a difference between the General and the Admiral, and that the army in general are disheartened and uneasy; other letters are full of invectives against the poor *Yankees*, as they call us ——We hear the Provincial Congress will keep Temple as an hostage, but I hope they will let the vessel go, with the above letters."

We hear a man of war is stationed off Portsmouth, has taken two vessels laden with provisions and has orders to take all such, and all that have West India goods on board, &c.

We hear that on Sunday last, the house of William Bayard, Esq; at Greenwich was struck with lightning, when several looking glasses were shattered, other furniture damaged, and a Negro woman hurt, but not dangerously. It is supposed the lightning was conducted into every room in the house by the means of a bell wire.

The following Extract of a letter, dated the first of June instant, in the Provincial Camp, at Cambridge from a gentleman of undoubted veracity and intelligence, gives a more authentic, and in many respects, a more particular account of the late action at Noddle's and Hog-Islands, than any that has appeared in the public papers, and therefore will doubtless be acceptable to the reader.

"When our people were engaged in taking the stock, &c. from Noddle's and Hog-Islands the king's troops made an attack upon them. On Hog Island, the combat began about 5 o'clock in the afternoon, and continued almost incessantly till midnight. The attack was made with cannon, swivels and small arms, from an armed schooner, sloop, and eight or ten barges, upon our people, who had small arms only, but were very advantageously posted by Colonel Putnam who got to them just in season to station and command them properly. He placed them in a ditch, up to their waists in water, and covered by the bank, to their

hout effect. This pro-
perated the people, that
eft in the province, and
gotted, have quitted the
the people, and join
pirited measures, &c."
expedition was on foot,
ived no news of its suc-
miscarried."
rning a quantity of mi-
ken from what are called
Turtle Bay, and car-

'Donald, who it is said
inlisting men to serve
e, against their country,
ody, and conducted by
Grenadiers, before the
this sitting, where he
returned in custody.—
ortant discoveries were

6th instant there was
ners at Cambridge, be-
ls and Regulars, which
en. Putnam on the one
onchief on the other.
revents the publication of
articles.]

E LET,
f a genteel house, neatly
the Coffee-House.——
er, 93—

who is in every
, offers his service to any
entlemen in the country, to
outh; and instruct them,
methods, in every essential
nglish education.
e most satisfactory testimo-
moral character, a genteel
otherwise, to G. D. at the
936

h Castle, May the 25, 1775.
ng now in actual confine-
onse, do hereby notify my
on to present a petition to
f this colony, at their next
of an insolvent act; and
y debts, agreeable to what
d to make in my favour.
ICHABOD OGDEN.

...oods, ... were imported in ship Lilly, on her last arrival here, deponent's knowledge, or belief: ...e owners of said ship gave strict or-...at no trunks, bales, or packages ... put on board the said ship, with-...examination; and that if any came ...d containing merchandize, they ...e relanded, which orders were ...mplied with, and further saith not.

Thomas Cochran.

...is 13th day of June, 1775,
...me *David Matthews.*

...lford, Litchfield County, Connecticut, May 29th, 1775.

...OLT.

...insert the following in your next ... and you will serve the public in ..., and oblige many of your constant ...rs in particular.

...Committee of observation, for said ...w Milford, having duly notified ... *Ferriss, Joseph Ferriss, jun.* ...*borne, Daniel Taylor, Nathaniel* ...*Hezekiah Stevens jun.* all of said ...ord, to appear before said Com-... day, to give reason, if any they ...they, and each of them, should ...ertised, as FOES to the rights of ...erica and said *Zechariah Ferriss,* ...*iss, jun James Osborne, Daniel* ...*Hezekiah Stevens, jun.* having ... appear, and to give any satis-...said Committee; and said *Na-*...*lor* having appeared, and decla-...osition to the doings of the Con-...ongress, and said Committee ...deliberated upon, and finding ...aforenamed persons obstinately ...eir opposition to the doings of ...ss, and the (now bleeding) cause ...; thinks itself in duty bound, to ...ublication, that each of said per-...universally neglected, and treat-...igible enemies to the rights of ...rica according to the eleventh ...he association, entered into by ...ss.

...of the Committee,
...UEL CANFIELD, Com. Clk.

...the above, have made ...ssion, and signed a compliance in ...the doings of the Congress...

necks: The schooner, sloop and boats fi... of them, came within 12 or 15 rods of them, and gave our people a fine opportunity to place their shot well. About midnight the fire ceased a little, and our people retreated to the main land, where they were soon after joined by Capt Foster with two field pieces, which were planted on the way of Winnesimit ferry. At day light the combat was renewed,—as the schooner passed the ferry way, she was briskly attacked by our people, with the field pieces and small arms; which soon clearing her deck, she drifted on shore, where our people set fire to her, and she blew up, notwithstanding the utmost endeavours of the people in the boats, &c. to tow her off, and save her from destruction —In this they exposed themselves much to our fire, and suffered greatly. When they found the schooner was lost, they with difficulty towed off the sloop, much disabled, and retired to their den; and thus ended the combat, at about 7 o'clock in the morning. In the afternoon, (Sunday) our people got out of the wreck, 12 four pounders, 6 swivels, and every thing else that was valuable, without molestation; they afterwards removed or destroyed from both the Islands, all the stock, &c. viz. about 5 or 600 sheep, 30 horses, about as many cattle, a large quantity of hay, and burned all the barns and houses."

"All this was done in sight, and as we may say, under the noses of the whole fleet and army at Boston, without molestation.— The killed of the enemy (*viz. Gen. Gage's crew of enemies to the English constitution*) they themselves allow to be more than 100, besides wounded; others who have good opportunity to know, say, their killed and wounded, exceed 300, and I believe they have suffered as much as in their precipitate flight from Lexington, on the memorable 19th of April." Our killed, none! wounded, three! "Heaven apparently, and most evidently fights for us; covers our heads in the day of battle, and shields our people from the assaults of our common enemies.— What thanks can speak our gratitude."

"These interpositions, and our determined resolutions, may perhaps ... a cooler and more calm retreat, in some distant quarter of the globe ... and leave us peaceably to enjoy th...

REPORTING THE BATTLE OF BUNKER HILL

By Don N. Hagist

Surrounded by an increasing number of colonists coalescing into an army, the British in Boston welcomed the mid-June arrival of two thousand reinforcements that would allow them to conduct offensive operations. Situated on a peninsula that projected into the harbor like a leaf from a tree, Boston was flanked by two other peninsular hills that would threaten the town if not secured. General Thomas Gage intended to occupy Bunker Hill to the north, then Dorchester Heights to the south, starting June 18. But British plans had a way of instantly reaching American ears, and the nascent colonial army made the bold stroke of seizing Bunker Hill during the night of June 16, 1775, building a redoubt on the summit, fortifying a rail fence that led down the slope on one side, and securing the town of Charlestown on the other side. Separated from Boston by a quarter-mile of water, these hastily built fieldworks were an affront that the British army could not allow to stand.

News of the first major battle in a new and unintended war spread quickly throughout America and to England.

The ensuing battle is well known: the early morning discovery by British warships, rapidly assembled British boats landing troops at the hill's base, a failed attempt by British light infantry to outflank the rail fence, the British grenadiers' frontal assault bogged down by terrain obstacles and murderous musketry, harassing American shots from Charlestown silenced by incendiary mortar shells that burned the town to ashes, and a final columnar assault on the redoubt's weak right corner that carried it at bayonet point, resulting in carnage among the defenders. All of this is well chronicled in numerous histories and continued modern scholarship.

News of the first major battle in a new and unintended war spread quickly throughout America and to England, but none of the news bearers had the clear and detailed understanding of events that we have today. The battle dominated colonial newspapers in late June and early July; by August, accounts began to appear in the British press. As such, it provides an excellent case study of how news traveled and the challenges readers faced in understanding events based on accounts that were partial in terms of completeness and perspective. Newspapers published what information they could obtain from letters and travelers, with no means of verification.

Supporters of both sides viewed the epic fight as a victory. The June 29, 1775, *Pennsylvania Evening Post* carried news from a person who arrived outside of Boston while the battle was in progress. The spirited writer overstates by a factor of two the number of regulars engaged while indicating only a quarter of the actual colonial force; considering that he was in the American camp, it is interesting that his estimate of British casualties is quite accurate while he understates American losses. Two famous fatalities are singled out: Major Pitcairn of the British Marines, known for his role on April 19, and Joseph Warren, the doctor-cum-soldier-statesman whose death in the redoubt made him a battlefield hero. The same day's *New-England Chronicle* was informed by an escapee from Boston and included a eulogy to America's new hero. Surely the British army would hesitate to face such staunch opponents again.

The Edinburgh Advertiser of August 1, 1775, broke the news with General Gage's official report on the front page and four further pages of extracts from letters by witnesses and participants. Their military terminology gives credibility to the accounts, with talk of fascines and gabions (bundles of saplings and brush used to reinforce fortifications), light infantry and grenadiers (specialized troops detached from their regiments and formed together to lead the assault), battalions (the main portion of a regiment), carcasses (incendiary shells thrown by mortars), and three-, six-, and twelve-pounders (cannons defined by the weight of iron ball they fired). They emphasize the courage of outnumbered troops who stormed a fortified position in spite of fearsome casualties. Surely the rebellious colonists would hesitate to face such determined professionals again.

A remarkable piece of journalism appeared in Dixon and Hunter's *Virginia Gazette* on August 26, 1775. The illustrations that dotted newspapers of the era were mostly generic images complementing advertisements or decorative nameplates similar to the one atop the front page of the *Gazette*. Skilled hands could typeset text quickly, but it was not feasible to illustrate a current event because of the time required to prepare a printing block. However, based on an eyewitness description, the Virginia publishers ingeniously and quite accurately rendered a schematic diagram of the battlefield of Breed's Hill using only standard typesetting components. This is the only known newspaper illustration of a current event during the entire American Revolution and the only illustration in any period source—newspaper, book, magazine, or other—to use this diagrammatic technique.

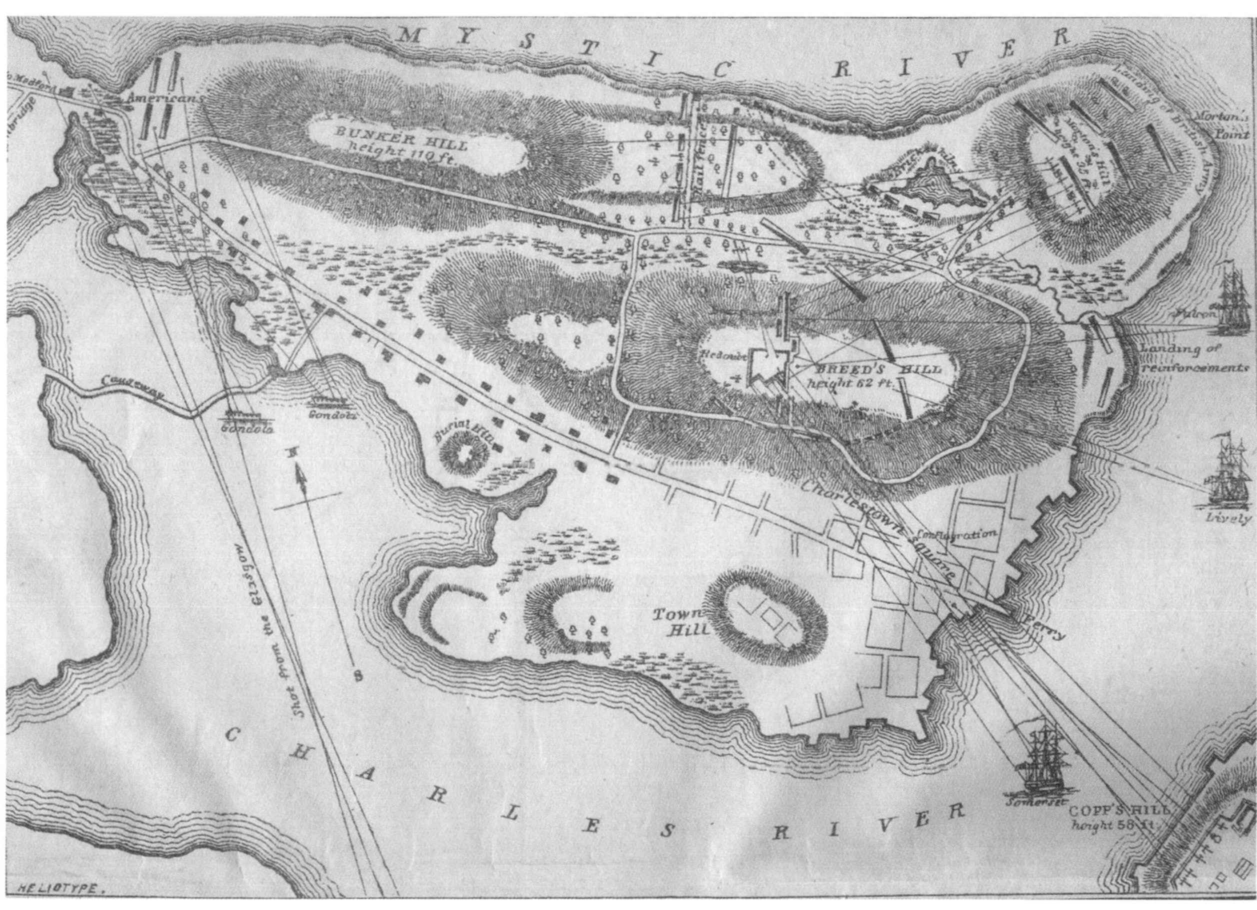

Battle of Bunker Hill
George E. Ellis,
U.S. Army Images

An illustrated map of the battleground on Charlestown peninsula, encompassing Bunker and Breed's Hills.

(272)

Lord Dunmore's *answer to the address of the* House *of* Burgesses *of* Virginia. *(See page 259.)*

IT is with real concern I can discover nothing in your address that I think manifests the smallest inclination to, or will be productive of, a reconcilation with the mother country.

PHILADELPHIA, *June* 29.

Extract of a letter from Watertown, dated June 21.

"I arrived at this spot on Saturday last in good health, though much exhausted with a rapid and lengthy journey in so warm a season. The thunder of cannon reached my ears some miles before I got here; the army of Britain had sallied out, and were then engaging our people, who had attempted a lodgment on Bunker's Hill; the line of battle ships, one frigate, the batteries from Boston, a number of floating batteries, and the musquetry of 5000 British troops were discharging incessant torrents of shot, for the space of six hours on about 1200 Americans, without any artillery except three three-pounders: And what renders the matter more remarkable, the regulars were twice repulsed with excessive slaughter, and finally gained the lines with the loss of seventy officers killed and wounded, and 1000 men. Our men have entrenched on an eminence in Charlestown, about three quarters of a mile from the enemies encampment. We have lost sixty men, and upwards of an hundred wounded. Our troops are in high spirits, and eagerly wish for another trial. We have met with one capital loss; our worthy friend Doctor Warren was slain in the trenches, bravely struggling for the liberties of his country. We have lost a few brave officers. On the part of the British troops Major Pitcairn, and a number of capital officers are among the dead."

Extract of a letter from a Gentleman at Stockbridge (Massachusetts-Bay) to a Gentleman of the Congress, dated June 22.

"A firm foundation now turns up to view, for the influence of the Stockbridge Indians amongst the SIX NATIONS, and matters stand well with the Canadian Indians. If I had time, I would relate to you every particular of what befel the messengers of our Indians to the Six Nations and the Canadian Indians. To be short, they were taken and bound by the regulars, and carried into Montreal, where, by a court

PENNSYLVANIA EVENING POST (PHILADELPHIA)

June 29, 1775

A common propaganda tactic was to inflate the enemy's numbers while deflating yours. This spirited writer overstates by a factor of two the number of regulars engaged, while indicating only a quarter of the actual colonial force.

offered us money to fight for you, but we would not take it, as

hang these our brothers, that came a great way to see us, do it, but remember we shall not forget it. Upon these threatenings

have taken Mr. Gibbs's brig, with a load of flour from [Phi]ladelphia, and have taken her cargo on board for fear [it] should be retaken."

COMMITTEE CHAMBER, *June* 26, 17[75].

A quantity of salt and a box of wine glasses having [been] imported in the ship Albion, Thomas Crippen, master, [from] Liverpool, it was resolved, that the said ship and cargo o[ught] to be returned forthwith, and that the Captain have n[otice] thereof immediately.

Ordered, That the District Committee see the above [reso]lution complied with.

On Motion, *Resolved*, That Mr. Joseph Whittall, [one] of the owners of the ship Albion, does not appear to h[ave] had any knowledge of or concern in the shipping the salt, [&c.] in said vessel.

Resolved, That Mr. Henry Cour, merchant, of Liverp[ool] in Great Britain, half owner of the ship Albion, has kn[ow]ingly violated the Association of the American Congress, [by] shipping the salt to America; and that it is the duty of [this] Committee to advertise him accordingly.

Resolved, That Nicholas Ashton, Esq; of or near Liv[er]pool, in the county of Lancaster, in Great-Britain, owner [of] the abovementioned salt, has wilfully violated the Associat[ion] of the American Congress by shipping the said salt to A[me]rica, and that it is the duty of this Committee to adver[tise] his conduct herein.

Resolved unanimously, That, agreeable to the resolutions [of] the Grand American Congress, it is the duty of us and of our constituents the inhabitants of the City and Liberties [of] Philadelphia, *from henceforth not to have any commercial int[er]course whatsoever* with the said Henry Cour and Nicholas A[sh]ton: And it is recommended that an inviolable regard [be] paid to this resolution.

Extract from the minutes.

J. B. SMITH, Secretary.

☞ Genteel BOARDING and LODGINGS to be had [in] a public Part of the City, on reasonable Terms. Inquire [of] the Printer.

Just PUBLSHED (Price 1s. 6d.)

By Robert Bell and Benjamin Towne,

THE CHRONICLE OF THE KINGS OF ENGLAND, from the Reign of William the Conquero[r] first King of England, down to his present Majesty Georg[e] III. containing a true History of their Lives, and the Chara[c]ter which they severally sustained, whether in Church an[d] State, in the Field, or in private Life.

This Book, though published under the fictitious Title [of] Nathan Ben-Saddi, was wrote by the ingenious Author of th[e] ECONOMY of HUMAN LIFE, and has gone through a[l]most every Press in Europe.

TO be SOLD by HENRY DAUGHERTY, at [his] GROCERY STORE at Cuthbert's Wharf, next [to] Willing and Morris's.

NEW-ENGLAND CHRONICLE (CAMBRIDGE, MA)

June 29, 1775

Following the Battle of Bunker Hill, the colonial militiamen retreated three miles to their headquarters at Cambridge, the same town where the *New-England Chronicle* was printed. In its second weekly issue to print since the battle, the *Chronicle* published several verses related to the battlefield death of Patriot Major General Joseph Warren.

---

he magazine, who have placed a ... be concerted for its better security.

NEW-YORK, June 22.

Extract of a letter from London, dated April 25, 1775.

"A steady friend to America called upon me this afternoon, to acquaint me with the following intelligence, communicated to him by ------- this day, which you may rely upon as a fact. The ------ said that Administration on Friday received advices from General Gage, to the 18th of March, where he acknowledges the receipt of the King's order to apprehend Messrs. Cushing, Adams, Hancock, &c. and send them over to England to be tried; but that the second orders, which were to hang them in Boston, he said the General had not then received. The General expressed his fears on the occasion, and in hopes of their being reversed he should delay the execution a while longer; because he must, if the orders were fulfilled, come to an engagement,---the event of which, he had every reason to apprehend would be fatal to himself, and the King's troops; as the Massachusetts Government had at least 15,000 men, ready trained for the onset,---and besides, had every public and private road occupied by the militia, so as to prevent his marching into the country, and which were at the same time ready to facilitate any attempt against the army: On which unwelcome situation he earnestly wished for a reinforcement, if that disagreeable order must be effected. The General also wrote that the standard was hoisted by the people at Salem, and multitudes flocked to it, which would not be the case should the royal standard be erected---added, that he now believed America would carry their point---That many of the Administration were of the same mind, and sincerely wished they had pursued more gentle measures with the Colonies.——

He said Lord North was evidently uneasy, and that Government dreaded the news by the April packet---that they suppressed this intelligence from General Gage, because of the instant effect it would have on the stocks. He acknowledged the nation was ready for a revolution, if any enterprising genius would step forth, and which would certainly be the case, if blood was ever drawn in America. He blames Hutchinson much, and says Administration charges him with duplicity, in telling them they ought to have been more active, and that they would have made the Massachusetts submit. To others, that Administration had gone much further than he advised: Be this as it may, he added that the King consults him, places a confidence in what he says, and has actually fixed his salary at 2000l. per annum *for life*, which had much chagrined some of the Administration, who ardently wished him given up, as a sacrifice to both countries. My intelligencer wishes, if this letter should be published, that ----- name might be omitted as the information was confidential. I shall only add, that my country may be free if she will; and that she may have the virtue to play the man, is the aspiration of Sir, your most obedient servant."

Extract of a letter from St. John's, Newfoundland, May 30th, 1775, to his friend in this city.

"Here we are starving for bread and flour, and no hopes of redress,---and the ports in America being shut up, we are at a loss what to do."

A Gentleman that come in the Coach from Philadelphia, last Saturday Evening, informs us, That a Letter had been just received there from Virginia, acquainting them, That his Excellency Lord Dunmore, with all his Family had retired on board a Man of War in Consequence of some Guns that were fixed in such a Position in the Provincial Magazine there, that as soon as the Door was opened several went off, and wounded three Men.

Yesterday, we hear General Haldiman, who, it is reported, is re called to England, ...

our Men were killed, and five wounded.

Mr. Robert Avery, of Norwich, in Connecticut, who was on board the Tender, a Prisoner, was unhappily ...

CA...

Generals W... from the Sout... Writs are i... tinental Cong... Watertown u... The Gene... met at Portsm... Day to the 1... A Man of ... the Time of ... from Admira... took the Opp... rived there the ... Day of the Battle ... brought over in Boats, to the Amount of at least 500; that 30 of them died before they arrived at the Hospital; that 84 Officers were killed and wounded, 3 of which were Field Officers; and that the whole of the Killed and Wounded amounted to 13 or 1400.

Various other Accounts confirm Mr. King's Intelligence, and give us great Reason to conclude that the Havoc among the ministerial Troops was very considerable. The Loss on our Side is not yet ascertained; but at the most is supposed to be from 150 to 200 killed and wounded. Major-General WARREN, late President of the Provincial Congress, is among the Slain. Col. Parker of Chelmsford, and 27 Privates from different Towns, are Prisoners in Boston Gaol.

The Hon. JAMES WARREN, Esq; is chosen President of the Provincial Congress, in the Room of the late Major-General Warren, slain in Battle.

On Saturday the 17th June, 1775,
fell in Battle,
in the American Army,
Major-General JOSEPH WARREN,
A Gentleman worthy that Office, to which, the Day before,
by the free Votes of his Countrymen,
he was honourably elected.
As a Friend to Britain, he wished the mutual Happiness
of her and America:
And conscious their Interests were inseparable,
He strenuously opposed the unjust Claims
of a venal Parliament,
Who attempted to ruin the latter, by depriving them of their Rights
sacred by Charter.
Twice, to crowded Audiences,
He wail'd the Fate of those massacred March 5, 1770;
and twice
receiv'd the Thanks of his Fellow Citizens therefor.
To enumerate his Virtues
would be a Subject worthy of an abler Pen.
Sufficient for us, we add,
He by them has laid the Foundation of a Fame
that shall not be impaired
by the Tooth of Time.

Over his Grave his mourning Countrymen may justly say,

Here lies the Body of a worthy Man;
Whose Name shall live and fill the World with wonder,
Although his Ashes scarcely fill an Urn.
His Virtues shall remain when we have left the Stage:
His Praises shall be spoke for many an Age to come.

Since the Battle of the 17th Instant, a considerable Body of the Army have been employed in fortifying Prospect-Hill, Winter-Hill, and other Eminences near Charlestown. The former, which is a very fine Situation, and in full View of the Enemy on Bunker Hill, is said to be now rendered almost impregnable.----

place. She left that place the 21st of June; and by a letter come in the above ship we hear, that not more than 300 of the provincials were killed in the late skirmish of the 17th of June, and that they behaved with the greatest courage.

Yesterday it was currently reported, and it is imagined not without some foundation, that an eminent American house in this city had a letter from Boston, dated the 26th of last month, which gives an account, the provincials had actually began bombarding Boston; and that General Gage had sent over an express to government, that he was under some apprehension that the rebels would certainly make themselves masters of Boston, or burn it down.

The day after the late battle in America, some of the regulars searched the pockets of Dr. Warren, who was killed, and found three letters sent to him from some spies at Boston, which were immediately sent there, and the writers being soon discovered were sent to prison, and it is said they were to be hanged next day.

During the late engagement, thirty of the provincials who were taken prisoners, and brought to Boston, desired to be shot, but were confined in a prison, and attended by a clergyman, to whom they declared they were led on entirely by their ministers enforcing the doctrine of resistance.

The news of a battle between General Carleton and the provincials is hourly expected.

Extract of a private letter from an officer in the engagement of the 17th of last month, near Boston, to his friend an eminent merchant in London.

"The engagement, whilst it lasted, was the hottest, I ever saw, and in all the actual service I ever was in, I never saw troops keep up a more constant fire than the provincials.

"The left wing of our troops gave way, a little and it is not to be wondered at considering what numbers they had firing at them; at this time our regiment came up very fortunately to support them, and our men behaved with great intrepidity; they had seen, that nothing was to be done but by continuing a brisk fire, which they did with great spirit, and at length drove the provincials off the field in the utmost confusion. Their loss must be very considerable; and as they seemed afraid of us in the field, and kept in their entrenchments in this engagement, in which they have sustained great loss, I am of opinion, they will not be desirous of meeting the King's troops again; but we are preparing for another rencounter, though it is uncertain where is to be the scene."

Part of a genuine letter from Boston, dated July 23, 1775, brought by the Cerberus.

"There is no instance in history of the mother country knowing so little of her colonies, as Great Britain does of America. At least, this is the best excuse that can be made for your conduct. Our troops are as well disciplined as your s; and they are better marksmen, as your officers know very well. An account of the late action you will have in a minute he was quite alone. His Aid de Camp was killed at his side. The officers brought up the men, and suffered for their temerity. General Clinton, with another corps, presently followed. General Putnam, who had not quite four thousand Connecticut men, thought the whole army was coming, and without the least disorder, or even being pursued a single step, left Bunker's hill, and went to another hill about half a mile further; where he has remained ever since, without the least disturbance. If the mercenaries had offered to march a yard after him General Ward, with his New-England men, was ready to give a good account of them. General Howe is come back to Boston, having had better than two thirds of his men killed and wounded.

"General Howe will do justice to the bravery of our troops. He makes no secret of saying he never saw troops behave better during the whole war. It has been proposed to attack Roxbury-hill; but the design is laid aside. The officers all declare, it will cost more men than the post is worth. So the army must remain cooped-up in Boston, or go on board the ships."

Extract of a letter from Plymouth, July 24.

"This morning a snow arrived in the Sound from Boston; what news she has brought we cannot tell, no person belonging to her being suffered to come on shore; the Captain is gone for London in a post chaise and four; it is said here that Boston has been burnt down, but by whom we do not know."

During the engagement near Charlestown, Gen. Ward, with the grand provincial army, remained quiet within his lines on Roxbury hill.

Major Pitcairn, of the marines, who was killed in the late action in America, has left eight children—Four balls were lodged in his body, and he was taken off the field upon his son's shoulders.

A very promising youth, cousin to General Gage's lady, who was an officer under General Putnam, was killed in the late battle between the regulars and the provincials.

Our letter from Portsmouth, of this day, says, we hear by the Cerberus, that about 700 provincials were killed and wounded, in the engagement near Charlestown.

Yesterday, at two o'clock, an express arrived at Lord Dartmouth's office, from General Gage, which was laid before the cabinet at St. James's; afterwards Lord Dartmouth held a conference with the King.

The watch word of the provincial detachment, in the morning of the 17th, we are told was *Wilkes*; the next hour it was *Bull*.

From the NEW-YORK GAZETTE *of June* 19.

Providence, June 10. Sunday last the schooner Pelican, Capt. Tucker, arrived at Marblehead from London, in ballast, and brought dispatches for Gen. Gage and Admiral Graves, which were immediately secured by the committee of that place, and sent to the Provincial Congress at Watertown. The contents of them have not yet transpired.

Cambridge, June 8. Whereas the Provincial Congress, on the 3d day of May ult. empowered and directed the receiver general of this colony to borrow the sum of one hundred

Yesterday both Houses of Parliament met, and were further prorogued until Thursday the 14th day of September next.

Advice is received in town of a dreadful engagement between the Spanish fleet and the Emperor of Morocco's, reinforced by other Barbary states, wherein several of the Spanish men of war were sunk, amongst which was the Spanish Admiral's ship. It is said the Moors obtained a complete victory, and that with a savage brutality peculiar to those infidels, they massacred numbers of the Spaniards in cool blood.

Yesterday, after the usual business was over, the Lady who has been suspected of contributing to the death of the late —— Scawen, Esq; was examined before Sir John Fielding in the parlour, at the public office in Bowstreet, where Mr. Scawen, the member for Surrey, an eminent counsel for the prisoner, and a great number of gentlemen attended. She denied any knowledge of the circumstance of Mr. Scawen's being poisoned, and behaved with great propriety and composure. After a short hearing she was committed on suspicion to Tothill fields Bridewell, for further examination. She was elegantly dressed in mourning for the deceased Mr. Scawen, is remarkably handsome, and appears to be about five or six and twenty years of age.

Bank stock, 141 7-8 India ditto, —

Lottery tickets, 12l. 18s.

EDINBURGH.

Extract of a letter from London, July 28.

"Many letters are received from Boston, but there is no particular account yet come of the loss on the side of the rebels, neither has the colony agents here received any accounts of the late action at Charlestown; but it is generally believed that the provincials must have suffered more than the King's troops.——The general proposed that the ships' boats, well manned and armed, should attack the rebels on both sides of Boston neck, which at last the admiral ordered to be done, but they came rather too late, to do effectual service: had the boats arrived sooner, it is supposed that all the rebels who were first engaged must have been cut off. Charlestown, which contained near a thousand houses, is entirely destroyed: as all the American ports were to be shut up the 1st of July, no accounts can come but by ships of war, or government packets.—It is confidently reported that more troops will be sent over soon to Boston, the army there being found by much too small for the service: this reinforcement cannot be great, till after the meeting of parliament, there being no funds for raising more men, which makes the situation of the army at Boston very critical, as it is probable the rebels will take advantage of the smallness of their number.

"Letters received this day from Carolina mention, that that province has agreed to raise two regiments of foot and one of horse, to join the rebels; Georgia has also acceded to the alliance, so that all America, Canada excepted, is leagued together.

"Last week Lieutenant General Houston was appointed to the command of one of the

The Death of General Warren at the Battle of Bunker's Hill, June 17, 1775, by John Trumbull
Museum of Fine Arts, Boston (current location)

EDINBURGH ADVERTISER

August 1, 1775

This eight-page newspaper issue is loaded with page after page of details about the biggest and bloodiest confrontation yet experienced in the American Revolutionary War.

AUGUST 26, 1775

The VIRGINIA GAZETTE

PHILADELPHIA, August 2.

Another Account of the late Action at BUNKER'S hill.

As to camp news, I was there for the first time last Saturday. Our people appear hearty and very happy. The great numbers who crowd to view it, and see their friends, and the parading of the regiments upon the commons, make a grand appearance. The famous Prospect hill is just by the stone house, on the left hand as you go to Charlestown. I believe the regulars will hardly venture out, for they must lose a vast many men if they should, and they cannot afford to purchase every inch of ground as they did at Charlestown. The number the regulars lost, and had wounded, you have seen in the account taken from the orderly serjeant, which agrees pretty nearly with a variety of accounts we have received from people, who have come here from Boston, in fishing boats. They must have suffered greatly, for the first continued with small arms sixty one minutes, and the great part of the time very close fighting. My classmate, Col. ——, was in the entrenchment, and was wounded in the head and leg. He says there was no need of waiting for a chance to fire, for as soon as you had loaded, there was always a mark at hand, and as near as you pleased. His description of the entrenchment, &c. was this:

[see map]

The square, or fort, had about one hundred and fifty men in it. The breastwork about two hundred. The rail fence stuffed with straw four or five hundred. The reason why the square was so thinly manned on the side toward Boston, was because the fire from Cop's hill poured in so thick that there was no living in it. The regulars when they found the fire slacked for want of ammunition, pushed over the walls with their guns in their left hand, and their swords in the right, for it was such an unfinished piece of work that they ran over it. Part of them had come round on the side next Charlestown, so as to fire on the back of our people, when they began to leave the entrenchment, and it was then we lost our men. The ships and floating batteries prevented any assistance, or support of consequence, being given to our men; the fire from Cop's hill ceased when that with small arms began, but that from a ship off New Boston killed and raked our men quite up to the Sun tavern.—— thinks there was more than three thousand of the regulars landed. They advanced in open order, the men often twelve feet apart in the front, but very close after one another in extraordinary deep or long files. As fast as the front man was shot down, the next stepped forward into his place; but our men dropt them so fast, they were a long time coming up. It was surprising how they would step over their dead bodies, as though they had been logs of wood. Their officers, it is said, were obliged to push them on behind, notwithstanding which they once ran and filled some of the boats, the fire was so hot. One of ——'s Captains told me he fired about thirty five times, and after that threw stones. —— says when they pushed over the breastwork, what with the smoke and dust, it was so dark in the square, that he was obliged to feel about for the outlet, the earth, which they threw up for a breastwork, being very dry and loose, for they had only one of these short nights to execute it in.

VIRGINIA GAZETTE (WILLIAMSBURG) (DIXON AND HUNTER)
August 26, 1775

Truly one of a kind, this issue of the *Virginia Gazette* contains the only known newspaper illustration of a current event published during the entire American Revolution. It depicts the battlefield at Breed's Hill, based on an eyewitness account, and is made entirely of standard typesetting components found in a print shop.

suffer me to entreat you to STAY the SWORD, and suspend any further operations against the colonies, until some happy conciliating means may be devised, some fortunate expedient may be hit upon to heel the bleeding wounds, and re-unite us again with that un-
ortunate and distracted country. It is, my Lord, the sincere wish
f every true friend of freedom, who are too sensibly afflicted,
lequately to express their feelings on the above most melancholy
vent.

As a well-wisher to your Lordship and all mankind, I entreat
ou, from every motive of humanity, to listen to the dictates of
und reason and policy, and you cannot fail of being convinced
f the justice and expediency of a measure so essentially requisite to
op the further effusion of the BLOOD of our COUNTRYMEN,
nd prevent us from being engaged in all the horrors of a civil
nd intestine war; the bare apprehension of which, my Lord,
lls me with the most poignant anxiety, and makes me dread the
npending consequences, with a torture of mind utterly impossible
be described.

If by those extraordinary exertions, which have often proceeded
om people contending for their liberties, or by any of those ac-
dents which have frequently decided the fate of battles and of
npires, taking the victory from the strong, and the race from
e swift, we should be REPULSED, to what a state of humilia-
on should we be reduced? Such is the insuperable absurdity of
e measure, that whether victors, or vanquished, we are sure of
eing sufferers.

With ties so strong to bind us to each other, is it not strange,
it not deplorable, that we should differ? Do they who talk of
hastising our colonies, and reducing them to obedience, consider
ow much we hazard when we dissolve those ties? What are we
substitue in their place, FORCE and FEAR, which Tacitus
isely tells us are insecure restraints, and always succeeded by in-
eterate hatred? When these consequences follow from the coer-
ve measures we are now pursuing, will the counsellors who have
npelled us to them by representations, not, I am sure, very fair,
efend us from their fatal effects?

It is from experience only, my Lord, that men learn wisdom,
ut unhappily, sometimes the injury of the experiment is irre-
ievable; we have too much reason, I think, to apprehend that
is will be the event of our present contest with America.

I acknowledge, I admire the bravery of our troops; what men
n do, they will do; but in a country furnished with fastnesses
nd defiles without number, intimately known to the enemy you
e to combat, where discipline is unavailing or embarrassing, and
lour useless, it requires more than human power to succeed to
ny permanent purpose. Heaven forbid that the bravery of such
oops as the English should be so vainly, so fatally employed;
ey who remember the fatal overthrow of BRADDOCK by a
w Indians in ambush, an overthrow incurred by the very disci-
ine in which he vainly put his trust, will be apt to doubt the fa-
lity of reducing the colonies by military force; they who re-
ect that the united aid and efforts of all the colonies were
ecessary to give success to our arms in the late war against the
anadians, will be still more doubtful of this expedient.

But, my Lord, so much having been already said on the sub-
ct, I will not take up more of your valuable moments, which I
n persuaded must now be fully employed; indulge me, how-
er, once more to entreat your most serious attention to the true
terest and happiness of this country, and to the welfare of our bre-
ren in America, so shall you be revered and esteemed by all good
en, your name deservedly transferred with honour to posterity,
d the tribute of gratitude, affection, and esteem, be echoed
om every quarter of this great and extensive empire.

MEMENTO.

on the left hand as you go to Charlestown. I believe the regulars will hardly venture out, for they must lose a vast many men if they should, and they cannot afford to purchase every inch of ground as they did at Charlestown. The number the regulars lost, and had wounded, you have seen in the account taken from the orderly serjeant, which agrees pretty nearly with a variety of accounts we have received from people, who have come here from Boston, in fishing boats. They must have suffered greatly, for the fire continued with small arms sixty one minutes, and great part of the time very close fighting. My classmate, Col.———, was in the entrenchment, and was wounded in the head and leg. He says there was no need of waiting for a chance to fire, for as soon as you had loaded, there was always a mark at hand, and as near as you pleased. His description of the entrenchment, &c. was this:

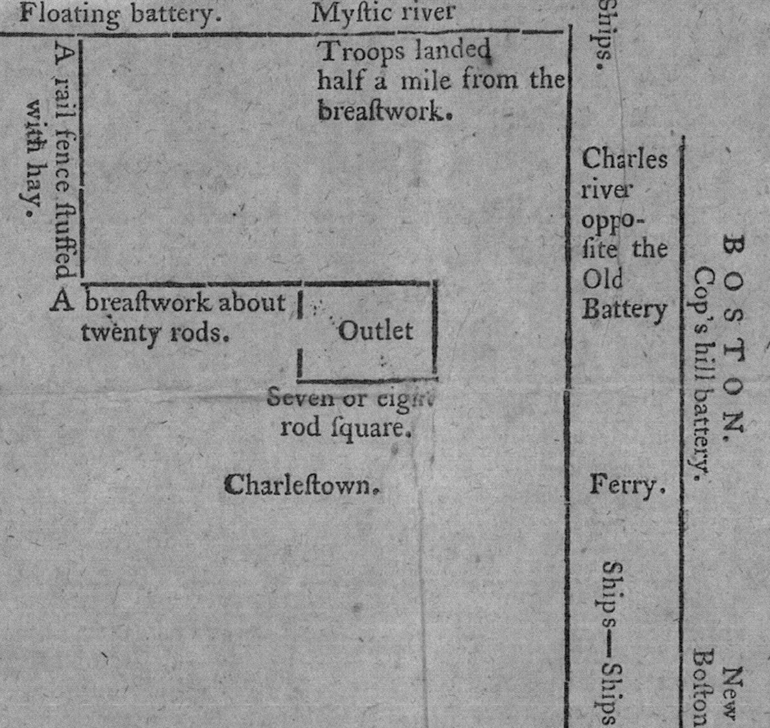

The square, or fort, had about one hundred and fifty men in it. The breastwork about two hundred. The rail fence stuffed with straw four or five hundred. The reason why the square was so thinly manned on the side toward Boston, was because the fire from Cop's hill poured in so thick that there was no living in it. The regulars when they found the fire slacked for want of ammunition, pushed over the walls with their guns in their left hand, and their swords in the right, for it was such an unfinished piece of work that they ran over it. Part of them had come round on the side next Charlestown, so as to fire on the back of our people, when they began to leave the entrenchment, and it was then we lost our men. The ships and floating batteries prevented any assistance, or support of consequence, being given to our men; the fire from Cop's hill ceased when that with small arms began, but that from a ship off New Boston killed and raked our men quite up to the Sun tavern. —— thinks there was more than three thousand of the regulars landed. They advanced in open order, the men often twelve feet apart in the front, but very close after one another in extraordinary deep or long files. As fast as the front man was shot down, the next stepped forward into his place; but our men dropt them so fast, they were a long time coming up. It was surprising how they would step over their dead bodies, as though they had been logs of wood. Their officers, it is said, were obliged to push them on behind, notwithstanding which they once ran and filled some of the boats, the fire was so hot. One of———'s Captains told me he fired about thirty five times, and after that threw stones. ——— says when they pushed over the breastwork, what with the smoke and dust, it was so dark in the square that he was obliged to feel about for the outlet, the

the navy and a
tion of the en
the General,
fact, it could
tions were im
lars from Quel
to obtain the n
can vessels at
cursed plan,
determination
acts of butche
50,000l. was
" The Gen
spike up the c
up the King's
this nation!
and the consol
threats, and
forming this i
Canada, they
they would d
lacious contra
believing that
cut off, or ign
board the men
" Such also
patched some
contradict the
men, cajole t
effection of the
expedients; f
supine landed
given to the fu
America, by
blish her righ
most flagitious
wisdom and c
" This eve
meet, revive a
consist of 800
in forcing a r
in supporting
nions."

SPEECH *of th*
mons, on the
affairs.

IT is but to
Ministers c
temper and fit
will be inevita
Gentlemen
favourite prop
duties; and, c
the other. N
protection to
no longer to b
zard of battle
the same acts
according to t
in the world.
conduct from
all the wars t
their own cou
that, in many
to the presen

REPORTING

GEORGE WASHINGTON TAKES COMMAND

By Robert J. Allison

BEFORE LEAVING VIRGINIA ON MAY 4, 1775, TO ATTEND the Congress in Philadelphia, Washington heard that British marines raided the Williamsburg gunpowder depot; the next day, he heard about the battle at Lexington and Concord. The political crisis had turned violent. Still, he expected to be home by July to attend to his own business. Instead, by early July, he was in Massachusetts taking command of an army.

Congress had him chair the committees to plan New York's defenses, to supply the army, and to devise rules for governing the army. Drawn from four different New England colonies, the army had no regular order. Men came and went at will, and men from one colony would not listen to orders issued by officers from another.

In the midst of this discussion, John Adams said he had a candidate to lead the army—"a gentleman of private fortune, a skilled, experienced officer, whose talents and character merited the praise of all America." Washington discretely left the room. The next day, June 15, Congress unanimously appointed him commanding general. It also appointed Charles Lee, a retired British officer who had served in Poland's army; Artemas Ward, the Massachusetts officer already in command in Cambridge; Philip Schuyler of New York; and Israel Putnam of Connecticut as major generals.

Washington wanted "it remembered by every Gentleman in the room" that he had not sought the position and did not "think myself equal to the command I am honoured with" (*New-England Chronicle and Essex Gazette*, January 11, 1776). He declined the $500 monthly salary and rode from Philadelphia on June 23 to take command. Three days later, he reached New York, whose provincial congress welcomed him, deploring "the calamities of this divided Empire," which forced them "to defend their dearest rights and privileges" and looked forward to an accommodation with England that would allow Washington to retire to private life (*New-England Chronicle*, July 6, 1775).

When "we assumed the Soldier," Washington told the Congress, "we did not lay aside the Citizen," agreeing on the goal of restored harmony between the colonies and England but pledging to fight for "the establishment of American Liberty, on the most firm and solid foundation" (*New-England Chronicle*, July 6, 1775). While in New York, he learned of Bunker Hill, which seemed to prove that the army would fight. He believed another such battle would convince the British public to give up the war.

He reached Cambridge on July 2, 1775, after briefly stopping in Watertown, where the Massachusetts Provincial Congress welcomed him. They told him his "naturally brave" soldiers had no real military experience and the "Youth in the Army are not possessed of the absolute necessity of Cleanliness in their Dress, and Lodging, continual Exercise, and strict Temperance" (*New-England Chronicle*, July 6, 1775).

Washington assured the Congress that in putting aside his private affairs to take on these duties, he emulated "the Virtue and publick Spirit of the whole Province of Massachusetts Bay," that his only ambition was to vindicate their rights and restore all to "Peace, Liberty, and Safety." Whatever his troops' deficiency, he was confident their "native Bravery and Spirit" would quickly end the "Distresses which now overwhelm this once happy Country" (*New-England Chronicle*, July 6, 1775).

But it would be Washington's task to organize this army; keep it fed, clothed, and armed; and turn it from an enthusiastic summertime encampment into a disciplined, effective fighting force.

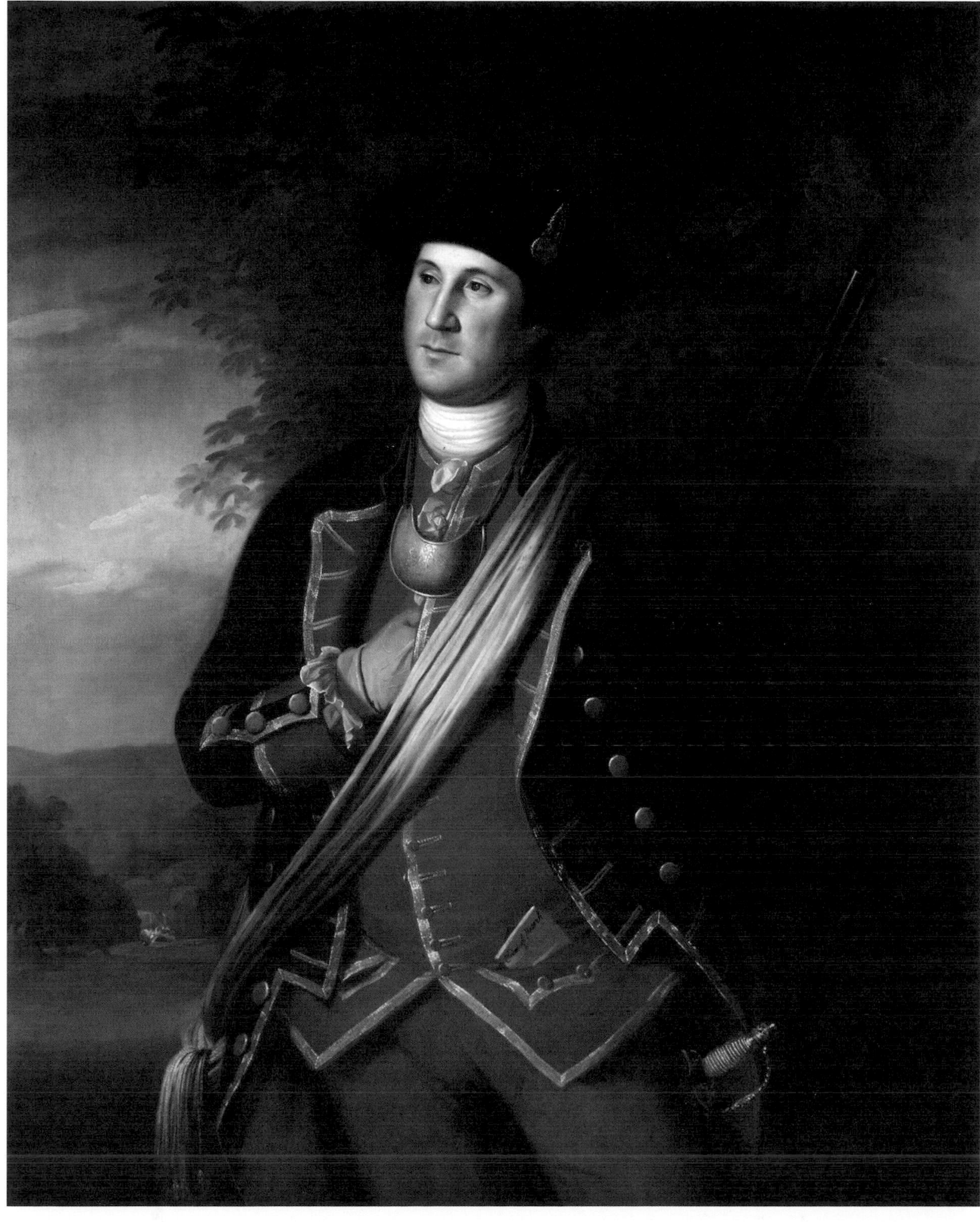

GEORGE WASHINGTON
Washington-Custis-Lee Collection, Washington and Lee University

The earliest portrait of George Washington wearing his colonel's uniform of the Virginia Regiment from the French and Indian War, likely the uniform he wore while accepting command of the Continental forces.

Subſcriber, it will be kindly received, but if it is detained with Deſign to defraud him, and any

NEW-ENGLAND CHRONICLE (CAMBRIDGE, MA)

January 11, 1776

As shown in the Congressional journal for June 16, 1775, printed a half-year later, Washington understood this was a "momentous duty." Demonstrating his character, Washington made sure everyone knew he did not "think myself equal to the command I am honoured with" and turned down the $500 monthly salary.

EXTRACTS from the JOURNAL *of the* CONGRESS.

In CONGRESS, JUNE 15, 1775.

Reſolved,

THAT a General be appointed to command all the Continental Forces raiſed or to be raiſed for the defence of American Liberty.

That five hundred dollars per month be allowed for the pay and expences of the General.

The Congreſs then proceeded to the choice of a General by ballot, and *George Waſhington*, Eſq; was unanimouſly elected.

JUNE 16, 1775.

The Preſident informed Col. Waſhington that the Congreſs had yeſterday unanimouſly made choice of him to be General and Commander in Chief of the American Forces, and requeſted he would accept of that employment; to which Col. Waſhington, ſtanding in his place, anſwered:

"*Mr. Preſident,*

"Though I am truly ſenſible of the high honour done me in this appointment, yet, I feel great diſtreſs from the conſciouſneſs, that my abilities and military experience may not be equal to the extenſive and important truſt: However, as the Congreſs deſire it, I will enter upon the momentous duty, and exert every power I poſſeſs in the ſervice and for ſupport of the glorious cauſe. I beg they will accept my moſt cordial thanks for this diſtinguiſhing teſtimony of their approbation.

"But leſt ſome unlucky event ſhould happen unfavourable to my reputation, I beg it may be

That [there] be one Comm[iſſ]ary-General of ſtores and proviſions.

That his pay be *Eighty Dollars* per month.

That there be one Quarter-Maſter-General [for th]e Grand Army, and one Deputy under him [for th]e ſeparate Army.

[Th]at the pay of the Quarter-Maſter-General [be E]ighty *Dollars* per month, and that of the De[puty] *Forty Dollars* per month.

[Th]at there be one Pay-Maſter-General, and [a De]puty under him for the army in a ſeparate [depar]tment; that the pay for the Pay-Maſter-[Gen]eral himſelf be *One Hundred Dollars* per month, [and f]or the Deputy Pay-Maſter under him *Fifty [Do]llars* per month.

That there be one Chief Engineer at the Grand Army, and that his pay be *Sixty Dollars* per month.

That two Aſſiſtants be employed under him, and that the pay of each of them be *Twenty Dollars* per month.

That there be one Chief Engineer for the Army in a ſeparate department, and two Aſſiſtants under him; that the pay of the Chief Engineer be *Sixty Dollars* per month, and the pay of the Aſſiſtants each *Twenty Dollars* per month.

That there be three Aids-de-Camp; and that their pay be *Thirty-three Dollars* per month each.

That there be a Secretary to the Major-General acting in a ſeparate department; and that his pay be *Thirty-three Dollars* per month.

That there be a Commiſſary of the Muſters.

JUNE 17, 1775.

The Committee appointed to draught a Commiſſion to the General, reported the ſame, which being read by paragraphs and debated, was agreed to as follows:

IN CONGRESS.

THE DELEGATES of the UNITED COLONIES of *New-Hampſhire, Maſſachuſetts-Bay, Rhode-Iſland, Connecticut, New-York, New-Jerſey, Pennſylvania*, the Counties of *New-Caſtle, Kent* and *Suſſex* on *Delaware, Maryland, Virginia, North-Carolina*, and *South-Carolina.*

To GEORGE WASHINGTON, ESQUIRE.

WE repoſing eſpecial truſt and confidence in your patriotiſm, valour, conduct and fidelity, do by theſe preſents conſtitute and appoint you, to be General and Commander in Chief, of the army

W-ENGLAND CHRONICLE
OR, THE
ESSEX GAZETTE.

VOL. VIII. NUMB. 389.

THURSDAY, *January* 4, to THURSDAY, *January* 11, 1776

RIDGE: Printed by SAMUEL and EBENEZER HALL, at their Office in Stoughton-Hall, HARVARD-COLLEG

Officers, non-commissioned Offi and Soldiers, belonging to any of the Corps of the Army of the United Co the immediate Command of his Ex neral WASHINGTON, who are absent gh, Recruiting, or by Permission of nding Officers, are to join their re ments by the first Day of February Officer neglects to pay due Obe is Order, he will be immediately nd any non-commissioned Officers, ffending therein, will be tried and Deserters.

is EXCELLENCY's Command,
TIO GATES, Adjutant-General.
s at Cambridge. *Jan.* 11, 1776.

NK OF LINNEN LOST.

End of May last, a TRUNK, con Table Cloths, Napkins, Towels, Cases, and sundry other Articles, om Boston, in a Vessel to Marble e taken away by some Person un-

has been made till now, because it have been put (by Mistake) on board bound for London, but it is now cer- s.

Goods brought for several People ssel, some of which went to the ater, and 'tis probable this Trunk Way.

possess of it, will send Word to the ill be kindly received, but if it is Design to defraud him, and any Information, that the Trunk may be recovered and the Thief ce, they shall receive a Reward of ARS, with Thanks.

SEPH BARRELL.

B
of the Linnen was mark't I A.

emembered by every Gentleman in the room, hat I this day declare with the utmost sincerity, I do not think myself equal to the command I am honoured with.

"As to pay, Sir, I beg leave to assure the Congress, that as no pecuniary consideration could have tempted me to accept this arduous employment, at the expence of my domestic ease and happiness, I do not wish to make any profit from it. I will keep an exact account of my expences.— Those I doubt not they will discharge, and that is all I desire."

Resolved, That a Committee be appointed to draught a Commission and Instructions for the General.

The persons chosen to compose the Committee were Mr. *Lee*, Mr. *E. Rutledge* and Mr. *J. Adams*.

The Congress resumed the consideration of the report from the Committee of the whole, and came to the following resolutions:

Resolved, That two Major-Generals be appointed for the American Army.

That the pay of each of the Major-Generals be *One Hundred* and *Sixty-six Dollars* per month.

That when any of these act in a separate department, he be allowed for his pay and expences *Three Hundred* and *Thirty-two Dollars* per month.

That there be eight Brigadiers-General.

That the pay of each of the Brigadiers-General be *One Hundred* and *Twenty five Dollars* per month.

That there be one Adjutant-General.

That his pay be *One Hundred* and *Twenty five Dollars* per month.

That there be one Commissary-General of stores and provisions.

That his pay be *Eighty Dollars* per month.

That there be one Quarter-Master-General for the Grand Army, and one Deputy under him for the separate Army.

That the pay of the Quarter-Master-General be *Eighty Dollars* per month, and that of the Deputy *Forty Dollars* per month.

of the United Colonies, and of all the forces ne raised or to be raised by them, and of all othe who shall voluntarily offer their service, and jo the said army for the defence of American libe ty, and for repelling every hostile invasion thereo And you are hereby vested with full power an authority to act as you shall think for the goo and welfare of the service.

And we do hereby strictly charge and requir all officers and soldiers under your command, t be obedient to your orders, and diligent in th exercise of their several duties.

And we do also enjoin and require you, to b careful in executing the great trust reposed in you, by causing strict discipline and order to be observ ed in the army, and that the soldiers be duly exercised and provided with all convenient necessaries.

And you are to regulate your conduct in every respect by the rules and discipline of war (as herewith given you) and punctually to observe and follow such orders and directions from time to time, as you shall receive from this or a future Congress of these United Colonies or Committee of Congress.

This Commission to continue in force, until revoked by this or a future Congress.

By order of the Congress.

Ordered, That the same be fairly transcribed, signed by the President, attested by the Secretary, and delivered to the General.

Resolved unanimously, Whereas the Delegates of all the Colonies from Nova Scotia to Georgia, in Congress assembled, have unanimously chosen *GEORGE WASHINGTON*, Esquire, to be General and Commander in Chief of such forces as are or shall be raised for the maintenance and preservation of American Liberty; this Congress doth now declare, that they will maintain and assist him, and adhere to him the said *George Washington* with their lives and fortunes in the same *rn, for the pay he gives them : loy'd that old mungy Jacobite ary Johnson, alias the Rambler, 's in a Pamphlet entitled, Tax- A piece full of sophistical guib- edantick bombast language. I answer to it; and am pleased to authors of the Monthly Review, (March) have cut him down in u ever see that periodical work , it will give you pleasure to read on the subject. If we may be- hings with you threaten war; in the standard of liberty had been m, and that it was repaired to by etermined to fight or die; should worsted in any general action, of is the greatest probability, what ake in England? And then let the . If the troops beat you, you can ey gain five battles and lose but them, so great is the disadvantage agage, besides what arises from the aate, and fighting against those who persuaded they fight* pro Aris et *n their own ground.*

Ambassador at the Hague applied id their subjects supplying the Ame- and ammunition. The states pub- under the penalty of a 1000 Guil- £ 90 Sterling: I leave you to com- ur leisure, and judge if where the are so great as a voyage of that s not worth the merchants while to

TON, Generalissimo of all the Forces raised, and to be raised in the Confederated Colonies of America.

May it please your Excellency,

AT a time when the most loyal of his Majesty's subjects, from a regard to the laws and constitution, by which he sits on the throne, feel themselves reduced to the unhappy necessity of taking up arms, to defend their dearest rights and privileges; while we deplore the calamities of this divided Empire, we rejoice in the appointment of a Gentleman, from whose abilities and virtue, we are taught to expect both security and peace.

Confiding in you, Sir, and in the worthy Generals, immediately under your command, we have the most flattering hopes of success, in the glorious struggle for American Liberty, and the fullest assurances that whenever this important contest shall be decided, by that fondest wish of each American soul, an accommodation with our Mother Country, you will cheerfully resign the important Deposit, committed into your hands, and re-assume the Character of our worthiest Citizen.

By Order,

P. V. B. LIVINGSTON, President.

June 26th, 1775.

His EXCELLENCY's Answer.

Gentlemen,

AT the same time that with you, I deplore the unhappy necessity of such an appointment, as that with which I am now honoured, I cannot but feel sentiments of the highest gratitude, for this affecting instance of distinction and regard.

The following Paragraph is inserted just as we recei

"We hear from Reading, that a Lad, about twelve climbed a Tree in order to catch a Squirrel, and he fell d the Top, about 35 Feet, amongst sharp Stones, and c Scalp all round to his Ears, so that it turned down o Side of his Neck, and fractured 3 of his Ribs: The on his Scalp, and sewed it on, and he told me he was Way of recovering, as he thought."

nocent in one , and for the y, distress and ose not your , and fellow

he power of tholic neigh- point of tax- fect humilia- prize would our national our liberties, emen. We ill somewhat you should vill you then

assist you in your determination on that point, it is own'd by our Ambassador at this place that a Dutch ship is lately got into Virginia where it has landed 400 Barrels Powder, and 1400 stands of arms. France was apply'd to, to forbid its subjects furnishing you with any military stores —— France it is well known could easily have crushed all such assistance by an express prohibition; but France knows better than to do it and therefore only tells its subjects, if they do it, it is entirely at their own risque, which is plainly saying, If you will venture you may. *Spain when applied to, roundly refused to give any hindrance to her subjects supplying you; and I dare say from present appearances will soon act openly against England. An article lately appeared in the English papers, that a Prussian ship sailed from Stettin to some part of America with 30 field pieces, a good store of Powder, Ball and small arms, and 6 or 7 Prussian Generals,*

May your warmest wishes be realized in the success of America, at this important and interesting period; and be assured, that every exertion of my worthy colleagues and myself, will be equally extended to the re-establishment of peace and harmony, between the Mother Country and these Colonies:—As to the fatal but necessary operations of War——————when we assumed the Soldier, we did not lay aside the Citizen, and we shall most sincerely rejoice with you, in that happy hour, when the establishment of American Liberty, on the most firm and solid foundations, shall enable us to return to our private stations, in the bosom of a free, peaceful, and happy Country.

G. WASHINGTON.

June 29th, 1775.

NEW-YORK, June 29.

On Tuesday General Wooster, with the advanced body of the Connecticut forces, arrived in the neighbourhood of this tended to.

We would not presume to prescribe to your Excellency, but supposing you would choose to be informed of the general Character of the Soldiers who compose this Army, beg Leave to represent, that the greatest Part of them have not before seen Service. And although naturally brave, and of good Understanding, yet for Want of Experience in military Life, have but little Knowledge of divers Things most essential to the Preservation of Health, and even of Life. The Youth in the Army are not possessed of the absolute Necessity of Cleanliness in their Dress, and Lodging, continual Exercise, and strict Temperance, to preserve them from Diseases frequently prevailing in Camps; especially among those, who, from their Childhood, have been used to a laborious Life.

We beg Leave to assure you, that this

...by private and public Distress.

GEO. WASHINGTON.

To the Honourable CHARLES LEE, Esq; Major-General of the Continental Army.

SIR,

THE Congress of the Massachusetts Colony, possessed of the fullest Evidence of your Attachment to the Rights of Mankind, and Regard to the Distresses which America in general, and this Colony in particular, are involved in, by the impolitic, wicked and tyrannic System, adopted by Administration, and pursued with relentless and savage Fury, do, with Pleasure, embrace this Opportunity to express the great Satisfaction and Gratitude they feel on your Appointment as a Major-General in the American Army.

We sincerely congratulate you on your safe Arrival here, and wish you all possible Happiness and Success in the Execution of so important a Trust. We admire and re-

...of the Enemy, including June 29. 1775.

Return of the Killed at C... an order

Commission Officers
Serjeants ---
Corporals
Rank and File ...

Total of killed
Wounded

Total of killed and w...

On Thursday, June 15th ... plexy, in the 68th Year of ... tuous Consort of AARON V... were happily united the ... pent Mistress, sincere Frie... Christian.-----Her Friends ... they rejoice in the Reason th... a World of Misery and Tro... --Her Remains were inter... Mark of Respect, and in a ... commended by the Honorabl...

STOLEN or lost, ... of June, a Pocket-Book, con... Bills, and some Notes of Han... said Bills and Notes, and deliv... Printers of this Paper, shall ... necessary Charges paid by

Cambridge, July 5, 17...

TO B...

A handsome new fal... ness. Inquire of Mr. F...

...resented to his Excellency ...or-General Lee.

...ency

...IGTON, Esq; *...Chief of the Con-...*

...ellency,

...e Massachusetts ...ith every Senti-...pect, beg Leave ...r safe Arrival: ...able Happiness ...n of the impor-... Station. While ...that Attention to the public ...sted in your Appointment, we ...re that disinterested Virtue, ...shed Patriotism, which alone ...from those Enjoyments of do-... which a sublime and manly ...with a most affluent Fortune, ...hazard your Life, and to en-...gues of War, in the Defence ...of Mankind, and the Good ...try.

...le Zeal for the common Cause ...and Compassion for the Dis-... Colony, exhibited by the great ...e in your Journey hither, fully ...niversal Satisfaction we have, ..., observed on this Occasion; ...ising Presages that the great ...formed from your personal ...d military Abilities, are well

...pointment, ... warmest Acknowledgments, and will ever be retained in grateful Remembrance.

In exchanging the Enjoyments of domestic Life for the Duties of my present honourable, but arduous Station, I only emulate the Virtue and publick Spirit of the whole Province of Massachusetts-Bay, which with a Firmness, and Patriotism without Example in modern History, has sacrificed all the Comforts of social and political Life, in Support of the Rights of Mankind, and the Welfare of our common Country. My highest Ambition is to be the happy Instrument of vindicating those Rights, and to see this devoted Province again restored to Peace, Liberty and Safety.

The short Space of Time which has elapsed since my Arrival does not permit me to decide upon the State of the Army. The Course of human Affairs forbids an Expectation, that Troops formed under such Circumstances, should at once possess the Order, Regularity and Discipline of Veterans — Whatever Deficiencies there may be, will I doubt not, soon be made up by the Activity and Zeal of the Officers, and the Docility and Obedience of the Men. These Qualities united with their native Bravery and Spirit will afford a happy Presage of Success, and put a final Period to those Distresses which now overwhelm this once happy Country.

I most sincerely thank you, Gentlemen,

...bation of your own Conscience, and eternal Happiness hereafter.

His Honour's Answer.

To the Gentlemen of the Provincial Congress of Massachusetts.

Gentlemen,

NOTHING can be so flattering to me as the good Opinion and Approbation of the Delegates of a free and uncorrupt People. I was educated in the highest Reverence for the Rights of Mankind, and have acquired by a long Acquaintance a most particular Regard for the People of America. You may depend therefore, Gentlemen, on my Zeal and Integrity.——I can promise you nothing from my Abilities. God Almighty grant us Success equal to the Ri...

from ... Treasurer, for what Money he had by him, belonging to the Province, and received from him 1500 £. which was safely conveyed to Exeter.

NEW-ENGLAND CHRONICLE (CAMBRIDGE, MA)

July 6, 1775

Washington's travel from Philadelphia to Cambridge to assume command of the Continental Army is documented in this issue. On July 2, he reached the army's headquarters at Cambridge, where this newspaper was printed.

...Discipline already established as may be agreeable to your The Hurry with which it

Duties of my Station; they are so complicated, and extended, that I shall need the Assistance of every good Man, and Lover

...heavy Fire upon the Town of Roxbury both from their Cannon and Mortars. They set one House on Fire, which was consumed; but did little other Damage.

Four of the Enemy's Horses strayed from Charlestown, on

REPORTING THE BATTLE OF GREAT BRIDGE AND BURNING OF NORFOLK

By John W. Hall

In 1775, few cities could claim the strategic significance of Norfolk. Virginia's largest and wealthiest city, it commanded one of the finest anchorages on the eastern seaboard and riverine access to the interior of the colony. It was also a Loyalist stronghold to which Tories from across the colony fled in the autumn of 1775. Among these was the Royal Governor John Murray, better know as Lord Dunmore and reviled throughout the region for offering freedom to slaves who would take up arms against their masters. This "cruel policy" horrified Virginians, who disingenuously accused Dunmore of exploiting African Americans. Those who answered Dunmore's call saw things in a different light, as they formed the Royal Ethiopian Regiment and embroidered "Liberty to Slaves" on their uniforms. Nevertheless, not enough Tories—black or white—responded to Dunmore's call to arms, leaving Norfolk ripe for Patriot picking.

Surrounded by water or low ground on nearly every side, Norfolk was most vulnerable from the south, where a single highway ran through the Great Dismal Swamp and on to Suffolk. Approximately nine miles south of Norfolk, the road crossed the Elizabeth River at the village of Great Bridge, incongruously named for the simple wooden structure that spanned this waterway. Realizing its importance, both the British and the Americans sent forces to defend the crossing. In mid-November, the British constructed a paltry stockade (Fort Murray) on the eastern bank; by month's end, Lieutenant Colonel Charles Scott and 215 men of the 2nd Virginia Regiment occupied the town on the opposite shore. On December 2, Colonel William Woodford arrived with the remainder of the regiment. Although he commanded seven hundred "shirtmen" (so-called because of their hunting shirts), Woodford did not realize that he faced fewer than one hundred British defenders and hesitated to await the arrival of artillery.

Lord Dunmore better appreciated the vulnerability of his little post, however, and sent reinforcements to mount a preemptive attack on the morning of December 9. Unfortunately for the British, little went according to plan. Two companies of the Ethiopian Regiment that were to conduct a feint downstream never received their orders. Meanwhile, the British tactical commander, Captain Samuel Leslie, assumed he outnumbered the Americans about 350 to three hundred when reinforcements had swollen Woodford's ranks to nearly nine hundred men. Mitigating this disparity was the geography of Great Bridge, which lay astride a narrow causeway scarcely wider than the road itself. While this prevented the Americans from bringing their superior numbers to bear, it confined attackers to a predictable, exposed approach.

The ensuing battle was one of few that conformed to subsequent American mythology about the superiority of the American rifleman over his red-coated antagonist. Although Leslie's light infantry replanked the bridge and secured its far side without being detected, the grenadiers commenced their attack just after Patriot drummers beat reveille. Unable to either surprise the Americans or envelop them, the grenadier commander, Captain Charles Fordyce, committed his men to a frontal assault across 150 yards of a narrow causeway against prepared defensive works. After withstanding a withering fire and losing perhaps thirty men (including Captain Fordyce), the British fell back to their bridgehead. There, they traded long-range shots with the Americans, eventually losing this contest to Virginia's Culpepper Minutemen, who wielded their Pennsylvania long rifles with deadly accuracy. With half of his 120 regulars dead, wounded, or captured, Captain Leslie abandoned not merely the attack, but also Fort Murray; he spiked his guns and retired to Norfolk. In his after-action report (reproduced in the *New-England Chronicle* of January 11, 1776), Woodford gloated that he had won "a second Bunker's-hill affair" in which American amateurs fighting from prepared positions had once again bested His Majesty's regulars.

But whereas the British continued to occupy Boston for nine months following the Battle of Bunker Hill, the much smaller fight at Great Bridge had more immediate consequences. Realizing that Norfolk was indefensible, Dunmore immediately withdrew his forces and Norfolk's Loyalist population to ships in Hampton Roads. When the Americans denied Dunmore access to provisions, he threatened to bombard the city—and did so New Year's Day. Landing parties also set fire to port facilities that sheltered snipers, which the Patriots used as a pretext to burn much of the hated city to the ground. American commanders omitted this fact in their reports (see the *New-England Chronicle*, February 1, 1776), creating the impression that the British had burned the city in a fit of vengeance. When Patriot forces withdrew in February, they razed whatever remained of the town.

The loss of Norfolk—a direct consequence of the Patriot victory at Great Bridge—was a serious blow to the British. Dunmore not only lost a precious port and bastion of Loyalist support, but also handed the Patriots one of the most significant propaganda victories of the war. Writing under the pseudonym "An American" in the *Virginia Gazette* (reprinted in the *New-England Chronicle*, February 1, 1776), Patrick Henry used the destruction of Norfolk to argue for independence. Outraged by these latest "specimens of British cruelty" and simultaneously moved by Thomas Paine's *Common Sense*, most Americans agreed.

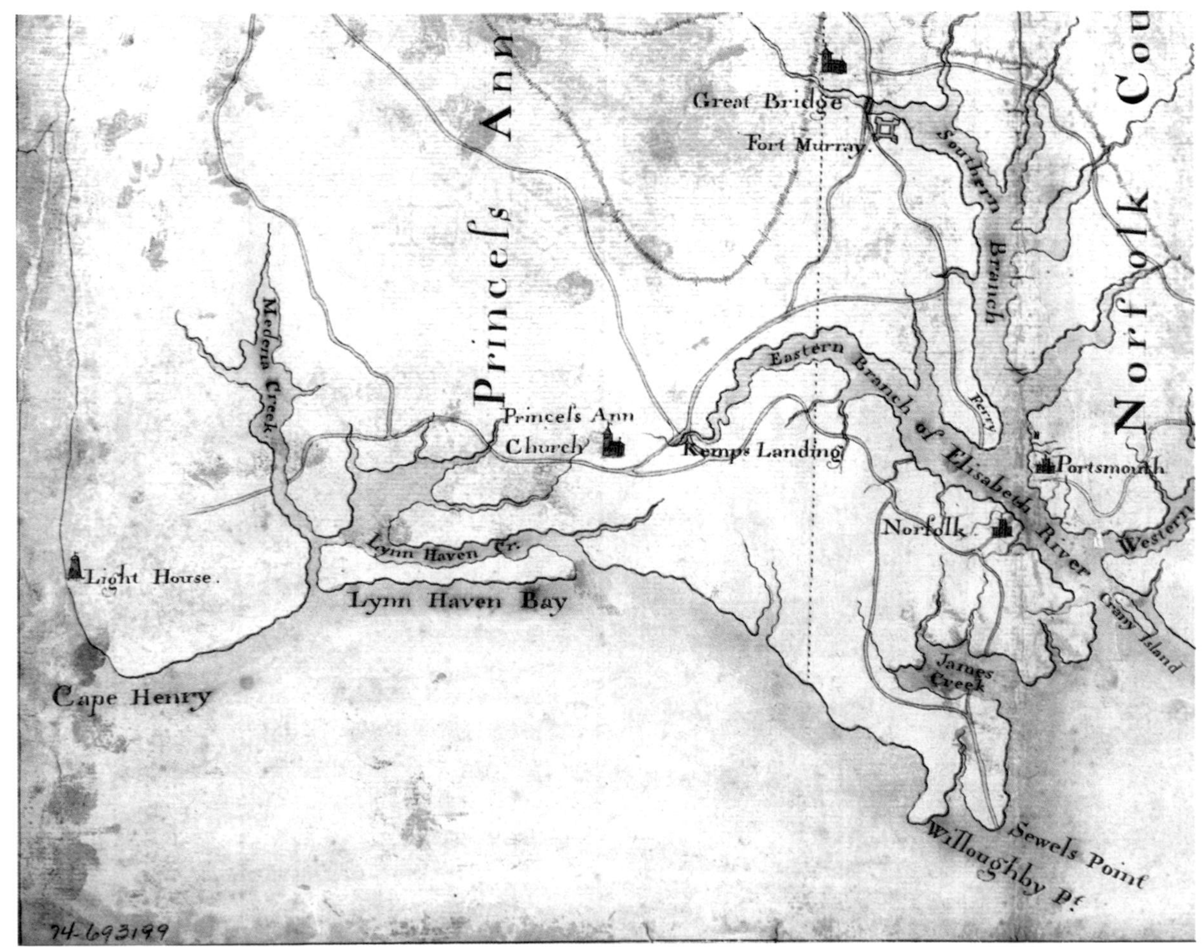

Eastern Virginia
Library of Congress

Detail of a 1770s map of eastern Virginia, oriented with north to the bottom and south to the top.

NEW-ENGLAND CHRONICLE (CAMBRIDGE, MA)

January 11, 1776

In his after-action report, Col. William Woodford gloated that he had won "a second Bunker's-hill affair" in which American amateurs fighting from prepared positions had once again bested His Majesty's regulars. But whereas the British continued to occupy Boston for nine months following the Battle of Bunker Hill, the much smaller fight at Great Bridge had more immediate consequences.

General Convention.

"A ſervant belonging to Major Marſhall, who deſerted the other night from Col. Scott's

and Capt. Fordyce, of the grenadiers, led the van with his company, who, for his coolneſs and bravery, deſerved a better fate, as well as the brave fellows who fell with him, who behaved like heroes. They marched up to our breaſt-work with fixed bayonets, and perhaps a hotter fire never happened, or a greater carnage, for the number of troops. None of the blacks, &c. in the rear with Capt. Leſlie, advanced farther than the bridge. I have the pleaſure to inform you, that the victory was complete, and that moſt of the dead and wounded, with two pieces of cannon, were carried off under cover of their guns from the fort. We buried 12, beſides the Captain (him with all military honours due to his rank) and have priſoners Lieut. Batut and 16 privates, all wounded; 35 ſtands of arms and accoutrements, 3 officers fuſees, powder, ball and cartridges, with ſundry other things, have likewiſe fallen into our hands. This was a ſecond Bunker's-hill affair, in miniature, with this difference, that we kept our poſt, and had only one man wounded in the hand."

On Tueſday laſt, a large ſchooner from the Weſt-Indies bound for Norfolk, was taken and bro't into Hampton by our men ſtationed there. She was laden with rum and ſugar, and had 2,700 dollars on board, for the uſe of our enemies.

Lord Dunmore, we hear, ſwears moſt furiouſly, that he will bombard Norfolk, ſhould the *ſhirt men* come into it. They moſt certainly will, ſo that we need not be amazed to hear ſoon, of that place's being laid in aſhes.

NEW-YORK, January 4.

Dear Sir,

"I wrote you the 21ſt ult. which make no

... that place but 14 days ago, that 7000 French troops, and nine ſail of the line were arrived there; that two veſſels belonging to North-America were at that place, but not having any credentials from the Congreſs, the inhabitants refuſed to trade with them; and that the Congreſs was in high eſteem there.

We hear, that yeſterday came to town, a gentleman from Canada, who has brought letters from thence to ſeveral gentlemen in town, ſignifying, that on the 5th ult. Gen. Montgomery with his army were on the heights of Abraham, that he had taken into pay 2500 Canadians, that his army conſiſted of near 5000 men, and that he had inveſted the city of Quebec on every ſide.

By the lateſt Accounts from Williamſburgh, in Virginia, we learn, That Lord Dunmore intends ſhortly for the Weſt-Indies, with his Cargo of Slaves, to make the moſt of them before his Departure for England; as by Letters lately received, it is affirmed, that he would be ſpeedily recalled, his Conduct in Virginia being much cenſured by the Miniſtry.—That 6 Men had deſerted from the Otter Man of War; who, when they were aſked, what induced them to leave Dunmore? Anſwered, *Hungry Bellies, naked Backs, and no Fuel*; *beſides, in other Reſpects, the moſt cruel and inhuman Treatment*.—That Lord Dunmore had requeſted an Exchange of Priſoners; and that the King's Soldiers killed and wounded in the Battle amounted to 102.

CAMBRIDGE, January 11.

Laſt Monday evening Major Knowlton was diſpatched with 100 *men, to make an incurſion into Charleſtown. He croſſed the Mill Dam, which lays between Cobble Hill and Bunker's Hill, about nine o'clock, and immediately proceeded down the ſtreet on the weſterly ſide of Bunker's-Hill; a part of the men, under the command of Capt. Kyes, at the ſame time were ordered to take poſt on the Eaſt ſide of the ſtreet, juſt under the hill, in order to intercept any perſons who might eſcape from the houſes in the ſtreet, ſome of which were occupied by the enemy. Theſe houſes, which were a little without the compact part of the town, the enemy ſuffered to remain unburnt in June laſt, for their own conveniencé.—They were now ſurrounded and ſet fire to by our men. In one of them they found ſix ſoldiers and one woman, all of whom, except one refractory fellow, who was killed, were brought off. In another of the houſes, according to the information of the priſoners, ...*

... this houſe, in order to borrow ſ... nothing, juſt before our men arrived; but ſeeing no light, and not being able to get into that part of the houſe where ...

THIS DAY IS ... by S. and E. ... and I. THO... North-...

By SAMUEL ...

LEFT on ... longing to the F... 4th inſtant, a fi... name Moſes Pe... leave it at Meſſ... two dollars.— ... in the afternoon

FOUND, ... quire of the P. ...

The whole ... conſiſting of a ... every utenſil fo... be ſold for the ...

To be ...

Good RA... ſweet OYL; ... particularize.

A neat ho... about an acre ... vard college, on ... pleaſantly ſituat... a very convenie... fruit trees, viz. ... particulars, inq...

STOLEN ... ſcriber, a ſilver ... 2120, with a c... ever will bring ... houſe, ſhall rec... N. B. Wat... take particular ... brought them f...

NOTICE ... of LEVI WILL... Maſſachuſetts ... in ſaid Lancaſte... company affairs ... fore all perſons ... payment to me ... Mrs Katharine ... of the ſaid Levi ... eſtate may be in... Lancaſter, D...

A FARM ... with a wood lot ... &c. Any perſo... a purchaſer, pro... printers.—

... demands on the ... Beverly, deceaſe... MIN JONES ...

WILLIAMSBURG, January 5.

A letter from Cols. Howe and Woodford, to the Hon. the President of the Convention, dated Norfolk, 10 o'clock at night, January 1, 1776.

"BEtween 3 and 4 o'clock a severe cannonade began from all the shipping, under cover of which they landed small parties, and set fire to the houses on the wharves. The wind favoured their design, and we believe the flames will become general. In the confusion which they supposed would ensue, they frequently attempted to land; but this, by the bravery of our officers and men, we have hitherto prevented, with only a few men wounded on our side, and we persuade ourselves with a good deal of loss on theirs. Their efforts, and our opposition, still continue. We have stationed ourselves in such a manner as will, we believe, render every thing but burning the houses ineffectual. We wait with impatience your farther orders, and are respectfully, &c.

Extract of a letter from Col. Howe, to the President of the Convention, January 2.

"The burning of the town has made several avenues, which yesterday they had not, so that they may now fire with greater effect. The tide is now rising, and we expect at high water another cannonade. I have only to wish it may be as ineffectual as the last; for we have not one man killed, and but a few wounded. I cannot enter into the melancholy consideration of the women and children running through a crowd of shot to get out of the town, some of them with children at their breast. A few have, I hear, been killed. Does it not call for vengeance, both from God and man! It is but justice to inform you, that I had the pleasure to find every officer ready to execute orders at a moment's warning, and that the men behaved with steadiness and spirit. Col. Stevens went down at my command, and headed some men near the water, where he engaged a party who had landed, with the spirit and conduct of a good officer. Of my friend Colonel Woodford, it is almost needless to speak; but I cannot avoid expressing, that I received from him every assistance which conduct and spirit could give me."

Extract of a letter from Col. Elliott, to Col. Patrick Henry, dated Hampton, January 5, 1776.

"Inclosed you have the copy of a letter from Col. Woodford to me, dated 3 o'clock yesterday, since which a snow and two small vessels have gone up to Norfolk. She appeared to have a great many men on board, but was not a vessel of

Great-Bridge, with 17 To[ries], and 11 negroes, arrived in town, under [a strong] guard, from Norfolk. The wounded soldiers are sent to the hospital, most of the tories and negroes lodged in the publick jail, and Lieut B[a]tu[t], with a few others, admitted on their parole.

Yesterday afternoon an express arrived from

From the Virginia Gazette, January 5.

I HOPE our countrymen will not be at all dispirited at the destruction of Norfolk, but rather rejoice that half the mischief our enemies can do us is done already. They have destroyed one of the first towns in America, and the only one (except 2 or 3) in Virginia, which carried on any thing like a trade. We are only sharing part of the sufferings of our American brethren, and can now glory in having received one of the keenest strokes of the enemy, without flinching. They have done their work, and to no other purpose than to harden our soldiers, and learn them to bear, without dismay, all the most formidable operations of a war carried on by a powerful and cruel enemy; to no other purpose than to give the world specimens of British cruelty, and American fortitude, unless it be to force us to lay aside that childish fondness for Britain, and that foolish tame dependence on her. We had borne so long with the oppression of an ungenerous restriction of our trade, of a restriction, in some instances, which seemed calculated merely as badges of our subjection, and had been contented so long with

without the assistance of Roman Catholicks and Indians, and endeavouring to raise amongst us a domestick enemy? Was this like a brave and generous nation! If they were lost to all the feelings of Britons, for men contending for the support of the British constitution, if they were

NEW-ENGLAND CHRONICLE (CAMBRIDGE, MA)

February 1, 1776

Landing parties also set fire to port facilities that sheltered snipers, which the Patriots used as a pretext to burn much of the hated city to the ground. American commanders omitted this fact in their reports, creating the impression that the British had burned the city in a fit of vengeance. When Patriot forces withdrew in February, they razed whatever remained of the town.

REPORTING THE

INVASION OF CANADA

By Tabitha Marshall

In early September 1775, Benedict Arnold and about 1,100 American soldiers marched out of Cambridge, Massachusetts. Sent by General Washington, their objective was to capture Quebec City as part of a two-pronged attack aimed at wresting control of the colony of Quebec (or "Canada") from the British. The other "arm"—about two thousand men led by Richard Montgomery—had left Ticonderoga in late August, bound for Montreal. After taking the forts of Chambly and St. John's, Montgomery and his men reached Montreal; the British fled before their advance, and the Americans entered the town on November 12. After fortifying Montreal, Montgomery and three hundred of his men proceeded to Quebec to join Arnold and his troops. However, the campaign against Quebec would not meet with the same success.

The failure of the Battle of Quebec and the march on Canada was a serious setback for the American cause, ensuring that Canada would remain a British stronghold throughout the war.

In the first place, Benedict Arnold had lost many of his men en route to Quebec, an arduous journey that took them through the forests and swamps of northern New England. Clothes torn and boots worn out from the hard march, the men suffered from exposure, sickness, and dwindling provisions; some were even forced to eat their dogs. By the time Arnold arrived at Quebec, he had only about six hundred men left; many had died from starvation, exposure, or disease, and about three hundred deserted. Given their reduced strength, Arnold decided to withdraw to Pointe-aux-Trembles to await the arrival of Montgomery in early December. The Americans had no heavy artillery, nor were they able to construct any siege lines, owing to the ground being frozen solid.

The British defenders were only slightly better off. There were only seventy British regular troops in Quebec and about 1,200 defenders in total. There was also some doubt concerning the loyalty of the local French-speaking inhabitants, some of whom resented their new British governors. Indeed, revolutionary leaders were counting on support from the local population (see letter from Arnold, November 1775, published in the *New-England Chronicle*, December 28, 1775). However, while some of the Canadiens aided the revolutionary army, others supported the British defenders, and many more remained neutral. This was partly because the British commander, General Carleton, had supported the passage of the Quebec Act of 1774, which guaranteed the right of the inhabitants to practice Catholicism.

In contrast to the optimistic tone of the letter written December 6 (published January 11, 1776, in the *New-England Chronicle*), the revolutionaries under Arnold and Montgomery were not in a strong position. However, they decided to launch an attack in late December, due in part to concern that many of their men would leave—a significant number had only enlisted until the end of the year. Thus, Arnold and Montgomery launched their attack during a snowstorm on December 31, 1775, hoping the weather conditions would provide some cover for their men. The attack was a failure: British fire repulsed the Americans, killing about fifty men, including Montgomery, and wounding Arnold and more than thirty others, while more than four hundred were taken prisoner. Despite this setback, the Americans remained encamped outside of Quebec for months, suffering from serious food shortages and outbreaks of smallpox and other diseases.

As the months passed, the chances of victory decreased. When spring arrived, the ice that had blocked the St. Lawrence River started to melt; this opened the way for reinforcements from Britain. On May 6, 1776, British ships arrived at Quebec, and the Americans were forced to withdraw. With the British in pursuit, they retreated along the St. Lawrence and Richelieu rivers until they reached Crown Point at the southern tip of Lake Champlain, where they began to build a fleet. The British began similar construction at the northern end of the lake. On October 11, 1776, the two fleets met in action in the Battle of Valcour Island. The American fleet suffered significant damage, and Arnold decided to retreat to Fort Ticonderoga farther south. The British did not follow but withdrew to Canada due to the approach of winter. Had Carleton and the British forces continued their pursuit, the outcome of the war may have been very different. As it was, the failure of the Battle of Quebec and the march on Canada was a serious setback for the American cause; not only was it their first significant military defeat, but it also ensured that Canada would remain a British stronghold throughout the war. Indeed, no significant attempts were made to invade Canada again until the War of 1812. The fate of the Revolution would be decided farther south.

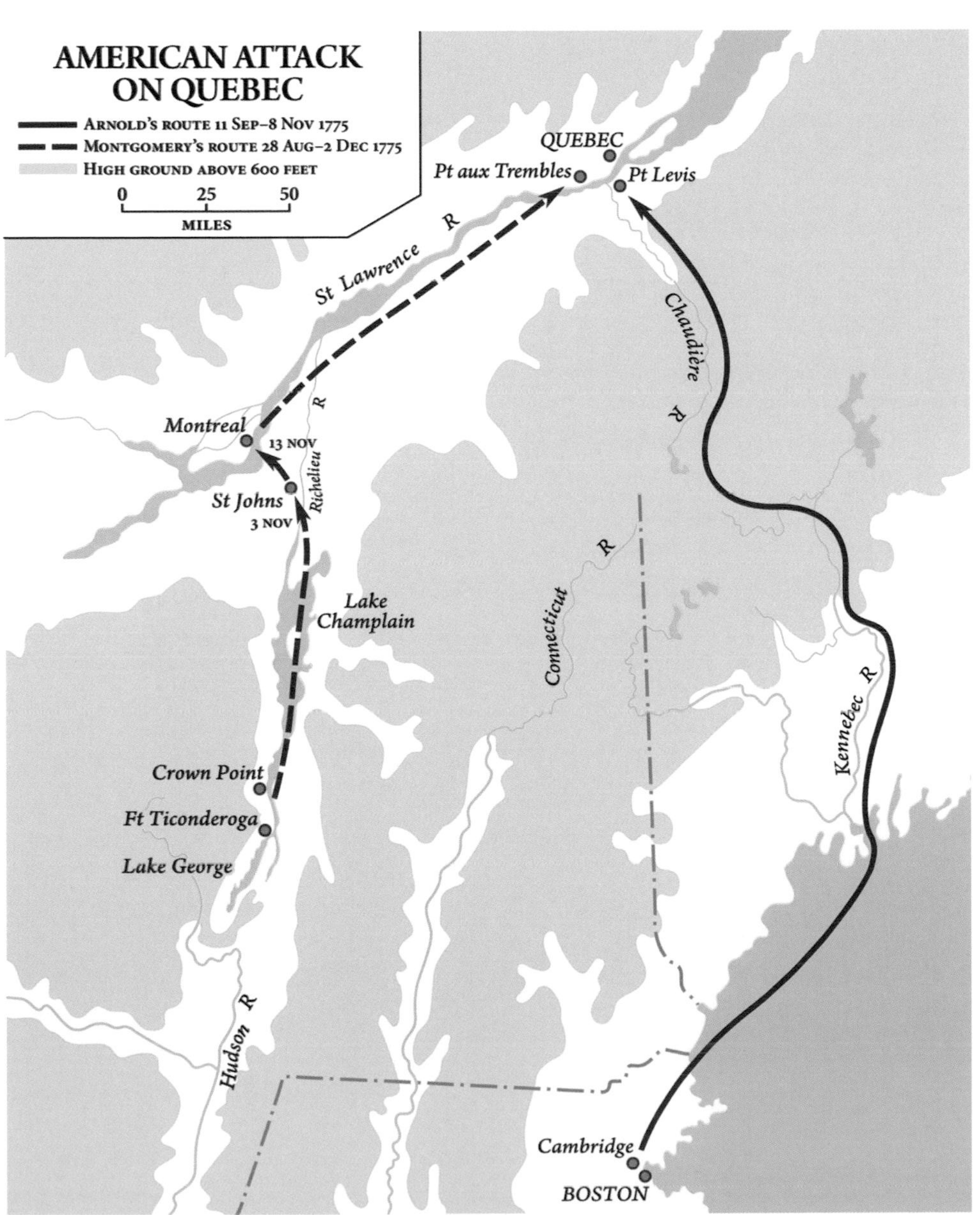

American Attack on Quebec
United States Army Center of Military History

Map showing the routes taken by the Benedict Arnold and Richard Montgomery expeditions into Quebec.

NUMB. 387.

NEW-ENGLAND CHRONICLE (CAMBRIDGE, MA)

December 28, 1775

In late 1775 and early 1776, despite frequent reports about the Continental Army's attack on Quebec, newspapers rarely featured details of Benedict Arnold's arduous expedition. A few particulars emerged in December 1775 when the Continental Congress ordered a series of letters by Montgomery, Schuyler, and Arnold to be published. At least a half-dozen newspapers from Philadelphia to Newburyport published the letters, including the December 28, 1775, *New-England Chronicle*. In the front page printing of the letters, Arnold hints at the exhausting terrain while adding some spin about the army's happy and healthy condition.

Newbury-Port, on Friday, the week before last, a pair of SADDLE BAGS, almost new, very large, with a linen lining.--Whoever has found the same, and will send them to Col. Joseph Gerrish's of Byfield, or to the Printers hereof, shall be entitled to one dollar, paid by NATH. PEIRCE.

Jamaica Rum, Sugar, and English Goods, to be sold cheap. Apply to the red shop next to the Blue Anchor Tavern in Cambridge.

STOLEN from me the subscriber, on Saturday evening, the 16th inst. a brownish grey Horse, about 14 hands high, paces and trots, a small white spot in his forehead, one hind foot white, his right hind foot something broke. Whoever will take up said horse, and convey him to the subscriber in Attleborough, shall be handsomely rewarded, and all necessary charges paid by LEVI MAXCY. Dec. 16, 1775.

STOLEN, on Monday evening last, from the door of Mr. Vose, innholder in Milton, a redish Mare, whitish mane and tail, about 8 years old, natural pacer, a white strip in her forehead, carries a high dock, with her head something low, about 13 hands and half high, had on a redish saddle and housing, and a poor bridle. Whoever takes up said mare shall have two dollars reward upon conveying her to my dwelling-house in Taunton, and all necessary charges paid by GEORGE REED.

N. B. Two old shirts and an old grey coat were fastened on the saddle with 2 garters. Cambridge, 18th Dec. 1775.

PHILADELPHIA, December 15.

The following LETTERS are published by order of the Hon. Continental Congress.

" My dear General, Montreal, Nov. 17

" With great pleasure I transmit you a letter from Col. Arnold for Gen. Washington, together with the copy of his letter to me. Col. Easton has six guns mounted on shore, three twelve pounders, one nine ditto, and two sixes, at the Sorrel, and the two row gallies. Mr. Carlton, with his 11 sail, has not yet been able to pass him by. Indeed Easton has obliged him twice to weigh anchor, and remove higher up the river. I am making all dispatch to attack him on my side, with field artillery mounted in batteaus. I have had great difficulty about the troops. I am afraid many of them will go home; however, depending on my good fortune, I hope to keep enough to give the final blow to ministerial politics in this province, as I hope effectual measures will be taken to prevent their laying hold of it again.

... of the difficulties we had to encounter, of which I cannot at present give a particular detail. Can only say we have hauled our batteaus up over falls, up rapid streams, over carrying places, and marched through morasses, thick woods, and over mountains, about three hundred and twenty miles, many of which we had to pass several times to bring over our baggage. These difficulties the soldiers have with the greatest fortitude surmounted, and about two thirds of the detachment are happily arrived here, and within two days march, most of them in good health and high spirits.

" The other part, with Col. Enos, returned from the Dead river contrary to my expectation, he having orders to send back only the sick, and those that could not be furnished with provisions. I wrote General Schuyler the thirteenth of October, by an Indian I thought trusty, inclosed to my friend in Quebec, and as I have had no answer from either, and he pretends being taken at Quebec, I make no doubt he has betrayed his trust, which I am confirmed in as I find they have been some time apprised of our coming to Quebec, and have destroyed all the canoes at Point Levy, to prevent our passing. This difficulty will be obviated by birch canoes, as we have about twenty of them, with forty Savages who have joined us, and profess great friendship, as well as the Canadians, by whom we have been very friendly received, and who will be able to furnish us with a number of canoes.

I am informed by the French there are two frigates and several small armed vessels lying before Quebec, and a large ship or two lately arrived from Boston; however I propose crossing the St. Lawrence as soon as possible; and if any opportunity offers of attacking Quebec with success shall embrace it, otherwise shall endeavour to join your army at Montreal. I shall as often as in my power advise you of my proceedings, and beg the favour of hearing from you by every opportunity.

The inclosed letter to his Excellency Gen. Washington beg the favour of your forwarding by express.

I am very respectfully, dear Sir,

Your most obedient humble servant,

...es and c[h]ildren, under pain of being treated as Rebels and Spies. In consequence of which, a great number of the principal inhabitants came out with their families, but were obliged to leave all their property behind, except some wearing apparel, and a little houshold furniture, &c —— Our men are in high spirits, being now well clothed with the regimentals destined for the 7th and 26th regiments, who were taken prisoners at St. John's.—This is a circumstance, which, I believe the like never before happened to the British troops, as two regiments of them to be made prisoners at one time. Providence smiles on us in a most remarkable manner. The Canadians say, 'Surely God is with this people, or they could never have done what they have done.'—They are all astonished at our march through the wilderness, which they say was impossible, and would not believe our coming, until they had ocular demonstration of it. I hope the next time I write you, it will be from Quebec, for if the in-

...the Lord Lieutenant made a speech to both houses, in which he tries to persuade the poor Irish (notwithstanding the many oppressions continually heaping upon them by the "*best of Sovereigns*" and his *blessed ministry*) that they were the happiest people under heaven. Respecting America, his Lordship said,---"I am persuaded that you entertain a grateful sense of the blessings you enjoy under the mild and firm government of the best of Sovereigns; and his Majesty relies on the known zeal and loyalty of his subjects of Ireland, that, whilst his government is disturbed by a rebellion existing in a part of his American dominions, you will be ready to shew your unavoidable attachment to his person and government, in the assertion of his just rights, and in the support of his legal authority."

We hear from Groton, that Mr. Amos Farnsworth, 70 years of age, and his son, aged 18, in attempting to cross a river in that town, in a canoe, on the 5th ult. were both unhappily drowned. The former has left a wife and five children.

Mr. Joseph Loring jun. of Lexington, lately had a child baptized by the name of JOHN HANCOCK.

Last Sabbath se'nnight died at Wenham, Mrs. MARY HALL, aged 21, Wife of Ebenezer Hall, one of the Printers of this Paper, and Daughter of the late Capt. Josiah Orne of Salem. Her remains were interred at Salem the Thursday following.

As several persons of the name of *Brimmer*, friends to the country, have lately come out of Boston, we are desired to insert, that the cargo of a vessel, sometime since taken by Capt. Manly, was not consigned to one *Brimer* in Boston, (as mentioned in a late paper) but to *Alexander Brymer*, a Scotchman, agent to the victuallers of the navy.

...MSBURG, (Virginia) Dec. 15.

...letter from Col. William Woodford to ...dward Pendleton, Esq; President of the ...vention.

...nt belonging to Major Marshall,
the other night from Col. Scott's
...ompletely taken his Lordship in.—
...who is wounded, and at present my
...ms, that this fellow told them that
...an three hundred shirtmen were
...t imprudent man catched at the
...ng Capt. Leslie with all the regu-
...o) who arrived at the bridge about
...e morning, joined by about 300
...ite slaves, laid planks upon the
...ssed just after our revaille had beat;
... us, and you'll say rather an im-
...er them to made ...
...ur men must be ...
...nt commanded ...
...yce, of the gr...
...any, who, for...
...ed a better fate, ...
...l with him, w...
...rched up to ou...
and perhaps ...
greater carnage, ...
...e of the blacks, &c. in the rear
...e, advanced farther than the
the pleasure to inform you, that
complete, and that most of the
...ed, with two pieces of cannon,
...nder cover of ...

...sulting foe does not surrender shortly, I believe it is the General's intention to carry the town by storm."

A gentleman from Hispaniola informs, he left that place but 14 days ago, that 7000 French troops, and nine sail of the line were arrived there; that two vessels belonging to North-America were at that place, but not having any credentials from the Congress, the inhabitants refused to trade with them; and that the Congress was in high esteem there.

We hear, that yesterday came to town, a gentleman from Canada, who has brought letters from thence to several gentlemen in town, signifying, that on the 5th ult. Gen. Montgomery with his army were on the heights of Abraham, that he had taken into pay 2500 C...

...Other Man of War; who, when they were asked, what induced them to leave Dunmore? Answered, *Hungry Bellies, naked Backs, and no Fuel; besides, in other Respects, the most cruel and inhuman Treatment.*—That Lord Dunmore had requested an Exchange of Pri...

Last Lord's-Day se'nnight, Lieut. Jonathan W... baptized, by the Rev. Mr. M'Gregore of Londo... JOHN SULLIVAN.

THIS DAY IS PUBLISHED, *and to be sold, by S. and E. HALL, in Cambridge; B. EDES, and I. THOMAS, in Worcester*,----The *North-American's* Alm...
For 1776.
By SAMUEL STEARNS, Student in Physic an...

LEFT on the seat of a necessary ... longing to the Free-Mason's arms tavern in Camb... 4th instant, a silver WATCH, china face, almost ... name Moses Peck. Whoever has taken up the ... leave it at Messrs. Halls' printing-office, shall receiv... two dollars.———N.B. The watch was left at ab... in the afternoon.

FOUND ...

...particularize. ... other articles too n...

To be SOLD on reasonable terms.
A neat house, with a shop, almost ne... about an acre and an half of good land, just 3 miles ...vard college, on the great road, in a good place for bu... pleasantly situated, with a small barn near the house ... a very convenient ...

NEW-ENGLAND CHRONICLE (CAMBRIDGE, MA)

January 11, 1776

In contrast to the optimistic tone of the letter written December 6, published January 11, 1776, in the *New-England Chronicle*, the revolutionaries under Arnold and Montgomery were not in a strong position. However, they decided to launch an attack in late December, due in part to concern that many of their men would leave – a significant number had only enlisted until the end of the year. The failure of the Battle of Quebec and the march on Canada was a serious setback for the American cause. It was their first significant military defeat.

REPORTING

Native Americans Choosing Sides

By Daniel J. Tortora

When the American Revolution began, Native Americans had to choose sides. The British, Patriots, and Tories coveted the services of Native American guides, interpreters, and spies, and they valued their bravery and intimidation in battle. Native American warriors played vital roles in the struggle for independence, but the Revolution devastated Native American lives and communities.

In the spring of 1775, when councils of safety pressed them to join the Patriot cause, Native Americans began to pick sides. The Continental Congress sent presents, letters, and wampum to the tribes in the east during the summer of 1775, reports the *Connecticut Journal* of August 23, 1775. The tribes of the Iroquois Confederacy initially declared neutrality as the same *Connecticut Journal* indicates, but most Native Americans sided with the British. Since 1763, they had seen white settlers overrun their lands. Natives believed that if Britain won, the Crown would limit white settlement in the west. Some fought with the Americans. They did so to escape poverty, pushed by family tradition and Christian missionaries, and the hopes, as one Mashpee Wampanoag put it, that the colonists' sufferings "would naturally lead them to respect and relieve ours."

Dozens of Native American Patriots fought in the siege of Boston, as the *Pennsylvania Evening Post* of June 29, 1775, reveals. Fifteen Native Americans saw action at Bunker Hill. Maine Native Americans escorted Benedict Arnold to Quebec in 1775. "Stockbridges" from western Massachusetts and eastern New York fought with the Continental Army from 1775 to 1778. On August 31, 1778, the Queen's Rangers decimated the Stockbridge unit in a battle in the Bronx.

Along the New York and Pennsylvania frontier, the Revolution devastated Native American communities. By 1777, a civil war broke out between, and even within, the six tribes of the Iroquois Confederacy. Mohawks, Senecas, Onondagas, and Cayugas joined the British. They raided and fought Patriot militias and Continental troops and provided food for British armies in New York, New Jersey, and Pennsylvania. Oneidas and Tuscaroras fought with Patriot militias.

Four hundred natives served with British General John Burgoyne. They pillaged, scalped, and killed without restraint. After suffering massive casualties, most of them deserted before the Battle of Saratoga. From late 1777 through summer 1779, hundreds of Native Americans and Tories, led by Mohawk Joseph Brant, Colonel John Butler, and Captain William Butler, raided the frontier along the Cherry Valley, Mohawk Valley, and the Wyoming Valley in New York and Pennsylvania. They seized supplies for the British Army and intimidated Patriot-leaning settlers and Native Americans.

In the south, Catawbas aided the American defense of Sullivan's Island, South Carolina, in 1776. At the same time, British agents incited Cherokees led by Dragging Canoe to attack the southern frontier. But southern militias and Catawbas destroyed most of the Cherokee settlements in response. Cherokee survivors ceded large tracts of land. Cherokee resistance was limited to sporadic raiding. Creek Native Americans helped the British defend the Gulf Coast region in 1780 and 1781. Catawbas defended Charleston in May 1780. They fought with General Thomas Sumter at King's Mountain and at Eutaw Springs. Lumbees, Pamunkeys, and other Native Americans fought in militia, state, and continental units.

In the west, George Rogers Clark and his Virginia militia took white settlements in Indiana and Illinois and quelled Shawnee resistance.

At war's end, it did not matter which side Native Americans had chosen. Tradition and grief led them to plunder, scalp, and mutilate. This reinforced land-hungry Americans' perceptions of Native Americans as "savage" and inhuman. With few exceptions, Patriot Native American veterans faced discrimination and marginalization. Massachusetts sold Maine Native American lands to pay white soldiers. Frontiersmen rapidly overtook Native American lands. Driven from their homelands, most Iroquois moved to Canada. Native communities reeled from the loss of their hunting grounds, men, and dignity. Survivors slipped into poverty, alcoholism, and despair, but they continued to fight to preserve their cultures.

PENNSYLVANIA EVENING POST (PHILADELPHIA)

June 29, 1775

Dozens of Native American Patriots fought in the siege of Boston, as this newspaper reveals. Fifteen saw action at Bunker Hill, and some from Maine escorted Benedict Arnold to Quebec in 1775.

CONNECTICUT JOURNAL (NEW HAVEN)

August 23, 1775

When the American Revolution began, Native Americans had to choose sides. The British, Patriots, and Tories coveted the services of Native American guides, interpreters, and spies and valued their bravery and intimidation in battle. The Continental Congress sent presents, letters, and wampum to the tribes in the east during the summer of 1775. The tribes of the Iroquois Confederacy initially declared neutrality as the same *Connecticut Journal* indicates, but most Indians sided with the British.

fetts-Bay) to a Gentleman of the Congrefs, dated June 22.

"A firm foundation now turns up to view, for the influence of the Stockbridge Indians amongft the SIX NATIONS, and matters ftand well with the Canadian Indians. If I had time, I would relate to you every particular of what befel the meffengers of our Indians to the Six Nations and the Canadian Indians. To be fhort, they were taken and bound by the regulars, and carried into Montreal, where, by a court martial they were condemned to be hanged, for a flight fufpicion that they were fent to engage the Indians to fall upon the regulars. This event turned much to our advantage, and has fully fixed the minds of the Indians there againft the regulars. High threatening words paffed between the General and the Indian Sachems, who were raifed far and near on the occafion, and a wonderful fpirit of benevolence appeared towards the young men that were taken by the Indians there. They told them, in the ftrongeft terms, *That they would take their place, they would die for them.* The whole ftory is very affecting. The Indian Sachems told the General, *You have offered us money to fight for you, but we would not take it, as we would have nothing to do with your quarrel, but now we fhall know who are our enemies. If you think it beft for you to hang thefe our brothers, that came a great way to fee us, do it, but remember we fhall not forget it.* Upon thefe threatenings they thought it beft to let the prifoners go, who got away with fome difficulty. The Canadian Indians farther told our Indians, *That if they did fight at all, they would* FIGHT AGAINST *the* REGULARS, *for they did not like them.*"

Extract of a letter from Providence, June 20.

"Our government have ordered two cruizers to be equipped and fent out to protect the trade. They have retaken Lindfay's packet in fight of the men of war. The men of war

August 10—13. THE LONDON CHRONICLE for 1776.

Commiſſion ſuperſeded.

John Carr, of Scotland-yard, Coal-merchant, (Partner in Trade with James Farrer and Edward Arrowſmith, of the ſame Place, Coal-merchants.)

Bankruptcy enlarged.

James Farrer, Edward Arrowſmith, and John Carr, of Scotland-yard, Coal-merchants and Partners, to ſurrender Aug. 29, at Guildhall.

Dividends to be made.

Sept. 3. John Gardner, late of Romſey, in Hants, Clothier, at the Angel in Romſey.

11. Richard Ford, of Coalbrookdale, in the County of Salop, Ironmaſter, at Mary Corbett's, in High-ſtreet, Bridgnorth, Salop.

20. Benjamin Cooper, late of Walſall, in Stafford-ſhire, and Joſeph Hodgkin, late of Aldridge, in the ſaid County, Merchants and Traders, at the King's-head in New-ſtreet, Birmingham.

Certificate to be granted.

Aug. 31. William Richardſon, of Fenchurch ſtreet, London, Linen-draper.

LONDON.

Advice is received that the Congreſs reſolved upon independence the 4th of July; and, it is ſaid, have declared war againſt Great Britain in form.

When General Thompſon was conducted in the guard-room at Montreal with the reſt of th… priſoners of that day, he reque… of his brother General, … tern waited on him wi… Carleton refuſed compl… for anſwer, "that he n… tion with rebels."

A letter from … ſays, "that the … refuſed to give a…

On Tueſday laſt was married at Aſh, in Kent, the Rev. Mr. Hutchinſon of Norbourn, to Miſs Elizabeth Beale Pery, of Aſh.

On Saturday laſt was married at Crayford, in Kent, Mr. Eſſex, of Southampton-ſtreet, Covent-Garden, to Miſs Nancy Wright, of Crayford.

Yeſterday was married Mr. Samuel Fenn, of this City, to Miſs Tate of the Old Change.

On Friday laſt died at Greenwich, Captain Francis Minſhull.

On Saturday laſt died, at his houſe in St. James's-ſtreet, Mr. Matthew Crane, Apothecary to the Houſhold.

At Shrewſbury aſſizes John Herbert for ſheep-ſtealing, was capitally convicted, but afterwards reprieved.

H. M. The Nabob, with Taſte.

This Day was publiſhed, Price 1s 6d.

A New Edition, corrected to the preſent time, on a broad ſheet of elephant paper, proper for framing, with an elegant engraved border,

A COMPLETE TITHE-TABLE: Wherein the nature of tithes, and all things tithable, are ſhewn at one view. With an account of compoſitions, cuſtom, preſcription, and privilege, diſtin…hed under their proper heads; with reference to …dged caſes, and ſtatutes relating to tithes. …oper f… Veſtries, Halls of Clergymen and …ntleme… ell as Attornies.

Printe… and C. Rivington, No. 62, in St. …

…hom may be had, …anner above-menti… Wherein all the … w. Price …

SOCIETY for the Diſcharge and Relief … impriſoned for Small Debts.

Craven-ſtreet, Strand, July …

BEnefactions ſince the laſt report, viz.

W. W. a Lady
Lord Chief Baron Smythe, annual
Lady Smythe, ditto
Mr. Hull, ditto
W. J. 3d benefaction
A. B.
D. B.
D. C. July 10
J. H. by J. R.

Diſcharged from the ſeveral priſons in …polis, and other parts of the kingdom, 2… who could not be relieved by the Inſolve… 39 l. 6s. 2d.

Approved the recommendations of 24 …

Referred for Enquiry 19 Petitions.

The books may be ſeen by any perſon … promote this undertaking, between th… Eleven and Three, at No. 7, Craven-ſt… benefactions are received, and where the … meet on Wedneſday the 22d of Aug… in the Afternoon.

…factions are alſo received by Mr. …atch'd-houſe … London … Compan… Nield, … St. Ja… Meſſ… Finch… Meſſ…

CHAPTER VII

THE SPIRIT OF LIBERTY

Introduction

As the snow began melting in the early months of 1776, colonists warmed to the idea of independence thanks to a forty-eight-page pamphlet titled *Common Sense* that colonial presses printed in unprecedented quantities. Early military engagements in North Carolina, Georgia, and South Carolina reinforced the Patriot spirit while Washington's troops fortified the heights around Boston and successfully forced the British to withdraw from town. In June 1776, a committee of five legislators drafted and presented the Declaration of Independence to the Continental Congress. On July 2, Congress voted for independence, and two days later it approved the text of its official Declaration. Celebrations were short-lived as General Washington's focus quickly turned to New York and the middle colonies for what was certain to be a large-scale retaliation attack by the British.

London Chronicle
August 13, 1776

Declaration of Independence
by John Trumbull
Architect of the Capitol

REPORTING

COMMON SENSE AND THE *AMERICAN CRISIS*

By Jim Piecuch

At the start of 1776, many American colonists had begun to believe that independence might be the only solution to their decade-long dispute with the British government. However, the prospect appeared daunting. Independence not only meant challenging the military might of the world's most powerful empire, but also rejecting the authority of a king who many believed ruled by divine right and replacing monarchy with a new system of government. That January, Thomas Paine published *Common Sense* in Philadelphia. More than one hundred thousand copies of the pamphlet were sold, and it was also serialized or excerpted in many American newspapers. Using a variety of clearly stated arguments based on history, biblical scripture, and Enlightenment rationalism to appeal to the widest possible audience, Paine convinced a large number of Americans that independence was necessary and attainable (noted in the *New-England Chronicle* of March 27, 1776). He denounced the institution of monarchy, offered an alternative form of government, and asserted that the colonists had the means to defeat the British armed forces. Although the ringing words of Thomas Jefferson's Declaration of Independence are better remembered, it is possible that without *Common Sense*, the Declaration would never have been written. Later, when military reverses raised questions about the ability of the colonists to triumph, Paine wrote a series of essays, *The American Crisis*, to boost morale and urge Americans to persist in their struggle.

Although the ringing words of Thomas Jefferson's Declaration of Independence are better remembered, it is possible that without Common Sense, *the Declaration would never have been written.*

When King George III advocated tougher policies toward the colonies following the publication of *Common Sense*, Paine's arguments appeared to have been validated. The colonial press took up the cause of independence, using Paine's arguments (as stated in the *New-England Chronicle*, March 27, 1776).

Some Americans disagreed with Paine and published their own essays challenging *Common Sense*. One religious group, the Quakers (Society of Friends), argued against independence based on their pacifist tenets. Paine responded by appending an address to the Quakers to later editions of *Common Sense* that countered the points they had raised (this address was reprinted in the *New-England Chronicle* of April 4, 1776). Paine asserted that those Quakers who opposed independence misunderstood both the principles of their own religion and the serious political situation.

British writers also disputed Paine's contention that the colonies could defeat the British armed forces. Challenging Paine's statement that New England shipyards had the capability to build a fleet that could challenge the Royal Navy, Admiral Clark Gayton declared that New England had thus far produced only two large warships and that these had been of such poor quality that British naval authorities quickly condemned both (Gayton's letter appeared in the *London Chronicle*, August 29, 1776).

After the Continental Congress declared independence and the war dragged on, Paine wrote his *American Crisis* essays exhorting Americans to continue the struggle. The first appeared in December 1776, when the Continental Army was in full retreat across New Jersey following a series of disastrous defeats around New York City. Like *Common Sense*, the *Crisis* essays were widely reprinted in American newspapers. In the third essay, published in the spring of 1777, Paine reminded Americans of the reasons why they had declared independence, accused the opponents of independence of acting from fear, laziness, and greed, and urged Americans to risk everything for their cause (see the *Independent Chronicle*, May 22, 1777). Three years later, in *The American Crisis No. VIII*, Paine reminded Americans of how, despite the "wanton cruelty" of the British army in its efforts to subdue the rebellion, five years had elapsed since the fighting had begun and the Americans remained unconquered.

Having played a crucial role in convincing the colonists to declare independence, Paine remained a steadfast advocate of the American cause throughout the Revolution. His writings not only helped give birth to the United States, but also nurtured the infant nation during the difficult wartime years until independence was finally attained.

THOMAS PAINE
National Portrait Gallery, London (current location)

Thomas Paine wrote *Common Sense*, which sold more than one hundred thousand copies and used clearly stated arguments to convince the widest possible audience that independence was necessary and attainable.

MARCH 27, 1776

The

NEW-ENGLAND CHRONICLE

The public in general having read, and (excepting a few timid Whigs or disguised Tories) loudly applauded that *truly excellent pamphlet, intitled,* COMMON SENSE*; our readers will doubtless be pleased with the perusal of the following* APPENDIX *written by the same ingenious author, and printed in Philadelphia since the publication of the second edition of* Common Sense.

SINCE the publication of the first edition of this pamphlet, or rather, on the same day on which it came out, the King's Speech made its appearance in this city.---- Had the spirit of prophecy directed the birth of this production, it could not have brought it forth at a more seasonable juncture, or a more necessary time. The bloody-mindedness of the one, shows the necessity of pursuing the doctrine of the other. Men read by way of revenge. And the Speech, instead of terrifying, prepared a way for the manly principles of Independence.

Ceremony, and even silence, from whatever motive they may arise, have a hurtful tendency, when they give the least degree of countenance to base and wicked performances ; wherefore, if this maxim be admitted, it naturally follows, that the King's Speech, as being a piece of finished villany, deserved, and still deserves, a general execration both by the Congress and the people.—Yet, as the domestic tranquility of a nation depends greatly on the *chastity* of what may properly be called NATIONAL MANNERS, it is often better to pass some things over in silent disdain, than to make use of such new methods of dislike, as might introduce the least innovation, on than guardian of our peace and safety. And, perhaps, it is chiefly owing to this prudent delicacy, that the King's Speech hath not, before now, suffered a public execution. The Speech, if it may be called one, is nothing better than a willful audacious libel against the truth, the common good, and the existence of mankind ; and is a formal and pompous method of offering up human sacrifices to the pride of tyrants. But this general massacre of mankind, is one of the privileges, and the certain consequence of Kings; for as nature knows them *not*, they know *not her;* and although they are beings of our *own* creating, they know not *us,* and are become the gods of their creators. The Speech hath one good quality, which is, that it is not calculated to deceive, neither can we, even if we would, be deceived by it. Brutality and tyranny appear on the face of it. It leaves us at no less : And every line convinces, even in the moment of reading, that He, who hunts the woods for prey, the naked and untutored Indian, is less a Savage than the King of Britain.

Sir John Dalrymple, the putative father of a whining jesuitical piece, fallaciously called, "*The address of the people of* ENGLAND *to the inhabitants of* AMERICA," hath, perhaps, from a vain supposition, that the people *here* were to be frightened at the pomp and description of a king, given, (though very unwisely on his part) the real character of the present one: "But," says this writer, "if you are inclined to pay compliments to an administration, which we do not complain of," (meaning the Marquis of Rockingham's at the repeal of the Stamp-Act) "it is very unfair in you to withhold them from that prince, *by whose* NOD ALONE *they were permitted to do any thing.*" This is toryism with a witness! Here is idolatry even without a mask: And he who can calmly hear, and digest such doctrine, hath forfeited his claim to rationality—an apostate from the order of manhood; and ought to be considered—as one, who hath not only given up the proper dignity of man, but sunk himself beneath the rank of animals, and contemptibly crawl through the world like a worm. [...]

NEW-ENGLAND CHRONICLE (CAMBRIDGE, MA)
March 27, 1776

Even at the start of 1776, the prospect of independence appeared daunting, but Thomas Paine's pamphlet, *Common Sense*, which was excerpted in many American newspapers, helped convince a large number of Americans that independence was necessary and attainable.

NEW-ENGLAND CHRONICLE:
OR, THE
ESSEX GAZETTE.
VOL. VIII. NUMB. 399.
From THURSDAY, *March* 21, to THURSDAY, *March* 27, 1776.

CAMBRIDGE: Printed by SAMUEL HALL, at his Printing-Office in Stoughton-Hall, HARVARD-COLLEGE.

The public in general having read, and (excepting a few timid Whigs or disguised Tories) loudly applauded that truly excellent pamphlet, intitled, COMMON SENSE; *our readers will doubtless be pleased with the perusal of the following* APPENDIX *written by the same ingenious author, and printed in Philadelphia since the publication of the second edition of* Common Sense.

SINCE the publication of the first edition of this pamphlet, or rather, on the same day on which it came out, the King's Speech made its appearance in this city.—Had the spirit of prophecy directed the birth of this production, it could not have brought it forth at a more seasonable juncture, or a more necessary time. The bloody-mindedness of the one, shews the necessity of pursuing the doctrine of the other. Men read by way of revenge. And the Speech, instead of terrifying, prepared a way for the manly principles of Independance.

Ceremony, and even silence, from whatever motive they may arise, have a hurtful tendency, when they give the least degree of countenance to base and wicked performances; wherefore, if this maxim be admitted, it naturally follows, that the King's Speech, as being a piece of finished villany, deserved, and still deserves, a general execration both by the Congress and the people.—Yet, as the domestic tranquility of a nation depends greatly on the *chastity* of what may properly be called NATIONAL MANNERS, it is often better to pass some things over in silent disdain, than to make use of such new methods of dislike, as might introduce the least innovation, on than guardian of our peace and safety. And, perhaps, it is chiefly owing to this prudent delicacy, that the King's Speech hath not, before now, suffered a public execution. The Speech, if it may be called one, is nothing better than a willful audacious libel against the truth, the common good, and the existence of mankind; and is a formal and pompous method of offering up human sacrifices to the pride of tyrants. But this general massacre of mankind, is one of the privileges, and

they are beings of our *own* creating, they know not *us*, and are become the gods of their creators.

wickedly broken through every moral and human obligation, trampled nature and conscience beneath his feet; and by a steady and constitutional spirit of insolence and cruelty, procured for himself an universal hatred. It it *now* the interest of America to provide for herself. She hath already a large and young family, whom it is more her duty to take care of, than to be granting away her property, to support a power who is become a reproach to the names of men and christians.—YE, whose office it is to watch over the morals of a nation, of whatsoever sect or denomination ye are of, as well as ye, who are more immediately the guardians of the public liberty, if ye wish to preserve your native country uncontaminated by European corruption, ye must in secret wish a separation.—But leaving the moral part to private reflection, I shall chiefly confine my farther remarks to the following heads.

First. That it is the interest of America to be separated from Britain.

Secondly: Which is the easiest and most practicable plan, RECONCILIATION OF INDEPENDANCE? with some occasional remarks.

In support of the first, I could, if I judged it proper, produce the opinion of some of the ablest and most experienced men on this continent; and whose sentiments, on that head, are not yet publickly known. It is in reality a self evident position: For no nation in a state of foreign dependance, limited in its commerce, and cramped and fettered in its legislative powers, can arrive at any material eminence. America doth not yet know what opulence is; and although the progress which she hath made stands unparalleled in the history of other nations, it is but childhood, compared with what she would be capable of arriving at, had she, as she ought to have, the legislative powers in her own hands. England is, at this time, proudly coveting what would do her no good, were she to accomplish it; and the Continent hesitating on a matter, which will be her final ruin if neglected. It is the commerce and not the conquest of America, by which England

of each other as France and Spain; because in many articles, neither can go to a better market. But it is the independance of this country on

tremes, in which a sufficiency of the former remains, and a proper increase of the latter is obtained; And that point of time is the present time..

The reader will pardon this digression, as it does not properly come under the head I first set out with, and to which I again return by the following position, viz.

Should affairs be patched up with Britain, and she to remain the governing and sovereign power of America, (which, as matters are now circumstanced, is giving up the point intirely) we shall deprive ourselves of the very means of sinking the debt we have, or may contract. The value of the back lands which some of the provinces are clandestinely deprived of, by the unjust extention of the limits of Canada, valued only at five pounds sterling per hundred acres, amount to upwards of twenty-five millions, Pennsylvania currency; and the quit-rents at one penny sterling per acre, to two millions yearly.

It is by the sale of those lands that the debt may be sunk, without burthen to any, and the quit-rent reserved thereon, will always lessen, and in time, will wholly support the yearly expence of government. It matters not how long the debt is in paying, so that the lands when sold be applied to the discharge of it, and for the execution of which, the Congress for the time being, will be the continental trustees.

I proceed now to the second head, viz. Which is the easiest and most practicable plan, RECONCILIATION OF INDEPENDANCE; with some occasional remarks.

He who takes nature for his guide is not easily beaten out of his argument, and on that ground, I answer *generally---That* INDEPENDANCE *being a* SINGLE SIMPLE LINE, *contained within our selves; and reconciliation, a matter exceedingly perplexed and complicated, & in which a treacherous capricious court is to interfere, gives the answer without a doubt.*

The present state of America is truly alarming to every man who is capable of reflection. Without law, without government, without any other mode of power than what is founded on, and

nevertheless subject to change, and which, every secret enemy is endeavouring to dissove. Our

NEW-ENGLAND CHRONICLE (CAMBRIDGE, MA)

March 27, 1776 (continued)

this production, it could not have brought it forth at a more seasonable juncture, or a more necessary time. The bloody-mindedness of the one, shews the necessity of pursuing the doctrine of the other. Men read by way of revenge. And the Speech, instead of terrifying, prepared a way for the manly principles of Independance.

Ceremony, and even silence, from whatever motive they may arise, have a hurtful tendency, when they give the least degree of countenance to base and wicked performances; wherefore, if this maxim be admitted, it naturally follows, that the King's Speech, as being a piece of finished villany, deserved, and still deserves, a general execration both by the Congress and the people.—Yet, as the domestic tranquility of a nation depends greatly on the *chastity* of what may properly be called NATIONAL MANNERS, it is often better to pass some things over in silent disdain, than to make use of such new methods of dislike, as might introduce the least innovation, on that guardian of our peace and safety. And, perhaps, it is chiefly owing to this prudent delicacy, that the King's Speech hath not, before now, suffered a public execution. The Speech, if it may be called one, is nothing better than a willful audacious libel against the truth, the common good, and the existence of mankind; and is a formal and pompous method of offering up human sacrifices to the pride of tyrants. But this general massacre of mankind, is one of the privileges, and the certain consequence of Kings; for as nature knows them *not*, they know *not her*; and although they are beings of our *own* creating, they know *not us*, and are become the gods of their creators. The Speech hath one good quality, which is, that it is not calculated to deceive, neither can we, even if we would, be deceived by it. Brutality and tyranny appear on the face of it. It leaves us at no loss: And every line convinces, even in the moment of reading, that He, who hunts the woods for prey, the naked and untutored Indian, is less a Savage than the King of Britain.

Sir John Dalrymple, the putative father of a whining jesuitical piece, fallaciously called, "*The address of the people of* ENGLAND *to the inhabitants of* AMERICA," hath, perhaps, from a vain supposition, that the people *here* were to be frightened at the pomp and description of a king, given, (though very unwisely on his part) the real character of the present one: "But," says this writer, "if you are inclined to pay compliments to an administration, which we do not complain of," (meaning the Marquis of Rockingham's at the repeal of the Stamp-Act) "it is very unfair in you to withhold them from that prince, *by whose* NOD ALONE *they were permitted to do any thing*." This is toryism with a witness! Here is idolatry

world like a worm.

However, it matters very little now, what the king of England either says or does; he hath

to preserve your native country uncontaminated by European corruption, ye must in secret wish a separation.—But leaving the moral part to private reflection, I shall chiefly confine my farther remarks to the following heads.

First. That it is the interest of America to be separated from Britain.

Secondly. Which is the easiest and most practicable plan, RECONCILIATION or INDEPENDANCE? with some occasional remarks.

In support of the first, I could, if I judged it proper, produce the opinion of some of the ablest and most experienced men on this continent; and whose sentiments, on that head, are not yet publickly known. It is in reality a self-evident position: For no nation in a state of foreign dependance, limited in its commerce, and cramped and fettered in its legislative powers, can ever arrive at any material eminence. America doth not yet know what opulence is; and although the progress which she hath made stands unparalleled in the history of other nations, it is but childhood, compared with what she would be capable of arriving at, had she, as she ought to have, the legislative powers in her own hands. England is, at this time, proudly coveting what would do her no good, were she to accomplish it; and the Continent hesitating on a matter, which will be her final ruin if neglected. It is the commerce and not the conquest of America, by which England is to be benefited, and that would in a great measure continue, were the countries as independant of each other as France and Spain; because in many articles, neither can go to a better market. But it is the independance of this country on Britain or any other, which is now the main and only object worthy of contention, and which, like all other truths discovered by necessity, will appear clearer and stronger every day.

First. Because it will come to that one time or other.

Secondly. Because, the longer it is delayed the harder it will be to accomplish.

I have frequently amused myself both in public and private companies, with silently remarking, the specious errors of those who speak without reflecting. And among the many which I have heard, the following seems the most general, viz. that had this rupture happened forty or fifty years hence, instead of *now*, the Continent would have been more able to have shaken off the dependance. To which I reply, that our military ability, *at this time*, arises from the experience gained in the last war, and which in forty or fifty years time, would have been totally extinct. The Continent would not, by that time, have had a General, or even a military officer left; and we, or those who may

been as ignorant of mar-

ent Indians: And this

nded to, will unanswer-

nt time is preferable to

ent turns thus—at the

ar, we had experience,

; and forty or fifty years hence, we should have numbers, without experience; wherefore the proper point of time must be some particular point between the two ex-

of the back lands which some of the provinces are clandestinely deprived of, by the unjust extention of the limits of Canada, valued only at five pounds sterling per hundred acres, amount to upwards of twenty-five millions, Pennsylvania currency; and the quit-rents at one penny sterling per acre, to two millions yearly.

It is by the sale of those lands that the debt may be sunk, without burthen to any, and the quit-rent reserved thereon, will always lessen, and in time, will wholly support the yearly expence of government. It matters not how long the debt is in paying, so that the lands when sold be applied to the discharge of it, and for the execution of which, the Congress for the time being, will be the continental trustees.

I proceed now to the second head, viz. Which is the easiest and most practicable plan, RECONCILIATION or INDEPENDANCE; with some occasional remarks.

He who takes nature for his guide is not easily beaten out of his argument, and on that ground, I answer *generally*.---*That* INDEPENDANCE *being a* SINGLE SIMPLE LINE, *contained within our selves; and reconciliation, a matter exceedingly perplexed and complicated, & in which a treacherous capricious court is to interfere, gives the answer without a doubt.*

The present state of America is truly alarming to every man who is capable of reflection. Without law, without government, without any other mode of power than what is founded on, and granted by courtesy. Held together by an unexampled concurrence of sentiment, which is nevertheless subject to change, and which, every secret enemy is endeavouring to dissolve. Our present condition, is, legislation without law; wisdom without a plan; a constitution without a name; and, what is strangely astonishing, perfect independance contending for dependance.—The instance is without a precedent; the case never existed before; and who can tell what may be the event? The property of no man is secure in the present unbraced system of things. The mind of the multitude is left at random, and seeing no fixed object before them, they pursue such as fancy or opinion starts. Nothing is criminal; there is no such thing as treason; wherefore, every one thinks himself at liberty to act as he pleases. The Tories dared not have assembled offensively, had they known that their lives, by that act, were forfeited to the laws of the state. A line of distinction should be drawn, between English soldiers taken in battle, and inhabitants of America taken in arms. The first are prisoners, but the latter traitors. The one forfeits his liberty, the other his head.

Notwithstanding our wisdom, there is a visible feebleness in some of our proceedings which gives encouragement to dissentions. The Continental Belt is too loosely buckled. And if something is not done in time, it will be too late to do any thing, and we shall fall into a state, in which, neither *Reconciliation* nor *Independance* will be practicable. The king and his worthless adherents are got at their old game of dividing the Continent, and there are not wanting among us, Printers, who will be busy in spreading specious falsehoods. The artful and hypocritical letter which

THE

NEW-ENGLAND CHRON[ICLE]

OR, THE

ESSEX GAZET[TE]

VOL. VIII. NUMB.

From THURSDAY, *March* 28, to THURSDAY, *Apr[il]*

CAMBRIDGE: Printed by SAMUE[L]

NEW-ENGLAND CHRONICLE (CAMBRIDGE, MA)

April 4, 1776

Some Americans disagreed with Paine. One religious group, the Quakers, argued against independence based on their pacifist tenets. Paine responded by appending an address to the Quakers to later editions of *Common Sense* that countered the points they had raised.

The following Address was lately published in Philadelphia, as an Addition to "COMMON SENSE."

Representatives of the religious Society of the people called Quakers, or to so many of them as were concerned in publishing a late piece, entitled, "THE ANTIENT TESTIMONY and PRINCIPLES of the people called QUAKERS renewed, with respect to the KING and GOVERNMENT, and touching the COMMOTIONS now prevailing in these and other parts of AMERICA, addressed to the PEOPLE IN GENERAL."

THE writer of this, is one of those few, who never dishonours religion either by ridiculing or cavelling at any denomination whatsoever. To God and not to man, are all men accountable on the score of religion. Wherefore, this epistle is not so properly addressed to you as a religious, but as a political body, dabbling in matters, which the professed quietude of your principles instruct you not to meddle with.

As you have, without a proper authority for so doing, put yourselves in the place of the whole Body of the Quakers, so, the writer of this, in order to be on an equal rank with yourselves, is under the necessity of putting himself in the place of all those who approve the very writings and principles against which, your testimony is directed: And he hath chosen this singular situation, in order, that you might discover in him that presumption of character which you cannot see in yourselves. For neither he nor you can have any claim or title to *political representation.*

When men have departed from the right way, it is no wonder they stumble and fall. And it is evident from the manner in which ye have managed your testimony, that politics (as a religious body of men,) is not your proper walk; for however well adapted it might appear to you, it is, nevertheless, a jumble of good and bad put un-

...

hope, end, and aim. *Our plan is peace for ever.* We are tired of contention with Britain, and can see no real end to it but in a final separation. We act consistently, because for the sake of introducing an endless and uninterrupted peace, do we bear the evils and burdens of the present day. We are endeavouring, and will steadily continue to endeavour, to separate and dissolve a connection which hath already filled our land with blood, and which, while the name of it remains, will be the fatal cause of future mischiefs to both countries.

We fight neither for revenge nor conquest; neither from pride nor passion; we are not insulting the world with our fleets and armies, nor ravaging the globe for plunder. Beneath the shade of our own vines are we attacked; in our own houses, and on our own lands, is the violence committed against us. We view our enemies in the character of highwaymen and housebreakers, and having no defence for ourselves in the civil law, are obliged to punish them by the military one, and apply the sword in the very case where you have, before now, applied the halter.---Perhaps we feel for the ruined and insulted sufferers in all and every part of the continent, with a degree of tenderness which hath not yet made its way into some of your bosoms. But be ye sure that ye mistake not the cause and ground of your testimony. Call not coldness of soul, religion; nor put the *Bigot* in the place of the *Christian.*

...

tite as keen as death.

...

the exciting and stirring u[p]

CHRONICLE:

THE

GAZETTE.

NUMB. 400.

THURSDAY, *April* 4, 1776.

at his Printing-Office in Stoughton-Hall, HARVARD-COLLEGE.

work, to be managed by himself? These very principles instruct you to wait with patience and humility, for the event of all public measures, and to receive *that event* as the divine will towards you. *Wherefore*, what occasion is there for your *political testimony* if you fully believe what it contains? And the very publishing proves, that either ye do not believe what ye profess, or have not virtue enough to practise what ye believe.

The principles of Quakerism have a direct tendency to make a man the quiet and inoffensive subject of any, and every government *which is set over him*. And if the setting up and putting down of kings and governments is God's peculiar prerogative, he most certainly will be robbed thereof by us; wherefore, the principle itself leads you to approve of every thing which ever happened, or may happen to Kings as being his work. OLIVER CROMWELL thanks you. CHARLES, then, died not by the hands of man; and should the present proud imitater of him, come to the

possibly stand, east and west, from every part of the old, doth, nevertheless, disapprove of its being independent of the corrupt and abandoned court of Britain; unless I say, ye can shew this, how can ye on the ground of your principles, justify the exciting and stirring up of the people,

tains, to applaud the fact. Kings are not taken away by miracles, neither are changes in governments brought about by any other means than such as are common and human; and such as we are now using. Even the dispersion of the Jews, though foretold by our Saviour, was effected by arms. Wherefore as ye refuse to be the means on one side, ye ought not to be meddlers on the other; but to wait the issue in silence; and unless ye can produce divine authority, to prove, that the Almighty, who hath created and placed this *new* world, at the greatest distance it could possibly stand, east and west, from every part of the old, doth, nevertheless, disapprove of its being independent of the corrupt and abandoned court of Britain; unless I say, ye can shew this, how can ye on the ground of your principles, justify the exciting and stirring up of the people, "firmly to unite in the *abhorrence* of all such *writings* "and *measures*, as evidence a desire and design to "break off the *happy* connection we have hitherto enjoyed, with the kingdom of Great-Britain, and our just and necessary subordination "to the King, and those who are lawfully placed "in authority under him." What a slap of the face is here! the men, who in the very paragraph before, have quietly and passively resigned up the ordering, altering, and disposal of kings and governments, into the hands of God, are now, recalling their principles, and putting in for a share of the business. Is it possible, that the conclusion, which is here justly quoted, can any ways follow from the doctrine laid down? The inconsistency is too glaring not to be seen; the absurdity too great not to be laughed at; and such as could only have been made by those, whose understandings were darkned by the narrow and crabby spirit of a disparing political party; for ye are not to be considered as the whole body of the Quakers, but only as a factional and fractional part thereof.

Here ends the examination of your testimony; (which I call upon no man to abhor, as ye have done, but only to read and judge of fairly;) to which I subjoin the following remark; "That the setting up and putting down of kings," most certainly mean, the making him a King, who is yet not so, and the making him no King who is already one. And pray what hath this to do in the present case? We neither mean to *set up* nor to *put down*, neither to *make* nor to *unmake*, but to have nothing to *do* with them. Wherefore, your testimony, in whatever light it is viewed, serves only to dishonour your judgment, and for many other reasons had better have been let alone than published.

First, Because it tends to the decrease and reproach of all religion whatever, and is of the ut-

NEW-ENGLAND CHRONICLE (CAMBRIDGE, MA)

April 4, 1776 (continued)

Samuel Hall moved his press out of Cambridge, headquarters of Washington's army, after printing this issue of the *New-England Chronicle: Or, the Essex Gazette* (full title). On April 25, he resumed publication in Boston, which the British had evacuated in March, now calling his paper simply the *New-England Chronicle*.

LONDON CHRONICLE

August 29, 1776

British writers also disputed Paine's contention that the colonies could defeat the British armed forces. Challenging Paine's statement that New England shipyards had the capability to build a fleet that could challenge the Royal Navy, Admiral Clark Gayton declared that New England had thus far produced only two large warships and that these had been of such poor quality that British naval authorities quickly condemned both.

---

morning through the Downs, for the River, the Ankerwyke Eaſt Indiaman; and the Anne, Kennedy, for Jamaica; the Golden Fleece, Dixon, for Corke; the Succeſs Increaſe, Tiſdale, for Halifax; and the Grange, Parker, for Liverpool. Remain in the Downs, the Prince Frederick, Sawyer; and the Amity's Experiment, Moore, for orders.

LONDON.

Extract of a Letter from Jamaica, dated June 29, 1776.

" A pamphlet has been circulated here under the title of " Common Senſe," which was ſent hither from America. It is written with great virulence againſt the Engliſh adminiſtration; and its deſign is to ſtir up the coloniſts to aſſert their independency on the mother country. There are many falſe aſſertions in it, one of which Admiral Gayton has thought proper to contradict in the Jamaica Gazette, in the following words:

" I have ſeen a pamphlet publiſhed in Philadelphia, under the title of *Common Senſe*, wherein the Author ſays, that 40 years ago there were 70 and 80 gun ſhips built in New England: In anſwer to which I do declare, that, at that very period of time I was in New England, a midſhipman on board his Majeſty's ſhip Squirrel, with the late Sir Peter Warren, and then there never had been a man of war built of any kind. In 1747 (after the reduction of Louiſburgh) there was a ſhip of 44 guns ordered to be built at Piſcataqua by one Mr. Meſſervey, ſhe was called the America, and ſailed for England the following year; when ſhe came home, ſhe was found ſo bad, that ſhe never was commiſſioned again. There was afterwards another ſhip of 20 guns built at Boſton, by Mr. Benjamin Hollwell, which was called the Boſton, ſhe run but a ſhort time before ſhe was condemned, and thoſe were the only two ſhips of war ever built in America; therefore I thought it my duty to publiſh this, to undeceive the Public in general, to ſhew that what the Author has ſet forth is an abſolute falſity. CLARK GAYTON."

On Monday their Majeſties viſited Lady Suſanna Clayton, at her ſeat near Great Marlow in Bucks; and Tueſday they paid a viſit to Lady Effingham Howard, at her ſeat at Stowe-Green, near Windſor.

Yeſterday (and not before) the Earl of March kiſſed his Majeſty's hand, on being appointed Lord High Commiſſioner to the General Aſſembly of the Church of Scotland, and Firſt Commiſſioner of the Police in that kingdom, in the room of Lord Cathcart, deceaſed.

The ſame day Baron D'Airing, lately arrived here from the Electorate of Hanover, was introduced by Baron Alvenſleben, the Hanoverian Miniſter, to his Majeſty.

Yeſterday John Hely Hutchinſon, Provoſt of

Charleſtown Bar to attack the town, and cover the landing of the army. In conſequence thereof the ſquadron weighed, conſiſting of the Briſtol, Experime[...]
There were 10[...]
Briſtol was lig[...]
The cannonad[...]
hours; but th[...]
board the Act[...]
At low water[...]
heeled into th[...]
kept up by th[...]
with ſuch acti[...]
the whole ſqu[...]
fort. The ſp[...]
ſhot away, ſh[...]
the fort; and[...]
the tranſports[...]
able to get ac[...]
conſtructed o[...]
the batteries l[...]
ſhips went ove[...]
16 men, and 13[...]
tified in the ſame way, and is capable of making an equal reſiſtance. Gen. Lee with his army attacked the flying rear of Gen. Clinton's army, and defeated them. If they had not made a precipitate retreat and embarkation, they had been all cut off. Gen. Lee was ſeen to command on Sullivan's Iſland; and till he came into the province they were in no ſtate of defence. The Ranger, which came home with this expreſs, was attacked by a one maſt ſloop privateer an hour and 40 minutes, and got off. The pilots were quite unacquainted with the navigation of Charleſtown River."

Another account ſays, that when the Ranger ſailed, General Lee was then engaged with Clinton's army; and thoſe troops who were embarked were ordered to land again; the fire obſerved by the Ranger's people appeared to be very hot, and conſiſted of muſquetry and field pieces.

The rebel army at preſent at Boſton, it is ſaid, does not exceed 7000 men, the others have been ſent in detached parties, from Cambridge to New York, and other places.

All the officers allow, that if it had not been for the intrepid conduct of Capt. Scot, of the Active, and Lieutenant Reddall, that the ſquadron had been quite deſtroyed.

By a letter from an Officer in Canada, it appears, that the article in the London Papers, which ſays that the Indians had murdered all the rebels that were taken at the Cedars, is not true. The following is an extract from a genuine letter. " Capt. Foſter, of the 8th regiment, on his way down the river St. Lawrence from Oſwegatchey, with his company of light infantry, 200 Indians, and a few Canadians, attacked a rebel poſt at the Cedars that conſiſted of 500 men, which he carried, after killing ſome and making the reſt priſoners. The In-

of war.

Extract of a Letter from Portſmouth, Aug.

" Yeſterday ſeveral of the ſhips from [...]

der convoy from St. Kitts, is ſafe arrived Dover, after being chaſed by an American [...]vateer, but outſailed her.

The Holland, Capt. Taylor, from Jamai[...] which is one of the miſſing ſhips, on which [...] per cent. was given, was ſpoke with by [...] Taunton, Capt. Fowler, the 10th of July, [...] the Colleradoes, all well.

Capt. Young, of the Matthew, who arri[...] at Dover on the 26th of July, in Lat. 34. ſa[...] ſhip taken by a Provincial privateer.

The Seahorſe, Collinſon, from Greenland, [...] three fiſh, and the Ankerwyke, Barwell, fr[...] Bengal, are arrived in the River.

A gentleman juſt arrived from Derbyſ[...] ſays, that they have had fourteen days co[...]nual rain there, which has damaged imme[...] quantities of hay. He adds, that the crops [...] wheat and oats are greater than ever reme[...]bered, but that hands are ſo ſcarce, they k[...] not how they ſhall get in the harveſt.

The Court of Directors of the Eaſt I[...] Company will nominate writers this ſeaſo[...] the preſidencies of Bengal, Madraſs, and B[...]bay. It is aſtoniſhing the intereſt that is [...]ing at the Weſt end of the town for the n[...]nations of the Bengal writers; and ſo diffi[...] has it been to ſucceed, that, it is ſaid, 4o[...] was actually offered laſt week by a gentle[...] near St. James's for an appointment to a Be[...] writerſhip for his ſon, owing, it is ſuppo[...] to a determination not to ſend out any [...] for theſe three years to come; and alſo to [...] ſons of the firſt gentry in the kingdom g[...]thither ſince the eſtabliſhment of the ſupr[...] council.

A diſpenſation has paſſed the great ſeal, [...]bling the Rev. James Topham, M. A. C[...]lain to Sir John Shelley, Treaſurer of his [...]jeſty's houſhold, to hold the united rectori[...]

INDEPENDENT CHRONICLE (BOSTON)

May 22, 1777

After the Continental Congress declared independence and the war dragged on, Paine wrote his *American Crisis* essays exhorting Americans to continue the struggle. In the third essay, published in the spring of 1777, Paine reminded Americans of the reasons why they had declared independence, accused the opponents of independence of acting from fear, laziness, and greed, and urged Americans to risk everything for their cause.

men began to think ferioufly on the matter; and their reafon being thus ftript of the falfe hope which had long encompaffed it, became approachable by fair debate; yet ftill the bulk of the people hefitated; they ftartled at the novelty of Independence, without once confidering that our getting into arms at firft was a more extraordinary novelty, and that all other nations had gone through the work of Independence before us. They doubted, likewife, the ability of the Continent to fupport it, without reflecting, that it required the fame force to obtain an accommodation by arms as an Independence. If the one was acquireable, the other was the fame; becaufe, to accomplifh either, it was neceffary that our ftrength fhould be too great for Britain to fubdue; and it was too unreafonable to fuppofe, that with the power of being mafters, we fhould fubmit to be fervants.* Their

* *In this ftate of political fufpenfe the pamphlet* Common Senfe *made its appearance, and the fuccefs it met with does not become me to mention. Dr. Franklin, Mr. Samuel and John Adams were feverally fpoken of as the fuppofed Author. I had not, at that time, the pleafure either of perfonally knowing or being known to the two laft Gentlemen. The favour of Dr. Franklin's friendfhip I poffeffed in England, and my introduction to this part of the world was through his patronage. I happened, when a fchool boy, to pick up a pleafing natural hiftory of Virginia, and my inclination from that day of feeing the weftern fide of the atlantic never left me. In October, Seventy-five, Dr. Franklin propofed giving me fuch materials as were in his hands, towards compleating a hiftory of the prefent tranfactions, and feemed defirous of having the firft volume out by the next fpring. I had then formed the outlines of Common Senfe, and finifhed nearly the firft part; and as I fuppofed the Doctor's defign in getting out a hiftory, was to open the new year with a new fyftem, I expected to furprize him with a production on that fubject much earlier than he thought of; and without informing him of what I was doing, got it ready for the prefs as faft as I conveniently could, and fent him the firft pamphlet that was printed off.*

took into keeping a fifter of their fociety, is reverenced and fupported with repeated teftimonies, while the friendly noddle from whom fhe was taken (and who is now in this city) continues a drudge in the fervice of his rival, as if proud of being cuckolded by a creature called a king.

Our fupport and fuccefs depend on fuch a variety of men and circumftances, that every one, who does but wifh well, is of fome ufe: There are men who have a ftrange awkwardnefs to arms, yet have hearts to rifk every fhilling in the caufe, or in fupport of thofe who have better talents for defending it. Nature, in the arrangement of mankind, has fitted fome for every fervice in life: Were all foldiers, all would ftarve and go naked, and were none foldiers, all would be flaves. As *difaffection* to Independence, is the badge of a Tory, fo *affection* to it is the mark of a Whig; and the different fervices of the Whigs down from thofe who nobly contribute every thing, to thofe who have nothing to tender but their wifhes, tend all to the fame centre, though with different degrees of merit and ability. The larger we make the circle, the more we fhall harmonize, and the ftronger we fhall be. All we want to fhut out, is difaffection, and *that excluded*, we muft accept from each other fuch duties as we are beft fitted to beftow. A narrow fyftem of politics, like a narrow fyftem of religion, is calculated only to four the temper, and live at variance with mankind.

All we want to know in America is fimply this, Who is for Independence, and who is not? Thofe who are for it, will fupport it, and the remainder will undoubtedly fee the reafonablenefs of their paying the charges; while thofe who oppofe, or feek to betray it, muft expect the more rigid fate of the jail and the gibbet. There is a kind of baftard generofity, which, by being extended to all men, is as fatal to fociety, on one hand, as the want of true generofity is on the other. A lax manner of adminiftring juftice, falfely termed moderation, has a tendency both to difpirit public virtue and promote

POWARS ...

THE AMERICAN CRISIS.

NUMBER III.

By the Author of COMMON SENSE.

(Continued from our laft.)

HAVING thus gone over fome of the principal points in fupport of Independence, I muft now requeft the reader to return back with me to the period when it firft began to be a public doctrine, and examine the progrefs it has made among the various claffes of men. The era I mean to begin at, is the breaking out of hoftilities, April 19th, 1775. Until this event happened, the Continent feemed to view the difpute as a kind of lawfuit for a matter of right, litigating between the old country and the new; and fhe felt the fame kind and degree of horror, as if fhe had feen an oppreffive plaintiff, at the head of a band of ruffians, enter the court, while the caufe was before it, and put the judge, the jury, the defendant and his council to the fword. Perhaps a more heart-felt convulfion never reached a country with the fame degree of power and rapidity before, and never may again. Pity for the fufferers, mixt with indignation at the violence, and heightened with apprehenfions of undergoing the fame fate, made the affair of Lexington, the affair of the Conti-

in England. But the principal fcheme, and that which has marked their character in every part of their conduct, was a defign of precipitating the Colonies into a ftate which they might afterwards deem rebellion, and under that pretence put an end to all future complaints, petitions and remonftrances, by feizing the whole at once. They had ravaged one part of the globe, till it could glut them no longer; their prodigality required new plunder, and through the Eaft-India article TEA, they hoped to transfer their rapine from that quarter of the world to this. Every defigned quarrel has its pretence and the fame barbarian avarice accompanied the *Plant* to America, which ruined the country that produced it.

That men never turn rogues without turning fools, is a maxim, fooner or later, univerfally true. The commencement of hoftilities, being in the beginning of April, was, of all times, the worft chofen: The Congrefs were to meet the tenth of May following, and the diftrefs the Continent felt at this unparalleled outrage gave a ftability to *That Body*, which no other circumftance could have done. It fuppreffed too all inferior debates, and bound them together by a neceffitous affection, without giving them time to differ upon trifles. The fuffering likewife, foftened the whole body of the people into a degree of pliability, which laid the principal foundation ftone of union, order and government; and which, at any other time, might only have fretted and then faded away unnoticed and unimproved: But Providence, who beft knows how to time her misfortunes as well as her immediate favours, chofe this to be the time: And who dares difpute it?

It did not feem the difpofition of the people at this crifis to heap petition upon petition, while the former remained unanfwered: The

caution, at this time, was e... able to defend their property... they confequently were able t... and in proportion as thefe me... meafure, they honeftly and ... part they have acted fince, h... lifhed their characters. Erro... with it, that the foremoft po... time be reached by the fudden... happens in fentimental differe... fome forcible reafon, quickly c... neither argument nor exampl...

I find it impoffible in the ... out the progrefs which Indep... different claffes of men, and ... moved. With fome, it wa... king of England and his mini... thefe men, governed by the a... ing every thing to hope and ... With others, it was a growin... Britifh court was to create, fer... of confifcated plunder: Men ... in proportion as the evidence ... ceiving it was the true intere... to be her own mafter, gave ... ftep, as they faw her abilitie... it was a compound of all the ... callous to be reached by neith...

REPORTING THE
BATTLE OF MOORE'S CREEK BRIDGE

By William P. Tatum III

Fought on February 27, 1776, the Battle of Moore's Creek Bridge effectively ended major organized resistance to the American Revolution in North Carolina. The engagement played on imperial and local divisions, pitting resettled Scots Highlanders and backcountry Regulators against Tidewater Whig militia. The former hailed from the north of Scotland and had resettled in America following their defeat during the Jacobite Uprising of 1745–46. Before immigrating, the Scots swore oaths of loyalty to the Crown, which they now honored. The Regulators had rebelled against the colonial assembly between 1769 and 1771 over taxation issues but were crushed by the Tidewater elites in a pitched battle at Alamance (near modern Burlington, North Carolina).

In early 1775, Royal Governor Josiah Martin of North Carolina laid the groundwork for the battle to come by organizing the Loyalists. After escaping from a Whig mob in April, Martin continued to coordinate resistance from his headquarters on HMS *Cruiser*. In the latter half of 1775, the Scottish settlements in the interior began mobilizing and were soon joined by British army officers. Among these officers was Donald MacDonald, who would lead the Loyalist forces during the ensuing campaign. In early 1776, Martin received word of a major British relief expedition bound for the Carolinas, which he ordered MacDonald to rendezvous with in February.

Events began to move quickly, as seen in the March 23, 1776, issue of the *Providence Gazette*. Following a meeting at Cross Creek on February 5, the Loyalist forces began their march to the coast. This news reached the Whig authorities by February 13, though the initial strength of the Loyalist force was closer to 3,500 men than the seven hundred reported. A steady stream of desertions weakened MacDonald's ranks throughout the march. By February 19, the opposing forces faced off at Rockfish Creek, where MacDonald began an exchange of letters with Whig General James Moore, which were later published in the April 25, 1776, issue of the *New-England Chronicle*. MacDonald's force slipped away the next day, crossing the Cape Fear River and continuing toward the coast. The Loyalists found their path unavoidably blocked at Moore's Creek Bridge by entrenched militia under Colonels Alexander Lillington and Richard Caswell. After sending an envoy to spy on the Whig camp, MacDonald elected to storm the position early on February 27, directing Lieutenant Colonel Donald MacLeod to lead the assault.

Shortly after dawn that morning, the Loyalist force of about seven hundred men advanced toward the bridge. Finding a redoubt on the west bank unoccupied, the mostly Scottish force quickly moved toward the bridge and exchanged fire with Whig sentries. Unbeknownst to MacLeod, Caswell's force had changed their position from the preceding day, redeploying in earthworks on the far side of the creek, supported by two small cannon. The militia had also removed the planks from the bridge and greased the rails that remained. As the April 4, 1776, issue of the *New-England Chronicle* reported, the Loyalist army attempted to storm across the bridge, led by a company of hand-picked swordsmen with MacLeod at their head. A withering volley of Whig musketry and cannon fire stopped the attack, killing MacLeod and upward of fifty soldiers. The surviving Loyalists fled, with the Whig militia in hot pursuit. Moore's Creek Bridge quickly became an irrecoverable strategic defeat: Whig forces arrested hundreds of Loyalists in its aftermath and confiscated

PROVIDENCE GAZETTE (RHODE ISLAND)
March 23, 1776

Fought on February 27, 1776, the Battle of Moore's Creek Bridge effectively ended major organized resistance to the American Revolution in North Carolina.

thousands of weapons, crippling any potential further attempts at resistance.

The Loyalist defeat at Moore's Creek Bridge revealed that southern Loyalists could not operate effectively against their Whig counterparts without support from British regular troops. The Scottish contingent had suggested as much at the Cross Creek meeting, where they argued for delaying the march until British troops were in a position to provide immediate aid. Unsupported Loyalist uprisings throughout South Carolina and Georgia repeatedly failed throughout the rest of the war. Thus, in the greater scheme of the American Revolution, the Battle of Moore's Creek Bridge stands out as the archetype for the majority of subsequent significant confrontations between Whig and Loyalist militias in the South.

The following letters passed between General Moore, and the Tory General M'Donald, before the late battle in North-Carolina.

A letter from Donald M'Donald, Esq; lately erected Brigadier General in the Tory army by Governor Martin, to Brigadier General Moore.

SIR,

I herewith send the bearer, Donald Morrison, by advice of the Commissioners appointed by his Excellency Josiah Martin, and in behalf of the army now under my command, to propose terms to you as friends and countrymen. I must suppose you unacquainted with the Governor's proclamation, commanding all his Majesty's loyal subjects to repair to the King's royal standard, else I should have imagined you would ere this have joined the King's army now engaged in his Majesty's service. I have therefore thought it proper to intimate to you, that in case you do not, by 12 o'clock to morrow, join the royal standard, I must consider you as enemies, and take the necessary steps for the support of legal authority.

I beg leave to remind you of his Majesty's speech to his Parliament, wherein he offers to receive the misled with tenderness and mercy, from motives of humanity. I again beg of you to accept the proffered clemency. I make no doubt, but you will shew the gentleman sent on this message every possibly civility; and you may depend in return, that all your officers and men, which may fall into our hands, shall be treated with an equal degree of respect. I have the honor to be, in behalf of the army, Sir, Your most obedient humble servant,

DON. M'DONALD.

Head Quarters, Feb. 19, 1776.

His Excellency's proclamation is herewith inclosed.

Brigadier General Moore's answer.

SIR,

Your's of this day I have received, in answer to which, I must inform you that the terms which you were pleased to say, in behalf of the army under your command, are offered to us as friends and countrymen, are such as neither my duty or inclination will permit me to accept, and which I must presume you too much of an officer to expect of me. You were very right when you supposed me unacquainted with the Governor's proclamation, but as the terms therein proposed are such as I hold incompatible with the freedom of Americans, it can be no rule of conduct for me. However, should I not hear farther from you before twelve o'clock to morrow, by which time I shall have an opportunity of consulting my officers here, and perhaps Col. Martin, who is in the neighbourhood of Cross-creek you may expect a more particular answer: mean time you may be assured that the feelings of humanity will induce me to shew that civility to such of your people as may fall into our hands, as I am desirous should be observed towards those of our's, who may be unfortunate enough to fall into your's. I am, Sir, your most obedient, and very humble servant,

JAMES MOORE.

Camp at Rockfish, Feb. 19. 1776.

From Brigadier General Moore, to Brigadier General M'Donald.

SIR,

Agreeable to my promise of yesterday, I have consulted the officers under my command, respecting your letter, and am happy in finding them unanimous in opinion with me. We consider ourselves engaged in a cause the most glorious and honourable in the world, the defence of the liberties of mankind, in support of which we are determined to hazard every thing dear and valuable, and in tenderness to the deluded people under your command, permit me, Sir, through you to inform them, before it is too late, of the dangerous and destructive precipice on which they stand, and to remind them of the ungrateful return they are about to make for their favourable reception in this [illegible] is not sufficient to recall them to the duty which they owe themselves and their posterity, inform them that they are engaged in a cause in which they cannot succeed, as not only the whole force of this country, but that of our neighbouring provinces, is exerting and now actually in motion to suppress them, and which must end in their utter destruction. Desirous, however, of avoiding the effusion of human blood, I have thought proper to send you a test recommended by the Continental Congress, which if they will yet subscribe we are willing to receive them as friends and countrymen. Should this offer be rejected, I shall consider them as enemies to the constitutional liberties of America, and treat them accordingly.

I cannot conclude without reminding you, Sir, of the oath which

...their utter destruction. Desirous, however, of avoiding the effusion of human blood, I have thought proper to send you a test recommended by the Continental Congress, which if they will yet subscribe we are willing to receive them as friends and countrymen. Should this offer be rejected, I shall consider them as enemies to the constitutional liberties of America, and treat them accordingly.

I cannot conclude without reminding you, Sir, of the oath which

you and some of your officers took at Newbern, on your arrival to this country, which I imagine you will find it difficult to reconcile to your present conduct. I have no doubt that the bearer, Capt. James Walker, will be treated with proper civility and respect in your camp. I am, Sir, your most obedient, and very humble servant,

Camp at Rockfish, Feb. 20, 1776. — JAMES MOORE.

From Brigadier General M'Donald to Brigadier General Moore.

SIR,

I received your favour by Capt. James Walker, and observed your declared sentiments of revolt, hostility, and rebellion to the King, and to what I understand to be the constitution of the country. If I am mistaken, future consequences must determine; but while I continue in my present sentiments, I shall consider myself embarked in a cause which must, in its consequences, extricate this country from anarchy and licentiousness. I cannot conceive that the Scotch emigrants, to whom I imagine you allude, can be under greater obligations to this country than to the King, under whose gracious and merciful government they alone could have been enabled to visit this western region: And I trust, Sir, it is in the womb of time to say, that they are not that deluded and ungrateful people which you would represent them to be. As a soldier, in his Majesty's service, I must inform you, if you are to learn, that it is my duty to conquer, if I cannot reclaim, all those who may be hardy enough to take up arms against the best of masters, as of kings. I have the honour to be, in behalf of the army under my command, Sir,

Your most obedient servant,

DON. M'DONALD.

To the commanding officer at Rockfish.

To be sold by Doc. ZECHARIAH HARVEY, of Westminster, in the county of Worcester, the FARM he now lives on, which is situated in the middle of the town, near the Meeting-House, lies on the great road that leads from Boston to Deerfield, and is well situated for public business of any sort. Said farm has a large new House on it, almost finished, with five fire places. On the farm is a good young orchard of about 180 acres, two barns, and a shop suitable for a trader. The land all under good improvement, well fenced, and excellent land for mowing, and pasturage, well watered in every part; a good place for a corn-mill or fulling-mill. Said Harvey has also 400 acres of other lands in town to sell, very good and suitable for settlements, and will be sold in such parcels as will suit the purchaser. All which will be sold very cheap for cash or short credit. Any person inclining to purchase, by applying to said Harvey, will be well used in the affair.

DESERTED from the Continental Hospital, [illegible] JOEL PIRKINS, belonging to Captain Sayer's company, in [illegible] Paterson's regiment; he is about five feet two inches high

... miles fr[illegible] is better [illegible] and by her [illegible] now is; which is not inconsiderable; and he himself has been absent almost the whole of the time (except in the winter, when there was little or nothing to be done;) so that it appears in fact, that she has maintained him, herself, and family, almost entirely since they were unhappily joined. And now, instead of her forsaking him, he has forsaken her, and his family, and let out the farm to a stranger (upon terms which he denied their own son) and seems to request her to remove to a place, (where all things con-

NEW-ENGLAND CHRONICLE (BOSTON)

April 25, 1776

By February 19, the opposing forces faced off at Rockfish Creek, where MacDonald began an exchange of letters with Whig General James Moore, which were later published in this newspaper.

Extract of a letter from Brigadier General James Moore, in the Continental service, to the Honourable Cornelius Harnet, Esq; President of the Provincial Council, North-Carolina, dated Wilmington, March 2d, 1776.

THE 25th of February, by four o'clock, we arrived at Dollison's landing, but as we could not possibly march that night, for want of horses for the artillery, I despatched an express to Moore's creek bridge, to learn the situation of affairs there, and was informed that Col. Lillington, who had the day before taken his stand at the bridge, was that afternoon reinforced by Col. Caswell, and that they had raised a small breast-work, and destroyed a part of the bridge. The next morning, the twenty-seventh, at break of day, an alarm gun was fired, immediately after which, scarce allowing our people a moment to prepare, the Tory army with Capt. M'Cloud at their head, made their attack on Col. Caswell and Col. Lillington, & finding a small intrenchment next to the bridge on our side empty, concluded that our people had abandoned their post, and in the most furious manner advanced within thirty paces of our breast work and artillery, where they met a very proper reception. Capt. McCloud and Captain Campell fell within a few paces of the breast-work, the former of whom received upwards of twenty balls through his body; and in a very few minutes their whole army was put to the flight, and most shamefully abandoned their General, who was next day taken prisoner. The loss of the enemy in this action, from the best accounts we have been able to learn, is about 30 killed and wounded; but as numbers of them must have fallen into the creek, besides many more that were carried off, I sup-

by the men of war, who now lie just below the town, gave the inhabitants reason to apprehend every thing that could be suffered from their disappointed vengeance; however the committee have most spiritedly determined rather to suffer the

His Excellency's ANSWER,

To the Select-men and Citizens of Boston.

GENTLEMEN,

YOUR congratulations on the success of the American arms, gives me the greatest pleasure.

I most sincerely rejoice with you on your being once more in the quiet possession of your former habitations; and, what greatly adds to my happiness, that this desirable event has been effected with so little effusion of human blood.

I am exceedingly obliged by the good opinion you are pleased to entertain of my conduct. Your virtuous efforts in the cause of freedom, and the unparralleled fortitude with which you have sustained the greatest of all human calamities, justly entitle you to the grateful remembrance of your American brethren; and I heartily pray that the hand of tyranny may never more disturb your repose; and that every blessing of a kind Providence may give happiness and prosperity to the town of Boston.

GEO. WASHINGTON.

Thursday last the Lecture, which was established, and has been observed from the first settlement of Boston, without interruption, until within these few months past, was opened by the Rev. Dr. Elliot. His Excellency General Washington, the other General Officers and their suites, having been previously invited, met in the Council Chamber, from whence, preceded by the Sheriff with his Wand, attended by the Members of the Council who had had the Small Pox, the Committee of the House of Representatives, the Selectmen, the Clergy, and many other Gentlemen, they repair'd to the Old Brick Meeting-House, where an excellent and well adapted Discourse was delivered from the 33 chap. Isaiah, 20 verse.

After Divine Service was ended, his Excellency, attended and accompanied as before, returned to the Council Chamber, from whence they proceeded to the Bunch of Grapes Tavern, where an elegant Dinner was provided at the Public Expence; after which many very proper and pertinent Toasts were drank.

Joy and gratitude sat on every countenance, & smiled in every eye. The whole was conducted and concluded to the satisfaction of all.

The Sukey, a large Transport Ship, with 4 Tories at least on board, is ashore on George's Island, and 'tis said cannot be got off.

We hear the Baron De WOEDLKE, formerly a General Officer in the Prussian Service, and lately arrived in Philadelphia, is appointed a Brigadier-General in the Continental Service, and is to do duty in Canada.

A favourite toast, in the best companies, is, "May the INDEPENDENT principles of COMMON SENSE be confirmed throughout the United Colonies."

We hear that about 10 or 12 transport vessels, supposed to be from England, arrived, last Tuesday, in Nantasket road, where 4 or 5 of the enemy's ships of war remain.

The Honourable Continental Congress have declared and resolved, That all ships and other vessels, and all goods, wares and merchandizes, belonging to any inhabitants of Great-Britain, taken on the high seas, or between high and low water mark, shall be deemed and adjudged to be lawful prize.

The Resolves of Congress, respecting the above, will be inserted in our next. Some further accounts from N. Carolina, new advertisements, &c. must also be deferred.

Last Tuesday died at Littleton, aged 38 years, Capt. EBENEZER SYMMES, of Boston. He has left a tender wife, and one daughter, an aged father and a great number of other near relatives to lament the loss of a kind husband, a tender father, a dutiful child and a very affectionate brother and sincere friend. He was a warm friend to his oppressed country, and consequently a determined opposer of the measures pursuing by its present unnatural and cruel enemies, by whom he [were] drove from his habitation in the capital, (where he lived in affluent circumstances) to seek an asylum in the country.

PUBLIC NOTICE is hereby given to such of the Colonels of the Militia ...

NEW-ENGLAND CHRONICLE (CAMBRIDGE, MA)

April 4, 1776

The Loyalist defeat at Moore's Creek Bridge revealed that southern Loyalists could not operate effectively against their Whig counterparts without support from British regular troops. Unsupported Loyalist uprisings throughout South Carolina and Georgia repeatedly failed throughout the rest of the war.

REPORTING THE

BATTLE OF THE RICE BOATS

By Hugh T. Harrington

After the battle of Lexington and Concord and its long wretched retreat, the British were confined to Boston, under siege. It was immediately apparent that food would soon become scarce.

In December 1775, General William Howe ordered a small fleet to Savannah in search of rice and other provisions. The intent was to purchase the supplies rather than antagonize and alienate the population by confiscation. However, use of force was authorized if necessary.

The May 2, 1776, edition of the *New-England Chronicle*, in splendid detail, describes the events. The appearance of the British fleet caused the government, controlled by the Whigs whose Provincial Congress and Council of Safety had replaced the Royal Assembly, to put Royal Governor James Wright under house arrest. Wright believed that the fleet would help restore him and Royal government to power over the Whigs. The Whigs called up the militia and asked for military assistance from South Carolina because it was feared that the British intended to seize Savannah.

Wright, fearing for his safety, fled along with several members of his Royal Council to one of the British ships. When the British Commander, Captain Andrew Barclay, communicated to the Whigs that he wished to negotiate for the sale of food, the Whigs refused and moved twenty rice-filled merchant vessels, referred to as the "rice boats," upriver in hopes of preventing their capture. Barclay went on the offensive, sending ships upriver to Savannah to capture the rice boats.

Musket and light artillery fire erupted as the Whigs tried to protect Savannah while retaining control of the boats. Men were captured on both sides. The British were successful, however, in securing most of the rice boats. The Whigs, without the artillery power needed to halt the British, intentionally set other ships on fire and drifted them down the river in attempts to burn the captured rice boats. Their efforts were only marginally successful.

In the end, the British made off with most of the rice boats. Savannah had never been their objective, nor was restoring Governor Wright and Royal government to Georgia. Captain Barclay did not have the resources and the time required to subdue the Whigs and reestablish the Royal government. Governor Wright sailed away with the British fleet, ending the Royal presence in Georgia. Temporarily, Georgia was in the hands of the Whigs.

The hastily assembled militia could boast that they had saved Savannah from the marauding British. While they had lost the rice boats, they had given up nothing of value to the Revolution. In fact, it was a time for celebration. The president of the Council of Safety wrote that the burning vessels, "passed and re-passed [Savannah] with the tide, which in any other but the present times would be truly horrible, but is now a subject only of gratulation [sic] and applause."

The *New-England Chronicle* accurately reported and concentrated on the dishonorable accounts of the British firing on unarmed Whig representatives and taking other envoys prisoner. Such spotlighting of these events would enflame readers and discredit the British.

The British had suffered a significant defeat as news of the Battle of the Rice Boats emerged as both a military and political victory for the Whig forces. The British had been repulsed from the vicinity of Savannah and had taken the remnants of the Royal government with them. The attack at Savannah transformed Georgia from being on the sidelines in the war to a colony in opposition to British authority.

your province, in a particular manner, renders it necessary, to acquaint you with the occurrences in the former, since the date of our last; to which, and the dispatches proceeding, we refer you.

"Our dispositions in the evening of the 2d, were such as appeared to our officers the most likely to prevent the landing of our enemy; and so as, if they should make their landing good, either above or below the town, to prevent their getting in; however, notwithstanding our vigilance, they, by collusion with the masters and others on board the merchant shipping, which hawled near the shore of Hutchinson's Island in the night time, got on board these ships, about four o'clock yesterday morning; to the number, as far as we are competent to judge, from observations we made, and the intelligence we received, of between two and three hundred, where they affected to conceal themselves.

"We had our fears respecting these shipping, and therefore kept a good watch upon them; but it was impossible for centinels, on this shore, to descry them in boarding from the other, the vessels being betwixt.

"Captain Rice, who commanded a boat of observation, was sent on board the shipping about nine o'clock, to order the rigging on shore, and was, without any noise, or the smallest knowledge of us, kidnapped. This we did not know, till about half an hour afterwards: Two sailors, under pretence of coming on shore for cloaths, gave information of the troops being on board the shipping, and of Rice's being taken: about three hundred were then immediately marched to Yaker, by a discharge down directly upon them of near two hundred shot, both from swivels and small arms; which was kept up while they were in reach; the Captains and men in the boat, not in the smallest degree confused, or even, perhaps, disappointed by the attack, fired their rifles, most of them three several times, and as they say, not without execution: And, wonderful to tell! not a man of them killed; one man only received a slug in the fleshy part of his shoulder, which was immediately cut out, without the smallest inconvenience or danger. The spectators all declare, as we now do, that such a providential deliverance has not yet been known. This unmanly attack, upon a few men in an open boat, produced a general fire from our field pieces and intrenchments; and a smart return from two four pounders and several swivels from the shipping; which lasted from about twelve o'clock to four; and, although they often fired langridge, which continually whistled about our men, not a single man was even touched; but we have no doubt a number of the enemy met with a worse fate, as they were seen frequently to fall.

"About four o'clock, we called a Council, and determined to have the vessels immediately burnt; and issued orders to Col. M'Intosh accordingly, whereupon the Inverness, late Capt. M'Gillivray, loaded with rice and deer-skins, was set on fire, and cut loose, to the amount of 15,000l sterl. Upon this the soldiers, in the most laughable confusion, got ashore in the marsh; while our rifle-men, and field-pieces, with grape shot, were incessantly galling them. The shipping were now also in confusion, some got up the river, under cover of

Colony of the MASSAC
A libel is filed b
named the INDUST
manded by JAMES FUR
supplies to the fleet and
nies, and brought into
Court erected to try and
infesting the sea-coast of
counties of Suffolk, Mid
House in Boston, in said
day of May, 1776, at th
justice of the said captur
suant to the laws of the
vessel, or any person conce
if any they have, why t
tenances, should not be
TIMO

NEW-ENGLAND CHRONICLE (BOSTON)

May 2, 1776

The British had suffered a significant defeat as news of the Battle of the Rice Boats emerged as both a military and political victory for the Whig forces. This edition of the *New-England Chronicle* describes the events of the battle in splendid detail. It accurately reports and concentrates on the dishonorable accounts of the British firing on unarmed Whig representatives and taking other envoys prisoner. Such spotlighting would enflame readers and discredit the British.

NEW-ENGLAND CHRONICLE.

(Vol. VIII.) *THURSDAY, May 2, 1776.* (Numb. 402.)

BOSTON: Printed by SAMUEL HALL, at his Office next to the Oliver Cromwell Tavern, in School-Street.

SAVANNAH, [*Georgia*,] February 7.

THE petition from the Congress of this province to the King, was presented to his Majesty by Governor Johnstone, on the 3d of November last.

February 14. Last Friday arrived a large transport with soldiers from Boston.

February 21. The ship which arrived at Cockspur, on Monday the 12th instant, proves to be a transport from Boston with more soldiers.

On the 12th instant, our Governor and his family took themselves on board the Scarborough, from which he has wrote a letter, to endeavour to persuade us to let the officers, lately arrived in our river, land in this town, and declaring the fleet only want water and fresh provisions, which they will pay for, with a great deal of stuff, to lull the people asleep.

February 28. The Cherokee, the two transports from Boston, a sloop and three small vessels, are now laying at anchor within three miles of this town.

Besides the militia of the town and district of Savannah, there are a number of companies from the country now in this place.

CHARLESTOWN, (S. Carolina) Feb. 16.

We hear from Georgia, that the Scarborough man of war, of 20 guns, lately arrived in Savannah river, with a prize schooner, having 4000lb. of gunpowder on board.

March 8. On Sunday a detachment of 120 men of the Charlestown volunteer companies, set out for Savannah.

We hear from Savannah, that two armed schooners and a sloop had got above the town, through Back River, and had taken a brig and a schooner lying there; that the Syren was arrived in the river; and that some more large vessels were in the offing; that the troops, said to be about 5 or 600, were in transports near the town; That it was expected they would attempt to land, to prevent which, upwards of 1000 Georgia and Carolina militia-men were in Savannah; and that there is too great reason to fear there will be much blood shed.

The troops are said to be the 40th regiment, and a detachment of marines; Majors Grant and Maitland are among them, also Capt. Pitcairn.

Copy of a letter just received, by express, from Georgia.

In the Council of Safety, Savannah, March 4, 1776.

"THE intimate connection between this and your province, in a particular manner, renders it necessary, to acquaint you with the occurrences in the former, since the date of our last; macraw, opposite the shipping, with three fourpounders, and threw up a breast-work. The armed schooner, Hinchinbrook, of — guns, with a number of men on board, which with others, went up the Back river in the afternoon of the day preceding, about this time set sail down the South River, with intent, no doubt, of covering the landing of the troops, from on board the merchant shipping: But being continually fired at, by two companies of rifle-men who were placeed in ambuscade, she was obliged to come very slowly, and [illegible] came to, and returned a very smart fire at every place where the rifle-men fired from, until the tide was spent, and she could not get down. During the course of their firing, only one of our men got wounded, and that slightly in the thigh; but on board, several were seen to fall.

"In town we had exhibited a still more interesting scene; we found the officers and men clamorous, about the capture and detention of Rice; and two gentlemen, Lieut. Daniel Roberts, of the St. John's rangers, and Mr. Raymond Demere, of St. Andrew's parish, solicited and were permitted to go on board, to demand a surrender of Rice and his people. They accordingly divested themselves of arms, and were rowed by a negro on board a vessel, in which were Captain Barclay, the Commodore, and Major Grant; and these officers, contrary to all the principles which cement society, and govern mankind, immediately arrested our deputies, and yet detain them as prisoners. We waited with anxious expectation for near half an hour, when we demanded our deputies, by the help of a trumpet, without getting any other but insulting answers; whereupon we fired two fourpounders directly into them; and then they informed us, that they would send an answer in writing; which they presently after did, signed by Lieutenant Roberts and Mr. Demere, purporting, that if we would send two of the persons in whom the people most confided, they would treat with them.

"Capt. Screven, of the St. John's rangers, and Capt. Baker, of the St. John's rifle-men, chagrined, no doubt (the former particularly, on account of his Lieutenant) by the detention of our deputies, took about a dozen of rifle men in a boat, and rowed directly under the stern of Capt. Inglis, in whose vessel were a great part of the soldiery, and, in peremptory terms, demanded the deputies, and were answered, after one shot from Capt. Baker, by a discharge down directly upon them of near two hundred shot, both from swivels and small arms; which was kept up while they were the armed schooner, while others caught the flame, and as night approached exhibited a scene, as they passed and repassed with the tide, which in any other but the present times would be truly horrible, but is now a subject only of gratulation and applause.

"The ships of Captains Inglis and Wardell neither got up the river, or on fire, they were ordered on shore, and are now prisoners of Captain Screven in the country, and their vessels brought down close into a wharff. They were permitted to write to Capt. Barclay in the evening, to inform of their situation, and to request an exchange of prisoners, which the latter peremptorily refused.

"We have thus given you a particular detail of things, as they really happened, to prevent the belief of any erroneous intelligence; and, from which, you will be competent to judge of our situation.

"Col. M'Intosh laid before the board a resolution of your Congress to aid us, accompanied by a letter from Mr. Lowndes; and we are very glad that you have determined to afford us farther assistance. We wish it may arrive in time.

By order of the Council of Safety,

WILLIAM EWEN, President."

To the Hon. the Congress, or Council of Safety, for South-Carolina.

BOSTON VIEWED FROM DORCHESTER HEIGHTS
North Wind Picture Archives

(*left*) Using the artillery that Henry Knox helped procure from Fort Ticonderoga, General Washington fortified the hill just south of Boston known as Dorchester Heights, which gave the Continental Army a military advantage by placing key British positions within range of bombardment.

WASHINGTON WATCHING EVACUATION OF BRITISH TROOPS FROM BOSTON
North Wind Picture Archives

(*right*) Threatened with destruction, the British army hastily evacuated the city by sea, taking along numerous loyal Bostonians. By March 17, 1776, the last British troops boarded ships, and Boston was again in colonial hands.

REPORTING THE

FORTIFICATION OF DORCHESTER HEIGHTS

By Don N. Hagist

THE STALEMATE HAD TO BE BROKEN. FOR NEARLY A YEAR the British army had been holed up in Boston, surrounded by a determined pro tem military of American inhabitants. The Boston garrison was too strong to dislodge, too weak to take the offensive; the besieging colonists were numerous but had neither a navy to blockade the city nor sufficient artillery to bombard it. Each side could only harass the other. British reinforcements would surely arrive in the spring. The Americans needed a decisive blow before then.

A substantial quantity of artillery had fallen into American hands when Fort Ticonderoga was seized in May 1775. It was, however, three hundred miles away; conventional transport by sea was impossible due to British naval dominance. Instead, General Washington's staff formulated a bold plan to move the ordnance over land during the coldest part of winter, when snow would allow transportation on sleds over the rugged New England terrain. Young Henry Knox was sent in November to carry out this scheme and masterfully assembled the necessary men, oxen, and equipment to haul some sixty tons of heavy guns and stores.

After ten weeks of toil over ice and snow, the guns arrived outside of Boston in late January. Preparations and planning proceeded apace; by March Washington's army was ready to commence a bombardment. Their existing positions were in range of British defenses, but the outcome of the siege hinged on a hill called Dorchester Heights. This prominence allowed artillery to bombard troops in the city and ships in the harbor. The British had moved to take the Heights immediately after storming Bunker Hill; after failing to seize it immediately, American troops occupied it. British officers, including Lieutenant-General John Burgoyne, repeatedly recommended taking the Heights, but their army lacked the strength to risk incurring heavy casualties.

The March 6, 1776, edition of the *New-England Chronicle* recounted the American stratagem: Beginning on March 2, guns in existing fortifications began an incessant bombardment of British positions, creating a distraction and drawing return fire. On the night of March 4, Washington's army fortified Dorchester Heights. When the works were discovered at dawn, they quickly organized an assault, but inclement weather made it impossible to ferry troops across the channel between the city and the Heights. By the time favorable conditions were present, so too were American guns; an assault was impossible. Threatened with destruction, the British army hastily evacuated the city by sea, taking along numerous loyal Bostonians. By March 17, the last British troops boarded ships. Boston was in colonial hands. The fleet stood for a week by Castle William, a British-held fortified island in the harbor, awaiting fair weather. They stocked their transports with water and destroyed the Castle's fortifications, all the while under threat of American guns. On March 27, they departed Boston harbor, never to return.

Americans were jubilant. It was common for newspapers to enumerate the spoils of a great victory; readers of the March 23, 1776, *Providence Gazette* saw for the first time a tally of weapons and supplies captured by a wholly American army. There were no ministerial troops remaining in the thirteen colonies. Rhode Island would soon declare independence, followed by a similar declaration from Congress itself. But the exhilaration would be short-lived; British reinforcements were on the way, and few foresaw the long war that was just beginning.

NEW-ENGLAND CHRONICLE (CAMBRIDGE, MA)

March 6, 1776

Utilizing a substantial quantity of artillery from the capture of Fort Ticonderoga, Washington's army fortified a strategic hill just south of town called Dorchester Heights. Threatened with destruction, the British army hastily evacuated Boston by sea, taking along many Loyalists.

was one of memorable minority of five, in the house of Lords, on the question some time ago, that the British parliament had no right to tax

is, to treat with each province separately about an accommodation, and to dispatch the business:—they are not now to treat with the Congress, as was first reported.

A plan is now under consideration, for all criminals in Great-Britain, sentenced for transportation, to be sent to the British settlements on the coast of Africa.

Mr. Glover has formed a calculation upon undoubted authority of the national loss for the present year owing to the American quarrel, and he makes it twenty-seven millions sterling.

Gov. Cornwallis is making the necessary preparations for the spring campaign, to go to Virginia with 5000 men.

Dec. 8. In pursuance of an advertisement for a meeting of the West-India merchants at the London tavern, a very numerous and opulent assembly met yesterday. Administration, through their emissaries, hoped for a petition in conformity to what the minister had thrown out in the House lately, that he expected an application for bounties from *Nova-Scotia*, Canada, and both Floridas, and the regions of Nova-Zembla; yet no sooner was this business opened by Mr. Edwards and Mr. Walker, than the attention of all present was engaged by the alarming danger of the Colonies from the purport of the bill now pending in Parliament, which denounces famine, and utter destruction to 500,000 of his Majesty's quiet subjects, concerned in the West-Indies.——A bill which inflicts the same punishment alike on the innocent subjects of the islands, as was in mockery of human woes held forth to the interested, yet infatuated landed interests of Britain, as a measure that would reduce America into subjugation; but which failing hitherto of that effect in America,

ative justice in all the colonies.

Should the consequence of the present ruinous

vided; ayes for admitting the troops 68, noes 106. Majority against admitting the foreign troops 38.

We are informed that 600 Georgian troops had marched for St. Augustine, to reduce that important place to the obedience of

COLONIES.

...ult. a Schooner from Hingham, bound to Wil...oad of Corn, was taken by a Tender, and car...k.

Jacob Rush, Esq; is appointed Secretary to the CONGRESS.

...ince, the Yankey-Hero sent into *Newbury-*...e, a fine Brig, of about 200 tons burthen, laden ...e, &c. bound from *White-Haven*, for the use of ...tchers, under the command of General Howe, ...on. This is the fifth prize out of eight which ...bove Port, and we are in hopes of giving a good ...ree remaining.

...which arrived at Cape-Cod last week from London, came passengers, Capt. Samuel Carlton, Capt. John Battin, and Mr. Samuel Bacon, of Salem, Capt. Holmes of Ipswich, Capt. Wyer of Cape-Ann, Capt. Nutter and Capt. Shores of Portsmouth, Capt. Smallcorn of Kittery, Capt. Hatch of Old-York, and John Greenough, Esq; of Wellfleet.

The Continental Army, assisted by a large body of Militia, are now carrying on the siege of Boston with great vigor. Last Saturday night our artillery at the fortresses of Cobble-Hill *and* Lechmere's-Point, *below this town, and at* Lamb's-Dam *in* Roxbury, *bombarded and cannonaded the town; the following night the same was continued with great briskness; and the whole of Monday night the artillery from all the above fortresses played incessantly. Our shot and shells were heard to make a great crashing in the town, but we have not learnt any particulars of the execution done thereby. The enemy returned the fire, from their batteries at* West-Boston, *and from their lines on the Neck, very vigorously. They threw many shells into the battery at* Lechmere's-Point, *one into the fort on* Prospect-Hill, *and one or two as far up as* fort No. 2, *within a quarter of a mile of the College. On Monday night we had two killed, Lieut. Mayo at* Roxbury, *by a cannon ball; and a man at* Lechmere's Point *by a shell, which, with one or two wounded, is all the loss, of any consequence, that we have sustained. We have had but little firing since Tuesday morning.*

On Monday night a body of the Continental troops took possession of two large hills at Dorchester, about a mile from the south part of Boston, where they are now strongly fortified.--These are two of the heights which General Burgoyne said, in a letter to a noble Lord, commanded the town of Boston, and which, he also said, it was absolutely necessary the British troops should be possessed of.

Yesterday was the anniversary of Preston's massacre, in King-Street, Boston, 1770, when Gray, Maverick, Caldwell, Carr and Attucks, were cruelly murdered by a band of ruffians, sent hither by George, the brutal tyrant of Britain, in order to execute his infernal plans for enslaving a free people. An Oration, to commemorate this event, and to impress upon our minds the fatal tendency of standing armies being posted in populous cities, in time of peace, was pronounced, at the meeting-house in Watertown, by the Rev. Mr. Thatcher of Malden, preceded by a prayer by the Rev. Doctor Cooper.

DIED.] At Danvers, last Sabbath, Mr. William Pool, of that place. His death is a great loss to the Town in which he lived, and much lamented by his numerous friends and acquaintance;---to his bereaved family, consisting of a widow and 7 or 8 children, it is inexpressibly distressing. He was son to Mr. Zechariah Pool of Medford, whose death was mentioned in our last.

----At Stoneham, Mrs. Osgood, the virtuous consort of Mr. John Fisk Osgood, of Boston.

----At Rowley, the 26th ult. Mrs. Mighill, widow of Captain Nathaniel Mighill, in her 92d year.---And, not long since, Mrs.

Adams, of said Rowley, in her 91st year.----There is yet living, in the said town of Rowley, twenty persons who are 80 years old and upward; one or two of them above 90, and a number more least Execution.—After dismantling the Castle, and burning the Barracks and other Buildings on the Island, they fell down to Nantasket Road, where they remained when the last Accounts came away.—So very precipitate was their Flight, that they left behind them a great Quantity of Ordnance, Stores, Provisions, &c. among which are the following.

100 Pieces of Cannon in the Town, from 9 to 32 Pounders.

100 Ditto at the Castle.

[illegible] Beds, weighing 5 Tons each.

2500 Chaldrons of Sea-Coal.

25000 Bushels of Wheat.

1300 Bushels of Barley.

600 Bushels of Oats in one Store.

100 Jars of Oil, containing one Barrel each.

150 Horses, marked G. R.

A Number of Cannon and Mortars have been since discovered in the Water.

Extract of a Letter from an Officer in the Continental Army, dated Boston, March 18.

"We are now in firm Possession of Boston and Charlestown.—On Sunday the 17th Instant (being just 9 Months since Bunker's Hill was taken) we observed a large Body of Troops move from thence to Boston. Many were the Conjectures concerning its being evacuated. Two Soldiers of our Company offered to ascend the Hill and examine, which they resolutely did, and discharged their Muskets as Signals for us to enter, when we found the Works extremely advantageous and strong. During this the Shipping in Boston sailed down to the Castle, and anchored.—General Putnam, with a large Party, entered Boston in Boats, by the Way of Cambridge River; a Party from Generals Green and Sullivan's Brigades entered by the Ferry-Way, and others by the Neck.—It would be difficult to describe the Joy of the Inhabitants on this Occasion. "My dear Countrymen and Friends, you are welcome—God bless you—now we are happy, notwithstanding our late unparalleled Distresses"—was the Cry of Fathers, Mothers, Children, &c.—Were I to attempt giving an Account of their truly deplorable Situation, the Cruelties they have experienced, together with the Destruction of Houses and other Property in many Parts of the Town, the Task would be arduous.—Let it suffice to say, they were not suffered by the ministerial Butchers to look out of their own Windows, or speak unless commanded—their Houses ravaged before their Eyes; their Property thrown into the Streets, and destroyed; Vessels scuttled; Masts, Yards and Rigging, wantonly demolished; Houses torn down, and the Furniture, of whatsoever excellent Kind, broke to Pieces, and strewed about the Streets.—The ministerial Army left a Number of Cannon, of various Sizes, which were spiked, and the Trunnions of many broke off. Those who were supposed to have been forward in the Cause of Liberty experienced their utmost Malice. They have likewise left behind them some Tories who

Congress; but said Bird soon after applied to the Committee, desiring their Pardon for [illegible] Crime, and promising Reformation: They therefore have stopped all Proceedings against him, and recommend him to the future good Opinion of the Continent, on his signing the following Paper. By Order of the Committee,

JAMES WILLIAMS, jun. Clerk.

Whereas I the Subscriber, a Shopkeeper in this Town, have been repeatedly guilty of [illegible] Paper Currency in Pay for my Goods, [illegible] find that [illegible] the Resolutions of the Continent, and [illegible] General Court of this Province, I therefore in this humble and public Manner ask the Forgiveness of my Country, and promise for the future to abide by and personally support the Resolutions of the Congress, and General Court of this Province, as far as lies in my Power.

N. BIRD.

Taunton, March 18, 1776.

A true Copy.

Attest. SAMUEL WILLIAMS, *jun. Clerk.*

LOST, on Monday the 18th Instant, a large black Hogskin Pocket-Book, containing sundry Accounts, Notes, &c. together with about Four or Five Pounds in Cash. As the Papers can be of no Use to any but the Owner, he would give a handsome Reward to any Person who will produce him the Book, and its Contents. DAVID LAWRENCE.

N. B. Among the Cash was a Maryland Bill of small Value, and one of the Currency of Pennsylvania.

To be SOLD or LETT,

A FARM, lying in the Northerly Part of Gloucester, containing 250 *Acres, adjoining on Herring Pond;* 150 *Acres are within good Fence,* 7 *or* 8 *Acres of Rye in the*

[illegible]

A Doctor James Howard, late of Cumberland, deceased, are hereby requested to make immediate Payment; and all Persons having any Demands against said Estate, are desired to come and receive their Dues.

of this To[wn]. The Sch[ool] ... reading, a[nd] with Prop[er] Arithmetic ... Parents or ... College Li[brary] ...

RIC[HARD] ...

HEreby ... lic, ... opposite to ... Store, in ... Flour, Ind[igo] ... late and C[o] ... few Englis[h] ...

DEsert[ed] ... Coc[k] ... Town, S... aged abou[t] ... ion, has l[ight] ... Inches hig[h] ... lightish c[omplexion] ... coat, whit[e] ... likewise to[ok] ... to Willian[...] ... ing the f... Silk and ... Waistcoats ... Worsted ... Shirts, fou[r] ... Ditto, fou[r] ... two Pair o[f] ... ed Ditto ...

A FAR[M] ... New-... Acres, wi[th] ... Stories high, ... Well of Wa[ter] ... and other O[ut-houses] ...

PROVIDENCE GAZETTE (RHODE ISLAND)

March 23, 1776

Americans were jubilant about the British army's evacuation of Boston. It was common for newspapers to enumerate the spoils of a great victory, and readers of the March 23, 1776, *Providence Gazette* saw for the first time a tally of weapons and supplies captured by the American army.

REPORTING THE

BATTLE OF SULLIVAN'S ISLAND

By David Lee Russell

Abandoning the Cape Fear region of North Carolina after the Loyalist defeat at Moore's Creek Bridge and "having received intelligence that the fortress erected by the rebels on Sullivan's Island...was in an imperfect and unfinished state" (*London Chronicle,* August 27, 1776), on June 1, 1776, Major General Henry Clinton and Commodore Sir Peter Parker, with a British Royal Navy fleet of forty ships and seven regiments under Major General Lord Earl Charles Cornwallis, weighed anchor and sailed away to Sullivan's Island.

Major General Charles Lee, commander of the Southern Department of the Continental Army, firmly held that Fort Sullivan, built at the entrance to Charleston Harbor, could not be defended, but Colonel William Moultrie, commanding the militia, disagreed. Clinton planned to wade across from Long Island to Sullivan's Island and attack the rear of the fort while Parker's naval forces simultaneously bombarded the fort from the channel side. On June 8, Clinton, with Lord Cornwallis's 2,200 redcoats, disembarked on Long Island from the British transports. On June 18, Clinton learned that that the low tide depth at Breach Inlet across to Sullivan's Island was not eighteen inches as expected but seven feet, which would force him to use his fifteen available flat boats to cross over only four hundred troops at a time.

The night before the battle there were 435 men at Fort Sullivan, but the fort was not completed in the rear, and on the front the logs were only seven feet high. On the northeastern point of Sullivan's Island were 780 Patriot Rangers commanded by Colonel William Thomson. Not counting his transports, Commodore Parker's attack fleet consisted of two fifty-gun ships, five frigates, and four other vessels, with a total of 270 naval guns.

At 9:00 a.m. on June 28, Commodore Parker ordered his men-of-war to begin moving to anchor off Fort Sullivan. By 11:30 a.m., Parker's First Division with four British warships—*Solebay, Experiment, Bristol*, and *Active*—moved into position at four hundred yards off the beach in seven fathoms of water. The bombship *Thunder* with the twenty-two-gun *Friendship* anchored to the southeast and began firing. Meanwhile, the Second Division, with the twenty-gun *Sphinx*, the twenty-eight-gun *Acteon*, and the twenty-eight-gun *Syren*, moved past the fort, raking it with fire as it tried to reach a position behind the fort. Two of these frigates soon ran aground.

As soon as the fleet began the bombardment of Fort Sullivan, Clinton began his attempt to cross Breach Inlet. Clinton's small boat flotilla rowed toward Thomson's men as they opened fire on the flotilla, raking their decks with grapeshot from the cannon and accompanying expert rifle fire. The flotilla dispersed in response to the deadly fire. Clinton and his men looked on in quiet disbelief. Discouraged, Clinton made the decision to abandon the crossing.

At 10:20 a.m., the rebels began to fire on the *Bristol* and then at all the British warships. The cannon battle was intense as the shells of the fleet landed in and around the fort, but it did no damage as the shells buried themselves in the loose sand of the fort, lodged in the soft Palmetto logs, or flew over the fort. At noon, the British fleet was fully engaged off the fort. By 2:00 p.m., Captain Morris reported: "we silenc'd the Fort until ½ past 3... during which time the Rebels fired one Gun" (*Journal of* HMS *Bristol, Captain John Morris, PRO, Admiralty 51/137*). Moultrie had decided to slow down his cannon firing to conserve his ammunition, but it restarted an hour later. The battle raged on the entire day as the fort and its men took their punishment. At 9:00 p.m., Parker's warships withdrew and moved to their former moorings. The twelve-hour battle was over.

It was a clear Patriot victory. As reported in the *London Chronicle* of August 27, 1776, the British suffered forty dead and seventy-one wounded aboard the *Bristol*, while there were twenty-three dead and fifty-six wounded on the *Experiment*. The *Solebay* lost eight wounded, and the *Active* saw one killed with six wounded. Colonel Moultrie had lost only twelve men and twenty-five wounded. On July 4, President Rutledge visited the garrison for a victory celebration, where he promoted William Moultrie to Brigadier General, and the fort was renamed Fort Moultrie.

With their defeat at the Battle of Sullivan's Island, the British expedition to establish a foothold in the south had failed, and the southern colonies would remain invasion-free for another thirty months.

American Defense of Fort Sullivan
North Wind Picture Archives

The cannon battle was intense as the shells of the fleet landed in and around the fort, but there was no damage.

LONDON CHRONICLE

August 27, 1776

Abandoning the Cape Fear region of North Carolina after the Loyalist defeat at Moore's Creek Bridge and "having received intelligence that the fortress erected by the rebels on Sullivan's Island...was in an imperfect and unfinished state," on June 1, 1776, Major General Henry Clinton and Commodore Sir Peter Parker, with a British Royal Navy fleet of forty ships and seven regiments under Major General Lord Earl Charles Cornwallis, sailed to Sullivan's Island. The Battle of Sullivan's Island was a clear Patriot victory and helped keep the southern colonies invasion-free for another two and a half years.

liberties of the Commons. And indeed we find the Peers ſometimes defending the liberties of the people, even when their own venal repreſentatives had given them up: for this

as uſeful as he could on this occaſion, and he merits every thing that can be ſaid in his favour. During the time of our being a-breaſt of the fort, which was near ten hours, a briſk fire

MONDAY, August 26.

The London Gazette. No. 11671.

Whitehall, Auguſt 24.

CAPTAIN Hope arrived on Wedneſday evening laſt from South Carolina with diſpatches from Commodore Sir Peter Parker and Lieutenant General Clinton.

Extract of a Letter from Sir Peter Parker to Mr. Stephens, Secretary of the Admiralty, dated within Charleſtown-bar, July 9, 1776.

"It having been judged adviſeable to make an attempt upon Charleſtown in South Carolina, the fleet ſailed from Cape Fear on the 1ſt of June, and on the 4th anchored off Charleſtown-bar. The 5th ſounded on the bar, and laid down buoys preparatory to the intended entrance of the harbour. The 7th all the frigates and moſt of the tranſports got over the bar into five fathom Hole. The 9th General Clinton landed on Long Iſland with about four or five hundred men. The 10th the Briſtol got over the bar with ſome difficulty. The 15th gave the Captains of the ſquadron my arrangement for the attack of the batteries on Sulivan's Iſland, and the next day acquainted General Clinton that the ſhips were ready. The General fixed on the 23d for our joint attack, but the wind proving unfavourable, prevented its taking effect. The 25th the Experiment arrived, and next day came over the bar, when a new arrangement was made for the attack. The 28th, at half an hour after nine in the morning, informed General Clinton by ſignal that I ſhould go on the attack. At half an hour after ten I made the ſignal to weigh; and about a quarter after eleven the Briſtol, Experiment, Active, and Solebay, brought up againſt the fort. Thunder Bomb, covered by the Friendſhip armed veſſel, brought the ſaliant angle of the eaſt baſtion to bear N. W. by N.

[Price Three-pence.]

for near an hour and a half; but the rebels finding that our army could not take poſſeſſion, about ſix o'clock a conſiderable body of people re-entered the fort, and renewed the firing from two or three guns, the reſt being, I ſuppoſe, diſmounted. About nine o'clock, it being very dark, great part of our ammunition expended, the people fatigued, the tide of ebb almoſt done, no proſpect from the eaſtward, and no poſſibility of our being of any farther ſervice, I ordered the ſhips to withdraw to their former moorings. Their lordſhips will ſee plainly by this account, that if the troops could have co-operated on this attack, his Majeſty would have been in poſſeſſion of Sulivan's Iſland. But I muſt beg leave here to be fully underſtood, leſt it ſhould be imagined that I mean to throw the moſt diſtant reflection on our army: I ſhould not diſcharge my conſcience, were I not to acknowledge, that ſuch was my opinion of his Majeſty's troops, from the general down to the private ſoldier, that after I had been engaged ſome hours, and perceived that the troops had not got a footing on the north end of Sulivan's Iſland, I was perfectly ſatisfied that the landing was impracticable, and that the attempt would have been the deſtruction of many brave men without the leaſt probability of ſucceſs; and this, I am certain, will appear to be the caſe, when General Clinton repreſents his ſituation.—The Briſtol had 40 men killed, and 71 wounded; the Experiment 23 killed and 56 wounded, and both of them ſuffered much in their hulls, maſts, and rigging; the Active had Lieutenant Pike killed, and 6 men wounded; and the Solebay 8 men wounded. Not one man who was quartered at the beginning of the action on the Briſtol's quarter-deck eſcaped being killed or wounded. Capt. Morris loſt his right arm, and received other wounds, and is ſince dead; the maſter is wounded in his right arm, but will recover the uſe of it: I received ſeveral contusions at different times, but as none of them are on any part where the least danger can be apprehended, they are not worth mentioning. Lieutenants Caulfield, Molloy, and Nugent, were the Lieutenants of the Bristol in the action; they behaved so remarkably well that it is impossible to say to whom the preference is due; and so indeed I may say of all the petty officers, ship's company, and volunteers. At the head of the latter I must place Lord **Wm.** Campbell, who was so condescending as to accept of the direction of some guns on the lower gun deck. His Lordship received a contusion on his left side, but I have the happiness to inform their Lordships that it has not proved of much consequence. Capt. Scott, of the Experiment, lost his left arm, and is otherwise so much wounded, that I fear he will not recover. I cannot conclude this letter without remarking, that when it was known we had many men too weak to come to quarters, almost all the seamen belonging to the transports offered their service with a truly British spirit, and a just sense of the cause we are engaged in. I accepted of upwards of fifty to supply the place of our sick. The Masters of many of the transports attended with their boats, but particular thanks are due to Mr. Chambers, the Master of the Mercury.

All the regiments will be embarked in a few days. The first brigade, consisting of four regiments, will sail in a day or two, under convoy, for New York; and the Bristol and Experiment will, I hope, follow with the remainder.

Sir Peter Parker's squadron consisted of the following ships and vessels:

Ships, &c.	Guns.	Commanders.
Bristol	50	Ad. Sir Peter Parker, Capt. John Morris.
Experiment	50	Alexander Scot.
Active	28	William Williams.
Solebay	28	Thomas Symonds.
Actæon	28	Christopher Atkins.
Syren	28	Tobias Furneaux.
Sphynx	20	Anthony Hunt.
Friendship	22	Charles Hope.
Ranger sloop	8	Roger Wills.
Thunder bomb	8	James Reid.
St. Laurence schooner	—	Lieut. John Graves.

Whitehall, August 24.

IT appears by Lieutenant General Clinton's letter to Lord George Germaine, dated July 8, 1776, from the camp on Long Island, province of South Carolina, that Sir Peter Parker and the General having received intelligence that the fortress erected by the Rebels on Sulivan's Island (the key to Charlestown harbour) was in an imperfect and unfinished state, resolved to attempt the reduction thereof by a coup de main; and that, in order that the army might co-operate with the fleet, the General landed his troops on Long Island, which had been represented to him as communicating with Sulivan's Island, by a ford passable at low water; but that he, to his very great mortification, found the channel, which was reported to have been eighteen inches deep at low water, to be seven feet deep; which circumstance rendered it impossible for the army to give that assistance to the fleet in the attack made upon the fortress, that the General intended, and which he, and the troops under his command, ardently wished to do.

St. James's, August 24. The King has been pleased to grant the dignity of a Baronet of the ... Great Britain, to them and their

George Baker, Doctor in Physic, and ... sician in ordinary to her Majesty.

St. James's, August 24. Mr. Robert Halifax and Mr. Edward Holdich are appointed joint Apothecaries to his Majesty's household.

The King has been pleased to grant unto Benjamin Wheeler, D. D. the office and place of Regius Professor of Divinity in the University of Oxford, together with the place and dignity of a Canon of the cathedral church of Christ in the said University, properly belonging to the Regius Professor of the said University; being both void by the death of Dr. Edward Bentham.

BANKRUPTS.

Richard Bishop, late of Holborn, Baker, to surrender Aug. 31, Sept. 14, Oct. 5, at Guildhall. Attorney, Mr. Jennings, of Shoe-lane.

David Riz, of Sweedland-court, in the Parish of St. Botolph Bishopsgate Without, London, Soap-maker, to surrender Sept. 3, 6, Oct. 5, at Guildhall. Attorney, Mr. Collet, Lamb's-conduit-street.

Samuel Cole, of Dartmouth, in Devonshire, Dealer, to surrender Sept. 9, 10, Oct. 5, at the Bear Inn in Southgate-street, Exeter. Attorney, Mr. Walter Prideaux, Dartmouth.

John Law, late of Strutton grounds, Westminster, Scrivener, to surrender Aug. 30, Sept. 11, Oct. 5, at Guildhall. Attorney, Mr. Wright, of Holborn-court, Gray's-inn.

William Holyland, of West Smithfield, London, Linen-draper, to surrender Aug. 31, Sept. 16, Oct. 5, at Guildhall. Attorney, Mr. Lowten, Middle Temple.

William Clarke and Robert Collins, of Paternoster-row, in the City of London, Booksellers, Dealers, and Chapmen, (surviving Copartners of Lacey Hawes, late of the same Place, Bookseller, deceased) to surrender Sept. 3, 6, Oct. 5, at Guildhall. Attorney, Mr. Edmunds, Cursitors-street, Chancery-lane.

Bankruptcy enlarged.

John Radenhurst, late of Dolgun Forge, in the Parish of Dolgelley, in Merionethshire, North Wales, Ironmaster, but now of the Parish of Heswall, in Cheshire, Merchant, to surrender Sept. 14, at Guildhall, London.

Dividends to be made.

Sept. 13. John Coster, jun. of Romsey, in the County of Southampton, and Matthew Jenkins, of the same Place, Common Brewers, at the Dolphin Inn in Romsey.

16. John Davy and Henry Hounsom, of Church-lane, near Whitechapel, Sugar-refiners, at Guildhall.

Certificate to be granted.

Sept. 14. David Goodsman, of the Strand, Bookbinder.

LONDON.

Last Saturday's Gazette contains his Majesty's Order in Council, that a former Order for prohibiting the exporting out of this kingdom, or carrying coastwise, gunpowder, saltpetre, or any sort of arms or ammunition, be continued for three months longer, to commence from the 23d of this inst. August.

A letter from Maryland mentions, "That the body of people which rose in arms against the congress grow every day stronger and stronger, as also that the latter has sent a considerable force to oppose them, and that the two parties lay intrenched at a few miles distance from each other; but unhappily the royalists, since the departure of the greater part of the British forces from the south, had little prospect of success, unless Lord Dunmore should leave his post, and attempt something for their assistance.

... the afternoon their Majesties ...

the crews.

The troops on the expedition at Charlestown, under General Clinton, consist of the 15th, 33d, 37th, 54th, and 57th regiments, and two companies of artillery, making in the whole 3395, to which the marines of the shipping may be added, who are about 300 in number.

General Lee is said to have commanded the Provincial forces at the attack of fort Sulivan.

A considerable number of the English troops were encamped on Long Island during the attack of fort Sulivan. Long Island is about a quarter of a mile distant from Sulivan's Island.

According to the plan of action, the English forces were to have forded from Long Island to Sulivan's Island, and to have attacked the Provincials by land, whilst the ships of war endeavoured to annoy them by a maritime attack. The Commodore was misinformed as to the depth of water between the two islands. The water was found to be seven feet deep.

Extract of a Letter from Amsterdam, Aug. 19.

"Several letters from Madrid, by yesterday's mail, have the following paragraph:—"It is universally reported here, that two members o
the Continental Congress of North America
have been at our court a few days ago; tha
they had several private audiences with ou
King, and actually concluded a treaty of alli
ance with Spain; and that orders were sent t
Don Michael de Caston in consequence there
to sail for North America with his fleet, and
act in conjunction with the Americans." B
how far this is grounded in truth, a very sho
time must discover."

On Friday a packet with letters was receiv
at Gloucester-house from his Royal Highn
the Duke of Gloucester, which bring advi
that the health of his Royal Highness was
so good as it was some months ago, and
a relapse of his former disorder was gre
feared.

An insurrection of the Negroes at Barba
is said to have happened, on account of
scarcity of provisions.

Extract of a Letter from Penzance, Aug

"Last Friday morning, about eight o'c
came in here the William and Mary, Wi
Phillips, Master, from Madeira, with
She was chased all the morning, and the
before, by two American privateers, one m
ing 12, the other 24 guns. When the
was given, all the inhabitants of Pen
Mousehole, &c. and all the adjacent parts b
ing on the Land's-end, went to see the
glasses. They were so near, that we
plainly see the men and guns; they stee
wards the Scilly Islands."

Extract of a Letter from Gosport, Au

"A letter from Capt. Dickson, Com
of the Greyhound, says, he had taken fiv
rican prizes, but has lost four of the
being retaken by the rebels, with his me
he had put on board to take care of th
they are made prisoners. He has but
left, which he kept by him. He sa
going to New York to join Lord Howe

"Thursday a company of the 4th
or King's own, arrived here from Hav
are to embark this day for America."

The Hero, Strivens, from Granada
don, was taken in lat. 21, by the Pro

Capt. Sumner, of the Sunbury,
rived in the river, met with a Frenc
had on board Capt. Strivens, and
English Captains; all three have
ships.

The Favourite man of war at Dep
... the comma

REPORTING THE

DECLARATION OF INDEPENDENCE

By Matthew P. Dziennik

AFTER THE EVACUATION OF BOSTON IN MARCH 1776, William Howe, commanding the British army in America, turned his attention toward the capture of New York. The battle of New York was to be the first military campaign undertaken by the independent United States of America.

In the months after April 1775, when tensions between the colonists and Great Britain had exploded into open hostilities, a series of events had pushed the United Colonies toward a formal declaration of independence. Until the autumn of 1775, many colonists still hoped that their grievances might still be addressed by a sympathetic king and that their troubles were primarily the result of corrupt ministers and the machinations of Parliament. As the November 16, 1775, *New-England Chronicle* had reported of a congressional investigation into British hostilities which would later make up part of the Declaration of Independence, atrocities had been committed by "ministerial troops," implicitly distinguishing between the king and his ministers. The King's Proclamation of August 23, 1775, which declared that the colonies were in "open and avowed Rebellion" and no longer subject to his protection, revealed the naivety of this line of thinking and pushed increasing numbers of colonists toward republicanism.

A new sense that the king was part of the problem was fully demonstrated by the phenomenal success of Thomas Paine's *Common Sense*, published in January 1776. In its bitter denunciation of the king, *Common Sense* both reflected and encouraged an increasing belief that independence was the only viable means of effecting change. Indeed, by the time Richard Henry Lee presented his resolution on independence to Congress on June 7 (following an earlier preamble by John Adams on May 15), the majority of colonists were probably already supportive of independence. At least ninety local "declarations" preceded the Declaration of Independence between April and July 1776. Congress formally declared independence on July 2 and on July 4 finalized the text of the Declaration, which was drafted by John Adams, Benjamin Franklin, Thomas Jefferson, Robert Livingston, and Roger Sherman. On the night of July 4, a handwritten copy of the document was rushed from Congress to a local printer, John Dunlap, who published the first broadsides the following day (the July 6, 1776, issue of the *Pennsylvania Evening Post*, printed by Benjamin Towne, was the first newspaper to publish the Declaration). John Hancock forwarded a copy of the Dunlap broadside to George Washington with instructions that it was to be read to the army defending New York.

While future generations have come to emphasize the stirring evocation of natural rights enshrined in the Declaration—"that all Men are created equal"—revolutionary leaders were intently aware of the Declaration's more immediate value. Washington hoped that it would improve enlistment and inspire his troops to face the regulars of the British army. As the report that appeared in the *London Chronicle* of September 26, 1776, makes clear, when the Declaration was officially read out on July 9, it had the desired effect. The reading was "everywhere received with loud huzzas, and the utmost demonstrations of joy." That same evening, a crowd gathered on the Bowling Green in lower Manhattan, where they proceeded to pull down and decapitate the equestrian statue of George III erected there in 1770. The statue was then delivered to Litchfield, Connecticut, where local women melted it down to make musket balls, something also referenced in the same report.

Most colonists, however, did not elevate the Declaration of Independence to the heights it has since attained. As the articles in the *New-England Chronicle* of August 29, 1776, and the *Pennsylvania Evening Post* of September 28, 1776, demonstrate, the revolutionaries did not idly congratulate themselves on a job well done but immediately turned to the question of the form of the new state and national governments. Much of the work done by Congress over the summer of 1776 was also directed toward international recognition of the United States. As the depth of analysis in the *Scots Magazine* of that August reveals, the audience for the Declaration was foreign as well as domestic. The Declaration was as much about declaring the United States to be a free and sovereign state within the international community as it was about appealing to the loyalties of the colonists. The appearance of the Declaration in the London newspapers is, therefore, significant. The small note contained in the *London Chronicle* from August 13, 1776, was likely a reprint of a government communique that had first appeared in numerous newspapers the previous day. More than half of the world's countries now have their own declarations of independence.

In a series of engagements in the autumn of 1776, Howe savaged the Continental Army and ejected it from New York. The riotous behavior reported on the evening of July 9, however, serves to demonstrate the significance of the Declaration of Independence, a work that would help sustain the revolutionary movement until Britain finally recognized that independence in 1783.

Americans Tearing Down Statue of George III
North Wind Picture Archives

The same evening the Declaration of Independence was read in New York, a crowd gathered in lower Manhattan to pull down and decapitate the equestrian statue of George III. The statue was later melted to make musket balls.

diſpatched to the aid of Hampton, and the Col. of the 2d regiment ſent to take the command of

NEW-ENGLAND CHRONICLE (CAMBRIDGE, MA)

November 16, 1775

As the November 16, 1775, *New-England Chronicle* had reported of a congressional investigation into British hostilities which would later make up part of the Declaration of Independence, atrocities had been committed by "ministerial troops," implicitly distinguishing between the king and his ministers.

ſwimming away with Mr. King's Negro man, who are on ſhore, and a purſuit, it is hoped, may overtake them. There were in the veſſel two men mortally wounded, one is ſince dead, and the other near his end; beſides which, we are informed nine men were ſeen to be thrown overboard from one of the veſſels. We have not a man even wounded. The veſſels went over to Norfolk, and we are informed the whole force from thence is intended to viſit Hampton to-day. If they come, we hope our brave troops are prepared for them, as we can with pleaſure aſſure the public that every part of them behaved with ſpirit and bravery, and are wiſhing for another ſkirmiſh.

PHILADELPHIA, November 4.

In CONGRESS, Wedneſday, Oct. 18, 1775.

RESOLVED, That a juſt and well authenticated account of the hoſtilities committed by the miniſterial troops and navy in America ſince March laſt, be collected, with proper evidence of the truth of the facts related, the number and value of the buildings deſtroyed by them. Alſo the number and value of the veſſels, inward and outward bound, which have been ſeized by them ſince that period, as near as the number and value can be aſcertained. Alſo the ſtock taken by them from different parts of the continent.

That Mr. Deane, Mr. John Adams, and Mr. Wythe, be a Committee for this purpoſe.

A true copy from the minutes,

CHARLES THOMSON, Secretary.

Capt. Stiles arrived here yeſterday from Bermuda. Coming out he ſpoke with a veſſel that left London the 10th of September, the Captain of whom informed him that he ſailed with three men of war and twenty five tranſports, with 5000 Hanoverians, bound for Charleſtown South Carolina,

...the Martiers; and out of five Galloons, that ſailed from Campeachy, four were diſmaſted, two of which put into Georgia, two more into South Carolina, and the fifth ſuppoſed to be loſt.

The Captain of the Tamar Frigate took the Powder and Caſh out of the Galloons, on their Arrival at Carolina; but the Spaniſh Capts in a few Days after took Charge of the Money themſelves.

CAMBRIDGE, November 16.

Yeſterday ſe'nnight Captain Robbins, bound from Ireland to Boſton, in a ſchooner, laden with Beef, Tongues, Butter, Potatoes, and Eggs, (all much wanted for the butchering aſſaſſins there) was taken by a two-maſt boat from Beverly, and carried in there. Capt. Robbins, who has been brought to town, informs us, that he left Ireland the 24th of September, at which time five regiments were embarking on board ſeven ſhips and one brig, for Boſton, and 'twas ſaid that thoſe were all the troops deſtin'd hence this fall, though a large reinforcement was to be ſent in the ſpring, to make up an army of 22,500 men. Capt. Robbins brought papers to the 16th of September, which are not come to hand; alſo the King's proclamation (inſerted in the laſt page) declaring the Coloniſts rebels. Capt. Robbins ſays, The common people of Ireland were almoſt unanimous in favour of the Americans, and that only thoſe in favour of government, appeared againſt us.

Thurſday laſt, at one o'clock P. M. about 300 of the enemy landed at Lechmere's point, covered by the guns of 2 or 3 men of war, which lay off the weſterly part of Boſton. The tide was very full, and our men were retarded in getting on to the point by being obliged to paſs a ford near breaſt high. The enemy (urged on by the proſpect of getting a little lean beef) took the advantage of ſtealing away 5 or 6 cows, and 2 or 3 horſes; and then, on diſcovering our men advancing towards them, run down to their boats with the greateſt precipitation. Our troops fired upon them as they went off, and killed and wounded ſeveral; but how many they loſt we have not been able to learn. Two of our ſoldiers were wounded by cannon balls from the ſhips, which kept up an inceſſant fire upon our men while in purſuit of the regulars.

A gentleman who lately came out of Boſton, aſſures, That the miniſterial rebels in Boſton, by order of their General, How, have taken down the pulpit and all the pews in the old ſouth meeting-houſe, and are uſing it for a riding ſchool;---this he ſaw. Thus we ſee the houſe once ſet apart for the true worſhip and ſervice of GOD, turned into a den for thieves!

Tueſday, laſt week, a privateer from Beverly, took and carried in there a veſſel, Richie maſter, bound from Boſton to Annapolis-Royal, laden with dry goods, &c. on a trading voyage.

Laſt week the privateers from Plymouth, took and carried in there ſeveral veſſels employed in the ſervice of the miniſterial butchers in Boſton; among others, Capt. Jabez Hatch of Boſton.

Governor Martin's proclamation of the 8th of Auguſt, was burnt at Hillſborough, in North-Carolina, by the hands of the common hangman, in purſuance of an order from the congreſs for that purpoſe.

Saturday laſt the general aſſembly of this colony adjourned to Wedneſday the 29th of November inſtant.

MARRIED.] At Eaſt-Greenwich, John Singer Dexter, Eſq; to Miſs Polly Pearce, of that Town.

STRAYED or ſtolen from the Subſcriber, in Salem, laſt Thurſday morning, a ſmall red HORSE, with a roan ſwaggle tail, and a white ſtar in his face. Whoever will return the ſaid horſe to the Subſcriber, or leave him with the Printers hereof, ſhall receive TWO DOLLARS reward, and be paid all neceſſary charges. JOSEPH HILLER.

Commiſſion ſuperſeded.

John Carr, of Scotland-yard, Coal-merchant, (Partner in Trade with James Farrer and Edward Arrowſmith, of the ſame Place, Coal-merchants.)

Bankruptcy enlarged.

James Farrer, Edward Arrowſmith, and John Carr, of Scotland-yard, Coal-merchants and Partners, to ſurrender Aug. 29, at Guildhall.

Dividends to be made.

Sept. 3. John Gardner, late of Romſey, in Hants, Clothier, at the Angel in Romſey.

11. Richard Ford, of Coalbrookdale, in the County of Salop, Ironmaſter, at Mary Corbett's, in High-ſtreet, Bridgnorth, Salop.

20. Benjamin Cooper, late of Walſall, in Staffordſhire, and Joſeph Hodgkin, late of Aldridge, in the ſaid County, Merchants and Traders, at the King's-head in New-ſtreet, Birmingham.

Certificate to be granted.

Aug. 31. William Richardſon, of Fenchurch ſtreet, London, Linen-draper.

LONDON.

Advice is received that the Congreſs reſolved upon independence the 4th of July; and, it is ſaid, have declared war againſt Great Britain in form.

When General Thompſon was conducted in the guard-room at Montreal with the reſt of the priſoners of that day, he requeſted an audience of his brother General, Carleton, and a ſubaltern waited on him with the meſſage, which Carleton refuſed complying with, and returned for anſwer, "that he never held any converſation with rebels."

A letter from Paris received on Saturday, ſays, "that the French Court have abſolutely refuſed to give any anſwer to the demand made by the Engliſh Ambaſſador, 'What they were arming for?"

A number of men, employed by the Board of Works, are now repairing and taking down the battlements at St. James's, to make the building more uniform, according to the preſent taſte.

Since the brigade of foot guards have embarked for America, upwards of 500 recruits have been raiſed and incorporated in the ſaid regiments; the remaining number to compleat the ſame to the full complement of men, are now raiſing.

The Jameſon and Peggy, the Kingſton, Benham, from London, and the Britannia, Sommers, from Waterford, are all arrived at Halifax.

Letters from Jamaica mention, that advice has been received there of the loſs of the Septentrion, a Spaniſh man of war of 74 guns, about 20 leagues from the Havannah (ſuppoſed by lightning) and all the crew periſhed.

The Ulyſſes, Littleton, from London, is loſt at Gambia.

The Thomas, Sides, from Newfoundland, foundered at ſea; the crew were ſaved.

The four 60 gun ſhips now fitting out for

On Tueſday laſt was married at Aſh, in Kent, the Rev. Mr. Hutchinſon of Norbourn, to Miſs Elizabeth Beale Pery, of Aſh.

On Saturday laſt was married at Crayford, in Kent, Mr. Eſſex, of Southampton-ſtreet, Covent-Garden, to Miſs Nancy Wright, of Crayford.

Yeſterday was married Mr. Samuel Fenn, of this City, to Miſs Tate of the Old Change.

On Friday laſt died at Greenwich, Captain Francis Minſhull.

On Saturday laſt died, at his houſe in St. James's-ſtreet, Mr. Matthew Crane, Apothecary to the Houſhold.

At Shrewſbury aſſizes John Herbert for ſheep-ſtealing, was capitally convicted, but afterwards reprieved.

H. M. The Nabob, with Taſte.

This Day was publiſhed, Price 1s 6d.

A New Edition, corrected to the preſent time, on a broad ſheet of elephant paper, proper for framing, with an elegant engraved border,

A COMPLETE TITHE-TABLE: Wherein the nature of tithes, and all things tithable, are ſhewn at one view. With an account of compoſitions, cuſtom, preſcription, and privilege, diſtinguiſhed under their proper heads; with reference to adjudged caſes, and ſtatutes relating to tithes.

Proper for all Veſtries, Halls of Clergymen and Gentlemen, as well as Attornies.

Printed for J. F. and C. Rivington, No. 62, in St. Paul's Church-yard.

Or whom may be had,

Printed in the manner above-mentioned,

A Sporting Table: Wherein all the laws touching game are ſhewn at one view. Price 1s. 6d.

For the TEETH and GUMS.

JACOB HEMET, Dentiſt to her MAJESTY, and the PRINCESS AMELIA, begs leave to recommend to the Public his ESSENCE of PEARL, and PEARL DENTIFRICE, which he has found to be greatly ſuperior, not only in elegance, but alſo in efficacy, plaint will p to ol out i as are becon cure t firm a breatl diſord Sol and r ſtreet, retail by ... and no where elſe in London. Sold alſo by Mr. Purdie, Perfumer, at Bath, price 2s. 6d. each.

For the COMPLEXION, and DISORDERS of the SKIN,

EAU DE FLEURS DE VENICE:

SOCIETY for the Diſcharge
impriſoned for Sm
Craven-ſtreet, St

BEnefactions ſince the laſ
viz.

W. W. a Lady
Lord Chief Baron Smythe, ann
Lady Smythe, ditto
Mr. Hull, ditto
W. J. 3d benefaction
A. B.
D. B.
D. C. July 10
J. H. by J. R.

Diſcharged from the ſeveral polis, and other parts of the ki who could not be relieved by th 39 l. 6 s. 2 d.

Approved the recommendati

Referred for Enquiry 19 Peti

The books may be ſeen by a promote this undertaking, b Eleven and Three, at No. 7, benefactions are received, and meet on Wedneſday the 22 o'Clock in the Afternoon.

Benefactions are alſo receive the Thatch'd-houſe Tavern; t Banking Company; and M ſurer, in St. James's-ſtreet; and Co. in Finch-lane, Cornh in Fleet-ſtreet; Meſſ. Biddul Charing Croſs; Meſſ. Fullers; Co. in Lombard-ſtreet; and ſeller, at Charing-Croſs.

DR. JAMES's ANAL

GEORGE the Thir ROBERT JAMES, of county of Middleſex, Doctor i repreſented unto us, that he h

year of our reign. By writ o

Theſe are the Pills which th ſo many years in his private pra been always in ſuch high eſtim tients. They are particularly

LONDON CHRONICLE

August 13, 1776

News that the United States had declared its independence first arrived in London on August 10, 1776. The printers of the *London Chronicle* finished typesetting the entire Declaration and printed it in the August 17, 1776, edition.

NEW-ENGLAND CHRONICLE (BOSTON)

August 29, 1776

—

Most colonists did not elevate the Declaration of Independence to the heights it has since attained. As the articles in the *New-England Chronicle* of August 29, 1776, and the *Pennsylvania Evening Post* of September 28, 1776, demonstrate, the revolutionaries did not idly congratulate themselves on a job well done but immediately turned to the question of the form of the new state and national governments.

THE

…ND CHRON…

…DAY, AUGUST 29, 1776.

…ILLIS, at their Office oppoſite the new COURT-…

For the NEW-ENGLAND CHRONICLE.

LETTER III.

To the PEOPLE of the MASSACHUSETTS-BAY.

Friends and Countrymen,

YOU are upon the eve of an event, that will prove of the utmoſt conſequence to the State. We congratulate ourſelves upon the Declaration of Independency: but the liberties of the preſent and future generations remain to be ſecured by a proper Form of Government. What we had taken up pro tempore by the advice of the Continental Congreſs is now neceſſarily expiring; for we no longer mean to receive a Governor from the King of Great-Britain, though he ſhould appoint one that would conform to the Charter. It might be queſtioned, whether the General Court can with conſiſtency paſs any new acts, till the Form of Government has been ſettled by the voice of the publick.—However, it may be proper enough, by reaſon of the times, to connive at their proceedings, till you can have digeſted matters, and prepared duly for the important ſervice before you: they being careful to act up to the *ſpirit* of liberty, and not to abuſe the confidence of the people. Suffer me to exhort you, upon every conſideration, not to be hurried or drawn in to any one particular Form of Government, without examining the nature and tendency of it with the greateſt accuracy. The weak and deſigning may tell you, that as you have the power of altering it when you find it defective, it does not ſo much ſignify what it is. The ſame ſet of perſons will argue againſt altering it, when once adopted, upon the plea of your not having given it a fair trial, and the inconvenience that ariſes from fre- … till they have got it eſtabliſhed

having received the inſtructions of their conſtituents upon the head. Whoever are appointed to form a Plan of Government would do well in conſulting the ſeveral Plans that have been already, or may be adopted by the other Colonies, ere they have finiſhed it. It would be well indeed were all theſe Plans publiſhed in each of our news-papers, that ſo you might have an opportunity of canvaſſing the ſubject in your own thoughts, and of culling out the excellencies, and marking the defects to be found in them.

I would now obſerve to you, my Friends and Countrymen, that I have reaſon to believe that there are ſome Gentlemen in the Houſe, who wiſh to have the legiſlature reſt in that body only, and to have no Council or any check upon them. Such Gentlemen may deſign well, but appear to me to be egregiouſly miſtaken. I do not ſay that the *Houſe* mean to engroſs the legiſlature: but they may poſſibly be led inſenſibly into the meaſure by thoſe that ſee further than the majority. They have been thought by ſome to have treſpaſſed already upon the right of the Council, to have leſſened their power, and to have encroached upon their authority as one Branch of the Conſtitution. This is certain, that they have neglected calling in the aſſiſtance of the Council in forming the Plan of Government, and taken the whole to themſelves. One reaſon aſſigned for this omiſſion, by a popular Member, (as I have been told) was very extraordinary, viz. that they were more the Repreſentatives of the people than the Council. Truly not in this caſe; for they were never elected by the people for that purpoſe, and therefore could be no more the Repreſentatives of the people in that, than the Council. Beſides, if the Council conſiſt of the ableſt perſons, whom we muſt ſup- …ſe the Houſe would be careful to elect annu-

a day of faſting, h…
Almighty GOD, ſhe…
imploring of his divi…
zation and eſtabliſhm…
ment for the ſecurit…
civil and religious ri…
kind; no leſs than…
protection in the…
America.

STATE of…

In COUNCI…

ORDERED, Th…
ble Congreſs of t…
ing Perſons app…
Letters of Marque and R…
ſeveral News-Papers in…
fitting out ſuch Veſſels…
plication for their Comm…
By Orde…
JOH…

In CONGR…

RESOLVED, Tha…
ſet forth and fit out…
War, and applying for…
Marque and Repriſal f…
a Writing, ſubſcribed…
and Tonnage or Burthe…
Number of her Guns,…
the Name and Place of…
Owners, the Names of…
cers, the Number of th…
Proviſions and Warlik…
be delivered to the Sec…
Clerk of the Houſe of…
or Council, or Commi…
which the Ship or Veſ…
the ſaid Secretary, a…
And that the Comman…
the Commiſſion or L…

Price THREE *Coppers.* Publiſhed every *Tueſday, Thurſday,* and *Saturday* Evenings.

Vol. II.] SATURDAY, SEPTEMBER 28, 1776. [Num. 264.

For the PENNSYLVANIA EVENING POST.

HOWEVER cenſurable a man may become, by differing in opinion with ſome part of the community, it ought not to leſſen his right and his duty to communicate his ſentiments, whenever he apprehends the happineſs and ſafety of the people to be in danger.

The right of publiſhing my ſentiments, I claim on the general principles of liberty and ſelf preſervation—The Convention for the ſtate of Pennſylvania have preſerved this right *defenſible*, by inſerting of it in the Declaration of Rights, and intending to admit it in their propoſed frame of government, to wit, "that the printing preſſes ſhall be free to every perſon who undertakes to examine the proceedings of the legiſlature, or *any part* of the government," &c. therefore I am induced to examine into *ſome* part of the proceedings of the Convention, and hope no evil tendency to the public will ariſe from the examination.

Public affairs being brought, by the American conteſt with Great-Britain, to a criſis, it was thought conducive to the people's ſecurity, that a change in the powers of government ſhould be made, without the interference of any other authority than the voice of the people.—A number of people were accordingly choſen, out of the ſeveral counties, to meet in Provincial Conference, in order to conſider, what meaſures might be judged beſt to be taken on the alarming occaſion—On conſultation, among other things, the Provincial Conference reſolved, N. C. D. "that it is neceſſary a Provincial Convention be called by this Conference, for the *expreſs purpoſe of forming a new government* in the province"—A Convention was therefore choſen and met, and although above one hundred days (at above 3000 pounds expence in wages) have expired ſince their firſt meeting, a frame of government hath not yet been concluded upon; but in the mean time, ſeveral ordinances have been paſſed by them, touching the liberty, property, and happineſs of the people in their moſt eſſential points—from the ſpirit and tenor of the powers given by the Provincial Conference, as well as by the reſolves of the ſeveral county Committees, it appears the Convention were only choſen to form a plan of government, *not to legiſlate*, or *execute* any laws or ordinances whatſoever.

This being premiſed, I ſhall beg leave to point out the ordinance paſſed Sept. 12th, wherein it is enacted, "that any perſon ſpeaking, &c. againſt the meaſures carrying on by the United States of America, on complaint and proof made on oath before any Juſtice or Juſtices, ſuch perſon ſo offending ſhall be committed to the common jail, for ſuch term as they ſhall deem proper, not exceeding the duration of the preſent war with Great-Britain," &c.

By virtue whereof, it is in the power of any two juſtices nominated by the Convention, on the evidence of a *ſingle* witneſs, without the leaſt *ſemblance* of trial by a jury, to abridge a freeman of his liberty, by committing of him to the common jail, perhaps forever. An appeal is indeed permitted to be made to the Council of Safety, who may *annul* or *confirm* the ſentence of the Juſtices aforeſaid. But who are the Council of Safety? They are nominated by the Convention, without order or authority, no code of laws to govern their proceeding, but left, like the Juſtices, to do as to them ſeem meet. "The ſuppoſed offender being in cloſe confinement, the writ of *Habeas Corpus*, the moſt *celebrated* writ in the law, is hereby rendered void, ſo that he has no other ſatiſfaction under the Ordinance before recited, than to reſt *there* in durance," till chance of war, or any other adventitiory circumſtance, may deliver him; that great oracle of the law, Judge *Blackſtone*, aſſerts, that "the perſonal liberty of the ſubject is a natural inherent right, which cannot be ſurrendered, or ought to be *abridged* in any caſe, without the ſpecial permiſſion of law." The Honorable Congreſs of the United States conſidered the form of trial by jury, and the benefits of a Habeas Corpus writ, to be of ſuch importance, to the preſervation of the liberty of the ſubject, that in their Declaration of Independance, they advance the breach of them as ſolemn teſtimonials of the tyranny and uſurpation of George III. Our wiſe anceſtors *fought, bled* and *conquered,* in ſupport of theſe grand bulwarks of liberty, and handed them down, notwithſtanding the violence of conqueſt, or the ferocity of the times; but why their poſterity ſhould eſteem them of leſs moment in this day, can only be accounted for by thoſe whoſe views and intereſts may be obtained by deſtroying of them.

Another Ordinance, paſſed in Convention in the ſame month, I ſhall next conſider—By authority of this Ordinance a tax and fines are impoſed on the eſtates and perſonal ſervice of the freemen of the province, who are above the age of fifty years, or do not either from conſcientious principles, or other ſolemn obligations, enter into a military ſtate of defence—the effects of which muſt, if carried into execution, be deſtructive to common juſtice, common honeſty, and the rights of mankind in general—the Convention have, in their Declaration, declared, that "no part of a man's property can be juſtly taken from him without his own conſent, or that of his *legal* repreſentatives"—and their intended frame of government expreſsly declares, "that no tax or contribution ſhall be *raiſed* or *paid* by *any* of the people of this ſtate, except by a *law* made for that purpoſe," and farther, "that it ſhall appear clearly to the legiſlature to be of more ſervice to the community than the money would be, if not collected."—The wildeſt enthuſiaſt for popular government will not be bold enough to prove, that the Convention is a *legiſlative body*, or that the money, when raiſed by virtue of the above intended Ordinance, will be better in coffers than circulating among its *proper owners*—there is not, and I hope will not be, any occaſion for the *uſe* of the money as *ſpecified* in the Ordinance, as from *experience* it has been found better to raiſe men into a well diſciplined ſtate of defence, to remain ſo during the preſent unhappy war, than by leading the inhabitants out of the province in a *militia* ſituation; though I admit that a militia, acting within its reſpective province, to be a good ſecurity.—I ſhall not at this time enter into the propriety, or otherways, of what may be moſt advantageous on this head; but, from the tenor of the above recited Ordinance, I ſhall beg leave to ob-

PENNSYLVANIA EVENING POST (PHILADELPHIA)
September 28, 1776

SCOTS MAGAZINE (EDINBURGH)

August 1776

This Scottish periodical was among the first of books, pamphlets, and periodicals to publish the Declaration of Independence in full. Unlike most other printings of the Declaration, *Scots Magazine* included extensive analysis, beginning with the question “In what are they created equal?”

“ In Congress, July 4. 1776.

A Declaration by the Representatives of the United

…

dent: That all men are created equal*; That they are endowed by their Creator with certain unalienable rights: That among theſe are life, liberty, and the purſuit of happineſs †: That to ſecure theſe rights,

* [In what are they created equal? Is it in ſize, ſtrength, underſtanding, figure, moral or civil accompliſhments, or ſituation of life? Every ploughman knows that they are not created equal in any of theſe. All men, it is true, are equally created: but what is this to the purpoſe? It certainly is no reaſon why the Americans ſhould turn rebels, becauſe the people of G. Britain are their fellow-creatures, *i. e.* are created as well as themſelves. It may be a reaſon why they ſhould not rebel, but moſt indiſputably is none why they ſhould. They therefore have introduced their ſelf-evident truth, either through ignorance, or by deſign, with a ſelf-evident falſehood; ſince I will defy any American rebel, or any of their patriotic retainers here in England, to point out to me any two men throughout the whole world of whom it may with truth be ſaid, that they are created equal.]

† [The meaning of theſe words the Congreſs appear not at all to underſtand; among which are life, liberty, and the purſuit of happineſs. Let us put ſome of theſe words together.—All men are endowed by their Creator with the unalienable right of life. How far they may be endowed with this unalienable right I do not yet ſay, but, ſure I am, theſe gentry aſſume to themſelves an unalienable right of talking nonſenſe. Was it ever heard ſince the introduction of blunders into the world, that life was a man's right? Life or animation is of the eſſence of human nature, and is that without which one is not a man; and therefore to call life a right, is to betray a total ignorance of the meaning of words. A living

3 I

434 America: Declaration of Independence, with Rem

rights, governments are inſtituted among men, deriving their juſt powers from the …t of the governed; and whenever
…n, *i. e.* a man with life, hath a right
…t many things; but to ſay that a man
… hath a right to be a man with life,
…urely American, that I believe the
…of no other brain upon the face of
…h will admit the idea. Whatever it
…, I have tried to make an idea out of
…wn I am unable. Prior to my ha-
…y right at all as a man, it is certain *I*
… a man, and ſuch a man *I* certainly
…e if I have no life; and therefore if
…d that *I* have a right to life, then
…d *I* muſt ſignify ſomething without
… and, conſequently, ſomething without life muſt be ſuppoſed to have a property, which without life it is not poſſible it can have.

Well, but they ſay, all men have not only a right to life, but an unalienable right. The word *unalienable* ſignifies that which is not alienable, and that which is not alienable is what cannot be transferred ſo as to become another's; ſo that their unalienable right is a right which they cannot transfer to a broomſtick or a cabbage-ſtalk; and becauſe they cannot transfer their own lives from themſelves to a cabbage-ſtalk, therefore they think it abſolutely neceſſary that they ſhould rebel; and, out of a decent reſpect to the opinions of mankind, alledge this as one of the cauſes which impels them to ſeparate themſelves from thoſe to whom they owe obedience.

The next aſſigned cauſe and ground of their rebellion is, that every man hath an unalienable right to liberty: and here the words, as it happens, are not nonſenſe; but then they are not true: ſlaves there are in America; and where there are ſlaves, their liberty is alienated.

If the Creator hath endowed man with an unalienable right to liberty, no reaſon in the world will juſtify the abridgement of that liberty, and a man hath a right to do every thing that he thinks proper without controul or reſtraint; and upon the ſame principle, there can be no ſuch things as ſervants, ſubjects, or government of any kind whatſoever. In a word, every law that hath been in the world ſince the formation of Adam, gives the lie to this ſelf-evident truth, (as they are pleaſed to term it); becauſe every law, divine or human, that is or hath been in the world, is an abridgement of man's liberty.

Their next ſelf-evident truth and ground of rebellion is, that they have an unalienable right to the purſuit of happineſs. The purſuit of happineſs an unalienable right! This ſurely is outdoing every thing that went before. Put it into Engliſh: The pur-

LONDON CHRONICLE

September 26, 1776

When the Declaration was officially read out in New York on July 9, it was "everywhere received with loud huzzas, and the utmost demonstrations of joy." That same evening, a crowd gathered on the Bowling Green in lower Manhattan, where they proceeded to pull down and decapitate the equestrian statue of King George III erected there in 1770.

---

for the government and im-
colony, adjourned themſelves
y in October next.

une 13, 1776. Reſolved, that
immediately eſtabliſhed, and
en thouſand men, to make up
reſolved, that the colony of
requeſted to furniſh of their
ryland, of their militia, 3400;
nent, of theirs, 600.
a be engaged to the firſt day
t, unleſs ſooner diſcharged by

of the militia commence from
arching from home, and that
one penny a mile, lawful mo-
ations for travelling expences,
for every 20 miles, between
eneral rendezvous, going and

provincial brigadier generals
the flying camp, two from
one from Maryland.
HARLES THOMPSON, Sec.

une 26, 1776. Reſolved, that
ollars be given to every non-
er and ſoldier who will enliſt
m of three years.
HARLES THOMPSON, Sec.

om Lieut. Colonel Campbell
General Howe.

Boſton, June 19th, 1776.
form you, that it has been
to have fallen into the hands
in the middle of Boſton har-
e circumſtances which have
fter are underſtood, I flatter
n will ariſe to myſelf or my
of it.
une, the George and Anna-
ith two companies of the
ghlanders, made the land of
paſſage of ſeven weeks from
e courſe of which we had
of ſpeaking to a ſingle veſſel
the ſmalleſt information of
aving evacuated Boſton. On
t we found ourſelves oppo-
mouth at Boſton, but from
as neceſſary to make ſeveral
Four ſchooners, which we
armed veſſels in the ſervice
which were afterwards found
privateers, of eight carriage
d 40 men each) were bear-
t four o'clock in the morn-
r thereafter two of them
out eleven o'clock the other
g-ſide. The George tranſ-
hich major Menzies and I,
2d battalion, the adjutant,
two lieutenants, five volun-
rs, had only ſix pieces of

receive protection either from a fort or from ſome ſhip of force ſtationed there for the ſecurity of our fleet.

"Toward the cloſe of the evening w... ceived the four ſchooners that were ... with us in the morning, joined by ... Defence, of 16 carriage guns, 20 ſwi... 117 men, and a ſchooner of 8 carria... 12 ſwivels, and 40 men, got under ... made towards us. As we ſtood up for ... road, an American battery opened ... which was the firſt ſerious proof we ... there could ſcarcely be many of our ... Boſton; and we were too far embay... treat, eſpecially as the wind had die... and the tide of flood not half expende... each of the veſſels had twice run a-gro... anchored at George's iſland, and prep... action; but the Annabella, by ſome miſf... or other, got a-ground ſo far a-ſtern of the George, we could expect but a feeble ſupport from her muſketry. About eleven o'clock four of the ſchooners anchored right upon our bow, and one right aſtern of us; the armed brig took her ſtation on our ſtarboard-ſide, at the diſtance of 200 yards, and hailed us to ſtrike the Britiſh flag. Although the mate of our ſhip, and every ſailor on board, (the captain only excepted) refuſed poſitively to fight any longer, I have the pleaſure to inform you, that there was not an officer, non-commiſſioned officer, or private man, of the 71ſt, but what ſtood to their quarters with a ready and cheerful obedience. On our refuſing to ſtrike the Britiſh flag, the action was renewed with a good deal of warmth on both ſides, and it was our misfortune, after a ſharp combat of an hour and an half, to have expended every ſhot that we had for our artillery. Under ſuch circumſtances, hemmed in as we were with ſix privateers, in the middle of an enemy's harbour, beſet with a dead calm, without the power of eſcaping, or even the moſt diſtant hope of relief, I thought it became my duty not to ſacrifice the lives of gallant men wantonly in the arduous attempt of an evident impoſſibility; in this unfortunate affair major Menzie and 7 private ſoldiers were killed; the quarter-maſter and 12 private ſoldiers wounded. The major was buried with the honours of war at Boſton.

"Since our captivity I have the honour to acquaint you, that we have experienced the utmoſt civility and good treatment from the people of power at Boſton, inſomuch, Sir, that I ſhould do injuſtice to the feelings of generoſity, did I not give this particular information with pleaſure and ſatisfaction.—I have now to requeſt of you, that ſo ſoon as the diſtracted ſtate of this unfortunate controverſy will admit, you will be pleaſed to take an early opportunity of ſettling a cartel for myſelf and officers.—I have the honour to be with great reſpect, Sir, your moſt obedient and moſt humble ſervant,

ARCHIBALD CAMPBELL,
Lieut. Col. of the 2d bat. 71ſt reg.

"P. S. On my arrival at Boſton I found that

volunteer, and acting ſerjeant major; James Flint, volunteer; Dougald Campbell, ditto; Donald M'Bane, John Wilſon, 3 ſerjeants, 4 corporals, 2 drummers, 90 private men.

ARCHIBALD CAMPBELL,
Lieut. col. of the 2d battal. 71ſt regiment."

NEW YORK, July 8.

A ſloop of 12 ſix-pounders, belonging to the fleet from Halifax, lying in the Kills, near Mr. Decker's ferry, was almoſt torn to pieces laſt Wedneſday morning, by a party under the command of general Herd, from the oppoſite ſhore, with two eighteen-pounders. The crew ſoon abandoned the ſloop, and we ſuppoſe ſhe is rendered entirely unfit for further ſervice.

July 11. On Wedneſday laſt, the declaration of independence was read at the head of each brigade of the continental army, poſted at and near New York, and every where received with loud huzzas, and the utmoſt demonſtrations of joy.

The ſame evening the equeſtrian ſtatue of George III. which tory pride and folly raiſed in the year 1770, was by the ſons of freedom laid proſtrate in the dirt. The lead wherewith this monument was made is to be run into bullets, to aſſimilate with the brains of our infatuated adverſaries, who to gain a peppercorn have loſt an empire. "*Quos Deus vult perdere prius dementat.*"

Trenton, (New Jerſey) July 8. The declaration of independence was proclaimed here, together with the conſtitution of the colony, of late eſtabliſhed, and the reſolve of the provincial congreſs, for continuing the adminiſtration of juſtice during the interim.

Princetown, New Jerſey, July 10.

"Laſt night Naſſau-hall was grandly illuminated, and independency proclaimed under a triple volley of muſketry, and univerſal acclamations for the proſperity of the united colonies. The ceremony was conducted with the greateſt decorum."

Williamſburgh, Aug. 3. Wedneſday an expreſs arrived here, with the following account of a battle fought by a party of the Fincaſtle militia, with a number of Cherokee and Creek Indians, near the Great-iſland of Holdein, the 20th of July ult.

"Our ſcouts returned and informed that they had diſcovered a large number of Indians

REPORTING THE

NEW YORK CAMPAIGN

By Barnet Schecter

At Boston and Charlestown in 1775–76, the narrow necks of the peninsulas had enabled the Americans to bottle up the king's powerful army, while the Charles and Mystic Rivers were too small for the navy's ships to penetrate the countryside. So the British shifted their focus to New York for a decisive blow against the American rebellion. By sending one army up from New York City and another down from Canada, they hoped to control the Hudson River, splitting New England from the rest of the colonies.

This misguided strategy, which focused on seizing territory instead of destroying the rebel army, was agreeable to General William Howe and Admiral Richard Howe, the co-commanders in chief. The two brothers were opposed to shedding American blood and had agreed to serve only if they were also named as peace commissioners, empowered to grant pardons and negotiate an end to the rebellion. Their older brother, George, was a popular officer who had been killed in the previous war while leading Massachusetts troops at Ticonderoga in 1758. The Massachusetts government funded a monument to him in Westminster Abbey, and his brothers remained grateful. In 1776, the Howes hoped to cow the Americans into submission, not crush them, with the largest expeditionary force Britain had ever assembled: more than thirty-four thousand troops and sailors—roughly the population of Philadelphia, America's largest city—aboard some 430 vessels, including thirty warships.

William Howe arrived in New York's Lower Bay with much of the fleet at the end of June, and on July 2, the day Congress voted for independence, he landed his troops on Staten Island. Richard was delayed in London by final discussions about the peace commission with the king and the secretary of state for the colonies, Lord George Germain, and did not arrive until July 12. The *London Chronicle* (September 26, 1776) describes the Americans' rejection of the admiral's peace initiative. For the next several weeks, the British probed the American defenses. A report in the *New-England Chronicle* (August 29, 1776) dated August 21 and a letter dated August 22 noted that the British were embarking their troops on flatboats, clearly preparing for an attack, and that a terrible storm on the night of August 21 seemed a portent of disaster for the Americans.

On the clear, bright morning of August 22, the British began landing troops on Long Island and soon had a total of twenty thousand ashore. On the night of August 26, the British flanked the American positions on Gowanus Heights and nearly surrounded them in the battle the following day—the largest of the war, with almost thirty thousand troops engaged. Describing the British victory in the Battle of Brooklyn in his report to Germain, printed in the *Continental Journal* (January 23, 1777), General Howe greatly exaggerates the number of Americans killed (see also the *London Chronicle*, October 10, 1776). Howe defends his puzzling decision—infuriating to his subordinates—not to press his advantage and overrun the American lines on Brooklyn Heights when half the rebel army was cornered, its back to the water. Then he explains, without comment, how the rebels escaped across the East River to Manhattan on the night of August 29. The British had lost their best chance to win the war at a stroke.

The Howes repeatedly launched amphibious assaults, beat the Americans on the battlefield, and then let them slip away: at Brooklyn in August, on Manhattan after the Kips Bay landing in September, and at White Plains in October. General Howe gave military explanations for pausing each offensive, but the American general Israel Putnam said it best: "He's either our friend, or he's no general." Despite the loss of 2,800 men taken prisoner at Fort Washington in November, enough of Washington's army escaped to carry on the war. With news often taking more than six weeks to cross the Atlantic, General Howe learned he had been knighted for the Battle of Brooklyn in December—just before Washington struck back at Trenton and Princeton. And the seven-year British occupation of New York would sap their efforts: while defending their principal base, the British failed to send timely support to Burgoyne at Saratoga and Cornwallis at Yorktown—the key turning points of the war.

Battle of Brooklyn
U.S. National Guard

The Battle of Brooklyn was the largest of the war, with almost thirty thousand troops engaged. The British were victorious but lost their best chance to win the war at a stroke.

Vol. XL. [297] The London Chronicle

... 26, 1776.

LONDON CHRONICLE

September 26, 1776

British General William Howe arrived in New York's Lower Bay with much of the fleet at the end of June, and on July 2, the day Congress voted for independence, he landed his troops on Staten Island. William's brother Admiral Richard Howe was delayed in London by final discussions about the peace commission with the king and the secretary of state for the colonies, Lord George Germain, and did not arrive until July 12. The *London Chronicle* describes the Americans' rejection of the admiral's peace initiative.

New York, July 15.

Yesterday Lord Howe sent up a flag, with the captain and lieutenant of the Eagle man of war. The adjutant general met them, after some little ceremony, but as the letter was directed to Geo. Washington, Esq; he could not receive it; the officers insisted much on his receiving it, saying it was of a civil nature, his lordship being invested with unlimited powers, and was sorry he had not arrived a few days sooner. This morning we have accounts that the ships, &c. which passed the town are 50 miles up, opposite to Tary-town, where the river is four miles wide, and they may be safe.

On Tuesday another flag from the fleet appeared, and was met as before, when a letter was again offered, but for the same reason as the former rejected.

Philadelphia: In Congress, July 19. Resolved, that general Washington, in refusing to receive a letter said to be sent from lord Howe, addressed to George Washington, Esq; acted with a dignity becoming his station, and therefore this congress do highly approve the same, and do direct that no letter or message be received, on any occasion whatever, from the enemy, by the commander in chief or other the commanders of the American army, but such as shall be directed to them in the characters they respectively sustain.——By order of the congress. JOHN HANCOCK, President.

Congress, July 19. Resolved, that a copy of the circular letters, and of the declarations they inclosed from Lord Howe to Mr. W. Franklin, Mr. Penn, Mr. Eden, Lord Dunmore, Mr. Martin, and Sir James Wright, late governors, sent to Amboy by a flag, and forwarded to congress by general Washington, be published in the several gazettes, that the good people of these united states may be informed of what nature are the commissioners, and what the terms,

province of New Jersey, as will render the same of the most public notoriety.

"Assured of being favoured with your assistance in every measure for the speedy and effectual restoration of public tranquillity, I am to request you will communicate, from time to time, such information as you may think will facilitate the attainment of that important object in the province over which you preside. I have the honour to be, with great respect and consideration, Sir, your most obedient humble servant, HOWE."

By *Richard Viscount Howe*, one of the King's commissioners for restoring peace to his Majesty's colonies and plantations in *America*, &c.

DECLARATION.

Whereas, by an act passed in the last session of parliament, to prohibit all trade and intercourse with the colonies of New Hampshire, Massachusetts Bay, Rhode Island, Connecticut, New York, New Jersey, Pennsylvania, the three lower counties on Delaware, Maryland, Virginia, North Carolina, South Carolina, and Georgia, and for other purposes therein mentioned, it is enacted, that "it shall and may be lawful to and for any persons or person appointed and authorised by his majesty, to grant a pardon or pardons to any number or description of persons by proclamation in his Majesty's name, to declare any colony or province to be at the peace of his majesty;" and that, "from and after the issuing of any such proclamation, in any of the aforesaid colonies or provinces, or if his Majesty shall be graciously pleased to signify the same by his royal proclamation," the said "act, with respect to such colony or province, colonies or provinces, county, town, port, district, or place, shall cease, determine, and be utterly void:"

And whereas the king, desirous to deliver all his subjects from the calamities of war, and other oppressions which they now undergo, and to restore the said colonies to his protection and peace, as soon as the constitutional authority of

... conducive to the ... ment and peace, ... most gracious p...

... rd his majesty's ... past of the province ... lett's-bay, the 20th day of Ju...

By order of the congress,
JOHN HANCOC...

From the Virginia Gazette, *W... July* 5.

The following are the appointme... new plan of governme...

Patrick Henry, junior, Esq; gov... Page, Dudley Digges, John Taylo... Benjamin Harrison of Berkeley, ... Dandridge, Charles Carter of Shirl... jamin Harrison of Brandon, couns... —Thomas Whiting, John Hutchi... Travis, Thomas Newton, jun. ... Webb, Esqrs. commissioners of ... James Husband, Joseph Prentis, a... ler, Esqrs. judges of admiralt... Randolph, Esq; attorney genera... Everard and James Cocke, Esqrs. c... for settling accounts.

GOD save the Con...

Upon Colonel Henry's being c... vernor by the honourable conven... mittee of the house was directed ... his excellency, to notify to him ... ment, to whom he delivered t... letter:

To the honourable the president ... convention.

"Gentlemen, The vote of t... pointing me governor of this co... has been notified to me, in the m... obliging manner, by Geo. Mason, ... Dudley Digges, John Blair, and ... Dandridge, Esqrs.

A sense of the high and unm... conferred upon me by the conven... heart with gratitude, which I tru... life will manifest. I take this ear... nity to express my thanks, wh... convey to you, gentlemen, in ... terms of acknowledgment.

When I reflect that the tyranny ...

All smuggled arts wou'd be expell'd the land!
Unsully'd Nature shou'd revive again,
And rosy Virtue bloom, without a stain!

Postscript.

FRESH ADVICES *from* AMERICA.

An express is arrived from Lord Howe, giving an account that on Aug. 22, he had obtained possession of Long Island; with the loss only of fifty men killed, and 200 slightly wounded. Of the Provincials 3500 were killed upon the spot, and above 1000 taken prisoners, among whom are Lord Sterling, and Generals Sullivan and Udal. The Rebels on this defeat were retreating from New York with the utmost precipitation; but two men of war were sent up East River to prevent their escape. On our side only Colonel Grant and two or three other Officers were killed, and Col. Monckton wounded, but not mortally.—It is not expected that the Provincials will set fire to New York, as they have no less than 4000 sick in that place, which it is expected soon after this action fell into our hands.—All the artillery of the Provincials were taken; and as there was an epidemical distemper in their camp, all their baggage was instantly burnt.

Several Merchants of this City have received letters of the above-mentioned defeat, which differ only in some trifling particulars. The Coffee-houses about the 'Change this morning were crowded with Merchants who expressed great joy on the occasion.

Private letters from a Gentleman of veracity in New York affirm, that the most horrid cruelties are inflicted on the American Loyalists. They are driven from their homes, on refusing to take the oaths of allegiance to the Congress, and are obliged to take shelter in the woods to escape loathsome gaols and the most horrid tortures; tortures peculiar to that country, of which tarring and feathering is the least. They oblige a man to ride on the ridge of a sharp rail, full of splinters, carried by two men, who take care to shake him so as to bruise him in a most shocking manner. That of carting is another species of torture; it consists in exposing the unfortunate sufferer to ride on a wooden horse, fixed in a cart, and to be pelted by the populace, while he is in this distressed attitude.

Dr. Auchmuty, the rector of New York, together with several other clergymen of that city, have been obliged to shut up their churches, as the leaving out the prayers for the King in the church service, and substituting the Congress, was required of them; and if they refused to comply, they were given to understand they must expect the consequences. So that the church of England is as much persecuted by American republican fanatics at this time, as it was in the days of Oliver in Britain.

Many of the zealous friends of liberty, such as have stood forth against American taxation by a British Parliament, are imprisoned and otherways persecuted, for refusing to renounce their allegiance to his Majesty.

...of Dartmouth, in New England, laden with flour and lumber, and bound to Hispaniola, taken by his Majesty's ship Galatea, is arrived here. On Saturday four seamen belonging to...

LONDON: Sold by J. WILKIE, No. 71, the *Bible*, in St. *Paul's Church-yard*, where Advertisements, a... Authors, are taken in: And where all Persons who chuse to be regularly served with this Paper, are desir...

LONDON CHRONICLE

October 10, 1776

The October 10, 1776, *London Chronicle* summarizes General Howe's exaggerated report of his lopsided victory in the Battle of Brooklyn on August 27, 1776 (see also the January 23, 1777, *Continental Journal*). The paper also emphasizes that New York's loyal merchants were celebrating the British victory. The next few paragraphs contain sharp descriptions of the cruelties inflicted on American Loyalists by the Whigs and assert that some of these persecuted Loyalists were outspoken friends of liberty, too: they opposed taxation by Parliament, without renouncing their loyalty to the king. The Revolution forced Americans to choose between king and country, creating divisions at every level of society and turning the struggle, in some areas, into a civil war.

cargo to ſome workers, who for fear of another female attack, forwarded the nefarious ſtuff to the North-River, precipitately; where it is now afloat, but the women have planted their guards on each ſide.

We can aſſure the public, that the foreigners, in Burgoyne's army, are beginning to de-

that cannot lie, hath promiſed, calmly ſubmitted to "the laſt Enemy, which will be deſtroyed —Death."

NEW-ENGLAND CHRONICLE (BOSTON)

August 29, 1776

A report in the *New-England Chronicle*, under the New-York August 21 dateline, and an "Extract of a letter from New-York, Aug. 22" noted that the British were embarking their troops on flatboats, clearly preparing for an attack, and that a terrible storm on the night of August 21 seemed a portent of disaster for the Americans.

after came to Anchor near Fiſher's Iſland.

Laſt Saturday a number of gentlemen were brought to this town from New-York, where they were lately taken up on ſuſpicion of enter- ... friendly to the American

Extract of a letter from New-York, Aug. 22.

"*I have but a moment in which to tell you what I have to ſay. It is ſaid the enemy are now attempting to land on Long-Iſland. There is a ſmoke there, from whence a General Officer told me he concluded that our people were burning dwelling-houſes, barns, grain and hay, for which orders have been ſome time iſſued in caſe the enemy ſhould attempt to land there. He told me they had certain intelligence that the enemy could not remain on Staten-Iſland, and they could not return to England; they were therefore under a neceſſity of attacking. They are expected here to-day if the wind ſhould favour; it is now a head. Laſt night was the moſt diſmal I ever ſaw. The Almighty appeared among us in terrible majeſty. The ſharpeſt and almoſt inceſſant lightning, from darkneſs thick as Egyptian, and accompanied with dreadful thunder, formed a moſt awful ſcene. A New-York Captain and two Lieutenants were killed in one tent; the Sentinel was ſtruck deaf and dumb, and ſtill continues ſo. A Private in town was killed.*"

trict, will be ... of Suffolk, or ... ber, 1776, to ... the Brigantin ... Tons Burth ... Dean, and ... againſt which ... Officers and ... named the ... the ſame Sloo ... Brig, or any ... appear and ſh ... the ſame Brig ... nances, ſhoul ...

TIM. PICKE...

To be Sold ...

TO-MO...

A Varie... Furnitu... Chairs, Lookin... Table Linnen, ... Stone Ware, ... bound and gil... Drawers, two ... ſix oared Pinna...

FIFTE...

PHILADELPHIA, Auguſt 20.

We are informed by a Captain of a veſſel belonging to this City, who eſcaped a few days ago from Staten-Iſland, that the German troops lately arrived from Halifax are landed on the iſland, where it is ſaid they are to wait the arrival of another reinforcement (which is hourly expected) before the attack will be made on New-York. He adds, that the Britiſh troops ſpeak with great contempt of General Waſhington's army, and are aſſured that they will have the pleaſure of ſoon meeting and ſpending the winter with General Burgoyne and his troops in New-York.

We hear that Lord Dunmore, with the remains of his Æthiopian regiment, joined his Britannic Majeſty's troops on Staten-Iſland, on the 13th of this month.

NEW-YORK, Auguſt 21.

For ſome days paſt, the Britiſh army, on Staten-Iſland, have been embarking on board the tranſports; ſo that we expect their whole force before this city every tide. We hope to give them a reception, worthy the free born ſons of America, and may every freeman of America make this his Toaſt, "That New York is now an aſſylum for American Liberty."

Yeſterday a number of the miniſterial fleet left their ſtation at Staten-Iſland, and went through the Narrows; it is ſuppoſed they mean to land part of their troops on Long-Iſland.

Extract of a letter from Ticonderoga, July 20.

"We have lately ...

On the 26th Inſt. Capt. Nott, of the Privateer Sloop Broome, of New-Haven, arrived at Dartmouth with 4 valuable Prizes, viz.—the Ship Charming Sally, John Stell, Captain, bound to Europe from Dominico; had on board 465 Hogſheads, 31 Teirces, 35 Barrels of Sugar and 25 Tons of Fuſtic:—The Snow Ann, John Bowes, Captain, from Tobago to Lancaſter; had on board 169 Hogſheads, 20 Teirces, 26 Barrels of Sugar, 40 Bags of Ginger and 118 Bales of Cotton:—The Brig Carolina Packet, Mark Towel, Captain, bound from Antigua to London; had on board 151 Hogſheads, 12 Teirces, 10 Barrels of Sugar, 2 Hogſheads of Rum, and 14 Tons of Lignum Vitæ and Fuſtic:—And the Brig John, Daniel McKay, Captain, from Grenada to Dublin; had on board 90 Hogſheads and 2 Teirces of Rum.

Yeſterdy the General Aſſembly of this State convened at Watertown, agreeable to Adjournment.

The Convention of the State of New-York, on the 17th Inſtant (Auguſt) Reſolved, "That the Women, Children and infirm Perſons, in that City, be immediately removed from the ſame, agreeable to a Requeſt of his Excellency General WASHINGTON."

One Day laſt Week, the Viper Sloop of War, belonging to the Royal Pirate, and which has been cruiſing off Cape-Ann ſome Days, took two Sloops, from the Eaſtward.

Laſt Sunday Morning ſafely arrived at Marblehead, a Prize Ship from Jamaica, with a Cargo of Sugars, Cotton, &c. She was chaſed in by the Milford Frigate, who being ...

State of the Maſſachuſetts Bay, Middle Diſtrict, ſſ.

NOTICE is hereb... Libels are filed before me ... ing Veſſels, their Cargoes and ... wit—in Behalf of Captain Jo... Company, and the Owners of ... Revenge, againſt the Ship ANN ... liam Pringle late Maſter; and ... POLLY, of about 170 Tons Burthe... Maſter:—In Behalf of the Cap... Skimmer and their Companies, o... armed Schooners Hancock and Fr... Brigantine PERKINS, burthened ... William Jenkins late Maſter:—In ... Wingate Newman and his Compan... of the Privateer Brigantine Hancoc... NANCY, burthened about 220 To... late Maſter; and againſt the Sloop ... burthened about 95 Tons:—In B... John Phillips and his Company, and ... the Privateer Sloop Warren, againſt ... burthened about 400 Tons, George A... ter: And in Behalf of Caleb Hog a... againſt the Schooner DEBORAH, ... 45 Tons, Samuel Nickerſon late Ma... Veſſels, their Cargoes and Appurtenan... are ſaid to have been taken and br... County of Eſſex. And another Libe... me by Bartholomew Putnam and ... againſt the Ship LORD DARTMOUT... Tons Burthen, her Boats, Sails, Ca... Rigging and Appurten...

... and put the whole army into high ſpirits. Our marine force conſiſts of eight gondolas and four ſchooners. W...

... (ſaid to be a Prize) bound for Salem) and a Schooner and Sloop from the Eaſtward, for this Port, laden with Lumber, &c. ...

... Lee, were, they ſay, by the ... taken in Danvers, in the County of E... of the Sea, between high ...

CONTINENTAL JOURNAL (BOSTON)

January 23, 1777

—

Describing the British victory in the Battle of Brooklyn in his report to Germain, printed in the *Continental Journal* (January 23, 1777), General Howe greatly exaggerates the number of Americans killed (see also the *London Chronicle*, October 10, 1776). Howe defends his puzzling decision—infuriating to his subordinates—not to press his advantage and overrun the American lines on Brooklyn Heights when half the rebel army was cornered, its back to the water. Then he explains, without comment, how the rebels escaped across the East River to Manhattan on the night of August 29. The British had lost their best chance to win the war at a stroke.

From the LONDON GAZETTE EXTRAORDINARY.

Whitehall, September 10, 1776.

THIS morning Major Cuyler, Firſt Aid de Camp to the honorable General Howe, arrived with the following letter from General Howe, to Lord George Germaine:

Camp at Newtown, Long-Iſland, Sep. 3, 1776.

My Lord,

ON the 22d of laſt month, in the morning, the Britiſh, with Colonel Donop's corps of Chaſſeurs and Heſſian grenadiers, diſembarked near Utrecht on Long-Iſland without oppoſition, the whole being landed, with forty peices of cannon, in two hours and an half, under the direction of Commodore Hotham; Lieutenant General Clinton commanding the firſt diviſion of the troops.

The enemy had only ſmall parties on the coaſt, who, upon the approach of the boats, retired to the woody heights, commanding a principal paſs on the road from Flat-Buſh to their works at Brooklyn. Lord Cornwallis was immediately detached to Flat-Buſh with the reſerve, two battalions of light infantry, and Colonel Donop's corps, with ſix field pieces, having orders not to riſk an attack upon the paſs, if he ſhould find it occupied; which proving to be the caſe, his Lordſhip took poſt in the Village, and the army extended from the Ferry to the Narrows, through Utrecht and Graveſend to the Village of Flatland.

On the 25th Lieutenent General de Heiſter, with two brigades of Heſſians from Staten-Iſland, joined the army, having one brigade of his troops, a detachment of the 14th regiment from Virginia, ſome Convaleſcents and recruits, under the command of Lieutenant Colonel Dalrymple, for the ſecurity of that Iſland.

On the 26th Lieutenant General de Heiſter took poſt at Flat-Buſh, and in the evening Lord Cornwallis with the Britiſh drew off to Flatland; about nine o'clock the ſame night the van of the army, commanded by Lieut. General Clinton, conſiſting of the light dragoons and brigade of light infantry, the reſerve, under the command of Lord Cornwallis, excepting the 42d regiment, which was poſted to the left of the Heſſians, the firſt brigade, and the 71ſt regiment, with fourteen field pieces began to move from Flatland, acroſs the country through the new lotts, to ſeize a paſs in the heights, extending from eaſt to weſt along the middle of the Iſland, and about three miles from Bedford, on the road to Jamaica, in order to turn the enemy's left, poſted at Flat-Buſh.

General Clinton being arrived within half a mile of the paſs about two hours before day-break, halted, and ſettled his diſpoſition for the attack. One of his patrols, falling in with a patrol of the enemy's officers, took them; and the General learning from their information that the rebels had not accupied the paſs, detached a battalion of light infantry to ſecure it, and advancing with his corps upon the firſt appearance of day, poſſeſſed himſelf of the hights, with ſuch a diſpoſition as muſt have inſured ſucceſs, had he found the enemy in force to oppoſe him.

The main body of the army, conſiſting of the guards, 2d, 3d, and 5th brigades, with 10 field pieces, led by Lord Percy, marched ſoon after General Clinton, and halted an hour before day in his rear. This column (the country not admitting of two columns of march) was followed by the 46th regiment, with four medium twelve pounders, and the baggage cloſed the rear with a ſeparate guard.

As ſoon as theſe corps had paſſed the heights, they halted for the ſoldiers to take a little refreſhment, after which the march was continued, and about half an hour paſt 8 o'clock, having got to Bedford, in the rear of the enemy's left, the attack was commenced by the light infantry and light dragoons upon large bodies of the rebels, having cannon, who were quitting the woody heights beforementioned to return to their lines upon deſcovering the march of the army, inſtead of which they were drove back, and the army ſtill moving on to gain the enemy's rear, the grenadiers and 33d regiment being in front of the column, ſoon approached within muſquet ſhot of the enemy's lines at Brooklyn, from whence theſe battalions, without regarding the fire of cannon and ſmall arms upon them, purſued numbers of the rebels that were retiring from the heights ſo cloſe to their principal redoubt, and with ſuch eargerneſs to attack it by ſtorm, that it required repeated orders to prevail upon them to deſiſt from the attempt. Had they been permitted to go on, it is my opinion they would have carried the redoubt; but it was apparent the lines muſt have been ours, at a very cheap rate by regular approaches. I would not riſk the loſs that might have been ſuſtained in the aſſault and ordered them back to a hollow way, in front of the works, out of the reach of muſquetry.

Lieut. Gen. de Heiſter began ſoon after day-break to cannonade the enemy in his front, and, upon the ap-

fered conſiderably: Numbers of them however did get into the Moraſs, where many were ſuffocated or drown'd.

The force of the enemy detached from the lines where General Putnam commanded, was not leſs, from the accounts I have had, than 10,000 men, who were under the orders of Major Gen. Sullivan, Brigadier Generals Lord Stirling and Udell. Their loſs is computed to be about 3,300 killed, wounded, priſoners, and drowned; with five field pieces, and one howitzer taken.——A return of the priſoners is incloſed.

On the part of the king's troops, five officers, and ſixty ſix non-commiſſioned officers and rank and file killed; twelve officers and 245 non-commiſſioned officers, and rank and file wounded: One officer and 20 Grenadiers of the Marines taken by miſtaking the enemy for the Heſſians.

The Heſſians had two privates killed, three officers, and twenty-three rank and file wounded. The wounds are in general very ſlight. Lieut. Col. Monckton is ſhot through the body, but there are the greateſt hopes of his recovery.

The behaviour of both officers and ſoldiers, Britiſh and Heſſians, were highly to their honour. More determined courage and ſteadineſs in troops have never been experienced, or a greater ardour to diſtinguiſh themſelves, as all thoſe who had an opportunity have amply evinced by their actions.

In the evening of the 27th the army encamped in front of the enemy's works. On the 28th, at night, broke ground 600 yards diſtant from a redoubt upon their left, and on the 29th at night, the rebels evacuated their entrenchments, and Redhook, with the utmoſt ſilence, and quitted Governor's Iſland the following evening, leaving their cannon and a quantity of ſtores in all their works. At day break on the 30th, their flight was diſcovered, the pickets of the line took poſſeſſion; and thoſe firſt advanced reached the ſhore oppoſite to New-York, as their rear guard was going over, and fired ſome ſhot among them.

The enemy is ſtill in poſſeſſion of the town and iſland of New-York, in force, and making demonſtrations of oppoſing us in their works on both ſides of King's-Bridge.

The inhabitants of this Iſland, many of whom had been forced into rebellion, have all ſubmitted, and are ready to take the oaths of allegiance.

This diſpatch will be delivered to your Lordſhip by Major Cuyler, my firſt Aid de Camp, who I truſt will be able to give your Lordſhip ſuch further information as may be required. I have the honour to be, &c.

W. HOWE.

P. S. I have omitted to take notice, in its proper place, of a movement made by the King's ſhips, towards the town on the 27th, at day break, with a view of drawing off the attention of the enemy from our real deſign, which I believe, effectually anſwered the intended purpoſe.

Return of Priſoner[...]

Three Gener[...]
Colonels; thre[...]
Lieutenants; e[...]
one hundred an[...]
ninety-ſeven.
Privates, of th[...]

Return of braſs[...]
in the engag[...]
found in the[...]
Governor's-I[...]
Cam[...]

Braſs ordnan[...]
1776, 1 five-a[...]
1 three-pounde[...]
Iron ordnanc[...]
Iſland and Gov[...]
1 twenty four p[...]
ers; 3 three po[...]
A quantity o[...]
tools, ſmall ar[...]
on carts, and m[...]
(Signed)[...]
Commande[...]

Return of kille[...]

1 Lieutenant[...]
Serjeants, 53 rank[...]
3 Captains, 8 Lieutenants, 11 Serjeants, 3 Drummers, 231 rank and file wounded; 1 Lieutenant, 1 Serjeant 330 rank and file miſſing.

Liſt of Officers killed, wounded and miſſing.

KILLED,

Captain Sir Alexander Murray, 17th regiment.
Lieutenant Colonel Grant, 40th ditto.
Captain Nelſon 52d ditto.
Captain Logan, 2d regiment marines.

NEW-YORK, *December* 23.

The brave Col. Harcourt of Burgoyne's light horſe, took LEE the deſerter from the king's ſervice and late rebel general, with a party of leſs than 50 Men, in the face of all his vagabond retinue, without the loſs of a ſingle man. The Col. by ſeveral circumſtances, found out his quarters, rode up to the houſe, and ſurrounded it. Lee, fearful of being put to the ſword, begged his life in a manner, which ſhews that, where juſt and loyal principles are not, true courage is never to be found. His life was granted by the brave commander, for further conſideration. Lee was brought to Brunſwick, and is now confined under a ſtrong guard at that place.

Gen. Clinton, Lord Percy, and the troops under their command, have taken poſſeſſion of Rhode-Iſland without firing a ſingle gun. Sir Peter Parker, Commodore Hotham, and his majeſty's ſhips under their command are ſafely moored in Newport harbour.

The rebels are every where mouldering away like a rope of ſand. With the moſt impudent bravadoes, they have not yet had the ſpirit to make any thing like a ſtand in a ſingle encounter. The New-England people have neither money nor recruits; and the reſt of the colonies are nearly drained of their reſources. Ruin, therefore, and deſtruction muſt be the conſequence to them of continuing the War any longer.

Mr. Waſhington, with about two thouſand poor wretches, who can get no ſubſiſtance but by following him, has fled to Lancaſter in Pennſylvania. Many people of Philadelphia have retired with their goods and effects into the back country, with but little proviſion for the winter.

The chain of poſts, formed by the Britiſh troops, reach within 17 miles of Philadelphia upon the banks of the Deleware; and the firſt ſtrong froſt will afford them a natural bridge over it.

The *Allens* and ſome other principal people of Philadelphia, are come in, and have claimed the protection of his majeſty's army.

Great numbers in the Jerſies have likewiſe come in, and taken the oaths; and two whole counties have laid down their arms together, and ſubſcribed the teſts required in the commiſſioner's proclamation. Moſt of them expreſs the deepeſt ſorrow for their late deluſion, and freely acknowledge that when they loſt Britiſh protection, they fell into real ſlavery, and into ſlavery of the worſt kind—the ſlavery of weak and wicked men.

It is reported, that ſome of the coal ſhips from Louiſburg are taken by rebel privateers, fitted out from the coaſts of New-England. Thoſe unhappy people will ſoon ſee, that ſuch ill gotten and pirated goods will only lay the foundation of their own ruin.

Several captures have been ſent in by the men of war in the courſe of laſt week.

We hear that the colony of Connecticut have ſcarce[...]

Newport. Theſe were the only buildings that remained on the iſland after Wallace's expedition up the bay laſt winter.

Capt. Ayres, who lately went with a flag of truce to Newport, returned on Wedneſday, and brought with him about 50 Americans, in exchange for a number of priſoners he delivered there.

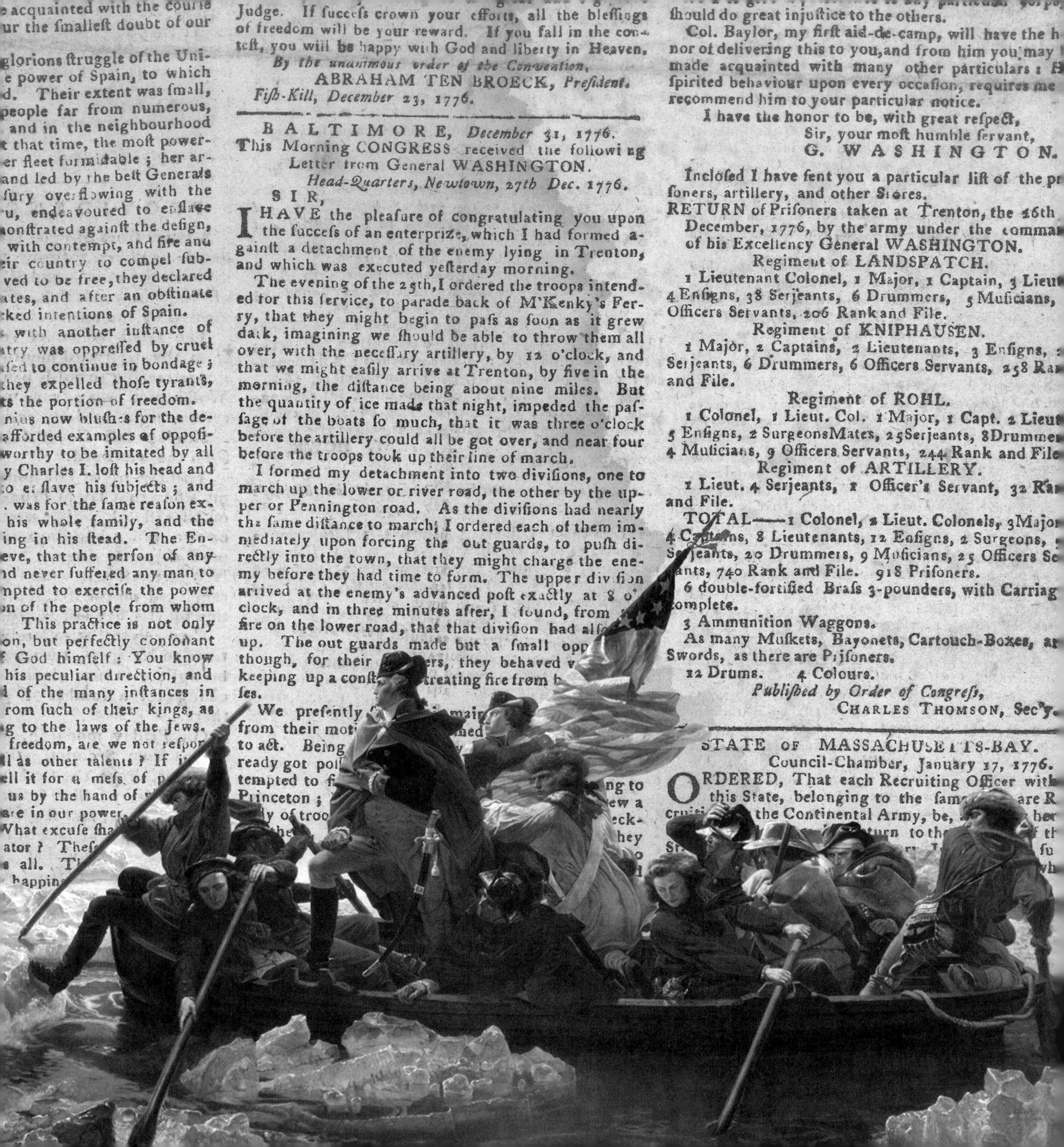

e acquainted with the courſe
ur the ſmalleſt doubt of our

glorious ſtruggle of the Uni-
e power of Spain, to which
d. Their extent was ſmall,
people far from numerous,
and in the neighbourhood
t that time, the moſt power-
er fleet formidable; her ar-
and led by the beſt Generals
fury overflowing with the
u, endeavoured to enſlave
monſtrated againſt the deſign,
with contempt, and fire and
eir country to compel ſub-
ved to be free, they declared
ates, and after an obſtinate
ked intentions of Spain.
with another inſtance of
try was oppreſſed by cruel
ſed to continue in bondage;
they expelled thoſe tyrants,
ts the portion of freedom.
nius now bluſhes for the de-
afforded examples of oppoſi-
worthy to be imitated by all
y Charles I. loſt his head and
o enſlave his ſubjects; and
was for the ſame reaſon ex-
his whole family, and the
ing in his ſtead. The En-
eve, that the perſon of any
nd never ſuffered any man to
mpted to exerciſe the power
on of the people from whom
This practice is not only
on, but perfectly conſonant
God himſelf: You know
his peculiar direction, and
l of the many inſtances in
rom ſuch of their kings, as
g to the laws of the Jews.
freedom, are we not reſpon
ll as other talents? If i
ell it for a meſs of p
us by the hand of
are in our power.
What excuſe ſha
ator? Theſ
s all. Th
happin

Judge. If ſucceſs crown your efforts, all the bleſſings of freedom will be your reward. If you fall in the conteſt, you will be happy with God and liberty in Heaven.

By the unanimous order of the Convention,

ABRAHAM TEN BROECK, *Preſident.*

Fiſh-Kill, December 23, 1776.

BALTIMORE, *December 31, 1776.*

This Morning CONGRESS received the following Letter from General WASHINGTON.

Head-Quarters, Newtown, 27th Dec. 1776.

SIR,

I HAVE the pleaſure of congratulating you upon the ſucceſs of an enterprize, which I had formed againſt a detachment of the enemy lying in Trenton, and which was executed yeſterday morning.

The evening of the 25th, I ordered the troops intended for this ſervice, to parade back of M'Kenky's Ferry, that they might begin to paſs as ſoon as it grew dark, imagining we ſhould be able to throw them all over, with the neceſſary artillery, by 12 o'clock, and that we might eaſily arrive at Trenton, by five in the morning, the diſtance being about nine miles. But the quantity of ice made that night, impeded the paſſage of the boats ſo much, that it was three o'clock before the artillery could all be got over, and near four before the troops took up their line of march.

I formed my detachment into two diviſions, one to march up the lower or river road, the other by the upper or Pennington road. As the diviſions had nearly the ſame diſtance to march, I ordered each of them immediately upon forcing the out guards, to puſh directly into the town, that they might charge the enemy before they had time to form. The upper diviſion arrived at the enemy's advanced poſt exactly at 8 o' clock, and in three minutes after, I found, from fire on the lower road, that that diviſion had alſ up. The out guards made but a ſmall opp though, for their ers, they behaved v keeping up a conſt treating fire from h ſes.

We preſently mai from their mot med to act. Being ready got poſ tempted to f ng to Princeton; ew a dy of troo eck- the hey

ſhould do great injuſtice to the others.

Col. Baylor, my firſt aid-de-camp, will have the honor of delivering this to you, and from him you may be made acquainted with many other particulars: His ſpirited behaviour upon every occaſion, requires me to recommend him to your particular notice.

I have the honor to be, with great reſpect,

Sir, your moſt humble ſervant,

G. WASHINGTON.

Incloſed I have ſent you a particular liſt of the priſoners, artillery, and other Stores.

RETURN of Priſoners taken at Trenton, the 26th December, 1776, by the army under the command of his Excellency General WASHINGTON.

Regiment of LANDSPATCH.

1 Lieutenant Colonel, 1 Major, 1 Captain, 3 Lieut. 4 Enſigns, 38 Serjeants, 6 Drummers, 5 Muſicians, Officers Servants, 206 Rank and File.

Regiment of KNIPHAUSEN.

1 Major, 2 Captains, 2 Lieutenants, 3 Enſigns, Serjeants, 6 Drummers, 6 Officers Servants, 258 Rank and File.

Regiment of ROHL.

1 Colonel, 1 Lieut. Col. 1 Major, 1 Capt. 2 Lieut. 5 Enſigns, 2 SurgeonsMates, 25Serjeants, 8Drummers 4 Muſicians, 9 Officers Servants, 244 Rank and File

Regiment of ARTILLERY.

1 Lieut. 4 Serjeants, 1 Officer's Servant, 32 Rank and File.

TOTAL——1 Colonel, 2 Lieut. Colonels, 3Majors 4 Captains, 8 Lieutenants, 12 Enſigns, 2 Surgeons, Serjeants, 20 Drummers, 9 Muſicians, 25 Officers Servants, 740 Rank and File. 918 Priſoners.

6 double-fortiſied Braſs 3-pounders, with Carriages complete.

3 Ammunition Waggons.

As many Muſkets, Bayonets, Cartouch-Boxes, and Swords, as there are Priſoners.

12 Drums. 4 Colours.

Publiſhed by Order of Congreſs,

CHARLES THOMSON, Sec'y.

STATE OF MASSACHUSETTS-BAY.

Council-Chamber, January 17, 1776.

ORDERED, That each Recruiting Officer within this State, belonging to the ſame are Recruiting the Continental Army, be, her turn to th f th

CHAPTER VIII

CUT TO PIECES

Introduction

After crushing, lopsided defeats in New York, General Washington's war-torn army retreated to New Jersey, where the pivotal day-after-Christmas victory against German mercenaries inspired the American troops to persevere. Confidence in Washington and the Continental Army is restored, but enlistment goals are increasingly difficult to achieve and an alliance with France is needed more than ever. While the French remain noncommittal, British General John Burgoyne returns to America in hopes of delivering a quick and decisive blow by taking the Hudson River, the strategic artery separating the north and south colonies. Fort Ticonderoga and Philadelphia, America's political capital, fall into British hands. Without aid, General Burgoyne surrenders at Saratoga to American Generals Horatio Gates and Benedict Arnold, changing the face of the war.

Continental Journal
January 23, 1777

Washington Crossing the Delaware by Emanuel Leutze
Metropolitan Museum of Art (current location)

REPORTING THE BATTLES OF TRENTON AND PRINCETON

By Bruce Chadwick

The fabled nighttime crossing of the Delaware River by George Washington's army on Christmas Day 1776 in a blizzard and freezing cold has long been a part of American legend. In truth, it was not a flag-waving, drums-beating crossing at all but a quiet, difficult sail across turbulent, freezing waters filled with large, heavy, flat chunks of ice and riverbanks covered with glistening snow.

After the treacherous crossing, the Continental Army, with men hauling just eight cannon, trudged some nine miles south on the New Jersey side of the river and surprised the Hessians at Trenton, attacking them through the snowstorm shortly before 8 a.m. The Hessians, reportedly England's toughest soldiers, were startled. Their colonel, Johann Rall, was shot dead during the assault and his troops had no one to lead them. They were defeated in a battle that lasted less than an hour. Near the end of the war, British General Charles Lord Cornwallis told his American captors that the crossing of the Delaware turned the tide of the war in favor of the Americans.

The story was well told—with sizable gaps—by George Washington in his letter to Congress, which was reprinted in many American newspapers and badly told by British sympathizers writing in their newspapers.

Near the end of the war, British General Charles Lord Cornwallis told his American captors that the crossing of the Delaware turned the tide of the war in favor of the Americans.

Washington, who saw most of the battle as he raced back and forth through Trenton on his horse with musket balls flying through the air around him, wrote a colorful and explosive letter that was published in the January 23, 1777, *Continental Journal*. It was written not only to state the facts, but also to drum up Congressional, press, and public support for his army. Washington offered a straightforward account of the battle. He wrote near the end of it that the Hessians surrendered because they knew they were about to be "cut to pieces," a dramatic phrase. He did not know the extent of the Hessians killed or wounded and did not exaggerate, as the British always did. He praised his men, writing that their behavior reflected "the highest honor" upon them and that they had passed over an entire river, faced a violent snow and ice storm, and marched a great distance.

The British press dismissed the battle and the Continental Army. The editor of one pro-British paper called the American army a "vagabond retinue." He also wrote that the army was comprised of "Mr. Washington (they often disdainfully called him "mister" and not General) and his two thousand poor wretches."

In its story, the *London Chronicle* (February 25, 1777) acknowledged that Washington had defeated the Hessians, but in the next line reminded readers that the British army, strong as ever, was marching throughout New Jersey and had nothing more to fear. It also wrote that many of Washington's ten thousand men were deserting. (He actually had about five thousand men but had spies feeding the British the much higher figure.)

A remarkable story from the January 13, 1777, *New-York Gazette*, reprinted in the March 4, 1777, *London Chronicle*, wrote of the British defeat ten days later at Princeton in such a way that any reader would have thought they had won the battle. The writer invented quotes from the dying American General Hugh Mercer that the British were even braver than he had heard and from British troops hailing their redcoat toughness and ability to conduct a very orderly retreat. Conversely, an American soldier sent a letter to an American paper in which he correctly described the Princeton engagement as a huge victory for the Americans, adding, as General Washington often told people, that if they only had more men they might have moved on to New Brunswick, defeated another British army there, and possibly won the war (see extract of letter from "Morris Town," January 8, in the January 23, 1777, *Continental Journal*).

Following his surprising two victories in ten days, George Washington realized that his army might win the war and that the public would now flock to its cause. Over the next few weeks, as word of the victories spread throughout the country, dozens of other newspapers agreed.

And James Rivington, the editor of the strong pro-British newspaper the *New-York Gazette* and who was close friends with all the British generals and insulted the Americans in all of his stories? One year later, he agreed, too, and became Washington's top spy.

Trenton, 1776
U.S. Army Center of Military History

George Washington witnessed most of the battle as he raced back and forth through Trenton on his horse with musket balls flying through the air around him.

JANUARY 23, 1777

The CONTINENTAL JOURNAL

BALTIMORE, *December 31, 1776.*

This Morning CONGRESS received the following Letter from General WASHINGTON.

Head-Quarters, Newtown, 27th Dec. 1776.

SIR,

I HAVE the pleasure of congratulating you upon the success of an enterprize, which I had formed against a detachment of the enemy lying in Trenton, and which was executed yesterday morning.

The evening of the 25th, I ordered the troops intended for this service, to parade back of M'Kenky's Ferry, that they might begin to pass as soon as it grew dark, imagining we should be able to throw them all over, with the necessary artillery, by 12 o'clock, and that we might easily arrive at Trenton, by five in the morning, the distance being about nine miles. But the quantity of ice made that night, impeded the passage of the boats so much, that it was three o'clock before the artillery could all be got over, and near four before the troops took up their line of march.

I formed my detachment into two divisions, one to march up the lower or river road, the other by the upper or Pennington road. As the divisions had nearly the same distance to march, I ordered each of them immediately upon forcing the out-guards, to push directly into the town, that they might charge the enemy before they had time to form. The upper division arrived at the enemy's advanced post exactly at 8 o'clock, and in three minutes after, I found, from the fire on the lower road, that the division had also got up. The out guards made but a small opposition, though, for their numbers, they behaved very well, keeping up a constant retreating fire from behind houses.

We presently saw their main body formed, but, from their motions, they seemed undetermined how to act. Being hard pressed by our troops, who had already got possession of part of their artillery, they attempted to file off by a road, on their right leading to Princeton ; but perceiving their intention, I threw a body of troops in their way, which immediately checked them. Finding, from our disposition, that they were surrounded, and they must inevitably be cut to pieces, if they made any further resistance, they agreed to lay down their arms. The number submitted, in this manner, was 23 officers, and 886 men. Col. Rohl, the commanding officer, and seven others, were found wounded in the town. I do not exactly know how many they had killed ; but I fancy not above twenty or thirty, as they never made any regular stand. Our loss is very trifling indeed ; only two officers and one or two privates wounded.

I find that the detachment of the enemy consisted of the three Hessian regiments of Landspatch, Kniphausen, and Rohl, amounting to about 1500 men, and a troop of British light-horse, but immediately upon the beginning of the attack, all those who were not killed or taken, pushed directly down the road towards Borden-town. These would likewise have fallen into our hands, could my plan have been completely carried into execution. Gen. Ewing was to have crossed before day at Trenton ferry, and taken possession of the bridge leading out of town ; but the quantity of ice was so great, that though he did every thing in his power to effect it, he could not get over. This difficulty also hindered Gen. Cadwallader from crossing, with the Pennsylvania militia, from Bristol ; he got part of his foot over, but finding it impossible to embark his artillery, he was obliged to desist. I am fully confident, that could the troops under Generals Ewing and Cadwallader have passed the river, I should have been able, with their assistance, to have driven the enemy from all their posts below Trenton ; but the numbers I had with me being inferior to theirs below me, and a strong battalion of light infantry being at Princeton, above me, I thought it most prudent to return the same evening with the prisoners, and the artillery we had taken. We found no stores of any consequences in the town. [...]

I have the honor to be, with great respect,

Sir, your must humble servant,
G. WASHINGTON.

THE
CONTINENTAL JOURNAL, AND WEEKLY ADVERTISER.

Address of Newyork Convention to the people

THURSDAY, JANUARY 23, 1777. [NUMB. XXXV.

BOSTON: PRINTED BY JOHN GILL, IN QUEEN-STREET.

☞ THE ENTIRE PROSPERITY OF EVERY STATE, DEPENDS UPON THE DICIPLINE OF ITS ARMIES. *The KING of PRUSSIA.*

he remainder of the Address of the Convention of th Representatives of the State of New-York to their Constituents, began in our last.

WHOEVER therefore considers the natural strength and advantages of this country, the distance it is moved from Britain, the obvious policy of many European owers, the great supplies of arms and ammunition chearlly afforded us by the French and Spaniards, and the eble and destitute condition of Britain: That she is ained of men and of money, obliged to hire foreign ercenaries for the execution of her wicked purposes; arrears to her troops for a twelve month's pay, which e cannot or will not discharge; her credit sunk; her ade ruined; her inhabitants divided; her king unpopu-r, and her ministers execrated: That she is overhelmed with a monstrous debt; cut off from the vast venue heretofore obtained by taxes on American oduce; her West-India islands in a starving conditi on; her ships taken; her merchants involved in nkruptcy; her designs against us wicked, unjust, uel, contrary to the laws of God and man, pursued th implacable, unrelenting vengeance, and in a manr barbarous, and opposed to the usage of civilized tions: Whoever considers that we have humbly ight peace, and been refused; that we have been deed even a hearing; all our petitions rejected; all our monstrances disregarded; that we fight not for conest, but only for security; that our cause is the cause God, of human nature and posterity: Whoever, we , seriously considers these things, must entertain very proper ideas of the divine justice, to which we have pealed, and be very little acquainted with the course human affairs, to harbour the smallest doubt of our ing successful.

Remember the long and glorious struggle of the Uni- Netherlands, against the power of Spain, to which y had once been subjected. Their extent was small, eir country poor, their people far from numerous, d unaccustomed to arms, and in the neighbourhood their enemies. Spain, at that time, the most power- kingdom in Europe; her fleet formidable; her ar-es great, inured to war, and led by the best Generals the age; and her treasury overflowing with the alth of Mexico and Peru, endeavoured to enslave em. They dutifully remonstrated against the design, eir petitions were treated with contempt, and fire and ord were carried into their country to compel subssion. They nobly resolved to be free, they declared emselves Independent States, and after an obstinate uggle, frustrated the wicked intentions of Spain.

Switzerland presents us with another instance of agnanimity. That country was oppressed by cruel rants, but the people refused to continue in bondage; th arms in their hands they expelled those tyrants, d left to their descendants the portion of freedom.

Even England, whose genius now blushes for the deneracy of her sons, hath afforded examples of opposin to tyranny which are worthy to be imitated by all tions. His sacred majesty Charles I. lost his head and s crown, by attempting to enslave his subjects; and s sacred majesty James II. was for the same reason exlled the kingdom with his whole family, and the ince of Orange chosen king in his stead. The Enish were too wise to believe, that the person of any rant could be sacred; and never suffered any man to ar the crown, who attempted to exercise the power royalty to the destruction of the people from whom ose powers were derived. This practice is not only nsistent with human reason, but perfectly consonant the will and practice of God himself: You know at the Jews were under his peculiar direction, and u need not be informed of the many instances in ich he took the crown from such of their kings, as used to govern according to the laws of the Jews. If then God has given us freedom, are we not responle to him for that, as well as other talents? If it e birth-right, let us not sell it for a mess of pottage, suffer it to be torn from us by the hand of violence! the means of defence are in our power, and we do make use of them; What excuse shall we make to children and our Creator? These are questions the deepest concern to us all. These are questions ich materially affect our happiness, not only in this rld, but in the world to come. And surely, "if r a test for the trial of spirits can be necessary, it is w. If ever those of liberty and faction ought to be inguished from each other, it is now. If ever it is umbent on the people to know truth and to follow it is now."

Rouze, therefore, brave citizens! Do your duty like n! And be persuaded, that divine Providence will permit this western world to be involved in the horrs of slavery. Consider! That from the earliest ages of the world, religion, liberty and empire have been bending their course toward the setting sun. The holy gospels are yet to be preached to those western regions, and we have the highest reason to believe, that the Almighty will not suffer slavery and the gospel to go hand in hand. It cannot! It will not be!

But if there be any among us, dead to all sense of honor and love of their country; if deaf to all the calls of liberty, virtue and religion; if forgetful of the magnanimity of their ancestors, and the happiness of their children: If neither the examples and success of other nations, the dictates of reason and nature, or the great duties they owe to their God, themselves and their posterity have any effect upon them: If neither the injuries they have received, the prize they are contending for, the future blessings or curses of their children, the applause or reproach of all mankind, the approbation or displeasure of their great Judge, or the happiness or misery consequent upon their conduct, in this and a future state can move them: Then let them be assured that they deserve to be slaves, and are entitled to nothing but anguish and tribulation. Let them banish from their remembrance, the reputation, the freedom and happiness which they have inherited from their forefathers: Let them forget every duty human and divine, remember not that they have children, and beware how they call to mind the justice of the Supreme Being: Let them go into captivity like the idolatrous and disobedient Jews, and be a reproach and a bye-word among the nations.

But we think better things of you. We believe, and are persuaded, that you will do your duty like men, and cheerfully refer your cause to the great and righteous Judge. If success crown your efforts, all the blessings of freedom will be your reward. If you fall in the contest, you will be happy with God and liberty in Heaven.

By the unanimous order of the Convention,

ABRAHAM TEN BROECK, *President.*

Fish-Kill, December 23, 1776.

BALTIMORE, *December 31, 1776.*

This Morning CONGRESS received the following Letter from General WASHINGTON.

Head-Quarters, Newtown, 27th Dec. 1776.

SIR,

I HAVE the pleasure of congratulating you upon the success of an enterprize, which I had formed against a detachment of the enemy lying in Trenton, and which was executed yesterday morning.

The evening of the 25th, I ordered the troops intended for this service, to parade back of M'Kenky's Ferry, that they might begin to pass as soon as it grew dark, imagining we should be able to throw them all over, with the necessary artillery, by 12 o'clock, and that we might easily arrive at Trenton, by five in the morning, the distance being about nine miles. But the quantity of ice made that night, impeded the passage of the boats so much, that it was three o'clock before the artillery could all be got over, and near four before the troops took up their line of march.

I formed my detachment into two divisions, one to march up the lower or river road, the other by the upper or Pennington road. As the divisions had nearly the same distance to march, I ordered each of them immediately upon forcing the out guards, to push directly into the town, that they might charge the enemy before they had time to form. The upper division arrived at the enemy's advanced post exactly at 8 o'clock, and in three minutes after, I found, from the fire on the lower road, that that division had also got up. The out guards made but a small opposition, though, for their numbers, they behaved very well, keeping up a constant retreating fire from behind houses.

We presently saw their main body formed, but, from their motions, they seemed undetermined how to act. Being hard pressed by our troops, who had already got possession of part of their artillery, they attempted to file off by a road, on their right, leading to Princeton; but perceiving their intention, I threw a body of troops in their way, which immediately checked them. Finding, from our disposition, that they were surrounded, and they must inevitably be cut to pieces, if they made any further resistance, they agreed to lay down their arms. The number that submitted, in this manner, was 23 officers, and 886 men. Col. Rohl, the commanding officer, and seven others, were found wounded in the town. I do not exactly know how many they had killed; but I fancy not above twenty or thirty, as they never made any regular stand. Our loss is very trifling indeed; only two officers and one or two privates wounded.

I find that the detachment of the enemy consisted of the three Hessian regiments of Landspatch, Kniphausen, and Rohl, amounting to about 1500 men, and a troop of British light-horse; but immediately upon the beginning of the attack, all those who were not killed or taken, pushed directly down the road towards Bordentown. These would likewise have fallen into our hands, could my plan have been completely carried into execution. Gen. Ewing was to have crossed before day at Trenton ferry, and taken possession of the bridge leading out of town; but the quantity of ice was so great, that though he did every thing in his power to effect it, he could not get over. This difficulty also hindered Gen. Cadwallader from crossing, with the Pennsylvania militia, from Bristol; he got part of his foot over, but finding it impossible to embark his artillery, he was obliged to desist. I am fully confident, that could the troops under Generals Ewing and Cadwallador have passed the river, I should have been able, with their assistance, to have driven the enemy from all their posts below Trenton; but the numbers I had with me being inferior to theirs below me, and a strong battalion of light infantry being at Princeton, above me, I thought it most prudent to return the same evening with the prisoners, and the artillery we had taken. We found no stores of any consequence in the town.

In justice to the officers and men I must add, that their behaviour upon this occasion reflects the highest honor upon them. The difficulty of passing the river, in a very severe night, and their march through a violent storm of snow and hail, did not in the least abate their ardour; but when they came to the charge, each seemed to vie with the other in pressing forward, and were I to give a preference to any particular corps, I should do great injustice to the others.

Col. Baylor, my first aid-de-camp, will have the honor of delivering this to you, and from him you may be made acquainted with many other particulars: His spirited behaviour upon every occasion, requires me to recommend him to your particular notice.

I have the honor to be, with great respect,
Sir, your most humble servant,
G. WASHINGTON.

Inclosed I have sent you a particular list of the prisoners, artillery, and other Stores.

RETURN of Prisoners taken at Trenton, the 26th of December, 1776, by the army under the command of his Excellency General WASHINGTON.

Regiment of LANDSPATCH.

1 Lieutenant Colonel, 1 Major, 1 Captain, 3 Lieuts. 4 Ensigns, 38 Serjeants, 6 Drummers, 5 Musicians, 9 Officers Servants, 206 Rank and File.

Regiment of KNIPHAUSEN.

1 Major, 2 Captains, 2 Lieutenants, 3 Ensigns, 15 Serjeants, 6 Drummers, 6 Officers Servants, 258 Rank and File.

Regiment of ROHL.

1 Colonel, 1 Lieut. Col. 1 Major, 1 Capt. 2 Lieuts. 5 Ensigns, 2 Surgeons Mates, 25 Serjeants, 8 Drummers, 4 Musicians, 9 Offi[...]

Regim[...]

1 Lieut. 4 Ser[...] and File.

TOTAL—[...] 4 Captains, 8 [...] Serjeants, 20 [...] vants, 740 Ra[...] 6 double-fo[...] complete. 3 Ammunit[...] As many M[...] Swords, as th[...] 12 Drums.

Pe[...]

STATE [...]

ORDERE[...] this Stat[...] cruising for th[...] by are direct[...] State, by the [...] Men as they h[...] Company and [...] A tr[...] Attest.

Every Finger a Fish-Hook.

TAKEN by accident from SPEAR's wharf a few days since, a single fortified four pounder. The persons who took it are desired to return it on said wharf; if they do not they will soon repent it. *Boston, December 23, 1776.*

[...]y 4. [...] Trenton, [...]ting in the [...] this city, [...] most of [...]ities by a [...] every ge[...]ry power. [...] 26th of [...]ngagement

[...]a, we are [...]n, a party [...] in with a[...]ated them, [...] horses:— [...]hiladelphia

[...]parties met [...], in New-

17. [...] in a sloop [...] of Novem[...] he put into [...]hip arrived [...] which in[...] taken place [...] was daily [...] The cargo [...] ng of blan[...] n into New[...]caped being [...] the harbour

[...] gentleman [...]-York, dated

[...] communi[...] lie in heaps [...] have died by [...] common ne[...] the boasted [...]erished unde[...] e no idea of [...] such treatment [...] revenge, but [...] and necessary, [...] antrym n, and [...] like situation, [...] and insults, [...] I am, &c. [...] io. 20.

[...]ding our arms [...] been received

[...]rs and soldiers [...] 160 more are [...] f the 500 who [...] as mentioned

[...]hibited of the [...]ily boast being [...]alian and Wal[...] Jersey, it gives [...] outraged the [...] were to unhap[...]tly the fair sex, [...] power of lan[...] the curious va[...]ublic library at [...] y the celebrated [...]ge at Princeton, [...] tutored savage, [...] ve beheld with [...] s are our cruel [...] and the arts and

[...]ry 23.

Sloop Union's [...]n'd with 600

[...] they were to be [...]t Capt. Johnson [...] France; that he [...] November; and [...]ance of a French [...] was 3000 Seamen

Extract of a another Letter from Morris Town, Jan. 8.

The 17th Regiment used their Bayonets with too much severity upon a Party they put to Flight, but they now paid for it in proportion, very few escaping, near 60 were killed on the Spot, besides the wounded; we have taken between 3 and 400 Prisoners, all British Troops, they must have lost very considerable in this Affair.——We lost several gallant Officers. Brigadier General Mercer was wounded, he had three Stabs with a Bayonet, but will get better. The Enemy took his Parole after we left Princeton; a Lieutenant Colonel Flemming was killed, and a Captain Neil of the Artillery. We took their Cannon, which consisted of two Brass 6 pounders, a considerable Number of Military Stores, Blankets, Guns, &c. They lost among a Number of other Officers, a Captain Leslie, Son to the Earl of Leven, and Nephew to General Leslie; him we buried with the Honors of War. After we had been about two Hours at Princeton, Word was bro't that the Enemy was advancing from Trenton. As we had other Objects in View, viz. of beating up their Quarters, we pursued our March to Somerset Court-House, where we had been informed there were 1300 Men Quartered; they however had marched off, and joined the Army at Trenton. We at first intended to have made a forced March to Brunswick, at which Place was the Baggage of their whole Army and General Lee; but our Men having been without either Rest, Rum or Provisions for two Days and Nights, were unequal to the Task of marching 17 Miles further. If we could have procured 1000 fresh Men at Princeton, to have pushed for Brunswick, we should have struck one of the most brilliant Strokes in all History. However our Advantages are very great already; they have collected their whole Force, and drawn themselves to one Point, viz. Brunswick. A Party of ours two Days ago attacked 60 Waldeckers, who were all killed or taken in Monmouth County, in the lower Part of the Jerseys. Another Party have routed a Party of Tories, killed and taken 200 Prisoners. They have sent their Baggage to Staten Island from the Jerseys, and we are very well informed they are doing the same from New-York.

Extract of a letter from Morris-Town, Jan. 9.

"The enemy have abandoned Elizabeth-Town. Our people have entered it and taken 50 Waldeckers and 50 Highlanders, and about 30 Baggage Waggons fully loaded—The enemy who had all the Jersies, are now only in possession of Amboy and Brunswick—this is a great reverse in the course of a fortnight, to the British power—Whether they mean to collect their whole force at Brunswick and give us battle, or whether they mean to push for Staten-Island, and abandon the Jersies entirely is matter of doubt—We shall make a move towards them to day, with a view to avail ourselves of circumstances—The enemy appear to be pannic struck in the extreme—God prospers our arms in an extra manner—there is to be an eclipse of the Sun to day—We mean if possible to attack the Germans as soon as it begins, and take the advantage of their ignorant superstition.—Endeavour to animate and awaken all ranks of people.—Let them view the distressed and lately subjugated people of the Jersies, complaining of their property being wrested from them by the lawless banditti that have infested these places.—Husbands and Fathers being oblig'd to be witnesses of the lustful Brute ravishing the dear object of their affections before their eyes.—These enormities have been committed and will be again committed, where tyranny reigns uncheck'd, and uncontroul'd.—May God give my countrymen to see those things necessary for their polical salvation, and may he avert from their country the horrid calamities of war."

We learn by the Hartford post, that the British

[...]

Which hangs out DEATH in one eternal night,
A night which glooms us in the Morning Ray
And wraps our tho'ts at banquets in a shroud."

THE sale of the remaining part of the cargo of the brig Countess of Eglington, as advertised in our last will certainly begin at Taunton on Tuesday next, at ten o'clock in the morning.

A [...] York [...] ces in [...] on th[...] right [...] own [...]

An e[...]

A [...] of C[...] in O[...] the c[...] as we[...] nomy [...] kind [...] A[...] The [...]

T[...] plai[...] dero[...] gime[...] mali[...] and [...] expi[...] appo[...] the [...] will [...] P[...]

T[...] Gen[...] in hi[...] jari[...] sinc[...] disa[...]

R[...] cle[...] can[...] pos[...] sel[...] dir[...] pro[...] in [...] to [...] an[...] of [...] for [...] to [...] ou[...] na[...] to [...] eff[...] to [...] su[...]

O[...]

I[...]

CONTINENTAL JOURNAL (BOSTON)

January 23, 1777

A letter published in the January 23, 1777, *Continental Journal*, written by General George Washington himself, who saw most of the battle as he raced back and forth through Trenton on his horse, musket balls flying through the air around him, was colorful and explosive. It was written, as were all of his letters, to drum up Congressional, press, and public support.

Christian Majesty's flag, and the Bey caused the accustomed presents to be carried on board. Some days after, Mr. de Saizieu, Consul and Chargé des Affaires of his most Christian Majesty at this place, presented the Chevalier de Coriolis d'Espinouse, and the officers of the frigate to the Bey, who gave them a most distinguished reception. At the close of the audience, the Bey notified to his Court that he had resolved to send an Envoy to his most Christian Majesty, and had conferred this very important commission on Suleiman Aga, general of the cavalry, his relation, who was then standing at the side of the Bey's throne, and who, after returning thanks to that Prince, received the compliments of the Grandees of the country. He is now preparing for his departure.

"The Bey hath already ordered a vessel to sail for France, which he hath freighted with slaves, horses, lions, and divers effects, intended to be presented to his Most Christian Majesty by his Envoy."

Extract of a Letter from Portsmouth, Feb. 24.

"The Bristol man of war arrived here, brings a confirmation of General Lee being a prisoner at Brunswick in the Jerseys, where it is said he will remain till orders are sent how he is to be disposed of."

The North Star, Sanders; Henry, Stuart, King George, Redmond, Concord, Randal, Unity, Moore, Stag, French, Favourite, Cousins, William and Ann, Seal, Bridget, Gilbody, Betsey, Wolfe, and Nancy, Sellers, transports, from Corke, are all safe arrived at New York, with provisions, &c. for the use of his Majesty's forces.

The Thomas and William, Smith, from New York to Corke, and Friendship, Shotten, from Quebec to Barcelona, are retaken by our men of war, and carried into Halifax.

Extract of a Letter from Newcastle, Feb. 22

"Wednesday morning there was a very nu-

British were ordered to advance, to bring off Dunhoff's corps, which they effected, but with great loss. The left of our army is now at Princess-town, in the mid-way between New York and Philadelphia, and about twenty miles from Trentown. He further adds, that Gen. Lee was made prisoner by Col. Harcourt, who had marched near forty miles from the army with his party of forty light dragoons, who surrounded the head quarters of the rebel Gen. about three miles from the provincial army, which was guarded by near fifty men; that on hearing the firing, Gen. Lee ran to the door, with two French officers, one of whom was shot dead by his side: that being thus taken by surprise, he was put upon a horse, and galloped off with, in despite of all his overtures for a parley; that Lee, when he was brought in, demanded to be received under the proclamation; but on being refused the benefit thereof, and told that he would be tried as a deserter, he flew into the most unbounded rage, and exclaimed against the repeated acts of false faith, and treachery, which had reduced him to his present situation.—He is now a close prisoner at Brunswick.

Col. White further says, that the Congress had removed from Philadelphia on the approach of Gen. Howe to Lancaster, about forty-five miles distant from their late place; that it was now rendered very contemptible by the divisions that had long agitated it, and the revolt of several of its principal members, particularly the family of the Alleynes, who had all quitted their seats in this congressional senate, come into government, and taken the benefit of the proclamation;—that Gen. Washington continues to occupy the heights with a reduced and mutinous force of about 10,000 men; for that the time being up of the principal part of the rebel army, they were quitting the service, and returning home in a state the most wretched and discontented, &c.

Extract of a Letter from Deal, Feb. 24.

LONDON CHRONICLE
February 25, 1777

In its story, the *London Chronicle* acknowledged that Washington had defeated the Hessians but in the next line reminded readers that the British Army, strong as ever, was marching throughout New Jersey and had nothing more to fear. It also wrote that many of Washington's ten thousand men were deserting (he actually had about five thousand men but had spies feed the British the much higher figure).

Sir Gilbert Elliott, Bart. who vacated his seat for that borough to stand for the shire of Roxbrough."

Yesterday Lieut. Col. White, aid de camp to Gen. Howe, arrived at Lord George Germain's office from America, with the following intelligence:—That about Christmas last Gen. Washington, at the head of a large body of Provincials, attacked the left wing of the King's forces near Trentown in New Jersey, consisting of several brigades of Hessians. The night preceding the grand affair, they drove in our advanced posts, and the next morning began their attack very briskly about six o'clock, when, after a smart engagement, the Hessians, who were unfortunately detached, were routed, 700 of whom were taken prisoners, and their Col. Reyne killed. The 49th, and 17th regiments of

was an uncommon quantity of corn brought in; which shews there is great plenty in the country.

Winchester, Feb. 22. At our fair on Monday last, we had a great quantity of cheese pitched, which sold from 29s. to 36s. per cwt.

A farmer coming to the said fair with cheese, fell from his horse, and died on the spot.

STOCKS.

Bank Stock, 138	Dit. Ind. An.—
India Ditto, 169 1/2	3 1/2 per Ct. 1758, —
South-Sea Ditto, —	4 per Ct. con. 1762, —
Do. Old An. 79 1/2	Ind. Bonds, 16s. a 17s. Prem.
Ditto New Ann. —	
3 per Ct. Bank red. 81	Navy and Vict. Bills, 3/4 per cent. dis.
3 per Ct. conf. 80 3/4	
3 per Cent. 1726, —	Long Annuities, —
Ditto 1751, —	

LONDON.

From the New York Gazette, *Jan. 13.*

Several skirmishes between the King's troops and the rebels have lately happened in the Jerseys. But the most distinguished rencounter occurred on the 3d instant near Prince-town. The 17th regiment, consisting of less than 300 men fell in with the rebel army of very superior force, whom they attacked with all the ardour and intrepidity of Britons. They received the fire from behind a fence, over which they immediately leaped upon their enemies, who presently turned to the right about with such precipitation as to leave their very cannon behind them. The soldiers instantly turned their cannon, and fired at least twenty rounds upon their rear; and had they been assisted with another regiment or two, the rebels would have found it rather difficult to make good their retreat. This has been one of the most splendid actions in the whole campaign, and has given a convincing proof that British valour has not declined from its antient glory. Of Col. Mawhood, their gallant commander, and of his conduct in the affair, too many encomiums cannot be said. The loss was about 20 killed and 80 wounded, of the troops. Of the rebels above 400 were killed and wounded. Among their slain were eleven officers. Mr. Mercer (one of the wounded rebel officers, since dead) when he was taken up by our people, asked how many the numbers were who had thus attacked him, and upon being told, he cried out with astonishment, "My God; is it possible? I hav often heard of British courage; but never could have imagined to find such an instance as this!"

Another account says, that the 17th regiment just before they charged the rebels, deliberately pulled off their knapsacks, and gave three cheers, then broke through the rebels, faced about, attacked, and broke through them a second time. Col. Mawhood then said, it would be prudent, as they were so few, to re-

LONDON CHRONICLE
March 4, 1777

A remarkable story from the January 13, 1777, *New-York Gazette*, reprinted in the March 4, 1777, *London Chronicle*, wrote of the British defeat ten days later at Princeton in such a way that any reader would have thought they had won the battle.

men, lying at Raway. They were bravely repulsed, with the loss of one man killed and three slightly wounded. The rebels left nine killed behind them. They fled with the more precipitation upon seeing Lieut. Col. Dongan with about 20 Jersey volunteers, belonging to Col. Lucee's battalion, coming up to Lieutenant Cameron's assistance.

A party of highlanders, about fifty in number, escorting some waggons and baggage, fell in with 3 or 400 rebels, who commanded them to surrender by a flag of truce. But the soldiers instead of surrendering gave them a salute of cannon which they had with them, drove them off with some precipitation, and brought their convoy safe to the next post.

PROCLAMATION.

By Major-general James Robertson.

WHEREAS there is ground to believe, that the rebels, not satisfied with the destruction of part of the city, entertain designs of burning

REPORTING THE

SIEGE OF FORT TICONDEROGA

By Eric H. Schnitzer

No one reading the *London Gazette Extraordinary*'s headline report for August 25, 1777, could have interpreted the news as being anything less than a complete victory for British arms in the northern New York theater of military operations. Lieutenant-General John Burgoyne's glowing—and generally accurate—descriptions of events for the opening phase of his campaign in June and July no doubt left readers with an assurance that everything was going perfectly as planned for the British general.

Burgoyne's army from Canada was a multinational force of nearly ten thousand officers and men from Great Britain and Ireland, the German states of Braunschweig and Hessen-Hanau, warriors from dozens of First Nations, Royalist Americans, and French-Canadians, with an extensive mechanism of army support personnel, and women, children, refugee, and sutler followers. His plan was to invade New York from Canada, moving south on Lake Champlain, after which he would put his army onto Lake George and Wood Creek, eventually recombining his forces at Fort Edward on the Hudson River. Then, marching his army south alongside the river, he planned to capture the city of Albany and there receive further instructions from the British commander in chief of America, General Sir William Howe. The distance of nearly two hundred miles across lakes and rivers, over mountains and hills, through old-growth forests, deep ravines, and valleys dotted with small industry and farming communities was not going to be an easy task. Further, in order to achieve complete victory, a number of forts needed to be captured and the Northern Department of the Army of the United States defeated. With initial British tactical dominance in those late June and early July days—the conquering of Forts Crown Point, Ticonderoga, Independence, and Anne, the routing of Revolutionary forces at Hubbardton and Skenesborough, and the capture of hundreds of tons of ordnance, armed vessels, provisions, and all manner of war matériel—seemed to make Burgoyne's plans for domination a certainty.

But these substantial victories were misleading. At the time Burgoyne's report to Lord George Germain was written on July 11, the army from Canada's rapid progress slowed to a crawl, in great part due to American troops destroying bridges, flooding streams, and blocking roads. This gave time for the army of the United States, commanded by Major General Philip Schuyler, to withdraw further south, receive reinforcements, and plan new defensive strategy. As the campaign wore on into August, Burgoyne's army effectively stalled when it reached the Hudson River as attempts were made to bring its disparate and far-flung parts—infantry, artillery, provisions, naval department, baggage, heavy baggage, and more—together. This considerable delay of nearly one and a half months bought Schuyler, and afterward his congressionally appointed replacement Major General Horatio Gates, even more time. When the report of Burgoyne's decisive successes was being read in the *London Gazette Extraordinary* on August 25, 1777, detachments of his army had already suffered major defeats near Bennington, Vermont (August 16), and in western New York a small supporting army intending to cooperate with Burgoyne retreated back to Canada after its unsuccessful siege of Fort Stanwix (August 23). Although Burgoyne still held the initiative and the dismal situation of his army as described in the November 8, 1777, issue of the *London Chronicle* was exaggerated, transportation delays, battle defeats, and isolation of communication were setting the stage for a complete reversal of fortune for the British general.

The London Gazette Extraordinary.

Publiſhed by Authority.

MONDAY, AUGUST 25, 1777.

Whitehall, Auguſt 25, 1777.

THE following Letter from Lieutenant-General Burgoyne to Lord George Germain was received the 23d Inſtant, by Captain Gardner, Firſt Aid de Camp to Lieutenant-General Burgoyne, who arrived in the Royal George Armed Tranſport from Quebec.

Head Quarters, Skeneſborough Houſe,
July 11, 1777.

MY LORD,

I HAVE the Honour to acquaint your Lordſhip, that the Enemy diſlodged from Ticonderoga and Mount Independance on the 6th Inſtant, and were driven on the ſame Day beyond Skeneſborough on the Right, and to Huberton on the Left, with the Loſs of 128 Pieces of Cannon, all their Armed Veſſels and Batteaux, the greateſt Part of their Baggage and Ammunition, Proviſion and Military Stores to a very large Amount.

This Succeſs has been followed by Events equally fortunate and rapid. I ſubjoin ſuch a Detail of Circumſtances as the Time will permit; and, for His Majeſty's further Information, I beg Leave to refer your Lordſhip to Captain Gardiner, my Aid de Camp, whom I have thought it neceſſary to diſpatch with News ſo important to the King's Service, and ſo honourable to the Troops under my Command.

Journal of the late principal Proceedings of the Army.

HAVING remained at Crown Point Three Days, to bring up the Rear of the Army, to eſtabliſh the Magazines and the Hoſpital, and to obtain Intelligence of the Enemy, on

June 30, I ordered the advanced Corps, conſiſting of the Britiſh Light Infantry and Grenadiers, the 24th Regiment, ſome Canadians and Savages, and Ten Pieces of Light Artillery, under the Command of Brigadier-General Frazer, to move from Putnam Creek, where they had been encamped ... Days, up the Weſt Shore of the Lake to Four ...

... tance of the Fort of Ticonderoga ... Reſerve, conſiſting of the Brunſwick Chaſſeurs, Light Infantry and Grenadiers, under Lieutenant- ...

Artillery, and a large Square of Barracks within it.

The Foot of the Mount, which projects into the Lake, was intrenched and covered with a ſtrong Abattis cloſe to the Water. This Intrenchment was lined with heavy Artillery pointing down the Lake, flanking the Water-battery above deſcribed, and ſuſtained by another Battery about half-way up the Mount. On the Weſt Side the Mount runs the main River, and in its Paſſage round is joined by the Water which comes down from Lake George. On the Eaſt Side of the Mount the Water forms a ſmall Bay, into which falls a Rivulet, after having encircled in its Courſe Part of the Mount to the South Eaſt. The Side to the South could not be ſeen, but was deſcribed as inacceſſible, There was a Bridge between the Mount and Ticonderoga, which alſo was unſeen.

July 2. About Nine in the Morning a Smoke was obſerved towards Lake George, and the Indians brought in a Report that the Enemy had ſet Fire to their further Blockhouſe and had abandoned the Saw Mills; and that a conſiderable Body were advancing from the Lines towards a Bridge upon the Road which led to the Right of the Britiſh Camp. A Detachment of the advanced Corps was immediately put in March under Brigadier Frazer, ſupported by a Brigade of the Line and ſome Artillery, under the Command of Major-General Phillips, with Orders to proceed towards Mount Hope, which is to the North of the Lines, to reconnoitre the Enemy's Poſition, and to take Advantage of any Poſt they might abandon or be driven from.

The Indians under Captain Frazer, ſupported by his Company of Markſmen, were directed to make a Circuit to the Left of Brig. Frazer's Line of March, and endeavour to cut off the Retreat of the Enemy to their Lines; but this Deſign miſcarried through the Impetuoſity of the Indians, who attacked too ſoon, and in Front, and the Enemy were thereby able to retire with the Loſs of one Officer and a few Men killed, and one Officer wounded. Major- ...

... tageous Poſt of Mount Hope ... Enemy were thereby entirely cut off from a Communication with Lake George.

LONDON GAZETTE EXTRAORDINARY

August 25, 1777

No one reading the *London Gazette Extraordinary*'s headline report for August 25, 1777, could have interpreted the news as being anything less than a complete victory for British arms in the northern New York theater of military operations. But the news was misleading, as Burgoyne's army slowed to a crawl and the American troops were posturing for a new defensive strategy.

---

ported this Hill to have the entire Command of the Works and Buildings both of Ticonderoga and Mount Independence; that the Ground might be levelled ſo as to receive Cannon; and that a Road to convey them, though difficult, might be made practicable in Twenty-four Hours. This Hill alſo entirely commanded in Reverſe the Bridge of Communication, ſaw the exact Situation of the Veſſels, nor could the Enemy during the Day make any material Movement or Preparation without being diſcovered, and even having their Numbers counted

It was immediately determined that a Battery ſhould be raiſed upon Sugar Hill for Eight Twenty-four Pounders, medium Twelves, and Eight-Inch Howitzers. This very arduous Work was carried on ſo rapidly that the Battery would have been ready the next Day.

It is a Duty in this Place to do ſome Juſtice to the Zeal and Activity of Major-General Phillips, who had the Direction of the Operation; and having mentioned that moſt valuable Officer, I truſt it cannot be thought a Digreſſion to add, that it is to his judicious Arrangements and indefatigable Pains, during the general Superintendency of Preparations which Sir Guy Carleton entruſted to him in the Winter and Spring, that the Service is indebted for its preſent Forwardneſs; the Prevalence of contrary Winds and other Accidents having rendered it impoſſible for any Neceſſaries prepared in England for the Opening of the Campaign yet to reach the Army.

July 6. Soon after Day-light an Officer arrived expreſs on board the Royal George, where in the Night I took my Quarters as the moſt centrical Situation, with Information from Brigadier Frazer that the Enemy were retiring, and that he was advancing with his Piquets, leaving Orders for the Brigade to follow as ſoon as they could accoutre, with Intention to purſue by Land. This Movement was very ſoon diſcernable, as were the Britiſh Colours which the Brigadier had fixed upon the Fort of Ticonderoga Knowing how ſafely I could truſt to that Officer's Conduct, I turned my chief Attention to the Purſuit by Water, by which Route I had Intelligence One Column were retiring in Two Hundred and Twenty Batteaux, covered by Five Armed Gallies.

The great Bridge of Communication, through which a Way was to be opened, was ſupported by Twenty-two ſunken Piers of large Timber at nearly equal Diſtances: The Spaces between were filled by ſeparate Floats, each about Fifty Feet long and Twelve Feet wide, ſtrongly faſtened together by Chains and Rivets, and alſo faſtened to the ſunken Piers. Before this Bridge was a Boom made of very large Pieces of round Timber, faſtened together by rivetted Bolts and double Chains made of Iron an Inch and Half Square.

The Gun Boats were immediately moved forward, and the Boom and one of the intermediate Floats

---

Activity, and Bra... upon all Occaſions, and ... racter upon all Occaſions ... recommended in the moſt particular Manner to ... The other Officers and Soldiers ... any Diſtinctions of Spirit.

by that Ro... of the Mag... intended at

Colonel Hill, comman... forced in t... he could the Enemy had been rei forced ... conſiderable Body of freſh Troops; that he could not retire before them with his Regiment, but would maintain his Ground. The two remaining Regiments of the Firſt Brigade under Brigadier Powell were ordered to quicken their March; and, upon ſecond Intelligence of the Force of the Enemy, and Firing being heard, the 20th Regiment was ordered forward, and Major General Phillips, with ſome Pieces of Artillery, was ſent to take the Command. A violent Storm of Rain, which laſted the whole Day, prevented theſe Troops from getting to Fort Anne ſo ſoon as was intended; but the Delay gave the 9th Regiment an Opportunity of diſtinguiſhing themſelves by ſtanding and repulſing an Attack of ſix Times their Numbers. The Enemy finding the Poſition not to be forced in Front, endeavoured to ſurround it; and, from the Superiority of their Numbers, that Inconvenience was to be apprehended, and Lieutenant-Colonel Hill therefore found it neceſſary to change his Ground in the Heat of Action. So critical an Order was executed by the Regiment with the greateſt Steadineſs and Bravery. The Enemy, after an Attack of Three Hours were totally repulſed with great Loſs. They fled towards Fort Edward, ſetting Fire to Fort Anne but leaving a Saw Mill and Block Houſe in goo Repair, which latter was afterwards poſſeſſed by th King's Troops. The 9th Regiment acquired, d ing their Expedition, about Thirty Priſoners, ſo Stores and Baggage, and the Colours of the Sec Hampſhire Regiment. The Accidents to coun ballance theſe ſeveral Succeſſes are few. The vice has loſt an Officer of great Gallantry and perience in Major Grant. The other Officers k are alſo to be much regretted. Captain Mont mery of the 9th Regiment, an Officer of Merit, was wounded in the Leg early in the A and was in the Act of being dreſſed by the Su when the Regiment changed Ground; being to help himſelf, he and the Surgeon were tak ſoners. I hear he has been well treated, a ...f recovering at Albany. The w ... here are alſo

450 THE LONDON CHRONICLE for 1777. Nov. 6—8.

LONDON CHRONICLE

November 8, 1777

Although Burgoyne still held the initiative and the dismal situation of his army as described in the November 8, 1777, issue of the *London Chronicle* was exaggerated, transportation delays, battle defeats, and isolation of communication were setting the stage for a complete reversal of fortune for the British general.

"In that trunk (ſaid I) Amelia, I have, with- [...]

[...] ſcruples had there been any feathers of objection remaining. I could eaſily ſee, that ſide of the heart was touched which contains thoſe veſſels that feed the paſſions of pleaſure —I ſaw conſent bloomingly written on every feature—I took my little cabinet under my arm, handed Amelia into the chaiſe, and heard, with pleaſure, the wheels rattle over the pavement."

FRIDAY, NOVEMBER 7.

COUNTRY NEWS.

Leeds, Nov. 4.

ON Thurſday laſt, as an Auctioneer was ſelling ſome houſhold goods at Blackhouſe-lane, near Colne, the chamber-floor gave way, bruiſed a number of perſons in the fall, and among the reſt the Auctioneer; happily no lives were loſt.

The ſame kind of caterpillars which have been found in the hayſtacks and mows in the neighbourhood of Otley, Bradford, &c. are alſo found in the ſtacks in this neighbourhood.

LONDON.

NEWS *from* AMERICA.

State of MASSACHUSETTS-BAY.

Council-Chamber, Sept. 1, 1777.

WHEREAS it is repreſented to this board, that ſome men who were drafted in conſequence of the reſolution of the general court, of the 8th of Auguſt laſt have not marched, although they have received orders,

Therefore ordered, That the militia officers in each town, where any perſon dwells that has been drafted, and agrreeable to the reſolves of the general court, of the 8th of Auguſt laſt, be and they hereby are directed to apprehend all ſuch perſons in their reſpective towns, as have been drafted, ordered to march, and have neglected as aforeſaid, and forward them, under guard, to the regiment to which they belong, without delay, and take a receipt of the commanding officer of the regiment to which ſaid delinquents belong, and return the ſame, with the account of the expences, into the ſecretary's office.

A true copy.

Atteſt, JOHN AVERY, Dep. Sec.

From the MARYLAND JOURNAL, Aug. 26.

counties, where they ſhall receive orders.—To [...] quires our exertions; our [...] our country, implore [...] mply ſufficient to arm [...] led a man.

[...] is 22d day of Auguſt, [...] rd, one thouſand ſeven [...] -ſeven.

T. JOHNSON.

Auguſt 26. [...] part of the continental [...] out 10,000 men, with [...] hington at their head, [...] ity, and immediately [...] Scuyikill, on their way [...] Maryland, where the [...] ely been ſeen, and it is thought will make a deſcent upon that ſtate. And yeſterday morning Gen. Naſh's brigade of North Carolina forces, and Col. Proctor's regiment of artillery, paſſed through this city. They are to purſue the ſame route, in order to join our moſt illuſtrious General.

On the enemy's fleet appearing off Baltimore, the diſaffected inhabitants were all ſeized and ſent under a ſtrong guard to Fredericktown.

Auguſt 28. Congreſs proceeded to the election of a committee to collect evidence and facts reſpecting the evacuation of Ticonderoga, and the ballot being taken, Mr. Laurens, Mr. R. Henry Loyde, and Mr. John Adams, were elected.

A letter received from a young gentleman who went to America with Gen. Burgoyne in a private capacity, tranſmitted to his father, Mr. C——, at Hackney, gives a moſt diſmal picture of the ſtate of that General's army: the troops are in ſo great diſtreſs for want of proviſions, that the gentleman who wrote the letter, though he dines at the ſecond table immediately after the General, has not been able, by reaſon of the ſcarcity of the fare, to make a hearty meal for ſeveral weeks. What then, may we ſuppoſe, muſt be the ſituation of the inferior officers and the common ſoldiers? The letter proceeds, thet the troops lay for a month upon the bare earth, which has greatly emaciated them; that the foraging parties had proved ſo very unſucceſsful, as to be almoſt cut off to a man; that a party of 800 were ſurrounded, and only three returned alive.

By the laſt returns made to the Adjutant-general's office from Sir William Howe, it appears, that there were above 900 of the rank and file incapable of duty, from a violent flux, which they got ſoon after landing in the ſouthward.

A letter was yeſterday received by a gentleman of conſideration in office from Corke, written by a perſon that landed there from Cheſapeak-bay, the 29th of Oct. which mentions, that the battle between Gen. Howe's army and Waſhington's happened on the 11th of Sept. that Waſhington's army was entirely routed, with the loſs of near 5000 killed and taken priſoners; and that Gen. Howe took poſſeſſion of Philadelphia on the 14th.

Yeſterday there was a very numerous and ſplendid Court at St. James's, when his Majeſty [...]

conſiſted of Engliſh property, conſigned to Spaniſh Merchants."

Extract of a Letter from Bilboa, Oct. 15.

"An American ſhip has brought in a prize loaded with 3000 quintals of fiſh, and as ſhe brings none of her real crew, we do not know what veſſel ſhe is. Yeſterday we received advice from Capt. Salmon, of the brig Peter, who was coming conſigned to us with 2600 quintals of cod fiſh: In his letter he ſays, that in lat. 44, long. 9, he was taken the 5th inſt. by an American privateer, bound from Bourdeaux to Philadelphia, who, after having plundered him of all his ſails, rigging, ſhip's ſtores, and a large quantity of fiſh, returned him the veſſel, not being capable of manning her, and ſhe has ſince got ſafe into this port."

Extract of a Letter from Bourdeaux, Oct. 23.

"This city is as much the ſeat of American politics as ever, though the privateering is not ſo briſk as formerly. Trade, however, was never briſker, as a proof of which the Officers of the King's Cuſtoms here are augmented, there not being enough before to do the buſineſs."

Extract of a Letter from St. Euſtatia, Aug. 12.

"An Engliſh armed veſſel belonging to Barbadoes chaſed an American brig into this harbour two days ago. Two American veſſels were taken juſt without this port, about a fortnight ago, and carried off, which has made the Engliſh cruiſers frequent this iſland, in hopes of meeting ſome more of them. Martinico has been ſo well watched lately, that the Provincials have paid us more viſits than they were uſed to to do, and Surinam has had ſome trade with them."

Extract of a Letter from Beerhaven, Oct. 22.

"An American privateer, which had been cruiſing for ſome time off Cape Clear, put in here two days ago, in order to heel ſhip, on account of a leak. They gave out that they were a letter of marque belonging to London, and on a cruiſe; this took with the common people, and many others; they bought a great quantity of live ſtock, and ſome ſpirits, for which they paid in dollars, and after lying here almoſt 24 hours, put again to ſea."

They write from Halifax in Nova Scotia, that a large French ſhip had lately been wrecked in the Gulph of St. Lawrence, and deſerted by the crew, on board of which were found a large quantity of gunpowder, a great number of fire-arms, and divers other military ſtores, ſuppoſed to be intended for the Americans.

The Brothers, Kelly, from Dublin to Oporto, is taken by Capt. Cunningham, off the coaſt of Portugal.

Extract of a Letter from Chatham, Nov. 4.

"Yeſterday ſailed from hence for Blackſtakes, the Sultan, Capt. Farker, a new ſhip of 74 guns; ſhe is to take in her powder and guns at Blackſtakes, after which ſhe is to proceed to Spithead.

"Tueſday ſailed from this port to the Nore, the Conqueſtadore of 74 guns, Capt. Thompſon; ſhe is to be ſtationed at the Nore, to receive impreſt men.

"Mr. John Blackmore is appointed Inſpector of the new work of his Majeſty's dock-yard at this place, in the room of Mr. Foot [...]

PROCLAMATION.

THIS ſtate being now actually invaded by a formidable land and ſea force, and the enemy, [...]

of another Princeſs.

Yeſterday a prodigious number of perſons partook of cake and caudle at St. James's; the [...]

of the Marines quartered in this town."

Extract of a Letter from Portſmouth, Nov. 5.

"We have juſt now heard the Monarque is [...]

REPORTING THE

BATTLE OF ORISKANY

By Daniel J. Tortora

By June 1777, General John Burgoyne had recruited four hundred Indian auxiliaries to join his campaign. He gave each warrior a silver medallion, explains the *Independent Chronicle* of September 11, 1777. Silver medallions symbolized the shine and luster of the idealized British-Iroquois alliance.

Burgoyne soon grew frustrated with the Indians. He could not stop them from plundering and killing. The warriors resented British officers' arrogance and hierarchy. Iroquois families were destitute, and the British paid for scalps. Further, by killing non-Indians, native warriors satisfied the evil spirits and honored their war dead. When the Indians murdered Jane McCrea, the fiancée of a Loyalist, Burgoyne feared alienating Loyalists and the uncommitted, so he stopped rewarding the Indians for taking colonists' scalps. However, he still threatened New Yorkers with Indian violence. The British used their native warriors in dangerous roles.

As Burgoyne advanced south, Lieutenant Colonel Barry St. Leger left Montreal. St. Leger aimed to take the forts in New York's Mohawk Valley and then to meet Burgoyne at Albany. The colonel led 1,500 men—half were Indian allies; half were Canadians, British and Hanau regulars, and Tory militiamen.

Colonel Peter Gansevoort commanded 750 militiamen at Fort Schuyler (formerly Fort Stanwix). In mid-June, Iroquois scouts killed five workers outside the fort and captured eight more. The prisoners exaggerated the fort's defenses and manpower. St. Leger delayed. The colonel finally arrived on August 3, 1777. Gansevoort refused to surrender. St. Leger commenced bombardment, and his Indian snipers picked off Gansevoort's men.

General Nicholas Herkimer left Fort Dayton on August 4 to reinforce Gansevoort. He led eight hundred Tryon County militiamen and some Oneida scouts. The *Independent Chronicle* of September 11, 1777, reveals that St. Leger's troops attacked a detachment sent from Fort Schuyler to meet Herkimer. Herkimer feared that his impatient men would mutiny, so he continued. Four hundred Iroquois and four hundred Tories under Mohawk Joseph Brant, Colonel John Butler, and Sir John Johnson lay in wait six miles from Fort Schuyler, near the Indian village of Oriskany. On August 6, 1777, they attacked after most of Herkimer's army had crossed a marshy ravine.

The Battle of Oriskany evolved into hand-to-hand combat. British officers had incited the Indians with liberal doses of rum. Many fought clumsily, but many American officers fell dead in the first few minutes of the chaos. Herkimer was shot in the leg. Many militiamen fled. A sudden thunderstorm enabled American forces to regroup on high ground. Herkimer organized his men into a defensive circle as he smoked a pipe, propped up on his saddle. Tory commander Colonel John Butler briefly breached the Patriot defenses, ordering his men to turn their green coats inside out so that they resembled American uniforms. Britain's Indians, fearing a rear attack and discouraged by their heavy losses, retreated. Tories Butler and Johnson then had to withdraw.

Both sides sustained heavy casualties in the six-hour-long battle. One Indian recalled that blood flowed in a stream down the battlefield. More than half of Herkimer's command were killed, wounded, or captured, so he retreated to Fort Dayton. He died there eleven days later. Of the Tory forces, at least sixty to eighty Indians—many of them Senecas—and a handful of Loyalists were killed or wounded. Neither side won, though both claimed victory.

St. Leger threatened that if Fort Schuyler refused to surrender, his Indians, "much exasperated and mortified from their losses," would destroy white settlements along the Mohawk River. Meanwhile, the article shows that Tories recruited for Burgoyne by threatening to unleash the natives against any who refused. St. Leger's subordinate, Colonel Daniel Claus, sought native allies in Canada.

Major General Benedict Arnold, already on his way from Saratoga to relieve the beleaguered fort, took prisoners and forced them to give misleading information to St. Leger. St. Leger's Indians fled. The colonel lifted the siege on August 22 and returned to Canada. The November 15, 1777, *London Chronicle* reflects his frustration. The British questioned the Indians' "bravery," without acknowledging the opportunistic nature of Indian warfare. Denied payment and discouraged by high casualties at Freeman's Farm, Burgoyne's Indians deserted. This contributed to the American victory at Saratoga.

Thereafter, brutal raids and ambushes pitted white and Indian brothers and neighbors against each other for months and even years. General Sullivan destroyed dozens of villages and fields in 1779.

L O N D O N.

May 30. Yesterday Lord North paid into the Treasury the sum of 200l. which he lately received by an unknown hand, towards defraying the expences of the American war; the above sum was sent in a letter by the penny-post.

By the last packet from New-York, which sailed the 11th of April, we have the following advices:

From Connecticut, that the jails in that Colony are filled with loyal Americans, who are treated in the most barbarous manner. Some are chained on their backs to the floor, and others so loaded with irons, that they can hardly walk. *A well-known lie!*

Extract of a letter from Sweden.

"We have four men of war building and almost finished here, for the service of the French, and two for Spain, all of fifty guns each; they will be ready to launch by the beginning of June, and are to take the routs of Brest and Ferrol, after being laden with a considerable quantity of iron, cannon, &c."

It is believed we have now 60,000 men in arms in North-America. The armies which last year were 25,000 under General Howe, and 11,000 under General Carleton, are still more numerous this year, independent of Canadians, and 7000 New-Yorkers. We have also 70 ships of war upon the coast, which, at 200 men to each, contain 14,000 seamen and marines.

Army under Gen. Howe -	26,000
Army from Canada -	13,000
New-Yorkers - -	7,000
On board 70 ships of war -	14.000
	60,000

Our loss in the last campaign was, rendered ineffective before the affair of the Hessians -	830
Hessians taken prisoners at Trenton -	700
Rendered ineffective in the subsequent skirmishes in the Jerseys - -	200
	1730

The Indians are exceeding fond of our copper-money, which they string round their necks, which it is said has lately occasioned a great number of silver medals to be struck with an impression on them of his Majesty on horse back. Several hundreds of which General Burgoyne took to Quebec, to make presents to the Indians of Canada.

P H I L A D E L P H I A, August 20.

Last week divers persons who have last been in office under the late hereditary government of Pennsylvania, or otherwise in the service of the king of Great-Britain, were arrested, and indulged on parole, with a convenient degree of liberty; they however consider themselves as prisoners of war. This was done for the public security, by his Excellency the president in council, in his character of commander in chief. These gentlemen are to be considered as servants and subjects of the enemy; at least they had not renounced him, nor given any pledge or assurance of their fidelity to the state. They must be subjects of the one or the other. There can be no neutrals. It was not fit they should go longer at large.

We hear that John Penn, Esq; late governor of Pennsylvania, and of the counties of New-Castle, Kent, Sussex upon Delaware; and Benjamin Chew, Esq; late chief justice, register general of wills, &c. and of the council of Pennsylvania, having declined signing paroles, are to be secured at Fredericksburg in Virginie.

While effectual measures are taking with our principal Tories among the men, the women seem to be neglected. But it is time to let the Tory ladies know, that their behaviour is under consideration; and the ringleaders of them will be noticed as soon as their names can be obtained.

Extract of a letter from a gentleman in Charlestown, to his friend at Newbern, dated July 20.

"A brig from Londonderry, mounting 12 guns, bound for St. Augustine, with a valuable cargo (by the description of the men I believe Lofthouse Master) is taken by our state brig of war Notre Dames, Capt. Seymore, and carried into George Town; she arrived off there last Monday, and I believe is got in to day. A French sloop from Cape Francois, with 90 barrels of gunpowder, 11 brass field pieces, with all their appurtenances, 152 bomb-shells, about 1500 shot, a quantity of soldiers cloathing, 30 tons of salt, and 8 officers of artillery, came in last Thursday without a pilot; two men of war at anchor a-breast and close to the bay, and another cruizing in sight: I saw a sloop next day run into Stone. Five or six North

KINGSTON, August 25.

By a gentleman from Albany, we are favoured with the following anecdote.---That at the late battle between General Harkman and the enemy, at Oneyda Creek, there was a friendly Indian, with his wife and son, who distinguished themselves remarkably on the occasion. The Indian killed nine of the enemy, when having received a ball through his wrist that disabled him from using his gun, he then fought with his tomahawk. His son killed two, and his wife on horseback, fought by his side, with pistols, during the whole action, which lasted six hours. That in this and Lieut. Col. Willet's action near the fort, three hundred and fifty Indians were killed, a greater number than they ever lost in any battle during the last war. That they having discovered some reluctance to engage our troops, were plied with liquor till they were half intoxicated, to highten their courage, and prepare them for the slaughter they meditated against us, but suffered themselves, in much greater numbers. This circumstance occasioned their standing the battle with such unusual perseverance. That upon the arrival of a troop of our light horse, at Schenectady, our friends there (who lately had been menaced by the Indians, and worse Savages the Tories) joined the troop in great numbers, and soon put the infamous M'Donald and his base, ungrateful clan, to the rout. That General Arnold, with about a thousand men, above half of whom were Continental troops, having a few days since, marched from Albany for the relief of Fort Stanwix, he was daily joined on the way, by great numbers of volunteers, and by Wednesday it was expected he arrived in the neighbourhood of the more than Savage Butler, and his tawny companions. It is greatly to be feared that this motly banditti of Indians, Tories, Bastards and Britons will retreat to their boats, and escape before our forces can come up with them.

That a son of Butler, with eighteen other ... vages, came a few days ago to the Germa ... recruits, and threatened the inhabitants, ... did not turn out immediately to join the ... bloody tyrant of Britain, a party of Indian ... sent to their houses, who should not spare ... infants in the cradle. But the brave and ... men there, disdaining their brutal threa ... surrounded, and took them all prisoners. ... soon after sent off for Albany, where pr ... are now confined.

[Has not Providence delivered these ... our hands, as hostages for the security of ... fenceless inhabitants, whose fears must be ... leviated by this happy event ?]

That at Bennington, in the battle of S ... 16th inst. when the enemy made their fe ... they received a reinforcement, headed by ... mock Governor, named Skeene, [*since dead*] on seeing our troops file off to the right and left, with a view to flank him, had so little penetration, as to imagine they were flying before him, when he insultingly bawled out, "Stand Yankies, stand, don't run away." They very soon got into the position they intended, bravely attacked the enemy, and gal-

dence, Fort Schuyler, &c. were all his, and as soon as his army appeared before them, would be delivered to his commanders, without firing a gun. And he, Col. Clause, only told them these things, because he had a good will to them, and wanted to keep them from hurting themselves by joining the Rebels, but that if they did join them, it would not make the least alteration in the King's affairs, nor stop him a moment from taking all that the Rebels had, whenever he had a mind to it.

That this speech was delivered with so much confident assurance, that many believed it on that account, while others doubted it. But that on the strange and shameful delivery of Ticonderoga, and all its Stores, Fort Independence, &c. all the rest that Clause had asserted was generally believed, both by Indians and Tories. But they have now reason to think they shall find all the rest of the speech to be false.

Col. Baum, who commanded the whole of the enemy's forces at the late battle near Bennington, is among the slain. We have taken 900 swords of the dragoons, upwards of 1000 stands of arms, four brass field-pieces, viz. one 12, two 9, and one 4 pounders. Our loss 20 or 30 killed, and not more than 50 wounded.

INDEPENDENT CHRONICLE (BOSTON)

September 11, 1777

By June 1777, General John Burgoyne had recruited four hundred Indian auxiliaries to join his campaign. He gave each warrior a silver medallion, which symbolized the shine and luster of the idealized British-Iroquois alliance. The *Independent Chronicle* reveals that Lieutenant Colonel Barry St. Leger's troops attacked a detachment sent from Fort Schuyler to meet General Nicholas Herkimer. Four hundred Iroquois and four hundred Tories lay in wait six miles from Fort Schuyler, near the Indian village of Oriskany.

To the PRINTER *of the* LONDON CHRONICLE

SIR,

WHEN the ſcheme was firſt adopted of taking a body of Indian ſavages to aſſiſt the Britiſh army, it was very generally affirmed, and almoſt as generally believed, that this circumſtance alone would decide the controverſy againſt the Americans; for nothing, it was ſaid, could exceed the terror which the Americans entertained of theſe ſame ſavages. At that time I wrote you a letter contradicting the report, and aſſuring you, from my own perſonal knowledge, that nothing could be worſe founded.

As individuals indeed, and man oppoſed to man, the ſavages are dreadful to the peaceable inhabitants of the Colonies; but as an open enemy, and forming an army, they are juſtly held in the moſt ſupreme contempt. In a word, the ſavages have all the cunning of the fox, and all the cruelty of the tyger; but they have none of the open bravery of the lion. And this opinion of mine is now confirmed by authority; for Colonel St. Leger, in his laſt diſpatches, ſays that the Indians in his army were ſo alarmed at the report of the approach of a body of Continental forces, that they could not be perſuaded to continue the attack upon Fort Stanwix, but immediately abandoned his colours, and took to their heels. R. M.

To be Sold by private Contract,

ALL that the Manor, or reputed Manor, or Lordſhip, of Stallington in the pariſh of Stone, in the county of Stafford.

Alſo all that capital and elegantly finiſhed Manſion-houſe called Stallington-hall, now in the poſſeſſion of Thomas Aſhwood, Eſq; ſituate in Stallington aforeſaid, with a good kitchen garden, pleaſure grounds, fiſh ponds, and all manner of convenient offices thereunto belonging, together with 78 acres, 3 roods, 24 perches of rich arable, meadow, and paſture land, tythe-free, lying round the ſaid Manſion-houſe.

Alſo all that capital Meſſuage called Leacroft-hall, and convenient outbuildings thereunto belonging, ſituate in Fulford in the pariſh of Stone afore-

lington aforeſaid.

And alſo ſeveral Chief Rents ariſing in the ſame Manor or Lordſhip, amounting in the whole to 18 l. per annum, together with ſuch herriotts and rights of common as will be ſpecified in the particular.

The Manſion-houſe is moſt agreeably ſituated, being very contiguous to ſeveral good turnpike roads

STATE LOTTERY, 1777.

RICHARDSON and GOODLUCK reſpectfully acquaint the Public, that the Tickets in the preſent State Lottery are ſold and divided into Shares, Chances, and Shares of Chances, from a Half to a Sixteenth Part, at their Offices in the Bank-buildings, Cornhill, and No. 8, facing the King's Mews, Charing-croſs, where every legal buſineſs of the Lottery is tranſacted with correctneſs and fidelity.

The Chances and Shares of Chances intitle the Purchaſers to every Prize in the Lottery above 20 l. for more than One-third leſs than the price of a Ticket.

Chances at One Guinea each are alſo ſelling at the above Offices, by which the fortunate Purchaſers will gain the following large ſums, viz.

l.			l.
2,000	if the number of the Chance is a Prize of	-	20,000
1,000	- - if a Prize of	-	10,000
500	- - if a Prize of	-	5,000
200	- - if a Prize of	-	2,000
100	- - if a Prize of	-	1,000
50	- - if a Prize of	-	500
10	- - if a Prize of	-	100
5	- - if a Prize of	-	50

The above plan is by much the moſt advantageous to Adventurers of any ever offered, as they will have the Chance of 768 Prizes, and may gain the ſum of Two Thouſand Pounds for the trifling conſideration of One Guinea.—The money for the above Chances will be paid to the fortunate Adventurers as ſoon as drawn, without any deduction, the Original Tickets being in the poſſeſſion of Meſſrs. Richardſon and Goodluck, purſuant to Act of Parliament.

The Lottery will begin drawing on Monday next.

LEGAL CHANCES for the STATE LOTTERY, 1777, at One Pound each; and at Four Shillings each, are now ſelling by HORNSBY and Co. Stock brokers, at the Original King's Arms State Lottery Office, No. 19, corner of Pope's-head-alley, Cornhill, and No. 16, near the Saracen's-head-inn, Aldgate; and No. 5, Bridges-ſtreet, oppoſite Drury-lane Theatre, where the following Capital Prizes were ſold, ſhared, and regiſtered, 10,000 l. in Cox's Muſeum, 20,000 l. in the State Lottery for 1774, 5,000 l. 2,000 l. and 1,000 l. in the laſt State Lottery.

r ONE POUND:

rchaſers will gain the following ſums, viz:

	l.
the Chance is Prize of -	20,000
Prize of -	10,000
Prize of -	5,000
Prize of -	2,000
Prize of -	1,000
Prize of -	500
Prize of -	100
Prize of -	50

UR SHILLINGS:

			l.
	ither of the	2	20,000
	ither of the	3	10,000
	ither of the	4	5,000
	ither of the	8	2,000
	s either of the	11	1,000
5	if the number is either of the	40	500
2 2	if the number is either of the	200	100
1 1	if the number is either of the	500	50

Total 768

The advantages ariſing to the Purchaſers of Chances on the above Plans are ſuperior to any thing yet offered to the Public, as they will have the

SOCIETY for the Diſcharge and Relief of Perſons impriſoned for Small Debts.

Craven-ſtreet, Strand, Nov. 5, 1777.

BEnefactions ſince the laſt report, viz.

	l.	s.	d.
M. S. a Jew Lady - - - -	2	2	0
A. B. - - - - -	2	2	0
Capt. Hooper, of Margate, 2d benefaction	1	1	0
	5	5	0

Diſcharged from the ſeveral priſons in the metropolis 23 Debtors, for 42l. 7s.

Approved the recommendations of 23 Petitioners.

Referred for Enquiry 15 Petitions.

The books may be ſeen by any perſon inclined to promote this undertaking, between the hours of Eleven and Three, at No. 7, Craven-ſtreet, where benefactions are received, and where the Society will meet on Wedneſday the 19th Inſtant, at Six o'Clock in the Afternoon.

Benefactions are alſo received by Mr. Willis, at the Thatch'd-houſe Tavern; the London Exchange Banking Company; and Mr. Nield, the Treaſurer, in St. James's-ſtreet; by Meſſrs. Dorrien and Co. in Finch-lane, Cornhill; Meſſrs. Hoares, in Fleet-ſtreet; Meſſ. Biddulph and Cocks, at Charing Croſs; Meſſ. Fullers in Lombard ſtreet; and Mr. Leacroft, Bookſeller, at Charing-Croſs.

A NEW SYSTEM OF HUSBANDRY.

This Day was publiſhed,

Printed on a new type, and fine paper, in Quarto, Price 10 s 6 d. in Boards,

CLARKE's TRUE THEORY and PRACTICE of HUSBANDRY, deduced from Philoſophical Reſearches, and Experience.—This Work conſiſts of Three Parts or Sections.—Sect. I. Contains a philoſophical and practical inveſtigation of the moſt eſſential matters in the walk of huſbandry; a fair and impartial method of eſtimating the value of land; the education of youth deſigned for Huſbandmen, &c. &c. II. The elements of mechanics illuſtrated with plates, and ſo explained and applied, as to enable the Huſbandman to direct the making and repairing his various utenſils in a true mechanical manner. III. Conſiſts of, 1ſt—An explanation of the figures contained in the five demy folio plates given in the Work, viz. Exact drawings of the beſt natural and artificial graſſes for paſture, meadow, and pleaſure grounds; two drain ploughs; a trenching plough; a paring plough; a turn-wriſt plough, or plough for banky land; the common plough; a plough that requires the leaſt force poſſible to draw it; an improved drill plough, &c. for the invention of which the Author has had the firſt premiums given by the Honourable Society, inſtituted in London, for the Encouragement of Arts. 2d—Full directions for making and managing a cheap and durable machine for threſhing corn, which may be worked by wind, water, horſes, or men, to great advantage.

Printed for the Author, and ſold by G. Robinſon, Pater-noſter-row; and T. Slack, Newcaſtle.

For the TEETH, SCURVY in the GUMS, and TOOTH ACH,

Mr. GREENOUGH's TINCTURES.

THESE Tinctures have now been in general uſe for more than thirty years paſt, and as the ſtanding the teſt of time and experience is the ſtrongeſt proof of real excellence, it is hoped the univerſal eſteem they have acquired during that period, is a ſufficient evidence of their merit, efficacy, and ſafety: But as their ſucceſs has occaſioned many counterfeits, Mr. Greenough requeſts, that every purchaſer will obſerve, that his genuine Tinctures are in oblong ſquare bottles, on each of which is a label with the following words, PREPARED BY T. GREENOUGH;

LONDON CHRONICLE

November 15, 1777

Colonel Daniel Claus, St. Leger's subordinate, lifted the siege of Fort Schuyler on August 22 and returned to Canada. The November 15, 1777, *London Chronicle* reflects his frustration. The British questioned the Indians' "bravery," without acknowledging the opportunistic nature of Indian warfare. Denied payment and discouraged by high casualties at Freeman's Farm, Burgoyne's Indians deserted. This contributed to the American victory at Saratoga.

REPORTING THE

BATTLES OF BRANDYWINE AND GERMANTOWN

By Bruce E. Mowday

ON THE MORNING OF SEPTEMBER 11, 1777, AMERICAN General George Washington's troops were well entrenched behind the banks of the Brandywine River near Chadds Ford, Pennsylvania. Washington picked the Brandywine as the perfect place to defend the young nation's capitol of Philadelphia against the British and to defeat King George III's army.

Late in August 1777, General William Howe's British army landed at the Head of the Elk in Maryland and began a campaign to capture Philadelphia. Howe's planning for the operation began in the waning months of 1776 and was approved by his superior Lord George Germain in London. The campaign had three objectives. The first was to capture Philadelphia, the second was to deprive Washington's army of supplies furnished by the inhabitants of the region, and the third was to rally citizens loyal to King George III to fight the rebels.

Before daybreak on the day of the Battle of Brandywine, Howe split his army into two segments. Howe and General Charles Cornwallis led more than half of the British army on a seventeen-mile march to flank Washington. The remaining segment of the British army under General Wilhelm Knyphausen was ordered to march from Kennett Square, Pennsylvania, and force Washington's light infantry back to the Brandywine. Knyphausen was ordered to cross the river and attack the rebels when Howe attacked the rear portion of Washington's army.

The plan almost worked perfectly for the British. Several British officers wrote after the battle that if they had an hour's additional daylight, Washington's army would have been destroyed. The Continental Congress fled Philadelphia after the defeat at Brandywine, and on September 26, 1777, the British took control of one of America's most important cities.

The Philadelphia campaign was a disaster for Washington, including General Anthony Wayne's defeat at Paoli on the evening of September 21, 1777. Washington attempted to surprise the British army at Germantown on October 4, 1777, and had initial success. Fog, friendly fire, and a stubborn British defense at the Cliveden mansion contributed to Washington's withdrawing from Germantown.

The early reporting on the Battle of Brandywine in the October 28, 1777, edition of the *London Chronicle* had few details and overstated the number of casualties of both armies. The paper estimated Washington's losses at two thousand and the British at seven hundred to eight hundred. The Americans actually lost about 1,300 and the British almost six hundred. The same newspaper on November 15, 1777, again inflated losses for Washington's army and reported that the British took possession of a city in ruins after rebels set fire to Philadelphia. While some supplies were destroyed, no widespread destruction of the city was done before the British took control.

A report from an American officer that first appeared in the *New-York Gazette* on September 22, 1777, was reprinted in the *London Chronicle* on November 8, 1777. That report was written at 5:00 p.m. on the day of the Battle of Brandywine, and the author didn't have a complete view of what was taking place that day. He wrote about his limited experiences and was overly optimistic about the American fortunes.

The *London Chronicle* reprinted a letter from a British officer attached to Hessian troops at Germantown that contained a great amount of details on the fighting. The letter was penned a week after the battle and was printed on January 6, 1778.

The Philadelphia campaign was a triumph for the British army as Howe's forces forced the Americans to retreat to Valley Forge, where Washington's army suffered through a hard winter.

Tueſday, Oct. 28.

IRELAND.

Tralee, Oct. 6.

A FEW days ago a Gentleman of Tubridbeg gave an order on one of his tenants to two brothers, Smiths, with power to diſtrain: accordingly they

LONDON CHRONICLE
October 28, 1777

The early reporting on the Battle of Brandywine in the October 28, 1777, edition of the *London Chronicle* had few details and overstated the number of casualties of both armies.

SCOTLAND.

Edinburgh, Oct. 22. Thurſday laſt were interred in the church-yard of Aberdeen a man and a woman, whoſe ages amounted to 190.

At Haddington, on the 19th inſt. died, Dr. James Lundie, Phyſician there, in the 92d year of his age.

COUNTRY NEWS.

Liverpool, Oct. 24. Yeſterday the John and Sally arrived from the Smalls, with Mr. Whiteſides and the workmen ſhe took from hence, and thoſe who went down before her, in perfect health. It is remarkable, that this is the fourth ſeaſon the people have returned from this ſuppoſed hazardous enterprize, without hurt or blemiſh. We hear, the building was left in a condition to ſtand the winter, though not habitable.

Briſtol, Oct. 25. Thurſday evening the Birmingham diligence returning to the White Hart in this city, was ſtopped within 100 yards of Stokes Croft Turnpike by two footpads, who robbed the paſſengers of between 5l. and 6l. On the arrival of the carriage, Mr. White informed Mr. Weekes of the event, who, anxious for the ſafety of his own diligence expected in, ordered a whiſkey, and, accompanied by a friend, with only a brace of piſtols, proceeded that road himſelf. Juſt at the croſs poſts, between the turnpike and Redland, the ſame two footpads ordered them to ſtop, when Mr. Weekes's companion rather too precipitately diſcharged his piſtol, on which the fellows inſtantly fired a brace of blunderbuſſes, but happily without effect. The horſe on the diſcharge of the fire arms ſet out full ſpeed, and the Gentlemen thought it moſt expedient to haſten home by another road, when they procured more aſſiſtance, and again ſallied out in purſuit of the offenders, but they eluded a diligent ſearch of ſeveral hours.

Saliſbury, Oct. 27. Laſt week the unanimous thanks of the pariſh of Milton was ſent to Philip Pulſe, Eſq; Patron of that church, for

Oxford, Oct. 25. Laſt Saturday morning a coach and a diligence were robbed between four and five o'clock; one of them near the Obſer-

Reading, Oct. 25. On Wedneſday laſt a gentleman of Savernacle Park, near Marlborough, aged 72, was married to Miſs Molly Tuch, aged 27. The coming of this couple together was not a little ſingular, and is as follows: The old gentleman was paying his addreſſes to a widow in Marlborough, on whom he had offered to ſettle 50l. a year for her life, beſides leaving her a conſiderable ſum at his deceaſe, which ſhe rejected, when the above young lady falling into their company, and Mr. Tarrant ſubmitting to

...he propoſals he had made
... and honourable? ſhe
... ſuch an offer." The
... the young woman,
...s her candour, and in
...ſervice to her, which

...E W S.

...d and ſailed for the
...dſhall, from Oporto;
...m Briſtol; the Plenty,
... and the Dublin, Rider,

from Cheſter. Remain in the Downs the ſhips as before, and the Nile, Goldſmith, for orders; the Duke of Cumberland, Paſſmore, for Ancona; the Princeſs Mary, Arthur, for Jamaica; the ——, Wilſon, for St. Ube's; and the Fleece, Moore, for Plymouth. Wind South Weſt, blows hard.

LONDON.

Accounts received yeſterday by the way of France ſay, that there has been a general engagement between Waſhington and Gen. Howe, near Philadelphia. On the approach of the Britiſh army Gen. Waſhington called a counſel of war, whether they ſhould defend their magazines, which was agreed to, the conſequence of which was a total defeat, with the loſs of 2000 men killed and wounded, and all their magazines. About ſeven or eight hundred of the Britiſh troops fell in the action. Policies were opened at Lloyd's to receive fifteen guineas to pay an hundred if the above is not true.

A report prevails that Lieut. Kniphauſen inſiſted on the releaſe of the Heſſian officers taken at Trenton laſt December, according to the terms propoſed by Mr. Waſhington; in conſequence of which Gen. Lee was given in exchange for them, and for Col. Campbell an Engliſh officer taken in his paſſage to America two years ſince. Sir Wm. Howe is ſaid to have been unwilling to part with Lee, but the Heſſian General inſiſting on having his officers, he was under the neceſſity of complying.

Yeſterday ſome diſpatches were received at the Admiralty from Admiral Montague on the Newfoundland ſtation, brought by the Active frigate, arrived at Portſmouth, which are to be laid before the Privy Council.

The army in America is to be reinforced next campaign with 17,000 troops, and early in the ſeſſions the Houſe of Commons is to be moved for ſupplies, to enable government to defray the expence. The minority Members are buſy collecting all their ſtrength.

Yeſterday his Majeſty took an airing on horſeback to Windſor, and returned to the Queen's Palace at three o'clock.

...ceſter Houſe.

It is ſaid Lord North intends to raiſe the principal additional ſupplies next ſeſſion, by

lings. By this a
collected withou
Yeſterday th
Cofferer's and o
hold a quarter's
It is ſaid that
powers to trea
Princes, and to
ſervice for next
It is ſaid that
for the America
cluded with th
body of troops
it be found nece
A letter from
tenant of a ma
having boarded
Ireland, the cr
cheſt, and ſhot
Advice is ſai
town, South C
very great diſtu
cipal inhabitant
properties ſeize
priſon, becauſe
currency iſſued
The Iriſh nat
veral eſtabliſhm
ing Lady-day 1
the two years e
to 2,561,065l. a
at the former p
the latter amou
The firſt regi
by his Majeſty
next week; as
ſoon after; wh
from each regi
America.
Extract of a
" Arrived th
from Plymout
here this even
ſhips, viz. on
ſhip Squirrel,
with about 16
under his conv
the Hero, Cap
lona; on the 1
Alarm, off Liſ
Extract of a
" Yeſterday
ſeveral paſſenge
of the Weſt I
was taken off
of 36 guns.
tacked the D
ſailer, and was
rica, in 63 v
prizes, among
from Jamaica
mouth, for
ſchooner, con
New York, w
Jamaica fleet.
on board a Fre
they obtained
Extract of a
" Arrived t
jeſty's ſhip th
Capt. William
cher cutter,
with eight fa
laden with li

Saturday, Nov.

Yeſterday arrived the Mails from
HOLLAND, *and* FLANDERS

Warſaw, Oct. 25.

WE have accounts her
Porte has declared w
the Tartars, becauſe
choſen a new Chan,
in conſequence of
Ruſſians have ſent 12
to their aſſiſtance,
Romanzow is to command the Ruſſ
It is added, that if war is declared th
will act upon a new plan, which will
Turks very much; but we do not hear
plan is.
Madrid, Oct. 30. By advices fro
we hear, that the coaſts of Biſcay ar
with American privateers, which ta
Engliſh veſſels, and that Capt. John F
the Succeſs privateer has taken ſeve
veſſels in one month.
Naples, Oct. 21. We have the ſatis
hear that all the royal children, who w
inoculated, are perfectly recovered,
gained great honour to Dr. Gaſkin,
given the utmoſt ſatisfaction to the C
the Public.
Rome, Oct. 25. Our letters fro
mention, that a violent ſhock of an ea
had been felt there, without mentio
conſequences of it, only that it had
general alarm throughout that city.
ſhocks have alſo been felt in the prov
patrimony of St. Peter, but happily d
mage.
Marſeilles, Oct. 23. The following
of the letter written by the Miniſter of
rine Department, and ſent to all the
France.
" You could not, Gentlemen, be ig
the orders ſo often renewed by his M
the fittings of the different Admiralti
ports, not to permit the ſale of any pri
by foreign privateers, or to ſuffer th
and their prizes to remain any long
ports than is abſolutely neceſſary to
them the proviſions and aſſiſtance t
might want. This prohibition, which
from a principle of faithfully obſerving
once made, ought not to be eluded on
tence whatever; and it is not without g
pleaſure, that his Majeſty hears that n
gal methods have been made uſe of to
vigilance of his Officers, and to buy
the goods belonging to the above-m
prizes; and I am charged by the King
give notice to the Chambers of Tr
through them to the Merchants, that th
not directly or indirectly buy any of t
chandizes which in any ſhape belong
prizes brought into any of his ports,
of anſwering for it perſonally, and being
to return the goods or their value.
" I deſire you will make theſe inten
his Majeſty known to the Merchants,
the ſame time that the King will not pe
leaſt evaſion of his orders to go unpu
and, I am perſuaded, that the Mercha
ſhew the utmoſt alacrity to prove th
miſſion to the King's pleaſure. I am
order you, that thoſe who counteract t
ders be rigorouſly proceeded againſt; a
further to add, that as the ports of th
dom are open for the trade of all nati
Merchant ſhips from North America ma
mitted with their cargoes, which they r
poſe of, and take in return any merc
which is permitted to be exported, exc
munition, &c. and his Majeſty particular
all Merchants to avoid the introducing
American prizes, under pretence of the
Merchantmen."

... hat the ueen of Portugal h... ed to accede to e Family Compact.

IRELAND.

Dublin, Nov. 8. The Lord Mayor, Sheriffs, ldermen, and Common Council of the county the town of Drogheda, having unanimously oted the freedom of said town, in an elegant ver box, unto Lambert Brabazon, Esq; of his lajesty's navy, in consideration of his intrepid nd attentive conduct, in protecting the trade nd commerce of this kingdom, whilst the coast as infested with American privateers; at the quest of their corporation, Wm. Mead Ogle, q; one of their representatives in parliament, Tuesday last delivered Lieut. Brabazon this stinguishing mark of their approbation.

And the principal Merchants of the city of ublin have also presented by their representa- e, Dr. Wm. Clement, a memorial to his Ex- llency the Lord Lieutenant, representing the irited and active conduct of Lieut. Brabazon, d the essential service rendered by him to the mmercial and trading interest of this kingdom, d in particular to the merchants of this city, aying that their representation be laid before Majesty that this officer might receive a re- rd equal to his merit and services.

The Lord Lieutenant has appointed the Right n. urrough Earl of Inchiquin, to be Go- nor of the County of Clare, in the room of late Earl of Inchiquin.

Wednesday Walter Hussey Burgh, Esq; Prime jeant at Law in this kingdom, and John ott, Esq; Attorney General, were sworn of Majesty's most Hon. Privy Council.

Letters by Thursday's post from Kilkenny ad- , that one Magher, a labouring man, was en and lodged in the county gaol there, rged with the murder and robbery of one lier, a lad, near Ballyragget, when he was to pay a sum of money.

Kilkenny, Nov. 5. Miss Vize has been res- d from the persons who forcibly took her y from the house of Mr. Parsons, of Bal- tten, near Clonmell, and restored to her fa- , by the activity of Lord Doneraile, the perary rangers, and many other gentlemen he counties of Tipperary and Corke.

COUNTRY NEWS.

enzance, Nov. 7. The beginning of this k a woman was committed to the county of Launceston from Liskeard, by the name ones, for horse-stealing.

SHIP NEWS.

eal, Nov. 13. Came down his Majesty's Boston, and remain in the Downs with the as before, and the Lapwing, Scott, for altar; the Hope, Warman, the Montserrat et, Clark, for Montserrat. Sailed for the the Allen, Liddey, from Dublin. Wind uth.

LONDON.

sterday morning his Majesty, attended by officers of the train, went on horseback oolwich to see a proof of several pieces nnon intended for New York; after which ajesty returned to the Queen's palace.

e same day, after breaking up of the Levee James's, a Privy-council was held, at all the great Officers of State assisted.

the House of Commons of Ireland on sday Nov. 6, Mr. Gorges Lowther moved quire into the state of the civil and mili- ensions.

e address of the house, thanking his ma- for his gracious answer to their former s, was presented by Mr. Charles Henry , and agreed to by the house,

e petition of Mr. Thomas Johnson, pray- lief for his losses incurred by his importa- f cattle for improving the live stock of d, was reported by Mr. Lodge Morris, as being fully proved, and the petitioner worthy of parliamentary aid.

Mr. Frederick Flood moved, that the proper officer do lay before the house a particular account of incidents on the civil establishment of this kingdom, from Lady-day 1775, to Lady-day, 1777, which was carried.

It appeared in the returns of the payments out of the concordatum, that Mr. Supple and Mr. Hackett had received money, and it had not been expressed in the warrant of the privy-council for what reason they had been paid the sums specified. To attain information on that head, Mr. Barry Barry moved that the report of the committee of the privy-council on which these warrants were grounded should be laid before the house. Mr. Prime Serjeant replied, though he would not wish any information should be withheld, yet the house was to judge what information was to be asked, and whether it was asked properly; which was not the present case, as the privy-council were all on oath.

Mr. Recorder, Mr. Daly, Mr. Grattan, and Mr. Barry, urged the right of members to call for any papers they pleased, and the latter made many remarks on the excesses on concordatum.

Mr. Leigh thought the motion improper; and Mr. Attorney General explained these two articles, by informing Mr. Barry that Mr. Supple had been very active in prosecuting to conviction some very atrocious criminals, and out of revenge their accomplices had set on him, and left him for dead, with 18 wounds. Still he survived, and successfully prosecuted the offenders; but had been long reduced to misery and distress, till the council had considered his case, and given him the above relief. As to Mr. Hackett, he was a messenger, and the money he had received was for travelling charges for his journey to London, and attendance there on Sir John Blaquiere. His information giving satisfaction, the motion was withdrawn.

General Cunningham informed the house, that for two journeys, one through all Ireland, and another to embark the troops at Corke, he had refused to receive any gratification, but it being insisted upon that his charges should be paid, he had received the expence of his post horses, which had been set down in the civil expences, without any explanation, and mixed with other accounts, that might induce the house to think he had charged for his trouble, which he scorned to do; and this matter had been thus set down by a person in office, in resentment for his not being so pliable as he could wish.

Mr. Gardiner also spoke concerning the money charged for works done in the Phœnix Park, and said he never had signed any paper for such works, and that the roads there were in very bad order.

On Friday, Nov. 7. The committee of accounts finished all its business previous to preparing their report.

Mr. Barry Barry began a revision of the case of Mr. Supple, as mentioned the day before, but being reminded it was time to go up with the address, he desisted, and the house adjourned, and went to present to his Excellency the address to his majesty, and request it may be transmitted to the king.

Some of the morning papers contain the following article: The Bienfaisant man of war, which arrived at Plymouth on Wednesday last, from Halifax, (from whence she sailed October 16,) at the mouth of Halifax harbour met the Grayhound frigate, the Capt. of which sent on board the Bienfaisant a Newport gazette extraordinary, of Sunday October 5, and another from New York of the same date, containing a letter from Gen. Howe, brought by a sloop of war from Chesapeak Bay to General Clinton, and also a letter from Lord Howe to Sir Peter Parker at Rhode Island, giving an account of what had happened since the disembarkation of the troops; viz. that General Howe came up with the rebels at Brandywine, on the

11th of September, about five o'clock in the afternoon, having had several skirmishes with the enemy's out-posts in the course of the day, and the rebels were at last brought to a general action, which lasted till dark, when Washington, taking the advantage of the night, made a precipitate retreat, leaving behind all his cannon, baggage, and 1800 of their dead on the field. That on the 17th another action had happened near the Schuyikill, where Washington was again defeated with great loss. That Gen. Howe took possession of Philadelphia the 24th, which the rebels instantly abandoned, setting it on fire in three places, but, from the vigilance of the troops, and the assistance afforded by the inhabitants, it was soon got under, with very little loss. The rebels likewise set fire to three frigates in the harbour, and several floating batteries. Gen. Howe left three regiments to garrison the town, and set off, full speed, with the grenadiers, light infantry, &c. into the Jerseys, after Washington. Provisions of all sorts have been sent into Philadelphia from the country around, and the inhabitants have promised to furnish the army with every necessary, in abundance. And the counties of Newcastle, Kent, and Sussex, had also sent delegates to the General, offering to supply him with provisions, if they could be protected, and that he had left a brigade there for that purpose. The Dispatch sloop of war had arrived at New York from Chesapeak-bay, and the Bristol and Experiment with their convoys from England.

When the Bienfaisant left Halifax, the reports were, that the provincials had set fire to Philadelphia in four places previous to their abandoning it. So that our troops are in possession only of the ruins of the city.

Philadelphia, Sept. 3.

In Congress, Sept. 1, 1777.

Resolved, That Gen. Washington be directed to appoint a court of enquiry relative to the late expedition by Gen. Sullivan, against the British forces on Staten-island.

Copy from the journals,

Wm. Ch. Houston, Dep. Sec.

A letter from Port Antonio, in the island of Jamaica, dated Sept. 2, says, "The 6th inst. two American privateers, both of them ships of considerable force, stood into, and cut three vessels out of this harbour; and a few days before, the same privateers took a large ship within a few miles of this place. There is at present nine of those provincial vessels of war cruising round this island, in defiance of the small squadron the Admiral has at Port Royal, which are too few in number to check their progress."

From New York, intelligence has been received, that Capt. T. was killed in a duel there, by Capt. P. of the guards, immediately after

the Mary Cutter, Lieutenant Donavan, are arrived from Dublin, having safely convoyed from thence to Dungeness, the London, Herd, the Success, Dunn, and the Allen, Liddey, all bound to London, loaded with linen for that port.

"Arrived about 14 sail of outward-bound ships from the Downs, and two large ordnance

dropped down to St. ship Ariel is put back to remains with the outw fleet."

Yesterday the Earl of Levee at St. James's, an with his Majesty.

On Thursday an extra of the Governors was hospital, St. George's- election (by ballot) of preachers. The candida Wm. Sellon, Minister o well; the Rev. Mr. Rich Brompton-chapel; the F ler, Preacher at Charlotte Mr. T. Bowen, Reader a ing up the ballot there a 180, Mr. Harrison 115, Bowen 30, whereupon t men were declared duly

Last week was married Bath, to Miss Eliz. Shern

On Wednesday died, Sir Lau. Dundas at Mo wood, Esq; of Soho-squa

On Tuesday last died, port, George Clarke, Es Justices of the Peace for and Lancaster.

On Thursday died, at Theamon, formerly an of

Yesterday died, at his Mr. Clarke, Builder.

Yesterday the body of a found drowned in the Tower. He was laid u to be owned.

D. L. The School for Scanda a Stage.

C. G. The Duenna, with T

LONDON CHRONICLE

November 15, 1777

—

The November 15, 1777, *London Chronicle* again had overinflated losses for Washington's army and reported that the British army took possession of a city in ruins after rebels set fire to Philadelphia. While some supplies were destroyed, no widespread destruction of the city was done before the British took control.

NOVEMBER 8, 1777

The LONDON CHRONICLE

From the New York Gazette, *Sept. 22.*

Yesterday the following account of the action of the 11th instant, between the King's troops under the command of his Excellency Sir Wm. Howe, and the rebel army under Mr. Washington, near Brandywine, came to hand, as the same was published by order of Congress.

Chad Ford, Sept. 11, 1777, 5 o'clock.

SIR,

WHEN I had the honour of advising you this morning, I mentioned that the enemy were advancing: I had begun a cannonade. I would now beg leave to inform you, that they have kept up a brisk fire from their artillery ever since their advanced party were attacked by our light troops under Gen. Maxwell, who hemmed the Brandywine for that purpose, and had posted his men on some high ground on each side the road. The fire from our people was not of long duration (as the enemy pushed on fast), but was very severe. What loss the enemy sustained cannot be ascertained with precision; but from our situation, and briskness of the attack, it is the general opinion (particularly those that were engaged) that they had at the least 300 killed and wounded. Our damage is not exactly known, but from the best account we have been able to obtain, it does not exceed 50 in the whole. After this affair, the enemy halted upon the heights, where they have remained ever since, except a detachment of them which filed off about eleven o'clock from their left, and have since passed Brandywine at John's Ford, between five and six miles above Chad's; the amount of it is not known, accounts respecting it being various, some making it to be two or three thousand strong, and others more. Generals Sullivan, Stirling, and Stephens, with their divisions, are gone in pursuit of them, and to attack if they can with any prospect of success. There has been a scattering fire between our parties on each side the brook since the action in the morning, which just now becomes warm, when Gen. Maxwell pushed over with his corps, and drove them from their ground, with the loss of 30 men left dead on the spot, amongst them a Captain of the 49th, and a number of intrenching tools, with which they were turning up a battery. At half after four o'clock the enemy attacked Gen. Sullivan at the Ford, and above this, and the action has been violent ever since; it still continues a very severe cannonade, has begun here, and I suppose we shall have a very hot evening. I hope it will be a happy one. I have the honour to be, Robt. H. Hannison.

Hon. John Hancock, Esq;

Published by Order of Congress,

Charles Thomson Sec

LONDON CHRONICLE

November 8, 1777

A report from an American officer that first appeared in the *New-York Gazette* on September 22, 1777, was reprinted in the *London Chronicle* on November 8, 1777. That report was written at 5:00 p.m. on the day of the Battle of Brandywine, and the author didn't have a complete view of what was taking place that day. He wrote about his limited experiences and was overly optimistic about the American fortunes that day.

Saturday, Nov. 8.

Yesterday arrived the Mails from FRANCE *and* HOLLAND.

Petersburgh, October 10.

ON the 6th of this month we had another tempest here, but happily no inundation; we are daily more sensible of the effects of the last, which has occasioned the price of corn to be very high, as all that was in the magazines is spoiled.

Cologne, Oct. 30. It is said that the Prince of Anhalt Zerbst is to send a corps of his troops into the British service, and that some of his Officers are already gone to London.

Madrid, Oct. 14. We have accounts from South America, that a great difference has arisen there between the two Commanders of our fleet, Don Cevallos and the Marquis of Cassa Tilly, insomuch that the former has complained to the Court, who it is said has given orders for the command of the fleet to be given to a Commodore, till the arrival of another Lieutenant-general, whom the King shall appoint to take the command of that fleet.

Lisbon, Oct. 7. It is said that peace is concluded between Spain and Portugal, on condition that the Spaniards shall return the Island St. Catherine to the Portuguese, but that the former are to keep the colony of St. Sacrament.

The departure of the Queen Dowager for Spain is fixed for the 21st of this month. Their Majesties and the royal family will accompany her Majesty to Villa Viciosa.

A shock of an earthquake was felt here on the 1st of this month, at six o'clock in the morning, and a subterraneous noise was heard at the same time.

Paris, Oct. 31. The Cardinal de la Roche Aymon, Archbishop and Duke of Rheims, first Peer and Grand Almoner of France, &c. died on the 27th of this month.

SHIP NEWS.

Deal, Nov. 6. Came down and sailed this morning, with several of the outward-bound ships, the Trecothick, Moore, the St. James Planter, Steward, for Jamaica. Came down, and remain in the Downs with the rest of the ships as before, his Majesty's ship Cornwall, the Thomas, Mann, for Montserrat; and the Resolution, Cox, for Grenada. Wind W S.W.

LONDON.

Yesterday the Lord Mayor, Aldermen, and Common Council, attended his Majesty according to his royal will and pleasure, and presented the following address.

To the KING's Most Excellent Majesty.

The humble Address of the Lord Mayor, Aldermen, and Commons of the City of London, in Common Council assembled:

Most Gracious Sovereign,

"We your Majesty's most dutiful and loyal subjects the Lord Mayor, Aldermen, and Commons of the city of London, in Common Council assembled, humbly beg leave to express our unfeigned joy upon the happy delivery of our Most Gracious Queen, and the birth of another Princess: an event which we consider as an ad-

To which the King returned the following answer:

"I thank you for this dutiful address, and your loyal congratulations on the happy delivery of the Queen, and the birth of another Princess.

"It is my invariable object to preserve, and transmit entire, the constitutional liberties of my people, which I shall ever consider as forming the basis of my government."

The Lord Mayor, the Lord Mayor Elect, and the following Aldermen, were present on the above occasion, viz. Alsop, Kennett, Thomas, Hayley, Pugh, and about 130 Common Councilmen, in 33 coaches and chariots; the Chamberlain, the City Remembrancer, the Town Clerk, and other officers.

They were all received very graciously, and had the honour of kissing the King's hand. After which they were regaled with cake, wine, &c.

Yesterday some dispatches were received at St. James's from the Hon. Robert Walpole, Esq; his Majesty's Ambassador at the Court of Lisbon, brought by the Squirrel man of war, arrived at Portsmouth.

It is said that General Faucett, who is gone to Germany, has received orders to contract with the different German States for 7000 men, who are to be in readiness to embark for America on the first notice.

On Thursday evening their Graces the Dukes of Leeds and Chandos arrived in town from their respective country seats, and were yesterday at Court.

The William, Norris, from New York, is arrived at Liverpool.

From the ROYAL AMERICAN GAZETTE, *received yesterday.*

New York, Sept. 11. On Monday last a vessel, with a flag of truce, arrived here from Martinico. Their business, we hear, is to solicit the release of the French officers taken in the vessels trading with the rebels.

New York, Sept. 15. Wednesday arrived here from Tobago, the ship Catharine, John Freeman, Master, laden with rum and sugar; she was on the 13th ult. taken by a rebel privateer sloop called the Baltimore Hero, commanded by one Hasey, who put on board the ship one Lieutenant, a prize-master, and three hands. They kept possession of her nine days; but in the night of the 22d past, Capt. Freeman, being assisted by the hands left on board belonging to the ship, resumed the command, and brought her safe into his destined port.

We hear that Commodore Hotham has very generously given up the salvage of the above ship to the master and mariners that rescued her from the hands of the Rebels, and brought her into this port.

Tuesday last the ship Peace and Plenty, Capt. M'Kenzie, the ship King George, Capt. Redmond, and the ship Nelly, Capt North, arrived here from Corke, with provisions, &c. after a tedious passage of 10 weeks: They sailed from thence under convoy of the ship British King, and in company with the Jane, Diana, Unity, Walters, Mary and Anne, Stagg, Indian King, Union Island, Concord, and Lord Howe; and left them the 19th of August, in lat. 38. 30. long. 60. being ordered by the Commodore to give chace to a rebel privateer schooner of 12 guns, that appeared among the shipping; but after a pursuit of several hours, the wind falling away, the privateer took to her oars, and got

From the NEW YORK GAZETTE, *Sept.* 22.

Yesterday the following account of the action of the 11th instant, between the King's troops under the command of his Excellency Sir Wm. Howe, and the rebel army under Mr. Washington, near Brandywine, came to hand, as the same was published by order of Congress.

Chad Ford, Sept. 11, 1777, 5 o'clock.

SIR,

WHEN I had the honour of advising you this morning, I mentioned that the enemy were advancing: I had begun a cannonade. I would now beg leave to inform you, that they have kept up a brisk fire from their artillery ever since their advanced party were attacked by our light troops under Gen. Maxwell, who hemmed the Brandywine for that purpose, and had posted his men on some high ground on each side the road. The fire from our people was not of long duration (as the enemy pushed on fast), but was very severe. What loss the enemy sustained cannot be ascertained with precision; but from our situation, and briskness of the attack, it is the general opinion (particularly those that were engaged) that they had at the least 300 killed and wounded. Our damage is not exactly known, but from the best account we have been able to obtain, it does not exceed 50 in the whole. After this affair, the enemy halted upon the heights, where they have remained ever since, except a detachment of them which filed off about eleven o'clock from their left, and have since passed Brandywine at John's Ford, between five and six miles above Chad's; the amount of it is not known, accounts respecting it being various, some making it to be two or three thousand strong, and others more. Generals Sullivan, Stirling, and Stephens, with their divisions, are gone in pursuit of them, and to attack it if they can with any prospect of success. There has been a scattering fire between our parties on each side the brook since the action in the morning, which just now becomes warm, when Gen. Maxwell pushed over with his corps, and drove them from their ground, with the loss of 30 men left dead on the spot, amongst them a Captain of the 49th, and a number of intrenching tools, with which they were turning up a battery. At half after four o'clock the enemy attacked Gen. Sullivan at the Ford, and above this, and the action has been violent ever since; it still continues a very severe cannonade, has begun here, and I suppose we shall have a very hot evening. I hope it will be a happy one. I have the honour to be,

ROBT. H. HANNISON.

Hon. John Hancock, Esq;

Published by Order of Congress,

CHARLES THOMSON, Sec.

The following extraordinary news, dated Bourdeaux, Oct. 15, appeared in the Avignon Gazette, and arrived by yesterday's mail.

"Letters received yesterday from l'Orient advise, that two vessels dispatched by the Congress, had arrived in that port; the Captains of the ships say, that Gen. Washington having sent a reinforcement of troops under the command of Arnold to join the army of Gen. St. Clair, these two Generals attacked Gen. Burgoyne under the cannon of Fort Edward; that they entirely defeated his army, and took him prisoner. This news, which prudence should forbid us to believe until well authenticated, has had strange effects in this city: and though there are wanting the most essential marks of authenticity, such as dates, &c. yet there are numbers of people here who believe it ...

STATE OF MASSACHUSETTS-BAY.

COUNCIL-CHAMBER, October 20, 1777.

WHEREAS it appears to this Board that the Committees of Correspondence in some Towns where there is British Officers on Parole have permitted them and their Servants to ride about the Country without Leave first had and obtained from the Council, which renders the Parole of no Validity, and indangers the State:

Therefore *Ordered*, That the Committees of Correspondence in some Towns where there are Officers on Parole, be and hereby are strictly enjoined not to permit any Officers on Parole or their Servants to exceed the Limits set them in the respective Paroles; and in Case any Officers on Parole, or their Servants, shall be so daring as to leap the Bounds set them, the said Committee are hereby directed immediately to secure them and give Notice thereof to the Council, that they may take such Order respecting them, as they shall think proper. True Copy.

Attest. JOHN AVERY, D. Sec'y.

STATE OF MASSACHUSETTS-BAY.

In the House of Representatives, October 18, 1777.

WHEREAS this Court on the twenty-second day of November last, resolved that the Naval-Officers for the several ports in this State, should hold their offices only for the term of one year: And whereas the time for which the said Naval-Officers were chosen will expire in November next, and it is not probable this Court will be then sitting, and their choice cannot therefore be then renewed:

Resolved, That said Naval-Officers be, and hereby are severally impowered to hold and execute their offices, until they shall be re-chosen by this Court, or until others shall be chosen in their Stead.

Sent up for Concurrence.

J. WARREN, Speaker.

In COUNCIL, October 18, 1777.

Read and concurred. JOHN AVERY, D. Sec'y.

Consented to. A true copy,

Attest. JOHN AVERY, D. Sec'y

STATE OF MASSACHUSETTS-BAY.

COUNCIL-CHAMBER, Boston, October 21, 1777.

ORDERED, That the Sheriffs of the several counties within this State, be, and they hereby are directed to convey, without loss of time, all such persons as are now confined in the common goals in their respective counties (and belong to another county) by virtue of a general warrant, under the hand of the President of the Council; to the common goal in the county to which they respectively belong.

And the Sheriffs are hereby further directed forthwith to make a return to this Board of the names of all the prisoners committed as aforesaid, with the names of the towns to which they respectively belong.

A true copy,

Attest. JOHN AVERY, D. Sec'y.

BOSTON, [illegible]

An Express arrived here last Wednesday Evening from the honorable Major-General GATES, to the honorable the President of the COUNCIL of this State, with the following important Advices, viz.

Albany, 19th October, 1777.

SIR,

I HAVE the pleasure to send your honorable Council, the inclosed copy of a Convention, by which Lieutenant General Burgoyne, surrendered himself and his whole army, on the 17th instant, into my hands; they are now upon their march towards Boston; General [illegible] and General Whipple, with a proper

Great-Britain, upon condition of not serving again in North America during the present contest, and the port of Boston is assigned for the entry of transports to receive the troops, whenever General Howe shall so order.

ART. III. Should any cartel take place, by which the army under Lieutenant-General Burgoyne, or any part of it, may be exchanged, the foregoing article to be void as far as such exchange shall be made.

ART. IV. The army under Lieutenant General Burgoyne, to march to Massachusetts-Bay by the easiest, most expeditious and convenient route; and to be quartered in, near, or as convenient as possible to Boston, that the march of the troops may not be delayed when transports arrive to receive them.

ART. V. The troops to be supplyed on the march, and during their being in quarters, with provisions by General Gates's orders, at the same rate of rations as the troops of his own army, and if possible, the officers horses and cattle are to be supplyed with forage at the usual rates.

ART. VI. All officers are to retain their carriages, batt-horses, and other cattle, and no baggage to be molested or searched, Lieutenant General Burgoyne giving his honor there are no public stores secreted therein.—Major-General Gates will of course take the necessary measures for the due performance of this article; should any carriages be wanting during the march for the transportation of officer's baggage, they are if possible to be supplyed by the country at the usual rates.

ART. VII. Upon the march and during the time the army shall remain in quarters, in the Massachusetts-Bay, the officers are not as far as circumstances will admit, to be separated from their men.—The officers are to be quartered according to rank, and are not to be hindered from assembling their men for roll calling, and other purposes of regularity.

ART. VIII. All corps whatever of Gen. Burgoyne's army, whether composed of sailors, batteaumen, artificers, drivers, independent companies and followers of the army of whatever country, shall be included in the fullest sense and utmost extent of the above articles, and comprehended in every respect as British subjects.

ART. IX. All Canadians and persons belonging to the Canadian establishment, consisting of sailors, batteaumen, artificers, drivers, independent companies, and many other followers of the army who come under no particular description, are to be permitted to return there—they are to be conducted immediately by the shortest route to the first British port on Lake George, are to be supplyed with provisions in the same manner as the other troops, [illegible] not serving during the present contest in North-America.

ART. X. Passports are to be immediately granted for three officers not exceeding the rank of Captains, who shall be appointed by Lieut. Gen. Burgoyne, to carry dispatches to Sir William Howe, Sir Guy Carlton, and to Great-Britain by way of New-York—and Major General Gates engages the public faith that these dispatches shall not be opened, these officers are to be set out immediately after receiving their dispatches, and are to travel by the shortest routes, and in the most expeditious manner.

ART XI. During the stay of the troops in Massachusetts-Bay, the officers are to be ad-

[illegible] Commander and his Corps, [illegible] as can possibly be inroll'd in the Annals of America.

The Day following, at Noon, the Fortresses and Shipping in this Harbour discharged their Cannon; and the Companies of Independents and Light Infantry, together with the Train of Artillery being paraded in State-street, fired thirteen Times in Honor of the Thirteen United States.—In the Evening there were Illuminations, Bonfires, and other Demonstrations of Joy.

In consequence of the above most important intelligence, the Rev. Doctor COOPER, (at the desire of the Assembly) made an excellent Prayer of Praise and Thanksgiving in the Representatives Chamber.

By the return of an express, we have the following Copy of a letter from his Excellency General Washington to Congress.

Camp near Pennibacker's *Mill, Oct. 5, 1777.*

SIR,

HAVING received intelligence thro' two intercepted letters, that General Howe had detach'd a part of his force for the purpose of reducing Billings-Fort, and the Forts on Delewate; I communicated the accounts to my General Officers, who were unanimously of opinion, that a favourable opportunity offered to make an attack upon the troops, which were at and near Germantown. It was accordingly agreed, that it should take place yesterday morning, and the following dispositions were made. The divisions of Sullivan and Wayne, flanked by Conway's Brigade were to enter the town by the way of Chesnut-Hill, while Gen. Armstrong with the Pensylvania militia should fall down the Manatawney road by Vandeeringa-mills, and get upon the enemies left and rear. The divisions of Green and Stephens, flank'd by McDougal's brigade, were to enter by taking a circuit by way of the Lime Kiln road, at the market houses, and to attack their right wing, and the militia of Maryland and Jersey, under General's Smallwood and Freeman were to march by the old York road, and fall upon the rear of the right. Lord Sterling with Nash and Maxwell's brigades was to form a corpse de reserve. We marched about seven o'clock the preceding evening, and General Sullivan's advanced party drawn from Conway's brigade attacked their picket at mount Airy, at Mr. Allen's House, about sun rise the next morning, which presently gave way, and his main body, consisting of the right wing, following soon, engaged the light infantry and other troops encamped near the Picket, which they forced from the ground, leaving their baggage. They retreated a considerable distance, having previously thrown a party into Mr. Chew's house, who were in a situation not to be easily forced, and had it in their power, from the windows to give us no small annoyance, and in a great measure to obstruct our advance.

The attack from our left column under Gen. Green, began about three quarters of an hour after that from the right, and was, for some time equally successful. But I cannot enter upon the particulars of what happened in that quarter, as I am not yet informed of them with sufficient certainty and precision.

The morning was extremely foggy, which prevented our improving the advantages we gained so well as we otherwise should have done. This circumstance, by concealing from us the true situation of the enemy, obliged us to act with more caution, and less expedition than we could have wished, and gave the enemy time to recover from the effects of our first impression; and what was still more unfortunate, it served to keep our different parties in ignorance of each other's movements, and hindred their acting in concert. It also occasioned them to mistake one another for the enemy, which I believe more than any thing else contributed to the misfortune which ensued. In the midst of the most promising appearances, when every thing gave the most flattering hopes of victory, the troops began suddenly to retreat, and entirely left the field in spite of every effort that could be made to rally them.

Upon the whole, it may be said the day was rather unfortunate than injurious. We sustained no material loss of men, and brought off all our artillery, except one piece which was dismounted. The enemy are nothing the better by the event; and our troops who are not the least dispirited by it, have gained what all young troops gain, by being in action. We have had however several valuable officers killed and wounded, particularly the latter—Gen Nash is among the wounded, and his life is despaired of. As soon as it is possible to obtain a return of our loss, I will transmit it.

In justice to Gen. Sullivan and the whole right wing of the army, whose conduct I had an opportunity of observing, as they acted immediately under my eye, I have the pleasure to inform you, that both officers and men behaved with a degree of gallantry that did them the highest honor. I have the honor to be with great respect, Sir, your most obedient servant

GEORGE WASHINGTON.

P. S. As I have observed, I have not received a return of our loss, but from what I have just now learnt from Gen. Green, I fear it is more considerable than I at first apprehended. The cannon mentioned above, is said to have been brought off in a waggon.

To the Hon. JOHN HANCOCK, Esq; President of CONGRESS.

Another letter of the 8th instant says. "The enemy in the action of the 4th instant, have lost the following officers, viz. Gen. Agnew, kill'd, Colonels Abercombie, Bird, Walcot, and General De Heister's son. Gen. Knyphauson (the present Hession General) wounded in the hand. between 2 and 300 waggons loaded with wounded soldiers came into the city before Mr.—— left the city. Several Quakers who were at yearly meeting confirm the above, and further say, that 2000 Hessians were sent over Schuylkill towards Chester since the action, probably to secure a retreat. Our loss about 700, chiefly wounded and taken. Gen. Nash of the North-Carolina forces dead of his wounds. Dr. Witherspoon's son killed.—two Aids De Camp mortally wounded.—— White and Sherburne of Gen. Sullivan's family, Colonels Henrcks, Stone, and Lt. Col. Parker of Virginia included in the above.

Camp near Perkioming Creek, 6th October 1777.

DEAR SIR,

"Shortly after I wrote you last from Philadelphia the Congress were alarmed by an account received from Mr. Hamilton one of General Washington's aids-de-camp, that the enemy were at the Swedes ford and had possessed themselves of some boats by which they might pass a small party into the city and make them prisoners; they immediately pack'd up and decamped in the middle of the night—I accompanied Mr. Hancock to Bristol, where I left him and many other members of Congress, they have since proceeded to Lancaster and from thence to York where they intend to fix their residence.

The enemy, a day or two after, made a shew of passing higher up Schuylkill but suddenly return'd down again, crossed at the lower fords with little or no opposition, took possession of Chesnut hill and the heights in & about German town, and extended their right as far as Francksford——On the 26th ult. Mr. Howe made his *triumphal entry* into Philadelphia with a very small part of his army, where he was most cordially received by his very good friends the Quakers, and a few * rascally tories who were left behind.

Our army remain'd about 26 miles from Philadelphia, near a village call'd the Trap, waiting for a reinforcement which was expected from Peeks Kill—This reinforcement consisting of about 2000 men under General McDougal arriv'd the latter end of last month, and General Washington moved his army down towards the enemy and encamped about eight miles from German town where a strong body of the enemy were encampt——On the 2d. inst. the necessary orders were given for an attack, and our army were in motion about nine o'clock—At five in the morning of the 3d. inst. we attack'd the enemy in different quarters, drove in their piquets, and fell in upon their main body, which we also drove through their encampments. They left all their tents standing, their baggage and part of their park of artillary: victory now seem'd to hover on every American brow; but alas! all of a sudden, and without any visible cause, our people got into confusion, and begun to retreat: the enemy perceiv'd this and immediately rallied, and having receiv'd a considerable reinforcement from Philadelphia, they pursued us in their turn, and we were obliged to quit all our acquisitions. The action was very obstinate and bloody, it lasted upwards of five hours; we have lost 5 or 600 men, mostly wounded which we have brought off. General Nash's thigh is broke. Mr. Sherburne of Portsmouth & Mr. White of Philadelphia are mortally wounded, they both were aids-de-camp to Gen. Sullivan. Dr. Witherspoon's son is killed. Capt. Sluman of Providence badly wounded in the head; besides a number of others whose names I cannot recollect. Since the action we have received a considerable reinforcement from Virginia, and our excellent General Washington has collected his force at the place from whence I date this letter, and intends soon to try another bout with them. All our men are in good spirits and I think grow fonder of fighting the more they have of it.

[illegible] was very foggy. [illegible] of part of our army was occasioned by the appearance of General Green, who was coming towards their rear with his division to support them, which they mistook for a large body of the enemy, not being able to distinguish properly on account of the fog. It is a very mortifying circumstance, that when we had nearly gain'd a complete victory we should lose it again so unfortunately.

About the time that Congress left Philadelphia, the baggage and the military chest were ordered to Bethlehem, where I remain'd till the day before the last action, when I receiv'd an order to repair to head-quarters. I just got down time enough to meet our people on their retreat. This misfortune was doubly aggravating to me as I had just before been inform'd on the road, that we had drove the enemy and were in possession of German town.

* *You will, perhaps, be surprised to be informed that Dr. Morgan is one of the number.*

Extract of a Letter, dated, Greenbush, Octob. 22, 1777.

"I sincerely congratulate you upon the compleat Victory gained over our Enemy in the Northern Department; General Burgoyne's grand Army grounded their Arms and surrendered themselves Prisoners of War the 17th inst. at Saratoga, marched down to Stillwater and crossed Hudson's River the 18th in Order to march for Boston.

British Troops by Capitulation,	2442
Foreign Troops, ditto.	2198
Canadians, Volunteers, &c. sent to Canada,	1100
Staff, - - - -	12
Total included in the Capitulation,	5752
Prisoners taken at different Times,	400
Sick and Wounded,	528
Deserters, -	300
Lost at Bennington, -	1220
Kill'd since the 17th of September,	600
Kill'd and taken at Ticonderoga,	413
Amounting in the whole, killed and taken Prisoners, - -	9213

The wonderful goodness of God in delivering so many of our cruel unnatural Enemies into our Hands, and with so little Loss on our Side, I hope every Heart will be suitably affected with. And may that God who has granted us such signal Successes here, vouchsafe to grant similar Successes to our Arms in the Southern Department.

Pieces of Ordnance taken from the Enemy, all Brass.

Two 24 pounders, four 12, eighteen 6, four 3, five Royal Howitzers 5 & half Inch, and 2 8 Inch Mortars.

We have taken in all in this Department, including those taken at Bennington, 37 Pieces of Ordnance, —4 Members of Parliament among the Prisoners.

Married at Danvers, by the Rev. Mr. Wadsworth, Mr. JOHN KETTLE, to Miss LYDIA HOLTEN, eldest Daughter of the Honorable SAMUEL HOLTEN, Esq;

BOSTON GAZETTE

October 27, 1777

George Washington's after-action report, appearing on page two of the October 27, 1777, *Boston Gazette*, details the events at Germantown, acknowledging failure but emphasizing bravery. According to Washington, "it may be said the day was rather unfortunate than injurious." On the following page of the same issue is an anonymous letter from an officer in the Continental Army providing additional details about Germantown.

REPORTING THE

BATTLES OF SARATOGA

By Eric H. Schnitzer

THE NORTHERN CAMPAIGN OF 1777 ENTERED A NEW phase in September, during which time both armies prepared to confront each other; no longer was Major General Horatio Gates's Northern Department of the Army of the United States retreating, and Lieutenant-General John Burgoyne's army from Canada was finally prepared to make its push to capture the city of Albany. Gates's force, at first deployed near Albany itself, moved about twenty miles north to Bemis Heights. The Heights, overlooking the valley and Hudson River below, were part of a continuity of stunning natural defenses, made stronger by man-made ones. Gates commanded an army of nearly eight thousand officers and men from Massachusetts, New York, New Hampshire, Connecticut, Virginia, and Pennsylvania, the great majority of whom were Continentals.

On September 19, Burgoyne's slightly larger army advanced to attack the American defenses. Gates's second-in-command, Major General Benedict Arnold, took the initiative and brought the battle to the British in the farm fields and woods one and a half miles north of Bemis Heights, with the primary fighting occurring on American Royalist John Freeman's Farm. The battle ended in a tactical British victory, albeit a pyrrhic one—British casualties numbered 590 to the Americans' 325. After a day of resting his army following the hard-fought battle, Burgoyne received a message from the commander of the City of New York, Sir Henry Clinton, who offered to assist Burgoyne by making a diversion in the Hudson Highlands with the hope that Gates would be forced to split his army in two. Relying wholly on this new plan, Burgoyne built a fortified camp on and around Freeman's Farm and waited. The wait lasted for two and a half weeks, during which time Gates's army was joined by militia regiments and grew to over twelve thousand, whereas attrition dwindled Burgoyne's to nearly seven thousand.

On October 7, having heard nothing further of Clinton's movements, Burgoyne took the initiative and, with a probing force of 1,500, moved south to observe the American lines in search of a weakness that could be exploited. But neither he nor anyone in his detachment got close enough to see the Revolutionary army's defenses. Gates ordered an immediate and decisive attack on the British probing force, which in little more than one hour was beaten back to its fortified camp. In close pursuit, the Americans attacked two fortifications and captured one of them, Breymann's Post, at which place Arnold was severely wounded. Having suffered over six hundred casualties to the Americans' 150, and having lost one of his key forts, Burgoyne ordered a retreat.

Thunderstorms, fatigue, and poor coordination slowed the British withdrawal to Saratoga, eight miles north of Freeman's Farm. Gates belatedly ordered a pursuit on October 10 but quickly caught up with Burgoyne at Saratoga later that day. The small village was surrounded by the army of the United States, now numbering nearly seventeen thousand, and the British were forced to surrender—by the generally favorable terms outlined in the *Articles of Convention*—on October 17.

The *Articles of Convention*, a transcript of which was published in the December 11, 1777, issue of the *London Chronicle*, stated that Burgoyne's surrendered troops would be allowed to return to Europe. However, Congress interposed a series of objections to the *Articles* (as reported in the April 4, 1778, issue of the *Pennsylvania Ledger*) by questioning Burgoyne's integrity on account of supposedly missing arms, accoutrements, and other war matériel. Burgoyne's and Gates's responses to Congress's inquiries on the matter proved unsatisfactory, and Congress doomed the Convention Army (as Burgoyne's surrendered army was called) to de facto prisoner of war status on January 8, 1778.

Gates's capture of an entire army commanded by a British Lieutenant-General—something which was never done before—was astonishing and inspired the new nation's first day of Thanksgiving on December 18, 1777. But the greatest effect of the victory at Saratoga was the resultant February 6, 1778, Treaty of Alliance between the United States and France, the decisiveness of which came to fruition at Yorktown, Virginia, in 1781. That is why the victory at Saratoga is known as the great "Turning Point of the Revolutionary War."

Surrender of General Burgoyne
Architect of the Capitol

On October 10, 1777, British Lieutenant-General John Burgoyne found his army surrounded at Saratoga, New York, by American forces totaling nearly seventeen thousand. One week later, he surrendered.

DECEMBER 11, 1777

The LONDON CHRONICLE

Postscript.
LONDON.
ADVICES *from* AMERICA.
Albany, Oct. 19, 1777

SIR,

I Have the pleasure to send your honourable council the inclosed copy of a convention, by which lieutenant general Burgoyne surrendered himself and his whole army on the 17th instant into my hands. They are now upon their march towards Boston. General Glover and general Whipple, with a proper guard of militia, escort them, and are to provide all such necessary articles as may be wanted upon the march. I am so extremely busy in pushing the army forward to stop the cruel career of general Vaughan up Hudson's-river, that I have only time to acquaint you, that my friend general Lincoln's leg is in a fair way of doing well, and to testify with what respect I am, your much obliged and most obedient humble servant,

HORATIO GATES.

To the honourable the President of the Council of the State of Massachusetts Bay.

ARTICLES *of* CONVENTION *made between*
Lieutenant-general BURGOYNE, *and Major-general* GATES.

ARTICLE. I.

The troops under lieutenant-general Burgoyne, are to march out of their camp with the honours of war, and the artillery of the intrenchments, to the verge of the river where the old fort stood, where the arms and artillery are to be left.—The arms are to be piled by word command from their own officers.

II. A free passage to be granted to the army under lieutenant-general Burgoyne to Great Britain, upon condition of not serving again in North America, during the present contest; and the port of Boston to be assigned for the entry of transports, to receive the troops, whenever general Howe shall so order.

III. Should any cartel take place, by which the army under lieutenant-general Burgoyne, or any part of it, may be exchanged, the foregoing article to be void, as far as such exchange shall be made.

IV. The army under lieutenant-general Burgoyne is to march to Massachusetts-bay, by the easiest, most expeditious, and convenient route; and to be quartered in, near, or as convenient as possible to Boston, that the march of the troops may not be delayed when transports arrive to receive them.

V. The troops to be supplied on the march, and during their being in quarters, with provisions, by general Gates's orders, at the same rate of rations as the troops of his own army; and, if possible, the officers horses and cattle are to be supplied with forage at the usual rates.

VI. All officers are to retain their carriages, but horses and other cattle and no baggage to be molested or searched; lieutenant general Burgoyne giving his honour there are no public stores secreted therein. Major general Gates will of course take the necessary measures for the due performance of this article: should any carriages be wanted during the march for the transportation of officers baggage, they are, if possible, to be supplied by the country at the usual rates.

VII. Upon the march, and during the time the army shall remain in quarters, in the Massachusets Bay, the officers are not, as far as circumstances will admit, to be separated from their men. The officers are to be quartered according to rank, and are not to be hindered from assembling their men for roll calling, and other purposes of regularity.

VIII. All corps whatever of general Burgoyne's army, whether composed of sailors, batteaumen, artificers, drivers, independant companies and followers of the army of whatever country, shall be included in the fullest sense, and utmost extent of the above articles, and comprehended in every respect as British subjects.

[...]

(Signed) J. BURGOYNE.

Camp at Saratoga, Oct. 16, 1777.

upon the Effects of CALOMEL in the DROPSY; upon BATH WATERS; and upon the EPILEPSY: Being an APPENDIX to Eſſays on theſe Subjects, formerly publiſhed.

To which is added, A Letter to Dr. ADEE, upon

North America, during the preſent conteſt; and the port of Boſton to be aſſigned for the entry of tranſports, to receive the troops, whenever general Howe ſhall ſo order.

LONDON CHRONICLE

December 11, 1777

The Battles of Saratoga, fought eighteen days apart, resulted in the surrender of British Lieutenant-General John Burgoyne's entire army and helped convince France to ally with the United States. The favorable terms of Burgoyne's surrender were published in the December, 11, 1777, *London Chronicle*.

PENNSYLVANIA LEDGER (PHILADELPHIA)

April 4, 1778

Congress interposed a series of objections to the articles, or terms, of surrender by questioning Burgoyne's integrity on account of supposedly missing arms, accoutrements, and other war matériel. The objections are reprinted from "Rebel Papers" in this Tory newspaper, published in Philadelphia while occupied by the British.

kind of ſpot (even paint, although it may have been dried in for ſeveral weeks) without leaving the ſmalleſt trace behind. It is ſo eaſily uſed, that cloaths which are only ſoiled (and not ſpotted) require very little trouble to clean them, and it is bruſhed out as readily as the duſt after a day's wear. It being uſed dry does not make the cloth appear rough, but on the contrary, if the cloaths are carefully bruſhed (with the grain) they will be as ſmooth as when new.

It will be found exceedingly uſeful to gentlemen of the army and navy, as it makes white and buff-coloured cloth and kerſymier appear as beautiful as new.

It is alſo particularly recommended for the linings of carriages, &c.

By appointment of the Patentee this Powder is ſold wholeſale and retail only by W. Bayley, Perfumer, in Cockſpur-ſtreet; and Meſſ. Smyths, Perfumers to his Majeſty, in New Bond-ſtreet. Sold alſo retail by J. Price, Perfumer, in Leadenhall-ſtreet, price 2s. a box.

††† Proper bruſhes may be had at the ſame places.

Poſtſcript.

LONDON.

ADVICES *from* AMERICA.

SIR, Albany, Oct. 19, 1777.

I Have the pleaſure to ſend your honourable council the incloſed copy of a convention, by which lieutenant general Burgoyne ſurrendered himſelf and his whole army on the 17th inſtant into my hands. They are now upon their march towards Boſton. General Glover and general Whipple, with a proper guard of militia, eſcort them, and are to provide all ſuch neceſſary articles as may be wanted upon the march. I am ſo extremely buſy in puſhing the army forward to ſtop the cruel career of general Vaughan up Hudſon's-river, that I have only time to acquaint you, that my friend general Lincoln's leg is in a fair way of doing well, and to teſtify with what reſpect I am, your much obliged and moſt obedient humble ſervant,

HORATIO GATES.

To the honourable the Preſident of the Council of the State of Maſſachuſetts Bay.

ARTICLES *of* CONVENTION *made between Lieutenant-general* BURGOYNE, *and Major-general* GATES.

ARTICLE. I.

THE troops under lieutenant-general Burgoyne, are to march out of their camp with the honours of war, and the artillery of the intrenchments, to the verge of the river where the old fort ſtood, where the arms and artillery are to be left.—The arms are to be piled by word command from their own officers.

VI. All officers are to retain their carriages, but horſes and other cattle and no baggage to be moleſted or ſearched; lieutenant general Burgoyne giving his honour there are no public ſtores ſecreted therein. Major general Gates will of courſe take the neceſſary meaſures for the due performance of this article: ſhould any carriages be wanted during the march for the tranſportation of officers baggage, they are, if poſſible, to be ſupplied by the country at the uſual rates.

VII. Upon the march, and during the time the army ſhall remain in quarters, in the Maſſachuſets Bay, the officers are not, as far as circumſtances will admit, to be ſeparated from their men. The officers are to be quartered according to rank, and are not to be hindered from aſſembling their men for roll calling, and other purpoſes of regularity.

VIII. All corps whatever of general Burgoyne's army, whether compoſed of ſailors, batteaumen, artificers, drivers, independant companies and followers of the army of whatever country, ſhall be included in the fulleſt ſenſe, and utmoſt extent of the above articles, and comprehended in every reſpect as Britiſh ſubjects.

IX. All Canadians and perſons belonging to the Canadian eſtabliſhment, conſiſting of ſailors, batteaumen, artificers, drivers, and independant companies, and many other followers of the army who come under no particular deſcription, are to be permitted to return there. They are to be conducted immediately by the ſhorteſt route to the firſt Britiſh poſt on Lake George; are to be ſupplied with proviſions in the ſame manner as the other troops, and are to be bound by the ſame condition of not ſerving during the preſent conteſt in North America.

X. Paſſports are to be immediately granted, for three officers, not exceeding the rank of captains, who ſhall be appointed by lieutenant-general Burgoyne, to carry diſpatches to Sir William Howe, Sir Guy Carleton, and to Great Britain, by way of New York. And major-general Gates engages the public faith, that theſe diſpatches ſhall not be opened. Theſe officers are to ſet out immediately after receiving their diſpatches, and are to travel by the ſhorteſt routes, and in the moſt expeditious manner.

XI. During the ſtay of the troops in Maſſachuſets-bay, the officers are to be admitted on parole, and are to be allowed to wear their ſide-arms.

XII. Should the army under lieutenant general Burgoyne find it neceſſary to ſend for their clothing and other baggage to Canada, they are to be permitted to do it in the moſt convenient manner, and the neceſſary paſſports granted for that purpoſe.

538 THE LOND

The Capitulation between Generals Gates *and* Burgoyne *concluded from the preceding Page.*

XIII. Theſe articles are to be mutually ſigned and exchanged to-morrow morning at nine o'clock, and the troops under lieutenant-general Burgoyne are to march out of their intrenchments at three o'clock in the afternoon.

(Signed) J. BURGOYNE.

Camp at Saratoga, Oct. 16, 1777.

In conſequence of the foregoing convention at Saratoga the 17th Oct. 1777, the following numbers laid down their arms, and ſurrendered to Gen. Gates, viz. Britiſh troops 2442; Brunſwick and other German troops 2198; Canadians, volunteers, &c. 1100; ſtaff 12; total 5752.

Sick and wounded left in the Britiſh camp when general Burgoyne began his retreat 528. Beſides the above, there were killed, wounded, taken, and deſerted, of Britiſh, German, and Canadian troops under general Burgoyne, between the 6th July, and 16th Oct. 2933; in all 9213.

Account of Braſs Ordnance, &c. delivered up to General Gates on the 17th of Oct. viz.

Two 24 pounders, four 12 ditto, eighteen 6 ditto, four 3 ditto, Royal Howitzers five 5½ inch, braſs mortars, two inch; in all 35, all of braſs, beſides thoſe taken at Bennington.

Stands of arms complete, 7000, beſides the military cheſt, large quantities of ordnance ſtores, cloathing for 7000 Provincials, tents, &c. &c.

By the laſt accounts from America, received by a packet arrived in France, we learn, that General Gates had returned to Albany on the 19th of October, and was puſhing forward his army (conſiſting of 12,000 men) with all poſſible ſpeed to attack the Britiſh troops under General Vaughan, on the North-river: General Putnam was advancing up that river, in their rear, with 5000 men, ſo that it was ſcarce poſſible they could eſcape a diſaſter ſimilar to that of general Burgoyne. Generals Gates and Putnam, after having overcome gen. Vaughan's troops, were immediately to join general Waſhington, whoſe army, by various reinforcements, had been increaſed to 25,000 men, and was laying ſiege to Philadelphia.

This day arrived the mails from Flanders, but brought nothing new.

MARKET-DAY ADVERTISER.

SATURDAY, APRIL 4, 1778.

☞ *Philadelphia:* Printed by JAMES HUMPHREYS, Jun. in *Market-ſtreet*, between *Front* and *Second ſtreets*, and nearly oppoſite the *Guard-houſe*:—By whom Eſſays, Articles of News, Advertiſements, &c. are gratefully received and impartially inſerted: And where Subſcriptions are taken in for this Paper.

CITY VENDUE,

THIS DAY, preciſely at eleven o'clock, at the London Coffee-houſe, by public auction, will begin the ſale of

MUSCOVADO, } ſugar;
Single refined }

Rum,—*ſubject to the regulations in the proclamation;*

Madeira, Port, Sherry, Teneriff } wines, by the quarter-caſk, hogſhead and pipe;

Rice;
Soap;
Fine ſalt;
And a few hogſheads of very good tobacco.

N. B. The City Vendue-ſtore (between Cheſnut and Walnut-ſtreets, on the eaſt ſide of Front-ſtreet) will continue to receive all ſorts of goods and merchandize for public and private ſale; where they will be kept at a very moderate expence, and expoſed to the greateſt advantage, in an elegant room fitted up for that purpoſe; and where purchaſers will always have the advantage of chuſing out of a general and large aſſortment, on low terms.

Commiſſions for purchaſing or diſpoſing of any article, for the gentlemen of the army or navy, will be particularly attended to.

April 4. DAVID SPROAT, Vendue-Maſter.

By his Excellency Sir WILLIAM HOWE, K. B. General and Commander in Chief, &c. &c.

PROCLAMATION.

WHEREAS, by my proclamation bearing date the fourth day of this inſtant, "All maſters "of merchant ſhips were ordered and commanded "immediately on their arrival, to make entry of "the veſſels, and deliver in proper manifeſts of their "cargoes, on oath, at the Superintendent's office," and it was further ordered, that "No goods or "merchandize whatever ſhould be laden on board "any ſhip or veſſel, (ſuch as are in his Majeſty's "ſervice excepted) until permiſſion in writing ſhould "firſt be obtained from the ſaid Superintendent's "office, ſpecifying the quantity and quality of the "goods ſo intended to be laden, with the veſſel "and maſter's name, and where bound:" And, "That no ſhip or veſſel (ſuch as are in his Majeſty's "ſervice excepted) ſhould leave this port, until "the maſter ſhould deliver in, at the Superintendent's office, a manifeſt on oath, ſpecifying the "quantity and quality of the goods, and by whom "ſhipped, together with the permiſſion granted for "the lading the veſſels." And whereas, the maſters of tranſports, victuallers, and other veſſels in his Majeſty's ſervice, may conceive themſelves juſtified under the exceptions aforeſaid, in importing into, and exporting goods and merchandize from, this port, without complying with the regulations in my ſaid proclamation contained, whereby great frauds may be committed, and the true intent and meaning of the ſaid proclamation eluded: For prevention whereof, I do hereby declare and order, that the ſaid exceptions, relating to ſhips or veſſels in his Majeſty's ſervice, ſhall be void, and that all ſhips and veſſels whatever, that are now in, or may hereafter come in, or go out of, this port, and the maſters thereof, ſhall be liable to the ſame regulations, pains and penalties, as merchant ſhips are

The printer JAMES HUMPHREYS, jun. Has for ſale a few copies of

GAINE's UNIVERSAL REGISTER. OR, AMERICAN BRITISH KALENDER, For the year 1778;

Containing beſides a complete liſt of the army, a variety of very uſeful matter

Juſt publiſhed, and to be ſold by JAMES HUMPHREY's, jun. printer hereof, at his Stationary Store in Market-ſtreet,

(Price bound in leather Six Shillings and Six-pence, in vellum Five Shillings)

The GENTLEMAN and LADY's

Pocket Memorandum Book for 1778.

Containing a page for memorandums for every week in the year; and for accounts of monies received, paid, or lent. Alſo a table reducing ſterling money into Pennſylvania currency.—A table ſhewing the amount of any number of dollars at 4*s.* 8*d.* ſterling—Another ſhewing the amount of any number of dollars at 7*s.* 6*d.* currency; a table ſhewing the amount of any number of guineas at 35*s.* currency; and a table of the value and weight of coins

A Meeting of the Yorkſhire club will be held on Monday the 13ſt inſtant, at the bunch of grapes, Third ſtreet,

JOHN VEVERS, Secretary.

N. B. Any gentlemen of the county deſirous of being member's, are requeſted to leave their names at the bar, on Friday the 10th inſtant.

ANTI-VENERIAL ESSENCE,

Prepared and Sold by Dr. YELDALL, at his Medicinal Ware-houſe two doors from Walnut-ſtreet in Second-ſtreet.

THIS Eſſence not only cures the diſeaſe in all its degrees, and in ſuch manner that the patient need not be hindered from his buſineſs, or his condition be made known to his moſt intimate acquaintance, but will alſo effectually prevent catching the infection: Proper directions will be given in print, ſo that no queſtions need be asked, *(price two dollars.)* April 4.

To be ſold, wholeſale and retail, by Henry Johns, *four doors below the Friends meeting in Second-ſtreet,*

AN aſſortment of hard-ware:
Japanned & plated goods:
Jewellery, &c.
Table knives & forks in ivory, green wood and ſtag hafts:
Splitbone, ſham buck & various other ſorts of common ditto:
Carving knives and forks:
Fine convex, and Barlow's beſt penknives:
Fine pocket knives:
Sciſſors:
Lancets, and poliſhed warranted razors:
Scarificators for cupping:
Cork ſcrews:
Plated and ſteel ſpurs:
Sewing needles:
Ivory and horn combs:
Pomatum in caſes
Japanned waiters and tea trays:
Tin and japaned tea pots and coffee-pots:
Tin diſhes and plates for canteens in parcels:
Pontypool japaned tea kettles:
Tea kitchens and table croſſes:
Silver enamelled and japaned bottle labels:
Wine and beer glaſſes:
Leather bottle ſtands:
Braſs cocks:
Braſs and japanned table and tea candlekicks:
Chamber candleſticks, with ſnuffers and extinguiſhers.
Green and white wax tapers.
Pewter plates, baſons, & ſpoons.
Plated table ſpoons
Silver mounted etwee caſes.

Extracts from REBEL PAPERS.

In CONGRESS, *November* 8, 1777.

Reſolved,

THAT Major General Heath be directed forthwith to cauſe to be taken down the name and rank of every commiſſioned officer, and the name, former place of abode, occupation, ſize, age and deſcription of every non-commiſſioned officer and private ſoldier, and all other perſons comprehended in the Convention, made between Lieutenant-General Burgoyne, and Major-General Gates, on the 16th of October, 1777, and tranſmit an authentic copy thereof to the Board of War, in order that if any officer, ſoldier, or any other perſon as abovementioned of the ſaid army, ſhall hereafter be found in arms againſt theſe States in North-America, during the preſent conteſt, he may be convicted of the offence, and ſuffer the puniſhment in ſuch caſe inflicted by the law of nations.

That Major-General Heath be directed to take the parole in writing of the officers, according to the Convention, and tranſmit authenticated copies of ſuch paroles to the Board of War.

NOVEMBER 22, 1777.

The Committee to whom were referred the return of ordnance and ſtores, taken from the enemy ſince the 19th day of September, and the letter from the Council of Safety of New-York, and to whom their former report was recommitted, having taken the ſame into conſideration, beg leave to obſerve.

"That there is no mention in the ſaid return of ſtandards, military cheſt, medicines or tents.

"That the quantity of powder is very ſmall, being only fifteen barrels grained, and two barrels mealed, and the quantity of fixed ammunition very inconſiderable. That the muſkets amount only to 4647, a number not equal to the priſoners who ſurrendered agreeable to the Convention of Saratoga, and all theſe muſkets are returned "unfit for ſervice." That there are only 638 cartouch boxes. That the number of bayonets is greatly inferior to the muſkets, and theſe as well as the cutlaſſes, are returned "without ſcabbards" or belts. In ſhort, the whole return ſeems very inadequate to a well appointed army, and to what might be expected from the anſwers returned by Lieut. Gen. Burgoyne to the firſt propoſitions made by Major Gen. Gates.

"Your Committee therefore are of opinion, that an enquiry ought to be made into the cauſes of this deficiency," Whereupon,

Reſolved, That the Preſident immediately ſend an expreſs to Gen. Gates, and deſire anſwers to the following queſtions, viz.

What is become of the ſtandards belonging to the reſpective regiments in Gen. Burgoyne's army?
Where is the military cheſt and medicines?
What is become of the cartouch boxes?
How comes the quantity of powder and cartridges to be ſo ſmall?
How comes it that the number of muſkets is leſs than that of the priſoners, and that all the muſkets are unfit for ſervice?
How comes the number of bayonets to be ſo greatly inferior to that of muſkets?
Where are the ſcabbards and belts of the bayonets and cutlaſſes?
Was there any deſtruction, waſte, removal or concealment, of the arms, tents, colours, treaſure or other military ſtores belonging to Gen. Bur-

REPORTING

Women and Children on the War Front

By Eric H. Schnitzer

Revolutionary War armies generally included "followers"—noncombatants who were sutlers, refugees, or (most commonly) soldiers' wives and children. Women and children endured the same living conditions and suffered the same privations as the soldiers in an army, which sometimes included a lack of food, clothing, and shelter. Like soldiers, women labored intensely, fulfilling the roles of laundresses, seamstresses, and nurses. Children were expected to work as well.

But there were exceptions. In rare cases, followers included women and children of the middle or upper classes whose husbands formed part of an army's officer corps. Such was the case in Lieutenant-General John Burgoyne's army, in which six such women and five children followed the British forces as they attempted to make their way from Canada to Albany, New York. Their class protected them from the labors that the hundreds of soldier wives and children toiled upon. One upper-class woman, Lady Christian "Harriet" Acland, chose to brave the rigorous conditions of the Northern Campaign of 1777 in order to be with her husband, a major in the British army. Daughter of an Earl, Lady Acland suffered—she was almost burned to death when her tent caught fire from an overturned candle, and her husband was almost killed in the Battle of Bemis Heights (October 7, 1777). Both accounts of these events, and how Lady Acland dealt with them, were published in the February 29, 1780, edition of the *Edinburgh Advertiser*. However, other women suffered far worse; the husband of one of Lady Acland's traveling companions, Anne Reynell, was killed in the Battle of Freeman's Farm (September 19, 1777), leaving their four young children fatherless. Their stories are only two from the many followers whose husbands died in the service—in some cases, women and children lost their own lives while suffering an army life.

Molly Pitcher Firing Cannon at Battle of Monmouth
Library of Congress

Although women were not allowed to fight, some took the initiative to do so anyway. One of the most famous was Mary Hayes ("Molly Pitcher") who helped load a cannon in the 1778 Battle of Monmouth, NJ.

EDINBURGH ADVERTISER.

From FRIDAY FEBRUARY 25, to TUESDAY FEBRUARY 29, 1780.

The following true and affecting story, is taken from Lieutenant General Burgoyne's state of the expedition from Canada.

"BESIDES the continuation of difficulties and general fatigue, this day was remarkable for a circumstance of private distress too peculiar and affecting to be omitted. The circumstance to which I allude is Lady Harriet Ackland's passage through the enemy's army, to attend her wounded husband then their prisoner.

"The progress of this lady with the army could hardly be thought abruptly or superfluously introduced, were it only for the purpose of authenticating a wonderful story. It would exhibit, if well delineated, an interesting picture of the spirit, the enterprize, and the distress of romance, realized and regulated upon the chaste and sober principles of rational love and connubial duty.

"Lady Harriet Ackland had accompanied her husband to Canada in the beginning of the year 1776. In the course of that campaign she had traversed a vast space of county, in different extremities of season, and with difficulties that an European traveller will not easily conceive, to attend her husband, in a poor hut at Chamblee, upon his sick bed.

"In the opening of the campaign of 1777, she was restrained from offering herself to a share of the fatigue and hazard expected before Ticonderago, by the positive injunctions of her husband. The day after the conquest of that place, he was badly wounded, and she crossed the Lake Champlain to join him.

"As soon as he recovered, Lady Harriet proceeded to follow his fortunes thro' the campaign; and at Fort Edward, or at the next camp, she acquired a two-wheel tumbril, which had been constructed by the artificers of the artillery, something similar to the carriage used for the mail upon the great roads of England. Major Ackland commanded the British grenadiers, which were attached to General Fraser's corps, and consequently were alway the most advanced post of the army. Their situations were often so alert, that no person slept out of their clothes. In one of these situations a tent, in which the major and Lady Harriet were asleep, suddenly took fire. An orderly serjeant of grenadiers, with great hazard of suffocation, dragged out the first person he caught hold of. It proved to be the major. It happened, that in the same instant she had, unknowing what she did, and perhaps not perfectly awake, providentially made her escape, by creeping under the walls of the back part of the tent.

"The first object she saw, upon the recovery of her senses, was the Major on the other side, and in the same instant again in the fire, in search of her. The serjeant again saved him, but not without the major being severely burned in his face and different parts of the body. Every thing they had with them in the tent was consumed.

"This accident happened a little time before the army passed the Hudson's river. It neither altered the resolution nor the chearfulness of Lady Harriet; and she continued her progress, a partaker of the fatigues of the advanced corps. The next call upon her fortitude was of a different nature, and more distressful, as of longer suspense. On the march of the 19th, the grenadiers being liable to action at every step, she had been directed by the Major to follow the route of the artillery and baggage, which was not exposed. At the time the action began she found herself near a small uninhabited hut, where she alighted. When it was found the action was becoming general and bloody, the surgeons of the hospital took possession of the same place, as the most convenient for the first care of the wounded. Thus was this lady in hearing of one continued fire of cannon and musketry, for four hours together, with the presumption, from the post of her husband at the head of the grenadiers, that he was in the most exposed part of the action. She had three female companions, the Baroness of Reidesel, and the wives of two British officers, Major Harnage and Lieutenant Reynell; but in the event their presence served but little for comfort. Major Harnage was soon brought to the surgeons, very badly wounded; and a little time after came intelligence that Lieutenant Reynell was shot dead. Imagination will want no helps to figure the state of the whole groupe.

"From the date of that action to the 7th of October, Lady Harriet, with her usual serenity, stood prepared for new trials; and it was her lot that their severity increased with their numbers. She was again exposed to the hearing of the whole action, and at last received the shock of her individual misfortune mixed with the intelligence of the general calamity; the troops were defeated, and Major Ackland, desperately wounded, was a prisoner.

"The day of the 8th was passed by Lady Harriet and her companions in common anxiety, not a tent, nor a shed being standing, except what belonged to the hospital, their refuge was among the wounded and dying.

"When the army was upon the point of moving after the halt described, I received a message from Lady Harriet, submitting to my decision a proposal (and expressing an earnest solicitude to execute it, if not interfering with my designs) of passing to the camp of the enemy, and requesting General Gates's permission to attend her husband.

"Though I was ready to believe (for I had experienced) that patience and fortitude in a supreme degree, were to be found, as well as every other virtue, under the most tender forms, I was astonished at this proposal. After so long an agitation of the spirits, exhausted not only for want of rest, but absolutely for want of food, drenched in rains for twelve hours together, that a woman should be capable of such an undertaking as delivering herself to
probably in the night, and unce
hands she might first fall into, app
above human nature. The assista
bled to give was small indeed; I
cup of wine to offer her; but I w
found, from some kind and fort
litt'e rum and dirty water. All
to her was an open boat and a f
ten upon dirty and wet paper, to
recommending her to his protecti

SATURDAY's PO

From the LONDON PAPERS, *Feb.* 22.

LONDON.

HOUSE OF LORDS, *Feb.* 21.

THE *Marquis of Rockingham* when he brought up the petition from the planters and merchants trading to Jamaica, took notice of the shameful negligence of ministry, with respect to that valuable island, notwithstanding frequent representations from the Governor and Council which had been disregarded.—The dependence of that island on the crown of Great Britain could only be ascribed to the interposition of providence, as the expedition intended against it had proved abortive, by the troops being attacked with sickness. The petition stated three particulars. *First*, That no attention had been paid to frequent remonstrances by his Majesty's ministers. *Second*, That no force had been detached for defence of the island, and, *Third*, That its present situation was in the last degree precarious.

Lord Sandwich declared, that the three particulars stated in the petition were all false. He wished a day might be appointed to take it into consideration, when it would appear ministry had paid every attention to Jamaica, that at present it was in a state of security, and when the day of investigation did come, he and his colleagues in administration would, he trusted, be found to deserve honour in place of being found guilty of any neglect or criminality.

The *Marquis of Rockingham* replied, that Jamaica had been neglected, in proof of which he read part of a letter from Governor Dalling, to Sir Henry Clinton, which says, "D'Estaing is every day expected here. We rely upon you to send us the earliest assistance, as the military force at this time within the island is *extremely trifling, and entirely unequal to its defence.*"

Lord Sandwich said, that the Marquis should also have informed the house, that Sir H. Clinton had detached a proper naval and military force to the assistance of Jamaica, which was only stopt, on intelligence that D'Estaing had left these seas.

The *Marquis of Rockingham* maintained, that that detachment would have come too late had D'Estaing persisted in his attack.

Here a long altercation took place betwixt the Marquis and Lord Sandwich, upon stationing ships off the leeward and windward islands. Lord Sandwich said, he consulted Sir Hugh Palliser in most cases, and acted by his advice, as he always found it good. No man was better able to give good counsel. He did not care though all the world heard him say so, it was the truth.

The petition was ordered to lie on the table.

HOUSE of COMMONS, *Feb.* 21.

Mr. Smith member for Nottingham informed

which the old ground of the nature of the petitions and protests was once more travelled over. The ministry condemned the petitions and associations as factious, libellous, and tending to harass government. They maintained, that the protestors

EDINBURGH ADVERTISER

February 29, 1780

—

It was extremely rare for newspapers to report on women and children, who occasionally followed their officer husbands and fathers during the war.

Another winter is over, and nothing has been either attempted, or done of conſequence by his Excellency Gen. Howe. The Britiſh army, thank heaven, was in good health, and in good ſpirits, and the general continues to be preparing for ſomething, if we are to credit report but when any thing material is to be done, no common augur can tell. We were often told during the winter, that Mr. Waſhington's army was inferior in numbers to the Britiſh; ſickly, dying, ill clothed, ill fed, diſpirited, and by no means ſo well armed as our troops; all which I verily believe.

But what avails all this to us? although we might add, and with truth, that our troops are better officered, and better diſciplined, without diſreſpect to Mr. Waſhington's officers; ſtill it anſwers no good end to Britain, ſince the prudence of Gen. Howe does not think it fit to hazard a battle or diſperſe the rebels.

Neither ancient nor modern hiſtory can produce any thing equal to the campaigns ſpent in North America, ſince the ſword has been unſheathed againſt the inſurgents. Armies of regular, well diſciplined troops, furniſhed amply with all neceſſaries for war, offic...ed with a ſet of old experienced veterans, an... troops that never turned their backs when le... on! yet yea... after year goes on and no exertio... is attemp... to cruſh rebellion, and ... ack to their revolted ſubjects, that ... eſpeaks ... judgment, or ſpirit, in ... whole ... is to ſet t... whole in ...

Even t... graceful ſepara..., nor the unfor...ate, ſeem... on t... chief com... ... e ... rati...

we are on the eve of loſing an empire; unleſs ſome guardian ſpirit riſes amongſt us, like that which directed and conducted with honour and glory our laſt war with France and Spain.

PASTOR FIDO.

For the EDINBURGH ADVERTISER.

A REMEDY *for the* BITE *of a* MAD DOG.

Diſcovered by a GENTLEMAN *of* SILESIA, *and publiſhed by order of the* KING *of* PRUSSIA.

[*Sent to Scotland by Earl* MARSHAL, *and approved of by ſome eminent phyſicians of this place.*]

TWENTY-four of the inſect called *Meloë Majalis* or May-bug, cut into ſmall pieces:

Two drachms of ebony wood, finely ſcraped:

One drachm of *Serpentaria* or Virginia ſnakeroot, nicely pulverized.

One drachm of raſped lead.

Twenty grains of clunn cignn giglrium.

Two ounces of tre...cle; or, in place of it, the inſpiſſated jui... fruit of the ... ee.

All theſe ing... is well kneaded... er, and made into a ... aſte with the ho... in- ſects are kept in...

As the ... in this re... inſec... neceſſa... part... he m... the ... called ... he inſe... ds of ... e M...

with ſciſſars and thrown put into a glaſs with ſome be well covered, and ke place. If, after ſome tim to have dried up, ſome mo and thus, with proper keep for two or three yea the black-coloured inſects ſeventy-five of the gold quart of honey, meaſure o

DOS	
Age.	
From one to three years old	
—— three to ſix	
—— ſix to twelve	
—— twelve to twenty	
—— twenty to thirty	
—— thirty upwards	

N. B. This doſe to be di the conſtitution of the patie the breaſt, the nurſe is to t

When a perſon bit by a the medicine, as preſcribed, for twenty-four hou... and for twelve hou... om ... t time he finds ... f ... ſome tea ...

CHAPTER IX

GOOD AND FAITHFUL ALLIES

Introduction

During a harsh winter at the Valley Forge encampment, General Washington and Prussian military officer Baron von Steuben helped breathe new life into the American army with modernized drills, tactics, and disciplines. The poorly supplied soldiers began to see themselves as professionals. In spring 1778, British Commander William Howe returned to England with blame for the loss at Saratoga, an American victory that motivated a French alliance and further bolstered American confidence as demonstrated at the Battle of Monmouth, where the Patriots faced off against new British Commander Henry Clinton.

Edinburgh Advertiser
May 29, 1778

Washington and Lafayette
at Valley Forge
by John Ward Dunsmore
Library of Congress

REPORTING THE

VALLEY FORGE WINTER ENCAMPMENT

By Wayne Bodle

THE 1777–78 VALLEY FORGE WINTER CAMP WAS A harrowing experience for the Continental Army, but not one that brought it near the breaking point. It was neither the proverbial "darkest hour" nor the "turning point" of the Revolution. The operational effects of Friedrich Steuben's training of the troops at Valley Forge were real enough, but its decisive effect on the outcome of the Revolution has not been proven by historians. By July 1777, General Washington led a much different group of soldiers—newly recruited and inexperienced in combat—from the men who ended the 1776 campaign successfully at Trenton and Princeton. While losing battles at Brandywine and Germantown and surrendering the rebel capital at Philadelphia, they fought with spirit and some real effectiveness. Washington brought the army to Valley Forge in December as part of a political bargain to protect the fragile state government of Pennsylvania and persuade the Continental Congress to help professionalize the force.

At Valley Forge, the army experienced two brief periods of desperate material shortage for about ten days in late December and then for two weeks in February 1778. Fortunately for Washington, the second crisis hit during the two-month-long visit to camp by a committee from Congress. Sharing the crisis showed the politicians the weaknesses of America's first truly complex mass organization better than words ever could have. The May 12, 1778, *Edinburgh Advertiser* reprinted Washington's February 18 appeal to mid-Atlantic farmers to raise more cattle, reflecting hard realities. With the area near Valley Forge drained of provisions, flour and bread were imported from parts of the Chesapeake Region that had long since abandoned tobacco cultivation, while beef cattle were driven on the hoof from New England. Unless the middle states replenished their productive capacities, planning for a new campaign was futile. Washington's letter was written during the army's worst supply disruption of the year, however, which brought shared hardship to local civilians, and it is not clear what, if any, positive effects it had.

By July 1777, General Washington led a much different group of soldiers—newly recruited and inexperienced in combat—from the men who ended the 1776 campaign successfully at Trenton and Princeton.

The March 7, 1778, letter from a "Gentleman in Philadelphia," printed in the *London Chronicle* nearly two months later, was insightful on a local scale but quite inaccurate in strategic terms. General William Howe exploited the Continental Army's midwinter paralysis by supporting local Loyalists in a "kidnapping campaign" to break the political backbone of the American rebellion. Exactly the kinds of individuals mentioned ("tax-gatherers," "committee-men," and "justices") were targeted, and important local revolutionaries did not sleep quietly that spring. British forces had no realistic hope, however, of "large reinforcements." France's entry into the war on the American side led British planners to shift forces from North America to focus on a West Indian and Atlantic defensive strategy. The continental war moved into the southern states, and the rebels were offered generous terms of peace essentially to repeal the Declaration of Independence. Congress ignored the proposal with a kind of studied contempt.

Congress's May 27, 1778, agreement on a new "Establishment" for the army, as printed in the August 26, 1778, *New-Jersey Gazette*, was a broad compromise between the continued resistance by many of its members, especially New Englanders, to an expensive, dangerous, unrepublican "standing army" and the growing realization by many Americans that independence could not be won by minutemen. Friedrich von Steuben's training of the army that winter paid important morale and other dividends, but how effectively it would intersect with the reorganization plan was unknowable before the American victory at Yorktown in 1781.

General John Burgoyne, the British general defeated at Saratoga in October of 1777, arrived in Britain on May 13, 1778, to defend his conduct in that battle. Far from bringing "good news," his arrival presaged a growing sense in British circles that the effort to crush the rebellion was doomed. Ironically, on May 18, as "Pastor Fido" wrote the *Edinburgh Advertiser* to articulate that pessimism, the resigned British commander William Howe was feted by his officers in Philadelphia in a "Meschianza" as he left them to contest Burgoyne's account. Fido's morose predictions may seem quite recognizable to members of a modern global generation for whom counterinsurgency operations have often proved more frustrating than gratifying. For most Britons, however, the decades after 1783 brought increasing "glory." The British state defeated Napoleonic France, consolidated in Asia and Africa a "Second Empire" more valuable than the first, and led the world into an industrial epoch. For Americans, the fruits of perseverance at Valley Forge were still five long and mostly exhausting years in the future.

The March to Valley Forge,
December 16, 1777
by William B. T. Trego
American Revolution Center
(current location)

Valley Forge was not the proverbial "darkest hour," but the Continental Army did experience two brief periods of desperate material shortage.

…f defence, but it would appear in its pro-…ns, and then he would be ready to abide …dgment of the house, which he doubted …ould be in favour of the king's servants.

Pulteney observed, that the minister had …aid, that this country was in a state of de-…–did he mean the island of Britain alone, …ere all our dependencies to be left exposed? …id, he could prove that government had … of the sailing of the Toulon fleet on …y se'ennight; and though the wind had …air for some time, not a ship had been or-…to follow them, nor was even a council … upon so important a subject till Wednes-… This inactivity was the more inexcusable, … had actually at Spithead eighteen sail of …e fit to put to sea. He mentioned this re-…ircumstance, that it might be in the memo-… the house when it should come before them …other shape hereafter.

…e motion went in the affirmative.

Wednesday, May 6.

…e order of the day being read for a vote of … to his Majesty of 1,000,000 l. Mr. T. …send rose to oppose it upon the ground of …ation, and incapacity in the servants of the …; drew an exaggerated picture of our na-… defence, having, as he said, a militia …ut arms, who were going to be encamped …ut tent equipage; and a navy, either not …d or not victualled, but lying embayed at …ad for the mere parade of a naval review. … the Toulon fleet had sailed on its expedi-… which might prove fatal to the distant …ments of the British empire. As to Great …n, its situation must be deplorable when …oasts and towns are daily stripped, and the …e thrown into consternation by the enemies …ceers.

… *Fenton*, one of the lords of the admi… replied to that part which respected the …; said he had the happiness of assuring the …, that the fleet was both manned and vic-…d for any expedition. With regard to the …dations of the American privateer, it was …mptom of the national imbecility, as Thurot …e very height of our glory last war, an-… our coasts in a similar manner; but he … very reason to believe the American priva-…was by this time taken, four frigates having …despatched for that purpose.

… *C. Fox* censured the conduct of the mi-… in letting Monf. D'Estaing's fleet sail out time enough for the king to sign them, and that they had gone through all the official forms, and were despatched to Portsmouth before nine o'clock that evening: therefore he wished, that no *general* imputation might be thrown on the ministry, but that a proper inquiry might take place, and that the blame, if any there was, might fall only where it was found due. As to the sailing of any part of the fleet, it was judged improper to detach any squadron of it, till the internal safety of Great Britain could admit of it.

Mr. *Fox* confessed the candour of the noble lord, but urged, that the language of despondence now came from administration and not from opposition; reprobated the narrow policy that kept that vast fleet for the internal defence of this island, which, he said, had force and magnanimity enough still to repel any force France could land in it; said he should rather hear of a body of French troops having invaded it, than that the distant territories of the empire should be thus timorously sacrificed to her inglorious safety.

Lord G. Germaine said, he had spoken fairly and openly, nor did he mean to hold a language of despondency; so far from it, that should Monf. D'Estaing have sailed to America, he trusted our fleet would arrive in time to punish him for any attempt to oppose the British arms.

Mr. Burke spoke next, for near two hours, represented the premier as the man who had trifled away the favourable winds of fortune; the nodding Palinurus, who had lashed the rudder fast, and left the state vessel in the midst of the storm: he said Sir William Howe, with 36,000 men, was likely to be in a similar predicament with that of Mr. Burgoyne; for as they received their daily bread from the sea, who was their present mother and guardian, as soon as the French admiral domineered it over the American seas, which must soon be the case, as Lord Howe had no force to look him in the face, they must surrender to him at discretion. He concluded, by lamenting that we had nothing but prayers left for it, and that the only consolation we could find was, that the noble Lord was about to turn priest, when he found himself incapable of being any longer a minister.

Sir *Edward Astley* said, he should not give his assent to the vote of credit. He asked whether government were sure of the allegiance of Canada? and whether they had not received ac-… …volt: had …with the …ited the …heir re-… …tructions …Ameri-…admit of …ir assent

March 14.

The following letter was sent on the 18th ult. from Gen. Washington to the inhabitants of New Jersey, Pennsylvania, Delaware, Maryland, and Virginia.

"Friends, Countrymen, and Fellow Citizens,

"After three campaigns, during which the brave subjects of these States have contended, not unsuccessfully, with one of the most powerful kingdoms upon earth, we now find ourselves at least upon a level with our opponents; and there is the best reason to believe, that efforts adequate to the abilities of this country would enable us speedily to conclude the war, and to secure the invaluable blessings of peace, liberty, and safety. With this view it is in contemplation, at the opening of the next campaign, to assemble a force sufficient, not barely to cover the country from a repetition of those depredations which it hath already suffered, but also to *operate offensively* and to *strike a decisive blow*.

"In the prosecution of this object, it is to be feared that so large an army may suffer for want of provisions. The distance between this and the Eastern states, whence considerable supplies of flesh have been hitherto drawn, will necessarily render those supplies extremely precarious. And unless the virtuous yeomanry of New Jersey, Pennsylvania, Delaware, Maryland, and Virginia, will exert themselves to prepare cattle for the use of the army, during the months of May, June, and July next, great difficulties may arise in the course of the campaign; it is therefore recommended to the inhabitants of those states, to put up and feed immediately as many of their stock cattle as they can spare, so that they may be driven to this army within that period. A bountiful price will be given, and the proprietors may assure themselves that they will render a most essential service to the illustrious cause of their country, and contribute in a great degree to shorten this bloody contest. But should there be any so insensible to the common interest, as not to exert themselves upon these generous principles, the private interest of those whose situation makes them liable to become immediate subjects to the enemy's incursions should prompt them at least to a measure which is calculated to save their property from plunder, their families from insult, and their own persons from abuse, hopeless confinement, or perhaps a violent death.

GEORGE WASHINGTON.

Head quarters Valley Forge, Feb. 18.

In Congress Jan. 2. 1778. Congress having, no further occasion for the service of Esek Hopkins, Esq; who on the 22d of December 1775, was appointed commander in chief of the fleet fitted out by the naval committee,

Resolved, that the said Esek Hopkins, Esq be dismissed from the service of the United States.

CHARLES THOMPSON. Sec.

EDINBURGH ADVERTISER

May 12, 1778

The May 12, 1778, *Edinburgh Advertiser* reprinted Washington's February 18 appeal to mid-Atlantic farmers to raise more cattle, reflecting hard realities of the Valley Forge winter camp.

LONDON CHRONICLE

April 30, 1778

The March 7, 1778, letter from a "Gentleman in Philadelphia," printed in the *London Chronicle* nearly two months later, was insightful on a local scale but quite inaccurate in strategic terms. General William Howe exploited the Continental Army's midwinter paralysis by supporting local Loyalists in a "kidnapping campaign" to break the political backbone of the American rebellion. Exactly the kinds of individuals mentioned ("tax-gatherers," "committee-men," and "justices") were targeted, and important local revolutionaries did not sleep quietly that spring.

Of ſtarting 'fore he'd broke his faſt;
But having ſcap'd ſo well laſt night,
To yield this time he thought was right.
At Marlborough they ſtopt to dine,
Where Doctor Robert did not ſhine;
For tho' his faſt he had not broke,
He cou'd not eat, ſhe turn'd the joke:
And in the ſequel you will find
The Lady's joke and how they din'd.

[To be continued in our next.]

Thurſday, April 30.

SCOTLAND.

Edinburgh, April 25.

HE beating orders for the new regiments of Fencible Men are now come down from the War-office.

We are informed that Government have reſolved to give two guineas of levy-money in place of one, that being the price paid for Sutherland's Fenſibles laſt war.

On the 24th of March laſt died abroad, Sir James Kinloch, Bart. He is ſucceeded in his titles by David Kinloch, of Gilmerton, Eſq; his brother.

COUNTRY NEWS.

Northampton, April 27. Laſt Tueſday an inquiſition was taken by William Jackſon, Gent. at Mears-Aſhby in this county, on view of the body of one Roger Grove, who in attempting to ſteal ſome fowls out of a cow-houſe belonging to one William Bayley, where there were ſome looſe poles lay upon the beams on which the fowls rooſted, fell to the ground, by which he received a mortal concuſſion of the brain, and inſtantly died. The jury brought in their verdict Accidental Death.

Reading, April 25. Wedneſday laſt Meſſ. Ajax and Tomlinſon, Officers of Exciſe, and Mr. Smallbone, Clerk to Mr. Pierce, collector, ſeized 4157lb. of black and green tea, and 431lb. of coffee, valued at upwards of 1000l. in a houſe, near Lambourne, in this county, which they lodged the ſame evening in this Borough (52 miles diſtant from the place of ſeizure.) The officers of our militia favoured Mr. Pierce with a proper guard for its ſecurity.

SHIP NEWS.

Deal, April 28. Came down and ſailed immediately the Hercules, Ruſſell, for Antigua; the Elliott, Squires, for Barcelona. Remain in the Downs his Majeſty's ſhips Medway and Buffalo, the Ranger ſloop of war, and Grey-hound cutter. Wind E. N. E.

LONDON.

Yeſterday there was a very numerous Levee at St. James's to pay their compliments to his Majeſty on his arrival in town from ſurveying the dock-yard, &c. at Chatham.

... clear of incumbrances.

Extract of a Letter from Dantzick, April 10.

"The regiments in Pruſſia are upon the march, and there are ſaid to be great deſertions from them. The Pruſſian ... went a few days ago to Pu... ſeveral recruits, and as ot... at Schidlitz and other Pr... of them took refuge in th... zic, and concealed ther... threw the inhabitants in... that many of them fled w... were purſued to the very ... who ſeized thoſe they cam... The officers at Dantzick ... the gates ſent out ſome m... fire upon thoſe who comm... which obliged the Pruſſia... ſent however our inhabita... out on account of the inſ... but we hope our tranqu... when the detachment retu...

"The navigation of th... interrupted by the like ... be feared will alſo affect t... Viſtula, by which the produc... brought hither."

They write from Cadiz that the departure of the flota, which was fixed for the 16th of April, was ſtill further poſtponed by order from Court, and that it was not now to put to ſea without a ſtrong convoy, which would not be ready before the end of May.

Extract of a Letter from a Gentleman at Philadelphia, to his Father in Glaſgow, dated March 7.

"We are all much encouraged by the aſſurances from Britain of a large reinforcement of troops the enſuing ſummer, which, I hope, providence will make the happy means of cruſhing this unprovoked rebellion. The rebel army (and indeed the whole country) are in a moſt miſerable ſituation for want of almoſt every neceſſary. The King's troops in this city are uncommonly healthy. Sickneſs even to a contagion prevails in the rebel camp; and never a day paſſes but ſome deſerters come in here, ſometimes 40 or 50 together. Several thouſands have come in here within theſe laſt three months, many of them with their arms. The poor people are ſo oppreſſed by Congreſs and their minions, that we have had ſeveral inſtances lately of tax-gatherers, committee-men, juſtices, and military officers being brought in, and delivered up here, by the poor people whom they have oppreſſed. Theſe men have formed themſelves into volunteer companies, and have been ſo active in kidnapping theſe gentry, that any kind of officer under Congreſs is not ſafe to ſleep within 20 miles of this city. I think matters at preſent look very favourable, as the poor deluded people begin to ſee that they have made an unhappy choice, in renouncing Britiſh liberty in exchange for the moſt cruel ſlavery ever before exhibited in the large compaſs of the known world. They rob people indiſcriminately of every thing they want for their miſerable army;

ces this kingdom now labours under, is actually agitating in his Majeſty's cabinet; and that the firſt object of reformation is to be the aboliſhing the places of governors to diſmantled and nomi-

...

a mixture of rudeneſs and civility, who they were, and that all the plate muſt be delivered to them. Lady Selkirk behaved with great compoſure and preſence of mind. She ſoon directed her plate to be delivered, with which, without doing any other damage, or aſking for watches, jewels, or any thing elſe, (which is odd) the gentlemen made off. Something, however, had been ſaid about their returning; and the Kirkcudbright people were in expectation of a viſit laſt night. There is reaſon to think that there were ſome people among them acquainted with perſons and places, and in particular one fellow, ſuppoſed to have been once a waiter at an inn in Kirkcudbright. The leader of the party, who was not the Captain of the veſſel, told, that their intention was to ſeize Lord Selkirk, who is now in London; that two other privateers were at hand; and that they had been at Whitehaven, where they had burnt ſome ſmall veſſels, but did not get done what they intended. When the affair was ended, Lady Selkirk, with her family and viſitors, left the houſe. Her Ladyſhip remained laſt night at Carlingworth, in order to be near information.

"It appears, that the privateer which did the damage at Whitehaven, landed at one o'clock yeſterday morning, and did not ſail till ten, ſo that it could not be the ſame with the one which landed at the Iſle. It is ſaid there are ſome ſhips of force at Belfaſt."

Extract of a Letter from Glaſgow, April 23.

"On Friday and Saturday laſt the 70th regiment of foot arrived here in two diviſions from Edinburgh, and on the ſame days ſeveral additional companies belonging to different corps in America paſſed through here for Greenock in order to be embarked there.

"On Monday the new raiſed regiment of Argyleſhire highlanders marched for Greenock,

VOL. I.] THE [NUMB. 38.]

NEW-JERSEY GAZETTE.

WEDNESDAY, AUGUST 26, 1778.

To the PRINTER *of the* NEW-JERSEY GAZETTE.

SIR,

SOMETIME ago I had occaſion to extract the cube-root to four or five places of figures, but could not recollect the common methods for doing it; and not having logarithms at hand, I ſat down to make a rule to anſwer the preſent exigency: This led me to conſider the ſubject much further than I at firſt intended, and produced the following theorems, which may be uſeful to the mathematician; therefore their publication in your paper will greatly oblige EXPONENT.

The firſt and moſt ſimple that offered a'e,

$$\frac{d}{\frac{m}{r}+2rr}=e, \text{ or } \quad \frac{2m+r^3}{\frac{m}{r}+2rr}=R$$

m = Reſolvend given.
r = Root aſſumed.
e = Part ſought.
R = Root found, and
d = Difference between the reſolvend and r^3

Theſe theorems converge faſt, and may ſerve very well for common uſe, when no great exactneſs is required at one operation.

The third theorem is,

$$\frac{2:\overline{\frac{m}{r}}\big|^{\frac{1}{2}}+r}{3}=R \text{ for the cube root.}$$

$$\frac{2:\overline{\frac{m}{rr}}\big|^{\frac{1}{2}}+2r}{4}=R \text{ for the 4th power.}$$

$$\frac{2\,\overline{\frac{m}{r3}}\big|^{\frac{1}{2}}+3r}{5}=R \text{ for the 5th power, \&c. \&c.}$$

Theſe expreſſions always give the value of R too much, if not exactly true; but as the exceſs is in a

many of firſt figures in the quotient by 5 as there are correſpondent figures to the left hand, between $\frac{m}{r}+rr$, and $2r:\overline{\frac{m}{r}}\big|^{\frac{1}{2}}$.

But univerſally, the value of e may be found to ſix, eight, or ten places of figures, by the firſt and third theorems thus:

In CONGRESS, May 27, 1778.

ESTABLISHMENT of the AMERICAN ARMY.

I. INFANTRY.

RESOLVED, That each battalion of infantry ſhall conſiſt of nine companies, one of which ſhall be of light infantry; the light infantry to be kept complete by drafts from the battalion, and organized during the campaign into corps of light infantry:

That the battalion of infantry conſiſt of

Commiſſioned.	1 Colonel and Captain,	75 dollars per month.
	1 Lieut. Col. and Captain,	60
	1 Major and Captain,	50
	6 Captains, each - -	40
	1 Captain Lieutenant, -	26 2-3
	8 Lieutenants, each -	26 2-3
	9 Enſigns, each - -	20

Paymaſter,	To be taken from the line.	20	In addition to their pay as officers in the line.
Adjutant,		13	
Quartermaſter,		13	

1 Surgeon, - -	60
1 Surgeon's Mate, - -	40
1 Serjeant Major, - -	10
1 Quartermaſter Serjeant,	10
27 Serjeants, each - -	10
1 Drum Major, - -	9
1 Fife Major, - -	9
18 Drums and Fifes, each	7 1-3
27 Corporals, each - -	7 1-3
477 Privates, each - -	6 2-3

Each of the field officers to command a company.

The Lieutenant of the Colonel's company to have the rank of Captain Lieutenant.

II. ARTILLERY.

That a battalion of artillery conſiſt of

Commiſſioned.	1 Colonel, - -	100 dollars per month.
	1 Lieutenant Colonel, -	75
	1 Major, - -	62 1-2
	12 Captains, each - -	50
	12 Capt. Lieutenants, each	33 1-3

72 Gunners, each - -	8 2-3
24 Drums and Fifes, each	8 2-3
336 Matroſſes, each - -	8 1-3

III. CAVALRY.

That a battalion of cavalry conſiſt of

Commiſſioned.	1 Colonel, - -	93 3-4ths dollars per month.
	1 Lieutenant Colonel,	75

1 Captain, - -	50 dollars per month.
3 Lieutenants, each -	33 1-3
4 Serjeants, each -	10
4 Corporals, each -	9
60 Privates, each -	8 1-3

Theſe companies to be inſtructed in the fabrication of field works, as far as relates to the manual and mechanical part. Their buſineſs ſhall be to inſtruct the fatigue parties to do their duty with celerity and exactneſs; to repair injuries done to the works by the enemy's fire, and to proſecute works in the face of it. The commiſſioned officers to be ſkilled in the neceſſary branches of the mathematics; the non-commiſſioned officers to write a good hand.

Reſolved, That the Adjutant and Quartermaſter of a regiment be nominated by the field officers out of the Subalterns, and preſented to the Commander in Chief or the commander in a ſeparate department for approbation; and that, being approved of, they ſhall receive from him a warrant agreeable to ſuch nomination:

That the Paymaſter of a regiment be choſen by the officers of the regiment out of the Captains or Subalterns, and appointed by warrant as above; the officers are to riſque their pay in his hands; the Paymaſters to have the charge of the cloathing, and to diſtribute the ſame.

Reſolved, That the Brigade Major be appointed as heretofore by the Commander in Chief, or commander in a ſeparate department, out of the Captains in the brigade to which he ſhall be appointed:

That the Brigade Quartermaſter be appointed by the Quartermaſter General, out of the Captains or Subalterns in the brigade to which he ſhall be appointed.

Reſolved, That two Aids-de-Camp be allowed to each Major General, who ſhall for the future appoint them out of the Captains or Subalterns.

Reſolved, That in addition to their pay as officers in the line, there be allowed to

An Aid-de-Camp, -	24 dollars per month.
Brigade Major, -	24
	15

he Staff officers aped above the ranks eſpectively appoint-ll thereupon be va-

d Brigade Majors to ons.

Brigade Majors and ore appointed from anks, and be admiſame rank they held provided that no Aid, Brigade Major or Quartermaſter ſhall have the command of any officers who commanded him while in the line.

Reſolved, That whenever the Adjutant General ſhall be appointed from the line, he may continue to hold his rank and commiſſion in the line.

Reſolved, That when ſupernumerary Lieutenants are continued under this arrange ent of the battali-

NEW-JERSEY GAZETTE (TRENTON)

August 26, 1778

Congress's May 27, 1778, agreement on a new "Establishment" for the army was a broad compromise between the continued resistance by many of its members, especially New Englanders, to an expensive, dangerous, unrepublican "standing army" and the growing realization by many Americans that independence could not be won by minutemen. Friedrich Steuben's training of the army that winter paid important morale and other dividends, but how effectively it would intersect with the reorganization plan was unknowable before the American victory at Yorktown in 1781.

Vol. XXIX. THE No. 15[...]

EDINBURGH ADVERTISER.

From TUESDAY May 26, to FRIDAY May 29, 1778.

To the PRINTER.

SIR, *Hungerford Coffee-house, May* 18.

THE arrival of Gen. Burgoyne gave hopes to many loyal subjects, that he had come home with some good news from America.— But alas! nothing has transpired of the kind. Another winter is over, and nothing has been either attempted, or done of consequence by his Excellency Gen. Howe. The British army, thank heaven, was in good health, and in good spirits, and the general continues to be preparing for something, if we are to credit report but when any thing material is to be done, no common augur can tell. We were often told during the winter, that Mr. Washington's army was inferior in numbers to the British; sickly, dying, ill clothed, ill fed, dispirited, and by no means so well armed as our troops; all which I verily believe.

But what avails all this to us? although we might add, and with truth, that our troops are better officered, and better disciplined, without disrespect to Mr. Washington's officers; still it answers no good end to Britain, since the prudence of Gen. Howe does not think it fit to hazard a battle or disperse the rebels.

Neither ancient nor modern history can produce any thing equal to the campaigns spent in North America, since the sword has been unsheathed against the insurgents. Armies of regular, well disciplined troops, furnished amply with all necessaries for war, officered with a set of old experienced veterans, and troops that never turned their backs when led on! yet year after year goes on and no exertion is attempted to crush rebellion, and bring back to their duty revolted subjects, that either bespeaks wisdom, judgment, or spirit, in those whose province it is to set the whole in motion.

Even the disgraceful captivity of our whole separate army, nor their remaining in the same unfortunate state, seems to have the least effect on the British chief commander in America.— Nor does the declaration of France, of her avowing the American rebels to be an independent people, seem to have any more effect upon our ministers at home, than if such a declaration had never been made.

The business of this kind of war, seems to be nothing more than the sending, at an enormous expence to the nation, a great army and fleet to America, to spend millions of hard guineas amongst a people who have revolted from

himself in removing his head quarters from Boston to New York; and from New York to Philadelphia. Where he is next to go, God

him, will slip away where the prospect of less taxes and trade is apparent.

Good God, Mr. Printer, what times do we live in! Was the British spirit ever at such an ebb, or the British glory ever so sunk, for want of men of spirit, resolution and wisdom, to guide and conduct the national concerns? In 1764 we gained and secured an empire; in 1778 we are on the eve of losing an empire; unless some guardian spirit rises amongst us, like that which directed and conducted with honour and glory our last war with France and Spain.

PASTOR FIDO.

For the EDINBURGH ADVERTISER.

A REMEDY *for the* BITE *of a* MAD DOG.

Discovered by a GENTLEMAN *of* SILESIA, *and published by order of the* KING *of* PRUSSIA.

[*Sent to Scotland by Earl* MARSHAL, *and approved of by some eminent physicians of this place.*]

TWENTY-four of the insect called *Meloë Majalis* or May-bug, cut into small pieces:
Two drachms of ebony wood, finely scraped:
One drachm of *Serpentaria* or Virginia snakeroot, nicely pulverized.
One drachm of ra[...]
Twenty grains [...]
Two ounces o[...]
inspissated ju[...]
All these ing[...]
and made into [...]
sects are kept i[...]

As the princi[...] insect above me[...] particular descr[...] it is to be gathe[...] the patient.

The commor[...] *Scarabæus Melo*[...] use of is a *Mel*[...] indifferently. [...] *bæus*, also called [...] his Elem. Eutom. T[...] gives the best figure of this insect. It is almost as large as the finger, and an inch and a half long. The female is larger than the male. It has no wings, but small elytra, that is, a kind of strong hard wings, or rather sheaths, *(jus coleopter)*, which serve as a cover for their softer wings, not for flying with, and reach to the half length only of the body. They are softer than in other kinds, black, mark'd with points, without lustre; for this reason the insect cannot fly, but moves slowly. His body is in general soft, tender, and black, surrounded with blue, green, and

antennæ are composed of twelve articulations; the fore and middle feet have five of them, but the hinder feet have only four. Whenever it

are to be gathered in the month of May, in dry and warm day; but particular care must taken not to touch them with the fingers, b[...] cause they will immediately drop their juice, a[...] therefore they must be taken up with small b[...] of wood, or pincers, without squeezing the[...] and put into a vase. The heads are to be cut [...] with scissars and thrown away, and the bodi[...] put into a glass with some fine honey, which mu[...] be well covered, and kept in a dry tempera[...] place. If, after some time, the honey is foun[...] to have dried up, some more fresh may be adde[...] and thus, with proper care, the insects wi[...] keep for two or three years. Two hundred o[...] the black-coloured insects, or a hundred an[...] seventy-five of the gold coloured, require quart of honey, measure of Berlin.

DOSE.

Age.	Men.		Women	
	dra.	*gr.*	*dra.*	*gr*
From one to three years old	0	24	0	20
—— three to six	0	30	0	26
—— six to twelve	0	40	0	30
—— twelve to twenty	1	0	0	50
—— twenty to thirty				

[...] fed, or burnt.—In winter the chamber is to be kept warm. If the bite has caused a wound, it must be washed with some wine, beer, or vinegar, which last is to be mixed with fine salt, but salt-water alone will do as well. This to be repeated from time to time. The wounded part to be wrapped up in a linen cloth dipped in warm vinegar, and the wound dressed with a plaister of basilicon, or with fresh wet salt butter, and often touched with oil of scorpion, or with oil of olives wherein Meloës have been steeped. This is done in order to keep the wound open that it may be well cleaned; it will afterwards heal of itself.

[...] overheat him; all strong liquors, and, in general, all kinds of excess.

As to animals, the following rules are to be

EDINBURGH ADVERTISER

May 29, 1778

General John Burgoyne, the British general defeated at Saratoga in October of 1777, arrived in Britain on May 13, 1778, to defend his conduct in that battle. Far from bringing "good news," his arrival presaged a growing sense in British circles that the effort to crush the rebellion was doomed. Ironically, on May 18, as "Pastor Fido" wrote the *Edinburgh Advertiser* to articulate that pessimism, the resigned British commander William Howe was feted by his officers in Philadelphia.

REPORTING THE

FRENCH-AMERICAN ALLIANCE

By Julia Osman

THE FRENCH-AMERICAN ALLIANCE CONSISTED OF MORE than the Treaties of Amity and Commerce and of Alliance, signed on February 6, 1778. While the treaties stipulated that France would send America aid in its war against Great Britain, France had already been unofficially supporting the colonists for two years. With the support of King Louis XVI, Caron de Beaumarchais, the famous French playwright, had created a special merchant company specifically to send substantial amounts of military supplies and money to the American colonies. French officers, such as the Marquis de Lafayette, frustrated at the lack of opportunity to prove their worth in combat in Europe, sailed to America to offer their military expertise to the American Congress. The rebelling American colonies had excited the French state and its people for two major reasons: on one hand, Great Britain, France's greatest rival for European and global power, would suffer greatly if it lost its thirteen American colonies. Eager to incapacitate Britain, the French were happy for any reason to make "unjust seizures…upon the ships and goods" of the English king (*London Gazette*, August 1, 1778). While King George III took care to justify his decision to "procure reparation," the "two crowns" had never been interested in maintaining peace for too long. On the other hand, the possibility of an independent America generated a great deal of genuine excitement, as American colonists seemed to be pursuing a way of life and government that closely mirrored French Enlightenment ideals of virtue and patriotism.

The possibility of an independent America generated a great deal of genuine excitement, as American colonists seemed to be pursuing a way of life and government that closely mirrored French Enlightenment ideals of virtue and patriotism.

Adding fuel to the pro-American fire, Ben Franklin arrived in Paris in December 1776 to facilitate an alliance with France that would include supplies and military aid. He wooed the French court and intellectual circles by presenting himself as the quintessential "American" that French readers had come to expect. With the victory of the Battles of Saratoga, Louis XVI finally expressed his happiness in "acknowledging the Independence of America" in 1778 (*Continental Journal*, May 14, 1778). While desiring an American victory over Britain for years, France now felt for certain that it could enter the war on the side of the victors. Louis XVI resolved to send military aid. Initial attempts to land French troops in America under the command of General d'Estaing were unsuccessful, but the Comte de Rochambeau arrived with several French regiments in 1780 in Newport, Rhode Island. Rochambeau, in turn, served "under the orders of General Washington." While European armies had reputations as plunderers and looters, French troops did prove to be "under the strictest discipline" while in America, and relationships between American citizens and the French army were generally cordial (*London Chronicle*, October 17, 1780)

The treaty of Amity and Commerce sealed the French-American alliance, but it also hints at more revolution to come. Made "for reciprocal advantage of their subjects and citizens," the treaty itself recognized that "subjects" of a monarchy were becoming "citizens" in an American Republic, a condition that would soon apply to the French, just six years after the Treaty of Paris ended the American Revolution (*Independent Chronicle*, December 10, 1778). By pledging money, supplies, and troops, and by celebrating the American Revolution, France had set the stage for its own.

Numb. 11896.

The London Gazette.

Published by Authority.

From Tuesday July 28, to Saturday August 1, 1778.

AT the Court at *St. James's*, the 29th of *July*, 1778,

P R E S E N T,

The KING's Most Excellent Majesty in Council.

WHEREAS many Injuries and Acts of Hostility have been committed, and many unjust Seizures made, by the French King and his Subjects, unto and upon the Ships and Goods of His Majesty's Subjects, contrary to the Faith of Treaties; and whereas His Majesty has lately received Advice, that such Acts of Hostility are now Publickly encouraged and authorized by the French King's Orders: His Majesty has taken into Consideration these injurious Proceedings of the French Court; and His Majesty, being determined to take such Measures as are necessary for vindicating the Honour of His Crown, and for procuring Reparation and Satisfaction for His injured Subjects, is pleased, by and with the Advice of His Privy Council, to order, and it is hereby ordered, That General Reprizals be granted against the Ships, Goods and Subjects of the French King, so that as well His Majesty's Fleet and Ships, as also all other Ships and Vessels that shall be commissionated by Letters of Marque or General Reprizals, or otherwise by His Majesty's Commissioners for executing the Office of Lord High Admiral of Great Britain, shall and may lawfully seize all Ships, Vessels and Goods belonging to the French King or his Subjects, or others inhabiting within any the Territories of the French King, and bring the same to Judgment in any of the Courts of Admiralty within His Majesty's Dominions; and to that End His Majesty's Advocate-General, with the Advocate of the Admiralty, are forthwith to prepare the Draught of a Commission, and present the same to His Majesty at this Board, authorizing the Commissioners for executing the Office of Lord High Admiral, or any Person or Persons by them empowered and appointed, to issue forth and grant Letters of Marque and Reprizal to any of His Majesty's Subjects,
others whom the said Commissioners shall deer
qualified in that Behalf, for the appreher
seizing and taking the Ships, Vessels and
belonging to the French King, and the Vassa
Subjects of the French King, or any inha
within his Countries, Territories or Domi
and that such Powers and Clauses be inserted
said Commission as have been usual, and are a
ing to former Precedents: And His Majesty'
Advocate-General, with the Advocate of th
miralty, are also forthwith to prepare the Dr
of a Commission, and present the same to Hi
jesty at this Board, authorizing the said Co
sioners for executing the Office of Lord High
miral, to will and require the High Court of Ad
miralty of Great Britain, and the Lieutenant and Judge of the said Court, his Surrogate or Surrogates, as also the several Courts of Admiralty within His Majesty's Dominions, to take Cognizance of, and judicially proceed upon, all and all Manner of Captures, Seizures, Prizes and Reprizals of all Ships and Goods that are or shall be taken, and to hear and determine the same; and according to the Course of Admiralty, and the Laws of Nations, to adjudge and condemn all such Ships, Vessels and Goods as shall belong to the French King, or the Vassals and Subjects of the French King, or to any others inhabiting within any of his Countries, Territories and Dominions; and that such Powers and Clause be inserted in the said Commission as have been usual, and are according to former Precedents: And they are likewise to prepare, and lay before His Majesty at this Board, a Draught of such Instructions as may be proper to be sent to the Courts of Admiralty in His Majesty's Foreign Governments and Plantations, for their Guidance herein; as also another Draught of Instructions for such Ships as shall be commissionated for the Purposes afore-mentioned.

AT the Court at St. *James's*, the 10th of *July*, 1778,

P R E S E N T,

The KING's Most Excellent Majesty in Council.

WHEREAS the Names of many of the Officers serving in the respective Regiments and Battalions of Militia, within the several Counties in England and Wales, have been frequently returned by the Judges in the List of Persons proper to be appointed Sheriffs, notwithstanding such Officers are by Law exempted from serving the Office of Sheriff, during the Time of their Service in the Militia: And whereas the Impropriety of such Returns has proceeded from the Want of Information being given to the Judges of the Names of the several Officers serving in the Militia, from whence many Inconveniencies have arisen: His Majesty, in order to

Steph. Cottrell.

LONDON GAZETTE

August 1, 1778

The rebelling American colonies had excited the French state and French people. Eager to incapacitate Britain, the French were happy for any reason to make "unjust seizures . . . upon the ships and goods" of the English king.

MAY 14, 1778

The CONTINENTAL JOURNAL

Extract of a letter from a gentleman in Nantes, to another in this town, dated 25th March, 1778.

"It must undoubtedly give you great pleasure, my dear friend, to hear that our Independency is acknowledged in form by the Court of France. On the 20th instant, the Commissioners were received at Versailles as Ministers Plenipotentiary of the United States of America, and the next day the English Ambassador went off without taking leave. Orders are given to seize all English vessels that are found in any French port, and an open declaration of war is daily expected. At the reception of our ministers, the King (addressing himself to Dr. Franklin) said, he was happy in acknowledging the Independence of America, and that the conditions of the treaty on the part of France, should be faithfully observed: The Doctor answered to the same effect on the part of Congress. In England they are in the most humiliating confusion, they are driven to the last resource, and want to make peace with us at any rate; peace, peace is the cry of the nation; but as the weak ministers have still the foolish hope of persuading us to renounce our Independence, I imagine their plan will only be another public proof of their foolish obstinacy."

It is rumoured, That the late news from England, is very unpleasing to the Tories in New York--has fixed a surly gloom on their countenances---fear works so hard on some of them that they are privately packing up in order to decamp.

CONTINENTAL JOURNAL (BOSTON)
May 14, 1778

With the victory of the Battles of Saratoga, Louis XVI finally expressed his happiness in "acknowledging the Independence of America" in 1778.

NEW-HAVEN, May 6.

Monday last came to town, Major-General BENEDICT ARNOLD; he was met on the road by several Continental and Militia Officers, the Cadet Company, and a number of respectable inhabitants from this place, to testify their esteem for one who has, by his bravery, rendered his country many important services. On his arrival in town, he was saluted by a discharge of thirteen cannon.

PROVIDENCE, May 9.

Capt. Whipple, in the Providence frigate, who sailed from this port last week, in his passage down the Bay was fired on by the Lark frigate, which lay near Warwick Neck, and had got under way; Capt. Whipple returned the compliment with a broadside, and we since learn killed three and wounded seventeen of the Lark's crew; her hull and rigging were likewise much damaged. The Juno frigate, the lowermost of the enemy's ships, fired a broadside at the Providence as she passed, and received another, but with what effect we have not yet learnt. Capt. Whipple likewise poured a broadside into a tender that got under sail, and shattered her so much that the enemy were obliged to haul her to a wharf at Newport, where she sunk. The enemy's ships did not follow Capt. Whipple to sea as was reported.

BOSTON, May 14.

Yesterday being the annual meeting for the choice of Representatives for this town the ensuing year, the following Gentlemen were chosen, viz.—Hon. JOHN HANCOCK, Esq; Hon. WILLIAM PHILLIPS, Esq; Hon. JOHN PITTS, Esq; OLIVER WENDELL and CALEB DAVIS, Esq'rs; Mr. ELLIS GRAY and JOHN LOWELL, Esq;

Extract of a letter from a gentleman in Nantes, to another in this town, dated 25th March, 1778.

"It must undoubtedly give you great pleasure, my dear friend, to hear that our Independency is acknowledged in form by the Court of France. On the 20th instant, the Commissioners were received at Versailles as Ministers Plenipotentiary of the United States of America, and the next day the English Ambassador went off without taking leave. Orders are given to seize all English vessels that are found in any French port, and an open declaration of war is daily expected. At the reception of our ministers, the King (addressing himself to Dr. Franklin) said, he was happy in acknowledging the Independence of America, and that the conditions of the treaty on the part of France, should be faithfully observed: The Doctor answered to the same effect on the part of Congress. In England they are in the most humiliating confusion, they are driven to the last resource, and want to make peace with us at any rate; peace, peace is the cry of the nation; but as the weak ministers have still the foolish hope of persuading us to renounce our Independence, I imagine their plan will only be another public proof of their foolish obstinacy."

It is rumoured, That the late news from England, is very unpleasing to the Tories in New York--has fixed a surly gloom on their countenances---fear works so hard on some of them that they are privately packing up in order to decamp.

Tuesday last arrived a Ship from Nantz in five weeks.

A Letter from Head-Quarters, dated May 2d, mentions as a report, that General Amherst and Admiral Kepple were arrived at Philadelphia.

The lengthiness of the Valuation Act, obliges us to omit several articles of intelligence, particularly the late patriotic exertions of the ladies in the towns of Andover and Mendon, towards their pastors.

STATE of MASSACHUSETTS BAY.

A Proclamation for Dissolving the Great and General Court of said State.

WHEREAS the Great and General Court of

STATE OF MASSACHUSETTS BAY.

In COUNCIL, Roxbury, April, 6 1778.

WHEREAS it is represented to this Court, that some of the Men inlisted into the public Service for the Defence of Rhode-Island, are not possessed of Fire Arms, but are willing to furnish themselves, if they knew where to purchase them:

Therefore, RESOLVED, That the Board of War, be, and they hereby are impowered and directed to sell Fire Arms to any such Persons as are, or may be engaged in the public Service of this State, and shall apply to them for the same, at such Price as they may judge reasonable. And the Secretary is directed to publish this Resolve in the next Thursday News Papers.

Sent down for Concurrence.

JNo. AVERY, Dep. Sec'y.

In the House of REPRESENTATIVES, April 29, 1778. Read and concurr'd.

J. PITTS, Speak. pro Tem.

Consented to by the Council,

A true Copy. Attest J. AVERY, D. Sec'ry.

STATE OF MASSACHUSETTS-BAY.

IN THE HOUSE OF REPRESENTATIVES, APRIL 28, 1778.

WHEREAS it appears by the Returns made into the Secretary's office, that in many instances the same men have been returned for several towns as one seventh part of their male inhabitants for the Continental army, by which means the compleating this State's quota of said army has been greatly delayed. For remedy whereof, and in order that the deficiencies of each town may be exactly and speedily known:

RESOLVED, That Daniel Perry, Abner Ellis, and Thomas Crane, Esq'rs; be a committee for the county of Suffolk; Samuel Osgood, Esq; Col. Israel Hutchinson and Major Joseph Page, a committee for the county of Essex; Col. Eleazer Brooks, Capt. Joseph Hosmer and Col. Cyprian Howe, a committee for the county of Middlesex; Mr. Willis Hall, Israel Nichols, Esq; Col. Jacob Davis, Dr. William Dunsmore and Capt. Timothy Page, a committee for the county of Worcester; Justin Ely, Esq; Mr. Elijah Hunt and Col. Ruggles Woodbridge, a committee for the county of Hampshire; John Turner, Esq; Mr. Benjamin Thomas and Col. John Gray, a committee for the county of Plymouth; John Greenough, Solomon Freeman, Esq'rs; and Mr. Joseph Snow, a committee for the county of Barnstable; Thomas Durfee, Shubael Peck and Samuel Toby, Esq'rs; a committee for the county of Bristol; Joseph Simpson, John Frost and Thomas Cutts, Esq'rs; a committee for the county of York; John Waite, Esq; Mr. Paul Little, and John Lewis, Esq; a committee for the county of Cumberland; Dummer Sewall, Esq; Col. Samuel McCobb, and Nathaniel Thwing, Esq; a committee for the county of Lincoln; and Capt. William Bacon, Joel Woodbridge, Esq; and Capt. William King, a committee for the county of Berkshire.

And it is further RESOLVED, That said committees be, and hereby are invested with full powers to hear and determine all disputes arising from returns made in manner aforesaid, between the several towns and companies within the county for which they are respectively appointed; and said committees are hereby directed as soon as may be to notify by writing the time and place at which they will meet the selectmen and military officers of the several towns within the county for which they are respectively appointed; and in case the officers or selectmen of any such town or company as shall have made returns in manner aforesaid, shall refuse or neglect to appear and defend their claims before said committees, they shall nevertheless proceed to hear and determine the cause upon such evidence as they shall be able to obtain; and said committees are hereby directed to transmit to the Secretary's office on or before the 20th of June next, a particular account of their proceedings, together with the number of men each town within their county is deficient, in order to compleat one seventh part of their male inhabitants, in consequence of having made such wrong returns as aforesaid. And it is further

Resolved, That there be allowed said committee for each man per day the sum of eighteen shillings for his time and expences (including horse-hire) whilst attending said service; which together with all other charges arising thereon, shall be paid as the General Court shall hereafter order.

And whereas it is represented to this Court that several towns or companies have returned men as part of their respective quotas of the Continental army, who were inlisted or drafted to do duty as guards, or otherwise for short terms in Continental pay:

Resolved, That the aforesaid committees be directed to make full enquiry into this matter, and make report to this Court of those towns or captains of companies who have returned such men, and order said captains immediately to detach other men, agreeable to the true intent of the resolves of this Court for filling

NOTICE is hereby given that the proprietors unimproved Land belonging to THOMAS FLUKER, Esq; and the heirs of Col SAMUEL WALDO, deceased, lying in *Warren*, in the county of *Lincoln*, are taxed in the sum of *thirty five pounds four shillings and three pence*; the owners of said Lands are requested to pay the same speedily, to prevent further proceeding according to law. JOSEPH COPELAND, Constable.

PUBLIC NOTICE.

TAKEN into Custody by Jonas Dix and Leonard Williams, Esqrs; of Waltham, in the County of Middlesex, a Person, with two Pieces of 7/8 Linnen Cloth, not of the best Kind, loose roll'd, and which no doubt were stolen. The Owner by applying to the Justices, may serve both himself and the Public.

IN the County of *Hampshire*, in the *Province* of the *Massachusetts* Bay.

AGreeable to the Directions given in the present Tax-Bill,—Public Notice is hereby given, That the non-resident Land hereafter named, lying in the Town of Leverett, are indebted by a Tax in equal Proportion to the other Lands in said Town, (viz.) Mr. Thomas Dickenson for Lot No. 12, £.1 0 3. Hoppin's Heirs for Lot No. 15, £.1 6 10, and Lot No. 16, £.1 10 10. Owners not known, Lot No. 19, £.0 16 8. Lot No. 50, £.1 1 8. Captain Ayres's Land, £.2 9 2. George Nye's Land, £.3 10 10.—Samuel Hinckley's Land, £.1 0 0. James Convus's Land, £.0 9 2. Mr. Chandler's Land, £.0 12 0.—The above Sums are to be paid to Joseph Smith and Moses Keep. The Owners of which are requested immediately to pay the Sums above set against their

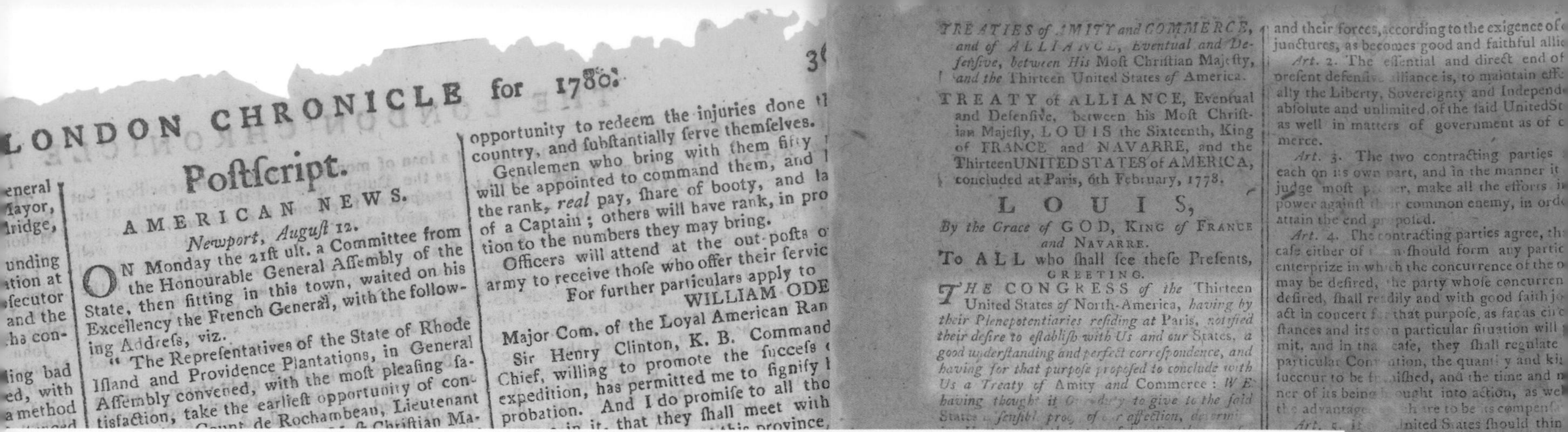

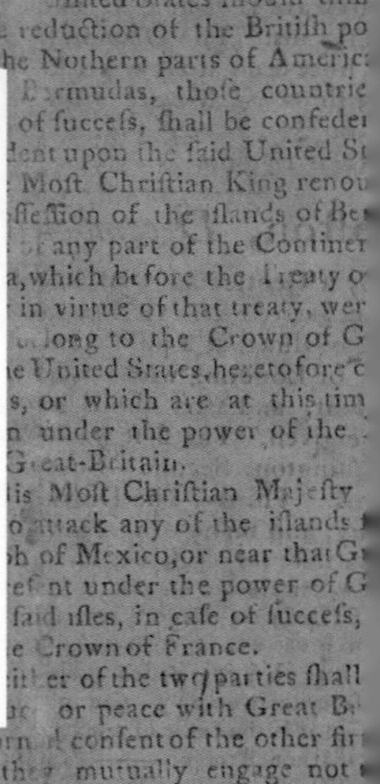

LONDON CHRONICLE

October 17, 1778

While European armies had reputations as plunderers and looters, French troops did prove to be "under the strictest discipline" while in America, and relationships between American citizens and the French army were generally cordial.

INDEPENDENT CHRONICLE (BOSTON)

December 10, 1778

On February 6, 1778, the French signed two treaties: the Treaty of Alliance and the Treaty of Amity and Commerce, which officially sealed the French-American alliance with political and commercial support. However, France had been unofficially supporting the colonists for two years already with military supplies, money, and French officers, such as the Marquis de Lafayette.

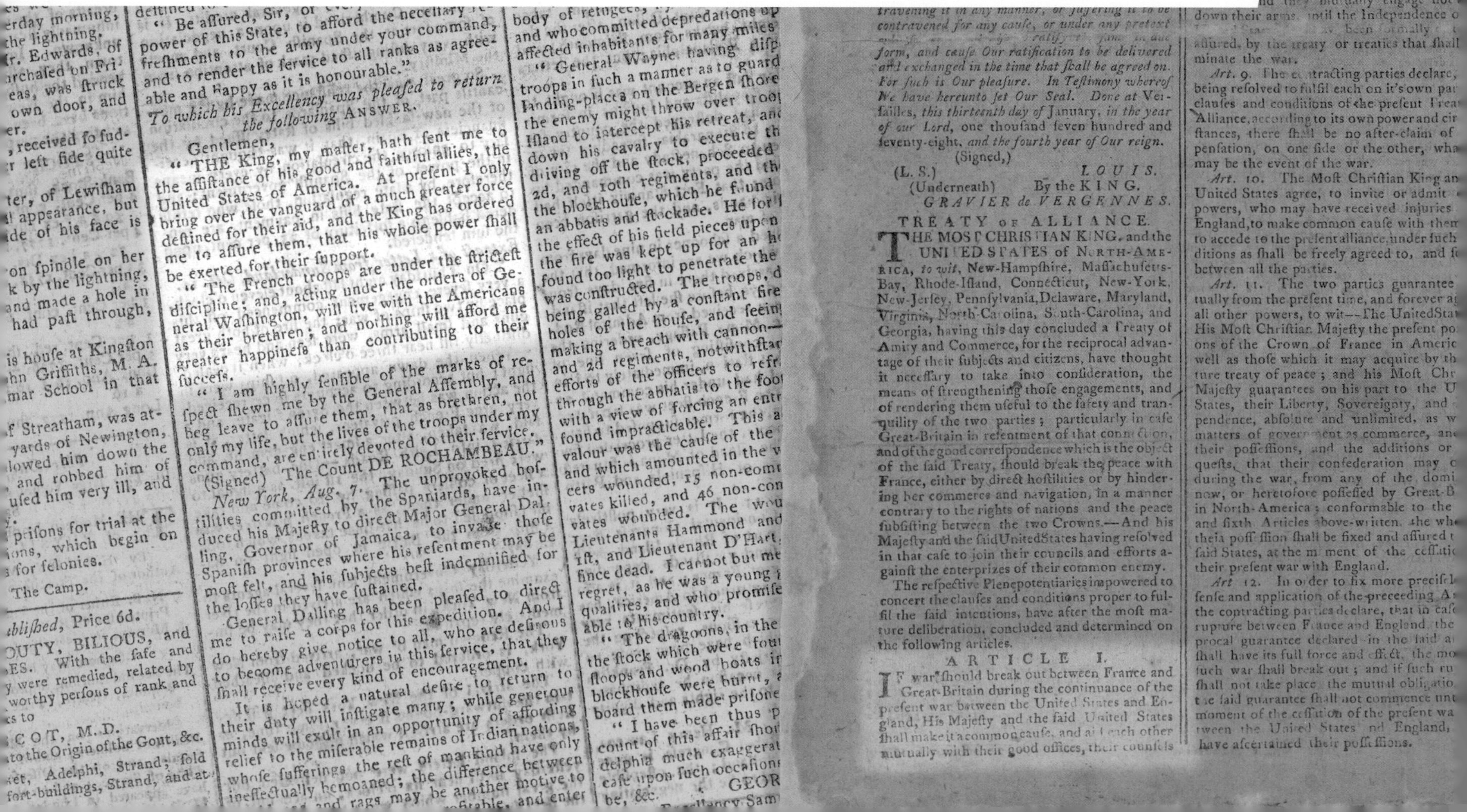

REPORTING THE

BATTLE OF MONMOUTH

By Michael S. Adelberg

THE AMERICAN REVOLUTION FUNDAMENTALLY changed for the British in 1778. France's entry into the war forced the British to shift military resources elsewhere in the Empire and shift from an offensive to a defensive posture in America. The first task of the new British commander, Henry Clinton, was quitting Philadelphia and consolidating forces in New York.

In June, the British army began its march across New Jersey. The march was slow and difficult from the start. In his July 5, 1778, report (printed in the *London Gazette Extraordinary* on August 24, 1778), Clinton complained "the obstructions we met with were frequent," as the New Jersey Militia felled bridges, fouled wells, and skirmished with their advance parties. Clinton also reported being "encumbered by an enormous provision train" that "extended near 12 miles." Another report suggested fourteen miles. On June 27, Clinton paused at Freehold (Monmouth Court House) to rest his weary troops.

After enduring the famous winter encampment at Valley Forge, the Continental Army was improved by newly arrived European drill masters—such as Baron von Steuben—and fresh recruits. Under command of the Marquis de Lafayette and then Charles Lee, the vanguard of the Continental Army marched into New Jersey with the main body of the army, commanded by George Washington, trailing behind.

On the morning of June 28, Clinton sent his provision train east toward Sandy Hook and turned to face the gathering Continentals. The British drove the Continentals back through the morning, but the Continental lines stiffened when Washington arrived with more men. Well-positioned artillery gave the Continentals the upper hand in the late afternoon. Lee was blamed for disorderly leadership that morning and court-martialed shortly after the battle (see December 22, 1778, *London Chronicle*). Clinton ignored all of this in his report, claiming instead that his men halted because they "were so over-powered with fatigue" and heat. Indeed, officers from both armies claimed that the heat took as many lives that day as the enemy.

At sundown, the battlefield quieted. Clinton reported taking "advantage of the moonlight" to retreat and reunite with his provision train. The evacuation to New York was completed without serious opposition. Clinton's report downplayed the high cost of the Monmouth Campaign, omitting mention of the massive desertions (reportedly 1,800 men) and the humiliation of leaving behind forty-five wounded at Freehold. He also neglected to mention soldier misconduct during the march, including the arson of a dozen homes near Freehold.

After the battle, stories swirled about the wife of a Continental soldier who risked her life carrying water and munitions to the men during the battle and taking her husband's place at his cannon when he fell. Tales of heroic women at different Revolutionary War battles mixed together, resulting in the Molly Pitcher legend. Though much of the Molly Pitcher legend is unlikely, it is well understood that hundreds of women—wives, daughters, mistresses, and refugees—followed the armies and performed important support roles throughout the war.

Both commanders claimed victory after the Battle of Monmouth. Clinton reported that his strategic objective—reaching New York—was achieved. He claimed that he merely wished to protect his provision train, but the British maneuvers at the Battle of Monmouth suggest he was trying to rout the Continentals. Though the Battle of Monmouth is often discussed as a draw, it marked the first time that the main body of the Continental Army engaged the main body of the British army and held the battlefield. It was also reported as a Continental victory throughout America, persuading wavering Americans to support the war effort.

The London Gazette
EXTRAORDINARY.

Publiſhed by Authority.

MONDAY, AUGUST 24, 1778.

Whitehall, Auguſt 24, 1778.

THE following Letter from Lieutenant-General Sir Henry Clinton, Knight of the Bath, to Lord George Germain, One of His Majeſty's Principal Secretaries of State, was received on Saturday Night by Colonel Patterſon, who arrived in the Grantham Packet from New York.

New York, July 5, 1778.

MY LORD,

I Have the Honor to inform your Lordſhip, that, purſuant to His Majeſty's Inſtructions, I evacuated Philadelphia on the 18th of June, at Three o'Clock in the Morning, and proceeded to Glouceſter Point without being followed by the Enemy. Every Thing being from thence paſſed, in Safety acroſs the Delaware, through the excellent Diſpoſition made by the Admiral to ſecure our Paſſage, the Army marched at Ten o'Clock, and reached Haddonfield the ſame Day. A ſtrong Corps of the Enemy having, upon our Approach, abandoned the difficult Paſs of Mount Holly, the Army proceeded without any Interruption from them, excepting what was occaſioned by their having deſtroyed every Bridge on our Road. As the Country is much interſected with marſhy Rivulets, the Obſtructions we met with were frequent, and the exceſſive Heat of the Seaſon rendered the Labour of repairing the Bridges ſeverely felt.

The advanced Parties of our Light Troops arriving unexpectedly at Croſſwicks on the 23d, after a trifling Skirmiſh, prevented the Enemy from deſtroying the Bridge over a large Creek at that Village, and the Army paſſed it the next Morning. One Column, under the Command of his Excellency Lieutenant-General Knyphauſen, halted near Amely's Town; and as the Proviſion Train and heavy Artillery were ſtationed in that Diviſion, the other Column, under Lieutenant-General Earl Cornwallis, took a Poſition at Allen's Town, which

LONDON GAZETTE EXTRAORDINARY

August 24, 1778

France's entry into the war forced the British to shift military resources elsewhere in the Empire and shift from an offensive to a defensive posture in America. The British army's march from Philadelphia across New Jersey to New York was slow and difficult.

[Price Three-pence Halfpenny.]

join them on the Rariton. As I could not hope that, after having always hitherto ſo ſtudiouſly avoided a general Action, General Waſhington would now give into it againſt every Dictate of Policy; I could only ſuppoſe that his Views were directed againſt my Baggage, &c. in which Part I was indeed vulnerable. This Circumſtance alone would have tempted me to avoid the difficult Paſſage of the Rariton; but when I reflected that from Sandy Hook I ſhould be able, with more Expedition, to carry His Majeſty's further Orders into Execution, I did not heſitate to order the Army into the Road which leads through Freehold to the Naveſink. The Approach of the Enemy's Army being indicated by the frequent Appearance of their Light Troops on our Rear, I requeſted his Excellency Lieutenant General Knyphauſen to take the Baggage of the whole Army under the Charge of his Diviſion, conſiſting of the Troops mentioned in the Margin.* Under the Head of Baggage was comprized, not only all the Wheel Carriages of every Department, but alſo the Bât Horſes; a Train which, as the Country admitted but of one Route for Carriages, extended near 12 Miles. The indiſpenſible Neceſſity I was under of ſecuring theſe is obvious; and the Difficulty of doing it, in a moſt woody Country, againſt an Army far ſuperior in Numbers, will, I truſt, be no leſs ſo.

I deſired Lieutenant-General Knyphauſen to move at Day-Break on the 28th; and, that I might not preſs upon him in the firſt Part of the March, in which we had but one Route, I did not follow with the other Diviſion† till near Eight o'Clock. Soon after I had marched, reconnoitring Parties of the Enemy appeared on our Left Flank. The Queen's Rangers fell in with and diſperſed ſome Detachments among the Woods in the ſame Quarter. Our Rear Guard having deſcended from the Heights above Freehold into a Plain near Three Miles in Length, and about One Mile in Breadth, ſeveral Columns of the Enemy appeared likewiſe deſcending into the Plain, ... annonade our ... ought me, ... in Force ... our Baggage ... Juncture ... for ſome ... he Blow, ... our Rear, ... achments ...

I had

* ... Infantry. ... Stern's and ... nts. West ... Battalion Britiſh Grenadiers. 2d Ditto. 1ſt Battalion of Light Infantry. Heſſian Grenadiers, Guards, 3d, 4th, 5th Brigades Britiſh.

formed, of near 12,000 Men, from two ſtrong Poſitions; but it will, I doubt not, be conſidered as doubly creditable, when I mention, that they did it under ſuch Diſadvantages of Heat and Fatigue, that a great Part of thoſe we loſt fell dead as they advanced, without a Wound.

Fearing that my firſt Order had miſcarried, before I quitted this Ground I ſent a ſecond, for a Brigade of Infantry, the 17th Light Dragoons, and 2d Battalion of Light Infantry, to meet me on the March, with which additional Force, had General Waſhington ſhewn himſelf the next Day, I was determined to attack him; but there not being the leaſt Appearance of an Enemy, I ſuſpected he might have puſhed a conſiderable Corps to a ſtrong Poſition near Middletown; I therefore left the Rear Guard on its March, and detached Major General Grant to take Poſt there, which was effected on the 29th. The whole Army marched to this Poſition the next Day, and then fell back to another, near Naveſink, where I waited two Days, in the Hope, that Mr. Waſhington might have been tempted to have advanced to the Poſition near Middletown, which we had quitted; in which Caſe I might have attacked him to Advantage.

During this Time the Sick and Wounded were embarked, and Preparations made for paſſing to Sandy Hook Iſland by a Bridge, which by the extraordinary Efforts of the Navy was ſoon compleated, and over which the whole Army paſſed in about two Hours Time; the Horſes and Cattle having been previouſly tranſported.

Your Lordſhip will receive herewith a Return of the Killed, Wounded, Miſſing, &c of His Majeſty's Troops on the 28th of laſt Month. That of the Enemy is ſuppoſed to have been more conſiderable, eſpecially in Killed.

The Loſs of Lieutenant Colonel Monckton, who commanded the 2d Battalion of Grenadiers, is much to be lamented.

I am much indebted to Lord Cornwallis for his zealous Services on every Occaſion; and I found great Support from the Activity of Major General Grey, Brigadier Generals Mathew, Leſlie, and Sir William Erſkine.

I beg Leave to refer your Lordſhip for any other Particulars, which you may wiſh to be informed of, to Colonel Patterſon, who will have the Honor of delivering theſe Diſpatches, and whoſe Services in this Country entitle him to every Mark of your Lordſhip's Favor.

I have the Honor to be, &c.

H. CLINTON.

Return of the Killed, Wounded, Miſſing, &c. of the Troops under the Command of General Sir Henry Clinton, in an Engagement with the Rebel Army, on the Heights of Freehold, County of Monmouth, New Jerſey, the 28th of June, 1778.

TOTAL *BRITISH*.

1 Lieutenant-Colonel, 1 Captain, 2 Lieutenants, 4 Serjeants, 56 Rank and File, *killed*; 3 Serje- ...

File, *wounded*; 3 Serjeants, 61 Rank and File, *miſſing*.

LONDON CHRONICLE

December 22, 1778

Despite a strong engagement and demonstration of America's more professional army, the Battle of Monmouth resulted in the court-martial of American Major General Charles Lee for disorderly leadership.

EXTRACT *from the* TRIAL *of* MAJOR-GENERAL LEE.

Major-general Lord STIRLING, *Preſident.*—*Brigadier-generals*, Smallwood, Poor, Woodford, *and* Huntington. *Colonels*, Irvine, Shepherd, Swift, Wiggelſworth, Angel, Clarke, Williams, Febiger, *Members.*

JOHN LAWRENCE, *Judge Advocate.*

Brunſwick, July 4, 1778.

THE Judge Advocate produces the General's orders (Waſhington) for the court to ſit. The Preſident, Members, and Judge Advocate, being ſworn, the Judge Advocate proſecuting in the name of the United States of America, the court proceed to the trial of Major-general Lee, who appears before the court, and the following charges are exhibited againſt him: Firſt, for diſobedience of orders, in not attacking the enemy on the 28th of June, agreeable to repeated inſtructions. Secondly, for miſbehaviour before the enemy on the ſame day, by making an unneceſſary, diſorderly, and ſhameful retreat. Thirdly, for diſreſpect to the Commander in Chief in two letters, dated the 1ſt of July and the 28th of June.

Major-general Lee pleads, Not Guilty.

[The letters on which the third charge is founded are as follow:]

Sir, *Camp, Engliſh Town, July* 1.

FROM the knowledge I have of your Excellency's character, I muſt conclude, that nothing but the miſinformation of ſome very ſtupid or miſrepreſentation of ſome very wicked perſon, could have occaſioned your making uſe of ſo very ſingular expreſſions as you did, on my coming up to the ground where you had taken poſt: they implied, that I was guilty either of diſobedience of orders, of want of conduct, or want of courage: your Excellency will therefore infinitely oblige me, by letting me know on which of theſe three articles you ground your charge, that I may prepare for my juſtification, which I have the happineſs to be confident, I can do to the army, to the Congreſs, to America, and to the world in general. Your Excellency muſt give me leave to obſerve, that neither yourſelf nor thoſe about your perſon could, from your ſituation, be in the leaſt judges of the merits or demerits of our manœuvres, and, to ſpeak with a becoming pride, can aſſert, that to theſe manœuvres, the ſucceſs of the day was entirely owing: I can boldly ſay, that had we remained on the firſt ground, or had we advanced, or had the retreat been conducted in a manner different from what it was, the whole army and the intereſts of America would have riſked being ſacrificed. I ever had (and I hope ever ſhall have) the greateſt reſpect and veneration for Gen. Waſhington; I think him endued with many great and good qualities, but in this inſtance, I muſt pronounce, that he has been guilty of an act of cruel injuſtice towards a man, who certainly has ſome pretenſions to the regard of every ſervant of this country; and, I think, Sir, I have a right to demand ſome reparation for the injury committed; and unleſs I can obtain it, I muſt in juſtice to myſelf, when the campaign is cloſed (which I believe will cloſe the war), retire from a ſervice, at the head of which is placed a man, capable of offering ſuch injuries; but, at the ſame time, in juſtice to you, I muſt repeat, that I from my ſoul believe, that it was not a motion of your own breaſt, but inſtigated by ſome of thoſe *dirty earwigs*, who will for ever inſinuate themſelves near perſons in high office; for I am really convinced that, when Gen. Waſhington acts from himſelf, no man in his army will have reaſon to complain of injuſtice or indecorum.

His Excellency Gen. Waſhington.

Head Quarters, Engliſh Town, June 28.

Sir,

I RECEIVED your letter (dated through miſtake the 1ſt of July) expreſſed, as I conceive, in terms highly improper. I am not conſcious of having made uſe of any very ſingular expreſſions at the time of my meeting you, as you intimate. What I recollect to have ſaid, was dictated by duty, and warranted by the occaſion. As ſoon as circumſtances will permit, you ſhall have an opportunity, either of juſtifying yourſelf to the army, to Congreſs, to America, and to the world in general; or of convincing them, that you were guilty of a breach of orders, and of miſbehaviour before the enemy on the 28th inſtant, in not attacking them as you had been directed, and in making an unneceſſary, diſorderly, and ſhameful retreat. I am, Sir, your moſt obedient ſervant,

GEORGE WASHINGTON.

General Lee.

Sir, *Camp, June* 30.

SINCE I had the
letter by Col. Fi
have reflected on
and beg leave to
mutual convenie
ſhould be immedi
it might be a Cou
drawn into length
the neceſſary evid
on a paper war b
parties, which m
feuds on the conti
nor all your admi
from your love of
diately exhibit your
halt, I may be brough
your moſt obedient humble ſervant,

CHARLES LEE.

His Excellency General Waſhington.

The Court met by ſeveral adjournments till the 12th of Auguſt.

The Court having conſidered the firſt charge againſt Major General Lee, the evidence, and his defence, are of opinion, that he is guilty of diſobedience of orders, in not attacking the enemy on the 28th of June, agreeable to repeated inſtructions; being a breach of the latter part of article 5, ſec. 2, of the articles of war.

The Court having conſidered the ſecond charge againſt Major General Lee, the evidence and his defence, are of opinion he is guilty of miſbehaviour before the enemy on the 28th of June, by making an unneceſſary, and in ſome few inſtances a diſorderly retreat, being a breach of the 13th article, of the 13th ſec. of the articles of war.

The Court having conſidered the 3d charge againſt Major General Lee, are of opinion, that he is guilty of diſreſpect to the Commander in Chief in two letters dated 1ſt July and 28th of June, being a breach of the 2d art. 2d ſec. of the articles of war.

The Court do ſentence Major General Lee to be ſuſpended from any command in the armies of the United States of North America, for the term of 12 months.

STIRLING,
M. G. and Preſident.

The Court adjourn without day.

---

h ult. arrived here a Virginia pilot boat, which was cut out ur last Friday night, by 38 Bri- ho had effected their escape from here. The schooner had lately e West Indies, and had part of her d. These brave men, rendered e by the hard usage they receiv- els, had, some time before, pro- for their deliverance, and were ve boarded and brought off the , of 36 guns; but that vessel be- e draught of water, and all of inted with the channel, they to desist from the enterprize: wen, late prize-master of the formerly of this port having to get on shore last Thursday, iday night a large boat along-side hip, with which they boarded the re they found three rebels, (now hip here) a very small quantity and only ten gallons of wa- ork, and only ten gallons of wa- wever, on their passage, boarded el schooners, and obliged them to t of their provisions. Off the back d, they were chased by two rebel the southward of Barnegat, but n."

MERICA.

Aug. 18. It is reported tha tely concerted a plan to cut a woods from the Upper Caho river, to Canada, in order to arties into that province; a gly sent out, under the comma rk, but before they had m s they were surrounded b and totally routed: those ing in almost famished, in

or fo

from LLOYD'S LIST

Sir Charles Hardy ha all officers to be and prepare for wind, and fe

New-York; the proceeds with a fleet of victuallers.

"The Alexander, Monkhouse, from Granada to Halifax, was taken the 14th of July, by three American privateers, and carried into Casco Bay.

"The St. Carolo and Pedro, a Genoese ship, from Sallo to Ferrol, with 340 pipes of wine, designed for the use of the Spanish fleet, is taken and sent into Falmouth by the Union and Phœnix cutters belonging to Folkstone.

"The brig Hazard from Scotland, and a brig from Liverpool, the one of 18 and the other of 16 guns, are taken by Captain Manley, and sent into Boston.

"The Nancy privateer of New London, of 16 six-pounders, is taken by the Greyhound man of war, and sent into New York.

"The Snow Bristol Packet, loaded with dry goods, and the Dashwood Packet, Captain Roberts, who sailed from Falmouth with the June mail, are retaken by the Perseus man of war, Capt. Elphinston, and sent into New York; the mail thrown overboard.

Bank stock, $111\frac{7}{8}$. India ditto, $142\frac{3}{4}$. 3 per ct. b. red. —— Do. con. $61\frac{1}{4}$ a $\frac{3}{8}$. L. t. Tick. 13l. 14s. od Dub. Ex. $7\frac{5}{8}$.

EDINBURGH.

Extract of a letter from London, Oct.

Several letters from Amsterdam me Paul Jones was arrived in the Texel, Serapis and his other prizes, in a s

rliament, which is to meet on t mber, will only sit for a few supplies, and then adjourn for th

is still talked off, the terms o will be, to make America in altar to Spain, and G

ot has agreed to wo hundred thousan of Pondic

party of them had the assurance to come within a mile of this city, at a place called Paulus Hook, surprised and carried off with them a number of British and Hessian soldiers. Within these few days two rebel privateers have been sent in here by the Greyhound, frigate."

The following particulars, relative to the late engagement between Paul Jones and the Serapis man of war, may be depended on as authentic: when Jones first attacked the Serapis, he was a-head of his little fleet several leagues; notwithstanding this, he engaged with all the fury of a man determined to conquer or die. The engagement soon grew desperate, and Jones, besides having a great part of his crew shot round him, had his rigging on fire for about seven minutes. In this interval, the Captain of the Serapis, who was so near him as to be audible, called out to him to strike, or he must infallibly go to the bottom. Jones replied, with an oath, "I may sink, but I'll be d—d if I strike." At this instant, one of his men attempted to strike the colours, when Jones, turning round, shot him dead on the spot. Two more attempted the same thing, and met with the same fate; a mutiny then was expected to take place, as the ship was appr inking, when, fortunately for Jones, his squadron immediately came up t ce, which turned the ta- s on t and she was obliged to e, af degree of co uld, ty, have ssful enemy. A le ton in

CHAPTER X

CONQUER OR DIE

Introduction

Beyond the Atlantic coast of North America, important battles of the Revolutionary War were also fiercely fought in remote forts of the frontier, as far west as the Mississippi River, and even at the doorstep of Great Britain. George Rogers Clark, older brother to William Clark of Lewis and Clark fame, led the militia actions against British posts and their Indian allies in territories of modern day Ohio, Kentucky, Michigan, Indiana, and Illinois. Also on the western front, General John Sullivan led a force of 4,000 on a scorched-earth campaign through Iroquois country. Across the globe, American naval captain John Paul Jones, commanding the forty-two-gun *Bonhomme Richard*, was leading an effective maritime terror campaign against the British.

Edinburgh Advertiser
October 12, 1779

John Paul Jones's
Bonhomme Richard
vs the British *Serapis*
Library of Congress

REPORTING THE

REVOLUTIONARY WAR IN THE WEST AND GEORGE ROGERS CLARK

By John Reda

IN THE AUTUMN OF 1777, SEVERAL AMERICAN SETTLEMENTS in the future state of Kentucky were under siege. Hostile Indians, supplied and encouraged by British officials in Detroit, posed an ongoing threat to the very lives of the Americans. In desperation, twenty-six-year-old George Rogers Clark started for Virginia—where he had been born and raised—to pitch a desperate plan by which the American settlements might be protected. On his way east, Clark joined a party of seventy-six men and women who had given up on the West and were returning to their old homes.

Once in Virginia, Clark huddled with a group including Virginia's governor, Patrick Henry, as well as Thomas Jefferson, George Mason, and George Wythe. Clark had met a year earlier with these same men to request five hundred pounds of powder desperately needed for the defense of the western settlements. Now his plan involved a daring attack on British holdings in the Illinois Country. Clark explained to Virginia's leaders that spies he had sent to Illinois had returned with the news that the British fort in Kaskaskia was undefended and that the mostly French inhabitants of the scattered Illinois villages were lukewarm in their support of the British. Clark's ultimate target was Detroit, where Lieutenant Governor Henry Hamilton was coordinating the Indian attacks that were ravaging the frontier. Known to settlers as the "Hair Buyer," Hamilton was rumored to be paying a bounty for scalps taken in the raids. Clark's plan was to occupy Illinois as a stepping-stone to an attack on Detroit that might stop the Indian raids at their source.

With no hope of receiving help from the near destitute Continental Congress, Clark's appeal to Virginia's leaders reflected that state's claim on much of the West—based on its original colonial charter. Armed with the authorization for an expedition described to Virginia's Assembly as a defense of Kentucky, Clark headed west to recruit volunteers. His efforts met with meager results as most men already in the West were more concerned with protecting their families and farms than attacking British holdings.

When Clark set out on June 26, 1778, from the Falls of the Ohio (present-day Louisville), his forces numbered just 175 men, although all were buoyed by the recent news that France had formally agreed to join the American war against Great Britain. After traveling ten miles down the Ohio River, Clark and his men set off on foot on a 120-mile overland march to Kaskaskia, where they arrived on July 4, 1778, surprising the fort's commander, Rocheblave, and taking the town without losing a man. In fact, Clark's men did not even fire a shot. Gathering the inhabitants the next morning, Clark offered American citizenship to all willing to take an oath in support of the United States. The Kaskaskians, relieved to learn that the feared Americans meant them no harm, accepted Clark's offer and sent representatives ahead to the other Illinois villages where similar scenes ensued.

Two months later, Clark convened a council of Indians where he bluntly offered them a choice between war and peace. Although many would later again take up arms against the people they called the "Long Knives," the American Indians accepted Clark's offer and the winter of 1778–79 saw a marked decrease in Indian attacks against American settlements. In the meantime, however, Henry Hamilton led a British and Indian force down from Detroit to capture the American-held fort at Vincennes on the Wabash River.

In February 1779, Clark responded to Hamilton's move by collecting ninety American and eighty French volunteers for an excruciating 180-mile march across waterlogged lands to come to the relief of Vincennes. Wading for days through water often up to their chests, Clark's force surprised Hamilton and forced his surrender. The fort, now renamed Patrick Henry, was again in American hands.

Because of the distances involved, numerous inaccuracies about Clark's exploits made it into eastern newspapers. Contrary to an item in the *Connecticut Journal* (June 9, 1779), Clark did not put Hamilton to death, but rather placed him in custody and sent him east to be held as a prisoner of war at Virginia's capital of Williamsburg. Nor did Clark and his men move on to capture Fort Detroit, as claimed by the *Boston Gazette* (January 18, 1779). In fact, Clark spent much of the next three years trying to organize an expedition against Detroit but failing at any point to gather the necessary men or supplies to do so. Instead, as printed in Clark's own words by the *Pennsylvania Gazette* (October 25, 1780), the Americans had to settle for a 1780 attack against Indian villages north of the Ohio River. Clark led another such attack in 1782 before the 1783 Treaty of Paris brought the Revolutionary War to an end.

George Rogers Clark
and the March to Vincennes
North Wind Picture Archives

In February 1779, George Rogers Clark, with ninety American and eighty French volunteers, marched 180 miles across waterlogged lands to Vincennes.

WEDNESDAY, June 9, 1779. THE [NUMB. 603.

CONNECTICUT JOURNAL.

NEW-HAVEN: Printed by THOMAS and SAMUEL GREEN, near the College.

WILLIAMSBURG, (Virginia) May 15.

Extract of a letter from Col. Lawson, to his Excellency the Governor, dated Smithfield May 13.

"I Presume your Excellency by this time, is pretty well informed of the strength and movements of the enemy. From accounts which I have received, the cruel and horrid depredations and rapine committed on the unfortunate and defenceless inhabitants who have fallen within their reach, exceed almost every thing yet heard of within the circle of their tragic display of savage barbarity!—Houshold furniture, stock of all kinds, houses, and in short almost every species of perishable property, are effectually destroyed, with unrelenting fury, by those devils incarnate; murder, rape, rapine and violence, fill up the dark catalogue of their detestable transactions!—They surprised and took a small body of Frenchmen, at the Great-Bridge, whom they murdered immediately on the spot, to the amount of seven.—The feelings of humanity are deeply wounded with reflections, on the various and pointed cruelties exercised towards our suffering countrymen, and call aloud for the most strenuous exertions."

Extract of another letter from the same gentleman.

"On my way down from Smithfield, towards Suffolk, I met numbers of the unfortunate inhabitants flying from the rapid approach of the enemy, with such circumstances of distress, as language cannot paint.—I feel no pleasure (I believe your Excellency will think) in numerating and dwelling upon the distresses of our countrymen and fellow creatures; but on the present occasion, they exceed any thing in imagination. The enemy are now in possession of Suffolk, a part of

taing, who is constantly watching his motions, and will not quit it till he sees the end of it."

On the 6th instant, the brig Monmouth, Captain Ingersol, took the brig Constance, Capt. Devereaux, from N York to Surrinham; and the sloop Nancy, Capt. Bunyan, from Providence for New York; and the same

intercepted by the militia, fourteen killed & sixteen taken prisoners. The enemy have with them three thousand men only; and I have the pleasure to inform you that the militia of the lower counties are turning out with great alacrity."

Published by order of Congress,
CHARLES THOMSON, Secr'y.

MAY 25.

Extract of a letter from Baltimore, dated May 23.

"The town is nearly clear of all kinds of goods, and many families have moved out; many more daily moving. The militia are getting under arms, and march in freely if required. Our last advices from below are from Hampton, dated on Tuesday night after burning Suffolk and some Whig's houses in its vicinity, the enemy divided their force there, and marched part for South-Quay, and part for Smithfield, a little town higher up James's river. At the latter place our militia were collecting, tolerably well armed, and to all appearance anxious to meet the barbarians, who were commiting th... and wanton outrages on the... neighbours and countrymen. ... unjustly to brand an enemy wi... inhumanity, but alas! stubborn... ly justify the charge.—A ge... near Suffolk, assures me, they d... tleman of consequence, in bot... private life, (who is an inhabit... mond county and an old ac... yours, therefore it would be pa... particularize him) together wi... ters from their house, and car... board their shipping, and th... wretched father was loaded w... on board the same vessel, the still more wretch- ... were pos- ... of those ... as shot ... family, ... —s, ... as car- ... ot been ... 't rouse ... s. Ar- ... but is ... he Vir- ... ter, and ... enemy, ... aken in ... foregoing ... Goodrich is with them, and as insolent as ever. Our town will be cleared of stores and goods in a day or two, and then, if they visit us, we will give them a warm reception. It is time the Whigs should rouse; we have been too long languid and supine."

MAY 26.

post St. Vincent, was surprized in the garrison, by a party of Col. Clarke's men, and taken prisoner with all his people and stores; that the Governor and some others were certainly put to death, in consequence of their former cruelties; that a party of wariors, twenty in number, who had been sent to Kentuckey settlement, happened soon after to return, and not knowing of the Fort being re-taken, marched boldly within a few yards of it, expecting that their father (the Governor) was still there ready to receive them with open arms; but were prepared for their reception, killed eighteen the first fire, the other two made their escape with the news to Detroit. This is the third time we have received these accounts, and from different quarters."

In CONGRESS, May 28, 1779.

The Board of Treasury having reported, "That in their opinion it will be impracticable to carry on the war by paper emissions, at the present enormous expences of the

MAY 27.

Extract of a letter from Fort Pitt, dated May 14.

"The 11th inst. four Delaware Indians arrived here from Muskingum, and brought letters for Col. Broadhead; they say, that Henry Hamilton, Lieut. Governor of Detroit, having some time ago got possession of

four top-sail
sloops, about
number of sl
Last Lord
eight miles b
consisting of
infantry, wit

Committee of three, and ... they be directed to report a plan for the purpose.

The Members chosen, Mr. Dickenson, Mr. Huntington, and Mr. Burke.

Extract from the Minutes,
CHARLES THOMSON, Sec'ry.

In CONGRESS, May 28 1779.

WHEREAS, it is indispensibly necessary that the greatest oeconomy should be introduced in public expenditures.

Resolved, That a Committee of three be appointed to make strict enquiry into the establishments and contingent expences of the respective Boards and Departments, and to consider and report the retrenchments and reformations which shall appear to be practicable and expedient, and that they have power to call for returns from the offices, and for information from the officers of any Department, and to confer thereupon with the Commander in Chief.

The Members chosen, Mr. Dickenson, Mr. Sherman, and Mr. Scudder.

Extract from the Minutes.
CHARLES THOMSON, Sec'ry.

In CONGRESS, May 28 ...

CONNECTICUT JOURNAL (NEW HAVEN)

June 9, 1779

Because of the distances involved, numerous inaccuracies about George Roger Clark's exploits in the western frontier made it into eastern newspapers. Contrary to an item in the *Connecticut Journal* (June 9, 1779), Clark did not put Hamilton to death, but rather placed him in custody and sent him east to be held as a prisoner of war at Virginia's capital of Williamsburg.

WILLIAMSBURG, (Virginia) Nov 20.

Major Rogers Clark, the conqueror of the Illinois, has sent in the late Governor of the British settlement there, a Frenchman by birth, who is now in this city upon his parole, where he will be able to form a judgment of the friendly intentions of his nation to the United States of America, and see clearly the declining state of his employer's power on this continent, now ready to expire.—Major Clark, after regulating the affairs of his late conquest, and having received the submission of sundry Indian nations (many of them hitherto unknown to us) had marched with a chosen body of men and a number of Indian warriors, against Fort D'Etroit, which, from the best accounts, being in a very defenceless condition, and in great want of provisions, there is good reason to conclude is now reduced to the obedience of these States, which will put a finishing stroke to the British interests in these parts, and secure to us the friendship of all the Indian nations who have been chiefly issued out on their scalping expeditions from that abominable magazine. And indeed it appears, that the savages themselves began to suspect the boasted strength of the British Worthies, and to slacken in their readiness to serve them; for some time ago, on being summoned against our settlements, which they were told they could easily plunder and destroy, for that the Big Knives, as the Indians call the Americans, were no more to be dreaded than flies, one of their chiefs, to keep up the allegory, told them, that he had lately seen those very harmless flies turn into wasps and hornets, and sting the Great King's men most severely, and he should not be surprised to behold them quickly turn into snakes and swallow them up, as those animals are accustomed to serve the miserable and helpless frogs.

BOSTON GAZETTE

January 18, 1779

While George Roger Clark's ultimate target was Detroit, Clark and his men did not move on to capture Fort Detroit, as claimed by the *Boston Gazette* (January 18, 1779). In fact, Clark spent much of the next three years trying to organize an expedition against Detroit but failing at any point to gather the necessary men or supplies to do so.

is a man of nice ho-
the temptation was
ver his error.
ton and others were
, that Andre came
th a passport from a
consequently could
deputation compos-
Mr. Elliot, and Mr.
id, the true state of
m t Robinson, and
ch he reiterated the
ase as a personal fa-
l any friend of ours
g could have been
was used. The fact
and object of the
circumstances, there
with flags; and the
t to Mr. Anderson.
all the formalities,
y, the sanction of a

will not suffer themselves to be *persuaded to give up*, what they have thus become possessed of by virtue of one of the *wisest* laws of this State. A law essentially necessary to the safety of the lives and property of the people, who have a right to insist on the strictest adherence to it.

Oct. 12. Yesterday a ship of 20 guns, prize to the Mifflin privateer, arrived safe in port. She was bound from New-York to Newfoundland.

N E W - H A V E N, *October* 12.

Monday and Tuesday last, Admiral Arbuthnot's fleet left Gardner's-Bay, and stood to the eastward;—their destination not known, but supposed to be for Newport.

F I S H - K I L L, *October* 19.

By the arrival of yesterday's post from Albany, we have it reported, That Sir John Johnston had, with a party, said to be about 500 men, come down the Mohawk river, and advanced within six miles of Johnstown; when, hearing that a party of our three month's men lay there, he contented himself with burning a few houses, killing and carrying off some inhabitants—Another party of about 800, commanded by Major Carleton, nephew to Gen. Carleton, came down the Lakes from St. John's and

the enemy, are to be included.

R I C H M O N D, *(Virginia) October* 4.

Extract of a letter from Colonel George Rogers Clarke, to his Excellency the Governor, dated Louisville, August 22, 1780.

By every possible exertion, and the aid of Colonel Slaughter's corps, we compleated the number of 1000, with which we crossed the river at the mouth of Licking on the 1st day of August, and began our march the 2d. Having a road to cut for the artillery to pass for seventy miles, it was the 6th before we reached the first town, which we found vacated, and the greatest part of their effects carried off. The general conduct of the Indians on our march, and many other corroborating circumstances, proved their design of leading us on to their own ground and time of action. After destroying the crops and buildings of Chelcauthy, we began our march for the Picawey settlements, on the waters of the Big Miame, the Indians keeping runners continually before our advanced guards. At half past two in the evening of the 8th, we arrived in sight of the town and forts, a plain of half a mile in width laying between us. I had an opportunity of viewing the situation and motions of the enemy, near their works.

"I had scarcely time to make the necessary dispositions, before the action commenced on our left wing, and in a few minutes became almost general, with a savage fierceness on both sides. The confidence the enemy had in their own strength and certain victory, or the want of generalship, occasioned several neglects, by which those advantages were taken that proved the ruin of their army, being flanked two or three different times, drove from hill to hill in a circuitous direction for upwards of a mile and a half; at last took shelter in their strong holds and woods adjacent, when the firing ceased for about half an hour, until necessary preparations were made for dislodging them. A heavy firing again commenced, and continued severe until dark, by which time the enemy were totally routed. The cannon playing too briskly on their works, they could afford them no shelter. Our loss was about 14 killed and 13 wounded, theirs at least triple that number. They carried off their dead during the night, except 12 or 14 that lay too near our lines for them to venture. This would have been a most decisive stroke to the Indians, if unfortunately the right wing of our army had not been rendered useless for some time by an uncommon chain of rocks, that they could not pass, by which means part of the enemy escaped through the ground they were ordered to occupy.

"By a French prisoner we got the next morning, we learn that the Indians had been preparing for our reception ten days; moving their families and effects; that the morning before our arrival, they were 300 Warriors, Shawanese, Mingoes, Wiandatts, and Delawares. Several reinforcements coming that day, he did not know their numbers; that they were sure of destroying the whole of us; that the greatest part of the prisoners taken by Byrd were carried to Detroit, where there were only 200 regulars, having no provisions except green corn and vegetables. Our whole store at first setting out being only 300 bushels of corn, and 1500lb. of flour, having done the Shawanese all the mischief in our power, after destroying Picawey settlements, I returned to this post, having marched, in the whole, 480 miles in 31 days. We destroyed upwards of 800 acres of corn, besides great quantities of vegetables, a considerable proportion of which appear to have been cultivated by white men, I suppose for the purpose of supporting war parties from Detroit. I could wish to have had a small store of provisions, to have enabled us to have laid waste part of the Delaware settlements, and falling in at Pittsburgh, but the excessive heat and weak diet shewed the impropriety of such a step. Nothing could excel the few regulars and Kentuckyans that composed this little army, in bravery and implicit obedience to orders. Each company vying with the other who should be the most subordinate."

may if you can catch him."

The Governor of this State hath issued a proclamation,

P H I L A D E L P H I A, *October* 25.

Extract of a letter from his Excellency Governor Jefferson, of Virginia, to the President of Congress, dated Richmond, October 15, 1780, *six o'clock, P. M.*

S I R,

"I DO myself the pleasure of congratulating your Excellency on the small dawn of good fortune which at length appears in the south, as you will find by the dispatches I have the honour of inclosing to you, and which I this moment received from General Gates."

S I R, *Burk county, 2d October,* 1780.

"I am, at present, about 70 miles from Salisbury, in the fork of the Catabaw, with about 450 horsemen, in pursuit of Colonel Ferguson. On my crossing the Catabaw river I dispatched to different quarters for intelligence, and this evening I was favoured with this news, which you may depend on: That Colonel Clark, of the State of Georgia, with 100 riflemen, forced his way through South-Carolina to Georgia. On his route thither, being joined by 700 men, he proceeded to the town of Augusta, and has taken it with a large quantity of goods; but not finding it prudent to continue there, he has retreated to the upper parts of South-Carolina, in Ninety-six district, and made a stand with 800 brave men.

"This moment another of my expresses is arrived from

PENNSYLVANIA GAZETTE (PHILADELPHIA)

October 25, 1780

As printed in Clark's own words by the *Pennsylvania Gazette*, the Americans had to settle for a 1780 attack against Indian villages north of the Ohio River rather than continue on to Detroit. Clark led another such attack in 1782 before the 1783 Treaty of Paris brought the Revolutionary War to an end.

bert, Esquires.

Burlington county. Council, Peter Tallman, Esquire. Assembly, Thomas Fenimore, William Trent, William Hough, Esquires.

Gloucester county. Council, John Cooper, Esquire. Assembly, John Sparks, Thomas Rennard, Isaac Kay, Esquires.

Adjutant General, to &c. &c.

eptember 29, 1780.

OCTOBER 25, 1780

The PENNSYLVANIA GAZETTE

RICHMOND *(Virginia) October 4.*

Extract of a letter from Colonel George Rogers Clarke, to his Excellency the Governor, dated Louisville, August 22, 1780.

By every possible exertion, and the aid of Colonel Slaughter & corps, we completed the number of 1000, with which we crossed the river at the mouth of Licking on the 1st day of August, and began our march the 2d. having a road to cut for the artillery to pass for seventy miles, it was the 6th before we reached the first town, which we found vacated, and the greatest part of their effects carried off. The general conduct of the Indians on our march, and many other corroborating circumstances, proved their design of leading us on to their own ground and time of action. After destroying the crops and buildings Chelcauthy, we began our march for the Picawey settlements, on the waters of the Big Miame, the Indians keeping runners continually before our advanced guards. At half past two in the evening of the 8th, we arrived in sight of the town and forts, a plain of half a mile in width laying between us. I had an opportunity of viewing the situation and motions of the enemy, near their works.

"I had scarcely time to make the necessary dispositions, before the action commenced on our left wing, and in a few minutes became almost general, with a savage fierceness on both sides. The confidence the enemy had in their own strength and certain victory, or the want of generalship, occasioned several neglects, by which those advantages were taken that proved the ruin of their army, being flanked two or three different times, drove from hill to hill in a circuitous direction for upwards of a mile and a half; at last took shelter in their strong holds and woods adjacent, when the firing ceased for about half and hour, until necessary preparations were made for dislodging them. A heavy firing again commenced, and continued severe until dark, by which time the enemy were totally routed. The cannon playing too briskly on their works, they could afford them no shelter. Our loss was about 14 killed and 13 wounded, theirs at least triple that number. They carried off their dead during the night, except 12 or 14 that lay too near our lines for them to venture. This would have been a most decisive stroke to the Indians, if unfortunately the right wing of our army had not been rendered useless for some time by an uncommon chain of rocks, that they could not pass, by which means part of the enemy escaped through the ground they were ordered to occupy.

"By a French prisoner we got the next morning, we learn that the Indians had been preparing for our reception ten days; moving their families and effects; that the morning before our arrival, they were 300 Warriors, Shawanese, Mingoes, Wiandatts, and Delawares. Several reinforcements coming that day, he did not know their numbers; that they were sure of destroying the whole of us; that the greatest part of the prisoners taken by Byrd were carried to Detroit, where there were only 200 regulars, having no provisions except green corn and vegetables. Our whole store at first setting out being only 300 bushels of corn, and 1500lb. of flour, having done the Shawanese all the mischief in our power, after destroying Picawey settlements, I returned to this post, having marched, in the whole, 480 miles in 31 days. We destroyed upwards of 800 acres of corn, besides great quantities of vegetables, a considerable proportion of which appear to have been cultivated by white men, I suppose for the purpose of supporting war parties from Detroit. I could wish to have had a small store of provisions, to have enabled us to have laid waste part of the Delaware settlements, and falling in at Pittsburgh, but the excessive heat and weak diet shewed the impropriety of such a step. Nothing could excel the few regulars and Kentuckyans that composed this little army, in bravery and implicit obedience to orders. Each company vying with the other who should be the most subordinate.

REPORTING THE

SULLIVAN EXPEDITION

By Daniel J. Tortora

Britain recruited Indian allies with generous gifts and promised to halt the white settlers that overran native lands. Of the six members in the Iroquois Confederacy, Senecas, Mohawks, Onondagas, and Cayugas joined the British. Christian Tuscaroras and Oneidas sided with the Americans. Since the Battle of Oriskany, Colonel John Butler and Captain William Butler and their Tory militias, along with Mohawk Joseph Brant and his Iroquois, had decimated New York's Cherry Valley and Pennsylvania's Wyoming Valley. Frontiersmen refused to join the Continental Army because they feared for their families' safety, and Indian villages in the region fed and supplied the British army.

General George Washington wanted revenge. He wished to cut off the supplies of Indians and the British, to end the devastating frontier raids, and to free up land for American settlers. In 1779, he ordered an invasion of Indian towns in Northern Pennsylvania, the Finger Lakes, and the Genesee Valley in New York. The *London Chronicle* of October 19, 1779, details the pivotal events of the "Sullivan Expedition" of 1779.

With preparations for the campaign underway, on July 20, Mohawk Joseph Brant, with Indians and Tories, attacked Minisink (letter dated Philadelphia, August 19). A militia company overtook the attackers and a bloody engagement followed.

Major General John Sullivan marched from Easton, Pennsylvania. He traveled across the Poconos to Wyoming. He then followed the Susquehanna River north to Tioga. Brigadier General James Clinton marched west from Schenectady to Otsego Lake. The forces then combined. They had orders to "lay waste" to Indian villages and fields.

On August 11, Sullivan arrived at Tioga. The next day, Sullivan sent a detachment to burn the Indian town of Chemung. When the men completed their task, they chased some Iroquois. The Iroquois ambushed the soldiers, killing several and wounding fourteen.

On August 22, Clinton arrived at Tioga. The combined force of three thousand to four thousand left four days later. On August 29, near the Indian village of Newtown, 1,200 Tories and Indians hid in a breastworks concealed by saplings. Pennsylvania Continentals under Brigadier General Edward Hand, with some Virginia riflemen, detected the intended ambush. Sullivan ordered an attack. The *London Chronicle*'s coverage (October 19, 1779, dateline New York, September 1) exaggerates. In the battle that followed, Sullivan suffered three dead and thirty-nine wounded. The Tories and Iroquois narrowly escaped as the Americans took the high ground, but a dozen of the Tory-Indian force died, and two fell captive.

Sullivan's army then traversed dangerous terrain, burning Indian villages and destroying crops and orchards. Its only major setback involved an ambush set by Colonel John Butler and his Indians. They killed and mutilated most of the men in a small American detachment. Some reports claimed that the killers had even resorted to ritual cannibalism.

Meanwhile, Colonel Daniel Broadhead led Pennsylvanians up the Allegheny from Fort Pitt on August 11. The October 26, 1779, *Maryland Journal* details the expedition. Broadhead's men drove off Indian attackers fifteen miles north of Venango. They advanced "without the least interruption," destroying ten Indian villages before returning to Fort Pitt thirty-three days later.

Citing a shortage of supplies and fearing the dangerous paths, Sullivan ended his campaign in late September without linking up with Clinton and without attacking Fort Niagara. Sullivan, Clinton, and Broadhead destroyed fifty villages, 1,200 houses, vast cornfields, two hundred thousand bushels of grain, and ten thousand fruit trees.

Indians raided the frontier in 1780 and 1781, killing two hundred settlers, but Sullivan's expedition had permanently crippled the Iroquois. The expedition destroyed Britain's food supplies, and the British struggled to support five thousand Indian refugees. It prevented a British campaign in the region and also underscored the divisions that were not unique to New York: brother fought brother. Tribesman fought tribesman. And it secured land along the frontier for American settlers. Many Iroquois settled in Canada and never returned. The British ceded Iroquois lands to the Americans in the 1784 Treaty of Fort Stanwix. Patriot soldiers and speculators soon populated the Indian lands cleared by the Sullivan Expedition.

THE LONDON CHRONICLE for 1779. 375

...nse of the whole of the ...x against Mr. Tuffnell's ...e still continues to offer ...he county. ...his canvass, I do not ...for me to take any step ...n I made to Mr. Byng, ...of this month. I have ...the greatest respect, ...mble servant, &c.

NORTH."

...iverted on the conduct ...id, that it seemed the ...was shut against the ...and that his Lordship ...ownshend then came ...ery largely and freely ...oble Lord, and con... ...serving that his Lord... ...al to the county of ...ouse-tax bill, to which ...ur of being in op... ...and 200,000l. was ...ark, and Middles...

...ne through. Mr. ...ly voted into the ...nd proposed Tho. ...a candidate, who ...But Mr. Wood ...onour, on account ...e, which he...

unless it be drawn a prize of 500l. or upwards, in which case it will be entitled to a prize of

ONE THOUSAND POUNDS.

If the number is first drawn upon any of the first eight days of drawing, it will also be entitled to a prize of

FIVE HUNDRED POUNDS.

And if last drawn, to Sixty State Lottery Tickets, the numbers of which are printed, by which the

TWENTY THOUSAND POUNDS,

or any other prizes may be gained.

Mr. Sharman has procured a separate cheque for the Eight Guinea whole Classes of Half Guinea Policies, which explains, in the clearest manner, that most advantageous and much-approved adventure, by which the purchaser, at the expence of only EIGHT GUINEAS, has a chance equal to that of Six Whole Tickets, which cost above 80l. and may receive any of the following numerous and capital benefits, viz.

		£.
2 Prizes of	- -	20,000
3 ditto	- -	10,000

...er of ...bers ...two ...has ...nber ...chance

Besides the chance of the whole of both the *Twenty Thousand Pounds*, or any other prizes, and considerable benefits for every prize above 20l. through the whole Drawing, the single Half Guinea Policies have in the average value of the real Tickets allotted, and unquestionably...

AMERICAN NEWS.

YESTERDAY morning the New York Mail, which was brought by the Grenville packet-boat to Falmouth, was brought up to the General Post Office.

From the NEW YORK GAZETTE.

Philadelphia, Aug. 19. The following is an extract of a letter to Gen. Sullivan, dated Minisink, July 28. "I embrace the earliest opportunity to inform you, that on the 20th of this instant Joseph Brant, with a party of Tories and Indians, made an attack on Minisink killed four men, took 15 prisoners, burnt 10 dwelling-houses, one church, 11 barns, and one grist-mill, a large quantity of hay and grain, took a great quantity of horses and cattle, and much other plunder. The militia soon collected and pursued them, overtook them about 25 miles up Delaware, upon which a most bloody engagement began, which was continued at least four hours; the enemy were reinforced during the action, upon which our people were obliged to give way, with the loss of 40 of our best men; to wit, one Colonel, six Captains, seven or eight Lieutenant, and one Justice of Peace, who was my own son, and whom you was acquainted with."

Copy of a Letter to the Hon. Major General Sullivan, at Wyoming, dated Northumberland, July 29.

"The enemy yesterday made themselves masters of Fort Freeland, on the west branch of Susquehanna, upon terms of capitulation, viz. The garrison to remain prisoners of war, the whole garrison to be plundered by the Indians, and the women to go free.

"The number of the enemy appearing before the fort about 250; one third British, the residue savages, together with a corps de reserve at some distance of 100 men. The whole under the command of Capt. M'Donald.

"We have at Northumberland about 150 to oppose the enemy, and protect the women and children, whom it is impossible...

LONDON CHRONICLE

October 19, 1779

General George Washington wished to cut off the supplies of Indians and the British, to end the devastating frontier raids, and to free up land for American settlers. In 1779, he ordered an invasion of Indian towns in Northern Pennsylvania, the Finger Lakes, and the Genesee Valley in New York. Major General John Sullivan and Brigadier General James Clinton had orders to "lay waste" to Indian villages and fields.

MARYLAND JOURNAL (BALTIMORE)

October 26, 1779

Simultaneous to Sullivan's expedition, Colonel Daniel Broadhead led Pennsylvanians up the Allegheny from Fort Pitt on August 11. Broadhead's men drove off Indian attackers fifteen miles north of Venango. They advanced "without the least interruption," destroying ten Indian villages before returning to Fort Pitt thirty-three days later.

---

ormed, that the fleet under the
es Hardy, had put into Torbay
to wait for a reinforcement of
, which are to join him from
uth. The sudden return of our
sioned by their having received
united squadrons of France and
ips of the line, besides frigates.
Majesty last Tuesday sent for the
Lord Howe, and having closet-
jointly the command of the
Admirals demanded an hour's
ich they returned, and thank-
jesty's offer, on condition that
moved from the board of Admi-
nder his auspices they must ever
eir King and Country.

---

th-Carolina *Gazette*.

STOWN, *Sept.* 22.

ve had no direct advices from
ployed upon the Southern ex-
ly know, is, That Count d'Es-
troops as he thought necessary,
site to the Orphan-House, 12
in the night between the 11th
out the least opposition; and
ad been opened between him
that General Lincoln had been
intosh; and that the Head-
a week ago, were at Cherokee-
annah: That General Count
ith the cavalry, and had not
picket of the enemy, but also
aptains and three privates at
Maitland had abandoned Port-
whole force he had there, on
king off the trunnions from the
ied upwards of 200 men, leav-
groes, for want of means of
is embarkation was made ra-
he Vigilante, the Gallies, and
with an intent to push through
General Prevost at Savannah:

perintendant of Indian affairs)
ped falling into the General's

possible he could have any objection to what concerned the Lady; but the plate, he had been informed, was obtained in such a way from the Allies of his King, that he was confident the General could not mean to disgrace himself with keeping possession of it."

PHILADELPHIA, October 16.

Last Sunday arrived from Bordeaux (Old France) the ship General Mercer, Captain Robinson, and bro't in with her the ship Minerva, Capt. ———, from Halifax bound to Surinam, loaded with fish, &c.

Extract of a letter from Nantz, dated July 3, 1779.

"The French have 32,000 men at St. Malo, ready to embark; it is said they only wait the arrival of Compte D'Orvilliers in the Channel, accounts of which may be daily expected, as the wind has been for 36 hours past from the westward, and likely to continue. It is supposed that there is a descent intended on England or Ireland. It is reported that the ships the Spaniards were to furnish by compact, which is ten sail of the line, have joined D'Orvilliers, and that the Cadiz fleet sailed about the fifth ult. The sailing of the English fleet you'll find by the papers. The French have an army of 40,000 men on the frontiers of Holland, which will keep the Dutchman quiet, if even his inclination was to be troublesome."

Extract of a letter from a Gentleman in Bordeaux, dated July 22, 1779.

"We have no certain advices from the combined fleets, expect some very interesting; if any arrives before the present conveyances leave the river, shall embrace the opportunity to forward them. Mr. Wedderburne is nominated to succeed Lord Suffolk; other new nominations are daily expected in the different ministerial departments of that Kingdom.

"Advices from Spain agree in the determination of that Court on the blockade of Gibraltar.

"An army is marching into Flanders, under the command of Monsieur, said to pay a visit to Hanover, and thereby oblige that Electorate to recal her troops in the pay of Britain from Minorca and Gibraltar, or to watch the Dutch, and hold them to a strict neutrality."

Extract of a letter from Bordeaux, dated July 20, 1779.

"The grand French fleet, consisting of 32 sail of the
th of June.
coast of
e Dutch
he coast
as a de-
l of the
he line,
adiz the
ish Am-
ain have
he line,
nation not
known.

"On the ninth of July arrived at Brest, a fleet of

our route upon its banks. But here our march was rendered still more difficult by the mountains which jutted close upon the river, forming a continued narrow defile, allowing us only the breadth of an Indian path to march upon. In the midst of one of these defiles, our advanced party, consisting of 15 white men & Delawares, discovered between 30 landing from their canoes, who having also seen part of our troops, immediately stripped themselves and prepared for action. Lieutenant Harding, who commanded our advance, disposed his men in a semicircular form, and began the attack with such irresistible fury, tomahawk in hand, that the Savages could not long sustain the charge, but fled with the utmost horror and precipitation, some plunging themselves into the river, and others, favoured by the thickness of the bushes, made their escape on the main, leaving five dead on the field, without any loss on our side, except three men slightly wounded. Upon the first alarm, supposing it to be more serious, the army was arranged for fight, both officers and men, enraged at their former cruelties, and animated by the calmness, resolution and intrepidity of the commandant, shewed the utmost ardor to engage; and had the action been general, we had every prospect of the most ample success from a brave commander, at the head of brave men. Continuing our march, we arrived the same day at Buchaloons, where leaving our baggage, stores, &c. under a guard, proceeded to their towns with the utmost despatch, which we found at the distance of about twenty miles farther, with extensive corn-fields on both sides of the river, but deserted by the inhabitants on our approach. Eight towns we set in flames, and committed their pagod and war posts to the river; the corn was our next object, which, in three days, we cut down and piled into heaps, amounting in the whole to near 600 acres, without the least interruption from the enemy.

"Upon our return we several times crossed a creek about ten miles above Venango, remarkable for an oily liquor, which oozes from the sides and bottom of the channel, and the adjacent springs, much resembling British oil, and if applied to woolen cloth, burns it in an instant.

"After burning the old towns of Conauwago and Mahusquachiakoeken, we arrived at Pittsburgh the 14th inst. with the scalps we had taken, and 30,000 dollars worth of plunder, having in the course of 33 days compleated a march of near 400 miles, through a country the Indians had hitherto thought impenetrable by us, and considered as a sufficient barrier for the security of their towns, and indeed nothing but the absolute necessity of such a measure, and a noble spirit of enterprize, could be a sufficient inducement to undertake so arduous a task, and encounter those difficulties and obstacles which require the most consummate fortitude to surmount."

IN CONGRESS, October 14, 1779.

Resolved, That the thanks of Congress be given to His Excellency General Washington, for directing, and to Major-General Sullivan, and the brave officers and soldiers under his command, for effectually executing

OCTOBER 26, 1779

The MARYLAND JOURNAL

Extract of a letter from Pittsburgh, September 16, 1779.

"The many savage barbarities and horrid depredations, committed by the Seneca and Muncy Nations upon the Western frontiers, had determined Col. Broadhead, as the most effectual way to prevent such hostilities in the future, and revenge the past, to carry the war into their own country, and strike a decisive blow at their towns.

"On the 11th of August, our little army, consisting only of six hundred and five, rank and file, marched from Pittsburgh with one month's provision; at Mahoning, 15 miles above the Old Kittanning, we were detained four days by the excessive rains, from whence (leaving the river which rolls in a thousand meanders) we proceeded by a blind path leading to Cuscushing, thro' a country almost impassible, by reason of the stupendous heights and frightful declivities, with a continued range of craggy hills, overspread with fallen timber, thorns and underwood, here and there an intervening valley, whose deep impenetrable gloom has always been impervious to the piercing rays of the warmest sun. At Cuscushing (which is 15 miles above Venango) we crossed the Alleghany, and continued our route upon its banks. But here our march was rendered still more difficult by the mountains which jutted close upon the river, forming a continued narrow defile, allowing us only the breadth of an Indian path to march upon. In the midst of one of these [...] our advanced party, consisting of 15 white men [...] Delawares, discovered between [...] landing from their canoes, who having also seen part of our troops, immediately stripped themselves and prepared for action. Lieutenant Harding, who commanded our advance, disposed his men in a semincircular form, and began the attack with such irresistible fury, tomahawk in hand, that the Savages could not long sustain the charge, but fled with the utmost horror and precipitation, some plunging themselves into the river, and others, savoured by the thickness of the bushes, made their escape on the main, leaving five dead on the field, without any loss on our side, except three men slightly wounded. Upon the first alarm, supposing it to be more serious, the army was arranged for fight, both officers and men, enraged at their former cruelties, and animated by the calmness, resolution and intrepidity of the commandant, shewed the utmost ardor to engage; and had the action been general, we had every prospect of the most ample success from a brave commander, at the head of brave men. Continuing our march, we arrived the same day at Buchaloons, where leaving our baggage, stores, &c. under a guard, proceeded to their towns with the utmost dispatch, which we found at the distance of about twenty miles farther, with extensive corn fields on both sides of the river, but deserted by the inhabitants on our approach. Eight towns we set in flames, and committed their pagod and war posts to the river; the corn was our next object, which, in three days, we cut down and piled into heaps, amounting in the whole to near 600 acres, without the least interruption from the enemy.

"Upon our return we several times crossed a creek about ten miles above Venango, remarkable for an oily liquor, which ouzes from the sides and bottom of the channel, and the adjacent springs, much resembling British oil, and if applied to woolen cloth, burns it in an instant.

"After burning the old towns of Conauwago and Mahusquachiakouken, we arrived at Pittsburgh the 14th inst. with the scalps we had taken, and 30,000 dollars worth of plunder, having in the course of 33 days compleated a march of near 400 miles, through a country the Indians had hitherto thought impenetrable by us, and considered as sufficient barrier for the security of their towns, and indeed nothing but the absolute necessity of such a measure, and a noble spirit of enterprize, could be a sufficient inducement to undertake so arduous a task, and encounter those difficulties and obstacles which require the most consummate fortitude to surmount."

Courses of John Paul Jones's Ships
North Wind Picture Archives

John Paul Jones's two cruises into British waters with Continental ships *Ranger* (1778) and *Bonhomme Richard* (1779).

Reporting the

Battle of Flamborough Head and John Paul Jones

By Dennis M. Conrad

Joseph Callo, a recent biographer of John Paul Jones, has written of the battle between the Continental ship *Bonhomme Richard* and HMS *Serapis* that took place on September 23, 1779, off Flamborough Head, a promontory on England's Yorkshire coast:

> *"It was an isolated struggle, albeit a particularly bloody one, between two ships that weren't even large enough to be classified as capital ships in the age of sail.... [but it] was to the naval component of the American Revolution what the battle of Saratoga was to the land campaign—it changed everything. The battle's unlikely outcome broadcast to the world that the American Continental Navy not only could fight, it could fight and win."*

John Paul Jones was "projecting power" and bringing the war to England. The October 4, 1779, *Birmingham Gazette* report is correct in suggesting that Jones had planned to capture a British city or port town and hold it hostage for ransom. Earlier in the cruise, Jones had tried to capture Leith, the port city for Edinburg, and when thwarted by bad weather had sailed to Newcastle-on-Tyne with the intention of seizing its waterfront and burning the British collier fleet loading there but was dissuaded by the captains of other vessels in his squadron who argued that the attempt was too risky. By the time of the battle, Jones had given up his plans and was preparing to sail to Texel, where a French fleet of merchantmen awaited escort, when his lookouts spied the Baltic fleet approaching Flamborough. This fleet was valuable as it carried naval stores—canvas, rope, and timber—essential to equip the Royal Navy, so Jones decided to attack it.

As the newspaper accounts indicate, the action was long, obstinate, and bloody, although whether the *Alliance* helped or hurt the American cause is still debated. Jones's answer when asked if he was prepared to surrender is probably what was reported in the *Edinburg Advertiser* of October 12, 1779. However, Richard Dale, an officer serving with Jones, in a book written long after the battle, quoted Jones as saying "I have not yet begun to fight," and those words are now immortalized. Contrary to the report in the *Birmingham Gazette* of October 4, 1779, Jones did not shoot members of his crew. When he found two petty officers trying to lower the flag, he ran at them shouting "stop them, shoot them," but when he discovered his pistols were unloaded he threw them at the sailors, knocking one senseless, but he did not shoot or kill them. Portraying Jones as a merciless brute and pirate was a staple of British press coverage of him.

Finally, the newspaper accounts are correct that the shaken Royal Navy leadership sent warships—at least eight—to capture Jones. Arriving at Flamborough Head after Jones had departed, some of the British warships sailed northeast toward Scandinavia, others southeast toward France, and still others cruised British waters, but none spotted Jones's squadron, which zigzagged in the North Sea for ten days and then sailed directly to Texel, the deep-water anchorage for Amsterdam, a neutral, and therefore safe, port.

SATURDAY's POST.

LONDON, Thursday, Sept. 30.

Some Particulars of the Proceedings of PAUL JONES's *Squadron.*

A LETTER from Bridlington, dated Sept. 24, ſays, "I doubt not but you have heard of the alarming Situation we have been in ſince Tueſday Night; but thank God, as yet we have been only terrified by this Paul Jones. An Engagement took Place at ſeven laſt Night, and continued till two this Morning, between the Serapis Frigate of 44 Guns, aſſiſted by the Counteſs of Scarborough armed Ship of 22 Guns, and Paul Jones's Ship, the Bonne Homme of 44 Guns, with ſome ſmaller Veſſels, off Flamborough head, and I am ſorry to ſay that Jones hath now our two Ships with their Commanders, who diſtinguiſhed themſelves in a moſt gallant Manner, though obliged at laſt to ſurrender to ſuperior Force, after having made almoſt a Wreck of Jones's own Ship. The Serapis had her Maſts ſhot away. Several Sailors made their Eſcape, and have been examined this Afternoon at the Key, but their Stories are different as to Jones's Loſs; ſome of them ſay he had 140 Men killed, and his Ship quite a Wreck. They ſay his Deſign was to deſtroy Scarborough, Bridlington, and Hull, with ſome other Places; and that he intended landing at Flamborough Yeſterday Morning, but the Sea ran too high."

A Letter from Hull, dated Sept. 26, which may be depended on, ſays, "A little paſt five this Afternoon an Expreſs arrived from Mr. Foſter, of Bridlington, to the Mayor of this Place, which relates, that between Eight and Nine this Morning, Paul Jones, with his Fleet, was ſeen off Flamborough Head, ſteering to the Northward; that he was ſcarcely out of Sight, when three Frigates, two large armed Ships, and two Sloops appeared there, (ſent by the Admiralty) who immediately purſued the ſame Courſe after him, and we are in the moſt ſanguine Expectation of hearing an Account of Jones and his

BIRMINGHAM GAZETTE (ENGLAND)
October 4, 1779

John Paul Jones was "projecting power" and bringing the war to England. The *Birmingham Gazette* report is correct in suggesting that Jones had planned to capture a British city or port town and hold it hostage for ransom. Contrary to the report, Jones did not shoot members of his crew.

Service, made the Remainder drunk, ſent them on Shore by their own Deſire, brought the Ship into the Humber, and ſhe is now in our Dock. We are this Day (Sunday) at Work in mounting 28 Pieces of Cannon, viz. 20 Eighteen pounders, the reſt of a ſmaller Size. The Marquis

On Tueſday morning his
of Wales, and the Biſhop
the Diverſion of Stag-hunti
reſt.

Monſ. le Comte D'Orvilli
ſigned the Command of the c
France and Spain, as ſome Tin
in this Paper, it being confirm
Journal of the 15th Inſtant.
Article. viz-

"Monſ. le Comte d'Orvilli
ed the Kings Permiſſion to re
of the Naval Armament, h
cepted of his Reſignation; an
Duchauffault is named his S
Command: this Officer w
vered of the Wound he rece
ment off Uſhant, arrived h

Lord S——— has aſſure
within theſe few Days, t
reſpecting the home Defe
engage to have 64 Ships c
proceed to Sea by the 15t

According to Letters fr
have been given there for
of the Troops of that Elec
embark for America early i
Prince Charles of Meckle
Brother, goes along with t

A Letter from Portſmo
ſays, "This Day arrived ſ
The reſt of the Convoy, c
100 Sail, were left well 20
of Scilly, under the Care o
and a Sloop of War. Th
Capt. Cornwallis, put into
40 Men killed in the Acti

Another Letter from Po
Pearl Frigate, of 32 Guns,
George Mountagu, from
in here, a Spaniſh Frigate,
ers, and two ſix Pounders,
the St. Dominique. She
tern Iſlands after a bloody
Hours and a Half, in whic
had 18 Men killed and 5
wounde

TS
gh H
s of
. 9, a
of Ne
Wigan
Herm
Wm.
r.—J
rchant
Andi
ilſon
Fryer o
Cheeſemonger.

DIVIDENDS *to be ma*

Oct. 15, Peter Nouaille of
Silk-merchant.——8, Nathan
Lancaſhire, Fuſtian-manufactu
mas late of Briſtol, but now o
Dealer.—11, George Hudſon

into the Humber, and ſhe is now in our Dock. We are this Day (Sunday) at Work in mounting 28 Pieces of Cannon, viz. 20 Eighteen pounders, the reſt of a ſmaller Size. The Marquis of Rockingham has been here ſome Days, and has had ſeveral Meetings with the Gentlemen of the Town reſpecting its defenceleſs State. A Man who eſcaped from Jones's Ship has made Oath before the Mayor, that Jones ſtood on the Quarter-Deck with a Brace of Piſtols, and ſhot ſome of his own Men during the Action."

By an Affadavit made by Thomas Berry on 24th Inſtant, before Humphrey Oſbaldiſton, one of his Majeſty's Juſtices of the Peace for the Eaſt-Riding of Yorkſhire, it appears, that Paul Jones's Squadron had been ſix Days between Berwick and the Humber, and his declared Intentions were to make a Deſcent ſomewhere on the Coaſt; that on Tueſday he ordered all his Oars to be muffled, and the Boats ready to be hoiſted out; that on Wedneſday Morning the Alliance and Pallas rejoined Jones off Flamborough-Head: and on Thurſday Evening about ſeven o'Clock, they met with the Eaſt-Country Fleet, convoyed by a 40 Gun Ship, and an armed Ship, the 40 Gun Ship engaged Jones alone about 4 Hours, till Jones's Fire ceaſed; having been ſeveral Times on Fire and very near ſinking, he called to the Alliance for Aſſiſtance, which came up, and gave the 40 Gun Ship a Broadſide, which being totally diſabled ſtruck. Jones's Officers called to the Alliance to hoiſt out their Boats, as their Ship was ſinking, in one of which the Deponent and Six other Men made their Eſcape to Filey.

In the Engagement between the Serapis and Paul Jones, his Veſſel was ſo diſabled, that the Captain of the Serapis called out to Jones to ſtrike, or elſe he would ſink him. To which the latter replied, "that he might if he could; for whenever the Devil was ready to take him, he would rather obey his Summons, than ſtrike to any one." And if another of Jones's Squadron had not come to his Aſſiſtance, he would ſoon have gone to the Bottom. The foregoing Account is from the Affidavits of ſeven Seamen who made their Eſcape after the Engagement, before the Mayor of Hull; and they add, that during the Engagement, **Paul Jones** (who was dreſſed in a ſhort Jacket and long Trowſers, with about a Dozen of charged Piſtols ſlung in a Belt round his Middle, and a Cutlaſs in his Hand) ſhot ſeven of his Men for deſerting from their Quarters; and to his Nephew whom he thought a little daſtardly, he ſaid, that "D—n his Eyes, he would not blow his Brains out, but he would pepper his Shins," and had actually the Barbarity to ſhoot at the Legs of the Lad, who is a Lieutenant on board Jones's Ship.

It was this Morning aſſerted as a Fact in the City, that Paul Jones's Ship abſolutely ſunk before the Engagement with the Seraphis was over, and that he got on board another Ship, of equal Force, not above three Minutes before his Ship went to the Bottom.

No Accounts whatever were received of Paul Jones by the ſeveral Mails which came to the Poſt Office this Day, nor by any Expreſs or other-

Silk-mercha
Lancaſhire,
mas late of
Dealer.—1
Ironmonger
London, Gl
ſquare, Lon
ter, Suſſex,
and Nathan
19, Wm. F
21, Thomas
Wm. Hook
Cooper.—1
Maſter, Ma
of Rippon,
Wood-ſtree
and Wright
ler.——8,
church-ſtree
Mumford-c
Certificat
minſter, Gr
ceſter, Wo

STA

The T
ſtamped at
liament, ar
NICHOLS
Lottery Off
where ſix C
and ſhared
No. 31,591,
each, beſide
Alſo thei
Guinea, H
each, ſimil
(on which
of upwards
liament-ſtre
Farmer, at
to Mr. Lan
proved for t
more from
gained in a
as theſe Pla
leaſt Riſk b
preſumed w
Adventurer
be had grat
to any Th
Whole Tin
others are.
THE
l.
Half, 7
Quarter, 3
Eighth, 1
Sixteenth
Beſides the
Schemes
neſs relative
with that
that cannot
Public.
The Lotte

HOR
mov
Cornhill, t
near the S
ſincere tha
in the laſt
candid plan
advantageo
cure and be
gain a conſ
SHILLIN
the courſe
ſuch polic

OCTOBER 4, 1779

Aris's

BIRMINGHAM GAZETTE

SATURDAY's POST.

LONDON, Thursday, Sept. 30.

Some Particulars of the Proceedings of Paul Jones's *Squadron.*

A LETTER from Bridlington, dated Sept. 24, says, " I doubt not but you have heard of the alarming Situation we have been in since Tuesday Night ; but thank God, as yet we have been only terrified by this Paul Jones. An Engagement took Place at seven last Night, and continued till two this Morning, between the Serapis Frigate of 44 Guns, and Paul Jones's Ship, the Bonne Homme of 44 Guns, with some smaller Vessels, off Flamborough head, and I am sorry to say that Jones hath now our two Ships with their Commanders, who distinguished themselves in a most galant Manner, though obliged at last to surrender to superior Force, after having made almost a Wreck of Jones's own Ship. The Serapis had her Masts shot away. Several Sailors made their Escape, and have been examined this Afternoon at the Key, but their Stories are different as to Jones's Loss ; some of them say he had 140 Men killed, and his Ship quite a Wreck. They say his Design was to destroy Scarborough, Bridlington, and Hull, with some other Places ; and that he intended landing at Falmborough Yesterday Morning, but the Sea ran too high. "

A Letter from Hull, dated Sept. 26, which may be depended on says, "[...] A Man who escaped from Jones's Ship has made Oath before the Mayor, that Jones stood on the quarter-Deck with a Brace of Pistols, and shot some of his own Men during the Action."

By an Affadavit made by Thomas Berry on 24th Instant, before Humphrey Osbaldiston, one of his Majesty's Justices of the Peace for the East-Riding of Yorkshire, it appears, that Paul Jones's Squadron had been six Days between Berwick and the Humber, and his declared Intentions were to make a Descent somewhere on the Coast ; that on Tuesday he ordered all his Oars to be muffled, and the Boats ready to be hoisted out ; that on Wednesday morning the Alliance and Pallas rejoined Jones off Flamborough-Head : and on Thursday Evening about seven o'Clock, they met with the East-Country Fleet, convoyed by a 40 Gun Ship, and an armed Ship, the 40 Gun Ship engaged Jones alone about 4 Hours, till Jones's Fire ceased ; having been several Times on Fire and very near sinking, he called on the Alliance for Assistance, which came up, and gave the 40 Gun Ship a Broadside, which being totally disabled struck. Jones's Officers called to the Alliance to hoist out their Boats, as their Ship was sinking, in one of which the Deponent and Six other Men made their Escape to Filey.

In the Engagement between the Serapis and Paul Jones, his Vessel was so disabled, that the Captain of the Serapis called out to Jones to strike, or else he would sink him. To which the latter replied, " That he might if he could ; for whenever the Devil was ready to take him, he would rather obey his summons, than strike to any one." And if another of Jones's Squadron had not come to his Assistance, he would soon have gone to the Bottom. The foregoing Account is from the Affidavits of seven Seamen who made their escape after the Engagement, before the Mayor of Hull ; and they add, that during the Engagement, Paul Jones (who was dressed in a short Jacket and long Trowsers, with about a Dozen of charged Pistols slung in a Belt round his Middle, and a Cutlass in his Hand) shot seven of his Men for desrting from their Quarters ; and to his Nephew whom he thought a little dastardly, he said, that " D—n his Eyes, he would not blow his Brains out, but would pepper his Shins," and had actually the Barbarity to shoot at the Legs of the Lad, who is a Lieutenant on board Jones's Ship.

convoy of the Jaſon of 34 guns, the Queen of 20, and Beaver's prize of 14."

Extract of a letter from New-York, dated Aug. 12.

" I arrived here about a month ago, to a very glutted market for proviſions. The Yankies are perplexing us greatly ; a few nights ago, a party of them had the aſſurance to come within a mile of this city, at a place called Paulus Hook, ſurpriſed and carried off with them a number of Britiſh and Heſſian ſoldiers. Within theſe few days two rebel privateers have been ſent in here by the Greyhound, frigate."

The following particulars, relative to the late engagement between Paul Jones and the Serapis man of war, may be depended on as authentic : when Jones firſt attacked the Serapis, he was a-head of his little fleet ſeveral leagues ; notwithſtanding this, he engaged with all the fury of a man determined to conquer or die. The engagement ſoon grew deſperate, and Jones, beſides having a great part of his crew ſhot round him, had his rigging on fire for about ſeven minutes. In this interval, the Captain of the Serapis, who was ſo near him as to be audible, called out to him to ſtrike, or he muſt infallibly go to the bottom. Jones replied, with an oath, " I may ſink, but I'll be d—d if I ſtrike." At this inſtant, one of his men attempted to ſtrike the colours, when Jones, turning round, ſhot him dead on the ſpot. Two more attempted the ſame thing, and met with the ſame fate ; a mutiny then was expected to take place, as the ſhip was apparently ſinking, when, fortunately for Jones, another of his ſquadron immediately came up to his aſſiſtance, which turned the tables on the Serapis, and ſhe was obliged to ſtrike, after exerting a degree of courage which would, in all probability, have made her ſucceſsful with any other enemy.

A letter from Preſton in Lancaſhire, dated

grain, wool, &c. made a conſiderable abatement in their rents, to the inexpreſſible joy of them all.

The Hazard letter of marque belonging to Glaſgow, and a Liverpool ſhip, are taken by the rebel Captain Manley, and carried into Boſton.

EDINBURGH ADVERTISER

October 12, 1779

As the newspaper accounts indicate, the action was long, obstinate, and bloody. Jones's answer when asked if he was prepared to surrender is probably what was reported in the *Edinburgh Advertiser* of October 12, 1779. However, Richard Dale, an officer serving with Jones, in a book written long after the battle, quoted Jones as saying "I have not yet begun to fight," and those words are now immortalized.

The

EDINBURGH ADVERTISER

Extract of a letter from New-York, dated Aug. 12.

" I arrived here about a month ago, to very glutted market for provisions. The Yankies are perplexing us greatly ; a few nights ago, a party of them had the assurance to come within a mile of this city, at a place called Paulus Hook, surprised and carried off with them a number of British and Hessian soldiers. Within these few days two rebel privateers have been sent in here by the Greyhound, frigate."

The following particulars, relative to the late engagement between Paul Jones and the Serapis man of war, may be depended on as authentic : when Jones first attacked the Serapis, he was a-head of his little fleet several leagues; notwithstanding this, he engaged with all the fury of a man determined to conquer or die. The engagement soon grew desperate, and Jones, besides having a great part of his crew shot round him, had his rigging on fire for about seven minutes. In this interval, the Captain of the Serapis, who was so near him as to be audible, called out to him to strike, or he must infallibly go to the bottom. Jones replied, with an oath, " I may sink, but I'll be d—d if I strike. " At this instant, one of his men attempted to strike the colours, when Jones, turning round, shot him dead on the spot. Two more attempted the same thing, and met with the same fate ; a mutiny then was expected to take place, as the ship was apparently sinking, when, fortunately for Jones, another of his squadron immediately came up to his assistance, which turned the tables on the Serapis, and she was obliged to strike, after exerting a degree of courage which would, in all probability, have made her successful with any other enemy.

A LIST of SHIPS TAKEN or DESTROYED by our ENEMIES or by ACCIDENT, within the Space of the last five Years.

Guns.	Ships Names.	Year.	Where, and by whom, taken, or destroyed.
14	Ferret	1774	On the Jamaica station, lost with all the crew.
14	Pomona	1776	On the Antigua station, lost with all the crew.
32	Repulse		On her passage from New York to the West Indies, lost, all her crew.
28	Actæon		Burnt near Charlestown, having run ashore.
64	Augusta	1777	Burnt near Philadelphia, a few of the crew perished.
20	Vestal		Lost on the Newfoundland station, with their crews.
16	Pegasus		
16	Merlin		Burnt near Philadelphia, the crew saved.
8	Cruiser		Burnt on the coast of Carolina, the crew saved.
8	Savage		Lost near Louisburgh, the crew saved, except two.
70	Somerset	1778	Lost near Boston, with part of the crew.
32	Minerva		Taken on the Jamaica station, by a French ship of 50 guns.
32	Flora		Burnt at Rhode Island, to prevent their falling into the hands of the French fleet, the crews saved.
32	Juno		
32	Lark		
32	Orpheus		
28	Cerberus		Ditto.
28	Mermaid		Lost near Philadelphia, attempting to escape the French fleet, the crew saved.
28	Liverpool		Lost near New York, the crew saved.
28	Syren		Lost near Rhode Island, the crew saved.
28	Active		Taken on the Jamaica station by two French frigates.
28	Fox		Taken in the Channel by a French frigate of 36 guns.
20	Lively		Taken by several French frigates.
20	Mercury		Lost near New York, the crew saved.
16	King's Fisher		Burnt at Rhode Island, to prevent her falling into the hands of the French, the crew saved.
16	Otter		Lost near St. Augustine, the crew saved.
16	Senegal		Taken by the French fleet near Rhode Island.
16	Drake		Taken by Paul Jones near Belfast.
16	Thunder Bomb		Taken by the French fleet near Rhode Island.
8	Zephyr		Taken by the French in the Mediterranean.
64	Ardent	1779	Taken by the combined fleets near Plymouth.
44	Serapis		Taken by Paul Jones near Hull.
32	Quebec		Burnt near Ushant, in an engagement with a French frigate of 40 guns, and only 30 of the crew saved.
32	Montreal		Taken by two French 74 gun ships in the Mediterranean.
32	Arethusa		Lost near Brest, the crew saved.
26	Supply storeship		Burnt in the West Indies, the crew saved.
20	Glasgow		
20	Countess of Scarborough		Taken by Paul Jones near Hull, the crew saved.
16	Ceres		Taken on the Antigua station by a French frigate of 36 guns.
16	Weazle		Taken near St. Eustatia.
12	York		Taken at the Grenades by the French.

Total number, one of 70 guns, two of 64, one of 44, nine of 32, seven of 28, one of 26, five of 20, eight of 16, two of 14, one of 12, three of 8, and one bomb.

I believe the Zebra of 16 guns was lost with the Somerset, and the Swift of 16, since, near Virginia. There are also several armed vessels, such as brigs, schooners, cutters, &c.

A LIST of SHIPS TAKEN or DESTROYED from the FRENCH, SPANIARDS and AMERICANS.

AMERICANS.

Guns.	Ships Names.	Year.	Where, and by whom, taken, or destroyed.
32	Delaware	1777	Taken near Philadelphia, by the army.
32	Hancock		Taken near Halifax, by the Rainbow of 44 guns.
36	Randolph	1778	Blown up near Barbadoes, in an engagement with the Yarmouth of 64 guns, and only five of the crew saved.
32	Raleigh		Taken near Boston, by the Experiment of 50 guns, and Unicorn of 20, the crew saved.
26	Warren	1779	Burnt, with sixteen others of inferior force, at Penobscot, by Sir George Collier's fleet.
40	Bon Homme Richard		Sunk in an engagement with the Serapis of 44 guns, which she took before she went down.

FRENCH.

Guns.	Ships Names.	Year.	Where, and by whom, taken, or destroyed.
32	Licorne	1778	Taken by Admiral Keppel's fleet in the Channel.
32	Pallas		

Tuesday, the 16th Nov. will be published,

plate,

Also a New London Sheet Almanack, printed o aRoyal Paper. To which is added, The Court an City Register for 1780; containing the names o the Lords and Commons in Parliament, and thei town residences. With other useful Lists an Tables.

And the following BOOK ALMANACKS,

The Gentleman's Diary	Season on the Seasons
The Ladies Diary	Tycho Wing's Almanac
Fran. Moore's Almanack	White's Cœlestial Atlas or New Ephemeris
Jo. Partridge's Almanack	
Parker's Ephemeris	Cardanus Rider's Britis Merlin
Poor Robin's Almanack	
Saunders's English Apollo	Goldsmith's Almanack.

All the Almanacks printed for the Company o Stationers are to be known by the following words:

Printed for the COMPANY of STATIONERS. And sold by George Hawkins, at their Hall i Ludgate-street.

LOTTERY POLICIES, at Half a Guinea One Guinea, and Two Guineas, which last fo the whole time of drawing, are now delivering b JOHN BARNES PEARCE and Co. at their offic (licensed agreeable to act of parliament), No. 19 the corner of Pope's Head-alley, Cornhill; where during the six last lotteries, the following capita prizes have been sold, viz. four of 20,000l. three o 10,000l. four of 5000l. two of 2000l. six of 1000 and twenty of 50l.

The following prizes are to be gained, besides th twenty thousands, ten thousands, five thousands and every other prize, by these policies:

2	prizes	of	1400 £.
5	——	of	1000
3	——	of	700
5	——	of	500
5	——	of	300
10	——	of	200
8	——	of	160
12	——	of	120
20	——	of	100
135	——	of	60
420	——	of	50
625			

By the policies at two guineas, the adventurer ha 145 more chances, for prizes of 50l. and upwards than by a whole ticket at 14l. exclusive of th chances for the two twenty thousands, and ever other prize in the lottery.

The policies at one guinea have the same propor tion of 145 chances, for 25l. and upwards, mo than a half ticket, which costs 8l.

The policies at half a guinea have the same 14 chances more than a quarter ticket, which costs 4l. 4s

N. B. As there are other policies at half a guine advertised, it is necessary to observe to the Public that, by sixteen of those policies, price eight guineas they have no more than 1024 prizes above 20l. but by four of Pearce and Co's policies at two guineas eight policies at one guinea, or sixteen policies a half a guinea, 2500 prizes of 50l. and upwards ma be gained.

Tickets, shares, and chances, are now selling, i

They arrived in the houſe juſt before day & ſtay'd there until the next evening, when Major Andre became extremely ſollicitous to return by the way he came, but that was impoſſible, for the two men who Arnold and Smith had ſeduced to bring on ſhore, refuſed to carry him back. It then was abſolutely neceſſary he ſhould return to New-York by land. He chang'd his dreſs and name, and thus diſguiſed, paſſed our poſt of Stoney and Verplank's Points, on the evening of the 22d ult. in company with the ſaid Joſhua Smith, brother to William Smith, Eſq; Chief Juſtice within the Britiſh lines; he lodged that night at Cron Pond, with Smith, and in the morning left Smith, and took the road to Tarry-Town, where he was taken by ſome militia lads about 15 miles from Kings Bridge. He offered them any ſum of money, and goods, if they would permit him to eſcape, but they readily declared and inflexibly adhered to it, that 10 000 guineas, or any other ſum, would be no temptation to them. It was this virtue as glorious to America as Arnold's apoſtacy is diſgraceful, that his abominable crimes were diſcovered.

"The lads, in ſearching him found concealed under his ſtockings, in his boots, papers of the higheſt importance, viz.

1 Returns of the ordnance and its diſtributions at Weſt-Point and its dependencies.

2. Artillery orders, in caſe of an alarm.

3. Returns of the number of men neceſſary to man the works at Weſt-Point and its dependencies.

4 Remarks on ... at W... with the ſtrength an... of each

5. Returns ... and their diſtrib...

6. State o... neral Waſhi... which ſtate ha... officers i...

"Beſid... carried ... of Weſt...

Gen. Robertſon, Andrew Eliot and William Smith, Eſqrs; the two latter were not permitted to land. General Greene met Gen. Robertſon; he had nothing material to urge—' but that Andre had come on ſhore under the ſanction of a flag, and therefore could not be conſidered as a ſpy:" But this is not true, for he came at night, had no flag, and on buſineſs totally incompatible with the nature of a flag. He alſo ſaid they ſhould retaliate on ſome people at New-York and Charleſtown; but he was told that ſuch converſation could neither be heard nor underſtood. After which he urged the releaſe of Andre on motives of humanity, and becauſe Sir Harry Clinton was much attached to him; and other reaſons equally abſurd

"I have been particular in this narration, well knowing what ſtrange ſtories you will have on the ſubject."

The following is a Copy of a Letter from Major Andre to his Excellency General Waſhington.

SIR,

"Buoyed above the fear of death, by the conſciouſneſs of a life ſpent in the purſuit of honor, and fully ſenſible that it has at no time been ſtained by any action, which at this ſerious moment could give me remorſe—I have to ſollicit your Excellency if there is any thing in my character which excites your eſteem; if aught in my circumſtances can impreſs you with compaſſion; that I may be permitted to die the death of a ſoldier:—It is my laſt requeſt and I hope it will be granted." I have the honor to be, &c.

in the old C... an Hundred... Agents appo... are hereby d... Money at th... agreeable to ... lutions, for f... tation ſhall f... Rate aforeſai... fore the Thi... after which T... ther Directio... determine no... that Time,

And the A... to tranſmit a... receive on th... to the Comm... Orders.

CHAPTER XI

MARKS OF HEROISM

Introduction

Hoping to stir Loyalist support and restore British authority in the South, the British army realigns its strategy and shifts more than ten thousand troops loyal to the Crown, under the command of Henry Clinton, southward. In scorching heat and humidity, the Patriot-Loyalist civil war is fierce. Many of the bloodiest scenes unfold, including some of the worst Patriot defeats as well as the most pivotal victories. Despite the heroism of Patriot forces, "treason of the blackest dye" is uncovered among America's highest ranks and sends a shock wave through the Continental Army.

Boston Gazette
October 16, 1780

Capture of John André and discovery of Benedict Arnold's treason
North Wind Picture Archives

REPORTING THE

SIEGE OF SAVANNAH

By Rita Folse Elliott

BUNKER HILL, SARATOGA, YORKTOWN. WHILE SOME think the American Revolution happened only in New England and the mid-Atlantic, southern landscapes were also deadly scenes of strategic battles, with Georgia serving as the springboard for British military operations in the second half of the war. Casualties were not limited to the military, as civilians suffered intensively in what amounted to civil war. A Georgian's eyewitness account in the *London Chronicle* on October 26, 1779, stated, "the whole country to within 25 miles of Savannah has been plundered in the most cruel manner." The British taking of Savannah in December 1778 set the stage for one of the most decisive American defeats. The epic 1779 saga involved eight thousand to twelve thousand multinational forces consisting of American, African, British, French, Haitian, Hessian, Irish, Scottish, and Native American troops.

The British taking of Savannah in December 1778 set the stage for one of the most decisive American defeats.

Southern colonial importance is reflected in British Lieutenant Colonel Archibald Campbell's proclamation printed March 18, 1779, in the *American Journal*, three months after British troops took Savannah in little more than a heavy skirmish. The proclamation mentioned "all his Majesty's faithful subjects of the southern provinces," and the British mistakenly believed that applied to most residents. Perhaps for that reason, Major General Augustin Prevost seemed in no hurry to reinforce the city's weak defenses, even when word arrived that French Admiral Count Charles Henri d'Estaing's fleet was in route to America from the nearby West Indies.

While Prevost remained composed, British political and military figures from Florida to Rhode Island were fearful of being d'Estaing's target. A *Maryland Journal* article printed October 26, 1779, is a typical compilation of fact, fiction, and biased optimism. It correctly reported Count d'Estaing landing troops downstream from Savannah but failed to mention why d'Estaing was so terrifying. He brought one of the world's largest military flotillas: twenty-two ships of the line. The article mentioned American Major General Benjamin Lincoln, commander of the war's southern theater. The 1779 battle represented the first time French and American forces allied in ground combat. Lincoln and d'Estaing proved a disastrous combination of character flaws, cultural incompatibility, and poor judgment.

Unbeknownst at the time of the article, British Lieutenant Colonel John Maitland mustered eight hundred troops in Beaufort, South Carolina. Contrary to the article, he did "effect a junction with General Prevost" by slogging through back swamps and inlets through enemy lines. Meanwhile, Prevost ordered engineers, five hundred African Americans, militia, and regulars to reinforce four redoubts and construct nine new ones surrounding the city. Inside, Royal Georgia Governor James Wright and petrified civilians, including Prevost's wife Anne and children, waited. Prevost bought time with a twenty-four-hour truce. The same newspaper article optimistically stated "officers gave their opinions publicly that [Savannah] must capitulate." This may have happened had the allies attacked immediately in lieu of laying a siege. The allies bombarded Savannah for two weeks with little effect, other than torching houses and killing women and children cowering in basements. The futile siege ended with an unsuccessful attack on October 9, 1779.

It would be weeks before George Washington learned

of the catastrophic loss at Savannah. French and American military casualties numbering eight hundred contrasted with fifty British. D'Estaing himself was among officers wounded. Count Casimir Pulaski, mentioned in the newspaper as victoriously taking the picket, suffered mortal wounds leading a cavalry charge. This loss was significant as the Polish Pulaski had created America's first cavalry.

The *London Chronicle* celebrated the British victory in its December 28, 1779, issue more than seventy days after the battle. It published an accurate battle account by Prevost. The 1779 battle of Savannah, Georgia, resulted in a rift in the fragile Franco-American alliance and a strategic victory for the British, enabling them to hold Georgia, take Charleston, South Carolina, and launch an attack from the southern front.

Siege of Savannah,
by A. I. Keller
North Wind Picture Archives

The epic 1779 Siege of Savannah, one of the most decisive American defeats, involved eight thousand to twelve thousand multinational forces consisting of American, African, British, French, Haitian, Hessian, Irish, Scottish, and Native American troops.

LONDON CHRONICLE

October 26, 1779

A Georgian's eyewitness account in the *London Chronicle* on October 26, 1779, stated, "the whole country to within 25 miles of Savannah has been plundered in the most cruel manner." The British taking of Savannah in December 1778 set the stage for one of the most decisive American defeats.

LONDON.

Extract of a Letter from a Gentleman of the firſt Diſtinction in Georgia, dated Savannah, July 27.

" During near three months that the royal army was in South Carolina, the whole province, excepting our three poſts of Savannah, Ebenezer, and Sunbury, was entirely in the rebels power; and the conſequence has been, that the whole country to within 25 miles of Savannah has been plundered in the moſt cruel manner, and almoſt every man who had ſubmitted to, and received the protection of government, either killed or taken priſoners, and the few that have eſcaped that fate have been obliged to ſubmit to ſuch terms as the rebels pleaſed to preſcribe.

" On the 26th ult. we were alarmed with accounts of a large body of horſe having penetrated into the heart of our lower ſettlements; having a few days before received a ſmall reinforcement from our army, a detachment of about 50 men was ſent out from this garriſon to watch their motions, but by very bad conduct they fell in with and were ſurpriſed by upwards of 100 of the enemy, within 17 miles of Savannah; in conſequence of which the Commanding Officer, Capt. Muller, and ſeveral privates, were killed, and the remainder of the detachment made priſoners.

" Col. Maitland now commands at Beaufort, with about 1500 men; the reſt of the army is here with Gen. Prevoſt. We have force enough to defend the part of the country that we are in poſſeſſion of, until the ſeaſon will admit of operations in the field, for at preſent the weather is ſo exceſſive hot that nothing material could be attempted. Our reinforcements, we doubt not, will be with us early enough to complete the work we have ſo happily begun in theſe ſouthern provinces.

" Our worthy Governor, Sir James Wright, arrived here in the Experiment, Commodore Sir James Wallace, on the 13th inſt. He was much diſappointed on finding a deſcent had been made upon Carolina, which, it was hoped in England, would have been deferred till the arrival of the

and when Capt. Delmley brought to, all his own topmaſts fell over the ſide; the lower maſts would likewiſe have gone, had not the weather proved fine."

Three battalions, making upwards of 2500 men, will go out to the Leeward iſlands, in the fleet now getting ready to ſail, and which is ex-

taking ſoundings of the coaſt along ſhore under Engliſh colours."

Extract of a Letter from Milford Haven, dated Oct. 19.

" A coaſter from the northward was chaſed in here on the 17th by a large cutter; ſhe is ſaid to be one of thoſe fitted out at Dunkirk as ſmugglers, or privateers; they are commanded by an American, and have a commiſſion from the Congreſs, and the crew are Iriſh, Engliſh, and French, and, in ſhort, whatever they can get: ſhe had 18 guns, and was full of men."

Extract of a Letter from Weymouth, Oct. 20.

" This morning was brought in here a French privateer belonging to Cherburg, mounting 12 guns, called the St. Amiand, taken by the Rover privateer, after an engagement of two hours, in which the French had 12 men killed and 20 wounded. The Rover had only two men killed and three wounded."

Extract of a Letter from Goſport, Oct. 22.

" His Majeſty's ſhip Garland is appointed convoy to Newfoundland, and is this day ſailed; ſhe gave inſtructions to all ſhips that would go with her, bound to New York; accordingly the Hannah, Watſon, and the ——, Moor, with a ſhip bound to Bermuda, and ſeveral others, are all this day ſailed under her convoy, with a fine N. E. wind."

Extract of a Letter from Dunwich, in Suffolk, October 19.

" The violent blowing weather we have had for ſeveral days has done a great deal of damage amongſt the ſhipping on our coaſt; every tide preſents to our view a melancholy ſcene of dead bodies, and pieces of wrecks thrown on the ſands. It likewiſe did great havoc on ſhore, blowing down rows of large trees, barns, outhouſes, &c. and unroofing dwelling houſes; in ſhort, the damage done amounts to many thouſands of pounds. A man, his wife, and ſeveral children, were buried under the ruins of a houſe, and all killed."

A Captain of a ſhip arrived from Yarmouth mentions, that the whole of the Society's buſſes are ſafely arrived at Southwold from the Shetland fiſhery, with full cargoes.

urday laſt, at one o'clock, William
; finding that moſt of his friends
d to poll for Henry Kitchen, Eſq;
licited their favours, he therefore
ng on with the poll, and deſired that
ight be finally cloſed, to prevent the
r and the Gentlemen of the Ward
further trouble; which requeſt was
th, and thereupon the Lord Mayor
nry Kitchen, Eſq; duly elected Al-
Farringdon Ward within, in the
late Wm. Bridgen, Eſq.

nday laſt as ſome workmen were ſinking a grave in the north ayle of the pariſh church of Danbury in Eſſex, they diſcovered a leaden coffin, which encloſed a ſtout elm coffin, about one inch and a quarter thick, in which was a ſhell of about half that thickneſs, containing the body of a Knight Templer, ſuppoſed to be of the family of the Sancto Clare's, or St. Clare's

Shoe-lane, Fleet-ſtreet.

On Saturday laſt died, at Ba
ham, Surry, Mrs. Elizabeth Scr

On Tueſday laſt died, at Cam
Thomas Hooper, A. M. a pre
and Rector of Barley, in Hertfo

Saturday morning at 1 o'clock
of the Royal George Weſt India
ped near the end of Virginia-
fellows, who beat him moſt cru
him of near 30l. which he had
afternoon received from his own

On Saturday nine priſoners w
Old Bailey, one of whom was c
ed, viz. Wm. Ruſſell, for bre
dwelling-houſe of Mr. James E
court, in the night-time, with
five were convicted of grand la
of petit larceny.

Lea Joſepha Salomons was c
lawfully ſetting fire to a wooden
ers, in her dwelling-houſe, in th
inu-paſſage, in Warwick-lane,
burn and deſtroy the ſaid hou
ſentence to be impriſoned two
gate, and pay a fine of 100l.
victed on his own confeſſion fo
rupt perjury, and his ſentence

The ſame day the ſeſſion e
priſoners received ſentence of de

The Recorder, in paſſing ſe
laſt Saturday, addreſſed himſelf
Mr. Taylor. He ſaid, it was
courſe of his trial that he had
function, the more eaſily to
world; that a man capable of
a character with any ſort of ſu
ſuppoſe, was poſſeſſed of ſome
from a liberal education, and
conſidered the unfortunate con
was far from his wiſh to aggrav
of a man in ſo deplorable a
crime of the priſoner was ſo d
comercial intereſts of this king
could be no expectation of m
thoſe feelings which a ſenſible
would make a proper impreſſion
and diſpoſe him to think ſeriou
of the ſtate of his ſoul, in order
employ the ſhort time he had
manner as to entitle him to th
ven.—This ſerious addreſs, h
to be thrown away upon the
appeared very inattentive and
ſpoke not a word. The other p
with a becoming decency.

The Seſſions of the Peace is
the 3d of November at Guildha
ſions of Gaol Delivery of Newg
of December at the Old Bailey.

D. L. Love in a Village, with
C. G. Macbeth, with Plymouth

For DISORDERS in the BO

THE ſudden alteration of the
produced a ſtate of air ver

CHARLESTOWN, *January* 12.

The commanders of the British armament in Georgia, in humble imitation of their superiors to the northward, have entertained the good people of the southern states with a proclamation; which, notwithstanding it militates directly against the cause of America, in order to shew how little apprehension is entertained of its producing the effect the framers of it have in view, is here published: Indeed those who at this time can put any confidence in their promises would richly merit that share of misery and want, which has invariably attended all those Americans who have been apostates to the cause of freedom, and inlisted themselves under the banners of their country's foes.

By HYDE PARKER, *jun. Esquire, Commodore of a Squadron of his Majesty's Ships of War; and Lieut. Col.* ARCHIBALD CAMPBELL, *commanding a Detachment of the Royal Army, sent for the Relief of his Majesty's faithful Subjects in North and South-Carolina and Georgia.*

A PROCLAMATION.

WHereas the blessings of peace, freedom, and protection, most graciously tendered by his Majesty to his deluded subjects of America, have been treated by Congress with repeated marks of studied disrespect, and to the disgrace of human nature have had no effect in reclaiming them from the bloody persecutions of their fellow citizens: BE IT THEREFORE KNOWN to all his Majesty's faithful subjects of the southern provinces, that a fleet and army, under orders, are actually arrived in Georgia for their protection, to which they are desired to repair without loss of time, and, by uniting their force under the royal standard, rescue their friends from oppression, themselves from slavery, and obtain for both the most ample satisfaction for the manifold injuries sustained.

To all other well disposed inhabitants, who, from a just regard to the blessings of peace, reprobate the idea of supporting a French league, insidiously framed to prolong the calamities of war, and who, with his Majesty's faithful subjects wish to embrace the happy occasion of cementing a firm and perpetual coalition with the parent state, free from the imposition of taxes by the Parliament of Great-Britain, and secured in the irrevocable enjoyment of every privilege, consistent with that union of interests and force on which their mutual advantage, religion and liberties depend. WE offer the most ample protection to their families and effects, on condition they shall immediately return to the class of peaceful citizens, acknowledge their just allegiance to the crown, and with their arms support it.

To those who shall attempt to oppose the reestablishment of legal government, or who shall presume to injure such whom the dictates of reason, honor and conscience prompt to embrace it; WE lament the necessity of exhibiting the rigours of war, and call God and the world to witness, that they only shall be answerable for all the miseries which may ensue.

Deserters of every description, who, from a due sense of their error, wish to return to their colours, have also our pardon, provided they return within the space of three months from the date of this proclamation.

GIVEN at Head-Quarters at Savannah, this 4th day of January 1779, and in the nineteenth year of his Majesty's reign,

HYDE PARKER,

ARCHIBALD CAMPBELL.

PHILADELPHIA, Feb. 22.

We beg leave further to observe to Excellency, that the people expect, on cess of the Assembly, to have a full and p account of what may be determined c which there can be no medium observed. must either have a clear mode of obt provisions pointed out, or must be tol nothing can be done: --They must q island, or depend on Providence alone.

By order of the House.

By order of the Board.

Jan. 15, 1779. *Cornelius Hinson*, Speaker.

James Jones, President.

The foregoing is a true copy.

pendence of America, have agreed to assist France with 30 sail of the line, and lend the United States of America thirty millions of dollars, as they can better spare money than their troops at so great a distance. The other is, that the Dutch have agreed to supply the

AMERICAN JOURNAL (PROVIDENCE, RI)

March 18, 1779

Southern colonial importance is reflected in British Lieutenant Colonel Archibald Campbell's proclamation printed March 18, 1779, in the *American Journal*, three months after British troops took Savannah in little more than a heavy skirmish.

MARYLAND JOURNAL (BALTIMORE)

October 26, 1779

This *Maryland Journal* article is a typical compilation of fact, fiction, and biased optimism. It correctly reported Count d'Estaing landing troops downstream from Savannah but failed to mention why d'Estaing was so terrifying. He brought one of the world's largest military flotillas—twenty-two ships of the line.

---

have deſerted into the city to their friends, perhaps half as many more.

(To be continued.)

LEGHORN, *June* 15.

ACCORDING to a private letter from an officer on board the Chatham, ſix French ſhips of the line keep Gibraltar blocked up; that fortreſs is provided with ammunition and proviſions for nine months, with a garriſon of 8000 men. That letter adds, that Admiral Roddam has been ſeen off Cape St. Vincent, making proper diſpoſitions to clear the Streights of Gibraltar.

DUBLIN, July 3.

The Amſterdam Gazette, which arrived here yeſterday, in the Paris article contains a regulation of the ceremonial obſerved at the junction of the French and Spaniſh fleets, and the diſpoſition for embarking the army under M. de Vaux, which the French affectedly call L'Armee Irlandoiſe. This army, which conſiſts of 30,000 foot, and 1000 horſe, were on the 20th of June to go on board 300 tranſports, which had been ſome time waiting for them. The ſame Gazette gives an account of the arrival of a frigate at Breſt, which had left the ſquadron under the command of M. de la Mothe Piquet off the Azores, where they had captured ſix Engliſh privateers, which they ſay were lying in wait for the French homeward-bound Weſt-India ſhips.

July 13. By Gentlemen who are arrived here in the laſt packet we are informed, that the fleet under the command of Sir Charles Hardy, had put into Torbay the 5th inſtant, there to wait for a reinforcement of eight ſhips of the line, which are to join him from

CHARLESTOWN, *Sept.* 22.

Since our laſt, we have had no direct advices from either of the armies employed upon the Southern expedition. All we certainly know, is, That Count d'Eſting did land as many troops as he thought neceſſary, at Beulah, nearly oppoſite to the Orphan-Houſe, 12 miles from Savannah, in the night between the 11th and 12th inſt. and without the leaſt oppoſition; and that a communication had been opened between him and General Lincoln; that General Lincoln had been joined by General Mackintoſh; and that the Head-Quarters of our army, a week ago, were at Cherokee-hill, 9 miles from Savannah: That General Count Pulaſki was advanced with the cavalry, and had not only taken an advanced picket of the enemy, but alſo ſurprized one of their captains and three privates at Ebenetzer. That Col. Maitland had abandoned Port-Royal Iſland, with the whole force he had there, on the 12th inſt. after breaking off the trunnions from the cannon, and having buried upwards of 200 men, leaving behind alſo 300 negroes, for want of means of tranſportation: That his embarkation was made rather haſtily, on board the Vigilante, the Gallies, and ſome other ſmall craft, with an intent to puſh through Skull-Creek, and join General Prevoſt. Savannah: tachments, one at Brewton's plantation, with 36 pieces of braſs cannon, the other at Girardeau's point: That the active and enterprizing General Count Pulaſki, with the cavalry, had ſo thoroughly cleared the way, and broke up all the enemy's advanced poſts, as to afford Major-General Lincoln the opportunity of an interview with the French General, at the Orphan-houſe, on the 16th, when and where the plan of operations was ſettled: That ſome of the French men of war had got into the harbour, and poſſeſſed themſelves of all the Britiſh ſhipping below Brewton's, amongſt them the Fowey man of war, which, tho' grounded, had all been got off and into the fleet: That the fortifications at Savannah were but trifling, conſiſting only of 9 redoubts (no lines) and abbatis: That the force to defend theſe, conſiſted of about 1000 regulars, and 1200 militia, refugees, and protection gentry: That Sir James Wright, governor, &c. was in Savannah: That Col. Maitland had not been able to effect a junction with General Prevoſt, and it was ſuppoſed had been repulſed in an attempt to get thro' Skull-creek, yeſterday morning, when we heard a heavy cannonade: That the enemy's ſoldiery, in general, were much diſſatiſfied; and tho' it was pretended, that Savannah would be defended, even the officers gave their opinions publicly, that it muſt capitulate. And that General Prevoſt had applied to the Count d'Eſtaing, for a ſafe conduct and permiſſion to remove his lady, plate and effects, to Florida; to which the gallant French General politely replied, "*That it was impoſſible be could have any objection to what concerned the Lady; but the plate, he had been informed, was obtained in ſuch a way from the Allies of his King, that he was confident the General could not mean to diſgrace him-* [illegible] *poſſeſſion of it.*"

[illegible]ELPHIA, October 16.

[illegible]ived from Bordeaux (Old France)
[illegible]ercer, Captain Robinſon, and bro't
[illegible] Minerva, Capt. ——, from Ha-
[illegible]am, loaded with fiſh, &c.
[illegible] *from Nantz, dated July* 3, 1779.
[illegible]e 32,000 men at St. Malo, ready to
[illegible]ey only wait the arrival of Compte
[illegible]e Channel, accounts of which
[illegible]ected, as the wind has been for 36
[illegible] weſtward, and likely to continue.
[illegible]here is a deſcent intended on Eng-
[illegible] It is reported that the ſhips the

Spaniards were to furniſh by compact, which is ten ſail of the line, have joined D'Orvilliers, and that the Cadiz fleet ſailed about the fifth ult. The ſailing of the Engliſh fleet you'll find by the papers. The French have an army of 40,000 men on the frontiers of Holland, which will keep the Dutchman quiet, if even his inclination was to be troubleſome."

Extract of a letter from a Gentleman in Bordeaux, dated July 22, 1779.

"We have no certain advices from the combined fleets, expect ſome very intereſting; if any arrives before the preſent conveyances leave the river, ſhall embrace the opportunity to forward them. Mr. Wedderburne is nominated to ſucceed Lord Suffolk; other new nominations are daily expected in the different miniſterial departments of that Kingdom.

"Advices from Spain agree in the determination of that Court on the blockade of Gibraltar.

"An army is marching into Flanders, under the command of Monſieur, ſaid to pay a viſit to Hanover, and thereby oblige that Electorate to recal her troops in the pay of Britain from Minorca and Gibraltar, or to watch the Dutch, and hold them to a ſtrict neutrality."

Extract of a letter from Bordeaux, dated July 20, 1779.

"The grand French fleet [illegible]

ſhortly be on that coaſt. They are fortifying
all poſſible expedition, every advantageous place
about the city, and have eleven veſſels rea
ſink in the channel at the Hook. Every poſſibi
tion is making on board their ſhipping, in caſe o
tack. In ſhort, the whole city is one ſcene c
fuſion and fear."

Extract of a letter from Pittſburgh, September 16,

"The many ſavage barbarities and horrid
dations, committed by the Seneca and Muncy N
upon the Weſtern frontiers, had determinec
Broadhead, as the moſt effectual way to prever
hoſtilities in future, and revenge the paſt, to ca
war into their own country, and ſtrike a deciſiv
at their towns.

"On the 11th of Auguſt, our little army, co
only of ſix hundred and five, rank and file, m
from Pittſburgh with one month's proviſion;
honing, 15 miles above the Old Kittanning, w
detained four days by the exceſſive rains, from v
(leaving the river which rolls in a thouſand mea
we proceeded by a blind path leading to Cuſc
thro' a country almoſt impaſſible, by reaſon of t
pendous heights and frightful declivities, with
tinued range of craggy hills, overſpread with
timber, thorns and underwood, here and there an
vening valley, whoſe deep impenetrable gloo
always been impervious to the piercing rays
warmeſt ſun. At Cuſcuſhing (which is 15 miles
Venango) we croſſed the Alleghany, and con
our route upon its banks But here our mar
rendered ſtill more difficult by the mountains
jutted cloſe upon the river, forming a continued
defile, allowing us only the breadth of an India
to march upon. In the midſt of one of theſ
our advanced party, conſiſting of 15 white m
Delawares, diſcovered between 30 [illegible]
landing from their canoes, who having alſo [illegible]
of our troops, immediately ſtripped themſelves a
pared for action. Lieutenant Harding, who
manded our advance, diſpoſed his men in a ſemic
form, and began the attack with ſuch irreſiſtib
tomahawk in hand, that the Savages could nc
ſuſtain the charge, but fled with the utmoſt horr
precipitation, ſome plunging themſelves into th
and others, favoured by the thickneſs of the
made their eſcape on the main, leaving five d
the field, without any loſs on our ſide, except thr
ſlightly wounded. Upon the firſt alarm, ſuppc
to be more ſerious, the army was arranged fo
both officers and men, enraged at their forme
ties, and animated by the calmneſs, reſolution
trepidity of the commandant, ſhewed the utmo
to engage; and had the action been general,
every proſpect of the moſt ample ſucceſs from
commander, at the head of brave men. Con
our march, we arrived the ſame day at Buch
where leaving our baggage, ſtores, &c. under a
proceeded to their towns with the utmoſt de
which we found at the diſtance of about twent
farther, with extenſive corn-fields on both ſides
river, but deſerted by the inhabitants on our ap
Eight towns we ſet in flames, and committed th
god and war poſts to the river; the corn was ou
object, which, in three days, we cut down and pi
to heaps, amounting in the whole to near 600
without the leaſt interruption from the enemy.

"Upon our return we ſeveral times croſſed a
about ten miles above Venango, remarkable for
liquor, which ouzes from the ſides and bottom
channel, and the adjacent ſprings, much reſe
Britiſh oil, and if applied to woolen cloth, burr
an inſtant.

"After burning the old towns of Conauwag

voſt, commanding his Majeſty's Forces in the Province of Georgia, to the Right Honourable Lord George Germaine, one of his Majeſty's Principal Secretaries of State, dated Savannah, November 1, 1779: Received by Captain Shaw, Aid de Camp to Major General Prevoſt.

AS I look upon it to be always of Importance, and my indiſpenſable Duty, that your Lordſhip ſhould directly be made acquainted with every material Occurrence in this Quarter affecting his Majeſty's Service; and as it is robable the very unexpected Viſit of the ount d'Eſtaing to this Coaſt, with ſo powerful a Squadron, and a conſiderable Body f Land Troops, when known, would have xcited ſome Uneaſineſs for our Safety; it is with very ſincere Pleaſure I do myſelf the Hoour to inform you, that we have ſeen the laſt f the French Fleet this Day depart,—we hope ff the Coaſt,—got both them and their Amecan Allies off our Hands, in a Manner which e humbly hope our gracious Sovereign will ot think unhandſome.

September 4th. When Intelligence was reeived from Tybee, that five Sail of French Men of War, with ſome Sloops and Schooners, vere off the Bar, as it was impoſſible to deternine whether this was a Whole or only Part f a larger Force; whether they had landed Troops in Carolina, or this was their firſt Apearance on the Coaſt; Orders were ſent to all he Out-Poſts to hold themſelves in Readineſs o join: And as it was very poſſible that the Enemy might puſh their Frigates into Port Royal Bay, and cut off the Communication ith Beaufort, an Order was ſent to the HoourableColonel Maitland, commanding there, orthwith to evacuate that Place, and croſs to Hilton Head Iſland, from whence, if he was ot ſtopped by a further Order, he was to proeed to this Place. The Officer who was harged with this Order was taken by the Reels, going through Skull Creek; but this Accident was then judged of no other Conſeuence, as the French diſappearing, and their oming on the Coaſt being hoped, for various Reaſons, to be only accidental, Colonel Maitnd was next Day directed to remain; but nbarking all his heavy Baggage and other Inumbrances, to hold himſelf in conſtant Readieſs to come away on the ſhorteſt Notice: Or , through any other Channel, he received ntelligence which ſhould induce that Meaure, he was immediately to adopt it, without aiting the Ceremony of Orders, as beſt for is Majeſty's Service; his great Care being alays to run no Riſque, poſſibly to be avoided, f being cut off from this Place, which was ur principal Concern.

6th. The French Ships re-appeared with ne of Addition, and from the Northward. Captain Moncrief, the Commanding Engieer, with one hundred Men and a Howitz, as ſent to Tybee to reinforce the Poſt and attery there; and an Order to be forwarded Colonel Maitland to join, without Loſs of make other neceſſary Diſpoſitions for ſuſtaining an Attack.—Repair and ſtrengthen the Abbatis.—A very ſuperior Force approaching the Bar, our Ships, the Fowey and Roſe, of twenty Guns each, the Keppel and Germain armed Veſſels, obliged to retire towards Town. The Battery on Tybee deſtroyed, the Guns ſpiked, and the Howitz and Stores carried off. Four large Frigates came over the Bar.

10th. All the Out-poſts in Georgia join. Lieutenant-Colonel Cruger from Sunbury came by Land with all his Men able to march; his Sick and Convaleſcents he embarked on board an armed Veſſel to come inland.—By contrary Winds they were detained till the Paſſage was ſeized by the Enemy. They however put up Ogechy River, where, finding the Communication by Land alſo cut off, Captain French (commanding) landed and took Poſt, and for many Days continued to defend himſelf, until obliged, by Want of Proviſions, to capitulate to a very ſuperior Force. Began new Redoubts and Batteries, and ſtrengthen the Abbatis. The Troops encamped.

11th. Buſy in landing Cannon from the Shipping.—Making Faſcines.—The Engineer hard at Work.

12th. Several French and Rebel Veſſels come over Oſſiban Bar.—At Ten o'Clock, Evening, the French landed at Beaulieu.

13th. Having confined our Views to the Defence of the Town, as our ſole Object, which we determined, by the Bleſſing of God, to be vigorous, and worthy of Britiſh Troops, continued our Works with unremitting Ardour. Captains Henry, Brown, and Fiſher came on Shore, their Aſſiſtance being required in the Defence of the Place, on which every Thing depended.—They chearfully agreed, and proceeded directly to land their whole Force, Men, Guns, &c. Some Maſters of Tranſports, and a Privateer with their Men, made voluntary Offers of their Services. Capt. Watſon of the Tweed, Tate, Nancy, Higgins, Betſey, Mr. Manley, Merchant of Jamaica, all had their Poſts aſſigned; the Seamen on the Batteries, the Marines joined to the 60th Grenadiers.—Report, that the Rebels from Auguſta were at Hudſon's, and General Lincoln from Carolina approaching Zubly's Ferry.

14th. The Engineer hard at Work.—Certain Intelligence that Lincoln was croſſing at Zubly's Ferry, from intelligent Spies, who croſſed with him.—His Numbers about 1500. More on their Way from all Parts of Carolina. Polaſki, already croſſed and joined by the Horſe from above, advanced to within eight Miles of the Town.

15th. Some French and Polaſki's Lighthorſe appear in Front. Force in a Subaltern's Piquet, of which ſix are taken: They are forced to retire in Turn with ſome killed, and an Officer taken. No further Loſs on our Side, our Men not being ſuffered to paſs beyond the Cover of our Cannon.

16th. Receive a Summons (No. I.) from the Count d'Eſtaing, *To ſurrender to the Arms of France.* No Stranger to the unanimous Opinion of the Army; but, for Form's Sake, aſſemble the Field Officers at the Governor's—twenty-four Hours to deliberate, which is agreed to (No. IV. and No. V.).

17th. By Noon, and in the Night before, all the reſt of the Army fit for Duty from Beaufort arrive, and take their Poſts in the Line. The Enemy being in Poſſeſſion of the Ship Channel, Colonel Maitland had been obliged to come round Dawfuſkie, and land on the Marſhes; and dragging his Boats empty thro' a Cut, got into Savannah River above the Enemy, and ſo to this Place.—Again aſſemble the Field Officers, Sea and Land, with the Governor and Lieutenant Governor in Camp.—Unanimouſly determined to defend ourſelves to the laſt Man, which is communicated to Count d'Eſtaing, (No. VI.) Our Evening Gun fired an Hour before Sunſet, to be the Signal for recommencing Hoſtilities.—Review the Troops under Arms at their Poſts, all in high Spirits, and the moſt pleaſing Confidence expreſſed in every Face—The Sailors not to be prevented from giving Three Cheers.

18th and 19th. We continue to work hard on Redoubts and Batteries—Further ſtrengthen the Abbatis.

20th. A Frigate and Gallies at Four Mile Point. Captain Moncrief prepares Fire Rafts. The Roſe and Savannah ſunk in the Channel.

21ſt. A new Work for ſeven 6 and 9 pounders begun in Front of the Barracks—Hearing the Rebels were making Fire Rafts above the Town, we get the Boom acroſs, and Veſſels ready to be ſunk, a ſmall Galley, and the Germain to cover the Boom, and occaſionally to ſcour Yamacraw Swamp on our Right.—Some Houſes and Barns on our Flanks, judged too near, are burnt, unfortunately the Property of Friends.

22d. The Enemy appear in Force all along our Front—In Readineſs to fight, but continue our Works—Boats and other Craft of the Enemy go up Auguſtine Creek, probably with Cannon and Stores.

23d. As the Day before.

24th. The Enemy had been hard at Work the whole Night; and when the Morning Fog cleared off, were diſcovered to have puſhed a Sap to within Three Hundred Yards of our Abbatis, to the Left of the Center.—At Nine o'Clock Three Companies of Light Infantry (97 Rank and File) were ſent out under Major Graham, of the 16th, to give an Opportunity of reconnoitring, and probably judging of the Enemy's Force, and to draw them expoſed to our Cannon. It had been once intended to ſend the whole Light Infantry with Major G[illegible]

7[illegible]

b[illegible]

T[illegible]

A[illegible]

o[illegible]

and the Vicinity of the French Camp, which was diſcovered to be very near, there was Reaſon to apprehend an Affair more general than we wiſhed for, might be brought on; it was judged ſufficient to draw the remaining Three Light Companies along the Abbatis, and the Highlanders concealed behind the Barracks, in

LONDON CHRONICLE

December 28, 1779

REPORTING THE

SIEGE OF CHARLESTON

By David Lee Russell

On March 8, 1778, Lord Germain, the secretary of state for the American Department, signed final directives to General Henry Clinton specifying his future military operations against the colonies, revealing that "it is the King's intention that an attack should be made upon the southern colonies, with a view to the conquest and possession of Georgia and South Carolina." This "Southern Strategy" as it became known, led to the British capture of Savannah on December 29, 1778, and the defeat of a Franco-American siege against British-held Savannah in October of the following year led by General Benjamin Lincoln and French Admiral Charles Henri d'Estaing. Clinton's next target was Charleston, South Carolina.

At 10:00 the morning after Christmas in 1780, British Vice Admiral Arbuthnot's fleet of ninety-six ships (eighty transports), with General Clinton's 6,975 British and German Hessian troops, sailed from Sandy Hook, New York, for Charleston. The British landed below the city on Simmons Island (Seabrook Island) on February 11, and by the afternoon of March 31, they broke ground on their siege works 1,200 yards from the Patriot main defensive line opposite Charleston.

It was the greatest victory in the war for the British, and there was great celebration in England over the fall of the city.

When the British works reached only 250 yards off the city's works on April 21, General Lincoln sent a flag of truce with his terms consisting of articles of surrender. Clinton rejected Lincoln's terms and asked for the immediate surrender of the city. The Patriot Council refused, and the bombardments began again.

By May 8, the British held all escape routes from Charleston. That day, Clinton sent a summons to General Lincoln to surrender, as recorded in the *New-Jersey Gazette* of June 28, 1780:

> *Circumstanced as I now am with respect to the place invested, humanity only can induce me to lay within your reach the terms I had determined should not again be proffered* [...] *By this last summons therefore, I throw to your charge whatever vindictive severity exasperated soldiers may inflict on the unhappy people, whom you devote by preserving in a fruitless defence. I shall expect your answer until eight o'clock, when hostilities will commence again, unless the town be surrendered.*

Again Clinton rejected Lincoln's revisions, and when that time arrived on May 9, Hessian Captain Hinrichs recorded in his diary, "The enemy rang all the bells in the city and after a threefold 'Hurray!' opened a cannonade more furious than any before." On May 11, the British crossed the lines within twenty-five yards of the Patriot works. Hinrichs noted, "At two o'clock in the afternoon the enemy hoisted a large white flag on the hornwork and dispatched a second flag, offering the capitulation of the city."

The *London Chronicle* dated June 17, 1780, printed Sir Henry Clinton's account of the May 12 surrender of Charleston:

> *On the 12th Major-General Leslie took possession of the town. There were taken seven general officers, a commodore, ten continental regiments, and three battalions of artillery, together with town and country militia, French and seamen, making about six thousand men in arms. The titular deputy governor, council, and civil officers, are also prisoners. Four frigates and several armed vessels, with a great number of boats, have*

likewise fallen into our possession, and about four hundred pieces of canon.

Clinton continued with his warm appreciations to Lieutenant-General Earl Cornwallis, his army corps, and to Admiral Arbuthnot's fleet for their service. The British and German Hessian losses were "2 ensigns, 1 sergeant, 73 rank and file, killed; 1 captain, 7 lieutenants, 2 sergeants, 179 rank and file, wounded."

This was a tragic end to the Siege of Charleston. King George III was out riding when Clinton's aide, the Earl of Lincoln, told him of the good news. It was the greatest victory in the war for the British, and there was great celebration in England over the fall of the city. The returning British troops were paraded before their cheering citizens. Charleston remained under British control until they evacuated it in 1782. It was the largest surrender of an American armed force until the 1862 surrender of Union forces at Harper's Ferry during the Civil War.

Siege of Charleston
North Wind Picture Archives

By May 8, 1780, the British held all escape routes from Charleston, and British General Henry Clinton sent a summons to American General Benjamin Lincoln to surrender.

NEW-JERSEY GAZETTE.

[NUMB. 131.]

WEDNESDAY, JUNE 28, 1780.

PHILADELPHIA, June 17.

Last Wednesday evening arrived Lieutenant Colonel Ternant, with the following Dispatches from Major-General Lincoln to Congress.

SIR, Charlestown, May 24, 1780.

THE enclosed papers will inform Congress of each important circumst nce which has occurred in this department since I did myself the honor to write them on the 9th ult. by Mr. Cannon.

They will hereby observe, that after every effort and exertion made by a handful of brave troops, contending with numberless hardships and difficulties, (to all which they most chearfully submitted) we were reduced to the sad necessity of treating with Sir Henry Clinton, and acceding to the terms of capitulation, which accompany this letter.

I shall not at present go into a detail of the matter as I expect to reach Congress before this—but should I not, Lieutenant Colonel Ternant, who is the bearer of this letter, will be able to give a minute state of things: I must beg leave therefore to refer Congress to that gentleman, and to assure them, that his steady attention to duty, and zeal for the service, entitle him to every respect.

I have the honor to be, with the highest regard and esteem, your Excellency's most obedient servant, B. LINCOLN.

Lieutenant-Colonel Ternant will be able to inform Congress what has caused so much delay in getting off the dispatches.

His Excellency Samuel Huntington, Esq. President of Congress.

No. I.

Camp, before Charlestown, April 10th, 1780.

SIR Henry Clinton, K. B. General and Commander in Chief of his Majesty's forces, in the colonies lying on the Atlantic, from Nova Scotia, &c. &c. &c. and Vice-Admiral Arbuthnot, Commander in Chief of his Majesty's ships in North-America, &c. &c. &c. regretting the effusion of blood, and the distresses which must now commence, deem it consonant to humanity to warn the town and garrison of Charlestown of the havock and desolation with which they are threatened from the formidable force surrounding them by land and sea.

An alternative is offered at this hour to the inhabitants of saving their lives and property (contained in the town) or of abiding by the fatal ...

... in Charlestown.

No. II.

Head-Quarters, (Charlestown) April 10, 1780.

Gentlemen,

I HAVE received your summons of this date. Sixty days have passed since it has been known that your intentions against this town were hostile, in which, time has been afforded to abandon it; but duty and inclination point to the propriety of supporting it to the last extremity.

letter, and my request that the battery on James island may desist firing. I have the honor to be, &c.

(Signed) H. CLINTON.

Major-General Lincoln.

No. V.

Articles of Capitulation proposed by Major-Gen. Lincoln.

Art. 1. That all acts of hostility and works shall cease between the naval and land forces of Great-Britain and America, in this state, until the articles of capitulation shall be agreed on, signed and executed, or collectively rejected.

2. That the town, forts, and fortifications belonging to them, shall be surrendered to the Commander in Chief of the British forces such as they now stand.

3. That the several troops garrisoning the town and forts including the French and American sailors, the French invalids, the North-Carolina and South-Carolina militia, and such of the Charlestown militia as may choose to leave this place, shall have thirty-six hours to withdraw to Lampriere's after the capitulation has been accepted and signed on both sides—and that those troops shall retire with the usual honours of war, and carry off during that time their arms, field artillery, ammunition, baggage, and such of their stores as they may be able to transport.

4. That after the expiration of the thirty-six hours mentioned in the preceding article, the British troops before the town shall take possession of it, and those now at Wappetaw shall proceed to Fort Moultrie.

5. That the American army, thus collected at Lampriere's, shall have ten days, from the expiration of the thirty-six hours before-mentioned, to march where-ever General Lincoln may think proper to the eastward of Cooper River, without any movement being made by the British troops, or part of them out of the town, or Fort Moultrie.

6. That the sick and wounded of the American and French hospitals, with their medicines, stores, the Surgeons, and Director-General, shall remain in the town, and be supplied with the necessaries requisite, until provision can be made for their removal, which will be as speedily as possible.

7. That no soldier shall be encouraged to desert, or permitted to enlist on either side.

8. That the French Consul, his house, papers, and other moveable property, shall be protected and untouched, and a proper time granted him for retiring to any place that may afterwards be agreed upon be- ... et of the Bri- ... rovidence, ... with the ... ave liberty ... on board, ... iladelphia, ... French in- ... ir persons ... as do not ... ment, to ... n the state, ... remove such part thereof as they chuse, as well as themselves and families, and that during that time, they or any of them may have it at their option to reside occasionally in town or country.

12. That the same protection to their persons and properties, and the same time for the removal of their effects, be given to the subjects of France and Spain, residing amongst us, as are required for the citizens in the preceding articles.

No. VII.

SIR, Camp before Charlestown, May 8, 1780.

CIrcumstanced as I now am with respect to the place invested, humanity only can induce me to lay within your reach the terms I had determined should not again be proffered.

The fall of Fort Sullivan, the destruction (on the 6th instant) of what remained of your cavalry, the critical period to which our approaches against the town have brought us, mark this as the term of your hopes of succour, (could you ever have formed any) and as an hour, beyond which resistance is temerity.

By this last summons therefore, I throw to your charge whatever vindictive severity exasperated soldiers may inflict on the unhappy people, whom you devote by persevering in a fruitless defence.

I shall expect your answer until eight o'clock, when hostilities will commence again, unless the town be surrendered, &c. &c.

(Signed) H. CLINTON.

Major-General Lincoln.

No. VIII.

SIR, Charlestown, May 8, 1780.

YOUR letter to me of this date is now under consideration—there are so many different interests to be consulted, that I have to propose that hostilities do not again commence till twelve.

(Signed) B. LINCOLN.

His Excellency Sir Henry Clinton.

No. IX.

SIR, May 8, 1780.

I CONSENT that hostilities shall not again commence before the hour of twelve, as you desire.

I have the honour to be, Sir, &c.

(Signed) H. CLINTON.

Major-General Lincoln.

No. X.

SIR, May 8, 1780.

AS more time has been expended in consulting the different interests than I supposed there would be, I have to request that the truce may be continued until four o'clock.

(Signed) B. LINCOLN.

His Excellency Sir Henry Clinton.

No. XI.

Articles of Capitulation proposed by Major-Gen. Lincoln.

Art. 1. That all acts of hostility and work shall cease between the besiegers and besieged, until the articles of capitulation shall be agreed on, signed, and executed, or collectively rejected.

2. The town and fortifications shall be surrendered to the Commander in Chief of the British forces, such as they now stand.

3. The continental troops and sailors, with their baggage, shall be conducted to a place to be agreed on, where they will remain prisoners of war, until exchanged—While prisoners, they shall be supplied with good and wholesome provisions, in such quantity as is served out to the troops of his Britannic Majesty.

4. The militia now in garrison shall be permitted to return to their respective homes, and be secured in their persons and property.

5. The sick and wounded shall be continued under the care of their own Surgeons, and be supplied with medicines, and such necessaries as are allowed to the British hospitals.

6. The officers of the army and navy shall keep their horses, swords, pistols and baggage, which shall not be searched, and retain their servants.

NEW-JERSEY GAZETTE (TRENTON)

June 28, 1780

By Monday, May 8, the British held all escape routes from Charleston. That day, Clinton sent a summons to General Lincoln to surrender, as recorded in the *New-Jersey Gazette*.

LONDON CHRONICLE

June 17, 1780

—

The *London Chronicle* dated June 17, 1780, printed Sir Henry Clinton's account of the May 12 surrender of Charleston. Charleston remained under British control until they evacuated it in 1782. It was the largest surrender of an American armed force until the 1862 surrender of Union forces at Harper's Ferry during the Civil War.

---

nain.

Charles Town, May 13, 1780.

trouble your Lordſhip with a repe- delays and difficulties which pro- us operation until the 29th of hich day the landing on Charles was effected.

e a depot was formed; the Admi- the Bar, and I had the eſſential officers and ſeamen of the Royal operations. I was alſo ſtrengthened s from Georgia, under Brigadier- rſon, which, through a country in- rivers, and rendered more difficult s, had advanced, not unoppoſed, f twelve days, from Savannah to

e of Aſhley, under the conduct of inſtone, and by the good ſervice and ſailors of the fleet, was ac- ith order and expedition, and nce on the part of the enemy. ucceeding it the army mo ed to- Town, and on the night of the broke ground within 800 yards of s.

our guns were mounted in bat- ad the ſatisfaction to ſee the Ad- Charles Town Harbour, with conduct deſerved, though under re from Sullivan's Iſland. riod we judged it adviſeable to ſed ſummons to the place, which nſwer I have the honour to tranſ-

ies were opened the next day. fect we ſoon obſerved the fire of dvanced works to abate conſide- tention of the engineers, and di- troops but encreaſing as they pro- cond parallel was completed on pril, and ſecure approaches open- were now within 450 yards of

nications had hitherto required ttention. They had been choſen u's landing in Stono River acroſs and by ſmall inlets, leaving only carriage into the part of Aſhley our camp. the protection of the ſtores and tono, others on the communica- veral redoubts and batteries on the labours neceſſary to give ſe- portant a point. e of the fleet in the harbour re- n apprehenſion on that part, and

vers to croſs, and other difficult operations to effect, in preſence of a very ſuperior cavalry, which might haraſs him much. It was there- fore of the utmoſt importance to ... corps, and, as ſuddenly as poſſ... principal paſſes of the country.

The ſurprize and defeat of ... valry and militia of the rebels, a... Biggin's Bridge over Cooper by ... lonel Tarleton with the horſe, ... Major Ferguſon's detachment, ... mand of the country to Colonel ... into his hands great ſupplies of ... enabled him to take a poſt n... Wandoo River, forbidding by ... acceſs to the town from Coope... Navigation. An armed naval fo... Admiral ſent into Sevee Bay, and another ſtationed in Spencer's Inlet, completed the in- veſtiture to the ſea.

A conſiderable reinforcement joining me from New York the 18th of April, I immediately ſtrengthened the corps beyond Cooper river, which, thus augmented, I requeſted Lieutenant General Earl Cornwallis to take under his com- mand.

On the 6th of May the third parallel was compleated cloſe to the edge of the rebel canal, and a ſhip carried to the dam, which contained its water on the right, by which means a great part was drained to the bottom.

We could now form juſter opinions of the de- fences of the town towards the land, which ex- tended in a chain of redoubts, lines and batte- ries, from Aſhley to Cooper. In front of either flank of the works, ſwamps, which the canal connects, ooze to each river; betwixt theſe im- pediments and the place are two rows of abba- tis, various other obſtructions, and a double pic- ketted ditch; a horn work of maſonry, which, during the ſiege, the enemy cloſed as a kind of citadel, ſtrengthened the center of the line and the gate, where the ſame natural defences were not found as nearer the water: eighty pieces of cannon or mortars were mounted in the extent of theſe lines.

On the 6th of May our batteries were ready in the third parallel.

New and very forcible motives now prevailed to induce the place to capitulate. Admiral Arbuthnot had landed a force of ſeamen and mariners on Sullivan's Iſland under Captain Hudſon, to whom, on the threat that ſhips ſhould batter the fort, the garriſon delivered themſelves up on terms.

Lieutenant-General Earl Cornwallis had been no leſs ſucceſsful in the country. The ca- valry under Lieutenant-Colonel Tarleton had

the enemy ſolicited, they had ſhewn in their propoſals for a ſurrender far too extenſive pre- tenſions, the Admiral and myſelf could not re-

quieſcence in the terms he had two days before objected to. Whatever ſevere juſtice might dictate on ſuch an occaſion, we reſolved not to preſs to unconditional ſubmiſſion a reduced ar- my, whom we hoped clemency might yet re- concile to us. The articles of capitulation were therefore ſigned, ſuch as I have the honor to incloſe them.

On the 12th Major-General Leſlie took poſ- ſeſſion of the town.

There are taken ſeven general officers, a commodore, ten continental regiments, and three battalions of artillery, together with town and country militia, French and ſeamen, mak- ing about ſix thouſand men in arms. The ti- tular deputy governor, council, and civil offi- cers, are alſo priſoners.

Four frigates and ſeveral armed veſſels, with a great number of boats, have likewiſe fallen into our poſſeſſion, and about four hundred pieces of canon.

Of the garriſon, artillery, and ſtores, your Lordſhip will have as perfect returns as I ſhall be able to collect.

I have yet, my Lord, to add to this letter the expreſſions of gratitude I owe to the army, whoſe courage and toil have given me ſuc- ceſs.

I have moſt warmly to thank Lieutenant General Earl Cornwallis, Major Generals Leſ- lie, Huyne, and Koſborth, and Brigadier-Ge- neral Paterſon, for their animated aſſiſtance.

I truſt I do no not flatter myſelf vainly, that the good ſervices during the ſiege of the officers and ſoldiers of the royal artillery, of Captain Elphinſtone, and the officers and ſeamen of the royal navy ſerving with us on ſhore, of the corps of engineers, of the officers and ſoldiers of every corps, Britiſh and Heſſian, and particularly the Yager detachment, will receive his Majeſty's gra- cious approbation.

[Price Threepence.]

REPORTING THE

CAROLINA BACKCOUNTRY MILITIA ACTIONS

By Charles B. Baxley

The British southern strategy was paying off in the summer of 1780—Georgia and the South Carolina coast were again under the Crown's control. Lord Cornwallis established his inland posts at Camden and Ninety Six in the South Carolina backcountry and reestablished Royal governance and militias to subdue the rebellion in North Carolina. Ninety Six controlled the route into Cherokee country linking the British with her Native American allies. Camden controlled the roads to central North Carolina and Virginia.

A December 5, 1780, letter from Charlotte, North Carolina, printed in the February 15, 1781, **Connecticut Journal** *accurately summarized the summer's actions: "Such a train of important victories obtained by raw militia, has no parallel in history."*

The infamous British Legion, a Loyalist-American-comprised infantry and cavalry commanded by Banastre Tarleton, raced through Camden to catch the last remnant of Continentals commanded by Colonel Abraham Buford as he retreated from the South Carolina Lowcountry in late May 1780. Tarleton caught Buford at the Waxhaws near the North Carolina border. While it was a British victory, "massacre" echoed through the Carolina backcountry. British overall commander General Henry Clinton's political proclamations also polarized the backcountry militiamen: loyal British citizens to arm and put down this rebellion. It was civil war.

Backcountry Patriot militia leaders from both Carolinas and Georgia, alive with zeal for liberty and self-determination, cooperated. North Carolina acted as the safe base for organization and recruitment and as a source of money and supply for South Carolina militiamen like Cols. Thomas Sumter, John Thomas Jr., and James Williams. They cooperated with the North Carolina leaders Colonel Charles McDowell in the west, General Griffith Rutherford in the central area, and General Henry William Harrington in the east.

Sumter's troops countered the British raids into the New Acquisition District of South Carolina by annihilating Captain Christian Huck's British Legion detachment at Williamson's Plantation in July. Sumter, supported by North Carolina militia, next attacked the strongly fortified British outpost at Rocky Mount, South Carolina, on July 30, 1780. Volunteers of New York and South Carolina Loyalists commanded by Lieutenant Colonel George Turnbull garrisoned Rocky Mount. Sumter's troops withdrew after a five-hour fight, without artillery to force the fortifications, when a rainstorm soaked the fire set by two intrepid soldiers to burn the British-occupied buildings. Although the August 29, 1780, excerpt from "Robertson's *New-York Gazette*," printed in the *Providence Gazette* of September 16, 1780, reported a general bayonet charge by the British, this refers to the British sally out of the defensive works to drive back the two flame throwers.

Again on the offensive a week later, Sumter's troops with North Carolina militia attacked the main British outpost at Hanging Rock. The Americans dispersed Colonel Samuel Brian's North Carolina Loyalist militia regiment and so severely damaged the Prince of Wales's American (Loyalist) Regiment, it would never fight again. After almost five hours of combat, which pushed the surviving British into a defensive square, the combat ended upon the arrival of some British Legion cavalry and Sumter's troops exhausting all of their ammunition. Sumter withdrew with many prisoners and military supplies, militia having taken on British regulars and defeated them. Bias is again evident in the report of this battle in the September 16, 1780, *Providence Gazette* acknowledging that the partisans claimed victory but disputed Sumter's claim by relating that some Legion cavalry "dashed among the rebels, put them to flight, and pursued them some a considerable distance." Sumter's men controlled the battlefield for over four hours, marched through three regimental camps, took prisoners and supplies from all of the British camps, and captured the British artillery; his six hundred men did not decide to withdraw because thirty or forty cavalrymen arrived.

A December 5, 1780, letter from Charlotte, North Carolina, printed in the February 15, 1781, *Connecticut Journal*, accurately summarized the summer's actions: "Such a train of important victories obtained by raw militia, has no parallel in history."

Into this cauldron marched the new American Southern Army commander, General Horatio Gates, the hero of Saratoga, supported by militia from North Carolina and Virginia. He relied on the partisans who secured his flanks, but the Battle of Camden a week later was an unmitigated disaster.

THURSDAY, FEBRUARY 15, 1781. [NUMB. 694.

CONNECTICUT JOURNAL.

NEW-HAVEN: Printed by THOMAS and SAMUEL GREEN, near the College.

St. John's, in Antigua, December 9.

"Although ſome pains has been taken to aſperſe the militia of this, as well as our ſiſter States, on account of what happened on the memorable 16th and 18th of Auguſt; yet, I hope, that an impartial world will not looſe ſight of thoſe ſtriking marks of heroiſm diſplayed at Ramſour's, on the 20th of June, where Col. Locke commanded; at Packelet, in the night of the 15th of July, where Col. M'Dowel commanded; at Coleſon's, the mouth of Rockey river, on the 21ſt of July, where Col. now General Davidſon commanded, in which he was wounded; at Rocky-Mount, on the 23d of July, where the heroic Gen. Sumpter commanded; at Hanging-Rock, on the 6th of Auguſt, where General Sumpter commanded; at Enoree, the 19th of Auguſt, where the late intrepid Col. Williams commanded; at Auguſta, in Georgia, on the 12th of September, where Col. Clarke commanded; at King's Mountain, on the 7th of October, where Col. Campbell commanded; at Broad-River, on the 9th of November, where Gen. Sumpter commanded, & where Maj. Wemyſs was made priſoner; at Blackſtocks, on Tyger river, on the 20th of November, where Gen. Sumpter commanded, and was unfortunately wounded; beſides ſeveral other rencounters. Such a train of important victories obtained by raw militia, has no parrallel in hiſtory.

"The firmneſs of the people in Mecklenburg, and Rowan counties, when the enemy advanced to Char-

... ment, and conceived himſelf reinſtated. The people generally abandoned their habitations, ſome fled with what of their property they could carry, others took the field,

CONNECTICUT JOURNAL (NEW HAVEN)
February 15, 1781

A December 5, 1780, letter from Charlotte, North Carolina, printed in the February 15, 1781, *Connecticut Journal*, accurately summarized the summer's actions: "Such a train of important victories obtained by raw militia, has no parallel in history."

SEPTEMBER 16, 1780

The PROVIDENCE GAZETTE

CHARLES-TOWN (South-Carolina) July 19.

From different parts of the province we have the most agreeable accounts of there being every appearance of a very plentiful harvest. There has not been in the memory of the oldest planter a more favourable season.

July 26. On Thursday last arrived here his Majesty's ship Hydra, with five sail of transports under convoy, from Savannah, having on board the Hessian regiment of Trambach.

August 9. On Friday the 28th ult. the privateer schooner Highland Lass, Capt. Sloo, returned to Savannah. On the 12th of June, she was taken by the brigantine Wasp, formerly belonging to this port, but then in possession of Spaniard. Next day she fell in with and was retaken by his Majesty's ships Richmond and Camilla, who also took the Wasp the same day. On the day following, the men of war captured 4 vessels out of 25 that had come out from the Capes of Virginia.

The following are the particulars we have been able to procure of the action on the 30th of last month: Col. Turnbull receiving intimation of the approach of a large body of rebels, said to be led by Sumpter, formerly a Lieutenant-Colonel in one of the South-Carolina Continental battalions, retired with his men, consisting of the New-York volunteers, and some loyal militia, into a block-house of stockade, at Rocky Mount, where on the 30th he was summoned to surrender. Returning a defiance in answer, a considerable firing commenced, and continued for some hours; but the enemy hearing that a reinforcement was coming from a post 9 miles distant, made a precipitate retreat, in which their speed was encreased by Col. Turnbull's dashing his corps with fixed bayonets amongst them. A number of their killed and wounded were left on the field; among the former a Colonel Neil.

Some banditti from North-Carolina, and the northern parts of this province, have been lately skulking and plundering about the Cheraws, and towards Georgetown, and have kidnapped several gentlemen, who were friends to government. They are encouraged to make these inroads by the hopes of indiscriminate plunder, held out to them by the leaders of a desperate faction.

August 10. Yesterday intelligence was brought to town, that a body of rebels, consisting of about five thousand, attacked one of our posts near the Hanging Rock, thirty miles above Camden, on Sunday last, but were repulsed. The report is, that the rebels charged our brave troops, who consisted of about two hundred and fifty men, two different times, but were drove back with great loss; and on making the third, with their whole force, were so confident of victory, that the officer who was leading them on exclaimed with great vociferation, that the day was their own; at that instant, a detachment of the cavalry of the legion arrived, dashed in amongst the rebels, put them to flight, and pursued them a considerable distance.

PROVIDENCE GAZETTE (RHODE ISLAND)

September 16, 1780

Bias is evident in the Hanging Rock battle report in the *Providence Gazette*. It acknowledged that the partisans claimed victory but disputed Sumter's claim by relating that some Legion cavalry "dashed among the rebels, put them to flight, and pursued them some a considerable distance." Sumter's men controlled the battlefield for over four hours, marched through three regimental camps, took prisoners and supplies from all of the British camps, and captured the British artillery; his six hundred men did not decide to withdraw because thirty or forty cavalrymen arrived.

ely harsh and

as warm, but,
d much the best
imed the out of
y averse to the
was his enemy,
nended him, as
any command,
by reciting his
answer to his
d directed him
mediate trial,
e; and in the
negyric on his

, and a mark-
difference be-
man in office.
y agreed with

make what he
declaring that
ave the House
n from attend-
le friend, the
ichmond) and
elf to the after-
to that House
a greater like-
purpose. His
at ability, and
e said of him,
is voice like a
t. His Lord-
venal House of
lty man, and
the Tower.
to order, and
grounds, de-
, and shewing
ually contrary
y to liberality.
l very ably.
for, and the

ents, 42.
ndwich.
were then cal-
very distinctly
at of his hav-
to prepare the
the civil pow-
the preceding

nt of his con-
, that he had
rth, and that
ay, as a Ma-
es to preserve

his manner of rejecting the bill.

At length it was read a first time, and on the motion of Lord Stormont the bill was rejected.

The second reading of the bill to amend an act of the 3d of the present King, intituled, "an act to prevent occasional freemen from voting at elections of members to serve in Parliament for cities and boroughs," was, upon motion, on Friday last, in the House of Commons, put off till to-morrow.

The House rose between ten and eleven o'clock.

June 6.

The idea of appointing Commissioners, who shall cross the Atlantic, and treat for peace with the Americans, is again revived. It is proper (from an authority that cannot be overthrown) to warn the public, that such a measure will only serve to aggravate the burthen of national expences. Mr. Adams (a Plenipotentiary now at Paris) is near at hand; and, although not permitted to make the first propositions, is *totally* and *absolutely* empowered to listen, in the name of the United States, to general (but not *particular*) overtures.

Extract of a letter from Chatham, May 18.

"We have had several riots this week, in this town and neighbourhood, between the naval, military, and dock-yard men. Scarce a night passes without hearing of three or four of them being dangerously wounded; and on Thursday night three of these desperate wretches received their death wounds in an affray on the fair ground, and are since dead."

From the ROYAL MAGAZINE.

A short Account of the Origin, ecclesiastical Government, and Religion, of the RUSSIAN EMPIRE.

THE Russians are originally from Sclavonia, a province in Hungary. Ancient history says, that in the fifth century, three Princes went with their followers to seek new habitations, their native country being too narrow for them. It is said they were brothers, and the eldest, named Chech, settled in Bohemia, and he and his successors reigned Kings there many ages; Lech, the second brother, proceeded yet further east, and settled in Poland, and there erected a kingdom; and Rus, the third brother, went still further east, and settled a principality at Muscow.

It is observed, that in the Sclavonic language, the Bohemians are called Chechy, the Poles Lechy, and the Russians Russy. The language of these three countries is the same, and only differ in dialect, as the High Dutch from the Low Dutch. The Bohemians and Poles about the year 800 embraced the Christian religion, at the persuasion of some Romish Priests, and consequently the rites and ceremonies of that church, which they observe to this day, and make use of Latin characters in writings. But the Russians, who embraced the Christian religion much about this time, were instructed by Greek monks from Constantinople, and adhered strictly to the doctrines of the Greek church. In printing and writing they make use of Greek characters. They never acknowledged the

in the memory of the oldest planter a more favourable season.

July 26. On Thursday last arrived here his Majesty's ship Hydra, with five sail of transports under convoy, from Savannah, having on board the Hessian regiment of Trambach.

August 9. On Friday the 28th ult. the privateer schooner Highland Lass, Capt. Sloo, returned to Savannah. On the 12th of June, she was taken by the brigantine Wasp, formerly belonging to this port, but then in possession of a Spaniard. Next day she fell in with and was retaken by his Majesty's ships Richmond and Camilla, who also took the Wasp the same day. On the day following, the men of war captured 4 vessels out of 25 that had come out from the Capes of Virginia.

The following are the particulars we have been able to procure of the action on the 30th of last month: Col. Turnbull receiving intimation of the approach of a large body of rebels, said to be led by Sumpter, formerly a Lieutenant-Colonel in one of the South-Carolina Continental battalions, retired with his men, consisting of the New-York volunteers, and some loyal militia, into a block-house or stockade, at Rocky Mount, where on the 30th he was summoned to surrender. Returning a defiance in answer, a considerable firing commenced, and continued for some hours; but the enemy hearing that a reinforcement was coming from a post 9 miles distant, made a precipitate retreat, in which their speed was encreased by Col. Turnbull's dashing his corps with fixed bayonets amongst them. A number of their killed and wounded were left on the field; among the former a Colonel Neil.

Some banditti from North-Carolina, and the northern parts of this province, have been lately skulking and plundering about the Cheraws, and towards Georgetown, and have kidnapped several gentlemen, who were friends to government. They are encouraged to make these inroads by the hopes of indiscriminate plunder, held out to them by the leaders of a desperate faction.

August 10. Yesterday intelligence was brought to town, that a body of rebels, consisting of about five thousand, attacked one of our posts near the Hanging Rock, thirty miles above Camden, on Sunday last, but were repulsed. The report is, that the rebels charged our brave troops, who consisted of about two hundred and fifty men, two different times, but were drove back with great loss; and on making the third, with their whole force, were so confident of victory, that the officer who was leading them on exclaimed with great vociferation, that the day was their own; at that instant, a detachment of the cavalry of the legion arrived, dashed in amongst the rebels, put them to flight, and pursued them a considerable distance.

BALTIMORE, August 29.

An embarkation of troops lately took place at Charlestown, South-Carolina, it is said, for St. Au-

REPORTING THE

BATTLE OF CAMDEN

By Jim Piecuch

On August 16, 1780, American and British forces engaged in one of the largest battles of the Revolution in an open pine forest eight miles north of Camden, South Carolina. The engagement, which lasted nearly an hour, resulted in a crushing American defeat.

The Continental Congress responded to the British capture of Charleston on May 12, 1780, by appointing Major General Horatio Gates, hero of Saratoga, to take command of a new southern army. Gates assembled eight Continental regiments and contingents of North Carolina and Virginia militia twenty miles north of the British post at Camden. He intended to occupy a strong position about six miles north of Camden while partisans cut the town's supply lines. The British would then be forced either to attack Gates or abandon Camden.

The British commander in the south, Lieutenant General Charles, Earl Cornwallis, recognized the danger and chose to fight (as he explained in his report published in the *London Chronicle* on October 10, 1780). At 10:00 p.m. on August 15, Cornwallis marched from Camden to attack the Americans in their camp. Coincidentally, Gates marched at the same hour to occupy the position he had selected.

The vanguards of both armies met at about 2:00 a.m., and after some inconclusive fighting both commanders deployed their troops to resume the battle at daylight (the *Providence Gazette* of September 16, 1780, correctly reported the time of the initial encounter, but the main battle did not begin at that time). The exact strength of the American army is unknown. The best estimate of American strength is about 4,100. American press accounts (such as that in the *Gazette*) tended to understate the numbers of their own army and exaggerate those of the British. A field return for Cornwallis's army listed 2,239 men present at the battle.

Gates deployed the militia on his left flank, a Continental brigade on his right, and held his second brigade of Continentals in reserve. Cornwallis positioned his regular British regiments on his right, his Loyalist (provincial) units on his left, and kept two regular battalions and his cavalry in reserve.

At first light Gates ordered the militia on his left to charge the British in their front. He also ordered the reserve Continental brigade to occupy the space vacated by the militia and instructed the commander of the other Continental brigade, Major General Johann de Kalb, to make a supporting attack. Cornwallis's orders mirrored those of Gates. He instructed his right under Lieutenant Colonel James Webster to attack the militia and his left under Lieutenant Colonel Francis, Lord Rawdon, to advance in support of Webster.

The attacking North Carolina and Virginia militiamen met the British regulars rushing toward them and panicked. Throwing away their muskets, the militia fled with the exception of one North Carolina regiment (the September 16, 1780, *Providence Gazette* accurately described the militia's flight but incorrectly credited the South Carolina militia as having fought well). Gates tried to rally the fugitives but was caught up in the mob and swept from the battlefield. Webster wheeled to meet the reserve Continental brigade, and the veterans of both armies exchanged volleys with neither side able to gain an advantage. Cornwallis reinforced Webster with a reserve battalion, yet the Continental line held (Cornwallis noted their strong resistance in the October 10, 1780, *London Chronicle*).

On the American right, the Continentals drove Rawdon's line back, captured a British cannon (as the

Gazette recounted), and nearly seized Rawdon himself. Cornwallis's other reserve battalion stabilized the line. Finally, Cornwallis ordered the cavalry to charge through a gap between the two wings of the American line. Threatened with encirclement, the Continentals fled. British cavalry pursued the Americans for twenty-two miles (as reported in the *Chronicle*).

British casualties totaled 324 killed, wounded, and missing. American losses can only be estimated. Cornwallis reported capturing 695 Americans, and at least three hundred were killed, including de Kalb (heavier casualties than reported in the *Gazette*).

Congress responded by dismissing Gates and appointing Major General Nathanael Greene to replace him. Because Cornwallis lacked supplies, he could not pursue his beaten opponent. The Americans used the reprieve to regroup in preparation for the next British move.

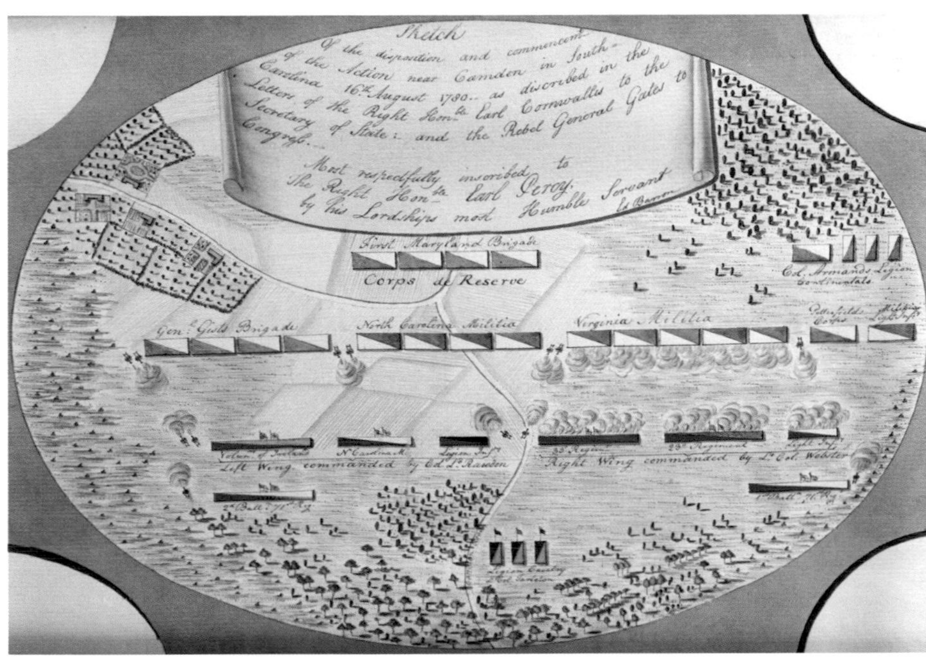

BATTLE OF CAMDEN, 1780
The Bridgeman Art Library

The Battle of Camden was fought in an open pine forest eight miles north of Camden, South Carolina.

BATTLE OF CAMDEN,
DEATH OF DE KALB
North Wind Picture Archives

The Battle of Camden was one of the largest battles of the Revolution and resulted in a crushing American defeat that included the death of Major General Johann de Kalb.

MEMBERS *elected for the ensuing* PARLIAMENT, *continued.*

ABERDENSHIRE. Alexander Gordon, Esq.

Anstruther, Pittenweem, and *Kilrenny.* Sir John Anstruther, Bart.

St. Andrews, Forfar, Coupar, Perth, and *Dundee.* George Dempster, Esq.

Dumfermline, Culross, Stirling, and *Queensferry.* Major Campbell.

Dunbar, Lauder, North Berwick, Haddington, and *Jedburgh.* Francis Charteris of Beanston, Esq.

Rossshire. George Graham, Esq.

Rutherglen, Dumbarton, Glasgow, and *Renfrew.* James Crawford, of Auchinames, Esq.

Selkirk. John Pringle, Esq.

Wigtown, Whitehorn, New Galloway, and *Stranrawer.* William Adams, Esq.

Postscript.

THE LONDON GAZETTE EXTRAORDINARY.

Whitehall, October 9, 1780.

THIS Morning Captain Ross, Aid de Camp to Lieutenant-General Earl Cornwallis, arrived in Town from South-…

LONDON CHRONICLE

October 10, 1780

The Continental Congress responded to the British capture of Charleston on May 12, 1780, by appointing Major General Horatio Gates, hero of Saratoga, to take command of a new southern army. Gates assembled his forces twenty miles north of the British post at Camden and planned to occupy a strong position about six miles north of town. British commander in the South, Lieutenant General Charles, Earl Cornwallis, recognized the danger and chose to fight.

… Sumpter, who, after having in vain attempted to force the Posts at Rocky Mount and Hanging Rock, was believed to be at that Time trying to get round the Left of our Position, to cut off our Communication with the Congarees and Charles-Town; that the disaffected Country between Pedee and Black River had actually revolted; and that Lord Rawdon was contracting his Posts, and preparing to assemble his Force at Camden.

In consequence of this Information, after finishing some important Points of Business at Charles-Town, I set out on the Evening of the 10th, and arrived at Camden on the Night between the 13th and 14th, and there found Lord Rawdon with our whole Force, except Lieutenant Colonel Turnbull's small Detachment, which fell back from Rocky Mount to Major Ferguson's Posts of the Militia of Ninety-six on Little River.

I had now my Option to make, either to retire or attempt the Enemy; for the Position at Camden was a bad one to be attacked in, and by General Sumpter's advancing down the Wateree, my Supplies must have failed me in a few Days.

I saw no Difficulty in making good my Retreat to Charles-Town with the Troops that were able to march; but in taking that Resolution, I must have not only left near 800 Sick and a great Quantity of Stores at this Place, but I clearly saw the Loss of the whole Province, except Charles-Town, and of all Georgia, except Savannah, as immediate Consequences, besides forfeiting all Pretensions to future Confidence from our Friends in this Part of America.

On the other Hand, there was no Doubt of the Rebel Army being well appointed, and of its Number being upwards of 5000 Men, exclusive of General Sumpter's Detachment, and of a Corps of Virginia Militia of 12 or 1500 Men, either actually joined, or expected to join the main Body every Hour; and my own Corps, which never was numerous, was now reduced, by Sickness and other Casualties, to about 1400 Fighting Men of Regulars and Provincials, with 4 or 500 Militia and North Carolina Refugees.

However, the greatest Part of the Troops that I had being perfectly good, and having left Charles-Town sufficiently garrisoned and provided for a Siege, and seeing little to lose by a Defeat, and much to gain by a Victory, I resolved to take the first good Opportunity to attack the Rebel Army.

Accordingly, I took great Pains to procure … Course of the Night.

I had proceeded nine Miles when about Half an Hour past Two in the Morning my advanced Guard fell in with the Enemy. By the Weight of the Fire I was convinced they were in considerable Force, and was soon assured by some Deserters and Prisoners that it was the whole Rebel Army on its March to attack us at Camden. I immediately halted, and formed, and the Enemy doing the same, the Firing soon ceased. Confiding in the disciplined Courage of his Majesty's Troops, and well apprized by several intelligent Inhabitants, that the Ground on which both Armies stood, being narrowed by Swamps on the Right and Left, was extremely favourable for my Numbers, I did not chuse to hazard the great Stake for which I was going to fight, to the Uncertainty and Confusion to which an Action in the Dark is so particularly liable: But having taken Measures that the Enemy should not have it in their Power to avoid an Engagement on that Ground, I resolved to defer the Attack till Day. At the Dawn I made my last Disposition, and formed the Troops in the following Order: The Division of the Right, consisting of a small Corps of Light Infantry, the 23d and 33d Regiments, under the Command of Lieutenant Colonel Webster; the Division of the Left, consisting of the Volunteers of Ireland, Infantry of the Legion, and Part of Lieutenant Colonel Hamilton's North Carolina Regiment, under the Command of Lord Rawdon, with two Six and two Three Pounders, which were commanded by Lieutenant M'Leod. The 71st Regiment, with two Six Pounders, was formed as a Reserve, one Battalion in the Rear of the Division of the Right, the other of that of the Left, and the Cavalry of the Legion in the Rear, and the Country being woody, close to the 71st Regiment, with Orders to seize any Opportunity that might offer to break the Enemy's Line, and to be ready to protect our own, in case any Corps should meet with a Check.

This Disposition was just made when I perceived that the Enemy, having likewise persisted in their Resolution to fight, were formed in two Lines opposite and near to us; and observing a Movement on their Left, which I supposed to be with an Intention to make some Alteration in their Order, I directed Lieutenant Colonel Webster to begin the Attack, which was done with great Vigor, and in a few Minutes the Action was general along the whole Front. It was at this Time a dead Calm, with a little Haziness in the Air, which, preventing the Smoke from rising, occasioned so thick a Darkness, that it was difficult to see the Effect of a very heavy and well supported Fire on both Sides. Our Line continued to advance in good Order, and with the cool Intrepidity of experienced British Soldiers, keeping up a constant Fire, or making Use of Bayonets, as Opportunities offered; and, after an obstinate Resistance during Three Quarters of an Hour, threw the Enemy into total Confusion, and forced them to give Way on all Quarters.

At this Instant I ordered the Cavalry to complete the Route, which was performed with their usual Promptitude and Gallantry; and after doing great Execution on the Field of Battle, they continued the Pursuit to Hanging Rock, 22 Miles from the Place where the Action happened, during which many of the Enemy were slain, a Number of Prisoners, near 150 Waggons (in one of which was a Brass Cannon, the Carriage of which had been damaged in the Skirmish of the Night), a considerable Quantity of Military Stores, and all the Baggage and Camp Equipage of the Rebel Army, fell into our Hands.

The Loss of the Enemy was very considerable; a Number of Colours, and seven Pieces of Brass Cannon (being all their Artillery that were in the Action), with all their Ammunition Waggons, were taken; between Eight and Nine Hundred were killed, among that Number Brigadier-General Gregory, and about One Thousand Prisoners, many of whom wounded, of which Number were Major-General Baron de Kalb, since dead, and Brigadier General Rutherford.

I have the Honour to inclose a Return of Killed and Wounded on our Side. The Loss of so many brave Men is much to be lamented; but the Number is moderate in Proportion to so great an Advantage.

The Behaviour of his Majesty's Troops in general was beyond all Praise; it did Honour to themselves and to their Country.

I was particularly indebted to Colonel Lord Rawdon and to Lieutenant Colonel Webster for the distinguished Courage and Ability with which they conducted their respective Divisions; and the Capacity and Vi-

arliament for cities and bo-
ation, on Friday laſt, in the
ut off till to-morrow.
een ten and eleven o'clock.
une 6.
ing Commiſſioners, who ſhall
reat for peace with the Ame-
.' It is proper (from an au-
verthrown) to warn the pub-
will only ſerve to aggravate
expences. Mr. Adams (a
Paris) is near at hand; and,
to make the firſt propoſitions,
empowered to liſten, in the
ates, to general (but not *par-*

rom Chatham, May 18.
veral riots this week, in this
d, between the naval, mili-
n. Scarce a night paſſes with-
our of them being dangerouſ-
hurſday night three of theſe
ved their death wounds in an
nd, and are ſince dead."

AL MAGAZINE.
Origin, eccleſiaſtical Govern-
the RUSSIAN EMPIRE.
originally from Sclavonia, a
gary. Ancient hiſtory ſays,
three Princes went with their
bitations, their native coun-
them. It is ſaid they were
named Chech, ſettled in Bo-
cceſſors reigned Kings there
econd brother, proceeded yet
n Poland, and there erected
the third brother, went ſtill
principality at Muſcow.
in the Sclavonic language,
Chechy, the Poles Lechy,
The language of theſe three
only differ in dialect, as the
w Dutch. The Bohemians
800 embraced the Chriſtian
of ſome Romiſh Prieſts, and
ceremonies of that church,
s day, and make uſe of La-
. But the Ruſſians, who
igion much about this time,
monks from Conſtantino-
the doctrines of the Greek
writing they make uſe of
never acknowledged the
the church, but the Patri-
ll the time Conſtantinople
and the Ruſs clergy elected
reſidence at Muſcow, and
er in all eccleſiaſtical mat-
t thinking too great, depoſ-
nſelf head of the church.
ent in ſecular and monaſtic
are Archbiſhops, Biſhops,
ecular order of prieſts may
die, they cannot officiate in
to a monaſtery; which is
ind to their wives. The
. Baſil, whereof there are
; each monaſtery has a
ndit. The monks are not
are two or three nunne-
are not very regular, for
ceive company.

August 9. On Friday the 28th ult. the privateer ſchooner Highland Laſs, Capt. Sloo, returned to Savannah. On the 12th of June, ſhe was taken by the brigantine Waſp, formerly belonging to this port, but then in poſſeſſion of a Spaniard. Next day ſhe fell in with and was retaken by his Majeſty's ſhips Richmond and Camilla, who alſo took the Waſp the ſame day. On the day following, the men of war captured 4 veſſels out of 25 that had come out from the Capes of Virginia.

The following are the particulars we have been able to procure of the action on the 30th of laſt month: Col. Turnbull receiving intimation of the approach of a large body of rebels, ſaid to be led by Sumpter, formerly a Lieutenant-Colonel in one of the South-Carolina Continental battalions, retired with his men, conſiſting of the New-York volunteers, and ſome loyal militia, into a block-houſe or ſtockade, at Rocky Mount, where on the 30th he was ſummoned to ſurrender. Returning a defiance in anſwer, a conſiderable firing commenced, and continued for ſome hours; but the enemy hearing that a reinforcement was coming from a poſt 9 miles diſtant, made a precipitate retreat, in which their ſpeed was encreaſed by Col. Turnbull's daſhing his corps with fixed bayonets amongſt them. A number of their killed and wounded were left on the field; among the former a Colonel Neil.

Some banditti from North-Carolina, and the northern parts of this province, have been lately ſkulking and plundering about the Cheraws, and towards Georgetown, and have kidnapped ſeveral gentlemen, who were friends to government. They are encouraged to make theſe inroads by the hopes of indiſcriminate plunder, held out to them by the leaders of a deſperate faction.

Auguſt 10. Yeſterday intelligence was brought to town, that a body of rebels, conſiſting of about five thouſand, attacked one of our poſts near the Hanging Rock, thirty miles above Camden, on Sunday laſt, but were repulſed. The report is, that the rebels charged our brave troops, who conſiſted of about two hundred and fifty men, two different times, but were drove back with great loſs; and on making the third, with their whole force, were ſo confident of victory, that the officer who was leading them on exclaimed with great vociferation, that the day was their own; at that inſtant, a detachment of the cavalry of the legion arrived, daſhed in amongſt the rebels, put them to flight, and purſued them a conſiderable diſtance.

BALTIMORE, Auguſt 29.

An embarkation of troops lately took place at Charleſtown, South-Carolina, it is ſaid, for St. Auguſtine, which it is apprehended will be ſhortly inveſted by the Spaniards.

Several valuable bay craft, ſome of them richly laden, have, within a few days, been captured by the enemy's ſmall privateers, which are cruiſing between the Capes and the mouth of Patuxent. One of the captured veſſels was commanded by Capt. Joſeph White, of this town, and had effects on board worth upwards of 100,000 l.

We are aſſured, by good authority, that on the 16th inſt. at 2 o'clock, A. M. a bloody battle was fought within 8 miles of Camden, South-Carolina, between his Excellency General Gates, at the head of about 3000 men, 900 of whom were regulars, and the Britiſh forces, under the command of Earl Cornwallis, conſiſting of 1800 regulars, and 2400 refugees, &c. The contending armies engaged each other with the greateſt fury, and the proſpect, for ſome time, was extremely favourable to the American troops, who charged bayonets on the enemy, which obliged them to give ground, and leave ſome of their artillery in the poſſeſſion of our advancing troops—But unfortunately, at this critical moment, the premature flight of the militia terminated the conflict in favour of the enemy—an event which hath proved fatal to many of our brave countrymen of the regular troops, 4 or 500 of whom having been killed and taken—amongſt them are ſeveral valuable officers, whoſe names we think it prudent to omit for the preſent. The enemy's loſs hath been much more conſiderable. Lord Cornwallis, or ſome other Britiſh General, it is conjectured, is amongſt the ſlain.——Notwithſtanding this misfortune, General Gates, whoſe Head-Quarters are at Hillſborough, is collecting a force much ſuperior to his late army, and appears reſolved to try the fortune of another day.

The Virginians have compleated their quota of 5000 men, who are marching, in detachments of 500 men each, to reinforce General Gates.

About 300 cavalry, under the Colonels White and Waſhington, left Halifax, North-Carolina, a few days ago, to join General Gates, at Hillſborough.

In juſtice to the South-Carolina militia, it muſt be mentioned, that they greatly diſtinguiſhed themſelves in the late action.

PHILADELPHIA, Auguſt 23.

A letter from Pittſburgh, of the 4th ult. ſays, that a party of 600 Indians, with 150 Engliſh and French, marched from Detroit, with four field-pieces, to take poſſeſſion of Kaintuck, in Virginia; when information being given, Major Lanckton, Superintendent of Indian affairs, went and met them privately, and ſoon perſuaded the Indians to lay down their arms, which they did; and two days after, the guide came in, leaving the Britiſh to find their way back to Detroit in the beſt manner they could—but 'tis generally believed they would all periſh, unleſs they came and ſurrendered themſelves.

September 2. Captain Montgomery, who lately arrived here from L'Orient, left the coaſt of France about the 10th of July. He ſays, that the Britiſh channel fleet had been ſeen near Uſhant, about the laſt of June. Some days after his departure, about 150 leagues from the land, juſt before day, he fell in with 16 ſail of large ſhips, and 2 frigates, lying too; they chaſed him for ſome time. Perhaps they may be a Spaniſh ſquadron, bound from Cadiz to Breſt, which had left the coaſt of Europe to avoid the northern winds, common in ſummer on the coaſt of

which the inhabitants of the neighbourhood regularly attended; and the reſpect paid to private property was ſuch, that all the damage done in three weeks did not amount to more than fifty pounds ſpecie, agreeable to an appraiſement made by two freeholders of New-Jerſey. They were well provided with tents, and all other neceſſaries for actual field ſervice. In a few days more the whole with

the brig Phœnix, b
her in.
At a Town-Mee
John Hancock, Eſq
Governor of this C
We hear from Po
night the tories bur
that place, whom th
PROVID
At the Superior C
than Carpenter an
been charged, as m
glary, in breaking
Nathaniel Sprague,
quitted ſaid Carpente
a *Nolle Proſequi* up
for the ſame Offenc
alſo for Larceny, they
and on pleading gu
for that Crime, rece
That they ſhould p
the Value of the Mo
of One Thouſand On
and all Coſts of Proſe
caſe the ſame ſhould
ſtant, each to be whi
Stripes, at a Cart's
Providence, between
of that Day; that if d
ſtolen, and all Coſts o
were not paid by the
be reſpectively ſold b
the 1ſt Day of Octobe
not to exceed three Y
and that each ſhould r
Thouſand Pounds, with
in the Sum of Five Th
haviour for one Year,
tence ſhould be perform
A Letter from Philad
mentions, that in the
South-Carolina, Genera
land Line, was kille
wounded, and taken Pri
Sunday laſt arrived h
from Cape Francois, wh
Company with a French
a Number of Frigates, a

tain Lot of Land, ſituate
about Four Acres, bounded
John Uſher, and partly by
Eaſt, Weſt and South, by
otherwiſe the ſaid Lot may
to be bounded.
Therefore Notice is here
who have Claim to ſaid L

PROVIDENCE GAZETTE (RHODE ISLAND)

September 16, 1780

The vanguards of both armies met at about two a.m., and after some inconclusive fighting both commanders deployed their troops to resume the battle at daylight (the *Providence Gazette* of September 16, 1780, correctly reported the time of the initial encounter, but the main battle did not begin at that time). Also, American press accounts (such as that in the *Gazette*) tended to understate the numbers of their own army and exaggerate those of the British.

REPORTING THE BATTLE OF KINGS MOUNTAIN

By Jim Piecuch

In September 1780, the British army under Lieutenant General Charles, Earl Cornwallis, occupied Charlotte, North Carolina. Opposed by only a few partisans in South Carolina and the remnants of Major General Horatio Gates's Continental Army, defeated the previous month at the Battle of Camden, Cornwallis seemed on the verge of completing the conquest of the southern states. Then, at the Battle of Kings Mountain on October 7, 1780, the tide of war suddenly shifted in the Americans' favor.

Scottish Major Patrick Ferguson had been assigned the task of organizing South Carolina Loyalists into an effective militia. With a core of about one hundred veteran Loyalist troops from the north, Ferguson began training volunteers in the northwestern part of the state, where a large percentage of the populace remained loyal to Britain. While undertaking this task, Ferguson also conducted operations against American partisans.

Rebel partisans attacked the British-held town of Augusta, Georgia, in September 1780 (contrary to the report in the *Pennsylvania Gazette* of October 25, 1780, the Americans failed to capture the town). When the Americans abandoned the siege and withdrew northward, Ferguson received orders to intercept their retreat.

Cornwallis seemed on the verge of completing the conquest of the southern states, but the American victory at Kings Mountain marked a turning point in the campaign.

Ferguson took his one hundred provincials and seven hundred militia into western North Carolina. There they recruited about two hundred Loyalists but failed to catch the Americans. On several previous occasions, Ferguson had battled Americans who had come from west of the Appalachians to harass the British, and since he was close to their settlements, he sent them a message threatening to raze their homes if they continued to fight.

The western settlers, called the "Overmountain Men," lived illegally on lands reserved to the Indians by the British government's Proclamation of 1763. Knowing that a British victory would result in their removal from the territory, the Overmountain Men opted to attack Ferguson. Colonels Isaac Shelby, John Sevier, William Campbell, and Benjamin Cleveland (as reported in the October 25, 1780, *Pennsylvania Gazette*) led the Overmountain Men, and Colonel James Williams joined them with a force of South Carolinians. Their strength was about three thousand men, although just over half were able to reach Kings Mountain in time to engage Ferguson (these figures were accurately reported in the *Gazette*).

Learning that this force was pursuing him, Ferguson retreated to Kings Mountain, about twenty-five miles from the main British army in Charlotte, on October 6. He occupied the hilltop and asked Cornwallis for reinforcements. Apparently Ferguson hoped to trap the Americans between his own force and British troops from Charlotte. Cornwallis, however, did not send Ferguson any aid, despite the pleas of his cavalry commander, Lieutenant Colonel Banastre Tarleton, that he be permitted to lead a detachment to assist Ferguson.

On the afternoon of October 7, the Americans surrounded Ferguson's Loyalists. Repeated assaults on the hill were repulsed by bayonet charges that dispersed the attackers (noted in the *London Chronicle* of January 13, 1781, although the report understated Ferguson's strength and exaggerated the Americans' numbers). After nearly an hour of fighting, the Americans gained a foothold on the southeastern end of Kings Mountain, and Ferguson ordered a desperate bayonet charge in an attempt to break out. He was killed in the effort (which was not a reconnaissance as stated in the *Chronicle*), and his troops surrendered.

About 135 Loyalists were killed and six hundred captured (fewer than claimed by the *Gazette*, but more than reported in the *Chronicle*). Americans losses were officially reported at twenty-eight killed, including Colonel Williams, and sixty-two wounded (the *Gazette* accurately noted Williams's death but understated American casualties); however, Loyalist prisoners estimated American casualties as equal to their own.

The American victory at Kings Mountain marked a turning point in the southern campaign. Cornwallis was forced to withdraw to South Carolina (as stated in the *Chronicle*), and the Americans soon seized the opportunity to mount their own offensive operations.

and land, have reſolved, and do, by and with the advice of our Privy Council, hereby command, That a Public Faſt and Humiliation be obſerved throughout that part of our kingdom of Great Britain called England, our dominion of Wales, and town of Berwick upon Tweed, upon Wedneſday the 21ſt day of February next; that ſo both we and our people may humble ourſelves before Almighty God, in order to obtain pardon of our ſins; and may, in the moſt devout and ſolemn manner, ſend up our prayers and ſupplications to the Divine Majeſty, for averting thoſe heavy judgments which our manifold ſins and provocations have moſt juſtly deſerved, and imploring his bleſſing and aſſiſtance on our arms, and for reſtoring and perpetuating peace, ſafety, and proſperity, to us and our kingdoms: And we do ſtrictly charge and command, that the ſaid Public Faſt be reverently and devoutly obſerved by all our loving ſubjects in England, our dominion of Wales, and town of Berwick upon Tweed, as they tender the favour of Almighty God, and would avoid his wrath and indignation; and upon pain of ſuch puniſhment as we may juſtly inflict on all ſuch as contemn and neglect the performance of ſo religious and neceſſary a duty. And for the better and more orderly ſolemnizing the ſame, we have given directions to the moſt Reverend the Archbiſhops, and the Right Reverend ... a form of ... be uſed in ... f public ... be timely ... dioceſes. ..., the 12th ... ear of our

LONDON CHRONICLE

killed and took upwards of three hundred. This ſtroke obliged Lord Cornwallis to return into South Carolina, and by the laſt accounts from him, he was returning near Waxſaws towards Ninety Six.

"The rebels made an unſucceſsful attempt upon Auguſta. The garriſon was relieved by a

Yeſterday there was a levee at St. James's, when the Hon. Mr. North, ſon of Lord North, kiſſed his Majeſty's hand on being appointed Secretary and Comptroller of her Majeſty's houſehold, in the room of James Harris, Eſq; deceaſed.

Yeſterday a deputation of the Weſt India merchants waited on Lord Sandwich, at his houſe in the Admiralty, with whom they had an hour and an half's conference, when his Lordſhip aſſured them of every aſſiſtance in his power towards the relief of the Weſt India Iſlands.

Extract of a Letter from New York, Nov. 30.

"After the battle of Camden, Lord Cornwallis advanced into North Carolina, and Col. Ferguſon attempting to join him from Ninety Six, with about 400 militia, was attacked at King's Mountain by near 2000 rebels. He twice repulſed them, and went out with 30 men to reconnoitre, when he was unfortunately killed. This diſpirited his party. The rebels made a third attack, and ſucceeded. They

LONDON CHRONICLE

January 13, 1781

On the afternoon of October 7, 1780, the Americans surrounded Ferguson's Loyalists. Repeated assaults on the hill were repulsed by bayonet charges that dispersed the attackers (noted in the *London Chronicle* of January 13, 1781, although the report understated Ferguson's strength and exaggerated the Americans' numbers). After nearly an hour of fighting, the Americans gained a foothold on the southeastern end of Kings Mountain.

OCTOBER 25, 1780

The PENNSYLVANIA GAZETTE

PHILADELPHIA, *October 25.*

Extract of a letter from his Excellency Governor Jefferson, of Virginia, to the President of Congress, dated Richmond, October 15, 1780, six o'clock, P. M.

SIR,

" I DO myself the pleasure of congratulating your Excellency on the small dawn of good fortune which at length appears in the south, as you will find by the dispatches I have the honour of inclosing to you, and which I this moment received from General Gates."

SIR, *Burk county, 2d October, 1780.*

" I am, at present, about 70 miles from Salisbury, in the fork of the Catabaw, with about 450 horsemen, in pursuit of Colonel Ferguson. On my crossing the Catabaw river I dispatched to different quarters for intelligence, and this evening I was favoured with this news, which you may depend on: That Colonel Clark, of the State of Georgia, with 100 riflemen, forced his way through South Carolina to Georgia. On his route thither being joined by 700 men, he proceeded to the town of Augusta, and has taken it with a large quantity of goods; but not finding it prudent to continue there, he has retreated to the upper parts of South-Carolina, in Ninety-six district, and made a stand with 800 brave men.

" This moment another of my expresses is arrived from Colonels M'Dowell and Shelby: They were on their march, near Burk Court-house, with 1500 brave Mountain-men, and Colonel Cleveland was within 10 miles of them with 800 men, and was to form a junction with them this day. I expect to join them to morrow, in pursuit of Colonel Ferguson, and under the direction of Heaven, I hope to be able to render your Honour a good account of him in a few days. I am, &c.

(Signed) JAMES WILLIAMS."

Major General GATES

SIR, *Hillsborough, 12th October, 1780.*

" This instant I received the great and glorious news contained in the inclosed letter from Brigadier General Davidson to General Sumner, who directly dispatched it to me by express. We are now more than even with the enemy. The moment the supplies for the troops here arrive from Taylor's Ferry, I shall proceed with the whole to Yadkin. General Smallwood and Colonel Morgan are on their way to that post; the latter, with the light-infantry, was yesterday advanced 18 miles beyond Guilford Court-house; the former, with the cavalry, lay, last night, 13 miles on this side that place. I desire your Excellency will forthwith dispatch copies of all the letters I now send you to the President of Congress. I am, &c.

HORATIO GATES."

Governor JEFFERSON.

[...]

SIR, *Camp, Rocky-river, October 10, 1780.*

" I have the pleasure of handing you very agreeable intelligence from the west Ferguson, the great partisan, has miscarried. This we are assured of by Mr. Tate, Brigade Major in General Sumpter's late command: The particulars from that gentleman's mouth stand thus: That Colonels Campbell, Cleaveland, Shelby, Seveer, Williams, Brandon, Lacey, &c. formed a conjunct body, near Gilbert-Town, consisting of 3000; from this body were selected 1600 good horse, who immediately went in pursuit of Colonel Ferguson, who was making his way to Charlotte. Our people overtook him well posted on King's Mountain, and on the evening of the 7th inst. at 4 o'clock, began the attack, which continued 47 minutes. Colonel Ferguson fell in the action, besides 150 of his men; 810 were made prisoners, including the British; 150 of the prisoners are wounded; 1500 stand of arms fell into our hands. Colonel Ferguson had about 1400 men. Our people surrounded them, and the enemy surrendered. We left about 20 men, among whom is Major Chronicle of Lincoln county. Colonel Williams is mortally wounded. The number of our wounded cannot be ascertained. This blow will certainly affect the British very considerable. The Brigade Major who gives us this was in the action. The above is true. The blow is great. I give you joy upon the occasion. I am, &c.

(Signed) WILLIAM DAVISON."

Honourable General SUMNER.

PENNSYLVANIA GAZETTE (PHILADELPHIA)

October 25, 1780

—

Rebel partisans attacked the British-held town of Augusta, Georgia, in September 1780 (contrary to the report in the *Pennsylvania Gazette* of October 25, 1780, the Americans failed to capture the town). When the Americans abandoned the siege and withdrew northward, Ferguson received orders to intercept their retreat but failed to catch the Americans. Three thousand "Overmountain Men" then opted to attack Ferguson.

I could wiſh to have had a ſmall ſtore of proviſions, to have enabled us to have laid waſte part of the Delaware ſettlements, and falling in at Pittſburgh, but the exceſſive heat and weak diet ſhewed the impropriety of ſuch a ſtep. Nothing could excel the few regulars and Kentuckyans that compoſed this little army, in bravery and implicit obedience to orders. Each company vying with the other who ſhould be the moſt ſubordinate."

PHILADELPHIA, *October* 25.

Extract of a letter from his Excellency Governor Jefferſon, of Virginia, to the Preſident of Congreſs, dated Richmond, October 15, 1780, *ſix o'clock, P. M.*

SIR,

"I DO myſelf the pleaſure of congratulating your Excellency on the ſmall dawn of good fortune which at length appears in the ſouth, as you will find by the diſpatches I have the honour of incloſing to you, and which I this moment received from General Gates."

SIR, *Burk county, 2d October*, 1780.

"I am, at preſent, about 70 miles from Saliſbury, in the fork of the Catabaw, with about 450 horſemen, in purſuit of Colonel Ferguſon. On my croſſing the Catabaw river I diſpatched to different quarters for intelligence, and this evening I was favoured with this news, which you may depend on: That Colonel Clark, of the State of Georgia, with 100 riflemen, forced his way [illegible] being joined by 700 men, he proceeded to the town of Auguſta, and has taken it with a large quantity of goods; but not finding it prudent to continue there, he has retreated to the upper parts of South-Carolina, in Ninety-ſix diſtrict, and made a ſtand with 800 brave men.

"This moment another of my expreſſes is arrived from Colonels M'Dowell and Shelby: They were on their march, near Burk Court-houſe, with 1500 brave Mountain-men, and Colonel Cleveland was within 10 miles of them with 800 men, and was to form a junction with them this day. I expect to join them to-morrow, in purſuit of Colonel Ferguſon, and under the direction of Heaven, I hope to be able to render your Honour a good account of him in a few days. I am, &c.

(Signed) JAMES WILLIAMS."

Major General GATES.

SIR, *Hillſborough, 12th October*, 1780.

"This inſtant I received the great and glorious news contained in the incloſed letter from Brigadier General Davidſon to General Sumner, who directly diſpatched it to me by expreſs. We are now more than even with the enemy. The moment the ſupplies for the troops here arrive from Taylor's Ferry, I ſhall proceed with the whole to the Yadkin. General Smallwood and Colonel Morgan are on their way to that poſt; the latter, with the light-infantry, was yeſterday advanced 18 miles beyond Guilford Court-houſe; the former, with the cavalry, lay, laſt night, 13 miles on this ſide that place. I deſire your Excellency will forthwith diſpatch copies of all the letters I now ſend you to the Preſident of Congreſs. I am, &c.

HORATIO GATES."

Governor JEFFERSON.

DEAR SIR,

"I have the pleaſure to encloſe to you a large packet of diſpatches taken yeſterday, at M'Cappin's Creek, on the way to Camden, by a ſmall party of my brigade. A detachment of 120 horſe, under Rutledge and Dickſon, almoſt ſurrounded Charlotte yeſterday, attacked a picket at Col. Polk's mill, and at a certain Mr. Elliot's, brought off a centinel and eight tories, who are now on their way to you. A ſmall party of riflemen brought off 50 horſes from the tories at Col. Polk's plantation laſt night. I have the honour to be, &c. WILLIAM DAVISON.

Rocky-river, Sunday, 2 o'clock, 10th October, 1780.

"*P. S.* Dickſon loſt one man killed, and one officer wounded."

General SUMNER.

SIR, *Camp, Rocky-river, October* 10, 1780.

"I have the pleaſure of handing you very agreeable intelligence from the weſt. Ferguſon, the great partizan, has miſcarried. This we are aſſured of by Mr. Tate, Brigade Major in General Sumpter's late command: The particulars from that gentleman's mouth ſtand thus: That Colonels Campbell, Cleaveland, Shelby, Seveer, Williams, Brandon, Lacey, &c. formed a conjunct body, near Gilbert-Town, conſiſting of 3000; from this body were ſelected 1600 good horſe, who immediately went in purſuit of Colonel Ferguſon, who was making his way to Charlotte. Our people overtook him well poſted on King's Mountain, and on the evening of the 7ht inſt. at 4 o'clock, began the attack, which continued 47 minutes. Colonel

vain. This horſe is
t De Lancey 200l.—
he brought him in.--
nter of all his cattle
er went down with a
of taking his cattle,
s horſe by way of re-
ingly replied, "You

ſued a proclamation,
his State, to obſerve
ber next, as a day of
ty God, for the re-
rought in behalf of
this State in particu-
le conſpiracy for be-
lands into the hands
n for the evils preva-
ore a continuance of

October 18.
election in this State,
t the ſeveral counties
during the enſuing
were choſen.
-Stevens, Eſquire.

Tallman, Eſquire.
am Trent, William

ooper, Eſquire. Aſ-
ard, Iſaac Kay, Eſ-

ripps, Eſquire. Aſ-
eton, jun. William

min Manning, Eſq.
uydam, Melancthon

Lawrence, Eſquire.
aniel Scudder, Tho-

itherſpoon, Eſquire.
patrick, Chriſtopher

are not yet come to

moved from Tapan
ergen county, previ-
e marched four bri-

tant ſays, that "On
oſt at Bergen Point,
omas Ward, was at
and horſe, conſiſting
a ſmart fire from the
ees, aſſiſted by a can-
forced to retreat."
e above, that the aſ-
Refugees.
ners has lately been
an troops, now with

ia) October 4.
ge Rogers Clarke, to
Louiſville, Auguſt 22,

the aid of Colonel
he number of 1000,
he mouth of Licking
n our march the 2d.
to paſs for ſeventy
ched the firſt town,
reateſt part of their
nduct of the Indians
borating circumſtan-
us on to their own
deſtroying the crops
an our march for the
the Big Miame, the
before our advanced
ening of the 8th, we
ts, a plain of half a
had an opportunity
of the enemy, near

ne neceſſary diſpoſi-
n our left wing, and
eral, with a ſavage

Ferguſon fell in the action, beſides 150 of his men; 810 were made priſoners, including the Britiſh; 150 of the priſoners are wounded; 1500 ſtand of arms fell into our hands. Colonel Ferguſon had about 1400 men. Our people ſurrounded them, and the enemy ſurrendered. We loſt about 20 men, among whom is Major Chronicle of Lincoln county. Colonel Williams is mortally wounded. The number of our wounded cannot be aſcertained. This blow will certainly affect the Britiſh very conſiderably. The Brigade Major who gives us this was in the action. The above is true. The blow is great. I give you joy upon the occaſion. I am, &c.

(Signed) WILLIAM DAVISON."

Honourable General SUMNER.

Camp, Yadkin-Ford, October 10, 1780.

SIR, *Eight o'clock, evening.*

"With great ſatisfaction I inform you of the defeat of Major Ferguſon, on King's Mountain, 4 o'clock, Saturday afternoon. The particulars I incloſe you as I received them a few minutes ago: Alſo a letter from General Daviſon, of his ſecuring 29 barrels of powder, which were ſecreted, ſome time ſince, near Charlotte. I am, Sir,

With great reſpect, your very humble ſervant,

JETHRO SUMNER."

Publiſhed by Order of Congreſs,

CHARLES THOMSON, *Secretary.*

On the above important intelligence being circulated in the city, the chearful countenances of the honeſt and virtuous part of the community fully evinced the heart-felt ſatisfaction they experienced on the joyful occaſion; whilſt the malignant aſpects of the diſaffected ſufficiently betrayed their chagrin and diſappointment.

Extract of a letter from Cadiz, dated Auguſt 16, 1780.

"The pleaſure of communicating intelligence, that I ſuppoſe may prove intereſting or acceptable, induces me to give you the following:

PROCLAM

WHEREAS it hath ple
Father of all mercies, ar
calamities of war, to beſtow bl
theſe ſtates, which call for their
knowledgments, more eſpecially
interpoſition of his watchful pro
perſon of our commander in ch
imminent dangers, at the mome
ened for execution: in proſpering
bandmen, and cauſing the earth
plentiful harveſts; and above all,
enjoyment of the goſpel of peace
It is therefore recommended t
apart Thurſday, the ſeventh day
obſerved as a day of public thank
all the people may aſſemble on
praiſes of our Divine Benefactor
thineſs of the leaſt of his favours,
ſupplications to the God of all g
him to pardon our heinous tranſ
hearts for the future to keep all
relieve our brethren who are anyw
to ſmile upon our huſbandry and t
lic councils and lead our forces by
to take our illuſtrious ally unde
and favour our joint councils a
bliſhment of ſpeedy and perman
ſchools and ſeminaries of educa
knowledge of Chriſtianity to ſpre
Done in Congreſs, this eightee
and in the fifth year of the
States of America.
Atteſt. SAMUEL HUNT
CHARLES THOMSON, *Secretary.*

CITY OF PHILADELPHIA,

EXECUTION OF
MAJOR JOHN ANDRÉ
The Bridgeman Art Library

Major John André, British army officer, hanged October 2, 1780, by the Continental Army for spying.

REPORTING THE TREASON OF BENEDICT ARNOLD AND HANGING OF JOHN ANDRÉ

By Dennis M. Conrad

To this day, Benedict Arnold's attempt to treasonously surrender the American bastion at West Point to the British is considered an act of the vilest nature, and Arnold continues to be considered one of America's greatest villains. How Arnold's well-conceived plans were disrupted is laid out in the *Boston Gazette* article of October 16, 1780. Almost immediately, the British launched an attempt to save Adjutant-General of the British army, Major John André, who had served as Arnold's go-between and had been arrested out of uniform. The letters by Beverly Robinson, Sir Henry Clinton, and Arnold arguing that André was acting under a flag of truce and should not be considered a spy, which are printed in the *London Chronicle* of December 2, 1780, were part of that effort. They were presented to General Nathanael Greene, acting as Washington's representative, in a clandestine meeting with three important British officials on October 1. Greene countered with the letter from André of September 24, also printed in the *London Chronicle*. In that letter, conceded the Royal Governor of New York writing to Henry Clinton immediately after the meeting, André, admitted his actions were criminal. The British delegation then offered to release anyone in British possession in exchange for André, and Greene countered by saying that only by returning Arnold could the British secure André's release. Not surprisingly, the British found such an exchange to be unacceptable, and the Americans proceeded to hang André as a spy, releasing the documents printed in the *London Chronicle* of December 2 to justify their action.

As can be seen in the proclamations issued in Arnold's name printed in the *London Chronicle* of November 14 and December 2, the British hoped to capitalize on the defection of Arnold and appointed him a brigadier general in the British army and authorized him to raise an armed force comprised of American deserters and Loyalists. Arnold's efforts to spark wholesale defection were unsuccessful, and Arnold himself, though he became an active and successful leader for the British in America, was never embraced nor trusted by his new compatriots, who treated him with cold politeness. After the war, he was quickly shunted aside by British authorities and never again given a position of any importance. Legend has it that on his deathbed he said: "Let me die in this old uniform in which I fought my battles. May God forgive me for ever having put on another," though the story is probably apocryphal.

"It is an irony among ironies that Benedict Arnold managed to do what no one else had. He revitalized the Revolution."

According to historian Dave R. Palmer in his book *George Washington and Benedict Arnold: A Tale of Two Patriots*, reaction to Arnold's treason among Americans followed three distinct waves. First was "surprise, disbelief, and shock," followed quickly by "biting anger" and sheer hatred. "Arnold became almost at once a figure despised and reviled as none other has been in the entire history of the United States." The third wave concerned the nation itself. Seeing the "hand of Providence" in the foiling of the treasonous plot, Americans experienced something akin to a "religious revival." Palmer notes: "It is an irony among ironies that Benedict Arnold managed to do what no one else had. He revitalized the Revolution."

OCTOBER 16, 1780

The BOSTON GAZETTE

BOSTON, October 16.

Extract of a letter from a gentleman, dated Tapan, *October 2, 1780.*

" You will have heard before you can receive this, of the *infernal* villainy of Arnold. It is not possible for human nature to receive a greater quantity of guilt than he possesses : Perhaps there is not a single obligation, moral or divine, but what he has broken thro'. It is deserved now, that in his most early infancy, hell mark'd him for her own, and infus'd into him a full proportion of her diabolical malice.

" His late apostacy is the summit of his character. He began his negotiations with the enemy, to deliver up West Point to them, long before he was invested with the command of it, and whilst he was still in Philadelphia ; after which he solicited the command of that post, for the ostensible reason, that the wound in his leg incapacitated him for active command in the field : It was granted him on the 6th of August last.—Since which he has been as assiduous as possible in ripening his plans, but the various positions the army assumed, prevented their being put into execution.

" On the night of the 21st ultimo, he had an interview with Major Andre, the Adjutant-General of the British army. This gentleman came on shore from the Vulture man of war, which lay not far from Taller's Point, to a place on the banks of the river, near to the Haverstraw mountain, where he met Arnold, who conducted him to the house of Joshua Smith (the white house) within our lines, and only two miles from Stony-Point. They arrived in the house just before day & stay'd there until next evening, when Major Andre became extremely sollicitous to return by the way he came, but that was impossible, for the two men who Arnold and Smith had seduced to bring on shore, refused to carry him back. It then was absolutely necessary he should return to New-York by land. He chang'd his dress and name, and thus disgused, passed our post of Stoney and Verplank's Points, on the evening of the 22d ult. in company with the said Joshua Smith, brother to William Smith, Esq; Chief Justice within the British lines ; he lodged that night at Cron Pond, with Smith, and in the morning left Smith, and took the road to Tarry-Town, where he was taken by some militia lads about 15 miles from Kings Bridge. He offered them any sum of money, and goods, if they would permit him to escape, but they readily declared and inflexibly adhered to it, that 10,000 guineas, or any other sum, would be no temptation to them. It was this virtue as glorious to America as Arnold's apostacy is disgraceful, that his abominable crimes were discovered.

" The lads, in searching him, found concealed under his stockings, in his boots, papers of the highest importance, viz.

1. Return of the ordnance and its distributions at West-Point and its dependencies.

2. Artillery orders, in case of an alarm.

3. Returns of the number of men necessary to man the works at West-Point and its dependencies.

4 Remarks on the works at West Point with the strength and working of each.

5. Returns of the troops at West Point and their distribution.

6. State of our army &c transmitted by General Washington to Arnold for his opinion, which state had been submitted to all the general officers in the Camp, for their opinions.

" Besides which it appears, that Arnold had carried with him to the interview, a general plan of West Point and its vicinity, and all the works, and also particular plans of each work, on a large scale,—all elegantly drawn by the engineer at that post. But these were not delivered to Major Andre, and from their requiring much time to copy, it was supposed they were not to be delivered until some future period.

From some circumstances it appears, that it was not Arnold's intention to have deserted, but that he meant to be taken at his post, which, from his distributions of the troops, was very easy to have seized. [...]

trary notwithstanding.

[*This Act passed September 29, 1780*]

BOSTON, October 16.

Extract of a letter from a gentleman, dated Tappan, *October 2, 1780*

"You will have heard before you can receive this, of the *infernal* villainy of Arnold. It is not possible for human nature to receive a greater quantity of guilt than he possesses: Perhaps there is not a single obligation, moral or divine, but what he has broken thro'. It is discovered now, that in his most early infancy, hell mark'd him for her own, and infus'd into him a full proportion of her diabolical malice.

"His late apostacy is the summit of his character. He began his negotiations with the enemy, to deliver up West Point to them, long before he was invested with the command of it, and whilst he was still in Philadelphia; after which he sollicited the command of that post, for the ostensible reason, that the wound in his leg incapacitated him for an active command in the field: It was granted him on the 6th of August last—Since which he has been as assiduous as possible in ripening his plans, but the various positions the army assumed, prevented their being put into execution.

"On the night of the 21st ultimo, he had an interview with Major Andre, the Adjutant-General of the British army. This gentleman came on shore from the Vulture man of war, which lay not far from Taller's Point, to a place on the banks of the river, near to the Haverstraw mountain, where he met Arnold, who conducted him to the house of Joshua Smith (the white house) within our lines, and only two miles from Stony-Point. They arrived in the house just before day & stay'd there until the next evening, when Major Andre became extremely sollicitous to return by the way he came, but that was impossible, for the two men who Arnold and Smith had seduced to bring on shore, refused to carry him back. It then was absolutely necessary he should return to New-York by land. He chang'd his dress and name, and thus disguised, passed our post of Stoney and Verplank's Points, on the evening of the 22d ult. in company with the said Joshua Smith, brother to William Smith, Esq; Chief Justice within the British lines; he lodged that night at Cron Pond, with Smith, and in the morning left Smith, and took the road to Tarry-Town, where he was taken by some militia lads about 15 miles from Kings Bridge. He offered them any sum of money, and goods, if they would permit him to escape, but they readily declared and inflexibly adhered to it, that 10 000 guineas, or any other sum, would be no temptation to them. It was this virtue as glorious to America as Arnold's apostacy is disgraceful, that his abominable crimes were discovered.

"The lads, in searching him found concealed under his stockings, in his boots, papers of the highest importance, viz.

1 Returns of the ordnance and its distributions at West-Point and its dependencies.

2. Artillery orders, in case of an alarm.

3. Returns of the number of men necessary to man the works at West Point and its dependencies.

4 Remarks on the works at West Point, with the strength and working of each.

5. Returns of the troops at West Point and their distribution.

6. State of our army, &c transmitted by General Washington to Arnold for his opinion, which state had been submitted to all the general officers in the Camp, for their opinions.

"Besides which it appears, that Arnold had carried with him to the interview, a general plan of West Point and its vicinity, and all the works,

"The General proceeded to view the works, wondering where Arnold should be; but about 4 o'clock in the afternoon he was undeceived, by an express with the papers taken on Andre. The apostate at this time was on board the Vulture, which lay about 5 or 6 miles below Stoney and Verplank's Points.

"Major Andre was brought to the General at West Point, and from thence he was brought to this camp. A board of general officers have examined into his case, and upon his own most candid confession, were of opinion that he was a spy, and according to the custom & usages of nations, he ought to suffer death; and about two hours ago he was executed.

"This gentleman was in the highest degree of reputation in the British army, of the most polite and accomplished manners, extremely beloved by Sir Henry Clinton. His deportment while a prisoner was candid and dignified. He requested no favour, but to die the death of a soldier, and not on a gibbet. Rigorous policy forbid granting a favour which at first flush seems immaterial. Our army sympathizes in the misfortunes of *this Chesterfield of the day*: But if he possessed a portion of the blood of all the Kings on earth justice and policy would have dictated his death.

The enemy from hints that some of the officers dropped, appeared to be inclined to deliver Arnold into our hands for Major Andre: But they have since declared it was impossible. If it could have been effected, our desire to get Arnold would have rendered the exchange easy on our part.

"The British army are in the utmost affliction on the account of Major Andre and have sent repeated flags on the subject. Yesterday they sent Gen. Robertson, Andrew Eliot and William Smith, Esqrs; the two latter were not permitted to land. General Greene met Gen. Robertson; he had nothing material to urge—'but that Andre had come on shore under the sanction of a flag, and therefore could not be considered as a spy:" But this is not true, for he came at night, had no flag, and on business totally incompatible with the nature of a flag. He also said they should retaliate on some people at New-York and Charlestown; but he was told that such conversation could neither be heard nor understood. After which he urged the release of Andre on motives of humanity, and because Sir Harry Clinton was much attached to him; and other reasons equally absurd

"I have been particular in this narration, well knowing what strange stories you will have on the subject."

The following is a Copy of a Letter from Major Andre to his Excellency General Washington.

SIR,

"Buoyed above the fear of death, by the consciousness of a life spent in the pursuit of honor, and fully sensible that it has at no time been stained by any action, which at this serious moment could give me remorse—I have to solicit your Excellency if there is any thing in my character which excites your esteem; if aught in my circumstances can impress you with compassion; that I may be permitted to die the death of a soldier:—It is my last request and I hope it will be granted." I have the honor to be, &c.

By their Honors Command,
JOHN AVERY, Dep. Sec.
GOD save the United States of AMERICA.

STATE OF MASSACHUSETTS BAY.
Council-Chamber, *October* 10th, 1780.

WHEREAS *this Board have received intelligence from the Quarter Master General of the United States, that the Army have had a sufficient supply of Horses for the present Campaign:*

Therefore *Ordered*, That the Agents appointed to procure Horses from the several Counties in this State, who were directed by the Resolve of the General Court of the twenty third of *June* last, to procure Horses within the limits of their appointment for the use of the Army of the United States, be, and they are hereby directed to surcease all further proceedings on the aforesaid Resolve, and that no more Horses be procured or sent on to the Committee appointed to receive them at *Springfield*, in consequence of the Resolve aforesaid.

True Copy, Attest.
JOHN AVERY, Dep. Sec'y.

COMMITTEE-OFFICE, *Springfield, Oct.* 11, 1780.

WHEREAS *by the Resolutions of the General Court of the 25th of* September *last the several Towns in this State are ordered to furnish a Quantity of Beef for the Use of the Army, or to pay so much Money as in the Judgment of the Committee for superintending Purchases, may be sufficient to purchase the same:*

THIS is therefore to GIVE NOTICE, That the Committee are of Opinion, that *Three Pounds* in New Money, or an *Hundred and Twenty Pounds* in the old Currency, may be received in Lieu of an Hundred Weight of Beef at present: And the Agents appointed by us in the several Counties, are hereby directed to receive the old or the new Money at the aforesaid Rate, and give Discharges agreeable to the Directions of the aforesaid Resolutions, for so much Beef as any Town or Plantation shall furnish Money to purchase, at the Rate aforesaid; provided the Money is paid before the Thirty first Day of this Instant *October*; after which Time, the Agents will wait the farther Directions of the Committee, as they cannot determine now, at what Price Beef may be at that Time,

And the Agents aforesaid are hereby directed to transmit all such Sums of Money as they may receive on the above Account, as soon as possible, to the Committee at *Springfield*, untill further Orders.

SAMUEL OSGOOD, ELIJAH HUNT, OLIVER PHELPS, } Committe for superintending Purchases

BOSTON GAZETTE
October 16, 1780

LONDON CHRONICLE

December 2, 1780

The letters by Beverly Robinson, Sir Henry Clinton, and Arnold arguing that Major John André was acting under a flag of truce and should not be considered a spy, which are printed in the *London Chronicle* of December 2, 1780, were part of an effort by the British to save André from being hanged.

---

the British Army, Sept. 29,

at West Point; whither I pro- in order to visit the post. I nold had not been there during on my return to his quarters, he . In the mean time, a packet m Lieutenant Colonel Jamieson, e capture of a John Anderson, avouring to go to New York teresting and important papers, -writing of Gen. Arnold. This npanied with a letter from the ving himself to be Major John nt General to the British army, nner of his capture, and endea- v that he did not come under of a spy. From these several and information that the Ge- o be thrown into some degree of eceiving a letter a little time be- from his quarters, I was led to ediately that he had heard of captivity, and that he would, if to the enemy, and accordingly sures as appeared the most pro- end him; but he had embarked nd proceeded down the river, the Vulture ship of war, which les below Stoney and Verplank's ote me a letter after he got on Andre is not arrived yet; but I ure, and that he will be here e been, and am taking precau trust will prove effectual, to pre- rtant consequences which this e part of Gen. Arnold, was in- uce. I do not know the party or Andre; but it is said that it of a few militia, who acted in upon the occasion, as does them our, and proves them to be men

As soon as I know their names, easure in transmitting them to

Paramus, Oct. 7, 1780.

e honour to inclose Congress a oceedings of a Board of General cause of Major Andre, Adjutant British army. This officer was ursuance of the sentence of the

Major General GREEN, President.

Maj. Gen. Ld. Stirling	Brig. Gen. Knox
Major Gen. St. Clair	Brig. Gen. Glover
	... Patterson
	...Hand
	Hunting-
	...tarke

...s, Judge ... General ... the Bri- ...oard, and ...hington to ...ppan, Sep- ...hem, and

"Major Andre, Adjutant General to the British army, will be brought before you for your examination. He came within our lines in the night, on an interview with Major General Arnold, and in an assumed character, and was taken within our lines, in a disguised habit, with a pass under a feigned name, and with the inclosed papers concealed upon him. After a careful examination, you will be pleased, as speedily as possible to report a precise state of his case, together with your opinion of the light in which he ought to be considered, and the punishment that ought to be inflicted. The Judge Advocate will attend to assist in the examination, who has sundry other papers relative to this matter, which he will lay before the Board.

"I have the honour to be, Gentlemen, your most obedient humble servant,

G. WASHINGTON."

The Board of General Officers, convened at Tappan.

The names of the officers composing the Board were read to Major Andre, and on his being asked whether he confessed the matters contained in the letter from his Excellency General Washington to the Board, or denied them, *he said, in addition to his letter to General Washington, dated Salem, the 24th of September* 1780, which was read to the Board, and acknowledged by Major Andre to have been written by him, which letter is as follows:

Sir, *Salem, 24th Sept* 1780.

"What I have as yet said concerning myself, was in the justifiable attempt to be extricated; I am too little accustomed to duplicity to have succeeded.

"I beg your Excellency will be persuaded, that no alteration in the temper of my mind, or apprehension for my safety, induces me to take the step of addressing you, but that it is to secure myself from an imputation of having assumed a mean character for treacherous purposes or self interest. A conduct incompatible with the principles that actuated me, as well as with my condition in life.

"It is to vindicate my fame that I speak, and not to solicit security.

"The person in your possession is Major John Andre, Adjutant General to the British army.

me back the next night as I had been brought. Thus become a prisoner, I had to concert my escape; I *quitted my uniform*, and was passed another way in the night without the American posts to neutral ground; and informed I was beyond all armed parties, and left to press for New York. I was taken at Tarry Town by some volunteers.

"Thus, as I have had the honour to relate, was I betrayed (being Adjutant General of the British army) into the vile condition of an enemy in disguise within your posts.

"Having avowed myself a British officer, I have nothing to reveal but what relates to myself, which is true on the honour of an officer and a gentleman.

"The request I have to make to your Excellency, and I am conscious that I address myself well, is, that in any rigour policy may dictate, a decency of conduct towards me may mark, that though unfortunate, I am branded with nothing dishonourable; as no motive could be mine, but the service of my King, and as I was involuntarily an impostor.

"Another request is, that I may be permitted to write an open letter to Sir Henry Clinton, and another to a friend for clothes and linen.

"I take the liberty to mention the condition of some gentlemen at Charlestown, who being either on parole or under protection, were engaged in a conspiracy against us. Though their situation is not similar, they are objects who may be sent in exchange for me, or are persons whom the treatment I receive might affect.

"It is no less, Sir, in a confidence in the generosity of your mind, than on account of your superior station, that I have chosen to importune you with this letter. I have the honour to be, with great respect, Sir, your Excellency's most obedient, and most humble servant,

JOHN ANDRE, Adj. Gen."

His Excellency Gen. Washington, &c. &c.

That he came on shore from the Vulture sloop of war *in the* night of the 21st of September instant, somewhere under the Haverstraw Mountain. That the boat he came on shore in carried *no flag*, that he had on a surtout coat over his regimentals, and that he wore his surtout coat when he was taken. That he met General Arnold on the shore, and had an interview with him there. He also said, that when he left the Vulture sloop of war, it was understood he was to return that night; but it was then doubted, and if he could not return, he was promised to be *concealed on* shore in a place of safety, until the next *night*, when he was to return in the same manner he came on shore; and when the next day came, he was solicitous to get back, and made enquiries in the course of the day how he should return, when he was informed he could not return that way, and he must take the route he did afterwards. He also said, that the first notice he had of his being within any *of our posts*, was, being challenged by the sentry, which was the first night

" Sir, *New York, Sept.* 7, 1780.

" I am told *my name* is made known to you, and that I may hope your indulgence in permitting me to meet a friend near your out poſts. I will endeavour to obtain permiſſion to go out *with a flag* which will be ſent to Dobb's Ferry on Monday next, the 11th, at 12 o'clock, when I ſhall be happy to meet Mr. G—— †. Should I not be allowed to go, the officer who is to command the eſcort, between whom and myſelf no diſtinction need be made, can ſpeak on the affair.

" Let me entreat you, Sir, to favour a matter ſo intereſting to the parties concerned, and which is of ſo private a nature, that the public on neither ſide can be injured by it.

" I ſhall be happy on my part, of doing any act of kindneſs to you, in a family or property concern of a ſimilar nature.

" I truſt I ſhall not be detained; but ſhould any old grudge be a cauſe for it, I ſhould rather riſk that, than neglect the buſineſs in queſtion, *or aſſume a myſterious character*, to carry on an innocent affair; and, as friends have adviſed, get to your lines by ſtealth. I am, Sir, with all regard, your moſt obedient humble ſervant, JOHN ANDERSON."

Colonel Sheldon.

Major Andre obſerved, that this letter could be of no force in the caſe in queſtion, as it was written in New York, when he was under the orders of General Clinton; but that it tended to prove that it was not his intention to come within our lines.

The Board having interrogated Major Andre about his conception of coming on ſhore under the ſanction of a flag, *he ſaid, that it was impoſſible for him to ſuppoſe he came on ſhore under that ſanction;* and added, that if he came on ſhore under that ſanction, he certainly might have returned under it.

Major Andre having acknowledged the preceding facts, and being aſked whether he had any thing to ſay reſpecting them, anſwered, he left them to operate with the Board.

---

* Leſt it ſhould be ſuppoſed that Col. Sheldon, to whom the above letter is addreſſed, was privy to the plot carrying on by General Arnold, it is to be obſerved, that the letter was found among Arnold's papers, and had been tranſmitted by Col. Sheldon; who, it appears from a letter, on the 9th of September to Arnold, which incloſed it, had never heard of John Anderſon before. Arnold, in his anſwer on the 10th, acknowledged he had not communicated it to him, though he had informed him that he expected a perſon would come from New York, for the purpoſe of bringing him intelligence.

† It appears, by the ſame letter, that Arnold had written to Mr. Anderſon, under the ſignature of Guſtavus. His words are, " I was obliged to write with great caution to him, my letter was ſigned Guſtavus, to prevent any diſcovery, in caſe it fell into the hands of the enemy."

too often experienced the ingratitude of my country to attempt it; but from the known humanity of your Excellency, I am induced to aſk your protection for Mrs. Arnold, from every inſult and injury that a miſtaken vengeance of my country may expoſe her to. It ought to fall only on me; ſhe is as good and as innocent as an angel, and is incapable of doing wrong. I beg ſhe may be permitted to return to her friends in Philadelphia, or to come to me, as ſhe may chooſe. From your Excellency I have no fears on her account, but ſhe may ſuffer from the miſtaken fury of the country.

I have to requeſt that the incloſed letter may be delivered to Mrs. Arnold, and ſhe permitted to write to me.

I have alſo to aſk that my clothes and baggage, which are of little conſequence, may be ſent to me; if required, their value ſhall be paid in money. I have the honour to be, with great regard and eſteem, your Excellency's moſt obedient humble ſervant, B. ARNOLD."

His Excellency Gen. Waſhington.

N. B. In juſtice to the Gentlemen of my family, Col. Warrick and Major Franke, I think myſelf in honour bound to declare, that they, as well as Joſhua Smith, Eſq; (who I know is ſuſpected) are totally ignorant of any tranſactions of mine, that they had reaſon to believe were injurious to the public.

Sir, *Vulture, off Sinſink, Sept.* 25, 1780.

" I am this moment informed that Major Andre, Adjutant General of his Majeſty's army in America, is detained as a priſoner by the army under your command. It is therefore incumbent on me to inform you of the manner of his falling into your hands:—He went up with a flag at the requeſt of General Arnold, on public buſineſs with him, and had his permit to return by land to New York. Under theſe circumſtances Major Andre cannot be detained by you, without the greateſt violation of flags, and contrary to the cuſtom and uſage of all nations; and, as I imagine you will ſee this matter in the ſame point of view as I do, I muſt deſire you will order him to be ſet at liberty, and allowed to return immediately. Every ſtep Major Andre took, was by the advice and direction of Gen. Arnold, even that of taking a feigned name, and of courſe not liable to cenſure for it. I am, Sir, not forgetting our former acquaintance, your very humble ſervant.

BEV. ROBINSON, Col. Loy. Americ."

His Excellency Gen Waſhington.

Sir, *New York, Sept.* 26, 1780.

" Being informed that the King's Adjutant General in America has been ſtopped, under Major General Arnold's paſſports, and is detained a priſoner in your Excellency's army, I have the honour to inform you, Sir, that I permitted Major Andre to go to Major General Arnold, at the particular requeſt of that General Officer. You will perceive, Sir, by the in

relating to myſelf, and which I wiſhed to communicate, through that officer, to your Excellency.

I commanded at the time at Weſt Point, and had an undoubted right to ſend my flag of truce for Major Andre, who came to me under that protection; and having held my converſation with him, I delivered him confidential papers in my own hand writing, to deliver to your Excellency; thinking it much properer he ſhould return by land, I directed him to make uſe of the feigned name of John Anderſon, under which he had by my direction come on ſhore, and gave him my paſſports to go to the White Plains on his way to New York. This officer cannot therefore fail of being immediately ſent to New York, as he was invited to a converſation with me, for which I ſent him a flag of truce, and finally gave him paſſports for his ſafe return to your Excellency; all which I had then a right to do, being in the actual ſervice of America, under the orders of General Waſhington, and Commanding General at Weſt Point and its dependencies.

I have the honour to be your Excellency's moſt obedient and very humble ſervant.

B. ARNOLD."

His Excellency Sir Henry Clinton.

The Board having conſidered the letter from his Excellency General Waſhington reſpecting Major Andre, Adjutant General to the Britiſh army, the confeſſion of Major Andre, and the papers produced to them,—*Report* to his Excellency the Commander in Chief the following facts which appear to them relative to Major Andre:

Firſt, That he came on ſhore from the Vulture ſloop of war, in the *night* of the 21ſt of September inſtant, on an interview with General Arnold, *in a private and ſecret manner.*

Secondly, That he changed his dreſs within our lines, and under a feigned name, and in a diſguiſed habit, paſſed our *works at Stoney and Verplanks Points,* the evening of the twenty-ſecond of September, inſtant, and was taken the morning of the twenty third of September inſtant, *at Tarry-town, in a diſguiſed habit,* being then on his way to New York, *and when taken* he had in his poſſeſſion ſeveral papers, which contained intelligence *for the enemy.*

The Board having maturely conſidered theſe facts, *Do alſo report* to his Excellency General Waſhington, that Major Andre, Adjutant General to the Britiſh army, ought to be conſidered as a SPY from the enemy and that, agreeable to the law and uſage of nations, it is their opinion, he ought to ſuffer death.

Nathaniel Green,	M. General, Preſident.
Stirling, M. G.	John Starke, B. G.
R. Howe, M. G.	Edw. Hand, B. G.
Ar. St. Clair, M. G.	Sam. H. Parſons, B. G.
La Fayette, M. G.	John Glover, B. G.
Stuben, M. G.	Artillery:
H. Knox, B. G.	J. Huntington, B. G.
James Clinton, B. G.	J. Lawrens, J. A. G.
John Paterſon, B. G.	

LONDON CHRONICLE

November 14, 1780

As can be seen in the proclamations issued in Arnold's name printed in the *London Chronicle* of November 14 and December 2, 1780, the British hoped to capitalize on the defection of Arnold and appointed him a brigadier general in the British army and authorized him to raise an armed force comprised of American deserters and Loyalists.

Plymouth; and remain in the Downs ſhips as per laſt. Arrived the Shark Nimble cutter from a cruize. Wind

LONDON.

ay a Chapter of the Order of the held at St. James's, and the fol- nights attended the ceremony, viz Irvin, Sir Charles Frederick, Sir ne, Sir Robert Gunning, and Lords and Amherſt; when General Ri- erſon, who commanded the camp at laſt Summer; Thomas Wroughton, Majeſty's Ambaſſador at the Court of and Admiral Sir George Brydges Bart. were the three new-elected the two laſt by proxy.

ndia Company have received advice gal, by the way of Holland, that a edition is now fitting out in the Gan- s ſuppoſed to be deſtined either againſt or the Manillas. They have the moſt hopes of ſucceſs from this expedition, great force, both naval and military, collected, and they have even preſſed n from the India ſhips.

of a Letter from Corke, Nov. 5.

day arrived here his Majeſty's ſhip , of 48 guns, the Ranger ſloop of war, rince George armed ſhip, with a fleet ders from Plymouth, bound to New ſire; from Nantz, bound to the Weſt

of Broad-ſtreet.

ednesday laſt died, at his houſe on green, William Donaldſon, Eſq.

y died, at Marlborough, James Houb- lyne, Eſq.

y died, at Tottenham, Charles Dower,

day died, in Bloomſbury-Square, Ar- ings, Eſq.

y died, in Wimpole-Street, Cavendiſh- dward Clutterbuck, Eſq.

urday laſt died at Packington in War- in the 21ſt year of his age, the Hon.

iel Hankerſon, Knt.

y laſt died, at Newton-Houſe near

taken from RIVINGTON'S ROYAL NEW YORK GAZETTE, *of Oct. 21, 1780.*

To the INHABITANTS *of* AMERICA.

I SHOULD forfeit, even in my own opinion, the place I have ſo long held in yours, if I could be indifferent to your approbation, and ſilent on the motives which have induced me to join the King's arms.

A very few words, however, ſhall ſuffice upon a ſubject ſo perſonal; for to the thouſands who ſuffer under the tyranny of the uſurpers in the revolted provinces, as well as to the great multitude who have long wiſhed for its ſubverſion, this inſtance of my conduct can want no vindication; and as to the claſs of men who are criminally protracting the war from ſiniſter views at the expence of the public intereſt, I prefer their enmity to their applauſe. I am, therefore, only concerned in this addreſs, to expalin, myſelf to ſuch of my countrymen, as want abilities, or opportunities, to detect the artifices by which they are duped.

Having fought by your ſide when the love of our country animated our arms, I ſhall expect, from your juſtice and candour, what your deceivers, with more art and leſs honeſty, will find it inconſiſtent with their own views to admit.

When I quitted domeſtic happineſs for the perils of the field, I conceived the rights of my country in danger, and that duty and honour called me to her defence. A redreſs of griev- aim; however, I thought precipi- ence: to juſtify ons were urged, hen Great Bri- parent, offered ant the wiſhed- ies are in her principles, if I ourſelves being becauſe fellow foe? You have raiſed our arms e the guilty protectors of theſe unnatural diſſentions to reſign their ambition, and ceaſe from their deluſions, in compaſſion to kindred blood!

I anticipate your queſtion, Was not the war a defenſive one, until the French joined in the combination? I anſwer, that I thought ſo. You will add, Was it not afterwards neceſſary, till the ſeparation of the Britiſh empire was complete? By no means; in contending for the welfare of my country, I am free to declare my opinion, that this end attained, all ſtrife ſhould have ceaſed.

I lamented, therefore, the impolicy, tyran-

glected to take their collective ſentiments of the Britiſh propoſals of peace, and to negociate, un-

of intemperate paſſion, to give up their felicity to ſerve a nation wanting both the will and the power to protect us, and aiming at the deſtruction both of the mother country and the provinces. In the plainneſs of common ſenſe, for I pretend to no caſuiſtry, did the pretended treaty with the Court of Verſailles, amount to more than an overture to America? Certainly not, becauſe no authority had been given by the people to conclude it, nor to this very hour have they authoriſed its ratification. The articles of confederation remain ſtill unſigned.

In the firm perſuaſion, therefore, that the private judgement of an individual citizen of this country is as free from all conventional reſtraints, ſince as before the inſidious offers of France, I preferred thoſe from Great Britain; thinking it infinitely wiſer and ſafer to caſt my confidence upon her juſtice and generoſity, than to truſt a monarchy too feeble to eſtabliſh your independency, ſo perilous to her diſtant dominions; the enemy of the Proteſtant faith and fraudulently avowing an affection for the liberties of mankind, while ſhe holds her native ſons in vaſſalage and chains.

I affect no diſguiſe, and therefore frankly declare, that in theſe principles I had determined to retain my arms and command for an opportunity to ſurrender them to Great Britain; and in concerting the meaſures for a purpoſe, in my opinion, as grateful as it would have been beneficial to my country, I was only ſolicitous to accompliſh an event of deciſive importance, and to prevent as much as poſſible, in the execution of it, the effuſion of blood.

With the higheſt ſatiſfaction I bear teſtimony to my old fellow ſoldiers and citizens, that I find ſolid ground to rely upon the clemency of our Sovereign, and abundant conviction that it is the generous intention of Great Britain not only to leave the rights and privileges of the colonies unimpaired, together with their perpetual exemption from taxation, but to ſuperadd ſuch further benefits as may conſiſt with the common proſperity of the empire. In ſhort, I fought for much leſs than the parent country is as willing to grant to her colonies as they can be to receive or enjoy.

Some may think I continued in the ſtruggle of theſe unhappy days too long, and others that I quitted it too ſoon.—To the firſt I reply, that I did not ſee with their eyes, nor perhaps had ſo favourable a ſituation to look from, and that to our common maſter I am willing to ſtand or fall. In behalf of the candid among the latter, ſome of whom I believe ſerve blindly but honeſtly—in the bands I have left, I pray God to give them all the lights requiſite to their own ſafety before it is too late; and with reſpect to that herd of cenſurers, whoſe enmity to me originates in their hatred to the principles by which I am now led to devote my life to the re-union of the Britiſh

they may be aſſured, that, conſcious of the rectitude of my intentions, I ſhall treat their malice

From RIVINGTON'S NEW YORK ROYAL GAZETTE, *Nov.* 1.

By Brigadier General ARNOLD.

A PROCLAMATION.

To the Officers and Soldiers of the Continental Army, who have the real Intereſt of their Country at Heart, and who are determined to be no longer the Tools and Dupes of Congreſs, or of France.

HAVING reaſon to believe, that the principles I have avowed, in my addreſs to the public of the 7th inſtant, animated the greateſt part of this Continent, I rejoice in the opportunity I have, of inviting you to join his Majeſty's arms.

His Excellency Sir Henry Clinton has authorized me to raiſe a corps of cavalry, and infantry, who are to be clothed, ſubſiſted, and paid as the other troops are in the Britiſh ſervice; and thoſe who bring in horſes, arms, or accoutrements, are to be paid their value, or have liberty to ſell them: To every non-commiſſioned officer and private, a bounty of three guineas will be given; and as the Commander in Chief is pleaſed to allow me to nominate the officers, I ſhall with infinite ſatisfaction embrace the opportunity of advancing men, whoſe valour I have witneſſed, and whoſe principles are favourable to an union with Britain, and true American Liberty.

The rank they obtain in the King's ſervice, will bear a proportion to their former rank, and the number of men they bring with them.

It is expected that a Lieutenant Colonel of cavalry will bring with him, or recruit in a reaſonable time, 75 men.

Major of horſe	50 men.
Captain of ditto	30
Lieutenant of ditto	15
Cornet of ditto	12
Serjeant of ditto	6
Lieutenant-colonel of infantry	75 men.
Major of ditto — —	50
Captain of ditto — —	30
Lieutenant of ditto — —	15
Enſign of ditto — —	12
Serjeant of ditto —	6

N. B. Each field officer will have a company.

Great as theſe encouragements muſt appear to ſuch as have ſuffered every diſtreſs of want of pay, hunger, and nakedneſs, from the neglect, contempt, and corruption of Congreſs, they are nothing to the motives which I expect will influence the brave and generous minds I hope to have the honour to command.

I wiſh to lead a choſen band of Americans to the attainment of peace, liberty, and ſafety (the firſt objects in taking the field), and with them to ſhare in the glory of reſcuing our native country from the graſping hand of France, as well as from the ambitious and intereſted views of a deſperate party among ourſelves, who, in liſtening to French overtures, and rejecting thoſe from Great Britain, have brought the Colonies to the very brink of deſtruction.

Friends, fellow ſoldiers, and citizens, arouſe, and judge for yourſelves—reflect on what you

threatens you.

Your country once was happy; and had the proffered peace been embraced, your laſt two

you to the field of battle, and is daily deluging your country with your blood?

You are flattered with independency as preferable to a redreſs of grievances, and for that ſhadow, inſtead of real felicity, are ſunk into all the wretchedneſs of poverty by the rapacity of your own rulers. Already are you diſqualified to ſupport the pride of character they taught you to aim at, and muſt inevitably ſhortly belong to one or other of the great powers, their folly and wickedneſs have drawn into conflict. Happy for you that you may ſtill become the fellow ſubjects of Great Britain, if you nobly diſdain to be the vaſſals of France.

What is America now but a land of widows, orphans, and beggars?—and ſhould the parent nation ceaſe her exertions to deliver you, what ſecurity remains to you, even for the enjoyment of the conſolations of that religion, for which your fathers braved the ocean, the heathen, and the wilderneſs? Do you know that the eye, which guides this pen, lately ſaw your mean and profligate Congreſs at maſs, for the ſoul of a Roman Catholic in Purgatory, and participating in the rites of a church, againſt whoſe antichriſtian corruptions, your pious anceſtors would have witneſſed with their blood.

As to you, who have been ſoldiers in the Continental Army, can you at this day want evidence, that the funds of your country are exhauſted, or that the managers have applied them to their own private uſes? In either caſe, you ſurely can no longer continue in their ſervice with honour or advantage; yet you have hitherto been their ſupporters in that cruelty, which, with an equal indifference to your's, as well as to the labour and blood of others, is devouring a country, that, from the moment you quit their colours, will be redeemed from their tyranny.

But what need of arguments to ſuch as feel infinitely more miſery than tongue can expreſs? I therefore only add my promiſe of the moſt affectionate welcome and attention, to all who are diſpoſed to join me in the meaſures neceſſary to cloſe the ſcene of our afflictions, which, intolerable as they are, muſt continue to increaſe until we have the wiſdom (ſhewn of late by Ireland) in being contented with the liberality of the Parent Country, who ſtill offers her protection, with the immediate reſtoration of our ancient privileges, civil and ſacred, and a perpetual exemption from all taxes, but ſuch as we ſhall think fit to impoſe on ourſelves.

B. ARNOLD.

New York, Oct. 20, 1780.

For Ink Spots, Iron Moulds, Stains, &c.

The true eſſential SALT of LEMONS.

THIS SALT is infinitely preferable to any other thing whatever for diſcharging of Iron Moulds, Ink Spots, Red Wine, and Stains of every kind out of Lace, Muſlin, Lawn, Cambrick, and Linen immediately, and without any trouble, whitening them to admiration, if grown yellow, and rendering them as beautiful as when quite new. It is alſo excellent for all the purpoſes which the Lemon itſelf is uſed for, being nothing more than the pure acid part of that fruit, ſeparated from the pulp and

and ſauces, and has the advantage over the fruit itſelf, in being always ready, and never ſpoiling in keeping.

N. B. As ſome perſons may apprehend that this

FOURTEENTH DAY's DRAWING.

Prize of 1000l.
No. 13,790.

Prizes of 100l. each.
No. 21,902, 38,214.

Prizes of 50l. each.
No. 357, 2,964, 5,537, 5,802, 6,147, 9,211, 11,453, 21,855, 21,910, 27,736, 40,159, 44,366.

Prizes of 20l. each.

102	184	418	525	583	940	1127
1311	1439	1620	1622	1652	1782	1956
1974	1983	2102	2146	2391	2483	2509
2521	2614	2623	2870	2939	2955	3105
3197	3328	3381	3575	3843	3887	4101
4198	4288	4420	4459	4465	4587	4632
4690	4722	4810	4832	4882	4892	4898
5084	5095	5120	5217	5618	5651	5706
6031	6083	6502	6525	6560	6581	6702
6819	6889	6995	7044	7177	7214	7215
7223	7351	7425	7523	7776	7785	8038
8237	8319	8355	8376	8387	8635	8994
9242	9312	9446	9488	9795	9816	9977
10050	10399	10476	10481	10850	10866	10928
11130	11143	11203	11279	11433	11492	11627
11766	11809	11874	11975	12029	12039	12319
12444	12706	12737	12800	12808	12883	12952
12968	13045	13080	13085	13225	13329	13344
13372	13467	13533	14099	14129	14131	14339
14414	14512	14529	14530	14556	14635	15005
15157	15187	15188	15272	15309	15528	15832
15837	15920	15975	16207	16288	16466	16665
16848	16861	16931	16959	17128	17157	17745
18141	18385	18544	18597	18677	18716	19129
19262	19486	19497	19619	19793	19917	20066
20162	20240	20244	20254	20351	20400	20666
20811	20861	20941	21035	21036	21117	21152
21242	21341	21516	21834	21994	22156	22234
22304	22333	22461	22469	22572	22608	22626
22839	22887	22977	23063	23306	23326	23404
23648	23747	23754	23874	23893	23937	23939
23998	24218	24311	24333	24526	24551	24603
24613	24687	25051	25185	25195	25302	25383
25441	25634	25655	25715	25731	25784	25836
25929	26065	26077	26094	26138	26150	26152
26154	26213	26224	26228	26241	26282	26311
26579	26653	26779	27001	27038	27074	27126
27203	27333	27377	27418	27672	27813	27890
27918	27987	28031	28175	28275	28475	28890
28995	29157	29353	29755	30031	30188	30268
30353	30403	30423	30492	30512	30552	30555
30604	30778	30811	31043	31077	31277	31318
31324	31617	31674	31764	31861	31911	32006
32132	32142	32354	32398	32427	32455	32503
32558	32968	33035	33078	33146	33513	33726
33738	34485	34498	34676	34750	34761	35001
35054	35263	35382	35417	35435	35513	35713
35720	35861	35887	36000	36070	36357	36490
42130	42239	42294	42441	42500	42659	42787
44668	44710	44938	45113	45388	45425	45552
45631	45800	45811	45819	45974	46103	45203
46286	46338	46364	46430	46459	46617	46987

LONDON CHRONICLE

December 2, 1780

The enemy were under the command of the
amous General Arnold, and by the best accounts
nsisted of from 1500 to 2000 men——They
re burnt the greatest part of the towns of New-
ndon, and Groton, near the water——The
rison at Fort-Trumbull evacuated the fort and
nt over to Fort Griswold, where Colonel Led-
d made a noble defence——repulsed the enemy
or three times, but at last was obliged to surren-
the fort to superiour force. The enemy,
r Col. Ledyard had surrendered, murdered him
a number of others; they left 73 of our men
d, and between 30 and 40 wounded in the fort;
also carried off about 40 prisoners, among
ch last number is Ebenezer Ledyard, Esquire.
y evacuated the fort about 10 o'clock, in the e-
ing. They blew up the magazines in both forts
lid very little other damage to either of them.
The enemy this morning were at the har-
's mouth on board their shipping, and came to
about eight o'clock; they are still just out be-
d the Light-House, as the wind is against them.
r shipping consists of about 30 sail, two of which
ar to be about 20 guns each.
We cannot ascertain the loss the enemy sus-
d, but by the best accounts imagine it must be
ge as ours if not larger. We have taken on
de a few prisoners, among which is an Ensign,
ally wounded.
The loss sustained in goods, pro-
s, stores, shipping, & at——A
derable number of vess scape up
vich River."
oth letter, dated For riswold, ton, 7th
10 clock, A. M. says, "That the enemy
d at New-London and Groton yesterday morn-
nd took possession of the works on New-
on one in the after-
to wold, in Groton,
resistance

A New-York city paper of the 30th ult. mentions the arrival of Rear Admiral Hood, at Sandy-Hook, from the West-Indies, with 14 sail of the line, four frigates, one sloop, and a number of troops, consisting of the first battalion of the royal, the 13th and 69th regiments. We are informed that these ships, together with the fleet which were before at New-York, amounting in the whole to 35 sail, under the command of Admiral Graves, have taken their departure from Sandy-Hook, bound to the Chesapeake, in order to give battle to the French squadron, which arrived there from Rhode-Island the latter end of last month, and are much inferiour in force to the British; the whole French squadron is said to consist of only 23 sail including frigates and inferiour vessels. The English fleet consist of one ship of 98 guns, one of 90, one of 70, eleven of 74, four of 64, two of 50, four of 44, three of 32, five of 28, one of 24, one Fire-ship of 8, and a sloop of war. All the British line of battle ships except one are said to be copper-bottomed.

It is not doubted but that his Excellency General Washington has marched, with 8000 choice troops including the French, to Virginia, where the troops in that quarter will join him; Lord Cornwallis is blocked up by the French fleet;—by the present appearance of things we are at the eve of some important event, which God grant may be propitious to the United States.

It is said that Sir George Rodney and General Vaughan have gone for England from the W. Indies.

We hear that Arnold when he landed at New-London, dined at a gentleman's house with whom he was formerly acquainted. After dinner he ordered the house to be plundered and sat on fire. The traitor carried off all the plunder in the town that his short stay wo rmit him to take. Had he tarried in order to e taken breakfast the ne morning, it is likely have been reward for all his villanies.

A la quantit ney, lately from st carr

in Worcester. Those gentlem
to favour him with their comma
ed that his utmost endeavours sh
them with fidelity and dispatch.

S A D D L
MEN's and Women's SADI
made and sold by
NATHANIEL CO
At his Shop in Worcester, near t
He begs leave to inform the Pub
on the Saddler's business in all it
tlemen and Ladies who will plea
with their custom, may depend
with fidelity on reasonable terms

Wine Glas
Genteel WINE GLASSES,
JOSEPH TRUM
At his Store near the Court-H
Where may be had choice MA
TER, &c. &c.

STRAYED or stolen from the
about the 26th day of last m
brown COW, low in flesh, the
horns a little broke, and about ei
old. Whoever will give inform
scriber, of Cow, so that he ma
shall h OLLARS re
le the thief, so tha
vi entitled to a furth
G JOS
September 11, 78

DESERTED betw
fie
aged
plex

CHAPTER XII

CONQUEST AND CAPTURE

Introduction

Propelled by success at Kings Mountain and a decisive American victory under Daniel Morgan at Cowpens, General Nathanael Greene begins a strategic retreat, leading Cornwallis's forces northward. As commander of the Southern Army, Greene safely establishes himself as one of America's greatest military minds, helping set the stage for a series of climactic battles, by land and sea, in Virginia. A remarkable American victory at Yorktown in October 1781 was a key step toward ending the American Revolution. With its military overextended around the globe, Britain began peace talks with America, France, and Spain a few months later.

Massachusetts Spy
September 13, 1781

Surrender of Lord Cornwallis
Architect of the Capitol

REPORTING THE

BATTLE OF COWPENS

By John Buchanan

January 1781. Early the previous year, a British expeditionary force invaded South Carolina and won two big battles and some smaller actions. But throughout the Carolina Backcountry, mounted partisan militia rose and in a sweeping guerilla war of movement forced a stalemate. Then the new American commander in the south, Major General Nathanael Greene, sent the cream of his little army, six hundred light troops under the command of his brilliant deputy, Brigadier General Daniel Morgan, westward beyond the Catawba River, with orders "to give protection to that part of the country and spirit up the people, to annoy the enemy in that quarter." Lord Cornwallis, believing that Morgan endangered the key British strongpoint of Ninety Six, sent against him his own light troops commanded by a cavalry officer with a fearsome reputation: Lieutenant Colonel Banastre Tarleton. With about 1,100 infantry and cavalry, Tarleton, bold and confident, drove his men through the rain-soaked Carolina Backcountry in pursuit of Morgan's six hundred.

While the British won most of the battles during the Revolutionary War, the Americans won the key battles, including Cowpens.

Morgan met his pursuer on the ground called Cowpens. It was a location familiar to backcountry militia, and during the night before the battle hundreds rode in to join Morgan, until his force numbered 1,500 to 1,600, perhaps more. Yet in his report to Greene published in the *New-Jersey Gazette,* Morgan claimed he had only eight hundred men, thus drawing attention largely to his light troops, especially his regulars. But the militia, though untrained in formal warfare, was a vital element at Cowpens, and Morgan was the right man to instruct guerilla warriors on how to fight British regulars in an open field.

Before Cowpens, American generals often placed militia in the front line and expected them to behave as regulars. Morgan also placed them in the front line, but he did not ask them to stand fast in the face of advancing British regulars wielding fixed bayonets. He deployed militia skirmishers supported by a militia line behind them. "Boys, give me three fires," Morgan told the militia, then they could retire behind the Continentals on the third line and form as a reserve. The third line was commanded by the cool, unflappable Lieutenant Colonel John Eager Howard of Maryland, and in reserve behind Howard was Colonel William Washington with eighty-two Continental Light Dragoons and forty-five mounted militiamen.

Tarleton reached Cowpens at dawn on January 17, 1781, and immediately attacked. The militia behaved well and delivered a "heavy and galling fire" before retiring behind the Continentals. The British came on and exchanged volleys with the third line. Then a misunderstood order led to a rearward movement that Morgan in his report incorrectly described as planned. Howard's entire command about-faced and marched to the rear—but in good order. As the British, certain of victory, came on in disorder, the Americans marched to a spot chosen by Morgan. Suddenly, upon command, the American regiments faced about and at short range delivered destructive volleys in sequence into the stunned British. Howard ordered a bayonet charge. Washington's cavalry also charged, and Colonel Andrew Pickens's militia came storming back into the fight. The British regulars collapsed and, in the words of a teenager fighting with Washington's cavalry, "did the prettiest sort of running." Of Tarleton's 1,100, some eight hundred were casualties, while the Americans suffered about twenty-four killed and more than one hundred wounded, double what Morgan reported.

With the exception of the two-hundred-man British Legion Horse, which refused Tarleton's order to charge and fled the field, Cornwallis had lost his light troops, the eyes and ears of his army, and in his fury he would pursue first Morgan, then Greene, and in the process ruin his army. During the Revolutionary War, the British won most of the battles, but the Americans won the key battles. Cowpens was one of those key battles, the beginning of the road to Yorktown and the British loss of America—the real jewel in the crown.

BATTLE OF COWPENS
North Wind Picture Archives

Of Tarleton's 1,100 infantry and cavalry, some eight hundred were casualties, while the Americans suffered about twenty-four killed and more than one hundred wounded.

FEBRUARY 14, 1781

The NEW-JERSEY GAZETTE

PHILADELPHIA, February 8.

[...]

His Excellency
The President of Congress.
General MORGAN's letter to General GREENE.
Camp, near Cain-creek, January 19, 1781.

Dear Sir,

THE troops I have the honour to command have gained a complete victory over a detachment from the British army, commanded by Lieut. Col. Tarleton. The action happened on the 17th instant, about sunrise, at a place called the Cowpens, near Pacolet river.

On the 14th, having received intelligence that the British army were in motion, and that their movements clearly indicated their intention of dislodging me, I abandoned my encampment at Grendales Ford, and on the 16th, in the evening, took possession of a post about 7 miles from the Chrokee Ford, on Broad River. My former position subjected me at once to the operations of Lord Corwallis and Col. Tarleton, and in case of a defeat my retreat might easily have been cut off. My situation at the Cowpens enabled me to improve any advantages that I might gain, and to provide better for my security should I be unfortunate. These reasons induced me to take this post, notwithstanding it had the appearance of a retreat.

[...]

The enemy drew up in one line, 400 yards in front of our advanced corps. The first battalion of the 71st regiment was opposed to our right, the 7th to our left, the Legion Infantry to our centre, and two companies of light troops of 100 each on our flanks.

In their front they moved two pieces of artillery, and Lieut. Col. Tarleton, with 280 cavalry, was posted in the rear of his line. The disposition being thus made, small parties of riflemen were detached to skirmish with the enemy, on which their whole line advanced with the greatest impetuosity, shouting as they advanced. Majors M'Dowal and Cunningham gave them a heavy and galling fire, and retreated to the regiments intended for their support; the whole of Col. Picken's command then kept up a fire by regiments, retreating agreeably to orders. When the enemy advanced to our line, they received a well directed and incessant fire, but their numbers being superior to ours, they gained our flanks, which obliged us to change our position. We retired in good order about fifty paces, formed, advanced on the enemy, and gave them a brisk fire, which threw them into disorder. Lieutenant Colonel Howard observing this, gave orders for the line to charge bayonets, which was done with such address that the enemy fled with the utmost precipitation. Lieut. Col. Washington discovering that the cavalry were cutting down our riflemen on the left, charged them with such firmness as obliged them to retire in confusion. The enemy were entirely routed, and the pursuit continued upwards of 20 miles. Our loss was inconsiderable, not having more than 12 killed and 60 wounded. The enemy's loss was 10 commissioned offecers, and upwards of 100 rank and file killed, 200 wounded, 29 commissioned officers, and above 500 privates, prisoners, which fell into our hands, with two pieces of artillery, two standards, eight hundred muskets, one travelling forge, thirty-five baggage-waggons, seventy Negroes, and upwards of one hundred dragoon horses, with all their musick. They destroyed most of their baggage, which was immense.

Although our success was complete, we fought only eight hundred men, and were opposed by upwards of one thousand of chosen British troops.

Such was the inferiority of our numbers, that our success must be attributed, under God, to the justice of our cause, and the bravery of our troops. My wishes would induce me to mention the name of every private centinel in the corps. In justice to the bravery and good conduct to the officers, I have taken the liberty to enclose you a list of their names, from a conviction that you will be pleased to introduce such characters to the world.

[...]

I am, Sir, your obedient servant,
DAN. MORGAN.

NEW-JERSEY GAZETTE (TRENTON)

February 14, 1781

Nathanael Greene's after-action report and Daniel Morgan's letter provided readers of the *New-Jersey Gazette* with vivid detail about the Battle of Cowpens. During the Revolutionary War, the British won most of the battles, but the Americans won the key battles. Cowpens was one of those key battles, the beginning of the road to Yorktown.

BALTIMORE, January 30.

On Monday, the 22d inſtant, the brig Hawk, Captain Bull; the brig Cato, Captain Weeks; and the ſchooner Nautilus, Capt. Kerſtead, outward bound from this port, were chaſed on ſhore in Roman bay, a little below Cedar Point, by the Iris frigate and other veſſels of war. The enemy immediately boarded the Cato, who, by ſome accident, took fire, and blew off her quarters. Fifteen of the enemy and 8 of her people periſhed. They ſet the Hawk on fire, and ſhe burnt to the water's edge. The Captain of the Nautilus landed his guns, and prevented the enemy from boarding his veſſel, and in all probability ſhe and her cargo will be ſaved. The Britiſh left Cedar Point on Wedneſday.

Extract of a letter from Richmond, dated the 19th of January, 1781.

"I am this moment informed that the enemy landed at Hardy's ferry, and marched from thence to Smithfield, and thence to Mackie's mills, where they ſtaid ſome time, and then returned to Smithfield. Some of their veſſels are up Nanſemond river, as high as Sleepy-Hole ferry."

PHILADELPHIA, February 8.

This morning arrived here Major Giles, Aid de Camp to General Morgan, with diſpatches to Congreſs, containing the following

Important Intelligence.

Camp, South-Carolina, on Pee-Dee, January 24, 1781.

SIR,

I HAVE the honour to encloſe, for the information of Congreſs, the copy of my letter to his Excellency General Waſhington, with the encloſures, announcing the defeat of a detachment of the Britiſh army, under Lt. Col. Tarleton. The action was important, and reflects the higheſt honour on General Morgan, and the troops under his command.

Major Edward Giles will deliver theſe diſpatches, and have the honour to give Congreſs ſuch further information as they may requeſt.

The Deputy Commiſſary General of Priſoners will, as ſoon as poſſible, tranſmit a particular return of the priſoners taken on the 17th, by which conveyance I will forward the ſtandards, to be laid at the feet of Congreſs.

I have the honour to be, with ſentiments of the greateſt eſteem and reſpect,

Your Excellency's
Moſt obedient humble ſervant,
NATHANIEL GREENE.

His Excellency
The Preſident of Congreſs.

General MORGAN's letter to General GREENE.

Camp, near Cain-creek, January 19, 1781.

Dear Sir,

THE troops I have the honour to command have gained a complete victory over a detachment from the Britiſh army, commanded by Lieut. Col. Tarleton. The action happened on the 17th inſtant, about ſunriſe, at a place called the Cowpens, near Pacolet river.

On the 14th, having received intelligence that the Britiſh army were in motion, and that their movements clearly indicated their intention of diſlodging me, I abandoned my encampment at Grendales Ford, and on the 16th, in the evening, took poſſeſſion of a poſt about 7 miles from the Chrokee Ford, on Broad River. My former poſition ſubjected me at once to the operations of Lord Cornwallis and Col. Tarleton, and in caſe of a defeat my retreat might eaſily have been cut off. My ſituation at the Cowpens enabled me to improve any advantages that I might gain, and to provide better for my ſecurity ſhould I be unfortunate. Theſe reaſons induced me to take this poſt, notwithſtanding it had the appearance of a retreat.

On the evening of the 16th the enemy occupied the ground we had removed from in the morning. An hour before daylight one of my ſcouts informed me that they had advanced within five miles of our camp. On this information the neceſſary diſpoſitions were made, and, from the alacrity of the troops, we were ſoon prepared to receive them. The light-infantry, commanded by Lieut. Col. Howard, and the Virginia militia under Major Triplett, were formed on a riſing ground; the third regiment of dragoons, con-

In their front they moved two pieces of artillery, and Lieut. Col. Tarleton, with 280 cavalry, was poſted in the rear of his line. The diſpoſition being thus made, ſmall parties of riflemen were detached to ſkirmiſh with the enemy, on which their whole line advanced with the greateſt impetuoſity, ſhouting as they advanced. Majors M'Dowal and Cunningham gave them a heavy and galling fire, and retreated to the regiments intended for their ſupport; the whole of Col. Picken's command then kept up a fire by regiments, retreating agreeably to orders. When the enemy advanced to our line, they received a well directed and inceſſant fire, but their numbers being ſuperior to ours, they gained our flanks, which obliged us to change our poſition. We retired in good order about fifty paces, formed, advanced on the enemy, and gave them a briſk fire, which threw them into diſorder. Lieutenant Colonel Howard obſerving this, gave orders for the line to charge bayonets, which was done with ſuch addreſs that the enemy fled with the utmoſt precipitation. Lieut. Col. Waſhington diſcovering that the cavalry were cutting down our riflemen on the left, charged them with ſuch firmneſs as obliged them to retire in confuſion. The enemy were entirely routed, and the purſuit continued upwards of 20 miles. Our loſs was inconſiderable, not having more than 12 killed and 60 wounded. The enemy's loſs was 10 commiſſioned officers, and upwards of 100 rank and file killed, 200 wounded, 29 commiſſioned officers, and above 500 privates, priſoners, which fell into our hands, with two pieces of artillery, two ſtandards, eight hundred muſkets, one travelling forge, thirty-five baggage-waggons, ſeventy Negroes, and upwards of one hundred dragoon horſes, with all their muſick. They deſtroyed moſt of their baggage, which was immenſe.

Although our ſucceſs was complete, we fought only eight hundred men, and were oppoſed by upwards of one thouſand of choſen Britiſh troops.

Such was the inferiority of our numbers, that our ſucceſs muſt be attributed, under God, to the juſtice of our cauſe, and the bravery of our troops. My wiſhes would induce me to mention the name of every private centinel in the corps. In juſtice to the bravery and good conduct of the officers, I have taken the liberty to encloſe you a liſt of their names, from a conviction that you will be pleaſed to introduce ſuch characters to the world.

Major Giles, my Aid de Camp, and Capt. Brooks, acting as my Brigade-Major, deſerve and have my thanks, for their aſſiſtance and behaviour on this occaſion. The Baron de Glabuck, who accompanies Major Giles with theſe diſpatches, ſerved with me as a volunteer, and behaved in ſuch a manner as to merit your attention.

I am, Sir, your obedient ſervant,
DAN. MORGAN.

tence of death for horſeſtealing. There
others that eſcaped who were charged
offences; one of whom, of the name of D
gether with a Negro man) is retaken.
On the 6th inſtant, about 11 o'clock
noon, a certain Samuel Reed, of Philad
on his way to Freehold in Monmouth
robbed by three villains, diſguiſed in froc
ſers, of ſixty Guineas, twenty Half-Joe
hundred Continental dollars, at the Sand-
half a mile this ſide Lawrence Taylor's ta

To the Printer of the NEW-JERSEY G
SIR,
AS it is a matter of the utmoſt importa
value of the new money ſhould be e
culating medium to gold and ſilver, and
citizen ſhould endeavour to prevent its d
it behoves us to enquire why the county
are authorized to give higher prices for
as they purchaſe for the public, than was
value of them in gold or ſilver. They gi
the amount, and by this means the mon
ciated before it comes into circulation.
ably certain that grain can be purchaſed e
new money or the old continental at ſever
lars inſtead of one, at leaſt thirty or fort
leſs than is allowed by the public. The p
fore appears like a merchant whoſe circu
deſperate, and therefore offers a much
than common, in order to obtain credit.
proper that the money ſhould be immediat
into circulation, yet as we ſuppoſe it wi
paid in value equal to gold and ſilver, wh
public be burthened with a debt of at lea
part more than is neceſſary? This, Sir, i
of importance to all who have taxes to
behoves our Repreſentatives to inform
public money is thus to be ſquandered.
February 1, 1781. A F

Mr. COLLINS,
VIRGINIA has at laſt communicated t
her reſolution of ceding to the Unite
the land on the weſt of the Ohio river, pro
greſs will pay her the expence of conqueri
conquered country, furniſh land for the ſ
her troops, and guaranty to her all the
eaſt of the ſaid river Ohio.
The ſharper has her own conſent for a
She will give Congreſs the Indian country
of the Ohio river, to which ſhe has no rig
greſs will pay her the expence of ſending
thoſe woods to hunt for and make enemie
might have the better pretence to add to h
ed chartered claim, that of conqueſt, at
deficient quota was wanted in the field to
tled property and eſtabliſh independence

REPORTING THE

RACE TO THE DAN

By Dennis M. Conrad

THE RACE TO THE DAN WAS A REMARKABLE STRATEGIC retreat that saved the American Continental Army in the south and shifted momentum to the Americans in the bitterly contested war in that region. This retreat began immediately after the Battle of Cowpens on January 17, 1781, and continued until Nathanael Greene's army crossed the Dan River into Virginia on February 14.

It was a rugged retreat for both armies, but especially for the Americans. Having divided his army in order to feed and reform it while still maintaining a presence in the western Carolinas, Greene had to reunite his ill-supplied army in the face of the British advance. One officer observed that you could track Greene's army "by the Blood from the feet of the men."

It was a reluctant retreat on Greene's part. Twice he engaged or tried to engage his British pursuers. The first time was at Cowan's Ford. With militia led by William Lee Davidson, Greene tried to defeat the British as they crossed the swollen Catawba River. That effort failed because Davidson, contrary to Greene's advice, posted most of his force away from the river. Thus, despite what Lord Cornwallis writes in his account of the crossing in his report published in the *Massachusetts Spy* of September 13, 1781, the British vanguard was able to cross the river against weak resistance. When Davidson arrived with reinforcements, he was killed, which demoralized his men, who broke and ran.

Again at Guilford Court House, Greene tried to stop and fight Cornwallis, but, as Cornwallis correctly noted in his after-action report, the militia of North Carolina and Virginia did not assemble, and after consulting a Council of War, the American general decided to abandon North Carolina and move his army across the Dan River into Virginia.

The newspaper report printed in the March 15, 1781, *Connecticut Journal* is taken from Greene's letter to George Washington of February 9, which was written during the race. Therefore, the successful conclusion is not given. As he reported here, Greene again split his army and created a light infantry unit, which marched off in a northwesterly direction toward Virginia. Cornwallis, unaware that Greene's quartermaster was collecting boats at Irwin's and Boyd's Ferries at South Boston, Virginia, and therefore convinced that Greene's army would be forced to use the shallower, upper fords of the Dan River, pursued Colonel Otho H. Williams's diversionary force, buying time for the slower-moving main force, which marched directly to Boyd's and Irwin's Ferries.

Although initially fooled, Cornwallis soon saw through the American deception and moved in direct pursuit of the American army with Williams's force between them. The race began in earnest. For three days, the van of Cornwallis's army and the rearmost unit of Williams's light infantry remained in almost constant sight of each other. At one point, Williams spied campfires ahead and, believing he had overtaken the main army, contemplated a suicidal attack in an attempt to save the main force. Before issuing those fateful orders, Williams discovered that the fires had been left burning for the use of his men. More telling is that the British pursuers were so near that Williams's troops were unable to halt and cook a meal.

On February 14, after averaging over thirty miles per day, the rear of Greene's army crossed the Dan just as the first troops of Cornwallis's army arrived on the opposite bank. Greene, not convinced that the race was over, prepared to retreat farther into Virginia, but as Cornwallis reported in his letter published in the September 13, 1781, *Massachusetts Spy*, his army being "ill suited to enter by that quarter so powerful as Virginia," he moved away from the Dan toward Hillsborough, North Carolina, where he "erected the King's standard," hoping to attract local Loyalists.

Greene was active as well. Recognizing the retreat as an opportunity to defeat Cornwallis, who was now far from reinforcements and his supply lines, Greene wrote local militia leaders begging them to reinforce him and promising that they would "injure" Cornwallis or "effect his ruin." The result was the Battle of Guilford Courthouse, covered in the next section of this chapter.

Along with the account of the Race to the Dan, the March 15, 1781, *Connecticut Journal* contains reports of the activities of Francis Marion, a partisan leader operating in northeastern South Carolina. The letters of January 31 and February 2 detail successful raids conducted against the British supply line up the Santee River by Marion's subordinates, Major James Postell and Captain John Postell. The letter from Colonel Henry "Light Horse Harry" Lee discusses a joint attack on Georgetown, South Carolina, by Marion and Lee. It was an ingenious and complicated effort that failed when the British garrison, instead of trying to move to the brick redoubt, barricaded themselves in their quarters outside of the fort. As mentioned, Captain Patrick Carnes captured Colonel George Campbell, whose quarters were also in the town. The British considered the operation inconsequential. Lee's failure to mention Marion's role in the Georgetown operation is inexplicable.

Finally, there are two reports of a British expedition, commanded by Major James Craig, which captured Wilmington, North Carolina. That capture was intended to support Cornwallis's planned invasion of North Carolina by providing a supply depot for Cornwallis on the North Carolina coast. The opposition of local militia, however, prevented Craig from moving up the Cape Fear River as planned to set up a line of communication and supply as far as Cross Creek (Fayetteville).

General Nathanael Greene
North Wind Picture Archives

Despite having no decisive victories on his resumé, Nathanael Greene is widely regarded as America's most gifted military strategist.

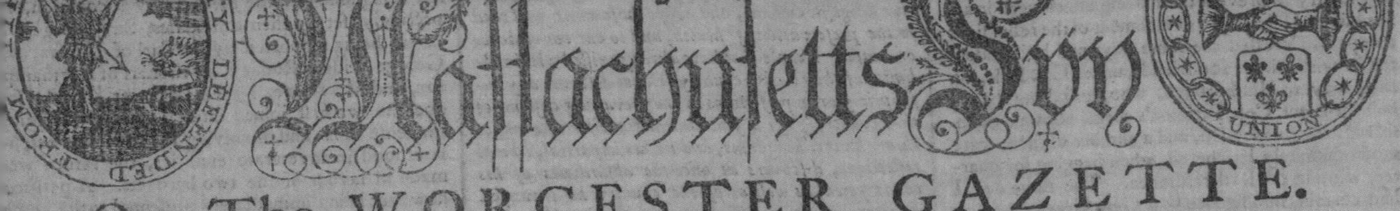

Or, The WORCESTER GAZETTE.

The noble Efforts of a Virtuous, Free and United People, ſhall extirpate TYRANNY, and eſtabliſh LIBERTY and PEACE.

VOL. XI.) THURSDAY, SEPTEMBER 13, 1781. (No. 540.

The following is taken from a Charleſtown Paper of July 26, 1781.

From the LONDON GAZETTE.

WHITEHALL, June 4, 1781.

THIS morning Captain Brodrick, Aid-de-camp to Lieut. Gen. Cornwallis, arrived from Charleſtown, South-Carolina, with diſpatches from his Lordſhip, and Lieutenant Colonel Balfour, to the Right Honourable Lord George Germaine, one of his Majeſty's principal Secretaries of State, of which the following are copies and extracts:

My LORD, *Guilford, March 17, 1781.*

HAVING occaſion to diſpatch my Aid-de-camp Capt. Brodrick, with the particulars of the action of the 15th, in compliance with general directions from Sir Henry Clinton, I ſhall embrace the opportunity to give your Lordſhip an account of the operations of the troops under my command, previous to that event, and of thoſe ſubſequent, until the departure of Capt. Brodrick.

My plan for the winter's campaign was to penetrate into North-Carolina, leaving South-Carolina in ſecurity againſt any probable attack in my abſence.

Lord Rawdon, with a conſiderable body of troops, had charge of the defenſive, and I proceeded about the middle of January upon the offenſive operations. I decided to march up the upper, in preference to the lower roads, leading into North-Carolina, becauſe fords being frequent above the forks of the rivers, my paſſage there could not eaſily be obſtructed; and General Greene having taken poſt on the Pedee, and there being few fords in any of the great rivers of this country below their forks, eſpecially in the winter, I apprehended being much delayed, if not entirely prevented from penetrating by the latter route. I was the more induced to prefer this route, as I hoped in my way to be able to deſtroy or drive out of South-Carolina the corps of the enemy, commanded by Gen. Morgan, which threatened our valuable diſtrict of Ninety-Six; and I likewiſe hoped by rapid marches, to be between Gen. Greene and Virginia, and by that means force him to fight without receiving any reinforcement from that province; or failing of that to oblige him to quit North-Carolina with precipitation, and thereby encourage our friends to make good their promiſes of a general riſing to aſſiſt me in the re-eſtabliſhing his Majeſty's government.

The unfortunate affair of the 17th of January, was a very unexpected and ſevere blow; however, being thoroughly ſenſible that defenſive meaſures would be certain ruin to the affairs of Britain in the ſouthern colonies, this event did not deter me from proſecuting the original plan.

That General Greene might be uncertain of my intended route as long as poſſible, I had left Gen. Leſlie at Camden, until I was ready to move from Winnſborough, and he was now within a march of me. I employed the 18th in forming a junction with him, and in collecting the remains of Lieutenant Colonel Tarleton's corps, after which great exertions were made by part of the army without baggage, to retake our priſoners, and to intercept General Morgan's corps, on its retreat to Catawba; but the celerity of their movements, and the ſwelling of the numberleſs creeks in our way, rendered all our efforts fruitleſs. I therefore aſſembled the army on the 25th, at Ramſoure's mill, on the ſouth fork of the Catawba; and as the loſs of my light troops could not be remedied by the activity of the whole corps, I employed a halt of two days in collecting ſome flour, and in deſtroying ſuperfluous baggage, and all my waggons, except thoſe loaded with hoſpital ſtores, ſalt and ammunition, and four reſerved empty, in readineſs for ſick or wounded. In this meaſure, though at the expence of a great deal of officers baggage, and of all proſpect in future of rum, and even a regular ſupply of proviſions to the ſoldiers, I muſt, in juſtice to this army, ſay, that there was the moſt general and chearful acquieſcence.

In the mean time the rains had rendered the North-Catawba impaſſible, and Gen. Morgan's corps, the militia of the rebellious counties of Rowan and Mecklenburg, under Gen. Davidſon, or the gang of plunderers uſually under the command of General Sumpter, not then recovered from his wounds, had occupied all the fords in a ſpace of more than forty miles upwards from the fork. I approached the river, during its heighth, by ſhort marches, ſo as to give the enemy equal apprehenſions for ſeveral fords; and after having procured the beſt information in my power, I reſolved to attempt the paſſage at a private ford (then ſlightly guarded) near M'Cowan's ford, on the morning of the firſt of February.

Lieutenant-Colonel Webſter was detached with part of the army, and all the baggage to Battle's ford, ſix miles above M'Cowan's, where General Davidſon was ſuppoſed to be poſted with 500 militia, and was directed to make every poſſible demonſtration, by cannonading and otherwiſe, of an intention to force a paſſage there; and I marched at one in the morning with the brigade of guards, regiment of Boſe, 23d regiment, 200 cavalry, and two 3-pounders, to the ford fixed upon for the real attempt. The morning being very dark and rainy, and part of our way through a wood, where there was no road, one of the three pounders, in front of the 23d regiment and the cavalry, overſet in a ſwamp, and occaſioned thoſe corps to loſe the line of march; and ſome of the artillery men belonging to the other gun (one of whom had the match) having ſtopped to aſſiſt were likewiſe left behind. The head of the column, in the mean while, arrived at the bank of the river, and day began to break. I could make no uſe of the gun that was up, and it was evident, from the number of fires on the other ſide, that the oppoſition would be greater than I had expected. However, as I knew that the rain, then falling, would ſoon render the river again impaſſible, and I had received information the evening before, that General Greene had arrived in General Morgan's camp, and that his army was marching after him with the greateſt expedition, I determined not to deſiſt from the attempt; and therefore, full of confidence in the zeal and gallantry of Brigadier General O'Hara, and of the brigade of guards under his command, I ordered them to march on; but to prevent confuſion, not to fire until they gained the oppoſite bank. Their behaviour juſtified my high opinion of them; for a conſtant fire from the enemy, in a ford upwards of 500 yards wide, in many places up to their middle, with a rocky bottom and ſtrong current, made no impreſſion on their cool and determined valour, nor checked their paſſage. The light infantry, landing firſt, immediately formed, and in a few minutes killed or diſperſed every thing that appeared before them, the reſt of the troops forming and advancing in ſucceſſion. We now learned that we had been oppoſed by about 300 militia, that had taken poſt there only the evening before, under the command of General Davidſon. Their General and two or three other officers were among the killed; the number of wounded was uncertain, and a few were taken. On our ſide, Lieutenant-Colonel Hall and three men were killed, and 36 wounded, and all of the light infantry and grenadiers of the guards. By this time the rear of the column had joined, and the whole having paſſed with the greateſt diſpatch, I detached Lieut. Col. Tarleton, with the cavalry and 23d regiment, to purſue the routed militia; a few were ſoon killed or taken; and Lieut. Col. Tarleton having learned that 3 or 400 of the neighbouring militia were to aſſemble that day at Tarrank's houſe, about ten miles from the ford, leaving his infantry, he went on with the cavalry, and finding the militia as expected, he with excellent conduct and great ſpirit, attacked them inſtantly, and totally routed them, with little loſs on his ſide, and on theirs between forty and fifty killed, wounded or priſoners. This ſtroke, with our paſſage of the ford, ſo effectually diſpirited the militia, that we met with no farther oppoſition on our march to the Yadkin, through one of the moſt rebellious tracts in America.

During this time, the rebels having quitted Beattie's ford, Lieut. Col. Webſter was paſſing his detachment and the baggage of the army: This had become tedious and difficult by the continuance of the rain and the ſwelling of the river; but all joined us ſoon after dark, about ſix miles from Beattie's ford. The other fords were alſo abandoned by the enemy. The greateſt part of the militia diſperſed; and Gen. Morgan, with his corps, marched all that afternoon, and the following night, towards Saliſbury. We purſued next morning, in hopes to intercept him between the rivers, and after ſtruggling with many difficulties, ariſing from ſwelled creeks and bad roads, the guards came up with his rear, in the evening of the third, routed it, and took a few waggons at the trading ford of the Yadkin. He had paſſed the body of his infantry in flats, and his cavalry and waggons by the ford, during that day and the preceeding night; but at the time of our arrival the boats were ſecured on the other ſide, and the ford had become impaſſible. The river continuing
to riſe, and th
termined
ing a ſmal
and the h
me two d
the banks
friends, w
army wa
form a ju
had time
having r
conclude
er to avo
and it b
made gr
the uppe
fords are
could no
was in g
receivin

Noth
of the o
hardſhi
him ; l
exceedi
bad ro
and bri
rendered
val at Boy
guard had got over the night before, his baggage and main body having paſſed the preceeding day, at that and a neighbouring ferry, where more flats had been collected than had been repreſented to me as poſſible. My force being ill ſuited to enter by that quarter ſo powerful a province as Virginia, and North-Carolina being in the utmoſt confuſion, after giving the troops a halt of one day, I proceeded by eaſy marches to Hillſborough, where I erected the King's ſtandard, and invited by proclamation, all

MASSACHUSETTS SPY (BOSTON)

September 13, 1781

The Race to the Dan was a remarkable strategic retreat that saved the American Continental Army in the south and shifted momentum to the Americans in the bitterly contested war in that region. This retreat began immediately after the Battle of Cowpens on January 17, 1781, and continued until Nathanael Greene's army crossed the Dan River into Virginia on February 14. It was a reluctant retreat on Greene's part. Twice he engaged or tried to engage his British pursuers. Lord Cornwallis's account of the crossing is published in the *Massachusetts Spy* of September 13.

CONNECTICUT JOURNAL (NEW HAVEN)

March 15, 1781

—

The report printed in the March 15, 1781, *Connecticut Journal* is taken from Greene's letter to George Washington of February 9, which was written during the race. Therefore, the successful conclusion is not given. Along with the account of the Race to the Dan, the *Connecticut Journal* contains reports of the activities of Francis Marion, a partisan leader operating in northeastern South Carolina.

PHILADELPHIA, February 28.

Intelligence from the Southward.

BY authentic advices we learn, That General Morgan collected near one hundred prisoners, by parties sent out for the purpose, after the account given in his letter to General Greene, dated the 19th of January last. That upon receiving the news of Tarleton's defeat, Lord Cornwallis marched in pursuit of the light infantry and the prisoners. As soon as Gen. Greene was informed of the movements of Lord Cornwallis, he put the army in motion on Pedee, and, leaving it under the command of Gen. Huger, set out to join the light-infantry, in order to collect the militia & embarrass the enemy, until he could affect a junction of his forces. Gen. Morgan, after the defeat of Tarleton, had very judiciously made forced marches up into the country, and happily crossed the Catawba the evening before a great rain, which swelled the rivers to such a degree as prevented the enemy from crossing, for several days, during which time the prisoners were got over the Yadkin, and on their march for Dan river, which they likewise passed, on the 14th of this month had reached Bedford Court-house, in the State of Virginia.

Gen. Greene, on the latter end of January, arrived at the light infantry camp at Sherard's ford, on the Catawba. The enemy were a little lower down the river at M'Cowan's ford, and the river was still so high that they could not cross. They had [...]s, and equip[...]y as light [...]onsisted of [...]roops, in[...]s & their [...]e first of [...]an's ford, [...]ty of mili[...]der to op[...] falling by [...]my made [...]he militia [...]ndezvous [...]tia to col[...] up and [...]hem halt[...]rt of the [...]were over[...] dispersed. [...]t night at [...]nding the [...] the light infantry the next morning continued their march to Salisbury, and crossed the Yadkin. Before they got over all the baggage and stores, the ene[...] enemy near the ford. The boats being secured, and the river continu[...]

[...] junction as soon as was expected. Gen. Greene therefore, fearing that the river might fall so as to be fordable, ordered the army to file off to Guilford Court-House, where part of them arrived on the evening of the 8th, and the rest were expected to be in on the 9th. The enemy, finding they could not pass at the Trading ford, near Salisbury, marched up the south side of the Yadkin, and on the night of the 7th crossed at the Shallow-ford, and had on the 9th advanced towards Salem, one of the Moravian towns, within 25 or 30 miles of Guilford Court-House.

These rapid movements having prevented the junction of the militia, Gen. Greene ordered the stores and heavy baggage to be removed to Prince Edward Court-House, in the State of Virginia; and having formed a light army, composed of the cavalry of the 1st and 3d regiments, and Lieut. Col. Lee's legion, a detachment of light infantry under Col. Howard, and some few Virginia riflemen, making in the whole 700, ordered them with the militia to harrass the enemy in their advance, and check their progress, while he with the rest of the army crossed the Roanoke. In the mean while, Gen. Sumpter was ordered to collect the militia in the upper part of South-Carolina, and Gen. Pickens had orders to take the command of the men in arms in the rear of the enemy. Such was the situation of the two armies at the date of the last dispatches, which was the 10th of this month.

Extract of a letter from General Marian to General Greene, dated Santee, January 31.

"On the 29th inst. I sent over the Santee river two parties of horse, consisting of 30 each, one under the command of Major Postil, the other under Capt. Postil. The first to burn the enemy's stores at Thompson's; the other to burn those at Watboo-bridge. The Captain has executed his orders with great spirit and good conduct. At Watboo there were 15 hogsheads of rum, a quantity of pork, flour, rice, salt and turpentine. He marched from there to Keithfield, near Monk's Corner, attacked a British guard, killed two, wounded three, took and brought off two surgeons, one Quarter-Master, one Waggon-Master, seven Waggons, one Steward, and twenty five non-commissioned officers and privates of the 7th, 23d, 33d, 63d, and 71st regiments. He had not one [...] cloathing and baggage, 20 hogsheads of rum, and retired with his prisoners."

[...] away some days before. But on his return he heard of a great quantity of rum, sugar, salt, flour, pork, soldiers cloathing and baggage, at Maringault's Ferry. The guard had gone after Capt. Postil, and left only four men in a redoubt of wood, which the Major took, and entirely destroyed all the stores and redoubt, without receiving any loss or hurt."

Extract of a letter from Major General Greene, dated at Sherrad's Ford, on Catawba River, Jan. 31.

"I have received intelligence that 400 troops have sailed from Charlestown for Wilmington in North-Carolina."

Extract of a letter from Col. Drayton, to Major General Greene, dated Feb. 2.

"On Monday evening the 12th ult. the enemy's fleet appeared off. On Tuesday part got in, and the Thursday following the whole of them reached the first flatts. The inhabitants then held a consultation on the propriety of meeting their foes with a flag and concluded on it. In consequence they insisted on Col. Young, who commanded the militia, to withdraw the few he had (not more than fifty) and leave the town to make their own terms. This he did, and on Saturday a flag was sent, with an offer to surrender as prisoners of war, until exchanged. This the British answered, by taking possession of the town with two gallies and about 200 infantry on Monday the 19th, at 12 o'clock.

Extract of a letter from Major General Greene, to Congress, dated January 31, 1781.

"I HAVE the honor to enclose a copy of a letter from Lieut. Col. Lee, announcing the partial success of an enterprise against George-Town, which does honor to his corps.

Legion camp, on Sampit river, Jan. 25.

"SIR,

"I have the honor to advise you of the compleat surprise of the post at George-Town, this morning, by the infantry of the legion; Captain Carnes, who conducted this enterprise, has claim, to great merit, for the address exhibited on the occasion; the officers and soldiers under him distinguished themselves by their gallantry and firmness. My force was inadequate to the assault of the enemy's inclosed works, nor was the possession equivalent to the certain loss to be expected from such a measure; I therefore determined to pursue my principal object, by means more certain and less destructive to [...] prevented a full correspondence in the movements of the cavalry and infantry, by which mistakes we were, [...]

Reporting the Battle of Guilford Courthouse

By Dennis M. Conrad

The battle, fought at current-day Greensboro, North Carolina, is the pivotal contest of the war in the south. While the British army commanded by Earl Cornwallis won a tactical victory, it was so crippled in the battle that it retreated to the coast, eliminating any British presence from the interior of North Carolina and giving the Americans an important strategic victory. In its aftermath, Cornwallis decided to abandon the contest in North Carolina and march instead into Virginia, where later in 1781 his army was captured at Yorktown. In discussing that capture, Greene wrote that although Washington's army had "bagged" the bird, it was the Southern Army that had "flushed" it at Guilford Courthouse.

While Greene provides a good overview of the battle, his report published in the *Independent Chronicle* of April 19, 1781, written in haste and with incomplete knowledge, contains omissions, errors, and inconsistencies. For example, Greene does not give the size of his force, which is now estimated as having numbered 4,000 to 4,400 men, with over half being militia. Cornwallis's army numbered about 2,000 men, all regulars. Cornwallis's after-action report, published in the *London Chronicle* of June 7, 1781, is equally flawed. For example, he reported that Greene's army "exceeded 7000 men."

Greene erred in describing his arrangement of the Southern Army in the battle. He states that there were 300 yards between the three American lines, but scholars have found that there were 400 yards between the first (North Carolina militia) and second line (Virginia militia) and 600 yards between the second and third (Continental troops). Some have argued that this distancing led the militia, particularly the North Carolinians, to feel unsupported and vulnerable.

Another point of controversy is the conduct of the North Carolina militia. Greene's assessment of their performance grew increasingly more critical from what he wrote in the after-action report that appeared in the *Independent Chronicle* on April 19, 1781. For example, on March 20, he wrote General Daniel Morgan that they "deserted the most advantageous post I ever saw & without scarsely firing a gun." Other battle participants, however, remember the North Carolinians discharging at least two volleys and inflicting a considerable number of casualties on the British. Moreover, while Greene praised the conduct of the North Carolina militia officers in the piece that appeared in the *Independent Chronicle*, Colonel William Davie, another participant in the battle, wrote that the militiamen were "wretchedly officered." Cornwallis's report is no more helpful as he summarizes the contest involving the two militia lines with the phrase, "[Major General Alexander Leslie] soon defeated every Thing before him."

Finally, the number of American casualties, compiled by Greene's adjutant general Otho H. Williams and published in the *Independent Chronicle,* was understated by as much as 20 percent in terms of killed and wounded. Though the official British casualty report, which is printed in the *London Chronicle* of June 7, 1781, listed 28 percent of Cornwallis's army as killed, wounded, or captured, historians believe that even that devastatingly high number is understated.

There is no argument, however, with Greene's contention that his army conducted an orderly retreat to a prearranged position and was willing and able to renew the contest. In fact, after the battle, it was the British who precipitously retreated—though Cornwallis maintained it was because his army needed to find provisions—and the Americans who pursued, at least until the time of service of the militiamen expired.

The battle's result may be best summed up in the words

of Cornwallis's second-in-command, General Charles O'Hara, who wrote his patron, the Duke of Grafton, that "nearly one half of our best Officers and Soldiers, were either Killed or Wounded, and what remains are so completely worn out. . . [that] *entre nous*, the Spirit of our little Army has evaporated a good deal."

LONDON CHRONICLE

June 7, 1781

Though the official British casualty report printed in the *London Chronicle* listed 28 percent of Cornwallis's army as killed, wounded, or captured, historians believe that even that devastatingly high number is understated.

June 5—7. THE LONDON CHR

Attack was directed to be made in the following Order:

On the Right the Regiment of Bose, and the 71st Regiment, led by Major General Leslie, and supported by the 1st Battalion of Guards; on the Left the 23d and 33d Regiments, led by Lieutenant Colonel Webster, and supported by the Grenadiers and 2d Battalion of Guards, commanded by Brigadier General O'Hara; the Yagers and Light Infantry of the Guards remained in the Wood on the Left of the Guns; and the Cavalry in the Road, ready to act as Circumstances might require. Our Preparations being made, the Action began about Half an Hour past One in the Afternoon; Major General Leslie, after being obliged, by the great Extent of the Enemy's Line, to bring up the 1st Battalion of Guards to the Right of the Regiment of Bose, soon defeated every Thing before him; Lieutenant Colonel Webster having joined the Left of Major General Leslie's Division, was no less successful in his Front, when, on finding that the Left of the 33d was exposed to a heavy Fire from the Right Wing of the Enemy, he changed his Front to the Left, and being supported by the Yagers and Light Infantry of the Guards, attacked and routed it; the Grenadiers and 2d Battalion of Guards moving forward to occupy the Ground left vacant by the Movement of Lieut. Colonel Webster.

All the Infantry being now in the Line, Lieutenant-Colonel Tarleton had Directions to keep his Cavalry compact, and not to charge without positive Orders, except to protect any of the Corps from the most evident Danger of being defeated. The excessive Thickness of the Woods rendered our Bayonets of little Use, and enabled the broken Enemy to make frequent Stands, with an irregular Fire, which occasioned some Loss, and to several of the Corps great Delay, particularly on our Right, where the first Battalion of Guards and Regiment of Bose were warmly engaged in Front, Flank, and Rear, with some of the Enemy that had been routed on the first Attack, and with Part of the Extremity of their left Wing, which by the Closeness of the Wood had been passed unbroken. The 71st Regiment and Grenadiers, and second Battalion of Guards, not knowing what was passing on their Right, and hearing the Fire advance on their Left, continued to move forward, the Artillery keeping Pace with them on the Road, followed by the Cavalry. The second Battalion of the Guards first gained the clear Ground near Guildford Court-house, and found a Corps of Continental Infantry, much superior in Number, formed in the open Field on the Left of the Road. Glowing with Impatience to signalize themselves, they instantly attacked and defeated them, taking two Six-pounders, but, pursuing into the Wood with too much Ardour, were thrown into Confusion by a heavy Fire, and imme-

cond Battalion of Guar
lied, and, supported by
returned to the Charge with
city. The 23d Regiment
Instant from our Left, and
nel Tarleton having advan
the Cavalry, the Enemy v
Flight, and the 2 Six-poun
into our Hands; 2 Ammu
and 2 other Six-pounders, bein
tillery they had in the Field, were likewise taken. About this Time the 33d Regiment and Light Infantry of the Guards, after overcoming many Difficulties, completely routed the Corps which was opposed to them, and put an End to the Action in this Quarter. The 23d and 71st Regiments, with Part of the Cavalry, were ordered to pursue; the Remainder of the Cavalry was detached with Lieutenant Colonel Tarleton to our Right, where a heavy Fire continued, and where his Appearance and spirited Attack contributed much to a speedy Termination of the Action. The Militia, with which our Right had been engaged, dispersed in the Woods; the Continentals went off by Reedy Fork, beyond which it was not in my Power to follow them, as their Cavalry had suffered but little. Our Troops were excessively fatigued by an Action which lasted an Hour and a half; and our numerous Wounded, dispersed over an extensive Space of Country, required immediate Attention. The Care of our Wounded, and the total Want of Provisions in an exhausted Country, made it equally impossible for me to follow the Blow the next Day. The Enemy did not stop till they got to the Iron Works on Troublesome Creek, 18 Miles from the Field of Battle.

From our own Observation, and the best Accounts we could procure, we did not doubt but the Strength of the Enemy exceeded 7000 Men; their Militia composed their Line, with Parties advanced to the Rails of the Fields in their Front; the Continentals were posted obliquely in the Rear of their Right Wing. Their Cannon fired on us whilst we were forming from the Center of the Line of Militia, but were withdrawn to the Continentals before the Attack.

I have the Honour to inclose your Lordship the List of our Killed and Wounded. Captain Schutz's Wound is supposed to be mortal; but the Surgeons assure me, that none of the other Officers are in Danger, and that a great Number of the Men will soon recover. I cannot ascertain the Loss of the Enemy, but it must have been considerable; between 2 and 300 Dead were left upon the Field; many of their Wounded that were able to move, while we were employed in the Care of our own, escaped, and followed the routed Enemy; and our Cattle-Drivers and Foraging Parties have reported to me, that the Houses in a Circle of six or eight Miles round us are full of others; those that

and Spirit of Brigadier General O'Hara merit my highest Commendations; for, after receiving two dangerous Wounds, he continued in the Field whilst the Action lasted. By his earnest Attention on all other Occasions, seconded by the Officers and Soldiers of the Brigade, his Majesty's Guards are no less distinguished by their Order and Discipline, than by their Spirit and Valour.

The Hessian Regiment of Bose deserves my warmest Praise for its Discipline, Alacrity, and Courage, and does Honour to Major du Buy, who commands it, and who is an Officer of superior Merit.

I am much obliged to Brigadier-General Howard, who served as a Volunteer, for his spirited Example on all Occasions.

Lieutenant-Colonel Webster conducted his Brigade like an Officer of Experience and Gallantry. Lieutenant Colonel Tarleton's good Conduct and Spirit in the Management of his Cavalry was conspicuous during the whole Action; and Lieutenant Macleod, who commanded the Artillery, proved himself upon this as well as on all former Occasions, a most capable and deserving Officer. The Attention and Exertion of my Aids de Camp, and of all the other public Officers of the Army, contributed very much to the Success of the Day.

I have constantly received the most zealous Assistance from Governor Martin during my Command in the Southern District. Hoping that his Presence would tend to excite the loyal Subjects in this Province to take an active Part with us, he has chearfully submitted to the Fatigues and Dangers of our Campaign; but his delicate Constitution has suffered by his public Spirit, for, by the Advice of the Physicians, he is now obliged to return to England for the recovering his Health.

This Part of the Country is so totally destitute of Subsistence, that Forage is not nearer than nine Miles, and the Soldiers have been two Days without Bread; I shall therefore leave about 70 of the worst of the wounded Cases at the New Garden Quaker Meeting-house, with proper Assistance, and move the Remainder with the Army To-morrow Morning to Bell's Mill. I hope our Friends will heartily take an active Part with us, to which I shall continue to encourage them, still approaching our Shipping by easy Marches, that we may procure the necessary Supplies for further Operations, and lodge our Sick and Wounded where proper Attention can be

INDEPENDENT CHRONICLE (BOSTON)

April 19, 1781

While Greene provides a good overview of the battle, his report published in the *Independent Chronicle* of April 19, 1781, written in haste and with incomplete knowledge, contains omissions, errors, and inconsistencies. For example, Greene does not give the size of his force, which is now estimated as having numbered 4,000 to 4,400 men, with over half being militia. Cornwallis's army numbered about 2,000 men, all regulars.

PHILADELPHIA, April 4.

Head Quarters, Iron Works, North-Carolina, March 10.

SIR,

SINCE I had the honour of addreſſing your Excellency laſt, there has been ſome changes in our circumſtances. On the ſecond, Lieut. Col. Lee, with a detachment of riflemen, attacked the advance of the Britiſh army, under Col. Tarleton near Allamance and killed and wounded, by report, about thirty of them. On the 6th the Britiſh moved down towards High Rock, either with a view to intercept our ſtores, or cut off the light infantry from the main body of the army, then advanced near ſeven miles; but they were handſomely oppoſed, and ſuffered conſiderably without effecting any thing.

This manœuvre occaſioned me to retire over the Haw river, and move down the north ſide of it, with a view to ſecure our ſtores, coming to the army, and to form a junction with ſeveral conſiderable reinforcements of Carolina and Virginia militia, and one regiment of Virginia eighteen months men, on the march from Hillſborough to High Rock. I effected this buſineſs, and retired towards Guilford Court-houſe.

Our militia had been on ſuch a looſe and uncertain foot

North-Carolina. After this junction, finding that our force was much more reſpectable than it had been, and that there was a much greater probability of its declining than increaſing, and that there would be the greateſt difficulty of ſubſiſting it long in the field in this exhauſted country, I took the reſolution of attacking the enemy without loſs of time, and made the neceſſary diſpoſition accordingly; being perſuaded that if we were ſucceſsful it would prove ruinous to the enemy, and if otherwiſe, would only prove a partial evil to us.

The enemy marched from the High Rock-Ford on the 12th, and on the 14th arrived at Guilford.—The enemy lay at the Quaker Meeting-Houſe, on Deep-River, eight miles from our camp. On the morning of the 15th our reconnoitring parties reported the enemy advancing on the great Saliſbury road. The army was drawn up in three lines. The front line was compoſed of the North-Carolina militia, under the command of Generals Butler and Eaton—the ſecond line of Virginia militia, commanded by Generals Stevens and Lawſon, forming two brigades—the third line conſiſting of two brigades, one of Virginia and one of Maryland Continental troops, commanded by General Hugar and Col. Williams. Lieut. Col. Waſhington, with the dragoons of the 1ſt and 3d regiments, a detachment of light infantry, compoſed of Continental troops, and a regiment of riflemen under Col. Lynch formed a corps of obſervation for the ſecurity of our right flank. Lieut. Col Lee, with his legion, a detachment of light infantry and a corps of riflemen under Col. Campbell formed a corps of obſer-

The action commenced by a cannonade which laſted about twenty minutes, when the enemy advanced in three columns; the Heſſians on the right, the guards in the center, and Lieut. Col. Webſter's brigade on the left. The whole moved through the old fields to attack the North Carolina brigades, who waited the attack until the enemy got within about one hundred and forty yards, when part of them began a fire, but a conſiderable part left the ground without firing at all. The Generals and field officers did all they could to induce themen to ſtand their ground; but neither the advantages of the poſition nor any other conſideration could induce them to ſtay. Gen. Stephens and Gen. Lawſon, and the field officers of thoſe brigades, were more ſucceſsful in their exertions. The Virginia militia gave the enemy a warm reception, and kept up a heavy fire for a long time; but being beat back the action became general almoſt every where. The corps of obſervation under Waſhington and Lee were warmly engaged, and did great execution. In a word, the conflict was long and ſevere, and ... [...] their point by ſuperior diſ... [...] broke the ſecond Maryland ... [...] ir left flank, and got into ... [...] brigade, and appearing ... [...] which would have encir... [...] tinental troops, I thought ... [...] er a retreat. About this ... [...] rton made charge with the ... [...] e brigade of guards; and ... [...] rylanders, commanded by ... [...] d by Lieut. Col. Howard, ... [...] their bayonets; near the ... [...] a ſacrifice. General Hu... [...] as engaged, and gave the ... [...] reated in good order to the ... [...] croſſed at the ford, about ... [...] l of action, and there halt... [...] roops, until we collected moſt of our ſtragglers. We loſt our artillery and two ammunition waggons, the greateſt part of the horſes being killed before the retreat began, and it being impoſſible to remove the pieces but along the great road. After collecting our ſtragglers, we retired to this camp, ten miles diſtant from Guilford.

From the beſt information I can get the enemy's loſs is very great, not leſs in killed and wounded than 600 men beſides ſome few priſoners that we brought off.

Incloſed I ſend your Excellency a return of killed, wounded and miſſing; moſt of the latter have gone home as is but too cuſtomary with militia after an action. I cannot learn that the enemy have got any conſiderable number of priſoners. Our men are in good ſpirits for another field day. I only lament the loſs of ſeveral valuable officers who were killed and wounded in the action. Among the latter is General Stevens ſhot through the thigh, and General Huger in the hand, and among the former is Major Anderſon of the Maryland line.

The firmneſs of the officers and ſoldiers during the whole campaign has been almoſt unparalleld. Amidſt innumerable difficulties they have diſcovered a degree of magnanimity and fortitude that will forever add luſtre to their military reputation.

I have the honour to be &c.

NAT. GREENE.

His Excellency SAMUEL HUNTINGTON, *Eſq; Preſident of Congreſs.*

Continentals. Killed. 1 Major, 1 Captain, 3 ſubalterns, 5 ſergeants 47 rank and file. Wounded. 8 Captains, 4 ſubalterns, 6 ſergeants, 93 rank and file. Miſſing. 3 ſergeants, 8 drummers, 150 rank and file. Total. 1 Major, 9 Captains, 7 ſubalterns, 14 ſergeants, 8 drummers, 290 rank and file.

"What a glorious opportunity ... an end to the war—The enemy in this country by victories and defeats, have loſt two thirds of their army ſince the taking of Charleſtown, and a little exertion of the States would totally deſtroy them. I fear you will not make theſe exertions before you are ſcourged to it by the enemy. It is a very fooliſh way to ruin an enemy by allowing him to obtain expenſive victories when we might ſo eaſily do it by defeats, though I am certain his ruin is inevitable."

We hear that the Honorable Robert Morris, Eſq; hath been appointed, by Congreſs, Superintendant-General of the Finances of America; and that the abilities, integrity and patriotiſm of this gentleman, give room to hope, that ways and means will now be found to remove many of the embarraſſments of this country, by furniſhing her with the ſinews of war, &c.

Capt. Cames in a privateer from Salem, has taken two prizes, one a brig with 200 pipes Madeira wine, which he ordered home; the other a ſchooner with fiſh, which was ſent for Martinico.

By a veſſel arrived at Beverly ſince our laſt, in 28 days from Port Dauphen, we learn it was reported there, that a French fleet, conſiſting of 17 ſail of the line and a large number of tranſports, had arrived at St. Piers in Martinico.

By Capt. Thorndike, who alſo arrived at Beverly ſince our laſt, we learn, that the iſland of Curaſſow was in quiet poſſeſſion of the Dutch the 1ſt March.

Arrived in a ſafe port, a ſhip from Cork, bound to New-York, laden with pork, flour, butter, peas and cordage; prize to the ſnow Rochambeau, Capt. Melally.

Monday laſt arrived here the Continental frigate Deane, Capt. Nicholſon, from the Weſt-Indies.

☞ *The Sale of ſeveral Abſentees Eſtates, as advertiſed in our preceeding Paper to have been at the Bunch of Grapes Tavern in State-Street, Boſton, on the 3d of May, is by order of the Committee adjourned to Friday the 4th, at 11 o'Clock, at the ſame Place—Thurſday being appointed, by Authority, a Day of public Humiliation, Faſting and Prayer.*

Commonwealth of Maſſachuſetts.

Boſton, April 18, 1781.

The abſent Members of the honorable Houſe of Repreſentatives are required to give immediate Attendance on the Houſe, as Matters of the greateſt Importance are to be acted upon.

By Order of the Houſe.

G. R. MINOT, Clerk pro tem.

APRIL 19, 1781

The

INDEPENDENT CHRONICLE

PHILADELPHIA, April 4.

[...]

His Excellency Gen. Washington.

Camp at the Iron-Works, 10 miles from Guilford Court-House, March 16, 1781.

SIR,

ON the 10th I wrote to his Excellency General Washington, from the High-Rock Ford, on the Haw-River, a copy of which I enclosed your Excellency, that I had effected a junction with a Continental regiment of 8 months men, and two considerable bodies of militia belonging to Virginia and North-Carolina. After this junction, finding that our force was much more respectable than it had been, and that there was a much greater probability of its declining than increasing, and that there would be the greatest difficulty of subsisting it long in the field in this exhausted country, I took the resolution of attacking the enemy without loss of time, and made the necessary disposition accordingly; being persuaded that if we were successful it would prove ruinous to the enemy, and if otherwise, would only prove a partial evil to us.

The enemy marched from the High Rock-Ford on the 12th, and on the 14th arrived at Guildford.—The enemy lay at the Quaker Meeting-House, on Deep-River, eight miles from our camp. On the morning of the 15th our reconnoitering parties reported the enemy advancing on the great Salisbury road. The army was drawn up in three lines. The front line was composed of the North-Carolina militia, under the command of Generals Butler and Eaton—the second line of Virginia militia, commanded by Generals Stevens and Lawson, forming two brigades—the third line consisting of two brigades, one of Virginia and one of Maryland Continental troops, commanded by General Hugar and Col. Williams. Lieut. Col. Washington, with the dragoons of the 1st and 3d regiments, a detachment of light infantry, composed of Continental troops, and a regiment of riflemen under Col. Lynch formed a corps of observation for the security of our right flank. Lieut. Col. Lee, with his legion, a detachment of light infantry and a corps of riflemen under Col. Campbell, formed a corps of observation for the security of our left flank.

The greater part of this country is a wilderness, with a few cleared fields interspersed here and there. The army was drawn up upon a large hill of ground, surrounded by other hills, the greater part of which was covered with timber and thick under brush—The front line was posted with two field pieces just in the edge of the woods, and the back of a fence which run parallel with the line, with an open field directly in their front. The second line was in the woods about 300 yards in the rear of the first; and the Continental troops about 300 yards in the rear of the second, with a double front as the hill drew to a point where they were posted, and on the right and left were two old fields.

In this position we waited the approach of the enemy, having previously sent off the baggage to this place, appointed to rendezvous at in case of a defeat. Lieut. Col. Lee with his legion, his infantry, and part of his riflemen, met the enemy on their advance, and had a very severe skirmish with Lieut. Col. Tarleton, in which the enemy suffered greatly. Capt. Armstrong charged the British legion and cut down near 30 of their dragoons; but the enemy reinforced their advanced party, Lieut. Col. Lee was obliged to retire, and take his position in the line.

The action commenced by a cannonade which lasted about twenty minutes, when the enemy advanced in three columns; the Hessians on the right, the guards in the center, and Lieut. Col. Webster's brigade on the left. The whole moved through the old fields to attack the North Carolina brigades, who waited the attack until the enemy got within about one hundred and forty yards, when part of them began a fire, but a considerable part left the ground without firing at all. The Generals and field officers did all they could to induce the men to stand their ground; but neither the advantages of the position nor any other consideration could induce them to stay.

[...]

I have the honour to be &c.

NAT. GREENE.

REPORTING THE

BATTLE OF HOBKIRK'S HILL

By John Buchanan

In March 1781, following a long, debilitating pursuit, Lord Cornwallis defeated Major General Nathanael Greene at Guilford Courthouse, North Carolina. But though he was the tactical victor, Cornwallis's losses were so heavy that he was forced to withdraw to Wilmington on the coast to rest and refit his army. Greene, his army intact and ready to fight again, marched for South Carolina, his twin goals to drive the British from the state and restore civil government. Thus began the second phase of the Carolina campaign.

Greene bivouacked at Hobkirk's Hill, about a mile and a half north of a key British post, Camden, South Carolina, then occupied by some nine hundred British and Provincial regulars under a fine officer, Lieutenant Colonel Francis, Lord Rawdon, now commanding British troops in the Carolinas. Greene, with about 1,500 men, was not strong enough to assault Camden and waited for Rawdon to attack him. Rawdon bided his time until he learned that Greene's artillery had left. On April 25, 1781, Rawdon marched to the attack. He eluded observation until his advance bumped into Greene's pickets.

Rawdon had taken Greene by surprise, which Greene failed to mention in his report to Samuel Huntington, president of the Continental Congress, as printed in the *Connecticut Journal* (June 14, 1781). The troops had been eating breakfast and washing clothes when the firing at the picket line alerted them. But the Americans formed quickly "& received us bravely," Rawdon wrote. Greene decided to attack with his infantry while sending Colonel William Washington and his dragoons on a swing to get behind Rawdon and charge from the rear. It was Rawdon's turn to be surprised when American artillery that was supposed to have left appeared and shook his advance with grapeshot. Greene ordered his regiments to charge with the bayonet. The Americans appeared to be on the verge of victory, then a company commander of First Maryland was killed by musket fire and some of his men were felled by a volley. This threw his troops and another company into confusion, whereupon Colonel John Gunby, commanding First Maryland, blundered. He ordered the entire regiment to retire and reform about fifty yards to the rear. This threw the entire American line out of kilter, the British again advanced, and Greene was forced to order a general retreat.

Colonel Washington had also committed a serious error of judgment. On his ride to Rawdon's rear, he encountered wounded British soldiers and surgeons and ignored his mission in order to take them captive. Yet in his report to Huntington, Greene said that the behavior of Washington and his regiment "did them the highest honour," which was not true, and his claim that Washington found the British "retiring with the greatest precipitation toward the town" was also untrue.

Rawdon suffered more than Greene, taking over 28 percent casualties. He awaited reinforcements before pursuing Greene, and when they arrived, he set out once more to bring the American general to battle but found his prey in too strong a defensive position. Meanwhile, the brilliant partisan commander General Francis Marion, in concert with Lieutenant Colonel "Light Horse Harry" Lee's Continental Legion of horse and foot, was operating in Rawdon's rear between Camden and Charleston. They had taken Fort Watson, one of a string of forts protecting the British supply line, and were now besieging Fort Motte. Rawdon, the tactical victor, was in strategic peril: a beaten but unbroken foe before him, hostile territory swarming with partisans behind him. It was an old story in this frustrating war. With the exception of the Saratoga campaign, British armies marched where they pleased and won most of their battles along the way. But after they passed, implacable enemies who had gotten out of the way reappeared from their sanctuaries and once again took control of the countryside.

On May 10 and 11, Rawdon evacuated Camden and marched for Charleston, and Nathanael Greene once again went on the offensive.

Battle of Hobkirk's Hill
North Wind Picture Archives

The troops had been eating breakfast and washing clothes when the firing at the picket line alerted them. But the Americans formed quickly and Greene attacked with his infantry while sending Colonel William Washington and his dragoons on a swing to get behind Rawdon and charge from the rear.

THURSDAY, JUNE 14, 1781.

CONNECTICUT JOURNAL

NEW-HAVEN: Printed by THOMAS and SAMUEL GREEN, near the Colle[ge]

Philadelphia, May 26.

Camp, Sander's Creek, April 27, 1781.

SIR,

I Did myself the honor to address your Excellency on the 2d, and informed you that we lay before Camden, having found it impracticable to storm the town with a prospect of success, and nothing left but to make a position to induce the enemy to sally. We chose a hill about one mile from the town, on the main road leading to the Waxhaws. It was covered with timber, and flanked on the left by an impassible morass. The country between that and the town is covered by heavy wood and under brush. In this situation we lay constantly upon our arms, ready for action at a moment's warning.

About eleven o'clock on the morning of the 25th, our advanced pickets were fired upon, who gave the enemy a warm reception.

The line was formed in an instant, General Huger's brigade upon the right of the road, Colonel Williams's brigade of Marylanders on the left, and the artillery in the centre. Colonel Read, with a few militia, in the rear, as a second line. Captain Kirkwood and the light infantry lay in our front, and as the enemy advanced, he was soon engaged with them, and both he and his corps behaved with great gallantry.

The pickets, under the command of Captains Morgan and Benson, behaved with equal spirit, and good conduct.

As the enemy were found to be advancing only with a small front, Lieut. Col. Ford, with the Second Maryland regiment, had orders to advance and flank them upon the left. Lieut. Col. Campbell had orders to do the like upon the right. Col. Gunby, with the First Maryland regiment, and Lieut. Col. Haws, with the Second Virginia regiment, had orders to advance down the hill and charge them in the front. Lieut. Col. Washington had orders to turn the enemy's right flank, and charge them in the rear. The whole line was soon engaged in close firing, and the artillery under Col. Harrison playing on their front. The enemy were staggered in all quarters,

Lieut. Col. Washington had orders to turn the enemy's right flank, and charge them in the rear. The whole line was soon engaged in close firing, and the artillery under Col. Harrison playing on their front. The enemy were staggered in all quarters,
and upon the left were retiring, while our troops continued to advance, when unfortunately two companies of the right, of the First Maryland regiment, got a little disordered, & unhappily Colonel Gunby gave an order for the rest of the regiment, then advancing to take a new position in the rear, where the two companies were rallying. This impressed the whole regiment with an idea of a retreat, and communicated itself to the Second regiment, which immediately followed the first on their retiring. Both were rallied, but it was too late, the enemy had gained the hill, and obliged the artillery to retire. The Second Virginia regiment having advanced some distance down the hill, and the Maryland line being gone, the enemy immediately turned their flank, while they were engaged in the front. Lieut. Col. Campbell's regiment had got into some disorder and fallen back a little; this obliged me to order Lieut. Col. Haws to retire. The troops were frequently rallied but had got into too much disorder to recover the fortune of the day, which once promised us a complete victory, as Col. Washington found the enemy, both horse and foot, retiring with the greatest precipitation towards the town, and took upwards of 200 prisoners, and ten or fifteen officers, before he discovered our people had left the ground; more than 50 of which were brought off. The Colonel's behavior, and that of his regiment upon this occasion, did them the highest honour. We retired about two or three miles, without any loss of artillery or ammunition waggons, the baggage having been sent off at the beginning of the action. The enemy suffered very greatly. Our force was not materially different; but had we succeeded, from the disposition made, we must have had the whole prisoners, as well as full possession of Camden. Inclosed is the return of the killed and wounded. Among the former is Captain Beaty of the Maryland line, a most excellent officer, and an ornament to his profession. Our army is in good spirits, and this little repulse will make no alteration in our general plan of operations. Inclosed I send your Excellency the conditions of the capitulation and surrender of fort Watson, which, I hope, will be followed by others.

I have the honour to be,
With the greatest respect,
Your Excellency's most obedient,
And most humble servant,
NATH. GREENE.

P. S. The horse and part of the infantry at the close of the eve[ning] ...

[...]rously wounded, elbow. Lt. Col. Cam[p]bell, Virginia, slight contusion, thi[gh]. Capt. William Beaty, Maryland, [kil]led. Capt. S. Smith. 3d Maryla[nd] prisoner. Capt. Denholm, Virgi[nia] slight contusion. Captain-Lieut. Br[...] Maryland, wounded in both ankles, prisoner on parole. Lieut. M. Ga[...]way, slightly wounded. Lieut. [...] Virginia, dangerously in the leg.

O. H. WILLIAMS, D. A[...]

RETURN of the killed and wounde[d in] the action.

Killed: 1 sergeant, 17 rank & [file].

Wounded: 7 sergeants, 101 r[ank] and file.

Missing: 3 sergeants, 133 rank [and] file.

Most of the missing mistook the o[rder] to rally, at Saunders creek, and to[ok a] different route; some are killed, [some] wounded and in the British hospit[al]; one third of the remainder have [been] heard of and expected to rejoin.

O. H. WILLIAMS, D. [...]

Fort Watson, April 23, 1[781].

" SIR,

" Lieutenant Colonel Lee ma[de a] junction with me on Santee, the [...] instant, after a rapid march from [...]sey's Mill on Deep river, whic[h was] performed in eight days.

" The 15th we marched to this [post] and invested it; our hope was [to cut] off their water; some riflemen [and] continentals immediately took p[ost be]tween the fort and the lake.

" The fort was situated on a [...] hill, forty feet high, stockaded, w[ith three] rows of abbatis around it, and no [...] near enough to cover our men from [their] fire.

" The third day after we had [invest]ed it, we found the enemy had [sunk a] well near the stockade, which we [could] not prevent them from, as we h[ad no] intrenching tools to make our appro[aches]. We immediately determined to r[aise a] work equal to the heighth of the [fort]. This arduous work was compleat[ed ...] morning by Major Maham, who [under]took it. We then made a lodgem[ent on] the side of the mount near the sto[ckade]; this was performed with great [...] and address, by Ensign Johns[on and] Mr. Lee, a volunteer in Colone[l Lee's] legion, who with difficulty ascen[ded the] hill and pulled away the abbatis [which] induced the commandant to hoist [a flag]. Inclosed is the capitulation, w[hich I] hope may be approved of by you.

CONNECTICUT JOURNAL (NEW HAVEN)

June 14, 1781

Despite a tactical victory, Cornwallis's losses were so heavy at Guilford Courthouse that he was forced to withdraw to Wilmington on the North Carolina coast to rest and refit his army. Greene, his army intact and ready to fight again, began the second phase of the Carolina campaign at Hobkirk's Hill. The *Connecticut Journal* prints Greene's report to Samuel Huntington, president of the Continental Congress.

"The officers and men performed every thing that could be expected, and Major Mahan, of my brigade, had in a particular manner a great share in this success, by his unwearied diligence in executing a tower, which was the principal occasion of the reduction of the fort. In short, Sir, I have had the greatest satisfaction from every one under my command.

"Inclosed is a list of the prisoners & stores taken, I shall, without loss of time, demolish the fort; after which I shall proceed to the high hills of Santee, and halt at Captain Richardson's plantation till further orders.

I have the honor to be, with the greatest respect, Sir, your most obedient humble servant,

FRANCIS MARION, B. G."

TERMS of CAPITULATION proposed by Lieutenant M'Kay, commandant of Fort Watson.

I. The officers to be permitted their parole, to wear their side arms, and to possess their private baggage. Agreed.

II. The British soldiers to be permitted to march to Charlestown, where they are to continue perfectly out of service till exchanged, and liable to be ordered elsewhere by the commander in chief of the American southern army. Agreed.

III. The irregulars to be treated as prisoners of war. Agreed.

IV. All public stores to be delivered to the legion Quarter-master, and the fort to be delivered up to Captain Oldham, who will take possession this evening with a detachment of Marylanders.

The capitulation is acceeded to, as it now stands, in compliment to the gallantry with which it has been defended.

(Signed)

PATRICK CARNS, JAMES M'KAY
Capt. Leg. Infantry. Lieutenant.
April 23, 1781.

A LIST of PRISONERS taken at Scott's Lake, April 23, 1781.

Commanding Officers.

Lieutenant M'Kay, commandant of the fort. Surgeon Campbell, King's American regiment. Ensign Robinson, Loyal American regiment. Lieutenant Lewis, South Carolina rangers. Ensign and Quarter-master M'Kallam, ditto. 73 British privates. 36 Tories. Total, 5 commissioned officers, and 109 privates.

Extract of a letter from Gen. Marion, dated April 21, 1781.

"A small detachment which I sent to watch the enemy's movements in Camden, took, at the mouth of Kershaw's creek, a boat laden with corn, killed two, wounded four, and took 6 British soldiers and one Tory.

"Colonel Horry crossed the Pedee with seventy men to intercept the Tories, who I expected would join Colonel Watson in his march up Pedee; he fell in with a party of thirty foragers and as many more to cover them, he charged them on horseback, in Mr. M'Pherson's plantation, killed two and took 13 British soldiers, and two Tories, two negroes; without the loss of a man.

"General Lillington reports that the Bladen militia of North-Carolina, fell with great spirit on the rear of Lord Cornwallis's army, as he was retreating to Wilmington, and killed 13 men, and took between fifteen an ty prisoners.

"General Pickens rep Col. Clarke, on the 23d of an action with Major Du Ninety-Six, killed thirty-fo forty-two prisoners; among the Major himself is number

Published by order of Con

CHARLES THOMSC

May 29. Yesterday ar the prize sloop Jane, from town, bound to New-Y with rice, &c. sent in by th Sun privateer, of this port. been but a short time from town, and brings advice Rawdon's having burnt Ca retreated towards Charlesto that Lord Cornwallis had from Wilmington to the same place. Upwards of one hundred wounded British officers and soldiers had been shipped from Wilmington to Charlestown, supposed to have suffered at the late action at Guilford Court-House.

By a gentleman who left York-Town on Friday evening we learn, that four of the soldiers of the Pennsylvania line were shot at that place on Tuesday last for mutiny. Six had been condemned and two were pardoned by Gen. Wayne.

These men, each of them, at different times, had behaved in a very disorderly mutinous manner, discovering the most seditious temper, & calling upon their fellow soldiers of the several regiments to join them in their revolt. They found however no support from their comrades. The whole line were drawn up under arms at the execution, and behaved in the most orderly manner. A finer body of men never were collected. They were to have marched from that place on Wednesday, but were obstructed solely by the heavy rains. The men appear chearful and happy without the least appearance of tumult or discontent.

FISH-KILL, June 7.

We learn that the French & English fleets in the West-Indies have had a severe engagement; that the French have been victorious, and have taken two ships of the line. A New-York paper of the 2d instant says also, that the British lost two ships of the line; but reports from thence add further, that two are taken and three sunk.

Last Friday the post from this office to Morristown was taken, with the mail, by a party of the enemy, near Col. Soward's. His horse, saddle and holsters, are found. As he has not yet been heard of, it is supposed he is either murdered or carried to New-York.

NEWPORT, May 26.

Last Thursday night seven or eight prisoners made their escape from the prison ship in this harbour, boarded a schooner of about fifty tons lying in the road ready to sail the next morning, and carried her off.

Six of the above ships of the line were bound to the East-Indies, and the remainder to the windward islands.—And it is reported, that the French have the greatest prospect of a most advantageous campaign.

The same day Capt. Young arrived here in 20 days from Martinico: By him we have a confirmation that the French fleet lately arrived at Martinico, had been in pursuit of and drove the British from before St. Lucia, and landed 6000 troops there; and that there is no doubt but the island is now in possession of our allies.

Yesterday arrived here the Continental frigate Alliance, Capt. Barry, from France; he sailed in company with a French ship of 40 guns, which he parted with six weeks ago in a heavy gale of wind. Capt. Barry has captured on his passage six prizes, viz. Two privateers, as formerly mentioned, two Jamaica men, and two sloops of war, of 16 six-pounders, the two last he took about ten days ago, on the banks of Newfoundland, after a severe conflict, in which the Alliance had 8 men killed and 24 wounded. Capt. Barry is unfortunately among the latter. One of the prizes was sent to Newfoundland, with 300 prisoners, taking a receipt for them, and hostages for the return of the vessel.

The Thorn, Capt. Tucker, has sent into a safe port a prize, from Eustatia bound to Halifax, and was left in chase of four or five others.

A number of vessels were seen in the offing yesterday, supposed to be the French fleet which sailed from France in March last for this place.

Extract of a letter from a gentleman at Newbury-Port, to his friend in Salem, dated the 4th instant.

"This day arrived the brig Weasel, Capt. Combs, in 14 days from Port Louis, in Guadaloupe, by whom we learn that the French fleet and army had laid siege to St. Lucia, and that our informant on his passage, fell in with (as he supposed) Rodney's fleet beating up for it."

REPORTING THE

SIEGE OF NINETY SIX

By Robert M. Dunkerly

The Siege of Ninety Six, South Carolina, in the summer of 1781 was taxing for both sides. General Nathanael Greene led a small army into South Carolina to attack the various British-held posts across the state. With the main British army under General Lord Charles Cornwallis in Virginia (where other American forces were ready to receive him), Greene felt free to attack the many weakly defended forts and outposts here.

Ninety Six was a village on the Cherokee Trading Path in upper South Carolina. British forces occupied and fortified the site, with a large, earthen, star-shaped fort and a stockade around the town. They also converted its large brick jail into a fortress. Greene's army of Virginia, Maryland, and Delaware Continental troops, along with militia from both Carolinas, arrived and began to lay siege to the post. Defending Ninety Six was a garrison composed entirely of Loyalists led by Lieutenant Colonel John Cruger.

The July 19, 1781, *Independent Chronicle* reveals that at the same time as the Ninety Six operation, American forces were also attacking Augusta, Georgia, just seventy miles to the south. In fact, after capturing the important Georgia town, Lieutenant Colonel "Light Horse Harry" Lee brought his forces to Ninety Six to assist Greene. They arrived in time for the final assault on June 18. It was a tremendous effort, as the Americans charged through obstructions and up to the very walls of the star fort, but they could go no farther and suffered heavy losses.

The Siege of Ninety Six illustrates an important fact about the fighting in the Carolinas: it was a brutal civil war.

This article, written by an unidentified American officer, is optimistic as it was written in late May before many of the challenges of attacking Ninety Six surfaced. In fact, the article later proclaims that "the above post has surrendered." Inaccuracies have obviously crept into the reports coming out of South Carolina.

The August 16, 1781, *Continental Journal* reports the news using General Greene's letter—no better source could be found for a summary of the siege. As the writer notes, Greene knew that British reinforcements had landed in Charleston and were on the way to relieve the beleaguered garrison. General Thomas Sumter had been dispatched to delay their march but could not impede their progress. Unable to take the fort and with enemy reinforcements closing in, Greene had no choice but to pull back after investing much time, effort, and resources. It was extremely frustrating for the commander, his officers, and the common soldiers who struggled there. Greene later recorded, "Our poor fellows are worn out with fatigue."

The small American army tried everything to capture Ninety Six: artillery to batter it, infantry assaulting it, and even tunneling under it. Despite their efforts under grueling conditions, Cruger's stubborn Loyalist defenders held on.

The Siege of Ninety Six illustrates an important fact about the fighting in the Carolinas: it was a brutal civil war. The defending garrison contained not one British soldier: they were all Loyalist Americans fighting for the King. Many communities in the Carolinas were split, and rival militias sprang up across the region. The war here was much more bitter and personal than in other regions.

Greene's letter in the August 16, 1781, *Continental Journal* is dated June 20, but the news it conveys is obviously not printed until mid-August in Boston, illustrating how slowly news traveled and the uncertainty of reports. These newspaper accounts, fragmentary and sometimes inaccurate, illustrate how uncertain good news was in the eighteenth century. It took many months, and often from many sources, for contemporaries to piece together the facts of distant occurrences. Imagine the shock of readers who saw the July 19, 1781, *Independent Chronicle* article only to learn later that Greene not only failed to take the fort, but also was repulsed handily.

Of little help to historians is that there were no American newspapers active in the Carolinas in 1781. Newspapers came and went with frequency here during the colonial period, and to make matters worse, only fragments of issues survived.

It is a good reminder to us in the "information age," with infinite access to news and data, that it was not always so; that our ancestors struggled to understand their world and make good decisions based on what they obtained. Period newspapers are thus not only a wonderful primary source, but also a window into how we construct and understand the past.

BALTIMORE, June 19.

LETTERS from Fredericksſburg, dated on Tueſday laſt, mention, that the Britiſh army had viſited Goochland and Amelia counties, the former on the North, and the latter on the South ſide of James river, and that it was hoped they were on their retreat ſtill more Southerly.---That their cavalry had made a rapid march, in two diviſions, under command of Colonels Tarlton and Simcoe, one to Charlotteſville, and the other to a place called "Point of Fork," where they had committed great exceſſes, the particulars of which had not been received.

A poſtcript to one of the above-mentioned letters, adviſes, that intelligence had juſt been received from the Southward, that the Britiſh forces were in march for Richmond.

JUNE 26.

Extract of a letter from an officer of diſtinction in General Greene's army, dated camp before Ninety-Six, South-Carolina, May 24, 1781.

"Lord Rawdon has retreated to Charleſtown. Fort-Watſon, on Santee, forts Mott and Granby, on Congary, Camden and Nelſon's-ferry, are in our poſſeſſion. General Pickens and Lieut. Col. Lee are before Auguſta: General Marian is below, manœuvering towards Charleſtown, and General Greene has inveſted Ninety-Six. It is only poſſible we may not ſucceed. I expect ſoon to hear of the reduction of Auguſta. What General Phillips is doing, or Lord Cornwallis intends to do, I cannot inform you; you will have it from better authority. We fear nothing before us."

Extract of a letter from Frederickſburg, dated on Tueſday laſt.

"It is ſaid the enemy were, on Saturday laſt, at Richmond, deſtroying the tobacco and houſes.---The Marquis, by the laſt accounts, lay 12 or 15 miles from them,"

A letter from George-Town, dated on Sunday laſt, mentions, that the Baltimore and Frederick-Town troops of light-dragoons, were to croſs Patowmack the next day, on their way to join the Marquis de la Fayette.

PHILADELPHIA, July 4.

On the 28th ult. His Excellency JOHN RUTLEDGE, Eſq; ſet out from this city, in order to reſume the reins of his government, where, we hear,

have the pleaſure to ...
good authority, that that State and Georgia are now entirely in the poſſeſſion of the Americans
... and Savannah excepted) and as ſoon

him, the paragraph in laſt Saturday's paper, wherein that gentleman is named, ought to be conſidered as a ſlander, circulated to injure his character.

Extract of a letter, (found on board the ſchooner Dolphin, taken by Capt. Angus) from Colonel Brathwaite to Mr. Mayne, of Liſbon, dated Madras, October 10 1781.

"IN July laſt, Hyder Ally entered the Carnatick with 60,000 horſe, 20,000 foot, 20 battering guns and 40 field pieces. The country fell before him like ripe corn before the reaper's ſickle. We had no where 3500 men. In the face of this army we were to make a junction to form any thing to oppoſe. I had with me about the number above mentioned, with 10 field pieces; I was ordered to join the General at the Preſidency; I was at Pondicherry; on accout of rivers I was obliged to go inland, and the enemy was ſo ſituated that his ſecond days march would have croſſed my fourth, but by marching always ſuddenly in the night, and ſending people to clear one road when I meant to take another, I made good my junction, with only the loſs of a little baggage, which I could not protect from his numerous horſe. I joined the General, and we marched to join Lieutenant-Colonel Bailie coming from the northward, and with ſuch a force as I had, we got within ten miles of him, and even reinforced him by a detachment. The enemy, on this occaſion, ſhewed a great piece of generalſhip, for he made as if he meant to attack us,
ſlipt by us in the
whole force,
braveſt condu
er of our arm
there was ſca
tale; ſo com
happened to
ſuppoſe, had
about 4000
to believe th
horſes. Th
the ammunit
anſwering ſc
ſome of our
to ſee, for o
marched to
about 4 miles
gitives met us, told us ...
moving off as faſt as they could. As our's,
... the remains of an
... gage, tents, &c. The enemy has began the ſiege of Arcot, in which he makes neither figure nor progreſs, and as the periodical rains have now

means to ſend him to the Weſt-Indies, as there is no Britain on the Continent who will ſerve with a man ſo infamous. O Arnold! doſt thou think to find the Britiſh in the Iſlands, more hardened to diſhonour than thoſe at New-York? O wretched Arnold! the opprobium of thy country---the ſcorn of nations---doſt thou think there is any corner of the univerſe, where thou canſt find a ſhelter from devouring remorſe, and from vengefull deſpair?

In Rivington's New-York Gazettee of June 30, the following is inſerted in a letter from London, dated May 5. "Our Court, to pleaſe the Northern Powers, have iſſued Proclamations forbidding privateers and letters of marque from ſtopping or moleſting any veſſels, though belonging to our enemies, in the Baltic, ſo we keep them in good humor with us."

Yeſterday was the anniverſary commencement at Harvard-College, Cambridge, which being the firſt public one ſince the preſent war, a very great concourſe of all ranks of people were collected on the occaſion. The names of the young gentlemen who took their degrees, will be inſerted in our next.

A ſmall boat, one of the noted Shaving-Mills which continually infeſt our bay, was captured by two or three whale-boats, and ſent in here laſt Saturday.

The privateer ſhip Rover, of 20 guns, from Salem---privateer ſloop Kingbird, of 10 guns, from Providence---and the brig Good-Intent, Captain Trott, from this port, bound to St. Croix, ...

GREENLEAF'S Office, ...
Broad-Cloths, German Serges, ...
Callicoes, Chintzes, Muſlins, ...
lands and Cottons, China Cups and Sau...
Starch, Hair-Powder, Nails of many Sizes, a...
... Knives and Forks, Cuttos,

INDEPENDENT CHRONICLE (BOSTON)

July 19, 1781

The July 19, 1781, *Independent Chronicle* reveals that at the same time as the Ninety Six operation, American forces were also attacking Augusta, Georgia, just seventy miles to the south. In fact, after capturing the important Georgia town, Lieutenant Colonel "Light Horse Harry" Lee brought his forces to Ninety Six to assist Greene.

THE CONTINENTAL JOURNAL, AND WEEKLY ADVERTISER.

THURSDAY, August 16, 1781. [Numb. CCLXXXVI.]

BOSTON: Printed by JOHN GILL, in Court-Street.

THE ENTIRE PROSPERITY OF EVERY STATE DEPENDS UPON THE DISCIPLINE OF IT'S ARMIES. *The* KING *of* PRUSSIA.

PAILADELPHIA, July 25.

The following are copies of ſome of the Letters found in a packet from England bound to N York, but taken on her paſſage and carried into France.

(Duplicate) Parliament-ſtreet, 17 Feb. 1781.

Dear Sir,

WITH this letter I ſend a copy of account between you and Mr. Murray of Quebec, by which I find you had drawn yourſelf, from New-York in May for l.206: 16: 3, the ſum for which you left with me a ſet of bills, and which I had negociated through my friend Captain Matthews, General Haldimand's ſecretary, not knowing you had drawn again. I alſo ſend Meſſrs. Roſs and Gray's account, in which I obſerve, what ſeems to me extraordinary, that you are credited only l.85: 14: 6, for deficiences in appointments on receiving the battallion, and charged with l.613: 14: 2, for deficiences on your getting the 16th regiment. I have wrote fully to General Arnold, that his money is inveſted in the ſtock he mentioned, which is a very deſirable inveſtment, and made at a good time; I did my beſt for him, and hope he will approve, I know it was as well laid out as poſſible.

I hope now all tumults are over. Lord G. Gordon was two days ago tried and acquitted for his ſhare in the riots in July 1780. Nothing yet from Lord Cornwallis, his army is in good ſpirits and no doubt reinforced by this time. I have nothing material to trouble you with. Mrs. Meyrick deſires me to offer her moſt reſpectful compliments, and joins me in ſincere wiſhes for your health and happineſs.

I am, dear Sir, with the higheſt reſpect,
your obedient and moſt humble ſervant,
(ſigned) JAMES MEYRICK.

His Excellency General Robertſon.

(Duplicate) Parliament ſtreet, 30 Jan. 1781.

SIR,

I AM honored with your ſeveral letters, incloſing bills on Harley and Drummond, to amount of 5000l. the receipt of which I have regularly, by packet, acknowledged. On the day they were paid, I inveſted the amount in the fund you mentioned, and as it was a very favourable time, I flatter myſelf it will meet your approbation, alſo the mode in which it was done.

As it is poſſible ſome directions might come from you for diſpoſing of the money in ſome other mode, I thought it might not be ſo advantageous to lock it up totally, as it might be a long while before I could receive a power from you to transfer, had I put it in your name, and in the mean time the dividends could not be received for your uſe. The mode I have adopted has been uſed in like caſes, and can be inſtantly altered to any you direct, on your favouring me with a letter. The account is as follows, viz.

Brought by Samuel and William Scholey, ſtock brokers, for Major General Arnold, 7000l. in new 4 per cents, at 71 1 4 new 1-4 as follows.

In the name of Major General Benedict Arnold 100l. ſtock at 71 1 4 new 4 per cents conſols 6900 ſtock at 71 1 4do.	paid	4987 10
In the name of James Meyrick, Esq;		
7000 commiſſions paid the brokers		8 15
power of attorney to receive dividends		1 6
		4996 6 6

There remains therefore 3l. 13s. 6 of the 5000l.

By this method in caſe I receive my inſtructions from you from a different application of your money, I can ſell out the 6900l. ſtock, and follow them before you receive this letter, and if you wiſh to continue in this fund, it may, if you prefer, be all placed in your own name, by transferring the 6900l. to your 100l. and it was for the purpoſe of your having an account there, I bought the 100l in your name. Alſo the power of attorney now incloſed will enable me to receive the dividends on the whole 7000l. ſtock, after I have made the transfer, ſhould you chooſe I ſhould do for. I hope I have made myſelf properly underſtood, and can aſſure you I have to the beſt of my abilities acted for you as for myſelf.

I have the honour to be, Sir,
Your obedient and humble ſervant,
(Signed) JAMES MEYRICK.

Major Gen. Arnold.

[*Judas Iſcariot betrayed his maſter for thirty pieces of ſilver, but repenting of his guilt, returned the money into the treaſury, and went and hanged himſelf.*

Judas Arnold *received five thouſand pounds ſterling for his treachery, and we find has lodged the money in the Britiſh funds, but he has not ſpirit enough to purſue the character in the only part worthy of imitation.*]

(No. 82.) Whitehall, March 7, 1781.

SIR,

YOUR letter, No. 123, incloſing a general ſtate of his Majeſty's provincial forces ſerving under your command, and the report of the deputy inſpector general of provincial forces, of nine battalions, which you have thought worthy of being recommended to his Majeſty for half pay and permanent rank in America, has been received and laid before the king.

The encouragement held out to the officers of the provincial troops, of having their ranks made permanent in Ameirica, and of being entitled to half pay upon the reduction of their regiments, as ſtated in my letter of the 23d January, 1779, was meant as a reward and compenſation to thoſe of his Majeſty's faithful American ſubjects as had ſuffered the loſs of their property on account of their loyalty, and had taken or ſhould take arms in his Majeſty's ſervice, and ſhould exert themſelves in raiſing and compleating provincial regiments: but it never was the king's intentions that thoſe indulgencies ſhould be extended generally to all thoſe who held or who ſhould hold commiſſions in the provincial corps, nor even to all thoſe who came within this deſcription of loyal American ſufferers; but to ſuch regiments only as ſhould be compleated to the then eſtabliſhment of the Britiſh regiments of foot, and ſhould be recommended to his Majeſty by his commander in chief, as being properly officered and fit for ſervice.

It is true, this rule was in ſome meaſure departed from, in the inſtance of the eſtabliſhment of the queen's rangers, and the New-York volunteers, neither of which regiments were compleat when they were recommended to the king; and alſo in the caſe of the volunteers of Ireland, as many of the officers of that regt. were neither Americans, nor had property or connections in that country: but then it was done on account of the diſtinguiſhed merit of thoſe corps, and upon your particular recommendation; but in caſes in general, where there is no ſuch extraordinary merit to claim particular and diſtinguiſhed marks of favor, it is expected by his majeſty that all the conditions ſpecified in my letter of the 23d January, 1779, before-mentioned, ſhould be complied with in order to the officers of the Provincial regiments availing themſelves of the advantages there held out to them.

With reſpect to the Britiſh legion, which you recommended to his Majeſty's favour in your ſeparate letter of the 1ſt June, 1780, and which you again mention in your letter of the 18th December, as it appears by a return of that corps, dated the 31ſt Dec. laſt, which I have lately received from South Carolina, that their numbers at that time amounted to more than 600 rank and file; and as they would long ſince have been greatly over complete, but for the loſſes they have ſuſtained in the very active and important ſervice in which they have been employed; upon theſe conſiderations, and as a mark of his Majeſty's royal approbation of the gallant behaviour of this corps, and of the ſervices of that very deſerving officer Lieut. Col. Tarleton, who commands it, the king has been graciouſly pleaſed to approve of your recommendation of the Britiſh legion for permanent rank in America; and the officers will be recommended to Parliament for half-pay, whenever the corps ſhall be reduced; and it is his Majeſty's pleaſure, that you do take the earlieſt opportunity of making known to them theſe his gracious intentions.

And as it appears by the deputy inſpector general's report, that the king's American regt. (which ſtands firſt upon the liſt of thoſe you have recommended) was raiſed at a very early period of the rebellion, and was nearly compleated in a ſhort time, and has ſince been conſtantly employed in active ſervice in the field, where it has more than once been diſtinguiſhed for its gallant and ſpirited behaviour in action, particularly at the affair of Rhode-Iſland, on the 29th of Auguſt, 1778, under the command of Major General Pigot, his Majeſty has been pleaſed to approve of your recommendation of that regiment to be put upon the American eſtabliſhment, and you will pleaſe to notify it accordingly.

But in future it is his Majeſty's pleaſure, that no provincial regiment ſhould be recommended to him for permanent rank and half pay, that is not actually compleat to ten companies, conſiſting of 70 men rank and file each, with a due proportion of officers; and whenever any regiment ſhall be ſo recommended, I am to deſire you will give directions to the inſpector general of Provincial forces, or his deputy, to report ſpecially upon the merit of each commiſſioned officer, ſtating the place of his birth; the time of his reſidence in North-America, if not a native of that country; his former occupation and place of reſidence; and whether he has ſuffered in his property on account of his loyalty; in order that the king may ſee how far the eſtabliſhing of ſuch regiments will come up to the original intention of the encouragement held out to the Provincials by the new regulations.

I am Sir, your moſt obedient humble ſervant,
(Signed) GEO. GERMAIN.

Sir Henry Clinton.

Extract of a letter from Maj. Gen. *Greene*, dated Camp, at Little river, near Ninety-Six, June 20.

IN my letter of the 9th I informed your Excellency that the enemy had received a conſiderable reinforcement at Charleſtown, and that I was aprehenſive they would march out and interrupt our operations. On the 11th I got intelligence that they were advancing: I immediately detached the cavalry, with orders to General Sumpter to collect all the force he could, and keep in their front, and by every means in his power retard their march. The enemy paſſed him at Congaree before he got his troops in motion; afterwards he found it impracticable to gain their front. It was my intention to have fought them before they arrived at Ninety-Six, could I have collected a force ſufficient for the purpoſe.

"We had puſhed on our approaches very near to the enemy's works. Our third parellel was formed round their abbatis: A mine and two approaches were within a few feet of their ditch. Theſe approaches were directed againſt the ſtar fort, which ſtands upon the left of the town, as we approached it from the Saluda. On the right our approaches were very near the enemy's redoubt; this was a

[*For remainder ſee laſt Page.*]

strong stockade fort, with two block-houses in it. These two works flanked the town, which is picketed in with strong pickets, a ditch round the whole, and a bank raised near the height of a common parapet. Besides these fortifications, were several little flushes in different parts of the town, and all the works communicated with each other by covered ways. We had raised several batteries for cannon, one upwards of twenty feet high, within one hundred and forty yards of the star fort, to command the works, and a rifle battery also within thirty yards, to prevent the enemy from annoying our workmen. For the last ten days not a man could shew his head but he was immediately shot down, and the firing was almost incessant day and night. In this stage of the approaches I found the enemy so near us that it would be impossible to reduce the place without hazarding a storm. This, from the peculiar strength of the place could not be warranted by the success of a partial attempt to make a lodgment on one of the *curtains* of the star redoubt, and a vigorous push to carry the aright-hand work. The disposition was accordingly formed, and the attack made. Lieutenant Colonel Lee, with his legion infantry, and Capt. Kirkwood's light infantry, made the attack on the right; and Lieut. Colonel Campbell, with the first Maryland & first Virginia regiments, was to have stormed the star redoubt, which is their principal work, and stands upon the left. The parapet of this work is near 12 feet high, and raised with sand bags near 3 feet more. Lieut. Duval, of the Maryland line, and Lieut. Selden of the Virginia line, led on the forlorn hope, followed by a party with hooks to pull down the sand bags, the better to enable them to make the alodgment. A furious cannonade preluded the attack. On the right the enemy were driven out of their works, and our people took possession of it. On the left never was greater bravery exhibited than by the parties led on by Duval, and Selden, but they were not so successful. They entered the enemy's ditch, and made every exertion to get down the sand bags, which from the depth of the ditch, height of the parapet, and under a galling fire, was rendered difficult. Finding the enemy defended their works with great obstinacy, & seeing but little prospect of succeeding without heavy loss, I ordered the attack to be pushed no farther.

"The behaviour of the troops on this occasion deserves the highest commendation; both the officers that entered the ditch were wounded, and the greater part of their men were killed or wounded. I have only to lament that such men fell in an unsuccessful attempt.

"Capt. Armstrong, of the first Maryland regiment, was killed, and Capt. Benson, who commanded the regiment, was wounded at the head of the trenches. In both attacks we had upwards of 40 men killed and wounded; the loss was principally at the star fort, and in the enemy's ditch, the other parties being all under cover. The attack was continued three quarters of an hour, and as the enemy were greatly exposed to the fire of the rifle battery and artillery, they must have suffered greatly. Our artillery was well served, and I believe did great execution.

"The troops have undergone incredible hardships during the siege, and though the issue was not successful, I hope their exertions will merit the approbation of Congress.

"We continued the siege until the enemy got within a few miles of us, having previously sent off all our sick, wounded and spare stores.

"Inclosed is a list of our killed and wounded during the siege."

RETURN *of the killed, wounded and missing, during the siege of Ninety-Six, in South Carolina.*

The 6th, I detached an advance corps under General Wayne, with a view of reconnoitring the enemy's situation. Their light parties being drawn in; the picquets, which lay close to their encampment, were gallantly attacked by some riflemen, whose skill was employed to great effect.

Having ascertained that Lord Cornwallis has sent off his heavy baggage under a proper escort, and posted his army in an open field- fortified by the shipping, I returned to the detachment which I found more generally engaged. A piece of cannon had been attempted by the vanguard under Major Galvan, whose conduct deserves high applause. Upon this the whole British army come out and advanced to the thin wood occupied by General Wayne. His corps chiefly composed of Pennsylvanians and some light infantry, did not exceed 800 men, with three field pieces, but notwithstanding their number, at sight of the British army the troops ran to the rencounter; a short skirmish ensued with a close warm and well directed fire; but as the enemy's right and left of course greatly out flanked ours, I sent General Wayne orders to retire half a mile to where Colonels Vose and Barber's light infantry battalions had arrived by a most rapid move, and where I directed them to form. In this position they remained till some hours in the night. The militia under Gen. Lawson had been advanced and the continentals were at Norrell's mill, when the enemy retreated during the night, to James Island, which they also evacuated, crossing over to the south side of the river. Their ground at this place and the Island was successively occupied by General Muhlenberg. A number of valuable horses were left on their retreat. From every account the enemy's loss has been very great and much pains taken to conceal it. Their light infantry, the brigade of guards, and two British regiments, former the first line; the remainder of their army the second.—The cavalry were drawn up but did not charge.

By the inclosed return you will see what part of General Wayne's detachment suffered most. The services rendered by the officers make me happy to think that although many were wounded we lost none. Most of the field officers had their horses killed; the same accident to every horse of two field pieces, made it impossible to move them, unless men had been sacrificed. But it is enough for the glory of General Wayne and the officers and men he commanded, with a reconnoitering party only, to have attacked the whole British army close to their encampment, and by this severe skirmish hastened their retreat over the river.

Colonel Boyer of the riflemen is a prisoner.

I ha...

Major Genera...

RETUR...

detachment ... mish with t... in Virginia

Total 4 ... tains, 1 Ca... and file wo...

NA...

Capt. Vanl...

Montgome...

Lieutenants. P... prisoner) Capt. Lieut. Crossly, of artillery.

STOP THIEF!

TWENTY GUINEAS REWARD.

STOLEN from the Store of

EATON & BENSO

At STORE No. 5, *Butler's Row*

HAVE FOR SALE,

On the most reasonable Terms,

European and West-India Goo

SPERMACETI CANDLE

WINES, &c. &c. &c.

JUST IMPORTED,

And now ready for SALE,

By M. BROWN & J. THORNDIK

The following Articles, viz.

Broad Cloths of different colou

Knit Patterns, Velvets, Spotted Jeans, Linens, Dia Table Cloths and Napkins, Calicoes, Tapes, Silk Thread Hose, Cambricks, black and white Gau Gauze Handkerchiefs, black, green, crimson and w Modes, Damascus, a beautiful assortment of Lutestri black, white and crimson, plain and sprigg'd Sa Taffities, Padusoys, black and white Lace of diffe prices, Sewing Silks, Buttons, Ribbons, Calimance Shalloons, Durants, Looking-Glasses, Men's and B Hatts, a small but pretty assortment of Cutlery W Green and Bohea Tea, &c. &c.

N. B. As the above Goods belong to a Gentle in Europe, they will be Sold by wholesale only, bu parcels suitable for Gentlemen Shopkeepers in Country, unless some person should incline to purch the whole, in which case the time of payment will made easy for the purchaser.

Beverly, July 31, 1781.

To-Morrow, (FRIDAY 17th instan

Precisely at ONE o'CLOCK,

WILL BE SOLD,

By PUBLIC VENDUE

At the AMERICAN COFFEE-HOUSE,

The swift-sailing Ship JAC

lately captured by the British and re captu by his most Christian Majesty's Frigates *Astrea* & *Hermoine*, built on the new construction, mou 16 six and 9-pounders, and has every thing nec sary for an immediate cruise.—She was la captured by said frigates, after being fr port 5 or 6 days, and will be sold as she arri from sea.—She now lays in this harbour, may be viewed any time previous to the Inventory of the above Ship may be seen the time and place of sale.

... and is supposed to be stolen from some other person. Whoever takes up said Horse and the thief, and re them to said *Dalton*, shall have FIVE GUIN reward and all charges paid, or TWO GUIN and charges for the Horse only.

MICHAEL DALTO

Londonderry, July 19, 1781.

These may notify the persons hereof

CONTINENTAL JOURNAL (BOSTON)

August 16, 1781

The August 16, 1781, *Continental Journal* reports the news of the Siege of Ninety Six using General Greene's letter. No better source could be found for a summary of the siege.

REPORTING THE

RAID ON NEW LONDON

By Matthew Reardon

No man was hated more in Connecticut in 1781 than its native son turned traitor, Benedict Arnold. In September, Arnold met with British General Sir Henry Clinton at his headquarters in New York City. Clinton had been meticulously planning a combined land-naval attack on Newport, Rhode Island, where a sizable French army and naval squadron were stationed. He had hoped to deal a decisive blow to the Franco-American alliance. However, before he could set his plan in motion, he learned that a British ship carrying messages related to the attack had been captured by an American privateer. With the element of surprise gone, the attack was cancelled.

In retaliation, Clinton attempted to deal a blow to the American privateer fleet. American privateers had been a constant nuisance to the British high command since the beginning of the war. Arnold was given 1,700 men and orders to attack New London, Connecticut. New London was, according to the Loyalist newspaper *Rivington's Gazette*, "a nest of pirates." Once there, they were to destroy the privateers and any military stores they could locate.

Arriving at the mouth of the Thames River in the early hours of September 6, the force divided into two divisions. The first landed on the west side of the river to march on New London, while the second landed on the east side with orders to secure Fort Griswold. The first division met little resistance and quickly occupied the town. Detachments of soldiers began setting fire to many of the warehouses and privateers along the riverfront. Others struck at the homes of rebel leaders and in the process discovered military stores hidden in several private barns, which were also burned. Despite attempts to prevent looting and extensive damage, chaos soon erupted. Some British soldiers disobeyed orders and, along with several unlawful citizens, began looting abandoned houses. The wind picked up off the river, which only helped spread the fires.

Arnold was supposedly witnessed to be in several locations throughout New London during the day. Many citizens would try to place the blame of the fire and looting on him personally, even though he had issued strict orders beforehand not to do so. In his report, he would credit one of his staff officers for "his endeavors to prevent plundering...and the destruction of publick buildings."

One example of this was included in the September 13, 1781, *Massachusetts Spy*. The newspaper wrote that he dined at a house of an acquaintance and then ordered the house to be plundered and burned. This claim cannot be substantially proven. Arnold was hated, and people were eager to put him in any situation that would make him appear worse. It is very difficult to find any contemporary American accounts that are unbiased and do not refer to him as "Traitor Arnold" or "the Traitor" or his troops as "Arnold's murdering corps."

However, there are a few accounts of British soldiers doing the exact opposite of what so many are accused of doing. When writing her *History of New London*, Frances Caulkins wrote about a story of a daughter of a militia captain who pleaded with a British officer not to burn their home. She told him that her father was very ill and could not leave the house. The officer stepped in and ordered the house to be spared. It is impossible to draw any conclusion as to what Arnold or any individual British soldier was doing that day and is unjustifiable to accuse every British soldier of committing heinous acts.

The September 13, 1781, *Massachusetts Spy* also reported that "after Colonel Ledyard had surrendered [Fort Griswold, he was] murdered." This was a rumor that came about after the battle and has remained around even until today. New research suggests that Ledyard was actually attempting to lead a counterattack and was killed in the melee that ensued. The *Spy* also reported that the powder magazine in the fort was destroyed and that a British ensign was captured. The British did make an attempt to destroy the powder magazine, but the fuse that was set was put out before it reached the magazine. In his official report written the day after the battle, Arnold does not list any missing or captured officers. Neither do the official rosters of the regiments engaged.

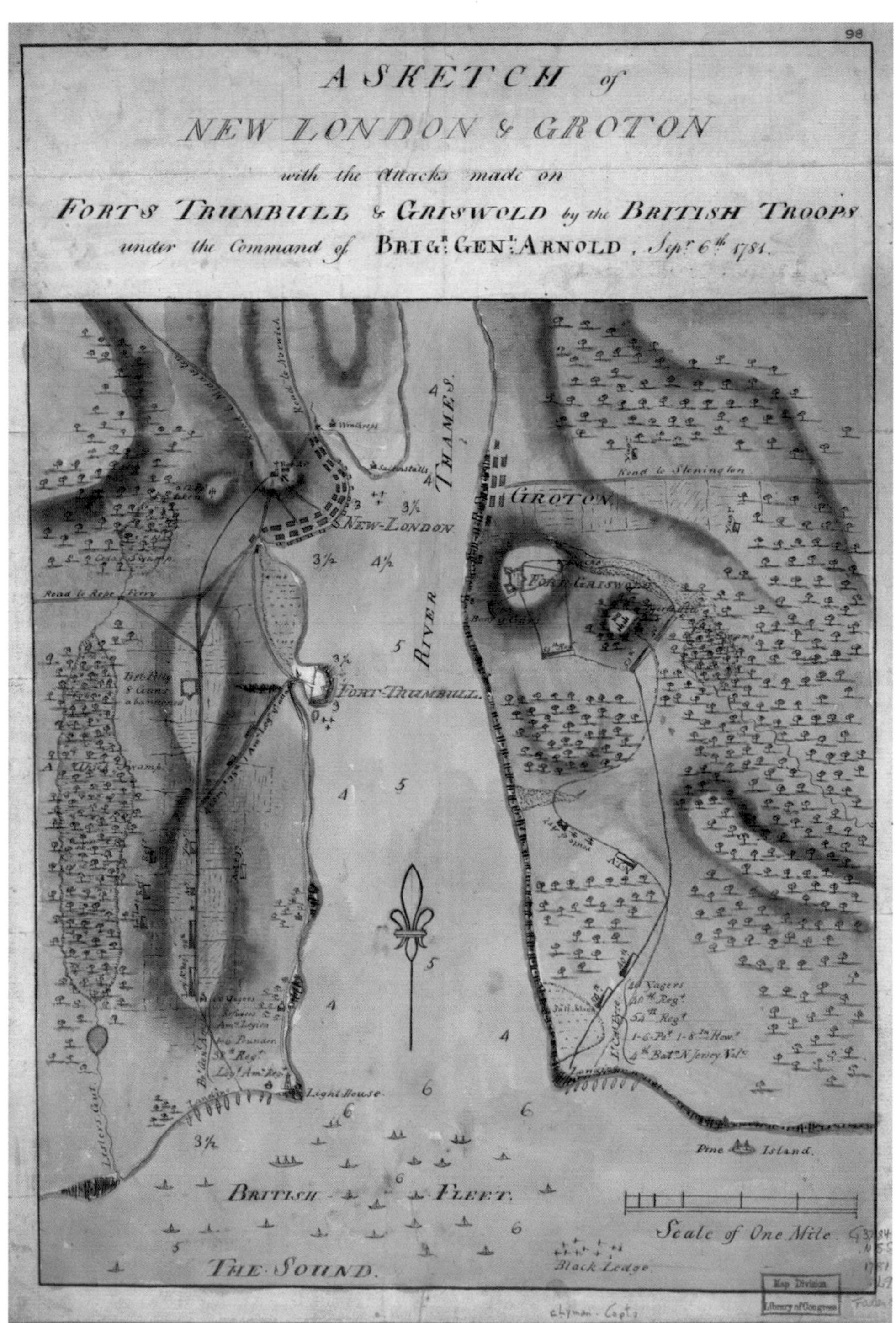

Sketch of New London & Groton
Library of Congress

The British targeted privateers and military stores in New London, Connecticut, which one Loyalist newspaper labeled "a nest of pirates."

ſaid to have on board 19 head of cattle, which being to leeward, was the cauſe of her loſs.

HARTFORD, September 11.

Extract of a letter from an officer commanding militia, dated New-London, Friday, 9 o'clock September 7, 1781.

"Yeſterday morning at 10 o'clock, I received advice that the enemy were landing at New-London Harbour's mouth——I immediately ordered the regiment under my command to march to New-London for its defence. I arrived here, but it was too late to afford any great aſſiſtance in repelling the enemy, as they landed at 6 o'clock, and it was ſo late before I received advice of their arrival, that before the regiment could poſſibly get down, they were embarking.

"The enemy were under the command of the infamous General Arnold, and by the beſt accounts conſiſted of from 1500 to 2000 men——They have burnt the greateſt part of the towns of New-London, and Groton, near the water——The garriſon at Fort-Trumbull evacuated the fort and went over to Fort Griſwold, where Colonel Ledyard made a noble defence——repulſed the enemy two or three times, but at laſt was obliged to ſurrender the fort to ſuperiour force. The enemy, after Col. Ledyard had ſurrendered, murdered him and a number of others; they left 73 of our men dead, and between 30 and 40 wounded in the fort; they alſo carried off about 40 priſoners, among which laſt number is Ebenezer Ledyard, Eſquire. They evacuated the fort about 10 o'clock, in the evening. They blew up the magazines in both forts but did very little other damage to either of them.

"The enemy this morning were at the harbour's mouth on board their ſhipping, and came to ſail about eight o'clock; they are ſtill juſt out beyond the Light-Houſe, as the wind is againſt them. Their ſhipping conſiſts of about 30 ſail, two of which appear to be about 20 guns each.

"We cannot aſcertain the loſs the enemy ſuſtained, but by the beſt accounts imagine it muſt be as large as ours if not larger. We have taken on this ſide a few priſoners, among which is an Enſign, mortally wounded.

"The loſs ſuſtained in this town, in goods, proviſions, ſtores, ſhipping, &c. is very great——A conſiderable number of veſſels made their eſcape up Norwich River."

Another letter, dated Fort-Griſwold, Groton, 7th Sept. 10 o'clock, A. M. ſays, "That the enemy landed at New-London and Groton yeſterday morning, and ſoon took poſſeſſion of the works on New-London ſide the river; and about one in the afternoon took poſſeſſion of Fort-Griſwold, in Groton, by ſtorm, after a moſt ſevere and ſpirited reſiſtance from our troops.——About ſeventy-five of our men found dead in the fort, officers included, among whom is the worthy and brave Lieut. Col. Ledyard, with ſeveral other officers of diſtinguiſhed

dangerouſly wounded.

"The enemy embarked on board their ſhips at about 11 o'clock laſt night, after burning moſt of the houſes and other buildings on Groton bank, and many in New-London, among which are the Court-Houſe, Church, &c."

From RIVINGTON's ROYAL GAZETTE.

tions we can to give them a warm reception."

Yeſterday came up two victuallers, part of the fleet committed to the protection of his Majeſty's frigate Pegaſus, and diſpatched by Rear Admiral Sir Samuel Hood to New-York; the Pegaſus and her convoy on the paſſage fell in with a French ſquadron of eight line of battle ſhips, ſuppoſed to be Monſ. de Barras; it was apprehended the whole conſiſting of ſix victuallers, and a veſſel with the 40th regiment's cloathing, had fallen into the hands of the enemy, until happily thoſe two effected a ſafe arrival in our harbour.

WORCESTER, September 13.

A New-York city paper of the 30th ult. mentions the arrival of Rear Admiral Hood, at Sandy-Hook, from the Weſt-Indies, with 14 ſail of the line, four frigates, one ſloop, and a number of troops, conſiſting of the firſt battalion of the royal, the 13th and 69th regiments. We are informed that theſe ſhips, together with the fleet which were before at New-York, amounting in the whole to 35 ſail, under the command of Admiral Graves, have taken their departure from Sandy-Hook, bound
to the Cheſapeake, in orde
French ſquadron, which ar
Iſland the latter end of laſt
feriour in force to the Bri
ſquadron is ſaid to conſiſt o
frigates and inferiour veſſ
conſiſt of one ſhip of 98 g
70, eleven of 74, four of 6
three of 32, five of 28, one of 24, one fire-ſhip of 8, and a ſloop of war. All the Britiſh line of battle ſhips except one are ſaid to be copper-bottomed.

It is not doubted but that his Excellency General Waſhington has marched, with 8000 choice troops including the French, to Virginia, where the troops in that quarter will join him; Lord Cornwallis is blocked up by the French fleet;—by the preſent appearance of things we are at the eve of ſome important event, which God grant may be propitious to the United States.

It is ſaid that Sir George Rodney and General Vaughan have gone for England from the W. Indies.

We hear that Arnold when he landed at New-London, dined at a gentleman's houſe with whom he was formerly acquainted. After dinner he ordered the houſe to be plundered and ſet on fire. The traitor carried off all the plunder in the town that his ſhort ſtay would permit him to take. Had he tarried in order to have taken breakfaſt the next morning, it is likely he would have been rewarded for all his villanies.

A large quantity of hard money, lately arrived from France, was a few days paſt carried through town, under a ſtrong guard.

Laſt Friday Col. Armand, an active officer in the

old way, according to the number of colours, and the neatneſs of the flowers.

Any ſort of produce or money will be received as pay for work done. Buſineſs in this way which individuals may order, will be cheerfully entered upon, and faithfully executed by their humble ſervant, SAMUEL JENNISON.

Oxford, September 5th, 1781.

N. B. A variety of patterns with different colours and figures may be ſeen at the houſe aforeſaid.

BENJAMIN ANDREWS,
TAYLOR from BOSTON,

BEGS leave to inform the publick that he carries on his buſineſs near the Meeting-Houſe in Worceſter. Thoſe gentlemen who will pleaſe to favour him with their commands, may be aſſured that his utmoſt endeavours ſhall be uſed to ſerve them with fidelity and diſpatch.

SADDLES.

MEN's and Women's SADDLES, of all ſorts, made and ſold by
NATHANIEL COOLIDGE,
At his Shop in Worceſter, near the Meeting-Houſe.
ublick that he carries
its branches. Gen-
eaſe to favour him
nd on being ſerved
ms.

aſſes.
5, to be ſold by
JOSEPH TRUMBULL,
At his Store near the Court-Houſe in Worceſter, Where may be had choice MADDER and OTTER, &c. &c.

STRAYED or ſtolen from the Subſcriber, on or about the 26th day of laſt month, a very dark brown COW, low in fleſh, the end of one of her horns a little broke, and about eight or nine years old. Whoever will give information to the Subſcriber, of ſaid Cow, ſo that he may have her again, ſhall have TWO DOLLARS reward; and if ſtolen, will diſcover the thief, ſo that he may be convicted, ſhall be entitled to a further reward of one GUINEA. JOSEPH ALLEN.

Worceſter, September 11, 1781.

DESERTED between Leiceſter and Springfield, one ASA KNOWLTON, of Bolton, aged 22 years, five feet 11 inches high, dark complexion, a farmer, engaged for ſix months for the town of Bolton. Whoever will take up ſaid deſerter and bring him to me, or to Col. Shepard at Springfield, ſhall have a handſome reward, and all neceſſary charges paid.

SETH WASHBURN, Superintendant.

MASSACHUSETTS SPY (BOSTON)

September 13, 1781

The *Massachusetts Spy* provides early accounts of the Raid on New London from letters, including one by "an officer commanding militia." Letters like these were among the top sources of colonial news. In a separate report under the Worcester dateline, Benedict Arnold is rumored to have dined with a former acquaintance in New London before ordering his house to be plundered and burned. Most Americans despised Arnold after his defection and were eager to make him appear worse in any situation.

SEPTEMBER 13, 1781

The MASSACHUSETTS SPY

HARTFORD, September 11.

Extract of a letter from an officer commanding militia, dated New-London, Friday, 9 o'clock September 7, 1781.

"Yesterday morning at 10 o'clock, I received advice that the enemy were landing at New-London Harbour's mouth——I immediately ordered this regiment under my command to march on New-London for its defence. I arrived here, but it was too late to afford any great assistance in repelling the enemy, as they landed at 6 o'clock, and it was so late before I received advice of their arrival, that before the regiment could possibly get down, they were embarking.

"The enemy were under the command of the infamous General Arnold, and by the best accounts consisted of from 1500 to 2000 men——They have burnt the greatest part of the towns of New-London, and Groton, near the water——The garrison at Fort-Trumbull evacuated the fort and went over to Fort Griswold, where Colonel Ledyard made a noble defence——repulsed the enemy two or three times, but a last was obliged to surrender the fort to superiour force. The enemy, after Col. Ledyard had surrendered, murdered him and a number of others; they left 73 of our men dead, and between 30 and 40 wounded in the fort; they also carried off about 40 prisoners, among which last number is Ebenezer Ledyard, Esquire. They evacuated the fort about 10 o'clock, in the evening. They blew up the magazines in both forts but did very little other damage to either of them.

"The enemy this morning were at the harbour's mouth on board their shipping, and came to sail about eight o'clock; they are still just out beyond the Light-House, as the wind is against them. Their shipping consists of about 30 sail, two of which appear to be about 20 guns each.

"We cannot ascertain the loss the enemy sustained, but by the best accounts imagined it must be as large as ours if not larger. We have taken on this side a few prisoners, among which is an Ensign, mortally wounded.

"The loss sustained in this town, in goods, provisions, stores, shipping, &c. is very great—A considerable number of vessels made their escape up Norwich River."

Another letter, dated Fort-Griswold, in Groton, 7th Sept. 10 o'clock, A.M. says, "That the enemy landed at New-London and Groton yesterday morning, and soon took possession of the works on New-London side the river; and about one in the afternoon took possession of Fort-Griswold, in Groton, by storm, after most severe and spirited resistance from our troops.——About seventy-five of our men found dead in the fort, officers included, among whom is the worthy and brave Lieut. Col. Ledyard, with several other officers of distinguished merit. Captain Shapley of Fort Trumbull, is also dangerously wounded.

"The enemy embarked on board their ships at about 11 o'clock last night, after burning most of the houses and other buildings on Groton bank, and many in New-London, among which are the Court-House, Church, &c."

[...]

WORCESTER, September 13.

[...]

We hear that Arnold when he landed at New-London, dined at a gentleman's house with whom he was formerly acquainted. After dinner he ordered the house to be plundered and sat on fire. The traitor carried off all the plunder in the town that is short stay would permit him to take. Had he tarried in order to have taken breakfast the next morning, it is likely he would have been rewarded for all his villanies.

REPORTING THE

BATTLE OF EUTAW SPRINGS

By David Paul Reuwer

"We fight, get beat, rise, and fight again," General Nathanael Greene said of his Southern Army's 1781 defeats at Guilford Courthouse and Hobkirk's Hill. Following partisan militia campaigns, Greene led the Southern Continental Army on a dynamic offensive attack.

Leading 2,100 troops for twenty-two days and 120 miles, Greene's intention was to crush Lieutenant Colonel Alexander Stewart's 1,690-man British force and eliminate the British threat in the Carolinas once and for all. The Patriots marched from the Santee High Hills to Camden, crossing the Wateree and Congaree rivers, then toward the Eutaws—within four miles of the British without their detection. The wooded topography of soft rises, swales, sinks, and steep-banked Eutaw Creek and its blackjack thickets influenced this battle.

Cavalry and infantry clashed on the morning of September 8 on the river road to the British encamped at Eutaw Springs, South Carolina. Hundreds of British foragers were then captured. Patriots arrayed in three lines, and the militia advanced two miles out, firing seventeen volleys, driving in the British skirmish line. The Maryland and Virginia Continentals "advanced in the face of the enemy's fire, a terrible cannonade and shower of bullets overturned all that presented, and the enemy were put to a rout" (*Glasgow Mercury*, December 13, 1781). Greene's army wielded four artillery pieces and the British five cannon plus two swivels; some were disabled and captured. Both armies employed extensive and repeated tactical use of cavalry, artillery, and infantry. Resilient British officers Coffin, Marjoribanks, and Sheridan bought time for Stewart to reform ranks, launch counterattacks, and check the American advance. Continentals utilized the bayonet with agility, such that Greene's report, reprinted in the December 13, 1781, *Glasgow Mercury*, stated, "I owe the victory which I have gained, to the brisk use the Virginians, Marylanders, and one party of the infantry made of the bayonet."

The intense, pitched fighting with infantry, artillery, and cavalry lasted four struggling hours until both sides wore out. Many leading Southern theater commanders fought together here. The drunken brawl portrayed by secondary sources is mostly myth; closed lines could not hold order fighting through the tented British camp. The Americans did not breach or dislodge the British from the three-storied brick house. This citadel anchored the British defense together with blackjack thickets along the creek. Both sides looked at each other from across the eight cleared acres as the afternoon sun broiled the wounded and bloated the dead. Greene's main force retired several miles to water, rest, and reorganize at Burdell's. Stewart broke one thousand arms, emptied rum barrels, abandoned supplies, and proceeded to withdraw the rest of his men who had not already fled toward Moncks Corner. In the end, Americans slaughtered Americans and 204 soldiers from both sides were buried at the battlefield.

Greene wrote to Governor John Rutledge the next day:

> *"We have had a most Obstinate and Bloody action. Victory was ours. We drove the Enemy, more than four Miles. We took between three and four hundred prisoners, and had it not been, for the large Brick Building, at the Eutaw Spring, and the peculiar kind of Brush that surrounds it, we should have taken the whole Army prisoners."*

Marion, Lee, and Maham pursued and harassed Stewart's men retreating southeast toward Ferguson's Swamp even as British prisoners shuttled north to

Camden. Major Archibald McArthur's three hundred men up from Moncks Corner reinforced Stewart's retreat, but the whole army retired back there. Greene chased until September 13, short of Moncks Corner halfway to Charleston.

This fiercely fought engagement debilitated British field combat ability in the Carolinas. Unable to reinforce Cornwallis at Yorktown, the British ventured far from Charleston for more than another year, foraging and skirmishing at will. South Carolina Governor John Rutledge used this victory to declare qualified pardon to all those who had joined the British side. British officer Roderick Mackenzie journalized Greene in his diary: "the more he is beaten, the farther he advances in the end." Congress awarded Greene one of only six gold medals during the war for "a most signal victory" (*Pennsylvania Packet*, December 4, 1781) at Eutaw Springs.

order, on … THE VOICE OF THE PEOPLE, which ſupported thirteen columns, repreſenting the ſtates, ſupporting a frize, on which were wrote ILLUSTRIOUS SENATORS; and in a pediment, which covered the whole range of columns, were wrote, BRAVE SOLDIERY, with rays of light and ſupport from the ſenate; the pediment ornamented with the following ſtatues, Juſtice with her even ſcales, a flaming ſword, and thirteen ſtars in the glory around the figure, emblematical of the juſtice of Congreſs; on the right, the ſtatue of Hope, with her anchor; and on the left, the ſtatue of Induſtry, with her bee hive. The ſecond ſtory of the Corinthian order, with ſtatues in niches, with the words, HEROES FALLEN IN BATTLE; and an attic ſtory, as the work compleated with the words AGRICULTURE, ARTS AND COMMERCE, and repreſented by the following ſtatues: Agriculture, a figure holding a ſheaf of wheat on her left arm, a ſickle in her right hand, and a plow at her feet. The Arts repreſented by the ſtatues of painting, ſculpture, and architecture; Painting has a pallet and pencils in one hand, and the other ſupporting a picture; ſhe has a golden chain hanging from her neck, with a medal, on which is IMITATION; the ſeveral links allude to the many parts neceſſary to be ſtudied before a whole can be produced; or the combined qualifications of an able artiſt: and it being of gold, to ſhew that the art of painting cannot flouriſh without it is ſupported by the generoſity of the opulent. Sculpture is repreſented by a ſtatue, holding in one hand a mallet and chiſſel, and in the other a buſt, ornamented with laurels. Architecture by a ſtatue, having in one hand a plan of elevation, and in the other a ſquare and a plummet. Commerce by a ſtatue, holding a globe in one hand, and the other on the prow of a ſhip. A dome covers the building and finiſhes with the figure of Fame, blowing her trumpet to the eaſt; which may eaſily be comprehended.

And at another window the genius of America, trampling on Diſcord, eing a handſome female figure, the bigneſs of life, cloathed in white, a purple girdle with the word VIRTUE on it, and a blue mantle ſtrewed with ſtars, a fillet on her head, with the word PERSEVERANCE: She holds in one hand her bannor of thirteen ſtripes, with the words EQUAL RIGHTS, and in the other hand a globe with the word UNIVERSALITY on a circular index to the globe. The figure of Diſcord with his ſnakes inſtead of hair, and holding a torch, the flame of which turns down on himſelf.

By the UNITED STATES in CONGRESS aſſembled, October 29, 1781.

Reſolved,

THAT the thanks of the united ſtates in congreſs aſſembled, be preſented to major general Greene, for his wiſe, deciſive and magnanimous conduct in the action of the 8th of September laſt, near the Eutaw Springs in South-Carolina; in which, with a force inferior in number to that of the enemy, he obtained a moſt ſignal victory.

That the thanks of the united ſtates in congreſs aſſembled, be preſented to the officers and men of the Maryland and Virginia brigades, and Delaware battalion of continental troops, for the unparalleled bravery and heroiſm by them diſplayed, in advancing to the enemy through an inceſſant fire, and charging them with an impetuoſity and ardour that could not be reſiſted.

That the thanks of the united ſtates in congreſs aſſembled, be preſented to the officers and men of the legionary corps and artillery, for their intrepid and gallant exertions during the action.

To be Sold by
At William Cooper's Fer
Day of De

The Prize

With her Tackle, App
now lying oppoſite ſaid
Boards, Plank and Scant
preciſely at 10 o'clock in
muſt expect to pay the Ca
By
JO

Kaighn an

Have removed their STO
door below Arch ſtree
the following MER

A GENERAL Aſſort-
ment of ſuperfine a
ſecond Broadcloths of t
moſt faſhionable colours
Silk Serge and Rattin
Linings;
An elegant Aſſortment
gold and ſilver ſpang
Buttons,
Sewing Silk,
Scarf Twiſt,
Silk Knee-garters,
Serge Denim,
Sattinet,
Callimancoes,
White Modes,
White Barcelona ſilk,
muſlin and bord
gauze Handkerchief
Chineſe Ribbons,
Laval Linens,
Scotch Threads,
Blue Moreen,
Womens coloured
and lamb Mitts,
Small French Pins,
Quality Binding,
Red ell wide P rſi n
Apron Tapes and Bo
Striped Ginghams,

To be L E T, a

The Blac

in Market-ſtreet,
It is an excellent ſta
there was erected o
two ſtory FRAM
21 feet by 22 feet
ſtalls for each horſ
a loft that will ho
with a large and c
under the ſame roo
culars enquire o
place.

ALL perſons i
the Eſtate o
city, Gardener,
with the ſubſcribe
ROI

PENNSYLVANIA PACKET (PHILADELPHIA)
December 4, 1781

Congress awarded Greene one of only six gold medals during the war for "a most signal victory" at Eutaw Springs.

her, then pushed forward and closed the other which was engaged on our bow. In about thirty minutes she struck, sent a boat on board to take possession, and wore round after the other, who was making off, who also struck on our coming up. They proved to be the Hercules and Mars, two privateers belonging to Amsterdam, mounting 24 nine-pounders and 10 cohorns each, are perfectly new and alike, sail as fast as the Artois, and the compleatest privateers I ever saw, cost upwards of 20,000l. commanded by two Hogenboombes, father and son, inhabitants of Flushing. The father was well known last war, by the name of John Hardapple, had a schoote privateer, with a French commission, out of Flushing, and did much mischief to our trade; he was sent for on purpose to command these privateers. They sailed from the Texel the 30th of November, and had only taken one of our fishing smacks.

"The Hercules had 164 men on board; 13 were killed, and 20 wounded: the Mars 146 men, nine were killed, and 15 wounded. We had one man killed, and six wounded.

"I beg you to transmit to their Lordships, that I am much indebted to the attention of my officers and people in securing both these gentry. Our rigging and sails are cut, and fore-top mast unserviceable."

The capture of the two Dutch privateers by Capt. Macbride, most probably will prove of the happiest consequences to the trade. Their great force, and going in company, would have been very dangerous to the traders. The great object, we are informed, of these privateers, was to capture as many colliers as possible. The Hollanders are so very scarce of the article of coals, at present, that we are assured they sell at the amazing price of a penny the pound.

Yesterday the Lord Mayor held a common hall at Guildhall, in consequence of a requisition made for that purpose. Mr. Hurford came forward and moved that an address, petition, and remonstrance be presented to his Majesty on the present alarming state of affairs. The motion being seconded, the question was put and unanimously carried.

It concludes with beseeching his Majesty to abandon the attempt of reducing our fellow-subjects in America by force of arms, a fatal system, which he has been led to adopt from the misrepresentations and delusions of his ministers, and which, if persisted in, must terminate in the loss of all his possessions in the western world.—It declares to Europe, to America, the West-Indies, and the world in general, an abhorrence of the war against the Americans, with whom it re-

he would be graciously pleased to receive on his Throne, their humble petition, address, and remonstrance; to which his Majesty immediately replied in the following words.—

"*I shall take time to consider of the manner in*

Petitions and remonstrances to the throne, of the same nature as the city of London's, are meditating in all the principal counties and towns in England. The minority are the promoters of them.

AMERICA.

Extract of a letter from General Green, to the President of Congress, from his head-quarters, at Martin's Tavern, near Ferguson's Swamps, in South Carolina, the 11th of September, 1781.

"We marched to attack the English army encamped at M'Leod's Ferry at four o'clock in the morning of the 8th. Our front line was composed of four small battalions of militia, two of North and two of South Carolina, our second line consisted of three small brigades of Continental troops, one of North Carolina, one of Virginia, and one of Maryland; Lieut Colonel Lee, with his legion, covered our right flank: and Lieut. Colonel Henderson, with the state troops, our left. Lieut. Col. Washington with his cavalry, and the Delaware troops, formed the body of reserve. Two three-pounders were in the front of our line, and two six-pounders with the second line; the legion and the state troops formed our advanced guard, and were to retreat on our flanks when the enemy should form. We marched in this order to the attack. The legion and state troops met with a party of the enemy's horse and foot, about four miles from their camp, and put them to flight with fixed bayonets, having many killed and wounded. As we thought this was the van of the enemy, our first line was ordered to form, and the legion and state troops to take post on our flanks. From the place of action to Entow Springs, the whole country is covered with wood. The firing began at three miles from the English camp. The militia advanced firing, and the advanced posts of the enemy were routed; the fire redoubled, our officers behaved with the greatest bravery, and the militia gained much honour by their firmness; but the fire of the enemy, who continued to advance, being superior to ours, the militia were obliged to retreat.

The Carolina brigade, under General Sumner were ordered to support them, and though not above three months raised, behaved nobly. In this moment of action, the Virginans under Col. Campbell, and the Marylanders under Col. Williams advanced in the face of the enemy's fire, a terrible cannonade and shower of bullets overturned all that presented, and the enemy were put to the rout.

Lieutenant-Colonel Lee turned his left flank to the enemy, and charged them in the rear, while the troops of Maryland and Virginia charged them in the front. Col. Hampton, who commanded the troops of the State, charged one party, of whom he made 100 prisoners. Colonel Washington advanced with a corps-du-reserve upon the left, where the enemy appeared to prepare again to make resistance, and charged them so impetuously with his cavalry, and a body of infantry, that they had not time to rally.

We continued to pursue the enemy, after having broken them, until we attained their camp. A great number of prisoners fell into our hands, and some hundreds of fugitives escaped towards Charlestown: but a party having got into a brick house three stories high, and others took post in a pallisadoed garden, their rear being covered with springs and hollow ways, the enemy renewed the fight. Lieut. Col. Washington did his utmost to dislodge them from a thick wood, but found it impossible; his horse was killed under him, and himself wounded, and taken prisoner; four cannon were advanced against the house, but the fire from it was so brisk, that it was impossible to

forward under the fire of the house, and we returned to the bank, which we occupied in the morning, not finding water any where nearer, and our troops having great need for refreshment after a fight which had continued four hours. I left upon the field of battle a strong piquet. I shall send Colonel Lee, and General Marion, early to-morrow morning between Entow's and Charlestown, to pre-

guard, and compleat our success. We lost two pieces of artillery to the enemy, and we have taken one of theirs.

The night of the 9th, the enemy retired, leaving more than 70 of their wounded behind them, and more than 1000 arms, which they had broken, and concealed in the springs of the Entows; they staved 20 or 30 barrels of rum; and destroyed a large quantity of provisions, which they could not carry with them.

We pursued them as soon as we had notice of their retreat, but they joined Major Arthur; General Marion, and Colonel Lee, not having troops enough to hinder them. At our approach they retired to Charlestown. We took 500 prisoners, including the wounded they had left behind, and I reckon they had no less than 600 killed and wounded. The fugitives spread such an alarm, that the enemy burnt their provisions at Dorchester, and quitted their post at Fair Lawn. A great number of negroes and others have been employed to throw down trees across the roads, at some miles distance from Charlestown. Nothing but the brick house, and their strong post at Entows, hindered the remains of the English army from falling into our hands.

We have pursued them to the Entows, but could not overtake them. We shall rest here one or two days, and then retake our old position near the heights of Santee.

I think that I owe the victory which I have gained, to the brisk use the Virginians, Marylanders, and one party of the infantry, made of the bayonet. I cannot forbear praising the conduct and courage of all my troops.

Signed NATHANIEL GREEN.

State of the Continental troops.

Killed—1 Lieutetant Colonel, 6 Captains, 4 Subalterns, 4 Serjeants, 98 rank and file.

Wounded—2 Lieutenant-Colonels, 7 Captains, 20 Lieutenants, 24 Serjeants, 209 rank and file. Total 408 men.

State of the Continental troops of the state and militia.

Killed—1 Major, 4 Subalterns 4 Serjeants, 16 soldiers.

Wounded—3 Lieutenant-Colonels, 6 Captains, Subalterns, 8 Serjeants, 91 soldiers.

Missing—8 soldiers Total 146 men.

Total of killed, wounded, and missing of the continental troops of the state and militia, 554 men. Published by order of Congress, CHARLES THOMSON, Sec.

STATE LOTTERY.

Monday, December 3. No. 25,653, a prize of 2000 l.—No. 11,485, a prize of 500 l.—No. 46,985, 17,740, 47,884, prizes of 50l.

Tuesday, December 4. No. 31,217, a blank, but as first drawn 2,000 l.—No. 36,376, a prize of 10,000 l.—No. 3,810, a prize of 1,000 l.—No. 42,752, and 2,698, prizes of 500 l. each.—No. 39,605, and 34,613, prizes of 100l. each.—No. 6,838, 16,183, 26,019, 34,020, 41,732, 225, 2,049, 13,377, 21,640, and 45,102, prizes of 50l. each.

Wednesday, December 5. No. 37,991, as first drawn, 3000 l.—No. 17,459, 616, prizes of 100l.—No. 15,997, 9153, 38,565, 16,913, 5707, 33,982, 26,008, 22,490, 8242, 131, 728, 43,229, prizes of 50l.

Thursday, December 6. No. 21,044, a prize of 1,000 l. No. 10,684, 30,514, and 10,684, prizes of 50l.

Intelligence from Lloyd's List.

December 4.

The Magdalena, Hill, from Riga to Hull; the ——, Torres, from Riga to Oporto; and a ship from Bourdeaux to Stettin, are all lost in the Baltic.

The Henry Elisabeth, Shuttle, from London to Blackney, is taken and ransomed for 500 guineas; the Medway, Burches, from Arundel to Aberdeen, for 600 ditto; the William, Lamos, from Ostend to Overy, for 100 ditto;

flows over her every high water; they have scuttled her larboard side in two places, and work day and night to save as much of her cargo as possible.

The Ann and Francis, Thompson, of Whitbaven for the Baltic, is totally lost in the Lewes, and two hands perished.

The Amazon privateer, of London, Capt. Hughes, ar-

GLASGOW MERCURY

December 13, 1781

"We fight, get beat, rise, and fight again," General Nathanael Greene said of his Southern Army's 1781 defeats at Guilford Courthouse and Hobkirk's Hill. Following partisan militia campaigns, Greene led the Southern Continental Army on a dynamic offensive attack at the Battle of Eutaw Springs. Greene's after-action report, reprinted in the December 13, 1781, *Glasgow Mercury*, stated, "I owe the victory which I have gained, to the brisk use the Virginians, Marylanders, and one party of the infantry made of the bayonet."

DECEMBER 13, 1781

The GLASGOW MERCURY

AMERICA.

Extract of a letter from General Green, to the President of Congress, from his head-quarters, at Martin's Tavern, near Ferguson's Swamps, in South Carolina, the 11th of September, 1781.

" We marched to attack the English army encamped at M'Leod's Ferry at four o'clock in the morning of the 8th. Our front line was composed of four small battalions of militia, two of North and two of South Carolina, our second line consisted of three small brigades of Continental troops, one of North Carolina, one of Virginia, and one of Maryland; Lieut. Colonel Lee, with his legion, covered our right flank: and Lieut. Colonel Henderson, with the state troops, our left. Lieut. Col. Washington with his cavalry, and the Delaware troops, formed the body of reserve. Two three-pounders were in the front of our line, and two six-pounders with the second line; the legion and the state troops formed our advanced guard, and were to retreat on our flanks when the enemy should form. We marched in this order to the attack. The legion and state troops met with a party of the enemy's horse and foot, about four miles from their camp, and put them to flight with fixed bayonets, having many killed and wounded. As we thought this was the van of the enemy, our first line was ordered to form, and the legion and state troops to take post on our flanks. From the place of action to Entow Springs, the whole country is covered with wood. The firing began at three miles from the English camp. The militia advanced firing, and the advanced posts of the enemy were routed; the fire redoubled, our officers behaved with the greatest bravery, and the militia gained much honour by their firmness; but the fire of the enemy, who continued to advance, being superior to ours, the militia were obliged to retreat.

The Carolina brigade, under General Sumner were ordered to support them, and though not above three months raised, behaved nobly. In this moment of action, the Virginans under Col. Campbell, and the Marylanders under Col. Williams advanced in the face of the enemy's fire, a terrible cannonade and shower of bullets overturned all that presented, and the enemy were put to the rout. [...]

We collected all our wounded, except those who were too forward under the fire of the house, and we returned to the bank, which we occupied in the morning, not finding water any where nearer, and our troops having great need for refreshment after a fight which had continued four hours. I left upon the field of battle a strong piquet. I shall send Colonel Lee, and General Marion, early to morrow morning between Entow's and Charlestown, to prevent the reinforcements which may come to succour the enemy, or to retard their march, if they attempt to retreat; and to give room to the army to attack their rear guard, and compleat our success. We lost two pieces of artillery to the enemy, and we have taken one of theirs. [...]

We pursued them as soon as we had notice of their retreat, but they joined Major Arthur; General Marion, and Colonel Lee, not having troops enough to hinder them. At our approach they retired to Charlestown. We took 500 prisoners, including the wounded they had left behind, and I reckon they had no less than 600 killed and wounded. The fugitives spread such an alarm, that the enemy burnt their provisions at Dorchester, and quitted their post at Fair Lawn. A great number of negroes and others have been employed to throw down trees across the roads, at some miles distance from Charlestown. Nothing but the brick house, and their strong post at Entows, hindered the remains of the English army from falling into our hands.

We have pursued them to the Entows, but could not overtake them. We shall rest here one or two days, and then retake our old position near the heights of Santee.

I think that I owe the victory which I have gained, to the brisk use the Virginians, Marylanders, and one party of the infantry, made of the bayonet. I cannot forbear praising the conduct and courage of all my troops.

Signed NATHANIEL GREEN.

REPORTING THE

YORKTOWN CAMPAIGN

By Diane K. Depew

"WE ARE AT THE EVE OF SOME IMPORTANT EVENT, WHICH God grant may be propitious to the United States" (*Massachusetts Spy*, September 13, 1781).

Many Americans involved in the 1781 Siege of Yorktown anticipated the outcome could be crucial to the war, and when news of General Charles Lord Cornwallis's defeat at Yorktown reached Great Britain, the British government realized the war was over. But what is often lost in popular history of the war is the role France played. Without France, the siege and victory would not have happened.

In the summer of 1781, General George Washington, reinforced by a French army under General Jean-Baptiste Comte de Rochambeau, was planning an offensive against General Sir Henry Clinton's British garrison at New York City. Clinton, anticipating the attack, ordered Cornwallis, who was attempting to subdue Virginia, to establish a defensive naval base there and transfer some of his men to New York. Cornwallis moved his army to the port of Yorktown, on the York River, though his troops were never redeployed.

But for a chance at victory, Washington required a substantial navy. As he later wrote, "No land force can act decisively unless it is accompanied by a maritime superiority." On August 14, 1781, he learned a French battle fleet of twenty-eight ships of the line, commanded by Admiral François Joseph Paul Comte de Grasse, was sailing from the Caribbean to the Chesapeake Bay. Within less than five days, in an amazing accomplishment of logistics and organization, Washington changed his objective to Cornwallis and had most of his troops, including Rochambeau's army, headed south. It was a bold move. As Washington withdrew from New York, Clinton made no attempt to stop him, a decision at which, according to the December 13, 1781, *Glasgow Mercury*, "very sensible men express great surprise... [Clinton] did not offer him battle." Even some Americans were astonished, as the *Continental Journal* reported on October 18, 1781: "Sir Henry Clinton remains quiet in New York notwithstanding the imminent danger hanging over...Cornwallis."

When news of General Charles Lord Cornwallis's defeat at Yorktown reached Great Britain, the British government realized the war was over, but without France, the siege and victory would not have happened.

Even without hindrance from Clinton, Washington lacked crucial information—would de Grasse gain control of the Chesapeake Bay and York River? But France's alliance with Spain and their joint effort against the British in the Caribbean benefited Washington. The British, discovering de Grasse was headed north, incorrectly deduced that he would leave part of his fleet to defend the French islands, but Spain's Admiral Bernardo de Galvez covered de Grasse's absence. With only nineteen ships of the line, Rear Admiral Sir Thomas Graves sailed from New York to stop de Grasse. On September 5, 1781, off the Virginia coast, the two fleets fought the largest naval battle of the Revolutionary War. Grave's fleet, outgunned and badly mangled, returned to New York for repairs. De Grasse, joined by another French fleet of eight battleships, now blockaded the mouth of the Chesapeake Bay and the York River. Washington had his naval advantage over Cornwallis. And on September 28, 1781, the allied army reached Yorktown.

Over the next week, Washington's soldiers prepared to besiege Cornwallis, who had encircled Yorktown with substantial earthen fortifications. On October 9, French artillery began pummeling Yorktown; a few hours later, Washington fired the first American cannon shot as his artillery joined the French in bombarding the British round the clock.

Throughout the siege, Clinton, still in New York, sent Cornwallis messages that he was coming with five thousand reinforcements. But Clinton had no control over the speed of repairs to Grave's ships; and as an article in the November 22, 1781, *Glasgow Mercury* notes, there was a celebrity in New York—King George III's son, Prince William Henry. The prince's presence was a distraction from important military matters, including the urgency to relieve Cornwallis.

On October 19, with defenses crumbling, most cannon damaged, many of his men sick, any chance of escape gone, and having lost expectation of help from Clinton, Cornwallis surrendered. The Articles of Capitulation, as accurately reported in the December 18, 1781, *London Gazette*, confirms it was an American and French victory. The first article of the terms stated: "The garrisons of York & Gloucester...to surrender themselves prisoners of war to the combined forces of America and France."

The November 22, 1781, *Glasgow Mercury* revealed irony to the British defeat. The same day Cornwallis surrendered, Clinton sailed from New York with Admiral Graves and "19 frigates and 8 fire ships." Noted on the listing of Graves's ships in the *Glasgow Mercury* was the seventy-four-gun vessel *Canada*, with a commander named Cornwallis. This was General Cornwallis's younger brother, Captain Sir William Cornwallis. The relief fleet, and Cornwallis's brother, reached Virginia five days later and too late to change history. However, less than six months later, Captain Cornwallis helped defeat Admiral de Grasse at the Battle of the Saints. This British victory improved Great Britain's strategic position during peace negotiations with the French—the same negotiations that resulted in the Treaty of Paris in 1783, in which Great Britain recognized the independence of the United States.

Battle of the Virginia Capes
U.S. Naval History and Heritage Command

The French fleet successfully prevented the British fleet from entering the Chesapeake Bay and relieving Major General Lord Cornwallis's army at Yorktown.

ſaid to have on board 19 head of cattle, which being to leeward, was the cauſe of her loſs.

HARTFORD, September 11.

MASSACHUSETTS SPY (BOSTON)

September 13, 1781

"...we are at the eve of some important event, which God grant may be propitious to the United States."

arrival, that before the regiment could poſſibly get down, they were embarking.

"The enemy were under the command of the infamous General Arnold, and by the beſt accounts conſiſted of from 1500 to 2000 men——They have burnt the greateſt part of the towns of New-London, and Groton, near the water——The garriſon at Fort-Trumbull evacuated the fort and went over to Fort Griſwold, where Colonel Ledyard made a noble defence——repulſed the enemy two or three times, but at laſt was obliged to ſurrender the fort to ſuperiour force. The enemy, after Col. Ledyard had ſurrendered, murdered him and a number of others; they left 73 of our men dead, and between 30 and 40 wounded in the fort; they alſo carried off about 40 priſoners, among which laſt number is Ebenezer Ledyard, Eſquire. They evacuated the fort about 10 o'clock, in the evening. They blew up the magazines in both forts but did very little other damage to either of them.

"The enemy this morning were at the harbour's mouth on board their ſhipping, and came to ſail about eight o'clock; they are ſtill juſt out beyond the Light-Houſe, as the wind is againſt them. Their ſhipping conſiſts of about 30 ſail, two of which appear to be about 20 guns each.

"We cannot aſcertain the loſs the enemy ſuſtained, but by the beſt accounts imagine it muſt be as large as ours if not larger. We have taken on this ſide a few priſoners, among which is an Enſign, mortally wounded.

"The loſs ſuſtained in this town, in goods, proviſions, ſtores, ſhipping, &c. is very great——A conſiderable number of veſſels made their eſcape up Norwich River."

Another letter, dated Fort-Griſwold, Groton, 7th Sept. 10 o'clock, A. M. ſays, "That the enemy landed at New-London and Groton yeſterday morning, and ſoon took poſſeſſion of the works on New-London ſide the river; and about one in the afternoon took poſſeſſion of Fort-Griſwold, in Groton, by ſtorm, after a moſt ſevere and ſpirited reſiſtance from our troops.——About ſeventy-five of our men found dead in the fort, officers included, among whom is the worthy and brave Lieut. Col. Ledyard, with ſeveral other officers of diſtinguiſhed

lie in ſight of us. We are making all the preparations we can to give them a warm reception."

Yeſterday came up two victuallers, part of the fleet committed to the protection of his Majeſty's ...iſpatched by Rear Admiral ...-York; the Pegaſus and ...ge fell in with a French ...attle ſhips, ſuppoſed to be ... apprehended the whole ...s, and a veſſel with the ..., had fallen into the hands ...y thoſe two effected a ſafe

WORCESTER, September 13.

A New-York city paper of the 30th ult. mentions the arrival of Rear Admiral Hood, at Sandy-Hook, from the Weſt-Indies, with 14 ſail of the line, four frigates, one ſloop, and a number of troops, conſiſting of the firſt battalion of the royal, the 13th and 69th regiments. We are informed that theſe ſhips, together with the fleet which were before at New-York, amounting in the whole to 35 ſail, under the command of Admiral Graves, have taken their departure from Sandy-Hook, bound to the Cheſapeake, in order to give battle to the French ſquadron, which arrived there from Rhode-Iſland the latter end of laſt month, and are much inferiour in force to the Britiſh; the whole French ſquadron is ſaid to conſiſt of only 23 ſail including frigates and inferiour veſſels. The Engliſh fleet conſiſt of one ſhip of 98 guns, one of 90, one of 70, eleven of 74, four of 64, two of 50, four of 44, three of 32, five of 28, one of 24, one Fire-ſhip of 8, and a ſloop of war. All the Britiſh line of battle ſhips except one are ſaid to be copper-bottomed.

It is not doubted but that his Excellency General Waſhington has marched, with 8000 choice troops including the French, to Virginia, where the troops in that quarter will join him; Lord Cornwallis is blocked up by the French fleet;—by the preſent appearance of things we are at the eve of ſome important event, which God grant may be propitious to the United States.

It is ſaid that Sir George Rodney and General Vaughan have gone for England from the W. Indies.

We hear that Arnold when he landed at New-London, dined at a gentleman's houſe with whom he was formerly acquainted. After dinner he ordered the houſe to be plundered and ſat on fire. The traitor carried off all the plunder in the town that his ſhort ſtay would permit him to take. Had he tarried in order to have taken breakfaſt the next morning, it is likely he would have been rewarded for all his villanies.

A large quantity of hard money, lately arrived from France, was a few days paſt carried through town, under a ſtrong guard.

Laſt Friday Col. Armand, an active officer in the

account of her rudder. He concluded with pro-
feſſions of his integrity.

General Vaughan ſpoke to the ſame points; and ſaid they had brought the ſtores to ſale on account of the private plunder, and for fear that they ſhould be burnt by the wicked people in the iſland.

Lord Mahon recommended dividing the motion; as it ſtood, he thought it too complex.

Lord George Germain could not vote for the motion, becauſe it bore relation to the claims agitating by the courts below.

Colonel Barré removed all difficulties, by perſuading Lord Mahon to withdraw his amendment, which his Lordſhip did; the Colonel then moved as an amendment, to add the words, "excepting ſuch wares and merchandize as have been claimed in the Courts of Weſtminſter Hall."

This amendment was received by the Houſe, and the queſtion ſo amended being put, the Houſe divided,

Noes,	—	163
Ayes,	—	89

Wedneſday, December 5.

The Houſe having gone into a committee of ſupply,

Lord Liſburne ſtated the neceſſity of having a formidable navy in the preſent criſis. His Lordſhip moved, that 100,000 ſeamen, including 21,305 marines be voted for the year 1782, and that 4l. per man per month be granted for the ſame.

An amendment was propoſed to vote 110,000 men, which was oppoſed by *Lord North* as unneceſſary. The fact was, that the Admiralty employed as many men as they could get without regard to the vote of credit. His Lordſhip ſaid, ſome gentlemen might be afraid that great augmentations were to take place in the army, and conſequently that the American war was to be purſued with redoubled vigour. The largeneſs of the ſupply called for this day, might lull their apprehenſions on that head, for the motion without the amendment was ſtill for 10,000 ſeamen more than were called for laſt year, and conſequently the ſum of 520,000l. would be employed in the naval department more than laſt year.

At half after nine o'clock the Houſe divided,

For the amendment	—	73
For the original motion	—	143

Advices have been received at the Admiralty, that the grand armament preparing at Breſt had not failed from that harbour ſo late as the 21ſt of November laſt, owing to an unexpected difficulty in obtaining the neceſſary equipment of men. It was owing to this information, that Admiral Kempenfelt's departure was accelerated, his inſtructions being to cruize, for the preſent, off the port of Breſt; and, as he has a larger force with him than any the enemy poſſeſs in that quarter, it is expected he will be able to prevent the execution of their intended ſcheme for this ſeaſon, which is ſtrongly believed, though not poſitively known by Adminiſtration, to be directed againſt our Weſt India iſlands.

Government have received, by the laſt packet from the Leeward Iſlands, the moſt alarming accounts from the Governors reſpecting the dangers that threaten them, and their incompetency for making any material reſiſtance. Information has been received from St. Lucia and Jamaica, been indefatigable in his exertions for putting the iſland in the beſt ſtate of defence poſſible; but the great misfortune, which it is feared will render all his efforts abortive, is, that a ſtrong ſpirit of party prevails amongſt the people there, and many of the moſt wealthy inhabitants in the iſland are the avowed patrons of the American defection. On this account the Governor finds great difficulty to ſtimulate the natives and eſtabliſhed inhabitants, to take any ſhare in the military preparations which are making on the part of this country; and Government at home have therefore determined to ſend out 2000 men with the fleet that goes under the command of Admiral Rodney, for the further ſecurity of this valuable iſland.

It has been ſtrongly reported and believed, that the French fleet, immediately upon the capture of Lord Cornwallis, failed to the Weſt Indies, as they had no further buſineſs in America. The probability of their purſuing this ſtep greatly alarms the Weſt India merchants, as at preſent we have no force there equal to cope with them, and therefore, although Jamaica is too ſtrong for a detachment of the fleet, yet there is great reaſon to be alarmed for its ſafety, when inveſted, as it probably may be, by the whole force of the enemy.

By a Gentleman lately arrived from Quebec, who made a very extenſive journey upon commercial buſineſs through the back ſettlements of New England, New York, Jerſey, Pennſylvania, and Virginia, we learn, that almoſt the whole Interior of the Colonies, out of the reach of the coaſt and its immediate communication, are in aſſociation armed to reſiſt the Congreſs, whoſe meaſures are execrated among them, for not making peace. No recruiting officer, nor one in any civil employment, much leſs a tax-gatherer, dares to appear there. In the country between Fort Pitt and the Ohio, there are not leſs than 300,000 inhabitants ſettled, who fly to arms on any appearance of their own perfect independence being infringed. It is expected, that theſe and other territories, peopled with men of the ſame principles, will be the means of forcing the Congreſs to treat for a peace, on much more reaſonable terms than have yet been mentioned.

Tueſday advice was received expreſs from France, of the Andromaque frigate being arrived at Breſt from the Cheſapeak.—She ſailed from thence on the 12th of November, in company with De Graſſe's fleet, conſiſting of thirty-five ſail of the line, and three thouſand five hundred troops, which were bound to Martinico; Waſhington and Rochambeau w[...]
turn to the Jerſeys, havi[...]
ment under Monſ. Le Fa[...]
to join Green in South C[...]

The many idle reports [...]
ſtate of the Eaſt India C[...]
Carnatic, which have be[...]
vailed on a gentleman wh[...]
a later date than any oth[...]
from Madras, to commu[...]
friends; and we have h[...]
get the following extrac[...]
pended upon as authenti[...]

Mad[...]

"I have the pleaſure to [...] ſituation of our public affairs is much mended ſince my laſt to you. Sir Eyre Coote took the

"Hyder, with his collected force, marched out of Arcot, and encamped on the plain between Wandewaſh and Arnee, ſo that we may ſoon expect to hear of an engagement between the two armies; which, in all likelihood, will decide the great conteſt, which has ſubſiſted near ſeven months, and laid the whole Carnatic in flames.

"Six French ſhips of the line, the Caſolante of 40 guns, the Subtile of 22, and another little veſſel of 14, made their appearance in our road on the 27th of laſt month. Our apprehenſions at firſt were very great, as we had near 200 Paddy veſſels laden with proviſions lying in the road, an accident to which muſt have reduced the ſettlement to great diſtreſs; but they paſſed on quietly without attempting any thing; we had the five Indiamen lately arrived, and ſeveral country ſhips lying in the road.

"There was a degree of ſtupidity and indifference in their conduct, which is entirely unaccountable, but it was moſt fortunate for us, for they might have rode triumphant on the coaſt, deſtroying our trade, and intercepting all ſupplies of proviſions; and if they had put a number of their marines aſhore to join Hyder, would have rendered the diſpute more unequal; whereas we are now freed from the continual apprehenſion of the French fleet coming, and this muſt naturally diſpoſe Hyder againſt them, and may probably have the good effect to make him alter his plan of conqueſt; he is too wiſe not to ſee the impracticability of keeping the Carnatic, unleſs ſtrongly ſupported by an European power. No peace with the Marattas yet, notwithſtanding our ſucceſſes on the other coaſt."

Many very ſenſible men expreſs great ſurpriſe that when Mr. Waſhington made his *feint* towards New York, the Commander in Chief did not offer him battle; or, at leaſt that upon his retreat, he did not make a vigorous ſally in purſuit of him. Had either of theſe meaſures been purſued, or due care been taken to obtain information of the enemy's route, the brave Cornwallis and his army would moſt probably have been preſerved, and the triumph of rebellion prevented.

Sir Henry Clinton, though with no leſs than 20,000 of the fineſt troops in Europe, wrote to the gallant and unſupported Cornwallis, for the loan of 2000 of his little army, to protect him from the threatened attacks of the rebels, conſiſting of no more than 7000 men.

WEDNESDAY's POST.

[...] fall in with them. At ten o'clock yeſterday morning ſaw them: they ſtood for us with much

GLASGOW MERCURY

December 13, 1781

As George Washington withdrew from New York, Clinton made no attempt to stop him, a decision that, according to the December 13, 1781, *Glasgow Mercury,* "very sensible men express great surprise…[Clinton] did not offer him battle."

Extracts from the Leyden Gazettes, of July 1781.

MADRID, June 26th. The crew of the Dutch frigate la-Bruis, complain bitterly of the English for having had the cruelty to fire on them with guns charged with pieces of broken glass and earthen ware; by means of which the wounded have suffered the utmost torture, and their wounds rendered incurable.

PETERSBURGH, July 3d. The ratification of the King of Prussia's accession to the armed neutrality was exchanged on the 29th of last month. On this occasion the usual presents have been sent to the Plenipotentaries who signed the accession. The magnificent presents from our Court, to the two Ministers of State, Count Finckenstein and Baron Hertsberg, & also those to the three first Secretaries of the Cabinet, to his Prussian Majesty, will be transmitted to Berlin by a courier, who will be sent off in three days. The Minister from Berlin will send the ratification to his Court by the same conveyance.

PHILADELPHIA, October 3.

We have the pleasure to congratulate the public on the complete re-establishment of American government in the state of Georgia.

Advices from South-Carolina inform that Major General Leslie (who some time since left Virginia in the Carysfort frigate, and arrived in Wilmington, in North Carolina, from whence he departed in the Blond frigate to take the command of the British forces in South-Carolina) was lost at sea, the frigate having foundered in a storm, and every soul on board perished.

We hear that General Washington began his operations against York, about the 25th ult. and that two French 64's have forced their way up the river a considerable distance above York.

Extract of a letter from Count de Grasse to the Hon. the Chevalier de la Luzerne, Minister Plenipotentiary of France.

Cape Henry, Sept. 13, 1781.

"*Nothing gave me greater pleasure than the approach of the armies under General Washington and the Count de Rochambeau. In order to hasten their arrival I had selected out seven vessels that drew the least water to transport them from the mouth of*

I could. My putting to sea facilitated the entrance of M. de Barras, and our junction has added much to our strength—I fell in with two of the enemy's frigates, the Iris and the Richmond, of 32 guns each They had been sent by the English Admiral to cut away the buoys of our anchors—They have

time closely penned up in York-Town, which, it appears, he has rendered very strong by numerous fortifications; though it was said considerable impression was made on his works by the fire of our heavy cannon, &c. We shall very probably soon have agreeable accounts from that quarter.

Sir Henry Clinton remains quiet in NewYork, notwithstanding the imminent danger hanging over the head of his colleague in wickedness Lord Cornwallis; but it is presumed the presence of his YOUNG MASTER will at once dissipate his Fears, and that he, as a "man of spirit," "will be proud to fight in a cause for which the young Gentleman exposes his life."

Extract of a letter from Richmond, dated Sept. 26.

"The following are extracts from letters wrote by Doctors Brown and Johnstone, of the southern army, and handed me by a gentleman at this place.

"At Hutah, near Santee, 53 miles from Charlestown, on the 8th of September, an engagement commenced between Gen. Greene and the main body of the enemy's army, in which the former lost from 250 to 300; the enemy's loss, killed 300, wounded and taken 60, taken, not wounded 340, total 700.

"These letters add, that all the officers in Col. Washington's corps were either killed, wounded or taken, except Capt. Clarke. The Colonel was missing, but returned slightly wounded.

"Monday the 10th a heavy firing was heard, but no account of the event. As Gen. Greene had sent a detachment of fresh troops after the enemy's flying army, there is no doubt of a total defeat.

A list of the officers killed and wounded on our part.

K I L L E D.

Col. Campbell, Virginia; Maj. Rutherford, N. C. Capts. Dobson, Maryland, Goodman, N. Carolina; Lieuts. Potterfield, do. Goodwin, do. Polk, do. Luss, Dayton, do.

W O U N D E D.

Gen. Pickens, S. Carolina; Cols. Henderson, do. Middleton, do. Howard, Maryland, Polk, do. Maj's. Edmonds, Virginia, Erving, Maryland, Martin, S. C. Giles do. Moore, do. Lieuts. Finn, Virginia, Dickson, do. Dudley, do.

October 8.

Extract of a letter from Williamsburg, dated September 29.

I have seen a letter from Brigadier General Jones, of North Carolina, to the Marquis de la Fayette, which says, that on the 8th of September, Gen. Green had a very severe action with the British, commanded by Col. Stewart, at the Eutaw Springs, 60 miles from Charlestown.—Our troops were hard pushed at first, and lost two field pieces; ...aking a spirited stroke, ... and took two others ... followed up the blow, ...ed them 6 miles: Col. ... regiments was pushed ... came up with them, ...eard the next morning. ... the field 250 killed, ...0 prisoners were taken, ...5 commissioned officers. ...oss was 250 killed and ...m some valuable offi... ...ngton's cavalry behaved bravely, but are mostly cut to pieces.

HARTFORD, October 16.

Extract of a letter dated head-quarters, Williamsburgh (Virginia) Sep. 24.

"We are at present within six miles of the British army, commanded by Lord

BOSTON, October 18.

A Spanish news-paper of a late date, brought by the vessel arrived at Newbury-Port from Bilboa, contains an account that stock had fallen 17 pr cent. owing to advices lately received, which, though the ministry endeavoured to suppress, had yet obtained credit; that Hyder Ally had taken Madrass, and cut to pieces a body of British troops that had been newly sent to that quarter. The same paper mentions an account, received in Europe by a Danish East-Indiaman, that Commodore Johnstone had arrived with part of his squadron at St. Helena, in a most shattered condition, having had a second engagement, in which the French had taken two ships belonging to the East-India company, and a transport, and taken or sunk a ship of the line.

The Brig Spanish Fame, James Rob, Commander, was lost upon the South Shoal of Hog-Island the 21st September, six Souls perished, two of them of this town, Mr. Chickley and Mr. Prince.

On Sunday evening expir'd after a short illness, in the 14th year of her age, and on Tuesday was interred, Miss *Mary Greene*, eldest daughter of Mr. *Joseph Greene*, merchant, of this town. An amiable and benevolent disposition of mind, a grave and serious deportment, and most engaging manners had greatly endeared her to her parents and friends, whose pleasing hopes of future comfort and happiness in her are thus suddenly blasted, and the bereavement peculiarly heavy and afflictive.

"She drops a smile my weeping friends she cries,
What mean the tears that trickle from your eyes,
O! my lov'd Parents could I but reveal
The vast unutterable Bliss I feel,
The glorious vision would your souls inspire,
And warm your bosoms with celestial fire.
Then cease the unavailing flood to pour
The curtain soon will drop-your grief be o'er
And we shall meet again to part no more."

CONTINENTAL JOURNAL (BOSTON)

October 18, 1781

Even some Americans were astonished with Clinton's lack of movement, as the *Continental Journal* reported on October 18, 1781: "Sir Henry Clinton remains quiet in New York notwithstanding the imminent danger hanging over…Cornwallis."

374 THE GLASGOW MERCURY.

the ſaid Thomas Lonnergan was guilty of the murder.—Margaret Murry, a ſervant in the family, and indicted for aiding abetting this horrid crime, will be tried on Friday next.

" Saturday laſt, between 11 and 12 o'clock, an accidental fire broke out in the Cuſtom-houſe, which burned for ſome time with great violence; but, by the aſſiſtance of the firemen and engines, the fire was happily got under without doing ſo much miſchief as it was natural to expect. The Right Hon. the Lord Mayor and the High Sheriffs attended on the firſt alarm, and continued there till the fire was extinguiſhed; and the different officers and clerks of the Cuſtom-houſe removed, on the firſt intimation of the fire, all the books and papers to a place of ſafety. It was very fortunate that the fire was got under before it reached the ſpirits, &c. in the ſtores, as the conſequences muſt have been dreadful."

The Counteſs of Donegal, Captain Reed, has arrived in Loughfoil from Charleſtown. In her paſſage ſhe touched at Madeira, where a Portugueze ſhip, from Goa for Liſbon, brought intelligence, that the Swallow packet, with Lord Macartney, and ſeveral Gentlemen, bound to Madras, arrived at Surat, on the Malabar coaſt, about the 29th or 30th of May, in a very bad condition, with ſeveral feet water in her hold, and the loſs of all her guns, which were thrown over-board in a dreadful monſoon or hurricane, in the gulf of Baſſora. The paſſengers and crew were in tolerable health. After refitting, they proceeded for the Coromandel coaſt, which it is ſuppoſed they made in about three weeks.

We hear from Saltcoats, that, on Friday laſt, a ſmuggling veſſel from Dunkirk, bound for the Trun, ſtruck upon a rock, about a mile from that place, and ſunk: the water was about eight feet above her deck. She mounted 12 guns, and had 32 men on board, who were all ſaved. Her cargo conſiſted of above 500 caſks of brandy, and a conſiderable quantity of tea. The brandy will turn out a very good prize to the revenue-officers on that coaſt.

Extract of a letter from Whitehaven, Nov. 13.

" Three boats, with each ſix men on board, which were fiſhing near Peeletown when the gale came on, on Tueſday evening, were driven aſhore, and by the violence of the breakers were beat to pieces, and all hands periſhed before any aſſiſtance could be given them."

Extract of a letter from Aberdeen, Nov. 19.

" We are informed that the veſſel de Gunſt van Goede Vrienden, brought in here in April laſt, as prize to the Tarter privateer, having been claimed as Pruſſian by the maſter, and by the Pruſſian ambaſſador; The judge admiral, on the 16th inſt. ordered her to be reſtored to the owners, who are Pruſſians, and reſerves to them to inſiſt afterwards for the damages occaſioned by the capture."

ARRIVALS in CLYDE.

Nov. 15. Fanny, Campbell, Jamaica, ſugar and rum.
Minerva, Speirs, do. do.
Mary, Hunter, do. do.
Commerce, Symonds, do. do.
Argyle, Campbell, Dublin, goods.
Greenock, M'Kinlay, do. do.
10. St. Andrew, Scott, Jamaica, ſugar and rum.

Nov. 17. Phenix, Cuninghame, Dublin, ſugar.
Jenny, M'Lean, Highlands, ſalt and tree.
Arrivals at the Weſt End of the Canal.

Thurſday's Expreſs.

This day arrived the Mails from France *and* Flanders.

From the LONDON GAZETTE, *Nov.* 17.
Admiralty-Office.

THE following ext... Admiral Graves... his Majeſty's ſhips in... Stephens, were receiv... Captain Manly, of his M...

London, at New Y...

BE pleaſed to acqua... the Santa Marga... inſtant, with her conv... of forty-two ſail, for N... had parted company.

The Caryſfort, whi... returned the 8th, and ... good fortune to meet with ... Cape François, on the French King's account, with a conſiderable quantity of maſts for large ſhips.

The Torbay and Prince William arrived here the 11th, having parted from the Jamaica convoy the 21ſt of September.

The Nymphe returned from cruizing off Cape Henry, and brought in five prizes, taken by her and the Amphion.

London, off Sandy Hook, October 19, 1781.

MY laſt letter could not fix the time of my ſailing, the ſhips were however moving down as they could be got ready, and on the 17th, ſo ſoon as the tide ſerved, I got under ſail with the remainder of the ſquadron, except the Shrewſbury, Montagu, and Europe, and got down with the help of the afternoon tide to Sandy Hook.

The next morning we embarked all the troops on board the men of war from the tranſports, to the amount of 7149 (officers included;) and this morning the whole fleet ſailed and got ſafe over the Bar, conſiſting of 25 ſail of the line, two fifties, and eight frigates, and the whole are now under ſail for the Cheaſapeak.

A numerous convoy appears off, which we judge to be the Engliſh convoy, as they are making for this place, and the moſt advanced ſhew Engliſh colours.

The fleet above-mentioned proves to be the Centurion and her convoy, which are all arrived (except eight private traders,) and are now ſtanding in for the Hook. [*See page* 370.]

PROMOTIONS.—*War-Office, Nov.* 17, 1781.

22d Regiment of Light Dragoons, Quarter-Maſter John Anderſon is appointed to be Adjutant, vice Thomas Walker.

15th Regiment of foot, Enſign James Gilleſpie to be Lieutenant in one of the additional companies, vice Michael Jackſon.

97th Regiment of foot, John Ware, gent. to be Enſign, vice Charles Mac Vicar.

101ſt Regiment of foot, Enſign William Ryan, of Captain A. Campbell's Independent Company, to be Enſign, vice John Quinn.—Enſign William Dane, of Captain Cowan's Independent Company, to be Enſign, vice Robert Robinſon.

Independent Company of foot, Lieutenant James Abercrombie, of 71ſt foot, to be Captain.—Enſign William Whatley, of 97th foot, to be Lieutenant.—Enſign Robert Robinſon, of 101ſt foot, to be Enſign in Captain Andrew Cowan's Independent Company of foot, vice

dent Company of foot, vice William Ryan.

From the LONDON PAPERS, *November* 17.

Barcelona, Oct. 17. The officers of a frigate

directed againſt a poſt where it was known that M. de Crillon had placed an hundred of his fineſt grenadiers.

The convoy from the Havannah did not arrive the day after the regiſter ſhips, as was ſaid in

only 100 men, of which the enemy had intelligence, gave them every hope of ſucceſs; but the beſieged lying upon their arms till the French were within piſtol-ſhot, and then ſupported their fire with ſuch unabated vigour, that the Frenchmen gave way on all ſides, and in their retreat were almoſt to a man cut off.

Captain Manly ſays, that Sir Henry Clinton and the fleet expected, when he left them, to reach the Cheſapeak by the 22d of October; and in that caſe he hoped to relieve Cornwallis by the 26th at fartheſt.

We are informed that his Royal Highneſs Prince William Henry, when he delivered his letters to Captain Manly, of the Lively ſloop, who arrived with the diſpatches from America, ſaid to him, " Here's a letter for my father, another for my mother, and letters for as many of my brothers and ſiſters as I had time to write to, and pray give my compliments to Sandwich, and tell him, we are juſt going to fight the French *in earneſt.*"

There is an account from New York, that Gen. Arnold arrived there the 6th of October, and was preparing to execute an expedition up the North River, in the abſence of Waſhington's army. Gen. Robertſon commands at New York during the abſence of the Commander in Chief.

The annals of hiſtory do not exhibit a more important period than the preſent. The honour, the intereſt, of the nation are in a ſtate of temporary ſuſpenſion. Our hopes, derived from the known courage of our commanders in America, are highly raiſed; but it is very much to be feared that the cunning wary Frenchmen will ſteal out of the Cheſapeak before we ſhall be able to prevent them.

Fourteen ſhips of the line of battle are preparing, with all poſſible expedition, for ſome ſecret and important expedition, the command of which is to be given to Sir John Lockhart Roſs, or Adm. Kempenfelt. The Edgar and another ſhip of the line are alſo fitting out, and, as report ſays, are intended for America.

STATE-LOTTERY.

Nov. 16. This day the following numbers were drawn prizes at Guildhall, viz. No. 42,794, as firſt drawn, 500l.—Nos. 28,128, 2,005, and

35,537, prizes of 50l.

Nov. 17. No. 29,817, as firſt drawn, 500l.—No. 756, a prize of 2,000l.—No. 46,905, a

GLASGOW MERCURY

November 22, 1781

The November 22, 1781, *Glasgow Mercury* notes there was a celebrity in New York: King George III's son, Prince William Henry. The prince's presence was a distraction from important military matters, including the urgency to relieve Cornwallis.

LONDON GAZETTE

December 18, 1781

The Articles of Capitulation, as accurately reported in the December 18, 1781, *London Gazette*, confirms Yorktown was an American and French victory.

which left New York the 17th of November.

New York, November 13, 1781.

MY LORD,

IN my laſt Diſpatch I had the Honor to acquaint your Lordſhip with my Fears reſpecting the Fate of the Army in Virginia.

It now gives me the deepeſt Concern to inform you, that they were but too well founded, as your Lordſhip will perceive by Lord Cornwallis's Letter to me of the 20th ult. a Copy of which, and the Papers accompanying it, being incloſed for your Information.

Had it been poſſible for the Fleet to have ſailed from hence at the Time it was firſt imagined they would have been able to do, I have not the leaſt Doubt that Lord Cornwallis would have been relieved by the joint Exertions of the Navy and Army; and I therefore cannot ſufficiently lament that they could not have been made ſooner.

Your Lordſhip will be informed by Lord Cornwallis's Letter to me, (a Copy of which accompanies this Diſpatch) of the Force that was oppoſed to his Lordſhip in Virginia; beſides which, by Rebel Accounts, which I have the Honor to incloſe for your Lordſhip's Information, General Green ſeems ſtill to have an Army acting in that Quarter; and there are, at this Inſtant, above 3000 Continental Troops at Weſt Point and in its Vicinity.

My Diſpatches will be delivered to your Lordſhip [illegible] Lordſhip, without teſtifying to you the high Opinion I have of his Merit, and my entire Approbation of his Conduct ſince he has been on this Service, acting as one of my Aides de Camp, having always ſhewn the greateſt Attention to me, and highly diſtinguiſhed his Spirit, by attending as a Volunteer upon every Expedition and Excurſion which have taken Place ſince his being here.

Copy of a Letter from Lieutenant-General Earl Cornwallis to Sir Henry Clinton, dated York Town in Virginia, October 20, 1781.

SIR,

I HAVE the Mortification to inform your Excellency, that I have been forced to give up the Poſts of York and Glouceſter, and to ſurrender the Troops under my Command, by Capitulation, on the 19th Inſtant, as Priſoners of War to the Combined Forces of America and France.

I never ſaw this Poſt in a very favorable Light; but when I found I was to be attacked in it, in ſo unprepared a State, by ſo powerful an Army and Artillery, nothing but the Hopes of Relief would have induced me to attempt it's Defence; for I would either have endeavoured to eſcape to New York, by rapid Marches, from the Glouceſter Side, immediately on the Arrival of General Waſhington's Troops at Williamſburgh, or I would, notwithſtanding the Diſparity of Numbers, have attacked them in the open Field, where it might have been juſt poſſible that Fortune would have favored the Gallantry of the Handful of Troops under my Command: But being aſſured by your Excellency's Letters, that every poſſible Means would be tried by the Navy and Army to relieve us, I could not think myſelf at Liberty to venture on either of thoſe deſperate Attempts: Therefore, after remaining Two Days in a ſtrong Poſition in Front of this Place, in Hopes of being attacked, upon obſerving that the Enemy were taking Meaſures which could not fail of turning my Left Flank in a ſhort Time; and receiving, on the Second Evening your Letter of the 24th of September, informing me, that the Relief would ſail about the 5th of October, I withdrew within the Works on the Night of the 29th of September, hoping, by the Labour and Firmneſs of the Soldiers, to protract the Defence until you could arrive.

Every Thing was to be expected from the Spirit of the Troops, but every Diſadvantage attended their Labour, as the Works were to be continued under the Enemy's Fire, and our Stock of Intrenching Tools, which did not much exceed 400, when we began to work in the latter End of Auguſt, was now much diminiſhed.

The Enemy broke Ground on the Night of the 30th, and conſtructed, on that Night and the Two following Days and Nights, Two Redoubts, which, with ſome Works that had belonged to our outward Poſition, occupied a Gorge between Two Creeks or Ravines, which come from the River on each Side of the Town. On the Night of the 6th of October they made their firſt Parallel, extending from it's Right on the River to a deep Ravine on the Left, nearly oppoſite to the Center of this Place, and embracing our whole Left, at the Diſtance of 600 Yards. Having perfected this Parallel, their Batteries opened on the Evening of the 9th againſt our Left; and other Batteries fired at the ſame Time againſt a Redoubt advanced over the Creek upon our Right, and defended by about 120 Men of the 23d Regiment and Marines, who maintained that Poſt with uncommon Gallantry. The Fire continued inceſſant from heavy Cannon, and from Mortars and Howitzers throwing Shells from

remain Priſoners to the United States, the Navy to the naval Army of His Moſt Chriſtian Majeſty.

Article I. Granted.

Article II. The Artillery, Arms, Accoutrements, Military Cheſt, and public Stores of every Denomination, ſhall be delivered, unimpaired, to the Heads of Departments appointed [illegible]

Article [illegible]. At Twelve O'Clock this Day the two Redoubts on the Left Flank of York to be delivered, the one to a Detachment of American Infantry, the other to a Detachment of French Grenadiers. The Garriſon of York will march out to a Place to be appointed, in Front of the Poſts, at Two o'Clock preciſely, with ſhouldered Arms, Colours caſed, and Drums beating a Britiſh or German March; they are then to ground their Arms, and return to their Encampment, where they will remain, until they are diſpatched to the Places of their Deſtination. Two Works on the Glouceſter Side will be delivered at One o'Clock to Detachments of French and American Troops appointed to poſſeſs them; the Garriſon will march out at Three o'Clock in the Afternoon; the Cavalry with their Swords drawn, Trumpets ſounding; and the Infantry in the Manner preſcribed for the Garriſon of York: They are likewiſe to return to their Encampment, until they can be finally marched off.

Article III. Granted.

Article IV. Officers to retain their Side Arms;

the Redoubts that covered them, ſpiking 11 Guns, and killing or wounding about 100 of the French Troops who had the Guard of that Part of the Trenches, and with little Loſs on our Side. This Action, though extremely honorable to the Officers and Soldiers who executed it, proved of little Public Advantage; for the Cannon having been ſpiked in a Hurry, were ſoon rendered fit for Service again, and before Dark the whole Parallel and Batteries appeared to be nearly complete. At this Time we knew that there was no Part of the whole Front attacked, in which we could ſhew a ſingle Gun, and our Shells were nearly expended. I had therefore only to chuſe between preparing to ſurrender next Day, or endeavouring to get off with the greateſt Part of the Troops; and I determined to attempt the latter, reflecting, that though it ſhould prove unſucceſsful in it's immediate Object, it might at leaſt delay the Enemy in the Proſecution of further Enterprizes. Sixteen large Boats were prepared, and upon other Pretexts were ordered to the lungs are entirely exhauſted, the tongue bliſtered and inflamed, the ſtomach cloſed up, and the heart oſſified!—This ſubject is ſuppoſed to have died through want and vexation, and is a ſtriking inſtance of miniſterial inflexibility!

WEDNESDAY's POST.

No foreign Mails.

From the LONDON PAPERS, *November* 16.

A Letter from Holland of a very late date, ſays, that the defamatory libels, &c. againſt the Duke of Brunſwick are entirely the production of the French faction there, who ſtill rule with an uncontrolled ſway the councils of Holland. The French antipathy to the Duke of Brunſwick ſprings from the open manner in which he has always ſpoken of the political duplicity of the French, who in almoſt every alliance, both ancient and modern, have either betrayed or deſerted their allies. This letter adds, that a pamphlet has been diſtributed throughout the Provinces, compoſed by Van Berkel and the ſecretary of the French ambaſſador, diſplaying in a very pompous manner the courage and ſeamanſhip of the Dutch in their former wars with England, magnifying the preſent power of France, Spain, and America, and diminiſhing that of Great Britain, while it encourages the Dutch to perſiſt in their warlike operations only for a little time, and the allies will monopoliſe the whole of the American trade amongſt them, and ruin that of England in every part of the globe.

By the laſt accounts from America, the French and Americans had broken up all the roads, and thrown up every poſſible impediment that induſtry could produce, to prevent Lord Cornwallis from making a ſally. It is alſo known, that a number of officers, and many of the American loyaliſts, have gone upon the expedition from New York, and the Britiſh Admiral has taken three light faſt ſailing veſſels with him, in order to give the earlieſt intelligence to Government here. The above facts were given us by a Gentleman, whoſe veracity may be depended upon.

The fleet under the command of Admiral Graves, which ſailed for the Cheſapeak on the 19th of October, conſiſted of the following veſſels, viz.

	Guns.		Guns.
* London, Ad. Graves, Capt. Graves	98	* Shrewſbury, Robinſon	74
Prince George, Rear Ad. Digby, C. Williams	98	Torbay, Gidoin —	74
* Barfleur, Ad. Hood, C. Hood — —	90	* Princeſſa, Knatchbull	74
Canada, Cornwallis	74	Robuſt, Croſby —	74
* Alfred, Bayne —	74	Ramilies — —	74
* Invincible, Saxton	74	Prudent, Burnett —	64
* Monarch, Reynolds	74	Lion, Fooks — —	64
* Centaur, Inglefield	74	Prince William, Wilkinſon — —	64
* Reſolution, Manners	74	* Belliqueux, Brine	64
* Bedford, Graves	74	* America, Thompſon	64
* Royal Oak, Ardeſoif	74	* Europe, Child —	64
* Montague, Bowen	74	* Intrepid, Molloy —	64
* Ajax, Turrington	74	* Adamant — —	50
* Alcide, Thompſon	74	* Centurion — —	50
		* Chatham — —	50
		* Warwick — —	50

19 Frigates, and 8 fire-ſhips.

Thoſe marked * were with Admiral Graves when he engaged de Graſſe.

Admiral Rodney will ſail for the Weſt Indies about the end of this month with fifteen ſail of the line. Sir Richard Bickerton will ſail at the ſame time, as Commodore, with ſix ſail of the line to the Eaſt Indies. The Eaſt India ſhips will alſo ſail under his convoy.

tion of three to one; they are now in poſſeſſion of the greateſt part of the Levant and Mediterranean trade. The trade to the port of Oſtend has encreaſed ſo ago above 40 that place.

The follow pany's ſhips, the next con barked the re have been ra his Britannic of the Compar Worceſter, C Henry, Dund bot, Taylor; Alfred, Brow Dampier.

Moſt peopl fleet either ha it, before the although they h tiſh, yet it is ſcarcely to be ſuppoſed they will riſk a battle, after having avoided it ſo ſkilfully in nine different actions this war, in moſt of which they had a ſuperiority. They will probably keep to their old plan of going off in a line of battle, and ſo ſpin out the war, unleſs they had a certainty of obtaining a victory.

By letters from Peterſburgh, of the 19th of September, we are informed, that the Britiſh had this ſeaſon four-fifths of the trade to Peterſburgh. On the 11th of September 460 Britiſh veſſels had been there. The Dutch had three veſſels which came there laſt ſeaſon, and had not ſailed on the 11th of September; and no other veſſel from Holland had arrived at that time, nor could this ſeaſon; ſo that the Britiſh muſt be in poſſeſſion of moſt of the naval ſtores, ſuch as hemp, iron, &c. From this account, which may be depended on as authentic, the great advantage reſulting from Admiral Parker's engagement with the Dutch fleet may be eaſily conceived.

The Treaſury and Secretary of State's office in Cleveland Row, have been buſily employed during the courſe of the laſt fortnight, in diſpatching their circular *billets-doux* to ſuch peers and members of the lower Houſe as are conceived to be their particular friends in parliament, in which they ſtrongly requeſt their attendance at the opening of the ſeſſion, as affairs of the higheſt importance to the ſtate are expected to be agitated the firſt week after its commencement.

This morning ſome diſpatches were received from Newfoundland, by which we are informed, that upwards of twenty ſail of American privateers were cruizing on that ſtation, four of which are taken by his Majeſty's cruizers, and carried into St. John's.

A dreadful contagion now rages in this metropolis. On Wedneſday evening laſt, and yeſterday morning, ſeveral thouſand perſons were ſeized with it, and are in a very dangerous way. It is called the " Lottery Peſtilence."

It is imagined there are not leſs than one hundred thouſand perſons afflicted with the above malady. Its ſymptoms are a giddineſs of head, a wildneſs of countenance, a reſtleſſneſs of body, a high pulſe, and a total loſs of natural reaſon.——People in health are adviſed not to go near the ſick, leſt the effluvia of the diſorder ſhould infect them, for 'tis full of contagious particles.

A countryman a few days ſince going into a lottery-office, and a profuſion of policies being

a fortune may be gained."——" *Policies!*" cry'd the countryman; " methinks the beſt *Policy* for me will be to keep my money in my

GLASGOW MERCURY

November 22, 1781 (continued from page 337)

The November 22 *Mercury* also revealed irony. The same day Cornwallis surrendered, Clinton sailed from New York with Admiral Graves and "19 frigates and 8 fire ships." Noted on the listing of Graves's ships was the seventy-four gun vessel *Canada*, with a commander named Cornwallis. This was General Cornwallis's younger brother, Captain Sir William Cornwallis. The relief fleet, and Cornwallis's brother, reached Virginia five days later and too late to change history.

Thurſday, Nov. 15. This morning the Lottery began drawing at Guildhall, when No. 27,684 was drawn a blank, but as firſt drawn is entitled to 500l.—Nos. 41,620, and 6,016, 500l. each.—Nos. 6,037, 17,269, and 35,470, 100l. each.—Nos. 15,328, 41,310, 2,747, 10,579, 34,672, 25,826, 21,003, and 38,330, prizes of 50l. each.

Intelligence from LLOYD'S LIST.

November 13.

The Norfolk, ———, with maſts, &c. is loſt on the rocks near Norway.

The Albion, Oglen, from Liverpool to Cork, and the Rodney, Bramwell, from Waterford to ditto, are taken and carried into Morlaix.

The Nelly, Owen, from Tortola and Cork to Liverpool, is arrived at Milford, after being taken by a Dunkirk privateer, and ranſomed for 5000 guineas.

The John, Urry, from London to America, retaken by the Adventure privateer of Weymouth, is arrived at Portſmouth.

The Bee, ———, from Newfoundland to Oporto, was taken off Oporto bar.

The Charming Kitty, Roche, from Tortola and Cork, is on ſhore at Liverpool, but is expected to be got off without damage.

The Minerva, Squarey, from London to Quebec, is retaken and carried into Halifax.

The Two Brothers, Hans Crow, from Cadiz to Oſtend, is loſt near Ilfracombe, and only ſaved 1 hide, 5 bags red wool, 46 barrels cochineal, and 3 bags of indigo.

Two Danes and a Swede are ſtranded on the coaſt of Cornwall.

The Brayton, Harriſon, from Liverpool to Quebec, with ſalt, after being retaken, drove on ſhore near Louiſburgh, on her paſſage to Halifax, and loſt her anchors and cables, and received other damage.

The Felicity, Mourant, from Peterſburg to Jerſey, is loſt in the Baltic near Libau; only a ſmall part of the cargo ſaved.

The Sarah, Newby (or Gale,) from Jamaica to England, which ſailed with the fleet and ſeparated, afterwards ſprung a leak and put back to Jamaica, where ſhe was to unload and repair, and would then proceed for England.

The Antigallican, Butler, from Liverpool to Charleſtown, is on ſhore near Holyhead.

Portſmouth, Nov. 11. Arrived from Topſham, the Charlotte, Punſhon, after engaging a French privateer, and beating her off: The Charlotte had two killed.

Downs, Nov. 12. Sailed to the northward the Sampſon and Artois men of war, and Shark ſloop.

November 16.

The following ſhips of war are now at Spithead, viz.

Royal George, Dublin, Monſieur, Britannia, Defence, Juno, Victory, Valiant, Anſon, Lynx, Defiance, Yarmouth, Tiſiphone, Arrogant, Prothée, Furnace, Stag, Queen, Diligente, Succeſs, Duke, Inflexible, Alarm, Union, Sceptre, Daphne, Courageux, Alexander, Agamemnon, Lightning, Cumberland, Renown, Conqueror, Minerva, Edgar, La Prudente, Harpy.

The Edward, Peoples, from New York to Halifax and Quebec, was taken the 11th of Auguſt laſt by the Grayhound privateer, of Portſmouth in New Hampſhire.

The Emulation, Simonds, from Quebec to Newfoundland, is taken by the Americans.

ae Mharattas disallowed ...
e peace, and behaved with the
elty. Before the 28th of May,
s taken by Tippoo Saib. His army
more than one hundred thousand
er surrendering, on condition of
onours of war, he forced the gar-
down their arms. Accounts of
urope were then received. Sir Eyre
at Madras on the 26th of April.
been another drawn action between
nd Sir Edward Hughes. General
as before Cuddalore, when he recei-
gence of the news of Peace in Europe.
e intelligence was received by the
with the greatest alarm: for though
of France had effected nothing, the
gement of affairs in the country had
ly left our whole possessions on the
destruction. The dispatches are
th the mutual accusations of the se-
mmanders.
following, as a true state of the news
dia, is sent to us by a gentleman who
sent in the General Court when it
d, and pledges himself for the truth
Sir Eyre Coote arrived at Madras in
with ten lacks of rupees, from Bengal,
aving been chased by four French ships:
most unfortunately, this old hero died
ays after he landed. The grand army
Coast of Coromandel, after Tippo Sa-
quitted the Carnatic, marched to at-
he French troops at Cuddalore: they
orced the outworks, and there was no
of their success against the place, when
igence arrived at Cuddalore of the peace,
hen all hostilities ceased. There was an
n between the two fleets in June, but

... on the shoulders of Mr. Fox: and ...
bour is indeed Herculean.

TO BE SOLD,

By PUBLIC VENDUE,

At the AMERICAN Coffee-House,
In State-Street,

On THURSDAY next, 22d Inst.

THE GOOD BRIGANTINE

VICTORY,

Burthen 120 Tons, more or less,
European built, and well found as she came
from Sea, with all her Appurtenances.

N. B. Said BRIGANTINE now lying at
Governor HANCOCK's Wharf.

The SALE beginning at ONE o'Clock.

The INVENTORY to be seen any time
before the Sale, at JOHN JUTAU's Office in
State Street.

BRIG NEW-YORK PACQUET.

THE brig NEW YORK PACQUET,
WILLIAM MORTON, Master, will sail
with all possible dispatch, for NEW-YORK.

For FREIGHT or PASSAGE, apply to the
Master on board, at GRAY's wharf; or at
WILLIAM SHATTUCK's store, in State-street.

N. B.—Said BRIG has excellent accommodations for PASSENGERS.

BOSTON, January 16, 1784.

Having ...
this new world--having taught a lesson ...
ful to those who inflict, and to those who feel
oppression, you retire from the great theatre
of action with the blessings of your fellow
citizens. But the *glory* of your virtues will
not terminate with your military command--
it will continue to animate remotest ages.

We feel with you our obligations to the army in general, and will particularly charge
ourselves with the interest of those confidential officers who have attended your person to
this affecting moment.

We join with you in commending the interests of our dearest country to the protection
of Almighty God, beseeching him to dispose
the hearts and minds of its citizens to improve the opportunity afforded them of becoming a happy and respectable nation.--And
for *You*, we address to *Him* our warmest prayers, that a life so beloved, may be fostered
with all his *care*---that your days may be
happy as they have been *illustrious*, and that
he will finally give you that reward which
this world cannot give.

Extract from the Minutes,
CHARLES THOMSON, Secretary.

Here we must let fall the scene---few tragedies ever drew more tears from so many
beautiful eyes, as were affected by the moving
manner in which his Excellency took his final
leave of Congress. After which he immediately set out for Virginia, accompanied ...
South river by his Excellency ou...
with the warmest wishes of the ...
repose, health, and happiness ...
may be enjoy them!

CHAPTER XIII

DELIVERED WITH ELOQUENCE

Introduction

As British troops and Loyalists evacuated key port towns, peace negotiations in Paris delivered a treaty containing several favorable terms for America. With American independence officially recognized, all eyes turned to the commander in chief, George Washington, who resigned his commission, retired to his farm home at Mount Vernon, Virginia, and formally concluded the Revolution. His return to civilization was a powerful gesture of character and leadership that helped build the foundation for a new nation.

American Herald (Boston)
January 19, 1784

General George Washington
Resigning His Commission
Architect of the Capitol

REPORTING THE

PERILS OF PEACE

By Thomas Fleming

MAKING PEACE TURNED OUT TO BE ALMOST AS DIFficult as making war. The instructions a supine Congress sent to Europe—that American negotiators were to do nothing without the consent of France—put Benjamin Franklin and his two associates, John Jay and John Adams, in a dangerous bind. France had her own territorial goals, mostly in the West Indies. Spanish politicians were making noises about claiming control of the Mississippi and title to all the territory between the Allegheny Mountains and the great river.

Franklin, who conducted the first round of negotiations alone early in July 1782, had no intention of playing second fiddle to the French, no matter what Congress said. He had declared the year prior that he would never sell a drop of the Mississippi. "A neighbor might as well ask me to sell my street door," he said. Moreover, his relationship with the French foreign minister, the Count de Vergennes, was good. When he told the Count that he was going to try for the best possible bargain with the British, Vergennes made no objection.

The seventy-six-year-old American ambassador's opening gambit was nothing short of breathtaking. He informed the chief British negotiator that there were four necessary articles to the treaty of peace: (1) Recognition of American independence and the withdrawal of all British troops. (2) An agreement on the Mississippi as the western boundary, plus the right to use the river. (3) A return of the Canadian boundary to the Great Lakes. (4) The right of Americans to fish in freedom and safety on the Newfoundland Grand Banks. To these four, Franklin added several "advisable" articles—the chief one being the cession of Canada to the United States. He also urged the British to issue a public apology to the people of the United States to restore genuine peace between the two nations.

Franklin, who conducted the first round of negotiations alone early in July 1782, had no intention of playing second fiddle to the French, no matter what Congress said. He had declared the year prior that he would never sell a drop of the Mississippi.

When Jay and Adams entered the negotiations, matters grew confused. Both suspected the French to the point of paranoia, and this inspired the English to drag their feet and try one last time to divide the two allies. During this wasted interval, victories on distant fronts toughened the British stand. In mid-September 1782, the garrison of Gibraltar beat off a combined Spanish-French assault. In the West Indies, the British thrashed Admiral de Grasse's fleet and captured the admiral.

The revitalized British brushed aside the idea of apologizing for the war, refused to cede Canada, insisted on the payment of all prewar American debts to British merchants, and demanded compensation for the Loyalists whose homes and property had been seized by the rebels. The Americans conceded Canada and the debts, but reimbursing the Loyalists was unacceptable. Franklin maintained they deserved nothing. They had gambled their estates against the rebels' estates and lost. The negotiations teetered toward stalemate.

Franklin proposed requiring Parliament to compensate the Americans for all the seaports the British Navy had burned and for the hundreds of houses their troops had plundered in the previous six years.

The king's negotiators swallowed hard and agreed to a compromise. Congress would ask the states to make some compensation to Loyalists who did not bear arms in the war. At this point, the bankrupt Congress's influence with the states was close to zero. It was a gesture that meant nothing, and everyone knew it.

With the terms settled, the Americans signed the agreement on November 30, 1782, without consulting the French. This was perilously close to violating the terms of America's treaty with France and unquestionably ignored the instructions from Congress. Jay and Adams exulted over this display of American independence. Ambassador Franklin had the task of soothing the Count de Vergennes's extremely ruffled feathers. He not only managed this feat with finesse, but also persuaded the irked foreign minister to agree to one last loan to keep the penniless American government afloat.

On January 20, 1783, the French and the British agreed on terms. Vergennes, pointedly reminding Franklin of the courtesy the Americans had not offered him, invited the ambassador to sign the document with him. Franklin swallowed the rebuke and signed without a murmur. Only one thing mattered to him: the war was over. Later that day, when he arrived at the home of the Duc de la Rochefoucauld for dinner, he threw his arms around this staunch supporter of America and exclaimed, "My friend, could I have hoped, at my age, to enjoy such happiness?"

Independent Ledger (Boston), August 18, 1783
Todd Andrlik

This engraving of thirteen hands grasping one ring adorns the masthead of the *Independent Ledger* and is accompanied by the slogan "All Hands With One Inflamed Enlightened Heart."

France
Spain &
The United States —

THURSDAY, APRIL 10, 1783.

THE Pennsylvania Packet, OR, THE GENERAL ADVERTISER.

VOL. XII.] PUBLISHED EVERY TUESDAY, THURSDAY AND SATURDAY.—Price SIX-PENCE. [NUMB. 1026.

By the February Packet from Falmouth, the ship Vigilant from London, and other late arrivals at New-York from Europe, we have British Prints to the beginning of February, from which the following are taken—

Authentic Copies OF THE PRELIMINARY ARTICLES OF PEACE, BETWEEN His Britannic Majesty, the Most Christian King, His Most Catholic Majesty, and The United States of America.

Signed at Versailles, the 20th of January, 1783.

Translation of the Preliminary Articles of Peace, between His Britannic Majesty and the Most Christian King; signed at Versailles the 20th of January, 1783.

In the Name of the Most Holy TRINITY.

THE KING of GREAT-BRITAIN and the MOST CHRISTIAN KING, equally animated with a desire of putting an end to the calamities of a destructive war, and of re-establishing union and good understanding between them, as necessary for the good of mankind in general as for that of their respective kingdoms, states and subjects, have named for this purpose, viz. on the part of his Britannic Majesty Mr. Alleyne Fitz-Herbert, Minister Plenipotentiary of his said Majesty the King of Great Britain; and on the part of His Most Christian Majesty, Charles Gravier, Comte de Vergennes, Counsellor in all his councils, Commander of his Orders, Counsellor of State, Minister and Secretary of State, and of the Commands and Finances of his said Majesty, for the department of Foreign Affairs; who, after having duly communicated to each other their full powers in good form, have agreed on the following Preliminary

Art. 7. The King of Great Britain shall restore to France the island of St. Lucia, and shall cede and guarantee to her that of Tobago.

Art. 8. The Most Christian King shall restore to Great Britain the islands of Grenada and the Grenadines, St. Vincent, Dominica, St. Christopher's, Nevis, and Montserrat; and the fortresses of those islands conquered by the arms of Great Britain and by those of France, shall be restored in the same condition in which they were when the conquest of them was made, provided that the term of eighteen months, to be computed from the time of the ratification of the definitive treaty, shall be granted to the respective subjects of the Crowns of Great Britain and France, who may have settled in the said islands, and in other places which shall be restored by the definitive treaty, to sell their estates, recover their debts, and to transport their effects and retire without being restrained, on account of their religion, or any other whatever, except in cases of debt or of criminal prosecutions.

Art. 9. The King of Great Britain shall cede and guarantee in full right to his Most Christian Majesty the river of Senegal and its dependencies, with the forts of St. Louis, Podor, Galam, Arguin and Portendu. His Britannic Majesty shall restore, likewise, the island of Goree, which shall be given up in the condition in which it was when the British arms took possession of it.

Art. 10. The Most Christian King shall on his side, guarantee to his Majesty, the King of Great Britain, the possession of Fort James, and of the river Gambia.

Art. 11. In order to prevent all discussions in that part of the world, the two Courts shall agree, either by the definitive treaty, or by a separate act, upon the boundaries to be fixed to their respective [...] The gum trade shall be carried on in future as [...] and French nations carried it on before the [...]

Art. 12. In regard to the rest of the coast [...] ca, the subjects of both powers shall conti[...] quent them, according to the custom whi[...] vailed hitherto.

Art. 13. The King of Great-Britain shal[...] His Most Christian Majesty all the esta[...] which belonged to him at the commencem[...] present war on the coast of Orixa, and in Be[...] liberty to surround Chandernagor with [...] draining the waters; and his Britannic Maje[...] to take such measures as may be in his power for [...] curing to the subjects of France, in that part of India, as also on the coast of Orixa, Coromandel, and Malabar, a safe, free, and independent trade, such as was carried on by the late French East India Company, whether it be carried on by them as individuals or as a company.

Art. 14. Pondicherry, as well as Karical, shall likewise be restored, and guaranteed to France; and

Majesty, or by those of his Most Christian Majesty, and which are not included in the present articles, shall be restored without difficulty, and without requiring compensation.

Art. 20. As it is necessary to assign a fixed epoch for the restitutions and the evacuations to be made by each of the high contracting parties, it is agreed, that the King of Great-Britain shall cause to be evacuated the Islands of St. Pierre and Miquelon, three months after the ratification of the definitive treaty, or sooner if it can be done; St. Lucia in the West-Indies, and Goree in Africa, three months after the ratification of the definitive treaty, or sooner if it can be done. The king of Great Britain shall, in like manner, at the end of three months after the ratification of the definitive treaty, or sooner if it can be done, enter again into possession of the Islands of Grenada, the Grenadines, St. Vincent, Dominica, St. Christopher's, Nevis, and Montserrat.

France shall be put into possession of the towns and comptoirs, which are restored to her in the East-Indies, and of the territories which are procured for her, to serve as dependencies round Pondicherry, and round Karical, six Months after the ratification of the definitive Treaty, or sooner if it can be done.

France shall at the end of the same term of six months, restore the towns and territories which her arms may have taken from the English or their allies in the East-Indies.

In consequence whereof, the necessary orders shall be sent by each of the high contracting parties, with reciprocal passports for the ships which shall carry them, immediately after the ratification of the defini-[...]

[...]ly by the [...] Christian [...]ed recipro-[...]ratification [...]nd on pay-[...]uring their [...] reimburse [...]r the sub-[...] by the So-[...]e been de-[...]d accounts, [...]oduced on [...]each side.

Translation of the Preliminary Articles of Peace, between His Britannic Majesty and the Most Catholic King; signed at Versailles the 20th of January, 1783.

In the Name of the Most Holy TRINITY.

THE King of Great Britain and the King of Spain, equally animated with a desire of putting an end to the calamities of a destructive war, and of re-establishing union and good understanding between them, as necessary for the good of mankind in general, as for that of their respective kingdoms, states, and sub-

Art. 22. In order to prevent all causes of complaint and dispute which may arise on account of prizes which may be made at Sea after the signing of these preliminary articles, it is reciprocally agreed, that the vessels and effects which may be taken in the Channel and the North Seas, after the space of twelve days, to be computed from the ratification of the present preliminary articles, shall be restored on each

PENNSYLVANIA PACKET (PHILADELPHIA)

April 10, 1783

The January 20, 1783, preliminary terms of peace between Great Britain and France, and Great Britain and Spain, were shipped across the Atlantic and published in American newspapers, such as the April 10, 1783, issue of the *Pennsylvania Packet*, which also reprinted the November 30, 1782, terms with America. The treaty with the United States was approved by the Congress of the Confederation on April 15, 1783, signed in Paris on September 3, and ratified by Congress on January 14, 1784, to officially conclude the American Revolutionary War.

Torres, of Villan[...] Yoch; Baron of [...] mola, Enipol, Tr[...] Antillon, La Alm[...] bovillet; Oreau, [...] the Tenance, and [...] Rodellar, the Caſt[...] Tiurana, de Villa[...] Rico Hombre in [...] of the firſt Claſs, [...] Fleece, and of th[...] the King's Bed-ch[...] neral of his Armies [...] Chriſtian Majeſty, wi[...] cated to each other their full powers in good form, have agreed on the following Preliminary Articles:

Art. 1. AS ſoon as the Preliminaries ſhall be ſigned and ratified, ſincere friendſhip ſhall be eſtabliſhed between his Britannic Majeſty and his Catholic Majeſty, their kingdoms, ſtates and ſubjects, by ſea and by land, in all parts of the world Orders ſhall be ſent to the armies and ſquadrons, as well as to the ſubjects of the two powers, to ſtop all hoſtilities, and to live in the moſt perfect union, forgetting what has paſſed, of which their Sovereigns give them the order and example, and for the execution of this article, ſea paſſes ſhall be given on each ſide for the ſhips which ſhall be diſpatched to carry the news of it to the poſſeſſions of the ſaid Powers.

Art. 2. His Catholic Majeſty ſhall keep the iſland of Minorca.

Art. 3. His Britannic Majeſty ſhall cede to his Catholic Majeſty Eaſt Florida, and his Catholic Majeſty ſhall keep Weſt Florida, provided that the term of eighteen months, to be computed from the time of the ratification of the Definitive Treaty, ſhall be granted to the ſubjects of his Britannic Majeſty who are ſettled as well in the iſland of Minorca as in the two Floridas, to ſell their eſtates, recover their debts, and to tranſport their effects, as well as their perſons, without being reſtrained on account of their religion, or under any other pretence whatſoever, except that of debts and criminal proſecutions; and his Britannic Majeſty ſhall have power to cauſe all the effects that may belong to him in Eaſt Florida, whether artillery or others, to be carried away.

Art. 4. His Catholic Majeſty ſhall not for the future, ſuffer the ſubjects of his Britannic Majeſty, or their workmen, to be diſturbed or moleſted, under any pretence whatſoever, in their occupation of cutting, loading and carrying away logwood, in a diſtrict of which the boundaries ſhall be fixed, and for this purpoſe they may build without hindrance, and occupy without interruption, the houſes and magazines neceſſary for them, for their families and for their effects, in a place to be agreed upon, either in the definitive treaty, or within ſix months after the exchange of the ratifications; and his ſaid Catholic Majeſty aſſures to them, by this article, the entire enjoyment of what is above ſtipulated; provided that theſe ſtipulations ſhall not be conſidered as derogatory in any reſpect from the rights of his ſovereignty.

Art. 5. His Catholic Majeſty ſhall reſtore to Great-Britain, the Iſlands of Providence and the Bahamas, without exception in the ſame condition in which they were, when they were conquered by the arms of the King of Spain.

Art. 6. All the countries and territories which may have been, or may be conquered in any part of the world whatſoever, by the arms of his Britannic Majeſty, or by thoſe of his Catholic Majeſty, and which are not included in our preſent articles, ſhall be reſtored without difficulty, and without requiring compenſations.

Art. 7. By the definitive Treaty, all thoſe which have exiſted till now between the two High contracting parties, and which ſhall not be derogated from either by the ſaid Treaty, or by the preſent Preliminary Treaty, ſhall be renewed and confirmed; and the two Courts ſhall name Commiſſioners to enquire into the ſtate of the commerce between the two nations, in order to agree upon new arrangements of trade, on the footing of reciprocity and mutual convenience; and the two ſaid Courts ſhall [...]

Done at Verſailles, the 20th day January, 1783.

ALLEYNE FITZ-HERBERT, (L. S.)
LE COMTE D'ARANDA, (L. S.)

Articles agreed upon by and between Richard Oſwald, eſquire, the Commiſſioner of his Britannic Majeſty, for treating of Peace with the Commiſſioners of the United States of America, in behalf of his ſaid Majeſty, on the one part, and John Adams, Benjamin Franklin, John Jay, and Henry Laurens, four of the Commiſſioners of the ſaid States for treating of Peace with the Commiſſioner of his ſaid Majeſty, on their behalf, on the other part; to be inſerted in and to conſtitute the Treaty of Peace propoſed to be concluded between the Crown of Great Britain and the ſaid United States; but which Treaty is not to be concluded until terms of a Peace ſhall be agreed upon between Great Britain and France; and his Britannic Majeſty ſhall be ready to conclude ſuch Treaty accordingly.

WHEREAS reciprocal advantages and mutual convenience are found by experience to form the only permanent foundation of peace and friendſhip between States, it is agreed to form the Articles of the propoſed Treaty on ſuch principles of liberal equity and reciprocity, as that partial advantages, thoſe ſeeds of diſcord, being excluded, ſuch a beneficial and ſatisfactory intercourſe between the two countries may be eſtabliſhed as to promiſe and ſecure to both perpetual peace and harmony.

Art. 1. His Britannic Majeſty acknowledges the ſaid United States, viz. New-Hampſhire, Maſſachuſetts-Bay, Rhode-Iſland and Providence Plantations, Connecticut, New-York, New-Jerſey, Pennſylvania, Delaware, Maryland, Virginia, North Carolina, South Carolina, and Georgia, to be Free, Sovereign, and Independent States: that he treats with them as ſuch; and for himſelf, his heirs and ſucceſſors, relinquiſhes all claim to the government, proprietary, and territorial rights of the ſame, and every part thereof: and that all diſputes which might ariſe in future, on the ſubject of the boundaries of the ſaid United States, may be prevented, it is hereby agreed and declared, that the following are and ſhall be their boundaries, viz.

Art. 2. From the north weſt angle of Nova Scotia, viz. that angle which is formed by a line drawn due north from the ſource of Saint Croix River to the Highlands; along the ſaid iſlands, which divide thoſe rivers that empty themſelves into the River Saint Laurence from thoſe which fall into the Atlantic Ocean, to the north-weſternmoſt head of Connecticut River, thence down along the middle of that river to the forty-fifth degree of north latitude, from thence by a line due weſt on ſaid latitude, until it ſtrikes the River Iroquois or Cataraquy; thence along the middle of ſaid river into Lake Ontario, through the middle of ſaid lake, until it ſtrikes the communication by water between that lake and Lake Erie; thence along the middle of ſaid communication into Lake Erie, through the middle of ſaid lake until it arrives at the water communication between that lake and Lake Huron; thence along the middle of ſaid water communication into the Lake Huron; thence through the middle of ſaid lake to the water communication between that lake and Lake Superior; thence through Lake Superior, northward of the Iſles, Royal and Phelipeaux, to the Long Lake, thence through the middle of ſaid Long Lake, and the water communication between it and the Lake of the Woods, to the ſaid Lake of the Woods; [...]

[...] States, to provide for the reſtitution of all eſtates, rights, and properties, which have been confiſcated, belonging to real Britiſh ſubjects, and alſo of the eſtates, rights, and properties of perſons reſident in diſtricts, in the poſſeſſion of his Majeſty's arms, and who have not borne arms againſt the ſaid United States. And that perſons of any other deſcription ſhall have free liberty to go into any part or parts of any of the Thirteen United States, and therein to remain twelve months unmoleſted in their endeavours to obtain the reſtitution of ſuch of their eſtates, rights, and properties, as may have been confiſcated; and that Congreſs ſhall alſo earneſtly recommend to the ſeveral States a reconſideration and reviſion of all acts or laws regarding the premiſes, ſo as to render the ſaid laws or acts perfectly conſiſtent, not only with juſtice and equity, but with that ſpirit of conciliation, which on the return of the bleſſings of peace ſhould univerſally prevail. And that Congreſs ſhall alſo earneſtly recommend to the ſeveral States, that the eſtates, rights, and properties of ſuch laſt mentioned perſons ſhall be reſtored to them; they refunding to any perſons who may be now in poſſeſſion the bona fide price (where any has been given) which ſuch perſons may have paid on purchaſing any of the ſaid lands or properties ſince the confiſcation.

And it is agreed, That all perſons who have any intereſt in confiſcated lands, either by debts, marriage ſettlements, or otherwiſe, ſhall meet with no lawful impediment in the proſecution of their juſt rights.

Art. 6. That there ſhall be no future confiſcations made, nor any proſecutions commenced againſt any perſon or perſons for or by reaſon of the part which he or they may have taken in the preſent war; and that no perſon ſhall, on that account, ſuffer any future loſs or damage, either in his perſon, liberty, or property, and that thoſe who may be in confinement on ſuch charges, at the time of the ratification of the Treaty in America, ſhall be immediately ſet at liberty, and the proſecutions ſo commenced be diſcontinued.

Art. 7. There ſhall be a firm and perpetual peace between his Britannic Majeſty and the ſaid States, and between the ſubjects of the one and the citizens of the other, wherefore all hoſtilities both by ſea and land ſhall then immediately ceaſe: all priſoners on both ſides ſhall be ſet at liberty, and his Britannic Majeſty ſhall, with all convenient ſpeed, and without cauſing any deſtruction, or carrying away any negroes, or other property of the American inhabitants, withdraw all his armies, garriſons, and fleets from the ſaid United States, and from every port, place, and harbour within the ſame; leaving in all fortifications the American artillery that may be therein: and ſhall alſo order, and cauſe all archives, records, deeds, and papers, belonging to any of the ſaid States, or their citizens, which in the courſe of the war may have fallen into the hands of his officers, to be forthwith reſtored and delivered to the proper States and perſons to whom they belong.

Art. 8. The navigation of the Miſſiſſippi, from its ſource to the ocean, ſhall for ever remain free and open to the ſubjects of Great-Britain and the citizens of the United States.

Art. 9. In caſe it ſhould ſo happen, that any place or territory belonging to Great-Britain or to the United States, ſhould be conquered by the arms of either from the other, before the arrival of theſe articles in America, it is agreed, that the ſame ſhall be reſtored without difficulty, and without requiring any compenſation.

Done at Paris, the thirtieth day of November, in [...]

Last boat of British troops leaving New York City, 1783
North Wind Picture Archives

Along with British troops, some 29,200 Loyalist refugees evacuated New York, scattering far and wide.

REPORTING THE

BRITISH AND LOYALIST EVACUATIONS OF AMERICA

By Dennis M. Conrad

As can be seen from the newspaper articles printed here, British evacuation of its remaining outposts in the United States was a complex and protracted operation complicated by poor planning on the part of the British ministry, lack of adequate shipping, and the large number of white and black Loyalists and slaves (estimates range from fifty thousand to one hundred thousand—roughly 2 to 3 percent of the population of the United States) that swelled the ranks of those needing transportation. As a result, evacuation dates that were initially set ended up being pushed back for months, and plans that were made initially, such as to evacuate St. Augustine in 1782, were cancelled.

Nonetheless, despite mutual frustration, the handover was done peacefully. The guarantee given by General Anthony Wayne concerning the evacuation of Savannah, which is published in the *Pennsylvania Packet* (August 3, 1782), included an agreement not to attack the retreating British troops. This arrangement was duplicated when Charleston and New York were evacuated so that the turnover of power was done peacefully and order was maintained so there was no looting or civil disturbance.

In defense of the British, a large number of Loyalists chose to leave the United States, which greatly complicated the evacuation process. This outflow of Loyalists was a product of their concern that they would be punished, either personally or through confiscation of their property, by the victorious state governments. For example, Anthony Wayne, in addition to the guarantee he gave to British merchants in Savannah that is published in the August 3, 1782, *Pennsylvania Packet*, issued a proclamation granting amnesty to all Loyalists, except murderers, if those Loyalists would agree to serve in the Georgia Continental line for two years. The Georgia legislature initially agreed to accept this policy but then quickly reneged on it. The Georgia lawmakers were not, in the words of a Wayne biographer, willing to allow "bygones be bygones, as Wayne wished." The passions created by years of civil war were too great to be smoothed over by "easy proclamation."

As a result of such attitudes, which were to be found in every state, Loyalists felt compelled to flee. Some 6,600 Georgia Loyalists and their slaves sought transportation, an estimated 9,127 people (including 5,333 slaves) had to be transported from Charleston, and some 29,200 refugees left New York. These refugees scattered far and wide. Most went to Canada, particularly New Brunswick and Nova Scotia, but others went to Bermuda, to the British Caribbean Islands, especially Jamaica, to England, to East and West Florida (until the Spanish took possession of those territories shortly after the war), and even to the British colony of Sierra Leone in Africa.

It was this outflow of humanity that slowed and complicated the evacuation process. While the author of the "Evacuation Anecdote" published in the *American Herald* (February 16, 1784) could congratulate America on the conduct of its citizens during the turnover of power and argue that it demonstrated the superiority of the American system, the process could have been much quicker and easier had Americans truly practiced the "Clemency and generosity" that the writer claims for them.

AUGUST 3, 1782

The PENNSYLVANIA PACKET

Philadelphia, August 3.

The ship Nonsuch, captain Wells, is arrived in our river from Nantz, which she left about the middle of June. By her we have European papers as late as the 1st of June, from which the most material articles are copied into this paper.

Yesterday morning the brig Mercury, captain Faris, arrived here from Bilboa, after a passage of 50 days. At the time of her sailing a large fleet of French and Spanish ships lay in the bay of Cadiz with a body of 8000 French and 22000 Spanish troops, commanded by the duke de Crillon. This powerful armament was destined for a fresh attack upon Gibraltar, a new plan having been adopted for carrying on the siege of that fortress, which it was not doubted would finally be compelled to surrender.

Besides the account given in our last, of the evacuation of Savannah, we have the pleasure of assuring our readers, that the garrison had arrived at Charlestown before some persons (who arrived in town yesterday from that place, by way of a flag) left it, which was on the 11th ult. They also say, that St. Augustine was certainly abandoned by the enemy.

In addition to the above article our informant says, that a number of heavy cannon, &c. were embarked on board some vessels in Charlestown harbour, and that every appearance indicated a speedy removal of all the British forces from the quarter.

On Tuesday last a court of oyer and terminer, and general gaol delivery, was opened at Newtown, for the county of Bucks, when John Lowright and Jesse Lowright was brought to trial, but acquitted, notwithstanding direct and positive proof, that he was one of the burglars, strong evidence being adduced on his part, that he was at another place when the offence was committed. Next day Vickars was convicted on the full and satisfactory testimony of two persons of undoubted character, although there was an attempt to support an ALIBI in this café also. The persons, whose houses had been broke open were, in both instances, collectors of the public taxes. It is hoped that the conviction of Vickars will curb the disaffected, and disappoint the base arts by which our enemy carries on the war against us.

The following is said to be a copy of an application from some persons in Savannah, to brigadier general Wayne; and of his answer.

SIR,

AS there is reason to believe it is the intention of the British troops to evacuate the town and garrison of Savannah. We are deputed by different classes of inhabitants to wait upon you, as the commander of the army, and also governor Martin, to know whether such of them as are inclined to remain will be protected in their persons and properties, and for more fully discusing this business, we are entrusted with the honour of requesting a conference.

We have the honour &c.

JNO IRVINE,
ANDREW M'LEAN,
JNO WALLACE,
HENRY KEALL,
LD. CECILL.

General WAYNE.

ANSWER.

Should the garrison eventually effect an evacuation, the persons and properties of such inhabitants, or others as chuse to remain in Savannah will be protected by the military, and resigned inviolate to the hands of the civil authority of this state which must ultimately decide.

Given at Head-Quarters, 17th June, 1782.

PENNSYLVANIA PACKET (PHILADELPHIA)

August 3, 1782

The guarantee given by Gen. Anthony Wayne concerning the evacuation of Savannah, which is published in the *Pennsylvania Packet*, included an agreement not to attack the retreating British troops. This arrangement was duplicated when Charleston and New York were evacuated so that the turnover of power was done peacefully.

---

and the Ruſſian plenipotentiary at the Hague. It was then thought proper, under a plauſible pretext to ſend to Paris the honourable Mr T. Grenville, who is now there, continually receives and diſpatches meſſengers, relative to that great affair.

The 12th inſt. Mr. Laurens left England. He is ſuppoſed to be now near the place where the negociations are to be deciſive. It is ſaid they are on the following terms:

All our iſlands, that of Grenada excepted, ſhall be reſtitured by France, which ſhall again be in poſſeſſion of St. Lucia, Pondicherry, and all her other ſettlements in India.

Minorca to be ceded to Spain, who ſhall give us Porto Rico, renounce her pretenſions to Jamaica, in conſideration of which ſhe ſhall be put in full poſſeſſion of Gibraltar.

Florida to be ceded to the Americans.

We ſhall reſtitute to the Dutch all their poſſeſſions taken during the war, and ſecure to them the exerciſe of a free and neutral trade, on the terms of the armed neutrality.

America will be granted her independency, and a general liberty of trade. England on her part will equally divide with her the fiſheries of Newfoundland and New-England; preſerve the peaceable poſſeſſion of Canada to its old limits, and all the lands to the northward of that province. We ſhall, in conſequence of this give up New-York to the Americans, and whatever we poſſeſs to the ſouthward.

Lord Keppel moved yeſterday in the houſe of peers, a vote of thanks to admiral Rodney. It paſſed unanimouſly; but lord Sandwich ſeized this opportunity for obſerving, that the ſervices done the country by this fortunate commander, were not due to the new adminiſtration, which, far from acknowledging them, did in a manner puniſh the author of them by recalling him. He demanded lord Keppel's declaration of the motive for that recall; but this firſt lord of the admiralty refuſed complying.

May 29. The king has created ſir George B. Rodney, baronet and knight of the Bath, barron of the kingdom of Great-Britain, under the ſtile of baron Rodney, of Rodney Stoke, in Somerſetſhire; and ſir F. S. Drake, baronet of Great-Britain; as alſo captain Edmund Afflick. The king has likewiſe created ſir Samuel Hood, baronet, an Iriſh peer, under the title of baron Hood, of Cathrington.

The kings of France and Sardinia have ſent troops to Geneva, to reſtore public tranquility in that unfortunate republic; and at the ſame time took the moſt effectual ſteps to perſuade the Halvetic body that it was not their intention to make any attempt on the independence of that city.

General Monckton, governor of Portſmouth, died 23d May. Lord George Lenox is to ſucceed him.

All the meaſures of the new adminiſtration are equally oppoſed; that, for inſtance, which puts arms into the hands of the people, has occaſioned the following paragraph: "When it was propoſed to a certain great perſonage to arm the people, he diſcovered the greateſt repugnance, and made the moſt ſenſible repreſentations againſt it. The chancellor declared, he conſidered that meaſure as the moſt proper for deſtroying the very foundation of government: he obſerved, that the loſs of America had been effected by armed aſſociations; that with the ſame aſſiſtance Ireland had diſengaged herſelf from all her connections with England, except thoſe which ſuited her; and that from the ſame cauſes, the ſame effects ought to be expected from England. The majority carried it in the council, and the king's acquieſcence was founded but on the hopes of ſeeing the plan miſcarry."

It is ſaid lord North has been ſomewhat nigardly in arranging the prince of Wales's ſettlement; that young dauphin of England, who is doubtleſs more taken up with his pleaſures than politics, is ſuppoſed to tread in the ſteps of his predeceſſors; to have the ſame principles, and holding neceſſarily, by his ſituation, to the whig party. The better to keep him in ſuch pretended diſpoſitions, it is given out that the new miniſtry out-bid each other for him.

The marquis of Rockingham, ſay they, is for ſettling upon him an yearly income of 30,000l. ſterling. Lord Shelburne would have him to be allowed 45,000l.

G E N E V A, May 10.

By advices from Turin we learn, that a body of 4500 Sardinian forces, to be joined by 6000 French, are on their march to quell the diſorders in this city. This has raiſed great ... are leaving this plac... lar party are prepari... have begun to repair... &c. The ſituation ...

Philadelp...

The ſhip Nonſuch ... river from Nantz, w... June. By her we ha... 1ſt of June, from wh... copied into this pape...

Yeſterday mornin... ris, arrived here from... At the time of her ... Spaniſh ſhips lay in th... French and 22000 S... duke de Crillon. Th... ed for a freſh attack upo... been adopted for carrying on the ſiege of that fortreſs, which it was not doubted would finally be compelled to ſurrender.

Beſides the account given in our laſt, of the evacuation of Savannah, we have the pleaſure of aſſuring our readers, that the garriſon had arrived at Charleſtown before ſome perſons (who arrived in town yeſterday from that place, by way of a flag) left it, which was on the 11th ult. They alſo ſay, that St. Auguſtine was certainly abandoned by the enemy.

In addition to the above article our informant ſays, that a number of heavy cannon, &c. were embarked on board ſome veſſels in Charleſtown harbour, and that every appearance indicated a ſpeedy removal of all the Britiſh forces from that quarter.

On Tueſday laſt a court of oyer and terminer, and general gaol delivery, was opened at Newtown, for the county of Bucks, when John Lowright and Jeſſe Vickars were indicted for burglary. On Wedneſday Lowright was brought to trial, but acquitted, notwithſtanding direct and poſitive proof, that he was one of the burglars, ſtrong evidence being adduced on his part, that he was at another place when the offence was committed. Next day Vickars was convicted on the full and ſatisfactory teſtimony of two perſons of undoubted character, although there was an attempt to ſupport an ALIBI in this caſe alſo. The perſons, whoſe houſes had been broke open were, in both inſtances, collectors of the public taxes. It is hoped that the conviction of Vickars will curb the diſaffected, and diſappoint the baſe arts by which our enemy carries on the war againſt us.

The following is ſaid to be a copy of an application from ſome perſons in Savannah, to brigadier general Wayne; and of his anſwer.

S I R,

AS there is reaſon to believe it is the intention of the Britiſh troops to evacuate the town and garriſon of Savannah. We are deputed by different claſſes of the inhabitants to wait upon you, as the commander of the army, and alſo governor Martin, to know whether ſuch of them as are inclined to remain will be protected in their perſons and properties, and for more fully diſcuſſing this buſineſs, we are entruſted with the honour of requeſting a conference.

We have the honour &c.

JNO. IRVINE,
ANDREW M'LEAN,
JNO. WALLACE,
HENRY KEALL,
LD. CECILL.

General WAYNE.

A N S W E R.

Should the garriſon eventually effect an evacuation, the perſons and properties of ſuch inhabitants, or others as chuſe to remain in Savannah will be protected by the military, and reſigned inviolate to the hands of the civil authority of this ſtate which muſt ultimately decide.

Given at Head-Quarters, 17th June, 1782.

The plague alſo rages at Angora, a city much connected in trade with Europe, from whence great quantities of yarn are imported via Smyrna.

AMERICAN HERALD (BOSTON)

February 16, 1784

While the author of the "Evacuation Anecdote" published in the *American Herald* could congratulate America on the conduct of its citizens during the turnover of power and argue that it demonstrated the superiority of the American system, the process could have been much quicker and easier had Americans truly practiced the "Clemency and generosity" that the writer claims for them.

oner, who had the *fortitude* to walk knee deep into the water, and then returned, having entirely ungarbed himſelf, on purpoſe to avoid the fury of a diſappointed rabble; however, a *lucky* brick-bat reached his head as he was getting into a boat, which had an *excellent* effect, its *ruby infuſion* being the only ſport left for the ſpectators.

Mangalore, which, according to the late overland expreſs from the Eaſt Indies, has been taken by the Eaſt India company's forces, under the command of Gen. Matthews and Col. M'Leod, is on the Malabar coaſt, about 50 leagues to the Southward of Onore, which was taken by ſtorm on the 5th of January laſt. Mangalore is one of the principal ſettlements in Heider Ali's country, but not his capital, which is called Seringa Patnam (an in land ſettlement) from which, however, it is diſtant only 60 miles. Before the Portugueſe eſtabliſhed themſelves at Goa, and made that ſettlement ſo capital, Mangalore was called the capital of the ancient kingdom of Viſiapoor, which is more than 300 miles in length. It lies in the ſame latitude as Madras, at oppoſite ſides of the peninſula of India, ſo that a line drawn from one to the other would paſs the heart of the country, the diſtance between them being upwards of 400 miles.

The Engliſh have had better ſucceſs againſt the Algerines than any of the other European powers. In 1655, the great admiral Blake entered their harbours, and deſtroyed their ſhips—in 1668 ſir Thomas Allen forced them to ſue for peace—in 1670 commodore Beach, with five men of war, engaged ſeven of their's, drove two of them on ſhore, and burnt the other five, clearing four hundred and thirty

him no information, threw it down with a ſmile. By this honeſt ſimplicity, which would have gained the affection of a generous mind, Father Vincenti was ſo enraged that he gave the word of command, crying out, "Kill
oot the word
could not
at indigna-
peared, that
rm exhibit-
that exe-
of a world
uffered as a
Such are
h fix an in-
eSpaniards,
has paſſed
s, that ſuch
oblivion, ra-
on they de-
able to the
e to embel-

pothecary who
o America, and who carried his medicinal bags on his ſhoulders from province to province, has lately made a claim on government for the loſs of poſſeſſion as a Loyaliſt to the amount of 16, 322l. The Commiſſioners, we underſtand, have allowed only the TWO POUNDS. The inveſtigation of the right of claimants is one of the beſt ſchemes ever adopted to get at the bottom of the fact; and it muſt turn out a ſaving to the kingdom that will aſtoniſh parliament, when they find how very much they have been impoſed upon in the diſtribution of the gratuities, and annual payments, to people calling themſelves Loyaliſts.

A M E R I C A.

NEW-YORK, January 15.

An EVACUATION ANECDOTE.

With ſome OCCASIONAL OBSERVATIONS.

A FEW days after the evacuation of New-York, and while the britiſh fleet, with the troops and refugees on board, lay within ſight of the city, a Britiſh officer was ſent on ſhore to remove ſome effects, which in the hurry of evacuation had been forgotten. Struck, no doubt, with the recollection of the tyrannical conduct of the Britiſh army for ſuch a length of time, and apprehenſive for his own ſafety, he applied to the government of the ſtate for a protection; and tho' he was told, that while he conducted himſelf peaceably and decently, he would meet with no ill uſage; he ſtill urged his requeſt, and to eaſe his fears, was I believe indulged with one.

... time of the evacuation, and the immediate repoſſeſſion of it by its exiled inhabitants, without experiencing a conflict of affecting paſſions. To ſee ſo many hundreds immediately happy, by a ſafe return to their long forſaken homes, and others made wretched by having new habitations to ſeek, in a comfortleſs region, and at a ſtormy ſeaſon, were circumſtances that by contraſting each other produced in the mind a diſquieting compound of joy and pity.

Diſtreſs in any ſhape it can be preſented to us, will in ſpite of reſentment find a way to ſoften it; and the difference between threatening revenge and acting it, is ſo exceedingly great, that thoſe who threaten the higheſt generally puniſh the leaſt.

A fallen enemy appears a different being to what he did before, and in our conqueſt over him, one half our reſentments are conquered with him.

Clemency and generoſity are as naturally the companions of a great mind, as revenge and cruelty are of a little one. The former diſdains to trample on the vanquiſhed, and the latter makes it his only ſcene of action. If we look into the characters that have been the moſt eminent throughout the whole of the conteſt, we ſhall find greatneſs and benevolence are united qualities. For the heart that can be generouſly warmed with the love and principles of liberty, feels its happineſs encreaſed, by ſharing it with the world.

COMMON SENSE.

WORCESTER, February 12.

Silas Deane, Eſq; has publiſhed at London, October 12th, 1783, "An addreſs to the free and independent citizens of the United States of North America;" in which Mr. Deane exhibits a ſtatement of his public accounts, and endeavours to wipe off the aſperſions thrown upon his character by his enemies.

It has been obſerved, that ſince the firſt ſettlement of this country, no two years have produced ſo many caſual deaths as the laſt twelve months: And it muſt wound the feelings of every rational being when he reflects that Unnatural and truly Horrible crime of SUICIDE has been more prevalent, not only in Europe, but in this Country, during the aforementioned period, than it has ever been remembered to be before in that ſpace of time.

By the ſouthern papers we learn, that ſome gentlemen in Trenton and Philadelphia, who have obſerved the Comet, ſuppoſe, that it is advancing towards the ſun, and that ſoon after its perihelion it will make a moſt ſplendid appearance in the morning before day break; but it is rather ſuppoſed by thoſe who have lately had an opportunity to obſerve it, that it has already paſt its perihelion, and is now on its receſs from the ſun.

forthwith, and lodged at the
Price, Eſq; in the State Hou
RICHARD C
(Agent fo
Braintree, February 9th, 1

TO BE SO
By JONAS MINOT, in
In the Maſſachuſ
NINETY thouſa
unimproved LAND
New-Hampſhire and
in Maſon, New-Ipſwich, Rin
Richmond, Marlborough, Du
Stoddard, Lyneſborough, Hil
Amherſt, Gofſtown, Notting
Bowwere, Newborton, Deari
Antrim, Waſhington, Bradfo
Goar, Kyahſavge-Goar, He
Saliſberry, Andover, New Ch
Alexandria, Grafton, Cardig
Lyme, Corniſh, Bath, Gunthw
Luningburg, Newbury, Put
Harwich, Glaſſenburg, and
Many Lots of which are kn
beſt quality, and ſundry lots
New-London, Maſon and P
der large and good improve
buildings, and are choice tav
Farm of 50 acres in Hollis,
meeting-houſe, choice land,
and a good orchard;——Al
Barn, &c. with ſix acres of
near Hollis meeting-houſe, b
for a trader or tavern, bot
formerly owned and occupie
WHITING, eſq; late of Holli
Alſo, a choice Farm of 100
and one of 120, in Concord,
ſetts, and ſundry other tracts
unimproved Lands, not here
Theſe Lands and Farms
ſonable for caſh, ſhort or lo
ſecurity, or country produc
thoſe lands will be ſold for i

THE Committee
receive the SUBSCRI
BANK, about to be eſtabliſh
—would inform the Gentle
that ſaid Committee are no
Buſineſs.
N. B. Said Committee
three or four IRON CHEST
Boſton, Feb 12, 1784.

WANTED in a ſmal
A WOMAN, who unde
and other Houſe Work
recommended, may hear of
Inquire of th
N. B. None other ne

christian slaves. The same year sir Edward Spragge destroyed nine of their ships near the castle of Burgia, in which conflict near 1800 of the Moors were killed and drowned. This last victory reduced those free booters to beg a treaty of pacification, and they have shown a proper regard to the British flag for a series of years.

The following is a copy of the will made by Lieutenant-Colonel Thomas the Evening previous to the fatal interview with Colonel Cosmo Gordon.

London, Sept. 3, 1783.

" I am now called upon, and, by the rules of what is called honour, forced into a personal interview with Colonel Cosmo Gordon —God only can know the event, and into his hands I commit my Soul, conscious only of having done my duty.

" I therefore declare this to be my last will and testament, and do hereby revoke all former wills, &c. I have made at any time.

" In the first place, I commit my Soul to Almighty God, in hopes of his mercy and pardon for the irreligious step I now (in compliance with the unwarrantable customs of this wicked world) put myself under the necessity of taking.

" I leave 150l. in Bank notes, enclosed, to my dear brother, John Thomas, Esq. I bequeath unto him whatever sums may be due to me from the agent of the 1st. regiment of guards, reserving a sufficient sum to pay my debts, which are inconsiderable; and I also give and bequeath unto him all my books and household furniture, and every thing else of which I am now possessed. I give and bequeath to Tho. Hobber, my servant, 50l. which I request my brother will pay him. What debts may be now owing, I request my brother will immediately discharge.

FRED. THOMAS.

Wednesday Night, Sept. 3, 1783.

" P. S. I commit this into the hands of my Friend, Captain Hill, of the 1st regiment of guards."

ANECDOTE.

When the Spaniards were invading Peru, after the inhabitants of that country were driven to the greatest extremity, one Friar Vincenti was sent by the Spaniards in order to treat with the vanquished. The behaviour of Ata-Nulpa, the last Inca of Peru, in his intercourse with Vincenti, appeared particularly striking. He heard the Spanish Missioner with calm attention, and replied, " That it was absurd on the part of the POPE to grant away a territory which did not belong to him, he would still continue to venerate the Gods of his ancestors; and if the Christians worshipped a God that died, he adored the Sun that never died." He viewed the Prayer-book, which was put into his hands by the Friar, and after saying, that it conveyed to him no information, threw it down with a smile. By this honest simplicity, which would have gained the affection of a generous mind, Father Vincenti was so enraged that he gave the word of command, crying out, " Kill the dogs who trample under foot the word of God." An incident like this could not fail to excite indignation, and that indignation rose still higher, when it appeared, that articles of high treason were in form exhibited against Ata Nulpa, and, after that execrable farce of a state, the Prince of a world just discovered by the Spaniards suffered as a

Observing afterwards that every thing in this city was civil and tranquil, no mobs—no riots—no disorders, he finished unmolested, the business he was sent upon, and prepared to return on board.

Well! said he to a gentleman in company, this is a strange scene indeed! Here, in this city, we have had an army for more than seven years, and yet could not keep the peace of it—scarcely a day or night passed without tumults. Now we are gone every thing is in quietness and safety. These Americans, continued he, are a curious original people, *they know how to govern themselves, but nobody else can govern them.*

Though this remark was produced by the force of immediate observation, and with very little reflection, it has something in it that is strong and striking.

To know how to govern ourselves is the nicest point of human wisdom. It is the foundation of character and greatness either in the individual or the nation collectively. The highest abilities or the best of causes without prudence and temper to manage them, lose, in a little time, their grace and influence, and the experience of the world has shewn us, that power without discretion undermines itself.

The British appear to have been exceedingly disappointed and mortified, at the order and regularity which immediately took place, upon the evacuation. They had predicted nothing but riots, revenge and tumults; and under this expectation, the last scene they were witness to in America, confounded them like a conquest.

It is melancholy to reflect (for reflection will find its way even to the severest heart) how many thousands their assuming arrogance and delusive proclamations have ruined, and how many more their false alarms have unnecessarily frightened away. Hundreds who might have staid in safety, and many no doubt, remain, who can have no good pretensions to be here.

When an enemy suddenly extends his arms and authority over a country, it is impossible for every one to get out of his way. The incumbrance of children and families, the insurmountable difficulty of procuring conveyance for so many thousands at once, the embarrassment of private circumstances which none but themselves can know, the intricacy and influence of dependent connections, the want of money to move with, and, at last, the not knowing where to go, or how to live, will unavoidably leave numbers within their power whose situation being blended with the voluntary traitor, exposes them alike to indiscriminate suspicion. All are not friends or enemies who at first appear so. Misfortune may have the resemblance of guilt, and guilt assume the stile of misfortune; and to distinguish between them, requires observation, temper and prudence.

It was impossible to view this city at the time of the evacuation, and the immediate repossession of it by its exiled inhabitants, without experiencing a conflict of affecting passions To see so many hundreds immediately happy, by a safe return to their long forsaken homes, and others made wretched by having new habitations to seek, in a comfortless region, and at a stormy season, were circumstances that by contrasting each other produced in the mind a disquieting compound of joy and pity.

Distress in any shape it can be presented to us, will in spite of resentment find a way to soften it; and the difference between their

THE Selectmen of the several Towns in the County of Suffolk, are desired to take Notice, That Returns of the Monthly Prices of Indian Corn, Beef, Sheep's Wool and Sole Leather, are to be made to the Agent of the said County, within the course of the present Month of February. The Subscriber therefore requests, that the said Returns of Prices, from September last to the present Month inclusive, may be sent forthwith, and lodged at the Office of Ezekiel Price, Esq; in the State House, Boston.

RICHARD CRANCH,
(Agent for said county.

Braintree, February 9th, 1784.

REPORTING THE

Resignation of George Washington as Commander in Chief

By Robert J. Allison

King George III asked American-born portrait painter Benjamin West what Washington would do after the war. The United States had no effective government. Would the victorious general use his army to hold onto power? No, West said. Washington would return to his farm. "If he does that," the King said, "he will be the greatest man in the world."

As it became clear the war was ending, it also was clear the United States did not have an effective government. Disgruntled Pennsylvania soldiers demanding their pay drove Congress from Philadelphia. Some of Washington's officers plotted to overthrow the ineffective Congress. Washington denounced their threat against the civil power, warning officers not to betray the cause they had served. Washington wrote to state governors urging their support for a stronger union but insisted that citizens, not soldiers, governed.

Facing down a coup d'état, lobbying for a more effective elected government, Washington as commander had to ensure that the British army left. When news that the treaty was signed reached him in October, he wrote to the British commander, General Guy Carleton, about his plans to evacuate New York City. On November 20, Washington accompanied New York governor George Clinton as he crossed into Harlem. Washington and his men were there to restore legitimate civil power. On November 23, the British were on their ships, and the American flag rose at New York's battery. After an emotional farewell to his officers, Washington began his journey home, stopping in Philadelphia to settle his accounts, then on to Annapolis, where Congress met.

As it became clear the war was ending, it also was clear the United States did not have an effective government.

Washington notified Congress of his arrival on December 20; Congress agreed to receive him at noon on December 23. Congress hosted a banquet for Washington and two hundred guests on December 22, and afterward the Maryland government sponsored a gala ball at the State House. To give every lady "the pleasure of dancing with him," Washington danced every set.

At noon the next day, he returned to the State House. The nineteen members of Congress, representing only seven states, remained seated, with their hats on, as Washington entered. Once he was seated, "respectable citizens of Annapolis," the French consul, Governor William Paca, members of the assembly, and "a beautiful group of elegant ladies" filled the gallery and the House floor (*Massachusetts Spy*, January 29, 1784). President Thomas Mifflin told Washington that "the United States in Congress assembled, were prepared to receive his communications." Washington rose and bowed; the members raised their hats. He read his statement, resigning "with satisfaction" the appointment "accepted with diffidence" (*American Herald*, January 19, 1784).

Washington recommended Congress's "favourable notice" to the officers who had formed his official family and commended the "interests of my dearest country to the protection of Almighty God." Now having "finished the work assigned me," he retired "from the great theatre of action," taking "leave of all the employments of public life" (*American Herald*, January 19, 1781). From his pocket he took the commission the Congress of the United Colonies had issued on June 17, 1775, presenting it to President Mifflin.

Virginia delegate Thomas Jefferson wrote the official reply, which Mifflin read with dignity but little feeling. Washington had "defended the standard of liberty in this new world" and "taught a lesson useful to those who inflict, and those who feel oppression."

"[F]ew tragedies ever drew more tears from so many beautiful eyes," the *American Herald* reported (January 19, 1784). All understood the symbolic significance as Washington surrendered military power back into the hands of the civil government, whose authority came from the American people. No one watching knew what their former King had said; but none who saw this remarkable scene would have disagreed, as Washington rode off in haste to spend Christmas as a civilian at home, that they had had a glimpse of the greatest man in the world.

Washington's farewell to his officers after the Revolution, Fraunces Tavern, NYC
North Wind Picture Archives

After an emotional farewell to his officers in New York, Washington began his journey home, stopping in Philadelphia to settle his accounts, then on to Annapolis, where Congress met.

JANUARY 29, 1784

The MASSACHUSETTS SPY

BOSTON, January 22.

Extract of a letter, dated Annapolis, 24th December, 1783.

" General Washington having requested to resign his commission, was admitted to a publick audience on Tuesday last. The gallery was filled with a beautiful group of elegant ladies, and some graced the floor of Congress. On this were likewise the Governor, Council and Legislature of the State, several general officers, the Consul General of France, and the respectable citizens of Annapolis. Congress were seated and covered, as Representatives of the sovereignty of the union, the spectators were uncovered and standing. The General was introduced to a chair by the Secretary, who after a decent interval ordered silence. The President then informed the General, That "the United States in Congress assembled were prepared to receive his communications," on which he rose with great dignity and delivered his address. This was followed by his advancing to the President and resigning his commission.—He resumed his place and received in a standing posture, the answer of Congress, which the President delivered with eloquence. The occasion produced a pleasing solemnity that may more easily be conceived than expressed.—To see on the one hand so great and good a man taking his leave of publick employments to spend the residue of his days in retirement, and his country on the other acknowledging his unprecedented merit, and with the most affectionate embraces, loading him with their blessings, exhibited a scene that drew tears from many of the spectators. He is now with his family, and may his rewards and enjoyments be in future adequate to his important services."

Since or last, Major General Knox arrived in Town from Head Quarters.

MASSACHUSETTS SPY (BOSTON)

January 29, 1784

King George III asked American-born portrait painter Benjamin West what Washington would do after the war. The United States had no effective government. Would the victorious general use his army to hold on to power? No, West said. Washington would return to his farm. "If he does that," the King said, "he will be the greatest man in the world."

full period of existence allotted them, and to die chiefly of old age: And, were any observations to be made among savages, perhaps the same would be found to be true of them.—Death is an evil to which the order of Providence has subjected every inhabitant of this earth; but to man it has been rendered unspeakably more an evil than it was designed to be. The greatest part of that black catalogue of diseases which ravage human life, is the offspring of the tenderness, the luxury, and the corruptions introduced by the vices and false refinements of civil society. That delicacy which is injured by every breath of air, and that rottenness of constitution which is the effect of intemperance and debauchery, were never intended by the Author of Nature; and it is impossible, that they should not lay the foundation of numberless sufferings, and terminate in premature and miserable deaths.—Let us then value more the simplicity and innocence of a life agreeable to Nature, and learn to consider nothing as savageness but malevolence, ignorance, and wickedness. The order of Nature is wise and kind. In a conformity to it consist health and long life; grace, honour, virtue, and joy. But Nature turned out of its way will always punish. 'The wicked shall not live out half their days.' Criminal excesses imbitter and cut short our present existence; and the highest authority has taught us to expect, that they will not only kill the body, but the soul; and deprive us of an Everlasting Existence.

HAMBOURG, (Russia) October 12.

A very extraordinary instance of fecundity has happened in Lower Austria, to the wife of one Langenloin. After being married a very long time, without having any children, on the 10th of September last she brought forth four. On the 17th she felt fresh pains, and was brought to bed of four more. The eight children, which are all boys, have been baptized, and seem likely to live; nor does the mother appear to be at all incommoded by this double delivery.

LONDON.

The following copy of a very extraordinary letter was received by a gentleman in London, from a respectable correspondent in Cambridge, who asserts that he has seen the original.

Provence, (France) July 12, 1779.

"SIR,

NOW *Mr. Dodd is beyond the reach of his enemies, you may acquaint them that he is here, in sound health, though melancholy spirits; depressed in mind, from the idea of quitting forever his native country, and being necessarily compelled to hide his head from publick conversation, which, in England, was his chief enjoyment. Gifted by nature with the most shining talents of speech, it must be a great mortification to him, that the courtship of popular applause is at an end; he must sink in obscurity, after raising himself to the pinnacle of admiration. He is at the house of Mr. De Pee, who being my particular friend and relation, I have had an opportunity of seeing the Doctor. The account he gives of his deliverance, which he gathered partly from the information of those to whom he is indebted for life, and partly from his own knowledge, is this:*

... pain, that he says, his life was not worth the purchase.

"*After the ceremony of congratulation, on one side and on the other, was over, the next affair to be considered (for before, nothing was considered by the Doctor's friends) was, how he should be disposed of, when it was proposed, that he should set off the next day for France. A subscription for present supply was entered into, and in the evening the Doctor went to his wife's lodgings, which she had quitted the evening before, opposite Stationer's-Hall. The next day he was equipped in women's apparel, by which, and the great alteration in his countenance, it was hardly possible for his most intimate friends to know him, unless he discovered himself by his speech. It was thought proper to conceal all this from Mrs. Dodd, as it might be too sudden a surprize, but bring her by degrees to the knowledge of her husband's existence. The next day the Doctor attended by his friend Mr. H——, went to Dover, and there met with a fair wind, which carried them to Calais, from whence they came here.*"

NOVEMBER 15.

Mr. Paine, the excellent author of Common Sense, is, we are told, preparing a history of the late War in America. Mr. Paine, obviously, with all his talents, cannot mount to the source and secret spring—and there is one, who can thus mount, and that is General Washington. What a desideratum must it be in the world of letters and political attainment, if the General would, without delay, enter on this great work?—Of his talents in literary composition, his circular letter alone is a sufficient proof.

Extract of a letter from an English gentleman at Paris, to his friend in Bristol, dated October 22.

"*The weather has been very cold and foggy in Paris till Sunday last, when to my great surprise, I saw an advertisement that Montgolfier and another gentleman were to go up with the globe that has been so much talked of, the next day. I went to the place, and was a witness, among many thousands, of their executing their promise. Mr. M. and no less a person than a Marquis, an officer in the King's service, went up 350 odd feet, and remained in the air some time, and afterwards descended without the least hurt or inconvenience. The place they were in was a kind of gallery, constructed below the globe.—The next experiment is to give it a direction at will, and mount higher: In short, this globe engrosses every conversation here.*"

Of all French commanders, not one has shown more determined bravery than M. Suffrein. In the engagement where his ship received so much damage, that she sunk going into Trincomale, his courage almost drove him into a phrensy; it being well authenticated, that some of his officers, thinking it impossible to carry the ship out of the line of battle, begun a murmur about striking, on which Suffrein instantly seized a lighted match, and making towards the powder room, declared that no enemy should capture him, and therefore they had no alternative to choose, but either to attempt carrying the ship into port, or be blown up in her. By this threat he preserved himself and crew from being made prisoners, though it proved afterwards impossible to save the ship.

Though the French claim the honour of the new invention of air-globes, there is little doubt but the English will be the men to make

An act for appraising personal estate taken by execution.

An act to repeal an act of this State, intitled an act in addition to an act passed November 28th, 1781, intitled, an act for preventing the subjects of his Britannick Majesty, and all other persons inimical to the United States of North-America, from prosecuting actions, serving as jurors, or acting as town officers within this State, passed the 21st day of June, A. D. 1782.

An act for the more speedy recovery of small debts, and to save the cost usually attending the recovery in the present course of the law.

A list of the members of the Counciland House of Representatives, who constituted the Assembly of this State, at their late Session in Concord, viz.

COUNCIL.

County of ROCKINGHAM. The Hon. Meshech Weare, Josiah Bartlett, John M'Clary, Woodbury Langdon, and Nathaniel Folsom, Esquires.

County of STRAFFORD. Hon. John Wentworth, and George Frost, Esqrs.

County of HILLSBOROUGH. Hon. Timothy Farrar, and Francis Blood, Esqrs.

County of CHESHIRE. Hon. T. Applin, and Enoch Hale, Esqrs.

County of GRAFTON. Hon. Moses Dow, Esquire.

The Hon. Meshech Weare, Esq; was unanimously chosen President of said Council. Ebenezer Thomson, Esq; Secretary; and Joseph Pearson, Esq; Deputy Secretary.

HOUSE OF REPRESENTATIVES.

COUNTY of ROCKINGHAM.

Portsmouth, George Atkinson, George Gains, and John Pickering, Esqrs.
Exeter, Joseph Gilman, Esq; and Mr. Jedediah Jewett.
Londonderry, Daniel Runnells, Esq; and Mr. Archibald M'Murphey.
Chester, William White, Esq; and Mr. Jabez Hoyt.
Hampton, Christopher Toppan, Esq;
Hampton-Falls, M. Abner Sandborn.
Brintwood, Capt. Levi Morrel.
Stratham, Mark Wiggin, Esq;
North-Hampton, Moses Leavitt, Esq;
Kensington, Mr. Moses Shaw.
Newmarket, Capt. Samuel Gilman.
Epping, Capt. Seth Fogg.
South-Hampton, and *Newtown*, Mr. Benjamin Clough.
Kingston, and *East-Kingston*, Capt. John Eastman.
Greenland, Mr. Stephen March.
Nottingham, Thomas Bartlett, Esq;
Hawke, and *Sandown*, Mr. Thomas Page.
Newington, Ephraim Pickering, Esq;
Rye, Samuel Jenness, Esq;
Atkinson, and *Plastow*, Nathaniel Peabody, Esq;
Hampstead, John Calf, Esq;
Raymond, John Dudley, Esq;
Deerfield, and *Northwood*, Jeremiah Eastman, Esq;
Salem, Captain John Allen.
Candin, Mr. Ezekiel Knowles.
Epsom, and *Chichester*, Capt. James Gray.
Pelham, James Gibson, Esq;
Windham, Mr. Gain Armour.
Pembrook, Samuel Daniel, Esq;
Concord, Timothy Walker, Esq;

...ge, and *Jaffery*, Mr. William Smiley.
Keene, Mr. Benjamin Hall.
Packersfield, Mr. William Barker.
Swanzey, and *Fitzwilliam*, Mr. Sam. Kindall.
Hindsdale, and *Chesterfield*, Mr. Sam. King.
Richmond, Mr. Oliver Caprice.
Surry, and *Alstead*, Nath. Sartill Prentice, Esq;
Newport, Benj. Giles, Esq;
Unity, and *Ackworth*, Mr. Elijah Frink.
Winchester, Mr. Simon Willard.
Granthan, and *Plainfield*, Mr. Nathan Young.
Charlestown, John Hubbard, Esq;
Cornish, Moses Chace, Esq;
Washington, and *Stoddard*, Captain Jacob Coptland.

COUNTY of GRAFTON.

Plymouth, Francis Wooster, Esq;
New Holderness, Samuel Livermore, Esq;
Haverhill, James Woodward, Esq;
Wentworth, and *Warren*, Captain Obadiah Clement.
New Chester, and *Andover*, Mr. Enoch Noyce.
Canaan, and *Cardigan*, Capt. Caleb Church.
Landaff, Mr. John Young.
Orford, Capt. John Mann.
Northumberland, Joseph Whipple, Esq;
Lebanon, and *Hanover*, Bezaleel Woodward, Esq;
Lyme, Capt. Ebenezer Green.

The Honourable John Dudley, Esq; was chosen Speaker, and John Calfe, Esq; Clerk of the Honourable House of Representatives; both of whom have been staunch friends to their country, and never deserted our councils in the worst of times.

The General Court of this State, after finishing their late session at Concord, adjourned to the last Tuesday of March next, then to meet at the Court-House in Exeter.

BOSTON, January 22.

Extract of a letter, dated Annapolis, 24th December, 1783.

"General Washington having requested leave to resign his commission, was admitted to a publick audience on Tuesday last. The gallery was filled with a beautiful group of elegant ladies, and some graced the *floor* of Congress. On *this* were likewise the Governor, Council and Legislature of the State, several general officers, the Consul General of France, and the respectable citizens of Annapolis. Congress were seated and covered, as Representatives of the sovereignty of the union, the spectators were uncovered and standing. The General was introduced to a chair by the Secretary, who after a decent interval ordered silence. The President then informed the General, That "the United States in Congress assembled were prepared to receive his communications," on which he rose with great dignity and delivered his address. This was followed by his advancing to the President and resigning his commission.—He resumed his place and received in a standing posture, the answer of Congress, which the President delivered with eloquence. The occasion produced a pleasing solemnity that may more easily be conceived than expressed.—To see on the one hand so great and good a man taking his leave of publick employments to spend the residue of his days in retirement, and his country on the other acknowledging his unprecedented merit, and with the most affectionate embraces, loading him with their blessings, exhibited a scene that drew tears from many of the spectators. He is now with his family, and may his

AMERICAN HERALD (BOSTON)

January 19, 1784

Washington rose and bowed; the members raised their hats. He read his statement, resigning "with satisfaction" the appointment "accepted with diffidence." The *American Herald* reported that "few tragedies drew more tears from so many beautiful eyes."

ORE, in the ship
assage of 34 days,
s to the 24th of

...

ir: the next day
reigning Duke,
his rout for Italy.
id that the King
f the Carnival at

M. Le Febvre
d his post of Con-
nces to the King
was pleased to
The Count de
ng sent to know
quired a pension,
that "he should

nt of Lisle, was
ontroller-General
w Minister is ex-
ing

EMBER 13.

ibraltar mention,
ingly healthy and
tranquility, new
for their accom-
olerable cheap.
d will not return
eutenant-General
Lieutenant-Go-

s introduced on
t St. James's, was
ability, and con-
ds of an hour.
fifty years in the
acquitted himself
the late reign to
of the Prince of
a letter to King
mending him to
strongest terms.

r necessity, in any
maintaining our
esent——Laws
d almost to have
e owe our conse-
most every great

asis of our great
ommerce of the
at (which is said
y permitting the
te to trade with
ies, or by suffer-
this country any
ll desert the na-
marine of Great

ote his celebrated
navigation had
speaking of that
s, "I am of opi-
, shipping, profit
hoicest and most
ade in England,
not been owners
ipping or trade;

---

or authority can he now shelter himself? Truly the Court of Proprietors here interpose, vote thanks to the Governor General

...

terance, and I could scarce congratulate these more than conquerors, in the name of every loyal, every honest heart. Well, my lads, you fought well; how welcome you are to every Englishman! You have a grateful country to reward your services, which have been long, laborious, and faithful; you'll be promoted.——Sir, interrupted one of [illegible], you are mistaken; no man has yet noticed us but yourself; we have done our duty, Sir, the King, God bless him, THANKED us for it. As to promotion, that is at an end [illegible] were relieved, brought to Portsm[illegible] dis[illegible]nded: when we [illegible] to Scotl[illegible] wives, our children, and our mothers [illegible] rush upon us with open arms. No indifferent man notices individuals. The glory of the British arms gradually tarnished in my eyes: the honour of my country sunk away in a moment; and though I bore no share in that *negligence* which disgraces this æra, I felt my self *less than a man in being a* BRITON!

NOV. 17. It is reported, in the vicinity of St. James's, that David Hartley, Esq. will go before Christmas to America in a public capacity; but whether as Ambassador, or Envoy Extraordinary, is not yet determined.

They write from Paris, that an express is arrived from Monf. de Suffrein at Trincomale, who had been informed of the peace by a frigate in June last; and that he had sent the same vessel as a flag of truce to all the English settlements with the grateful news.

The emigrators to America may, in the *back* settlements, get *land* almost *for nothing*! And there, with nature in all her sublimity of dimension,

"Each like an ocean, each parterre a down,"

they will have the greatest attitude of things, and may revel in each natural delight! it is a *sporting country*, such as a mere European has no idea of! *Foxes, wolves, bears*, &c. are put up at every turn! Then as to *society*, when they understand them, the *natives* will delight them infinitely! And when, with the help of bark, and molasses spirits (which are always at hand in the *adjoining places*, New-England and Peru) they shall have weathered but the *first ten or twelve years*, they will be thoroughly seasoned to the climate, and *ague-proof* at every pore! A *family* will be established after their own name [illegible] do not relapse into [illegible] habits and [illegible] of the aborigines of the country) their *great grand children* may, perhaps, become *great fortunes*!

LONDON, NOVEMBER 22.

IT is with the truest concern we inform the public, that the advices received yesterday over land from India, are of a most melancholy complexion indeed! The Mharattas have entered into new engagements with the French, and have already infringed their recent treaty with us. Tippoo Saib continues a most formidable enemy. Mangalore has surrendered to him, and General Mathews and his whole

---

not decisive. Colonels Macleod and Humberstone were attacked by the Mharratta fleet and taken before the Mharatta peace was [illegible] latter unfortunately [illegible] former was releas[illegible] ay. The Mha[illegible] d, and Madajee [illegible] re complete sa[illegible] ccident, from the [illegible] ondence had been [illegible] d the Mharattas, [illegible] ng the countries [illegible] ty. General Ma[illegible] ore, returned to [illegible] acked by Tippo [illegible] as compelled to [illegible] e attacked Man[illegible] h very great loss [illegible], and there was no [illegible] holding out, till reinforced. Three hundred Europeans had sailed from Madrass, for the purpose, and a strong detachment from Bombay. No recent accounts from Bengall——all well there by the last letters.

To-morrow morning the Duke and Duchess of Cumberland will set off to Brightelmstone, where they are to embark for France.

The Crocodile frigate, which sailed in February for the East-Indies, carried out an account of the peace; and the Eurydice, which has since sailed, carried instructions to Sir [illegible]ward Hughes for such ships as are to return home.

The Prince of Capers, Monarch of the Graces, and Emperor of taste——the most puissant and much renowned Monsieur VESTRIS, junior, arrived yesterday, at 3 o'clock in Great Pultney-street, from France, being engaged at the Opera-House for the ensuing season.

The system of East-India Government, proposed on Tuesday last by Mr. Fox, is perhaps one of the completest efforts of human policy that was ever devised by the ingenuity of man, and will probably, when the rage of party acrimony has a little subsided, and the effects of personal enmity are also past, transmit him to posterity, with the brighest character of ancient political wisdom, and invest him with the glorious titles to which he has proved indisputable pretensions, of being the saviour of his country, and the general friend of mankind.

Mr. Fox assigned as one reason for fixing the scence of Indian Administration here at home, that Parliament might have their eye upon the conduct of the Commissioners, and that the House of Commons might watch it, and be ready to check each appearance of misrule or mistake, and keep the current of the Company's affairs pure, and equally free from the foulness of corruption, or being diverted from its proper channel by weak management.

The speech of Mr. Fox on Tuesday did the highest credit to his abilities, but still more to his force of mind and resolution. His sentiments declaring his readiness to take every degree of responsibility upon himself for the bold and arduous attempt of reforming and regulating India, did him the highest credit [illegible]h all who heard him. There is not a doubt that this measure is completely calculated to put the affairs of India in a situation of being substantially useful to this country. It is manly, vigorous, and comprehensive, and accompanied with a degree of responsibility both from the nature of the measure and manner of opening it, that gave a high opinion of the boldness of the Minister, and his confidence in the plan.

It is evident from the conclusion of Mr. Fox's speech on Tuesday, that there is not the most distant foundation for the reports that Opposition have wished to propagate relative to dissension among the Administrati-

---

AMERICA.

ANNAPOLIS, Dec. 25.

The UNITED STATES in CONGRESS Assembled, December 23, 1783.

According to order, his Excellency the Commander in Chief was admitted to a public audience, and being seated, the President after a pause, informed him, that the United States in Congress Assembled, were prepared to receive his communications; whereupon he rose and addressed Congress as follows:

MR. PRESIDENT,

THE great events on which my resignation depended, having at length taken place; I have now the honour of offering my sincere congratulations to Congress, and of presenting myself before them to surrender into their hands the trust committed to me; and to claim the indulgence of retiring from the service of my country.

Happy in the confirmation of our independence and sovereignty, and pleased with the opportunity afforded the United States of becoming a respectable nation, I resign with satisfaction the appointment I accepted with diffidence; a diffidence in my abilities to accomplish so arduous a task, which, however, was superceded by a confidence in the rectitude of our cause, the support of the supreme power of the union, and the patronage of heaven.

The successful termination of the war has verified the most sanguine expectations; and my gratitude for the interposition of providence, and the assistance I have received from my countrymen, increases with every review of the momentuous contest.

While I repeat my obligations to the army in general I should do injustice to my own feelings not to acknowledge, in this place, the peculiar services, and distinguished merits, of the gentlemen who have been attached to my person during the war.

It was impossible the choice of confidential officers to compose my family, should have been more fortunate.

Permit me, sir, to recommend in particular, those who have continued in the service to the present moment, as worthy of the favourable notice and patronage of Congress.

I consider it as an indispensible duty to close this last act of my official life, by commending the interests of our dearest country to the protection of Almighty God, and those who have the superintendence of them to his holy keeping.

Having now finished the work assigned me, I retire from the great theatre of action; and bidding an affectionate farewell to this august body, under whose orders I have so long acted.

I here offer my commission, and take my leave of all the employments of public life.

He then advanced and delivered to the President his commission, with a copy of his address, and having resumed his place, the president returned him the following answer:

SIR,

THE United States in Congress assembled, receive with emotions too affecting for utterance, the solemn resignation of the authorities under which you have led their troops with success through a perilous and doubtful war.

Called upon by your country to defend its invaded rights, you accepted the sacred charge before it had formed alliances, and whilst it was without funds or a government to support you.

You have conducted the great military contest with wisdom and fortitude, invariably regarding the rights of the civil powers thro' all disasters and changes. You have, by the

---

he W
o brin
s own,
d sacri

shua C
ade, t
or 18 y
lladium
lation
s one
at eve
which
our pre
one h
nt."
been,
on n
n as t
e of G
ompar
a Char
aritim
An ord
ndenc
he Re
entar
g befo
who a
e Hag
had b
bassad
tes in
rdere
iately
kept

ia Co
heir lo
o Dec
some
arlian
d, in
ay be
ame ti
inistr
House
is m
refuse
n of t
r!
which
uns,
rt of
asting
is the
Parli
recom
tings

r trade with
r by suffer-
country any
sert the na-
ine of Great

is celebrated
igation had
king of that
am of opi-
oping, profit
st and most
in England,
seen owners
g or trade ;
amen which

oreign and
h and pow-
urce of the
. By some
of impor-
ervedly en-

or copies of
his Majesty's
lland, dur-
to be pre-
es.
n on Wed-
some dis-
there from
which had
lternation,
f troops to
rticulars of
owledge of

rawing up
e war, from
n order to
before the
tes are al-
e whole of
fore both

hemselves
they could
ng, a cer-
nen them
rs, as per-

ent of In-
of atten-
their or-
to obey
he holds
House of
direction
at superi-

(do not relapse into the habits and [illegible] of the aborigines of the country) their *great grand children* may, perhaps, become *great fortunes*!

LONDON, November 22.

IT is with the truest concern we inform the public, that the advices received yesterday over land from India, are of a most melancholy complexion indeed! The Mharattas have entered into new engagements with the French, and have already infringed their recent treaty with us. Tippoo Saib continues a most formidable enemy. Mangalore has surrendered to him, and General Mathews and his whole army are prisoners, on the most ignominious terms. This event happened on the 9th of March. The Mharatta fleet had taken the Ranger, and almost all our party are killed or wounded. Colonel Humberstone is slain, and Colonel Macleod had received three wounds. At Geriah the Mharattas disowned all knowledge of the peace, and behaved with the greatest cruelty. Before the 28th of May, Bidnore was taken by Tippoo Saib. His army consisted of more than one hundred thousand men. After surrendering, on condition of receiving honours of war, he forced the garrison to lay down their arms. Accounts of peace in Europe were then received. Sir Eyre Coote died at Madras on the 26th of April. There had been another drawn action between Suffrein and Sir Edward Hughes. General Stewart was before Cuddalore, when he received intelligence of the news of Peace in Europe. The above intelligence was received by the Directors with the greatest alarm: for though the arms of France had effected nothing, the mismanagement of affairs in the country had apparently left our whole possessions on the brink of destruction. The dispatches are filled with the mutual accusations of the several Commanders.

The following, as a true state of the news from India, is sent to us by a gentleman who was present in the General Court when it was read, and pledges himself for the truth of it: Sir Eyre Coote arrived at Madras in April, with ten lacks of rupees, from Bengal, after having been chased by four French ships: but, most unfortunately, this old hero died two days after he landed. The grand army on the Coast of Coromandel, after Tippo Saib had quitted the Carnatic, marched to attack the French troops at Cuddalore: they had forced the outworks, and there was no doubt of their success against the place, when intelligence arrived at Cuddalore of the peace, and then all hostilities ceased. There was an action between the two fleets in June, but

[illegible] all who heard him. There is not a doubt that this measure is completely calculated to put the affairs of India in a situation of being substantially useful to this country: It is manly, vigorous, and comprehensive, and accompanied with a degree of responsibility both from the nature of the measure and manner of opening it, that gave a high opinion of the boldness of the Minister, and his confidence in the plan.

It is evident from the conclusion of Mr. Fox's speech on Tuesday, that there is not the most distant foundation for the reports that Opposition have wished to propagate relative to dissension among the Administration, but, on the contrary, Lord North and Mr. Fox, are as much agreed upon this great essential measure for India, and upon every other relative to the good of the country, as ever Ministers were at any period.

Lord North's illness renders him wholly incapable of attending to business of any kind, so that the whole weight of public affairs lies on the shoulders of Mr. Fox: and the labour is indeed Herculean.

THE United States in Congress assembled, receive with emotions too affecting for utterance, the solemn resignation of the authorities under which you have led their troops with success through a perilous and doubtful war.

Called upon by your country to defend its invaded rights, you accepted the sacred charge before it had formed alliances, and whilst it was without funds or a government to support you.

You have conducted the great military contest with wisdom and fortitude, invariably regarding the rights of the civil powers thro' all disasters and changes. You have, by the love and confidence of your fellow citizens, enabled them to display their martial genius, and transmit their fame to posterity.

You have persevered, till these United States aided by a magnanimous King and nation) have been enabled, under a just providence, to close the war in freedom, safety and independence; on which happy event we sincerely join you in congratulations.

Having defended the standard of liberty in this new world -- having taught a lesson useful to those who inflict, and to those who feel oppression, you retire from the great theatre of action with the blessings of your fellow citizens. But the *glory* of your virtues will not terminate with your military command -- it will continue to animate remotest ages.

We feel with you our obligations to the army in general, and will particularly charge ourselves with the interest of those confidential officers who have attended your person to this affecting moment.

We join with you in commending the interests of our dearest country to the protection of Almighty God, beseeching him to dispose the hearts and minds of its citizens to improve the opportunity afforded them of becoming a happy and respectable nation. -- And for *You*, we address to *Him* our warmest prayers, that a life so beloved, may be fostered with all his *care*---that your days may be happy as they have been *illustrious*, and that he will finally give you that reward which this world cannot give.

Extract from the Minutes,
CHARLES THOMSON, Secretary.

Here we must let fall the scene---few tragedies ever drew more tears from so many beautiful eyes, as were affected by the moving manner in which his Excellency took his final leave of Congress. After which he immediately set out for Virginia, accompanied to South river by his Excellency our Governor, with the warmest wishes of the city for his repose, health, and happiness. Long, long may he enjoy them!

EPILOGUE

By Todd Andrlik

In 1783, after a bitter eight-year war against Great Britain, America won its liberty, ushering in a new era of hope and optimism. Celebrations were soon tempered by harsh economic realities and the obstacles of a fledgling nation. The world watched with great anticipation.

Among the first major tasks was to create an enduring constitution that enabled a fully functional nation. Under the Articles of Confederation, the first constitution, the Continental Congress had just enough power to fight a war but not enough to run a country. Soaring war debts, coupled with no power to tax, severely depreciated Continental currency and caused colossal inflation.

In the weeks following May 14, 1787, fifty-five delegates convened in the State Hall in Philadelphia for a Federal Convention, presided over by George Washington, to confront the crisis and rewrite a national constitution. Four months later, on September 17, after great debate and compromise among the states, the Convention closed with the introduction of the United States Constitution.

Within weeks, "We the People" was splashed across the pages of newspapers around the globe, including Canada, where the *Quebec Gazette* began publishing the entire Constitution, with French translation, in its November 8, 1787, issue. Through newspaper printings of the Constitution, people learned the construction and powers of the United States's new executive, legislative, and judicial branches of government.

On June 21, 1788, New Hampshire became the ninth and decisive state to ratify the Constitution. Less than a year later, on April 30, 1789, George Washington was sworn in as the first president of the United States. Washington, a leader who Americans trusted to stay true to a constitutional republic, took the oath shortly after noon from the second-floor balcony of Federal Hall in New York City. According to an eyewitness report in the May 6, 1789, *Massachusetts Centinel*:

> *At 9 o'clock, all the churches were opened—and the people, in prodigious numbers, thronged these sacred temples—and, with one voice, put up their prayers to Almighty God for the safety of the President. At 12, the procession moved to the Federal State-House, where in the gallery front Broad-Street, in the presence of an immense concourse, his Excellency took the oath, the book being placed on a velvet cushion. The Chancellor then proclaimed him President—and in a moment the air trembled with the shouts of the citizens, and the roar of artillery. His Excellency, with that greatness of soul—that dignity and calmness, which are his characteristicks—then bowed to his 'fellow citizens'—who again huzzaed.*

Following the ceremony, Washington stepped into the Senate chamber and delivered the first inaugural address to a joint session of both Houses of Congress, the text of which was also published in the May 6, 1789, *Massachusetts Centinel.*

Nearing the end of two terms as president, Washington knew it was time to resign from public office. With input from James Madison and Alexander Hamilton, Washington penned his thirty-two-page farewell address, declaring he would not seek reelection for a third term.

The sixty-four-year-old Washington never publicly read his farewell address. Instead it was sent directly to newspapers and first published in Philadelphia, then the capital of the United States, on September 19, 1796, in the *American Daily Advertiser*. The milestone address was widely circulated and reprinted in many newspapers, including *The Herald* (New York) on September 21, 1796.

After the Revolutionary War, Washington voluntarily retired as commander in chief of the Continental Army. Now, after two terms as president, Washington was voluntarily retiring from public life again.

Washington used his last public address to impart his wishes, wisdom, and warnings for the fledgling nation. He stressed "unity of government" and "preserving the Union of the whole," cautioning about evident North and South separatism, which escalated and eventually led to the American Civil War. He warned of the effects of political parties and permanent foreign alliances. As a critical source of strength and security, Washington counseled Americans to "cherish public credit. One method of preserving it is, to use it as sparingly as possible."

By the end of 1796, America's republican spirit stretched throughout the colonies and across the globe. America had proved to the world its ability to find great leaders as well as its strength and resolve—militarily, politically, economically, and socially.

NEW-YORK, September 22.

Copy of the Reſult of the Deliberations of the FEDERAL CONVENTION.

In Convention, September 17, 1787.

SIR,

WE have now the honor to ſubmit to the conſideration of the United States in Congreſs aſſembled, that Conſtitution which has appeared to us the moſt adviſeable.

The friends of our country have long ſeen and deſired, that the power of making war, peace and treaties, that of levying money and regulating commerce, and the correſpondent executive and judicial authorities ſhould be fully and effectually veſted in the general government of the Union: but the impropriety of delegating ſuch extenſive truſt to one body of men is evident—Hence reſults the neceſſity of a different organization.

It is obviouſly impracticable in the fœderal government of theſe States, to ſecure all rights of independent ſovereignty to each, and yet provide for the intereſt and ſafety of all—Individuals entering into ſociety, muſt give up a ſhare of liberty to preſerve the reſt. The magnitude of the ſacrifice, muſt depend as well on ſituation and circumſtance, as on the object to be obtained. It is at all times difficult to draw with preciſion the line between thoſe rights which muſt be ſurrendered, and thoſe which may be reſerved; and on the preſent occaſion this difficulty was encreaſed by a difference among the ſeveral States as to their ſituation, extent, habits, and particular intereſts.

In all our deliberations on this ſubject we kept ſteadily in our view, that which appears to us the greateſt intereſt of every true American, the conſolidation of our Union, in which is involved our proſperity, felicity, ſafety, perhaps our national exiſtence. This important conſideration, ſeriouſly and deeply impreſſed on our minds, led each State in the Convention to be leſs rigid on points of inferior magnitude, than might have been otherwiſe expected; and thus the Conſtitution, which we now preſent, is the reſult of a ſpirit of amity, and of that mutual deference and conceſſion which the peculiarity of our political ſituation rendered indiſpenſible.

That it will meet the full and entire approbation of every State is not perhaps to be expected; but each will doubtleſs conſider, that had her intereſts been alone conſulted, the conſequences might have been particularly diſagreeable or injurious to others; that it is liable to as few exceptions as could reaſonably have been expected, we hope and believe; that it may promote the laſting welfare of that country ſo dear to us all, and ſecure her freedom and happineſs, is our moſt ardent wiſh.

With great reſpect, we have the honor to be,

SIR,

Your Excellency's moſt obedient and humble ſervants,

GEORGE WASHINGTON, Preſident.

By unanimous Order of the Convention.

HIS EXCELLENCY
The Preſident of Congreſs.

WE the People of the United States, in order to form a more perfect Union, eſtabliſh Juſtice, inſure domeſtic Tranquility, provide for the common Defence, promote the general Welfare, and ſecure the Bleſſings of Liberty to ourſelves and our Poſterity, do ordain and eſtabliſh this CONSTITUTION *for the United States of America.*

ARTICLE I.

Sect. 1. ALL legiſlative powers herein granted ſhall be veſted in a Congreſs of the United States, which ſhall conſiſt of a Senate and Houſe of Repreſentatives.

Sect. 2. The Houſe of Repreſentatives ſhall be compoſed of members choſen every ſecond year by the people of the ſeveral ſtates, and the electors in each ſtate ſhall have the qualifications requiſite for electors of the moſt numerous branch of the ſtate legiſlature.

No perſon ſhall be a repreſentative who ſhall not have attained to th
age of twenty-five years, and been ſeven years a citizen of the U
States, and who ſhall not, when elected, be an inhabitant of that ſt
which he ſhall be choſen.

Repreſentatives and direct taxes ſhall be apportioned among the ſ
ſtates which may be included within this Union, according to the
ſpective numbers, which ſhall be determined by adding to the whole
ber of free perſons, including thoſe bound to ſervice for a term of
and excluding Indians not taxed, three-fifths of all other perſons.
actual enumeration ſhall be made within three years after the firſt me
of the Congreſs of the United States, and within every ſubſequent
of ten years, in ſuch manner as they ſhall by law direct. The nu
of repreſentatives ſhall not exceed one for every thirty thouſand, bu
ſtate ſhall have at leaſt one repreſentative; and until ſuch enume
ſhall be made, the ſtate of New-Hampſhire ſhall be entitled to chuſe
Maſſachuſetts eight, Rhode-Iſland and Providence Plantations one,
necticut five, New-York ſix, New-Jerſey four, Pennſylvania eight
laware one, Maryland ſix, Virginia ten, North-Carolina five, S
Carolina five, and Georgia three.

When vacancies happen in the repreſentation from any ſtate, the Ex
ecutive authority thereof ſhall iſſue writs of election to fill ſuch vacancies.

and each ſenator ſhall have one vote.

Immediately after they ſhall be aſſembled in conſequence of the firſt election, they ſhall be divided as equally as may be into three claſſes. The

NOUVELLE-YORK, 22 Septembre.

Copie du Réſultat des délibérations de la CONVENTION FEDERALE.

En Convention, 17 Septembre, 1787.

MONSIEUR,

NOUS avons actuellement l'honneur de ſoumettre à la conſidération des Etats Unis aſſemblés en congrès, la conſtitution qui nous a paru la plus convenable.

Les amis de notre Païs ont longtems vu et deſiré, que le pouvoir de faire la guerre, la paix et les traités, celui de lever l'argent et de régler le commerce, ainſi que les autorités exécutives et judiciaires correſpondantes ſoient pleinement et effectivement confiés au Gouvernement général de l'Union: mais l'impropriété de déléguer un pouvoir ſi étendu à un tel corps eſt évidente. De là réſulte la néceſſité d'une organiſation differente.

Il eſt évidemment impraticable dans le Gouvernement fédérale de ces Etats, d'aſſurer tous les droits d'une ſouveraineté indépendante à chacun en pourvoyant en même tems aux intérêts et à la ſureté de tous. Lorſque les hommes entrent en ſociété il leur faut ſacrifier une partie de leur liberté pour conſerver le reſte—la grandeur de ce ſacrifice doit dépendre autant de la ſituation et des circumſtances que l'objet qu'on veut obtenir. Il eſt toujours difficile de ſeparer avec preciſion les droits qu'on doit abandonner de ceux qu'on peut réſerver—mais dans l'occurence préſente cette difficulté ſe trouve plus grande par la différence qu'il y a entre les Etats relativement à leur ſituation, étendue, coutumes et intérêts particuliers,

Nous avons eu conſtamment en vue dans toutes nos délibérations ſur cet objet, ce qui nous paroit être le plus grand intérêt de chaque véritable Amériquain, la conſolidation de notre Union, d'où dépend notre proſpérité, félicité, ſureté, et peut-être notre exiſtence nationale. Cette importante conſidération, ſérieuſement et profondement imprimée dans nos eſprits, a induit chaque Etat de la convention à être moins rigide relativement à des points moins importans, qu'on eut pû autrement l'eſperer. Ainſi la conſtitution que nous préſentons maintenant eſt le reſultat d'un eſprit d'amitié, et de cette deférence et conceſſion mutuelles, que la particularité de notre ſituation politique a rendu indiſpenſable.

On ne doit peut-être pas eſperer qu'elle ſera entierement approuvée de tous les Etats; mais ſans doute chacun d'eux conſiderera, que ſi on n'eut conſulté que ſon intérêt particulier, les conſéquences auroient été particuliérement déſagréables ou préjudiciables à d'autres. Nous eſperons et croyons qu'elle eſt ſujette à auſſi peu d'exception qu'on peut raiſonnablement l'eſperer. Quelle puiſſe contribuer au bien-être durable de ce païs, ſi cher à nous tous, et aſſurer ſa liberté et ſa félicité, eſt notre vœu très ſincère.

Nous avons l'honneur d'être, avec beaucoup de reſpect,

MONSIEUR,

de votre Excellence, les très humbles et obéiſſants ſerviteurs

GEORGE WASHINGTON, Préſident.

Par ordre unanime de la Convention,

SON EXCELLENCE
Le Préſident du Congrès.

Nous, les peuples des Etats Unis, afin de former une union plus parfaite, établir la juſtice, aſſurer la tranquilité domeſtique, pourvoir à la défenſe commune, promouvoir le bien-être général et aſſurer les avantages de la liberté à nous et à notre poſterité, ordonnons et établiſſons la préſente Conſtitution pour les Etats Unis d'Amérique.

ARTICLE I.

Sec. 1. TOUS pouvoirs légiſlatifs par le préſent accordés ſeront commis à un Congrès des Etats Unis, qui ſera compoſé d'un Sénat et chambre de Répréſentans.

Sec 2. La Chambre des Répréſentans ſera compoſée de membres choiſis tous les deux ans par les peuples des divers états; et les electeurs de

Lorſqu'il arrivera des vacances dans la Répréſentation de quelque état, l'autorité exécutive d'icelle émanera des *writs* ou ordres d'élection

chaque état, choiſis par la légiſlature d'icelui, pour ſix ans, et chaque ſénateur aura une voix.

Immédiatement après qu'ils feront aſſemblés en conſéquence de la pre-

QUEBEC GAZETTE

November 8, 1787

Soon after the Constitutional Convention closed on September 17, "We the People" was splashed across the pages of newspapers around the globe, including Canada, where the *Quebec Gazette* began publishing the entire U.S. Constitution, with French translation, in its November 8, 1787, issue.

BOSTON, WEDNESDAY, MAY 6, 1789.

RECEIVED YESTERDAY AT NOON.

PROVIDENCE, MAY 4, 1789.

MR. RUSSELL,

A perſon leaving this place for Boſton in the morning, I encloſe a New-York paper containing the Preſident's Speech, &c.—I ſhall be happy if it ſhould give you the lateſt intelligence from that quarter. I am, your humble ſervant, CHARLES BULFINCH.

NEW-YORK, MAY 1.

YEſterday the great and illuſtrious WASHINGTON, the favourite ſon of liberty, and deliverer of his country, entered upon the execution of the office of Firſt Magiſtrate of the United States of America; to which important ſtation he had been unanimouſly called by the united voice of the people. The ceremony which took place on this occaſion was truly grand and pleaſing, and every heart ſeemed anxious to teſtify the joy it felt on ſo memorable an event. His Excellency was eſcorted from his houſe, by a troop of Light Dragoons, and the Legion under the command of Col. LEWIS, attended by a Committee of the Senate and Houſe of Repreſentatives, to Federal Hall, where he was formally received by both Houſes of Congreſs, aſſembled in the Senate Chamber; after which he was conducted to the gallery in front of the Hall, accompanied by all the Members, when the oath preſcribed by the Conſtitution was adminiſtered to him by the Chancellor of this State, who then ſaid—

"*Long live* GEORGE WASHINGTON, Preſident of the United States;" which was anſwered by an immenſe concourſe of Citizens, aſſembled on the occaſion, by the loudeſt plaudit and acclamation, that love and veneration ever inſpired. His Excellency then made a ſpeech to both Houſes, and then proceeded, attended by Congreſs, to St. Paul's Church, where Divine Service was performed by the Right Rev. SAMUEL PREVOST, after which his Excellency was conducted in form to his own houſe. In the evening a moſt magnificent and brilliant diſplay of Fire-Works was exhibited at the Fort, under the direction of Col. BEUMAN. The houſes of the French and Spaniſh Miniſters were illuminated in a ſuperb and elegant manner; a number of beautiful tranſparent paintings were exhibited, which did infinite credit to the parties concerned in the deſign and execution.

His Excellency's Speech to both Houſes of Congreſs.

FELLOW-CITIZENS OF THE SENATE, AND OF THE HOUSE OF REPRESENTATIVES,

AMONG the viciſſitudes incident to life, no event could have filled me with greater anxieties than that of which the notification was tranſmitted by your order, and received on the 14th day of the preſent month.—On the one hand, I was ſummoned by my country, whoſe voice I can never hear but with veneration and love, from a retreat which I had choſen with the fondeſt predilection, and, in my flattering hopes, with an immutable deciſion as the aſylum of my declining years:—A retreat which was rendered every day more neceſſary as well as more dear to me, by the addition of habit to inclination, and of frequent interruptions in my health to the gradual waſte committed on it by time. On the other hand, the magnitude and difficulty of the truſt to which the voice of my country called me, being ſufficient to awaken in the wiſeſt and moſt experienced of her citizens, a diſtruſtful ſcrutiny into his qualifications, could not but overwhelm with deſpondence, one, who

Such being the impreſſions under which I have, in obedience to the publick ſummons, repaired to ... it would be peculiarly im-

... ver the Univerſe— ... of nations—and whoſe providential aids can ſupply every human defect—that his benediction may conſecrate to the liberties and happineſs of the ... Government inſti-

... ſeems to have ... of providential agency. And in the important revolution juſt accompliſhed in the ſyſtem of their United Government, the tranquil deliberations and voluntary conſent of ſo many diſtinct communities, from which the event has reſulted, cannot be compared with the means by which moſt governments have been eſtabliſhed, without ſome return of pious gratitude along with an humble anticipation of the future bleſſings which the paſt ſeem to preſage. Theſe reflections, ariſing out of the preſent criſis, have forced themſelves too ſtrongly on my mind to be ſuppreſſed. You will join with me I truſt in thinking, that there are none under the influence of which, the proceedings of a new and free government can more auſpiciouſly commence.

By the article eſtabliſhing the Executive Department, it is made the duty of the Preſident "to recommend to your conſideration, ſuch meaſures as he ſhall judge neceſſary and expedient." The circumſtances under which I now meet you, will acquit me from entering into that ſubject farther than to refer to the Great Conſtitutional Charter under which we are aſſembled; and which, in defining your powers, deſignates the objects to which your attention is to be given. It will be more conſiſtent with thoſe circumſtances, and far more congenial with the feelings which actuate me, to ſubſtitute in place of a recommendation of particular meaſures, the tribute that is due to the talents—the rectitude, and the patriotiſm which adorn the characters ſelected to deviſe and adopt them. In theſe honourable qualifications, I behold the ſureſt pledges, that as on one ſide, no local prejudices or attachments—no ſeparate views nor party animoſities, will miſdirect the comprehenſive and equal eye which ought to watch over this great aſſemblage of communities and intereſts: ſo, on another, that the foundations of our national policy will be laid in the pure and immutable principles of private morality; and the pre-eminence of a free government be exemplified by all the attributes which can win the affections of its citizens, and command the reſpect of the world.

I dwell on this proſpect with every ſatisfaction which an ardent love for my country can inſpire: ſince there is no truth more thoroughly eſtabliſhed, than that there exiſts in the economy and courſe of nature, an indiſſoluble union between virtue and happineſs—between duty and advantage—between the genuine maxims of an honeſt and magnanimous policy, and the ſolid rewards of publick proſperity and felicity. Since we ought to be no leſs perſuaded that the propitious ſmiles of Heaven can never be expected on a nation that diſregards the eternal rules of order and right, which Heaven itſelf has ordained.—And ſince the preſervation of the ſacred fire of liberty, and the deſtiny of the republican model of government, are juſtly conſidered as *deeply*, perhaps as *finally* ſtaked, on the experiment intruſted to the hands of the American people.

Beſides the ordinary objects ſubmitted to your care, it will remain with your judgment to decide how far an exerciſe of the occaſional power delegated by the Fifth Article of the Conſtitution is rendered expedient at the preſent juncture by the nature of objections which have been urged ... y the degree of inquietude ... them. Inſtead of un... ommendations on this ... be guided by no lights ... rtunities, I ſhall again ... fidence in your diſcern... ublick good: For I aſ... u carefully avoid every ... ndanger the benefits of ... government, or which ... leſſons of experience; ... cteriſtick rights of free... publick harmony, will ... r deliberations on the ... rmer can be more im... latter be ſafely and ad...

... obſervations I have one to add, which will be moſt properly addreſſed to the Houſe of Repreſentatives. It concerns my... ſelf ... if ... poſſible ...

... duous ſtruggle for its liberties, the light ... I contemplated my duty, required that I ſhould renounce every pecuniary compenſation. From this reſolution I have in no inſtance departed.

... the Being ... ſupplication, that ſince he has been pleaſed to favour the American People with opportunities for deliberating in perfect tranquillity, and diſpoſitions for deciding with unparalleled unanimity on a form of government for the ſecurity of their Union, and the advancement of their happineſs; ſo his divine bleſſing may be equally conſpicuous in the enlarged views—the temperate conſultations—and the wiſe meaſures on which the ſucceſs of this government muſt depend.

George Washington.

FROM NEW-YORK.

APRIL 30. We have had this day one of thoſe impreſſive ſights which dignify and adorn human nature. At 9 o'clock, all the churches were opened—and the people, in prodigious numbers, thronged theſe ſacred temples—and, with one voice, put up their prayers to Almighty God for the ſafety of the Preſident.

At 12 the proceſſion moved to the Federal State-Houſe, where in the gallery fronting Broad-Street, in the preſence of an immenſe concourſe, his Excellency took the oath, the book being placed on a velvet cuſhion. The Chancellor then proclaimed him Preſident—and in a moment the air trembled with the ſhouts of the citizens, and the roar of artillery. His Excellency, with that greatneſs of ſoul—that dignity and calmneſs, which are his characteriſticks—then bowed to his "fellow-citizens"—who again huzzaed.

☞ *In having it in our power—through the goodneſs of our correſpondents—to announce thus early the Speech of our beloved Preſident—the congratulatory addreſſes of the Pennſylvanians, and the anſwers thereto—as well as the pathetick and elegant valedictory addreſs of the Alexandrians—with its equally pathetick and elegant anſwer—we feel a felicity which can only be equalled by that which muſt animate our readers on peruſing what we preſent this day.*

SHIP NEWS.

Capt. Gage arrived here yeſterday from N. Carolina—The 29th ult. in lat. 39. long. 71 30. ſpoke the Brig ——, Capt. Killam, from Newbury-Port, bound to Philadelphia—out 20 days—who informed, that he had ſprung his foremaſt and maintopmaſt—and had continual gales of wind moſt of his paſſage.

NAVAL-OFFICE, Entered ſince our laſt,

		from
Schooner 2-Friends,	Knights,	St. Thomas
Schooner Harmony,	Phinney,	N. Carolina
Sloop Nancy,	McElroy,	Demarara

CLEARED,

		for
Brig Liſbon-Packet,	Rob.	Liſbon
Brig Dædalus,	Crocker,	Baltimore
Sloop Betſy,	Stetſon,	Virginia
Sloop Phœnix,	Loring,	Philadelphia
Sloop Friendſhip,	Stetſon,	Philadelphia

On TUESDAY next, 13th inſt.

Will be ſold by PUBLICK VENDUE, as ſhe now lays at WOODWARD'S wharf,

THE Brigantine HANNAH, with all her appurtenances as ſhe lately came from ſea, burthen about 150 tons, more or leſs, a very faſt ſailer, and well calculated for the Whaling Fiſhery, Straights or any other trade, and may be ſent to ſea, with a very little expenſe.

For Inventory, condition of Sale, &c. apply to LEWIS HAYT, State-Street.

The ſale will be on board preciſely at half paſt XII.

COTTON WOOL.

A Quantity of excellent COTTON, juſt imported in the Ship FRIENDSHIP, Capt. ROBERTS, from India, to be ſold cheap, at

John Codman, jun's Store,

South ſide of the TOWN-DOCK.

At the ſame place may be had,

A few ſets of very handſome Tea China, at 48*ſ.* per ſet. *May 6, 1789.*

APPLETON PRENTISS

INFORMS his friends and cuſtomers, that he has REMOVED from Shop, No. 28, CORNHILL, to No. 21, MARLBOROUGH-STREET;

Where may be had,

... ENGLISH GOODS as ...

May 6, 1789.

Gilbert Deblois, jun.

INTENDS in a few weeks for England, ...

MASSACHUSETTS CENTINEL (BOSTON)

May 6, 1789

On April 30, 1789, George Washington was sworn in as the first president of the United States. Washington, a leader that Americans trusted to stay true to a constitutional republic, took the oath shortly after noon from the second-floor balcony of Federal Hall in New York City.

...tity of cheese, and after greatly diminishing the lump, by eating alternately from her scale, in order to distribute impartial justice, at length retains the remainder for trouble of settling the difference.

NEW-YORK.

SATURDAY, SEPTEMBER 17.

The opposition papers, for such there must be under the *best government on earth*, begin to vent their spleen against John Adams, Vice President of the United States, with a view to influence the election of President. The Aurora attacks him, as a friend of ranks and *hereditary distinctions!* This calumny is grown *stale*; but as it is the most effectual weapon to be wielded against that old patriot—the *very man* that *planned* our Independence, long before the battle of Lexington, we expect that those papers will continue to dwell on that point, till the election is decided.

The truth is, Mr. Adams is so great an enemy to *orders and hereditary distinctions*, that he spent years in writing his "Defence of the American Constitutions," on purpose to persuade the Americans so to organize their government as forever to *prevent such distinctions* and *guard against* all *aristocratical influence*.

To accomplish this point, Mr. Adams begins with a fact that cannot be denied, viz. that there is in every human society such a thing as a *Natural Aristocracy*, that is, *men of wealth, education*, and *the born of parents who have been very very distinguished*, will pride themselves on these advantages, and claim a kind of superiority over their fellow citizens. On the other hand, the people are naturally inclined to pay to such men *more respect*, than to those who have no such advantages. This is so obvious a thing, that every man sees it—he knows it—he *feels it to be true*.

Now, says Mr. Adams, these men who have such advantages, will always be making use of them to extend their power and influence, and will seek themselves into places of trust and profit. The business of the framers of a free Constitution, is to *balance* the different branches, as to check such men, and guard the state from any undue influence of theirs.

In short, the whole tenor of Mr. Adams Defence, is, to inculcate the danger of *aristocracy* and ... ; to show from what principles of human nature and society, these scourges of freedom, ... proceed; to illustrate his doctrines by facts and examples drawn from history; and to point out the barriers which ought to be erected in a republican government, to *guard against aristocracy and faction*. He is in truth, the most decided *foe of aristocracy* that this country ever produced. ... who give him a different character, neither ... the man, nor have read his book.

Mr. Adams is a friend to a strong and Independent Executive Power. On this subject many ... men differ. But it remains to be proved that his ideas on this point go too far ... The fact is certain, and let our democrats be ... on this score, the *leading principles* of the *present French Constitution*, were borrowed from Mr. Adams Defence of the American Constitutions; one of the Framers of it and the Reporter of the first draft, Boissy d'Anglas, does Mr. Adams justice to acknowledge it. Indeed the French ... uniformly appeared *more friendly* to our government, than our *own Democrats*.

The French have imposed on the city of Frankfort a contribution of 37 millions of florins; about ... millions and a half sterling.

Accounts from Genoa state that the French government has demanded of the Genoese government to shut all their ports against all English ... of war and merchantmen. It is added the demand is made of Spain, and that the court ... disposed to comply.

Genoa is a *neutral State*. We may expect the ..., in the career of her conquests, may find it convenient to make the same demand of the United States.

The abject condition of the states of Italy—not only the fiefs of the emperor, but neutral states, and even the *allies* of France, under the insolent conduct of Buonaparte, is indeed deplorable. Not only under contribution, as usual by laws of war, but robbed of those elegant monuments of the fine arts, which are the pride and boast of the country. This despotic ... of power will go farther than any ..., perhaps, in exciting resentment in Italians; as it is taking from them what peculiarly their *own*; the fruits of their *genius*; and these elegant attractions ... lead men of taste from all the world, ... Italy.

20th August, which after mentioning the affair of Captain Jessop, his cruel treatment by Captain Pigot, &c. which have already been fully detailed in this Gazette, goes on to state—that "all at once the proceedings against Pigot were stopped, and report says, that "*the Root of all evil*" softened all the stripes and healed Jessop's beaten back—800 glittering golden guineas said to be the cure. We hope on his arrival in America, he will be able to shew that he is not that despicable wretch we here take him to be."

It is said, that Lieut. Cudwith was lately killed in a duel by Lieut. Geddes, at West-Point.

In the letter from Favarat, French commissioner, giving an account to the Directory of the surrender of the rebels in Morbihan, published in the Minerva of Tuesday, the last paragraph deserves particular remark.

"These deluded men do not dissemble, that it was the *atrocities of government which armed them against the Republic; and that a wise and paternal government has induced them to return to its bosom.*"

This is precisely conformable to the opinions repeatedly published in this paper, "That the opposition made to the establishment of a republic in France, proceeded very much from the sanguinary measures of the government under the domination of the clubs. The severe despotism of Robespierre, and his jacobin agents, has been the principal cause of the factions, massacres and civil war that have distressed that nation. Since that party has been subdued, and kept under the law; since a division of the legislature has placed that body out of the reach of demagogues and intriguers, *government has assumed a milder aspect*—life and property are respected, and the *rebels return to their allegiance and duty*. Such facts as these are a volume of instruction, not only to the French, but to the Americans, who have been in eminent hazard from *private associations of men of the same sanguinary temper*, as those who deluged France with blood.

A member of one of the clubs lately declared in the presence of witnesses, that "he wished the motion made in the Convention of France two or three years ago, to form a band of two thousand assassins, and dispatch them to massacre the kings of Europe, had prevailed and been carried into effect. He thought it would be an act of *humanity*, to murder all those tyrants."

This is exactly the temper of a violent jacobin or democrat. It is precisely, *in politics*, what the *bigotry of religious fanatics*, Popes, Cardinals, and Priests has been in *religion*. The *same* spirit, with a *different* education, would preside with zeal in a court of inquisition and burn heretics at the stake.

It is a remark of Condorcet, in his elegant book, on the "Progress of the Human Mind," that the Monks, under the Papal Hierarchy, were so many armies of the Roman Pontiff, spread over Europe, to aid the cause of his despotism. An excellent remark.

Popular societies or clubs, formed for political purposes, and affiliated to a mother club, answer the same purposes in Government, as the monasteries did in religion. They are the *monks of civil society*; scattered thro a country, and corresponding, they form so many different corps of partizans, ready on a call from their chief, to second all his projects, good or bad. The papal power was augmented principally and a long time supported, by these *cloistered* instruments of superstition and sacerdotal tyranny.

The enormous power of the Jesuits, was originally erected and maintained in the same manner, by *detached corps* of their order, established in different countries, but subject to *one head*, acting in close concert! By these simple means, that society had raised a despotism that became formidable to Europe; government took the alarm, and suppressed them, as it had Popular Societies in France, and for similar reasons.

Resignation of the President.

To the PEOPLE *of the* UNITED STATES:

FRIENDS AND FELLOW-CITIZENS,

THE period for a new election of a Citizen, to administer the executive government of the United States, being not far distant, and the time actually arrived, when your thoughts must be employed in designating the person, who is to be cloathed with that important trust, it appears to me proper, especially as it may conduce to a more distinct expression of the public voice, that I should now apprise you of the resolution I have formed, to decline being considered among the number of those, out of whom a choice is to be made.

I beg you, at the same time, to do me the justice to be assured, that this resolution has not been taken, without a strict regard to all the considerations appertaining to the relation, which binds a dutiful citizen to his country; and that, in withdrawing the tender of service which silence in my situation might imply, I am influenced by no diminution of zeal for your future interest; no deficiency of grateful respect for your past kindness; but am supported by a full conviction that the step is compatible with both.

The acceptance of, and continuance hitherto in the office to which your suffrages have twice called me, have been a uniform sacrifice of inclination to the opinion of duty, and to a deference for what appeared to be your desire. I constantly hoped, that it would have been much earlier in my power, consistently with motives, which I was not at liberty to disregard, to return to that retirement, from which I had been reluctantly drawn. The strength of my inclination to do this, previous to the last election, had even led to the preparation of an address to declare it to you; but mature reflection on the then perplexed and critical posture of our affairs with foreign nations, and the unanimous advice of persons entitled to my confidence, impelled me to abandon the idea.

I rejoice, that the state of your concerns, external as well as internal, no longer renders the pursuit of inclination incompatible with the sentiment of duty, or propriety; and am persuaded whatever partiality may be retained for my services, that in the present circumstances of our country, you will not disapprove my determination to retire.

The impressions with which I first undertook the arduous trust, were explained on the proper occasion. In the discharge of this trust, I will only say, that I have with good intentions, contributed towards the organization and administration of the government, the best exertions of which a very fallible judgment was capable. Not unconscious in the outset, of the inferiority of my q...

and which appear to me all important to the permanency of your felicity as a people. These will be offered to you with the more freedom, as you can only see in them the disinterested warnings of a parting friend, who can possibly have no personal motive to bias his counsel. Nor can I forget, as an encouragement to it, your indulgent reception of my sentiments on a former and not dissimilar occasion.

Interwoven as is the love of liberty with every ligament of your hearts, no recommendation of mine is necessary to fortify or confirm the attachment.

The unity of government which constitutes you one people, is also now dear to you. It is justly so; for it is a main pillar in the edifice of your real independence, the support of your tranquility at home, your peace abroad; of your safety; of your prosperity; of that very liberty which you so highly prize. But as it is easy to foresee, that from different causes and from different quarters, much pains will be taken, many artifices employed, to weaken in your minds the conviction of this truth; as this is the point in your political fortress against which the batteries of internal and external enemies will be most constantly and actively (though often covertly and insidiously) directed, it is of infinite moment, that you should properly estimate the immense value of your national Union, to your collective and individual happiness; that you should cherish a cordial, habitual, and immoveable attachment to it; accustoming yourselves to think and speak of it as of the Palladium of your political safety and prosperity; watching for its preservation with jealous anxiety; discountenancing whatever may suggest even a suspicion that it can in any event be abandoned; and indignantly frowning upon the first dawning of every attempt to alienate any portion of our country from the rest, or to enfeeble the sacred ties which now link together the various parts.

For this you have every inducement of sympathy and interest. Citizens by birth or choice, of a common country, that country has a right to concentrate your affections. The name of AMERICAN, which belongs to you, in your national capacity, must always exalt the just pride of Patriotism, more than any appellation derived from local discriminations. With slight shades of difference, you have the same religion, manners, habits and political principles. You have in a common cause fought and triumphed together; the Independence and Liberty you possess are the work of joint councils, and joint efforts, of common dangers, sufferings and successes.

But these considerations, however powerfully they address themselves to your sensibility, are greatly outweighed by those which apply more immediately to your interest.—Here every portion of our country finds the most commanding motives for carefully guar...

THE HERALD (NEW YORK CITY)

September 21, 1796

Nearing the end of two terms as president, Washington knew it was time to resign from public office. With input from James Madison and Alexander Hamilton, Washington penned his 32-page farewell address, declaring he would not seek reelection for a third term. The sixty-four-year-old Washington never publicly read his farewell address. Instead it was sent directly to newspapers.

REVOLUTIONARY PRESS IMPACT

By Carol Sue Humphrey

Newspapers were absolutely essential for Americans in their struggle for independence. Before the fighting started in 1775, newspapers provided information about the arguments with Great Britain and the various protests related to those arguments. During the years of fighting, the press provided news about the war itself, but the press also encouraged the people to support the war effort. Thus, newspapers became the primary morale boosters throughout the Revolutionary War. Printers such as Benjamin Edes and Isaiah Thomas used many means to lift public confidence in the drive for independence. Essays and news stories emphasized the tyranny of the British and the righteousness of the Americans. Patriot newspapers sought to destroy any remaining colonial ties to Great Britain as well as point out American successes and future prospects. Printers filled their productions with material on the justness of the American cause and the success of the Continental Army in battle. Newspapers continually worked to increase public resolve by urging readers to put the war above all other concerns.

Printers personally suffered because of the fighting in the Revolution. Many faced problems because of the activities of the armies. Several printers had to move their offices in the face of the approach of the enemy—Isaiah Thomas moved his printing press from Boston to Worcester following the Battle of Lexington and Concord. But other printers moved their operation to better serve the public. For example, Samuel Hall moved around to accommodate the government of Massachusetts. He had founded the *Essex Gazette* in Salem in 1768, and he moved to Cambridge in 1775 to better serve the state convention and the army. He then moved to Boston after the British left in 1776.

The press played an important role during the Revolution by keeping Americans engaged in the war even when the fighting occurred far away. Some writers used the newspapers to stir up people's passions against Britain, but the press served primarily to keep Americans informed about the progress of the fight for independence. Americans did gain some information from personal letters, broadsides, and pamphlets, but none of these media circulated as widely as newspapers. From the moment that the colonials received word of Britain's new taxes in 1764 until news of the peace treaty arrived in 1783, newspapers constituted the primary source of information about the conflict with the mother country. Without the press, many Americans would have known practically nothing about what was happening and could have lost their interest in the outcome of the war. For example, large-scale fighting ended in New England when the British army withdrew from Boston in March 1776. The public remained interested in what was going on in the war with Great Britain for a number of reasons, but constant discussion of battles in the newspapers constituted the major reason for many people. Newspaper printers included as much information about the fighting as they could get. Knowledge produces involvement, and Patriot printers worked hard to make sure that a loss of interest in the Revolution did not occur among the readers of their newspapers.

Patriot newspaper printers also sought to keep people encouraged about how the Revolution was progressing. Thus, they often put a positive spin on reports they published. Military victories and successes were extolled and expanded while defeats and setbacks were downplayed and minimized. For example, printers lavishly praised George Washington and the Continental Army for the relatively small victory at Trenton, New Jersey, in December 1776 while passing off the loss of a five-thousand-man army at Charleston, South Carolina, in May 1780 as a minor setback that would quickly be overcome. Through the use of such reporting techniques, newspaper printers helped to boost morale and keep people engaged in the war.

Newspapers have been a major source of information for Americans for a long time. This proved true for the first time during the American Revolution. There is little doubt that newspapers played an important role during the war. When people wanted information about how the war was going elsewhere, they turned to their local newspaper. Thus, these weekly news-sheets constituted the primary sources of news about the conflict. Their reports were not always accurate, but printers hoped they would boost morale by helping to maintain interest in, and support for, the war effort. By publishing accounts from throughout the colonies, newspapers helped foster a sense of unity and solidarity of purpose that was essential if Americans were going to win their fight for independence.

Contemporaries on both sides believed that the newspapers played an essential role in the war. For example, in 1776, Loyalist Ambrose Serle reported on the potential impact of the press in a letter to Lord Dartmouth: "Among other Engines, which have raised the present Commotion next to the indecent Harangues of the Preachers, none has had a more extensive or stronger Influence than the Newspapers of the respective Colonies. One is astonished to see with what Avidity they are sought after, and how implicitly they are believed, by the great Bulk of the People... Government may find it expedient, in the Sum of things, to employ this popular Engine." And in a 1782 letter to Richard Price, Benjamin Franklin commented on the role of the newspapers during the Revolution: "The ancient Roman and Greek orators could only speak to the number of citizens capable of being assembled within the reach of their voice. Their *writings* had little effect, because the bulk of the people could not read. Now by the press we can speak to nations; and good books and well written pamphlets have great and general influence. The facility, with which the same truths may be repeatedly enforced by placing them daily in different lights in *newspapers,* which are everywhere read, gives a great chance of establishing them. And we now find, that it is not only right to strike while the iron is hot, but that it may be very practicable to heat it by continually striking."

Most Americans concluded that the efforts of Patriot newspaper printers to keep readers informed about the war helped ensure ultimate success by boosting people's morale and rallying Americans to the cause until victory was achieved. By keeping people informed about the war's progress, newspapers made winning independence possible. Newspapers were essential in the fight to win independence and thus were essential in the creation of the United States.

THE VALUE OF PRIMARY SOURCES

By Michelle A. Larson

It should be no surprise that American history books glorify the Revolution. We believe so strongly in the ideals of that Revolutionary spirit that we allow our textbooks to ignore the complexities that led to the hotly debated decision to declare our independence and the difficult and protracted war that arose afterward. Our education distills nearly twenty years of history down to a handful of momentous events and famous names but glosses over the process by which the colonies shared information and galvanized the population.

While there are many important events in history to cover, no other period is more critical to understanding ourselves as Americans. It is the birth of everything we believe as a nation. While history books credit Thomas Paine and Thomas Jefferson as the major voices of Revolutionary thought, their contributions came about after years of debate. Hundreds of writers had already contributed to the argument. It was the newspapers that provided the platform for that debate and generated the fervor necessary to ignite and sustain the flame of independence where Paine and Jefferson would eventually flourish.

As a teacher, I can't help but encourage the analysis of these valuable primary source documents. Not only do they provide us with a way to help students understand the deeper issues that affected the time, but they also provide us with a way to develop the skills these students need to critically evaluate modern issues.

One of the biggest reasons to read these newspapers is to understand more deeply the issues that the Revolutionaries faced. Since many of the papers included in this volume originate on both sides of the Atlantic, it is possible to evaluate the wide variety of viewpoints as a class. For example, as Americans were resisting attempts to be taxed without representation, members of Parliament disagreed over how to deal with the "childish" Americans. The *New-Hampshire Gazette* of April 14, 1775, published a speech of Lord Chatham arguing for a more reasoned approach but follows it up with a summary from London of the various dissenting attitudes.

Another valuable purpose is to add a dose of reality to our views of the time. The Patriots were not always the "good guys," and their zeal was rife with irony. Several papers in 1765–66 and 1774–75, for example, gleefully describe mobs converging on Loyalists and compelling them to resign their posts or issue apologies for their point of view—not exactly the hallmark of a society that values free speech. Rousing diatribes against colonists serving as slaves to Britain ran side by side with advertisements offering rewards for escaped slaves and indentured servants.

These newspapers also help us to see historical figures as people. Letters in the November 29, 1774, *Essex Gazette* show that General Gage had no real desire to serve as a commander against

America. Benedict Arnold's letter to the Americans in the *London Chronicle* (November 14, 1780) expresses his disillusionment of the goals of the American resistance, but also belies a certain pettiness. Furthermore, the letters exchanged in regards to his captured British accomplice, Major André, show that Washington respected André despite his decision to have him executed as a spy.

There are also many parallels between the American Revolution and the conflicts occurring in our world today. Discussing these issues together can help students gain a greater understanding of media bias. After all, we teach history from an American perspective, so we talk of "revolutionaries," while the British referred to "rebels" and "rabble-rousers." Militias didn't stand much of a chance at fighting the British soldiers in straight lines on formal battlefields, so they shot at the enemy from hidden vantage points. The British considered this barbaric. Taught in concert with a discussion about the "Arab Spring" or the war on terror, for example, we open up a dialogue in which students may begin to look more closely at all sides of modern conflict as well.

As an English teacher, I can't overlook the value of using these articles to discuss literary analysis and writing skills. The *New-Hampshire Gazette* of February 17, 1775, provides a treasure trove of well-constructed arguments and scathing sarcasm. The *Massachusetts Gazette; and the Boston Post-Boy* of January 2, 1775, published a letter by Massachutensis, which argues against the actions of the Americans in response to the British duties on tea. His letter alone provides enough literary devices, formal arguments, and satirical wit to keep a class digging for weeks.

I am also fascinated with the evolution of the printed language in these papers. At the beginning of the Revolution, the language in American papers referring to the King—and Britain in general—is practically dripping with sweetness. This continues until the eve of war. However, in mid-1775, they are referred to as a "crew of enemies to the English constitution." Early papers made veiled attempts to "protect" the identities of those whom they were criticizing by replacing some or nearly all of a person's name with dashes. But as tensions flared, the dashes slowly disappeared and by beginning of the war had vanished almost completely, leaving readers with no doubt as to the target of criticism. Last, early newspapers show inconsistencies in spelling, punctuation, and capitalization, which become almost completely standardized by the end of the Revolutionary period.

As a high school English teacher, I've had my nose in textbooks practically my entire life, so I can say unequivocally that these newspapers are far more interesting reading than anything I have seen in a textbook. They give a glimpse into the daily life, dreams, and desires of the people who gave birth to this nation. Textbooks sanitize and summarize all the juicy bits out of history. Reading a few primary source documents just might reconstitute it!

CONTRIBUTORS

Todd Andrlik

Todd Andrlik is the primary architect of *Reporting the Revolutionary War*. In addition to providing the initial vision for the project, Andrlik authored several sections of the book, recruited more than three dozen contributors, directed more than sixty essays, produced supplemental video, and conceived many of the project's print and digital components. Among America's leading Revolutionary War newspaper archivists, Andrlik built one of the most significant collections of American Revolution newspapers, containing the earliest printed reports of practically every major event and battle from 1763 through 1783. This once-private archive is now publicly exhibited in *Reporting the Revolutionary War*.

Andrlik is curator and publisher of RagLinen.com, an online museum of historically significant newspapers dating back to the sixteenth century. Collaborating with individuals and institutions, including the Library of Congress, Andrlik helps others build private and public collections of these treasured relics. Beyond the acquisition, research, and digital preservation of early newspapers, Andrlik also takes an active role in their physical conservation. Through a partnership with one of the world's top paper conservators, Andrlik helps save damaged newspapers from loss and restores the artifacts as close as possible to original condition.

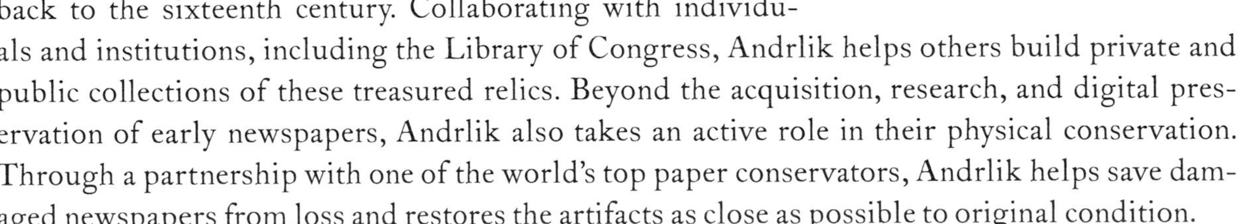

His passion for newspaper history stems from a career in media and marketing. Andrlik heads the marketing and media operations for Leopardo Companies, one of the nation's largest construction, design-build, and commercial real estate development firms. Andrlik has written or ghostwritten thousands of published articles and, as a social media pioneer, created the *Advertising Age* Power 150, a global ranking of the top marketing and media blogs. It was after Andrlik's success in new media that he made a 180-degree turn and focused his attention on old media.

Andrlik earned a bachelor's degree in public relations from Illinois State University and an MBA from Roosevelt University. He studied international business at Salzburg College, Austria. Andrlik serves on the advisory board of the Printing Office of Edes & Gill, the only colonial-era printing experience along Boston's Freedom Trail. He frequently writes for *American Revolution* magazine and is a member of the American Journalism Historians Association (AJHA), the American Revolution Association (ARA), and the Associates of the Omohundro Institute of Early American History and Culture (OIEAHC).

Michael S. Adelberg

Michael S. Adelberg is author of *The American Revolution in Monmouth County: The Theatre of Spoil and Destruction* (History Press, 2010), *The Razing of Tinton Falls: Voices from the American Revolution* (History Press 2012), scholarly articles published in the *Journal of Military History*, the *Journal of the Early Republic*, and *New Jersey History*, and the novel *A Thinking Man's Bully* (Permanent Press, 2011). His historical research has been recognized by the NJSAA, NJTV, and the *Wilson Quarterly*. To learn more about Adelberg, visit www.michaeladelberg.com. Garry Wheeler Stone, historian at Monmouth Battlefield State Park, is thanked for his contributions to this article.

Robert J. Allison

Robert J. Allison, professor of history at Suffolk University in Boston, also teaches at the Harvard Extension School. He is the author of *The American Revolution: A Concise History* (Oxford University Press, 2011), *Stephen Decatur: American Naval Hero* (University of Massachusetts Press, 2005), as well as several books on Boston and the American Revolution. He is vice president of the Colonial Society of Massachusetts, a trustee of the USS *Constitution* Museum, and a consultant to the Commonwealth Museum in Boston.

Charles B. Baxley

Charles B. Baxley earned a BA and JD from the University of South Carolina. He is a practicing attorney in Lugoff, South Carolina, and is the publisher and editor of the magazine *Southern Campaigns of the American Revolution.* Charles has served as president of the Kershaw County Historical Society, as host of several American Revolution symposia, and a guide of Revolutionary War sites. He is the cofounder of the Southern Campaigns Roundtable, Corps of Discovery tour group, and the Archaeological Reconnaissance and Computerization of Hobkirk's Hill battlefield (ARCHH, Inc.) project. Charles is chair of the Battle of Camden battlefield preservation project advisory council.

J. L. Bell

J. L. Bell maintains the Boston1775.net website, dedicated to history, analysis, and unabashed gossip about the start of the American Revolution in New England. Reflecting his interest in the experiences of young people, his study of Boston's Revolutionary youth appeared in *Children in Colonial America* (New York University Press, 2007). He has also published articles about colonial boys' diaries, town watchmen at the Boston Massacre, the wave of bankruptcies in 1765, and the town's raucous Pope Night celebration and has lectured at numerous historical sites in greater Boston.

Wayne Bodle

Wayne Bodle teaches early American history at Indiana University of Pennsylvania. He is the author of *The Valley Forge Winter: Civilians and Soldiers in War* (Penn State Press, 2002) and of a forthcoming monograph on the Middle Colonies of British North America from first European settlement to 1776. He is also working on a biographical account of the American adventures of Charles Wollstonecraft—the youngest brother of the English feminist writer Mary Wollstonecraft—from his arrival in Philadelphia in 1793 until his death in New Orleans in 1817, and another on the life and career of a reputedly "rogue" British colonial governor in America.

John Buchanan

John Buchanan is a military historian who spent almost thirty years on the staff of the Metropolitan Museum of Art, where he was museum archivist, special assistant to the director, and for over twenty years, chief registrar in charge of worldwide art movements. Since his retirement in 1993, he has published three books on early American history, including *The Road to Guilford Courthouse: The American Revolution in the Carolinas* (Wiley, 1999); a novel, *The Rise of Stefan Gregorovic* (iUniverse, 2010), about rebellion in Communist Eastern Europe; and short stories. For more information, visit www.jackbuchanan.net.

Benjamin L. Carp

Benjamin L. Carp is an associate professor of history at Tufts University, where he teaches the history of early America. He has published two books: *Rebels Rising: Cities and the American Revolution* (New York: Oxford University Press, 2007) and *Defiance of the Patriots: The Boston Tea Party and the Making of America* (New Haven: Yale University Press, 2010). He has a BA from Yale University and a PhD from the University of Virginia, and he previously taught at the University of Edinburgh. He has received the Leverhulme Research Fellowship and the Charlotte W. Newcombe Doctoral Dissertation Fellowship.

Bruce Chadwick

Bruce Chadwick, who lives in New Jersey right next door to the winter encampment of the Continental Army, has written five books on the American Revolution and lectures about the war around the world. Chadwick, a former journalist, has also written extensively about the Civil War. He has appeared as a guest scholar on a number of productions for the History Channel and the National Geographic Channel. The historian has also authored a series of books on the history of baseball. He is a history professor at New Jersey City University and an American studies lecturer at Rutgers.

Dennis M. Conrad

Dennis M. Conrad is a historian with the Naval History and Heritage Command in Washington, D.C., and is one of the editors of the series *Naval Documents of the American Revolution*, Vol. 12, which is forthcoming. He is former editor and project director of *The Papers of General Nathanael Greene*, published by the University of North Carolina Press. He has authored an essay on Greene's generalship style for *General Nathanael Greene and the American Revolution in the South*, forthcoming, University of South Carolina Press, and on the career of John Paul Jones in *Sea Raiders of the American Revolution: The Continental Navy in European Waters*.

Diane K. Depew

Diane K. Depew holds a BS in park administration from Shepherd College and an MA in history from Texas A&M University. With over thirty years of National Park Service experience, she previously worked on the Natchez Trace Parkway, Eisenhower National Historic Site, and Gettysburg National Military Park. She started working for Colonial National Historical Park at Yorktown Battlefield in 1988. With a strong interest in military history and having ancestors who served on both sides of the American Revolutionary War, she continues to research and uncover archival material to better tell the Yorktown story.

Robert M. Dunkerly

A native of Lewisburg, Pennsylvania, Robert M. Dunkerly is a park ranger at Richmond National Battlefield Park in Virginia. He holds a degree in history from St. Vincent College and a master's degree in public history from Middle Tennessee State University. He has authored six books and numerous articles on the American Revolution, including *Old Ninety Six* (History Press, 2006). Dunkerly is active in historic preservation and research, promoting the preservation and interpretation of historic sites. He assisted in the 2005 archaeological investigations at Ninety Six and has given many tours of Revolutionary War sites in the Carolinas.

Matthew P. Dziennik

Matthew P. Dziennik is currently a postdoctoral fellow at the New York Historical Society. He was awarded his PhD from the University of Edinburgh with a thesis on the Gaelic military diaspora in the age of the American Revolution. He has held numerous fellowships in Britain, the United States, and Canada and has articles published or forthcoming in the *Journal of British Studies, Historical Research, and Past & Present*. He is currently working on a social and cultural history of revolutionary political organizations in the middle colonies.

Rita Folse Elliott

Rita Folse Elliott (MA, RPA) is an archaeologist, exhibit designer, and former museum curator. She led crews in the archaeological discovery of the 1779 Savannah Battlefield. She has twenty-five years of archaeological and museum experience in eleven states, the Caribbean, three U.S. territories, and several countries. Elliott has authored over fifty monographs and articles and served as a guest editor and reviewer. She participates on committees for museum and archaeology organizations at the state, regional, and national levels. Elliott received the Governor's Award in the Humanities and serves as the education coordinator/research associate for the LAMAR Institute.

Thomas Fleming

Thomas Fleming is one of the most distinguished and productive historians and novelists of our time. He has written twenty nonfiction books that have won prizes and praise from critics and fellow historians, many with a special focus on the American Revolution. His twenty-three novels, many of them bestsellers, explore the lives of men and women in vivid narratives that range from the raw America of the 1730s to the superpower that confronted World War II and endured Korea and Vietnam. He has written frequently for *American Heritage* and many other magazines and is often a guest on C-Span, the History Channel, and PBS.

Don N. Hagist

Don N. Hagist is an independent researcher and author who specializes in the demographics of the British army during the American Revolution. He has written several books and numerous articles concerning the 1775–83 era, including *A British Soldier's Story: Roger Lamb's Narrative of the American Revolution* (Ballindalloch Press, 2004) and *British Soldiers: American War* (Westholme Publishing, 2012). He is also an engineer for a major electronics company and writes humor for several syndicated and freelance cartoonists.

John W. Hall

John W. Hall is the Ambrose-Hesseltine Assistant Professor of U.S. Military History at the University of Wisconsin at Madison. He holds a BS in history from the U.S. Military Academy at West Point and a PhD in history from the University of North Carolina–Chapel Hill. He specializes in early American military history with particular emphasis on partisan and Native American warfare. He is the author of *Uncommon Defense: Indian Allies in the Black Hawk War* (Harvard University Press, 2009) and numerous essays on early American warfare, including "Washington's Irregulars" in *A Companion to George Washington*, edited by Edward Lengel (Wiley-Blackwell, 2012).

Hugh T. Harrington

Hugh T. Harrington is an independent researcher and author whose books include *Remembering Milledgeville* (History Press, 2005), *More Milledgeville Memories* (History Press, 2006), *Civil War Milledgeville* (History Press, 2005), and biography of 1890s magician *Annie Abbott, "The Little Georgia Magnet"* (Createspace, 2010). His articles have appeared in the *Journal of Military History*, *Georgia Historical Quarterly*, *America's Civil War*, *Southern Campaigns of the American Revolution*, *American Revolution*, *Muzzle Blasts*, and others. He has written extensively on Sherlock Holmes and is a member of the Baker Street Irregulars. He lives in Milledgeville, Georgia.

Carol Sue Humphrey

Carol Sue Humphrey has been interested in the Revolutionary War since childhood. She narrowed her interest to the role of the press during the Revolution while in graduate school at the University of North Carolina. She is the author or editor of five books related to the history of the media in the United States, including *This Popular Engine: New England Newspapers During the American Revolution, 1775–1789* (University of Delaware Press, 1992), *Debating Historical Issues in the Media of the Time: The Revolutionary Era* (Greenwood, 2003), and *The Greenwood Library of American War Reporting: The Revolutionary War* (Greenwood, 2005). She currently teaches history at Oklahoma Baptist University.

Neal Thomas Hurst

For nearly a decade, Neal Thomas Hurst has studied and researched all aspects of eighteenth-century history with a focus on colonial men's clothing. Many of his publications and research examine the unique American hunting shirt. Hurst completed a seven-year apprenticeship at the Colonial Williamsburg Foundation as a tailor. He is currently studying history at the College of William and Mary in Virginia, where his primary interests are in early Virginia history and the events and actions leading up to the Williamsburg gunpowder incident.

Benjamin H. Irvin

Benjamin H. Irvin, associate professor of history at the University of Arizona, is a social and cultural historian of early America and the United States, working primarily in the Revolutionary period. His book, *Clothed in Robes of Sovereignty: The Continental Congress and the People Out of Doors*, published by Oxford University Press in April 2011, examines the material culture and ceremonies of state—including, for example, fast days, funeral processions, diplomatic protocols, and presentment swords—by which Congress promoted republicanism and revolution. Central to his study are the many ways that the American people challenged Congress and its vision of the United States.

Michelle A. Larson

Michelle A. Larson is a Pennsylvania high school English teacher and freelance writer who served as transcriptionist on *Reporting the Revolutionary War*. She has twelve years experience teaching British and American literature from a historical perspective. She holds a BSEd in English from Millersville University and an MEd in technology in the classroom from Wilkes University.

Tabitha Marshall

Tabitha Marshall was awarded a PhD in history (2006) by McMaster University in Hamilton, Ontario, Canada, for work on the health of British soldiers during the American Revolution. Current research interests include the health of sailors, as well as a study of the Royal Canadian Army Medical Corps during World War II. After teaching history at Memorial University of Newfoundland and McMaster University, Tabitha now works as an independent scholar and freelance writer in Hamilton, Ontario.

Bruce E. Mowday

Bruce E. Mowday is an award-winning journalist and author from Chester County, Pennsylvania. He has authored books on local history, the American Revolution, and the Civil War. He has also written books on the notorious Johnston gang and on baseball great Richie Ashburn of the Philadelphia Phillies. He was named a local Literacy Hero in 2008. For more than twenty years, he was a newspaper reporter and editor before founding his own media relations firm, the Mowday Group, Inc. For more information on Bruce, see www.mowday.com.

James L. Nelson

James L. Nelson spent a number of years at sea working aboard traditional sailing ships until he decided it would be easier to write about them than work on them. He has since written sixteen works of fiction and nonfiction, including *Glory in the Name* (Harper Perennial, 2004), which won the American Library Association/William Young Boyd Award for best military fiction, and *George Washington's Secret Navy* (Ragged Mountain Press, 2008), winner of the Naval Order's Samuel Eliot Morison Award. He currently lives on the coast of Maine with his former shipmate, now wife, Lisa and their four children.

Julia Osman

Julia Osman is an assistant professor at Mississippi State University, specializing in French, military, and Atlantic history. She received her PhD from the University of North Carolina at Chapel Hill in May 2010. Her work focuses primarily on the French army and its challenges and changes during the seventeenth and eighteenth centuries, as well as North American influences on French military reform. Her current book project, *The Citizen Army of Old Regime France*, traces the intellectual and cultural prehistory of the French Revolutionary army.

Steven H. Park

Steven H. Park wrote his doctoral dissertation on the *Gaspee* Affair and now teaches U.S. history and maritime studies at the University of Connecticut in Storrs and at UConn's campus-by-the-sea at Avery Point. Steve is a sought-after historical speaker for audiences young and mature alike. He teaches a popular class called "Pirates of the Caribbean" that engages undergraduate students in maritime history. He has published in a variety of scholarly print and electronic formats covering mutiny, seamen's missions, seafaring religion, piracy, and privateering. Please see www.stevenpark.org.

Jim Piecuch

Jim Piecuch earned his BA and MA degrees in history at the University of New Hampshire and his PhD at the College of William and Mary. He is an associate professor of history at Kennesaw State University and has published several articles on colonial and Revolutionary history. He is also the author of six books including: *The Battle of Camden: A Documentary History* (History Press, 2006); *Three Peoples, One King: Loyalists, Indians, and Slaves in the Revolutionary South* (University of South Carolina Press, 2008); *"Cool Deliberate Courage": John Eager Howard in the American Revolution* (Nautical & Aviation Pub, 2009), co-authored with John Beakes; and *"The Blood Be Upon Your Head": Tarleton and the Myth of Buford's Massacre* (Southern Campaigns of the American Revolution, 2010).

Ray Raphael

Ray Raphael, author of fifteen books, turned his attention to the Revolutionary Era in the mid-1990s. His several books in that field include *A People's History of the American Revolution*; *Founding Myths: Stories that Hide Our Patriotic Past* (Harper Perennial, 2002); and a detailed study of the Massachusetts Revolution of 1774, *The First American Revolution: Before Lexington and Concord* (New Press, 2002). A complete list of his books and articles, as well as some key historical documents not published elsewhere, can be found at www.rayraphael.com.

Matthew Reardon

Matthew Reardon earned a BA in history and an MA in education from Sacred Heart University. His primary interest lies with early American Military History, focusing on the American Revolution and the Civil War. He currently serves as the executive director of the New England Civil War Museum in Rockville, Connecticut. His first book, *"A Most Desperate Defence": An Interpretive Guide to the Battle of Groton Heights* is forthcoming. Matt resides in Tolland, Connecticut.

John Reda

John Reda is an assistant professor of history at Illinois State University, specializing in colonial and early national American history. He received his PhD from the University of Illinois at Chicago in 2009. His article, "From Subjects to Citizens: Two Pierres and the French Influence on the Transformation of the Illinois Country," appears in the anthology *French and Indians in the Heart of North America, 1630–1815* (Michigan State University Press, 2013). He is currently working on a book for NIU Press entitled *From Furs to Farms: Land, Race, and Sovereignty in the Mississippi Valley, 1762–1825*.

David Paul Reuwer

David Paul Reuwer is editor of *American Revolution* magazine. He earned a JD from Pepperdine University and a BA from Towson University and is currently a historian and practicing attorney, emphasizing historic preservation law. He was an adjunct professor of historic preservation at the College of Charleston. He was the lead investigator of the initial Eutaw Springs battlefield survey and is the plenipotentiary of the magazine *Southern Campaigns of the American Revolution*. David is also a battlefield tour guide.

J. Dennis Robinson

J. Dennis Robinson writes books about American history for young and old. He works from an office in historic Portsmouth, New Hampshire, near the swirling Piscataqua River, where he is also a popular columnist, lecturer, and editor of the award-winning history website SeacoastNH.com. His work includes AASLH award-winning books on the Strawbery Banke Museum and the historic Wentworth by the Sea Hotel, plus juvenile biographies of Jesse James and Lord Baltimore. His most recent books are *America's Privateer: Lynx and the War of 1812* (Lynx Educational Foundation, 2011) and *Under the Isles of Shoals: Archaeological Discovery at Smuttynose Island* (Portsmouth Marine Society, 2012).

David Lee Russell

David Lee Russell was born in Wilmington, North Carolina. After receiving his BS in aerospace engineering from North Carolina State University, he attended the Naval Aviation Officer's Candidate School in Pensacola. Commissioned as an Ensign-Special Duty Intelligence, he served as a Naval Air Intelligence Officer in the Pacific, Southeast Asia, and the Indian Ocean. After leaving active duty service, David began a long career in information technology. He is the author of *The American Revolution in the Southern Colonies* (McFarlard, 2009), *Victory on Sullivan's Island: The British Cape Fear/Charles Town Expedition of 1776* (Infinity Publishing, 2002), *Oglethorpe and Colonial Georgia: A History, 1733–1783* (McFarland, 2006), and *The Duke of Southbourne* (CreateSpace, 2011). David resides in Milton, Georgia.

Barnet Schecter

Barnet Schecter, an independent historian, is the author of *George Washington's America: A Biography Through His Maps* (Walker Publishing, 2010), *The Devil's Own Work: The Civil War Draft Riots and the Fight to Reconstruct America* (Walker Publishing, 2007), and *The Battle for New York: The City at the Heart of the American Revolution* (Walker Publishing, 2002). A contributing editor of the three-volume *Encyclopedia of the American Revolution and Landmarks of the American Revolution*, he is also a contributor to the *Encyclopedia of New York City*. In addition to lecturing and leading tours and military staff rides, he has appeared in a variety of television documentaries.

Eric H. Schnitzer

Eric H. Schnitzer, park ranger/historian at Saratoga National Historical Park, has dedicated his life's study to the organization, personnel, and material culture of the British and American armed forces of the Revolution, especially as it relates to the Northern Campaign of 1777. He has written articles for journals such as *The Hessians* and created illustrations for books such as *Philadelphia 1777* and *Wenches, Wives, and Servant Girls*. He and his wife, Jenna, are members of the re-created British 62nd Regiment and live in an eighteenth-century house in the White Creek Historic District near Bennington Battlefield, New York, where they spend much of their time sewing reproduction eighteenth-century garments.

William P. Tatum III

William P. Tatum III is the director of programs and research at the Historical Society of Newburgh Bay and the Hudson Highlands, previously worked at the David Library of the American Revolution, and is an advanced PhD candidate at Brown University. His work focuses on the eighteenth-century British army in its imperial context, as well as larger issues of social control and civil-military relations. He is the author of several articles on the British army during the era of the American Revolutionary War and is currently completing his dissertation, *For the Good of the King's Service: British Military Justice, Society, and Empire, 1715–1785*.

Daniel J. Tortora

Daniel J. Tortora is assistant professor of history at Colby College, where he teaches Native American and early American history. He is writing a book about the Anglo-Cherokee War of 1759–61 and its influence on the American Revolution. He speaks extensively on the South during the French and Indian War era, on Native American military history, and leads battlefield tours. He is currently working on a project in Winslow, Maine, to expand Fort Halifax Park, a reconstructed 1754 blockhouse and the site of an encampment for Benedict Arnold's Quebec campaign.

ACKNOWLEDGMENTS

THIS BOOK IS THE CULMINATION OF FIVE YEARS OF RESEARCH, CURATING, WRITING, AND EDITING. As such, I am indebted to numerous people for their support and contributions along the way.

My parents, Sharon and Robert, taught me to be ambitious, resourceful, creative, and determined, all of which I needed to successfully complete this project, so I am eternally grateful for their love and life instruction. Likewise, my grandmothers, siblings, nieces, nephews, in-laws, and close friends provided tremendous encouragement throughout the whole process, and I owe many thanks to all of them.

To help kick-start the publishing process, book illustrator Leslie Harrington introduced me to book packager Janice Shay, who served as the matchmaker with Sourcebooks. Janice believed in the project from the start and helped convince Sourcebooks that this was a book for them, so a big thank-you to Leslie for making the introduction and to Janice for getting things off the ground.

Sourcebooks instantly recognized the educational importance of historical newspapers and quickly latched on to the concept. I was fortunate to have a publisher so strongly committed to the project from the get-go and who offered a bottomless pit of forward-thinking ideas to help me bring the eighteenth century to the twenty-first. They made the process of publishing my first book a truly wonderful experience. I owe special thanks to Dominique Raccah, Peter Lynch, Todd Stocke, Kelly Bale, Liz Kelsch, Valerie Pierce, Lindsey Tom, Heather Hall, Melanie Jackson, and the entire Sourcebooks team for all their hard work.

Several people provided helpful consulting and aid to various elements of the project, so my sincerest appreciation goes to Ray Raphael, J. L. Bell, David Reuwer, Carol Humphrey, Bob Allison, Ben Carp, Ben Irvin, Will Tatum, Don Hagist, Ben Edwards, Gary Gregory, Danny Maiello, Ernest Kramer, Benjamin Smith, Jaime Ferguson, Craig Bloomfield, Lou Mongello, Brett Sneed, Gil Perez, Matthew Wilding, Jimi Allen, Adam Kelsey, and Hillary Andrlik. I am also extremely grateful to Joyce and Marlon Herring and their family, who provided me with superb hospitality and creative isolation in coastal North Carolina during the early writing and planning stages.

Many thanks to Michelle Larson, a Pennsylvania high school teacher who transcribed several of the newspapers featured in this book and provided an important educational perspective on the project that lent itself to a valuable essay contribution and several of the reading tips featured at the front of the book. Also, thank you to Andrea Wasilko and Karen Vanderzanden, who assisted in the transcriptions.

I would like to give very special thanks to those in and around the historical newspaper community who taught me so much as well as helped me to build and shape the collection featured in this book, including Tim Hughes, Guy Heilenman, Eric Caren, Steve Goldman, Steve Hanly, Mark Mitchell, Joe Felcone, Bob Ward, Brian Zak, Robert Heron, Sam Best, Rick Brown, Phil Barber, Vince Golden, Richard Robinson, Seth Kaller, Will Steere, John Reznikoff, Jim Arsenault, Bill Reese, Rick Mohovich, Scott Nason, Kathy Novak, Matthew Needle, Clarence Wolf, Bob Oswald, Doreen Mileto, Rodger Friedman, Andrew Robinson, Robert Hamm, William Butts, Charles Signer, Rick Stattler, Steve Alsberg, Ed Lake, and Ed King. Also, many thanks to Georgia Higley, Teri Sierra, and Mark Sweeney at the Library of Congress for their support and encouragement over the years.

To help save dozens of the newspapers from loss, I turned to J. Franklin Mowery for his expert paper conservation. Thanks to his collaboration, we restored many of the extremely fragile and tattered papers close to their original condition (many more to go).

This book was made exponentially better by the important essay contributions of 37 professors, scholars, and experts in the field. They helped put the newspaper accounts in context, provided valuable analysis and perspective, and bridged the eighteenth and twenty-first centuries for readers. Their passion for and lifelong commitments to the subject matter is admirable, and I am forever grateful for their generosity and time spent on the project. A full list of contributors and their bios is available within the book.

Thank you to my brothers from Illumination Lodge No. 5 and all my colleagues at Leopardo Companies for their support, especially Jim Leopardo, Rick Mattioda, and John Ward.

Finally, this book is dedicated to Hillary, Rory, and Lincoln, my wife, daughter, and son. I am the luckiest man on earth to be married to such a patient, creative, and helpful wife. Her enduring support helped me get through many long nights and weekends. Thankfully, we share an addiction to hard work and commitment to innovation in both our full-time jobs as well as our hobbies. More importantly, Hillary's objective opinions, sound counsel, artistic talents, and educational acumen helped steer me on several aspects of this project. She is my Abigail Adams. My daughter, Rory, went off to kindergarten, and my son, Lincoln, was born just as this book was being published. They inspire me every day, and when they get older I look forward to sharing all the exciting discoveries and valuable lessons about our nation's founding that I learned from reading eighteenth-century newspapers.

INDEX

M

N

O

P

Q

R

S

T

V

W

Y